Penn State ACCTG 211

Course Version 3

Taken from:

Financial Accounting: A Business Process Approach, Third Edition
by Jane L. Reimers

Managerial Accounting, Third Edition
by Karen Wilken Braun and Wendy M. Tietz

Cover Art: Courtesy of Glowimages Getty Images.

Excerpts taken from:

Financial Accounting: A Business Process Approach, Third Edition
by Jane L. Reimers
Copyright © 2011, 2008, 2003 by Pearson Education, Inc.
Published by Prentice Hall
Upper Saddle River, New Jersey 07458

Managerial Accounting, Third Edition
by Karen Wilken Braun and Wendy M. Tietz
Copyright © 2013, 2010, 2008 by Pearson Education, Inc.
Upper Saddle River, New Jersey 07458

This special edition published in cooperation with Pearson Learning Solutions.

All trademarks, service marks, registered trademarks, and registered service marks are the property of their respective owners and are used herein for identification purposes only.

Pearson Learning Solutions, 501 Boylston Street, Suite 900, Boston, MA 02116
A Pearson Education Company
www.pearsoned.com

Printed in the United States of America

6 7 8 9 10 V092 16 15 14

000200010271847295

JAG

ISBN 10: 1-269-62623-X
ISBN 13: 978-1-269-62623-1

For my son

Brief Contents

Chapter 1   Business: What's It All About?   1

Chapter 2   Qualities of Accounting Information   51

Chapter 3   Accruals and Deferrals: Timing Is Everything
in Accounting   97

Appendix B: The Mechanics of an Accounting System   563

Chapter 5   The Purchase and Sale of Inventory   201

Chapter 6   Acquisition and Use of Long-Term Assets   267

Chapter 8   Accounting for Shareholders' Equity   371

Chapter 9   Preparing and Analyzing the Statement of Cash Flows   415

Chapter 10   Using Financial Statement Analysis to Evaluate Firm
Performance   461

Glossary   609
Index   615

Contents

Chapter 1   Business: What's It All About?   1

Purpose and Organization of a Business   2
What Is a Business All About?   3
The Nature of Business Operations   3
Ownership Structure of a Business   4
Sole Proprietorships   4
Partnerships   5
Corporations   6
Limited Liability Partnerships (LLP) and Corporations (LLC)   8

Business Activities and the Flow of Goods and Services   8

Information Needs for Decision Making in Business   10
Who Needs Information about Transactions of the Business?   11
Setting Guidelines   11
International Financial Reporting Standards   11
Other Users of Accounting Information   12
Accounting Information: A Part of the Firm's Information System   13

Overview of the Financial Statements   13
Balance Sheet   13
Income Statement   17
The Difference between the Balance Sheet and the Income Statement   18
Statement of Changes in Shareholders' Equity   19
Statement of Cash Flows   20
Flow of Information and the Financial Statements   23

Real Company Financial Statements   23

Business Risk, Control, and Ethics   26

Chapter Summary Points   28   •   Chapter Summary Problems   28   •   Key Terms for
Chapter 1   29   •   Answers to YOUR TURN Questions   30   •   Financial Statement
Analysis   47   •   Critical Thinking Problems   49   •   Internet Exercise: Disney
Corporation   49

Chapter 2   Qualities of Accounting Information   51

Information for Decision Making   52

Characteristics of Accounting Information   53
What Makes Information Useful?   53
Relevant   53
Reliable   53
Comparable   53
Consistent   54
Assumptions Underlying Financial Reporting   54
Principles Underlying Financial Reporting   55

Elements of the Financial Statements   56
Transactions for the Second Month of Business   56
Assets   62
Liabilities   62
Shareholders' Equity   64
Measurement and Recognition in Financial Statements   64
Measuring Assets   64
Recognizing Revenues and Expenses   65

Accruals and Deferrals   66
Accrual Basis Accounting   66

Cash Basis versus Accrual Basis Accounting   66
Accounting Periods and Cutoff Issues   67
How Investors—Owners and Creditors—Use Accrual Accounting Information   67
An Example to Illustrate the Information Financial Statements Provide   68

Putting It All Together—The Objectives of Financial Statements   72
Real Company Financial Statements   73

Applying Your Knowledge: Ratio Analysis   75

Business Risk, Control, and Ethics   75
Internal Controls—Definition and Objectives   76
Special Internal Control Issues Related to Financial Statements   76
Preventive Controls   76
Detective Controls   76
Corrective Controls   77

Chapter Summary Points   77   •   Chapter Summary Problems   77   •   Key Terms for
Chapter 2   81   •   Answers to YOUR TURN Questions   81   •   Financial Statement
Analysis   94   •   Critical Thinking Problems   96   •   Internet Exercise: MSN Money
and Merck   96

Chapter 3   Accruals and Deferrals: Timing Is Everything in Accounting   97

Measuring Income   98
The Income Statement   98

Accruals   99
Accrued Revenue   99
Accrued Expenses   101
Reporting Interest Expense   102
Other Accrued Expenses   102

Deferrals   104
Deferred Revenue   104
Subscriptions   105
Gift Cards   105
Deferred Expenses   106
Insurance   106
Rent   107
Supplies   108
Equipment   109

Effects of Accruals and Deferrals on Financial Statements   112
Team Shirts Transactions for March   112
Adjustments to the Accounting Records   115
Preparing the Financial Statements   116
Accruals and Deferrals on Real Firms' Financial Statements   119

Applying Your Knowledge: Ratio Analysis   121
Profit Margin on Sales Ratio   121

Business Risk, Control, and Ethics   122
Errors in Recording and Updating the Accounting Records   123
Unauthorized Access to the Accounting Information   123
Loss or Destruction of Accounting Data   123

Chapter Summary Points   124   •   Chapter Summary Problems   124   •   Key Terms for
Chapter 3   126   •   Answers to YOUR TURN Questions   126   •   Financial Statement
Analysis   150   •   Critical Thinking Problems   152   •   Internet Exercise: Darden   152

Appendix B: The Mechanics of an Accounting System   563

Chapter 5   The Purchase and Sale of Inventory   201

Acquiring and Selling Merchandise   202
An Operating Cycle   202
Acquiring Merchandise for Sale   202
Acquisition Process for Inventory   203
Recording Purchases   204
Who Pays the Freight Costs to Obtain Inventory?   204
Purchase Returns and Allowances   205
Purchase Discounts   206
Summary of Purchases for Quality Lawn Mowers   207

Selling Merchandise   207
   Sales Process   208
   Recording Sales   208
   Sales Returns and Allowances   209
   Sales Discounts and Shipping Terms   209
   Summary of Purchases and Sales for Quality Lawn Mowers   210
   Sales Taxes   210

Recording Inventory: Perpetual Versus Periodic Record Keeping   211
   Differences between Perpetual and Periodic Inventory Systems   211

Inventory Cost Flow Assumptions   211
   Specific Identification   212
   Weighted Average Cost   213
   First-In, First-Out Method (FIFO)   214
   Last-In, First-Out Method (LIFO)   215
   How Inventory Cost Flow Assumptions Affect the Financial Statements   217
      Differences in Reported Inventory and Cost of Goods Sold under Different Cost Flow
      Assumptions   217
      Conclusions about Inventory Cost Flow Assumptions   222
      Income Tax Effects of LIFO and FIFO   222
      How Do Firms Choose an Inventory Cost Flow Method?   223

   NEWS FLASH: **IFRS in the *News*   225**

Applying Inventory Assumptions to Team Shirts   225
Complications in Valuing Inventory: Lower-of-Cost-or-Market Rule   230
Financial Statement Analysis   231
   Gross Profit Ratio   231
   Inventory Turnover Ratio   232

Business Risk, Control, and Ethics   233
   Obsolescence   234
   The Ethics of Inventory Losses   234

Chapter Summary Points   234   •   Chapter Summary Problem   235   •   Key Terms for
Chapter 5   238   •   Answers to YOUR TURN Questions   238   •   Financial Statement
Analysis   259   •   Critical Thinking Problems   260   •   Internet Exercise: Gap   260
•   Appendix 5A: Inventory Errors   262   •   Appendix 5B: Gross Profit Method of
Estimating Ending Inventory   265

Chapter 6   Acquisition and Use of Long-Term Assets   267
Acquiring Long-Term Assets   268
   Types of Long-Lived Assets: Tangible and Intangible   268
   Acquisition Costs   268
   Basket Purchase Allocation   270

Using Long-Term Tangible Assets: Depreciation and Depletion   270
   Straight-Line Depreciation   272
   Activity (Units-of-Production) Depreciation   274
   Declining Balance Depreciation   276
   Depletion   278

Using Intangible Assets: Amortization   279
   Copyrights   279
   Patents   279
   Trademarks   280
   Franchises   280
   Goodwill   280
   Research and Development Costs   280

Changes after the Purchase of the Asset   281
   Asset Impairment   281
   Expenditures to Improve an Asset or Extend Its Useful Life   281
   Revising Estimates of Useful Life and Salvage Value   282

Selling Long-Term Assets   283
Presentation of Long-Term Assets on the Financial Statements   285
   Reporting Long-Term Assets   285

NEWS FLASH: **IFRS and Long-Lived Assets** 286
Preparing Statements for Team Shirts 286
Applying Your Knowledge—Ratio Analysis 289
Return on Assets 289
Asset Turnover Ratio 290
Business Risk, Control, and Ethics 291
Chapter Summary Points 291 • Chapter Summary Problems 292 • Key Terms
for Chapter 6 294 • Answers to YOUR TURN Questions 295 • Financial
Statement Analysis 314 • Critical Thinking Problems 314 • Internet Exercise:
Best Buy 315 • Appendix 6: Depreciation and Taxes 316

Chapter 8 Accounting for Shareholders' Equity 371
Components of Shareholders' Equity in a Corporation—Contributed Capital 372
Stock—Authorized, Issued, and Outstanding 372
Common Stock 373
Preferred Stock 376
Cash Dividends 376
Important Dates Related to Dividends 376
Declaration Date 376
Date of Record 377
Payment Date 377
Distribution of Dividends between Common and Preferred Shareholders 377
An Example of a Dividend Payment 378
Treasury Stock 379
Why Do Firms Buy Their Own Stock? 379
Accounting for the Purchase 380
Selling Treasury Stock 380
Reporting Treasury Stock 381
Stock Dividends and Stock Splits 382
Stock Dividends 382
Stock Splits 383
Retained Earnings 383
Team Shirts Issues New Stock 384
Applying Your Knowledge: Ratio Analysis 388
Return on Equity 388
Earnings Per Share 389
Business Risk, Control, and Ethics 391
Risks Faced by Owners 391
Chapter Summary Points 391 • Chapter Summary Problems 392 • Key Terms
for Chapter 8 393 • Answers to YOUR TURN Questions 394 • Financial
Statement Analysis 411 • Critical Thinking Problems 412 • Internet Exercise:
Hershey Foods Corporation 412

Chapter 9 Preparing and Analyzing the Statement of Cash Flows 415
The Importance of the Statement of Cash Flows 416
Two Methods of Preparing and Presenting the Statement of Cash Flows 417
Accrual Accounting versus Cash Basis Accounting 418
Sales versus Cash Collected from Customers 418
Salary Expense versus Cash Paid to Employees 419
Preparing the Statement of Cash Flows: Direct Method 420
Revenue → Cash Collected from Customers 420
Cost of Goods Sold → Cash Paid to Vendors 421
Other Expenses → Cash Paid for Other Expenses 422
Summary of Direct Method 422
Preparing the Statement of Cash Flows: Indirect Method 423
Start with Net Income 423
Examine Current Asset and Current Liability Accounts 423
Comparing the Direct and Indirect Methods 425
Cash from Investing and Financing Activities 425
Investing Activities 425
Financing Activities 425

Putting It All Together   426
Summary of Direct and Indirect Methods   427
Applying Your Knowledge: Financial Statement Analysis   427
Cash from Operating Activities—AutoZone   427
Cash from Investing Activities—AutoZone   427
Cash from Financing Activities—AutoZone   428
Other Characteristics of the Statement of Cash Flows   429
Free Cash Flow   429
Business Risk, Control, and Ethics   430
Chapter Summary Points   430   •   Chapter Summary Problems   431   •   Key Terms
for Chapter 9   434   •   Answers to YOUR TURN Questions   434   •   Financial
Statement Analysis   456   •   Critical Thinking Problems   459   •   Internet Exercise:
Carnival Corporation   459

**Chapter 10   Using Financial Statement Analysis to Evaluate Firm
Performance   461**
A Closer Look at the Income Statement   462
Discontinued Operations   462
Extraordinary Items   463
Horizontal and Vertical Analysis of Financial Information   463
Horizontal Analysis   464
Vertical Analysis   465
Ratio Analysis   466
A Review of All Ratios   466
Liquidity Ratio with Cash Flows   467
Market Indicator Ratios   468
Understanding Ratios   469
Using Ratio Analysis   470
Liquidity Ratios   470
Current Ratio   470
Cash from Operations to Current Liabilities Ratio   471
Inventory Turnover Ratio   472
Accounts Receivable Turnover Ratio   472
Profitability Ratios   474
Financial Statement Analysis—More than Numbers   474
Business Risk, Control, and Ethics   475
NEWS FLASH   475
Chapter Summary Points   476   •   Chapter Summary Problems   476   •   Key Terms
for Chapter 10   480   •   Answers to YOUR TURN Questions   480   •   Critical Thinking
Problems   503   •   Internet Exercise: Papa John's International   504   •
Appendix 10A: Comprehensive Income   505   •   Appendix 10B: Investments in
Securities   507

Glossary   609
Index   615

With
Financial Accounting:
A Business Process Approach
Student Text, Study Resources,
and MyAccountingLab
students will have more

"I Get It!"

moments.

A Business Process Approach

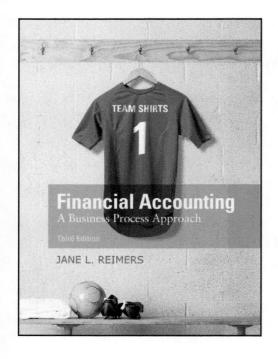

Financial Accounting: A Business Process Approach, Third Edition, explains accounting concepts in a way all majors can understand by organizing the material around how a business works. The business process approach in this text presents a business topic and then shows the accounting concepts behind that topic—rather than solely explaining accounting concepts based on the balance sheet order, a difficult approach for students who have yet to learn about the balance sheet. Overall, this text reinforces the big picture of how businesses operate while showing students how the corresponding accounting concepts work in context.

Jane Reimers' Unique Business Process Approach, in her own words...

More Important to Business Than Ever Before

In the past, one of the biggest challenges we have faced as accounting professors has been motivating our students to learn accounting. However, the business failures of the past decade, particularly those involving accounting irregularities and fraud, have done a great deal to provide needed motivation. In addition, the economic recession of 2008–09 has continued to keep accounting in the news. Most of our students today have no doubt that accounting is important to business. My approach to the first course in accounting is based on emphasizing this relationship between business and accounting.

www.pearsonhighered.com/reimers

Make Financial Statements Relevant to All Majors.

With a focus on what a business does and less of a focus on bookkeeping, the business process approach helps all majors understand financial statements. Although the mechanics of debits and credits are included in an appendix for professors who want to use this tool, the fundamental accounting equation and the path from business transactions to financial statements are at the heart of this approach.

Offer Hands-On Practice in Preparing Statements: Color-Coded Accounting Equation.

To become effective users of financial statements, students must understand how the statements are prepared—and nothing helps them understand this more than having them prepare the statements themselves. Students have had extremely positive reactions to the color-coded accounting equation, which enables them to see exactly how business transactions are summarized and presented on each of the four basic financial statements.

Color-Coded Accounting Equation

This color-coded accounting equation is a tool you will use throughout your financial accounting course. Fully explained in Chapter 1, this tool is so important that we have put it here for quick reference. You may find this helpful when preparing your homework assignments. Each financial statement has a unique color. You will see these colors throughout the chapters when we present a financial statement.

Transaction	Cash	All other assets	(Account)	All liabilities	(Account)	Common stock	(Account)
			Assets	**= Liabilities**		**+ Shareholders' Equity**	
						Contributed Capital	Retained Earnings
1.	$250					$250	
2.	850			850	Notes payable		
3.	(650)	650	Property, plant, and equipment				
4.	(25)						(25) Operating expenses
5.	(300)	300	Property, plant, and equipment				
6.	800						800 Service revenue
7.	(480)						(480) Salary expense
8.		20	Supplies	20	Accounts payable		
9.	(5)						(5) Dividends
	$440	+ $970		= $870		+ $250	+ $290

— Income Statement   — Statement of Changes in Shareholders' Equity   — Balance Sheet   — Statement of Cash Flows

■ Red identifies the income statement. The transactions that affect the income statement will have an amount in the red section on the accounting equation worksheet.

■ Yellow identifies the statement of shareholders' equity. The transactions that affect shareholders' equity will have an amount in the yellow section.

■ Blue identifies the balance sheet. Only the summary of the transactions—the ending balances in each account—will be shown on the balance sheet.

■ Green identifies the statement of cash flows. The cash inflows and outflows are all found in the cash column of the accounting equation worksheet. These inflows and outflows are explained in the statement of cash flows.

All of our students—both accounting and non-accounting majors—need to understand the basic relationship between business transactions and the financial statements. Overall, the approach in this text provides a strong foundation for accounting majors while keeping the content relevant for all majors. I hope this textbook provides your students with all of the tools they will need to truly understand accounting.

— *Jane L. Reimers*

New to the Third Edition

Understanding the Latest Potential Shift in Reporting Standards: International Financial Reporting Standards (IFRS).

Awareness of IFRS—including what it is, what it means, and when it's coming—is becoming increasingly important in our global economy. In the third edition, IFRS is introduced and explained in the first chapter. Then, throughout the book, differences between U.S. GAAP and IFRS are noted as they apply to the chapter's topic. A section on IFRS has been added to the capstone chapter (11), along with some examples of financial statements prepared according to IFRS.

Learning in the Right Sequence: Reordered Coverage of Operating and Investing Activities.

Operating topics, such as sales and inventory, are covered before the acquisition and use of long-term assets, consistent with a renewed emphasis on operating, investing, and financing activities by the FASB. This new order helps students because it's consistent with the statement of cash flows and the lifeblood of all business. This reorganization will also help prepare students for convergence with IFRS because it reflects how IFRS statements are organized.

Making Practice Easier: Revised Color-Coded Accounting Equation Worksheet.

We modified the color-coded accounting equation worksheet to make it easier to use. Rather than having a column for every asset and liability account used in a problem, there are just two asset columns—cash and all other assets—and just one column for liabilities. The new format provides space to include the name of the account next to each entry in the general asset and liability columns, making the worksheets larger and easier to read.

Panel A: Clean Sweep

	Assets			=	Liabilities		+	Owner's Equity		
	Cash	All other assets	(Account)		All liabilities	(Account)		Contributed Capital	Retained Earnings	(Account)
Beginning Balances	$ 900	$ 200	Supplies	$400	Notes payable			$700		
Transaction										
1. Earns revenue and collects fees in cash	750								$ 750	Revenue
2. Makes loan payment	(440)				(400)	Notes payable			(40)	Interest expense
3. Adjusts for supplies used		(175)	Supplies						(175)	Supplies expense
Ending Balances	$1,210	+ $ 25		=	0		+	$700	+	$ 535

— Income Statement   — Statement of Changes in Owner's Equity   — Balance Sheet   — Statement of Cash Flows

Panel B: Maids-R-Us

	Assets			=	Liabilities		+	Owner's Equity		
	Cash	All other assets	(Account)		All liabilities	(Account)		Contributed Capital	Retained Earnings	(Account)
Beginning Balances	$900	$200	Supplies	$400	Notes payable			$700		
Transaction										
1. Earns revenue and extends credit		750	Accounts receivable						$750	Revenue
2. Makes loan payment	(140)				(100)	Notes payable			(40)	Interest expense
3. Adjusts for supplies used		(175)	Supplies						(175)	Supplies expense
Ending Balances	$760	+ $775		=	$300		+	$700	+	$535

ETHICS Matters

Paying for Silence

With just two weeks until the start of his trial, Computer Associates International's former CEO, Sanjay Kumar, pleaded guilty to securities fraud and obstruction of justice. Not only did Kumar engage in a conspiracy to inflate the firm's 2000 and 2001 sales revenue, but he also authorized a $3.7 million payment to buy the silence of potential witnesses. In November 2006, he was sentenced to 12 years in prison and fined $8 million for his part in the $2.2 billion fraud.

As you will learn in this chapter, precisely *when* revenue is included on the income statement is one of the most crucial timing issues in accounting. Computer Associates included revenue on its income statement *before* the company actually earned the revenue. This violates one of the most significant accounting principles that forms the basis of U.S. GAAP and IFRS. Revenue must be earned before it can be included on the income statement for the period.

Emphasizing How Ethics Matters.

With the current scandals occurring in today's economy, ethics is one aspect of accounting that truly does matter. To help students avoid potential pitfalls and complications involved with ethics, this edition opens each chapter with a current, relevant example stressing the importance of ethics in accounting and business.

Including the Coverage You Want: Revised Time Value of Money Coverage.

Due to extensive reviewer feedback, time value of money and calculating proceeds from a bond issue have been moved to a chapter appendix. Now Chapter 7, long-term liabilities, can be covered without prior knowledge of present value concepts. The appendix, however, can easily be integrated into chapter coverage for those who prefer to include it.

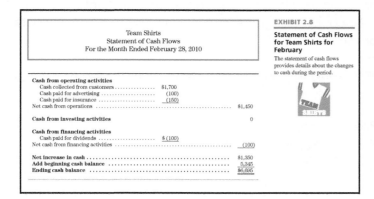

Team Shirts
Statement of Cash Flows
For the Month Ended February 28, 2010

EXHIBIT 2.8

Statement of Cash Flows for Team Shirts for February
The statement of cash flows provides details about the changes to cash during the period.

Cash from operating activities		
Cash collected from customers	$1,700	
Cash paid for advertising	(100)	
Cash paid for insurance	(150)	
Net cash from operations		$1,450
Cash from investing activities		0
Cash from financing activities		
Cash paid for dividends	$ (100)	
Net cash from financing activities		(100)
Net increase in cash		$1,350
Add beginning cash balance		5,345
Ending cash balance		$6,695

Connecting Accounting to Business: Continuing Case Example.

Seeing one example carried throughout the entire business process is a great way to help students connect accounting to the big picture of business. The previous edition's example, Tom's Wear, has been updated to Team Shirts, and the computations for depreciation, prepaid expenses, and cost of goods sold are easier to follow. The slow build of the continuing case and its computations in each chapter help students follow the progression of the calculations they're learning.

Keeping Up with the Trends: Updated Examples.

The third edition includes many opportunities to discuss the economic issues facing firms today. For example, in Chapter 3, the Understanding Business feature discusses the cost savings of "going green." Throughout the book, examples like this help students see how the changes in the economy are reflected in a firm's financial statements.

UNDERSTANDING → **Business**

Does Going Green Help a Company's Bottom Line?

The goal of a corporation is to make money for its shareholders—that is, to increase shareholders' value. It is the job of financial statements to report the corporation's financial performance. Where does a corporation's social responsibility fit in? Is there a relationship between financial performance and a corporation's social performance? For any company, part of being socially responsible is finding ways to reduce its negative impact on the environment. Everyone, it seems, is talking about "going green."

In his book, *What Matters Most: How a Small Group of Pioneers Is Teaching Social Responsibility to Big Business and Why Big Business Is Listening*, Jeffrey Hollander argues that "introducing social responsibility into day-to-day business operations is an effective way of creating long-term sustainable growth and improved financial performance." Many organizations agree. Staples, for example, reports that its switching from three-amp to two-amp light bulbs added $4.2 million to its bottom line. Dell's plan to neutralize its carbon footprint saved the company $3 million in 2008. Dell Inc. plans to reduce its waste and reuse 99% of its waste by 2013.

According to a recent study by A.T. Kearney, firms with a true commitment to corporate sustainability practices are achieving above-average performance in the financial markets in the current economic recession. John Mahoney, CFO at Staples, told the CFO Green Conference in March 2009 that being socially responsible should continue to reap financial benefits.

"While the economy is reeling today, we can afford to maintain our sustainability programs because of their measurable impact on our financial performance. I think the economic environment is going to really represent a turning point for many companies in thinking about how sustainability works."

Source: "Staples CFO: Going Green Means Saving Green," by David McCann, April 1, 2009, CFO.com

Promoting Practice: A Second Set of Short Exercises.

Included in each chapter of this edition, every Short Exercise, Exercise, and Problem in the Set "A" material has a "matching" exercise or problem in the corresponding Set "B" material. This provides students with even more practice to enhance their skills.

Student Resources

www.myaccountinglab.com

MyAccountingLab is Web-based tutorial and assessment software for accounting that gives students more "I Get It!" moments. **MyAccountingLab** provides students with a personalized, interactive learning environment where they can complete their course assignments with immediate tutorial assistance, learn at their own pace, and measure their progress.

In addition to completing assignments and reviewing tutorial help, students have access to the following resources in **MyAccountingLab**:

- Pearson eText
- Study Guide
- Excel in Practice
- PowerPoints
- Working Papers in both Excel and PDF
- Flash Cards

Study Guide

This chapter-by-chapter learning aid helps students learn financial accounting while getting the maximum benefit from study time.

Student Resource Website www.pearsonhighered.com/reimers

- Excel in Practice
- Working Papers

Student Reference Cards

International Financial Reporting Standards Student Reference Card

This four-page laminated reference card includes an overview of IFRS, why it matters and how it compares to U.S. standards, and highlights key differences between IFRS and U.S. GAAP.

Math for Accounting Student Reference Card

This six-page laminated reference card provides students with a study tool for the basic math they will need to be successful in accounting, such as rounding, fractions, converting decimals, calculating interest, break-even analysis, and more!

Instructor Resources

The primary goal of the Instructor Resources is to help instructors deliver their course with ease, using any delivery method—traditional, self-paced, or online. *Every instructor and student resource has been either written or reviewed by the author.*

MyAccountingLab®

www.myaccountinglab.com

MyAccountingLab is Web-based tutorial and assessment software for accounting that not only gives students more "I Get It!" moments, but also provides instructors the flexibility to make technology an integral part of their course or a supplementary resource for students. And, because practice makes perfect, **MyAccountingLab** offers all the Set A end-of-chapter material found in the text along with algorithmic options that instructors can assign for homework. **MyAccountingLab** also replicates the text's exercises and problems so that students are familiar and comfortable working with the material.

Instructor's Manual

The Instructor's Manual, available electronically or in print, offers course-specific content including a guide to available resources, a road map for using **MyAccountingLab**, a first-day handout for students, sample syllabi, and guidelines for teaching an online course, as well as content-specific material including chapter overviews, teaching outlines, student summary handouts, lecture outline tips, assignment grids, ten-minute quizzes, and more!

Instructor Resource Center www.pearsonhighered.com/reimers

For your convenience, many of our instructor supplements are available for download from the textbook's catalog page or from **MyAccountingLab**. Available resources include:
- **Solutions Manual** containing the fully worked-through and accuracy-checked solutions for every question, exercise, and problem in the text.
- **Test Item File with TestGen Software** providing over 1,600 multiple choice, true/false, and problem-solving questions correlated by Learning Objective and difficulty level as well as AACSB and AICPA standards.
- **Author-Reviewed PowerPoint Presentations.** There are 508 Compliant Instructor PowerPoints with extensive notes for on-campus or online classes, and Student PowerPoints.
- **Excel in Practice**
- **Image Library**
- **Working Papers and Solutions**
- **Instructors' Manual**

Course Cartridges

Course Cartridges for BlackBoard, WebCT, CourseCompass, and other learning management systems are available upon request.

Provide More "I Get It!" Moments.

New! End-of-Chapter Material Integrated with MyAccountingLab at: www.myaccountinglab.com
Students need practice and repetition in order to successfully learn the fundamentals of financial accounting. The **MyAccountingLab** course for *Financial Accounting: A Business Process Approach*, *third edition*, now contains book-match and algorithmic Short Exercises, Exercises, and Problems. This makes it easy to assign homework, and provides practice that's relevant to each chapter. In addition, IFRS coverage has been added so students can see how IFRS will impact decisions in accounting.

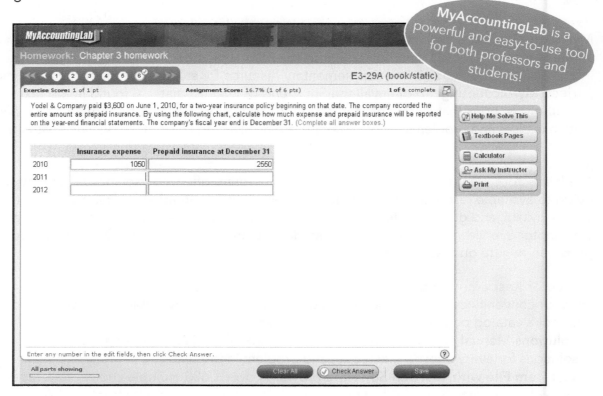

Powerful Homework and Test Manager
Create, import, and manage online homework assignments, quizzes, and tests that are automatically graded, allowing you to spend less time grading and more time teaching. Create assignments from online exercises directly correlated to the textbook. Homework exercises include guided solutions and other tools to help students understand and master concepts.

Comprehensive Gradebook Tracking
MyAccountingLab's online Gradebook automatically tracks your students' results on tests, homework, and tutorials, and gives you control over managing results and calculating grades. All **MyAccountingLab** grades can be exported to a spreadsheet program, such as Microsoft® Excel. The **MyAccountingLab** Gradebook provides a number of views of student data and gives you the flexibility to weight assignments, select which attempts to include when calculating scores, and omit or delete results for individual assignments.

About the Author

For the past six years, Jane Reimers has been a member of the faculty at the Crummer Graduate School of Business at Rollins College. Previously, she taught at Florida State University and Duke University.

Professor Reimers grew up in the Orlando area, earning her bachelor's degree at the University of Florida. She worked as a high school math teacher and as an auditor with a national accounting firm in Orlando before going on to the University of Michigan where she earned a Ph.D. in accounting. In 2009, she won the Cornell Outstanding Faculty in Crummer Award. She has published research in the *Journal of Accounting Research*, *The Accounting Review*, *Auditing: A Journal of Practice and Theory*, *Accounting Horizons*, *Decision Sciences*, and *Accounting, Organizations and Society*.

Acknowledgments

Instructors from colleges and universities across the country helped with the revision of *Financial Accounting: A Business Approach*. Their suggestions and comments were invaluable. All of the Prentice Hall people who worked on this edition also deserve my thanks. At the top of that list is Karen Misler, the developmental editor for this edition. Her skill, insight, and patience were astounding. I want to give special thanks to Christopher Evans, a friend and former graduate student of mine, for his invaluable help with this revision. I am grateful to all of the following people for their help.

Reviewers of the third edition:

Robert Derstine, Villanova University

Anthony Greig, Purdue University

John Hathorn, Metropolitan State College

Jeff Hillard, Baltimore County Community College

Nancy Lynch, West Virginia University

Joyce Middleton, Frostburg State University

Susan Minke, Indiana University – Purdue University Fort Wayne

Aamer Sheikh, Quinnipiac University

Pavani Tallapalli, Slippery Rock University of Pennsylvania

Craig Vilhauer, Merced College

Accuracy checkers:

Anthony Greig, Purdue University

Joyce Middleton, Frostburg State University

Richard J. Pettit, Mountain View College

Carolyn Streuly

To the loyal users of previous editions of my book: Your support has made this revision possible. You have inspired me with your dedication to finding the best ways to teach introductory financial accounting. Special thanks to the hundreds of students over the past 20 years who have inspired me to strive to be a better teacher and a better person. Thanks, too, for your specific suggestions for the book.

To my family and friends, including all of my colleagues at Rollins, thank you for all of the opportunities and support you have given me. I am grateful to a handful of special friends who, year after year, continue to go above and beyond anything I could expect from friends. You know who you are. Thank you.

Finally, to my son, thank you for the support and encouragement you have always given me. I continue to learn so much from you and the way you live your life. This book is definitely for you!

Jane L. Reimers
Professor, Crummer Graduate School of Business
Rollins College

1

Business: What's It All About?

LEARNING OBJECTIVES

When you are finished studying Chapter 1, you should be able to:

1. Describe what a business does and the various ways a business can be organized.

2. Classify business transactions as operating, investing, or financing activities.

3. Describe who uses accounting information and why accounting information is important to them.

4. Identify the elements of the four basic financial statements—the income statement, the statement of changes in shareholders' equity, the balance sheet, and the statement of cash flows, explain the purpose of each, and be able to use basic transaction analysis to prepare each statement.

5. Identify the elements of a real company's financial statements.

6. Describe the risks associated with being in business and the part that ethics plays in business.

ETHICS Matters

Ethical Decisions—As Easy as 1-2-3

When you are asked to do something you believe may be unethical, ask yourself the following questions: (1) Is it legal? (2) Will it harm anyone? (3) Would you mind reading about your decision in the morning newspaper? These are not ambiguous or theoretical questions. They are questions that should be part of everyone's decision-making process. An example follows of what can happen if you ignore them.

In 2009, Bernie Madoff pleaded guilty to 11 felony charges associated with a $50 billion Ponzi scheme that lasted for decades. In his own words, Madoff does a pretty good job of explaining what a Ponzi scheme involves:

> The essence of my scheme was that I represented to clients and prospective clients who wished to open investment advisory and individual trading accounts with me that I would invest their money in shares of common stock, options and other securities of large well-known corporations, and upon request, would return to them their profits and principal. Those representations were false because for many years up until I was arrested on December 11, 2008, I never invested those funds in the securities, as I had promised. Instead, those funds were deposited in a bank account at Chase Manhattan Bank. When clients wished to receive the profits they believed they had earned with me or to redeem their principal, I used the money in the Chase Manhattan Bank account that belonged to them or other clients to pay the requested funds. (Source: Document #09-Cr-213(DC) filed with the United States District Court Southern District of New York on March 12, 2009.)

Madoff's auditing firm, Friehling & Horowitz, CPAs, has been charged with failing to conduct meaningful, independent audits of Madoff's firm while falsely certifying that it had done so. As you will read later in this chapter, investors depend on auditors to provide an unbiased evaluation of a firm's financial position and performance. As in the big scandals of the early 2000s, such as Enron and WorldCom, people are asking why the auditors didn't find the problems.

Madoff's failure to address our initial three questions, combined with the auditor's failure to do a competent audit, resulted in thousands of people losing their life savings. Madoff's sentence of 150 years in prison will keep him in jail for the rest of his life. As of this writing, the case against the auditor has not been resolved. See if you can find out what happened.

Do you think accounting is important? Anyone who has a television or reads a newspaper is reminded almost every day of the importance of accounting. Now more than ever, it is crucial for people in business to understand basic accounting. In this chapter, you will start with a simple company to learn the basic ideas of how a business works and why the financial reporting for a business is so important to its success. As you learn about accounting, you will understand more and more about what has been happening in our economy and how it relates to accounting information. First, you must understand what a business is all about.

Purpose and Organization of a Business

Sara Gonzales loved to play basketball. She also wanted to start her own business. During years of playing on various teams organized by local recreation departments, she noticed that the teams did not have any identifying clothing—no matching outfits or T-shirts. She began her business by ordering T-shirts with a logo monogrammed on them, and the other teams in the area wanted matching T-shirts, too. Today, Sara runs a large Web-based T-shirt business that specializes in shirts for groups of any type. Her company, Team Shirts, has been growing every year in both sales and profit.

How does a business get started and, once started, how does it succeed? Generally, a business is formed to provide goods or services for the purpose of making a profit for its owner or owners. It begins by obtaining financial resources—and that means money. Team Shirts began as a business with $5,000 of Sara's own money and a $500 loan from her sister. The financial resources to start a business—called **capital**—come from the owners of the business (like Sara), who are investors, or from creditors (like Sara's sister), who are lenders.

Capital is the name for the resources used to start and run a business.

Why buy T-shirts from Team Shirts rather than from somewhere else? It's all about value. We order clothes from J.Crew because the company provides added value to us. Instead of going to the mall to buy our clothes, we may prefer the convenience of mail-order delivery. J.Crew's customers find value in this service. What all businesses have in common is that they provide their customers with something of value. A business may start from scratch and create something of value or it may simply add value to an existing product or service. For some customers, the value that J.Crew adds to the product may be its easy order and delivery procedures. For other customers, the added value may be in the specific styles available. Businesses create or add value to earn money for the owners.

A **for-profit firm** has the goal of making a profit for its owners.

An enterprise—another name for a business organization—with this goal is called a **for-profit firm**. In contrast, a firm that provides goods or services for the sole purpose of helping people instead of making a profit is called a **not-for-profit firm**. A not-for-profit firm is more likely to be called an organization or agency than a business. Even though it is called not-for-profit, this type of organization does not mind making a profit. The difference is that a not-for-profit organization uses any profit to provide more goods and services to the people it serves rather than distributing profits to its owners. Both for-profit organizations and not-for-profit organizations provide value. Throughout this book, we will be dealing primarily with for-profit organizations—businesses.

A **not-for-profit firm** has the goal of providing goods or services to its clients.

To be a viable business, Team Shirts needed to provide customers with something of value. Sara found a supplier to make shirts to order and then provided them to her customers.

What Is a Business All About?

A simple model of the firm is shown in Exhibit 1.1.

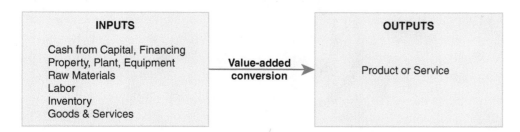

EXHIBIT 1.1

The Firm

A firm takes inputs, adds value, and provides the output to its customers.

The inputs in a firm include capital, equipment, inventory, supplies, and labor. The firm acquires goods and services and pays for them. The firm then takes these inputs and converts them into outputs by adding value. The outputs of a firm are its products or services. As the firm carries out these activities—acquiring inputs, converting them to outputs, and providing those outputs to customers—information about these activities is recorded in the company's information system. Both insiders (the owners and the firm's employees) and outsiders (the creditors, governmental agencies, and potential investors) use the information.

A business must successfully plan, control, and evaluate its activities. If it does these activities well, the business will survive. If it does them very well, it will make a profit. Profit is the difference between the revenue—the amount a business earns for the goods it sells or the services it provides—and the expenses of selling those goods or providing those services. When a company takes all of its revenue and subtracts all of the expenses of earning that revenue, the difference is called **net income**. This is a number and a concept that we will focus on throughout this book because of its importance to firms and to investors. The complexity of a company's planning, control, and evaluation processes depends on the type, size, and structure of the business. You will see this as we look at businesses in two ways: the nature of their operations and who owns them.

Net income equals all revenues minus all expenses for a specific period of time.

The Nature of Business Operations

The operation of a business depends on what the business has been formed to do. From that perspective, there are four types of businesses: service, merchandising, manufacturing, and financial services. Although most businesses can be classified as one of these four types, many large businesses are a combination of two or more.

A **service company** provides a service—it does something for you, rather than sells something to you. Services range from activities you cannot see, such as the advice provided by lawyers or tax consultants, to activities you can see, such as house cleaning or car washing. During the past two decades, our economy has been producing more services than goods. Google is an example of a service firm.

A **service company** does something for its customers.

A **merchandising company** buys goods, adds value to them, and then sells them with the added value. It does not make the goods, and it does not buy them to use. Instead, a merchandising business buys the goods for the purpose of adding its own particular value to them and, after adding value, sells them to another company or person.

A **merchandising company** sells a product to its customers.

There are two types of merchandising companies:

- A wholesale company buys goods, adds value, and sells them to other companies (business to business).
- A retail company buys goods, adds value, and sells them to customers who consume them, which is why you will see these customers referred to as "final consumers" (business to consumer). Target, shown in the photo on the following page, is an example of a retail company.

Both wholesale and retail merchandising companies add value to the goods they buy. Wholesale companies are often not familiar to us because we do not buy things from them. Typically, a wholesale firm sells to another business, like a company that sells computer chips to Dell or Apple. A retail firm, on the other hand, sells its products to the final consumer. However, as a result of the ability of firms to sell their products on the Internet, the line between wholesale and retail firms has become blurred. A decade ago you would have purchased this textbook from

Target is an example of a retail firm. It buys goods and sells them to the final consumer.

your school's bookstore—a retail business—and the bookstore would have purchased it from Pearson Education, operating in the role of a wholesale company. Now you can also buy your book directly from Pearson Education's Web site.

A **manufacturing company** makes the goods it sells.

A **manufacturing company** makes the products it sells. Manufacturing companies vary in size and complexity. Making clay pots and vases in a space no larger than a garage is a manufacturing business. Manufacturing giants such as Boeing and Lockheed Martin, owned by many thousands of people and employing hundreds of thousands of workers at all levels in enormous factories all over the world, are large and complex manufacturing businesses.

Financial services companies deal in services related to money.

Financial services companies do not make tangible products, and they do not sell products made by another company. They deal in services related to money. Banks are one kind of financial services company; they lend money to borrowers to pay for cars, houses, and furniture. Another type of financial services company is an insurance company, which provides some financial protection in the case of loss of life or property. Financial services firms, like Countrywide Mortgage and Merrill Lynch, have been at the center of the 2008 financial crisis.

Your Turn 1-1

1. What is the main purpose of a business?
2. Describe the four general types of businesses and what each does.

Ownership Structure of a Business

No matter what type of product or service it provides, a business must have an owner or owners. The government owns some businesses, but in the United States, an individual or a group of individuals owns most businesses. Business ownership generally takes one of three general forms: a sole proprietorship, a partnership, or a corporation.

A **sole proprietorship** is a company with a single owner.

SOLE PROPRIETORSHIPS. If a single person owns a business, like the clay pot maker in his garage, it is a **sole proprietorship**. A new business often starts as a sole proprietorship. In the course of running the business, a sole proprietorship accumulates financial information—such

(UNDERSTANDING →
Business

Starting A New Business: The Business Plan Includes Financial Statements

Have you ever considered starting your own business? According to the Small Business Administration (SBA*), small businesses—those with fewer than 100 employees—

- represent more than 99.7% of employer firms.
- employ half of all private-sector workers and 41% of workers in high-tech jobs.
- have provided 60%–80% of the net new jobs annually over the last decade.

The SBA was established by Congress in 1953 to assist small businesses. In addition to the many contributions SBA makes to ongoing businesses, the SBA provides information and guidance for starting a business. For example, before Sara started her T-shirt company, she found some terrific information on the SBA Web site, like the fact that she needed to start with a business plan. The SBA describes four sections to be included in the body of the business plan: the business description, marketing, finances, and management.

The business description is the foundation for the rest of the business plan. It should give the form of your business enterprise—a sole proprietorship, a partnership, or a

corporation. The business description should also describe the nature of your business—manufacturing, merchandising, or service. Then, more specific details should be explained— goals and objectives, operating procedures, location, personnel, marketing, licenses and insurance, and financing plans. Sara learned about many issues she needed to address before she could start her business, including state and local licensing requirements.

The section on finances should include a start-up budget and a detailed operating budget. The financial statements are prepared based on the budgets. The financial statements are a significant part of a business plan. Sara was lucky enough to learn about the financial statements in an accounting course she took in college. Fortunately, she still had the book on her shelf for reference.

A good business plan is essential for starting a successful company. For more information on the SBA and creating a business plan, visit the SBA Web site at www.sba.gov.

———
*Sources: U.S. Bureau of the Census; Advocacy-funded research. Data provided by the SBA.

as the cost of materials, equipment, rent, electricity, and income from sales—but is not required by law to make any of that financial information available to the public. That means the average person is not privy to this information. Naturally, the Department of Revenue in the states where the company operates will receive some of this information from the company's sales tax return.

A business in the form of a sole proprietorship is not separate from its owner in terms of responsibility and liability—the owner is personally responsible for all the decisions made for the business. For example, the income from the business is included as income on the owner's individual income tax return. The business does not have its own tax return.

Also, as a sole proprietor, you are responsible for your company's debts. Your company's bills are your bills; if there is not enough money in your company's "pockets" to pay its bills, then you must pay the bills from your pockets. Moreover, you own the company's assets, and your personal assets are the company's assets—even if those personal assets are the only way of paying your company's bills.

Even though the financial records of a business—the company's books—should always be kept separate from the owner's personal financial records, there is no separation of the sole proprietorship's books and its owner's books for tax and legal purposes. For example, your business checking account should be separate from your personal checking account, but the income you earn from your business and the income you earn from other sources must both be included on your individual, personal tax return.

You will see in Exhibit 1.2 on the following page that there are more sole proprietorships in the United States than any other form of business. Notice, however, that profits for sole proprietorships do not come close to the enormous profits earned by corporations.

PARTNERSHIPS. A business **partnership** is owned by two or more people, although it is similar to a sole proprietorship in the sense that the income both partners earn (or lose) from the business partnership is included on their own personal tax returns. When two or more people form a

A **partnership** is a company owned by two or more individuals.

EXHIBIT 1.2

Types of Firms and Their Profits

Although over two-thirds of U.S. firms are sole proprietorships, more than two-thirds of firm profits are made by corporations. Source: Internal Revenue Service Web site (www.irs.gov).

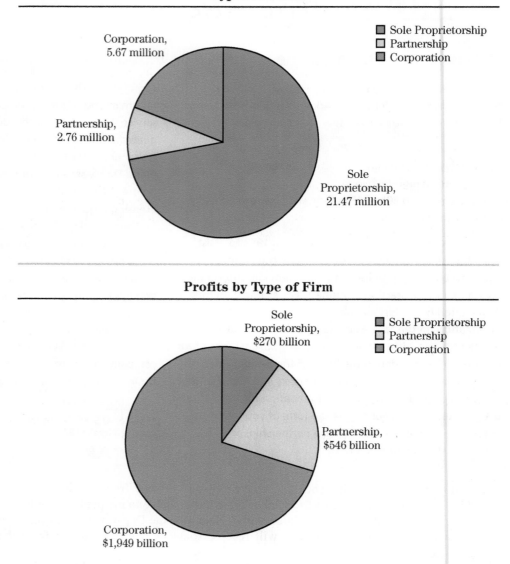

Types of Firms

- Sole Proprietorship
- Partnership
- Corporation

Corporation, 5.67 million

Partnership, 2.76 million

Sole Proprietorship, 21.47 million

Profits by Type of Firm

- Sole Proprietorship
- Partnership
- Corporation

Sole Proprietorship, $270 billion

Partnership, $546 billion

Corporation, $1,949 billion

business as partners, they usually hire an attorney to help them define the specific terms of their business relationship. Details regarding how much work each will do and how they will divide the profits from the business are specified in a document called a partnership agreement. Like a sole proprietorship, the owners—each of the partners—are responsible for everything the company does. For example, if the company is sued for violating an employee's civil rights, then the partners are legally liable. The company's assets are the partners' assets, and the company's debts are the partners' debts. Even so, as with a sole proprietorship, the financial records of a partnership should be separate from the partners' personal financial records.

CORPORATIONS. **A corporation** is legally separate and financially separate from its owners. Individual states control the rules for forming corporations within their boundaries. A company must have a corporate charter that describes the business, how the business plans to acquire financing, and how many owners it will be allowed to have. Ownership in a corporation is divided into units called **shares of common stock**, each representing ownership in a fraction of the corporation. An owner of shares of stock in a corporation is called a **stockholder** or a **shareholder**. Most corporations have many shareholders, although there is no minimum number of owners required. A corporation whose shares of stock are owned by a very small number of people is called a closely held corporation.

As legal entities, corporations may enter into contracts just like individuals. A corporation pays taxes on its earnings. A corporation's owners do not include the corporation's income in

A **corporation** is a special legal form for a business in which the business is a legal entity separate from the owners. A corporation may have a single owner or a large number of owners.

Shares of common stock are the units of ownership in a corporation.

Stockholders or **shareholders** are the owners of the corporation.

their personal tax returns—unlike the owner of a sole proprietorship or the partners in a partnership. Each individual corporation owner does not have individual legal responsibility for the corporation's actions, as is true for the owners of a sole proprietorship or partnership. For example, a shareholder cannot be sued for the illegal actions of the corporation. The managers are held responsible for the actions of the corporation, and only the corporation's assets are at risk.

Dell Inc. is one of America's best-known corporations. Dell Inc. was founded in 1984 by Michael Dell, currently the computer industry's longest-tenured chief executive officer, on this simple concept: By selling computers directly to customers, Dell Inc. could get a clear picture of its customers' needs and then efficiently provide the most effective products to meet those needs. The company has offered new shares of stock to anyone who is able and willing to invest in the company by making them available for sale on a stock exchange. A **stock exchange** is a marketplace for buying and selling shares of a publicly-traded corporation.

A **stock exchange** is a marketplace where buyers and sellers exchange their shares of stock. Buying and selling shares of stock can also be done on the Internet.

After the shares are issued—sold for the first time to the public—investors who want to become owners of a corporation may purchase the shares from people who want to sell the same shares. The buyers and sellers get together, usually through a stockbroker, by using a stock exchange. Stockbrokers represent people who want to buy shares and the people who want to sell shares of a corporation. Stockbrokers work for firms like Charles Schwab. There are several stock exchanges—known collectively as the **stock market**—in the United States; the New York Stock Exchange is the largest. If you wanted to be one of the owners of Dell Inc., you could purchase shares by contacting a stockbroker.

The **stock market** is the name for a collection of stock exchanges. It is a term generally used to designate any place where stock is bought and sold.

Another way to buy or sell shares of stock—also known as *trading*—is to use the Internet. Many companies now provide a way for investors to buy and sell stock without a stockbroker. As Internet usage continues to grow at an incredible pace, more and more people are taking advantage of electronic trading in shares of stock.

Regulation Shareholders usually hire people who are not owners of the corporation to manage the business of the corporation. This separation of ownership and management can create problems. For example, there may be a large number of owners, and they may be far away from the location of the business. How can the owners be sure that the managers are running the corporation the way the owners want it to be run? How do the owners monitor the managers to be sure they are not taking advantage of the power of being a manager of a large company, for example, buying expensive items like country club memberships and luxury cars for the business?

To protect the owners with respect to issues like these, the government created the **Securities and Exchange Commission (SEC)** to monitor the activities and financial reporting of corporations that sell shares of ownership on the stock exchanges. The SEC sets the rules for stock exchanges and for the financial reporting of publicly-traded corporations for the entire United States. The degree of regulation for corporations depends on the size and nature of the business. A business that provides an essential product or service, such as electric power generating companies, has more rules to follow than a business that provides something not essential, but discretionary, such as toys. Large companies have more rules than smaller companies because large companies provide more opportunities for managers to take advantage of the owners. Due to the financial crisis that began in 2008, financial firms like banks and mortgage companies will be subject to many new regulations in the future.

The **Securities and Exchange Commission (SEC)** is the governmental agency that monitors the stock market and the financial reporting of the firms that trade in the market.

Advantages of a Corporation Advantages of the corporate structure of a business organization include the following:

- Investors can diversify their financial risk. Being able to buy a small share in a variety of corporations means that persons are able to balance the risks they are taking as business owners. For example, an investor may own shares in a soft drink company and also own shares in a coffee company. If coffee companies have a bad year due to a shortage of coffee beans, people will be likely to buy more soft drinks. By owning a little of each type of company, an investor reduces overall risk.
- Owners have limited liability. Individual owners risk only the amount of money they have invested in the company, that is the amount they paid for the shares of stock. If the corporation is found legally responsible for injury to an employee or customer, or if the business fails, only the corporation's assets are at risk—not the owner's personal property. (In contrast, there is no limit to the legal liability of a sole proprietor or a partner. Both the assets of the business and the personal assets of the owner or owners are at risk.)

Disadvantages of a Corporation   Disadvantages of the corporate structure of a business organization include the following:

- Separation of management and ownership creates a difference in knowledge about the operations of the business. Suppose you own 100 shares of Dell Inc. stock. The managers of Dell will know many details of the business that you do not know. For example, the managers are aware of all possible investment options for the company's extra cash. They may select the option that minimizes clerical work, whereas an owner might prefer an option that involves more work but would secure a higher return.

  There are literally thousands of such details that owners do not know, many of which they do not even want to know. However, the owners want some assurance that managers are acting in the best interests of the shareholders. Owners need information about how well the business is doing to assess how the actions and decisions of the managers are affecting the business. The owners need some assurance that managers are providing complete and accurate information about the business. Both the individual states and the SEC at the federal level set rules for the financial reporting of corporations. A corporation's type of business and its size determine how extensive its reporting requirements are. We will come back to this subject many times throughout our discussions of financial accounting, especially given the current economic environment and the new reporting regulations that are certain to be developed in the next few years.

Dividends are the earnings of a corporation distributed to the owners of the corporation.

- Corporate income is taxed twice. Unlike a sole proprietorship or partnership, a corporation pays income taxes on its net income. Then, net income (or at least a part of it) may be divided by the number of shareholders of the corporation and distributed among shareholders as **dividends**. The shareholders must include the dividend income on their personal tax returns. This amounts to double taxation on the same income. The income of the corporation—which is owned by shareholders—is taxed as corporation income, and then the amount passed on to owners as dividend income is again taxed as personal income. (Current tax laws do allow some special treatment for dividend income to the shareholder, so this disadvantage can be reduced by a change in the tax law.)

LIMITED LIABILITY PARTNERSHIPS (LLP) AND CORPORATIONS (LLC). In the past 10 years, new business forms with some characteristics of a partnership and some characteristics of a corporation have become commonplace. Both LLPs and LLCs have the tax advantages of a partnership and the legal liability advantages of a corporation.

An LLP is a business form mostly of interest to partners in professions such as law, medicine, and accounting. An LLP's owners—who are the partners—are not personally liable for the malpractice of the other partners. They are personally liable for many types of obligations owed to the LLP's creditors, lenders, and landlords. Owners of an LLP report their share of profit or loss on their personal tax returns. The LLP form of business organization is not available in all states, and it is often limited to a short list of professions—usually attorneys and accountants. You will notice that the four largest international accounting firms have all taken this organizational form. The letters LLP will appear after the firm's name.

An LLC is a corporation that has characteristics of a partnership. It has the advantage of limited liability like a regular corporation with the tax advantage of a partnership. It generally requires less paperwork and documentation than a regular corporation.

Your Turn 1-2

1. What are the three major forms of business ownership?
2. From the owners' point of view, what are the advantages and disadvantages of each form of ownership?

L.O.2
Classify business transactions as operating, investing, or financing activities.

Business Activities and the Flow of Goods and Services

A person who takes the risk of starting a business is often called an *entrepreneur*. Our entrepreneur, Sara, started a T-shirt business. Exhibit 1.3 shows the events for Team Shirts that followed. Identifying those events and analyzing the transactions are the first steps in understanding how a business works.

EXHIBIT 1.3

How a Business Works

These business transactions show Team Shirts' first month of business.

| Sara **contributes** $5,000 of her own money to start her business. | Team Shirts **borrows** $500 from Sara's sister to help finance the business. | Team Shirts **purchases** 100 T-shirts from a T-shirt maker. | Team Shirts decides to **advertise** the new business. | Team Shirts **sells** 90 T-shirts. | Team Shirts **repays** the loan **plus interest** to Sara's sister. |

We can classify each step in the process of developing a business in terms of exchanges—who gets what and who gives what in return. One of the important functions of accounting is to provide information about these economic exchanges, also known as business transactions. In accounting, we often classify transactions as operating activities, investing activities, or financing activities. Operating activities are transactions related to the general operations of a firm—what the firm is in business to do. Investing activities are transactions related to buying and selling items that the firm will use for longer than a year. Financing activities are those that deal with how a business gets its funding—how it obtains the capital needed to finance the business.

The first exchange starts the business—Sara invests her own $5,000 in the business. From the perspective of the business, this is called a contribution. It is often called **contributed capital**. As with all transactions, we look at this from the point of view of the business entity. This transaction is the exchange of cash for ownership in the business. Because this transaction deals with the way Team Shirts is financed, it is classified as a financing transaction.

You may need to think about it to see the *give* part of this exchange—it is the business giving ownership to Sara. Because Sara has chosen to organize her business firm as a corporation, this share of ownership is called stock. For a sole proprietorship or a partnership, the ownership has no special name. Sara has chosen the corporate form of organization because of the limited legal liability of a corporation. The *get* part of the exchange is the business getting the $5,000 cash. Because Sara is the only shareholder, she owns 100% of the stock.

The second transaction is between Team Shirts and Sara's sister. The business borrows $500 from Sara's sister. Team Shirts gets an economic resource—cash—and in exchange Team Shirts gives an I-owe-you (IOU). From the perspective of Team Shirts, this transaction involves a cash receipt. Borrowing money to finance a business is the get side of the exchange. The give side is the IOU to Sara's sister. Technically, it is not really the give side until Sara repays the loan with cash. The IOU is useful for describing the timing difference between the time of the get and give sides of the exchange. We will see a lot of examples of this type of timing difference in accounting for business events. Again, this transaction is a financing activity.

The next transaction is the company's purchase of 100 T-shirts with unique logos on them. The get part of the exchange is when Team Shirts gets the shirts for the inventory. The give part of the exchange is when Team Shirts gives cash to the T-shirt manufacturer. Remember, the exchange is seen through the eyes of Team Shirts. The transaction would look different if we took the perspective of the T-shirt manufacturer. In business problems, we take one point of view throughout a problem or an analysis. This transaction is an operating activity.

The next transaction is the acquisition of a service. The economic resources exchanged in this transaction are advertising and cash. The get part is the acquisition or purchase of advertising brochures. The give part is a cash disbursement transaction. Again, this is an operating activity.

Team Shirts now sells the T-shirts, exchanging T-shirts for cash. Once again, the activity is an operating activity, precisely what Team Shirts is in business to do—sell T-shirts.

Finally, Team Shirts repays the $500 loan from Sara's sister plus interest. The company gives the economic resource of cash (amount of the loan, called the **principal**, plus **interest**, a cost of borrowing the money) to Sara's sister. Recall that the actual get part of this exchange occurred near the beginning of our story. The second transaction was when Team Shirts took the cash, as a loan, from Sara's sister. The IOU was a sort of marker, indicating that there would be a timing difference in the get and give parts of this transaction. Repayment of the principal of a loan is a financing activity. Payment of interest, on the other hand, is considered an operating activity.

Contributed capital is an owner's investment in a company.

The **principal** of a loan is the amount of money borrowed.

The **interest** is the cost of borrowing money—using someone else's money.

Your Turn 1-3

1. What are the two sources of financing for a business, both used by Team Shirts?
2. What do you call the cost of using someone else's money?

L.O.3
Describe who uses accounting information and why accounting information is important to them.

Revenue is the amount the company has earned from providing goods or services to customers.

Expenses are the costs incurred to generate revenue.

Information Needs for Decision Making in Business

To start a new business, Sara had many decisions to make. First, how would she finance it? What organizational form should it take? How many T-shirts should she buy? From whom should she buy them? How much should she pay for advertising? How much should she charge for the shirts?

After the first complete operating cycle, shown in Exhibit 1.4—beginning with cash, converting cash to inventory, selling the inventory, and turning inventory sales back into cash—Sara has more decisions to make. Should she buy T-shirts and do the whole thing again? If so, should she buy more T-shirts than she bought the first time and from the same vendor? To make these decisions, Sara must have information. The kind of information usually provided by accountants will provide the basis for getting a good picture of the performance of her business.

- What was the **revenue** from sales during the accounting period? An accounting period is any length of time that a company uses to evaluate its operating performance. It can be a month, a quarter, or a year.
- What **expenses** were incurred so those sales could be made?
- What was net income—the difference between revenues and expenses?
- What goods does Team Shirts have left at the end of the period?
- Should Sara increase or lower the price of the T-shirts she sells?

In addition to this kind of financial information, there is other information that can help Sara make decisions about her business. For example, Sara would want information on the reliability of different vendors and the quality of their merchandise to decide which vendor to use next

EXHIBIT 1.4

The Operating Cycle

The operating cycle shows how a firm starts with cash and, after providing goods to its customers, ends up with more cash.

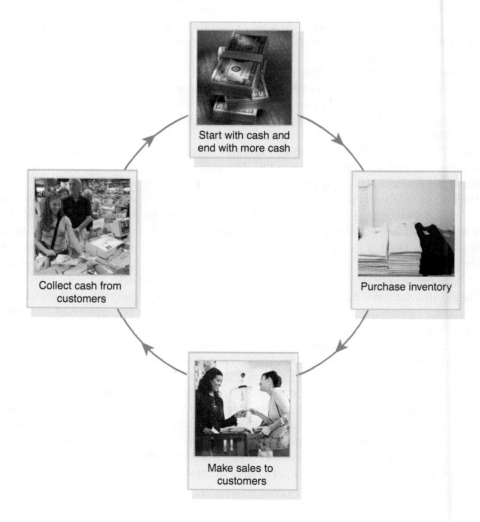

Start with cash and end with more cash

Purchase inventory

Make sales to customers

Collect cash from customers

Before the advances in computer technology that have enabled us to collect, organize, and report huge quantities of information, a company had only the basic financial information to help make its business decisions. Today, financial information is just a part of a firm's information system.

A modern supermarket is a great example of a business that collects a tremendous amount of information. With a simple, swift swipe of the grocery item bar code past the checkout scanner, the store information system collects product data, recording and tracking information about vendors, product shelf life, customer preferences and buying habits, and the typical financial information such as price and quantity of each item sold. As we look at business processes and the information needed to run a business, we will pay attention to the information reflected in the basic financial statements—the income statement, the balance sheet, the statement of changes in shareholders' equity, and the statement of cash flows. You will learn more about each of these statements soon.

Your Turn 1-4

1. What are revenues and expenses?
2. What are the four basic financial statements?

Who Needs Information about Transactions of the Business?

No part of any business can operate without information. The functions of the management of a company are to plan, to control, and to evaluate the operation of the business. To perform these functions effectively, management must have information about what the business has done, about what it is currently doing, and about where it looks like it is going or should be going. Traditionally, the accounting information system has provided only very general data about the past transactions of a business firm. A business firm used to keep at least two sets of records, each for specific purposes: one set for financial reporting and one set for internal decision making. Now, with modern computers and software that can organize information in a variety of ways with a few simple commands, one information system can accumulate and organize all data of a company. The managers of each business area—usually referred to as a department—can obtain and use whatever information is relevant to the decisions they make. Accountants, too, can obtain the information they need for preparing the basic financial statements.

SETTING GUIDELINES. The financial statements are based on a set of guidelines called **generally accepted accounting principles (GAAP)**. These guidelines are not exact rules. As you learn more about accounting, you will see that the amounts on the financial statements are not exact. To make the financial statements useful, we need to understand the guidelines and the choices used to construct them. Who sets the guidelines for financial reporting? As shown in Exhibit 1.5 on the following page, at the top of the authority chain is the Securities and Exchange Commission.

In the 1930s, Congress established the SEC to set the rules for corporations that trade on the public stock exchanges. The SEC has delegated much of the responsibility for setting financial standards to an independent group called the **Financial Accounting Standards Board (FASB)**. This is a group of professional business people, accountants, and accounting scholars who have the responsibility of setting current accounting standards. Accounting standards dictate the way business events are reported, so it makes sense that businesses are very interested in what the FASB does. The newest player in the rule-setting game is a group called the **Public Company Accounting Oversight Board (PCAOB)**. Mandated by the Sarbanes-Oxley Act in 2002, this independent board was created to oversee the auditing profession and public company audits.

INTERNATIONAL FINANCIAL REPORTING STANDARDS. Although U.S. GAAP are currently the set of standards used by U.S. firms, there is another widely used set of accounting standards called the **International Financial Reporting Standards (IFRS)**. These standards, similar in many ways to GAAP, are used in many other places around the world. They are set by a group called the **International Accounting Standards Board (IASB)**, similar to the FASB. As a matter of fact, there is a member of FASB who also sits on the IASB. In 2008, the SEC published a "roadmap to IFRS" that details how and when U.S. GAAP should converge with IFRS so that one global set of standards is used by all major economies. The SEC plan calls for implementation of IFRS in the United States by 2014. Currently, there is some resistance and a great deal of uncertainty regarding this change. Throughout this book, we will look at some of the ways GAAP and IFRS differ and the implications for firms' financial statements. This is an ongoing issue, so you should look for developments in the popular business press.

Generally accepted accounting principles (GAAP) are the guidelines for financial reporting.

The **Financial Accounting Standards Board (FASB)** is the group that sets accounting standards. It gets its authority from the SEC.

The **Public Company Accounting Oversight Board (PCAOB)** is a group formed to oversee the auditing profession and the audits of public companies. Its creation was mandated by the Sarbanes-Oxley Act of 2002.

The **International Financial Reporting Standards (IFRS)** are international guidelines for financial reporting, used in many places around the world.

The **International Accounting Standards Board (IASB)** is the group that sets international financial reporting standards.

Who Sets the Guidelines for Financial Reporting?

The U.S. Congress established the Securities and Exchange Commission (SEC) in 1934. Auditing standards are set by the Public Company Accounting Oversight Board (PCAOB), and accounting standards (GAAP) are set by the Financial Accounting Standards Board (FASB).

Securities and Exchange Commission (SEC)

Public Company Accounting Oversight Board (PCAOB)

In response to the 2001–2002 discovery of accounting scandals, the SEC created the PCAOB to oversee the auditing profession and the audit of public companies.

Financial Accounting Standards Board (FASB)

The SEC has delegated much of the standards-setting responsibility to the FASB. The SEC retains and sometimes exercises the right to set accounting standards.

In many industries, there are regulatory agencies that require specific information from companies, particularly corporations. For example, the SEC requires corporations that trade on the stock exchanges to file many different kinds of reports about the company's transactions. We will come back to this topic near the end of the chapter when we turn our attention to real company financial statements.

For all businesses, payroll taxes and sales taxes must be reported and paid to state revenue agencies. The **Internal Revenue Service (IRS)** requires information from businesses concerning income and expenses, even if the income from the business flows through to the owners as it does for sole proprietorships and partnerships.

The **Internal Revenue Service (IRS)** is the federal agency responsible for federal income tax collection.

When a company wants to borrow money, creditors—the people and firms who lend money—require information about the company before they will lend money. Banks want to be sure that the loans they make will be repaid. The creditworthiness—a term indicating that a borrower has in the past made loan payments when due (or failed to make them when due)—of a business must be supported with information about the business. This information is usually very specific and very detailed.

OTHER USERS OF ACCOUNTING INFORMATION. Who else needs information about the business? Potential investors are information consumers. Suppose Sara wanted to find additional owners for her T-shirt business. That means she would be looking for someone who wanted to invest money in her T-shirt business in return for a portion of ownership in the company. A potential owner would want some reliable information about the business before making a financial investment. Publicly-traded corporations—whose shares are traded on the stock exchanges— invite anyone willing and financially able to become an owner by offering for sale shares of stock in the corporation. Buying the stock of a corporation is investing in that corporation. Investors want information about a company before they will buy that company's stock. The SEC requires that the information provided by companies whose stock is publicly traded be accurate and reliable. That means the information in their financial statements must be audited. Audited information means it has been examined by professional accountants, called **certified public accountants (CPAs)**. We will talk more about that when we turn our attention to real company financial statements.

Finally, current and potential vendors, customers, and employees also need useful information about the company. They need to evaluate a company's financial condition to make decisions about working for, or doing business with, the company.

Accounting Information: A Part of the Firm's Information System

Have you ever filed an address change with a company only to find later that one department uses your new address, while another department of that same company continues to use your old address? Even with such common data as customer names and addresses, the information is often gathered and maintained in several different places within the same organization. As computers and databases become more common, central data information systems are replacing departmental systems and eliminating their inefficiencies.

Because accountants have traditionally been the recorders and maintainers of financial information, it makes sense that they have expanded their role as the keepers of business information systems to include more than financial information. The cost of obtaining and storing business information has decreased rapidly in the past few years. The financial accounting information a company reports is now just a part of the total available business information. For example, the information a firm uses to file its tax return is not the same information that shareholders need. People who know very little about accounting often think that accounting means taxes. This is not true. Tax accounting and financial accounting are very different. The goal of reporting to the IRS is usually to minimize the amount of taxes owed (within the law), and the goal of financial reporting is to provide useful information to the shareholders and other external parties (not including the IRS) to make investment and credit decisions. Financial accounting information is provided in four basic financial statements and supporting notes.

Generally, accounting is divided into two major areas: financial accounting and managerial accounting. Financial accounting deals with the financial reporting primarily for those outside the firm, like creditors and shareholders. Managerial accounting, on the other hand, deals with information needs and uses inside the firm. Managerial accounting is addressed in another course. In this textbook, we will be studying financial accounting.

Overview of the Financial Statements

There are four financial statements a company uses to report its financial condition at a point in time and operations for a period of time.

1. Balance sheet
2. Income statement
3. Statement of changes in shareholders' equity
4. Statement of cash flows

A company's set of financial statements includes these four basic statements as well as an important section called **notes to the financial statements**. These notes, sometimes referred to as *footnotes*, are an integral part of the set of financial statements. The notes describe the company's major accounting policies and provide other disclosures to help external users better understand the financial statements. As you learn about the four statements, remember that you will be able to find additional information about each in the notes.

In this chapter, we will look at each financial statement briefly. Later chapters will go into each in detail.

Balance Sheet

A **balance sheet** describes the financial situation of a company at a specific point in time. It is a snapshot that captures the items of value the business possesses at a particular moment and how the company has financed them. A balance sheet has three parts:

• Assets
• Liabilities
• Shareholders' equity

A **certified public accountant (CPA)** is someone who has met specific education and exam requirements set up by individual states to make sure that only individuals with the appropriate qualifications can perform audits. To sign an audit report, an accountant must be a CPA.

L.O.4
Identify the elements of the four basic financial statements—the income statement, the statement of changes in shareholders' equity, the balance sheet, and the statement of cash flows, explain the purpose each, and be able to use basic transaction analysis to prepare each statement.

Notes to the financial statements are information provided with the four basic statements that describe the company's major accounting policies and provide other disclosures to help external users better understand the financial statements.

The **balance sheet** shows a summary of each element of the accounting equation: assets, liabilities, and shareholders' equity.

Assets—economic resources owned or controlled by the business.

Liabilities—obligations of the business; amounts owed to creditors.

Shareholders' equity—the owners' claims to the assets of the company. There are two types: contributed capital and retained earnings.

Retained earnings is the total of all net income amounts minus all dividends paid in the life of the company. It is descriptively named—it is the earnings that have been kept (retained) in the company. The amount of retained earnings represents the part of the owner's claims that the company has earned (i.e., not contributed). Retained earnings is **not** the same as cash.

Assets are economic resources owned or controlled by a business. They provide future benefits to the firm. Cash and equipment are common assets. When a business has an asset, someone has the rights to, that is, a claim to, that asset. There is a claim on every asset in a business. There are two groups who might have claims to a company's assets—creditors and owners.

The claims of creditors are called liabilities. **Liabilities** are amounts the business owes to others outside the business—those who have loaned money to the company and have not yet been fully repaid. For example, the amount of a loan—like your car loan—is a liability.

The claims of the owners are called **shareholders' equity**. Stockholders' equity and owners' equity are other names for the claims of the owners. Shareholders' equity is also called net assets because it is the amount left over after the amount of the liabilities is subtracted from the amount of the assets. Another way to say this is that liabilities are netted out of assets.

There are two ways for the owners to increase their claims to the assets of the business. One is by making contributions, and the other is by earning a net income. When the business is successful, the equity that results from doing business and is kept in the company is called **retained earnings**. We will see the difference between contributed capital and retained earnings more clearly when we go through the first month of business for Team Shirts.

Together, assets, liabilities, and shareholders' equity make up the balance sheet, one of the four basic financial statements. The second equation below is called the accounting equation, and it is the basis for the balance sheet:

$$\text{Assets} = \overbrace{\hspace{3cm}\text{Claims}\hspace{3cm}}$$
$$\text{Assets} = \text{Liabilities} + \text{Shareholders' equity}$$

Each transaction that takes place in a business can be recorded in the accounting equation. In other words, every transaction changes the balance sheet; but the balance sheet must stay in balance. Look at the transactions for Team Shirts for January and see how each one changes the accounting equation.

Date	Transaction
January 1	Sara contributes $5,000 of her own money to start the business in exchange for common stock.
January 1	Team Shirts borrows $500 from Sara's sister for the business.
January 5	Team Shirts buys 100 T-shirts for inventory for $400 cash.
January 10	Team Shirts pays a public relations firm $50 cash for advertising brochures.
January 20	Team Shirts sells 90 of the T-shirts in inventory for $10 each (cash).
January 30	Team Shirts repays Sara's sister the $500 plus $5 interest.
January 31	Team Shirts declares and pays a $100 dividend.

Before the first transaction, there are no assets, no liabilities, and no shareholders' equity. So the accounting equation is as follows:

Assets	=	Liabilities	+	Shareholders' equity
0		0		0

Sara starts her company as a corporation. That means the owner's equity will be called shareholder's equity (note the singular form because there is only one owner), and her initial contribution will be classified as common stock. We will discuss the details of shareholder's equity in Chapter 8. This is how the first transaction affects the accounting equation:

Assets	=	Liabilities	+	Shareholder's equity
$5,000 cash		0		$5,000 common stock

Also on January 1, Team Shirts borrows $500. This is how the second transaction affects the accounting equation:

Assets	=	Liabilities	+	Shareholder's equity
$500 cash		$500 notes payable		0

A balance sheet can be prepared at any point in time to show the assets, liabilities, and shareholder's equity for the company. If Team Shirts prepared a balance sheet on January 2, 2010, these two transactions would be reflected in the amounts on the statement. Exhibit 1.6 shows the balance sheet at that time. With every subsequent transaction the balance sheet will change.

Team Shirts
Balance Sheet
At January 2, 2010

Assets		Liabilities and Shareholder's Equity	
Cash	$5,500	Note payable	$ 500
		Common stock	5,000
Total assets	$5,500	Total liabilities and shareholder's equity	$5,500

There are several characteristics of the balance sheet that you should notice in Exhibit 1.6. First, the heading on every financial statement specifies three things:

- The name of the company
- The name of the financial statement
- The date or time period covered by the statement

The date on the balance sheet is one specific date. If the business year for Team Shirts, also known as its **fiscal year**, is from January 1 to December 31, the balance sheet at the beginning of the first year of business is empty. Until there is a transaction, there are no assets, no liabilities, and no shareholder's equity.

The balance sheet in Exhibit 1.6 for Team Shirts is dated January 2, 2010. Team Shirts has been in business for only two days. Even though a business would be unlikely to prepare a balance sheet just two days after starting the business, this is what the balance sheet for Team Shirts would look like on January 2, 2010. The balance sheet shows the financial condition—assets, liabilities, and shareholder's equity—at the close of business on January 2, 2010. At this time, Team Shirts had received $5,000 from the owner, Sara, and had borrowed $500 from Sara's sister. The total cash—$5,500—is shown as an asset, and the liability of $500 plus the shareholder's equity of $5,000 together show who has claim to the company's assets.

Because the balance sheet gives the financial position of a company at a specific point in time, a new, updated balance sheet could be produced after every transaction. However, no company would want that much information! When a company presents its revenues and expenses for an accounting period, the information makes up the income statement. The company must show the balance sheet at the beginning of that period and the balance sheet at the end of that period. Those two balance sheets are called **comparative balance sheets**. For Team Shirts, the first balance sheet for the fiscal year is empty. That is, at the beginning of the day on January 1, 2010, the accounting equation was 0 = 0 + 0. Before we look at the balance sheet at January 31, 2010, we need to see the income statement for the month of January. We need the information on the income statement to see what happened during the time between the two balance sheets.

A **fiscal year** is a year in the life of a business. It may or may not coincide with the calendar year.

Comparative balance sheets are the balance sheets from consecutive fiscal years for a single company. The ending balance sheet for one fiscal year is the beginning balance sheet for the next fiscal year.

---

1. What are the two parts of shareholders' equity?
2. What is a fiscal year?

Your Turn 1-5

Before we prepare an income statement for January for Team Shirts or a balance sheet at January 31, 2010, we will look at each transaction that took place in January and see how each affects the accounting equation. This analysis is shown in Exhibit 1.7 on the following page.

EXHIBIT 1.7

Accounting Equation Worksheet for Team Shirts for January

All of a firm's transactions can be shown in the accounting equation worksheet. The income statement is made up of the transactions in the red box—everything that is in the retained earnings column EXCEPT dividends. The income statement transactions (revenues and expenses) are then condensed into one number (net income), which becomes part of the statement of changes in shareholder's equity, indicated by the yellow box. Then, the information from the statement of changes in shareholder's equity is summarized as part of the balance sheet, shown in blue. All of the transactions have directly or indirectly affected the balance sheet. The balance sheet reports the condensed and summarized information from the transactions, indicated by the amounts in the last row (balances at 1/31/2010). The fourth statement, the statement of cash flows, indicated by the green box, shows how the company got its cash and how it spent its cash during the accounting period.

Date	Transaction	Assets			= Liabilities		+	Shareholder's Equity	
								Contributed Capital	Retained Earnings
		Cash	All other assets	(Account)	All liabilities	(Account)		Common stock	(Account)
1/1/2010	Company receives $5,000 contribution from Sara in exchange for common stock.	$5,000						$5,000	
1/1/2010	Company borrows $500 from Sara's sister.	500			500	Notes payable			
1/5/2010	Company buys 100 shirts for inventory for $4 each.	(400)	400	Inventory					
1/10/2010	Company purchases advertising for $50 cash.	(50)							(50) Advertising expense
1/20/2010	Company sells 90 shirts for $10 each, cash. (Inventory goes down.)	900	(360)	Inventory					900 Sales revenue (360) Cost of goods sold
1/30/2010	Company pays off $500 loan plus $5 interest.	(505)			(500)	Notes payable			(5) Interest expense
1/31/2010	Company declares and pays $100 dividend.	(100)							(100) Dividends
Balances 1/31/2010		**$5,345**	**+ $ 40**		**= 0**		**+**	**$5,000**	**+ $385**

━ Income statement   ━ Statement of changes in shareholder's equity   ━ Balance sheet   ━ Statement of cash flows

When a business is started, it begins with an empty balance sheet. For Team Shirts, there are no assets, and therefore no claims at the start of business on January 1, 2010. The first two transactions that started the business, Sara's contribution of $5,000 and the loan from Sara's sister for $500, occurred on January 1, 2010. First, Sara's contribution increases assets by $5,000 and shareholder's equity by $5,000, because the owner, Sara, has claim to the new asset. Then, the loan increases assets by $500 and liabilities by $500. The company receives an asset (cash) and a creditor (Sara's sister) has claim to it. Following these two beginning transactions, the operations of the business begin. Each transaction that takes place during the month is shown as it affects the balance sheet. Study each transaction in Exhibit 1.7 as you read the following descriptions:

- On January 5, cash is decreased by $400 and inventory is increased by $400. This is called an asset exchange, because the company is simply exchanging one asset (cash) for another asset (inventory). Notice the entire effect of this exchange on the accounting equation is on one side of the equation. That is perfectly acceptable. Also notice an asset exchange has no effect on shareholder's equity. Sara still has claim to the same dollar amount of assets.

- On January 10, Sara pays $50 for advertising brochures. This is a cost Team Shirts has incurred to generate revenue. Assets are decreased and retained earnings, a component of shareholder's equity, is decreased. Why is retained earnings decreased? Because when assets are decreased by $50, someone's claim must be reduced. In this case, the shareholder's claims are reduced when assets are decreased. Retained earnings is the part of shareholder's equity that reflects the amount of equity the business has earned. (Throughout this book, as you study the transactions that take place in a business, you will see that all revenues increase retained earnings and all expenses decrease retained earnings.)
- On January 20, Team Shirts sells 90 T-shirts for $10 each. This sale increases assets (cash) by $900. Who has claim to this asset? The shareholder has this claim. Revenues increase retained earnings. At the time of the sale, an asset is reduced. The company no longer has 90 of the original 100 T-shirts in the inventory. Because each shirt costs $4 (and we recorded the T-shirts at their original cost), the firm now must reduce the asset inventory by $360. That reduction in assets is an expense and so shareholder's claims—via retained earnings—are reduced by the amount of that expense.
- On January 30, Team Shirts pays off the $500 loan with $5 interest. The repayment of the $500 principal reduces cash and eliminates the obligation that had been recorded as a liability. In other words, that liability is settled. The $500 reduction in assets is balanced in the accounting equation with a $500 reduction in the claims of creditors. However, the interest represents the cost of borrowing money. For a business, that is called interest expense. Like all expenses, it reduces the shareholder's claims by reducing retained earnings.
- On January 31, Team Shirts pays a $100 dividend. A dividend is a distribution paid to the shareholders of a corporation. That reduction in cash reduces the shareholder's claims to the assets of the firm, shown by the decrease in retained earnings. The $100, after it is distributed, is now part of Sara's personal financial assets, which are entirely separate from the business.

Using the accounting equation to keep track of the transactions of a business is a useful way to see how the financial statements are put together. Exhibit 1.8 shows how the statements are related to the basic accounting equation.

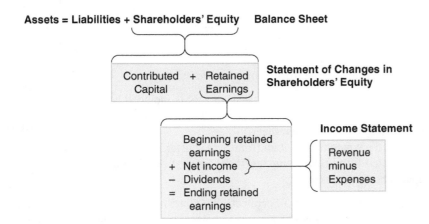

EXHIBIT 1.8

The Accounting Equation
This shows how the accounting equation forms the foundation of the financial statements.

The actual way a company keeps track of its financial transactions and its records—commonly called its **books**—can vary from a simple manual record-keeping system to a complex computerized system. No matter how a company keeps its records, the financial statements will look the same. The accounting equation is the basis for accumulating accounting information and communicating that information to decision makers. A company starts the year with a balance sheet (empty only at the start of the business firm), engages in business transactions during the year, and ends the year with a new, updated balance sheet. After a year of operations, the first statement a firm prepares is the income statement.

The **books** are a company's accounting records.

Income Statement

The most well-known financial statement is the **income statement**, also known as the statement of earnings, the statement of operations, or the profit and loss statement (P&L). The income statement is a summary of all the revenues (from sales or services) a company earns minus all the

The **income statement** shows all revenues minus all expenses for an accounting period—a month, a quarter, or a year.

expenses (costs incurred in the earning process) associated with earning that revenue. It describes the performance of a company during a specific period, which is called a fiscal period. Most often, the term fiscal period is used to describe the business year, which may or may not coincide with the calendar year. A fiscal year (not physical year) for a company may, for example, begin on July 1. That means the fiscal year of the business runs from July 1 of one year to June 30 of the next calendar year. Sometimes a company will end a fiscal year at a specific point in time that may result in slightly different dates for its year end from year to year. For example, Dell Inc. defines its fiscal year as the 52- or 53-week period ending on the Sunday nearest January 31.

Recall that the balance sheet gives the amount of assets, the amount of liabilities, and the amount of shareholders' equity of a business at a specific date. However, the first statement a firm prepares after completing an accounting period is the income statement. The income statement describes the operating performance of a company during a period. Look at the income statement for Team Shirts in Exhibit 1.9. It shows the amount of sales the company made during the month, from January 1, 2010, through January 31, 2010. The expenses shown are also for the same period. As noted earlier, the difference between the revenues and expenses is called net income, or net earnings.

EXHIBIT 1.9

Income Statement for Team Shirts for January

The income statement for the month of January shows all of the revenue and all of the expenses for the month.

Team Shirts
Income Statement
For the Month Ended January 31, 2010

Revenue		
Sales		$900
Expenses		
Cost of goods sold	$360	
Advertising	50	
Interest	5	
Total expenses		415
Net income		$485

Notice several things about the income statement:

- First, only the cost of the T-shirts that were sold is included as an expense—cost of goods sold, also called cost of sales. The cost of the T-shirts that were not sold is shown as an asset called inventory on the balance sheet.
- Second, the repayment of the loan from Sara's sister is not shown as an expense. The only expense related to borrowing money is the interest owed to the lender. The repayment of principal is not an expense.

Also notice that dividends, a corporation's distribution to owners, are excluded from the income statement. Sara could have paid herself a salary for running the business. That salary would have been an expense, but she decided not to do that. Instead, she decided to take cash out of the business as a dividend. Dividends are not a component of earnings; they are a distribution of earnings.

The Difference between the Balance Sheet and the Income Statement

You should get a better idea of the difference between the balance sheet and the income statement by thinking about your own personal finances. If you were asked to prepare a personal balance sheet, you would list all your assets, such as your cash on hand (no matter how little) and the cost of your car, clothes, computer, and cell phone. Then, you would list all the people to whom you owe money and how much money you owe to each. This might include some credit card companies and perhaps a bank for a car loan. All these assets and liabilities are measured in dollars. The specific point of time associated with a balance sheet must be given. For example, if you were listing your assets and liabilities on the last day of 2010, your balance sheet date would be December 31, 2010. Remember the accounting equation:

Assets   =   Liabilities   +   Shareholder's equity

If you subtract the amount of your liabilities—what you owe to others—from your assets, the difference is your equity. Shareholders' equity is sometimes called the residual, indicating that it is the amount left over after the claims of creditors are deducted from a company's assets.

In contrast, if you constructed a personal income statement, it would cover a period of time. For example, what was your net income total during the year 2010? You would list all revenue you received during the year and then subtract all your expenses during the same year. The difference would be your net income for the year. There is no equation to balance. The income statement lists all of your sources of revenue and subtracts the related expenses, leaving a difference, hopefully positive, called net income. If the subtraction of expenses from revenues results in a negative number, that amount is called a net loss.

> **Your Turn 1-6**
>
> 1. What is included on the income statement? What is included on the balance sheet?
> 2. Describe the difference in the time periods captured by the income statement and the balance sheet.

Statement of Changes in Shareholders' Equity

As its name suggests, the statement of changes in shareholders' equity shows the changes that have taken place in the amount of shareholders' equity during a period. For a corporation, the statement is called the **statement of changes in shareholders' equity** because the owners are known as shareholders. (When there is only one owner, use the singular "shareholder's equity." When there are two or more owners, use the plural "shareholders' equity." If you don't know the number of owners, using the plural is the accepted practice.) The statement starts with the amount of contributed capital on a given balance sheet date and summarizes the additions and subtractions from that amount during a specific period, usually a year. In this course, we will not see deductions from contributed capital. Contributed capital is reduced in only very special circumstances, and those will be studied in more advanced accounting courses. The second part of the statement starts with the beginning balance in retained earnings and then shows the additions (net income is the most common) and the deductions (dividends are the most common). Contributed capital and retained earnings are then added to show the total amount of shareholders' equity at the end of the accounting period. For demonstration purposes, we will look at monthly financial statements for Team Shirts throughout this book.

The statement of changes in shareholder's equity for Sara's first month of business is shown in Exhibit 1.10.

> The **statement of changes in shareholders' equity** starts with the beginning amount of contributed capital and shows all changes during the accounting period. Then the statement shows the beginning balance in retained earnings with its changes. The usual changes to retained earnings are the increase due to net income and the decrease due to dividends paid to shareholders.

Team Shirts
Statement of Changes in Shareholder's Equity
For the Month Ended January 31, 2010

Beginning contributed capital	$ 0	
Stock issued during the month	5,000	
Ending contributed capital		$5,000
Beginning retained earnings	$ 0	
Net income for the month	485	
Dividends	(100)	
Ending retained earnings		385
Total shareholder's equity		$5,385

EXHIBIT 1.10

Statement of Changes in Shareholder's Equity for Team Shirts for January

This statement shows all of the changes to shareholder's equity that occurred during the period.

The statement starts with the contributed capital at the beginning of the month. Team Shirts has nothing on the first day of the month, because the company is just getting started. Then, capital contributions—the owner's contributions to the business—made during the month are listed. Sara contributed $5,000 to the business. In a corporation, contributions take the form of shares of stock. Next, the statement shows beginning retained earnings, the equity that owners have as a result of the business earning income, rather than the equity from contributions. The beginning retained earnings balance is zero because January was the company's first month of doing business. Net income for the period—$485—is shown as an increase to retained earnings. The dividends of $100 are shown as a decrease to retained earnings. The amount of retained earnings at the end of the period is then added to the amount of contributed capital at the end of the period to give the total shareholder's equity at the end of the period.

After preparing the income statement for the month and the statement of changes in shareholder's equity for the same month, you will be able to prepare the end-of-the-month balance sheet. If you set up the balance sheet horizontally in the accounting equation format as shown in Exhibit 1.7, you can view the changes in assets, liabilities, and shareholder's equity from the beginning to the end of the month, with each transaction keeping the accounting equation in balance. The balance sheet for Team Shirts at January 31, 2010, is shown in Exhibit 1.11.

EXHIBIT 1.11

Balance Sheet for Team Shirts at January 31, 2010

After a month of transactions, this is the balance sheet for Team Shirts. Notice how all the information from the income statement and statement of changes in shareholder's equity is incorporated in the totals shown on the balance sheet.

Team Shirts			
Balance Sheet			
At January 31, 2010			

Assets		Liabilities and Shareholder's equity	
Cash	$5,345	Notes payable	$ 0
Inventory	40		
		Common stock	5,000
		Retained earnings	385
		Total liabilities and	
Total assets	$5,385	shareholder's equity	$5,385

Statement of Cash Flows

The **statement of cash flows** shows all the cash collected and all the cash disbursed during the period. Each cash amount is classified as one of three types:

1. **Cash from operating activities**—cash transactions that relate to the everyday, routine transactions needed to run a business.
2. **Cash from investing activities**—transactions involving the sale and purchase of long-term assets used in the business.
3. **Cash from financing activities**—transactions related to how a business is financed. Examples include contributions from owners and amounts borrowed using loans.

The **statement of cash flows** is needed to form a complete picture of a company's financial health. This statement is, in theory, the easiest to understand, and many people consider it the most important. It is a list of all the cash that has come into a business (its cash receipts) and all the cash that has gone out of the business (its cash disbursements) during a specific period. In other words, it shows all the cash inflows and all the cash outflows for a fiscal period. Compare the cash inflows and cash outflows for a specific period with the revenues and expenses for the same specific period on the income statement. Accountants measure revenue as what the company has earned during the period, even if it is not equal to the amount of cash actually collected. Accountants measure expenses as the costs incurred to generate those revenues, even if they are not the same as the amounts actually paid in cash. Because this way of measuring revenues and expenses may not have an exact correspondence to the amount of cash collected and disbursed, the statement of cash flows is necessary to get a complete picture of the business transactions for the period.

The statement of cash flows is divided into three sections:

• **Cash from operating activities**
• **Cash from investing activities**
• **Cash from financing activities**

These represent the three general types of business activities. Exhibit 1.12 shows some common transactions and how they fit into these classifications. Remember that the transactions must be cash transactions to be shown on the statement of cash flows.

	Operating Activities	Investing Activities	Financing Activities
Cash inflows...	From customers who purchase products From interest or dividend income earned from bank deposits	From sale of property and equipment	From issuing long-term debt From issuing stock
Cash outflows...	To suppliers for the purchase of inventory To employees in the form of salaries	To purchase plant and equipment To purchase investments in other firms	To repay long-term debt principal To pay dividends to owners

EXHIBIT 1.12

Types of Cash Flows

All transactions can be classified as one of these three types. When the transactions are for cash, they appear on the statement of cash flows.

Cash inflows and outflows from operating activities pertain to the general operating activities of the business. For Team Shirts, purchasing T-shirts is an operating activity. Look at the other cash flows from operations on the statement of cash flows in Exhibit 1.13.

Team Shirts
Statement of Cash Flows
For the Month Ended January 31, 2010

Cash from operating activities:

Cash collected from customers	$ 900	
Cash paid to vendors	(400)	
Cash paid for advertising	(50)	
Cash paid for interest	(5)	$ 445
Cash from investing activities:		0
Cash from financing activities:		
Contributions from owners	$5,000	
Cash from loan	500	
Cash to repay loan	(500)	
Cash paid for dividends	(100)	4,900
Increase in cash		$5,345
Add beginning cash balance		0
Ending cash balance		$5,345

EXHIBIT 1.13

Statement of Cash Flows for Team Shirts for January

The statement of cash flows shows all of the cash inflows and outflows during the period. At the end of the statement, the beginning cash balance is added to the change in cash to give the ending cash balance.

Cash inflows and outflows from investing activities are the cash flows related to the purchase and sale of assets that a firm uses for more than a year. If Sara decided to purchase a piece of equipment to silk screen her own shirts, that purchase would be an investing activity—not an operating activity—because Team Shirts is not in the business of buying and selling equipment. The purchase and sale of assets that last longer than a year—often called long-term assets—are investing activities.

Financing activities are related to a company's sources of capital. The two sources of capital, usually in the form of cash, for financing a business are contributions from owners and loans from creditors. Any cash inflows related to these transactions are classified as cash inflows from financing activities. Financing outflows include repayment of the principal of loans and distributions to owners. Team Shirts' repayment of the $500 loan is an example of a financing cash outflow.

You should begin to see the relationship between the four financial statements. Study Exhibit 1.14, where all of the statements for Team Shirts for January are shown with arrows

EXHIBIT 1.14

Summary of Team Shirts' Financial Statements and Their Relationships

This shows how the four financial statements are related.

Team Shirts Income Statement For the Month Ended January 31, 2010

Revenue	
Sales	$900
Expenses	
Cost of goods sold	(360)
Advertising expense	(50)
Interest expense	(5)
Net income	$485

Team Shirts Statement of Changes in Shareholder's Equity For the Month Ended January 31, 2010

Contributed capital		
Beginning balance	$	0
Stock issued during the month		5,000
Ending balance		5,000
Retained earnings		
Beginning balance	$	0
+ Net income		485
– Dividends		(100)
Ending balance		385
Total shareholder's equity		$5,385

Team Shirts Statement of Cash Flows For the Month Ended January 31, 2010

Cash from operating activities:		
Cash collected from customers ...	$ 900	
Cash paid to vendors	(400)	
Cash paid for advertising	(50)	
Cash paid for interest	(5)	$ 445
Cash from investing activities: ...		0
Cash from financing activities:		
Contributions from owners	$5,000	
Cash from loan	500	
Cash to repay loan	(500)	
Cash paid for dividends	(100)	4,900
Increase in cash		$5,345
Add beginning cash balance		0
Ending cash balance		$5,345

Team Shirts Balance Sheet At January 31, 2010

Assets	
Cash	$5,345
Inventory	40
Total assets	$5,385
Liabilities & Shareholder's Equity	
Liabilities	
Note payable	0
Shareholder's Equity	
Common stock	5,000
Retained earnings	385
Total liabilities and shareholder's equity	$5,385

indicating the relationships between the statements. All four financial statements will be discussed in detail in the chapters to follow. By the time you are finished, you will be able to read and understand what is on most financial statements. You will also be able to analyze business transactions and understand how they affect the financial statements of a business.

---

1. Refer to Exhibit 1.14. How is the income statement related to the balance sheet? In other words, how does the amount of net income affect the balance sheet?
2. Why is it necessary to have both an income statement and a statement of cash flows? Look at the statements for Team Shirts and explain why they are different.

Your Turn 1-7

Flow of Information and the Financial Statements

A company records and uses a large amount of information about its transactions. The amount of data and the way the information is collected and stored vary widely from company to company. The information contained in the four financial statements is a specific, well-defined part of the information available from a company's overall information system. The purpose of these four financial statements is to provide the financial information needed to represent and evaluate the transactions of the business. Investors, regulators, vendors, customers, and creditors rely on financial accounting information as a critical input for decision making.

Real Company Financial Statements

L.O.5
Identify the elements of a real company's financial statements.

All publicly-traded corporations—ones that sell their stock in the public stock exchanges such as the New York Stock Exchange (NYSE)—must prepare the four basic financial statements every year. Even though these statements are much more complicated than those of Team Shirts, they have all of the basic financial statement elements that were on the statements for Team Shirts.

The SEC requires these companies to regularly supply information about what is happening in their firms. Check out the SEC's Web site at www.sec.gov. Explore the links to see if you can find some recent corporate filings. One of the most important filings a company must make is the 10-K, an important report that companies file with the SEC. It provides a comprehensive overview of the registrant's business. An important part of a 10-K is a company's audited financial statements, without the company's sales pitch and story found in its glossy annual report. The 10-K report includes information you simply will not find in most annual reports, such as insider stock holdings and brief biographies of the management team. The report must be filed within 60 or 75 days after the end of the company's fiscal year (depending on the company's filing status).

Beginning in June 2009, firms that are required to file 10-K reports with the SEC will do so using a computer language called **XBRL (Extensible Business Reporting Language)**. This is a technology that enables firms to report information in a standardized way that makes the data immediately reusable and interactive. Take a test drive at www.sec.gov/spotlight/xbrl/viewers.shtml; click on *Interactive Financial Reports*. According to the SEC, the interactive data encoded with XBRL will make analyzing financial information more efficient and effective.

XBRL (Extensible Business Reporting Language) is a technology that enables firms to report information in a standardized way that makes the data immediately reusable and interactive.

Interactive data can create new ways for investors, analysts, and others to retrieve and use financial information in documents filed with us. For example, users of financial information will be able to download it directly into spreadsheets, analyze it using commercial off-the-shelf software, or use it within investment models in other software formats. Through interactive data, what is currently static, text-based information can be dynamically searched and analyzed, facilitating the comparison of financial and business performance across companies, reporting periods, and industries. (Source: SEC Release Nos. 33-9902; 34-59324; 39-2461.)

Look at the comparative balance sheets of Dell Inc., formerly called the Dell Computer Corporation (see Exhibit 1.15 on the following page). Notice the similarities between the real

EXHIBIT 1.15

Comparative Balance Sheets for Dell Inc.

This is Dell's balance sheet, taken from its annual report.

> **Dell Inc.**
> **Consolidated Statements of Financial Position**
> (in millions)

> Statement of Financial Position is just another name for the balance sheet.

> Assets are shown first on the balance sheet.

Assets	January 30, 2009	February 1, 2008
Current assets:		
Cash and cash equivalents	$ 8,352	$ 7,764
Short-term investments	740	208
Accounts receivable, net	4,731	5,961
Financing receivables, net	1,712	1,732
Inventories, net	867	1,180
Other current assets	3,749	3,035
Total current assets	20,151	19,880
Property, plant, and equipment, net	2,277	2,668
Investments	454	1,560
Long-term financing receivables, net	500	407
Goodwill	1,737	1,648
Purchased intangible assets, net	724	780
Other non-current assets	657	618
Total assets	$26,500	$27,561

> Liabilities and Stockholders' Equity are shown together.

Liabilities and Equity		
Current liabilities:		
Short-term debt	$ 113	$ 225
Accounts payable	8,309	11,492
Accrued and other	3,788	4,323
Short-term deferred service revenue	2,649	2,486
Total current liabilities	14,859	18,526
Long-term debt	1,898	362
Long-term deferred service revenue	3,000	2,774
Other non-current liabilities	2,472	2,070
Total liabilities	22,229	23,732
Commitments and contingencies (Note 10)		
Redeemable common stock and capital in excess of $.01 par value; shares issued and outstanding: 0 and 4, respectively (Note 4)	–	94
Stockholders' equity:		
Preferred stock and capital in excess of $.01 par value; shares authorized: 5,000; shares issued and outstanding: none	–	–
Common stock and capital in excess of $.01 par value; shares authorized: 7,000; shares issued: 3,338 and 3,320, respectively; shares outstanding: 1,944 and 2,060, respectively	11,189	10,589
Treasury stock at cost: 919 and 785 shares, respectively	(27,904)	(25,037)
Retained earnings	20,677	18,199
Accumulated other comprehensive income (loss)	309	(16)
Total stockholders' equity	4,271	3,735
Total liabilities and equity	$26,500	$27,561

> The balance sheet actually balances.

The accompanying notes are an integral part of these consolidated financial statements.

world of Dell and the fictitious world of Team Shirts—the balance sheets for both actually balance. Both companies list assets first, then liabilities and stockholders' equity. Both companies have used dollars to measure their balance sheet items. There are differences between the balance sheets of the real-world example and our not-so-real-world example that we will discuss in later chapters.

Dell's income statement (consolidated statements of income in Exhibit 1.16) does not look exactly like the Team Shirts' income statement (Exhibit 1.9). First, Dell Inc. provides three years of comparative income statements. Both Dell Inc. and Team Shirts have revenues and expenses, but the two companies have presented the data in a different order. Team Shirts lists revenue first and then groups all the expenses together. This is called a **single-step income statement**. Dell Inc. lists its largest revenue first and then subtracts the largest expense related to the revenue, *cost of revenue* (also known as *cost of goods sold*), which gives a subtotal called gross margin. This is called a **multistep income statement**. If we were to recast Team Shirts' income statement into a multistep income statement, we would subtract the cost of goods sold of $360 from the sales revenue of $900 to get a subtotal of $540 for the gross margin. Although Dell Inc. and Team Shirts have arranged their revenues and expenses differently, net income for each company is still the difference between all revenues and all expenses. Net income is always the same no matter how the revenues and expenses are grouped on the statement.

> A **single-step income statement** groups all revenues together and shows all expenses deducted from total revenue.

> A **multistep income statement** starts with sales and subtracts cost of goods sold to get a subtotal called gross profit on sales, also known as gross margin. Then, other operating revenues are added and other operating expenses are deducted. A subtotal for operating income is shown before deductions related to nonoperating items and taxes are deducted. Then, income taxes are subtracted, leaving net income.

EXHIBIT 1.16

Dell's Income Statements
This shows the income statements for Dell Inc. for three consecutive years.

Dell Inc.
Consolidated Statements of Income
(in millions, except per share amounts)

	Fiscal Year Ended		
	January 30, 2009	February 1, 2008	February 2, 2007
Net revenue	$61,101	$61,133	$57,420
Cost of revenue	50,144	49,462	47,904
Gross margin	10,957	11,671	9,516
Operating expenses:			
Selling, general, and administrative	7,102	7,538	5,948
In-process research and development	2	83	–
Research, development, and engineering	663	610	498
Total operating expenses	7,767	8,231	6,446
Operating income	3,190	3,440	3,070
Investment and other income, net	134	387	275
Income before income taxes	3,324	3,827	3,345
Income tax provision	846	880	762
Net income	$ 2,478	$ 2,947	$ 2,583
Earnings per common share:			
Basic	$ 1.25	$ 1.33	$ 1.15
Diluted	$ 1.25	$ 1.31	$ 1.14
Weighted-average shares outstanding:			
Basic	1,980	2,223	2,255
Diluted	1,986	2,247	2,271

The accompanying notes are an integral part of these consolidated financial statements.

A complete set of annual financial statements includes the four basic statements—balance sheet, income statement, statement of changes in shareholders' equity, and the statement of cash flows—as well as the Notes to the Financial Statements. Accompanying the annual financial statements in a public company's 10-K is an audit opinion. Exhibit 1.17 on the following page shows the audit opinion from the most recent annual report of Dell Inc. Independent auditors play a crucial role in making sure the financial statements provide data that investors can rely on.

EXHIBIT 1.17

Report of the Independent Auditor

Every public company is required to have an audit. Only part of the audit report is shown here.

Report of Independent Registered Public Accounting Firm

To the Board of Directors and Shareholders of Dell Inc.

In our opinion, the consolidated financial statements listed in the accompanying index present fairly, in all material respects, the financial position of Dell Inc. and its subsidiaries ("Company") at January 30, 2009 and February 1, 2008, and the results of their operations and their cash flows for each of the three years in the period ended January 30, 2009 in conformity with accounting principles generally accepted in the United States of America. In addition, in our opinion, the financial statement schedule listed in the accompanying index presents fairly, in all material respects, the information set forth therein when read in conjunction with the related consolidated financial statements. Also in our opinion, the Company maintained, in all material respects, effective internal control over financial reporting as of January 30, 2009, based on criteria established in *Internal Control — Integrated Framework* issued by the Committee of Sponsoring Organizations of the Treadway Commission (COSO). The Company's management is responsible for these financial statements and the financial statement schedule, for maintaining effective internal control over financial reporting, and for its assessment of the effectiveness of internal control over financial reporting included in Management's Report on Internal Control Over Financial Reporting appearing under Item 9A. Our responsibility is to express opinions on these financial statements, on the financial statement schedule, and on the Company's internal control over financial reporting based on our integrated audits. We conducted our audits in accordance with the standards of the Public Company Accounting Oversight Board (United States). Those standards require that we plan and perform the audits to obtain reasonable assurance about whether the financial statements are free of material misstatement and whether effective internal control over financial reporting was maintained in all material respects. Our audits of the financial statements included examining, on a test basis, evidence supporting the amounts and disclosures in the financial statements, assessing the accounting principles used and significant estimates made by management, and evaluating the overall financial statement presentation. Our audit of internal control over financial reporting included obtaining an understanding of internal control over financial reporting, assessing the risk that a material weakness exists, and testing and evaluating the design and operating effectiveness of internal control based on the assessed risk. Our audits also included performing such other procedures as we considered necessary in the circumstances. We believe that our audits provide a reasonable basis for our opinions.

PricewaterhouseCoopers LLP
Austin, Texas
March 26, 2009

> Consolidated means that any firms controlled by Dell are included in Dell's financial statements.

> What do you think it means for the statements to "present fairly"?

> What is a reasonable basis for an opinion?

Business Risk, Control, and Ethics

Starting a business is more than having a good idea about what it should be and obtaining the financing to get it going. Both are a good beginning, but they must be followed with sound business planning for acquiring goods and services and selling the company's products or services. Part of that planning is identifying the risks involved. Before we discuss the details of the business activities in the chapters to follow, we consider the risks of being in business and how we can minimize the negative consequences of those risks.

> A **risk** is a danger—something that exposes a business to a potential injury or loss.

A **risk** may be generally defined as anything that exposes us to potential injury or loss. In business, risks can turn into significant losses, scandals, or total company failure. There are hundreds of risks that any business faces. Some examples are

- the risk of product failure that might result in the death of consumers.
- the risk that someone will steal assets from the company.
- the risk that poor-quality inventory will be purchased and sold.

What losses could result? For a serious product failure, such as the Firestone tires on the Ford Explorers in the early 2000s, the financial losses of the business could amount to millions of dollars in lawsuit settlements. For employee theft, the potential losses range from significant financial losses to the loss of a company secret that could cause a business to fail. Poor-quality inventory could result in the loss of customers and reputation.

Risks relate to all aspects of the business, including the following:

- General strategic risks—for example, should we market our cigarettes to teenagers?
- Operating risks—for example, should we operate without a backup power supply?
- Financial risks—for example, should we borrow the money from the bank or get it from our shareholders?
- Information risks—for example, should we use a manual accounting system?

The potential losses from taking on business risks may be the loss of reputation, loss of customers, loss of needed information, or loss of assets. All the losses translate into monetary losses that can put the company at risk for total failure.

It is difficult to think of business risk without considering the relationship of risks to ethics. When the risks of business result in losses or legal exposure, a firm's managers want to minimize the damage to the firm. In such cases, the ethical standards of the firm and its managers become paramount. A manager must always put good ethical behavior above putting a good face on the firm's financial position or performance. Failure to do this has resulted in huge losses for employees and investors. See how many of the faces you recognize in Exhibit 1.18.

EXHIBIT 1.18

Accounting Frauds

Company	What Happened	The Legal Events	
Enron, an energy company	Firm filed for bankruptcy protection in December 2001, after massive fraud was uncovered by the SEC.	Andrew Fastow, former CFO, was sentenced to 10 years in prison; Jeff Skilling, former CEO and president, was sentenced to 24 years in prison.	
WorldCom, a telecommunications company	Firm filed for bankruptcy protection in July 2002 after disclosing it overstated profits by $3.8 billion.	Bernie Ebbers, former CEO, was sentenced to 25 years in prison.	
Computer Associates (CA), a computer company	Former CEO Sanjay Kumar was indicted in April 2004 for $2 billion fraud and obstruction of justice.	Kumar pleaded guilty in May 2006 and was sentenced to 12 years in prison.	
Monster Worldwide, Inc., a global online career company	Monster executives secretly backdated stock options granted to officers, directors, and employees, and overstated the company's annual earnings between 1997 and 2005 by $339.5 million (pretax).	Without admitting or denying liability, Monster agreed to pay a $2.5 million penalty. According to the SEC complaint, Monster cooperated with the investigation.	
Countrywide Financial, a mortgage lender	Countrywide Financial executives are charged with deliberately misleading investors about the credit risks they were taking in an effort to build the company's market share and maintain the stock price.	On June 4, 2009, the SEC filed fraud charges against former Countrywide Financial CEO, Angelo Mozilo, former COO and president, David Sambol, and former CFO, Eric Sieracki. These cases are pending.	

Why do people take risks? Every risk brings a potential reward. The reward is why we are in business. An entrepreneur like Sara has put her money and her reputation at risk to start a business. Why? For the potential of developing a successful business. To deal with the risks and increase the chances to reap the rewards, a firm must establish and maintain control over its operations, assets, and information system. A control is an activity performed to minimize or eliminate a risk. As we study the business processes that Team Shirts will be engaged in during its first year in business, we will look at how the firm can control the risk involved in each process.

Chapter Summary Points

- A business is started when investors are willing to risk their money to start a business—to provide something of value for customers and to make a profit.
- Investors, vendors, customers, and governmental agencies require financial information about businesses. There are four basic financial statements that provide the information: the income statement, the balance sheet, the statement of changes in shareholders' equity, and the statement of cash flows.
- The financial statements are based on a set of guidelines called generally accepted accounting principles (GAAP). The SEC and the FASB are currently the important players in the rule-setting game.
- The accounting equation, assets = liabilities + shareholders' equity, is the basis of the balance sheet. It is a snapshot of the business at a specific point in time.
- The income statement shows all revenues and expenses for a period of time, resulting in net income.
- The statement of changes in shareholders' (owners') equity shows the changes in shareholders' equity—both contributed capital and retained earnings—for a period of time.
- The statement of cash flows presents all the cash inflows and outflows for a period of time. It accounts for the difference between the balances in cash on the balance sheets at the end of two consecutive accounting periods.
- Notes to the financial statements are an important part of the financial information provided with a firm's four financial statements.

Chapter Summary Problems

Suppose the following transactions occurred during Lexar Computer's first month of business:

a. Two friends together contributed $50,000 from their savings to start Lexar Computer, Inc. In return, the corporation issued 100 shares of common stock to each of them.
b. The company paid $20,000 cash for parts for new computers that it planned to make during the next few months.
c. The company rented office space for the month for $350 cash.
d. The company hired and paid employees for work done during the month for a total of $1,500.
e. The company sold computers for $40,000 cash. (These computers were made from the parts the company purchased in item (b).)
f. The company declared and paid $400 in dividends to its shareholders.
g. On the last day of the month, the company purchased $12,000 worth of office furniture and equipment on credit. (Lexar signed a 60-day note—that is, borrowed the money—from the furniture company.)

Instructions

1. For each transaction, tell whether the related accounting information will be shown on the income statement, the balance sheet, or both. If it is on the income statement, tell whether it increases or decreases net income.
2. For each transaction, tell whether it is an operating, investing, or financing activity.
3. For each transaction, identify an asset or a liability that is affected by the transaction, and tell whether it is an increase or a decrease to the asset or liability you named.

Solution

Transaction	Which financial statements are affected?	Which type of activity is it?	Which asset or liability is affected?
a. Two friends together contributed $50,000 cash to start Lexar Computer, Inc. In return, the corporation issued 100 shares of common stock to each of them.	Balance sheet	Financing	Asset: Cash—increased
b. The company paid $20,000 cash for parts for new computers that it planned to make during the next few months.	Balance sheet	Operating	Assets: Inventory—increased; Cash—decreased
c. The company rented office space for the month for $350 cash.	Balance sheet and income statement (decreases income)	Operating	Asset: Cash—decreased
d. The company hired and paid employees for work done during the month for a total of $1,500.	Balance sheet and income statement (decreases income)	Operating	Asset: Cash—decreased
e. The company sold computers for $40,000 cash. (These computers were made from the parts the company purchased in item (b).)	Balance sheet and income statement (increases income)	Operating	Asset: Cash—increased; Inventory—decreased
f. The company declared and paid $400 in dividends to its shareholders.	Balance sheet	Financing	Asset: Cash—decreased
g. The company purchased $12,000 worth of office furniture and equipment on credit. (Lexar signed a 60-day note with the furniture company.)	Balance sheet	Investing	Asset: Office Furniture—increased; Liability: Notes payable—increased

Key Terms for Chapter 1

Assets (p. 14)
Balance sheet (p. 13)
Books (p. 17)
Capital (p. 2)
Cash from financing activities (p. 20)
Cash from investing activities (p. 20)
Cash from operating activities (p. 20)
Certified public accountant (CPA) (p. 13)
Comparative balance sheets (p. 15)
Contributed capital (p. 9)
Corporation (p. 6)
Dividends (p. 8)

Expenses (p. 10)
Financial Accounting Standards Board (FASB) (p. 11)
Financial services company (p. 4)
Fiscal year (p. 15)
For-profit firm (p. 2)
Generally accepted accounting principles (GAAP) (p. 11)
Income statement (p. 17)
Interest (p. 9)
Internal Revenue Service (IRS) (p. 12)
International Accounting Standards Board (IASB) (p. 11)

International Financial Reporting Standards (IFRS) (p. 11)
Liabilities (p. 14)
Manufacturing company (p. 4)
Merchandising company (p. 3)
Multistep income statement (p. 25)
Net income (p. 3)
Not-for-profit firm (p. 2)
Notes to the financial statements (p. 13)
Partnership (p. 5)
Principal (p. 9)
Public Company Accounting Oversight Board (PCAOB) (p. 11)

Retained earnings (p. 14)
Revenue (p. 10)
Risk (p. 26)
Securities and Exchange
  Commission (SEC) (p. 7)
Service company (p. 3)
Shareholder (stockholder)
  (p. 6)

Shareholders' equity (p. 14)
Shares of common stock
  (p. 6)
Single-step income statement
  (p. 25)
Sole proprietorship (p. 4)
Statement of cash flows
  (p. 20)

Statement of changes in
  shareholder's equity
  (p. 19)
Stock exchange (p. 7)
Stock market (p. 7)
XBRL (Extensible Business
  Reporting Language)
  (p. 23)

Answers to YOUR TURN Questions

Chapter 1

Your Turn 1-1

1. The main purpose of a business is to make a profit, increasing the value of the company for the owners.
2. The four general types of businesses are as follows:
   a. Service company: provides a service—it does something for its customers rather than selling them a tangible product.
   b. Merchandising company: buys goods, adds value to them, and then sells them with the added value.
   c. Manufacturing company: makes products and sells them to other companies and sometimes to the final consumers.
   d. Financial services company: provides services related to money—insurance, banking, etc.

Your Turn 1-2

1. The three general forms of business ownership are (1) sole proprietorships (single owner), (2) partnerships (multiple owners), and (3) corporations (potential for widespread ownership often with separation of ownership and management).
2. Some advantages and disadvantages of each business form are as follows:

	Sole Proprietorship	Partnership	Corporation
Advantages:	Owner control Taxes flow to proprietor's income	Owners control Taxes flow to partners' income	Limited liability for owners Often easier to raise capital For owners, they may diversify their investments across many different companies, often for a very small investment
Disadvantages:	Owner is liable for all business decisions Often difficult to raise capital	Partners are liable for all business decisions Often difficult to raise capital	Often, management and owners are separate, creating a conflict of interests Corporation pays taxes and then owners pay taxes again on the dividends they receive (unless the tax law provides special treatment for dividends)

Your Turn 1-3

1. The two sources of financing for a business are investments by owners (contributed capital) and loans from outsiders (liabilities).
2. Interest is the cost of using someone else's money.

Your Turn 1-4

1. Revenues are the amounts a company earns from providing goods or services to its customers. Expenses are the costs to earn those revenues.
2. The four statements include the income statement, balance sheet, statement of changes in shareholders' equity, and the statement of cash flows.

Your Turn 1-5

1. The two parts of shareholders' equity are contributed capital and retained earnings (earned capital).
2. A fiscal year is a year in the life of a business for financial reporting purposes. It may begin at any time and ends a year later.

Your Turn 1-6

1. The income statement contains revenues and expenses. The balance sheet contains assets, liabilities, and shareholders' equity.
2. The time period captured by the income statement is an accounting period, often a fiscal year. The statement covers a period of time. On the other hand, the balance sheet describes the financial position of a company at a given point in time.

Your Turn 1-7

1. The income statement gives the revenues and expenses for the period. The net amount, net income, is added to retained earnings. So the income statement number becomes part of the retained earnings total on the year-end balance sheet.
2. The income statement shows all revenues and expenses for a period of time—all the revenues that have been earned and expenses incurred to earn those revenues. The statement of cash flows simply lists the cash inflows and outflows during the period. The income statement and the statement of cash flows for Team Shirts are different because Team Shirts paid cash for some inventory that was not sold, so the cost of that inventory is not included in the income statement's cost of goods sold. Also, any transactions with owners (contributions and dividends) are not included on the income statement.

Questions

1. What is the purpose of a business?
2. Is the goal of all organizations to make a profit?
3. Name the three types of activities that make up most business transactions.
4. What are the possible ownership structures for a business?
5. What are the advantages of the corporate form of ownership?
6. What are the disadvantages of the corporate form of ownership?
7. Who are some of the people in need of business information and for what purposes?
8. What is the relationship between the information available to a business and the information provided in financial statements?
9. What are the basic financial statements? Describe the information that each provides.
10. What makes the income statement different from the statement of cash flows?
11. What is XBRL and why is the SEC mandating its use?

Multiple-Choice Questions

1. What type of activities relate to what the firm is in business to do?
   a. Investing activities
   b. Operating activities
   c. Financing activities
   d. Protection activities
2. Which financial statement is similar to the accounting equation?
   a. The income statement
   b. The balance sheet
   c. The statement of changes in shareholders' equity
   d. The statement of cash flows
3. The Pets Plus Superstore, Inc., acquires 50 doggie beds from a supplier for $500 in cash. What is the give portion of this transaction?
   a. Pets Plus giving the doggie beds to customers in return for cash
   b. The supplier giving the doggie beds to Pets Plus
   c. Pets Plus giving $500 in cash to the supplier
   d. The supplier giving $500 to Pets Plus

4. The two parts of shareholders' equity are
   a. assets and liabilities.
   b. net income and common stock.
   c. contributed capital and retained earnings.
   d. revenues and expenses.
5. Which financial statement is a snapshot of the financial position of a company at a specific point in time?
   a. Income statement
   b. Balance sheet
   c. Statement of changes in shareholders' equity
   d. Statement of cash flows
6. Online Pharmacy Company borrowed $5,000 cash from the National Bank. As a result of this transaction,
   a. assets would decrease by $5,000.
   b. liabilities would increase by $5,000.
   c. equity would increase by $5,000.
   d. revenue would increase by $5,000.
7. Accounting information is
   a. useful in profitable businesses only.
   b. considered the most important part of a company's information system by all managers.
   c. an integral part of business.
   d. used only by CPAs.
8. During its first year of business, West Company earned service revenues of $2,000. If the company collected $700 related to those sales, how much revenue would be shown on West's income statement for the year?
   a. $2,000
   b. $700
   c. $1,300
   d. Cannot be determined with the given information
9. Interest is the cost of
   a. purchasing inventory.
   b. making a sale.
   c. being in business.
   d. using someone else's money.
10. The balance sheet of United Studios at December 31 showed assets of $30,000 and shareholders' equity of $20,000. What were the liabilities at December 31?
    a. $30,000
    b. $10,000
    c. $20,000
    d. $50,000

Short Exercises
Set A

All of the A exercises can be found within MyAccountingLab, an online homework and practice environment.

SE1-1A. *Classify business transactions. (LO 2).* For each of the following cash transactions, identify whether it is better described as an operating, financing, or investing activity.

1. An entrepreneur contributes his own money to start a new business.
2. The business buys a machine.
3. The business purchases inventory.
4. The business sells inventory to customers.
5. The business repays a loan.

SE1-2A. *Identify balance sheet items. (LO 4).* Classify the items listed (1 to 6) under the following balance sheet headings:
A - Assets
L - Liabilities
SE - Shareholders' equity

1. _____ Cash
2. _____ Common stock
3. _____ Equipment
4. _____ Notes payable
5. _____ Retained earnings
6. _____ Accounts receivable

SE1-3A. *Calculate owners' equity. (LO 4).* Doughnut Company shows $130,000 worth of assets on its December 31, 2009, balance sheet. If the company's total liabilities are $55,800, what is the amount of owners' equity?

SE1-4A. *Calculate liability. (LO 4).* Given the following items on Tiffany Restoration Company's June 30, 2009, balance sheet, how much did the company owe its creditors on June 30, 2009?

Cash	$ 1,725	Liabilities	???
Inventory	205		
Equipment	10,636	Common stock	$7,600
Other assets	8,135	Retained earnings	7,450
Total	$20,701		

SE1-5A. *Income statement analysis. (LO 4).* For each of the following, calculate the missing amount:

1. Revenues $560; Expenses $300; Net Income = _____
2. Net Income $700; Expenses $485; Revenues = _____
3. Expenses $600; Revenues $940; Net Income = _____
4. Revenues $1,240; Net Income $670; Expenses = _____
5. Net Income $6,450; Expenses $3,500; Revenues = _____

SE1-6A. *Calculate owners' equity. (LO 4).* Pasta Enterprises has $42,000 in cash, $20,000 in inventory, $17,000 balance due to creditors, and $21,000 balance due from customers. What is the amount of owners' equity?

SE1-7A. *Calculate retained earnings. (LO 4).* Super Shop had a retained earnings balance of $1,000 on December 31, 2010. For year 2011, sales were $14,000 and expenses were $7,500. Cash dividends of $1,000 were declared and distributed on December 31, 2011. What was the amount of retained earnings on December 31, 2011?

Set B

SE1-8B. *Classify business transactions. (LO 2).* For each of the following cash transactions, identify whether it is better described as an operating, financing, or investing activity.

1. A firm pays dividends to its shareholders.
2. A firm provides services to its customers.
3. A firm sells inventory.
4. A firm pays its employees for work completed.
5. The business takes out a loan from the local bank.

SE1-9B. *Identify balance sheet items. (LO 4).* Classify the items listed (1 to 6) under the following balance sheet headings:

A - Assets
L - Liabilities
SE - Shareholders' equity

1. _____ Inventory
2. _____ Notes payable
3. _____ Cash
4. _____ Accounts payable
5. _____ Accounts receivable
6. _____ Common stock

SE1-10B. *Calculate owner's equity. (LO 4).* Breck Company shows $180,000 worth of assets on its December 31, 2011, balance sheet. If the company's total liabilities are $103,200, what is the amount of owners' equity?

SE1-11B. *Calculate liability. (LO 4).* Given the following items on Baldwin Company's December 31, 2011, balance sheet, how much did the company owe its creditors on December 31, 2011?

Cash	$ 2,000	Liabilities	???
Inventory	1,500		
Equipment	10,400	Common stock	$ 5,000
Other assets	8,100	Retained earnings	12,450
Total	$22,000		

SE1-12B. *Income statement analysis. (LO 4).* For each of the following, calculate the missing amount:

1. Revenues $860; Expenses $500; Net Income = _____
2. Net Income $300; Expenses $185; Revenues = _____
3. Expenses $360; Revenues $1,040; Net Income = _____
4. Revenues $2,240; Net Income $1,670; Expenses = _____
5. Net Income $5,450; Expenses $1,500; Revenues = _____

SE1-13B. *Calculate owners' equity. (LO 4).* Lasting Enterprises has $82,000 in cash, $30,000 in inventory, $37,000 balance due to creditors, and $11,000 balance due from customers. What is the amount of owners' equity?

SE1-14B. *Calculate retained earnings. (LO 4).* M Company had a retained earnings balance of $4,200 on June 30, 2010. For the fiscal year ended June 30, 2011, sales were $24,000 and expenses were $12,500. Cash dividends of $2,500 were declared and distributed on June 1, 2011. What was the amount of retained earnings on June 30, 2011?

MyAccountingLab

All of the A exercises can be found within MyAccountingLab, an online homework and practice environment.

Exercises
Set A

E1-15A. *Business exchanges. (LO 1, 2).* Identify the transactions from the following story. For each, identify the transaction as operating, investing, or financing.

Latasha Jones decided to go into business for herself. As a talented Web designer, she decided to open a small consulting firm with $5,000 of her own money, for which she received common stock. Latasha borrowed $500 from her best friend to help get the business started, and in exchange she gave her friend an I-owe-you (IOU). The company bought a state-of-the-art desktop computer, complete with the accessories and software needed to get the business off the ground, at a total cost of $6,000. The business required a separate phone line, which cost $450. Then, the company put an advertisement in the local newspaper, at a cost of $45 per month for weekly ads. The company was ready to go. All of the payments were cash.

E1-16A. *Analyze business transactions using the accounting equation. (LO 4).* John Weiss recently started a lawn care service named "The Grass Is Always Greener, Inc." The following transactions occurred during the company's first month of business. Enter each of the following transactions into the accounting equation and identify an increase or decrease to assets, liabilities, shareholder's equity, revenues, or expenses.

1. John contributed $16,500 of personal savings in exchange for common stock to start the business.
2. The company purchased $7,500 of inventory (plants and shrubs) from a gardening wholesaler in Kansas.
3. The company purchased three riding lawn mowers at a cost of $5,000 each.
4. The company paid rent expense of $500 the first month.
5. The company earned service revenue of $9,000 and sold the entire $7,500 of inventory it had purchased to customers for $13,250 cash.

All the transactions were for cash. Use the following format:

					Shareholder's equity		
Total assets	=	Total liabilities	+	Contributed capital	+	Retained earnings
Transaction 1: _____		_____		_____		_____

E1-17A. *Classify business transactions. (LO 2).* For each of the transactions in E1-16A, tell whether the transaction was an operating, investing, or financing activity.

E1-18A. *Analyze the balance sheet. (LO 3, 4).* Use the balance sheet for Leatherheads Football Gear, Inc., at August 31, 2010, to answer the following questions:

Leatherheads Football Gear, Inc.
Balance Sheet
At August 31, 2010

Assets		Liabilities and Shareholder's Equity	
Cash	$ 7,250	Accounts payable	$ 4,575
Short-term investments	400	Notes payable	11,570
Accounts receivable	275		
Inventory	490	Contributed capital	4,450
Prepaid insurance	345	Retained earnings	3,040
Prepaid rent	875		
Equipment (net)	14,000		
	$23,635		$23,635

---

1. List the assets the company had on August 31, 2010. Who has claim to these assets?
2. List the liabilities the company had on August 31, 2010.

E1-19A. *Analyze business transactions using the accounting equation. (LO 4).* Enter each transaction below into the accounting equation. Then, calculate (1) the amount of assets owned by Tommy's Irish Pub, Inc., at the end of its first month of business, and (2) the amount of net income for the month. All these transactions took place during the first 30 days of business.

1. Tommy started the pub by contributing $17,000 in exchange for common stock, and the business borrowed $12,750 from the bank.
2. The pub purchased $4,000 worth of beer and other items (its inventory) with cash.
3. The pub hired a bartender to assist Tommy and help run the new company. For this service, the pub paid $100 each day for 30 days.

4. The pub was popular with the local college and sold half of its inventory for total cash revenues of $8,500.
5. The pub paid rent expense of $725 the first month.
6. The pub repaid $1,500 of the bank loan along with $50 of interest for the first month.

E1-20A. *Classify business transactions. (LO 2).* Classify each of the transactions in E1-19A as an operating, investing, or financing activity.

E1-21A. *Business transactions effects on shareholders' equity. (LO 4).* For each of the transactions given, tell whether it increases, decreases, or has no effect on shareholders' equity. Consider both shareholders' equity components—contributed capital and retained earnings.

1. Two friends get together, each contributing $7,125, to start the Swing Right Golf Supplies Corporation in exchange for common stock.
2. Swing Right purchases equipment for $6,250 cash.
3. Swing Right purchases $3,000 worth of inventory for cash.
4. Swing Right pays expenses of $800 for electricity and phone for the month.
5. Swing Right makes cash sales to customers of $4,685 during the month.
6. Swing Right pays employees $2,000 for hours worked during the month.
7. Swing Right declares and pays $500 dividends to each of its owners at the end of the month.

E1-22A. *Classify cash flows. (LO 2, 4).* Classify each transaction as an operating, investing, or financing activity. Assume all transactions are for cash.

1. Jackie Benefield makes a contribution of $95,000 to start the Horse Trails & Stables from her personal funds in exchange for common stock.
2. The company purchases three horses and some equipment for $25,000 in cash.
3. The company purchases $5,000 worth of advertising with the local newspaper.
4. The company pays rent of $15,000 for barn and pasture space as well as use of 50 acres of land for riding trails.
5. The company hires several people to clean stables at a cost of $600 for the month.
6. The first customers pay Horse Trails & Stables $4,225 for six months' worth of riding lessons.

E1-23A. *Analyze business transactions using the accounting equation. (LO 4).* Enter each transaction into the accounting equation and identify its increase or decrease to assets, liabilities, shareholder's equity, revenues, or expenses of Green Trees & Lawn Corp.

1. Green Trees & Lawn earned and collected the cash for $15,000 in service revenues.
2. The business paid $2,000 cash for supplies.
3. Green Trees & Lawn paid $1,500 of a $4,000 note payable to creditors.
4. The company paid $1,100 for rent expense.
5. The company's owner provided $7,500 in additional financing in exchange for common stock.
6. The business declared and paid $2,100 in dividends.
7. Green Trees & Lawn loaned $2,225 cash to another company.

Use the following format:

					Shareholder's equity		
	Total assets	=	Total liabilities	+	Contributed capital	+	Retained earnings
Transaction 1:	_____		_____		_____		_____

E1-24A. *Changes in net income. (LO 4).* For each of the following transactions, determine if there is an increase, decrease, or no change on net income for Fun Movie Productions, Inc.

1. Fun Movie earned $10,000 in monthly sales.
2. The firm recorded a decrease in inventory of $6,000 due to the monthly sales.
3. The company paid current month's rent of $1,500.
4. The company paid employees $2,500 for work done in the current month.

5. The company purchased land for $7,500.
6. Fun Movie invested $4,000 in another company's stock.
7. The firm paid $1,000 in cash dividends.

E1-25A. *Relationship between income statement and balance sheet. (LO 4).* Fill in the amounts for X, Y, and Z in the following table. (The company started business on January 1, 2009.)

	December 31, 2009	December 31, 2010
Assets	$4,550	$5,225
Liabilities	X	$1,500
Contributed capital	$1,300	$1,300
Retained earnings	Y	Z
Revenue	$1,250	$2,575
Expenses	$ 225	$1,175

E1-26A. *Revenues and the statement of cash flows. (LO 4).* Bob started a pool cleaning business on the first day of March. He cleaned 15 pools in March and earned $225 for each cleaning. Most of his customers paid him at the time of cleaning, but one customer, Jeremy Thompson, asked Bob to mail him a bill and he would then send Bob a check. Bob sent Jeremy an invoice but had not yet received the payment by the end of March. When Bob prepares his first monthly income statement, how much will the statement show for revenue for the month ended March 31? How much will be shown on the statement of cash flows as cash collected from customers for the first month?

E1-27A. *Expenses and the statement of cash flows. (LO 4).* Naida decided to open a candle shop. During her first month of business, she purchased candles from the supplier for a total of $500 and paid in cash. She sold half of those candles during the month. On the income statement for the month, what amount would appear for the cost of goods sold expense? On the statement of cash flows for the month, what amount would appear as the cash paid to suppliers?

E1-28A. *Retained earnings and cash. (LO 4).* Checkmate Games, Inc., started business on April 1, 2011, with $7,500 cash contribution from its owners in exchange for common stock. The company used $2,225 of the cash for equipment for the new shop and $2,750 on games for its inventory. During the month, the company earned $4,275 of revenue in cash from the sale of the entire inventory. On April 30, 2011, the owners then spent $3,000 cash on more games for the inventory. What is the retained earnings balance on April 30, 2011? How much cash does the company have on hand on April 30, 2011?

E1-29A. *Classify cash flows. (LO 2, 4).* For E1-28A, what amounts would Checkmate Games show on its statement of cash flows for the month ended April 30, 2011? Classify each as an operating, investing, or financing cash flow.

Set B

E1-30B. *Business exchanges. (LO 1, 2).* Identify the transactions from the following story. For each, identify the transactions as operating, investing, or financing.

Bonnie Lawhon decided to start a business for herself breeding AKC miniature dachshunds. As a talented breeder who gave puppies to her friends and family, she decided to open a small kennel with $6,500 of her own money. She received common stock in exchange. The business had concrete poured and fences installed to give the dogs and puppies shelter at a cost of $3,250, paid in cash. Then, Bonnie's business hired a consultant to design and maintain a Web page for the company at a cost of $200 for the original design and $25 per month maintenance. She paid for the design and one month's maintenance fee. The business required a separate mobile phone to be purchased at a cost of $169 cash. Then, the business put an advertisement in the local newspaper, at a cost of $20 per month for weekly ads. The business paid cash for one month's advertising. The business was ready to go.

E1-31B. *Analyze business transactions using the accounting equation. (LO 4).*   Joe Evans opened a fishing supply store named Evans Bait & Tackle, Inc. The following transactions occurred during its first month. Enter each transaction into the accounting equation and identify an increase or decrease to assets, liabilities, shareholder's equity, revenues, or expenses.

1. Joe Evans used $100,000 of personal savings in exchange for common stock, and the business borrowed $50,000 from the bank to start the business.
2. The business purchased a small building for $75,000.
3. The business purchased $10,500 worth of inventory.
4. The business paid operating expenses of $1,315 the first month.
5. Evans Bait & Tackle, Inc., sold $5,250 of its inventory to customers for $7,875.

All the transactions were for cash. Use the following format:

				Shareholder's equity		
Total assets	=	Total liabilities	+	Contributed capital	+	Retained earnings
Transaction 1: _____		_____		_____		_____

E1-32B. *Classify business transactions. (LO 2).*   For each of the transactions in E1-31B, tell whether the transaction was an operating, investing, or financing activity.

E1-33B. *Analyze the balance sheet. (LO 3, 4).*   Use the balance sheet for Specialty Party Supplies, Inc., at December 31, 2011, to answer the following questions:

Specialty Party Supplies, Inc.
Balance Sheet
At December 31, 2011

Assets		Liabilities and Shareholders' Equity	
Cash	$ 5,000	Accounts payable	$ 1,770
Short-term investments	300	Notes payable (van)	12,500
Accounts receivable	465		
Inventory	825	Paid-in capital	4,000
Prepaid insurance	500	Retained earnings	4,120
Prepaid rent	300		
Mobile grooming van (net)	15,000		
	$22,390		$22,390

1. List the assets the company had on December 31, 2011. Who has claim to these assets?
2. List the liabilities the company had on December 31, 2011.

E1-34B. *Analyze business transactions using the accounting equation. (LO 4).*   Enter each transaction into the accounting equation. Then, calculate the (1) amount of assets owned by Izzy's Ice Cream Shop at the end of its first month of business and (2) the amount of net income for the month. All transactions took place during the first month; Izzy's was open for 25 days.

1. Izzy started the business by contributing $5,500 in exchange for common stock, and the firm borrowed $3,500 from the bank.
2. Izzy's Ice Cream Shop purchased an ice cream delivery truck for $4,500 cash.

3. The business purchased $1,200 worth of ice cream and other items (its inventory) for cash.
4. Izzy hired a delivery driver to work two days a week for a total of eight days the first month to help deliver ice cream for the new company. For this service, Izzy's paid $25 each day worked.
5. The ice cream delivery service was popular and Izzy's sold two-thirds of its inventory for total cash revenues of $3,600.
6. Izzy's paid operating expenses of $215 the first month.
7. Izzy's repaid $100 of the bank loan along with $5 of interest for the first month.

E1-35B. *Classify business transactions. (LO 2).* For each of the transactions in E1-34B, tell whether the transaction was an operating, investing, or financing activity.

E1-36B. *Business transactions effects on shareholders' equity. (LO 4).* For each of the transactions given next, tell whether it (1) increases, (2) decreases, or (3) has no effect on shareholders' equity. Consider both shareholders' equity components—contributed capital and retained earnings.

1. Two friends get together, each contributing $25,000 in cash, to start Luna's Pet Luau in exchange for common stock.
2. Luna's purchases a company van for $30,000 cash.
3. Luna's buys $2,250 worth of supplies for cash and uses them all right away.
4. Luna's pays cash expenses of $2,150 for gas and auto insurance.
5. Luna's earns service revenue from customers of $8,150 during the month and receives payment in cash.
6. Luna's pays its employees $465 cash for hours worked during the month.
7. Luna's declares and distributes $360 cash dividends to each of its owners at the end of the month.

E1-37B. *Classify cash flows. (LO 2, 4).* Classify each cash transaction for the statement of cash flows as an operating, investing, or financing activity.

1. William makes a contribution of $75,000 from his personal funds to start the Cookie Dough & More Ice Cream Co. and received common stock in exchange.
2. The company purchases a building and some equipment for $45,000 in cash.
3. The company purchases $5,500 worth of advertising time on a local television station for cash.
4. The company pays electricity and insurance expenses of $1,500 for the month.
5. The company hires several people to help make ice cream at a cost of $350 for the month and pays them in cash.
6. The National Bank pays $2,500 for ice cream and catering services for its grand opening.

E1-38B. *Analyze business transactions using the accounting equation. (LO 4).* Enter each transaction into the accounting equation and identify an increase or decrease to assets, liabilities, shareholders' equity, revenues, or expenses of Captured Memories Photography, Inc.

1. Captured Memories collected and earned $16,150 in sales revenues.
2. The firm paid $1,500 cash for supplies.
3. Captured Memories paid $1,000 of a $3,000 note payable to creditors.
4. The company paid $1,750 for operating expenses.
5. The company's owner provided $6,500 in additional financing in exchange for common stock.
6. The firm declared and paid $1,020 in dividends.

Use the following format:

					Shareholders' equity		
Total assets	=	Total liabilities	+	Contributed capital	+	Retained earnings
Transaction 1: _____		_____		_____		_____

E1-39B. *Changes in net income. (LO 4).* For each of the following transactions, determine if there is an increase, decrease, or no change on net income for Gardenia Lane Productions, Inc.

1. Gardenia Lane earned $12,000 in monthly sales.
2. The firm recorded a decrease in inventory of $7,500 due to the monthly sales.
3. Supplies were purchased for $50, and all of them were used.
4. The company paid employees $1,715 for current work done.
5. The company purchased land for $26,500.
6. Gardenia Lane paid rent of $2,500 for the current month.
7. The firm paid $1,000 in cash dividends.

E1-40B. *Relationship between income statement and balance sheet. (LO 4).* Fill in the amounts for X, Y, and Z in the table. The company started business on July 1, 2008.

	June 30, 2009	June 30, 2010
Assets	$2,000	$4,250
Liabilities	X	$2,500
Contributed capital	$ 500	$ 700
Retained earnings	Y	Z
Revenue	$ 800	$7,200
Expenses	$ 250	$6,700

E1-41B. *Revenues and the statement of cash flows. (LO 4).* Frank Frock started a consulting business on the first day of July. He provided consulting services for 30 hours in July and earned $150 per hour. Most of his clients paid him at the time he provided the services, but one customer, Ray Linch, asked Frank to send him a bill for the 5 hours he worked for him and he would then send the company a check. Frank sent Ray an invoice but had not received his payment by the end of July. When Frank prepares his first monthly income statement, how much will the statement show for revenue for the month? How much will be shown on the statement of cash flows for the month as cash collected from customers?

E1-42B. *Expenses and the statement of cash flows. (LO 4).* Lisa owns a jewelry shop. During her second month of business, she paid $150 of principal and $10 of interest on a loan from the bank. On the income statement for the month, what amount would appear as an expense? On the statement of cash flows for the month, what amount would appear as the loan payment to principal? Would each of these activities be classified as operating, financing, or investing?

E1-43B. *Retained earnings and cash. (LO 4).* Cookies & Pastries, Inc., started business on July 1, 2010, with a $16,000 cash contribution from its owners in exchange for common stock. The company used $7,500 of the cash for equipment for the new shop and $3,500 for cookies and pastries for its inventory. During the month, the company earned $7,000 cash revenue from the sale of the entire inventory. On July 31, 2010, the owners spent $5,000 for more cookies and pastries for the inventory. What is the balance in retained earnings on July 31, 2010? How much cash does the company have on hand on July 31, 2010? Use the accounting equation to help answer the questions.

E1-44B. *Classify cash flows. (LO 2, 4).* For E1-43B, what amounts would Cookies & Pastries, Inc., show on its statement of cash flows for the month ended July 31, 2010? Classify each as an operating, investing, or financing activity.

Problems
Set A

P1-45A. *Analyze income statement and balance sheet. (LO 4).* A set of financial statements for Gator Company follows:

Gator Company
Income Statement
For the Year Ended December 31, 2012

Sales	$600,000
Cost of goods sold	?
Gross profit on sales	375,000
Administrative expenses	54,000
Operating income	?
Interest expense	6,000
Income taxes expense	94,500
Net income	?

Gator Company
Balance Sheet
At December 31, 2012

Cash	$?		Accounts payable	$ 13,350
Accounts receivable	13,024		Notes payable	9,830
Inventory	43,271			
Equipment	972,684		Contributed capital	605,000
			Retained earnings	?
Total	$1,129,780		Total	?

Requirement

Fill in the missing amounts (indicated with question marks).

P1-46A. *Analyze business transactions using the accounting equation. (LO 3, 4).* The following transactions apply to Molly's Maid Service during April 2012:

a. Molly started the business by depositing $5,000 in a business checking account on April 1 in exchange for common stock.

b. The company provided services to clients and received $4,215 in cash.

c. The company borrowed $1,200 from the bank for the business by signing a note.

    d. The company paid $1,125 of operating expenses.

    e. The company purchased a new computer for $3,000 cash to use to keep track of its customers, starting next month.

    f. The company declared and distributed $1,050 to the owner as dividends.

Requirements

1. Enter the transactions into the accounting equation.
2. What are the total assets of the company at April 30, 2012?
3. Prepare a statement of cash flows for the month ended April 30, 2012.
4. What was net income for the month ended April 30, 2012?

P1-47A. *Analyze business transactions and the effect on the financial statements. (LO 2, 4).* The following business transactions occurred during Buck's Hunting Gear, Inc.'s first month of business:

    a. Buck began his business by depositing $25,000 into the business checking account. He received common stock in exchange.

    b. The company provided services to customers for $30,000 cash.

    c. The company paid travel expenses in the amount of $1,000 cash.

    d. The company borrowed $5,000 from the bank for operating capital.

    e. The company purchased $275 worth of office supplies (for future use) from Office Market for cash.

    f. During the month, the company paid cash of $5,000 for operating expenses.

    g. The company paid monthly rent on the retail space in the amount of $1,250.

    h. The company paid the staff $4,200.

    i. The company declared and paid a dividend of $1,000 to the owner, John Buck.

    j. On the last day of the month, Buck's purchased equipment costing $6,250 by signing a note payable with the bank.

Requirements

For each transaction in items (a)–(j), do the following:

1. Identify whether it is an operating, investing, or financing transaction.
2. Determine whether there is an increase, decrease, or no effect on the total assets of the business.
3. Determine whether there is an increase, decrease, or no effect on net income.
4. Indicate on which financial statement each amount would appear: the income statement (IS), the balance sheet (BS), the statement of changes in shareholder's equity (SE), or the statement of cash flows (CF). (Some will be shown on more than one statement.)

P1-48A. *Analyze business transactions and the effect on the financial statements. (LO 4).* Using transactions a–j in P1-47A, answer the following questions:

Requirements

1. What is the cash balance at the end of Buck's first month of business?
2. Does the company have any liabilities at the end of the first month of business? If so, how much?
3. Which assets will appear on the balance sheet at the end of Buck's first month of business?
4. Did the company generate a net income or a net loss for its first month of business? How much?

P1-49A. *Analyze effect of transactions on accounting equation. (LO 2, 4).* What will be the effects (increase, decrease, or no effect) on total assets, total liabilities, and total stockholders' equity in each of the following situations? When shareholders' equity changes, note whether it is contributed capital or retained earnings that changes. Identify whether each transaction is an operating, investing, or financing transaction.

	Total assets	=	Total liabilities	+	Shareholders' equity Contributed capital	+	Shareholders' equity Retained earnings
a. Received cash and issued shares of common stock	_____		_____		_____		_____
b. Purchased equipment with cash	_____		_____		_____		_____
c. Received cash from customers for services rendered	_____		_____		_____		_____
d. Borrowed money from the bank	_____		_____		_____		_____
e. Received a utility bill and paid cash for it	_____		_____		_____		_____

P1-50A. *Analyze business transactions and prepare the financial statements. (LO 4).* The following cash transactions took place during July 2010, the first month of business for Stay Bright Cleaning Supplies, Inc.:

a. Bill Lunden started a business, Stay Bright Cleaning Supplies, Inc., by contributing $7,500 cash. He received common stock in exchange.
b. The company earned and collected cash revenue of $2,500.
c. The company paid expenses of $1,250 in cash.
d. The company declared and paid dividends of $500.
e. On July 31, the company borrowed $4,375 from the local bank by signing a three-year note.

Requirements

1. Show how each transaction affects the accounting equation.
2. Prepare the income statement, statement of changes in shareholder's equity, and statement of cash flows for the month ended July 31, 2010, and the balance sheet at July 31, 2010.

P1-51A. *Retained earnings portion of the statement of changes in shareholders' equity. (LO 4).* The following information is for Rick's Bed and Breakfast:

a. Retained earnings on February 1, 2011, were $150,000.
b. In February, revenues were $35,000 and expenses were $65,000.
c. In March, revenues were $89,000 and expenses were $74,000.
d. In April, revenues were $73,000 and expenses were $62,000.
e. The only dividends declared and paid were in April for $5,000.

Requirements

1. Calculate the retained earnings balance for the three months ended April 30, 2011, for Rick's Bed and Breakfast.
2. Show the retained earnings portion of the statement of changes in shareholders' equity for the three months ended April 30, 2011.

Set B

P1-52B. *Analyze income statement and balance sheet. (LO 4).* A set of financial statements for Shelby's Music, Inc., follows:

Shelby's Music, Inc.
Income Statement
For the Year Ended June 30, 2012

Sales	?
Cost of goods sold	375,000
Gross profit on sales	525,000
Administrative expenses	?
Operating income	419,000
Interest expense	?
Income taxes	142,450
Net income	$264,550

Shelby's Music, Inc.
Balance Sheet
At June 30, 2012

Cash	$158,592	Accounts payable	$ 14,070
Accounts receivable	18,621	Notes payable	12,520
Inventory	?		
Equipment	895,895	Contributed capital	?
		Retained earnings	425,000
Total	?	Total	$1,231,000

Requirements

Fill in the missing amounts (indicated with question marks).

P1-53B. *Analyze business transactions using the accounting equation. (LO 3, 4).* The following transactions apply to Bostic's Auto Detail Service during November 2012:
   a. Xavier Bostic started the business by depositing $3,350 in a business checking account on November 1 in exchange for common stock.
   b. The company purchased a vacuum cleaner for $1,145 cash.
   c. The company borrowed $1,575 from the bank for the business by signing a note.
   d. The company provided services to clients and received $5,705 in cash.

e. The company paid $535 of operating expenses.
f. The company declared and made a distribution of $200 to the owner.

Requirements

1. Enter the transactions into the accounting equation.
2. What are the total assets of the company at November 30, 2012?
3. Prepare a statement of cash flows for the month ended November 30, 2012.
4. What was net income for the month ended November 30, 2012?

P1-54B. *Analyze business transactions and the effect on the financial statements. (LO 2, 4).*
The following business transactions occurred during Heidi's Smoothy Shop, Inc.'s first month
of business:

a. Heidi began her business by depositing $22,000 into the business checking account in exchange for common stock.
b. The shop paid travel expenses in the amount of $325.
c. The shop borrowed $12,000 from the bank for operating capital.
d. The shop purchased $600 worth of office supplies (for future use) from Office Supermarket for cash.
e. During the month, the shop earned revenue of $10,000 cash.
f. The shop paid the monthly rent on the retail space in the amount of $1,100.
g. The shop paid the staff $2,000.
h. Other operating expenses for the month were $1,375, which were paid in cash.
i. On the last day of the month, the shop purchased equipment costing $10,000 by signing a note payable with the bank.
j. The company declared and paid a dividend of $235 to Heidi, the firm's only shareholder.

Requirements

For each transaction in items (a)–(j), do the following:

1. Identify whether it is an operating, investing, or financing transaction.
2. Determine whether there is an increase, decrease, or no effect on the total assets of the business.
3. Determine whether there is an increase, decrease, or no effect on net income.
4. Indicate on which financial statement each amount would appear: the income statement (IS), the balance sheet (BS), the statement of changes in stockholder's equity (SE), or the statement of cash flows (CF). (Some will be shown on more than one statement.)

P1-55B. *Analyze business transactions and the effect on the financial statements. (LO 4).* Using
transactions (a)–(j) in P1-54B, answer the following questions:

Requirements

1. What is the cash balance at the end of Heidi's Smoothy Shop's first month of business?
2. Does the shop have any liabilities at the end of the first month of business? If so, how much?
3. Which assets will appear on the balance sheet at the end of the shop's first month of business?
4. Did Heidi's generate a net income or a net loss during its first month of business? How much?

P1-56B. *Analyze effect of transactions on accounting equation. (LO 2, 4).* What will be the
effects (increase, decrease, or no effect) on total assets, total liabilities, and total shareholders'
equity in each of the following situations? When shareholders' equity changes, note whether it is
contributed capital or retained earnings that changes. Identify whether each transaction is an operating, investing, or financing transaction.

	Total assets	=	Total liabilities	+	Contributed capital	+	Shareholders' equity Retained earnings
1. Purchased land with cash	_____		_____		_____		_____
2. Performed services and received cash from customers	_____		_____		_____		_____
3. Received cash from the issue of shares of common stock	_____		_____		_____		_____
4. Paid cash for inventory	_____		_____		_____		_____
5. Sold inventory for cash	_____		_____		_____		_____

P1-57B. *Analyze business transactions and prepare the financial statements. (LO 4).* The following cash transactions took place during August, the first month of business for Comfy Cushions Cleaning, a corporation:

   a. Justin Snyder started the company by contributing $30,000 cash and received common stock in exchange.
   b. The company earned and received $10,000 cash in service revenue.
   c. The company paid employees $3,000 cash.
   d. Miscellaneous expenses paid amounted to $725 cash.
   e. The company declared and paid cash dividends of $975.
   f. On August 31, the company borrowed $13,300 from the local bank, to be repaid at the end of December.

Requirements
   1. Show how each transaction affects the accounting equation.
   2. Prepare the income statement, statement of changes in shareholder's equity, and the statement of cash flows for the month ended August 31 and the balance sheet at August 31.

P1-58B. *Retained earnings portion of the statement of changes in shareholders' equity. (LO 4).* The following information is for Larry's Book Store:

   1. Retained earnings on January 1, 2010 were $127,000.
   2. In January, revenues were $15,000 and expenses were $10,000.
   3. In February, revenues were $17,500 and expenses were $20,000.
   4. In March, revenues were $19,225 and expenses were $13,000.
   5. The company declared and paid dividends in March of $1,000.

Requirement
Calculate the ending balance in retained earnings, and then prepare the retained earnings portion of the statement of changes in shareholders' equity for the quarter (three months) ended March 31, 2010.

Financial Statement Analysis

FSA1-1. *Identify items from the balance sheet. (LO 5).* Use Apple Inc.'s balance sheets given here to answer the questions that follow.

Apple Inc.
Consolidated Balance Sheets
(in millions, except share amounts)

	September 27, 2008	September 29, 2007
Assets:		
Current assets:		
Cash and cash equivalents	$11,875	$ 9,352
Short-term investments	12,615	6,034
Accounts receivable, less allowances of $47 in each period	2,422	1,637
Inventories	509	346
Deferred tax assets	1,447	782
Other current assets	5,822	3,805
Total currents assets	34,690	21,956
Property, plant, and equipment, net	2,455	1,832
Goodwill	207	38
Acquired intangible assets, net	285	299
Other assets	1,935	1,222
Total assets	$39,572	$25,347
Liabilities and Stockholders' Equity		
Current liabilities:		
Accounts payable	$ 5,520	$ 4,970
Accrued expenses	8,572	4,310
Total current liabilities	14,092	9,280
Non-current liabilities	4,450	1,535
Total liabilities	18,542	10,815
Commitments and contingencies		
Stockholders' equity:		
Common stock, no par value; 1,800,000,000 shares authorized; 888,325,973 and 872,328,972 shares issued and outstanding, respectively	7,177	5,368
Retained earnings	13,845	9,101
Accumulated other comprehensive income	8	63
Total shareholders' equity	21,030	14,532
Total liabilities and shareholders' equity	$39,572	$25,347

Requirements

1. What date marks the end of Apple's most recent fiscal year?
2. Did Apple earn a net income or net loss during the most recent fiscal year? How can you tell?
3. Did the owners of Apple make any capital contributions during the most recent fiscal year (or did Apple get some new owners)?
4. Did Apple buy or sell any property, plant, or equipment during the most recent fiscal year? How can you tell?
5. On the last day of the most recent fiscal year, did Apple have any debts? If so, what was the total amount?

FSA1-2. *Identify items from the statement of cash flows. (LO 5).* Use the statement of cash flows for Apple Inc. for the year ended September 27, 2008, given here to answer the questions that follow.

> **Apple Inc.**
> **Statement of Cash Flows**
> **For the Year Ended September 27, 2008**

(in millions)	
Cash and cash equivalents, beginning of the year	$ 9,352
Operating Activities:	
Net income	4,834
Adjustments to reconcile net income to cash generated by operating activities ...	4,762
Cash generated by operating activities	9,596
Investing Activities:	
Purchase of short-term investments	(22,965)
Proceeds from maturities of short-term investments	11,804
Proceeds from sales of short-term investments	4,439
Purchase of property, plant, and equipment	(1,091)
Other	(376)
Cash (used in) generated by investing activities	(8,189)
Financing Activities:	
Proceeds from issuance of common stock	483
Other financing activities (net)	633
Cash generated by financing activities	1,116
Increase in cash and cash equivalents	2,523
Cash and cash equivalents, end of the year	$11,875

Requirements

1. Did Apple purchase any property, plant, or equipment during the year?
2. If you were to examine Apple's balance sheet at September 27, 2008, what amount would be shown for cash and cash equivalents?
3. Was cash generated from operations or used by operations? By what amount?
4. Did Apple receive any new contributions from owners during the year? How can you tell?
5. What was the primary source of cash for Apple for the year ended September 27, 2008? What does this say to you about Apple's operations for this year?

FSA1-3. *Examine financial statements. (LO 2, 3, 5).* Use the selected pages from the annual report from Books-A-Million found in Appendix A to answer the following questions:

Requirements

1. What type of business is Books-A-Million and how is it organized?
2. Suppose you inherited $10,000 when your great-uncle passed away and you want to invest in a promising company. Would you invest in Books-A-Million? What information in the annual report would be useful in your decision? Be specific. Is there any information that is not provided in the annual report that you would want to have before making your decision?
3. What is your opinion of the information in the annual report? For example, do you think it is accurate? Useful? Interesting? Informative? Why or why not?

Critical Thinking Problems

Risks and Controls

Being in business is risky. Imagine that you are starting a business. What type of business would you start? What are the most significant risks you face with your business? What controls would you put into effect to minimize those risks?

Group Problem

Look at the four basic financial statements for Books-A-Million, found in Appendix A at the back of this book. Find the total assets, liabilities, and shareholders' equity for the two most recent years. As a group, discuss the change in the company's financial position without looking at the income statement. Jot down your opinions. Then, study the income statement for the most recent year. Do the results support your opinions about the balance sheet changes? What information do these statements provide for your analysis? What additional information would be useful? After answering these questions as a group, look at the notes to the financial statements. Do the notes help answer any of your questions?

Make a list of 10 questions you have about the financial statements. Try to answer them and discuss why you would like answers to these questions. Save the list so you can check to see how many of the questions you are able to answer at the end of the course.

Ethics

Does your school have an honor code? If it does, it very likely addresses the issue of cheating on assignments or exams. Have you ever cheated on an exam? Have you ever "borrowed" a friend's assignment and used it to help you complete yours? Have you ever been a witness to a violation of the honor code by your peers? Compare Target's code of ethics (called Business Conduct Guide and found at http://investors.target.com/phoenix.zhtml?c=65828&p=irol-govConduct) to your school's honor code. How are they similar in purpose and scope?

Internet Exercise: Disney Corporation

The Walt Disney Company is a diversified worldwide entertainment company with interests in ABC TV, ESPN, film production, theme parks, publishing, a cruise line, Infoseek, and the NHL Mighty Ducks. By using the Disney Web site, you can explore vacation options and get Disney's latest financial information.

Please go to the Disney Web site at http://corporate.disney.go.com/investors/

IE1-1. What is the Walt Disney Company's key objective?

Go to Financial Information and click on the most recent annual report.

1. What are the key businesses of the Walt Disney Company? Identify whether you think the primary business activity is manufacturing, merchandising, or servicing for each key business segment.
2. Use the site map to find Financial Highlights. Identify the amount of total revenues and operating income for the most recent year. On which financial statement will you find these amounts reported? Is the Walt Disney Company a proprietorship, a partnership, or a corporation? How can you tell?
3. Use the Site Map to find Financial Review. What key business segment was the largest driver of operating revenue and operating income growth for the past year? Does this order surprise you? Explain why or why not.

Please note: Internet Web sites are constantly being updated. Therefore, if the information is not found where indicated, please explore the annual report further to find the information.

2

Qualities of Accounting Information

ETHICS Matters

Paying for Silence

With just two weeks until the start of his trial, Computer Associates International's former CEO, Sanjay Kumar, pleaded guilty to securities fraud and obstruction of justice. Not only did Kumar engage in a conspiracy to inflate the firm's 2000 and 2001 sales revenue, but he also authorized a $3.7 million payment to buy the silence of potential witnesses. In November 2006, he was sentenced to 12 years in prison and fined $8 million for his part in the $2.2 billion fraud.

As you will learn in this chapter, precisely *when* revenue is included on the income statement is one of the most crucial timing issues in accounting. Computer Associates included revenue on its income statement *before* the company actually earned the revenue. This violates one of the most significant accounting principles that forms the basis of U.S. GAAP and IFRS. Revenue must be earned before it can be included on the income statement for the period.

Why would a smart and wealthy man falsify accounting records, taking the risk of a long prison sentence? Sometimes people in power begin to feel invincible. It is important for every individual to have a strong sense of ethical behavior and to apply high moral standards to every business decision, no matter how small. Too often a number of seemingly small decisions can add up to one big crime.

Information for Decision Making

After Sara sold her first batch of T-shirts, she had some decisions to make. The biggest one was whether or not to continue in business. What she needed to know to evaluate that decision was whether or not the company made a profit in January. **Net profit**, also known as net income, is the amount left after all expenses are deducted from all revenues.

For Team Shirts, the accounting period is the first month of doing business, January 1 through January 31. Information about the month's operations is summarized on the income statement—one of the four basic financial statements. The revenues for the period amounted to $900; this is the total amount the company earned when it sold 90 shirts. The expenses were the cost of the T-shirts sold, the cost of the advertising, and the interest paid on the loan from Sara's sister. The cost of the 90 T-shirts sold was $360, advertising expense was $50, and the cost of borrowing the money—interest expense—was $5. When those expenses, totaling $415, are deducted from the sales revenue of $900, the remaining $485 is net profit. Team Shirts added value by ordering shirts with a special logo and providing them to customers at a convenient time and place. And Team Shirts achieved its goal—to make a profit.

On the income statement in Exhibit 2.1, you will see $485 shown as net income, another name for net profit. The term profit can be applied to a single sale, a group of sales, or all the transactions for a period of time of business activity, whereas net income is a more specific term for describing a company's entire profit for a specific time period. The company made a gross profit of $540 ($900 sales − $360 cost of goods sold) on the sale of 90 T-shirts, and Team Shirts' net income for its first month of business activity was $485.

EXHIBIT 2.1

Income Statement for Team Shirts for January

This is a simple income statement for one month of business.

Team Shirts
Income Statement
For the Month Ended January 31, 2010

Revenue		
Sales		$900
Expenses		
Cost of goods sold	$360	
Advertising expense	50	
Interest expense	5	
Total expenses		415
Net income		$485

Financial reporting provides information for decision making. An income statement, like the one shown for Team Shirts, is one source of information. When the second month of business activity is complete, Sara will prepare another income statement and will be able to compare the two statements. To make such a comparison meaningful, Sara needs to use the same rules for preparing the two statements. If Sara wanted to compare her company's performance to the performance of another T-shirt company, she would need to be sure that the other company was using the same rules to prepare its income statement. For financial information to be useful for evaluating the performance of a business across time or for comparing two different companies, the same rules must be used consistently.

As you learned in Chapter 1, there is a set of guidelines called generally accepted accounting principles (GAAP) that a company must follow when preparing its financial statements; this helps ensure consistency. These guidelines—usually known as accounting principles—were historically developed through common usage. A principle was acceptable if it was used and acknowledged by most accountants. Today the process of establishing GAAP is more formal, with the SEC and the FASB responsible for setting accounting standards.

Setting accounting standards has become a widely discussed topic since the beginning of the 2008 financial crisis. As you read in Chapter 1, there is an international body called the International Accounting Standards Board (IASB) that sets international accounting rules and guidelines called International Financial Reporting Standards (IFRS). The general characteristics and qualitative characteristics of accounting information you are about to study are the same for U.S. GAAP and IFRS. Most differences that arise apply to specific assets and liabilities as well as to classifications of some transactions. Overall, U.S. GAAP are detailed and technical, with over 160 standards and even more interpretations and related guidance. It is often characterized as rule-based. IFRS, on the other hand, has much less detailed instruction and is often characterized as concept-based. Applying IFRS will require much more judgment and interpretation of circumstances than is required in the application of GAAP. As you learn more about these topics in the chapters to come, you'll read about some specific differences in the two sets of standards.

Most people who prepare and who use financial statements believe that having a single set of standards used worldwide is a good idea. With the technological advances of the past few decades, the world has become a global business market. Consider Fiat's 2009 purchase of Chrysler, formerly one of the big three U.S. automakers. As a member of the European Union, Italy, the home of Fiat, uses IFRS, while Chrysler has used GAAP for decades. If both companies had used the same set of accounting standards, the analysis that was done in the execution of this purchase could have been significantly easier. Relationships between U.S. businesses and businesses in the rest of the world have become the norm, and these relationships result in an obvious need for the use of the same accounting standards. Recall that the SEC has set forth a time table for the convergence of U.S. GAAP and IFRS, with the complete adoption of IFRS by the United States possible by 2014. For this reason, it is a good idea to stay abreast of the differences in the two sets of standards and how those differences will be reconciled in the next several years.

---

1. What does GAAP stand for? What does IFRS stand for?
2. Why are guidelines needed for financial reporting?

Your Turn 2-1

Characteristics of Accounting Information

What Makes Information Useful?

The most general and the most important objective of financial reporting is to provide useful information for making decisions. What makes information useful? According to the FASB, the information must be relevant, reliable, comparable, and consistent.

L.O.2
Explain the objective of financial reporting and the qualities of financial information necessary to achieve this objective.

RELEVANT. For information to be *relevant*, it needs to be significant enough to influence business decisions. The information should help confirm or correct the users' expectations. No matter how significant the information is, however, it must be timely to be relevant. For example, the price of fuel is extremely important information to an airline such as Southwest or JetBlue, and a manager needs this information to make decisions about ticket prices. However, if the firm reports fuel prices only monthly, the information will not be timely enough to be relevant. To be relevant, information must be useful in predicting the future. Currently, the SEC requires most firms to submit their financial information within 60 days of the end of the firm's fiscal year.

RELIABLE. When information is *reliable*, you can depend on it and you can verify its accuracy. The information is completely independent of the person reporting it. To be reliable, the information in the financial statements must be a faithful representation of what it intends to convey. For example, Darden Restaurants, Inc., parent company of Red Lobster and Olive Garden, reported $6.63 billion in sales for its fiscal year ended May 25, 2008. This amount must be true and verifiable; otherwise, the information could be misleading to investors. As you learned in Chapter 1, it is part of the auditors' job to make sure Darden has the documentation to confirm the accuracy of its sales amount. Anyone who examines Darden's sales records should come up with the same amount.

COMPARABLE. In addition to being relevant and reliable, useful information possesses *comparability*. This means investors will be able to compare corresponding financial information between two similar companies—how one company's net income compares with another company's net income. In putting together financial statements, accountants must allow for meaningful comparisons. Because there are often alternative ways to account for the same transaction within GAAP, companies must disclose the methods they select. The disclosures allow educated investors to adjust the reported amounts to make them comparable between different companies. As we learn more about the accounting choices involved in preparing the financial statements, you'll see how important comparability is to those who use financial statements.

CONSISTENT. To be useful, accounting information must be consistent. *Consistency* is the characteristic that makes it possible to track a company's performance or financial condition from one year to the next. Only if a company uses the same accounting methods from period to period are we able to make meaningful comparisons. For example, total revenues for Darden Restaurants were $6.63 billion for the fiscal year ended May 25, 2008, and $5.57 billion for the fiscal year ended May 27, 2007. Only when these two numbers are based on the same set of accounting methods can investors determine why sales increased. If the increase was caused partly or solely by the change in the way the company measured sales, then investors would be misled about the company's actual performance. Financial statement users want to rely on the firm's consistent application of accounting standards. Exhibit 2.2 summarizes the desired qualitative characteristics accounting information must have to be considered useful by GAAP.

EXHIBIT 2.2

Qualitative Characteristics of Accounting Information

Relevance:	**Reliability:**	**Comparability:**	**Consistency:**
Information that will provide a basis for forecasts of future firm performance by the CEO and CFO, among others. What's ahead for this company?	Information that is neutral and verifiable. Is the information independent of the specific person who prepared it?	Different companies use the same set of accounting rules. Does the information allow meaningful comparisons of two different companies?	A company uses the same rules from year to year. Does the information allow meaningful comparisons of a company's performance at different points in time?

Your Turn 2-2

1. What is the purpose of financial statements?
2. What four characteristics explain what GAAP mean by "useful" information?

Assumptions Underlying Financial Reporting

The **separate-entity assumption** means that the firm's financial records and financial statements are completely separate from those of the firm's owners.

The **monetary-unit assumption** means that the items on the financial statements are measured in monetary units (dollars in the United States).

Financial information pertains to only the firm, not to any other parties such as the firm's owners. This distinction between the financial information of the firm and the financial information of other firms or people is called the **separate-entity assumption**. It means that the financial statements of a business do not include any information about the finances of individual owners or other companies. Suppose Sara took a vacation to Hawaii at a cost of $3,000. No part of that transaction would be part of Team Shirts' financial reports because of the separate-entity assumption. Look at the income statement in Exhibit 2.1 on page 52, which summarizes the revenues and expenses for Team Shirts. You will notice that the items on the financial statements are expressed in amounts of money. This is called the **monetary-unit assumption**. Only items measured in monetary units, like dollars, are included in the financial statements.

At a minimum, firms prepare new financial statements every year. For internal use, financial statements are prepared more frequently. The SEC requires publicly-traded firms to prepare a new set of financial statements each quarter, which enables users to compare the company's performance from one quarter (every three months) to the next. Accountants divide the life of a business into time periods so they can prepare reports about the company's performance during those time periods. This creation of time periods is called the **time-period assumption**. Although most companies report financial information every three months, only the annual financial information is audited. Most companies use the calendar year as their fiscal year.

Accountants assume a company will continue to remain in business for the foreseeable future, unless they have clear evidence it will either close or go bankrupt. This is called the **going-concern assumption**. With this assumption, financial statement values are meaningful. Would the bank lend money to a firm if the firm were not going to continue operating in the foreseeable future? If the firm expects to liquidate, the values on the financial statements lose their meaning. If a company is not a going concern, the values on the financial statements would need to be liquidation values to be useful.

Principles Underlying Financial Reporting

In addition to these assumptions, there are four crucial principles that guide financial reporting. The first is called the **historical-cost principle**. Assets are recorded at their original cost to the company at the time of purchase. Accountants use cost because the cost of an asset is a reliable amount—it is unbiased and verifiable. After their original purchase, however, some assets and liabilities are revalued for the financial statements. You'll learn about assets that are originally recorded at historical cost but later adjusted to their fair market value—the amount the asset could be sold for in the marketplace under normal conditions—for presentation on the balance sheet. So, while the historical cost principle is still a basic accounting principle, both GAAP and IFRS have been increasing the use of fair value in the financial statements. The trade-off here is between information that is reliable (historical cost is exact and can be documented) and information that is relevant (fair value is often more useful to investors but may be harder to document and may not be exact).

The second principle is called the **revenue-recognition principle**. When should revenue be included on an income statement? GAAP say that revenue is **recognized** when it is earned—meaning that is when revenue should be recorded and included on the income statement. Recall that this is where Computer Associates went wrong. When Team Shirts delivers a shirt to a customer, the company has earned the revenue. When one of Sara's friends simply says she is going to buy a T-shirt next week, no revenue is recognized. When an exchange actually takes place, or when the earnings process is complete or "virtually complete," that is the time for revenue recognition. When Team Shirts and a customer exchange the cash and the T-shirt, there is no doubt the transaction is complete. However, even when Team Shirts only delivers the T-shirt and the customer agrees to pay for it later (the sale is on account), the company will consider the earnings process virtually complete. Team Shirts has done its part, so the sale is included on the income statement. The cash for the sale does *not* have to be received in order to recognize the revenue.

What about expenses? When an expense is recognized depends on when the revenue that results from that expense is recognized. Expenses are recognized—included on the income statement—when the revenue they were incurred to generate is recognized. This is the third principle, called the **matching principle**, and it is the basis of the income statement. Expenses are matched with the revenue they helped to generate. An example is the cost of goods sold. Only the cost of the T-shirts *sold* is recognized (e.g., included as an expense on the income statement). The expense is matched with the revenue from the sale of those shirts. The cost of the unsold T-shirts is not an expense—and will not be an expense—until those shirts are sold. An expense is a cost that has been used to generate revenue. If a cost has been incurred but it has not been used up, it is classified as an asset until it is used.

The fourth principle is called the **full-disclosure principle**. It essentially says that companies should disclose any circumstances and events that would make a difference to the users of the financial statements. As you might guess, there is a lot of judgment involved in applying this principle to the financial statements.

The **time-period assumption** means that the life of a business can be divided into meaningful time periods for financial reporting.

The **going-concern assumption** means that, unless there is obvious evidence to the contrary, a firm is expected to continue operating in the foreseeable future.

The **historical-cost principle** means that transactions are recorded at actual cost.

The **revenue-recognition principle** says that revenue should be recognized when it is earned and collection is reasonably assured.

Recognized revenue is revenue that has been recorded so that it will show up on the income statement.

The **matching principle** says that expenses should be recognized—shown on the income statement—in the same period as the revenue they helped generate.

The **full-disclosure principle** means that the firm must disclose any circumstances and events that would make a difference to the users of the financial statements.

As you have read about the four financial statements and the notes to the statements, you have learned about the qualities of financial information and the assumptions and principles that provide the foundation of financial reporting. Without these assumptions and principles, managers, investors, and analysts could not rely on the information to make decisions.

To complete the foundation for financial reporting and to enable you to gain a full understanding of the information contained in the financial statements, you will need to know about two constraints that apply to the preparation of the statements. A *constraint* in financial accounting is a limit or control imposed by GAAP. There are two types of constraints: materiality and conservatism.

Materiality refers to the size or significance of an item or transaction in relation to the company's overall financial performance or financial position. An item is material if it is large enough to influence investors' decisions. For example, the cost of fuel, the amounts paid to employees, and the cost of buying or leasing airplanes are all material items for JetBlue or Southwest Airlines. In contrast, an item is considered immaterial if it is too small to influence investors. GAAP do not have to be strictly applied to immaterial items (measured in total). For example, suppose JetBlue Airlines made an isolated error and failed to record the revenue from your $350 ticket purchased and used in 2008. Because JetBlue's total revenue was over $3.38 billion for its fiscal year ended December 31, 2008, the company would not need to correct this single error. The item is considered immaterial. (However, if there were lots of these errors, the total amount could be material and JetBlue would have to investigate the errors and correct them.)

Conservatism refers to the choices accountants make when preparing the financial statements. When there is any question about how to account for a transaction, the accountant should select the treatment that will be least likely to overstate income or assets. Accountants believe it is better to understate income or assets than it is to overstate either. As you learn more of the specific ways GAAP are applied, you will see how this conservatism constraint is embedded in many accounting principles. You'll learn, for example, that under specific circumstances a firm has to review its assets before a balance sheet is prepared to make sure none is valued at more than it is actually worth. For example, JetBlue's December 31, 2008, balance sheet shows total property and equipment of $4.47 billion. Under certain conditions, GAAP require JetBlue to evaluate these assets to make sure they are not overstated with respect to their future revenue-generating potential.

Elements of the Financial Statements

L.O.3
Identify the elements of the financial statements and describe their characteristics.

As you learned in Chapter 1, a complete set of financial statements includes the following:

1. Income statement (sometimes called the statement of earnings)
2. Balance sheet (sometimes called the statement of financial position)
3. Statement of changes in shareholders' equity (sometimes called the statement of changes in stockholders' equity)
4. Statement of cash flows
5. Notes to the financial statements

GAAP describe the individual items that are included in the financial statements. To learn what is shown on each financial statement, we will look at the second month of business for Team Shirts. We will take the second month's transactions and see how they affect the accounting equation and the financial statements. Then, we will relate the statements to the qualitative characteristics described by GAAP.

At the beginning of the second month, on February 1, 2010, Team Shirts has a balance sheet that is identical to the balance sheet dated January 31, 2010. Recall that the company's assets, liabilities, and shareholder's equity balances roll forward when the new period starts.

Transactions for the Second Month of Business

On account means *on credit*. The expression applies to either buying or selling on credit.

Accounts payable are amounts that a company owes its vendors. They are liabilities and are shown on the balance sheet.

The transactions for Team Shirts' second month of business are shown in Exhibit 2.3.

The first transaction in February is the purchase of 200 T-shirts, costing $4 each. Last month, Team Shirts paid cash for the purchase of the T-shirts. This month, the company buys them on credit, also known as **on account**. This means Team Shirts will pay for them later. The purchase increases the company's assets—$800 worth of T-shirts—and the $800 claim belongs to the vendor. When a company owes a vendor, **accounts payable** are the amounts the company

Date	Transaction
February 1	1. Team Shirts purchases 200 T-shirts for inventory at $4 each. They are purchased on account.
February 5	2. Team Shirts buys advertising for $150, paying $100 in cash and the remainder on account. The brochures are distributed and used up in February.
February 14	3. Team Shirts purchases three months' worth of insurance for $150 cash, with the policy beginning on the date of purchase.
February 23	4. Team Shirts sells 185 T-shirts for $10 each; 170 of these are sold for cash and the remainder on account.
February 28	5. Team Shirts declares and pays a dividend of $100.

EXHIBIT 2.3

Transactions for Team Shirts for February

owes. This is the first transaction shown in Exhibit 2.4 on the following page, where the transactions are presented in the accounting equation worksheet.

Next, Sara hires a company to advertise the business immediately. This cost is $150 for a service. Team Shirts pays $100 when the service is provided, so the company still owes $50. Like the first transaction, this one also postpones payment. However, in this transaction, Team Shirts has incurred an expense. In the first transaction—when the inventory was purchased—Team Shirts gained an asset. The cost of the shirts will become an expense when the shirts are sold. In contrast, the work done related to the advertising is complete, and that signals an expense. (The timing of recognizing expenses can be tricky; the next chapter will discuss timing in detail.) The $150 expense, like all expenses, reduces the owner's claims to the assets of the firm. Assets decrease by $100 (the cash paid for the advertising), and the remaining $50 increases creditors' claims (liabilities) because it will be paid later. It is shown as other payables because accounts payable is generally reserved for amounts a firm owes its vendors. This is the second transaction shown in Exhibit 2.4. Notice that the expense is recorded even though all of the cash has not yet been paid.

As her business grows, Sara decides the company needs some insurance. Team Shirts pays $150 for three months' worth of coverage, beginning February 14. When a company pays for something in advance, the item purchased is something of future value to the company. Because such an item provides future value, it is classified as an asset. Some items purchased in advance may seem like unusual assets, and often have the word *prepaid* with them to provide information about what sort of assets they are. Common prepaid items are insurance, rent, and supplies. In this case, Team Shirts has purchased an asset called **prepaid insurance**. Cash is decreased by $150, and the new asset—prepaid insurance—is increased by $150. Notice that insurance expense has not been recorded. Until some of the insurance is used up—and it can be used up only from one point in time to a subsequent point in time—there is no expense. Sometimes companies call these prepaid items *prepaid expenses*. Even though the word *expense* is used in its name, a prepaid expense is not an expense as we define it. In accounting, an expense is an item on the income statement. A prepaid expense is an asset, shown on the balance sheet. This is another case of the cash flow being different than the expense on the income statement. We'll cover this topic in more detail in the next chapter, but this should help you begin to think about the difference between spending cash for something for the business and actually recognizing an expense on the income statement.

The company's success continues with the sale of 185 more T-shirts at $10 each. Although Transaction 4 shows these sales as a single transaction, this is just the total of all of the month's sales. They are grouped together here to make the presentation simple. Of the 185 shirts sold, 170 were sold for cash of $1,700 (170 shirts at $10 each) and 15 were sold on account for $150 (15 shirts at $10 each). When a sale is made on account, **accounts receivable**, the amounts owed to the firm by customers, are recorded. Accounts receivable are assets—resources with economic value to a business. This is the fourth transaction shown in Exhibit 2.4. Notice that the rest of this transaction includes the decrease in inventory of $740 (185 shirts at $4 each) with a corresponding expense (cost of goods sold of $740), which decreases retained earnings by $740.

Prepaid insurance is the name for insurance a business has purchased but not yet used. It is an asset.

Accounts receivable are amounts customers owe a company for goods or services purchased on credit.

EXHIBIT 2.4

Accounting Equation Worksheet for Team Shirts for February

All of a firm's transactions can be shown in the accounting equation worksheet. The income statement is made up of the transactions in the red box—that is everything in the Retained Earnings column except the beginning and ending balances and dividends. The income statement transactions (revenues and expense) are then condensed into one number (net income), which becomes part of the statement of changes in shareholder's equity, indicated by the yellow box. Then, the information from the statement of changes in shareholder's equity is summarized as part of the balance sheet, shown in blue. All of the transactions either directly or indirectly affect the balance sheet. The balance sheet reports the condensed and summarized information from the transactions, the totals indicated by the amount in the last row (balances at 2/28/2010). The fourth statement, the statement of cash flows, indicated by the green box, shows where the company got its cash and how it used its cash during the accounting period. Don't forget the beginning balances carried over from the end of January.

		Assets		=	**Liabilities**	+		**Shareholder's Equity**	
							Contributed Capital	**Retained Earnings**	
	Cash	All other assets	(Account)	All liabilities	(Account)		Common stock		(Account)
Beginning Balances	$5,345	$ 40	Inventory				$5,000	$ 385	
Transactions									
1		800	Inventory	800	Accounts payable				
2	(100)			50	Other payables			(150)	Advertising expense
3	(150)	150	Prepaid insurance						
4	1,700	150	Accounts receivable					1,850	Sales revenue
		(740)	Inventory					(740)	Cost of goods sold
Adjustment		(25)	Prepaid insurance					(25)	Insurance expense
5	(100)							(100)	Dividends
Balances at 2/28/2010	$6,695	+ $375		= $850		+	$5,000	+ $1,220	

━ Income Statement   ━ Statement of Changes in Shareholder's Equity   ━ Balance Sheet   ━ Statement of Cash Flows

Details of Ending Balances:

Non-cash assets:		Liabilities	
Prepaid insurance......................	$125	Accounts payable	$800
Account receivable...................	150	Other payables	50
Inventory.....................................	100	Total...	$850
Total...	$375		

At the end of the second month of business, Team Shirts pays a dividend of $100 to its only stockholder, Sara. This transaction reduces assets—cash—by $100, and it reduces retained earnings by $100. This is Transaction 5 in Exhibit 2.4. Notice that it is not recorded with the other transactions. Because dividends are not a component of net income, we have to record a dividend payment *outside* the red (income statement) box.

The financial statements for February can be prepared with the information from these transactions. However, there is still one more step before accurate financial statements can be prepared. This step is called **adjusting the books**. A company must review the amount that has been recorded for each asset and each liability to make sure every amount correctly reflects the financial situation of the company on the specific date of the balance sheet—the last day of the fiscal period (month, quarter, or year). After reviewing the transactions for Team Shirts during the month, can you identify any amount that seems incorrect to you? Start at the beginning of the accounting equation worksheet in Exhibit 2.4 and look at each item that has been recorded. The assets are cash, $6,695; accounts receivable, $150; inventory, $100; and prepaid insurance, $150. Are these amounts accurate at February 28, 2010, the end of the second month of business? Is any asset likely to communicate incorrect information?

> **Adjusting the books** means to make changes in the accounting records, at the end of the period, just before the financial statements are prepared, to make sure the amounts reflect the financial condition of the company at that date.

Yes—prepaid insurance, as it currently appears in the company's records, will not express what it should. Because the balance sheet will have the date February 28, 2010, Team Shirts wants the amount of prepaid insurance to be accurate at that date. What is the amount of the asset—insurance that is still unused—at the date of the balance sheet? It is the $150, paid on February 14, applied to three months. On February 28, half a month's worth has passed. So, approximately one-sixth (half a month's worth) of the prepaid insurance has been used. An adjustment must be made to make sure the correct amount of prepaid insurance is shown on the balance sheet. Like routine transactions, adjustments must keep the accounting equation in balance. To record this adjustment in the accounting equation, subtract $25 ($1/6 \times \$150$) from the prepaid insurance column, reducing the amount of prepaid insurance, and then reduce owner's claims by the same $25 amount. This reduction in the owner's claims is an expense—insurance expense—so it will be shown in the red-boxed area in the accounting equation worksheet. This adjustment is shown on the worksheet in Exhibit 2.4. The correct amount of the asset—the unused portion—will be shown on the balance sheet at February 28, 2010, as $125.

A review of the other items on the balance sheet does not reveal any other needed adjustments on this particular balance sheet date. In the next chapter, you will learn about other situations requiring adjustments before the financial statements can be prepared. For now, this adjustment makes the accounting records ready for the preparation of the financial statements at the end of February.

The income statement, prepared first, lists the revenues and expenses for the period; you can find those in the red-boxed area in Exhibit 2.4. All revenues increase retained earnings; all expenses decrease retained earnings. The only item that we regularly find under retained earnings that is *not* included on the income statement is a distribution to the owners, *dividends* in a corporation. GAAP say that distributions are not expenses, so we will never record them in the income statement area (red box).

All of the items for the income statement are in the red-boxed area of the worksheet. We can simply take the amounts in the red box in the retained earnings columns and group the transactions into revenues and expenses to form an income statement. The accounts are considered income statement accounts, not balance sheet accounts, even though the amounts will eventually be included in the retained earnings balance. They are income statement accounts because we will see the individual accounts on the income statement. The first item on the income statement is revenue. For Team Shirts, the sales revenue, often simply called *sales*, is $1,850.

There are three types of expenses listed. One is the cost of goods sold—also known as cost of sales. Recall that this is the expense associated with selling something purchased from someone else. Team Shirts has cost of goods sold of $740. The other two expenses are $150 for the advertising and $25 for insurance. Be sure you see and understand that the insurance expense is not the amount Team Shirts actually paid to the insurance company. Instead, it is the cost of the insurance that was used during the period. The amount that has not been used as of February 28 remains on the balance sheet as an asset.

The net income for the period is $935—revenues of $1,850 minus expenses of $915. Check it out in Exhibit 2.5, the income statement for Team Shirts for the month of February.

EXHIBIT 2.5

Income Statement for Team Shirts for February

This is the income statement for the second month of business for Team Shirts.

> **Team Shirts**
> **Income Statement**
> **For the Month Ended February 28, 2010**

Revenue		
Sales		$1,850
Expenses		
Cost of goods sold	$740	
Advertising expense	150	
Insurance expense	25	
Total expenses		915
Net income		$ 935

The statement of changes in shareholder's equity is prepared next (shown in Exhibit 2.6).

EXHIBIT 2.6

Statement of Changes in Shareholder's Equity for Team Shirts for February

The statement of changes in shareholder's equity shows how all of the equity accounts have changed during the month.

> **Team Shirts**
> **Statement of Changes in Shareholder's Equity**
> **For the Month Ended February 28, 2010**

Beginning common stock	$5,000	
Common stock issued during the month	0	
Ending common stock		$5,000
Beginning retained earnings	$ 385	
Net income for the month	935	
Dividends declared	(100)	
Ending retained earnings		1,220
Total shareholder's equity		$6,220

This statement provides the details of the changes in shareholder's equity during the year. The information for this statement is found in the shareholder's equity columns of the worksheet in Exhibit 2.4, shown in the yellow-boxed area. Team Shirts began the month with $5,000 in contributed capital. No new stock was issued during the month. That means no new contributions were made during the month. Retained earnings began the month with a balance of $385. Net income of $935 increases retained earnings, and the dividend of $100 decreases retained earnings. Because we have already prepared the income statement to summarize what happened in the red-boxed area in the retained earnings column, we do not need to list all of the individual items again on the Statement of changes in shareholder's equity. We just need to add net income as a single amount. The amount of retained earnings at the end of the period is $1,220 ($385 + 935 − 100).

Next, Team Shirts prepares the balance sheet. The balance sheet was really prepared as the transactions were put in the accounting equation worksheet, but not in a way to communicate the information most effectively. The transactions need to be summarized and organized to communicate the information clearly and effectively. The total amounts at the end of the accounting equation worksheet will be the foundation for the balance sheet. Each asset owned at February 28 is listed, along with the claims to those assets. Notice the similarity between the list of transactions on the worksheet in Exhibit 2.4 and the balance sheet in Exhibit 2.7.

The assets are listed at their amounts on February 28, 2010. There is $6,695 cash. (The details of how this number was calculated will be shown on the statement of cash flows.) Team Shirts also

Team Shirts
Balance Sheet
At February 28, 2010

Assets		Liabilities and Shareholder's Equity	
Cash	$6,695	Accounts payable	$ 800
Accounts receivable	150	Other payables	50
Inventory	100		
Prepaid insurance	125	Common stock	5,000
		Retained earnings	1,220
		Total liabilities and	
Total assets	$7,070	shareholder's equity	$7,070

EXHIBIT 2.7

Balance Sheet for Team Shirts at February 28, 2010

The balance sheet at February 28 has incorporated the new retained earnings balance.

has accounts receivable of $150—the amount customers still owe the company for T-shirts purchased during the month. There are 25 shirts left in the inventory, each having a cost of $4, for a total of $100.

The last asset is prepaid insurance, and the amount shown is $125—the unused portion at February 28. The adjustment reduced prepaid insurance by $25 for the amount used up during the last half of February.

There are two liabilities at February 28, 2010—accounts payable of $800 and other payables of $50. These are amounts that Team Shirts still owes to creditors.

The last item is the amount of shareholder's equity. Because we have already prepared the statement of changes in shareholder's equity, we know that $5,000 is the total contributed capital—in the form of stock—and $1,220 is the amount of retained earnings. Together, the liabilities plus shareholder's equity add up to $7,070—the same amount as the total assets.

The statement of cash flows (shown in Exhibit 2.8) shows every cash collection and every cash disbursement for the month. Sometimes several cash flows are summed rather than individually listed if there are lots of cash transactions. Each cash transaction is classified as one of three types: operating, investing, or financing.

To prepare this statement, you need to use the items from the transactions in the cash column of the worksheet in Exhibit 2.4, shown in the green-boxed area. For each cash amount, ask yourself if it pertains to operating activities, investing activities, or financing activities.

Team Shirts
Statement of Cash Flows
For the Month Ended February 28, 2010

EXHIBIT 2.8

Statement of Cash Flows for Team Shirts for February

The statement of cash flows provides details about the changes to cash during the period.

Cash from operating activities
Cash collected from customers	$1,700	
Cash paid for advertising	(100)	
Cash paid for insurance	(150)	
Net cash from operations		$1,450

Cash from investing activities 0

Cash from financing activities
Cash paid for dividends	$ (100)	
Net cash from financing activities		(100)

Net increase in cash	$1,350
Add beginning cash balance	5,345
Ending cash balance	$6,695

The first cash amount in Exhibit 2.4 is the payment of $100 in cash for advertising; that was the second transaction. This $100 is an operating cash flow because it is a cash expense related to routine business activities.

The next cash transaction is the $150 paid to the insurance company. The purchase of insurance is an operating cash flow. Notice that the statement of cash flows shows the cash paid—with no regard for when the insurance is used.

Transaction 4 involves cash inflows, for a total of $1,700. This transaction was a sale, which is an operating cash flow. Notice the cash in Transaction 4 is $1,700, representing 170 T-shirts sold for cash. Although 185 were actually sold, the cash for 15 of them has not been collected yet. In the statement of cash flows, every item must be cash only.

The final cash transaction is the distribution of $100 to the owner as dividends. This is classified as a financing cash flow because it relates to how the business is financed.

Be sure you see that the statement of cash flows includes every cash inflow and every cash outflow shown on the accounting equation worksheet. Also notice that nothing else is included on this financial statement. The net amount is the change in the amount of cash during the period. The bottom of the statement of cash flows adds the beginning cash balance of $5,345 to the increase of $1,350 to get the ending cash balance of $6,695, shown on the February 28, 2010, balance sheet.

Notes to the financial statements are not included here for Team Shirts, but you should never forget that they are a crucial part of the financial statements. Look at the notes in the financial statements of Books-A-Million in the appendix of the book. The notes are longer than the statements! As you gain an understanding of the complexity of the choices accountants make in preparing financial statements, you will see the need for notes to give the financial statement users information about those choices. Remember that one of the four basic principles under GAAP is full disclosure.

Your Turn 2-3

Is prepaid insurance an expense or an asset? Explain.

Assets

Looking at the balance sheet at February 28, 2010, for Team Shirts, Exhibit 2.7, you see the company's assets, also referred to as economic resources, on the left. According to GAAP, *assets* are those items of value that belong to or are controlled by the company. They are on the balance sheet as a result of past transactions, but they do have value, which they will provide in the future when they will be used to help the business produce revenue.

The first asset on Team Shirts' balance sheet is cash. The amount has been determined by past transactions, and the money has value because of what it can buy in the future. Other common assets include accounts receivable (amounts owed to the company by customers) and inventory (items purchased for sale). The last asset shown is prepaid insurance. This is the unused portion of the insurance—it still has value on February 28.

Assets are listed on the balance sheet in order of **liquidity**. Liquidity refers to how easily an asset can be converted into cash. The assets that the firm expects to use within a year are called **current assets**. The assets that will not be used within a year are called **noncurrent assets**, or **long-term assets**. So far, Team Shirts has only current assets. Look at the balance sheet of The Home Depot, Inc., in Exhibit 2.9. The asset section of the balance sheet shows both current and long-term assets.

Assets are one of three classifications of items on the balance sheet. The other two classifications tell who—creditors or owners—has claim to these assets. Recall that the balance sheet is essentially the accounting equation:

$$\text{Assets} = \text{Liabilities} + \text{Shareholders' equity}$$

Liabilities

The January 2, 2010, balance sheet, shown in Exhibit 1.6, indicated that Team Shirts owed $500 to Sara's sister. On February 28, 2010, that is no longer the case. The debt was paid off in January. On February 28, 2010, the only liabilities Team Shirts has are accounts payable and other payables. *Liabilities* are amounts that the business owes. The word *payable* indicates a liability. Liabilities are the claims of creditors. Usually, these claims will be paid to creditors in

Liquidity is a measure of how easily an asset can be converted to cash. The more liquid an asset is, the more easily it can be turned into cash.

Current assets are the assets the company plans to turn into cash or use to generate revenue in the next fiscal year.

Noncurrent assets, or **long-term assets**, are assets that will last for more than a year.

EXHIBIT 2.9

Comparative Balance Sheets for The Home Depot

Here are comparative balance sheets taken from The Home Depot's recent annual report.

The Home Depot, Inc., and Subsidiaries
Consolidated Balance Sheets

amounts in millions, except share and per share data	February 1, 2009	February 3, 2008
Assets		
Current assets:		
Cash and cash equivalents	$ 519	$ 445
Short-term investments	6	12
Receivables, net	972	1,259
Merchandise inventories	10,673	11,731
Other current assets	1,192	1,227
Total current assets	13,362	14,674
Property and equipment, at cost:		
Land	8,301	8,398
Buildings	16,961	16,642
Furniture, fixtures, and equipment	8,741	8,050
Leasehold improvements	1,359	1,390
Construction in progress	625	1,435
Capital leases	490	497
	36,477	36,412
Less accumulated depreciation and amortization	10,243	8,936
Net property and equipment	26,234	27,476
Notes receivable	36	342
Goodwill	1,134	1,209
Other assets	398	623
Total assets	**$41,164**	**$44,324**
Liabilities and Stockholders' Equity		
Current liabilities:		
Short-term debt	$ —	$ 1,747
Accounts payable	4822	5,732
Accrued salaries and related expenses	1,129	1,094
Sales taxes payable	337	445
Deferred revenue	1,165	1,474
Income taxes payable	289	60
Current installments of long-term debt	1,767	300
Other accrued expenses	1,644	1,854
Total current liabilities	11,153	12,706
Long-term debt, excluding current installments	9,667	11,383
Other long-term liabilities	2,198	1,833
Deferred income taxes	369	688
Total liabilities	23,387	26,610
Stockholders' Equity		
Common stock, par value $0.05; authorized: 10 billion shares; issued 1.707 billion shares at February 1, 2009 and 1.698 billion shares at February 3, 2008; outstanding 1.696 billion shares at February 1, 2009 and 1.690 billion shares at February 3, 2008	85	85
Paid-in capital	6,048	5,800
Retained earnings	12,093	11,388
Accumulated other comprehensive income (loss)	(77)	755
Treasury stock, at cost, 11 million shares at February 1, 2009 and 8 million shares at February 3, 2008	(372)	(314)
Total stockholders' equity	17,777	17,714
Total liabilities and stockholders' equity	**$41,164**	**$44,324**

See accompanying Notes to Consolidated Financial Statements.

cash. Liabilities, like assets, are the result of past transactions or events. For example, a purchase of inventory items on account creates a liability called accounts payable. The balance sheet on February 28, 2010, was prepared after the purchase of the shirts but before the company paid for them, so the balance sheet shows the cost of the shirts as accounts payable. Once incurred, a liability continues as an obligation of the company until the company pays for it. The accounts payable amount for the T-shirts remains on the balance sheet until Team Shirts pays the bill for the shirts. Often, liabilities involve interest—payment of an additional amount for the right to delay payment. When Team Shirts repaid Sara's sister in January, the company paid $5 interest for the use of her money.

Current liabilities are liabilities the company will settle—pay off—in the next fiscal year.

Noncurrent liabilities, or **long-term liabilities**, are liabilities that will take longer than a year to settle.

A **classified balance sheet** shows a subtotal for many items, including current assets and current liabilities.

Liabilities can also be current or noncurrent. If a liability will be settled with a current asset, it is called a **current liability**. For practical purposes, you can think about a current liability as a liability that will be paid off in the next year. **Noncurrent liabilities**, or **long-term liabilities**, will be paid off over a period longer than one year. Most balance sheets show a subtotal for current assets and a subtotal for current liabilities. That format is called a **classified balance sheet**. Look at the balance sheet for Home Depot, shown in Exhibit 2.9. See if you can find the subtotals for current assets and current liabilities. This is a classified balance sheet because it has two classifications of assets and liabilities—short- and long-term.

Your Turn

1. What is the difference between a current asset and a long-term asset?
2. What is a classified balance sheet?

Shareholders' Equity

Shareholders' equity, sometimes called net assets, is the owners' claims to the assets of the company. There are two ways owners can create equity in a company. The first way is by making capital contributions—*contributed capital*. Usually, the capital is cash, but it could be equipment or other items of value. When Sara started her T-shirt business, she invested $5,000 of her own money. Sometimes this is called the owner's investment in the company. The term *investment* may be confused with investments that the company itself makes with its extra cash. For example, Apple may invest some of its extra cash in the stock of Google, which Apple would call an investment. To avoid that confusion, we will refer to owners' investments in the firm as capital contributions.

The second way to create equity in a business is to make a profit. (That is the preferred way.) When Team Shirts sells a shirt, the profit from that shirt increases the owner's equity in the company. In general, revenues increase shareholders' equity and expenses reduce shareholders' equity.

Paid-in capital, another name for contributed capital, is the owner's investment in the business.

In corporations, the two types of equity are separated on the balance sheet. The first type of equity is contributed capital, also known as **paid-in capital**, while the second is *retained earnings*. In a sole proprietorship or partnership, both types of equity are together called *capital*. Separating these amounts for corporations provides information for potential investors about how much the owners have actually invested in the corporation.

Measurement and Recognition in Financial Statements

We will now take a closer look at some of the features of the balance sheet and income statement. Recall that the balance sheet is simply a summary of the transactions from the accounting equation: **Assets = Liabilities + Shareholders' equity**. The three elements are major categories, each divided into subcategories.

MEASURING ASSETS. We will start with assets. The most well-known asset is cash. It is listed first on the balance sheet. As you will notice on Home Depot's balance sheet, all other assets are listed in order of their liquidity—how easily they can be converted to cash. A monetary value is computed for each asset. Cash, for example, is the total amount of money in checking and savings accounts. The next asset could be short-term investments, ones the company can easily sell for cash at any time. The next asset on the balance sheet is usually accounts receivable—the total amount that customers owe the company for credit sales. Inventory is another asset, measured at its cost. We saw that Team Shirts' balance sheet included the cost of the T-shirts still in the inventory on the balance sheet date. Statements prepared under GAAP almost always list assets in order of liquidity, starting with cash. However, under IFRS, the balance sheet often *ends* with current assets. This type of formatting difference is quite common between GAAP and IFRS financial statements.

Earlier you learned two characteristics of the way things are measured for the financial statements. First, they are measured in monetary units. For us, that means dollars. For example, the actual number of T-shirts in the inventory is not shown on the balance sheet; only the cost of the inventory is shown. Second, the items on the financial statements are reported at historical cost—what the company paid for them. They are not reported at the amount the company hopes to sell them for. Some assets continue to be shown at cost on the balance sheet, and others are revalued to a more current amount for each balance sheet. You will learn the details of which assets are revalued and which assets are not revalued in the chapters to come.

RECOGNIZING REVENUES AND EXPENSES. As you know, revenue is recognized when it is earned. Must the customer actually pay the company in cash before a sale can be counted as revenue? No. Notice that the sales of all the shirts are included in the sales total, even though 15 of the shirts have not been paid for yet. When a customer purchases an item on account, the earnings process is considered virtually complete, even though the cash has not been collected. Similarly, a cost incurred in the generation of revenue need not be paid to be included on the income statement. In calculating the revenue and expenses for an income statement, accountants do not follow the cash. Instead, they record revenue when the "economic substance" of the transaction is complete.

Accountants use the expressions *virtually complete* and *economic substance* to describe the same idea—that a transaction does not need to be technically complete to recognize the resulting revenue. If the transaction is substantially complete, the revenue is recognized. This is the revenue-recognition principle we discussed earlier. When Team Shirts sells T-shirts, delivering them and receiving the customers' promise to pay are considered the economic substance of that transaction. Cash may come before the transaction is complete or it may come afterward. This way of accounting for revenues and expenses—using the economic substance of the transaction to determine when to include it on the income statement instead of using the exchange of cash—is called **accrual basis accounting**. Exhibit 2.10 summarizes the assumptions, principles, and constraints of financial reporting.

Accrual basis accounting refers to the way we recognize revenues and expenses. Accountants do not rely on the exchange of cash to determine the timing of revenue recognition. Firms recognize revenue when it is earned and expenses when they are incurred—no matter when the cash is received or disbursed. Accrual accounting follows the matching principle.

EXHIBIT 2.10

Assumptions, Principles, and Constraints of Financial Reporting

Assumptions:	Time-period assumption	The life of a business can be divided into artificial time periods for financial reporting.
	Separate-entity assumption	Financial statements of a firm contain financial information about only that firm.
	Monetary-unit assumption	Only items that can be measured in monetary units are included in the financial statements.
	Going-concern assumption	A company will remain in business for the foreseeable future.
Principles:	Historical-cost principle	Assets are recorded at cost.
	Revenue-recognition principle	Revenue is recognized when it is earned and collection is reasonably assured.
	Matching principle	Expenses are recognized in the same period as the revenue they helped generate.
	Full-disclosure principle	A company should provide information about any circumstances and events that would make a difference to the users of the financial statements.
Constraints:	Materiality	Materiality refers to the size or significance of an item or transaction on the company's financial statements.
	Conservatism	When there is any question about how to account for a transaction, the accountant should select the treatment that will be least likely to overstate income or overstate assets.

When to recognize revenue is easy for some businesses and extremely difficult for others. There is a lot of disagreement among accountants about the timing of revenue recognition. Everyone agrees that the accounting standards say that revenue should be recognized when the revenue has actually been earned and it is reasonable to assume the customer will pay. That is, the transaction is virtually complete. But people often cannot agree on exactly when that has happened. This is an important topic that is regularly debated in the financial community. Unfortunately, improper revenue recognition has caused serious problems for many companies. Many of the accounting scandals in the last decade are related to revenue recognition.

Your Turn 2-5

Give an example of the matching principle from the income statement for Team Shirts for February.

L.O.4
Explain how accrual basis accounting differs from cash basis accounting, and identify examples of accrual basis accounting on actual financial statements.

Accruals and Deferrals

Accrual Basis Accounting

The term *accrual basis accounting* includes two kinds of transactions in which the exchange of cash does not coincide with the economic substance of the transaction. The revenues and expenses are recognized at a time other than the time when the cash is collected or paid.

One kind of accrual basis transaction is an **accrual** and the other is a **deferral**. The meaning of each kind of accrual basis transaction is shown in Exhibit 2.11.

EXHIBIT 2.11

Accrual Basis Accounting

Accrual basis accounting involves both accruals and deferrals.

An **accrual** is a transaction in which the revenue is earned or the expense is incurred before the exchange of cash.

A **deferral** is a transaction in which the exchange of cash takes place before the revenue is earned or the expense is incurred.

When the action comes before the cash, it is an *accrual*. When Team Shirts made a credit sale, it was an accrual. To accrue means to "build up" or "accumulate." In accounting, we are building up our sales or our expenses even though the cash has not been exchanged. The sale is completed first—merchandise is delivered to the customer—and the cash payment will come later. Instead of receiving the asset *cash* from the purchaser, the company records an asset called *accounts receivable*—meaning *cash* due from the purchaser. Accounts receivable is the amount owed to the company by customers. Because GAAP are based on accrual accounting, the necessary part of the transaction for recording the revenue is the actual sale of goods or services—that is the "action," not the cash receipt from the customers.

When the dollars come before the action, it is called a *deferral*. When Team Shirts paid for the insurance, it was an advance purchase—as we all pay insurance premiums up front, not after the expiration date of the policy. But the amount paid for the insurance was not considered an expense until it was actually used as indicated by time passing. To defer something, in common language, means to put it off—to delay or postpone it. In the language of accounting, a deferral means that the company will postpone recognizing the expense until the insurance is actually used. When Team Shirts paid the cash in advance of the period covered by the insurance, the company recorded the cash disbursement. In other words, Team Shirts recorded it in the business records as cash that had been spent. However, the expense was not recognized when the cash was paid. It will be recognized—and remember, that means included on the income statement—when the cost is actually used. That use is the "action" that signals expense recognition.

Cash basis accounting is a system based on the exchange of cash. In this system, revenue is recognized only when cash is collected, and an expense is recognized only when cash is disbursed. This is not an acceptable method of accounting under GAAP.

Cash Basis versus Accrual Basis Accounting

There is another type of accounting called **cash basis accounting**; revenue is recognized only when the cash is collected, and expenses are recorded only when the cash is paid. This is *not* a generally accepted method of accounting according to the FASB and the SEC. Using the exchange of cash as the signal for recognizing revenue and expense does not communicate the performance of the business in a way that allows us to evaluate its achievements. The cash flows are important, but alone they do not provide enough information for decision makers. This does not stop some businesses from using it as the basis of their own accounting records. Remember, some businesses are not required to follow GAAP. For example, doctors who are sole proprietors may use cash basis accounting in their businesses. This means they recognize only the cash they receive as revenue. If they provide services to someone who has not yet paid for those services at the time an income statement is prepared, they would not include the fee not yet received as revenue for that income statement. That is not GAAP. If the doctors were following GAAP, they would count it as revenue and as a receivable (accounts receivable).

Accounting Periods and Cutoff Issues

Why does it matter (for accounting purposes) if there is a difference between the time when the goods or services are exchanged (the economic substance of the transaction) and the time when the cash related to that transaction is received or disbursed? If a company makes a sale on account and the cash is collected later, why does it matter when the sale is recognized—included as revenue on the income statement? Studying Team Shirts will help you answer these questions.

When Sara began her business in 2010, she chose the calendar year as the company's fiscal year. Each of the company's annual income statements will cover the period from January 1 to December 31 of a specific year. It is important that what appears on the income statement for a specific year is only the revenue earned during those 12 months and only the expenses incurred to generate that revenue. What is included as a sale during the period? Accountants have decided to use the exchange of goods and services, not the cash exchange, to define when a sale has taken place. Expenses are matched with revenues, also without regard to when the cash is exchanged. This makes the financial statements of all companies that follow GAAP consistent and comparable.

Recall that the balance sheet is a snapshot view of the assets, liabilities, and shareholders' equity on a specific date. For a company with a fiscal year end on December 31, that is the date of the balance sheet. Remember, the end-of-the-year balance sheet for one year becomes the beginning-of-the-year balance sheet for the next year. When you are out celebrating New Year's Eve, nothing is happening to the balance sheet. When Sara goes to sleep on December 31, 2010, the cash on the December 31, 2010, balance sheet of Team Shirts is exactly the amount of cash that the company will have on January 1, 2011. So the final balance sheet amounts for one year simply roll forward to the next year.

Then, transactions start happening—exchanges take place. The revenues and expenses for the period of time are shown on the income statement. The income statement covers a period of time. A company may construct weekly, monthly, quarterly, or annual financial statements. Many companies prepare monthly and quarterly financial statements; all companies prepare annual financial statements. The income statement for a specific year gives the revenues and expenses for that year. It gives information about how the balance sheet has changed between the beginning of the year and the end of the year. The revenues increase owners' claims; expenses reduce owners' claims. If the difference between revenues and expenses is positive—if revenues are greater than expenses—the company has a net income. If the expenses are greater than revenues, the company has a net loss. The net income or net loss is sometimes called the *bottom line*.

What is the difference between cash basis and accrual basis accounting?

Your Turn 2-6

How Investors—Owners and Creditors—Use Accrual Accounting Information

Owners and creditors can both be considered investors in a business. Both invest their money to make money, and they both take a risk in investing their money in the business. In this context, you can think of risk as the uncertainty associated with the amount of future returns and the timing of future returns. Some investments are riskier than others. For example, when a bank makes a loan to a company, the banker evaluates the ability of the company to repay the loan amount—the principal—plus interest—the cost of borrowing the money. If the bank makes a loan to a company that does not do well enough to repay the debt, the company may need to sell noncash assets to raise cash to pay off the loan plus interest due. When lending money, the bank must compare the risk with the expected return.

Most often, the risk and return of an investment change value in the same direction—we say they are positively correlated. *Positively correlated* means they move in the same direction—higher risk means higher expected return for taking the higher risk; lower risk means lower expected returns. For higher investment risk, the potential for a higher return is needed to attract investors.

Investing in a company as an owner is riskier than investing as a creditor. A creditor's claim to the assets of a company has priority over an owner's claim. (Creditors have first claim to the assets.) If a company has just enough money either to pay its creditors or to make a distribution to its owner or owners, the creditors must be paid, and *they always must be paid* before anything—if there is anything left—is distributed to the owners. That translates into less risk for a creditor. The owner's risk is that the company will go out of business.

However, the owner, who takes more risk, has the right to share the profit. So the risk for the owner is accompanied by the potential for a higher return. A creditor, on the other hand, will never receive more than the amount of the loan, plus the amount of interest that is agreed on when the loan is made.

Financial information is useful for someone deciding whether or not to invest in a company. Suppose Team Shirts wanted to borrow money to expand. A bank would want to examine the company's income statement, balance sheet, and the statement of cash flows. The reason is to evaluate potential risk—the company's ability to make the required principal and interest payments.

The balance sheet shows a company's assets and who has claim to them. A bank loan officer would use the information on the balance sheet to evaluate Team Shirts' ability to repay the loan. He or she would want to be sure that the company did not have too many debts. The more debt a company has, the more cash it must generate to make the loan payments.

The information on the balance sheet would not be enough to assure the bank loan officer that Team Shirts would be able to repay the loan. Because a loan is repaid over several months or years, information about the future earning potential of the business is important. Studying the past performance of a business helps predict its future performance. That makes the profit the company earned during the past year relevant to the banker. Details about the sales revenue and expenses incurred to generate that revenue would help the bank evaluate the company's potential to generate enough cash to repay a loan.

Still, the information on these two financial statements, no matter how relevant to the bank's evaluation, would not be enough. Another piece of the puzzle is the way the company manages its cash. A company may have little debt and lots of earning potential. However, if the company does not have enough cash, the loan payments cannot be made. Because cash collection is the bank's primary concern, the statement of cash flows provides additional information for the bank.

An Example to Illustrate the Information Financial Statements Provide

We will compare two companies, each starting its fiscal year with an identical balance sheet. Then, during the first month of the year, they have very similar transactions. We will look at only a few of the transactions, and we will see that their income statements for the first month are the same. As you study the companies, try to figure out why their income statements are the same. Their ending balance sheets and statements of cash flows are not the same. Where do the differences show up in the financial statements?

The two companies are Clean Sweep and Maids-R-Us. Both are cleaning businesses and both are sole proprietorships. Judy Jones owns Clean Sweep, and Betty Brown owns Maids-R-Us. On January 1, 2011, the two companies have identical balance sheets. Look at each item on the balance sheet in Exhibit 2.12 and be sure you know what it means. Do this before you go on.

EXHIBIT 2.12

Beginning Balance Sheet for Clean Sweep and Maids-R-Us

At the beginning of the month, both companies have the same balance sheet.

Clean Sweep or Maids-R-Us
Balance Sheet
At January 1, 2011

Assets	
Cash	$ 900
Supplies	200
Total assets	$1,100
Liabilities	
Notes payable	$ 400
Owner's equity	
Capital, Owner's name (Jones or Brown)	700
Total liabilities and owner's equity	$1,100

Study each transaction and look at its effect on the accounting equation. Follow along using Exhibit 2.13 and 2.14 (on the following page).

Both Clean Sweep and Maids-R-Us	Clean Sweep	Maids-R-Us
1. Clean 10 houses for a fee of $75 per house	Collects the fees in cash at the time the services are rendered	Agrees to extend credit to the customers; fees will be collected after 30 days
2. Make a loan payment plus interest	Pays off the entire loan plus $40 interest	Pays only $100 of the loan plus $40 interest
3. Count the supplies on January 31 and find $25 worth left on hand	Both will make an adjustment to show $175 worth of supplies used	

EXHIBIT 2.13

Transactions for January 2011 for Clean Sweep and Maids-R-Us

Be sure to study how the transactions are different for the two companies.

Transaction 1: Each company earns $750 worth of revenue. Clean Sweep collects the cash, but Maids-R-Us extends credit to its customers. Clean Sweep records the asset cash, whereas Maids-R-Us records the asset *accounts receivable*. Both companies have earned the same amount of revenue, so each will show $750 revenue on its income statement for the month.

Transaction 2: Each company makes a loan payment. Clean Sweep pays the entire amount of the note payable, $400, plus interest of $40. Maids-R-Us pays only $100 of principal on the note payable, plus interest of $40. The only expense in this transaction is the interest expense of $40. Both companies have incurred the same amount of interest expense, so each will show $40 interest expense on its income statement. The repayment of the principal of a loan does not affect the income statement.

Adjustment: At the end of the period, each company will record supplies expense of $175, leaving $25 as supplies on hand on the January 31 balance sheet. Both income statements will show supplies expense of $175.

We can construct an income statement for each company from the numbers in the red-boxed area in Exhibit 2.14. Revenues for the month of January amounted to $750 and expenses were $215, so net income was $535. This is the case for both companies, as shown

EXHIBIT 2.14

Accounting Equation Worksheets for Clean Sweep and Maids-R-Us

The differences in the transactions between the two companies are reflected in the accounting equation worksheet.

Panel A: Clean Sweep

	Assets			**=** **Liabilities**		**+**	**Owner's Equity**		
							Contributed Capital	Retained Earnings	
	Cash	All other assets	(Account)	All liabilities	(Account)				(Account)
Beginning Balances	$ 900	$ 200	Supplies	$400	Notes payable		$700		
Transaction									
1. Earns revenue and collects fees in cash	750							$ 750	Revenue
2. Makes loan payment	(440)			(400)	Notes payable			(40)	Interest expense
3. Adjusts for supplies used		(175)	Supplies					(175)	Supplies expense
Ending Balances	$1,210 + $ 25			= 0		+	$700 +	$ 535	

— Income Statement   — Statement of Changes in Owner's Equity   — Balance Sheet   — Statement of Cash Flows

Panel B: Maids-R-Us

	Assets			**=** **Liabilities**		**+**	**Owner's Equity**		
							Contributed Capital	Retained Earnings	
	Cash	All other assets	(Account)	All liabilities	(Account)				(Account)
Beginning Balances	$900	$200	Supplies	$400	Notes payable		$700		
Transaction									
1. Earns revenue and extends credit		750	Accounts receivable					$750	Revenue
2. Makes loan payment	(140)			(100)	Notes payable			(40)	Interest expense
3. Adjusts for supplies used		(175)	Supplies					(175)	Supplies expense
Ending Balances	$760 + $775			= $300		+	$700 +	$535	

in Exhibit 2.15. Even though one company extended credit to its customers and the other collected cash for its services, the income statements are identical. The income statement is only concerned with revenues earned and expenses incurred, not with the timing of the related cash flows.

The balance sheet at January 31 for each company can be constructed by simply organizing the details of the ending balances of the accounting equation for each company in Exhibit 2.14. For a sole proprietorship, all owner's equity—contributed and earned—is added together and called *owner's capital*. Both types of equity—contributed capital and retained earnings—are shown on the worksheet, and their balances are added together when the balance sheet is prepared. The two balance sheets are shown in Exhibit 2.16. Notice the

Clean Sweep or Maids-R-Us
Income Statement
For the Month Ended January 31, 2011

Revenue		
Cleaning fees		$750
Expenses		
Supplies	$175	
Interest	40	
Total expenses		215
Net income		$535

EXHIBIT 2.15

Income Statement for Clean Sweep and Maids-R-Us for January

Look back at Exhibit 2.14 to the accounting equation worksheet, where you will see the transactions in the red-boxed area are the same for both companies. That means their income statements are identical.

EXHIBIT 2.16

Balance Sheets for Clean Sweep and Maids-R-Us at January 31, 2011

The balance sheets are not the same. The total assets are different because Clean Sweep paid $300 more than Maids-R-Us on the note payable. They have different assets also. Maids-R-Us has accounts receivable of $750, revenue it earned but did not collect in January.

Clean Sweep
Balance Sheet
At January 31, 2011

Assets		Liabilities and Owner's Equity	
Cash	$1,210		
Supplies	25	Capital, Jones	$1,235
Total assets	$1,235	Total liabilities and owner's equity	$1,235

Maids-R-Us
Balance Sheet
At January 31, 2011

Assets		Liabilities and Owner's Equity	
Cash	$ 760	Notes payable	$ 300
Accounts receivable	750		
Supplies	25	Capital, Brown	$1,235
Total assets	$1,535	Total liabilities and owner's equity	$1,535

differences. Assets and liabilities are different for the two companies, but the owner's equity amounts are the same.

It is important to understand why both companies have the same amount of owner's equity. Both had beginning equity of $700 plus net income for the month of $535, for a total of $1,235. That is the number you find on the January 31 balance sheet for owner's equity. The timing of cash receipts and disbursements does not affect owner's equity.

Finally, look at the statement of cash flows. As you have seen, the cash receipts and disbursements for the two companies were not the same. This shows up clearly on the statement of cash flows. The cash flows statement for each company shows all the cash received and all the cash disbursed for the month. The cash flows statements are shown in Exhibit 2.17 on the following page.

Your Turn 2-7

1. Explain how the revenues recognized on the income statement differ from the cash collected from customers shown on the statement of cash flows.
2. Suppose a company earns $50,000 in sales revenue, 20% of which is provided on account. How much revenue will be shown on the period's income statement? How much will be shown on the period's statement of cash flows? How much revenue will be included in the retained earnings total on the end-of-the-period balance sheet?

EXHIBIT 2.17

Statements of Cash Flows for Clean Sweep and Maids-R-Us

The differences in the cash transactions result in differences in the statements of cash flows.

Clean Sweep Statement of Cash Flows For the Month Ended January 31, 2011	Maids-R-Us Statement of Cash Flows For the Month Ended January 31, 2011

Clean Sweep

Cash from operating activities	
Cash collected from customers	$ 750
Cash paid for interest	(40)
Net cash from operations	$ 710
Cash from investing activities	0
Cash from financing activities	
Repayment of loan	(400)
Net cash from financing activities	(400)
Net increase in cash	$ 310

Maids-R-Us

Cash from operating activities	
Cash paid for interest	$ (40)
Net cash from operations	$ (40)
Cash from investing activities	0
Cash from financing activities	
Repayment of loan	$(100)
Net cash from financing activities	(100)
Net increase (decrease) in cash	$(140)

Putting It All Together—The Objectives of Financial Statements

Financial information should be useful. What makes it useful is the way the transactions of the business are organized into the four basic financial statements:

1. The income statement
2. The statement of changes in shareholders' equity
3. The balance sheet
4. The statement of cash flows

The ongoing life of a business is broken into discrete periods so that performance can be evaluated for a specific period. For our cleaning business example, the period is a month.

Income is measured in a way that captures the economic substance of earning revenue and incurring expenses; it is not based on cash collections and cash disbursements. Notice, the net incomes for Maids-R-Us and Clean Sweep for January are exactly the same, in spite of the differences in when the cash is collected and disbursed. Those timing differences are reflected on the balance sheet by the differences in cash and both receivables and payables; and differences are also shown on the statement of cash flows—the statement that provides the details of the timing of cash receipts and disbursements. The four statements have been designed to be relevant, reliable, consistent, and comparable.

In addition to these qualities, accounting information relies on the basic assumptions and principles we discussed earlier, shown in Exhibit 2.10. We can relate each of the assumptions and principles to the financial statements of Maids-R-Us.

- The separate-entity assumption means that only the business transactions of Maids-R-Us are shown in the financial statements—none of the owner's personal transactions are included.
- The going-concern assumption means we may assume that Maids-R-Us is an ongoing, viable business. According to GAAP, if it were not ongoing, the company would need to have all its assets appraised and listed at liquidation value.
- The monetary-unit assumption means everything shown on the financial statements is measured in monetary units; here we are using dollars.

UNDERSTANDING

Business

Accounting Is Accrual but Cash Is Important

In this chapter, you have learned that financial statements are prepared on an *accrual* basis, but that does not mean *cash* is not important. As a matter of fact, in the current economic environment, having enough cash is more important than ever. Business owners prepare and use historical cash flows statements to gain an understanding about where all of the cash came from and where all the cash went. Smart business owners also develop annual or even multiyear cash flow projections to make sure they can meet ongoing business needs. The goal of cash budgeting is to always have enough cash to keep your business running smoothly. If it turns out that you have more cash than you need, then you must figure out how best to use that extra cash—how to invest it. That is a cash flow problem that you definitely want!

Even in tough economic times, some companies might have too much cash. According to a 2009 *Wall Street Journal* article:

> Tech companies have traditionally held lots of cash because of the risk in developing new technologies. And right now, maintaining a healthy cash balance is prudent for anyone.

> But much of the tech industry is now mature and generating lots of cash. Many big tech names should have a plan for using the money.

Having enough cash to run a business is crucial, but having too much cash could be a poor use of a firm's financial resources. How much cash is enough?

Source: "Tech Companies Need a Cash Plan," by Martin Peers. *Wall Street Journal*, Heard on the Street, March 20, 2009.

- The historical-cost principle means the items on the financial statements are valued at cost. For example, the supplies on the balance sheet are not valued at what they might be worth if resold or at the current cost, which might be higher than the amount that Maids-R-Us paid for them. They are valued at the price Maids-R-Us paid when they were purchased.
- The revenue-recognition principle means the revenue on the income statement has been earned. The related cash may not have been collected, but the work of earning it has been completed and collection of the receivables is reasonably assured.
- The matching principle means related revenues and expenses should be on the same income statement. Only the supplies that are used to earn the revenue during the period are counted as supplies expense. The unused supplies are reported on the balance sheet, as an asset, until they are actually used.

Accrual basis accounting is an accounting system in which the measurement of income is not based on cash receipts and cash disbursements. Instead, revenue is included in the calculation of income when it is earned, and expenses are included as they are matched to revenue. Timing differences between the economic substance of a transaction and the related cash flows do not affect income. That is why both companies have the same net income even though the timing of the cash flows is different.

Real Company Financial Statements

Even though Team Shirts is a small, start-up company, its financial statements include the same types of financial statement items as large, well-established corporations. When Team Shirts sold shirts to customers on account, the balance sheet showed accounts receivable. Look at the balance sheet of FOSSIL, Inc., shown in Exhibit 2.18 on the following page. In the asset section, FOSSIL's balance sheet shows accounts receivable of $205,973,000 at January 3, 2009 (fiscal year 2008), its fiscal year end. Customers owe FOSSIL this amount for products and services the company provided to its customers on account.

Can you find another asset on the balance sheet that reflects the use of accrual basis, rather than cash basis, accounting? In the current assets section, the balance sheet lists prepaid expenses (and other current assets) of $60,084,000. Although the details of FOSSIL's prepaid expenses are not shown, the included items will be similar to prepaid insurance or prepaid rent—items the company has paid for but has not used yet. On the other side of the balance sheet, FOSSIL has

EXHIBIT 2.18

**Balance Sheet of
FOSSIL, Inc.**

Compare the balance sheet of
FOSSIL to that of Team Shirts.
See how many similarities you
can find.

FOSSIL, Inc.
Consolidated Balance Sheets
(dollars in thousands)

Fiscal Year	2008	2007
Assets		
Current assets:		
Cash and cash equivalents...............................	$ 172,012	$ 255,244
Securities available for sale..........................	6,436	12,626
Accounts receivable—net	205,973	227,481
Inventories—net.......................................	291,955	248,448
Deferred income tax assets—net	27,006	24,221
Prepaid expenses and other current assets.............	60,084	56,797
Total currents assets............................	763,466	824,817
Investments..	13,011	13,902
Property, plant, and equipment—net.....................	207,328	186,042
Goodwill	43,217	45,485
Intangible and other assets—net	60,274	52,382
Total assets	$1,087,296	$1,122,628
Liabilities and Stockholders' Equity		
Current liabilities:		
Short term debt..	$ 5,271	$ 9,993
Accounts payable	91,027	111,015
Accrued expenses:		
Compensation	34,091	44,224
Royalties..	17,078	22,524
Co-op advertising	21,869	17,769
Other...	30,306	32,833
Income taxes payable...................................	7,327	40,049
Total current liabilities........................	206,969	278,407
Long-term income taxes payable	38,784	38,455
Deferred income tax liabilities.......................	22,880	16,168
Long-term debt	4,733	3,452
Other long-term liabilities	8,567	8,357
Total long-term liabilities......................	74,964	66,432
Minority interest in subsidiaries.....................	3,219	6,127
Stockholders' equity:		
Common stock, 66,502 and 69,713 shares issued for		
2008 and 2007, respectively......................	665	697
Additional paid-in capital.............................	81,905	88,000
Retained earnings.....................................	695,427	646,492
Accumulated other comprehensive income	24,147	36,473
Total stockholders' equity	802,144	771,662
Total liabilities and stockholders' equity...........	$1,087,296	$1,122,628

accounts payable of $91,027,000. This represents what the firm owes to vendors for inventory items the company has purchased but has not yet paid for.

Check out the other things you learned in this and the previous chapter about the balance sheet. First, it balances—assets = liabilities + shareholders' equity. FOSSIL has a classified balance sheet. Current assets are shown first, with a subtotal, and current liabilities are also shown with a subtotal. Look at the stockholders' equity section. There is common stock and additional paid-in capital—both contributed capital amounts. Then, the balance sheet shows retained earnings, the amount of equity the shareholders have earned (reduced by any dividends paid) by FOSSIL's operations. Also, there are two balance sheets shown, which you will recall are called *comparative balance sheets*. Take notice of the dates of the balance sheets. This financial statement shows the financial position of the company at a single point in time. For FOSSIL, the last day of the most recent fiscal year shown was January 3, 2009, which FOSSIL refers to as fiscal

2008. A company selects its fiscal year for convenience and ability to compare its results with others in the industry.

Applying Your Knowledge: Ratio Analysis

Every business must pay its bills. Suppliers, in particular, want to evaluate a company's ability to meet its current obligations. Simply looking at how much cash a company has does not provide enough information. Using ratios often provides additional insights. A financial ratio is a comparison of different amounts on the financial statements. Several ratios measure the short-term liquidity of a company. The most common is the **current ratio**, which accountants compute by dividing the total amount of current assets by the total amount of current liabilities. The ratio gives information about a company's ability to fund its current operations in the short run.

$$\text{Current ratio} = \frac{\text{Current assets}}{\text{Current liabilities}}$$

Using the current ratio, investors can compare the liquidity of one company to that of other companies of different types and sizes. Recall that liquidity is a measure of how easily a company can turn its current assets into cash to pay its debts as they come due. This information would be important to a supplier considering extending credit to a company. The current ratio also provides information about the liquidity of a company over time.

Look at the balance sheet for Home Depot in Exhibit 2.9 on page 63. The current ratio at February 1, 2009, was

$$\$13{,}362 \text{ million} \div \$11{,}153 \text{ million} = 1.20$$

The current assets at February 3, 2008, totaled $14,674 million, and the current liabilities were $12,706 million. So the current ratio at February 3, 2008, was

$$\$14{,}674 \text{ million} \div \$12{,}706 \text{ million} = 1.15$$

Another way to think about the current ratio is to say that Home Depot had, at February 3, 2008, $1.15 of current assets with which to pay off each $1.00 of its current liabilities. Can you see why companies often strive to have a current ratio of 1 or greater? That would mean a firm has enough current assets to pay off its current liabilities. When using ratio analysis, it is often interesting to compare a firm's ratios to those of a competitor in the same industry. Lowe's, for example, had a current ratio of 1.15 at January 30, 2009, and 1.12 at February 1, 2008. For both firms, the current ratio has increased slightly over time. Also, for both companies, the current ratio has been above 1 for the past two years, so no trouble is indicated with respect to this ratio.

Looking at the current ratio for two consecutive years gives some information about Home Depot or Lowe's, but you would need much more information to reach any conclusions. As you learn more about financial statements, you will learn additional ratios and several ways to analyze a company's financial statements.

You might be surprised to know that some firms actually try to keep their current ratio *below* 1. If a firm generates a great deal of cash from operations, it may know that it will generate sufficient cash to pay its current liabilities as they come due. Darden Restaurants, owners of Olive Garden, Red Lobster, and LongHorn Steakhouse, had a current ratio of 0.41 at May 25, 2008. Here's what Darden's management had to say about the current ratio in the firm's annual report:

> Cash flows generated from operating activities provide us with a significant source of liquidity, which we use to finance the purchases of land, buildings and equipment and to repurchase shares of our common stock. Since substantially all our sales are for cash and cash equivalents and accounts payable are generally due in five to 30 days, we are able to carry current liabilities in excess of current assets.

Business Risk, Control, and Ethics

Now that we have discussed the general characteristics of accounting information and the information shown on the four basic financial statements, we will take a look at how companies make sure the information in those statements is reliable.

L.O.5
Compute and explain the meaning of the current ratio.

Current ratio is a liquidity ratio that measures a firm's ability to meet its short-term obligations.

L.O.6
Identify the risks and potential frauds related to financial accounting records, and explain the controls needed to ensure their accuracy.

Internal Controls—Definition and Objectives

Internal controls are a company's policies and procedures designed to protect the assets of the firm and to ensure the accuracy and reliability of the accounting records.

Internal controls are the policies and procedures the managers of a firm use to protect the firm's assets and to ensure the accuracy and reliability of the firm's accounting records. Internal controls are a company's rules to help it keep its assets safe and to make sure its financial records are accurate. By adhering to those rules, a firm minimizes the risks of being in business. These rules are called internal controls because they are put in place and controlled within the company. Controls imposed from outside the firm—laws and regulations, for example—are not internal controls because they are not rules that originated within the company.

Special Internal Control Issues Related to Financial Statements

Accountants are particularly concerned with the financial statements. Whether you are involved in preparing them or using them to make decisions, you must have confidence that the information in them is accurate and reliable. When you see cash on a company's balance sheet, you should be confident this is actually the amount of cash the company had on the balance sheet date. The sales shown on the income statement should be sales that have been completed—goods delivered to the customers.

Inaccurate information creates enormous problems. For example, the SEC filed charges against Computron for improperly recording more than $9 million in revenue on its financial statements contained in its reports to the SEC. Improperly recorded revenue was the focus of a recent SEC investigation of the Mexican unit of Xerox Corp. Xerox officials in Mexico failed to set up appropriate allowances for bad debts and improperly classified sales, leases, and rentals, violating GAAP. The causes cited were (1) failure (of the Mexican executives) to adhere to Xerox's corporate policies and procedures, and (2) inadequate internal controls.

Exhibit 2.19 summarizes three types of controls a company can use to minimize the risk of errors in the accounting system: preventive controls, detective controls, and corrective controls. This is just one possible way to classify internal controls.

EXHIBIT 2.19

Types of Internal Controls

A company's accounting information system consists of three major types of controls: ones that prevent errors, ones that detect errors, and ones that correct errors.

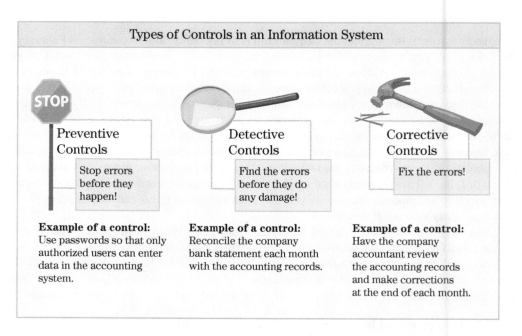

Types of Controls in an Information System

Preventive Controls
Stop errors before they happen!

Example of a control:
Use passwords so that only authorized users can enter data in the accounting system.

Detective Controls
Find the errors before they do any damage!

Example of a control:
Reconcile the company bank statement each month with the accounting records.

Corrective Controls
Fix the errors!

Example of a control:
Have the company accountant review the accounting records and make corrections at the end of each month.

PREVENTIVE CONTROLS. These types of controls help prevent errors in an accounting system. When you order something from Amazon.com, for example, the company gives you more than one chance to review and confirm your order. The computer program is designed to automatically insert the price of each item you order. These are controls that Amazon has put in place to help prevent errors from entering its accounting system.

DETECTIVE CONTROLS. Detective controls are those that help a company find errors. For example, at the end of every work day, a cashier at Target will count the money, ATM receipts, and credit card receipts in his or her drawer and compare the total to the total sales entered in the computer. This control will help Target find errors in its sales and receipts. Once the errors are found, they must be corrected.

CORRECTIVE CONTROLS. Corrective controls are policies and procedures that correct any errors that have been discovered. Target has a policy for handling cash shortages—perhaps the cashier must make up for any shortage.

As you learn more about accounting, you will see examples of preventive, detective, and corrective controls. Keep in mind that to be effective, a system of internal control must rely on the people who perform the duties assigned to them. An internal control system is only as effective as the people who execute it. Human error, collusion (two or more people working together to circumvent a policy or procedure), and changing conditions can all weaken a system of internal control.

Chapter Summary Points

- To make the financial statements useful, we need to understand the rules and the choices used to construct them. These rules are called generally accepted accounting principles (GAAP). In the future, the whole world may use a single set of standards known as International Financial Reporting Standards (IFRS).
- Accounting according to GAAP is accrual based. That means that revenues are recognized when they are earned (when the goods or services have been delivered), not when the cash is collected. Costs are matched to revenues so that they are recognized—put on the income statement as expenses—at the same time as the revenues they helped generate.
- Accrual basis accounting consists of two types of transactions—accruals and deferrals—in which the exchange of cash takes place at a different time than the exchange of goods or services.
- With accruals, the action takes place before the exchange of cash. An example is a credit sale. The sale is recorded, but the cash will be collected later. Remember, accrue means to "build up." When Team Shirts makes a sale on account, the company builds up sales, even though the cash has not been collected yet.
- With deferrals, the dollars are exchanged before the action occurs. An example is paying for something in advance. When Team Shirts paid for the insurance in advance, that was a deferral. Remember, defer means to "postpone." When Team Shirts purchases insurance in advance, prepaid insurance, the company postpones recognition of the expense. The action, in this case, is the passing of the time to which the insurance applies.
- Adjustments are made before financial statements are prepared. The amounts recorded throughout the year may need to be adjusted to make sure they accurately reflect the assets, liabilities, shareholders' equity, revenues, and expenses on the date of the statements. How we actually adjust the amounts to correctly reflect the financial position of a company depends on how we keep track of our business transactions.

Chapter Summary Problems

The following transactions took place during the first year of business for SW2 Company. (Dollars given are in millions. Use the numbers as shown, but make a note on your statements that the dollars are in millions.) The firm's year end is June 30.

a. Issued SW2 common stock (received contributions from owners) in the amount of $250
b. Borrowed $850 from a local bank with a 6-year note (ignore interest expense)
c. Purchased land for $650 cash
d. Paid $25 for operating expenses
e. Purchased new equipment for cash of $300
f. Collected $800 from customers for services provided
g. Paid salaries to employees of $480
h. Purchased supplies for $20 on account, to be used in the coming year
i. Declared and paid dividends to new shareholders of $5

Instructions

1. Set up an accounting equation worksheet like the one in Exhibit 2.4 and record each transaction on the worksheet. (Record the equipment purchase as an asset and ignore the fact that the equipment was probably used during the year. We will get to that topic in a later chapter. Also, ignore interest expense on the bank note.)
2. Prepare the four basic financial statements from the worksheet.

Solution

(dollars in millions)

		Assets		= Liabilities		+	Shareholders' Equity	
							Contributed Capital	Retained Earnings
Transaction	Cash	All other assets	(Account)	All liabilities	(Account)		Common stock	(Account)
a.	$250						$250	
b.	850			850	Notes payable			
c.	(650)	650	Property, plant, and equipment					
d.	(25)							(25) Operating expenses
e.	(300)	300	Property, plant, and equipment					
f.	800							800 Service revenue
g.	(480)							(480) Salary expense
h.		20	Supplies	20	Accounts payable			
i.	(5)							(5) Dividends
	$440	+ $970		= $870		+	$250	+ $290

━ Income Statement   ━ Statement of Changes in Stockholders' Equity   ━ Balance Sheet   ━ Statement of Cash Flows

From the accounting equation worksheet, you can prepare the financial statements. Start with the income statement. The red box indicates the revenues and expenses. In this case, it is a very condensed income statement. That is, the company would have many types of revenue accounts and many more expense accounts in its internal recordkeeping:

SW2 Company
Income Statement
For the Year Ended June 30
(in millions)

Service revenue	$ 800
Expenses	505
Net income	$ 295

The next statement you prepare is the statement of changes in shareholders' equity. Notice how net income is used in this statement:

SW2 Company
Statement of Changes in Shareholders' Equity
For the Year Ended June 30
(in millions)

Contributed Capital:	
Beginning balance, common stock	$ 0
Common stock issued	250
Ending balance, common stock	$250
Retained Earnings:	
Beginning balance	$ 0
+ Net income	295
– Dividends declared	(5)
Ending balance	290
Total shareholders' equity	$540

These amounts will go to the equity section of the balance sheet.

The balance sheet is the next statement that you prepare. Notice that revenues, expenses, and dividends are *not* shown on the balance sheet. Those amounts have been folded into the retained earnings balance.

SW2 Company
Balance Sheet
At June 30
(in millions)

Assets	
Cash	$ 440
Supplies	20
Property, plant, and equipment	950
Total assets	$1,410
Liabilities and Shareholders' Equity	
Liabilities	
Accounts payable	$ 20
Note payable	850
Shareholders' equity	
Common stock	250
Retained earnings	290
Total liabilities and shareholders' equity	$1,410

The change in cash from the beginning of the year (0 in this example) to the amount on the year-end balance sheet ($440) will be explained by the statement of cash flows.

These amounts came from the statement of changes in shareholders' equity.

Finally, you prepare the statement of cash flows. To do this, go down the list of transactions in the cash column of the worksheet and identify each as cash from operating activities, cash from investing activities, or cash from financing activities.

- All cash collected from customers and all cash paid for the expenses to run the day-to-day operations of the firm are cash flows from operations. For SW2, these are (d.) cash paid for operating expenses, (f.) cash collected from customers, and (g.) cash paid to employees for salaries.
- All cash paid for land and equipment (assets that last longer than a year) are cash flows from investing activities. For SW2, these are (c.) purchase of land and (e.) purchase of equipment.
- All cash used to finance the business—from owners and long-term creditors—are cash flows from financing activities. For SW2, these are (a.) issue of stock, (b.) receipt of proceeds from loan, and (i.) payment of dividends to shareholders.

Notice that Transaction 8, purchase supplies on account, does not affect the statement of cash flows. Why not? No cash is involved in the transaction. When the cash is paid in the next year, it will be an operating cash flow.

SW2 Company
Statement of Cash Flows
For the Year Ended June 30
(in millions)

Cash from operating activities:
Cash collected from customers	$ 800	
Cash paid for operating expenses	(25)	
Cash paid to employees	(480)	
Net cash from operations		$ 295

Cash from investing activities:
Cash paid for land	$(650)	
Cash paid for equipment	(300)	
Net cash used for investing activities		(950)

Cash from financing activities:
Cash from common stock issued	$ 250	
Cash proceeds from loan	850	
Cash paid for dividends	(5)	
Net cash generated by financing activities		1,095
Increase in cash		$ 440
Add beginning cash balance		0
Ending cash balance		**$ 440**

This is the cash balance found on the balance sheet.

Key Terms for Chapter 2

Accounts payable (p. 56)
Accounts receivable (p. 57)
Accrual (p. 66)
Accrual basis accounting (p. 65)
Adjusting the books (p. 59)
Cash basis accounting (p. 66)
Classified balance sheet (p. 64)
Current assets (p. 62)
Current liabilities (p. 64)
Current ratio (p. 75)
Deferral (p. 66)

Full-disclosure principle (p. 55)
Going-concern assumption (p. 55)
Historical-cost principle (p. 55)
Internal controls (p. 76)
Liquidity (p. 62)
Long-term assets (p. 62)
Long-term liabilities (p. 64)
Matching principle (p. 55)
Monetary-unit assumption (p. 54)

Net profit (p. 52)
Noncurrent assets (p. 62)
Noncurrent liabilities (p. 64)
On account (p. 56)
Paid-in capital (p. 64)
Prepaid insurance (p. 57)
Recognized revenue (p. 55)
Revenue-recognition principle (p. 55)
Separate-entity assumption (p. 54)
Time-period assumption (p. 55)

Answers to YOUR TURN Questions

Chapter 2

Your Turn 2-1

1. GAAP stands for generally accepted accounting principles. IFRS stands for International Financial Reporting Standards.
2. Guidelines are needed to ensure the usefulness of the information so that a firm's performance can be compared from period to period and compared to other firms' performances.

Your Turn 2-2

1. The purpose of financial statements is to provide information useful for decision making.
2. Useful information is relevant, reliable, comparable, and consistent.

Your Turn 2-3

Prepaid insurance is an asset until the time to which the policy applies has expired. Then, it becomes an expense.

Your Turn 2-4

1. A current asset is one that is expected to be converted to cash or used in the next year. A long-term asset is one that is expected to last longer than a year.
2. A classified balance sheet is one that has subtotals for both current assets and current liabilities.

Your Turn 2-5

An example of the matching principle is cost of goods sold and the related sales. The cost of the T-shirts sold is put on the same income statement as the sales revenue from the sale of those shirts.

Your Turn 2-6

The difference between cash basis and accrual basis accounting is the timing of recognizing revenues and expenses. Cash basis accounting recognizes revenue when the cash is collected and expenses when cash is disbursed. In accrual accounting, revenues are recognized in the period in which they are earned (by the completion of the work) and expenses are matched to the revenues they help create.

Your Turn 2-7

1. On the income statement, the revenues earned are shown. (That is called *recognizing* the revenue.) On the statement of cash flows, only the amount of cash collected from customers is included.
2. If a company earns $50,000 worth of revenue, then all of that will be recognized—included on the income statement. The amount of cash collected is given as 80%, so $40,000 would be shown on the statement of cash flows as cash collected from customers. The entire amount, $50,000, will be in the retained earnings balance because the retained earnings increase is the amount that is on the income statement.

Questions

1. What is GAAP? What is IFRS?
2. Name the four characteristics that help make accounting information useful.
3. What is the separate-entity assumption?
4. Why would the going-concern assumption be important to a bank giving a business a loan?
5. Explain materiality and give an example of both a material and an immaterial item.
6. What are the four basic financial statements?
7. Which financial statement pertains to a single moment in time?
8. What is a current asset? What is a current liability?
9. What are the two ways that shareholders' equity is generated in a business?
10. What does the income statement report about a firm? Name the types of accounts that appear on the income statement.
11. What is the purpose of the statement of cash flows? How are the cash flows categorized? What is the significance of classifying cash flows into these categories?
12. What is the full-disclosure principle?
13. What does *recognize revenue* mean in accounting?
14. What is the matching principle?
15. What is an accrual? What is a deferral?
16. Must a company collect the money from a sale before the sale can be recognized?
17. What is the cost of goods sold?
18. Explain the difference between cash basis accounting and accrual basis accounting.
19. How is the current ratio computed? What does it tell us about a company?
20. Define internal control and explain why it is important.
21. For each of the controls given, tell whether it is primarily a preventive control, a detective control, or a corrective control.
    a. Retro Clothing, Inc., has an online purchase system that automatically inserts the total price of each item a customer orders.
    b. The teller double-checks the account number on the loan payment before applying payment.
    c. External auditors are hired to audit the year-end financial statements.

Multiple-Choice Questions

1. If revenue exceeds expenses for a given period,
   a. total assets for the period will decrease.
   b. cash for the period will increase.
   c. the income statement will report net income.
   d. liabilities for the period will decrease.
2. The matching principle is best described as the process of
   a. matching assets to liabilities and owners' equity.
   b. recognizing a cost as an expense in the period in which it is used to generate revenue.
   c. matching cash collections to revenue.
   d. matching income to owners' equity.
3. Which of the following would never appear on a company's income statement?
   a. Prepaid insurance
   b. Cost of goods sold
   c. Interest expense
   d. Sales revenue
4. Which of the following statements is consistent with accrual basis accounting?
   a. Revenues are recorded when cash is received.
   b. Expenses are recorded when cash is paid.
   c. Expenses are recorded in a different period than the related revenue.
   d. Revenues are recorded when earned and expenses are matched with the revenues.
5. Sales revenue is most often recognized in the period in which
   a. the customer agrees to purchase the merchandise.
   b. the seller agrees to sell the merchandise to the customer at a specified price.
   c. the seller collects cash from the customer.
   d. the seller delivers the merchandise to the customer.
6. Which of the following is an example of a financing cash outflow?
   a. Borrowing money from a bank by signing a long-term note payable
   b. Financing the purchase of a new factory by issuing new shares of stock
   c. Paying a cash dividend to stockholders
   d. Purchasing a new delivery truck
7. How are assets reported in the balance sheet?
   a. Chronologically
   b. Alphabetically
   c. In the order of their liquidity
   d. In the order of their relative values
8. Which of the following financial statement elements is found on the balance sheet?
   a. Insurance expense
   b. Retained earnings
   c. Sales revenue
   d. All of the above
9. A company's current ratio is 1.85. You can safely conclude that
   a. the company is a good investment.
   b. the company will have no trouble paying its current obligations.
   c. the company has a short-term problem related to paying its bills.
   d. the company has a long-term problem related to meeting its obligations.
10. Which of the following is not a type of internal control?
    a. Preventive
    b. Corrective
    c. Collusion
    d. Detective

All of the A exercises can be found within MyAccountingLab, an online homework and practice environment.

Short Exercises
Set A

SE2-1A. *Elements of the financial statements. (LO 3).* For each item that follows, tell whether it is an asset, a liability, or a shareholders' equity item.

1. Automobile
2. Prepaid insurance
3. Common stock
4. Unearned revenue
5. Accounts payable
6. Retained earnings
7. Accounts receivable
8. Inventory
9. Cash

SE2-2A. *Elements of the financial statements. (LO 3).* For each of the following line items, give the financial statement on which it would appear.

Operating expense	Accounts payable
Sales revenue	Accounts receivable
Cost of goods sold	Net cash from operations
Equipment	Prepaid rent
Long-term debt	Advertising expense

SE2-3A. *Revenue recognition. (LO 3, 4).* Public Relations, Inc., managed a grand opening party on behalf of a new restaurant on April 15, 2009. Public Relations charged the restaurant $2,100. The restaurant paid for $1,800 of the bill from Public Relations, Inc., on April 20, 2009. The remaining balance was paid on May 5, 2009. How did these transactions affect Public Relations' income statement for the month of April and the balance sheet at April 30, 2009?

SE2-4A. *Accrual accounting versus cash basis accounting. (LO 4).* Missy & Adele Ice Cream, Inc., purchased inventory for its ice cream shop in August 2009 for $55,000 cash to sell in August and September. The company sold inventory that cost $35,000 in August and the remainder in September. What is the cost of goods sold for August 2009 and the cost of goods sold for September 2009 if Missy & Adele uses GAAP? What is the cost of goods sold for each month if Missy & Adele uses cash basis accounting?

SE2-5A. *Recording credit sales. (LO 4).* Wasil Company provided services on account for a customer that amounted to $1,000. How would this transaction be shown in the accounting equation?

SE2-6A. *Accounts payable versus accounts receivable. (LO 4).* Bolo Company purchased inventory on account in the amount of $500. Then, Bolo sold the inventory to a customer for $1,000. Bolo extended credit to this customer. In other words, the sale was made on account. Related to these two transactions, how much did Bolo record as accounts payable? How much did Bolo record as accounts receivable?

SE2-7A. *Cash versus credit sales. (LO 3, 4).* Company A had sales of $1,500 during the year and collected them all in cash. Company B, on the other hand, had sales of $1,500 during the year but collected only $1,000 cash with the remaining $500 sales on account. Both firms had expenses of $700, all paid in cash by both firms. What was Company A's net income for the year? What was Company B's net income for the year? What was Company A's net cash from operating activities during the year? What was Company B's net cash from operating activities during the year?

SE2-8A. *Costs versus expenses. (LO 3).* The cost of supplies purchased by the Decker Company was $5,000 during the year. Decker used $4,000 worth of those supplies during the year and still had $1,000 worth of them left at year end. What was the amount of Decker's supplies expense for the year?

SE2-9A. *Interest payment and cash flows. (LO 4).* Suppose Miller Hardware borrowed $10,000 from the local bank, with payments of principal and interest due each month. For April, Miller paid the bank $1,000 of principal and $50 interest. How would these cash flows be classified on the statement of cash flows?

SE2-10A. *Compute and explain current ratio. (LO 5).* Given the following information, compute the current ratio for the two years shown. Explain the trend in the ratio for both years and what you think it means.

From balance sheet at	06/30/2010	06/30/2011
Current assets	$300,000	$360,000
Current liabilities	$200,000	$300,000

Set B

SE2-11B. *Elements of the financial statements. (LO 3).* For each item that follows, tell whether it is an asset, a liability, or a shareholders' equity item.

1. Prepaid insurance
2. Accounts receivable
3. Retained earnings
4. Cash
5. Notes payable
6. Supplies

SE2-12B. *Elements of the financial statements. (LO 3).* For each of the following line items, give the financial statement on which it would appear.

Salary expense	Service revenue
Sales revenue	Accounts payable
Cost of goods sold	Net cash from financing activities
Land	Prepaid insurance
Notes payable	Marketing expenses

SE2-13B. *Revenue recognition. (LO 3, 4).* Myadd, Inc., spent $3,000 on catering for its grand opening. Myadd paid the caterer half of the bill at the event, and requested a bill for the remaining half. The following day, Myadd's accountant had to record the transaction. Show what he or she recorded by using the accounting equation.

SE2-14B. *Accrual accounting versus cash basis accounting. (LO 4).* At the beginning of January, Conway Coffee Bean Shop purchased inventory for $5,000 cash to sell in January and February. The shop sold inventory that cost $2,100 in January and the remainder in February. What is the cost of goods sold for January and the cost of goods sold for February if Conway Coffee uses GAAP? What is the cost of goods sold for each month if Conway Coffee uses cash basis accounting?

SE2-15B. *Recording credit sales. (LO 4).* Jaybee Company provided services on account for a customer that amounted to $400. How would this transaction be shown in the accounting equation?

SE2-16B. *Accounts payable versus accounts receivable. (LO 4).* Renata Jewels purchased inventory on account in the amount of $10,000. Then, the store sold the inventory to customers for $17,500. Renata extended credit to its customers. In other words, all sales were made on account. Related to these two transactions, how much did Renata Jewels record as accounts payable? How much did Renata Jewels record as accounts receivable?

SE2-17B. *Cash versus credit sales. (LO 3, 4).* Company X had sales of $7,500 during the year and collected half of them in cash. Company Y, on the other hand, had sales of $7,500 during the year and collected all in cash. Both firms had expenses of $2,400, paid in cash by both firms. What was Company X's net income for the year? What was Company Y's net income for the year? What was Company X's net cash from operating activities during the year? What was Company Y's net cash from operating activities during the year?

SE2-18B. *Costs versus expenses. (LO 3).* The cost of supplies purchased by the Alpha Company was $1,000 during the year. Alpha used $460 worth of those supplies during the year and still had $540 worth of them left at year end. What was the amount of Alpha's supplies *expense* for the year?

SE2-19B. *Interest payment and cash flows. (LO 4).* Suppose Betty's Beauty Supplies borrowed $40,000 from the local bank, with payments of principal and interest due each month. For the month of August, Betty's paid the bank $4,000 of principal and $200 interest. How would these cash flows be classified on the statement of cash flows?

SE2-20B. *Compute and explain current ratio. (LO 5).* Given the following information, compute the current ratio for the two years shown. Explain the trend in the ratio for both years and what you think it means.

From balance sheet at	09/30/2010	09/30/2011
Current assets	$13,000	$11,000
Current liabilities	$10,000	$10,000

All of the A exercises can be found within MyAccountingLab, an online homework and practice environment.

Exercises
Set A

E2-21A. *Elements of the financial statements. (LO 3).* The following accounts and balances were taken from the financial statements of Electronic Super Deals, Inc. For each item, identify the financial statement(s) on which the item would appear. Then, identify each balance sheet item as an asset, a liability, or a shareholders' equity account.

Equipment	$120,000
Accounts receivable	105,000
Inventory	225,000
Long-term notes payable	315,025
Net cash from operating activities	28,000
Common Stock	35,150
Land	575,000
Retained earnings	100,000
Cash	340,000
Interest payable	650
Long-term mortgage payable	85,000
Salaries payable	21,525
Net cash from financing activities	18,000

E2-22A. *Net income and retained earnings. (LO 3).* Jule's Dairy Farm, Inc., reported the following (incomplete) information in its records for 2010:

Net income	$ 25,000
Sales	115,000
Beginning balance—retained earnings	20,000
Cost of goods sold	45,000
Dividends declared and paid	2,250

1. If the sales revenue given is the only revenue for the year, what were the expenses for the year other than cost of goods sold?
2. What is the balance of retained earnings at the end of 2010?

E2-23A. *Elements of the financial statements. (LO 3).* Listed are elements of the financial statements discussed in this chapter. Match each element with the descriptions (use each as many times as necessary).

   a. Assets
   b. Liabilities
   c. Shareholders' equity
   d. Revenues
   e. Expenses

1. _____ Debts of the company
2. _____ Economic resources with future benefit
3. _____ Inflows of assets from delivering or producing goods or services
4. _____ Things of value a company owns
5. _____ The residual interest in the assets of an entity that remains after deducting its liabilities
6. _____ The difference between what the company has and what the company owes
7. _____ The owners' interest in the company
8. _____ Outflows or using up of assets from delivering or producing goods and services
9. _____ Costs that have no future value
10. _____ The amount the company owes
11. _____ Sales

E2-24A. *Balance sheet and income statement transactions. (LO 3, 4).* Unisource Company started the first year of operations with $2,000 in cash and common stock. During 2010, the Unisource Company earned $4,600 of revenue on account. The company collected $4,200 cash from accounts receivable and paid $2,850 cash for operating expenses. Enter the transactions into the accounting equation.

1. What happened to total assets (increase or decrease and by how much)?
2. What is the cash balance on December 31, 2010?
3. What is the total shareholders' equity on December 31, 2010?
4. What is net income for the year?

E2-25A. *Income statement preparation. (LO 3).* Use the following to prepare an income statement for Excel Technology, Inc., for the year ended June 30, 2011:

Service revenues	$62,675
Rent expense	12,000
Insurance expense	6,550
Salary expenses	18,625
Administrative expenses	5,720

E2-26A. *Classified balance sheet preparation. (LO 3).* The following items were taken from the December 31, 2012, financial statements of Whitehouse Corporation. (All dollars are in millions.) Prepare a classified balance sheet as of December 31, 2012.

Property and equipment	$15,225	Salaries payable	11,250
Common stock	15,895	Other noncurrent liabilities	1,445
Investment in land	13,215	Retained earnings	8,835
Short-term investments	1,900	Prepaid insurance	675
Cash	1,850	Other noncurrent assets	6,795
Accounts receivable	185	Interest payable	845
Supplies	110	Mortgage payable	1,685

E2-27A. *Current ratio. (LO 5).* Use the balance sheet you prepared in E2-26A to compute the current ratio at December 31, 2012.

E2-28A. *Current ratio. (LO 5).* The following data was taken from the 2009 and 2008 financial statements of Tasty Sweets Corporation. Calculate the current ratio for each year. What happened to the company's liquidity from 2008 to 2009?

	2009	2008
Current assets	384,728	385,642
Total assets	649,803	590,112
Current liabilities	151,084	157,990
Total liabilities	261,676	282,244
Total shareholders' equity	388,127	307,868

Set B

E2-29B. *Elements of the financial statements. (LO 3).* The following accounts and balances were taken from the financial statements of Books & Media, Inc. For each item, identify the financial statement(s) on which the item would appear. Then, identify each balance sheet item as an asset, a liability, or a shareholders' equity account.

Inventory	$ 81,250
Accounts payable	52,300
Cash	77,880
Short-term notes payable	32,200
Net cash from investing activities	49,300
Building	76,475
Common stock	105,000
Retained earnings	63,000
Net cash from financing activities	21,080
Accounts receivable	44,270
Long-term mortgage payable	54,000
Taxes payable	1,500
Net cash from operating activities	34,350

E2-30B. *Net income and retained earnings. (LO 3).* Donut Hole, Inc., reported the following (incomplete) information in its records for 2011:

Net income	$ 52,000
Sales	153,750
Beginning balance—retained earnings	15,445
Cost of goods sold	68,000
Dividends declared and paid	3,025

1. If the sales revenue given is the only revenue for the year, what were the expenses for the year other than cost of goods sold?
2. What is the balance of retained earnings at the end of 2011?

E2-31B. *Elements of the financial statements. (LO 3).* Listed are elements of the financial statements discussed in this chapter. Match each element with the descriptions (use each as many times as necessary).
   a. Assets
   b. Liabilities
   c. Shareholders' equity
   d. Revenues
   e. Expenses
   f. Retained earnings
   g. Common stock

1. _____ Note signed with a bank
2. _____ Rent paid a year in advance

3. _____ Items that make up net income that appear on the income statement
4. _____ Items that appear on the balance sheet
5. _____ A share of ownership in a corporation
6. _____ Equity that results from doing business and is kept in the company rather than paid out to stockholders
7. _____ Shareholders' interest in the company
8. _____ Costs of the daily operations of a business
9. _____ Salaries owed to employees
10. _____ Cost of inventory when it is sold
11. _____ Revenue received for services not yet provided
12. _____ Interest received on notes receivable

E2-32B. *Balance sheet and income statement transactions. (LO 3, 4).* Pet Caterers, Inc., started the first year of operations with $3,500 in cash and common stock. During 2012, Pet Caterers earned $6,500 of revenue on account. The company collected $5,900 cash from accounts receivable and paid $3,115 cash for operating expenses. Enter the transactions into the accounting equation.

1. What happened to total assets (increase or decrease and by how much)?
2. What is the cash balance on December 31, 2012?
3. What is the total shareholders' equity on December 31, 2012?
4. What is net income for the year?

E2-33B. *Income statement preparation. (LO 3).* Use the following to prepare an income statement for Grace's Landscape Service, Inc., for the year ended June 30, 2011:

Service revenue	$37,515
Rent expense	8,675
Insurance expense	2,125
Other operating expenses	12,075
Salary expense	10,650

E2-34B. *Classified balance sheet preparation. (LO 3).* The following items were taken from the December 31, 2012, financial statements of Organic Vegetables, Inc. (All dollars are in thousands.) Prepare a classified balance sheet as of December 31, 2012.

Land and building	$6,750	Accounts payable	4,125
Common stock	3,651	Other noncurrent liabilities	2,150
Long-term investments	2,175	Retained earnings	1,297
Short-term investments	615	Other current assets	1,100
Cash	1,260	Vehicles	3,267
Accounts receivable	575	Current portion of long-term debt	1,160
Inventories	505	Long-term debt	3,864

E2-35B. *Current ratio. (LO 5).* Use the balance sheet you prepared in E2-34B to compute the current ratio at December 31, 2012.

E2-36B. *Current ratio. (LO 5).* The following data was taken from the 2011 and 2010 financial statements of Shelby Pet Supplies Company. Calculate the current ratio for each year. What happened to the company's liquidity from 2010 to 2011?

	2011	2010
Current assets	105,000	142,000
Total assets	275,000	376,750
Current liabilities	55,000	115,000
Total liabilities	125,000	175,000
Total shareholders' equity	150,000	201,750

Problems
Set A

P2-37A. *Relationships between financial statement items. (LO 3).* Use the information from Shane and Lane, Inc., for the year ended December 31, 2011, to answer the questions that follow. Assume that the shareholders made new contributions of $25 to the company during the year.

    a. Expenses for the year ended December 31, 2011 = $625
    b. Net income for the year ended December 31, 2011 = $415
    c. Beginning balance (December 31, 2010, balance) in retained earnings = $215
    d. Ending balance (December 31, 2011, balance) in retained earnings = $500
    e. Total liabilities and shareholders' equity at December 31, 2011 = $875
    f. Beginning balance (December 31, 2010, balance) in total liabilities = $260
    g. Ending balance (December 31, 2011, balance) in total liabilities = $275

Requirements

    1. What were the company's total revenues during the year ended December 31, 2011?
    2. What was the amount of the dividends declared during the year ended December 31, 2011?
    3. What is the total that owners had invested in Shane and Lane as of December 31, 2011?
    4. What were total assets on the company's December 31, 2011, balance sheet?

P2-38A. *Analyzing transactions. (LO 3).* Accounting Services Corporation entered into the following transactions during 2010:

    a. The company started as a corporation with a $14,700 cash contribution from the owners in exchange for common stock.
    b. Service revenues on account amounted to $8,250.
    c. Cash collections of accounts receivable amounted to $6,875.
    d. Purchased supplies on account for $125 and used all of them.
    e. On December 15, 2010, the company paid $6,000 in advance for leased office space. The lease does not go into effect until 2011.

Requirements

Put each of the transactions in an accounting equation worksheet. Then, answer the following questions:

    1. What is the amount of cash flow from operating activities for 2010?
    2. What amount of total liabilities would appear on the December 31, 2010, balance sheet?
    3. What is the amount of contributed capital as of December 31, 2010?
    4. What amount of net income would appear on the income statement for the year ended December 31, 2010?

P2-39A. *Analyzing transactions and preparing financial statements. (LO 3).* The following transactions occurred during MP Public Relations Firm's first month of business:

    a. Marlene and Pamela opened up MP Public Relations Firm by contributing $22,750 on July 1, 2009, in exchange for common stock.
    b. The firm borrowed $15,000 from the bank on July 1. The note is a 1-year, 10% note, with both principal and interest to be repaid on June 30, 2010.
    c. The firm prepaid a year of rent for $1,200 that started August 1, 2009.
    d. The firm paid $1,050 cash for operating expenses for the first month.
    e. The firm earned $10,500 in revenue the first month. Of that amount, $7,500 was collected in cash.
    f. The firm hired an administrative assistant and paid $525 cash in salary expense for the first month.
    g. The firm declared and paid distributions to owners in the amount of $2,250 for the first month.
    h. At the end of the month, $125 of interest payable is due but not yet paid on the note from item (b).

Requirements

    1. Show how each transaction affects the accounting equation.
    2. Prepare the income statement, statement of changes in shareholders' equity, and statement of cash flows for the month of July. Also, prepare the balance sheet *at* July 31.

P2-40A. *Analyze transactions from the accounting equation and prepare the four financial statements. (LO 3).* The following accounting equation worksheet shows the transactions for Data Services for its first month of business, May 2010:

		Assets		=	Liabilities	+	Shareholders' Equity	
							Contributed Capital	Retained Earnings
Transaction	Cash	All other assets	(Account)		All liabilities	(Account)	Common stock	
a.	$ 5,000						$5,000	
b.	15,000				15,000	Notes payable (5-year)		
c.	(10,000)	10,000	Land					
d.		6,500	Accounts receivable					6,500 Revenue
e.	12,000							12,000 Revenue
f.	(8,000)	8,000	Land					
g.	3,500	(3,500)	Accounts receivable					
h.	(2,100)							(2,100) Expense
i.	(750)							(750) Dividends

Requirements

1. Analyze each transaction in the accounting equation worksheet and describe the underlying exchange that resulted in each entry.
2. Has the company been profitable this month? Explain.
3. Prepare an income statement for the month ended May 31, 2010.
4. Prepare a statement of shareholders' equity for the month ended May 31, 2010.
5. Prepare a statement of cash flows for the month ended May 31, 2010.
6. Prepare a balance sheet at May 31, 2010.

P2-41A. *Analyzing transactions and preparing financial statements. (LO 3, 5).* After Nate, Maggie, Nicol, and Lindsay finished medical school, they decided to open a new medical practice named New Beginnings. The graduates formed New Beginnings, Inc., as a corporation on January 1, 2011. Each graduate contributed $65,000 to the business in exchange for 2,500 shares of common stock. The company signed a note with Noble Bank for an additional $120,000. The company used available funds to purchase office space (building) for $216,000. The company also purchased medical equipment on account for $139,000, with payment due at the beginning of the following year.

• During the first year of business, New Beginnings earned $280,000 in service revenue, but collected only $215,000; the remaining $65,000 was due from customers early the next year.
• Salary expenses for the year were $115,000, of which $95,000 was paid in cash during the year; the remaining $20,000 was due to employees the first day of the next year.
• The company purchased an insurance policy for $40,000 cash of which $5,000 was for the current year and the remainder was for future years.
• The company paid operating expenses of $39,000 in cash during the year.
• The company sent a check during the last month of the year for $8,100 for interest expense due on the loan from Noble Bank.
• The company invested $22,000 of cash in short-term investments at the end of the year.
• New Beginnings declared and paid cash dividends of $10,500 during the year.

Requirements

1. Show how each transaction affects the accounting equation.

2. Prepare the income statement, the statement of changes in shareholders' equity, and the statement of cash flows for the year ended December 31, 2011. Prepare the balance sheet *at* December 31, 2011. Ignore depreciation expense on building and equipment.

3. Calculate the current ratio at December 31, 2011.

Set B

P2-42B. *Relationships between financial statement items. (LO 3).* Use the following information for Exotic Cruise Corporation for the year ended June 30, 2011, to answer the questions. Assume that the shareholders contributed $100 to the company during the year.

    a. Revenues for the year ended June 30, 2011 = $650
    b. Net income for the year ended June 30, 2011 = $215
    c. Beginning balance (June 30, 2010, balance) in retained earnings = $280
    d. Ending balance (June 30, 2011, balance) in retained earnings = $375
    e. Total liabilities and shareholders' equity at June 30, 2011 = $755
    f. Total liabilities at June 30, 2010 = $105
    g. Total liabilities at June 30, 2011 = $130

Requirements

1. What were Exotic Cruise's total expenses during the year ended June 30, 2011?
2. What was paid to shareholders during the year ended June 30, 2011?
3. What is the total that owners had invested in Exotic Cruise Corporation as of June 30, 2011?
4. What were total assets on Exotic Cruise's June 30, 2011, balance sheet?

P2-43B. *Analyzing transactions. (LO 3).* New Magazine Company entered into the following transactions during 2012:

    a. New Magazine Company started as a corporation with a $9,650 cash contribution from the owners in exchange for common stock.
    b. The company purchased supplies for $1,000 with cash and used all of them.
    c. Advertising revenues, all on account, amounted to $17,625.
    d. Cash collections of accounts amounted to $8,175.
    e. On October 15, 2012, the company paid $4,050 in advance for an insurance policy that does not go into effect until 2013.
    f. The company declared and paid dividends of $575.

Requirements

Put each of the transactions in an accounting equation worksheet. Then, answer the following questions:

1. What is the amount of net cash from financing activities for the year ended December 31, 2012?
2. What amount of total assets would appear on the December 31, 2012, balance sheet?
3. What amount of net income would appear on the income statement for the year ended December 31, 2012?
4. What is the amount of retained earnings as of December 31, 2012?

P2-44B. *Analyzing transactions and preparing financial statements. (LO 3).* The following transactions occurred during Bono Exterminators' first month of business:

    a. Joe Bono started a business, Bono Exterminators, by contributing $6,200 cash on January 1, 2010, in exchange for common stock.
    b. The company borrowed $18,000 from the bank in January. The note is a 1-year, 5% note, with both principal and interest to be repaid on December 30, 2010.
    c. The company paid $2,500 in cash for an insurance policy that begins February 1.
    d. The company earned $4,775 in revenues during January. Cash collections of revenue amounted to $4,270 during the month.
    e. The company paid operating expenses of $815 cash for the month of January.
    f. The company declared and made distributions to owners in the amount of $125 cash in January.
    g. At the end of January, $75 of interest payable is due on the note from item (b).

Requirements
1. Show how each transaction affects the accounting equation.
2. Prepare the income statement, statement of changes in shareholder's equity, and the statement of cash flows for the month of January and the balance sheet at January 31.

P2-45B. *Analyze transactions from the accounting equation, prepare the four financial statements, and calculate the current ratio. (LO 4, 5, 7).* The following accounting equation worksheet shows the transactions for Internet Advertising, a corporation, for the first month of business October 2009.

		Assets		= Liabilities		+	Shareholders' Equity		
							Contributed Capital	Retained Earnings	
Transaction	Cash	All other assets	(Account)	All liabilities	(Account)		Common stock		(Account)
a.	$17,250						$17,250		
b.	16,900			16,900	Long-term notes payable				
c.	(4,500)							(4,500)	Salary expenses
d.	1,500	1,500	Accounts receivable					3,000	Service revenue
e.		8,000	Supplies	8,000	Accounts payable				
f.	8,150	1,850	Accounts receivable					10,000	Service revenue
g.	1,000	(1,000)	Accounts receivable						
h.	(5,000)			(5,000)	Accounts payable				
i.	(4,100)							(4,100)	Operating expenses
j.	(165)							(165)	Dividends

Requirements
1. Analyze each transaction in the accounting equation worksheet and describe the underlying exchange that resulted in each entry.
2. Has the company been profitable this month? Explain.
3. Prepare an income statement for the month ended October 31, 2009.
4. Prepare a statement of shareholders' equity for the month ended October 31, 2009.
5. Prepare a statement of cash flows for the month ended October 31, 2009.
6. Prepare a balance sheet at October 31, 2009.
7. Calculate the current ratio at October 31, 2009.

P2-46B. *Analyzing transactions and preparing financial statements. (LO 3, 5).* Joanna Wu won a Web-designing contest and decided to start her own Web-design company. She contributed $200,000 in exchange for 1,000 shares of common stock and borrowed another $55,000 by signing a 4-year note with Quality Bank. She formed Wu Web Designs, Inc., on July 1, 2009. The business used available funds to purchase some land with an office building for $125,000 and office equipment and furniture for $25,000. The business also bought a computer system on account for $45,500; payment was due at the beginning of the following year.
- During the first year of business, Wu Web Designs earned $215,000 in service revenue, but had collected only $172,000; the remaining $43,000 was due early the next year.
- Salary expenses for the year were $95,000 of which the company paid $80,000 in cash during the year; the remaining $15,000 was due the first day of the next year.

- The company purchased an insurance policy for $24,000, of which $6,000 was for the current year and the remainder was for future years.
- The company paid operating expenses of $20,250 in cash during the year.
- Interest expense for the year was $7,175 but has not yet been paid.
- The company invested $20,000 of cash in a short-term investment at the end of the year.
- Wu Web Designs declared and paid dividends of $3,200 during the year.

Requirements

1. Show how each transaction affects the accounting equation.
2. Prepare the income statement, statement of changes in shareholder's equity, and statement of cash flows for the year ended June 30, 2010; and prepare the balance sheet at June 30, 2010. (Ignore depreciation.)
3. Calculate the current ratio at June 30, 2010.

Financial Statement Analysis

FSA2-1. *Identify items from the balance sheet. (LO 3, 5).* The balance sheets (adapted) for Tootsie Roll Industries, Inc., are shown here.

Tootsie Roll Industries, Inc.
Balance Sheet (adapted)
(in thousands)

	December 31, 2008	December 31, 2007
Assets		
Cash	$ 68,908	$ 57,606
Investments	17,963	41,307
Receivables	34,196	35,284
Inventory	55,584	57,402
Other current assets	11,328	8,127
Net property, plant, and equipment	217,628	201,401
Other noncurrent assets	406,485	411,598
Total assets	$812,092	$812,725
Liabilities and Shareholders' Equity		
Accounts payable	13,885	11,572
Dividends payable	4,401	4,344
Accrued liabilities	40,335	42,056
Deferred income taxes	631	0
Total current liabilities	59,252	57,972
Noncurrent liabilities	118,070	116,523
Total liabilities	177,322	174,495
Contributed capital	509,131	495,197
Retained earnings	142,872	156,752
Other shareholders' equity accounts, net*	(17,233)	(13,719)
Total shareholders' equity	634,770	638,230
Total liabilities and shareholders' equity	$812,092	$812,725

*This is an item you will learn about in a later chapter.

Requirements

1. What were the total current assets at December 31, 2007? December 31, 2008?
2. How are the assets ordered on the balance sheet?
3. What were the total current liabilities at December 31, 2007? December 31, 2008?
4. Calculate the current ratio at December 31, 2007, and December 31, 2008. What information do these numbers provide?

FSA2-2. *Evaluate liquidity from the balance sheet. (LO 3, 4, 5).* Selected information from the comparative balance sheets for Sears Holdings Corporation is presented here. Although some accounts are not listed, all of the current assets and current liabilities are given.

Sears Holdings Corporation
From the Consolidated Balance Sheets
(dollars in millions)

	January 31, 2009	February 2, 2008
Cash	$1,297	$ 1,622
Accounts receivable	839	744
Inventory	8,795	9,963
Other current assets	485	473
Property, plant, and equipment	8,091	8,863
Accounts payable	3,006	3,487
Other current liabilities	5,506	6,075
Long-term liabilities	7,450	7,168
Total shareholders' equity	9,380	10,667

Requirements

1. Provide the following values at the end of each given fiscal year:
   a. Current assets
   b. Current liabilities
   c. Current ratio
2. Based on your answers in part 1, discuss the change in liquidity between the two years.

FSA2-3. *Identify items from the statement of cash flows. (LO 3).* A condensed statement of cash flows for Apple Inc. for the year ended September 27, 2008, is shown here. Use it to answer the questions given after the statement.

Apple Inc.
Statement of Cash Flows (adapted)
For the Year Ended September 27, 2008
(in millions)

Cash and cash equivalents, beginning of the year	$ 9,352
Cash generated by operating activities	9,596
Investing Cash Flows:	
Purchase of short-term investments	(22,965)
Proceeds from maturities of short-term investments	11,804
Proceeds from sales of short-term investments	4,439
Purchase of property, plant, and equipment	(1,091)
Other	(376)
Cash (used in) generated by investing activities	(8,189)
Financing Cash Flows:	
Proceeds from issuance of common stock	483
Other (net)	633
Cash generated by financing activities	1,116
Increase in cash and cash equivalents	2,523
Cash and cash equivalents, end of the year	$11,875

Requirements

1. What was Apple's net cash flow related to operating activities during the year?
2. What was Apple's net cash flow related to investing activities during the year?
3. What was Apple's net cash flow related to financing activities during the year?
4. If you were to look at Apple's balance sheets for the two most recent fiscal years, what amount would be shown on each for cash (and cash equivalents)?

Critical Thinking Problems

Risk and Controls

Look at the information from the Books-A-Million annual report in Appendix A, paying special attention to the notes. What kinds of risks does Books-A-Million face? Use the information in the annual report and your own experience to answer this question.

Ethics

Ken Jones wants to start a small business and has asked his uncle to lend him $10,000. He has prepared a business plan and some financial statements that indicate the business could be very profitable. Ken is afraid his uncle will want some ownership in the company for his investment, but Ken does not want to share what he believes will be a hugely successful company. What are the ethical issues Ken must face as he prepares to present his business plan to his uncle? Do you think he should try to *emphasize* the risks of ownership to his uncle to convince him it would be preferable to be a creditor? Why or why not?

Group Assignment

Look at the four basic financial statements for Team Shirts in Exhibits 2.5, 2.6, 2.7, and 2.8. Work together to find numbers that show the links between the various financial statements. Then, write a brief explanation of how the statements relate to each other.

Internet Exercise: MSN Money and Merck

MSN Money offers information about companies, industries, people, and related news items. For researching a company, the Web site is a good place to start gathering basic information.
    Please go to http://moneycentral.msn.com.

IE2-1. In the *Symbol* box, enter MRK for Merck and Co., Inc.

1. What type of company is Merck?
2. List three products manufactured by Merck.

IE2-2. Click on Financial Results, and then on Statements.

1. For the most recent year list the amounts reported for sales, cost of goods sold, and total net income. Does the amount reported for revenue represent cash received from customers during the year? If not, what does it represent? What does the amount reported for cost of goods sold represent? Is Merck a profitable company? How can you tell?
2. For the most recent year list the amounts reported for total assets, total liabilities, and total shareholders' equity. Does the accounting equation hold true? Are assets primarily financed with liabilities or shareholders' equity?
3. Does Merck use accrual-based or cash-based accounting? How can you tell?

Please note: Internet Web sites are constantly being updated. Therefore, if the information is not found where indicated, please explore the Web site further to find the information.

3

Accruals and Deferrals: Timing Is Everything in Accounting

LEARNING OBJECTIVES

When you are finished studying Chapter 3, you should be able to:

1. Define accrual accounting and explain how income is measured.

2. Explain *accruals* and how they affect the financial statements; describe and perform the adjustments related to accruals.

3. Explain *deferrals* and how they affect the financial statements; describe and perform the adjustments related to deferrals.

4. Construct the basic financial statements from a given set of transactions that include accruals and deferrals and recognize the effect of these transactions on actual financial statements.

5. Compute and explain the *profit margin on sales* ratio.

6. Explain the business risks associated with financial records and accounting information.

ETHICS Matters

Cookie Sales Were Not So Sweet

Perhaps you've wondered what happened to the Archway cookies that used to be on your grocery store shelves. In 2008, daily sales reports looked pretty dismal. Then one evening, Keith Roberts, who had joined the Archway & Mother's Cookie Company in 2007 as the director of finance, found himself looking at some truly excellent sales figures. He was surprised, to say the least. After digging through the company's inventory, shipping, and sales records, Roberts determined that Archway had been recording fictitious sales.

You've read about Computer Associates recording sales before actually earning the revenue. Archway, in an even bolder fraudulent activity, simply made up sales that did not exist. According to one long-time distributor of Archway cookies, the company began billing him for $14,000 worth of cookies when they had only sent him $4,000 worth. He called it "hocus-pocus." You'll see in this chapter how Archway recorded this—by accruing revenue that did not exist.

Before this scandal resulted in Archway's bankruptcy, a private equity group owned the company. It was not traded on any stock exchange, so there was no need to produce false sales to maintain a stock price. Why, then, would a company simply falsify sales? Roberts concluded that it was done to maintain access to needed funds from its bank, Wachovia. After Roberts' discovery, the bank cancelled its funding of Archway, forcing the company into bankruptcy. Several members of Catterton Partners, the private equity firm that owned Archway, and former executives at Archway have been named in lawsuits brought by former employees and independent distributors.

Source: *"Oh, No! What Happened to Archway?" by Julie Creswell.* New York Times, *May 31, 2009.*

L.O.1
Define accrual accounting
and explain how income is
measured.

Measuring Income

After its first month, Team Shirts prepared a set of financial statements to measure and report the company's performance during that first month and to measure and report its financial position at the end of that month. Team Shirts did both again for the second month.

At different points of time in the life of a company, owners, investors, creditors, and other interested parties want to know the company's financial position and accomplishments in order to make all kinds of evaluations and decisions, including whether or not the company is meeting its goals. The main goal is usually to make a profit; so measuring the profit the company has made during a specified period plays a big role in evaluating how successfully a company has been doing its business.

THE INCOME STATEMENT. As you learned in Chapter 2, the income statement summarizes revenues and expenses for a period of time, usually a year. Net income can also be measured for a week, a month, or a quarter. For example, many companies provide quarterly financial information to their shareholders. That information would include net income for the quarter.

Accountants consider the continuous life of a business as being composed of discrete periods of time—months, quarters, or years. The way we divide the revenues and expenses among those time periods is a crucial part of accounting. That is why timing is everything in accounting. If revenue is *earned* (not necessarily *collected*) in a certain time period, you must be sure that it is included on the income statement for that period—not the one before and not the one after. If you have used some supplies during a period, then you need to include the cost of those supplies as part of the expenses on the income statement for that same period.

Sometimes you will see the income statement referred to as the *statement of operations* and other times as the *statement of earnings* or the *profit and loss statement*. However it is referred to, it will usually appear as the first financial statement in a company's annual report. Exhibit 3.1 shows the income statements for The Gap, Inc.

When you see total sales of $14,526,000,000 for the year ended January 31, 2009, you know that all the sales made in that fiscal year—a year of business for the company—are included in that amount, even if some of the cash has not been collected from the customers by January 31, 2009. Similarly, the expenses listed are only the expenses incurred in that fiscal year, whether or not the company has paid for those expenses by January 31, 2009. The Gap has to make sure the amounts are correct.

EXHIBIT 3.1

Income Statements for The Gap, Inc.

The Gap, Inc., had net sales of over $14.5 billion during the fiscal year ended January 31, 2009. Investors depend on that information, so The Gap works hard to get it right.

The Gap, Inc.
Consolidated Statements of Earnings
(dollars in millions)

	Fiscal Year		
	2008	2007	2006
Net sales	$14,526	$15,763	$15,923
Cost of goods sold and occupancy expenses	9,079	10,071	10,266
Gross profit	5,447	5,692	5,657
Operating expenses	3,899	4,377	4,432
Operating income	1,548	1,315	1,225
Interest expense	1	26	41
Interest income	(37)	(117)	(131)
Earnings from continuing operations before income taxes	1,584	1,406	1,315
Income taxes	617	539	506
Earnings from continuing operations, net of income taxes	967	867	809
Loss from discontinued operation, net of income tax benefit	—	(34)	(31)
Net earnings	$ 967	$ 833	$ 778

Timing differences in accounting are differences between

- the time when a company earns revenue by providing a product or service to customers and the time when the cash is collected from the customers,

and

- the time when the company incurs an expense and the time when the company pays for the expense.

You will see in this chapter how to identify timing differences and present them on the financial statements.

As discussed in the previous chapter, you can think of the timing problems in accounting in two simple ways:

- Action before dollars
- Dollars before action

Action refers to the substance of the transaction—the actual earning of the revenue or using the expense item. An example of action before dollars is when a sale is made *on account*. A customer buys on credit and agrees to pay later. The action of making the sale—the economic substance of the transaction—takes place before dollars are exchanged in payment. This type of transaction—action first, dollars later—is called an **accrual**.

In contrast, an example of dollars before action is when a firm buys insurance. By its nature, insurance must be purchased in advance of the time period to which it applies. Payment (when the dollars are exchanged) is made first, and the use of the insurance (the action provided by insurance protection) comes later. Dollars first, action later is called a **deferral**.

Accruals

When the substance of a business transaction takes place before any cash changes hands, the accountant includes that transaction in the measurement of income. That is, if a firm has earned revenue, that revenue must be included on the income statement. If the firm incurred an expense to earn that revenue, that expense must be included on the income statement. Accruals can pertain to both revenues and expenses.

Some accruals are the result of routine transactions like buying and selling items as you run your company. Other times revenue is earned or an expense is incurred without being captured by the accounting system in its everyday recordings. These will require an adjustment at the end of the accounting period, before the financial statements are prepared. First, let's talk about accruals related to revenue, and then we will turn our attention to accruals related to expenses.

Accrued Revenue

The most common accrual transaction is the *sale* of goods or services on account. You will recall that this transaction results in the firm recording revenue and accounts receivable. The cash will be collected later, but the revenue is recognized at the time the goods or services are delivered. Recording revenue with an increase to accounts receivable is called accruing revenue. In the chapter opener, you read about Archway recording fictitious revenue. This is how the company did it—with an increase in sales and an increase in accounts receivable. (Unfortunately, the company did not have valid sales to warrant recording revenue.) Recording revenue on account is a routine business transaction, not an adjusting entry in the accounting system.

However, there are other types of revenue that may have been earned but not recorded as a routine part of the accounting system. For example, interest revenue is an example of revenue that often must be accrued, recorded so that it will go on the income statement before the cash is actually collected at the end of the accounting period. Banks and other financial institutions make loans as a regular business activity, and other firms might lend money to another company or to an employee. A company that lends money earns interest revenue during the time the loan is outstanding. If the company has earned some interest revenue but not yet collected it at the date of the financial statements, the company will want to record that revenue. This is the formula for interest:

$$\text{Interest (I)} = \text{Principal (P)} \times \text{Rate (R)} \times \text{Time (T)}$$

Timing differences arise when revenues are earned in one accounting period and collected in a different accounting period. They also arise when expenses are incurred in one accounting period and paid for in another.

An **accrual** is a transaction in which the revenue has been earned or the expense has been incurred, but no cash has been exchanged.

A **deferral** is a transaction in which the cash is exchanged *before* the revenue has been earned or the expense has been incurred.

L.O.2
Explain *accruals* and how they affect the financial statements; describe and perform the adjustments related to accruals.

The amount of interest revenue will increase assets—interest receivable—and will increase retained earnings via interest revenue. Notice that making this accrual will have the same result that making a sale on account will have: Revenue is recorded along with a receivable.

Suppose a company lends $200 to an employee on October 1 at 10% interest, to be repaid on January 1 of the following year. The transaction on October 1 decreases assets (cash) and also increases assets (other receivables). Because firms generally use *accounts receivable* to describe amounts customers owe the company, we call the amounts owed by others—meaning anyone who is not a customer—*other* receivables.

Assets	=	Liabilities	+	Shareholders' equity		
				Contributed capital	+	Retained earnings
(200) cash						
+ 200 other receivables						

On December 31, the company will accrue interest revenue. Why? Because some time has passed and interest revenue has been earned during that period. With interest, the action is the passage of time, so the action has taken place, but the cash will not change hands until the following January 1. You would record interest revenue of $5 ($200 × 0.10 × 3/12). You would also record interest receivable of $5. By doing all this, the financial statements would accurately reflect the following situation on December 31:

- The company has earned $5 of interest revenue as of December 31.
- The company has not received the interest revenue at December 31.

Because all revenues increase retained earnings, the interest revenue will be recorded under retained earnings in the accounting equation:

Assets	=	Liabilities	+	Shareholders' equity		
				Contributed capital	+	Retained earnings
+ 5 interest receivable						+ 5 interest revenue

When the company actually receives the cash for the interest on January 1, along with repayment of the $200 principal, it will not be recorded as interest revenue. Instead, the total $205 cash is recorded as an increase in cash, a decrease in the asset *other receivables* by $200, and a decrease in the asset *interest receivable* by $5. The timing difference resulted in recording the interest revenue in one period and the cash collection in another.

There are other types of revenues that must be accrued at the end of the period so that the financial statements will accurately reflect the business transactions for that period. For example, if you have provided services for a customer during 2009 but have not recorded those services (perhaps because you have not billed the customer yet), you want to be sure to report the revenue on the 2009 income statement. Why report this on the 2009 income statement? Because the action of earning the revenue was completed in 2009. Even though you will not collect the cash until sometime in 2010, the revenue will be shown on the 2009 income statement.

To summarize, accrued revenue and receivables are often paired together in accruals. An increase in assets (accounts receivable) and an increase in retained earnings (revenue), both in the same amount, balance the accounting equation. Then, when the cash is actually collected—sometimes called **realized**—it is not recognized as revenue because it was already recognized in a previous period.

Realized means the cash is collected. Sometimes revenue is *recognized* before it is *realized*.

Exhibit 3.2 shows the current assets section of Talbots' balance sheet. At January 31, 2009, Talbots had accounts receivable amounting to $169,406,000. This is a significant amount of money! When you see receivables on a company's balance sheet, it means the related revenues have been earned and included on the income statement for that period even though the cash has not been collected yet.

EXHIBIT 3.2

Current Assets Section of Talbots' Balance Sheet

This is the current assets section of Talbots' balance sheet.

The Talbots, Inc., and Subsidiaries
From the Consolidated Balance Sheets
(amounts in thousands)

Assets	January 31, 2009	February 2, 2008
Current Assets:		
Cash and cash equivalents	$ 16,718	$ 25,476
Customer accounts receivable—net	169,406	210,853
Merchandise inventories	206,593	262,603
Deferred catalog costs	4,795	6,249
Due from related party	376	3,040
Deferred income taxes	—	25,084
Income tax refundable	26,646	—
Prepaid and other current assets	35,277	34,524
Assets held for sale—current	109,966	84,018
Total current assets	$569,777	$651,847

Your Turn 3-1

Suppose your firm loaned an employee $1,000 at 7% (interest rates are always assumed to be per year) on July 1. On December 31, the firm is preparing its year-end financial statements. What adjustment would the firm need to make to properly account for any interest revenue that had been earned prior to year end?

Accrued Expenses

If a firm buys goods or services from others (as opposed to selling them), and the firm uses those resources, an expense must be recognized even if the firm has not yet paid for the goods or services. Recording an expense along with an increase to a payable account, like salaries payable, is called accruing an expense.

Interest expense is often incurred before the firm actually pays the cash for it. Let's look at an example of borrowing money. Suppose you borrowed $500 from a bank on January 1, 2010, and agreed to repay it with 8% interest on January 1, 2011. On January 1, 2010, when you borrow the money, you get the $500 cash, an asset, and you increase your liabilities. The accounting equation is increased on both sides by $500.

Assets	=	Liabilities	+	Shareholders' equity	
				Contributed capital	+ Retained earnings
+ 500 cash		+ 500 notes payable			

When you get ready to prepare the financial statements for the year ended December 31, 2010, you see that this liability—notes payable—is still on the books and will be listed on the balance sheet. That is because on December 31, 2010, you still owe the bank the full amount of the loan. What about the $500 cash you received? You may still have it, but it is more likely you spent it during the year to keep your business running. That is why you borrowed it.

What about the cost of borrowing the money—the interest expense? On December 31, 2010, one full year has passed since you borrowed the money. The passing of time has caused interest expense to be incurred. Recall, however, that you aren't paying the interest until January when you repay the principal.

- Interest expense is the cost of using someone else's money.
- Time passing is the action related to interest expense.

Although the action of using someone else's money during the year has taken place, the dollars have not been exchanged—the interest payment for using that money. To make the December 31, 2010, financial statements correct, you must show the interest expense of $40 ($500 × 8% × 12/12, or $500 × 0.08 × 1) on the income statement. Also, you must show—on the balance sheet—the obligation called **interest payable**. It is a liability, indicating the bank's claim to the $40 as of December 31, 2010. The liability section of the balance sheet will show both the $500 loan and the $40 interest payable.

> **Interest payable** is a liability. It is the amount a company owes for borrowing money (after the time period to which the interest applies has passed).

Assets	=	Liabilities	+	Shareholders' equity		
				Contributed capital	+	Retained earnings
		+ 40 interest payable				(40) interest expense

Making this adjustment is called accruing interest expense; the expense itself is called an accrual. Sometimes a company will label the amount of interest expense accrued as *accrued liabilities* or *accrued expenses*. Each expression means the same thing—an expense that will be paid in the future. Notice that the interest expense will be on the income statement for the period, even though the cash has not been paid yet.

REPORTING INTEREST EXPENSE. Suppose you borrowed the $500 on July 1, 2010 (instead of January 1). In this case, you would have use of the money for only half of the year and therefore would have incurred only half a year of interest expense as of December 31, 2010. Remember that interest rates, like the 8% interest rate in this example, always pertain to a year. As of December 31, 2010, the interest payable on the note would be $500 × 0.08 × 6/12 = $20. The last part of the formula gives the time as a percentage of a year, or the number of months out of 12. Whenever you accrue interest, you must be careful to count the months that apply. That will help you make sure you put the right amount of interest expense on the income statement for exactly the period of time you had use of the borrowed money.

If you borrowed the $500 on January 1, 2010, for one full year, what would happen when you pay the bank on January 1, 2011? On one side of the accounting equation, you will reduce cash by $540. The equation will be balanced by a reduction of $500 in notes payable plus the reduction of $40 in interest payable. There will be no interest expense recorded when you actually pay the cash. Remember, the action has already taken place, and the action resulted in interest expense in 2010. There is no interest expense in 2011 because you paid off the loan on January 1, 2011.

This is how timing differences work. The expense is recorded in one period, but the cash is paid in another period.

Assets	=	Liabilities	+	Shareholders' equity		
				Contributed capital	+	Retained earnings
(540) cash		(40) interest payable (500) notes payable				

OTHER ACCRUED EXPENSES. In addition to interest, there may be other expenses that need to be accrued. When you get to the end of an accounting period—when you prepare financial statements—you examine your records and business transactions to find any expenses that might have been incurred but not recorded. These are the expenses you have not paid for yet. (If you paid for them, you would have recorded them when you gave the cash to pay for them.) When you receive a bill for some expenses such as utilities, you likely will record the expense and the related miscellaneous or other payable. If you already accrued the expense when you received the bill, you will not need to accrue it at the end of the period.

However, there are some typical expenses that companies do not record until the end of the period. These expenses will be accrued, recorded so that the result is an expense on the income statement and some sort of payable in the liabilities section of the balance sheet. These expenses have been recognized—shown on the income statement—but the cash has not been paid yet.

One of the most common accruals is salary expense. Typically, a company will record salary expense when it pays its employees. (In the accounting equation, that transaction would reduce assets—cash—and reduce retained earnings via salary expense.) What do you do if the end of an accounting period does not coincide with payday? You need to record the salary expense for the work that your employees have done since the last time you paid them. You want to be sure to get the correct amount of salary expense on the income statement for the period. This accrual will increase liabilities—salaries payable—and decrease retained earnings via salaries expense. The action—the employees performing the work—has already taken place; however, the cash will not be exchanged until the next payday, which will be in the next accounting period.

Suppose you are preparing the financial statements for the accounting period ended on December 31, 2012. That date is on a Monday. If you pay your employees every Friday, the last payday of the year is December 28, 2012. As of December 31, 2012, you will owe them for their work done on Monday, December 31, 2012. You will need to record the salary expense for that day, even though you will not pay the employees until Friday, January 4, 2013. Recording this salary expense so it is recognized on the correct income statement is called accruing salary expense. This adjustment will increase liabilities—salaries payable—and decrease retained earnings by increasing salary expense.

What happens when January 4, 2013, arrives and you actually pay the employees? You will pay them for the week from December 31, 2012, through January 4, 2013. (These employees are lucky enough to get paid for New Year's Day!) The expense for one day—December 31—was recorded on December 31, 2012, so that it would be on the income statement for the fiscal year ended December 31, 2012. The expense for the other four days—January 1, 2013, through January 4, 2013—has not been recorded yet. The expense for those four days belongs on the income statement for the fiscal year ended December 31, 2013. When you pay the employees on January 4, 2013, you will reduce liabilities—the amount of the salaries payable you recorded on December 31, 2012, will be deducted from that account—and you will reduce retained earnings by recording salary expense for those four days in 2013.

Putting numbers in an example should help make this clear. Suppose the total amount you owe your employees for a five-day workweek is $3,500. Look at the calendar in Exhibit 3.3—we are interested in the week beginning December 31.

EXHIBIT 3.3

Calendar for Accruing Salaries

If the firm's fiscal year ends on December 31 and payday is every Friday, then salary expense for December 31 must be accrued—even though it will not be paid to the employees until January 4.

Monday	Tuesday	Wednesday	Thursday	Friday
December 24	December 25	December 26	December 27	December 28
December 31	January 1	January 2	January 3	January 4

On December 31, you need to accrue one day's worth of salary expense. The $3,500 applies to five days, but you need to look at it as $700 per day. To accrue the salary expense for one day, you increase the liability salaries payable and decrease retained earnings via salary expense by $700. Why are you recording the salary expense and salaries payable even though you are not paying your employees until January 4? Because you want to have the expense for December 31 on the income statement for the year ended December 31, 2012. How does this adjustment affect the accounting equation? Both the income statement and the balance sheet are affected by this accrual.

Assets	=	Liabilities	+	Shareholders' equity		
				Contributed + capital		Retained earnings
		+ 700 salaries payable				(700) salary expense

On January 4, when you actually pay the employees for an entire week, you will give them cash of $3,500. How much of that amount is expense for work done in the year 2012 and how much is expense for work done in 2013? We already know that $700 is expense for 2012. The other four days' worth of work done and salary earned—$2,800—applies to 2013. Here is how the transaction on January 4—paying the employees for a full week of work—affects the accounting equation:

Cash is reduced, salaries payable is reduced, and retained earnings is reduced via salary expense.

Assets	=	Liabilities	+	Shareholders' equity		
				Contributed capital	+	Retained earnings
(3,500) cash		(700) salaries payable				(2,800) salary expense

Review the example and make sure you know why the adjustment on December 31 was necessary and how the amount was calculated. When the employees receive their pay on January 4, notice that the salary expense recorded is only the amount of the January work.

Your Turn 3-2

Suppose ABC Company pays its employees a total of $56,000 on the 15th of each month for work done the previous month. ABC generally records salary expense when the employees are paid. If the ABC fiscal year end is June 30, 2010, does any salary expense need to be accrued at year end? If so, how much?

L.O.3
Explain *deferrals* and how they affect the financial statements; describe and perform the adjustments related to deferrals.

Deferrals

The word *defer* means "to put off or to postpone." In accounting, a deferral refers to a transaction in which the dollars have been exchanged before the economic substance of the transaction—the action—has taken place. Just like accruals, deferrals can apply to both revenues and expenses. As you read and study the examples that follow, remember that you are taking the point of view of the business.

Deferred Revenue

One of the most common deferrals is called unearned revenue. That's when money has been collected before the firm has earned the revenue. Suppose a company sells a monthly magazine subscription to customers who pay in advance. Suppose a customer pays $60 cash for a 12-month subscription. Here's how the company would record the receipt of the $60:

Assets	=	Liabilities	+	Shareholders' equity		
				Contributed capital	+	Retained earnings
+ 60 cash		+ 60 unearned revenue				

Unearned revenue is a liability. It represents the amount of goods or services that a company owes its customers. The cash has been collected, but the action of *earning* the revenue has not taken place.

Unearned revenue is a balance sheet account—a liability. It represents amounts a company owes to others—customers. This is called a *deferral* because the company is *putting off* the recognition of the revenue, that is, not showing it on the income statement until the revenue is actually earned. Please notice that the name of this liability is a bit unusual. It has the word revenue in it, but it is *not* an income statement account.

When the items sold are actually delivered, the company will recognize the revenue. This will be done by decreasing unearned revenue and increasing retained earnings via revenue. In this example, the $60 payment buys 12 magazines, so each magazine is $5. Here is how the accounting equation will be affected after the first month's magazine has been delivered to the customer:

Assets	=	Liabilities	+	Shareholders' equity		
				Contributed capital	+	Retained earnings
		(5) unearned revenue				5 sales revenue

Now that one month's worth of the payment has been earned, the company can recognize $5 worth of the revenue. The unearned revenue for the remaining 11 months, $55, remains as a liability on the balance sheet.

SUBSCRIPTIONS. Subscriptions are a very common deferred revenue. For example, the current liabilities sections of the balance sheet for Time Warner at December 31, 2008 and 2007, shown in Exhibit 3.4, show $1,169 million of unearned revenue at the end of 2008 and $1,178 million at the end of 2007. The company calls it *deferred revenue*. It represents amounts Time Warner has collected from customers but has not yet earned by providing the related services. As the company earns those revenues, the earned amounts will be deducted from the liability and recognized as revenue.

EXHIBIT 3.4

Deferred Revenue from Time Warner

Time Warner has had over a billion dollars of deferred revenue at the end of each of the past two years, highlighted in the portion of its balance sheet shown here.

Time Warner
From the Consolidated Balance Sheets
At December 31, 2008 and 2007
(amounts in millions)

	2008	2007
Liabilities		
Current liabilities		
Accounts payable	$ 1,341	$ 1,470
Participations payable	2,522	2,547
Royalties and programming costs payable	1,265	1,253
Deferred revenue	1,169	1,178
Debt due within one year	2,067	126
Other current liabilities	5,610	5,611
Current liabilities of discontinued operations	2	8
Total current liabilities	$13,976	$12,193

GIFT CARDS. Another common deferred revenue relates to gift cards. Almost all retail firms are happy to sell gift cards. Suppose you decide to purchase a $50 gift card at Best Buy to give your cousin for his or her birthday. You want something easy to mail, and you are not sure what sort of gift he or she would like. When you pay $50 to Best Buy for a gift card, Best Buy records the cash (an asset) and a liability (unearned revenue). Some firms combine their liability for gift cards with other liabilities on their balance sheet. Others have such a significant amount that the liability for gift cards is shown as a line item on the balance sheet. Look at Best Buy's balance sheet in Exhibit 3.5 on the following page. You will see the liability *unredeemed* gift card liabilities for $479 million at February 28, 2009. As the gift cards are redeemed or as they expire, Best Buy will recognize the related revenue.

Your Turn 3-3

Living Time Magazine collected $300,000 for 12-month subscriptions before it published its first issue in June 2010. How much revenue should the magazine company recognize for the fiscal year ended December 31, 2010? Explain what it means to *recognize* revenue in this situation.

EXHIBIT 3.5

Liabilities from Best Buy's Balance Sheet

The highlighted line shows that Best Buy had a significant amount of outstanding gift cards at the end of each of the fiscal years shown.

Best Buy
From the Consolidated Balance Sheets
(dollars in millions)

	February 28, 2009	March 1, 2008
Liabilities and Shareholders' Equity		
Current Liabilities		
Accounts payable	$ 4,997	$ 4,297
Unredeemed gift card liabilities	479	531
Accrued compensation and related expenses	459	373
Accrued liabilities	1,382	975
Accrued income taxes	281	404
Short-term debt	783	156
Current portion of long-term debt	54	33
Total current liabilities	8,435	6,769
Long-Term Liabilities	1,109	838
Long-Term Debt	1,126	627
Minority Interests	513	40
Shareholders' Equity		
Preferred stock, $1.00 par value: Authorized—400,000 shares;		
Issued and outstanding—none	—	—
Common stock, $.10 par value: Authorized—1.0 billion shares;		
Issued and outstanding—413,684,000 and 410,578,000		
shares, respectively	41	41
Additional paid-in capital	205	8
Retained earnings	4,714	3,933
Accumulated other comprehensive (loss) income	(317)	502
Total shareholders' equity	4,643	4,484
Total Liabilities and Shareholders' Equity	$15,826	$12,758

Deferred Expenses

Four kinds of expenses are commonly paid in advance. We will first discuss expenses for insurance, rent, and supplies. The other is an advance payment for equipment used by a company for more than one fiscal period. All four expenses have in common that the timing of the cash disbursement precedes the actual use of the product or service purchased.

INSURANCE. Like any of us when we buy insurance, a company pays for insurance in advance of the service provided by the insurance company. In accounting, the advance payment for a service or good to be received in the future is considered the purchase of an asset. Recall from Chapter 2 that accountants call the asset for insurance paid in advance *prepaid insurance*. Remember, assets are items of value that the company will use up to produce revenue. Until it is actually used, prepaid insurance is shown in the current asset section of the balance sheet. Suppose a firm paid $2,400 for one year of insurance coverage, beginning on October 1, 2010, the date of the payment to the insurance company. Here is how the payment would affect the accounting equation:

Assets	=	Liabilities	+	Shareholders' equity		
				Contributed capital	+	Retained earnings
(2,400) cash						
+ 2,400 prepaid insurance						

Purchasing the insurance policy is an asset exchange: cash is exchanged for prepaid insurance. No expense is recorded when the payment is made because the benefit of the cost has not been used. The expense will be recognized when the company actually uses the insurance. The signal that the insurance is being used is the passing of time. As time passes, the insurance protection expires and the amount paid for insurance during that time becomes an expense. The firm will make the adjustment when it prepares the financial statements.

Suppose the firm wants to prepare the financial statements on December 31, 2010. How much of the insurance is still unused? That is the amount the firm must show as an asset on the December 31, 2010, balance sheet. How much has been used up? That is the amount the firm must show as an expense on the income statement.

Here is the adjustment the firm makes before preparing the December 31, 2010, financial statements:

Assets	=	Liabilities	+	Shareholders' equity		
				Contributed capital	+	Retained earnings
(600) prepaid insurance						(600) insurance expense

The firm has used up 3 months of the 12-month insurance policy already paid for. The firm paid $2,400 for the 12-month policy, so the monthly cost of insurance is $200. That means the total insurance expense for 3 months is $600, and the prepaid insurance remaining—insurance not yet used up—will be on the December 31, 2010, balance sheet in the amount of $1,800. Exhibit 3.6 shows how this works.

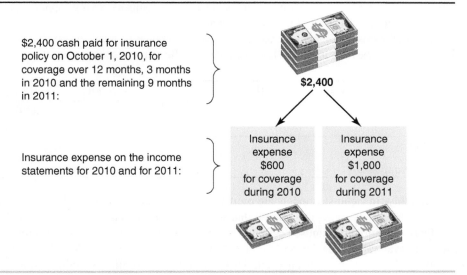

EXHIBIT 3.6

Deferred Expenses— Insurance

RENT. Rent is also usually paid in advance. In the accounting records, prepaid rent is treated exactly the same way as prepaid insurance. When the company pays the cash for rent in advance, an asset called **prepaid rent** is recorded. The disbursement of cash for prepaid rent is an asset exchange. Suppose a company paid $9,000 to rent a warehouse for three months, beginning on November 1, the date of the payment. The way it would affect the accounting equation follows:

Assets	=	Liabilities	+	Shareholders' equity		
				Contributed capital	+	Retained earnings
(9,000) cash						
+ 9,000 prepaid rent						

> **Prepaid rent** is an asset. It represents amounts paid for rent not yet used. The rent expense is deferred until the rented asset has actually been used—when the time related to the rent has passed.

The asset *prepaid rent* is increased, and cash is decreased. Notice, no expense is recognized when the company makes the payment for the rent. Until it is actually used, prepaid rent is an asset. When would the rent expense be recognized, that is, when would it be put on the income statement? When the company prepares financial statements, it wants to be sure that the rent expense is shown correctly on the income statement. The amount paid was $9,000 for a period of three months, which is $3,000 per month. When the financial statements are prepared on December 31, two months of rent has been used—$6,000. To make sure the income statement reflects the expense for the period ended December 31, the company makes the following adjustment:

Assets	=	Liabilities	+	Shareholders' equity		
				Contributed capital	+	Retained earnings
(6,000) prepaid rent						(6,000) rent expense

Notice that rent expense is shown as a reduction in retained earnings, like all expenses. That leaves one month of rent, $3,000, on the balance sheet as prepaid rent. The rent expense for November and December—$6,000—will be shown on the income statement for the year ended December 31.

Your Turn 3-4

Advantage Company paid the annual rent on its new office space on March 1. The total for a year of rent was $3,600. How much rent expense would be shown on the Advantage December 31 income statement?

In general, **supplies** are not called inventory. Supplies are miscellaneous items used in the business. When purchased, supplies are recorded as an asset. Supplies expense is recognized after the supplies are used. *Inventory* is a term reserved for the items a company purchases to resell.

SUPPLIES. **Supplies** are commonly purchased in advance. A company buying supplies is exchanging one asset for another. The cost of the supplies is not recognized as an expense until the supplies are actually used. Suppose a company started March with no supplies on hand and purchased $500 worth of supplies during the month. Here is how the purchase affects the accounting equation:

Assets	=	Liabilities	+	Shareholders' equity		
				Contributed capital	+	Retained earnings
(500) cash						
+ 500 supplies						

If monthly financial statements are prepared, the company will count the amount of unused supplies on March 31 to get the amount that will be shown as an asset on the March 31 balance sheet. Only the amount of unused supplies will be an asset on that date. The difference between the amount available to use during March and the amount remaining on March 31 is the amount of supplies that must have been used. This amount, representing supplies used, will be an expense on the income statement.

Suppose the company counts the supplies on March 31 and finds that there is $150 worth of supplies left in the supply closet. How many dollars worth of supplies must have been used? Five hundred dollars of supplies on hand minus $150 supplies remaining = $350 supplies used. After supplies have been counted, the company must make an adjustment to get the correct amounts for the financial statements. This is the necessary adjustment:

Assets	=	Liabilities	+	Shareholders' equity		
				Contributed capital	+	Retained earnings
(350) supplies						(350) supplies expense

That will leave $150 for the amount of supplies to be shown on the March 31 balance sheet. The income statement for the month of March will show $350 in supplies expense.

Suppose that during April the company purchases an additional $500 worth of supplies. Then, on April 30 as the company is preparing financial statements for April, the supplies left on hand are counted. If $200 worth of supplies are on hand on April 30, what adjustment should be made? Recall that at the end of March, there were supplies on hand amounting to $150. That means that April started with those supplies. Then, $500 worth of supplies were purchased. That means that the company had $650 of supplies available to use during April. What dollar amount of supplies was actually used? Because $200 worth of supplies are left, the company must have used $450 worth of supplies during April. The adjustment at the end of April would reduce the asset supplies by $450 and would reduce retained earnings by $450 via supplies expense.

Check out Exhibit 3.7 for another example of deferring supplies expense.

EXHIBIT 3.7

Deferred Expenses—Supplies

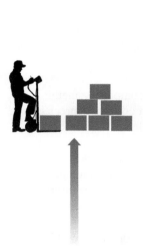

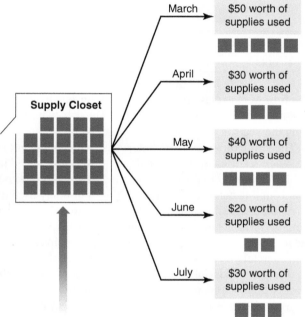

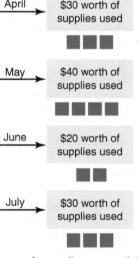

March — $50 worth of supplies used — Cost of supplies *used* in March will be on the income statement as *supplies expense of $50* for the month of March.

April — $30 worth of supplies used — Supplies expense for April will be $30.

May — $40 worth of supplies used — Supplies expense for May will be $40.

June — $20 worth of supplies used — Supplies expense for June will be $20.

July — $30 worth of supplies used — Supplies expense for July will be $30.

Supply Closet

| February 1: Company buys $240 worth of supplies and pays cash. This will be on the **statement of cash flows**. | Company puts the supplies in the supply closet. The cost of the supplies is recorded as an asset on the **balance sheet**. The company has something of value. Dollars have been exchanged before the action of using the supplies has taken place. This is a deferral: dollars first, action later. | As supplies are used, the cost of those used becomes supplies expense and will be on the **income statement** as an expense in the period the supplies are used. | There are supplies worth $70 in the supply closet at the end of July. That amount will remain on the balance sheet as an asset until the supplies are used. |

Konny Company started April with $500 worth of supplies. During the month, Konny purchased $650 worth of supplies. At the end of April, supplies on hand were counted, and $250 worth of supplies was left.

1. What amount of supplies would Konny put on its balance sheet at April 30?
2. What amount of supplies expense would appear on its income statement for the month of April?

Your Turn 3-5

EQUIPMENT. When a company purchases an asset that will be used for more than one accounting period, the cost of the asset is *not* recognized as an expense when the asset is purchased. The expense of using the asset is recognized during the periods in which the asset is used to generate revenue. When a firm buys an asset—such as a computer or office furniture—it will record the purchase as an asset. It is an asset exchange because the firm is exchanging one asset—cash—for another asset—equipment. Then, the firm will recognize a portion of that equipment cost each accounting period in which the equipment is used, hopefully to generate revenue.

The matching principle is the reason the cost of equipment is spread over several periods. Expenses and the revenues they help generate need to be on the same income statement—that is the heart of the matching principle. When it is hard to make a precise match with specific revenue (such as sales and cost of goods sold), the next best match is to put an expense on the income statement in the period in which the related asset is used. That is what you do with equipment—allocate the cost of the equipment to the periods in which the equipment is used.

Suppose a company purchases a computer for $5,000 cash. When the purchase is made, the company will record the acquisition of the new asset and the cash payment.

Assets	=	Liabilities	+	Shareholders' equity		
				Contributed capital	+	Retained earnings
(5,000) cash						
+ 5,000 computer						

If the firm were to classify the purchase as an expense at this point, it would be doing a very poor job of matching revenues and expenses. The firm wants to recognize the expense of the computer during the years in which it uses the computer.

The terminology that accountants use with equipment is different than the terminology used with other deferrals. Instead of calling the expense related to using the computer something logical like "computer expense," it is called **depreciation expense**. Do not confuse depreciation in this accounting context with depreciation commonly used to mean decline in market value.

As the asset is used and the firm wants to reduce its amount in the accounting records, the accountant will not subtract the amount of the expense directly from the asset's purchase price. Instead, per generally accepted accounting principles (GAAP), the firm will show the subtractions separately on the balance sheet. Exhibit 3.8 shows how Best Buy presents this information.

Using real financial information to first learn an accounting concept can be difficult. An example with a fictitious company will help explain the accounting treatment of the cost of equipment and its depreciation expense over time. Sample Company purchased a computer for $5,000 on January 1, 2011, and recorded the asset exchange shown in the preceding accounting equation. Then, when Sample Company prepares its year-end financial statements, depreciation expense must be recognized. The shareholders' claims to the company assets are reduced via depreciation expense.

To calculate how much the asset cost should be reduced each year, Sample Company first must deduct the value it believes the asset will have—what it will be worth—when the company is finished using it. That amount is called the **residual value**. In this example, Sample Company plans to use the computer until it is worth nothing; that means the residual value is zero. The cost of the asset minus any residual value is divided by the number of accounting periods that the asset will be used. Usually, the time period for depreciation expense is a year. Because Sample plans to use the $5,000 computer for five years and has estimated its residual value to be zero, the annual depreciation amount will be $1,000.

The total reduction in the dollar amount of equipment, at any particular point in time, is called **accumulated depreciation**. Each year, accumulated depreciation gets larger. Accumulated depreciation is not the same as depreciation expense. Accumulated depreciation is the total depreciation expense taken over the entire life of the asset, and depreciation expense is the amount of depreciation for a single year. Accumulated depreciation is called a **contra-asset** because it is the opposite of an asset. It is a deduction from assets. Accumulated depreciation is disclosed separately somewhere in the financial statements so that the original cost of the equipment is kept intact.

On the balance sheet, the original cost of the equipment is shown along with the deduction for accumulated depreciation—the total amount of depreciation that has been recorded during the time the asset has been owned. The resulting amount is called the **book value**, or **carrying value**, of the equipment. The book value is the net amount that is included when the total assets are added up on the balance sheet.

The **depreciation expense** is the expense for each period.

Residual value, also known as *salvage value*, is the estimated value of an asset at the end of its useful life. With most depreciation methods, residual value is deducted before the calculation of depreciation expense.

The **accumulated depreciation** is the reduction to the cost of the asset. Accumulated depreciation is a contra-asset, deducted from the cost of the asset for the balance sheet.

A **contra-asset** is an amount that is deducted from an asset.

The **book value** of an asset is the cost minus the accumulated depreciation related to the asset.

Carrying value is another expression for book value.

EXHIBIT 3.8

Assets from Best Buy's Balance Sheet

Best Buy has property and equipment that cost $6,940 million on February 28, 2009. The total amount of depreciation expense the firm has recorded over the life of these assets is $2,766 million.

Best Buy
From the Consolidated Balance Sheets
(dollars in millions)

Assets	February 28, 2009	March 1, 2008
Current Assets		
Cash and cash equivalents	$ 498	$ 1,438
Short-term investments	11	64
Receivables	1,868	549
Merchandise inventories	4,753	4,708
Other current assets	1,062	583
Total current assets	8,192	7,342
Property and equipment		
Land and buildings	755	732
Leasehold improvements	2,013	1,752
Fixtures and equipment	4,060	3,057
Property under master and capital lease	112	67
	6,940	5,608
Less accumulated depreciation	2,766	2,302
Net property and equipment	4,174	3,306
Goodwill	2,203	1,088
Tradenames	173	97
Customer Relationships	322	5
Equity and Other Investments	395	605
Other assets	367	315
Total assets	$15,826	$12,758

Here is the year-end adjustment to record depreciation of the asset after its first year of use:

Assets	=	Liabilities	+	Shareholders' equity	
				Contributed capital	+ Retained earnings
(1,000) accumulated depreciation					(1,000) depreciation expense

The accumulated depreciation is shown on the balance sheet as a *deduction* from the cost of the equipment. The depreciation expense is shown on the income statement. The book value of the asset is $4,000 (cost minus accumulated depreciation) at the end of the first year.

After the second year of use, Sample Company would again record the same thing—$1,000 more recorded as accumulated depreciation and $1,000 as depreciation expense. The amount of accumulated depreciation will then be $2,000. The amount of depreciation expense is only $1,000 because it represents only a single year—the second year—of depreciation expense. The accumulated depreciation refers to all the depreciation expense for the life of the asset through the year of the financial statement. The book value of the computer at the end of the second year is $3,000—$5,000 cost minus its $2,000 accumulated depreciation. See Exhibit 3.9 on the following page for another example.

Your Turn 3-6

Tango Company purchased a computer on July 1, 2011, for $6,500. It is expected to last for five years and have a residual value of $500 at the end of the fifth year. How much depreciation expense would appear on the Tango December 31, 2011, income statement? What is the book value of the computer at the end of 2012?

EXHIBIT 3.9

EXHIBIT 3.9

**Deferred Expenses—
Depreciation**

Truck purchased on
January 1, 2007. The
truck will last for seven
years. Cost is $49,000.
No residual value.

Cost of the truck will be spread over the
income statements of the seven years the
truck is used as depreciation expense. The
expense is being **deferred**, that is *put off*,
until the truck is actually used.

*The cost of the asset is spread—as an expense—evenly (in this
example) over the life of the asset.*

Year ended December 31	2007	2008	2009	2010	2011	2012	2013
Depreciation expense	$7,000	$ 7,000	$ 7,000	$ 7,000	$ 7,000	$ 7,000	$ 7,000
Accumulated depreciation	$7,000	$14,000	$21,000	$28,000	$35,000	$42,000	$49,000

L.O.4

Construct the basic financial
statements from a given set
of transactions that include
accruals and deferrals and
recognize the effect of these
transactions on actual
financial statements.

Effects of Accruals and Deferrals on Financial Statements

Now that you have learned the details of accruals and deferrals you are ready to put it all together in the construction of a set of financial statements. We will take Team Shirts through its third month of business to see how timing differences affect the firm's financial statements. Then we will look at some real firms' financial statements to identify the effects of accruals and deferrals.

Team Shirts Transactions for March

In Chapters 1 and 2, Team Shirts completed its first two months of operations. Exhibit 3.10 shows the company's balance sheet at the end of the second month, which we prepared in Chapter 2.

EXHIBIT 3.10

**Team Shirts' Balance Sheet
at February 28, 2010**

Team Shirts
Balance Sheet
At February 28, 2010

Assets		Liabilities and Shareholder's equity	
Cash	$6,695	Accounts payable	$ 800
Accounts receivable	150	Other payables	50
Inventory	100		
Prepaid insurance	125	Common stock	5,000
		Retained earnings	1,220
		Total liabilities and	
Total assets	$7,070	shareholder's equity	$7,070

These are the amounts that are carried over to the next month, so this is the March 1, 2010, balance sheet, too. We will now take Team Shirts through the third month of business, with the transactions shown in Exhibit 3.11.

At the end of the third month, Team Shirts prepares its financial statements to see how the business is progressing. We will see how each transaction affects the accounting equation. Then, we will look at the accounting equation worksheet in Exhibit 3.12 at the end of the example to see all of the transactions together.

Transaction 1: Purchase of a long-term asset Team Shirts purchases a fixed asset that will last longer than one year; therefore, it will be classified as a long-term asset. Remember, current assets will be used up or converted to cash within one year. If the

EXHIBIT 3.11

Transactions for Team Shirts for March

Date	Transaction
1. March 1	Purchased computer for $4,000 with $1,000 down and a three month, 12% note for $3,000. The computer is expected to last for three years and have a residual value of $400.
2. March 10	Paid the rest of last month's advertising bill, $50.
3. March 15	Collected accounts receivable of $150 from customers from February.
4. March 20	Paid for February purchases—paying off the accounts payable balance of $800.
5. March 24	Purchased 250 shirts @ $4 each for inventory for cash, $1,000.
6. March 27	Sold 200 shirts for $10 each, all on account, for total sales of $2,000.

cost of an asset needs to be spread over more than one year, it is considered long-term. The actual purchase of the asset is recorded as an asset exchange, not as an expense. Do not worry about depreciation expense and interest expense right now. That will be considered when it is time to prepare the financial statements. Here is how the purchase of the $4,000 computer with $1,000 down and a note payable of $3,000 with an annual interest rate of 12%, due in three months, affects the accounting equation:

Assets	=	Liabilities	+	Shareholder's equity		
				Contributed capital	+	Retained earnings
(1,000) cash + 4,000 computer		+ 3,000 notes payable				

The recognition of the expense related to the cost of the computer will be deferred—put off—until Team Shirts has used the asset and is ready to prepare financial statements. The cash portion of the payment for the computer will be shown as an investing cash flow on the statement of cash flows.

Transaction 2: Cash disbursement to settle a liability Last month, Sara hired a company to do some advertising for her business. On February 28, 2010, Team Shirts had not paid the full amount. Because the work was done in February, the expense was shown on the income statement for the month of February. In March, Team Shirts pays cash of $50 to settle—eliminate—the liability. Here is how the cash disbursement affects the accounting equation:

Assets	=	Liabilities	+	Shareholder's equity		
				Contributed capital	+	Retained earnings
(50) cash		(50) other payables				

The action took place during February, so the expense was shown on that month's income statement. The cash is now paid in March, but no expense is recognized in March because that would be double counting the expense. An expense is recognized only once. The cash payment is an operating cash flow for the statement of cash flows.

Transaction 3: Collection of cash to settle a receivable At the end of last month, Team Shirts had not received all the cash it was owed by customers. Because the sales were made during February, the revenue from those sales was shown on the income statement for the month of February. Because the cash for the sales was not collected at the time the sales were made, Team Shirts recorded accounts receivable. Accounts receivable is an asset that will be converted to cash within the next year. When customers pay their bills, Team Shirts records the receipt of cash and removes the receivable from its records. Here is how the collection of the cash affects the accounting equation:

Assets	=	Liabilities	+	Shareholder's equity		
				Contributed capital	+	Retained earnings
+ 150 cash (150) accounts receivable						

Revenue is not recorded when the cash is collected because the revenue was already recorded at the time of the sale. To count it now would be double counting. The cash collection is an operating cash flow for the statement of cash flows.

Transaction 4: Payment to vendor At the end of last month, the balance sheet for Team Shirts showed accounts payable of $800. This is the amount still owed to vendors for February purchases. Team Shirts pays this debt, bringing the accounts payable balance to zero. The cash payment is an operating cash flow for the statement of cash flows.

Assets	=	Liabilities	+	Shareholder's equity		
				Contributed capital	+	Retained earnings
(800) cash		(800) accounts payable				

Transaction 5: Purchase of inventory Team Shirts purchases 250 shirts at $4 each, for a total of $1,000 and pays cash for the purchase. The cash payment is an operating cash flow for the statement of cash flows.

Assets	=	Liabilities	+	Shareholder's equity		
				Contributed capital	+	Retained earnings
(1,000) cash						
+ 1,000 inventory						

Transaction 6: Sales Team Shirts sells 200 shirts at $10 each, all on account. That means the company extended credit to its customers and Team Shirts will collect the cash later.

Assets	=	Liabilities	+	Shareholder's equity		
				Contributed capital	+	Retained earnings
+ 2,000 accounts receivable						+ 2,000 sales revenue

At the same time sales revenue is recorded, Team Shirts records the reduction in inventory. The reduction in inventory is an expense called cost of goods sold.

Assets	=	Liabilities	+	Shareholder's equity		
				Contributed capital	+	Retained earnings
(800) inventory						(800) cost of goods sold

Notice that the sale is recorded at the amount Team Shirts will collect from the customer. At the same time, the reduction in the inventory is recorded at the cost of the inventory—200 shirts at a cost of $4 per shirt. This is a terrific example of the matching principle.

Notice that there is no explicit recording of profit in the company records. Instead, profit is a derived amount; it is calculated by subtracting cost of goods sold from the amount of sales. For this sale, the profit is $1,200. It is called the gross profit—also called gross margin—on sales. Other expenses must be subtracted from the gross margin to get to net profit, also called net income.

Up to this point, we have looked just at the routine transactions during the month ended March 31, 2010. At the end of the month, Team Shirts will adjust the company records for any accruals and deferrals needed for accurate financial statements. Look back over the transactions and see if you can identify the adjustments needed.

Adjustments to the Accounting Records

A review of the balance sheet at March 1 along with the transactions for March should reveal three adjustments needed at the end of March 2010:

1. Depreciation expense for the computer
2. Insurance expense for the month (recall that Team Shirts purchased three month's worth of insurance in the middle of February)
3. Interest expense on the note payable

We will now look at each of the adjustments and how the amounts for those adjustments are calculated.

> *Adjustment 1: Depreciation* The computer purchased on March 1 must be depreciated—that is, part of the cost must be recognized as depreciation expense during March. To figure out the depreciation expense, the residual value is subtracted from the cost of the asset, and then the difference is divided by the estimated useful life of the asset. In this case, the residual value is $400, so that amount is subtracted from the cost of $4,000. The remaining $3,600 is divided by three years, resulting in a depreciation expense of $1,200 per year. Because we are preparing monthly statements, the annual amount must be divided by 12 months, giving $100 depreciation per month. The adjustment is a reduction to assets and an expense.

Assets	=	Liabilities	+	Shareholder's equity		
				Contributed capital	+	Retained earnings
(100) accumulated depreciation						(100) depreciation expense

> The reduction to the cost of the computer accumulates each month, so that the carrying value of the asset in the accounting records goes down by $100 each month. In the accounting records, we do not simply subtract $100 each month from the computer's cost on the left side of the equation, because GAAP require the cost of a specific asset and the total accumulated depreciation related to that asset to be shown separately.
>
> The subtracted amount is called *accumulated depreciation*. After the first month, accumulated depreciation related to this particular asset is $100. After the second month, the accumulated depreciation will be $200. That amount—representing how much of the asset cost we count as used—is a contra-asset, because it reduces the recorded value of an asset.
>
> The cost of an asset minus its accumulated depreciation is called the *book value* or *carrying value* of the asset. Each time depreciation expense is recorded, the accumulated depreciation increases, and the book value of the asset decreases.
>
> Depreciation expense represents a single period's expense and is shown on the income statement.
>
> *Adjustment 2: Insurance expense* Remember that Team Shirts purchased three months' worth of insurance for $150, which is $50 per month, in mid-February. On the March 1 balance sheet, there is a current asset called prepaid insurance in the amount of $125. A full month

of insurance expense needs to be recorded for the month of March. That amount will be deducted from prepaid insurance.

Assets	=	Liabilities	+	Shareholder's equity		
				Contributed capital	+	Retained earnings
(50) prepaid insurance						(50) insurance expense

Adjustment 3: Accruing interest expense On March 1, Team Shirts signed a three-month note for $3,000. The note carries an interest rate of 12%. (Interest rates are typically given as an annual rate.) Because the firm is preparing a monthly income statement, it needs to accrue one month of interest expense. The interest rate formula—Interest = Principal × Rate × Time—produces the following interest computation:

$$\text{Interest} = \$3,000 \times 0.12 \times 1/12 \text{ (1 month out of 12)} = \$30$$

Assets	=	Liabilities	+	Shareholder's equity		
				Contributed capital	+	Retained earnings
		+ 30 interest payable				(30) interest expense

> Notice, the residual value is deducted only in the calculation of the amount of depreciation expense. It is not deducted from the cost of the asset in the company's formal records.
>
> Notice that the calculation of the interest expense does not take into consideration the length of the note. The interest expense would be the same if this were a six-month note or a two-year note, or a note of any other length of time. Interest expense is calculated based on the time that has passed as a fraction of a year because the interest rate used is an annual rate.

These are the needed adjustments at March 31, 2010, for Team Shirts to produce accurate financial statements according to GAAP.

Exhibit 3.12 shows all of the transactions and adjustments in the accounting equation worksheet. Notice how each financial statement is derived from the transactions.

Preparing the Financial Statements

First, Team Shirts prepares the income statement. Revenues and expenses are found in the red-boxed column on the accounting equation worksheet. Organized and summarized, they produce the income statement for Team Shirts for March, shown in Exhibit 3.13 on page 118. The income statement covers a period of time—in this case, it covers one month of business activity.

Second, Team Shirts prepares the statement of changes in shareholder's equity—a summary of what has happened to equity during the period. It is shown in Exhibit 3.14 on page 118. Like the income statement, the statement of changes in shareholder's equity covers a specific period of time—in this case, one month.

Third, Team Shirts prepares the balance sheet—composed of three sections: assets, liabilities, and shareholder's equity—with the amount of each on the last day of the period. The assets are arranged in order of liquidity—how easily the asset can be converted to cash. Remember that current assets will be used or converted to cash sometime during the next fiscal year, whereas long-term assets will last longer than one year.

Similarly, current liabilities are obligations that will be satisfied in the next fiscal year, whereas long-term liabilities are obligations that will not be repaid in the next fiscal year.

Shareholder's equity is shown in two parts—contributed capital and retained earnings. Because the balance sheet is a summary of all the transactions in the accounting equation, it should balance if there are no errors in your worksheet. The balance sheet is shown in Exhibit 3.15 on page 118.

Fourth, Team Shirts prepares the statement of cash flows. Because the first three financial statements (the income statement, statement of changes in shareholder's equity, and the balance sheet) are accrual based instead of cash based, these three financial statements do not provide detailed information about a company's cash—where it came from and how it was spent. The balance sheet gives only the total amount of cash on hand at the close of business on the last day of the fiscal period, and the income statement—the focus of financial reporting—gives no information about cash.

EXHIBIT 3.12

Accounting Equation Worksheet for Team Shirts for March

The income statement is prepared first. Then, the net income can be used on the statement of changes in shareholder's equity. The total contributed capital and retained earnings from that statement are then used on the balance sheet. Finally, the cash transactions are reorganized and summarized for the statement of cash flows.

	Assets		=	**Liabilities**	+	**Shareholder's Equity**	
	Cash	All other assets (Account)		All liabilities (Account)		Contributed Capital — Common stock	Retained Earnings (Account)
Beginning Balances	$6,695	$150 Accounts receivable 100 Inventory 125 Prepaid insurance		$800 Accounts payable 50 Other payables		$5,000	$1,220
Transaction							
1.	(1,000)	4,000 Computer		3,000 Notes payable			
2.	(50)			(50) Other payables			
3.	150	(150) Accounts receivable					
4.		(800) Accounts receivable		(800) Accounts payable			
5.	(1,000)	1,000 Inventory					
6.		2,000 Accounts receivable					2,000 Sales
Adjustment 1		(800) Inventory					(800) Cost of goods sold
Adjustment 1		(100) Accumulated depreciation					(100) Depreciation expense
Adjustment 2		(50) Prepaid insurance					(50) Insurance expense
Adjustment 3				30 Interest payable			(30) Interest expense
Ending Balances	$3,995	+ $6,275*	=	$3,030	+	$5,000	+ $2,240

— Income Statement   — Statement of Changes in Stockholders' Equity   — Balance Sheet   — Statement of Cash Flows

*All other assets (details)

$2,000	Accounts receivable
300	Inventory
75	Prepaid insurance
4,000	Computer
(100)	Accumulated depreciation, Computer
$6,275	Total

EXHIBIT 3.13

Income Statement for Team Shirts for March

Team Shirts
Income Statement
For the Month Ended March 31, 2010

Sales revenue		$2,000
Expenses		
Cost of goods sold	$800	
Depreciation expense	100	
Insurance expense	50	
Interest expense	30	980
Net income		$1,020

EXHIBIT 3.14

Statement of Changes in Shareholder's Equity for Team Shirts for March

Team Shirts
Statement of Changes in Shareholder's Equity
For the Month Ended March 31, 2010

Beginning common stock	$5,000	
Common stock issued during the month	0	
Ending common stock		$5,000
Beginning retained earnings	$1,220	
Net income for the month	1,020	
Dividends declared	0	
Ending retained earnings		2,240
Total shareholder's equity		$7,240

EXHIBIT 3.15

Balance Sheet for Team Shirts at March 31, 2010

Team Shirts
Balance Sheet
At March 31, 2010

Assets		Liabilities and Shareholder's equity	
Current assets		Current liabilities	
Cash	$3,995	Interest payable	$ 30
Accounts receivable	2,000	Notes payable	3,000
Inventory	300	Total current liabilities	3,030
Prepaid insurance	75	Shareholder's equity	
Total current assets	6,370	Common stock	5,000
Computer (net of $100		Retained earnings	2,240
accumulated depreciation)	3,900	Total shareholder's equity	7,240
		Total liabilities and	
Total assets	$10,270	shareholder's equity	$10,270

This is why the statement of cash flows is needed. Even though accrual accounting does not base the measurement of income on cash, there is no debate about the importance of the sources and uses of cash to a business. The statement of cash flows gives the details of how the cash balance has changed from the first day of the period to the last day. This statement is shown in Exhibit 3.16.

EXHIBIT 3.16

Statement of Cash Flows for Team Shirts for March

Team Shirts
Statement of Cash Flows
For the Month Ended March 31, 2010

Cash from Operating Activities:

Cash collected from customers............................	$ 150	
Cash paid to vendors..	(1,800)	
Cash paid for advertising	(50)	
Net cash used by operating activities..		$(1,700)
Cash from Investing Activities:		
Cash paid for computer*...		(1,000)
Cash from Financing Activities:...		0
Net decrease in cash...		$(2,700)
Beginning cash balance..		6,695
Ending cash balance		$ 3,995

*Computer was purchased for $4,000. A note was signed for $3,000 and cash paid was $1,000.

Accruals and Deferrals on Real Firms' Financial Statements

The most apparent place on a set of financial statements to identify accruals and deferrals is the balance sheet. Most often, the transactions have been summarized in such a way that the income statement does not make accruals and deferrals obvious. For example, if a firm shows sales revenue on the income statement, the firm may or may not have collected the related cash. The place to find that information is on the balance sheet.

Take a close look at Hormel Foods Corporation's balance sheets in Exhibit 3.17 on the following page. Although there are many items on these statements that you are not familiar with, you should be able to see how much you have learned about financial statements in three short chapters. For example, you know that it is a classified balance sheet because there are subtotals for current assets and current liabilities. The assets are ordered by liquidity, with cash and cash equivalents at the beginning of the assets. As you look at more real firms' financial statements, you will find that each firm will use some unique terminology. Usually, you will be able to figure out what sort of account or amount it is. If you cannot, take a look in the notes to the financial statements for more information.

Look down the balance sheet and see if you can identify specific accruals and deferrals that the company probably recorded when it was preparing its year-end balance sheet. Here are a few examples:

1. *Prepaid expenses*. This is listed as a current asset. It represents goods or services that have been paid for but not used. Putting this amount on the balance sheet is deferring the expense until the period in which the items are used. It is rare for the word *expense* to be on the balance sheet. Here it is the word *prepaid* that makes this an asset on the balance sheet rather than an expense on the income statement.

2. *Allowance for depreciation*. Hormel Foods has several types of property and equipment. Notice that *accumulated depreciation* is called *allowance for depreciation* here, and it has been deducted from the recorded cost of the assets to give the total book value of the assets. In the firm's accounting records, accumulated depreciation (or allowance for depreciation) is a contra-asset, representing the amount of the assets the company has recorded as depreciation expense over the life of the assets to the date of the balance sheet.

3. *Accrued expenses*. As part of the current liabilities, accrued expenses are amounts that the company has recognized as expenses (i.e., put on the income statement). The company purchased these things on account. That is, the company still owes someone for these things. It could be things such as utilities payable or salaries payable—anything the company has used to generate revenue but has not yet paid for. Again, there is the word *expense* on the balance sheet. Here it is preceded by the word *accrued*, which indicates that it is a liability on the balance sheet rather than an expense on the income statement.

EXHIBIT 3.17

Hormel Foods Corporation's Balance Sheets at October 26, 2008, and October 28, 2007

The three shaded items are just a few examples of accruals and deferrals that can easily be picked out from Hormel's balance sheet.

Hormel Foods Corporation
Consolidated Statements of Financial Position

(In Thousands)	October 26, 2008	October 28, 2007
Assets		
Current Assets		
Cash and cash equivalents	$ 154,778	$ 149,749
Accounts receivable [net of allowance for doubtful accounts of 3,144 at October 26, 2008 and 3,180 at October 28, 2007]	411,010	366,621
Inventories	784,542	646,968
Deferred income taxes	45,948	52,583
Prepaid expenses and other current assets	41,900	15,804
Total Current Assets	1,438,178	1,231,725
Deferred Income Taxes	89,249	66,220
Goodwill	619,325	595,756
Other Intangibles	151,219	162,237
Pension Assets	91,773	99,003
Investments in and Receivables from Affiliates	93,617	102,060
Other Assets	155,453	170,048
Property, Plant and Equipment		
Land	52,940	48,663
Buildings	662,519	615,245
Equipment	1,275,175	1,192,481
Construction in progress	78,083	114,415
	2,068,717	1,970,804
Less allowance for depreciation	(1,091,060)	(1,004,203)
	977,657	966,601
Total Assets	$3,616,471	$3,393,650
Liabilities and Shareholders' Investment		
Current Liabilities		
Accounts payable	$ 378,520	$ 290,919
Notes payable/Short-term debt	100,000	70,000
Accrued expenses	72,192	66,000
Accrued workers compensation	26,825	27,372
Accrued marketing expenses	60,223	67,260
Employee compensation	106,225	111,051
Taxes, other then federal income taxes	6,979	5,454
Dividends payable	24,946	20,745
Federal income taxes	5,323	5,927
Current maturities of long-term debt	0	49
Total Current Liabilities	781,233	664,777
Long-Term Debt – less current maturities	350,000	350,005
Pension and Post-Retirement Benefits	386,590	440,810
Other Long-Term Liabilities	91,076	53,275
Shareholders' Investment		
Preferred stock, par value $.01 a share – authorized 80,000,000 shares; issued – none		
Common stock, nonvoting, par value $.01 a share – authorized 200,000,000 shares; issued – none		
Common stock, par value $.0586 a share – authorized 400,000,000 shares; issued 134,520,581 shares October 26, 2008; issued 135,677,494 shares October 28, 2007	7,883	7,951
Additional paid-in capital	0	0
Accumulated other comprehensive loss	(113,184)	(101,811)
Retained earnings	2,112,873	1,978,643
Total Shareholders' Investment	2,007,572	1,884,783
Total Liabilities and Shareholders' Investment	$3,616,471	$3,393,650

See notes to consolidated financial statements.

Left margin note: Even though it is unusual to see the term "expenses" used on the balance sheet, you will often find it with the word "prepaid." A prepaid expense is NOT an expense; it's an asset.

Left margin note: Again, the term "expenses" is found on the balance sheet, but accrued expenses are NOT expenses. They are liabilities.

Right margin note: PPE assets are shown at cost, and then the accumulated depreciation is deducted. Allowance for depreciation means the same thing as accumulated depreciation.

UNDERSTANDING → # Business

Does Going Green Help a Company's Bottom Line?

The goal of a corporation is to make money for its shareholders—that is, to increase shareholders' value. It is the job of financial statements to report the corporation's financial performance. Where does a corporation's social responsibility fit in? Is there a relationship between financial performance and a corporation's social performance? For any company, part of being socially responsible is finding ways to reduce its negative impact on the environment. Everyone, it seems, is talking about "going green."

In his book, *What Matters Most: How a Small Group of Pioneers Is Teaching Social Responsibility to Big Business and Why Big Business Is Listening*, Jeffrey Hollander argues that "introducing social responsibility into day-to-day business operations is an effective way of creating long-term sustainable growth and improved financial performance." Many organizations agree. Staples, for example, reports that its switching from three-amp to two-amp light bulbs added $4.2 million to its bottom line. Dell's plan to neutralize its carbon footprint saved the company $3 million in 2008. Dell Inc. plans to reduce its waste and reuse 99% of its waste by 2013.

According to a recent study by A.T. Kearney, firms with a true commitment to corporate sustainability practices are achieving above-average performance in the financial markets in the current economic recession. John Mahoney, CFO at Staples, told the CFO Green Conference in March 2009 that being socially responsible should continue to reap financial benefits.

"While the economy is reeling today, we can afford to maintain our sustainability programs because of their measurable impact on our financial performance. I think the economic environment is going to really represent a turning point for many companies in thinking about how sustainability works."

Source: "Staples CFO: Going Green Means Saving Green," by David McCann, April 1, 2009, CFO.com

As you continue to learn about the underlying business transactions that are included in a company's financial statements, you will see more examples of accruals and deferrals that are an integral part of GAAP.

Applying Your Knowledge: Ratio Analysis

Profit Margin on Sales Ratio

In this chapter, we have discussed how firms measure profit with accounting net income. To evaluate the firm's profitability over time, the firm might use a ratio called **profit margin on sales**. Sometimes it is called the *net* profit margin on sales ratio or simply the profit margin ratio. It measures how much of the firm's sales revenue actually makes its way to the bottom line—net income. To calculate this ratio, simply divide net income by net sales:

$$\text{Profit margin on sales} = \frac{\text{Net income}}{\text{Net sales}}$$

As shown in Exhibit 3.18 on the following page, for its fiscal year ended October 26, 2008, Hormel Foods Corporation earned a net income of $285,500,000 with net sales of $6,754,903,000. That is a profit margin on sales ratio of 4.2%. Just a little over four cents of every dollar of sales makes its way to net income. Let's calculate the profit margin on sales ratio for the two prior fiscal years:

For fiscal year ended October 28, 2007: $301,892,000 ÷ $6,193,032,000 = 4.9%

For fiscal year ended October 29, 2006: $286,139,000 ÷ $5,745,481,000 = 5.0%

The trend shows that a smaller percentage of sales is making it all the way to net income each year. This means that a larger percentage of the firm's sales dollars are going toward covering the firm's costs. This is something that Hormel is definitely keeping an eye on, because it is a trend that the firm needs to either stop or reverse.

L.O.5
Compute and explain the *profit margin on sales* ratio.

Profit margin on sales is a ratio that measures how much of the firm's sales revenue actually makes its way to the bottom line—net income. To calculate this ratio, simply divide net income by net sales.

EXHIBIT 3.18

Income Statements for Hormel Foods Corporation

Hormel Foods Corporation
Statements of Operations

	Fiscal Year Ended		
(In Thousands, Except Per Share Amounts)	October 26, 2008	October 28, 2007	October 29, 2006
Net sales	$6,754,903	$6,193,032	$5,745,481
Cost of products sold	5,233,156	4,778,505	4,362,291
Gross Profit	1,521,747	1,414,527	1,383,190
Expenses:			
Selling and delivery	834,292	771,597	754,143
Administrative and general	178,029	162,480	182,891
Total Expenses	1,012,321	934,077	937,034
Equity in earnings of affiliates	4,235	3,470	4,553
Operating Income	513,661	483,920	450,709
Other income and expense:			
Interest and investment (loss) income	(28,102)	13,624	5,470
Interest expense	(28,023)	(27,707)	(25,636)
Earnings Before Income Taxes	457,536	469,837	430,543
Provision for income taxes	172,036	167,945	144,404
Net Earnings	$ 285,500	$ 301,892	$ 286,139
Net Earnings Per Share:			
Basic	$ 2.11	$ 2.20	$ 2.08
Diluted	$ 2.08	$ 2.17	$ 2.05
Weighted-Average Shares Outstanding:			
Basic	135,360	137,216	137,845
Diluted	137,128	139,151	139,561

Your Turn 3-7

Use the following information from Campbell Soup Company's income statements to calculate the company's profit margin on sales ratio. How does it compare with the ones calculated for Hormel?

Campbell Soup Company
(dollars in millions)

	For the year ended August 3, 2008	For the year ended July 29, 2007
Net sales	$7,998	$7,385
Net income	$1,165	$ 854

L.O.6
Explain the business risks associated with financial records and accounting information.

Business Risk, Control, and Ethics

In Chapters 1 and 2, we discussed the risks a business faces, particularly those risks associated with financial information. Now that you have learned how many transactions are reflected on the financial statements, we will look at the three most significant risks associated with this information:

1. Errors in recording and updating the financial accounting records
2. Unauthorized access to the financial accounting records
3. Loss of the data in the financial accounting records

No matter how transactions are recorded, the information system needs to address the risks of errors in recording the data, unauthorized access to the data, and potential loss of the data.

Errors in Recording and Updating the Accounting Records

Errors in recording transactions can lead to inaccurate records and reports. These errors can be costly, both for internal decision making and external reporting. The accuracy and completeness of the recording process are crucial for a firm's success. The controls that can minimize the risk of these errors include the following: (1) input and processing controls, (2) reconciliation and control reports, and (3) documentation to provide supporting evidence for the recorded transactions. These controls should be present in both manual and computerized accounting information systems.

- *Input and processing controls.* This control is designed to make sure that only authorized transactions are put into the system. For example, when a sales clerk enters a sale at a cash register, the clerk must put in an employee code before entering the data. Additional controls, such as department numbers and item numbers, help make sure that clerks enter the correct information. The computer program that controls this part of the accounting system may also have limits on the dollar amounts that can be entered. The design of the controls depends on the accounting information system and the business, but all firms should have controls to ensure the accuracy of the input and processing of the data that are recorded.
- *Reconciliation and control reports.* This control is designed to catch any errors in the input and processing of the accounting data. Computerized accounting systems are valuable because they make sure the accounting equation is in balance at every stage of the data entry. This type of equality with each entry is a control programmed into accounting software such as Peachtree and QuickBooks. Accounting software does not guarantee that all the transactions have been recorded correctly, but it does keep some errors from occurring.
- *Documentation to provide supporting evidence for the recorded transactions.* This control is designed to keep errors from occurring and also to catch errors that have occurred. The employee who puts the data into the accounting system will get that data from a document that describes the transaction. The information contained in the documentation can be compared to the data put into the accounting system. For example, when a book-publishing company such as Prentice Hall sends an invoice to Amazon.com for a shipment of books, Prentice Hall will keep a copy of this invoice to input the data into its accounting system. Prentice Hall may also use this invoice to verify the accuracy of the accounting entry by referring back to the original invoice.

Unauthorized Access to the Accounting Information

Unauthorized access is an obvious risk for any company's accounting system. Such access would expose a company to leaks of confidential data, errors, and the cover-up of theft. In manual systems, the records should be locked in a secure place so that they cannot be accessed by unauthorized employees. Computerized systems have user IDs and passwords to control access to the accounting system.

There are serious ethical issues related to a firm's data and computerized accounting systems. With the rapid expansion of the Internet and the development of wireless technologies, system-related fraud has been on the rise. Firms must carefully screen all employees, but particularly those who are involved with developing and securing the firm's computer systems. No system is totally safe from fraud.

Loss or Destruction of Accounting Data

Imagine that you are working for several hours on a report for your marketing class, and you save your work on your hard drive. You decide to step out for a coffee with friends before wrapping up. While you are gone, the computer shuts down, and you cannot reboot. If you backed up your file, you are okay. If you did not, you must start the report from scratch.

The accounting information system contains data that are crucial parts of a company's operations, so there must be a backup and disaster-recovery plan. According to the *Washington Post* (September 21, 2005, "Backups Enabled Systems to Survive," p. D05), disaster recovery related to computer records "has become a $6 billion share of the computer industry as companies and governments have taken to heart the lessons of lightning strikes, floods, and other incidents, such as the Sept. 11, 2001, terrorist attacks."

Chapter Summary Points

Accountants want the income statement to reflect the revenues and expenses for the period covered by the statement—none from the period before or the period after. Accountants also want the balance sheet to show the correct amount of assets and liabilities on the date of the statement. To do that, accountants must allocate revenues and expenses to the correct periods. This is done by making adjustments at the end of the accounting period.

- Sometimes a company purchases something and pays for it later. Sometimes a company earns revenue but collects the cash for that revenue later.
- Accountants do *not* base the recognition of revenues and expenses on the income statement on the collection of cash or on the disbursement of cash. Revenues and expenses are recognized—shown on the income statement—when the economic substance of the transaction has taken place. The economic substance of a transaction is the action of providing or receiving goods and services.
- When the action has been completed but the dollars have not yet changed hands, it is called an accrual. Action comes first, and payment for that action comes later. You accrue—build up or accumulate—revenue you have earned or expenses you have incurred, even though the cash has not been exchanged.
- In some situations, the payment comes first and the action for that payment comes later. Sometimes you pay in advance for goods or services; or sometimes your customers pay you in advance for those goods or services you will provide in a later period. These situations are called deferrals. Dollars are exchanged, but you defer recognition of the revenue or expense until the action of the transaction is complete.

Chapter Summary Problems

BB&B Decorating provides decorating services for a fee. Suppose BB&B Decorating began the month of January 2011 with the following account balances:

Cash	$200,000
Supplies	20,000
Equipment*	100,000
Accumulated depreciation	(10,000)
Total assets	$310,000
Miscellaneous payables	$ 40,000
Salaries payable	4,000
Long-term notes payable	50,000
Common stock	126,000
Retained earnings	90,000
Total liabilities and equity	$310,000

*Equipment is depreciated by $10,000 each year, which is $833 per month.

The following transactions occurred during January 2011:

- **a.** Purchased additional supplies for $12,000 on account (record the liability as miscellaneous payables)
- **b.** Paid salaries owed to employees at December 31, 2010
- **c.** Provided decorating services for $84,000 cash
- **d.** Paid entire balance in miscellaneous payables (including purchase in transaction (a))
- **e.** Purchased $15,000 worth of supplies on account (record as miscellaneous payables)
- **f.** Paid six months' worth of rent on buildings for $6,000, starting on January 1, 2011
- **g.** Made a payment on the long-term loan of $5,000, of which $4,950 was principal and $50 was interest for January

Additional information follows:

- There was $5,000 worth of supplies left on hand at the end of the month.
- The equipment is being depreciated at $833 per month.
- At month-end, the following expenses for January (to be paid in February) had not been recorded:
  Utilities $ 350
  Salaries $4,600

Requirements

1. Set up an accounting equation worksheet and enter the beginning balances. Then, record each transaction including the needed adjustments.
2. Prepare the four basic financial statements. For the statement of changes in shareholders' equity, prepare only the retained earnings portion of the statement.

Solution

	Cash	All other assets	(Account)	All liabilities	(Account)	Common stock	Retained Earnings	(Account)
Assets				**= Liabilities**		**+ Shareholders' Equity**		
						Contributed Capital	Retained Earnings	
Beginning Balances	$200,000	$ 20,000 100,000 (10,000)	Supplies Equipment Accumulated Depreciation	$40,000 4,000 50,000	Misc. payables Salaries payable Long-term notes payable	$126,000	$90,000	(Account)
Transaction a.		12,000	Supplies	12,000	Misc. payables			
b.	(4,000)			(4,000)	Salaries payable			
c.	84,000						84,000	Revenue
d.	(52,000)			(52,000)	Misc. payables			
e.		15,000	Supplies	15,000	Misc. payables			
f.	(6,000)	6,000	Prepaid rent					
g.	(5,000)			(4,950)	Long-term notes payable		(50)	Interest expense
Adjustment 1		(42,000)	Supplies				(42,000)	Supplies expense
Adjustment 2		(833)	Accumulated depreciation				(833)	Depreciation expense
Adjustment 3				350	Misc. payables		(350)	Utilities expense
Adjustment 4				4,600	Salaries payable		(4,600)	Salary expense
Adjustment 5		(1,000)	Prepaid rent				(1,000)	Rent expense
Ending Balances	$217,000 +	$99,167		= $65,000		+ $126,000 +	$125,167	

— Income Statement   — Statement of Changes in Shareholders' Equity   — Balance Sheet   — Statement of Cash Flows

BB&B Decorating
Income Statement
For the Month Ended January 31, 2011

Revenue	$84,000
Expenses	48,833
Net income	$35,167

BB&B Decorating
Statement of Retained Earnings
For the Month Ended January 31, 2011

Retained earnings:	
Beginning balance	$ 90,000
+ Net income	35,167
Ending balance	$125,167

BB&B Decorating
Statement of Cash Flows
For the Month Ended January 31, 2011

Cash from Operating Activities

Cash collected from customers	$ 84,000
Cash paid to suppliers	(52,000)
Cash paid for rent	(6,000)
Cash paid to employees	(4,000)
Cash paid for interest	(50)
Net cash from operating activities	$ 21,950
Cash from Investing Activities	0
Cash from Financing Activities	
Cash paid on loan principal	(4,950)
Net increase in cash	17,000
Add beginning cash balance	200,000
Cash balance at January 31, 2011	$217,000

BB&B Decorating
Balance Sheet
At January 31, 2011

Assets	
Cash	$217,000
Supplies	5,000
Prepaid rent	5,000
Total current assets	227,000
Equipment (net of $10,833 accumulated depreciation)	89,167
Total assets	$316,167
Liabilities and Shareholders' Equity	
Liabilities	
Miscellaneous payables	15,350
Salaries payable	4,600
Total current liabilities	19,950
Long-term notes payable	45,050
Shareholders' Equity	
Common stock	126,000
Retained earnings	125,167
Total liabilities and shareholders' equity	$316,167

Key Terms for Chapter 3

Accrual (p. 99)
Accumulated depreciation (p. 110)
Book value (p. 110)
Carrying value (p. 110)
Contra-asset (p. 110)

Deferral (p. 99)
Depreciation expense (p. 110)
Interest payable (p. 102)
Prepaid rent (p. 107)
Profit margin on sales (p. 121)

Realized (p. 100)
Residual value (p. 110)
Supplies (p. 108)
Timing differences (p. 99)
Unearned revenue (p. 104)

Answers to YOUR TURN Questions

Chapter 3

Your Turn 3-1

The firm has earned six months' worth of interest. The amount is $1,000 \times 0.07 \times 6/12 = \$35$. The firm would accrue the interest revenue with an increase to revenue (retained earnings column of the accounting equation) and an increase to an asset, interest receivable.

Your Turn 3-2

Yes, salary expense needs to be accrued. The expense for June would routinely be recorded on July 15 when the payment is made. To get the June salary expense on the income statement for the year ended June 30, ABC Company needs to accrue the expense. A month of salary expense for June is recorded as salary expense and salaries payable in the amount of $56,000.

Your Turn 3-3

Out of 12 months of magazines, seven months have been delivered at December 31. That means 7/12 of the $300,000 collected in advance has actually been earned by December 31. When the cash was collected, the recognition of the revenue was deferred—put off or postponed—because it had not been earned. At December 31, the company recognizes $175,000 worth of revenue. That means it will put $175,000 worth of revenue on the income statement and reduce the liability *unearned revenue* on the balance sheet.

Your Turn 3-4

When Advantage Company made the rent payment on March 1, the company recorded a decrease in cash and an increase in the asset *prepaid rent*. Now, it is 10 months later, and 10 months' worth of rent has been used. That means it should be recorded as rent expense. The March 1 payment was $3,600 for one year, which means $300 per month. Now, 10 months at $300 per month ($3,000) must be deducted from prepaid rent and added to rent expense. Then, $3,000 of rent paid on March 1 will be shown on the income statement as rent expense.

Your Turn 3-5

1. Konny started with $500 worth of supplies and then purchased an additional $650 worth, which made a total of $1,150 worth of supplies available for the company to use during the month. At the end of the month, there were $250 worth of supplies remaining. That means that the company must have used $900 worth ($1,150 − $250). Of the supplies remaining, $250 will be on the balance sheet as a current asset, *supplies*.
2. Supplies expense of $900 will be shown on the income statement for April.

Your Turn 3-6

The depreciable amount is the cost minus the residual (salvage) value, $6,500 − $500 = $6,000. The estimated life is five years. Thus, the depreciation expense per year is $6,000/5 = $1,200 per year. Because the computer was purchased on July 1, 2011, only half a year of depreciation expense, $600, will be shown on the income statement for the year ended December 31, 2011. The book value = cost less accumulated depreciation (all the depreciation that has been recorded on the asset during its life) = $6,500 − $600 (for 2011) − $1,200 (for 2012) = $4,700 at December 31, 2012.

Your Turn 3-7

For 2008: $1,165 ÷ $7,998 = 14.57%
For 2007: $854 ÷ $7,385 = 11.56%
These ratios are considerably better than the same ratios for Hormel. Additionally, the profit margin on sales ratio is growing, which is a good thing.

Questions

1. How does accrual basis accounting differ from cash basis accounting?
2. What is deferred revenue?
3. What is accrued revenue?
4. What are deferred expenses?
5. What are accrued expenses?
6. What is interest and how is it computed?
7. Explain the difference between liabilities and expenses.
8. Name two common deferred expenses.
9. What does it mean to recognize revenue?
10. How does matching relate to accruals and deferrals?
11. What is depreciation?

12. Why is depreciation necessary?
13. What is the profit margin on sales ratio and what does it indicate?
14. What risks are associated with the financial accounting records?

Multiple-Choice Questions

1. Which of the following accounts is a liability?
   a. Depreciation expense
   b. Dividends
   c. Accumulated depreciation
   d. Unearned advertising fees
2. Which of the following is an example of an accrual?
   a. Revenue collected in advance
   b. Supplies purchased for cash but not yet used
   c. Interest expense incurred but not yet paid
   d. Payment for insurance policy to be used in the next two years
3. Which of the following is an example of a deferral?
   a. Cash has not changed hands and services have not been rendered.
   b. Services have been rendered but nothing has been recorded.
   c. A business never has enough cash.
   d. Resources have been purchased for cash but not yet used.
4. The carrying (book) value of an asset is
   a. an account that increases an asset account on the balance sheet.
   b. the original cost of an asset minus the accumulated depreciation.
   c. the original cost of an asset.
   d. equivalent to accumulated depreciation.
5. Logan Company received $300 from a customer as payment for a credit sale made in a previous accounting period. Logan will record this as
   a. $300 in sales revenue.
   b. a $300 reduction in accounts payable.
   c. a $300 reduction in accounts receivable.
   d. a $300 increase in accounts receivable.
6. When a company pays cash in June to a vendor for goods purchased in May, the transaction will
   a. increase cash and decrease inventory.
   b. decrease accounts payable and decrease cash.
   c. decrease accounts receivable and decrease cash.
   d. increase accounts payable and increase inventory.
7. Z Company's accountant forgot to make an adjustment at the end of the year to record depreciation expense on the equipment. What effect did this omission have on the company's financial statements?
   a. Understated assets and liabilities
   b. Overstated assets and shareholders' equity
   c. Understated liabilities and overstated shareholders' equity
   d. Overstated assets and understated shareholders' equity
8. Phillip's Camera Store had a retained earnings balance of $1,000 on January 1, 2010. For the year 2010, sales were $10,500 and expenses were $6,500. The company declared and distributed cash dividends of $2,500 on December 31, 2010. What was the amount of retained earnings on December 31, 2010?
   a. $4,000
   b. $1,500
   c. $2,500
   d. $2,000
9. When prepaid insurance has been used, the following adjustment will be necessary:
   a. Increase insurance expense, decrease cash.
   b. Increase prepaid insurance, decrease insurance expense.
   c. Increase insurance expense, increase prepaid insurance.
   d. Increase insurance expense, decrease prepaid insurance.

10. The profit margin on sales ratio indicates how well the firm is
    a. marketing its products for sale.
    b. controlling its accounting records.
    c. managing its accruals and deferrals.
    d. controlling its costs.

Short Exercises
Set A

SE3-1A. *Analyze the effect of transactions on net income. (LO 1).* The following transactions occurred during a recent accounting period. For each, tell whether it (1) increases net income, (2) decreases net income, or (3) does not affect net income.
    a. Issued stock for cash
    b. Borrowed money from bank
    c. Provided services to customers on credit
    d. Paid rent in advance
    e. Used some supplies previously purchased
    f. Paid salaries to employees for work done this year

SE3-2A. *Calculate net income and retained earnings. (LO 1).* Capboy Company earned $5,000 of revenues and incurred $2,950 worth of expenses during the period. Capboy also declared and paid dividends of $500 to its shareholders. What was net income for the period? Assuming this is the first year of operations for Capboy, what is the ending balance in retained earnings for the period?

SE3-3A. *Account for interest expense. (LO 1, 2).* UMC Company purchased equipment on July 1, 2010, and gave a three-month, 9% note with a face value of $10,000. How much interest expense will be recognized on the income statement for the year ended December 31, 2010? What effect does the repayment of the note plus interest have on the statement of cash flows for 2010?

SE3-4A. *Account for supplies expense. (LO 1, 3).* MBI Corporation started the month with $800 worth of supplies on hand. During the month, the company purchased an additional $300 worth of supplies. At the end of the month, $150 worth of supplies was left on hand. What amount would MBI Corporation show as supplies expense on its income statement for the month? Is the needed adjustment related to an accrual or a deferral?

SE3-5A. *Account for insurance expense. (LO 1, 3).* Catrina Company was started on January 1, 2009. During its first week of business, the company paid $3,600 for 24 months' worth of fire insurance with an effective date of January 1, 2009. When Catrina Company prepares its income statement for the year ended December 31, 2009, how much prepaid insurance will be shown on the balance sheet at December 31, 2009, and how much insurance expense will be shown on the income statement? Is the needed adjustment at year end related to an accrual or a deferral?

SE3-6A. *Account for depreciation expense. (LO 1, 3).* Suppose a company purchases a piece of equipment for $30,000 at the beginning of the year. The equipment is estimated to have a useful life of three years and no residual value. Using the depreciation method you learned about in this chapter, what is the depreciation expense for the first year of the asset's life? What is the book value of the equipment at the end of the first year? What is the book value of the equipment at the end of the second year?

SE3-7A. *Account for unearned revenue. (LO 1, 3).* Able Company received $4,800 from a customer on April 1 for services to be provided in the coming year in an equal amount for each of the 12 months beginning April. In the Able information system, these cash receipts are recorded as unearned revenue. What adjustment will Able need to make when preparing the December 31 financial statements? What is the impact on the financial statements if the necessary adjustment is not made? Is this adjustment related to an accrual or a deferral?

SE3-8A. *Identify accounts. (LO 1, 2, 3).* From the following list of accounts (1) identify the assets or liabilities that commonly require an adjustment at the end of the accounting period, and (2) indicate whether the adjustment relates to a deferral or an accrual.

> Cash
> Prepaid insurance
> Inventory
> Supplies
> Accounts payable

SE3-9A. *Calculate net income. (LO 1, 4).* Suppose a company had the following accounts and balances at year end after all adjustments had been made:

Service revenue	$7,400
Interest revenue	$2,200
Unearned revenue	$3,250
Operating expenses	$1,500
Prepaid rent	$1,030

Prepare the income statement for the year.

SE3-10A. *Account for unearned revenue. (LO 1, 3).* On January 1, 2009, the law firm of Coats and Alday was formed with a contribution from each of the partners of $25,000. On February 1, 2009, the company received $24,000 from clients in advance for services to be performed monthly during the next 12 months beginning in February and recorded the full amount as unearned revenue. During the year, the firm incurred and paid expenses of $7,000. Is the adjustment to recognize the proper amount of service revenue related to an accrual or a deferral? Assuming that these were the only transactions completed in 2009, prepare the firm's income statement, statement of cash flows, statement of retained earnings for the year ended December 31, 2009, and balance sheet at December 31, 2009.

SE3-11A. *Calculate profit margin on sales ratio. (LO 5).* Suppose a firm had sales of $200,000 and net income of $7,000 for the year. What is the profit margin on sales ratio?

Set B

SE3-12B. *Analyze the effect of transactions on net income. (LO 1).* The following transactions occurred during a recent accounting period. For each, tell whether it (1) increases net income, (2) decreases net income, or (3) does not affect net income.
  a. Paid dividends
  b. Purchased inventory
  c. Made sales to customers on account
  d. Paid in advance for insurance policy
  e. Used some of the insurance purchased in item (d).
  f. Collected some cash from customers in item (c).

SE3-13B. *Calculate net income and retained earnings. (LO 1).* Petgirl Company earned $25,000 of revenues and incurred $12,950 worth of expenses during the period. Petgirl also declared and paid dividends of $1,500 to its shareholders. What was net income for the period? Assuming this is the first year of operations for Petgirl, what is the balance in retained earnings at the end of the period?

SE3-14B. *Account for interest expense. (LO 1, 2).* United Company purchased equipment on June 1, 2011, and gave a 10-month, 5% note with a face value of $20,000 with interest and principal payable at maturity. How much interest expense will be recognized on the income statement for the year ended December 31, 2011? What effect does the adjustment for interest have on the statement of cash flows for 2011? Is the adjustment to record the interest expense an accrual or a deferral?

SE3-15B. *Account for supplies expense. (LO 1, 3).* Peter's Pizza started the month with $500 worth of supplies. During the month, Peter's Pizza purchased an additional $300 worth of supplies. At the end of the month, $175 worth of supplies remained unused. Give the amount that would appear on the income statement for the month for supplies expense and the amount that would appear on the balance sheet at the end of the month as supplies on hand. Is the needed adjustment related to an accrual or a deferral?

SE3-16B. *Account for insurance expense. (LO 1, 3).* The correct amount of prepaid insurance shown on a company's December 31, 2011, balance sheet was $600. On July 1, 2012, the company paid an additional insurance premium of $1,440, recorded as more prepaid insurance. On the December 31, 2012, balance sheet, the amount of prepaid insurance was correctly shown as $720. What amount of insurance expense would appear on the company's income statement for the year ended December 31, 2012? Is the adjustment to record the insurance expense related to an accrual or a deferral?

SE3-17B. *Account for depreciation expense. (LO 1, 3).* Suppose a company purchases a piece of equipment for $80,000 at the beginning of the year. The equipment is estimated to have a useful life of five years and no residual value. Using the depreciation method you learned about in this chapter, what is the depreciation expense for the first year of the asset's life? What is the book value of the equipment at the end of the first year? What is the book value of the equipment at the end of the second year?

SE3-18B. *Account for unearned revenue. (LO 1, 3).* Kane Company received $7,200 from a customer on May 1 for services to be provided in the coming year in an equal amount for each of the 12 months beginning in May. In the Kane information system, these cash receipts are recorded as unearned revenue. What adjustment will Kane need to make when preparing the December 31 financial statements? What is the impact on the financial statements if the necessary adjustment is not made? Is this adjustment related to an accrual or a deferral?

SE3-19B. *Identify accounts. (LO 1, 2, 3).* From the following list of accounts (1) identify the assets or liabilities that commonly require an adjustment at the end of the accounting period, and (2) indicate whether the adjustment relates to a deferral or an accrual.

    Cash
    Accounts receivable
    Building
    Accumulated depreciation—building
    Unearned revenue
    Interest payable
    Salaries payable
    Common stock
    Retained earnings

SE3-20B. *Calculate net income. (LO 1, 4).* Suppose a company had the following accounts and balances at year end:

Sales revenue	$5,400
Interest revenue	$1,200
Rent expense	$1,240
Other operating expenses	$3,050
Dividends paid	$1,000

Calculate net income by preparing the income statement for the year.

SE3-21B. *Account for unearned revenue. (LO 1, 3).* On January 1, 2011, the accounting firm of Klindt & Smith was formed with a contribution from each of the partners of $50,000. On March 1, 2011, the company received $36,000 from clients in advance for services to be performed monthly during the next 12 months, beginning in March, and recorded the full amount as unearned revenue. During the year, the firm incurred and paid expenses of $17,500. Is the adjustment to recognize the proper amount of service revenue related to an accrual or a deferral? Assuming that these were the only transactions completed in 2011, prepare the firm's income statement, statement of cash flows, statement of retained earnings for the year ended December 31, 2011, and balance sheet at December 31, 2011.

SE3-22B. *Calculate profit margin on sales ratio. (LO 5).* Suppose a firm had sales of $35,750 and earned a net income of $1,430. What was the profit margin on sales ratio?

Exercises
Set A

E3-23A. *Account for salaries expense. (LO 1, 2).* Matrix Accounting pays all salaried employees biweekly. Overtime pay, however, is paid in the next biweekly period. Matrix accrues salary expense only at its December 31 year end. Information about salaries earned in December 2009 is as follows:

- Last payroll was paid on December 28, 2009, for the two-week period ended December 28, 2009.
- Overtime pay earned in the two-week period ended December 28, 2009, was $7,500.
- Remaining workdays in 2009 were December 29, 30, 31; no overtime was worked on these days.
- The regular biweekly salaries total $125,000.

Using a five-day workweek, what will Matrix's balance sheet show as salaries payable on December 31, 2009?

E3-24A. *Account for unearned revenue. (LO 1, 3).* The TJ Company collects all service revenue in advance. The company showed a $12,500 liability on its December 31, 2011, balance sheet for unearned service revenue. During 2012, customers paid $50,000 for future services, and the income statement for the year ended December 31, 2012, reported service revenue of $52,700. What amount for the liability unearned service revenue will appear on the balance sheet at December 31, 2012?

E3-25A. *Account for interest expense. (LO 1, 2).* Sojourn Company purchased equipment on November 1, 2010, and gave a three-month, 9% note with a face value of $20,000. On maturity, January 31, 2011, the note plus interest will be paid to the bank. Fill in the blanks in the following chart:

	Interest expense (for the month ended)	Cash paid for interest (during the month ended)
November 30, 2010	_____	_____
December 31, 2010	_____	_____
January 31, 2011	_____	_____

E3-26A. *Account for insurance expense. (LO 1, 3).* Vertigo Company paid $10,000 on July 1, 2009, for a two-year insurance policy. It was recorded as prepaid insurance. Use the accounting equation to show the adjustment Vertigo will make to properly report expenses when preparing the December 31, 2009, financial statements. (Assume no previous adjustments to prepaid insurance have been made.)

E3-27A. *Account for rent expense. (LO 1, 3).* Jayne rented office space for her new business on March 1, 2010. To receive a discount, she paid $3,600 for 12 months' rent in advance, beginning with March. How will this advance payment appear on the financial statements prepared at year end, December 31? Assume no additional rent was paid in 2011. Use the following chart for your answers:

	Rent expense for the year ended December 31	Prepaid rent at December 31
2010	_____	_____
2011	_____	_____

E3-28A. *Account for unearned revenue. (LO 1, 3).* In July of 2009, Wizard's Corporation, a newly developed internet game company, received $1,050,000 for 2,000 three-year subscriptions to a new online game priced at $175 per year. The subscriptions do not start until November of 2009. Fill in the following chart for each of the given years to show the amount of revenue to be recognized on the income statement and the related liability reported on the year-end balance sheet. Wizard's Corp fiscal year end is December 31.

	Revenue recognized during	Unearned revenue at December 31
2009	_____	_____
2010	_____	_____
2011	_____	_____
2012	_____	_____

E3-29A. *Account for insurance expense. (LO 1, 3).* Yodel & Company paid $3,600 on June 1, 2010, for a two-year insurance policy beginning on that date. The company recorded the entire amount as prepaid insurance. By using the following chart, calculate how much expense and prepaid insurance will be reported on the year-end financial statements. The company's fiscal year end is December 31.

	Insurance expense	Prepaid insurance at December 31
2010	_____	_____
2011	_____	_____
2012	_____	_____

E3-30A. *Account for depreciation expense. (LO 1, 3).* Maximus Dog Company purchased a new supply van on January 1, 2011, for $35,000. The van is estimated to last for five years and will then be sold, at which time it should be worth approximately $5,000. The company uses straight-line depreciation and has a fiscal year end of December 31.

1. How much depreciation expense will be shown on the income statement for the year ended December 31, 2011?
2. What is the book value (also called carrying value) of the van on the balance sheet for each of the five years beginning with December 31, 2011?

E3-31A. *Analyze timing of revenue recognition. (LO 1, 2, 3).* Show each of the following transactions in the accounting equation. Then, tell whether or not the original transaction as given is one that results in the recognition of revenue or expenses.
   a. Dell Inc. paid its computer service technicians $80,000 in salaries for the month ended January 31.
   b. Shell Oil used $5,000 worth of electricity in its headquarters building during March. Shell received the bill, but will not pay it until sometime in April.
   c. In 2011, Chico's, FAS had $22 million in catalogue sales. Assume all sales were recorded as credit sales.
   d. Home Depot collected $59 million in interest and investment income during 2010.

E3-32A. *Account for rent expense. (LO 1, 3).* Hobbs Company started the year with $6,000 of prepaid rent. During the year, Hobbs paid additional rent in advance amounting to $12,000. The rent expense for the year was $15,000. What was the balance in prepaid rent on the year-end balance sheet?

E3-33A. *Account for insurance expense. (LO 1, 3).* Center Corporation began the year with $9,250 prepaid insurance. During the year, Center prepaid additional insurance premiums amounting to $7,500. The company's insurance expense for the year was $6,000. What was the balance in prepaid insurance at year end?

E3-34A. *Account for rent expense and prepare financial statements. (LO 4).* On March 1, 2010, Quality Consulting, Inc., was formed when the owners contributed $35,000 cash to the business in exchange for common stock. On April 1, 2010, the company paid $24,000 cash to rent office space for the coming year. The consulting services generated $62,000 of cash revenue during 2010. Prepare an income statement, statement of changes in shareholders' equity, and statement of cash flows for the 10 months ended December 31, 2010, and a balance sheet at December 31, 2010.

E3-35A. *Account for depreciation expense and prepare financial statements. (LO 3, 4).* Southeast Pest Control, Inc., was started when its owners invested $20,000 in the business in exchange for common stock on January 1, 2011. The cash received by the company was immediately used to purchase a $15,000 heavy-duty chemical truck, which had no residual value and an expected useful life of five years. The company earned $13,000 of cash revenue during 2011 and had cash expenses of $4,500. Prepare an income statement, statement of changes in shareholders' equity, and statement of cash flows for the year ended December 31, 2011, and a balance sheet at December 31, 2011.

E3-36A. *Classify accounts. (LO 1, 4).* Tell whether each of the following items would appear on the income statement, statement of changes in shareholders' equity, balance sheet, or statement of cash flows. Some items may appear on more than one statement.

Interest receivable	Accounts payable
Salary expense	Common stock
Notes receivable	Dividends
Unearned revenue	Total assets
Net cash flow from investing activities	Net income
Insurance expense	Consulting revenue
Retained earnings	Depreciation expense
Prepaid insurance	Supplies expense
Cash	Salaries payable
Accumulated depreciation	Supplies
Prepaid rent	Net cash flow from financing activities
Accounts receivable	Land
Total shareholders' equity	Net cash flow from operating activities

E3-37A. *Analyze business transactions. (LO 1, 2, 3).* Analyze the following accounting equation worksheet for Starwood Yacht Repair Corporation and explain the transaction or event that resulted in each entry.

Transaction	Cash	All other assets	(Account)	All liabilities	(Account)	Common stock		(Account)
				= Liabilities		**Contributed Capital**	**+**	**Retained Earnings**
1.	$150,000					$150,000		
2.	(125,000)	125,000	Property, plant, and equipment					
3.	100,000			100,000	Notes payable			
4.	(500)	500	Supplies					
5.	(650)	650	Prepaid insurance					
6.	15,000							15,000 Service revenue
7.		(375)	Supplies					(375) Supplies expense
8.		(325)	Prepaid insurance					(325) Insurance expense
9.				500	Salaries payable			(500) Salary expense
10.		(1,000)	Accumulated depreciation					(1,000) Depreciation expense
11.				100	Interest payable			(100) Interest expense

— Income Statement   — Statement of Changes in Shareholders' Equity   — Balance Sheet   — Statement of Cash Flows

E3-38A. *Prepare financial statements. (LO 1, 2, 3, 4).* Refer to the worksheet in E3-37A. Assume all beginning balances are zero and the information pertains to a fiscal year ended December 31. Prepare the four financial statements from the data given in the worksheet.

E3-39A. *Compute profit margin on sales ratio. (LO 5).* Use the following information to calculate the profit margin on sales ratio for the two years provided. Is the change from 2010 to 2011 positive or negative? Why?

	For the year ended December 31, 2011	For the year ended December 31, 2010
Net sales	$6,626.5	$5,567.1
Net income	$ 377.2	$ 201.4

Set B

E3-40B. *Account for salaries expense. (LO 1, 2).* Alex's Editing Company pays all salaried employees monthly on the first Monday following the end of the month. Overtime, however, is recorded as vacation time for all employees. Alex allows employees to exchange all vacation time not used during the year for pay on May 31 and actually pays it on June 15. The company accrues salary expense only at its May 31 year end. Information about salaries earned in May 2009 is as follows:

- Last payroll was paid on May 1, 2009, for the month ended April 30, 2009.
- Vacation pay exchanged at year end totaled $250,000.
- The regular yearly salaries total $3,300,000.

Using a 12-month fiscal work year, what will Alex's Editing Company's balance sheet show as salaries payable on May 31, 2009?

E3-41B. *Account for unearned revenue. (LO 1, 3).* The Einstein Cable Company collects all service revenue in advance.Einstein showed a $16,825 liability on its June 30, 2010, balance sheet for unearned service revenue. During the following fiscal year, customers paid $85,000 for future services, and the income statement for the year ended June 30, 2011, reported service revenue of $75,850. What amount for the liability unearned service revenue will appear on the balance sheet at June 30, 2011?

E3-42B. *Account for interest expense. (LO 1, 2).* The Muzby Pet Grooming Company purchased a computer on December 31, 2012, and gave a four-month, 7% note with a face value of $6,000. On maturity, April 30, 2013, the note plus interest will be paid to the bank. Fill in the blanks in the following chart:

	Interest expense (for the month ended)	Cash paid for interest (during the month ended)
January 31, 2013	_____	_____
February 29, 2013	_____	_____
March 31, 2013	_____	_____
April 30, 2013	_____	_____

E3-43B. *Account for insurance expense. (LO 1, 3).* TJ's Tavern paid $10,800 on February 1, 2010, for a three-year insurance policy. In the company's information system, this was recorded as prepaid insurance. Use the accounting equation to show the adjustment TJ's will need to make to properly report expenses when preparing the July 31, 2010, financial statements. (Assume no adjustments have been made to prepaid insurance prior to July 31.)

E3-44B. *Account for rent expense. (LO 1, 3).* Utopia Dance Clubs, Inc., rented an old warehouse for its newest club on October 1, 2010. To receive a discount, Utopia paid $11,700 for 18 months of rent in advance. How will this advance payment appear on the financial statements prepared at year end, December 31? Assume no additional rent is paid in 2011 and 2012. Use the following chart for your answers:

	Rent expense (for the year ended)	Prepaid rent at December 31
2010	_____	_____
2011	_____	_____
2012	_____	_____

E3-45B. *Account for unearned revenue. (LO 1, 3).* In April 2010 Crummies, Inc., a newly organized style magazine, received $27,000 for 750 two-year (24-month) subscriptions to the new publication. The first issue will be delivered in August 2010. Fill in the following chart for each of the given years to show the amount of revenue to be recognized on the income statement and the related liability reported on the balance sheet. Crummies' fiscal year end is May 31.

	Revenue recognized (during the year ended May 31)	Unearned revenue at May 31
2010	_____	_____
2011	_____	_____
2012	_____	_____

E3-46B. *Account for insurance expense. (LO 1, 3).* All Natural Medicine Corporation paid $2,178 on August 1, 2009, for an 18-month insurance policy beginning on that date. The company recorded the entire amount as prepaid insurance. By using the following chart, calculate how much expense and prepaid insurance will be reported on the year-end financial statements. The company's year end is December 31.

	Insurance expense (for the year ended December 31)	Prepaid insurance at December 31
2009	_____	_____
2010	_____	_____
2011	_____	_____

E3-47B. *Account for depreciation expense. (LO 1, 3).* Trin's Freight purchased a new shipping truck on August 1, 2008, for $27,000. The truck is estimated to last for six years and will then be sold, at which time it should be worth nothing. The company uses straight-line depreciation and has a fiscal year end of July 31.

1. How much depreciation expense will be shown on the income statement for the year ended July 31, 2010?
2. What is the book value (also called carrying value) of the truck on the balance sheet for each of the six years beginning with July 31, 2008?

E3-48B. *Analyze timing of revenue recognition. (LO 1, 2, 3).* For each of the following transactions, tell whether or not the original transaction as shown is one that results in the recognition of revenue or expenses:

   a. On April 15, Mike's Pressure Cleaning Services, Inc., paid its employees $3,000 in salaries for services provided.
   b. Mister Hsieh Fencing Company used $1,000 worth of radio advertising during April. Mister Hsieh received the bill but will not pay it until sometime in May.

c. During the year, Tootie's Pet Training School, Inc., earned $125,000 in service revenues. Assume all services were provided on account.
d. Susan's Investment Company collected $130,000 in interest and investment income earned during the year.

E3-49B. *Account for rent expense. (LO 1, 3).* Roberto's Paper Supply started the year with $5,000 of prepaid rent. During the year, Roberto's paid $25,000 of additional rent in advance. The rent expense shown on the income statement for the year was $20,000. What was the balance in prepaid rent on the year-end balance sheet?

E3-50B. *Account for insurance expense. (LO 1, 3).* Eric's Coffee Shop began the year with $12,000 prepaid insurance. During the year, Eric's prepaid $75,000 in additional insurance premiums. According to the income statement, the company's insurance expense for the year was $62,000. What is the balance in prepaid insurance at year end?

E3-51B. *Account for rent expense and insurance expense and prepare financial statements. (LO 3, 4).* On February 1, 2010, Breeder's Choice Pet Trainers, Inc., was formed when the owners invested $25,626 cash in the business in exchange for common stock. On March 1, 2010, the company paid $22,212 cash to rent office space for the next 18 months and paid $3,414 cash for six months of prepaid insurance. The training services generated $115,725 of cash revenue during the remainder of the fiscal year. The company has chosen June 30 as the end of its fiscal year. Prepare an income statement, statement of changes in shareholders' equity, and statement of cash flows for the five months ended June 30, 2010, and a balance sheet at June 30, 2010.

E3-52B. *Account for depreciation expense and prepare financial statements. (LO 3, 4).* Northeast Termite Specialists, Inc., was started when its owners invested $32,685 in the business in exchange for common stock on July 1, 2010. Part of the cash received to start the company was immediately used to purchase a $19,875 high-pressure chemical sprayer, which had a $2,875 residual value and an expected useful life of 10 years. The company earned $68,315 of cash revenue during the year and had cash operating expenses of $27,205. Prepare an income statement, statement of changes in shareholders' equity, and statement of cash flows for the year ended June 30, 2011, and a balance sheet at June 30, 2011.

E3-53B. *Identify accounts. (LO 1, 4).* From the following list of accounts (1) identify the assets or liabilities that may require an adjustment at the end of the accounting period, and (2) indicate whether it relates to a deferral or an accrual.

Cash	Common stock
Accounts receivable	Retained earnings
Prepaid insurance	Sales revenue
Prepaid rent	Interest revenue
Supplies	Equipment
Depreciation expense	Accumulated depreciation—equipment
Insurance expense	Unearned revenue
Supplies expense	Interest payable
Utilities expense	Salaries payable
Rent expense	Accounts payable
Interest receivable	Other operating expense

E3-54B. *Analyze business transactions from the accounting equation. (LO 1, 2, 3).* Analyze the transactions for Information Resource Services, Inc., that appear in the worksheet on the following page and explain the transaction or event that resulted in each entry.

		Assets		= Liabilities		+	Shareholders' Equity		
							Contributed Capital	Retained Earnings	
Transaction	Cash	All other assets	(Account)	All liabilities	(Account)		Common stock		(Account)
1.	$115,000						$115,000		
2.	(112,500)	112,500	Property, plant, and equipment						
3.	85,000			85,000	Notes payable				
4.	(1,000)	1,000	Supplies						
5.	(825)	825	Prepaid rent						
6.		13,150	Accounts receivable					13,150	Service revenue
7.		(615)	Supplies					(615)	Supplies expense
8.		(275)	Prepaid rent					(275)	Rent expense
9.				795	Salaries payable			(795)	Salary expense
10.		(1,500)	Accumulated depreciation					(1,500)	Depreciation expense
11.				50	Interest payable			(50)	Interest expense

━ Income Statement   ━ Statement of Changes in Shareholders' Equity   ━ Balance Sheet   ━ Statement of Cash Flows

E3-55B. *Prepare financial statements. (LO 1, 2, 3, 4).* Refer to the worksheet in E3-54B. Assume all beginning balances are zero. Prepare the four financial statements using the data provided in the worksheet.

E3-56B. *Compute profit margin on sales ratio. (LO 5).* Use the following information to calculate the profit margin on sales ratio for the two years given. Is the trend positive or negative?

	For the year ended March 31, 2010	For the year ended March 31, 2009
Net sales	$45,015	$40,023
Net income	$ 1,003	$ 1,407

MyAccountingLab

All of the A problems can be found within MyAccountingLab, an online homework and practice environment.

Problems Set A

P3-57A. *Record adjustments and prepare income statement. (LO 1, 2, 3, 4).* Selected amounts (at December 31, 2010) from Solar Power, Inc.'s information system appear as follows:

Cash paid to employees for salaries and wages	$ 600,000
Cash collected from customers for service rendered	2,500,000
Long-term notes payable	225,000
Cash	375,000

Common stock	100,000
Equipment	750,000
Prepaid insurance	45,000
Inventory	175,000
Prepaid rent	75,000
Retained earnings	150,000
Salaries and wages expense	625,000
Service revenues	2,750,000

Requirements

1. There are five adjustments that need to be made before the financial statements can be prepared at year end. For each, show the adjustment in the accounting equation.
   a. The equipment (purchased on January 1, 2010) has a useful life of 10 years with no salvage value. (An equal amount of depreciation is taken each year.)
   b. Interest accrued on the notes payable is $2,500 as of December 31, 2010.
   c. Unexpired insurance at December 31, 2010, is $11,000.
   d. The rent payment of $75,000 covered the six months from December 1, 2010, through May 31, 2011.
   e. Employees had earned salaries and wages of $25,000 that were unpaid at December 31, 2010.
2. Prepare an income statement for the year ended December 31, 2010, for Solar Power, Inc.

P3-58A. *Record adjustments and calculate net income. (LO 1, 2, 3, 4).* The records of Poorman's, Inc., revealed the following recorded amounts at December 31, 2009, *before adjustments*:

Prepaid insurance	$ 2,700
Cleaning supplies	3,200
Unearned service fees	2,625
Notes payable	3,000
Service fees	125,000
Wages expense	90,000
Truck rent expense	6,500
Truck fuel expense	1,000
Insurance expense	0
Supplies expense	0
Interest expense	0
Interest payable	0
Wages payable	0
Prepaid rent—truck	0

Before Poorman's prepares the financial statements for the business at December 31, 2009, adjustments must be made for the following items:
   a. The prepaid insurance represents an 18-month policy purchased early in January so the policy has been in effect for the entire year.
   b. A physical count on December 31 revealed $500 of cleaning supplies on hand.
   c. On December 1, a customer paid for three months of service in advance (unearned service fees). One month's revenue has now been earned.
   d. The truck rent is $500 per month in advance. January 2010 rent was paid in late December 2009 and was included in truck rent expense for 2009.
   e. The bank loan was taken out October 1. The interest rate is 12% (1% per month) for 1 year. No interest expense has been accrued.
   f. On Wednesday, December 31, 2009, the company owed its employees for working three days. The normal workweek is five days with wages of $1,500 paid at the end of the week. No expense has been recorded for the last three days of 2009.

Requirements

1. For each item, show the adjustment in the accounting equation.
2. Prepare an income statement for the year ended December 31, 2009, for Poorman's, Inc.

P3-59A. *Account for depreciable assets. (LO 3).* Charlotte Motorcycle Repair Corporation purchased a machine on January 1, 2010, for $8,000 cash. The firm expects to use the machine for four years and thinks it will be worthless at the end of the four-year period. The company will depreciate the machine in equal annual amounts.

Requirements

1. Show the purchase of the machine and the first year's depreciation in the accounting equation.
2. Show how the machine will be presented in the asset section of the balance sheet at December 31, 2010, and December 31, 2011, after appropriate adjustments.
3. What amount of depreciation expense will be shown on the income statement for the year ended December 31, 2010? What amount will be shown for the year ended December 31, 2011?
4. Calculate the total depreciation expense for all four years of the asset's life. What do you notice about the book value of the asset at the end of its useful life?

P3-60A. *Record adjustments. (LO 1, 2, 3).* Following is a partial list of financial statement items from the records of Marshall's Company at December 31, 2010, before any adjustments have been made:

Prepaid insurance	$12,750
Prepaid rent	18,000
Interest receivable	0
Salaries payable	0
Unearned revenue	30,000
Interest revenue	10,000

Additional information includes the following:

- The insurance policy indicates that on December 31, 2010, only five months remain on the 24-month policy that originally cost $18,000 (purchased on June 1, 2009).
- Marshall's has a note receivable with $2,500 of interest due from a customer on January 1, 2011. This amount has not been recorded.
- The accounting records show that one-third of the revenue paid in advance by a customer on July 1, 2010, has now been earned.
- The company paid $18,000 for rent for nine months starting on August 1, 2010, recording the total amount as prepaid rent.
- At year end, Marshall's owed $7,000 worth of salaries to employees for work done in December 2010. The next payday is January 5, 2011. The salary expense has not been recorded.

Requirements

1. Use the accounting equation to show the adjustments that must be made prior to the preparation of the financial statements for the year ended December 31, 2010.
2. For the accounts shown, calculate the account balances that would be shown on Marshall's financial statements for the year ended December 31, 2010; balance sheet at December 31, 2010.

P3-61A. *Record adjustments. (LO 1, 2, 3).* Following is a list of financial statement items from Sugar & Spice Cookie Company as of December 31, 2010:

Prepaid insurance	$ 6,000
Prepaid rent	10,000
Wages expense	25,000
Unearned subscription revenue	70,000
Interest expense	38,000

Additional information is as follows:

- The company paid a $7,200 premium on a three-year business insurance policy on July 1, 2009. (Six months' worth was expensed on the income statement for the year ended December 31, 2009.) No expense has been recorded for the year ended December 31, 2010.

- Sugar & Spice borrowed $200,000 on January 2, 2010, and must pay 11% interest on January 2, 2011, for the entire year of 2010. The interest expense on this loan has not been recorded for 2010.
- The books show that $60,000 of the unearned subscription revenue has now been earned.
- The company paid 10 months of rent in advance on November 1, 2010. No rent expense has been booked for 2010.
- The company will pay wages of $2,000 for December 31, 2010, to employees on January 3, 2011. This amount is not included in the balance shown for wages expense.

Requirements

1. Use the accounting equation to show the adjustments that must be made prior to the preparation of the financial statements for the year ended December 31, 2010.
2. Calculate the account balances that would appear on the financial statements for the year ended December 31, 2010; balance sheet at December 31, 2010.

P3-62A. *Record adjustments. (LO 1, 2, 3).* The Gladiator Sports Company has the following account balances at the end of the year before any adjustments have been made:

Prepaid insurance	$9,000
Unearned revenue	5,300
Wages expense	7,590
Taxes payable	4,000
Interest revenue	2,000

The company also has the following information available at the end of the year:

- Of the prepaid insurance shown, $1,000 has now expired.
- Of the unearned revenue shown, $3,000 has been earned.
- The company must accrue an additional $2,250 of wages expense.
- The company has earned an additional $750 of interest revenue, not yet recorded or received.

Requirements

1. Use the accounting equation to show the adjustments needed at year end.
2. Calculate the balances in each account after the adjustments.
3. Indicate whether each adjustment is related to an accrual or a deferral.

P3-63A. *Record adjustments and prepare financial statements. (LO 1, 2, 3, 4).* The accounting records for Sony Snowboard Company, a snowboard repair company, contained the following balances as of December 31, 2008:

Sony Snowboard Company
Balance Sheet
At December 31, 2008

Assets		Liabilities and Shareholders' equity	
Cash	$40,000	Accounts payable	$17,000
Accounts receivable	16,500	Common stock	45,000
Land	20,000	Retained earnings	14,500
Totals	$76,500		$76,500

The following accounting events apply to Sony's 2009 fiscal year:

- a. January 1   The company received an additional $20,000 cash from the owners in exchange for common stock.
- b. January 1   Sony purchased a computer that cost $15,000 for cash. The computer had no salvage value and a three-year useful life.

c.	March	1	The company borrowed $10,000 by issuing a one-year note at 12%.
d.	May	1	The company paid $2,400 cash in advance for a one-year lease for office space.
e.	June	1	The company declared and paid dividends to the owners of $4,000 cash.
f.	July	1	The company purchased land that cost $17,000 cash.
g.	August	1	Cash payments on accounts payable amounted to $6,000.
h.	August	1	Sony received $9,600 cash in advance for 12 months of service to be performed monthly for the next year, beginning on receipt of payment.
i.	September	1	Sony sold a parcel of land for $13,000 cash, the amount the company originally paid for it.
j.	October	1	Sony purchased $795 of supplies on account.
k.	November	1	Sony purchased short-term investments for $18,000 cash. The investments pay a fixed rate of 6%.
l.	December	31	The company earned service revenue on account during the year that amounted to $40,000.
m.	December	31	Cash collections from accounts receivable amounted to $44,000.
n.	December	31	The company incurred other operating expenses on account during the year of $5,450.

- Salaries that had been earned by the sales staff but had not yet been paid amounted to $2,300.
- Supplies worth $180 were on hand at the end of the period.

Requirements

1. Prepare an accounting equation worksheet and record the account balances as of December 31, 2008 (beginning balances).
2. Using the worksheet, record the transactions that occurred during 2009 and the necessary adjustments needed at year end. (Based on the given transaction data, there are five additional adjustments [for a total of seven] that need to be made before the financial statements can be prepared.)
3. Prepare the income statement, statement of changes in shareholders' equity, and statement of cash flows for the year ended December 31, 2009, and the balance sheet at December 31, 2009.

P3-64A. *Record adjustments and prepare financial statements. (LO 1, 2, 3, 4).* Transactions for Pops Company for 2011 were as follows:
- a. The owners started the business as a corporation by contributing $30,000 cash in exchange for common stock.
- b. The company purchased office equipment for $8,000 cash and land for $15,000 cash.
- c. The company earned a total of $22,000 of revenue of which $16,000 was collected in cash.
- d. The company purchased $890 worth of supplies for cash.
- e. The company paid $6,000 in cash for other operating expenses.
- f. At the end of the year, the company owed employees $2,480 for work that the employees had done in 2011. The next payday, however, is not until January 4, 2012.
- g. Only $175 worth of supplies was left at the end of the year.

The office equipment was purchased on January 1 and is expected to last for eight years (straight-line depreciation, no salvage value).

Requirements

1. Use an accounting equation worksheet to record the transactions that occurred during 2011.
2. Record any needed adjustments at year end.
3. Prepare the income statement, statement of changes in shareholders' equity, and the statement of cash flows for the year ended December 31, 2011, and the balance sheet at December 31, 2011.

P3-65A. *Record adjustments and prepare financial statements. (LO 1, 2, 3, 4).* On May 1, Matt Smith started a consulting business as a corporation. Matt started the business by contributing $20,000 in exchange for common stock. On May 1, he paid three months of rent in advance totaling

$1,500. Rent starts May 1. On May 3, Matt purchased supplies for $700 and two computers at a total cost of $3,600. Matt expects the computers to last for two years with no residual value. Matt hired an office assistant, agreeing to pay the assistant $2,000 per month to be paid $1,000 on May 15 and May 31. On May 27, Matt paid $400 for a radio advertisement to run immediately to announce the opening of the business. Matt earned $6,000 revenue in May, of which he collected $4,200 in cash. At the end of the month, Matt had $300 worth of supplies on hand.

Requirements

1. Use an accounting equation worksheet to record the transactions that occurred during the month of May and the adjustments that must be made prior to the preparation of the financial statements for the month ended May 31.
2. Prepare the income statement, statement of changes in shareholder's equity, and statement of cash flows for Matt's company for the month ended May 31 and the balance sheet at May 31.

P3-66A. *Record adjustments and prepare financial statements. (LO 1, 2, 3, 4, 5).* The following is a list of accounts and their balances for Casa Bella Interiors at May 31 before adjustments and some additional data for the fiscal year ended May 31, 2010.

Casa Bella Interiors
Accounts and balances
May 31, 2010

Cash	$ 4,300
Accounts receivable	9,300
Notes receivable	1,000
Interest receivable	—
Prepaid rent	1,700
Supplies	400
Office equipment	23,400
Accumulated depreciation	(1,600)
(office equipment)	
Accounts payable	500
Salaries payable	—
Interest payable	—
Unearned service revenue	2,600
Long-term notes payable	8,400
Common stock	5,000
Additional paid-in capital	2,300
Retained earnings	5,000
Service revenue	19,800
Salary expense	4,650
Rent expense	
Depreciation expense	
Advertising expense	450

Additional data follow:

- Depreciation on the office equipment for the year is $500.
- Salaries owed to employees at year end but not yet recorded or paid total $750.
- Prepaid rent that has expired at year-end amounts to $800.
- Interest due at year end on the notes receivable is $120.
- Interest owed at year end on the notes payable is $840.
- Unearned service revenue that has actually been earned by year end totals $1,500.

Requirements

1. For each account, show the adjustment needed at year end.

2. Prepare an income statement for the year ended May 31, 2010, and a balance sheet at May 31, 2010.
3. Calculate the firm's profit margin on sales ratio for the year.

P3-67A. *Analyze business transactions and prepare financial statements. (LO 1, 2, 3, 4).* Drive Fast Car Rentals generates revenue by renting high speed sports cars to tourists in the area. When a reservation is made in advance, Drive Fast collects half the week's rent to hold the reservation. However, Drive Fast does not require reservations, and sometimes customers will come in to rent a unit the same day. The accounting department for Drive Fast recorded the following transactions for 2010, the first year of business. These types of transactions require that Drive Fast's accounting department record some cash receipts as unearned revenues and others as earned revenues.

| | | **Assets** | | **= Liabilities** | | **+** | **Shareholders' Equity** | |
| | | | | | | | Contributed Capital | Retained Earnings |
Transaction	Cash	All other assets	(Account)	All liabilities	(Account)		Common stock	(Account)
1.	$235,000						$235,000	
2.	(143,000)	143,000	Property, plant, and equipment					
3.	99,000			99,000	Notes payable			
4.	(3,000)	3,000	Supplies					
5.	(5,000)	5,000	Prepaid rent					
6.		17,000	Accounts receivable					17,000 Service revenue
7.		(925)	Supplies					(925) Supplies expense
8.		(800)	Prepaid rent					(800) Rent expense
9.				1,225	Salaries payable			(1,225) Salary expense
10.		(2,250)	Accumulated depreciation					(2,250) Depreciation expense
11.				225	Interest payable			(225) Interest expense

— Income Statement   — Statement of Changes in Shareholders' Equity   — Balance Sheet   — Statement of Cash Flows

Requirements

1. Explain the transaction or event that resulted in each entry in the accounting equation worksheet.
2. Did Drive Fast Car Rentals generate net income or net loss for the period ended December 31, 2010? How can you tell?
3. Prepare the income statement, statement of changes in shareholders' equity, and statement of cash flows for the year ended December 31, 2010, and the balance sheet at December 31, 2010.

Set B

P3-68B. *Record adjustments and prepare income statement. (LO 1, 2, 3, 4).* Selected amounts (at December 31, 2012) from the accounting records of Dan's Billiard Supply Company are shown here. No adjustments have been made.

Cash paid to employees for salaries and wages	$ 500,000
Cash collected from customers for services rendered	2,500,000
Long-term notes payable	425,000
Cash	375,000
Common stock	50,000
Equipment	850,000
Prepaid insurance	125,000
Inventory	200,000
Prepaid rent	175,000
Retained earnings	430,000
Salaries and wages expense	600,000
Service revenue	5,250,000

Requirements

1. Five adjustments need to be made before the financial statements for the year ended December 31, 2012, can be prepared. Show each in an accounting equation worksheet.
   a. The equipment (purchased on January 1, 2012) has a useful life of 10 years with no salvage value (equal amount of depreciation each year).
   b. Interest on the notes payable needs to be accrued for the year in the amount of $60,000.
   c. Unexpired insurance at December 31, 2012, is $25,000.
   d. The rent payment of $175,000 was made on May 1. The rent payment is for 12 months beginning on the date of payment.
   e. Salaries of $65,000 were earned but unrecorded and unpaid at December 31, 2012.
2. Prepare an income statement for the year ended December 31, 2012, for Dan's Billiard Supply Company.

P3-69B. *Record adjustments and calculate net income. (LO 1, 2, 3, 4).* The records of Thinker's School Supplies showed the following amounts at December 31, 2011, before adjustments:

Prepaid insurance	$ 2,400
Supplies	2,250
Unearned service fees (unearned revenue)	5,680
Notes payable	29,000
Service fees revenue	175,000
Salary expense	95,000
Prepaid rent	6,250
Insurance expense	0
Supplies expense	0
Rent expense	0
Interest expense	0
Interest payable	0
Wages payable	0

Before Thinker's prepares the financial statements for the business at December 31, 2011, adjustments must be made for the following items:
   a. The prepaid insurance is for a 12-month policy purchased on March 1 for cash. The policy is effective from March 1, 2011, to February 28, 2012.
   b. A count of the supplies on December 31 revealed $400 worth still on hand.
   c. One customer paid for four months of service in advance on December 1. By December 31, one month of the service had been performed by Thinker's.
   d. The prepaid rent was for 10 months of rent for the company office building, beginning August 1.

e. The company took out a bank loan on October 1, 2011. The interest rate is 6% (1/2% per month) for one year.

f. As of December 31, the company owed its employees $5,000 for work done in 2011. The next payday is in January 2012.

Requirements

1. Show the adjustments in the accounting equation.
2. Prepare an income statement for the year ended December 31, 2011, for Thinker's School Supplies.

P3-70B. *Account for depreciable assets. (LO 3).* Super Clean Dry Cleaning purchased a new piece of office equipment on January 1, 2009, for $18,000 cash. The company expects to use the equipment for three years and thinks it will be worthless at the end of the three-year period. The company depreciates the equipment in equal annual amounts.

Requirements

1. Show the adjustments in an accounting equation worksheet for the first two years of depreciation.
2. Prepare the asset section of the balance sheet at December 31, 2009, and December 31, 2010, after appropriate adjustments.
3. What amount of depreciation expense will be shown on the income statement for the year ended December 31, 2009? What amount will be shown for the year ended December 31, 2010?
4. Calculate the total depreciation for the life of the asset. What do you notice about the book value of the asset at the end of its useful life?

P3-71B. *Record adjustments. (LO 1, 2, 3).* Following is a partial list of financial statement items from the records of Starnes Company at December 31, 2012, before adjustments:

Prepaid rent	$20,000
Prepaid insurance	12,000
Service revenue	35,000
Wages expense	8,000
Unearned service revenue	18,000
Interest expense	5,000

Additional information includes the following:

- The insurance policy indicates that on December 31, 2012, only five months remain on the 12-month policy that originally cost $12,000.
- Starnes has a note payable with $2,500 of interest that must be paid on January 1, 2013. No interest expense has been recorded for this note.
- The accounting records show that two-thirds of the service revenue paid in advance by a customer on March 1 has now been earned.
- On August 1, the company paid $20,000 for rent for 10 months beginning on August 1.
- At year end, Starnes Company owed $500 worth of salaries to employees for work done in December. This has not been recorded or paid. The next payday is January 3, 2013.

Requirements

1. Use an accounting equation worksheet to record the adjustments that must be made prior to the preparation of the financial statements for the year ended December 31, 2012.
2. For the accounts shown, calculate the account balances that would be shown on Starnes' financial statements for the year ended December 31, 2012; balance sheet at December 31, 2012.

P3-72B. *Record adjustments. (LO 1, 2, 3).* Following is a list of financial statement items from Chunky Candy Company as of June 30, 2010. Chunky's fiscal year is from July 1 to June 30.

Prepaid insurance	$ 3,600
Prepaid rent	5,000
Wages expense	12,000
Unearned revenue	30,000
Interest expense	0

Additional information follows:

- The company paid a $3,600 premium on a three-year insurance policy on January 1, 2010, with the insurance coverage beginning immediately.
- Chunky borrowed $100,000 on July 1, 2009, with an interest rate of 11%. No interest has been paid as of June 30, 2010.
- The books show that $10,000 of the unearned revenue has now been earned.
- The company paid 10 months of rent in advance on March 1, 2010, for rent beginning in March.
- Wages for June 30, 2010, of $1,000 will be paid to employees on July 3, 2010 (the next fiscal year).

Requirements

1. Use the accounting equation to record the adjustments that must be made prior to the preparation of the financial statements for the fiscal year ended June 30, 2010.
2. For the accounts shown, calculate the balances that would appear on the financial statements for the year ended June 30, 2010; balance sheet at June 30, 2010.

P3-73B. *Record adjustments. (LO 1, 2, 3).* Summit Climbing Tours has the following amounts in its records at the end of the fiscal year:

Prepaid insurance	$9,000
Unearned revenue	2,500
Wages expense	9,500
Accounts payable	3,575
Interest revenue	2,250

The company also has the following information available at the end of the year:

- Of the prepaid insurance, $2,000 has now expired.
- Of the unearned revenue, $2,200 has been earned.
- The company must accrue an additional $3,275 of wages expense.
- A bill for $500 from the company that provides cleaning services to Summit arrived on the last day of the year. Nothing related to this invoice has been recorded or paid.
- The company has earned an additional $750 of interest revenue, not yet received (or recorded).

Requirements

1. Use an accounting equation worksheet to show the adjustments at the end of the year.
2. Calculate the balances in each account shown after the adjustments.
3. Indicate whether each adjustment is related to an accrual or a deferral.

P3-74B. *Record adjustments and prepare financial statements. (LO 1, 2, 3, 4).* The accounting records for Beta Company contained the following balances as of December 31, 2008, as shown on the year-end balance sheet:

Beta Company
Balance Sheet
At December 31, 2008

Assets		Liabilities and Shareholders' Equity	
Cash	$50,000	Accounts payable	$17,500
Accounts receivable	26,500		
Prepaid rent	3,600	Common stock	48,600
Land	10,500	Retained earnings	24,500
Totals	$90,600		$90,600

The following accounting events apply to Beta's 2009 fiscal year:

a.	January	1	Beta purchased a computer that cost $18,000 for cash. The computer had no salvage value and a three-year useful life.
b.	March	1	The company borrowed $20,000 by issuing a two-year note at 12%.
c.	May	1	The company paid $6,000 cash in advance for a six-month lease starting on July 1 for office space.
d.	June	1	The company declared and paid dividends of $2,000 to the owners.
e.	July	1	The company purchased land that cost $15,000 cash.
f.	August	1	Cash payments on accounts payable amounted to $5,500.
g.	August	1	Beta received $13,200 cash in advance for 12 months of service to be performed monthly for the next year, beginning on receipt of payment.
h.	September	1	Beta sold a parcel of land for $13,000, its original cost of the land.
i.	October	1	Beta purchased $1,300 of supplies on account.
j.	November	1	Beta purchased short-term investments for $10,000 cash. The investments earn a fixed rate of 5% per year.
k.	December	31	The company earned service revenue on account during the year that amounted to $50,000.
l.	December	31	Cash collections from accounts receivable amounted to $46,000.
m.	December	31	The company incurred other operating expenses on account during the year that amounted to $5,850.

Additional information follows:

- Salaries that had been earned by the sales staff but not yet paid amounted to $2,300.
- Supplies on hand at the end of the period totaled $200.
- The beginning balance of $3,600 in prepaid rent was completely used up by the end of the year.

Requirements

1. Set up an accounting equation worksheet and record the account balances as of December 31, 2008.
2. Record the transactions that occurred during 2009 and the necessary adjustments at year end.
3. Prepare the income statement, statement of changes in shareholders' equity, and statement of cash flows for the year ended December 31, 2009, and the balance sheet at December 31, 2009.

P3-75B. *Record adjustments and prepare financial statements. (LO 1, 2, 3, 4).* Following are transactions for Security Company for 2010:

- a. The owners started the business as a corporation by contributing $50,000 cash in exchange for common stock.
- b. Security Company purchased office equipment for $5,000 cash and land for $15,000 cash.
- c. The company earned a total of $32,000 of revenue of which $20,000 was collected in cash.
- d. The company purchased $550 worth of supplies for cash.
- e. The company paid $6,000 in cash for other operating expenses.
- f. At the end of the year, Security Company owed employees $3,600 for work that the employees had done in 2010. The next payday, however, is not until January 4, 2011.
- g. Only $120 worth of supplies was left at the end of the year.
- h. The office equipment was purchased on January 1 and is expected to last for five years. There is no expected salvage value, and the company wants equal amounts of depreciation expense each year related to this equipment.

Requirements

1. Use an accounting equation worksheet to record the transactions that occurred during 2010.
2. Record any adjustments needed at year end.
3. Prepare the income statement, statement of changes in shareholders' equity, and the statement of cash flows for the year ended December 31, 2010, and the balance sheet at December 31, 2010.

P3-76B. *Record adjustments and prepare financial statements. (LO 1, 2, 3, 4).* On October 1, Jill Jackson started Jill's Apple Farm as a corporation. Jill started the firm by contributing $50,000 in exchange for common stock. On October 1, the new firm paid six months of rent in advance totaling

$6,000 and paid eight months of insurance in advance totaling $3,000. Both rent and insurance coverage began on October 1. On October 6, the firm purchased supplies for $1,200. The firm hired one employee to help Jill and agreed to pay the worker $3,000 per month, paid on the last day of each month. Jill's Apple Farm paid $100 for a newspaper advertisement to announce the opening of the business. The farm earned revenue of $8,000 in October, of which $5,000 was in cash. At the end of the month, the firm had only $400 worth of supplies on hand.

Requirements

1. Using an accounting equation worksheet, record the transactions that occurred during the month of October and the adjustments that must be made prior to the preparation of the financial statements for the month ended October 31.
2. Prepare the income statement, statement of changes in shareholder's equity, and statement of cash flows for the month ended October 31 and the balance sheet at October 31.

P3-77B. *Record adjustments and prepare financial statements. (LO 1, 2, 3, 4, 5).* Puppy Studs, Inc., provides a stud service for serious dog breeders. The company's accountant prepared the following list of accounts with their unadjusted balances at the end of the fiscal year, March 31, 2011:

Cash	$ 52,200
Accounts receivable	47,500
Prepaid insurance	20,000
Prepaid rent	1,800
Supplies	10,350
Equipment	137,500
Accumulated depreciation	(1,700)
Accounts payable	3,500
Unearned service revenue	3,000
Long-term notes payable	35,000
Common stock	50,500
Additional paid-in capital	91,450
Retained earnings	87,120
Dividends	5,320
Service revenue	226,850
Miscellaneous operating expenses	149,450
Salary expense	75,000

Additional facts (related to adjustments that have not yet been made):
  a. The company owes its employees $2,500 for work done in this fiscal year. The next payday is not until April.
  b. $2,000 worth of the unearned service revenue has actually been earned at year end.
  c. The equipment is depreciated at the rate of $1,700 per year.
  d. At year end $600 worth of prepaid rent and $15,000 of prepaid insurance remains unexpired.
  e. Interest on the long-term note for a year at the rate of 6.5% is due on April 1.
  f. Supplies on hand at the end of the year amounted to $2,100.
  g. On the last day of the fiscal year, the firm earned $20,000. The customer paid $15,000 with cash and owed the remainder on account. However, the accountant left early that day, so the day's revenue was not recorded in the accounting records.

Requirements

1. For each account, show the adjustment needed at year end.
2. Prepare an income statement for the year ended March 31, 2011, and a balance sheet at March 31, 2011.
3. Calculate the firm's profit margin on sales ratio for the year.

P3-78B. *Analyze business transactions and prepare financial statements. (LO 1, 2, 3, 4).* The accounting department for Loud Noises Concerts (LNC) recorded the following transactions for the fiscal year ended April 30, 2009. LNC generates revenue by selling tickets for local concerts. Sometimes tickets are sold in advance and sometimes customers will purchase their tickets the same day as the event. These types of transactions require that the LNC accounting department record some cash receipts as unearned revenues and others as earned revenues.

		Assets		= Liabilities		+	Shareholders' Equity	
							Contributed Capital	Retained Earnings
Transaction	Cash	All other assets	(Account)	All liabilities	(Account)		Common stock	(Account)
1.	$175,000						$175,000	
2.		650	Office supplies	650	Accounts (or other) payable			
3.	(22,500)	22,500	Prepaid rent					
4.		439,000	Building	439,000	Long-term notes payable			
5.	20,000			20,000	Unearned ticket revenue			
6.	(675)							(675) Miscellaneous expense
7.	(650)			(650)	Accounts (or other) payable			
8.	70,000							70,000 Ticket revenue
9.				(18,000)	Unearned ticket revenue			18,000 Ticket revenue
10.		(275)	Office supplies					(275) Office supplies expense
11.		(11,000)	Prepaid rent					(11,000) Rent expense
12.				575	Interest payable			(575) Interest expense
13.		(3,500)	Accumulated depreciation					(3,500) Depreciation expense
14.				6,250	Salaries payable			(6,250) Salaries expense
15.	(8,250)							(8,250) Dividends

━ Income Statement   ━ Statement of Changes in Shareholders' Equity   ━ Balance Sheet   ━ Statement of Cash Flows

Requirements

1. Explain the transaction or event that resulted in each item recorded on the worksheet.
2. Did LNC generate net income or net loss for the fiscal year ended April 30, 2009? How can you tell?
3. Prepare the income statement, statement of changes in shareholders' equity, and statement of cash flows for the year ended April 30, 2009, and the balance sheet at April 30, 2009.

Financial Statement Analysis

FSA3-1. *Identify and explain accruals and deferrals. (LO 2, 3, 4, 5).* Use the selection from the annual report from Books-A-Million in Appendix A to answer these questions:

1. Does Books-A-Million have any deferred expenses? What are they, and where are they shown? (Ignore deferred taxes.)

2. Does Books-A-Million have accrued expenses? What are they, and where are they shown?
3. What is the difference between a deferred expense and an accrued expense?
4. Calculate the profit margin on sales ratio for the past two years. What information does this provide?

FSA3-2. *Identify and explain accruals and deferrals. (LO 2, 3, 4).* Use Hormel Foods' balance sheet in Exhibit 3.17 on page 120 to answer these questions:

1. The current asset section shows prepaid expenses. What might these pertain to? Have the "expenses" referred to here been recognized (i.e., included on the period's income statement)?
2. The liabilities section shows accrued expenses. What does this represent? Have the associated expenses been recognized?
3. The liabilities section shows accounts payable. Explain what this is and what Hormel Foods will do to satisfy this liability.

FSA3-3. *Identify and interpret expenses and liabilities. (LO 2, 3, 4).* Use Carnival Corporation's balance sheet to answer the questions that follow.

Carnival Corporation & PLC
Consolidated Balance Sheets
(amounts in millions, except par values)

	November 30,	
Assets	2008	2007
Current Assets		
Cash and cash equivalents	$ 650	$ 943
Trade and other receivables, net	418	436
Inventories	315	331
Prepaid expenses and other	267	266
Total current assets	1,650	1,976
Property and Equipment, Net	26,457	26,639
Goodwill	3,266	3,610
Trademarks	1,294	1,393
Other Assets	733	563
	$33,400	$34,181
Liabilities and Shareholders' Equity		
Current Liabilities		
Short-term borrowings	$ 256	$ 115
Current portion of long-term debt	1,081	1,028
Convertible debt subject to current put options	271	1,396
Accounts payable	512	561
Accrued liabilities and other	1,142	1,353
Customer deposits	2,519	2,807
Total current liabilities	5,781	7,260
Long-Term Debt	7,735	6,313
Other Long-Term Liabilities and Deferred Income	786	645
Commitments and Contingencies (Notes 6 and 7)		
Shareholders' Equity		
Common stock of Carnival Corporation; $.01 par value; 1,960 shares authorized; 643 shares at 2008 and 2007 issued	6	6
Ordinary shares of Carnival plc; $1.66 par value; 226 shares authorized; 213 shares at 2008 and 2007 issued	354	354
Additional paid-in capital	7,677	7,599
Retained earnings	13,980	12,921
Accumulated other comprehensive (loss) income	(623)	1,296
Treasury stock; 19 shares at 2008 and 2007 of Carnival Corporation and 52 shares at 2008 and 50 shares at 2007 of Carnival plc, at cost	(2,296)	(2,213)
Total shareholders' equity	19,098	19,963
	$33,400	$34,181

1. Which current asset reflects deferred expenses? Explain what it means to defer expenses, and give the adjustment to the accounting equation that was probably made to record this asset.
2. The liabilities section shows over $2.5 billion in customer deposits at November 30, 2008. Explain why this is a liability, and give the transaction (in the accounting equation) that resulted in this liability.

Critical Thinking Problems

Risk and Controls

Is there anything in the information about Books-A-Million given in Appendix A that addresses how the firm protects its accounting data?

Ethics

DVD-Online, Inc., is in its second year of business. The company is Web-based, offering DVD rental to online customers for a fixed monthly fee. For $30 per month, a customer receives three DVDs each month, one at a time as the previous one is returned. No matter how many DVDs a customer uses (up to three), the fee is fixed at $30 per month. Customers sign a contract for a year, so DVD-Online recognizes $360 sales revenue each time a customer signs up for the service. The owner of DVD-Online, John Richards, has heard about GAAP, but he does not see any reason to follow these accounting principles. Although DVD-Online is not publicly traded, John does put the company's financial statements on the company's Web page for customers to see.

1. Explain how DVD-Online would account for its revenue if it did follow GAAP.
2. Explain to John Richards why he should use GAAP, and describe why his financial statements may now be misleading.
3. Do you see this as an ethical issue? Explain.

Group Assignment

Use the balance sheet for Carnival Corporation shown in FSA3-3. For each of the current assets and current liabilities, prepare a brief explanation of the nature of the item. For each current liability, explain how you think the company will satisfy the liability.

Internet Exercise: Darden

Please go to www.dardenrestaurants.com.

IE3-1. If you were at a Darden property, what might you be doing? List two of the Darden chains.

IE3-2. Click on Investor Relations followed by Annual Report & Financials and then select the HTML version of the most recent annual report. Find the Balance Sheets under Financials, then Financial Review, by clicking next or using the "contents" scroll bar. Does Darden use a calendar year for its fiscal year? How can you tell?

IE3-3. Refer to the asset section.

1. List the title of one asset account that includes accrued revenue—amounts earned but not yet received in cash.
2. List the title of one asset account that includes amounts that have been paid for in cash but have not yet been expensed.
3. List the title of one asset account that includes amounts that will be depreciated.
4. For each account listed in 1 through 3, identify the amount reported for the most recent year. Do these amounts still need adjusting? Explain why or why not.

IE3-4. For the two most recent years list the amounts reported for total assets, total liabilities, and total stockholders' equity. For each type of account, identify what the trend indicates. Does the accounting equation hold true both years?

Please note: Internet Web sites are constantly being updated. Therefore, if the information is not found where indicated, please explore the Web site further to find the information.

Appendix B
The Mechanics of an Accounting System

LEARNING OBJECTIVES

When you are finished studying Appendix B, you should be able to:

1. Define the general ledger system and explain how it works.

2. Explain and perform the steps in the accounting cycle.

3. Identify the adjustments needed before preparing financial statements and make those adjustments.

4. Describe the closing process and explain why it is necessary.

Accounting Information Systems

Throughout the chapters of this book, you have been keeping track of Team Shirts' transactions using an accounting equation work sheet. We can do that in a simple world with a small number of transactions. In the real world, that wouldn't work very well. A company in the real world needs a better system to keep track of the large number of transactions represented in the four basic financial statements. A company may have an accounting system that gathers *only* accounting information—just recording the information that applies to the financial statements—and other information systems gathering information for marketing, production, and other parts of the company. Alternatively, a company may have a single, integrated information system in which all company information is recorded—data about suppliers, employees, operations; and the accounting information is simply a small part.

The firm's accounting information is kept in the firm's **general ledger**. The general ledger is the collection of a company's accounts where the amounts from the firm's transactions are organized and stored. You can think of it as a big book with a page for every asset, liability, equity, revenue, and expense account. Later in this appendix, you will learn how transactions get recorded in a company's general ledger. For years, the **general ledger system** was maintained by the accounting department as a separate information system; and the other functional areas of the business—marketing, production, sales, etc.—each had its own system for keeping track of the information it needed. Since the development of computers and software programs that can manage large amounts of information, more and more companies are using a single, integrated information system. Thus, instead of keeping their data separately, accountants may get

The **general ledger** is the collection of the company's accounts where the information from the financial transactions is organized and stored.

The **general ledger system** is the accountant's traditional way of keeping track of a company's financial transactions and then using those records to prepare the basic financial statements.

An **enterprise-wide resource planning system (ERP)** is an integrated software program used by large firms to manage all of a firm's information.

their information from the company's overall information system—often referred to as an **enterprise-wide resource planning system (ERP)**.

No matter how it is related to the rest of a firm's information system, the accounting system is still called the general ledger system. The same financial statements are produced with both the general ledger and the integrated types of information systems. In this appendix, we will use the general ledger system, which was designed as a manual system, to demonstrate how transactions are recorded, classified, and summarized for the financial statements.

L.O.1
Define the general ledger system and explain how it works.

Business transactions are first recorded in a **journal**. Then they are transferred to accounts in the general ledger through a process called posting.

The General Ledger Accounting System

Keeping track of financial information with a traditional record-keeping system is often called *bookkeeping*. As transactions occur, they are recorded chronologically by a bookkeeper in a book called a **journal**. When we prepare an accounting equation work sheet showing the effect of each transaction on the accounting equation, we are doing something similar to recording a transaction in a journal. The resources exchanged are shown with their dollar amounts. The journal contains a record of each transaction as it occurs. An example is shown in Exhibit B.1. In the next section, you'll learn how the "debits" and "credits" columns are used. For now, just notice that all of the accounts affected by the transaction are used in a journal entry. Most companies use more than one journal; each department may have its own journal. Common journals are the (1) sales journal, (2) cash receipts journal, and (3) cash disbursements journal. For simplicity, we'll use a single, general journal for all our transactions.

EXHIBIT B.1

An Example of a Journal

Page 4: General Journal

Ref.	Date	Journal entry	Debits	Credits
J-1	June 1	Cash	65,000	
		Sales		65,000
		To record the collection of cash for sales.		
J-2	June 4	Equipment	20,600	
		Cash		20,600
		To record the purchase of equipment for cash.		

The journal entries are recorded chronologically. Then, the individual items are "regrouped" by account as they are posted to the general ledger. Trace the cash amounts in the journal entries to the general ledger cash account shown in Exhibit B.2 on page 566. The amounts for sales and equipment will be posted to their own general ledger accounts.

Posting is the process of recording the transactions from the journal into the firm's general ledger so that the transactions will be organized by accounts.

Because a company may have hundreds or even thousands of transactions during an accounting period, it would be difficult, probably impossible, to try to gather and use the information from a chronological record such as the journal. To be useful, the information needs to be reorganized, grouping together transactions that involve the same account. For example, when all the transactions that involve cash are grouped together, then the company's cash balance can be easily determined. As you can see from that example, it is useful for similar transactions to be grouped together. The transactions from the journal or journals are transferred to another book called the general ledger through a process called **posting** the transactions to the general ledger. Posting is done periodically; it could be daily, weekly, or monthly, depending on the size of the company.

The general ledger is the primary record of the financial information of the business. It is organized by accounts. As you read earlier in this book, an account is the basic classification unit of accounting information. You can think of each financial statement item as an account, and each account as a page in the general ledger. On the page for a particular account, we record all the additions to, and deductions from, that account.

For example, one account in the general ledger is cash. On the cash page in the general ledger, we find every cash collection and every cash disbursement made by the company. If there are more disbursements or collections than can fit on one page, they will be recorded on as many following pages as needed, all comprising the cash account. To make it easy to find the amount of cash on hand, the cash account has a running balance. That means a new balance is calculated after every entry. Think about your own checkbook—that's the record you keep of each check you write (a subtraction); each deposit you make (an addition); and the resulting total remaining in your checking account (that's your running balance). If you keep a running balance, it is much faster to find out how much cash you have in your account. (Have you discovered what happens when you fail to keep your checkbook balance current?)

Accounts in the general ledger include cash, accounts receivable, inventory, prepaid insurance, equipment, accumulated depreciation, accounts payable, notes payable, contributed capital, and retained earnings. (Notice, these are given in the order in which they appear on the balance sheet.) How many accounts does a company have? Every company is different, and the number of accounts depends on the detail the company wants in its financial records. For example, one company could have an account called utilities expenses in which many different utility-related expenses could be accumulated. Another company might prefer to have a separate account for each type of utility expense—a separate page in the general ledger for electricity expense, gas expense, water expense, etc. The number of accounts is determined by the amount of detail a company wants to be able to retrieve from its records. If a company uses very little gas or water, it would be a waste of time and space to keep a separate account for those expenses. A company that uses water in its production process, on the other hand, would definitely want to keep a separate account for water purchases.

Companies also have subsidiary ledgers. These are detailed records that support the balances in the general ledger. For example, the *accounts receivable subsidiary ledger* will have details about the credit customers—sales, receipts, and account balances for every customer. The total dollar amount of accounts receivable in the accounts receivable subsidiary ledger will be the total in the general ledger.

Most companies have a large number of accounts, and they combine the similar ones for the financial statements. When we look at the financial statements, we can't really tell how many individual accounts a company has in its general ledger. Many smaller accounts may be combined for financial statement presentation.

Anyone in the firm with access to the accounting records who wants to know the balance in any account at any time can find it by looking in the general ledger. A list of the balances in all the accounts of a company is called a **trial balance**.

> A **trial balance** is a list of all the accounts of a company with the related balance.

Before the financial statements can be prepared, adjustments to the records must be made. We discussed those adjustments and how to make them in Chapter 3. Adjustments are needed because of the nature of accrual accounting. On the financial statements, we need to include revenues that have been earned and expenses that have been incurred, even if we have not yet received the cash earned or paid the cash for the expenses incurred during the accounting period. These adjustments are called accruals. The action has taken place, but the dollars have not been exchanged.

We also need to be sure to include on the income statement for the period any revenue we've earned or expenses we've incurred for which the dollars were exchanged at a previous time. These are called deferrals. The dollars were already exchanged, and we recorded the receipt of the cash when we received the cash. However, we did not recognize any revenue or expense at that time. At the end of the accounting period, we have to recognize any revenue we have earned and any expenses that we've incurred.

No matter what kind of accounting system a company uses, the information produced by that system must be adjusted before the financial statements can be prepared. After the adjustments are made, the financial statements are prepared. We have actually done all this—recording the transactions, making the adjustments, and preparing the financial statements—using the accounting equation work sheet. The general ledger system is simply a more feasible way to do it in an actual business.

Debits and Credits

To use the general ledger system and to understand the information it makes available, we must learn a bit more accounting language. Don't panic over the terms **debit** and **credit**. You will find them easy to understand, but only if first you get rid of any notions of what you already think debit and credit mean. In accounting, each term has a very specific meaning that should not be confused with its more general meaning.

> **Debit** means left side of an account.

> **Credit** means right side of an account.

In accounting, when we say *debit,* we mean the left side; when we say *credit,* we mean the right side. (This should be easy to remember.) Left is the only thing that the word *debit* means and right is the only thing that the word *credit* means—unless we apply the terms to specific accounts.

A general ledger has been traditionally composed of a multicolumn page, similar to the one shown in Exhibit B.2. The Debit column on the right shows the running balance in the cash account. You would almost never see a credit balance in this account. The general ledger is often computerized in a similar format.

EXHIBIT B.2

The General Ledger

Account: **Cash**					Account No. 1002	
					Balance	
Date 2011	Item	Jrnl. ref.	Debit	Credit	Debit	Credit
June 1		J–1, p. 4 65,000		....	**65,000**	
June 4		J–2, p. 4		20,600	.... **44,400**	

This is the **Cash** account. The cash amounts from all the journal entries are posted here. Trace these amounts back to the journal entries shown in Exhibit B.1.

In the balance columns, the column on the left is called the debit (DR) column, and the column on the right is called the credit (CR) column. As a shortcut to using formal preprinted two-column paper, accountants often draw a T-account to represent a page in the general ledger. T-accounts shown in Exhibit B.3 are our representation of the general ledger shown in Exhibit B.2.

EXHIBIT B.3

Debits and Credits in T-Accounts

Asset		Liability		Shareholders' Equity	
Debit increases (normal balance)	Credit decreases	Debit decreases	Credit increases (normal balance)	Debit decreases	Credit increases (normal balance)

Revenue		Expense	
Debit decreases	Credit increases (normal balance)	Debit increases (normal balance)	Credit decreases

One T-account such as cash, shown next, represents a single page in the general ledger. The left side of a T-account is the debit side, and the right side of a T-account is the credit side.

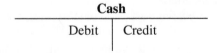

Cash	
Debit	Credit

Numbers we put on the left side of the account are called debits, and putting a number in the left column is called *debiting* an account. *Debit* is a wonderful word that can be an adjective, a noun, or a verb. The same goes for the word *credit*. The right side of the account is called the credit side, the numbers we put on the right side are called credits, and putting a number in the right column is called *crediting* an account.

In the fifteenth century, a monk named Fra Luca Paccioli wrote about a system that uses debits and credits with the accounting equation. In his system, the accounting equation stays in balance with each transaction *and* the monetary amounts of debits and credits are equal for each transaction. Here's how it works:

1. For the accounting equation, the balance in the accounts on the left side of the equation (*assets*) will increase with debits; and the balance in the accounts on the right side of the equation (*liabilities* and *shareholders' equity*) will increase with credits. It follows that the balance in an asset account will decrease with credits. Liability and equity account balances decrease with debits. Putting that together,

* asset accounts are increased with debits and decreased with credits.
* liability and shareholders' equity accounts are increased with credits and decreased with debits.

This means that when we want to add an amount to our cash balance, we put the number of that amount on the left (in the left column of the two columns in the general ledger account for cash)—so that's a debit. When we disburse cash and want to subtract the amount disbursed from the cash account, we put the number of that amount on the right side—so that's a credit. The *increase* side of an account is called its "normal" balance. Cash has a normal debit balance. Because we put the cash we receive on the debit side and the cash we disburse on the credit side, it makes sense that our cash account will normally have a debit balance. (It's not normal to disburse more cash than you have—it's pretty unusual.)

In accounting, we do not literally *add* and *subtract* from an account balance—we debit and credit an account to accomplish the same thing. If we make an error, we do not erase the mistake and replace it with the correct answer. Instead, we debit or credit the account to correct the error and make the account balance correct. When accounting records are kept by hand, all entries are made in ink so that no entries can be erased or changed. This has been traditional in accounting to keep the records from being altered. Recording every increase to, and decrease from, an account balance gives a complete record of every change made to the account.

2. Because shareholders' equity is increased with credits, all accounts that increase shareholders' equity will increase with credits. Revenue accounts increase with credits and decrease with debits. When we make a sale, we *credit* the sales account.

3. Because shareholders' equity is *decreased* with debits, all accounts that decrease shareholders' equity work in the opposite way as revenue accounts work. For example, expense accounts—where a list of our expenses is kept—increase with debits. As we incur expenses, we put the amounts on the left side of expense accounts.

Your Turn B-1

Indicate whether each of the following accounts normally has a debit (DR) or credit (CR) balance and what type of account it is.

Account Title	Expense	Revenue	Asset	Liability	Shareholders' Equity
Accounts payable				CR	
Accounts receivable					
Advertising expense					
Cash					
Depreciation expense					
Furniture and fixtures					
Accumulated depreciation					
Unearned fees					
Salary expense					
Common stock					
Rent expense					
Retained earnings					
(Earned) fees					
Land					
Building					

A summary of the use of debits and credits is shown in Exhibit B.3. Remember, it's just a clever system to be sure that, when we record a transaction, the accounting equation is kept in balance and, at the same time, debits = credits with every transaction. This system is called double-entry bookkeeping.

L.O.2
Explain and perform the
steps in the accounting cycle.

The **accounting cycle** begins with
the transactions of a new
accounting period. It includes
recording and posting the
transactions, adjusting the books,
preparing financial statements,
and closing the temporary
accounts to get ready for the next
accounting period.

The Accounting Cycle

The process that starts with recording individual transactions, produces the four basic financial statements, and gets our general ledger ready for the next accounting period is called the **accounting cycle**. Some of the steps in the accounting cycle won't make any sense to you yet, but this appendix examines each in detail. By the end of this appendix, you should be able to explain and perform each step. The steps in the accounting cycle follow:

1. Record transactions in the journal, the chronological record of all transactions, from source documents such as invoices. These are called journal entries.
2. Post the journal entries to the general ledger.
3. At the end of the accounting period, prepare an unadjusted trial balance.
4. Prepare adjusting journal entries and post them to the general ledger.
5. Prepare an adjusted trial balance.
6. Prepare the financial statements.
7. Close the temporary accounts.
8. Prepare a postclosing trial balance.

Let's look at each of these steps in detail.

Step 1: Recording Journal Entries

In the normal course of business, many transactions must be recorded in the accounting system. Let's look at how the transactions for a company's first year of business would be recorded in a journal. The transactions for the first year of Clint's Consulting Company, Inc., are shown in Exhibit B.4.

EXHIBIT B.4

Transactions for Clint's Consulting Company, Inc., during 2011

Date	Transaction
January 2	Clint contributes $2,000 of his own money to the business in exchange for common stock.
January 10	Clint's Consulting, Inc., borrows $4,000 from a local bank to begin the business.
February 4	Clint's buys supplies for $400 cash.
April 10	Clint's hires a company to prepare and distribute a brochure immediately for the company for $500 cash.
July 12	Clint's provides consulting services and earns revenue of $9,000 cash.
August 15	Clint's pays someone to do some typing, which costs $350 cash.
October 21	Clint's repays the $4,000 note along with $150 interest.
December 10	Clint's Consulting, Inc., makes a distribution to Clint, the only shareholder, for $600.

The first transaction in Clint's first year of business is his own contribution of $2,000 to the business in exchange for common stock. What a journal entry looks like on a journal page follows:

Date	Transaction	Debit	Credit
January 2, 2011	Cash	2,000	
	Common stock		2,000
	To record owner's cash contribution in exchange for common stock		1–1[a]

[a]This is a number we'll use to help us trace journal entries to the general ledger.

The cash account is increased by $2,000, so Clint's would debit the cash account for $2,000. Shareholders' equity is increased, so Clint's would credit common stock for $2,000. Notice, in this case two accounts are increased—one with a debit and one with a credit. In some transactions, both accounts are increased; in others, one account can be increased and one account can be decreased; or two accounts can be decreased. The only requirement for a journal entry is that the dollar amount of debits must equal the dollar amount of credits.

In the second transaction, Clint's Consulting Company borrows $4,000 from a local bank. Again, two different accounts are increased—one with a debit and one with a credit—in this transaction. Notice, debits ($4,000) = credits ($4,000).

Date	Transaction	Debit	Credit
January 10, 2011	Cash	4,000	
	Notes payable		4,000
	To record the loan from the bank		1-2

Debits are always listed first; credits are listed after all the debits—sometimes there is more than one account to debit or credit—and the accounts being credited are indented like the first sentence of a paragraph. Each page of the journal has a reference number that is used to trace journal entries to the general ledger. We'll see this number again when we post the journal entries to the general ledger.

The third transaction is the purchase of supplies for $400 cash. This is recorded with a debit to supplies and a credit to cash.

Date	Transaction	Debit	Credit
February 4, 2011	Supplies	400	
	Cash		400
	To record the purchase of supplies		1-3

Notice, this transaction increases one asset account (supplies) and decreases another asset account (cash). Because supplies is an asset, it is increased with a debit.

The fourth transaction is Clint's hiring a company to prepare and distribute a brochure immediately for its new consulting business. Clint's pays $500 for this service.

Date	Transaction	Debit	Credit
April 10, 2011	Advertising expense	500	
	Cash		500
	To record the cost of the brochures		1-4

In this transaction, an expense account, advertising expense, is increased by $500. Because expense accounts are eventually deducted from shareholders' equity, they increase with debits, the opposite of the normal balance in shareholders' equity accounts. Cash, an asset account, is decreased with a credit of $500.

Next, the company provides consulting services for $9,000 cash.

Date	Transaction	Debit	Credit
July 12, 2011	Cash	9,000	
	Consulting fees		9,000
	To record consulting revenue		1-5

In this transaction, cash is increased with a $9,000 debit. Consulting fees, a revenue account that will eventually be added to shareholders' equity, is increased with a $9,000 credit.

Clint has one employee who types for him occasionally, and he pays this person $350 for typing during his first year of business. This is an expense, which Clint categorizes as salary expense. Cash is reduced with a $350 credit, and salary expense is increased with a $350 debit.

Date	Transaction	Debit	Credit
August 15, 2011	Salary expense	350	
	Cash		350
	To record the cost of an employee to type		1-6

Next, the company repays the loan to the bank, with interest. The principal of the loan—the amount borrowed—was $4,000; the interest—the cost of using someone else's money—was $150. The journal entry for this transaction is an example of an entry with more than one debit.

Date	Transaction	Debit	Credit
October 21, 2011	Notes payable	4,000	
	Interest expense	150	
	Cash		4,150
	To record the repayment of a note plus interest		1-7

The debit to notes payable reduces the balance in that account. Before this transaction, it had a balance of $4,000. Now, when this debit is posted, the account will have a zero balance. The interest expense account will increase by $150 because expense accounts increase with debits. Cash is reduced by $4,150.

The final transaction of Clint's Consulting Company's first year of business is a $600 distribution to Clint, the only shareholder. In a sole proprietorship, a distribution is also called a **withdrawal**. Because Clint's Consulting Company is a corporation, the distribution is called a **dividend**. Corporations often use a special account to hold the amounts for dividends declared until it is time to prepare financial statements. The account is simply called dividends. The dividends account has a debit balance and will eventually reduce retained earnings. Paying a dividend reduces the cash balance. Remember, a dividend payment is not an expense.

> A distribution to the owner of a sole proprietorship is called a **withdrawal**; in a corporation, distributions to the shareholders are called **dividends**.

Date	Transaction	Debit	Credit
December 10, 2011	Dividends	600	
	Cash		600
	To record a dividend payment		1-8

Step 2: Posting Journal Entries to the General Ledger

Each of the journal entries a company makes must be posted to the general ledger. How often this is done depends on the number of journal entries a company normally makes. Some computerized systems post every journal entry automatically when it is entered into the system. Other companies post transactions to the general ledger daily or weekly.

The accounts for Clint's Consulting Company, Inc., all begin with a zero balance, because this is Clint's first year of business. Each journal entry has the reference number from the journal with it when the entry is posted in the general ledger. This provides a way to trace every entry in the general ledger back to the original record of the transaction in the journal. After all the journal entries are posted, it is easy to calculate the balance in any account. The accounts, shown in Exhibit B.5, are listed in the following order: assets, liabilities, shareholders' equity, revenues, and expenses.

Step 3: Prepare an Unadjusted Trial Balance

A trial balance is a list of all the accounts in the general ledger, each with its debit or credit balance. The reasons for preparing a trial balance are to confirm that debits equal credits and to have a way to quickly review the accounts for needed adjustments. Exhibit B.6 shows the unadjusted trial balance for Clint's Consulting at December 31, 2011.

Step 4: Adjusting Journal Entries

> L.O.3
> Identify the adjustments needed before preparing financial statements and make those adjustments.

Recording journal entries as transactions occur and posting them to the general ledger are routine accounting tasks. When a company gets ready to prepare financial statements at the end of the accounting period, there are more journal entries needed. These are not routine journal entries; they are called adjusting journal entries. As we discussed in Chapter 3, there are four situations

EXHIBIT B.5

Clint's Consulting Company, Inc., T-Accounts

ASSETS	=	LIABILITIES	+	SHAREHOLDER'S EQUITY

Cash
(asset)

1-1	2,000	400	1-3
1-2	4,000	500	1-4
1-5	9,000	350	1-6
		4,150	1-7
		600	1-8

| EB* | 9,000 | | |

Supplies
(asset)

1-3	400		
EB	400		

Notes payable
(liability)

1-7	4,000	4,000	1-2
		0	EB

Common stock
(shareholder's equity)

		2,000	1-1
		2,000	EB

Dividends
(a special temporary account)

1-8	600		
EB	600		

Consulting fees
(revenue)

		9,000	1-5
		9,000	EB

Advertising expense
(expense)

1-4	500		
EB	500		

Salary expense
(expense)

1-6	350		
EB	350		

Interest expense
(expense)

1-7	150		
EB	150		

*EB = ending balance

EXHIBIT B.6

Clint's Consulting Company, Inc., Unadjusted Trial Balance at December 31, 2011

Account	DR	CR
Cash	$ 9,000	
Supplies	400	
Notes payable		$ 0
Common stock		2,000
Dividends	600	
Consulting fees		9,000
Advertising expense	500	
Interest expense	150	
Salary expense	350	
	$11,000	$11,000

---

that require adjustments before the financial statements are prepared. We need to adjust our records for *accrued revenues, accrued expenses, deferred revenues,* and *deferred expenses.* Let's look at an example of each of those adjustments in a general ledger system.

ACCRUALS. **Accrued Revenue.** Suppose Clint's Consulting Company did some consulting for a fee of $3,000, but the company has not billed the client yet so the revenue has not been recognized—when it is recognized, it is put on the income statement. At December 31, Clint's will adjust the company's records to recognize this revenue, even though the company has not collected the cash. First, notice the effect of the adjustment on the accounting equation.

Assets	=	Liabilities	+	Contributed capital (CC)	+	Retained earnings
+3,000 Accounts receivable						+3,000 Consulting fees

The transaction increases assets—accounts receivable (AR). That means Clint's would debit AR, because assets are increased with debits. Clint's has also increased a revenue account, consulting fees. (The $3,000 is recorded in a revenue account, not directly into the retained earnings account. However, the revenue will end up increasing retained earnings on our balance sheet.) Revenue accounts increase with credits, so we would credit the revenue account consulting fees for $3,000. The accounting equation is in balance *and* debits = credits for our transaction. Here's what the journal entry would look like:

Date	Transaction	Debit	Credit
December 31, 2011	Accounts receivable	3,000	
	Consulting fees		3,000
	To accrue revenue earned in 2011		A-1

Accrued Expenses Another situation that requires an adjustment is accrued expenses. If we have incurred an expense (the dollar amount that *will* be paid for an item or a service that has already been used to produce revenue), the matching principle requires us to put that expense on the same income statement as the revenue it helped generate.

Sometimes matching an expense with a specific revenue is impossible to do. In that case, we record the expense in the time period when the expense item was used. For example, it is often impossible to match an employee's work with specific revenue the company earns. So the cost of the work done by an employee is put on the income statement as an expense in the accounting period when the work was done.

Let's look at an example of recording salary expense in the period in which the work was done. When companies pay their employees—on normal paydays during the year—they debit the account *salary expense* and credit the account *cash.* The salary expense account may have a significant balance at year end because the company has been recording salary expense as the employees have been paid throughout the year. To make sure we've included *all* the salary expense for the year, we must examine the time our employees have worked near the end of the year. The purpose is to be sure to include the cost of *all* work done during a year in the salary expense on that year's income statement.

If we owe employees for work done in December 2011, but we will not pay them until January 2012, we have to accrue salary expense when we are adjusting our accounts at December 31, 2011. Suppose Clint's owes its employee $50 for work done in 2011, but the next payday is in 2012. To get this salary expense on the income statement for the year, Clint's must debit salary expense for $50 and credit salaries payable for $50. The salary expense on the income statement for the year ended December 31, 2011, will now include this $50. Salaries payable on the balance sheet at December 31, 2011, will show the $50 obligation. Look at the adjustment in the accounting equation, and then look at the journal entry. Notice that in the adjusting entry, just like in a routine journal entry, debits = credits. The accounting equation remains in balance.

Assets	=	Liabilities	+	CC	+	Retained earnings
		+50 Salaries payable				(50) Salary expense

Date	Transaction	Debit	Credit
December 31, 2011	Salary expense	50	
	Salaries payable		50
	To accrue salary expense at year end		A-2

Suppose a company owes employees $300 on December 31, 2010, the date of the financial statements; and the next payday is January 3, 2011. Give the adjusting journal entry necessary on December 31, 2010. How much salary expense will the company recognize when it actually pays the $300 to the employees on January 3, 2011? Give the journal entry for the payment on January 3, 2011. (Ignore payroll taxes.)

DEFERRALS. **Deferred Revenue** Deferred revenue is revenue that hasn't been earned yet, so it is recorded as a liability in a company's records—an obligation—when the cash is collected. Because cash has been collected, it must be recorded; but the goods or services have not yet been provided. The company must defer—put off—recognizing the revenue. When the cash is received, the company increases cash and increases a liability called unearned revenue. In a general ledger system, the amount of cash received is recorded in the cash account, where it is shown as a debit—that's an increase because assets are increased with debits. The journal entry is balanced with a credit to unearned revenue—that's an increase because liabilities are increased with credits.

Suppose Clint's had received $4,000 on May 1 for consulting services to be provided over the next 16 months. This is how the receipt of the $4,000 cash for services to be provided in the future affects the accounting equation, followed by the journal entry for the receipt of the $4,000 cash:

Assets	=	Liabilities	+	CC	+	Retained earnings
+4,000 cash		+4,000 Unearned consulting fees				

Date	Transaction	Debit	Credit
May 1, 2011	Cash	4,000	
	Unearned consulting fees		4,000
	To record the receipt of cash for services to be provided		1-9

Notice that this is *not* an adjusting entry; it's a regular journal entry—made when it occurs during the year—to record the receipt of cash. When we look at the T-accounts again, we'll see it posted with the transactions we posted previously.

Whenever a company has recorded unearned revenue during the year, an adjustment will be necessary at year end to recognize the portion of the revenue that has been earned during the time between when the cash was received and year end. If, on that basis, any of the unearned revenue becomes earned revenue by year end, the unearned revenue account will be decreased and the revenue account will be increased with an adjustment. In terms of debits and credits, the unearned revenue account, which is a liability, will be decreased with a debit. In Clint's case, the credit corresponding to that debit will go to consulting fees, which means that the earned revenue will now show up on the income statement with the other consulting fees Clint's has earned during the year. This adjustment is necessary to be sure all the earned revenue for the year is recognized—meaning, put on the income statement. Suppose Clint's had earned half of the unearned revenue at year end. The adjustment in the accounting equation and the corresponding journal entry for this adjustment follow:

Assets	=	Liabilities	+	CC	+	Retained earnings
		(2,000) Unearned consulting fees				+2,000 Consulting fees

Date	Transaction	Debit	Credit
December 31, 2011	Unearned consulting fees	2,000	
	Consulting fees		2,000
	To record earned revenue at year end		A-3

DEFERRED EXPENSES. Deferred expenses may need to be adjusted before the financial statements are prepared. Recall, a deferred expense is something the company paid for in advance. One example is supplies, discussed in Chapter 3. Clint's paid $400 for supplies during the year, and the company recorded them as an asset. At the end of the year, the company must determine how many supplies are left and how many were used. Clint's counts the supplies on hand and then subtracts that amount from the amount purchased. Suppose Clint's finds that there is $75 worth of supplies left in the supply closet on December 31. Since the company purchased $400 worth, that means $325 worth of supplies must have been used during the year. Clint's wants to show supplies expense of $325 on the year's income statement; and the corresponding asset should show $75 on the balance sheet at year end. This is the adjustment to get the accounts to their correct year-end balances, first in the accounting equation and then as a journal entry:

Assets	=	Liabilities	+	CC	+	Retained earnings
(325) Supplies						(325) Supplies expense

Date	Transaction	Debit	Credit
December 31, 2011	Supplies expense	325	
	Supplies		325
	To record supplies expense for the year		A-4

The T-accounts with the adjusting entries posted to them are shown in Exhibit B.7.

Steps 5 and 6: Preparing the Adjusted Trial Balance and the Financial Statements

A trial balance is a list of all the accounts, each with its debit balance or its credit balance. An unadjusted trial balance is prepared before any adjustments have been made. An **adjusted trial balance** is prepared after adjustments have been made, and it can be used to prepare the financial statements.

After all the adjusting entries have been posted to the general ledger accounts and new balances have been computed in the general ledger, an **adjusted trial balance** is prepared. An adjusted trial balance is simply a list of all the general ledger accounts and their balances, to verify that debits = credits for all the company's accounts after all the adjustments have been made. The trial balance is an internal document, used in the process of preparing financial statements. Preparing an adjusted trial balance—and making sure it actually balances—helps ensure the accuracy of the recording process. If the adjusted trial balance *is* in balance—debits = credits—it can be used to prepare the financial statements.

The adjusted trial balance is shown in Exhibit B.8, and the financial statements are shown in Exhibit B.9 on page 576.

After the financial statements are prepared, we are *almost* ready to begin another accounting cycle. First, we must get our general ledger ready for a new fiscal year.

Step 7: Prepare Closing Entries

L.O.4
Describe the closing process and explain why it is necessary.

Temporary accounts are the revenue, expense, and dividends accounts.

Revenue accounts, expense accounts, and dividends are **temporary accounts**. The balances in those accounts will be transferred to retained earnings at the end of each period; therefore, they will start each new period with a zero balance.

Think about the accounting equation and the work sheet we've been using throughout this book to record transactions. We've been listing the revenues and expenses in the retained earnings column, because they increase and decrease the owner's claims to the assets of the business. The balance sheet will balance only when the revenue and expense amounts are incorporated into the retained earnings balance. The net amount of revenues minus expenses—net income—is incorporated into retained earnings when we prepare the statement of changes in shareholders' equity.

EXHIBIT B.7

Adjusted T-Accounts for Clint's Consulting Co., Inc.

ASSETS	=	LIABILITIES	+	SHAREHOLDER'S EQUITY

Cash
(asset)

1-1	2,000	400	1-3
1-2	4,000	500	1-4
1-5	9,000	350	1-6
1-9	4,000	4,150	1-7
		600	1-8
EB	13,000		

Accounts receivable
(asset)

A-1	**3,000**		
EB	3,000		

Supplies
(asset)

1-3	400	**325**	**A-4**
EB	75		

Notes payable
(liability)

1-7	4,000	4,000	1-2
		0	EB

Unearned consulting fees
(liability)

A-3	**2,000**	4,000	1-9
		2,000	EB

Salaries payable
(liability)

		50	**A-2**
		50	EB

Common stock
(shareholder's equity)

		2,000	1-1
		2,000	EB

Dividends
(a special temporary account)

1-8	600		
EB	600		

Consulting fees
(revenue)

		9,000	1-5
		3,000	**A-1**
		2,000	**A-3**
		14,000	EB

Advertising expense
(expense)

1-4	500		
EB	500		

Salary expense
(expense)

1-6	350		
A-2	**50**		
EB	400		

Interest expense
(expense)

1-7	150		
EB	150		

Supplies expense
(expense)

A-4	**325**		
EB	325		

EXHIBIT B.8

Adjusted Trial Balance for Clint's Consulting Company, Inc., for the Year 2011

Account	DR	CR
Cash	$13,000	
Accounts receivable	3,000	
Supplies	75	
Notes payable		$ 0
Salaries payable		50
Unearned consulting fees		2,000
Common stock		2,000
Dividends	600	
Consulting fees		14,000
Advertising expense	500	
Interest expense	150	
Salary expense	400	
Supplies expense	325	
	$18,050	$18,050

EXHIBIT B.9

**Financial Statements for
Clint's Consulting
Company, Inc., for 2011**

Clint's Consulting Company, Inc.
Income Statement
For the Year Ended December 31, 2011

Revenue
 Consulting fees $14,000
Expenses
 Advertising $500
 Salaries 400
 Supplies 325
 Interest 150
Total expenses 1,375
Net income $12,625

Clint's Consulting Company, Inc.
Statement of Changes in Shareholder's Equity
For the Year Ended December 31, 2011

Beginning common stock .... $ 0
 Common stock issued during the year 2,000
Ending common stock .... $ 2,000
Beginning retained earnings .... $ 0
Net income for the year 12,625
Dividends .... (600)
Ending retained earnings 12,025
Total shareholder's equity $14,025

Clint's Consulting Company, Inc.
Balance Sheet
At December 31, 2011

Assets		Liabilities and Shareholder's Equity	
Current Assets		Current Liabilities	
Cash	$13,000	Salaries payable	$ 50
Accounts receivable	3,000	Unearned consulting fees	2,000
Supplies	75	Total current liabilities	2,050
		Shareholder's equity	
		Common stock	2,000
Total assets	$16,075	Retained earnings	12,025
		Total shareholder's equity	14,025
		Total liabilities and	
		shareholder's equity	$16,075

Clint's Consulting Company, Inc.
Statement of Cash Flows
For the Year Ended December 31, 2011

Cash from operating activities
 Cash collected from customers $13,000
 Cash paid for supplies .... (400)
 Cash paid for interest .... (150)
 Cash paid to employees .... (350)
 Cash paid for advertising .... (500)
Net cash from operating activities $11,600
Cash from investing activities 0
Cash from financing activities
 Cash from issue of stock .... $ 2,000
 Proceeds from bank loan 4,000
 Repayment of bank loan .... (4,000)
 Cash dividends paid .... (600)
Net cash from financing activities 1,400
Net increase in cash $13,000
Beginning cash balance .... $ 0
Ending cash balance $13,000

From a bookkeeping perspective, **closing the accounts** is done—meaning to bring their balances to zero—with journal entries. Each account receives a debit or a credit to close it. For example, if a revenue account has a balance of $300—which would be a credit balance—the account is closed with a debit for $300. The corresponding credit in that closing journal entry is to retained earnings. Thus, closing the revenue account increases retained earnings. On the other hand, closing an expense account will decrease retained earnings. For example, if an expense account has a balance of $100—which would be a debit balance—the accounts is closed with a credit for $100. The corresponding debit for that closing journal entry is to retained earnings. Closing the expense accounts decreases retained earnings.

> **Closing the accounts** means bringing the balances in the temporary accounts to zero.

Keep in mind the reason for having revenue accounts and expense accounts. For a single accounting period, usually a year, the revenues and expenses are recorded separately from retained earnings so that we can report them on the year's income statement. Then we want those amounts included in retained earnings, and we want the revenue and expense accounts to be "empty" so they can start over, ready for amounts that will come during the coming year. Remember, the income statement covers a single accounting period. We don't want to mix up last year's revenue with this year's revenue in our revenue accounts or last year's expenses with this year's expenses in our expense accounts. The process of bringing these accounts to a zero balance is called closing the accounts, and the journal entries are called closing entries. We cannot close the revenue accounts and expense accounts until we have prepared the financial statements.

Asset accounts, liability accounts, and shareholders' equity accounts are **permanent accounts**, or **real accounts**. A balance in any of these accounts is carried over from one period to the next. For example, the amount of cash shown in the cash account will never be zero (unless we spend our last cent). Think about your own personal records. If you keep track of your cash (like your checking account), you will have a continuous record of your cash balance. On the date of a personal balance sheet, you would see how much cash you have on that particular date. As the next year begins, you still have that cash. It doesn't go away because a new year begins.

> **Permanent accounts** or **real accounts** are accounts that are never closed. They are the asset, liability, and shareholders' equity accounts.

To get a better idea of what we mean by the continuous record in a permanent account, let's consider a simple example of a *temporary* account. Suppose you were keeping a list of your grocery expenses for the year. At the end of the year, after you have reported the amount of those expenses on your annual income statement, you would want to start a new list for the next year. Because an income statement reports expenses for a period of time—a year, in this example—your grocery expenses for one year would be reported on *one* income statement, but those expenses would not apply to the following year. You would want the grocery expense account to be empty when you begin the next year. Expense amounts must apply to a specific time period for them to make sense.

Exhibit B.10 shows the closing journal entries for Clint's Consulting, which are recorded after the financial statements are prepared.

EXHIBIT B.10

Closing Entries

Ref.	Date	Journal entry	DR	CR
c-1	12/31	Consulting fees	14,000	
		Retained earnings		14,000
		To close revenue account		
c-2	12/31	Retained earnings	1,375	
		Advertising expense		500
		Salary expense		400
		Supplies expense		325
		Interest expense		150
		To close the expense accounts		
c-3	12/31	Retained earnings	600	
		Dividends		600
		To close dividends		

Your Turn B-3

Simple Company has one revenue account with a balance of $5,000 at year end and one expense account with a balance of $3,000. Prepare the closing journal entries for Simple Company.

MORE ABOUT CLOSING ENTRIES AND THE RELATIONSHIP BETWEEN THE INCOME STATEMENT AND THE BALANCE SHEET. Why do we bother with closing entries? They set the stage for the next accounting period by zeroing out the balances of all the temporary accounts. This is necessary because these accounts keep track of amounts that go to the income statement, which gives us the net income figure for *one specific period.* Without zeroing out the accounts, net income would include revenues or expenses for more than one period. Closing entries transfer the period's net income (or loss) to the retained earnings account (or to the owner's capital account in a sole proprietorship), so closing entries are the means by which net income flows downstream from the income statement through the statement of changes in shareholders' equity to the balance sheet.

Here's how the revenue amounts and expense amounts flow through the financial statements:

- *Income statement.* We present the details of net income—the revenues and expenses—on the income statement. The bottom line is net income.
- *Statement of changes in shareholders' equity.* We show net income as an addition to shareholders' equity on the statement of changes in shareholders' equity.
- *Balance sheet.* We present the total amount of shareholders' equity—which includes net income—on the balance sheet.

After we've used the revenue account balances and the expense account balances to prepare the income statement and after that information has flowed through to the balance sheet, we are ready to close the revenue accounts and expense accounts. That's the formal way of getting the correct balance in retained earnings. Here are the steps in detail to record closing entries:

1. Transfer all credit balances from the revenue accounts to retained earnings. This is done with a closing entry. The closing journal entry will have a debit to each of the revenue accounts for the entire balance of each—to bring them to a zero balance. The corresponding credit will be to retained earnings for the total amount of the period's revenue.

2. Transfer all debit balances from the expense accounts to retained earnings. This is done with a closing entry. The closing journal entry will have a debit to retained earnings and credits to all the expense accounts for their entire balances to bring them to a zero balance. The debit to retained earnings will be for the total amount of the period's expenses.

3. Transfer the dividends account balance to retained earnings. When a distribution is made to the shareholders of a corporation, a special account—dividends—is often used. This account is a temporary account that carries a debit balance. (When the dividends are declared and paid, dividends is debited and cash is credited.) The dividends account is closed directly to retained earnings. The amount of the dividends is not included on the income statement, but it is shown on the statement of changes in shareholders' equity. The journal entry to close this account will have a credit to dividends and a debit to retained earnings.

Look at the closing entries posted to Clint's T-accounts, shown in bold print in Exhibit B.11. Notice how the revenue and expense accounts have a zero balance.

When closing is done, there is one step left to completing our record keeping for the year. That step is preparing a postclosing trial balance.

Step 8: Preparing a Postclosing Trial Balance

A **postclosing trial balance** is a list of all the accounts and their debit balances or credit balances, prepared after the temporary accounts have been closed. Only balance sheet accounts will appear on the postclosing trial balance.

The final step in the accounting cycle is to prepare a **postclosing trial balance**. Remember, *post* means *after* (like *pre* means *before*). After the temporary accounts are closed, preparing a trial balance—a list of all the accounts with their debit or credit balances—accomplishes two things:

- It is a final check of the equality of debits and credits in the general ledger.
- It confirms that we are ready to start our next period with only real (permanent) accounts.

The postclosing trial balance for Clint's Consulting is shown in Exhibit B.12.

EXHIBIT B.11

T-Accounts with Closing Entries for Clint's Consulting Company, Inc.

ASSETS	=	LIABILITIES	+	SHAREHOLDER'S EQUITY

Cash
(asset)

1-1	2,000	400	1-3
1-2	4,000	500	1-4
1-5	9,000	350	1-6
1-9	4,000	4,150	1-7
		600	1-8
EB*	13,000		

Supplies
(asset)

1-3	400	325	A-4
EB	75		

Accounts receivable
(asset)

A-1	3,000		
EB	3,000		

Notes payable
(liability)

1-7	4,000	4,000	1-2
		0	EB

Unearned consulting fees
(liability)

A-3	2,000	4,000	1-9
		2,000	EB

Salaries payable
(liability)

		50	A-2
		50	EB

Common stock
(shareholder's equity)

		2,000	1-1
		2,000	EB

Retained earnings
(shareholder's equity)

C-2	**1,375**	**C-1**	**14,000**
C-3	**600**		
		EB	12,025

Dividends
(a special temporary account)

1-8	600	**C-3**	**600**

Consulting fees
(revenue)

		9,000	1-5
		3,000	A-1
		2,000	A-3
C-1	**14,000**	14,000	EB

Advertising expense
(expense)

1-4	500	**C-2**	**500**

Salary expense
(expense)

1-6	350		
A-2	50	**C-2**	**400**

Interest expense
(expense)

1-7	150	**C-2**	**150**

Supplies expense
(expense)

A-4	325	**C-2**	**325**

*EB=ending balance

Account	DR	CR
Cash	$13,000	
Accounts receivable	3,000	
Supplies	75	
Notes payable		$ 0
Salaries payable		50
Unearned consulting fees		2,000
Common stock		2,000
Retained earnings		12,025
Totals	$16,075	$16,075

EXHIBIT B.12

Postclosing Trial Balance for Clint's Consulting Company, Inc., at December 31, 2011

Review and Summary of the Accounting Cycle

To summarize, there are several steps in the process of preparing financial statements using a traditional general ledger system. Together, they are called the *accounting cycle.*

1. Record the transactions in the journal.
2. Post the journal entries to the ledger.
3. Prepare an unadjusted trial balance.
4. Adjust the accounts at the end of the period—record the adjusting journal entries and post them to the general ledger.
5. Prepare an adjusted trial balance.
6. Prepare the financial statements.
7. Close the temporary accounts to get ready for the next accounting period.
8. Prepare a postclosing trial balance.

UNDERSTANDING

Business

Enterprise Resource Planning Systems

Enterprise resource planning (ERP) systems are changing the way businesses manage, process, and use information. ERP systems are computer-based software programs designed to process an organization's transactions and integrate information for planning, production, financial reporting, and customer service. It is estimated that the majority of companies with annual revenues exceeding $1 billion have implemented ERP systems.

Exactly how ERP systems operate varies from company to company, depending on the company's needs.

- ERP systems are packaged software designed for business environments, both traditional and Web based. *Packaged software* means that the software is commercially available—for purchase or lease—from a software vendor, as opposed to being developed in-house.
- An ERP system is composed of modules relating to specific functions. There are modules for *accounting,* including financial, managerial, and international accounting; *logistics,* including materials requirement planning, production, distribution, sales management, and customer management; and *human resources,* including payroll, benefits, and compensation management.
- All the modules work together with a common database. This creates an enterprise-wide system instead of separate, independent systems for each function of the business.
- ERP systems are integrated in terms of software, but not hardware. So, even though two companies may buy ERP packages from the same vendor, the way the system is used will likely be very different.
- Because of their popularity and growth, the large ERP vendors are familiar to many of us—SAP, Oracle,

PeopleSoft, J.D. Edwards, and BAAN. Together these vendors hold a major share of the ERP market and provide their system packages along with training to their clients around the world.

Companies implement ERP systems to do the following:

- Consolidate their systems and eliminate redundant data entry and data storage
- Decrease their computer operating costs
- Better manage their business processes
- Accommodate international currencies and international languages
- Standardize policies and procedures
- Enhance and speed up financial reporting
- Improve decision making
- Improve productivity
- Improve profitability

In spite of all the potential benefits of ERP systems, there are drawbacks. ERP systems are costly to implement, with total implementation costs running into the millions of dollars. Switching to a new system requires extensive and costly training for those who will use the system.

Given the widespread adoption of ERP systems, it is apparent that the market perceives the ERP system benefits to outweigh the costs. Therefore, whether you choose to go into accounting, information technology, finance, marketing, or management, it is likely that you will encounter an ERP system. However, given the speed with which technology changes, the ERP systems that you will encounter will be even more complex with greater capacities than the ones in existence today.

Team Shirts Transactions for March 2010 in a General Ledger System

We've already analyzed the transactions for Team Shirts for the third month of business, and prepared the financial statements for March in Chapter 3. Let's repeat the accounting cycle for the same month, this time using debits and credits. The transactions for March are shown in Exhibit B.13. Each transaction is recorded as an entry in the general journal, chronologically as it occurs during the company's business activity. Then each transaction is posted to the general ledger (we'll use T-accounts). At March 31, we'll post the adjusting entries needed to prepare the four financial statements. After following along through the adjusted T-accounts, you will prepare the financial statements.

EXHIBIT B.13

Transactions for Team Shirts for March

March 1	Purchased computer for $4,000 with $1,000 down and a three-month, 12% note for $3,000. The computer is expected to last for three years and have a residual value of $400.
March 10	Paid the rest of last month's advertising bill, $50.
March 15	Collected accounts receivable of $150 from customers from February.
March 20	Paid for February purchases—paying off the accounts payable balance—of $800.
March 24	Purchased 250 shirts for the inventory @ $4 each for cash, $1,000.
March 27	Sold 200 shirts for $10 each, all on account, for total sales of $2,000.

To use a general ledger system, we need to set up the accounts with their balances on March 1, 2010. Exhibit B.14 on the following page shows all the accounts with their beginning balances (indicated with BB). Those accounts, in the Team Shirts general ledger, will remain with the beginning balances until we post journal entries from the month's transactions.

The first step in the accounting cycle is to record each transaction in chronological order in the journal—as each occurs in the business. Look at each transaction and its corresponding journal entry in Exhibit B.15 on page 583. Notice, for each journal entry there is the following:

- The date of the transaction
- The account names
- Equality between the debits and credits—in every journal entry
- A brief explanation of the transaction

Study each journal entry to make sure you understand how the transaction was recorded.

The remaining steps in the accounting cycle begin with posting journal entries to the general ledger. Some computerized accounting systems automatically do this. Because we are using T-accounts to represent the general ledger, that's where we will start. Here are the remaining steps to take us to the financial statements:

1. Post the journal entries for March using the T-accounts shown in Exhibit B.14.
2. Then prepare an unadjusted trial balance at March 31.
3. Make the necessary adjusting journal entries at March 31 and post them to the T-accounts. For Team Shirts, three adjustments need to be made before the financial statements can be prepared. The adjustments are as follows:
   a. Depreciation expense for the computer: $100
   b. Interest payable on the note: $30
   c. Insurance expense for the month: $50
4. Prepare an *adjusted* trial balance at March 31, 2010.
5. Use the adjusted trial balance to prepare the four basic financial statements.

EXHIBIT B.14

T-Accounts for Team Shirts at the Beginning of March

ASSETS	=	LIABILITIES	+	SHAREHOLDER'S EQUITY

Cash (asset)		Accounts payable (liability)		Common stock (shareholder's equity)
BB* 6,695		800 **BB**		5,000 **BB**

Accounts receivable (asset)		Other payables (liability)		Retained earnings (shareholder's equity)
BB 150		50 **BB**		1,220 **BB**

Inventory (asset)		Notes payable (liability)		Sales (revenue)
BB 100				

Prepaid insurance (asset)		Interest payable (liability)		Cost of goods sold (expense)
BB 125				

Computers (asset)				Insurance expense (expense)

Accumulated depreciation (contra asset)				Interest expense (expense)

				Depreciation expense (expense)

*BB = beginning balance

Journal Entries for March 2010

Ref.	Date	Journal entry	DR	CR
3-1	3/01/10	Computer	4,000	
		Cash		1,000
		Notes payable		3,000
		To record the purchase of a computer with a cash payment of $1,000 and a note payable of $3,000		
3-2	3/10/10	Other payables	50	
		Cash		50
		To record the payment of a liability for last month's advertising expense		
3-3	3/15/10	Cash	150	
		Accounts receivable		150
		To record the collection of accounts receivable		
3-4	3/20/10	Accounts payable	800	
		Cash		800
		To record payment to vendor for last month's purchase		
3-5	3/24/10	Inventory	1,000	
		Cash		1,000
		To record the purchase of 250 T-shirts at $4 each, paid for in cash		
3-6a	3/27/10	Accounts receivable	2,000	
		Sales		2,000
		To record the sale of 200 T-shirts, on account		
3-6b	3/27/10	Cost of goods sold	800	
		Inventory		800
		To record the expense *cost of goods sold* and reduce the inventory by 200 × $4		

Here are the details for each step:

1. T-accounts are shown in the answer to part (3).
2.

Team Shirts
Unadjusted Trial Balance
March 31, 2010

Cash	$ 3,995	
Accounts receivable	2,000	
Inventory	300	
Prepaid insurance	125	
Computer	4,000	
Notes payable		$ 3,000
Common stock		5,000
Retained earnings		1,220
Sales		2,000
Cost of goods sold	800	
Totals	$11,220	$11,220

3. Adjusting journal entries and explanations follow:

   a. The computer has been used for one full month, so you must record depreciation expense. The cost was $4,000, an estimated residual value of $400, and a three year useful life. Each year the equipment will be depreciated by $1,200 [($4,000 – $400)/3 years]. That makes the depreciation expense $100 per month.

Date	Transaction	Debit	Credit
March 31, 2010	Depreciation expense	100	
	Accumulated depreciation		100
	To record the depreciation expense for March		Adj-1

   b. Team Shirts signed a $3,000 note on March 1 to purchase the computer. A month has passed, and Team Shirts needs to accrue the interest expense on that note in the amount of $30 ($3,000 × 0.12 × 1/12).

Date	Transaction	Debit	Credit
March 31, 2010	Interest expense	30	
	Interest payable		30
	To record the interest expense for March		Adj-2

   c. In mid-February, Team Shirts purchased three months of insurance for $150, which is $50 per month. On the March 1 balance sheet, there is a current asset called prepaid insurance in the amount of $125. A full month's worth of insurance expense needs to be recorded for the month of March. That amount will be deducted from prepaid insurance.

Date	Transaction	Debit	Credit
March 31, 2010	Insurance expense	50	
	Prepaid insurance		50
	To record the insurance expense for March		Adj-3

Following are the T-accounts with adjustments for March 2010 posted. (Ending balances in each account are shown with a double underline.)

ASSETS	=	LIABILITIES	+	SHAREHOLDER'S EQUITY

ASSETS

Cash (asset)

*BB	6,695	1,000	3-1
		50	3-2
3-3	150	800	3-4
		1,000	3-5
**EB	3,995		

Accounts receivable (asset)

BB	150	150	3-3
3-6a	2,000		
EB	2,000		

Inventory (asset)

BB	100		
3-5	1,000	800	3-6b
EB	300		

Prepaid Insurance (asset)

BB	125	50	Adj-3
EB	75		

Computers (asset)

3-1	4,000	
EB	4,000	

Accumulated depreciation (contra asset)

	100	Adj-1
	100	EB

LIABILITIES

Accounts payable (liability)

3-4	800	800	BB
		0	EB

Other payables (liability)

3-2	50	50	BB
		0	EB

Notes payable (liability)

	3,000	3-1
	3,000	EB

Interest payable (liability)

	30	Adj-2
	30	EB

SHAREHOLDER'S EQUITY

Common stock (shareholder's equity)

	5,000	BB
	5,000	EB

Retained Earnings (shareholder's equity)

	1,220	BB
	1,220	EB

Sales (revenue)

	2,000	3-6a
	2,000	EB

Cost of goods sold (expense)

3-6b	800	
EB	800	

Insurance expense (expense)

Adj-3	50	
EB	50	

Interest expense (expense)

Adj-2	30	
EB	30	

Depreciation expense (expense)

Adj-1	100	
EB	100	

*BB = beginning balance
**EB = ending balance

4.

Team Shirts
Adjusted Trial Balance
March 31, 2010

Cash	$ 3,995	
Accounts receivable	2,000	
Inventory	300	
Prepaid insurance	75	
Computer	4,000	
Accumulated depreciation		$ 100
Interest payable		30
Notes payable		3,000
Common stock		5,000
Retained earnings		1,220
Sales		2,000
Cost of goods sold	800	
Insurance expense	50	
Depreciation expense	100	
Interest expense	30	
Totals	*$11,350*	*$11,350*

5. The financial statements are as follows:

Team Shirts
Income Statement
For the Month Ended March 31, 2010

Sales revenue		$2,000
Expenses		
Cost of goods sold	$800	
Depreciation expense	100	
Insurance expense	50	
Interest expense	30	980
Net income		$1,020

Team Shirts
Statement of Changes in Shareholder's Equity
For the Month Ended March 31, 2010

Beginning common stock	$5,000	
Common stock issued during the month	0	
Ending common stock		$5,000
Beginning retained earnings	$1,220	
Net income for the month	1,020	
Dividends declared	0	
Ending retained earnings		2,240
Total shareholder's equity		$7,240

Team Shirts
Balance Sheet
At March 31, 2010

Assets		Liabilities and Shareholder's equity	
Current assets		**Current liabilities**	
Cash	$ 3,995	Interest payable	$ 30
Accounts receivable	2,000	Notes payable	3,000
Inventory	300	Total current liabilities	3,030
Prepaid insurance	75	**Shareholder's equity**	
Total current assets	6,370	Common stock	5,000
Computer (net of $100		Retained earnings	2,240
accumulated depreciation)	3,900	Total shareholder's equity	7,240
		Total liabilities and	
Total assets	$10,270	shareholder's equity	$10,270

Team Shirts
Statement of Cash Flows
For the Month Ended March 31, 2010

Cash from operating activities:

Cash collected from customers	$ 150	
Cash paid to vendors	(1,800)	
Cash paid for advertising	(50)	
Net cash from operating activities		$(1,700)
Cash from investing activities:		
Purchase of computer*	$(1,000)	(1,000)
Cash from financing activities:		0
Net increase (decrease) in cash		$(2,700)
Beginning cash balance		6,695
Ending cash balance		$ 3,995

*Computer was purchased for $4,000. A note was signed for $3,000 and cash paid was $1,000.

You have seen these exact financial statements before. When we used the accounting equation to keep track of the transactions in Chapter 3, the results were the same as using the general ledger system here. No matter how we do the record keeping, the financial statements are the same. The mechanics of any accounting system—stand-alone or integrated with an enterprise resource planning system—must be designed to produce the information needed for the basic financial statements according to GAAP.

Key Terms for Appendix B

Accounting cycle (p. 568)
Adjusted trial balance
  (p. 574)
Closing the accounts (p. 577)
Credit (p. 565)
Debit (p. 565)
Dividend (p. 570)

Enterprise-wide resource
  planning system (ERP)
  (p. 564)
General ledger (p. 563)
General ledger system (p. 563)
Journal (p. 564)
Permanent accounts (p. 577)

Postclosing trial balance
  (p. 578)
Posting (p. 564)
Real accounts (p. 577)
Trial balance (p. 565)
Temporary accounts (p. 574)
Withdrawal (p. 570)

Answers to YOUR TURN Questions

Your Turn B-1

Account title	Expense	Revenue	Asset	Liability	Shareholders' equity
Accounts payable				CR (Credit)	
Accounts receivable			DR		
Advertising expense	DR				
Cash			DR		
Depreciation expense	DR				
Furniture and fixtures			DR		
Accumulated depreciation			(Contra) CR		
Unearned fees				CR	
Salary expense	DR				
Common stock					CR
Rent expense	DR				
Retained earnings					CR
(Earned) Fees		CR			
Land			DR		
Building			DR		

Your Turn B-2

Date	Transaction	Debit	Credit
December 31, 2010	Salaries expense	300	
	Salaries payable		300
	To accrue salary expense for December 2010		

No expense will be recognized in January 2011. It was recognized in December 2010, but will be paid in January 2011.

Date	Transaction	Debit	Credit
January 3, 2011	Salaries payable	300	
	Cash		300
	To record the cash payment of salaries payable		

Your Turn B-3

Date	Transaction	Debit	Credit
December 31, 2010	Revenue account	5,000	
	Retained earnings		5,000
	To close the revenue account to retained earnings		

Date	Transaction	Debit	Credit
December 31, 2010	Retained earnings	3,000	
	Expense account		3,000
	To close the expense account to retained earnings		

Questions

1. What is the general ledger system and what are its advantages?
2. What is an account?
3. What is the trial balance?
4. Which accounts are permanent and which are temporary?
5. What is the normal balance in each of these accounts?

Accounts receivable
Accounts payable
Common stock
Retained earnings
Sales revenue
Salary expense
Cash
Supplies expense
Distributions (dividends)
Inventory
Bonds payable
Cost of goods sold

6. What are the basic steps in the accounting cycle?
7. Can accounting transactions be recorded directly into the general ledger accounts? What is the advantage of using a journal first?
8. Is a credit a good thing or a bad thing? Explain.
9. What are adjusting entries and why are they necessary?

Multiple-Choice Questions

1. Evans Company completes a service engagement and bills a customer $50,000 on June 19, 2010. Included in the journal entry to record this transaction will be a:
   a. debit to cash, $50,000.
   b. credit to cash, $50,000.
   c. credit to accounts receivable, $50,000.
   d. credit to service revenue, $50,000.
2. A trial balance is a:
   a. list of all the accounts with a six-digit account number used by a business.
   b. place to record increases and decreases to a particular financial statement item's balance.
   c. chronological list of all recorded transactions.
   d. list of all the accounts used by the business along with each account's debit or credit balance at a point in time.
3. Bob Frederick, the owner of a delivery business, wants to know the balance of cash, accounts receivable, and sales on April 15 of the current period. Bob should look at what part of his accounting system?
   a. The journal
   b. The ledger
   c. The balance sheet
   d. The subsidiary journal
4. What is accomplished by preparing an unadjusted trial balance?
   a. A firm can make sure the debits equal the credits in the accounting system.
   b. A firm can make sure there are no errors in the accounting system.
   c. A firm can identify accruals and deferrals.
   d. All of the above
5. The data needed to prepare a trial balance comes from the
   a. journal.
   b. ledger.
   c. balance sheet.
   d. post-closing income statement.

6. If the income statement includes revenues earned even if the cash has not been collected from customers yet, it means that the
   a. closing entries have not been completed yet.
   b. journal has errors in it.
   c. accrual basis of accounting is being used.
   d. adjusting entries have not been done yet.

7. Myers Company pays its employees every Friday for a five-day workweek (Monday through Friday). The employees earn $3,000 per day of work. If the company pays the employees $15,000 on Friday, October 2, 2009, the entry into the journal would include
   a. a debit to wages expense for $15,000.
   b. a debit to cash for $15,000.
   c. a credit to wages payable for $15,000.
   d. a debit to cash for $3,000.

8. Jules, Inc., had a June 1, 2010, balance of office supplies of $100. During June, the company purchased $900 more of the office supplies in exchange for cash. On June 30, 2010, the supplies were counted and it was determined that $200 worth of office supplies were left unused. The adjusting journal entry should include a
   a. debit to supplies expense of $800.
   b. debit to office supplies of $900.
   c. credit to cash for $200.
   d. credit to supplies expense of $800.

9. Why should closing entries be completed at the end of each period?
   a. Certain accounts are not needed in the future.
   b. It allows the trial balance and financial statements to be prepared.
   c. All accounts must begin the next period at zero.
   d. Temporary accounts need to start the next period with a zero balance.

10. Which of the following accounts should NOT be closed?
    a. Accounts receivable
    b. Interest revenue
    c. Sales revenue
    d. Wages expense

MyAccountingLab

All of the A exercises can be found within MyAccountingLab, an online homework and practice environment.

Short Exercises
Set A

SEB-1A. *Normal account balances. (LO 1).* Given the following accounts, tell whether the normal balance of each account is a debit (DR) or a credit (CR):

1. _____ Supplies
2. _____ Insurance expense
3. _____ Income tax expense
4. _____ Salaries payable
5. _____ Retained earnings

SEB-2A. *Recognize revenue and record journal entries. (LO 1, 2, 3).* Indicate which of the following events would result in recognizing revenue for the year in which the described event takes place; indicate the amount and the account. Give the journal entry that would be made in each case. (Take the selling company's point of view.)

1. Seminole Boosters has received $75,000 in advanced ticket sales for next year's football games.
2. Comcast Cable collected several accounts that were outstanding from last year. Usually accounts are collected in advance; but in this case, the customer received the cable services last year but didn't pay until this year.
3. Customers paid $6,500 in advance for services to be rendered next year.

SEB-3A. *Recognize expenses and record journal entries. (LO 1, 2, 3).* Indicate which of the following events would result in recognizing expenses for the year in which the described event takes place; give the journal entry. (Take the company's point of view.)

1. Bright Shirts, Inc., sold 1,500 T-shirts to the FSU Bookstore for $16,500 cash. Bright origi-
   nally paid $4,500 for the shirts.
2. Home Industries, Inc., received a utility bill for the last month of the year in the amount of
   $575 but won't actually pay it until next year.
3. Waterline, Inc., paid $8,600 for a two-year insurance policy—for the current year and for
   next year.

SEB-4A. *Relate the accounting equation to debits and credits. (LO 1).* Following are selected
transactions for Ralph's Surfshop, Inc., that occurred during the month of December. For each
transaction, tell which accounts will be affected and how (debit or credit).

1. The company paid $650 cash for a truck rental for December.
2. The company purchased inventory for $4,500 on account.

SEB-5A. *Record journal entries. (LO 1).* The following selected transactions for ABC, Inc.,
occurred during the month of April. Give the journal entry for each.

1. The company incurred operating expenses for $800, paid in cash.
2. The company purchased supplies for $500 cash, to be used during May.

SEB-6A. *Effect of transactions on cash. (LO 1).* How do the following transactions affect Jolly,
Inc.'s cash account? (Tell if the result would be a debit or a credit.)

1. The firm gave customers $1,500 cash for returned merchandise.
2. The firm issued stock to investors for $7,750 cash.

SEB-7A. *Effect of transactions on the liability and shareholders' equity accounts. (LO 1).* How
do the following transactions affect the liability and shareholders' equity accounts for Slow
Pokes, Inc., during 2010? (Tell if the result would be a debit or a credit.)

1. The company earned $12,000 in sales for the year.
2. An estimated $2,500 will be due for yearly income taxes, payable in 2011.

SEB-8A. *Effect of transactions on accounts. (LO 1).* Determine how the accounts would be
affected (increase or decrease and debit or credit) for the following transactions occurring in April
2011 for Computer Solutions, Inc.:

1. The company paid $4,500 for next year's rent.
2. The company paid $2,000 of its accounts payable, owed for previously purchased inventory.
3. The company declared and distributed $500 of dividends.

SEB-9A. *Determine permanent or temporary accounts. (LO 4).* For each of the following
accounts, tell whether it is a permanent account or a temporary account:

1. _____ Merchandise inventory
2. _____ Insurance expense
3. _____ Interest expense
4. _____ Income taxes payable
5. _____ Common stock

Set B

SEB-10B. *Normal account balances. (LO 1).* Given the following accounts, tell whether the normal balance of each account is a debit (DR) or a credit (CR):

1. _____ Interest receivable
2. _____ Accounts payable
3. _____ Common stock
4. _____ Service revenue
5. _____ Prepaid rent

SEB-11B. *Recognize revenue and record journal entries. (LO 1, 2, 3).* Indicate which of the following events would result in recognizing revenue for the year in which the described event takes place; indicate the amount and the account. Give the journal entry that would be made in each case. (Take the selling company's point of view.)

1. Dell Inc. sold a computer system worth $10,000; the customer financed the purchase because he didn't have any cash.
2. Steel USA is producing 3 tons of steel for American Cans. It costs $4,500 per ton to produce, but American Cans has promised to pay $7,750 per ton when it receives the steel. Steel USA will probably ship it in the near future.

SEB-12B. *Recognize expenses and record journal entries. (LO 1, 2, 3).* Indicate which of the following events would result in recognizing expenses for the year in which the described event takes place; give the journal entry. (Take the T-shirt company's point of view.)

1. T-Shirts Plus, Inc., paid employees $6,000 for work performed during the prior year.
2. T-Shirts Plus, Inc., purchased 15,000 T-shirts for its inventory for $30,000 on account.
3. T-Shirts Plus, Inc., paid the factory cash for the 15,000 shirts purchased.

SEB-13B. *Relate the accounting equation to debits and credits. (LO 1).* Following are selected transactions for Jenna Enterprises, Inc., that occurred during the month of December. For each transaction, tell which accounts will be affected and how (debit or credit).

1. The company issued common stock to investors for $15,000 cash.
2. The company paid $1,500 cash for December rent for a warehouse.

SEB-14B. *Record journal entries. (LO 1).* The following selected transactions for Wilson's Consulting, Inc., occurred during the month of April. Give the journal entry for each.

1. The firm provided services to customers for $10,000. Seventy percent was paid with cash and thirty percent was on account.
2. The firm paid $1,000 for part of a $3,000 purchase made in March on account.

SEB-15B. *Effect of transactions on cash. (LO 1).* How do the following transactions affect Toys, Toys, Toys, Inc.'s cash account? (Tell if the result would be a debit or a credit.)

1. The company purchased $6,000 of baby cribs for cash.
2. The company sold one of its buildings, allowing the buyer to give it a short-term note for $135,000.
3. The employees were paid $5,400 cash in sales commissions.

SEB-16B. *Effect of transactions on the liability and shareholders' equity accounts. (LO 1).* How do the following transactions affect the liability and shareholders' equity accounts for Fast Signs, Inc., during 2010? (Tell if the result would be a debit or a credit.)

1. The company paid the remainder of a $3,000 loan.
2. The company obtained a loan for $10,000.

SEB-17B. *Effect of transactions on accounts. (LO 1).* Determine how the accounts would be affected (increase or decrease and debit or credit) for the following transactions occurring in January 2009 for Networking Solutions, Inc.:

1. The company received $25,000 cash from the owner in exchange for common stock.
2. The company purchased $10,000 of new office computers on account.
3. The company sold $2,500 of inventory for cash.

SEB-18B. *Determine permanent or temporary accounts. (LO 4).* For each of the following accounts, tell whether it is a permanent account or a temporary account:

1. _____ Cash
2. _____ Accounts payable
3. _____ Common stock
4. _____ Sales revenue
5. _____ Prepaid rent

Exercises
Set A

All of the A exercises can be found within MyAccountingLab, an online homework and practice environment.

EB-19A. *Record transactions to T-accounts. (LO 1, 2).* Record the following transactions for Bradford, Inc., in T-accounts and tell how each affects assets, liabilities, or stockholders' equity. The year end for Bradford, Inc., is June 30.

1. On September 1, the company issued a $6,000 note at 4%, both interest and principal due in one year.
2. On October 1, the company rented a copy machine and paid one year of rent in advance at a rate of $300 per month.
3. On December 30, the company purchased an insurance policy for a term of one year, beginning immediately. The cost was $600, paid in cash.
4. On March 1, the company purchased $600 worth of supplies for cash. The company started the year with $100 worth of supplies on hand.
5. Over the course of the year, the company earned $75,000 of service revenue, collected in cash.

EB-20A. *Record adjustments to T-accounts. (LO 1, 2, 3).* Use the information from EB-19A, including your answers to 1–5, to make the necessary adjustments to Bradford's accounts in preparation for the year-end financial statements. The company had $75 worth of supplies on hand at the end of the fiscal year.

EB-21A. *Record transactions to T-accounts and prepare an unadjusted trial balance. (LO 1, 2).* Matt opened a bookstore on April 1, 2011, selling new and used books. Matt contributed $4,000 in exchange for common stock to start the business, Matt's Books. Record each of the following transactions into T-accounts for the new company. Calculate the account balances and prepare an unadjusted trial balance at June 30, 2011.

1. On April 1, the company bought $2,000 of new books from its supplier with cash.
2. On April 30, customers brought in used books and the company purchased them for $550 cash.
3. On June 30, $1,000 of new books were sold for $3,000. Half of these sales were on account.
4. On June 30, the company sold all the used books for $1,500 cash.

EB-22A. *Record transactions to T-accounts and prepare an unadjusted trial balance. (LO 1, 2).* The trial balance of Whisper Lane Productions, Inc., on March 1, 2012, lists the company's assets, liabilities, and shareholders' equity on that date.

	Trial Balance	
Account Title	Debit	Credit
Cash	$15,000	
Accounts receivable	5,700	
Accounts payable		$ 3,200
Common stock		9,000
Retained earnings		8,500
Total	$20,700	$20,700

During March, Whisper Lane completed the following transactions:

1. The company borrowed $6,000 from the bank with a short-term note payable.
2. Whisper Lane paid cash of $12,000 to acquire land.
3. The company performed service for a customer and collected the cash of $3,500.
4. Whisper Lane purchased supplies on account, $225.
5. The company performed service for a customer on account, $1,800.

Set up T-accounts for the accounts given in the March 1 trial balance. Then post the preceding transactions to the accounts. Calculate the account balances and prepare an unadjusted trial balance at March 31.

EB-23A. *Recognize adjusting and closing entries. (LO 3, 4).* Use the information from EB-22A to identify the accounts that will likely need to be adjusted before the monthly financial statements are prepared. What additional information would you need in each case to make the appropriate adjustment? Which accounts will need to be closed at the end of the accounting period and why?

EB-24A. *Record closing entries and compute net income. (LO 4).* Given the following adjusted trial balance, record the appropriate closing entries. What is net income for the year?

Brett's Bait & Tackle, Inc.
Adjusted Trial Balance
June 30, 2011

	Debit	Credit
Cash	$ 13,000	
Accounts receivable	20,000	
Prepaid rent	28,000	
Supplies	21,500	
Equipment	20,000	
Accumulated depreciation		$ 9,000
Land	64,000	
Accounts payable		23,000
Notes payable		25,000
Interest payable		2,000
Common stock		51,000
Retained earnings		29,500[a]
Dividends	4,000	
Sales		94,000
Cost of goods sold	45,000	
Depreciation expense	3,000	
Salary expense	15,000	
Totals	$233,500	$233,500

[a]Retained earnings at July 1, 2010. (No accounts have been closed.)

EB-25A. *Record journal entries, record adjusting entries, and explain the accounting cycle. (LO 1, 2, 3, 4).* The Problem Solvers Consulting Corporation began business in 2010. The following transactions took place during January:

January	1	The owners invested $75,000 in exchange for common stock.
	1	The company borrowed $10,000 from a local bank with a 3% note and a six-month term. Both the principal and interest will be repaid in six months.
	1	The company purchased computer equipment for $13,200 cash. It should last four years, with no residual value.
	6	Supplies were purchased on account for $500.
	8	Office rent of $700 for January was paid in cash.
	20	The company received $3,150 from a customer for services to be performed in February.
	31	Consulting services performed during January on account totaled $12,000.

31   The company paid salaries of $6,500 to employees.

31   The company paid $300 to the supplies vendor as part of the $500 owed to the vendor from the purchase on January 6. The company only paid part of the invoice because it only used $300 worth of the supplies in January.

Give the journal entry for each transaction. Provide the reason for each entry. Then, make the necessary adjusting entries at January 31, 2010. What else should be done to finish the accounting cycle for the month?

EB-26A. *Record journal entries, post to T-accounts, and prepare an unadjusted trial balance. (LO 1, 2).* Ray & Peters CPAs decided to open its own tax practice, Tax Specialists, Inc. The following transactions are the events that occurred during May, the company's first month:

May 1   Ray and Peters each donated $20,000 cash in exchange for common stock. They also signed a note with National Bank for $25,000.

2   Tax Specialists paid $28,000 prepaid rent for the first year.

11   Office equipment was purchased on account for $17,500.

16   The company purchased insurance for two years with $6,500 cash. The policy was effective June 1.

18   A discolored piece of office equipment arrived and the supplier agreed to remove $3,500 from Tax Specialists' account.

25   The company purchased some office furniture on sale worth $10,000 on account.

28   Tax Specialists paid off balance owed on the equipment.

30   An office manager was hired at a rate of $110 a day. The start date is June 1.

Give the journal entry for each transaction. Set up the required T-accounts and post the entries to these accounts. Prepare an unadjusted trial balance.

Set B

EB-27B. *Record transactions to T-accounts. (LO 1, 2).* Record the following transactions for Krall Pianos, Inc., in T-accounts and tell how each affects assets, liabilities, or shareholders' equity. The year end for Krall Pianos, Inc., is December 31.

1. On March 1, Krall Pianos issued a $15,000 note at 6%, both interest and principal due in one year.
2. On May 1, Krall Pianos rented a warehouse and paid $6,750 for two years of rent in advance.
3. Krall Pianos purchased an insurance policy for a term of three years on July 1, beginning immediately. The cost was $5,400, paid in cash.
4. The company purchased $475 worth of supplies for cash on November 1. The company started the year with $375 worth of supplies on hand.
5. Over the course of the year, Krall Pianos earned $54,500 for cash sales of $15,000 worth of inventory, collected in cash. The company started the year with $20,000 in inventory.

EB-28B. *Record adjustments to T-accounts. (LO 1, 2, 3).* Use the information from EB-27B, including your answers to 1–5, to make the necessary adjustments to Krall Pianos' accounts in preparation for the year-end financial statements. At year end, there were $175 worth of supplies on hand.

EB-29B. *Record transactions to T-accounts and prepare an unadjusted trial balance. (LO 1, 2).* Flynt Freedman opened Flynt's Brew, Inc., on March 1, 2010, selling gourmet coffees, teas, and desserts. Flynt contributed $5,500 in exchange for common stock to start the business. Record the following transactions into T-accounts for Flynt's. Calculate the account balances and prepare an unadjusted trial balance at March 31, 2010.

1. On March 1, the company purchased $2,750 of inventory from the supplier with cash.
2. The company purchased equipment for $350 cash on March 15.
3. On March 30, the company paid $500 for operating expenses.
4. By the end of the month, the company had earned sales revenue of $6,500 by selling $2,000 of inventory. Cash sales were $6,000 and a local business who purchased items for a conference still owed Flynt's $500.

EB-30B. *Record transactions to T-accounts and prepare an unadjusted trial balance. (LO 1, 2).* The trial balance of Jewel's Diamond Dazzles, Inc., on November 1, 2011, lists the company's assets, liabilities, and shareholders' equity on that date.

Trial Balance

Account title	Debit	Credit
Cash	$18,000	
Accounts receivable	6,500	
Inventory	7,500	
Accounts payable		$11,700
Common stock		8,800
Retained earnings		11,500
Total	$32,000	$32,000

During November, Diamond Dazzles completed the following transactions:

1. The company borrowed $5,000 from the bank with a short-term note payable.
2. Diamond Dazzles paid cash of $8,500 to acquire land.
3. The company sold $5,000 of inventory to customers and collected the cash of $15,000.
4. Diamond Dazzles purchased supplies on credit, $375.
5. The company sold $1,000 of inventory to customers for $2,500 on account.

Set up T-accounts for the accounts given in the November 1 trial balance. Then post the preceding transactions to the accounts. Calculate the account balances and prepare an unadjusted trial balance at November 30.

EB-31B. *Recognize adjusting and closing entries. (LO 3, 4).* Use the information from EB-30B to identify the accounts that will likely need to be adjusted before the monthly financial statements are prepared. What additional information would you need in each case to make the appropriate adjustment? Which accounts will need to be closed at the end of the accounting period and why?

EB-32B. *Record closing entries and compute net income. (LO 4).* Given the following adjusted trial balance, record the appropriate closing entries. What is net income for the year?

SR Ski Shop, Inc.
Adjusted Trial Balance
December 31, 2011

	Debit	Credit
Cash	$ 15,000	
Accounts receivable	23,000	
Prepaid rent	19,600	
Supplies	21,750	
Equipment	18,000	
Accumulated depreciation		$ 10,000
Land	72,000	
Accounts payable		27,650
Notes payable		30,000
Interest payable		3,610
Common stock		45,500
Retained earnings		26,370[a]
Dividends	2,000	
Sales		69,220
Cost of goods sold	15,000	
Depreciation expense	5,000	
Salaries expense	21,000	
Totals	$212,350	$212,350

[a]Retained earnings at January 1, 2011. (No accounts have been closed.)

EB-33B. *Record journal entries, record adjusting entries, and explain the accounting cycle. (LO 1, 2, 3, 4).* Health & Nutrition Importance, Inc., began business July 1, 2012. The following transactions took place during July:

July 1   The owners invested $75,000 in exchange for common stock.

    1   The company borrowed $15,000 from a local bank with a 4% note and a six-month term. Both the principal and interest will be repaid in six months.

    1   The company purchased health equipment for $28,500 cash. It should last five years, with no residual value.

    5   The company purchased supplies on account for $750.

   15   The company paid rent of $675 for July in cash.

   23   The company received $3,500 in customer dues (service revenues) for the month of August.

   31   The company performed consulting services during July on account that totaled $15,000.

   31   The company paid salaries of $6,000 to employees.

   31   The company paid $500 to the supplies vendor as part of the $750 owed to the vendor from the purchase on July 5. The company only paid part of the invoice because it only used $500 worth of the supplies in July.

Give the journal entry for each transaction. Provide the reason for each entry. Then, make the necessary adjusting entries at July 31, 2012. What else should be done to finish the accounting cycle for the month?

EB-34B. *Record journal entries, post to T-accounts, and prepare an unadjusted trial balance. (LO 1, 2).* Julie Jones decided to open her own dry cleaning shop, Prestige Dry Cleaners, Inc. The following transactions are the events that occurred during April 2013, the company's first month:

April 1   Julie contributed $45,000 cash in exchange for common stock. She also signed a note with 1st Regional Bank for $30,000.

    3   The company rented a store at a shopping center and paid $14,400 prepaid rent for the first year.

   10   The company purchased dry cleaning equipment on account for $21,250.

   19   The company purchased insurance for three years with $5,400 cash. The policy was effective May 1.

   21   Part of the equipment purchased on April 10 was damaged. The supplier agreed to remove $3,150 from Prestige Dry Cleaners' account.

   24   The company purchased furniture for $6,000 for Julie's office on account.

   27   The company paid off the balance owed on the equipment.

   30   Three employees were hired at a rate of $56 a day each. Their start date is May 1.

Give the journal entry for each transaction. Set up the required T-accounts and post the entries to these accounts. Prepare an unadjusted trial balance.

Problems
Set A

PB-35A. *Prepare a trial balance and financial statements. (LO 1, 2).* The following is account information for Vision Corporation as of December 31, 2011, after all adjustments have been made:

Revenue	$20,000
Prepaid rent	1,000
Equipment	12,500
Accumulated depreciation, equipment	3,000
Common stock	4,000
Retained earnings	2,500[a]
Accounts receivable	5,000
Accounts payable	2,000
Salaries expense	2,000
Depreciation expense	1,000
Cash	1,000
Inventory	8,000
Dividends	1,000

[a]Balance at January 1, 2011.

Requirement

Prepare a trial balance at December 31, 2011, income statement and statement of changes in shareholders' equity for the year ended December 31, 2011, and balance sheet at December 31, 2011.

PB-36A. *Record journal entries, post to T-accounts, and prepare an unadjusted trial balance. (LO 1, 2).* Architectural Design and Associates, Inc., began business on May 1, 2011. The following transactions were entered into by the firm during its first two months of business, May and June:

May	1	Common stock was issued to investors in the amount of $275,000.
	1	Architectural Design signed a long-term note with 1st Regional Bank for $65,000.
	9	The company purchased an office building with cash for $130,500.
	13	Equipment was purchased on account for $35,000.
	20	Supplies worth $3,500 were purchased with cash.
	27	Architectural Design paid for equipment that was purchased on May 13.
	30	The company purchased a two-year insurance policy that began on June 1 with cash for $4,800.
	30	The city utility bill for $675 was received by Architectural Design. The utility bill is always due the 15th of the following month and will be paid then.
June	1	Architectural Design purchased some inventory on account for $50,000.
	3	The company purchased some advertising in a local newspaper and on a local radio station for $5,000 cash.
	15	May's utility bill for $675 was paid. (Note that the bill was recorded as a payable in May.)
	30	June salaries of $12,500 were owed to employees who started during the month. Salaries are always paid the last day of the month earned.
	30	Architectural Design earned service revenues of $60,000 for the month, of which $15,000 were on account.
	30	Architectural Design received the city utility bill for $625.

Requirements

1. Give the journal entry for each transaction.
2. Post each transaction to T-accounts.
3. Prepare an unadjusted trial balance.

PB-37A. *Prepare closing entries and financial statements. (LO 3, 4).* Tia's Cotton Fabrics, Inc., has the following account information on its adjusted trial balance:

Tia's Cotton Fabrics, Inc.
Adjusted Trial Balance
March 31, 2012

	Debit	Credit
Cash	$ 24,000	
Accounts receivable	28,000	
Prepaid rent	9,500	
Supplies	15,250	
Equipment	25,000	
Accumulated depreciation		$ 7,500
Land	44,000	
Accounts payable		24,805
Notes payable		17,650
Interest payable		2,175
Common stock		23,650[a]
Retained earnings		35,000[b]
Dividends	4,000	
Sales		97,675
Gain on sale of equipment		7,450
Cost of goods sold	51,475	
Depreciation expense	2,500	
Salaries expense	12,180	
Totals	$215,905	$215,905

[a]Balance at April 1, 2011. (No common stock has been issued during the year.)
[b]Balance at April 1, 2011. (No closing entries have been made.)

Requirement

Prepare the necessary closing entries and the income statement, statement of changes in share-holders' equity for the year ended March 31, 2012, and balance sheet as of March 31, 2012.

PB-38A. *Record adjusting journal entries, post to T-accounts, and prepare closing entries. (LO 1, 2, 3, 4).* Gourmet Teas & Coffee, Inc., has the following account balances at December 31, the end of the fiscal year:

Prepaid insurance	$ 4,000
Rental income	35,670
Unearned rental income	3,800
Accumulated depreciation	7,625
Salaries payable	5,550
Property tax expense	4,398
Depreciation expense	7,625
Salaries expense	10,400

The following information is available at the end of the year:
a. $1,000 worth of the prepaid insurance has not yet expired.
b. Of the unearned rental income only $1,500 remains unearned.
c. The business actually owes salaries of $5,500; the accountant recorded $50 extra by mistake.
d. The company owes an additional $4,700 in property taxes, not yet recorded.
e. Due to a clerical error, the depreciation expense amount is incorrect. It has been recalculated, and the total depreciation expense should be $8,750 for the year.

Requirements

1. Prepare the journal entries necessary to adjust the accounts.
2. Use T-accounts to compute and present the balances in these accounts after the adjustments have been posted.
3. Prepare the closing entries.

PB-39A. *Record business transactions and prepare financial statements. (LO 1, 2, 3, 4).* Sally opened a tropical fish store as a corporation and called it Exotic_Aquatics.com, selling only via the Internet. During 2011, the first year of business, Sally's company had the following transactions:

    a. The business was started with Sally's contribution of $16,500 in exchange for common stock on January 1.

    b. The company borrowed $10,000 from First American Bank at 7.5% for 12 months on January 1.

    c. The company purchased $6,000 in inventory for cash on February 15.

    d. The company paid $3,600 of rent to a Webmaster on June 30 for use of a maintained Web site for two years starting July 1.

    e. The company had cash sales of $11,100 for 2011 with cost of goods sold of $2,500.

    f. The company paid $1,050 in advertising fees.

Requirements

1. Post the preceding transactions to T-accounts to determine the balance of each account on December 31, 2011; include any adjusting entries necessary.
2. Prepare the adjusted trial balance at December 31, 2011, the income statement, statement of changes in shareholders' equity, and a statement of cash flows for the year ended December 31, 2011, and the balance sheet at December 31, 2011.
3. Prepare the closing entries and the postclosing trial balance at December 31, 2011.

PB-40A. *Record business transactions. (LO 1, 2, 3, 4).* A partial list of transactions from We Do Windows Company during 2010 follows:

    a. In January, Keith and Rachel each donated $22,500 in exchange for common stock to start the business.

    b. On February 1, the company paid $6,000 for two years rent in advance.

    c. During the year, the company purchased $10,000 of supplies for cash.

    d. On March 15, 2010, the shop obtained necessary equipment for $12,000 cash. The equipment should last for five years. The company will take a full year of depreciation in 2010.

    e. On April 1, 2010, the shop paid an annual insurance premium of $1,000, for coverage beginning April 1.

    f. On June 1, 2010, to increase business, the company paid for a year of advertising for $1,020.

    g. On November 1, 2010, the company obtained a three-month loan for $30,000 at 4.5% from Three Rivers Bank payable on February 1, 2011.

    h. As of December 31, 2010, cash revenues totaled $30,000.

    i. In December, the company entered into a contract with a local rental company to do all its window washing in 2011 for $8,000, payable in four installments. The first installment was collected from the rental company in December 2010.

    j. On December 31, the company paid $1,000 in cash dividends.

    Note: at the end of the year, remaining supplies totaled $2,000.

Requirements

1. Give the journal entries for the transactions; include any adjusting entries.
2. Post the transactions to T-accounts and prepare the adjusted trial balance at December 31, 2010.
3. Prepare the closing entries and post-closing trial balance for We Do Windows Company at December 31, 2010.

PB-41A. *Analyze business transactions and prepare financial statements. (LO 1, 2, 3, 4).* The accounting department for Fun in the Great Outdoors Resort, Inc., recorded the following journal entries for 2012, the first year of business:

	Description	Debit	Credit
a.	Cash	50,000	
	Common stock		50,000
b.	Office supplies	300	
	Accounts payable		300
c.	Prepaid rent	12,000	
	Cash		12,000
d.	Building	225,000	
	Note payable		225,000
e.	Cash	5,000	
	Unearned rent revenue		5,000
f.	Utilities expense	225	
	Cash		225
g.	Accounts payable	300	
	Cash		300
h.	Cash	12,000	
	Rent revenue		12,000
i.	Unearned rent revenue	3,000	
	Rent revenue		3,000
j.	Supplies expense	130	
	Supplies		130
k.	Rent expense	6,000	
	Prepaid rent		6,000
l.	Interest expense	100	
	Interest payable		100
m.	Depreciation expense	1,500	
	Accumulated depreciation—building		1,500
n.	Dividends	5,000	
	Cash		5,000
o.	Salary expense	1,200	
	Salaries payable		1,200

Fun in the Great Outdoors generates revenue by renting mountainside cottages to vacationers to the area. When a reservation is made in advance, Fun in the Great Outdoors collects half the week's rent to hold the reservation; however, Fun in the Great Outdoors does not require reservations, and sometimes customers will come in to rent a unit the same day. These types of transactions require that Fun in the Great Outdoors' accounting department record some cash receipts as unearned revenues and others as earned revenues.

Requirements

1. Explain the transaction or event that resulted in each journal entry.
2. Post entries (a) through (o) to T-accounts and calculate the balance in each account.
3. Did Fun in the Great Outdoors generate net income or net loss for the period ending December 31, 2012? How can you tell?
4. Prepare the four financial statements required at year end.
5. Prepare the closing entries.

PB-42A. *Record business transactions and prepare financial statements. (LO 1, 2, 3, 4).* The accounting records for Shelby & Sammy Pet Boarders, Inc., contained the following balances as of January 1, 2011:

Assets		Liabilities and Shareholders' Equity	
Cash	$40,000	Accounts payable	$17,000
Accounts receivable	16,500	Common stock	45,000
Land	20,000	Retained earnings	14,500
Totals	$76,500		$76,500

The following accounting events apply to Shelby & Sammy Pet Boarders, Inc.'s 2011 fiscal year:

January	1	The company acquired an additional $20,000 cash from the owners by issuing common stock.
	1	Pet Boarders purchased a computer that cost $15,000 for cash. The computer had no salvage value and a three-year useful life.
March	1	The company borrowed $10,000 by issuing a one-year note at 12%.
May	1	The company paid $2,400 cash in advance for a one-year lease for office space.
June	1	The company made a $5,000 cash distribution to the shareholders.
July	1	The company purchased land that cost $10,000 cash.
August	1	Cash payments on accounts payable amounted to $6,000.
	1	Pet Boarders received $9,600 cash in advance for 12 months of service to be performed monthly for the next year, beginning on receipt of payment.
September	1	Pet Boarders sold land for $13,000 cash. The land originally cost $13,000.
October	1	Pet Boarders purchased $1,300 of supplies on account.
November	1	Pet Boarders purchased a one-year, $20,000 certificate of deposit at 6%.
December	31	The company earned service revenue on account during the year that amounted to $40,000.
	31	Cash collections from accounts receivable amounted to $44,000.
	31	The company incurred other operating expenses on account during the year of $6,000.
	31	Salaries that had been earned by the sales staff but not yet paid amounted to $2,300.
	31	Supplies worth $200 were on hand at the end of the period.
	31	Based on the preceding transaction data, there are five additional adjustments that need to be made before the financial statements can be prepared.

Requirement

Post the journal entries directly to T-accounts, make the appropriate adjustments, prepare an adjusted trial balance, and prepare the financial statements (all four) for 2011. Then prepare the closing entries and the postclosing trial balance.

Set B

PB-43B. *Prepare a trial balance and financial statements. (LO 1, 2).* The following account information pertains to Dean Furniture, Inc., as of December 31, 2010, after adjustments:

Sales	$22,000	Other revenue	$13,000
Prepaid advertising	2,000	Equipment (net)	20,000
Common stock	14,000	Accounts receivable	2,500
Accounts payable	3,000	Cost of goods sold	11,000
Operating expenses	5,500	Cash	11,300
Inventory	15,200	Dividends	2,000
Retained earnings	17,500		

Requirement

Prepare a trial balance at December 31, 2010, income statement and statement of changes in shareholders' equity for the year ended December 31, 2010, and balance sheet as of December 31, 2010.

PB-44B. *Record journal entries, post to T-accounts, and prepare an unadjusted trial balance. (LO 1, 2).* Emerging Electronics, Inc., began business on February 1, 2012. The following transactions occurred during its first two months of business, February and March:

February	1	Common stock was issued to investors in the amount of $305,000.
	1	The company signed a long-term note with National Bank for $70,000.
	8	The company purchased a building with cash for $125,000.
	12	The company purchased equipment on account for $45,000.
	20	The company purchased supplies worth $4,300 for cash.
	28	The company paid for the equipment that was purchased on February 12.
	29	The company purchased a two-year insurance policy that began on March 1 with cash for $5,000.
	29	The company received the city utility bill for $475. The utility bill is always due the 12th of the following month and will be paid then.
March	1	The company purchased inventory on account for $65,000.
	3	The company purchased some advertising in a local newspaper and on a local radio station for $3,500 cash.
	12	February's utility bill for $475 was paid (note that the bill was recorded as a payable in February).
	31	The company paid employees for work done, $14,150 cash.
	31	The company earned sales revenues of $125,000 for the month, of which $35,000 were on account. Cost of inventory sold was $31,250.
	31	The company received the city utility bill for $425.

Requirement

Give the journal entry for each transaction. Post each transaction to T-accounts. Prepare an unadjusted trial balance at March 31, 2012.

PB-45B. *Prepare closing entries and financial statements. (LO 3, 4).* Following is an adjusted trial balance from Village Lighting Solutions, Inc.:

Village Lighting Solutions, Inc.
Adjusted Trial Balance
December 31, 2011

	Debit	Credit
Cash	$ 31,655	
Accounts receivable	52,000	
Prepaid rent	11,250	
Prepaid insurance	5,800	
Equipment	40,000	
Accumulated depreciation		$ 10,000
Land	25,755	
Salaries payable		1,250
Notes payable		16,875
Interest payable		1,820
Common stock		25,000[a]
Retained earnings		44,000[b]
Dividends	3,500	
Sales		151,595
Cost of goods sold	45,880	
Rent expense	13,000	
Insurance expense	1,200	
Depreciation expense	5,000	
Salaries expense	15,500	
Totals	$250,540	$250,540

[a]Balance at January 1, 2011. (No common stock has been issued during the year.)
[b]Balance at January 1, 2011. (No closing entries have been made.)

Requirement

Prepare the necessary closing entries, the income statement, and the statement of changes in shareholders' equity for the year ended December 31, 2011, and balance sheet as of December 31, 2011.

PB-46B. *Record adjusting journal entries, post to T-accounts, and prepare closing entries. (LO 1, 2, 3, 4).* Medical Massage, Inc., has the following account balances at the end of the year (partial list of accounts):

Service revenue	$34,320
Prepaid insurance	$4,000
Unearned service revenue	3,200
Salaries payable	2,550
Equipment	40,000
Accumulated depreciation	12,000
Taxes expense	3,650
Depreciation expense	5,000
Salaries expense	8,250

The following information is also available:
a. The company accountant forgot to depreciate a new deluxe massage table that was purchased at the beginning of the year. The table cost $4,000, has a useful life of four years, and has no expected residual value.
b. The unearned service revenue consists of gift certificates sold during the year. Medical Massage has lost track of customers redeeming certificates, but only $1,200 of the gift certificates have not been redeemed.
c. The company currently owes employees $200 of salaries in addition to the amount already recorded.
d. The company owes $1,075 in real estate taxes in addition to the taxes already recorded.
e. Half of the $4,000 insurance policy has expired.

Requirements
1. Prepare the adjusting journal entries necessary at year end.
2. Use T-accounts to compute and present the balances in these accounts after the adjustments have been posted.
3. Prepare the closing journal entries.

PB-47B. *Record business transactions and prepare financial statements. (LO 1, 2, 3, 4).* Gigi and Sue started Granny Apple Delicious, Inc., on January 1, 2011, to sell their famous applesauce. The following transactions occurred during the year:
a. Gigi and Sue started the business by contributing $15,000 each in exchange for common stock on January 1.
b. Also on January 1, the company borrowed $20,000 from Local Bank at 5.5%. The loan was for one year.
c. The company purchased $10,000 worth of apples and other inventory for cash during the year.
d. The company grew and needed to rent a shop. It paid $27,000 for rent on the shop for 18 months, beginning July 1.
e. Granny Apple Delicious, Inc., sold $36,000 worth of applesauce for cash during the first fiscal year. Of the inventory purchased in item (c) only $1,000 remained at year end.
f. During the year, Granny Apple Delicious, Inc., paid $1,525 in operating expenses.

Requirements
1. Post the preceding transactions to T-accounts to determine the balance of each account on December 31, 2011; include any adjusting transactions necessary.
2. Prepare the adjusted trial balance, the income statement, statement of changes in shareholders' equity, balance sheet, and a statement of cash flows at year end.
3. Prepare the closing entries and the postclosing trial balance at year end.

PB-48B. *Record business transactions. (LO 1, 2, 3, 4).* The following information is a partial list of transactions from Home Cleaning Service, Inc.:

  a. Tina, Don, and Daly each donated $5,000 in exchange for common stock to start the business on January 1, 2011.
  b. On March 1, Home Cleaning paid $3,000 cash for a two-year insurance policy that was effective immediately.
  c. On March 15, the company purchased $8,000 of supplies on account.
  d. On April 5, the company purchased some cleaning equipment for $10,000 cash. The equipment should last for five years with no residual value. Home Cleaning will take a full year of depreciation in 2011.
  e. On May 1, Home Cleaning purchased a year's worth of advertising in a local newspaper for $1,200 cash.
  f. On September 1, Home Cleaning obtained a nine-month loan for $15,000 at 5% from City National Bank, with interest and principal payable on June 1, 2012.
  g. On December 31, Home Cleaning paid $5,000 of what it owed on account for supplies from item (c); the company had $2,000 of the supplies still on hand at the end of the year.
  h. For the year ended December 31, 2011, Home Cleaning had revenues of $26,225. The cash had been received for all but $3,000.
  i. Home Cleaning paid $2,000 in cash dividends on December 31, 2011.

Requirements

  1. Give the journal entries for the transactions; include any adjusting entries.
  2. Post the transactions to T-accounts and prepare the adjusted trial balance at December 31, 2011.
  3. Prepare the closing entries and post-closing trial balance for Home Cleaning Service, Inc., at December 31, 2011.

PB-49B. *Analyze business transactions and prepare financial statements. (LO 2, 3, 4).* The accounting department for Entertainment Activities, Inc., recorded the following journal entries for the fiscal year ended June 30, 2012:

	Description	Debit	Credit
a.	Cash	150,000	
	Common stock		150,000
b.	Office supplies	475	
	Accounts payable		475
c.	Prepaid rent	18,000	
	Cash		18,000
d.	Building	375,000	
	Note payable		375,000
e.	Cash	16,000	
	Unearned ticket revenue		16,000
f.	Utilities expense	525	
	Cash		525
g.	Accounts payable	475	
	Cash		475
h.	Cash	50,000	
	Ticket revenue		50,000
i.	Unearned ticket revenue	10,000	
	Ticket revenue		10,000
j.	Office supplies expense	300	
	Office supplies		300
k.	Rent expense	7,000	
	Prepaid rent		7,000
l.	Interest expense	225	
	Interest payable		225

m.	Depreciation expense		2,000	
	Accumulated depreciation—building			2,000
n.	Dividends		7,500	
	Cash			7,500
o.	Salary expense		5,500	
	Salaries payable			5,500

Entertainment Activities generates revenue by selling tickets for local events such as concerts, fights, and sporting events. Sometimes tickets are sold in advance and sometimes customers will purchase their tickets the same day as the event. These types of transactions require that Entertainment Activities' accounting department record some cash receipts as unearned revenues and others as earned revenues.

Requirements

1. Explain the transaction or event that resulted in each journal entry.
2. Post entries (a) through (o) to T-accounts and calculate the balance in each account.
3. Did Entertainment Activities generate net income or net loss for the fiscal year ended June 30, 2012? How can you tell?
4. Prepare the four financial statements required at year end.
5. Prepare the closing entries.

PB-50B. *Record business transactions and prepare financial statements. (LO 1, 2, 3, 4).* The accounting records for Juan Electric Corporation contained the following balances as of December 31, 2010:

Assets		Liabilities and Shareholders' Equity	
Cash	$50,000	Accounts payable	$17,500
Accounts receivable	26,500	Common stock	48,600
Prepaid rent (through April 30, 2011)	3,600	Retained earnings	24,500
Land	10,500		
Totals	$90,600		$90,600

The following accounting events apply to Juan Electric Corporation's 2011 fiscal year:

January	1	Juan Electric purchased a computer that cost $18,000 for cash. The computer had no salvage value and a three-year useful life.
March	1	The company borrowed $20,000 by issuing a two-year note at 3%.
May	1	The company paid $6,000 cash in advance for an eight-month lease for office space. The lease started immediately.
June	1	The company paid cash dividends of $2,000 to the shareholders.
July	1	The company purchased land that cost $15,000 cash.
August	1	Cash payments on accounts payable amounted to $6,000.
	1	Juan Electric received $6,000 cash in advance for 12 months of service to be performed monthly, beginning on receipt of payment.
September	1	Juan Electric sold land for $13,000 cash. The land originally cost $15,000.
October	1	Juan Electric purchased $1,300 of supplies on account.
November	1	Juan Electric purchased a one-year, $10,000 certificate of deposit at 3%.
December	31	The company earned service revenue on account during the year that amounted to $50,000.
	31	Cash collections from accounts receivable amounted to $46,000.
	31	The company incurred other operating expenses on account during the year that amounted to $6,000.
Also:		Salaries that had been earned by the sales staff but not yet paid amounted to $2,300.
		There were $200 worth of supplies on hand at the end of the period.
		Based on the preceding transaction data, there are some additional adjustments that need to be made before the financial statements can be prepared.

Requirements
1. Give the journal entries for the transactions; include any adjusting entries.
2. Post the journal entries to T-accounts, prepare an adjusted trial balance, and then prepare the income statement, statement of changes in shareholders' equity, and statement of cash flows for the year ended December 31, 2011, and the balance sheet at December 31, 2011. Then, prepare the closing entries and the postclosing trial balance.

Financial Statement Analysis

Use the selection from the annual report of Books-A-Million, Inc., in Appendix A to answer the following questions:

1. When you look at the financial statements for Books-A-Million, can you tell if the company uses a general ledger accounting system? Explain.
2. Find at least four pieces of quantitative information contained in the selection from Books-A-Million's annual report that would not be found in a general ledger system.
3. Who are the auditors for Books-A-Million?
4. How does having an audit affect a firm's riskiness?

Critical Thinking Problem

Ethics

Companies often try to manage earnings by either recognizing revenue before it is actually earned according to GAAP or by deferring expenses that have been incurred. For example, to meet the targeted earnings for a specific period, a company may capitalize a cost that should be expensed. Read the following scenario and then decide how you would handle this opportunity to manage earnings.

You are a division manager of a large public company. Your bonus, as well as the bonuses of several of your best employees, is calculated on your division's net income targets that you must meet. This year that target is $1.5 million. You are authorized to sign off on any decision made within your division.

On December 15, 2011, your division of the company ordered $150,000 worth of supplies in anticipation of the seasonal rush. Most of them will be used by year end. These supplies were delivered on the evening of December 27. (Note that your company generally expenses supplies when purchased.) If you record this supplies expense this year, your net income will be $1.45 million and you will not meet the target and will therefore not receive your bonus of $25,000 that you have worked hard for. In addition, some of your key employees will not receive their bonuses. What would you do and why?

5

The Purchase and Sale of Inventory

LEARNING OBJECTIVES

When you are finished studying Chapter 5, you should be able to:

1. Calculate and record the purchase and sale of inventory.

2. Explain the two methods of inventory record keeping.

3. Define and calculate inventory using the four major inventory cost flow assumptions and explain how these methods affect the financial statements.

4. Analyze transactions and prepare financial statements after the purchase and sale of inventory.

5. Explain the lower-of-cost-or-market rule for valuing inventory.

6. Define and calculate the gross profit ratio and the inventory turnover ratio.

7. Describe the risks associated with inventory and the controls that minimize those risks.

8. (Appendix 5A) Describe and calculate the effect of inventory errors on the financial statements.

9. (Appendix 5B) Estimate inventory using the gross profit method.

ETHICS Matters

Watch Out for Disappearing Inventory

Firms lose billions of dollars from inventory theft. Individual firms, such as Bloomingdale's, Target, and Costco, will not talk about the numbers publicly, but the National Retail Federation gathers the data from hundreds of retailers. The bad news is that employee theft accounts for almost half of the over $30 billion annual losses from the disappearance of inventory.

What does that mean for a firm? Preston Turco, the owner of two specialty grocery stores in New York, uses elaborate security in his stores—special fraud detection software for cash registers, hidden cameras, store detectives, and an employee handprint identification device to clock his employees in and out. He has some other advice about reducing inventory theft: Hire and keep a happy and loyal staff.

We have all read about Bernie Madoff and John Sanford. They were at the center of frauds amounting to billions of dollars. But very few of us have read about the deli clerk who switched higher price tags for lower ones and tried to bribe a cashier to look the other way. That clerk is now in prison, according to Mr. Turco. It turns out that ethics matters at all levels of a business.

L.O.1
Calculate and record
the purchase and sale
of inventory.

Acquiring and Selling Merchandise

An Operating Cycle

The operating cycle for a merchandising firm is a series of business activities that describe how a company takes cash and turns it into more cash. Exhibit 5.1 shows the operating cycle for a typical merchandising firm. For example, Target Corporation starts with cash, buys inventory, sells that inventory to customers (creating accounts receivable if a person uses credit extended by Target), and then collects the cash from the customers. Not shown is the fact that the purchase of inventory will result in an accounts payable, which will reduce cash when paid. The operating cycle is complete when Target collects the cash.

EXHIBIT 5.1

An Operating Cycle

This diagram shows a typical operating cycle of a merchandising firm. The firm begins with cash, then it purchases inventory, sells the inventory, and ends with the collection of cash. Even though it is not shown here, accounts payable result from the purchase of inventory, and a cash outflow follows for its payment.

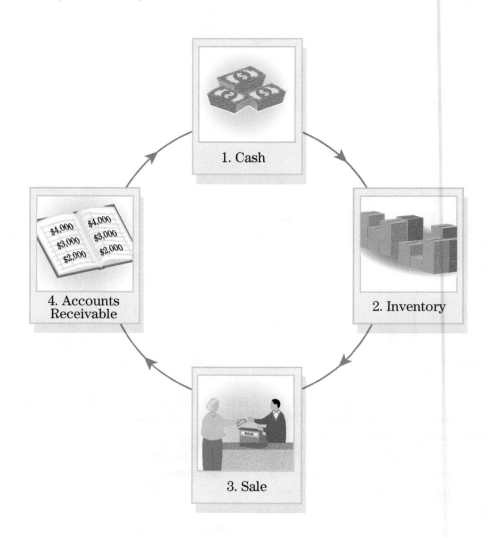

1. Cash

2. Inventory

3. Sale

4. Accounts Receivable

Acquiring Merchandise for Sale

Now that you know about the operating cycle of a business, we will focus on the activity of purchasing the inventory. Acquiring goods to sell is an important activity for merchandising firms. Stroll down the aisles of Staples, Inc., or OfficeMax Incorporated and imagine keeping track of all that merchandise. All goods owned and held for sale in the regular course of business are considered *merchandise* inventory. In contrast, supplies and equipment are used by most firms rather than sold by those firms. As a result, they are not considered inventory. Only the items a firm sells are considered inventory. Most large corporations have large purchasing departments dedicated exclusively to acquiring inventory. Regardless of their size, firms must keep meticulous track of their inventory purchases through their information systems. An information system refers to the way the firm records and reports its transactions, including inventory and sales.

A merchandising firm reports the inventory as a current asset until it is sold. According to the matching principle, inventory should be expensed in the period in which it is sold. So when it is sold, inventory becomes an expense—cost of goods sold. The revenue from the sales of particular goods and the cost of those goods sold during the period are matched—put on the same income statement. You can see that the value of the inventory affects both the balance sheet and the income statement. Does the value of inventory matter? On its January 31, 2009, balance sheet, Target had over $6.7 billion worth of inventory, making up over 15% of the company's total assets. That is a significant amount of the firm's assets.

We will look at the procedures for acquiring inventory and then focus on how to do the related record keeping.

Acquisition Process for Inventory

The process of acquiring inventory begins when someone in a firm decides to order merchandise for the inventory. The person requesting the purchase sends a document, called a purchase requisition, to the company's purchasing agent. For example, suppose that Office Depot, Inc., needs to order paper. The manager of the appropriate department would submit a purchase requisition in either hard copy or electronic form to the purchasing agent. The purchasing agent selects a vendor to provide the paper based on the vendor's prices, quality of goods or services needed, and the ability to deliver them in a timely manner. The purchasing agent specifies in a **purchase order**—a record of the company's request to a vendor for goods or services—what is needed, the prices, and the delivery time. A copy of the purchase order is sent to the vendor, and Office Depot keeps several copies for internal record keeping. However, no entry is made in the accounting system when a purchase order is submitted. The purchase won't be recorded until the goods are received. An example of a purchase order is shown in Exhibit 5.2.

A **purchase order** is a record of the company's request to a vendor for goods or services. It may be referred to as a P.O.

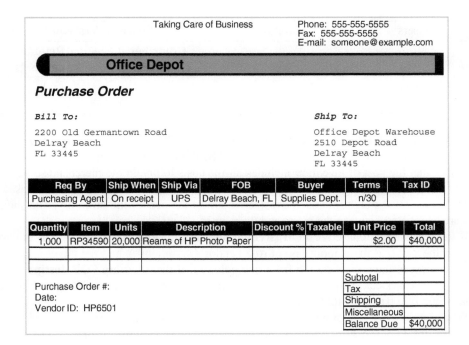

EXHIBIT 5.2

Purchase Order from Office Depot, Inc.

Office Depot's purchasing agent sends one copy of the purchase order to the receiving department and one to the accounts payable department. The receiving department will let the accounts payable department know when the goods have arrived. This is when the purchase will be recorded in the accounting records. Accounts payable will pay for the goods when it receives an invoice from the vendor to match with the purchase order. The process can be much more complicated, but it always includes cooperation between departments so that the company pays for only the goods ordered and received.

Modern technology has provided shorter and more efficient ways to manage inventory. At Wal-Mart Stores, Inc., for example, no one explicitly orders merchandise when it is needed. Using bar codes at the cash registers as each item is sold, the computerized inventory system is programmed to recognize when Wal-Mart should acquire more inventory, and the information goes directly to the vendor's computerized system. Even when the process is automated, the underlying transaction is the same: Inventory is acquired from a vendor to be available to sell to a firm's customers, and the firm wants to be sure it pays for only the merchandise it has received.

RECORDING PURCHASES. Now that you are familiar with the procedures for purchasing inventory, you are ready to learn to account for its cost. The cost of acquiring inventory includes all costs the company incurs to purchase the items and get them ready for sale. Many people in the firm need details about the cost of inventory, including the person requesting the goods, the CFO, and the CEO. This inventory information is also needed for the financial statements.

There are two ways for firms to record their inventory transactions—perpetual and periodic. These two different methods describe the timing of the firm's inventory record keeping. When a company uses a **perpetual inventory system**, the firm records every purchase of inventory directly to the inventory account at the time of the purchase. Similarly, each time an item is sold, the firm will remove the cost of the item—the cost of goods sold—from the inventory account. That is the way Team Shirts keeps track of its inventory. In the example that follows, Quality Lawn Mowers, a fictitious firm, will also use a perpetual inventory record-keeping system. We will discuss the **periodic inventory system** of record keeping—one in which the inventory account is updated only at the end of the period—later in the chapter.

We will use Quality Lawn Mowers for an example of how to account for the costs of inventory. Keep in mind that the company uses a perpetual inventory record-keeping system. Suppose that on June 1, Quality Lawn Mowers purchased 100 lawn mowers on account for $150 each from Black & Decker, a manufacturer of power tools and lawn mowers. This is how the transaction would be recorded in the accounting equation:

> The **perpetual inventory system** is a method of record keeping that involves updating the inventory account at the time of every purchase, sale, and return.

> The **periodic inventory system** is a method of record keeping that involves updating the inventory account only at the end of the accounting period.

Assets	=	Liabilities	+	Shareholders' equity		
				Contributed capital	+	Retained earnings
15,000 inventory		15,000 accounts payable				

WHO PAYS THE FREIGHT COSTS TO OBTAIN INVENTORY? The cost a company records in its inventory account is not always the amount quoted by the vendor. One reason is shipping costs. Remember that the cost of inventory includes all the costs to obtain the merchandise and get it ready to sell. When a merchandising firm pays the transportation costs for goods purchased, the freight cost is called freight-in and is considered part of the cost of the inventory. The shipping terms are negotiated between the buyer and the vendor.

If the terms of purchase are **FOB (free on board) shipping point**, the title to the goods passes to the buyer at the shipping point (the vendor's warehouse), and the buyer is responsible for the cost of the transportation from that point on. If the terms are **FOB destination**, the vendor—Black & Decker—pays for the transportation costs until the goods reach their destination, when title passes to the buyer.

When you are the vendor and you pay the shipping costs for goods to be delivered to your customers, the expense goes on your income statement as freight-out or delivery expense. Freight-out is an operating expense, whereas freight-in is part of the cost of the inventory. Exhibit 5.3 shows the relationships among the FOB shipping point, FOB destination, buyer, and vendor.

> **FOB (free on board) shipping point** means the buying firm pays the shipping costs. The amount is called freight-in and is included in the cost of the inventory.

> **FOB (free on board) destination** means that the vendor (selling firm) pays the shipping costs, so the buyer has no freight-in cost.

The details of inventory purchases, such as the shipping terms, can affect the cost of the inventory. A company must pay attention to these costs because such costs can make a difference in the profitability of the company.

Suppose the shipping cost for the 100 lawn mowers purchased by Quality Lawn Mowers was $343. If the shipping terms were FOB destination, then Black & Decker paid the shipping cost; and there is no record of the shipping cost in the books of Quality Lawn Mowers. However, suppose the terms were FOB shipping point. That means title changes hands at the point of shipping—the vendor's warehouse. Because Quality Lawn Mowers then owns the goods while they are in transit, Quality Lawn Mowers will pay the shipping costs. The $343 will be

EXHIBIT 5.3

Shipping Terms

Shipping terms determine who owns the goods, and at what point ownership of the goods changes. The firm that owns the goods while they are in transit must include the cost of those goods in its inventory.

Title passes here at *FOB shipping point*…or…Title passes here at *FOB destination*.

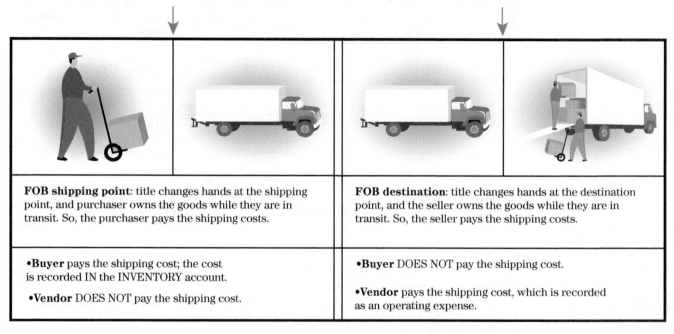

FOB shipping point: title changes hands at the shipping point, and purchaser owns the goods while they are in transit. So, the purchaser pays the shipping costs.	FOB destination: title changes hands at the destination point, and the seller owns the goods while they are in transit. So, the seller pays the shipping costs.
•**Buyer** pays the shipping cost; the cost is recorded IN the INVENTORY account. •**Vendor** DOES NOT pay the shipping cost.	•**Buyer** DOES NOT pay the shipping cost. •**Vendor** pays the shipping cost, which is recorded as an operating expense.

included as part of the cost of the inventory. Shipping costs are usually paid to the shipping company in cash. Here is how the transaction would be recorded in the accounting equation:

Assets	=	Liabilities	+	Shareholders' equity		
				Contributed capital	+	Retained earnings
343 inventory (343) cash						

In each separate situation, identify which company must pay the freight.

Your Turn 5-1

1. Company A purchased merchandise from Company X, FOB destination, for $10,000.
2. Company B purchased merchandise from Company Y, FOB shipping point, for $10,000.

PURCHASE RETURNS AND ALLOWANCES. Some goods may need to be returned to the vendor because the firm ordered too much inventory, ordered the wrong items, or found the goods slightly damaged. When a firm returns goods, the transaction is called a *purchase return*. In the firm's accounting system, the amount of purchase returns will be deducted from the cost of the inventory. Because the company puts the cost of the items in the inventory account, the balance in that account will be decreased when goods are returned. The details of the returns will be noted in another part of the company's information system. The firm wants to know exactly how much merchandise it is returning in any given accounting period. A firm should be sure it understands the vendor's return policy. Often, near the end of the year, a vendor will institute a very liberal return policy to make a sale. Nevertheless, the firm should buy only the amount of inventory it actually needs, not a larger amount with the idea of returning it when the next accounting period starts.

Goods damaged or defective may be kept by the purchaser with a cost reduction called a *purchase allowance*. When a company has a purchase allowance, it is like getting a discounted purchase price so the inventory account will be reduced. A purchase allowance is different from a purchase return because the goods are kept by the purchaser in the case of a purchase allowance.

When an item is returned, accounts payable, which shows the amount a firm owes its vendors, will be reduced. The inventory account will be decreased because the goods have been returned. Suppose Quality Lawn Mowers returned two of the lawn mowers because they were defective. This is how the transaction would be recorded in the accounting equation:

Assets	=	Liabilities	+	Shareholders' equity		
				Contributed capital	+	Retained earnings
(300) inventory		(300) accounts payable				

Similarly, if a vendor gives the firm a purchase allowance, the amount owed to the vendor is reduced by subtracting the amount from accounts payable. There will also be a reduction in the balance in the inventory account to reflect the reduced cost. Purchase returns and purchase allowances are often grouped together in one expression—**purchase returns and allowances**.

Purchase returns and allowances are amounts that decrease the cost of inventory due to returned or damaged merchandise.

PURCHASE DISCOUNTS. In addition to purchase returns and allowances, purchase discounts can also cause a difference between the vendor's quoted price and the actual cost to the purchasing firm. A **purchase discount** is a reduction in the purchase price in return for prompt payment. For example, a vendor offering a purchase discount for prompt payment from a customer would describe it in terms like this:

A **purchase discount** is a reduction in the price of an inventory purchase for prompt payment according to terms specified by the vendor.

2/10, n/30

This is read as "two-ten, net thirty" and means the vendor will give a 2% discount if the buyer pays for the entire purchase within 10 days of the invoice date. If not, the full amount is due within 30 days. A vendor may set any discount terms. What does 3/15, n/45 mean? The vendor will give a 3% discount if payment is made within 15 days. Otherwise, full payment must be made within 45 days. The number of days a customer has to pay an invoice starts on the day after the date of the invoice. For example, an invoice dated June 15 with the terms 2/10, n/30 gives the customer until June 25 to pay with the discount applied. The full amount is due by July 15.

A firm should take advantage of purchase discount offers from vendors whenever possible because they can amount to significant savings. If a vendor offers the terms 2/10, n/30, for example, the vendor is actually charging the firm 36% annual interest to use the money if the firm does not pay within the discount period and waits until the last day, the 30th day. Here is how we calculated the high interest rate of 36%. If the discount period expires, and the firm has not paid until the 30th day after the invoice date, the firm is "borrowing" the money from the vendor for an additional 20 days. Because the firm did not pay within the discount period, the vendor has earned 2% in 20 days. And, 2% interest on a "loan" over 20 days is the same as a 36% annual rate, determined with the help of a simple ratio:

$$2\% \div 20 \text{ days} = x \div 360$$

Solve for x and you get x = 36% annual interest—if you consider a year as having 360 days. Some companies borrow the money from the bank (at 10% or 12% annual interest) to take advantage of purchase discounts.

Suppose Black & Decker offers Quality Lawn Mowers the terms 1/10, n/30. Quality takes advantage of this discount and pays for the inventory on June 9. Recall that it purchased the inventory on June 1, so the payment is made within the discount period. Quality Lawn Mowers owes the vendor $14,700 because $300 worth of merchandise from the original purchase of $15,000 was returned. The 1% discount amounts to $147. That means that the company will pay the vendor $14,553 ($14,700 − $147). Here is the way the transaction would be recorded in the accounting equation:

Assets	=	Liabilities	+	Shareholders' equity	
				Contributed capital	+ Retained earnings
(14,553) cash		(14,700) accounts			
(147) inventory		payable			

Before the payment, the balance in accounts payable was $14,700. So the entire $14,700 must be subtracted out of accounts payable. Because only $14,553 was actually paid, this is the amount deducted from the cash account. That leaves the discount amount to balance the accounting equation. This decreases the inventory account because inventory purchase was recorded at $14,700, which turned out not to be the cost of the inventory. The reduction of $147 adjusts the inventory account balance to the actual cost of the goods purchased.

If Quality Lawn Mowers did not pay within the discount period, the payment would be recorded with a reduction in accounts payable for $14,700 and a reduction in cash for $14,700.

SUMMARY OF PURCHASES FOR QUALITY LAWN MOWERS. Let us review the activity in the inventory account for Quality Lawn Mowers. First, the original purchase of the 100 lawn mowers was recorded with an increase in inventory of $15,000. Then, Quality Lawn Mowers paid the shipping costs of $343. Next, Quality returned two lawn mowers—$300 worth of inventory. Finally, the company took advantage of the purchase discount. That reduced the value of the inventory by $147. The balance in the inventory account is now $14,896 for 98 lawn mowers. That is $152 per unit. This amount is called the **cost of goods available for sale**. If Quality had started the period with a beginning inventory, cost of goods available for sale would have included the amount of the beginning inventory. A simple way to think about the calculation of cost of goods available for sale is as follows:

> **Cost of goods available for sale** is the total of beginning inventory plus the net purchases made during the period (plus any freight-in costs).

Beginning inventory	$ 0
+ Net purchases (this is total purchases less returns and allowances and discounts) 15,000 − 300 −147	14,553
+ Shipping costs (freight-in)	343
= Cost of goods available for sale	$14,896

Your Turn 5-2

Jaden's Coffee Hut purchased 100 pounds of Columbian roast coffee beans to package and sell to its customers. The coffee cost $5 per pound, and Jaden's paid $100 for the bags in which to package the beans. When Jaden's received the invoice for $500 from the coffee importer, the accountant noticed that the payment terms were given as 2/10, n/30. The coffee beans were shipped FOB destination, and the shipping costs were $75. Jaden's accountant paid the coffee importer five days after the date on the invoice. The paper company that sold Jaden's the bags did not offer a discount, so Jaden's paid that firm a few weeks after receiving the invoice for $100. How much did Jaden's record in its inventory account related to these purchases?

Selling Merchandise

You now know how a company records the transactions related to the purchase of inventory. Now, we will look at what happens when the company sells the inventory.

Sales are reported net of returns, allowances, and any discounts given to customers. What you just learned about purchasing inventory also applies to selling the inventory, but everything is reversed. Instead of purchase returns and allowances, there will be *sales* returns and allowances. Instead of purchase discounts, there will be *sales* discounts.

Following are the typical business activities that take place when a firm makes a sale:

1. A customer places an order.
2. The company approves the order.
3. The warehouse packages the goods for shipment.
4. The company ships the goods.
5. The company bills the customer for the goods.
6. The company receives payment for the goods.

Computers can perform some of these steps. Whether a firm performs the steps manually or with a computer, the following objectives of those steps are the same:

• To ensure that the firm sells its goods or services to customers who will pay
• To ensure that the goods or services delivered are what the customers ordered
• To ensure that the customers are correctly billed and payment is received

SALES PROCESS. For sales, revenue is typically recognized when the goods are shipped or when they are delivered, depending on the shipping terms. For example, when Intel ships computer chips to IBM with the terms FOB shipping point, the time the shipment leaves Intel will be the point at which Intel recognizes the revenue, not when the order is placed, and not when IBM pays for the purchase. You know that the shipment of the goods is preceded by many crucial activities such as planning, marketing, and securing orders. Yet, no revenue is recognized until it is actually earned.

Exhibit 5.4 shows part of the note that IBM has included in the financial statements about its revenue recognition. Does payment need to be received before revenue is recognized at IBM? NO! Remember, GAAP (generally accepted accounting principles) are accrual accounting.

EXHIBIT 5.4

How Does IBM Recognize Revenue?

This is just a small part of IBM's note on revenue recognition.

The company recognizes revenue when it is realized or realizable and earned. The company considers revenue realized or realizable and earned when it has persuasive evidence of an arrangement, delivery has occurred, the sales price is fixed or determinable, and collectibility is reasonably assured. Delivery does not occur until products have been shipped or services have been provided to the client; the risk of loss has transferred to the client; and either client acceptance has been obtained, client acceptance provisions have lapsed, or the company has objective evidence that the criteria specified in the client acceptance provisions have been satisfied. The sale price is not considered to be fixed or determinable until all contingencies related to the sale have been resolved.

RECORDING SALES. When a sale is made, it is recorded as an increase in sales revenue, often simply called sales. Continuing our example with Quality Lawn Mowers, suppose the company sold 10 lawn mowers to Sam's Yard Service for $4,000 on account. This is the transaction in the accounting equation:

Assets	=	Liabilities	+	Shareholders' equity		
				Contributed capital	+	Retained earnings
4,000 accounts receivable						4,000 sales revenue

When a sale is made, the inventory will be reduced. Remember, this is called perpetual record keeping. Because Quality Lawn Mowers has sold 10 lawn mowers, the cost of those mowers will be deducted from the balance in the inventory account. Recall that each lawn mower had a cost of $152. Removing the 10 mowers from inventory will reduce the inventory by $1,520 ($152 × 10). Cost of goods sold, an expense account, will increase by $1,520. This is the transaction in the accounting equation:

Assets	=	Liabilities	+	Shareholders' equity	
				Contributed + capital	Retained earnings
(1,520) inventory					(1,520) cost of goods sold

SALES RETURNS AND ALLOWANCES. A company's customers may return items, and the company may provide allowances on items it sells. These amounts will be recorded either as a reduction to sales revenue or in a separate account called **sales returns and allowances**. This account is an example of a **contra-revenue**, which will be deducted from sales revenue for the income statement. Often, you will simply see the term *net sales* on the income statement. This is gross sales minus the amount of returns and allowances. When a customer returns an item to the company, the customer's account receivable will be reduced (or cash will be reduced if the refund is made in cash). The sales returns and allowances account will be increased, and the balance in the account will eventually be deducted from sales revenue.

Sales returns and allowances is an account that holds amounts that reduce sales due to customer returns or allowances for damaged merchandise.

Suppose Sam's Yard Service, the company that purchased the 10 lawn mowers, discovers that one of them is dented and missing a couple of screws. Sam's Yard Service calls Quality Lawn Mowers to complain, and the salesman for Quality Lawn Mowers offers Sam's Yard Service an allowance of $100 on the damaged lawn mower. Sam's Yard Service agrees to the allowance and will keep the lawn mower. Here is the transaction that Quality Lawn Mowers will record to adjust the amount of the sale and the amount Sam's Yard Service owes Quality Lawn Mowers:

A **contra-revenue** is an account that is an offset to a revenue account and therefore deducted from the revenue for the financial statements.

Assets	=	Liabilities	+	Shareholders' equity	
				Contributed + capital	Retained earnings
(100) accounts receivable					(100) sales returns and allowances

SALES DISCOUNTS AND SHIPPING TERMS. The terms of sales discounts, reductions in the sales price for prompt payment, are expressed exactly like the terms you learned for purchases. A company will offer **sales discounts** to its customers to motivate them to pay promptly.

A **sales discount** is a reduction in the sales price of a product offered to customers for prompt payment.

Suppose Quality Lawn Mowers offers Sam's Yard Service the terms 2/10, n/30 for the sale. If Sam's Yard Service pays its account within 10 days of the invoice date, Quality Lawn Mowers will reduce the amount due by 2%. This is an offer Sam's Yard Service should not refuse. Sam's Yard Service will pay $3,822, which is 98% of the amount of the invoice of $3,900. Recall the earlier $100 sales allowance that reduced the amount from $4,000 to $3,900.

Just as with sales returns and allowances, the amount of a sales discount could be subtracted directly from the sales revenue account, reducing the balance by $78. Whether or not you use a separate account to keep track of sales discounts, the income statement will show the net amount of sales. In this example, the calculation for net sales is

Sales revenue	$4,000
Sales allowance given	(100)
Sales discount	(78)
Net sales	$3,822

Here is how the collection of cash from the customer is recorded in the accounting equation:

Assets	=	Liabilities	+	Shareholders' equity		
				Contributed capital	+	Retained earnings
3,822 cash (3,900) accounts receivable						(78) sales discounts

Notice two important things about the way the payment from Sam's Yard Service is recorded.

1. Sales discounts is a contra-revenue account like sales returns and allowances. The amount in the sales discounts account will be subtracted from sales revenue along with any sales returns and allowances to get *net sales* for the income statement.
2. Accounts receivable must be reduced by the full amount that Quality Lawn Mowers has recorded as Sam's Yard Service's accounts receivable balance. Even though the cash collected is less than this balance, Sam's Yard Service's account is paid in full with this payment, so the entire balance in Quality Lawn Mowers' accounting records for accounts receivable for Sam's Yard Service must be removed from the accounting records.

In addition to sales returns and allowances and sales discounts, a company will be concerned with shipping costs. You already learned about identifying the firm that pays for shipping by examining the shipping terms: FOB destination and FOB shipping point. When paying the shipping costs, the vendor will likely set prices high enough to cover the shipping. When the vendor pays the shipping costs, those costs are classified as operating expenses. Look back over Exhibit 5.3 on page 205. When you are working an accounting problem with shipping costs, be careful to properly identify your company as the purchaser or the vendor of the goods being shipped.

SUMMARY OF PURCHASES AND SALES FOR QUALITY LAWN MOWERS. A firm starts with beginning inventory, purchases additional inventory, and then sells some of the inventory. The following calculation shows what happened with Quality Lawn Mowers, providing a summary of the purchase and sales transactions:

Beginning inventory	$ 0
Purchases (net)	
($15,000 – 300 – 147)	14,553
Freight-in	343
Cost of goods available for sale	14,896
Cost of goods sold	1,520
Ending inventory	$13,376

SALES TAXES. In addition to collecting sales revenue, most retail firms must also collect a sales tax for the state government. A sales tax is a percentage of the sales price. Suppose that Quality Lawn Mowers sold a mower to a customer for $400 and the sales tax rate is 4%. Quality collects the sales tax on behalf of the government, so it will owe the government whatever it collects. Here is how Quality Lawn Mowers would record receipt of $416 cash from the customer:

Assets	=	Liabilities	+	Shareholders' equity		
				Contributed capital	+	Retained earnings
416 cash		16 sales taxes payable				400 sales revenue

Your Turn 5-3

Fedco sold $3,000 worth of merchandise to a customer for cash. The sales tax was 5%. How much cash did Fedco receive? How much sales revenue did Fedco earn?

Recording Inventory: Perpetual Versus Periodic Record Keeping

L.O.2
Explain the two methods of inventory record keeping.

In our examples of buying and selling inventory so far, the company used a perpetual inventory record-keeping system. With every transaction related to inventory, the inventory records were updated. As you learned earlier in the chapter, this is called a perpetual inventory system because it requires a continuous updating of the inventory records at the time of every purchase, every return, and every sale.

The other method, mentioned briefly earlier in the chapter, is called periodic inventory record keeping. When a firm uses a periodic inventory system, the firm's accountant waits until the end of an accounting period to adjust the balance in the inventory account. The accounting system uses lots of different accounts to keep track of transactions related to inventory rather than recording the transactions directly to the inventory account.

Because of technology advances, an increasing number of companies are using perpetual inventory systems. For example, when you go shopping at Target and take your cart to the checkout counter, the cashier scans each of your items. The perpetual inventory record-keeping system enables Target and stores such as Kroger, Safeway, and Macy's to do the equivalent of making the cost of goods sold adjustment at the time of sale. Of course, much more information is captured for the information system at the same time. Many companies have systems so sophisticated that the supplier of specific items will have access to the purchasing company's inventory via the Internet so that the supplying company is able to deliver goods to the purchasing company automatically. For example, Wal-Mart has many suppliers that automatically deliver goods when Wal-Mart's inventory records show that the inventory has fallen to some preset level.

Differences between Perpetual and Periodic Inventory Systems

One of the primary advantages of a perpetual system is that inventory records are always current, and a physical count can be compared to the records to see if there is any inventory shrinkage. Inventory shrinkage is a reduction in the inventory by damage, loss, or theft by either employees or customers. A perpetual system allows a company to identify shrinkage. However, a perpetual system may be too cumbersome for firms that do not have up-to-date computerized support. A company may keep the physical count of its inventory current by recording each reduction in the amount of inventory sold without actually recording the cost of goods sold. That is a way to monitor the inventory for potential shrinkage without actually using a perpetual system for the accounting records. Using a perpetual system to track physical quantities of inventory while using a periodic system to track costs is sometimes considered a hybrid system. For financial statement purposes, however, this would be considered a periodic system because accountants report the cost of the inventory, not the quantity, on the balance sheet.

When a company uses a periodic system, the accounting records for the inventory account are updated only at the end of the period. The firm must count the ending inventory and then calculate the amount for cost of goods sold. In other words, if the inventory is gone, it must have been sold. That means that any inventory shrinkage is not separately identified from the inventory sold. All missing inventory is considered inventory sold, and its cost will be included in the firm's cost of goods sold expense for the period.

Suppose a firm is very concerned about inventory theft. Which method of record keeping would be the best choice for this firm? Explain.

Your Turn 5-4

Inventory Cost Flow Assumptions

L.O.3
Define and calculate inventory using the four major inventory cost flow assumptions and explain how these methods affect the financial statements.

So far in this chapter, you have learned about the costs that must be included in the inventory account. All costs to prepare the inventory for sale become part of the cost of the inventory and then, when the goods are sold, become part of the cost of goods sold expense. That is just the beginning of the story. Inventory costing gets more complicated when the cost of the merchandise changes with different purchases.

Suppose Oakley ships 120 pairs of its new sunglasses to Sunglass Hut. The cost to Sunglass Hut is $50 per pair. Then, suppose that just a month later, Sunglass Hut needs more of the popular sunglasses and buys another 120 pairs. This time, however, Oakley charges $55 per pair. If Sunglass Hut sold 140 pairs of Oakley sunglasses during the month to its customers, which ones did it sell? The problem is how to divide the cost of the inventory between the period's cost of goods sold and the ending (unsold) inventory.

We could determine the precise cost of goods sold if we knew how many pairs costing $50 were sold and how many pairs costing $55 were sold. Suppose Sunglass Hut has no method of keeping track of that information. The store simply knows 140 pairs were sold and 100 pairs are left in inventory. There were 240 pairs available for sale at a total cost of $12,600.

$$(120 \text{ pairs at } \$50 \text{ per pair}) + (120 \text{ pairs at } \$55 \text{ per pair})$$
$$= \$12,600 \text{ cost of goods available for sale}$$

How should the store allocate that amount—$12,600—between the 140 pairs sold (cost of goods sold) and the 100 pairs not sold (ending inventory) for the month?

Sunglass Hut will make an assumption about which pairs of sunglasses flowed out of inventory to customers and which pairs remain in inventory. Did the store sell all of the $50 pairs and some of the $55 pairs? Or did the store sell all of the $55 pairs and some of the $50 pairs? The assumption the store makes is called an inventory cost flow assumption, and it is made to calculate the cost of goods sold for the income statement and the cost of ending inventory for the balance sheet. The actual physical flow of the goods does not need to be consistent with the inventory cost flow assumption. The inventory manager could actually know that all of the $50 pairs could not have been sold because of the way shipments are stored below the display counter, yet the store is still allowed to use the assumption that the $50 pairs were sold first in calculating cost of goods sold. In accounting, we are concerned with inventory cost flow—that is, the flow of the costs associated with the goods that pass through a company—rather than with the actual physical movement of goods.

GAAP allow a company to select one of several inventory cost flow assumptions. Studying several of these methods will help you understand how accounting choices can affect the amounts on the financial statements, even when the transactions are identical. There are four basic inventory cost flow assumptions used to calculate the cost of goods sold and the cost of ending inventory.

1. Specific identification
2. Weighted average cost
3. First-in, first-out (FIFO)
4. Last-in, first-out (LIFO)

Specific Identification

The **specific identification method** is one way of assigning the dollar amounts to cost of goods sold and ending inventory. A firm that uses specific identification actually keeps track of which goods were sold because the firm records the actual cost of the specific goods sold.

With the specific identification method, each item sold must be identified as coming from a specific purchase of inventory, at a specific unit cost. Specific identification can be used for determining the cost of each item of a small quantity of large, luxury items such as cars or yachts. However, this method would take too much time and money to use to determine the cost of each item of many identical items, like pairs of identical sunglasses. Companies that specialize in large, one-of-a-kind products, such as Boeing's 787 Dreamliner airplane, will definitely use specific identification. However, when you go into Foot Locker to buy a pair of Nike running shoes, the store accountant will not know exactly what the store paid Nike for that specific pair of shoes. The cost of goods sold will be determined by a method other than specific identification.

We will use a simple example to show how specific identification works. Exhibit 5.5 shows how a car dealership identifies the cost of each car sold, which is the amount the dealership paid the car manufacturer. Suppose you own a Volkswagen car dealership. You buy one Volkswagen for $22,000, a second for $23,000, and a third for $25,000. These three items for the inventory may look identical to a customer, but each car actually has its own unique VIN (vehicle identification number). By checking the VIN, you will know exactly what your dealership paid the manufacturer for each car. Suppose you sold two cars during the accounting period. What is the cost of goods sold? You will specifically identify the cars sold and their cost. If you sold the $22,000 car and the $25,000 car, then cost of goods sold would be $47,000 and ending inventory would be $23,000. However, if you sold the $23,000 car and the $25,000 car, then cost of goods sold would be $48,000 and ending inventory would be $22,000.

The **specific identification method** is the inventory cost flow method in which the actual cost of the specific goods sold is recorded as cost of goods sold.

EXHIBIT 5.5

Inventory Cost Using Specific Identification

Each car's cost to the dealership is identified as the car is sold. The cost of goods sold will reflect the cost of each specific car sold.

Weighted Average Cost

Few firms use specific identification because it is costly to keep track of each individual item in inventory. Instead, most firms use one of the other inventory cost flow assumptions: weighted average cost, FIFO, or LIFO. A firm that uses **weighted average cost** averages the cost of the items available for sale and then uses that weighted average cost to value both cost of goods sold and the ending inventory. An average unit cost is calculated by dividing the total cost of goods available for sale by the total number of units available for sale. This average unit cost is weighted because the number of units at each different price is used to weight the unit costs. The calculated average unit cost is applied to all units sold to get cost of goods sold and applied to all units remaining to get a value for ending inventory. Companies such as Best Buy, Intel, Starbucks, and Chico's use the weighted average cost method to calculate the cost of goods sold and the cost of ending inventory. Exhibit 5.6 shows how the weighted average cost method works for a shop that sells sunglasses.

Weighted average cost is the inventory cost flow method in which the weighted average cost of the goods available for sale is used to calculate the cost of goods sold and the ending inventory.

EXHIBIT 5.6

Weighted Average Inventory Costing

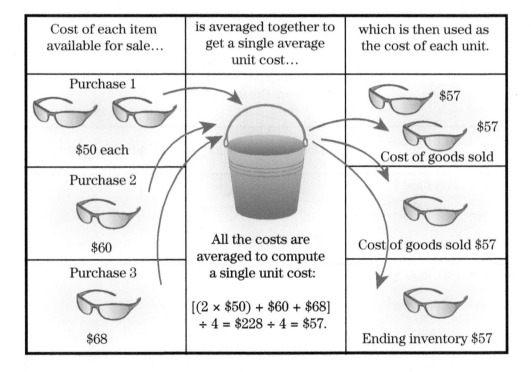

Consider the sunglasses shown in Exhibit 5.6. The store purchased four pairs from the manufacturer. The first two pairs cost $50, the third pair cost $60, and the fourth pair cost $68. The total cost of goods available for sale is

$$(2 \times \$50) + \$60 + \$68 = \$228$$

Averaged over four pairs, the weighted average cost per pair is $57.

$$\$228 \div 4 = \$57$$

If the store now sold three pairs to customers, the cost of goods sold would be as follows:

$$3 \times \$57 = \$171$$

The ending inventory would be $57. Notice that the cost of goods sold of $171 plus the ending inventory of $57 adds up to $228, the cost of goods available for sale.

$171 cost of goods sold
+ 57 ending inventory
$228 cost of goods available for sale

Your Turn 5-5

A firm starts with 10 tea cups in its beginning inventory at a cost of $1 each. During the first day of March, the firm purchases 20 tea cups at a cost of $2 each. No other purchases were made. Between the 2nd and 31st of the month, the firm sold 15 tea cups. How much was the cost of goods sold for those 15 tea cups if the firm uses weighted average cost as its inventory cost flow assumption?

First-In, First-Out Method (FIFO)

First-in, first-out (FIFO) is the inventory cost flow method that assumes the first items purchased are the first items sold.

The **first-in, first-out (FIFO)** method is the common assumption in inventory cost flow that the first items purchased are the first ones sold. The cost of the first goods purchased is assigned to the first goods sold. The cost of the goods on hand at the end of a period is determined from the most recent purchases. Apple, Barnes & Noble, and Wendy's all use FIFO.

We will use the four pairs of sunglasses we used earlier for the weighted average method to see how FIFO works. Suppose the glasses were purchased in the order shown in Exhibit 5.7. No

EXHIBIT 5.7

FIFO Inventory Cost Flow Method

	The actual order of the items sold is not necessarily known, but the costs flow "as if" this were the flow of the goods:	
Cost of goods available for sale	Cost of goods sold	Ending inventory
Purchase 1 $50 each		
Purchase 2 $60		
Purchase 3 $68		
$228	**$160**	**$68**

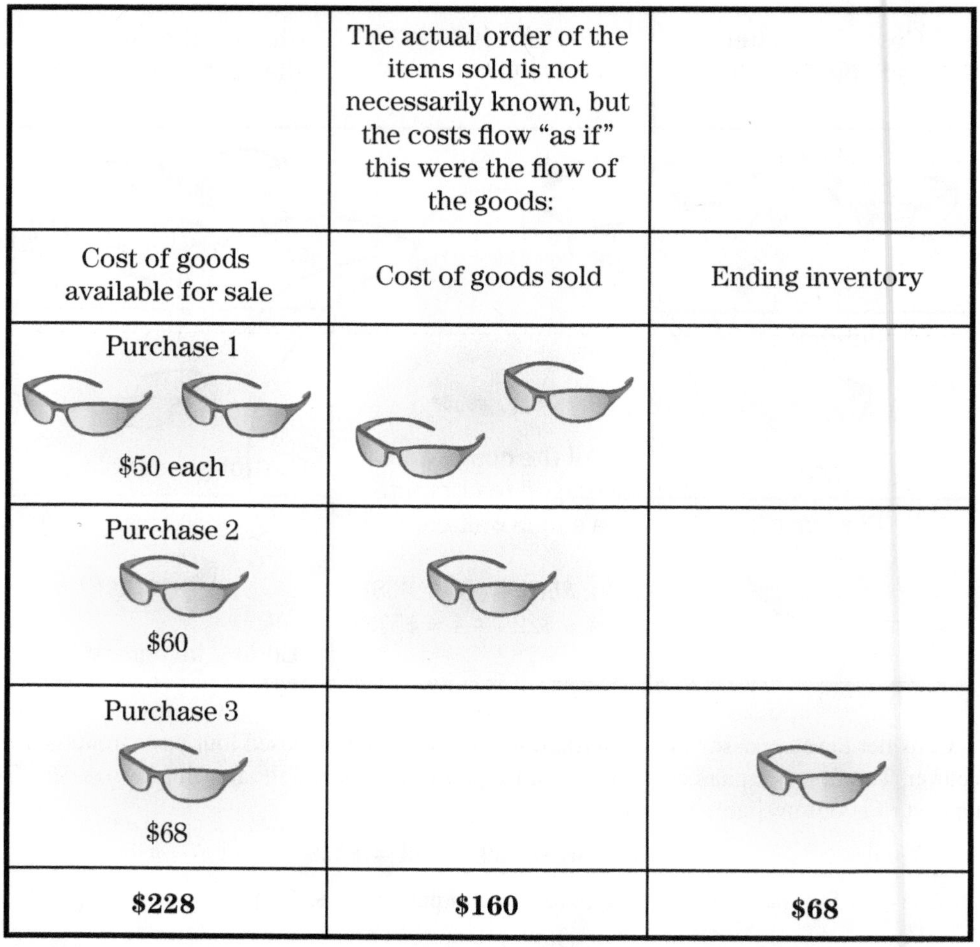

matter which ones were actually sold first, the costs of the oldest purchases will become cost of goods sold.

If the store sold three pairs, the cost of goods sold would be as follows:

$$\$50 + \$50 + \$60 = \$160$$

The ending inventory would be $68. Again notice that the cost of goods sold of $160 plus the ending inventory of $68 equals $228, the cost of goods available for sale.

$160 cost of goods sold
+ 68 ending inventory
$228 cost of goods available for sale

Last-In, First-Out Method (LIFO)

The **last-in, first-out (LIFO)** method is the inventory cost flow assumption that the most recently purchased goods are sold first. The cost of the last goods purchased is assigned to the cost of goods sold, so the cost of the ending inventory is assumed to be the cost of the goods purchased earliest. Firms from diverse industries use LIFO: Caterpillar, manufacturer of machinery and engines; Pepsico, the owner of PepsiCo Beverages North America and Frito-Lay; and McKesson Corporation, a pharmaceutical and health care company.

We will use the four pairs of sunglasses again to see how LIFO works. Suppose the glasses were purchased in the order shown in Exhibit 5.8.

Last-in, first-out (LIFO) is the inventory cost flow method that assumes the last items purchased are the first items sold.

EXHIBIT 5.8

LIFO Inventory Cost Flow Method

Cost of goods available for sale	The actual order of the items sold is not necessarily known, but the costs flow "as if" this were the flow of the goods: Cost of goods sold	Ending inventory
Purchase 1 $50 each		
Purchase 2 $60		
Purchase 3 $68		
$228	$178	$50

No matter which ones were actually sold first, the costs of the most recent purchases will become cost of goods sold. If the store sold three pairs, the cost of goods sold would be as follows:

$$\$68 + \$60 + \$50 = \$178$$

The ending inventory would be $50. Again notice that the cost of goods sold of $178 plus the ending inventory of $50 equals $228, the cost of goods available for sale.

$178 cost of goods sold
$+\ 50$ ending inventory
228 cost of goods available for sale

Firms that use LIFO must provide extra disclosures in their financial statements. Exhibit 5.9 shows an example of the disclosure about inventory provided by Tootsie Roll Industries.

EXHIBIT 5.9

LIFO Disclosure in Notes to the Financial Statements

From Note 1 in Tootsie Roll Industries' 2008 Annual Report (dollars in millions)

Inventories:

Inventories are stated at cost, not to exceed market. The cost of substantially all of the Company's inventories ($53,557 and $54,367 at December 31, 2008 and 2007, respectively) has been determined by the last-in, first-out (LIFO) method. The excess of current cost over LIFO cost of inventories approximates $12,432 and $11,284 at December 31, 2008 and 2007, respectively.

Although Tootsie Roll uses LIFO, it discloses information about the current cost of the ending inventory. Remember that LIFO inventory will be valued at the oldest costs because the more recent costs have gone to the income statement as cost of goods sold. The old inventory is often described as old "LIFO" layers. When a LIFO firm keeps a safety stock of inventory, never selling its entire inventory, those LIFO layers may be there for a long time. LIFO is controversial because a firm can make an extra purchase of inventory at the end of the period and change its cost of goods sold without making another sale. Whether or not it is ethical to buy extra inventory for the sole purpose of changing the period's cost of goods sold is something you should think about. Even if you believe it is not ethical, you should be aware that it can be done when using LIFO.

Take a look at Exhibit 5.10 for a comparison of three methods for calculating the cost of goods sold and the cost of ending inventory—weighted average cost, FIFO, and LIFO.

EXHIBIT 5.10

A Comparison of Weighted Average Cost, FIFO, and LIFO

This exhibit compares three methods for calculating the cost of goods sold and the cost of ending inventory—weighted average cost, FIFO, and LIFO—using the example with four pairs of sunglasses. The three pairs of sunglasses sold and the pair left in ending inventory are not identifiable as to cost to emphasize that the actual physical flow of goods does not matter to the inventory cost flow method.

Purchases	Cost of goods sold	Ending inventory
$50 each $60 $68		
Weighted average cost	$57 + $57 + $57 = **$171**	**$57**
FIFO	$50 + $50 + $60 = **$160**	**$68**
LIFO	$68 + $60 + $50 = **$178**	**$50**

Jayne's Jewelry Store purchased three diamond and emerald bracelets during March. The price of diamonds has fluctuated wildly during the month, causing the supplying firm to change the price of the bracelets it sells to Jayne's Jewelry Store.

Your Turn 5-6

- **a.** On March 5, the first bracelet cost $4,600.
- **b.** On March 15, the second bracelet cost $5,100.
- **c.** On March 20, the third bracelet cost $3,500.

Suppose Jayne's Jewelry Store sold two of these bracelets for $7,000 each.

1. Using FIFO, what is the cost of goods sold for these sales? What is the gross profit?
2. Using LIFO, what is the cost of goods sold for these sales? What is the gross profit?
3. Using weighted average cost, what is the cost of goods sold?

How Inventory Cost Flow Assumptions Affect the Financial Statements

Did you notice that the same set of facts and economic transactions in the examples you just studied resulted in different numbers on the financial statements for cost of goods sold and for ending inventory? In the following sections, you will learn how the firm's choice of inventory cost flow assumptions affects the financial statements.

DIFFERENCES IN REPORTED INVENTORY AND COST OF GOODS SOLD UNDER DIFFERENT COST FLOW ASSUMPTIONS. Exhibit 5.11 shows inventory records for Kaitlyn's Photo Shop. The shop sells a unique type of disposable camera that is relatively inexpensive. We will calculate the cost of goods sold and ending inventory for the month of January using weighted average cost, FIFO, and LIFO, first using periodic record keeping. Then, we will do each using perpetual record keeping.

January 1	Beginning Inventory	8 cameras	at $10 each
January 8	Sales	3 cameras	at $50 each
January 16	Purchase	5 cameras	at $12 each
January 20	Sales	8 cameras	at $55 each
January 30	Purchase	7 cameras	at $14 each

EXHIBIT 5.11

Inventory Records for Kaitlyn's Photo Shop

No matter which method a company selects, the cost of goods available for sale—beginning inventory plus purchases—is the same. Here is the calculation for cost of goods available for sale:

Cost of goods available for sale = Beginning inventory + purchases

For Kaitlyn's Photo Shop for January, the cost of goods available for sale is $238.

$80	+	$60	+	$98	= $238

(8 cameras × $10 each) + (5 cameras × $12 each) + (7 cameras × $14 each)

The inventory cost flow assumption and record-keeping method determine how that dollar amount of cost of goods available for sale is allocated between cost of goods sold and ending inventory.

Recall that a firm can update its accounting records with every sale (perpetual record keeping) or at the end of the accounting period (periodic record keeping). To keep the number of calculations to a minimum as you learn about inventory cost flow, we will start with periodic record keeping for the first examples. Then, we will repeat the examples using perpetual record keeping. No matter which record-keeping method a firm uses, the concept of cost flow differences between FIFO, LIFO, and weighted average cost is the same.

Weighted Average Cost—Periodic When the firm chooses a periodic record-keeping system, the computations for this method of keeping track of inventory are the simplest of all methods. Kaitlyn's adds up the cost of beginning inventory and the cost of all purchases to get the cost of goods available for sale. Kaitlyn's previously calculated that amount to be $238. Then, $238 is divided by the total number of cameras available for sale—that is the number of cameras that comprised the $238—to get a weighted average cost per camera. Kaitlyn's had a total of 20 (8 + 5 + 7) cameras available for sale. Dividing $238 by 20 cameras gives $11.90 per camera. That weighted average unit cost is used to compute cost of goods sold and ending inventory:

11	$\times$	$11.90	**$130.90** cost of goods sold
(Number of cameras sold)		(per unit cost)	
9	$\times$	$11.90	**$107.10** ending inventory
(Number of cameras in ending inventory)		(per unit cost)	

Cost of goods sold ($130.90) and ending inventory ($107.10) add up to $238.

FIFO—Periodic   At the end of the month, Kaitlyn's knows the total number of cameras sold in January was 11. Using FIFO, Kaitlyn's counts the oldest cameras in the inventory as sold. The first items to go in the inventory are the first to go out to the income statement as cost of goods sold. So the firm counts the beginning inventory of eight cameras at $10 each as the first part of cost of goods sold. On January 16, Kaitlyn's purchased five cameras, so the firm will include three of those as part of cost of goods sold, too. That makes 11 cameras sold during the month. The income statement will show $116 as expense, or cost of goods sold.

8 cameras $\times$ $10 per unit = $ 80

3 cameras $\times$ $12 per unit = $ 36

Cost of goods sold   = **$116**

What is left in inventory on the balance sheet?

2 cameras $\times$ $12 per unit = $ 24

7 cameras $\times$ $14 per unit = $ 98

Ending inventory   = **$122**

Notice that the cost of goods sold plus the ending inventory equals $238—the cost of goods available for sale during January. Exhibit 5.12 shows the FIFO inventory cost flow for Kaitlyn's Photo.

LIFO—Periodic   When you use any inventory cost flow method with periodic record keeping, you start by calculating the total number of cameras sold during the month. We know that in January, Kaitlyn's Photo sold 11 cameras. Using LIFO, Kaitlyn's counts cameras from the latest purchase as those sold first. The cost of the last items put in the inventory is the first to go to the income statement as cost of goods sold. For LIFO, we start at the bottom of the list of purchases in the sequence in which the cameras were purchased.

The purchase on January 30 was seven cameras, so Kaitlyn's counts the cost of those as part of cost of goods sold first.

The purchase on January 16 was five cameras, so the firm will count four of them in the cost of goods sold to get the total of 11 cameras sold.

7 cameras $\times$ $14 per unit = $ 98

4 cameras $\times$ $12 per unit = $ 48

Cost of goods sold   = **$146**

What is left in inventory on the balance sheet?

1 camera $\times$ $12 per unit = $12

8 cameras $\times$ $10 per unit = $80

Ending inventory   = **$92**

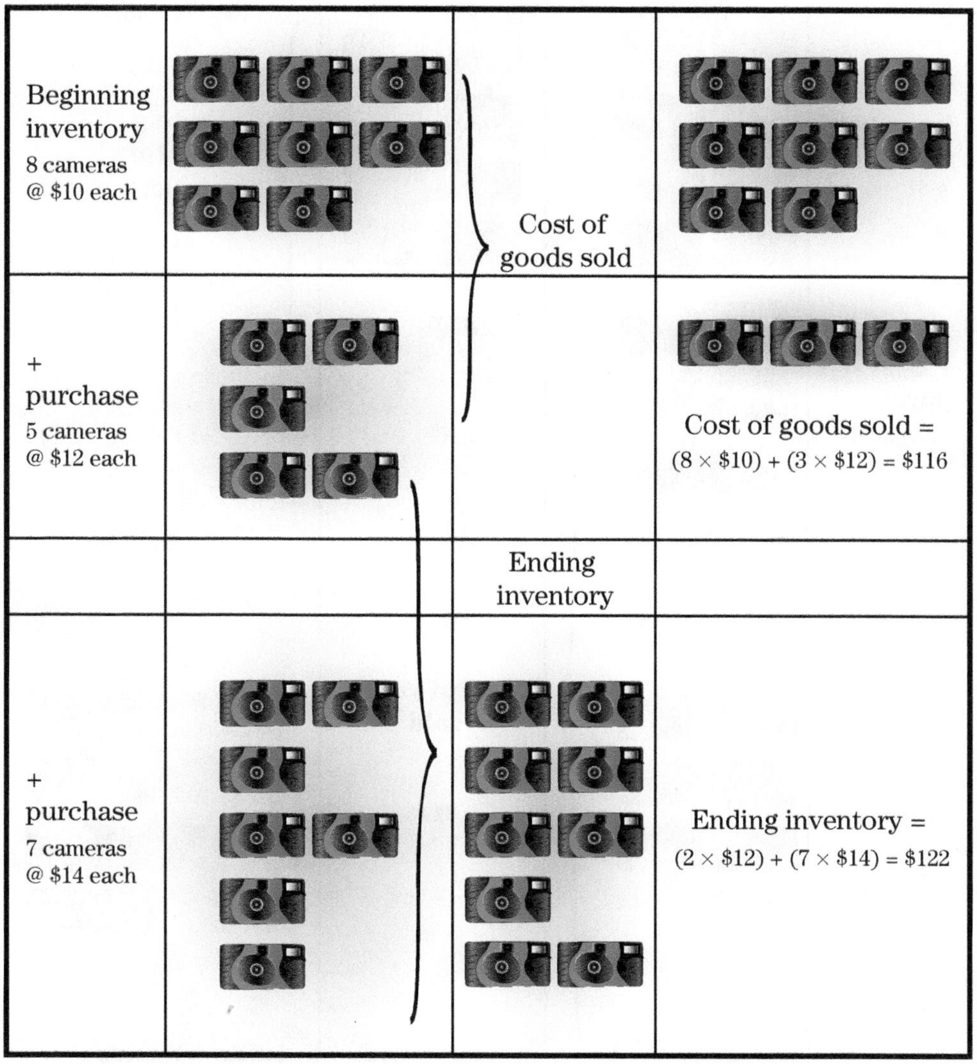

Cost of goods sold

Cost of goods sold =
$(8 \times \$10) + (3 \times \$12) = \$116$

Ending inventory

Ending inventory =
$(2 \times \$12) + (7 \times \$14) = \$122$

EXHIBIT 5.12

FIFO Inventory Cost Flow Assumption for Kaitlyn's Photo Shop

Even though an inventory cost flow assumption does not need to mimic the physical flow of goods, it is a useful way to visualize what is happening. In this exhibit, think of each color of camera as representing the particular cost of a camera in that purchase. The green cameras cost $10 each, the red cameras cost $12 each, and the blue cameras cost $14 each. Kaitlyn's Photo starts with 8 cameras, purchases 5 more and then 7 more, and sells 11 cameras. That leaves 9 cameras in the ending inventory—2 red and 7 blue.

Notice that the cost of goods sold ($146) plus the ending inventory ($92) equals cost of goods available for sale ($238). Exhibit 5.13 on the following page shows the LIFO inventory cost flow for Kaitlyn's Photo.

Weighted Average Cost—Perpetual   When a firm uses a perpetual inventory system, the inventory is reduced each time a sale is made. Technology makes it easy for a firm to use the perpetual system, but the calculations are a bit more complicated. Carefully trace the dates of the purchases and sales as you work through these examples.

If a company were to select perpetual record keeping with the weighted average inventory cost flow assumption, the accountant would calculate a new weighted average unit cost every time a purchase is made and every time a sale is made. The method is often called *moving* weighted average because the average changes with every transaction. A modern firm's computer system can handle this record keeping with ease. However, it can be pretty messy to use the weighted average perpetual system with only a calculator.

When Kaitlyn's Photo sells three cameras on January 8, the weighted average cost of a camera is simply the cost carried in the beginning inventory. So the cost of goods sold for the January 8 sale is $30. That leaves five cameras at a cost of $10 each in the inventory. On January 16, Kaitlyn's purchases five cameras at $12 each. The weighted average cost for a camera is now

$$\frac{(5 \times \$10) + (5 \times \$12)}{10 \text{ total}} = \$11 \text{ each}$$

On January 20, Kaitlyn's Photo sells eight cameras. The cost of goods sold is $88, and there are two cameras left in the inventory at a weighted average cost of $11 each.

EXHIBIT 5.13

LIFO Inventory Cost Flow Assumption for Kaitlyn's Photo Shop

Even though an inventory cost flow assumption does not need to mimic the physical flow of goods, it is a useful way to visualize what is happening. In this exhibit, think of each color of camera as representing the particular cost of a camera in that purchase. The green cameras cost $10 each, the red cameras cost $12 each, and the blue cameras cost $14 each. Kaitlyn's Photo starts with 8 cameras, purchases 5 more and then 7 more, and sells 11 cameras. That leaves 9 cameras in the ending inventory—8 green and 1 red.

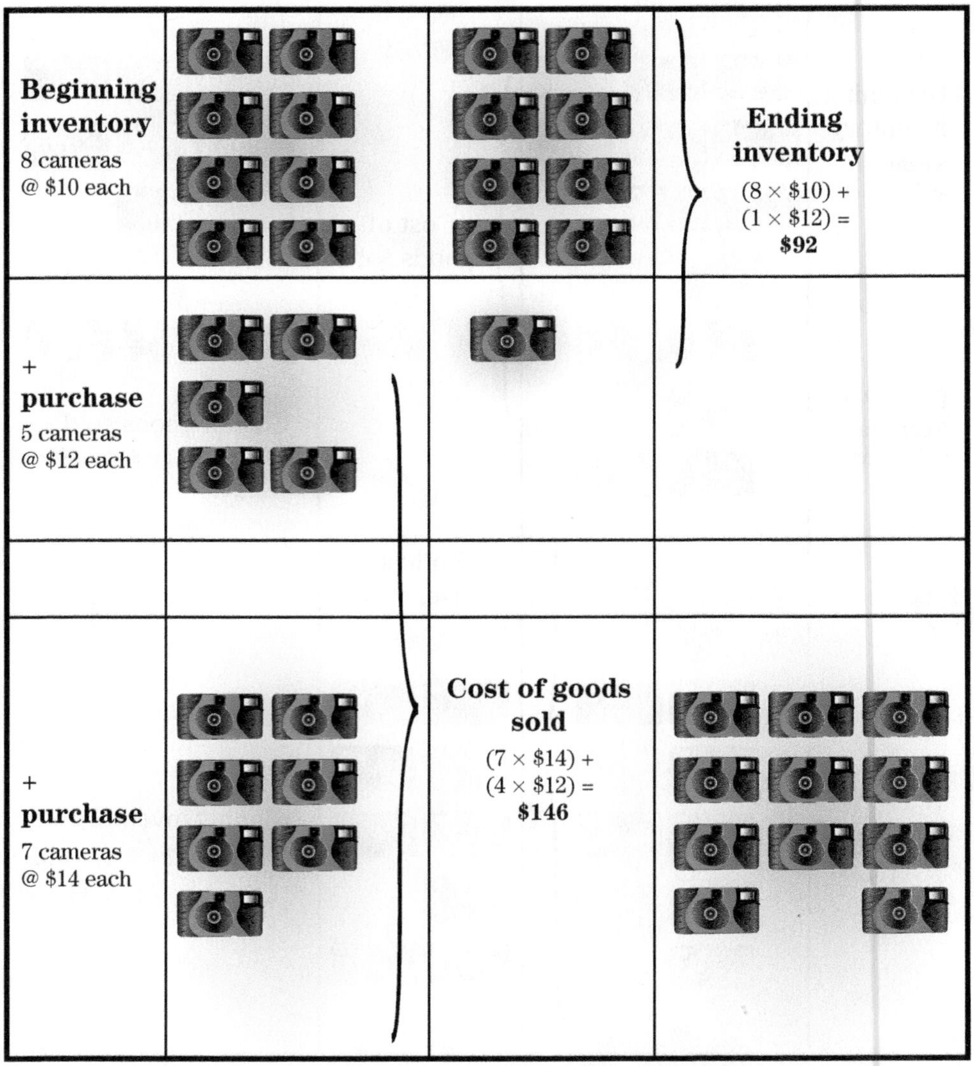

When the purchase of seven cameras at $14 each occurs on January 30, a new weighted average cost must be computed.

$$\frac{(2 \times \$11) + (7 \times \$14)}{9 \text{ total}} = \$13.33 \text{ each}$$

The cost of goods sold for the month of January is $88 + $30 = $118.

The ending inventory for the month of January is $120 (9 cameras × $13.33 each, rounded).

FIFO—Perpetual   When a perpetual record-keeping system is used, the cost of goods sold for each sale must be calculated and recorded at the *time of the sale*. Only the cameras from the purchases as of the date of a sale—meaning prior and up to the date of a sale—are available to become part of the cost of goods sold. Perpetual record keeping requires you to pay attention to the dates on which goods are purchased and sold. Kaitlyn's first sale is on January 8. Only cameras from the beginning inventory are available for Kaitlyn's to use to calculate the cost of goods sold for the January 8 sale. The other purchases are in the future, and Kaitlyn's does not know anything about them on January 8.

The cost of goods sold for the January 8 sale is

3 cameras × $10 per camera = $30

Next, eight cameras were sold on January 20. Because the inventory cost flow assumption is FIFO, Kaitlyn's uses the cameras left in the beginning inventory as part of the cost of goods sold. So the cost of goods sold for the January 20 sale must start with the five cameras remaining in the beginning inventory—that will be 5 × $10 each = $50. To get the other three needed to make the total of eight sold, Kaitlyn's will count three from the January 16 purchase. That is 3 × $12 each = $36. So, the total cost of goods sold for the January 20 sale is $86 ($50 + $36).

To summarize the cost of goods sold,

$$3 \text{ cameras} \times \$10 \text{ each} = \$\ 30$$
$$5 \text{ cameras} \times \$10 \text{ each} = \$\ 50$$
$$3 \text{ cameras} \times \$12 \text{ each} = \underline{\$\ 36}$$
$$\text{Total cost of goods sold} = \mathbf{\underline{\$116}}$$

What is left in inventory at the end of January?

$$2 \text{ cameras} \times \$12 \text{ each} = \$\ 24$$
$$7 \text{ cameras} \times \$14 \text{ each} = \underline{\$\ 98}$$
$$\text{Total ending inventory} = \mathbf{\underline{\$122}}$$

If you refer back to the FIFO periodic example, you will notice that doing all of the work to figure out the cost of goods sold using FIFO *perpetual* gives the same amount as FIFO *periodic*, which is much easier to calculate.

Is this coincidence, or is there a predictable pattern here? Look at the particular cameras that were assumed to be sold under the two methods. You will see that it is more than coincidence. No matter how the company does the actual record keeping, either FIFO method—perpetual or periodic—will give the same dollar amount of cost of goods sold and the same dollar amount of ending inventory for the period. Unfortunately, this is *not* true for LIFO or weighted average.

LIFO—Perpetual Choosing LIFO perpetual makes life a bit more difficult for the accounting system than choosing FIFO. Each time a sale is made, the cost of goods sold is determined by using the *last* purchase as of the date of the sale. The amounts may differ slightly between LIFO periodic and LIFO perpetual because of timing differences between sales and purchases.

Kaitlyn's first sale is on January 8. Only cameras from the beginning inventory are available for Kaitlyn's to use to calculate the cost of goods sold for the January 8 sale. The other purchases are in the future, and Kaitlyn's does not know anything about them on January 8! The cost of goods sold for the January 8 sale is 3 cameras × $10 per camera = $30.

Next, eight cameras were sold on January 20. Because the inventory cost flow assumption is LIFO, Kaitlyn's uses the cameras from the most recent purchase as of January 20 to determine the cost of goods sold. So the cost of goods sold for the January 20 sale starts with the five cameras from the January 16 purchase. That is 5 × $12 each = $60. To get the remaining three cameras she needs for the total eight sold on January 20, Kaitlyn's will need to pick up three from the beginning inventory: 3 × $10 each = $30. So the total cost of goods sold for the January 20 sale is $90 ($60 + $30).

To summarize the cost of goods sold,

$$3 \text{ cameras} \times \$10 \text{ each} = \$\ 30 \text{ Sale on January 8}$$
$$5 \text{ cameras} \times \$12 \text{ each} = \$\ 60 \text{ Sale on January 20}$$
$$3 \text{ cameras} \times \$10 \text{ each} = \underline{\$\ 30} \text{ Sale on January 20}$$
$$\text{Total cost of goods sold} = \mathbf{\underline{\$120}}$$

What is left in the inventory at the end of January?

$$2 \text{ cameras} \times \$10 \text{ each} = \$\ 20$$
$$7 \text{ cameras} \times \$14 \text{ each} = \underline{\$\ 98}$$
$$\text{Total ending inventory} = \mathbf{\underline{\$118}}$$

If you look back at the example of LIFO periodic, you will see that it resulted in a slightly higher cost of goods sold, $146. That is because, under periodic record keeping, Kaitlyn's was allowed to "pretend" to have sold the inventory purchased on January 30. That is, the inventory cost flow assumption allowed an assumed flow of goods that could not possibly have taken place.

CONCLUSIONS ABOUT INVENTORY COST FLOW ASSUMPTIONS.   Firms use all of the combinations of the three inventory cost flow assumptions (weighted average, FIFO, and LIFO) and the two record-keeping methods (perpetual and periodic). Accountants and firms have modified these methods to meet the needs of specific industries. Sometimes firms keep perpetual records of inventory in units but wait until the end of the period to calculate the cost of goods sold using the periodic method. You can see from the examples we have done that the method a company selects to account for inventory can make a difference in the reported cost of goods sold, inventory, and net income.

The cost of goods sold and ending inventory for our example are shown in Exhibit 5.14 for weighted average, FIFO, and LIFO—all using periodic record keeping. In every case, notice that cost of goods sold and ending inventory together total $238, the cost of the goods available for sale. That is true for FIFO, LIFO, and weighted average using either a perpetual or a periodic system. You can read about how a firm makes this important calculation in the notes to the financial statements.

EXHIBIT 5.14

Summary of Kaitlyn's Photo Inventory Data

Inventory Cost Flow Assumption	FIFO	LIFO	Weighted Average
Cost of goods sold	$116	$146	$131
Ending inventory	$122	$ 92	$107

Note: Amounts are rounded to the nearest dollar.

Your Turn 5-7

Jones Saddle Company had the following transactions during August 2011:

- Purchased 30 units at $20 per unit on August 10, 2011
- Purchased 20 units at $21 per unit on August 15, 2011
- Purchased 20 units at $23 per unit on August 21, 2011
- Sold 35 units at $30 per unit on August 30, 2011

Calculate the cost of goods sold using each of these inventory cost flow assumptions: (1) FIFO, (2) LIFO, and (3) weighted average cost. (In this case, perpetual and periodic produce the same answers because all purchases were made before any sales.)

INCOME TAX EFFECTS OF LIFO AND FIFO.   You see that the inventory cost flow assumption makes a difference in the amounts reported on the income statement for cost of goods sold and on the balance sheet for inventory. What effect do you think the inventory cost flow assumption has on the statement of cash flows? We will look at the income statement and the statement of cash flows for Kaitlyn's Photo for an explanation of what could make a company prefer one assumption over another. First, review Exhibit 5.14, which summarizes the calculation cost of goods sold under the three common methods.

Sales revenue and operating expenses are the same no matter what inventory cost flow assumption is used. Earlier we learned that sales revenue amounted to $590. Now, look at Exhibit 5.15. Notice that we have added two new numbers: Operating expenses, paid in cash, of $50 and income taxes of 30%. Exhibit 5.15 shows the income statement for each inventory cost flow assumption.

Before you decide that FIFO is best because it provides a higher net income, notice that this is true only in a period of increasing inventory costs. Additionally, we really need to look at the statement of cash flows to see what effect the inventory cost flow method has on cash flows. Exhibit 5.16 shows the statements of cash flow under each inventory cost flow assumption.

If you compare Exhibits 5.15 and 5.16, you will notice that although LIFO produces the lowest net income, it produces the largest net cash flow from operating activities. That is a direct result of the income tax savings from the lower net income. LIFO will yield the largest net cash flow in a period of rising costs of inventory. If Kaitlyn's uses LIFO instead of FIFO, it will save $9 on income taxes and have that money to spend on advertising or hiring new workers. Think of these savings in millions. Firms often save millions of dollars by using LIFO when inventory costs are rising. The disadvantage of using LIFO is that net income will be lower than it would have been with FIFO or weighted average cost.

EXHIBIT 5.15

Income Statements for Kaitlyn's Photo Using Periodic Inventory with Various Cost Flow Assumptions

Recall that the cost of the inventory has been rising. That means LIFO will yield a higher cost of goods sold and a lower taxable income. Cost of goods sold and income taxes are highlighted because those amounts are why LIFO income is lower than FIFO income.

Inventory Cost Flow Assumption	FIFO	LIFO	Weighted Average
Sales*	$590	$590	$590
Cost of goods sold	116	146	131
Operating expenses	50	50	50
Income before taxes	424	394	409
Income taxes (30%)	127	118	123
Net income	$297	$276	$286

(3 × $50) + (8 × $55) = $590

EXHIBIT 5.16

Statements of Cash Flows for Kaitlyn's Photo Using Various Inventory Cost Flow Assumptions

All inventory methods produce the same cash flows for all items except income taxes. This example assumes all transactions are cash.

Inventory Cost Flow Assumption	FIFO	LIFO	Weighted Average
Cash collected from customers	$590	$590	$590
Cash paid for inventory	(238)	(238)	(238)
Cash paid for operating expenses	(50)	(50)	(50)
Cash paid for income taxes	(127)	(118)	(123)
Net cash from operating activities	$175	$184	$179

HOW DO FIRMS CHOOSE AN INVENTORY COST FLOW METHOD? Now, think about some of the factors that might influence a firm's choice of inventory cost flow assumptions.

1. *Compatibility with similar companies.* A firm will often choose a method that other firms in the same industry use. Then, a manager can easily compare inventory levels to those of the competition. Also, investors like to compare similar companies without the complication of different inventory methods.
2. *Maximize tax savings and cash flows.* A firm may want to maximize tax savings and cash flows. As you saw in our analysis of Kaitlyn's Photo with various inventory methods, when inventory costs are rising, cost of goods sold is larger when a company uses LIFO rather than FIFO. There is a difference because the higher costs of the more recent purchases go to the income statement as cost of goods sold, and the older, lower costs are left on the balance sheet in inventory. A higher cost of goods sold expense results in a lower net income. **Although financial accounting and tax accounting are usually quite different, the IRS requires any company that uses LIFO for income taxes to also use LIFO for its financial statements. This is called the LIFO conformity rule.** So, if a firm wants to take advantage of lower income taxes when inventory costs are rising, the firm must also be willing to report a lower net income to its shareholders. Reducing income taxes is the major reason firms select LIFO. Read more about LIFO and taxes in Understanding Business on the following page.
3. *Maximize net income.* In a period of rising prices, a higher net income will come from using FIFO. That is because older, lower costs will go to the income statement as cost of goods sold. Suppose you are a CFO whose bonus depends on reaching a specific level of earnings. You may forego the tax benefits of LIFO to keep your net income higher with FIFO.

Whatever inventory cost flow method a firm uses, the method should be used consistently so that financial statements from one period can be compared to those from the previous period. A firm can change inventory cost flow methods only if the change improves the measurement of the firm's performance or financial position. Exhibit 5.17 gives an example of the type of disclosure a firm must make if it changes inventory cost flow methods.

EXHIBIT 5.17

Disclosure of a Change in Inventory Cost Flow Methods

This is just part of the inventory disclosure made by Avery Dennison Corporation in the notes to its December 29, 2007, financial statements. Notice the justification for the change in inventory methods, highlighted.

Change in Accounting Method

Beginning in the fourth quarter of 2007, the Company changed its method of accounting for inventories for the Company's U.S. operations from a combination of the use of first-in, first-out ("FIFO") and the last-in, first-out ("LIFO") methods to the FIFO method. The inventories for the Company's international operations continue to be valued using the FIFO method. The Company believes the change is preferable as the FIFO method better reflects the current value of inventories on the Consolidated Balance sheet; provides better matching of revenue and expense in the Consolidated Statement of Income; provides uniformity across the Company's operations with respect to the method of accounting for inventory accounting; and enhances comparability with peers.

If the Company had not changed its policy of accounting for inventory, pre-tax income would have been lower by $1.1 million for the year ended December 29, 2007.

UNDERSTANDING → Business

Inventory Cost Flow Assumptions and Taxes

Generally accepted accounting principles (GAAP) allow firms quite a bit of latitude in selecting a method of accounting for inventory costs. Last-in, first-out (LIFO) provides a tax benefit—lower taxes than first-in, first-out (FIFO)—in a period of rising prices. Taxes are computed based on a percentage of net income, and the cost of goods sold will be deducted in this calculation. The larger the cost of goods sold, the smaller the resulting taxable income. This is a real economic benefit that results from an accounting choice. In the past century, costs have been rising, so it would make sense for a company to take advantage of this tax savings by choosing LIFO for its inventory method. Yet, the most recent survey of accounting practices, reported in Accounting Trends & Techniques (2008), reports that only about 30% of firms use LIFO, many for only part of their inventories. What factors influence a firm's choice of inventory methods and why would a firm choose not to use LIFO?

Lower Earnings

As you just read, if a firm uses LIFO for taxes, the firm must also use LIFO for financial reporting. This is called the LIFO conformity rule. This is an exception to the general rule that a firm may use one accounting method for financial statements and a different method for taxes. With respect to inventory, this required consistency means that choosing LIFO for taxes in a period of rising prices will result in lower reported profits for both taxes and financial statements. Why is that a problem?

Managers may worry that lower earnings will have a negative effect on the firm's stock price. Managers may have a compensation contract that is tied to earnings; so lower earnings may mean a smaller bonus.

International Financial Reporting Standards

International Financial Reporting Standards (IFRS) do not allow the use of LIFO. So if a firm has international operations, the firm will not be able to use LIFO for those operations. Many firms use LIFO for domestic inventories, but they must use FIFO or weighted average for non-domestic divisions. As we move closer to convergence between GAAP and IFRS, inventory will become an important issue to any firm using LIFO.

Most of the time, the choice of an accounting method is difficult to trace to specific economic consequences. With inventory, however, the choice of accounting method can make a significant economic difference to a firm—real dollars. That makes selecting an inventory cost flow method an important business decision.

IFRS in the *News*

One of the most well known differences between U.S. GAAP and IFRS is related to inventory. IFRS do not allow the use of LIFO. Because of GAAP's LIFO conformity rule (LIFO for taxes means you must use LIFO for financial statements), eliminating LIFO will cause some very significant tax problems for firms that have been using LIFO while the cost of their inventories has been increasing.

Explain the LIFO conformity rule. What is the usual relationship between accounting under GAAP and the Internal Revenue Service (IRS) rules?

Your Turn 5-8

Applying Inventory Assumptions to Team Shirts

L.O.4
Analyze transactions and prepare financial statements after the purchase and sale of inventory.

Team Shirts began in January 2010 and has now completed four months of operations. As the company completes its transactions for May, inventory prices are changing. For Team Shirts, that means it must select an inventory cost flow assumption. If you look back at the first four months of transactions, you will see that inventory prices were constant at $4 per shirt. When inventory prices are constant, there is no need for a cost flow assumption. Every method produces the identical values for inventory and cost of goods sold. You will also recall that Team Shirts recorded the reduction in inventory at the same time as the related sale. You have now learned that this method is called perpetual inventory record keeping.

The balance sheet at May 1, 2010, is shown in Exhibit 5.18. As you know, it is the same as the balance sheet at April 30, 2010, from Exhibit 4.15.

EXHIBIT 5.18

Balance Sheet for Team Shirts at May 1, 2010

Team Shirts
Balance Sheet
at May 1, 2010

Assets

Current Assets:	
Cash	$ 3,295
Accounts receivable (net of allowance of $160)	7,840
Inventory	1,100
Prepaid expenses	1,825
Total current assets	14,060
Computer (net of accumulated depreciation of $200)	3,800
Total assets	$17,860

Liabilities & Shareholder's Equity

Current Liabilities:	
Accounts payable	$ 4,000
Interest payable	60
Notes payable	3,000
Total current liabilities	7,060
Shareholder's Equity:	
Common stock	5,000
Retained earnings	5,800
Total shareholder's equity	10,800
Total liabilities and shareholder's equity	$17,860

The transactions for May are shown in Exhibit 5.19.

EXHIBIT 5.19

Accounting Equation Worksheet for Team Shirts for May 2010

	Assets			= Liabilities		+ Shareholder's Equity		
						Contributed Capital	Retained Earnings	
	Cash	All other assets	(Account)	All liabilities	(Account)	Common Stock		(Account)
Beginning Balances	$ 3,295	$8,000 (160) 1,100 25 1,800 4,000 (200)	Accounts receivable Allowance Inventory Prepaid insurance Prepaid rent Computer Accumulated depreciation	$4,000 3,000 60	Accounts payable Notes payable Interest payable	$5,000	$5,800	
Transactions 1	(300)	300	Prepaid insurance					
2	7,900	(7,900)	Accounts receivable					
3	(4,000)			(4,000)	Accounts payable			
4		4,800	Inventory	4,800	Accounts payable			
5	9,900			9,900	Unearned revenue			
6		8,800 (3,200)	Accounts receivable Inventory				8,800 (3,200)	Sales Cost of goods sold
7	(500)	300	Prepaid Web design				(200)	Web design expense
8		(100) 100	Accounts receivable Allowance					
9		4,200	Inventory	4,200	Accounts payable			
10	(3,090)			(3,000) (60)	Notes payable Interest payable		(30)	Interest expense
11	(400)						(400)	Operating expenses
A-1		(75)	Prepaid insurance				(75)	Insurance expense
A-2		(1,200)	Prepaid rent				(1,200)	Rent expense
A-3		(50)	Prepaid Web design				(50)	Web design expense
A-4		(100)	Accumulated depreciation				(100)	Depreciation expense
A-5		(1,800)	Inventory	(4,950)	Unearned revenue		4,950 (1,800)	Sales Cost of goods sold
A-6		(116)	Allowance				(116)	Bad debts expense
	$12,805 +	$18,524		= $13,950		+ $5,000 +	$12,379	

▬ Income statement   ▬ Statement of changes in shareholder's equity   ▬ Balance sheet   ▬ Statement of cash flows

Assets (non cash)		Liabilities	
Accounts receivable	$ 8,800	Accounts payable	$ 9,000
Allowance	(176)	Interest payable	0
Inventory	5,100	Notes payable	0
Prepaid insurance	250	Unearned revenue	4,950
Prepaid rent	600	Total	$13,950
Prepaid Web design	250		
Computer	4,000		
Accum depreciation	(300)		
Total	$18,524		

First, we will record each transaction in the accounting equation. Then, we will review the records to identify any needed adjustments.

Transaction 1: Payment for insurance Team Shirts pays cash for insurance premium, $300 for three months; coverage starts May 15. The firm records all insurance payments to prepaid insurance. The expense will be recorded as an adjustment at the end of the month.

Assets	=	Liabilities	+	Shareholder's equity		
				Contributed capital	+	Retained earnings
(300) cash 300 prepaid insurance						

Transaction 2: Collection on accounts receivable Team Shirts collects $7,900 from customers who purchased shirts in prior months. No revenue is recognized because the revenue was already recognized when the sale was originally made. This collection simply exchanges one asset—accounts receivable—for another—cash.

Assets	=	Liabilities	+	Shareholder's equity		
				Contributed capital	+	Retained earnings
7,900 cash (7,900) accounts receivable						

Transaction 3: Payment on accounts payable Team Shirts makes a payment of $4,000 on accounts payable. This pays off the total amount of the obligation.

Assets	=	Liabilities	+	Shareholder's equity		
				Contributed capital	+	Retained earnings
(4,000) cash		(4,000) accounts payable				

Transaction 4: Purchase of inventory Team Shirts purchases 1,200 shirts at $4 each on account.

Assets	=	Liabilities	+	Shareholder's equity		
				Contributed capital	+	Retained earnings
4,800 inventory		4,800 accounts payable				

Transaction 5: Receipt of unearned revenue Team Shirts agrees to sell the local school system 900 shirts for $11 each. Team Shirts collects cash of $9,900 in advance of delivery. Half the shirts will be delivered on May 30, and the other half will be delivered in June.

Assets	=	Liabilities	+	Shareholder's equity		
				Contributed capital	+	Retained earnings
9,900 cash		9,900 unearned revenue				

Transaction 6: Sales Team Shirts sells 800 shirts at $11 each, all on account. That means the company extended credit to its customers, and Team Shirts will collect later.

Assets	=	Liabilities	+	Shareholder's equity		
				Contributed capital	+	Retained earnings
8,800 accounts receivable						8,800 sales revenue

At the same time sales revenue is recorded, Team Shirts records the reduction in inventory. As you know, the reduction in inventory is an expense called cost of goods sold. At this point, all of the items in inventory cost the same amount—$4. Team Shirts has decided to use FIFO, but there is no actual impact of that choice for this transaction. All of the shirts Team Shirts sold cost $4, so cost of goods sold is $3,200. There were 275 shirts at $4 each in the beginning inventory, so those are assumed to be sold first. The remaining 525 shirts come from the recent purchase of 1,200 shirts at $4 each.

Assets	=	Liabilities	+	Shareholder's equity		
				Contributed capital	+	Retained earnings
(3,200) inventory						(3,200) cost of goods sold

Transaction 7: Payment for Web design and for six months' worth of maintenance Team Shirts hires Web designers to start a Web page for the firm. The firm pays $200 for Web design and $300 for six months' worth of maintenance fees. A full month of maintenance will be charged for May.

Assets	=	Liabilities	+	Shareholder's equity		
				Contributed capital	+	Retained earnings
300 prepaid Web design (500) cash						(200) Web design expense

Transaction 8: Write off of a specific accounts receivable Team Shirts writes off the $100 accounts receivable balance of Ace Sports, a customer that has declared bankruptcy.

Assets	=	Liabilities	+	Shareholder's equity		
				Contributed capital	+	Retained earnings
(100) accounts receivable						
100 allowance for bad debts						

Transaction 9: Purchase of inventory Team Shirts purchases 1,000 shirts at a cost of $4.20 each, on account.

Assets	=	Liabilities	+	Shareholder's equity		
				Contributed capital	+	Retained earnings
4,200 inventory		4,200 accounts payable				

Transaction 10: Repayment of note with interest Team Shirts started the month with a short-term note payable of $3,000. It was issued on March 1, so three months' worth of interest is also paid. The interest rate on the note is 12%. Previously, at the end of March and again at the end of April, the interest for the month was accrued. That is, each month $30 of interest expense and interest payable was recorded. So the payment of interest here for three months is $90, $60 of which was interest payable and $30 will be recorded as interest expense for May. The payment of the note and the payment of the interest are shown separately because it will be easier to construct the statement of cash flows if these are separate. The repayment of the note is a financing cash outflow, whereas the interest payment is an operating cash flow. Interest payments and receipts are always classified as cash from operating activities on the statement of cash flows.

Assets	=	Liabilities	+	Shareholder's equity	
				Contributed capital	+	Retained earnings
(3,000) cash		(3,000) notes payable			
(90) cash		(60) interest payable			(30) interest expense

Transaction 11: Payment of operating expenses Team Shirts pays cash for other operating expenses of $400.

Assets	=	Liabilities	+	Shareholder's equity	
				Contributed capital	+	Retained earnings
(400) cash					(400) operating expenses

All of these routine transactions are recorded in the accounting equation worksheet in Exhibit 5.19. Now, Team Shirts must make several adjustments before it can prepare the financial statements for May. As you read about each adjustment, identify the entry in the accounting equation worksheet.

Adjustment 1: Insurance expense needs to be recorded. The total expense for May is $75. That is the total of $25 from the first half of the month (which uses up the beginning balance in prepaid insurance) and $50 for the second half of the month (from the new policy at $100 per month, beginning May 15).

Adjustment 2: Rent expense needs to be recorded. The amount is $1,200 for the month.

Adjustment 3: The Web service of $50 for May needs to be recorded.

Adjustment 4: Depreciation expense needs to be recorded on the computer, $100 per month.

Adjustment 5: Half of the 900 shirts were delivered to the schools, so half of the unearned revenue needs to be recognized. That is, $4,950 in revenue should be recorded. The reduction in inventory must also be recorded. Recall that Team Shirts is using FIFO. There are 675 shirts left that cost $4 each and a recent purchase of 1,000 shirts at $4.20 each. Using FIFO, the 450 shirts that were delivered (half of the 900 the school paid for in advance) are assumed to be from the oldest inventory, so the cost of goods sold is 450 × $4 = $1,800.

Adjustment 6: The firm must record bad debt expense based on the ending balance in accounts receivable. The ending balance is $8,800, and the firm estimates that 2% will be uncollectible. That is $176. However, the allowance account has $60 left from the prior month. The allowance balance started at $160. You can see this on the May 1 balance sheet. Then, in Transaction 8, a specific account for $100 was written off. This reduced the allowance balance to $60. Now, at the end of May, Team Shirts wants the balance to be $176 (2% of ending accounts receivable). That means that only $116 will be recorded as bad debts expense for May. The adjustment in the accounting equation will increase the allowance by $116 to an ending balance of the desired $176.

After the adjustments are made, the financial statements can be prepared. Make sure you can trace each amount on the financial statements in Exhibit 5.20 to the accounting equation worksheet in Exhibit 5.19.

EXHIBIT 5.20

Financial Statements for Team Shirts for May 2010

Team Shirts Income Statement For the month ended May 31, 2010		
Sales revenue		$13,750
Expenses:		
Cost of goods sold	$5,000	
Operating expenses	400	
Bad debts expense	116	
Insurance expense	75	
Rent expense	1,200	
Web design expenses	250	
Depreciation expense	100	
Interest expense	30	
Total expenses		7,171
Net income		$ 6,579

Team Shirts Statement of Changes in Shareholder's Equity For the month ended May 31, 2010	
Beginning common stock	$ 5,000
Common stock issued during the month	–
Ending common stock	$ 5,000
Beginning retained earnings	$ 5,800
Net income	6,579
Dividends	–
Ending retained earnings	$12,379
Total shareholder's equity	$17,379

Team Shirts Statement of Cash Flows For the month ended May 31, 2010	
Cash from operating activities:	
Cash collected from customers	$17,800
Cash paid to vendors	(4,000)
Cash paid for interest	(90)
Cash paid for operating expenses	(1,200)
Net cash from operating activities	$12,510
Cash from investing activities:	0
Cash from financing activities:	
Pay off Note Payable	(3,000)
Increase in cash	9,510
Beginning cash balance	3,295
Ending cash balance	$12,805

Team Shirts Balance Sheet At May 31, 2010	
Assets	
Current Assets:	
Cash	$12,805
Accounts receivable (net of allowance of $176)	8,624
Inventory	5,100
Prepaid expenses	1,100
Total current assets	27,629
Computer (net of accumulated depreciation of $300)	3,700
Total assets	$31,329
Liabilities and Shareholder's Equity	
Current Liabilities:	
Accounts payable	$ 9,000
Unearned revenue	4,950
Total current liabilities	13,950
Shareholder's Equity:	
Common stock	5,000
Retained earnings	12,379
Total shareholder's equity	17,379
Total liabilities and shareholder's equity	$31,329

L.O.5
Explain the lower-of-cost-or-market rule for valuing inventory.

Complications in Valuing Inventory: Lower-of-Cost-or-Market Rule

Inventory is an asset on the balance sheet, recorded at cost. As you have seen, that asset can be a significant amount. To make sure that inventory is not overstated, GAAP require companies to compare the cost of their inventory at the end of the period with the market value of that inventory, based on either individual items or total inventory. For the financial statements, the company must use the lower of either the cost or the market value of its inventory. This is called the **lower-of-cost-or-market (LCM) rule**. When you study any company's annual report, the note about inventory methods will almost always mention that the lower-of-cost-or-market valuation rule has been applied.

Estimating the market value of inventory is the difficult part of the LCM rule. The market value used is **replacement cost**. That is the cost to buy similar inventory items from the supplier to replace the inventory. A company compares the cost of the inventory, as it is recorded in the

The **lower-of-cost-or-market (LCM) rule** is the rule that requires firms to use the lower of either the cost or the market value (replacement cost) of its inventory on the date of the balance sheet.

accounting records, to the replacement cost at the date of the financial statements and uses the lower of the two values for the balance sheet. Although there are a few more complications in applying this rule, the concept is straightforward. There is a floor (lowest possible value) and a ceiling (highest possible value), but these computations are beyond the scope of an introductory course. The main point is that inventory must not be overstated. When the inventory value is reduced, the adjustment to reduce the inventory also reduces net income.

> **Replacement cost** is the cost to buy similar items in inventory from the supplier to replace the inventory.

Comparing the cost of inventory to its current replacement cost is more than a simple accounting requirement. Information about the current replacement cost of inventory is important for formulating sales strategies related to various items in inventory and for inventory-purchasing decisions.

It is common for the inventory of companies such as T-Mobile and Sony to lose value or quickly become obsolete because of new technology. These companies cannot know the value of the inventory with certainty, so they will often estimate the reduction in inventory. Sometimes this is shown on the financial statements as a "reserve for obsolescence." (Remember, a reserve like this is *not* cash.) Knowing how a company values its inventory is essential for analyzing a company's financial statements, and you will find this information in the notes to the financial statements.

Financial Statement Analysis

Gross Profit Ratio

Each of the four financial statements is useful to investors and other users. For example, the balance sheet tells investors about a firm's financial position and its ability to meet its short-term obligations. The current ratio you studied in Chapter 2 is calculated from amounts on the balance sheet. In addition to an analysis of a firm's financial position and ability to meet its short-term obligations, investors are very interested in a firm's performance. That information comes from the income statement. An important ratio for measuring a firm's performance is the **gross profit ratio**, also called the gross margin ratio. You know that gross profit equals sales minus cost of goods sold. The gross profit ratio is defined as gross profit divided by sales. The ratio measures the portion of sales dollars a company has left after paying for the goods sold. The remaining amount must cover all other operating costs, such as salary expense and insurance expense, and be large enough to have something left over for profit.

L.O.6
Define and calculate the gross profit ratio and the inventory turnover ratio.

> **Gross profit ratio** is equal to the gross profit (sales minus cost of goods sold) divided by sales. It is a ratio for evaluating firm performance.

$$\text{Gross profit ratio} = \frac{\text{Sales} - \text{Cost of goods sold}}{\text{Sales}}$$

We will calculate the gross profit ratio for Target from its income statement shown in Exhibit 5.21 on the following page. For its fiscal year ended January 30, 2009 (fiscal year 2008), Target's gross profit was $18,727 million ($62,884 million − $44,157 million). The gross profit ratio—gross profit as a percent of sales—was 29.8%.

The gross profit ratio is very important to a retail company. As with all ratios, it is useful to compare this ratio across several years. Look at Target's income statement, and compute the gross profit ratio for its fiscal year ended February 2, 2008 (fiscal year 2007). Divide the gross profit of $18,542 million by sales of $61,471 million for a gross margin ratio of 30.2%. From 2007 to 2008, Target's gross margin ratio decreased slightly.

A retail company is particularly interested in its gross profit ratio and how it compares to that of prior years or that of competitors. When managers talk about a product's margins, they are talking about the gross profit. There is no specific amount that signifies an acceptable or good gross profit. For example, the margin on a grocery store item is usually smaller than that of a new car because a grocery store turns over its inventory more frequently than does a car dealership. When a grocery store such as Kroger or Whole Foods Market buys a grocery item, such as a gallon of milk, the sales price of that item is often not much higher than its cost. Because a grocery store sells so many different items and a large quantity of each, the gross profit on each item does not need to be very big to accumulate into a sizable gross profit for the store. However, when a company sells larger items, such as cars, televisions, or clothing, and not so many of them, it needs to have a larger gross profit on each item. For its fiscal year ended September 28, 2008, Whole Foods' gross profit ratio was 34%, whereas Guess?, Inc., with fiscal year end February 2, 2008, had a gross profit ratio of 45%. (See Exhibit 5.22 on page 233.)

EXHIBIT 5.21

Target Corporation: Consolidated Statements of Operations

Target's year end for its fiscal year 2008 was January 31, 2009. Even though only a year is given at the top, you can find the exact date of the firm's year end on the balance sheet (not shown here).

Target Corporation
Consolidated Statements of Operations
(in millions)

	For fiscal years		
	2008	2007	2006
Sales	**$62,884**	$61,471	$57,878
Credit card revenues	**2,064**	1,896	1,612
Total revenues	**64,948**	63,367	59,490
Cost of sales	**44,157**	42,929	40,366
Selling, general and administrative expenses	**12,954**	12,670	11,852
Credit card expenses	**1,609**	837	707
Depreciation and amortization	**1,826**	1,659	1,496
Earnings before interest expense and income taxes	**4,402**	5,272	5,069
Net interest expense			
Nonrecourse debt collateralized by credit card receivables	**167**	133	98
Other interest expense	**727**	535	499
Interest income	**(28)**	(21)	(25)
Net interest expense	**866**	647	572
Earnings before income taxes	**3,536**	4,625	4,497
Provision for income taxes	**1,322**	1,776	1,710
Net earnings	**$ 2,214**	$ 2,849	$ 2,787

Inventory Turnover Ratio

Merchandising companies make a profit by selling their inventory. The faster they sell their inventory, the more profit they make. Buying inventory and then selling it makes the inventory "turn over." After a company sells its inventory, it must purchase new inventory. The more often this happens, the more profit a company makes. Financial analysts and investors are very interested in how quickly a company turns over its inventory. Inventory turnover rates vary a great deal from industry to industry. Industries with small gross margins, such as the candy industry, usually turn over their inventories more quickly than industries with large gross margins, such as the auto industry.

The **inventory turnover ratio** is defined as cost of goods sold divided by the average inventory on hand during the year. The ratio measures how many times a firm turns over its inventory during the year—how quickly a firm is selling its inventory.

The **inventory turnover ratio** is defined as cost of goods sold divided by average inventory. It is a measure of how quickly a firm sells its inventory.

$$\text{Inventory turnover ratio} = \frac{\text{Cost of goods sold}}{(\text{Beginning inventory} + \text{ending inventory}) \div 2}$$

We will compare the inventory turnover ratio for Whole Foods Market, Inc., a large grocery chain, with that for Guess?, Inc., a smaller specialty clothing store chain. The year's cost of goods sold for each firm is found on its income statement, and average inventory can be calculated from the beginning and ending inventory amounts shown on comparative balance sheets. To get the average, we will just add the beginning and year-end inventory balances and divide by two. The data and calculations are shown in Exhibit 5.22. Notice that although Whole Foods has a lower gross profit ratio than Guess, the firm turns over its inventory many more times each year than Guess.

Although managers want to turn over inventory rapidly, they also want enough inventory on hand to meet customer demand. Managers can monitor inventory by using the inventory turnover ratio to find out the number of days items stay in inventory. This is called the **average days in inventory**. For Whole Foods, 365 (days in a year) divided by 17.0 (inventory turnover ratio) = 21.5 days. For Guess, the average number of days in inventory is just over 77 days (365 ÷ 4.7).

The **average days in inventory** is the number of days it takes, on average, to sell an item of inventory.

(dollars in thousands) For fiscal year ended	Whole Foods Market, Inc. September 28, 2008	Guess?, Inc. February 2, 2008
(1) Sales	$7,953,912	$1,749,916
(2) Cost of goods sold	5,247,207	957,147
(3) Gross profit	2,706,705	792,769
Gross profit ratio (3) ÷ (1)	34%	45%
(4) Inventory, beginning of the year	288,112	173,668
(5) Inventory, end of the year	327,452	232,159
(6) Average inventory ((4) + (5)) ÷ 2	307,782	202,914
Inventory turnover ratio (2) ÷ (6)	17.0 times	4.7 times

EXHIBIT 5.22

Inventory Turnover Ratios for Whole Foods Market, Inc., and Guess?, Inc.

Managers closely watch both the inventory turnover ratio and average days in inventory. If a manager sees the average days in inventory increasing, indicating that items are being held in inventory longer, it could indicate potential problems with old or obsolete inventory.

Your Turn 5-9

Wal-Mart reported inventory of $35,159 and $34,511 on its balance sheets at the end of the fiscal years 2007 and 2008, respectively. During the 2008 fiscal year (ended on January 31, 2009), the company's cost of goods sold was $306,158. (All dollars are in millions.) What was Wal-Mart's inventory turnover ratio for the year? How many days, on average, did merchandise remain in the inventory?

Business Risk, Control, and Ethics

L.O.7
Describe the risks associated with inventory and the controls that minimize those risks.

Inventory is a very important asset and ties up a large percentage of a firm's cash. Managing inventory is important to a successful business. Making sure there is enough inventory on hand to meet demand, without having too much inventory because it is costly to store and maintain, is key for merchandising and manufacturing firms. Wal-Mart, for example, has spent millions of dollars to establish and maintain its state-of-the-art inventory system.

In addition to the routine management of inventory, however, the firm must also evaluate and control the risk of losing inventory. Have you ever read how much money retail companies lose from shoplifting? The 20th Annual Retail Theft Survey reported that over $6.7 billion was lost from shoplifting and employee theft in just 24 U.S. retail companies in 2007. It is no surprise that retail firms such as Macy's and Target are very concerned about inventory theft. All consumers pay for that loss in higher merchandise prices; therefore, good controls on inventory are important to both the company and the consumer.

Like any company asset, the inventory must be protected from damage and theft. The policies and procedures we have discussed can help reduce the risks associated with the actual purchase of the inventory—selecting a reliable vendor and making sure the items received are the ones ordered. To safeguard inventory from theft, companies can use controls such as locking storage rooms and limiting access to the inventory. When you buy clothes from Abercrombie & Fitch or The Gap, you might notice a sensor attached to the clothing that the salesclerk must remove before you leave the store. You may have experienced the unpleasant beeping of a sensor if a store clerk forgets to remove the device.

Segregation of duties is a control that helps companies minimize the risk of losing inventory to error or theft. The person who keeps the inventory records should not be the same person who has physical control of the inventory. This separation of record keeping and physical control of assets makes it impossible for a single individual to steal the inventory and cover it up with false record keeping. When this control is in place and functioning properly, it would take collusion— two or more people getting together on the plan—to lose inventory in this way.

Large retail firms such as Target have extensive inventory controls. There are many places— from the receiving dock to the front door of the store—where Target must keep an eye on its inventory. When goods arrive at the receiving dock, a clerk will make a record of the type and amount of merchandise that has arrived on a copy of the original purchase order without any quantities listed. The firm wants the receiving clerk to independently check the type and amount of goods that have been received. This record will be sent to the accounts payable department where a clerk in that department will compare the record of the goods received with the original purchase order, which was sent over earlier from the purchasing department. Do you see the controls in place to safeguard the incoming shipments of merchandise? Several different departments are keeping a record of the goods ordered and received. The receiving clerk sends the merchandise to the inventory department where physical custody of the goods is separate from the record keeping, which we have seen is verified by several departments.

Obsolescence

Inventory is such an important asset to a firm that financial analysts and investors are very concerned that it is properly reported on the financial statements. In addition to protecting inventory from damage and theft, firms risk losing inventory as a result of obsolescence. If you were the manager of Best Buy, you would hate to have a warehouse full of VHS tapes when DVDs are available.

Firms that deal with cutting-edge technologies are at most risk for having obsolete inventory. Sprint PCS or T-Mobile would not want to have a huge inventory of analog-only phones now that digital phones are the better choice. With the new Bluetooth technology, the cell phone business is at risk with its old inventories. Each year, a company's inventory is evaluated for obsolescence at the same time the lower-of-cost-or-market rule is applied. Inventory must be written off, which will increase the cost of goods sold, when it is deemed to be obsolete. For example, in the notes to its financial statements, shown in Exhibit 5.23, SanDisk Corporation, the manufacturer of flash storage, has a note about inventory obsolescence.

EXHIBIT 5.23

SanDisk Corporation's Note about the Risk of Inventory Obsolescence

SanDisk is in the technology business, so the company is especially concerned about inventory obsolescence.

The Company reduces the carrying value of its inventory to a new basis for estimated obsolescence or unmarketable inventory by an amount equal to the difference between the cost of the inventory and the estimated market value based upon assumptions about future demand and market conditions, including assumptions about changes in average selling prices. If actual market conditions are less favorable than those projected by management additional reductions in inventory valuation may be required.

The Ethics of Inventory Losses

Inventory losses have an ethical component. The obvious one is that unethical people may steal a firm's inventory. Less obvious is the opportunity that inventory provides for misstating the value of the firm's assets. Failure to write down inventory that has lost value means that earnings will be overstated by the amount of the decline in inventory. As you know by now, managers rarely want to recognize expenses that do not produce any revenue, and they often look for ways to boost earnings. Inventory valuation is an area where the flexibility of accounting standards can lead to manipulation of earnings. When you study a firm's financial statements, be sure to read the notes to the financial statements about the firm's policy on writing down its obsolete inventory.

Chapter Summary Points

- A firm records the purchase of inventory at cost. That includes all costs to get the inventory ready for sale. Shipping costs, purchase discounts, and purchase returns and allowances all must be considered in calculating the cost of inventory.
- When a firm sells the inventory, the firm must consider sales discounts and sales returns and allowances when calculating net sales revenue.
- Inventory record keeping can be done at the time of each sale (perpetual inventory system), or the record keeping can be done at the end of the period (periodic inventory system).
- If a firm does not specifically identify the inventory item sold at the time of the sale, the firm will select one of three common cost flow assumptions to value inventory sold. Making a cost flow assumption is necessary when inventory costs are not constant and the specific identification of inventory units sold is too costly. The three methods are weighted average cost;

first-in, first-out (FIFO); and last-in, first-out (LIFO). When costs of inventory are changing, these methods most often will produce different amounts for cost of goods sold.

- To avoid overvaluing inventory, firms must compare the cost of their inventory to the market value of the inventory and value the inventory at the lower of the two. This is called the lower-of-cost-or-market rule for valuing inventory.
- The gross profit ratio and the inventory turnover ratio are both useful in evaluating a firm's performance with respect to inventory. Gross profit ratio is equal to the gross profit divided by sales. The inventory turnover ratio is equal to cost of goods sold divided by average inventory.
- Firms face the risk of inventory being lost, damaged, and stolen. Controls include physically guarding the inventory (security services, locks, and alarms) and regular record keeping to identify potential problems. Many firms, high-tech firms in particular, run the risk of having obsolete inventory. Again, regular monitoring of purchases and sales will help control this risk.

Chapter Summary Problem

To compare the inventory methods for TV Heaven, a retail firm that specializes in high-end televisions, we will look at a single item to keep the analysis simple. Our results will apply to the other items in the inventory as well. Suppose TV Heaven started March with an inventory of 50 plasma TVs that cost $2,010 each, for a total beginning inventory of $100,500. During March, the firm made the following purchases:

March 2	200 TVs for $2,000 each
March 10	150 TVs for $1,800 each
March 20	100 TVs for $1,500 each
March 29	50 TVs for $1,000 each

During March, the firm made the following sales:

March 5	110 TVs for $4,000 each
March 12	160 TVs for $4,000 each
March 25	150 TVs for $4,000 each

Instructions

1. Using *periodic inventory record keeping*, calculate the cost of goods sold for the month and the inventory at the end of the month. Do these calculations using three methods: weighted average cost, FIFO, and LIFO. All other operating expenses amounted to $250,000. Assume these are the only transactions for the period. Calculate net income using each of the three methods. Which method provides the highest net income? What is causing this method to produce the highest net income?
2. Using *perpetual inventory record keeping*, calculate the cost of goods sold for the month and the inventory at the end of the month. Do these calculations using three methods: weighted average cost, FIFO, and LIFO. All other operating expenses amounted to $250,000. Assume these are the only transactions for the period. Calculate net income using each of the three methods. Which method provides the highest net income? Explain why weighted average cost and LIFO produce different amounts under perpetual than they do under periodic.

Solution

1. Periodic Inventory

Cost of Goods Sold

	No. of Units	Unit Cost	Total Cost
Beginning inventory	50	$2,010	$100,500
Purchases March 2	200	$2,000	$400,000
March 10	150	$1,800	$270,000
March 20	100	$1,500	$150,000
March 29	50	$1,000	$ 50,000
Goods available for sale	550		$970,500
Units sold	420		

Weighted average cost $970,500 ÷ 550 = $ 1,765 per unit (rounded)

Cost of goods sold = 420 units × $1,765 = $741,300   Ending inventory
                                      130 units × $1,765 = $229,450

FIFO				
	50 × $2,010 =	$100,500		
	200 × $2,000 =	$400,000		
	150 × $1,800 =	$270,000	80 × $1,500 =	$120,000
	20 × $1,500 =	$ 30,000	50 × $1,000 =	$ 50,000
Cost of goods sold	420 units	$800,500	Ending inventory	$170,000

LIFO				
	50 × $1,000 =	$ 50,000		
	100 × $1,500 =	$150,000		
	150 × $1,800 =	$270,000	80 × $2,000 =	$160,000
	120 × $2,000 =	$240,000	50 × $2,010 =	$100,500
Cost of goods sold	420 units	$710,000	Ending inventory	$260,500

TV Heaven
Income Statement
For the Month Ended March 31

	Weighted Average Cost	FIFO	LIFO
Sales revenue	$1,680,000	$1,680,000	$1,680,000
Cost of goods sold	741,300	800,500	710,000
Gross profit	938,700	879,500	970,000
Other operating expenses	250,000	250,000	250,000
Net income	$ 688,700	$ 629,500	$ 720,000

Net income is highest using LIFO because the cost of the inventory is going down. More often, costs go up so companies use LIFO to minimize net income. In this case, the technology advances are likely driving down the cost of plasma TVs.

2. Perpetual Inventory

Cost of Goods Sold

	No. of Units	Unit Cost	Total Cost
Beginning inventory	50	$2,010	$100,500
Purchases March 2	200	$2,000	$400,000
March 10	150	$1,800	$270,000
March 20	100	$1,500	$150,000
March 29	50	$1,000	$ 50,000
Goods available for sale	550		$970,500
Units sold March 5	110		
March 12	160		
March 25	150		
Ending inventory	130		

Weighted average (WA) cost		Average unit cost	Cost of goods sold
WA cost on March 5	50 at $2,010 ⎫ 200 at $2,000 ⎬ =	$500,500 ÷ 250 = $2,002 avg. cost	110 units × $2,002 = $220,220
WA cost on March 12	140 at $2,002 ⎫ 150 at $1,800 ⎬ =	$550,280 ÷ 290 = $1,898 average cost (rounded)	160 units × $1,898 = $303,680

		Average unit cost	Cost of goods sold
WA cost on March 25	130 at $1,898 ⎫ 100 at $1,500 ⎭ =	$396,740 ÷ 230 = $1,725 average cost (rounded)	150 units × $1,725 = $258,750
Total cost of goods sold			$782,650
(Ending inventory)	80 at $1,725 ⎫ 50 at $1,000 ⎭ =	$188,000 ÷ 130 = $1,446 per unit (rounded)	$188,000

Note: Under WA perpetual, the ending inventory plus cost of goods sold is $150 more than goods available for sale. This differential is due to rounding. If you carry out the calculations to several decimal places, you will eliminate this rounding error. This type of calculation is typically done in a computer program that will not round as we have done here.

FIFO

Sale on March 5 (110 units)	50 at $2,010 ⎫ 60 at $2,000 ⎭ =	$220,500
Sale on March 12 (160 units)	140 at $2,000 ⎫ 20 at $1,800 ⎭ =	$316,000
Sale on March 25 (150 units)	130 at $1,800 ⎫ 20 at $1,500 ⎭ =	$264,000
Cost of goods sold		$800,500
FIFO ending inventory	80 at $1,500 ⎫ 50 at $1,000 ⎭ =	$170,000

LIFO

Sale on March 5 (110 units)	110 at $2,000	$220,000
Sale on March 12 (160 units)	150 at $1,800 ⎫ 10 at $2,000 ⎭ =	$290,000
Sale on March 25 (150 units)	100 at $1,500 ⎫ 50 at $2,000 ⎭ =	$250,000
Cost of goods sold		$760,000
LIFO ending inventory	50 at $1,000 ⎫ 30 at $2,000 ⎬ = 50 at $2,010 ⎭	$210,500

```
                            TV Heaven
                        Income Statement
                For the Month Ended March 31
```

	Weighted Average Cost	FIFO	LIFO
Sales revenue	$1,680,000	$1,680,000	$1,680,000
Cost of goods sold	782,650	800,500	760,000
Gross profit	897,350	879,500	920,000
Other operating expenses	250,000	250,000	250,000
Net income	$ 647,350	$ 629,500	$ 670,000

Net income is highest under LIFO because the cost of the inventory is going down.

When a firm uses perpetual record keeping, it cannot assume to have sold units that were not purchased by the date of the sale. On the other hand, when a firm uses periodic record keeping, every purchase made during the period—no matter how the purchase dates match up to the sales dates—is part of the calculation of cost of goods sold. For weighted average cost, the average is different because the late purchase is included in the average cost calculation under periodic but not perpetual record keeping. For LIFO periodic, that last and cheapest purchase can be counted in the cost of goods sold. (Under perpetual, it could not be used because it had not been purchased at the time of the last sale.)

Key Terms for Chapter 5

Average days in inventory (p. 232)

Contra-revenue (p. 209)

Cost of goods available for sale (p. 207)

First-in, first-out (FIFO) (p. 214)

FOB destination (p. 204)

FOB shipping point (p. 204)

Gross profit ratio (p. 231)

Inventory turnover ratio (p. 232)

Last-in, first-out (LIFO) (p. 215)

Lower-of-cost-or-market (LCM) rule (p. 230)

Periodic inventory system (p. 204)

Perpetual inventory system (p. 204)

Purchase discount (p. 206)

Purchase order (p. 203)

Purchase returns and allowances (p. 206)

Replacement cost (p. 231)

Sales discount (p. 209)

Sales returns and allowances (p. 209)

Specific identification method (p. 212)

Weighted average cost (p. 213)

Answers to YOUR TURN Questions

Chapter 5

Your Turn 5-1

1. Company X pays the freight.
2. Company B pays the freight.

Your Turn 5-2

Coffee	98% of $500 =	$490
Bags		100
Total inventory cost		$590

Note: Shipping costs are not included because the purchase was FOB destination.

Your Turn 5-3

Cash collected: $3,150 ($3,000 + 5% of $3,000)
Revenue: $3,000

Your Turn 5-4

The firm should use perpetual. At the time of each sale, the inventory account will be reduced. When the period is over and the inventory is counted, any difference between the inventory amount shown in the records and the inventory amount identified by a physical count of the inventory will be the amount of inventory shrinkage. If the firm used a periodic system, all inventory not present at the end of the period is assumed to be part of cost of goods sold.

Your Turn 5-5

The weighted average cost of a unit is $[(($10 \times 1) + ($20 \times 2))/30] = 1.66667 per unit
Cost of goods sold = 15 units $\times$ $1.66667 = **$25**

Your Turn 5-6

1. Cost of goods sold is $4,600 + $5,100 = $9,700; and the gross profit is $14,000 – $9,700 = $4,300.
2. Cost of goods sold is $3,500 + $5,100 = $8,600; and the gross profit is $14,000 – $8,600 = $5,400.
3. Weighted average cost of the bracelets is $13,200/3 = $4,400. The cost of goods sold for the sale of two bracelets would be 2 $\times$ $4,400 = $8,800.

Your Turn 5-7

1. FIFO: $705 [(30 × $20) + (5 × $21)]
2. LIFO: $775 [(20 × $23) + (15 × $21)]
3. [(30 × $20) + (20 × $21) + (20 × $23)] ÷ 70 units = $21.143 (rounded)
   $21.143 × 35 = $740

Your Turn 5-8

The LIFO conformity rule says that if a firm uses LIFO for tax purposes, it must also use LIFO for accounting (GAAP) purposes. It is unusual for accounting and tax rules to overlap. Usually accounting rules (GAAP) do not follow tax law.

Your Turn 5-9

Inventory turnover ratio = $306,158 ÷ [(35,159 + 34,511) ÷ 2] = 8.79
Average days in inventory = 365 ÷ 8.79 = 41.5 days

Questions

1. Explain the terms *FOB shipping point* and *FOB destination.* What are the accounting and business implications of the shipping terms? Why is it important to know who owns goods during shipping?
2. What is the difference between freight-in and freight-out?
3. What is the difference between a purchase return and a purchase allowance? What is the effect of purchase returns and allowances on the overall cost of inventory to the buyer?
4. What is a purchase discount? What is the effect of a purchase discount on the overall cost of inventory to the buyer?
5. Explain the terms of a purchase described as *2/15, n/30.* Would you take advantage of this offer? Why or why not?
6. What is a contra-revenue account? Give two examples of contra-revenue accounts.
7. What is a sales discount? What is the effect of a sales discount on the total sales revenue of the seller?
8. What is the difference between a periodic and perpetual inventory system?
9. What is inventory shrinkage?
10. What is the difference between the physical flow of inventory and the inventory cost flow?
11. What are the common cost flow methods for accounting for inventory? Describe the differences.
12. If inventory costs are rising, which method (FIFO, LIFO, or weighted average cost) results in the highest net income? Explain your answer.
13. If inventory costs are rising, which method (FIFO, LIFO, or weighted average cost) results in the lowest net income? Explain your answer.
14. Does LIFO or FIFO give the best—most current—balance sheet value for the ending inventory? Why?
15. How do taxes affect the choice between LIFO and FIFO?
16. Does the periodic or perpetual choice affect the choice of a cost flow (LIFO versus FIFO) method? Explain.
17. What is the *lower-of-cost-or-market* rule and why is it necessary?
18. What does the gross profit percentage measure? How is it calculated?
19. What does the inventory turnover ratio measure? What does *average-days-in-inventory* mean?
20. What are some of the risks associated with inventory? How do managers minimize these risks?

Multiple-Choice Questions

1. When inventory is purchased, it is recorded as a(n) _____ and when sold it becomes a(n) _____.
   a. liability; withdrawal
   b. asset; expense
   c. liability; asset
   d. asset; contra-asset

Use the following information to answer questions 2–5:

Inventory data for Newman & Frith Merchandisers, Inc., is provided here. Sales for the period were 2,800 units. Each sold for $8. The company maintains a periodic inventory system.

Date		Number of Units	Unit Cost	Total Cost
January	Beginning inventory	1,000	$3.00	$ 3,000
February	Purchases	600	$3.50	$ 2,100
March	Purchases	800	$4.00	$ 3,200
April	Purchases	1,200	$4.25	$ 5,100
Totals		3,600		$13,400

2. Determine the ending inventory assuming the company uses the FIFO cost flow method.
   a. $3,400
   b. $2,400
   c. $9,200
   d. $10,000

3. Determine the cost of goods sold assuming the company uses the FIFO cost flow method.
   a. $3,400
   b. $10,000
   c. $10,200
   d. $2,400

4. Determine the ending inventory assuming the company uses the weighted average cost flow method. (Round average cost to two decimal places.)
   a. $2,300
   b. $3,300
   c. $9,800
   d. $2,976

5. Determine the gross profit assuming the company uses the LIFO cost flow method.
   a. $11,400
   b. $14,400
   c. $22,400
   d. $19,700

6. Using LIFO will produce a lower net income than using FIFO under which of the following conditions?
   a. Inventory costs are decreasing.
   b. Inventory costs are increasing.
   c. Inventory costs are not changing.
   d. Sales prices are decreasing.

Use the following information to answer questions 7–10:

Sales revenue	$480,000
Cost of goods sold	300,000
Sales discounts	20,000
Sales returns and allowances	15,000
Operating expenses	85,000
Interest revenue	5,000

7. What is the net sales revenue?
   a. $400,000
   b. $445,000
   c. $415,000
   d. $455,000

8. What is the gross profit?
   a. $145,000
   b. $105,000
   c. $140,000
   d. $90,000

9. What is the net income?
    a. $60,000
    b. $65,000
    c. $55,000
    d. $180,000
10. What is the gross profit percentage?
    a. 13.54%
    b. 14.61%
    c. 32.58%
    d. 21.67%

Short Exercises
Set A

SE5-1A. *Calculate cost of inventory. (LO 1).* Invoice price of goods is $5,000. Purchase terms are 2/10, n/30 and the invoice is paid in the week of receipt. The shipping terms are FOB shipping point, and the shipping costs amount to $200. What is the total cost of the inventory?

SE5-2A. *Record sale of merchandise inventory: perpetual inventory system. (LO 1, 2).* Brenda Bailey's Textiles, Inc., uses a perpetual inventory system. Enter the following transaction into the accounting equation:

In February, Brenda Bailey's sold $500,000 of merchandise on account with terms 2/10, n/30. The cost of the merchandise sold was $230,000.

SE5-3A. *Calculate gross profit and the gross profit ratio. (LO 1, 6).* Using the information in SE5-2A, calculate the gross profit from the sale and the gross profit ratio. Assume that the customer does not pay within the discount period.

SE5-4A. *Calculate cost of goods sold and ending inventory: weighted average cost. (LO 3).* Calculate the cost of goods sold and the cost of the ending inventory using the weighted average cost flow assumption. Assume periodic record keeping.

Sales	100 units at $15 per unit
Beginning inventory	90 units at $6 per unit
Purchases	60 units at $9 per unit

SE5-5A. *Calculate cost of goods sold and ending inventory: FIFO. (LO 3).* Using the data from SE5-4A, calculate the cost of goods sold and the cost of the ending inventory using the FIFO periodic cost flow assumption.

SE5-6A. *Calculate cost of goods sold and ending inventory: LIFO. (LO 3).* Using the data from SE5-4A, calculate the cost of goods sold and the cost of the ending inventory using the LIFO periodic cost flow assumption.

SE5-7A. *Analyze the effect of the cost flow method on net income. (LO 3).* Given the following information, calculate the amount by which net income would differ between FIFO and LIFO. Assume the periodic system.

Beginning inventory	3,000 units at $100 per unit
Purchases	8,000 units at $130 per unit
Units sold	6,000 units at $225 per unit

SE5-8A. *Analyze the effect of the cost flow method on gross profit. (LO 3, 4).* Given the following information, calculate the amount by which gross profit would differ between FIFO and LIFO. Assume the periodic system.

Beginning inventory	1,500 units at $55 per unit
Purchases	2,750 units at $58 per unit
Units sold	2,250 units at $99 per unit

SE5-9A. *Apply the lower-of-cost-or-market rule. (LO 5).* The following information pertains to item #007SS of inventory of Marine Aquatic Sales, Inc.:

	Per unit
Cost	$180
Replacement cost	181
Selling price	195

The physical inventory indicates 2,000 units of item #007SS on hand. What amount will be reported on the Marine Aquatic Sales, Inc.'s balance sheet for this inventory item?

SE5-10A. *Calculate the gross profit ratio, inventory turnover ratio, and average days in inventory. (LO 6).* Using the following information, calculate inventory turnover ratio, the average days in inventory, and the gross profit ratio for Barkley Company for the year ended December 31, 2012. (Round to two decimal places.)

Sales	$125,000
Cost of goods sold	75,000
Ending inventory, December 31, 2011	15,275
Ending inventory, December 31, 2012	18,750
Net income	26,500

Set B

SE5-11B. *Calculate cost of inventory. (LO 1).* Invoice price of goods is $1,000. Purchase terms are 1/10, n/30 and the invoice is paid in the week of receipt. The shipping terms are FOB shipping point, and the shipping costs amount to $200. What is the total cost of the inventory?

SE5-12B. *Record sale of merchandise inventory: perpetual inventory system. (LO 1, 2).* Sam's Supply, Inc., uses a perpetual inventory system. Enter the following transaction into the accounting equation:

In February, Sam's sold $320,000 of merchandise on account with terms 3/10, n/30. The cost of the merchandise sold was $100,000.

SE5-13B. *Calculate gross profit and the gross profit ratio. (LO 1, 6).* Using the information in SE5-12B, calculate the gross profit from the sale and the gross profit ratio. Assume the customer does not pay within the discount period.

SE5-14B. *Calculate cost of goods sold and ending inventory: weighted average cost. (LO 3).* Calculate the cost of goods sold and the cost of the ending inventory using the weighted average cost flow assumption. Assume periodic record keeping.

Sales	150 units at $5 per unit
Beginning inventory	100 units at $2 per unit
Purchases	60 units at $3 per unit

SE5-15B. *Calculate cost of goods sold and ending inventory: FIFO. (LO 3).* Using the data from SE5-14B, calculate the cost of goods sold and the cost of the ending inventory using the FIFO periodic cost flow assumption.

SE5-16B. *Calculate cost of goods sold and ending inventory: LIFO. (LO 3).* Using the data from SE5-14B, calculate the cost of goods sold and the cost of the ending inventory using the LIFO periodic cost flow assumption.

SE5-17B. *Analyze the effect of the cost flow method on net income. (LO 3).* Given the following information, calculate the amount by which net income would differ between FIFO and LIFO. Assume the periodic system.

Beginning inventory	2,000 units at $10 per unit
Purchases	5,000 units at $12 per unit
Units sold	6,500 units at $25 per unit

SE5-18B. *Analyze the effect of the cost flow method on gross profit. (LO 3, 4).* Given the following information, calculate the amount by which gross profit would differ between FIFO and LIFO. Assume the periodic system.

Beginning inventory	500 units at $50 per unit
Purchases	1,200 units at $48 per unit
Units sold	900 units at $60 per unit

SE5-19B. *Apply the lower-of-cost-or-market rule. (LO 5).* The following information pertains to item #3801B of inventory of Parts-A-Plenty:

	Per unit
Cost	$180
Replacement cost	170
Selling price	195

The physical inventory indicates 1,000 units of item #3801B on hand. What amount will be reported on Parts-A-Plenty's balance sheet for this inventory item?

SE5-20B. *Calculate the gross profit ratio, inventory turnover ratio, and average days in inventory. (LO 6).* Using the following information, calculate inventory turnover ratio, the average days in inventory, and the gross profit ratio for Howard Company for the year ended December 31, 2011. (Round to two decimal places.)

Sales	$225,000
Cost of goods sold	175,000
Ending inventory, December 31, 2011	15,275
Ending inventory, December 31, 2010	18,750
Net income	36,500

Exercises
Set A

All of the A exercises can be found within MyAccountingLab, an online homework and practice environment.

E5-21A. *Record merchandising transactions: perpetual inventory system. (LO 1, 2).* Assume the following transactions for Clark's Appliances, Inc., took place during May. Clark's Appliances uses a perpetual inventory system. Enter each of the transactions into the accounting equation.

May 2	Purchased refrigerators on account at a total cost of $500,000; terms 1/10, n/30
May 9	Paid freight of $800 on refrigerators purchased from GE
May 16	Returned refrigerators to GE because they were damaged; received a credit of $5,000 from GE
May 22	Sold refrigerators costing $100,000 for $180,000 to Pizzeria Number 1 on account, terms n/30
May 24	Gave a credit of $3,000 to Pizzeria Number 1 for the return of a refrigerator not ordered. Clark's cost was $1,200.

E5-22A. *Record merchandising transactions: perpetual inventory system. (LO 1, 2).* The Fedora Company had a beginning inventory balance of $25,750 and engaged in the following transactions during the month of June:

June 2	Purchased $4,000 of merchandise inventory on account from Plumes, Inc., with terms 2/10, n/30 and FOB destination. Freight costs associated with this purchase were $225.
June 4	Returned $400 of damaged merchandise to Plumes, Inc.
June 6	Sold $7,000 of merchandise to Fancy Caps on account, terms 1/15, n/30 and FOB shipping point. Freight costs were $125. The cost of the inventory sold was $3,500.
June 9	Paid the amount owed to Plumes, Inc.
June 10	Granted Fancy Caps an allowance on the June 6 sale of $300 for minor damage found on several pieces of merchandise

June 22	Received total payment owed from Fancy Caps
June 24	Paid sales salaries of $1,850
June 25	Paid the rent on the showroom of $1,200

Enter each of the transactions for the Fedora Company into the accounting equation, assuming it uses a perpetual inventory system.

Use the following data to answer the questions in E5-23A through E5-26A:

Box Office Projectors began the month of August with three movie projectors in inventory, each unit costing $350. During August, eight additional projectors of the same model were purchased.

August 11	Purchased four units at $400 each
August 13	Sold five units at $425 each
August 14	Purchased three units at $375
August 18	Sold two units at $425 each
August 21	Sold three units at $425 each
August 26	Purchased one unit at $380

E5-23A. *Calculate cost of goods sold and ending inventory: periodic FIFO. (LO 3, 4).* Assume Box Office uses a periodic record-keeping system and the FIFO cost flow method.

1. Calculate the cost of goods sold that will appear on the income statement for the month of August.
2. Determine the cost of inventory that will appear on the balance sheet at the end of August.

E5-24A. *Calculate cost of goods sold and ending inventory: periodic LIFO. (LO 3, 4).* Assume Box Office uses a periodic record-keeping system and the LIFO cost flow method.

1. Calculate the cost of goods sold that will appear on the income statement for the month of August.
2. Determine the cost of inventory that will appear on the balance sheet at the end of August.

E5-25A. *Calculate cost of goods sold and ending inventory: perpetual FIFO. (LO 3, 4).* Assume Box Office uses a perpetual record-keeping system and the FIFO cost flow method.

1. Calculate the cost of goods sold that will appear on the income statement for the month of August.
2. Determine the cost of inventory that will appear on the balance sheet at the end of August.

E5-26A. *Calculate cost of goods sold and ending inventory: perpetual LIFO. (LO 3, 4).* Assume Box Office uses a perpetual record-keeping system and the LIFO cost flow method.

1. Calculate the cost of goods sold that will appear on the income statement for the month of August.
2. Determine the cost of inventory that will appear on the balance sheet at the end of August.

E5-27A. *Calculate cost of goods sold and ending inventory: periodic weighted average cost. (LO 3, 4).* The Fancy Phones Company sells phones to business customers. The company began 2009 with 2,000 units of inventory on hand. These units cost $200 each. The following transactions related to the company's merchandise inventory occurred during the first quarter of 2009:

January 14	Purchased 750 units for $225 each
February 13	Purchased 500 units for $175 each
March 30	Purchased <u>200</u> units for $205 each
Total purchases	1,450 units

All unit costs include the purchase price and freight charges paid by Fancy Phones. During the quarter ending March 31, 2009, sales totaled 2,500 units, leaving 950 units in ending inventory.

Assume Fancy Phones uses a periodic record-keeping system and the weighted average cost flow method.

1. Calculate the cost of goods sold that will appear on Fancy Phone's income statement for the quarter ending March 31.
2. Determine the cost of inventory that will appear on Fancy Phone's balance sheet at the end of March.

E5-28A. *Calculate cost of goods sold and ending inventory: perpetual weighted average cost. (LO 3, 4).* Speedy Wireless, Inc., sells netbooks. The company began the fourth quarter of the year on October 1, 2009, with 500 units of inventory on hand. These units cost $250 each. The following transactions related to the company's merchandise inventory occurred during the fourth quarter of 2009:

October 3	Sold 400 units for $400 each
November 5	Purchased 600 units for $275 each
November 29	Sold 500 units for $425 each
December 1	Purchased 700 units for $260 each
December 24	Sold 600 units for $450 each

All unit costs include the purchase price and freight charges paid by Speedy Wireless.

Assume the company uses a perpetual record-keeping system and the weighted average cost flow method.

1. Calculate the cost of goods sold that will appear on the income statement for the quarter ending December 31, 2009.
2. Determine the cost of inventory that will appear on the balance sheet at December 31, 2009.

E5-29A. *Apply the lower-of-cost-or-market rule. (LO 5).* Use the data provided to answer the question that follows:

Ending inventory at cost, December 31, 2011	$ 17,095
Ending inventory at replacement cost, December 31, 2011	16,545
Cost of goods sold, balance at December 31, 2011	250,765
Sales revenue, balance at December 31, 2011	535,780
Cash, balance at December 31, 2011	165,340

What inventory amount will this firm report on its balance sheet at December 31, 2011?

E5-30A. *Apply the lower-of-cost-or-market rule. (LO 5).* In each case, indicate the correct amount to be reported for the inventory on the year-end balance sheet.

1. Ending inventory at cost $125,000
   Ending inventory at market $121,750
2. Ending inventory at cost $117,500
   Ending inventory at market $120,250

E5-31A. *Calculate gross profit and gross profit percentage: FIFO and LIFO. (LO 6).* Given the following information, calculate the gross profit and gross profit ratio under (a) FIFO periodic and under (b) LIFO periodic:

Sales	250 units at $100 per unit
Beginning inventory	75 units at $75 per unit
Purchases	300 units at $60 per unit

Set B

E5-32B. *Record merchandising transactions: perpetual inventory system. (LO 1, 2).* Assume the following transactions for Jennifer's Fix-It-Up, Inc., took place during March. Jennifer's uses a perpetual inventory system. Enter each of the transactions into the accounting equation.

March 3	Purchased televisions from Sanyo on account at a total cost of $650,000, terms 2/10, n/25
March 8	Paid freight of $1,000 on televisions purchased from Sanyo
March 16	Returned televisions to Sanyo because they were damaged. Received a credit of $15,000 from Sanyo.

March 22	Sold televisions costing $125,000 for $225,000 to Joe's Sports Bar & Grille on account, terms n/15
March 28	Gave a credit of $2,800 to Joe's Sports Bar & Grille for the return of a television not ordered. Jennifer's cost was $1,600.

E5-33B. *Record merchandising transactions: perpetual inventory system. (LO 1, 2).* Discount Wines, Inc., had a beginning inventory balance of $85,450 and engaged in the following transactions during the month of October:

October 2	Purchased $15,000 of merchandise inventory on account from Joe's Winery with terms 2/10, n/30 and FOB destination. Freight costs for this purchase were $750.
October 5	Returned $100 of damaged merchandise to Joe's
October 6	Sold $18,000 of merchandise to Tasty Catering Service on account, terms 2/15, n/30 and FOB shipping point. Freight costs were $155. The cost of the inventory sold was $10,500.
October 10	Paid the amount owed to Joe's
October 10	Granted Tasty an allowance on the October 6 sale of $200 for some soured wine
October 23	Received total payment owed from Tasty
October 29	Paid sales salaries of $1,500
October 31	Paid the rent on the warehouse of $1,450

Enter each of the transactions for Discount Wines, Inc., into the accounting equation, assuming it uses a perpetual inventory system.

E5-34B. *Calculate cost of goods sold and ending inventory: periodic weighted average cost. (LO 3, 4).* Tom's Trampoline Company sells commercial-size trampolines. The company's most recent fiscal year began on August 1, 2009, and ended July 31, 2010. The company began the year with 500 units of inventory on hand. These units cost $500 each. The following transactions related to the company's merchandise inventory occurred during the first quarter of the year:

August 14	Purchased 200 units for $525 each
September 12	Purchased 175 units for $490 each
October 20	Purchased <u>100</u> units for $510 each
Total purchases	475 units

During the quarter ending October 31, sales totaled 625 units.

Assume the company uses a periodic record-keeping system and the weighted average cost flow method.

1. Calculate the cost of goods sold that will appear on the company's income statement for the quarter ending October 31.
2. Determine the cost of inventory that will appear on the company's balance sheet at the end of October.

E5-35B. *Calculate cost of goods sold and ending inventory: perpetual weighted average cost. (LO 3, 4).* Bob's Barber Supplies sells hair clippers to local businesses. The company began the first quarter of the year January 1, 2009, with 1,000 units of inventory on hand. These units cost $50 each. The following transactions related to the company's merchandise inventory occurred during the first quarter of 2009:

January 12	Sold 800 units for $75 each
January 20	Purchased 500 units for $45 each
February 8	Sold 400 units for $75 each
March 5	Purchased 600 units for $60 each
March 19	Sold 500 units for $75 each

Assume the company uses a perpetual record-keeping system and the weighted average cost flow method.

1. Calculate the cost of goods sold that will appear on the income statement for the quarter ending March 31, 2009.
2. Determine the cost of inventory that will appear on the balance sheet at the end of March.

Use the following data to answer E5-36B through E5-39B:

Radio Tech Sales & Service, Inc., began the month of April with three top-of-the-line radios in inventory, Model # RD58V6Q; each unit cost $235. During April, nine additional radios of the same model were purchased.

April 9	Purchased three units at $230 each
April 11	Sold five units at $350 each
April 17	Purchased two units at $195 each
April 18	Sold one unit at $350
April 20	Sold two units at $350 each
April 28	Purchased four units at $180 each

E5-36B. *Calculate cost of goods sold and ending inventory: periodic FIFO. (LO 3, 4).* Assume Radio Tech uses a periodic inventory system and the FIFO cost flow method.

1. Calculate the cost of goods sold that will appear on Radio Tech's income statement for the month of April.
2. Determine the cost of inventory that will appear on Radio Tech's balance sheet at the end of April.

E5-37B. *Calculate cost of goods sold and ending inventory: periodic LIFO. (LO 3, 4).* Assume Radio Tech uses a periodic inventory system and the LIFO cost flow method.

1. Calculate the cost of goods sold that will appear on Radio Tech's income statement for the month of April.
2. Determine the cost of inventory that will appear on Radio Tech's balance sheet at the end of April.

E5-38B. *Calculate cost of goods sold and ending inventory: perpetual FIFO. (LO 3, 4).* Assume Radio Tech uses a perpetual inventory system and the FIFO cost flow method.

1. Calculate the cost of goods sold that will appear on Radio Tech's income statement for the month of April.
2. Determine the cost of inventory that will appear on Radio Tech's balance sheet at the end of April.

E5-39B. *Calculate cost of goods sold and ending inventory: perpetual LIFO. (LO 3, 4).* Assume Radio Tech uses a perpetual inventory system and the LIFO cost flow method.

1. Calculate the cost of goods sold that will appear on Radio Tech's income statement for the month of April.
2. Determine the cost of inventory that will appear on Radio Tech's balance sheet at the end of April.

E5-40B. *Apply the lower-of-cost-or-market rule. (LO 5).* Use the data provided to answer the question that follows:

Ending inventory at cost, June 30, 2010	$ 25,180
Ending inventory at replacement cost, June 30, 2010	25,130
Cost of goods sold, balance at June 30, 2010	150,550
Sales revenue, balance at June 30, 2010	275,625
Cash, balance at June 30, 2010	285,515

ASB Hardware, Inc., uses a perpetual inventory system and the FIFO cost flow method to account for its inventory. What inventory amount will ASB Hardware report on its balance sheet at June 30, 2010?

E5-41B. *Apply the lower-of-cost-or-market rule. (LO 5).* In each case, indicate the correct amount to be reported for the inventory on the year-end balance sheet.

1. Ending inventory at cost $275,000
   Ending inventory at market $271,250
2. Ending inventory at cost $185,250
   Ending inventory at market $187,550

E5-42B. *Calculate gross profit and gross profit ratio: FIFO and LIFO. (LO 6).* Given the following information, calculate the gross profit and gross profit ratio under (a) FIFO periodic and under (b) LIFO periodic:

Sales   300 units at $75 per unit
Beginning inventory   425 units at $40 per unit
Purchases   100 units at $50 per unit

Problems
Set A

MyAccountingLab

All of the A problems can be found within MyAccountingLab, an online homework and practice environment.

P5-43A. *Analyze purchases of merchandise inventory. (LO 1).* Rondo's Sports Wear made the following purchases in June of the current year:

June 7   Purchased $5,000 of merchandise, terms 5/15, n/60, FOB shipping point
June 15   Purchased $2,500 of merchandise, terms 3/10, n/30, FOB shipping point
June 25   Purchased $7,500 of merchandise, terms 2/10, n/30, FOB destination

Requirements

1. For each of the purchases listed, how many days does the company have to take advantage of the purchase discount?
2. What is the amount of the cash discount allowed in each case?
3. Assume the freight charges are 10% of the gross sales price. What is the amount of freight that Rondo's must pay for each purchase?
4. What is the total cost of inventory for Rondo's for the month of June, assuming that all discounts were taken?

P5-44A. *Analyze purchases of merchandise inventory. (LO 1)* Carrie & Runnels Bikes Plus, Inc., made the following purchases in December of the current year:

December 5   Purchased $2,600 of merchandise, terms 3/10, n/30, FOB destination
December 14   Purchased $6,150 of merchandise, terms 1/10, n/60, FOB shipping point
December 24   Purchased $8,375 of merchandise, terms 2/05, n/20, FOB destination

Requirements

1. For each purchase, by what date is the payment due, assuming the company takes advantage of the discount?
2. For each purchase, when is the payment due if the company does not take advantage of the discount?
3. In each case, what is the amount of the cash discount allowed?
4. Assume the freight charges are $365 on each purchase. For which purchase(s) is Bikes Plus responsible for the freight charges?
5. What is the total cost of inventory for Bikes Plus for the month of December, assuming that all discounts were taken?

P5-45A. *Record merchandising transactions, prepare financial statements, and calculate gross profit ratio: perpetual inventory system. (LO 1, 2, 4, 6).* At the beginning of February, Ace Distribution Company, Inc., started with a contribution of $10,000 cash in exchange for common stock from its shareholders. The company engaged in the following transactions during the month of February:

February 2	Purchased merchandise on account from Enter Supply Co. for $7,100, terms 2/10, n/45
February 5	Sold merchandise on account to Exit Company for $6,000, terms 2/10, n/30 and FOB destination. The cost of the merchandise sold was $4,500.
February 6	Paid $100 freight on the sale to Exit Company
February 8	Received credit from Enter Supply Co. for merchandise returned for $500
February 10	Paid Enter Supply Co. in full
February 12	Received payment from Exit Company for sale made on February 5
February 14	Purchased merchandise for cash for $5,200
February 16	Received refund from supplier for returned merchandise on February 14 cash purchase of $350
February 17	Purchased merchandise on account from Inware Distributors for $3,800, terms 1/10, n/30
February 18	Paid $250 freight on February 17 purchase
February 21	Sold merchandise for cash for $10,350. The cost of the merchandise sold was $8,200.
February 24	Purchased merchandise for cash for $2,300
February 25	Paid Inware Distributors for purchase on February 17
February 27	Gave refund of $200 to customer from February 21. The cost of the returned merchandise was $135.
February 28	Sold merchandise of $3,000 on account with the terms 2/10, n/30. The merchandise cost $2,300.

Requirements

1. Enter each transaction into the accounting equation, assuming Ace Distribution Company uses a perpetual inventory system. Start with the opening balances in cash and common stock described at the beginning of the problem.
2. Calculate the balance in the inventory account at the end of February.
3. Prepare a multistep income statement, the statement of changes in shareholders' equity, and the statement of cash flows for the month of February. Prepare a balance sheet at February 28.
4. Calculate the gross profit ratio.

P5-46A. *Record merchandising transactions, prepare financial statements, and calculate gross profit ratio: perpetual inventory system. (LO 1, 2, 4, 6).* The following transactions occurred during July 2010 at Tiny's Sports Shop:

July 2	Purchased weights on credit from Barbells Company for $900, with terms 3/10, n/30
July 4	Paid freight of $75 on the July 2 purchase
July 8	Sold merchandise to members on credit for $500, terms n/45. The merchandise sold cost $425.
July 9	Received credit of $50 from Barbells for damaged goods that were returned
July 11	Purchased workout equipment from Spinners for cash for $2,000
July 13	Paid Barbells Company in full
July 15	Purchased gloves and workout belts from Get Pumped on credit for $1,000, terms 5/15, n/60
July 17	Received credit of $25 from Get Pumped for damaged merchandise
July 19	Sold merchandise to members on account, $750, terms n/15. The cost of the merchandise sold was $250.
July 20	Received $700 in cash payment on account from members
July 23	Paid Get Pumped in full
July 27	Granted an allowance of $50 to members for gear that didn't work properly
July 29	Received $400 in cash payments on account from members
July 31	Paid cash operating expenses of $500 for the month

Requirements

1. Suppose Tiny's Sports Shop started the month with cash of $8,000, merchandise inventory of $2,000, and common stock of $10,000. Enter each transaction into the accounting equation, assuming Tiny's Sports Shop uses a perpetual inventory system.
2. Calculate the cost of goods sold for July and the ending balance in inventory.
3. Prepare the multistep income statement, and the statement of changes in shareholders' equity for the month of July, and the balance sheet at July 31.
4. Calculate the gross profit ratio for Tiny's Sports Shop for July. Explain what the ratio measures.

P5-47A. *Analyze accounting methods and prepare corrected income statement. (LO 1, 2, 4).* You are the accountant for Baldwin Company, and your assistant has prepared the following income statement for the year ended September 30, 2010:

Baldwin Company
Income Statement
For the Year Ended September 30, 2010

Sales revenue		$850,000
Sales returns and allowances	$ 22,500	
Freight costs	14,300	(36,800)
Net sales		813,200
Expenses		
Cost of goods sold	$540,000	
Selling expenses	150,000	
Insurance expense	20,000	
Administrative expenses	40,000	
Dividends	8,000	
Total expenses		758,000
Net income		$ 55,200

You have uncovered the following errors:

a. Sales revenue includes $5,000 of items that have been back-ordered. (The items have not been delivered to the customers, and the customers have not been billed for the items.)
b. Selling expenses include $250 of allowances that were given to customers who received damaged products.
c. Insurance expense includes $100 worth of insurance that applies to 2011.
d. Administrative expenses include a loan made to worker who had some serious financial trouble and needed $500 to pay a hospital bill. The worker plans to repay the money by the end of December.

Requirements

1. Prepare a corrected multistep income statement for the year. Baldwin shows sales as the net amount only on its income statement.
2. Write a memo to your assistant explaining why each error you found is incorrect and what the correct accounting treatment should be.

P5-48A. *Calculate cost of goods sold and ending inventory and analyze effect of each method on financial statements. (LO 3, 4).* Jefferson Company had the following sales and purchases during 2011, its first year of business:

January 5	Purchased 40 units at $100 each
February 15	Sold 15 units at $150 each
April 10	Sold 10 units at $150 each
June 30	Purchased 30 units at $105 each

| August 15 | Sold 25 units at $150 each |
| November 28 | Purchased 30 units at $110 each |

Requirements

1. Calculate the ending inventory, the cost of goods sold, and the gross profit for the December 31, 2011, financial statements under each of the following assumptions:
   a. FIFO periodic
   b. LIFO periodic
   c. Weighted average cost periodic
2. How will the differences between the methods affect the income statement for the year and balance sheet at December 31, 2011?

P5-49A. *Calculate cost of goods sold and ending inventory; analyze effects of each method on financial statements; apply lower-of-cost-or-market rule; calculate inventory turnover ratio. (LO 3, 4, 5, 6).* The following series of transactions occurred during 2009:

January 1	Beginning inventory was 70 units at $10 each
January 15	Purchased 100 units at $11 each
February 4	Sold 60 units at $20 each
March 10	Purchased 50 units at $12 each
April 15	Sold 70 units at $20 each
June 30	Purchased 100 units at $13 each
August 4	Sold 110 units at $20 each
October 1	Purchased 80 units at $14 each
December 5	Sold 50 units at $21 each

Requirements

1. Calculate the value of the ending inventory and cost of goods sold, assuming the company uses a periodic inventory system and the FIFO cost flow assumption.
2. Calculate the value of the ending inventory and cost of goods sold, assuming the company uses a periodic inventory system and the LIFO cost flow assumption.
3. Calculate the value of the ending inventory and cost of goods sold, assuming the company uses a periodic record-keeping system and the weighted average cost flow assumption.
4. Which of the three methods will result in the highest cost of goods sold for the year ended December 31, 2009?
5. Which of the three methods will provide the most current ending inventory value for the balance sheet at December 31, 2009?
6. How will the differences between the methods affect the income statement for the year and the balance sheet at year end?
7. Calculate the company's inventory turnover ratio and average days in inventory for the year for each method in items 1, 2, and 3.
8. At the end of the year, the current replacement cost of the inventory is $1,100. Indicate at what amount the company's inventory will be reported using the lower-of-cost-or-market rule for each method (FIFO, LIFO, and weighted average cost).

P5-50A. *Calculate cost of goods sold, ending inventory, and inventory turnover ratio. (LO 3, 6).* The following merchandise inventory transactions occurred during the month of May for the Super Stars, Inc.:

May 1	Inventory on hand was 2,000 units at $10 each
May 9	Sold 1,000 units at $15 each
May 15	Purchased 1,500 units at $11 each
May 21	Sold 1,250 units at $14 each
May 29	Purchased 3,000 units at $9 each

Requirements

1. Assume Super Stars uses a periodic record-keeping system and compute the cost of goods sold for the month ended May 31 and ending inventory at May 31 using each of the following cost flow methods:
   a. FIFO

b. LIFO

c. Weighted average cost

2. Using the information for item (1), calculate the inventory turnover ratio and average days in inventory for the month of May for each method.

3. Assume Super Stars uses the perpetual inventory system and compute the cost of goods sold for the month ended May 31 and ending inventory at May 31 using each of the following cost flow methods:

a. FIFO

b. LIFO

P5-51A. *Analyze effect of cost flow method on financial statements and inventory turnover ratio. (LO 2, 4, 6).* Green Bay Cheese Company is considering changing inventory cost flow methods. Green Bay's primary objective is to maximize profits. Currently, the firm uses weighted average cost. Data for 2011 are provided.

Beginning inventory (10,000 units)	$ 14,500
Purchases	
60,000 units at $1.50 each	$ 90,000
50,000 units at $1.60 each	80,000
70,000 units at $1.70 each	119,000
Sales	
130,000 units at $3.00 each	

Operating expenses were $120,000 and the company's tax rate is 30%.

Requirements

1. Prepare the multistep income statement for 2011 using each of the following methods:
   a. FIFO periodic
   b. LIFO periodic
2. Which method provides the more current balance sheet inventory balance at December 31, 2011? Explain your answer.
3. Which method provides the more current cost of goods sold for the year ended December 31, 2011? Explain your answer.
4. Which method provides the better inventory turnover ratio for the year? Explain your answer.
5. In order to meet its goal, what is your recommendation to Green Bay Cheese Company? Explain your answer.

P5-52A. *Calculate cost of goods sold and ending inventory; analyze effects of each method on financial statements; apply lower-of-cost-or-market rule; calculate inventory turnover ratio. (LO 3, 4, 5, 6).* The following information is for Leo's Solar Supplies for the year ending December 31, 2010.

At January 1, 2010:

- Cash amounted to $15,550.
- Beginning inventory was $20,000 (100 units at $200 each).
- Contributed capital was $19,000.
- Retained earnings was $16,550.

Transactions during 2010:

- Purchased 250 units for cash at $225 each
- Purchased 100 more units for cash at $250 each
- Cash sales of 300 units at $400 each
- Paid $11,500 cash for operating expenses
- Paid cash for income tax at a rate of 30% of net income

Requirements

1. Compute the cost of goods sold for the year and ending inventory at December 31, 2010, using each of the following cost flow methods:
   a. FIFO periodic
   b. LIFO periodic
   c. Weighted average cost periodic
2. For each method, prepare the balance sheet at December 31, 2010, a multistep income statement, statement of cash flows, and statement of changes in shareholders' equity for Leo's for the year ended December 31, 2010.
3. What is income before taxes and net income after taxes under each of the three inventory cost flow assumptions? What observations can you make about net income from the analysis of the three methods?
4. For each method, calculate the inventory turnover ratio and average days in inventory for the year ended December 31, 2010.
5. At the end of the year, the current replacement cost of the inventory is $35,000. Indicate at what amount the company's inventory will be reported using the lower-of-cost-or-market rule for each method (FIFO, LIFO, and weighted average cost).

P5-53A. *Calculate the gross profit ratio and inventory turnover ratio. (LO 6).* The following information is from the financial statements of Abby's International Pasta Corporation:

For year ended (amounts in thousands)	June 30, 2011	June 30, 2010	June 30, 2009
Sales	$416,049	$429,813	$445,849
Cost of sales	92,488	98,717	110,632
Inventory	17,030	16,341	12,659

Requirements

1. Calculate the gross profit ratio for the last two years shown.
2. Calculate the inventory turnover ratio for the last two years shown.
3. What information do these comparisons provide?

Set B

P5-54B. *Analyze purchases of merchandise inventory. (LO 1).* Deborah Hart's Professional Costumers, Inc., made the following purchases in November of the current year:

November 7	Purchased $2,500 of merchandise, terms 3/15, n/20, FOB shipping point
November 12	Purchased $4,300 of merchandise, terms 1/05, n/25, FOB destination
November 16	Purchased $6,200 of merchandise, terms 2/10, n/40, FOB shipping point

Requirements

1. For each of the listed purchases, how many days does the company have to take advantage of the purchase discount?
2. What is the amount of the cash discount allowed in each case?
3. Assume the freight charges are $115 on each purchase. What is the amount of freight that Professional Costumers must pay for each purchase?
4. What is the total cost of inventory for Professional Costumers for the month of November, assuming that all discounts were taken?

P5-55B. *Analyze purchases of merchandise inventory. (LO 1).* Cynthia's Pet Supplies, Inc., made the following purchases in March of the current year:

March 6	Purchased $3,500 of merchandise, terms 2/10, n/30, FOB shipping point
March 11	Purchased $5,250 of merchandise, terms 3/10, n/30, FOB destination
March 12	Purchased $4,000 of merchandise, terms 3/15, n/60, FOB shipping point

Requirements

1. For each purchase, by what date is the payment due, assuming the company takes advantage of the discount?
2. For each purchase, when is the payment due if the company does not take advantage of the discount?
3. In each case, what is the amount of the cash discount allowed?
4. Assume the freight charges are $100 on each purchase. For which purchase(s) is Cynthia's responsible for the freight charges?
5. What is the total amount of inventory costs for the month of March, assuming that all discounts were taken?

P5-56B. *Record merchandising transactions, prepare financial statements, and calculate gross profit ratio: perpetual inventory system. (LO 1, 2, 4, 6).* At the beginning of April, Morgan Parts Company, Inc., started with a contribution of $20,000 cash in exchange for common stock from its shareholders. The company engaged in the following transactions during the month of April:

April 3	Purchased merchandise on account from Thompson Supply Co. for $5,000, terms 1/10, n/30
April 4	Sold merchandise on account to Brown Company for $3,500, terms 2/10, n/30. The cost of the merchandise sold was $1,500.
April 7	Paid $100 freight on the sale to Brown Company
April 8	Received credit from Thompson Supply Co. for merchandise returned for $500
April 10	Paid Thompson Supply Co. in full
April 15	Received payment from Brown Company for sale made on April 4
April 16	Purchased merchandise for cash for $3,200
April 17	Received refund from supplier for returned merchandise on April 16 cash purchase of $350
April 19	Purchased merchandise on account from Kelsey Distributors for $4,100, terms 2/10, n/30
April 20	Paid $350 freight on April 19 purchase
April 21	Sold merchandise for cash for $12,170. The cost of the merchandise sold was $9,500.
April 24	Purchased merchandise for cash for $5,300
April 25	Paid Kelsey Distributors for purchase on April 19
April 27	Gave refund of $800 to customer from April 21. The cost of the returned merchandise was $535.
April 30	Sold merchandise of $2,000 on account with the terms 2/10, n/30. The merchandise cost $1,200.

Requirements

1. Enter each transaction into the accounting equation, assuming Morgan Parts Company, Inc., uses a perpetual inventory system. Start with the opening balances in cash and common stock described at the beginning of the problem.
2. Calculate the balance in the inventory account at the end of April.
3. Prepare a multistep income statement for the month of April and a balance sheet at April 30.
4. Calculate the gross profit ratio.

P5-57B. *Record merchandising transactions, prepare financial statements, and calculate gross profit ratio: perpetual inventory system. (LO 1, 2, 4, 6).* Wood Chuck Lumber Supplies is a finished wood provider for several local businesses. At the beginning of January, Wood Chuck had a $25,000 balance in cash and $25,000 in common stock. During the month of January, the following transactions took place:

January 2	Purchased $5,000 worth of lumber on account from a local lumberjack. The terms were 2/15, n/30, FOB shipping point. Freight costs were $100.
January 6	Sold $2,000 of lumber to Locked Up Fencing on account, with terms 1/05, n/25, FOB destination. Freight costs were $25. The cost of the inventory sold was $750.

January 12	Paid for the January 2 purchase
January 15	Received payment in full from Locked Up Fencing
January 18	Sold $3,000 worth of wood to Extreme Cabinet Makers on account, with terms 5/10, n/45, FOB shipping point. Freight costs were $75. The cost of the inventory sold was $2,000.
January 19	Returned a small amount of poor quality lumber to the lumberjack and received cash payment of $75
January 22	Purchased $7,000 of lumber from Tree Choppers on account. Terms were n/45, FOB destination. Freight costs were $100.
January 25	Sold $5,000 worth of lumber to Cabin Fever for cash. Cabin Fever picked up the order, so there were no shipping costs. The cost of the inventory sold was $2,750.
January 31	Paid for the purchase made on January 22.
January 31	Declared and paid cash dividends of $400

Requirements

1. Enter each transaction into the accounting equation, assuming Wood Chuck Lumber Supplies uses a perpetual inventory system. Start with the opening balances in cash and common stock described at the beginning of the problem.
2. Calculate the cost of goods sold for January and the ending balance in inventory.
3. Prepare the multistep income statement and the statement of changes in shareholders' equity for the month of January, and the balance sheet at January 31.
4. Calculate the gross profit ratio for Wood Chuck Lumber Supplies for the month of January. Explain what the ratio measures.

P5-58B. *Analyze accounting methods and prepare corrected income statement. (LO 1, 2, 4).* You are the accountant for Celebration Company, and your assistant has prepared the following income statement for the year ended December 31, 2010:

Celebration Company
Income Statement
For the Year Ended December 31, 2010

Sales revenue		$650,000
Sales returns and allowances	$ 18,100	
Freight expenses	2,000	
Selling expenses	48,300	(68,400)
Net sales		581,600
Expenses		
Cost of goods sold	350,000	
Salary expenses	82,000	
Rent expense	10,000	
Administrative expenses	23,500	
Dividends	4,000	
Total expenses		469,500
Net income		$112,100

You have uncovered the following facts:
   a. Sales revenue includes $6,000 of items that have been back-ordered. (The items have not been delivered to the customers, although the customers have paid for the items.)
   b. Selling expenses include $4,000 of allowances that were given to customers who received damaged products.
   c. Rent expense includes $400 worth of rent that applies to 2011.
   d. Salary expenses include $10,000 loaned to one of the executives for a boat.

Requirements

1. Prepare a corrected multistep income statement for the year. Celebration shows sales as the net amount only on its income statement.
2. Write a memo to your assistant explaining why each error you found is incorrect and what the correct accounting treatment should be.

P5-59B. *Calculate cost of goods sold and ending inventory and analyze effect of each method on the financial statements. (LO 3, 4).* Washington Company had the following sales and purchases during 2009, its first year of business:

January 8	Purchased 125 units at $100 each
February 20	Sold 75 units at $150 each
April 13	Sold 35 units at $150 each
June 28	Purchased 235 units at $105 each
August 2	Sold 175 units at $150 each
November 24	Purchased 140 units at $110 each

Requirements

1. Calculate the ending inventory, the cost of goods sold, and the gross profit for the December 31, 2009, financial statements under each of the following assumptions:
   a. FIFO periodic
   b. LIFO periodic
   c. Weighted average cost periodic
2. How will the differences between the methods affect the income statement for the year and balance sheet at December 31, 2009?

P5-60B. *Calculate cost of goods sold and ending inventory; analyze effects of each method on financial statements; apply lower-of-cost-or-market rule; calculate inventory turnover ratio. (LO 3, 4, 5, 6).* Kami's Pink Purses buys and then resells a special type of pink purse. Here is some information concerning Kami's inventory activity during the month of August 2010:

August 2	860 units on hand at a total cost of $51,600
August 6	Sold 400 units at $120 per unit
August 8	Purchased 640 units at $55 per unit
August 12	Purchased 425 units at $50 per unit
August 15	Sold 600 units at $120 per unit
August 21	Purchased 300 units at $50 per unit
August 24	Sold 800 units at $115 per unit
August 31	Purchased 100 units at $45 per unit

Requirements

1. Calculate the value of the ending inventory and cost of goods sold, assuming the company uses a periodic inventory system and the FIFO cost flow assumption.
2. Calculate the value of the ending inventory and cost of goods sold, assuming the company uses a periodic inventory system and the LIFO cost flow assumption.
3. Calculate the value of the ending inventory and cost of goods sold, assuming the company uses a periodic inventory system and the weighted average cost flow assumption.
4. Which of the three methods will result in the highest cost of goods sold for August?
5. Which of the three methods will provide the most current ending inventory value for Kami's balance sheet at August 31, 2010?
6. How would the differences between the methods affect Kami's income statement for August and balance sheet at August 31, 2010?

7. Calculate the company's inventory turnover ratio and average days in inventory for the month for each method in items (1), (2), and (3).
8. At the end of the month, the current replacement cost of the inventory is $32,000. Indicate at what amount the company's inventory will be reported using the lower-of-cost-or-market rule for each method (FIFO, LIFO, and weighted average cost).

P5-61B. *Calculate cost of goods sold, ending inventory, and inventory turnover ratio. (LO 3, 6).*
The following merchandise inventory transactions occurred during the month of June for Heavy Metal Guitars (HMG):

June 6	Inventory on hand was 500 units at a cost of $100 each
June 11	Sold 100 units for $200 each
June 15	Purchased 200 units at $125 each
June 21	Sold 300 units for $225 each
June 27	Purchased 100 units for $75 each

Requirements
1. Assume HMG uses a periodic inventory system and compute the cost of goods sold for the month ended June 30 and ending inventory at June 30 using each of the following cost flow methods:
   a. FIFO
   b. LIFO
   c. Weighted average cost
2. Using the information for item (1), calculate the inventory turnover ratio and average days in inventory for the month of June for each method.
3. Assume HMG uses the perpetual inventory system and compute the cost of goods sold for the month ended June 30 and ending inventory at June 30 using each of the following cost flow methods:
   a. FIFO
   b. LIFO

P5-62B. *Analyze effect of cost flow method on financial statements and inventory turnover ratio. (LO 2, 4, 6).* Castana Company is considering changing inventory cost flow methods. Castana's primary objective is to minimize its tax liability. Currently, the firm uses weighted average cost. Data for 2012 are provided.

Beginning inventory (2,000 units)	$ 10,000
Purchases	
5,000 units at $6 each	$ 30,000
4,000 units at $6.50 each	26,000
6,000 units at $7 each	42,000
Sales	
15,000 units at $10 each	$150,000

Operating expenses were $12,000 and the company's tax rate is 25%.

Requirements
1. Prepare the income statement for 2012 using each of the following methods:
   a. FIFO periodic
   b. LIFO periodic
2. Which method provides the more current balance sheet inventory balance at December 31, 2012? Explain your answer.

3. Which method provides the more current cost of goods sold for the year ended December 31, 2012? Explain your answer.
4. Which method provides the better inventory turnover ratio for the year? Explain your answer.
5. In order to meet its goal, what is your recommendation to Castana Company? Explain your answer.

P5-63B. *Calculate cost of goods sold and ending inventory; analyze effects of each method on financial statements; apply lower-of-cost-or-market rule; calculate inventory turnover ratio. (LO 3, 4, 5, 6).* The following information is for Falling Numbers Computers for the year ended December 31, 2010.

At January 1, 2010:

- Cash amounted to $20,000.
- Beginning inventory was $35,000 (1,400 units at $25 each).
- Contributed capital was $25,000.
- Retained earnings was $45,000.

Transactions during 2010:

- Purchased 1,250 units for cash at $30 each
- Purchased 750 more units for cash at $20 each
- Cash sales of 2,400 units at $50 each
- Paid $10,000 cash for operating expenses
- Paid cash for income taxes at a rate of 40% of net income

Requirements

1. Compute the cost of goods sold and ending inventory at December 31, 2010, using each of the following cost flow methods:
   a. FIFO periodic
   b. LIFO periodic
   c. Weighted average cost periodic
2. For each method, prepare the balance sheet at December 31, 2010, a multistep income statement, and statement of cash flows for the fiscal year ended December 31, 2010.
3. What is income before taxes and net income after taxes under each of the three inventory cost flow assumptions? What observations can you make about net income from the analysis of the three methods?
4. For each method, calculate the inventory turnover ratio and average days in inventory for the fiscal year ended December 31, 2010.
5. At the end of the year, the current replacement cost of the inventory is $33,000. Indicate at what amount the company's inventory will be reported using the lower-of-cost-or-market rule for each method (FIFO, LIFO, and weighted average cost).

P5-64B. *Calculate the gross profit ratio and inventory turnover ratio. (LO 6).* The following information is from the financial statements of Toys for Toddlers Company:

For year ended (amounts in thousands)	December 31, 2012	December 31, 2011	December 31, 2010
Sales	$2,534,135	$2,187,438	$1,925,319
Cost of goods sold	1,634,562	1,383,665	1,229,277
Inventory	54,353	47,433	45,334

Requirements

1. Calculate the gross profit ratio for the last two years shown.
2. Calculate the inventory turnover ratio for the last two years shown.
3. What information do these comparisons provide?

Financial Statement Analysis

FSA5-1. *Analyze income statement. (LO 6).* The income statements for Williams-Sonoma, Inc., for the fiscal years ended February 1, 2009, and February 3, 2008, are shown here. Compare the company's performance for the two years. Is the company controlling its cost of inventory? Is the company controlling its other expenses well? Be able to support your answers.

Williams-Sonoma, Inc.
Consolidated Statements of Earnings

	Fiscal Year Ended	
(Dollars in thousands)	Feb. 1, 2009 (52 Weeks)	Feb. 3, 2008 (53 Weeks)
Net revenues	$3,361,472	$3,944,934
Cost of goods sold	2,226,300	2,408,963
Gross margin	1,135,172	1,535,971
Selling, general and administrative expenses	1,093,019	1,222,573
Interest income	(1,280)	(5,041)
Interest expense	1,480	2,099
Earnings before income taxes	41,953	316,340
Income taxes	11,929	120,583
Net earnings	$ 30,024	$ 195,757

FSA5-2. *Analyze inventory management. (LO 6).* Use the following information from The Wet Seal, Inc., to analyze the firm's inventory management. Calculate the gross profit ratio and the inventory turnover ratio for each year. How do you think Wet Seal is managing its inventory? What other information would be useful in answering this question?

The Wet Seal, Inc.
Consolidated Statements of Operations
(In thousands)

	Fiscal Years Ended		
	January 31, 2009	February 2, 2008	February 3, 2007
Net sales	$592,960	$611,163	$564,324
Cost of sales	400,521	408,892	370,888
Gross margin	192,439	202,271	193,436
Selling, general, and administrative expenses	154,671	177,468	178,703
Store-closure costs	—	—	(730)
Asset impairment	5,611	5,546	425
Operating income	32,157	19,257	15,038
Interest income	2,182	5,489	4,387
Interest expense	(2,863)	(1,136)	(31,955)
Interest (expense) income, net	(681)	4,353	(27,568)
Income (loss) before provision for income taxes	31,476	23,610	(12,530)
Provision for income taxes	1,322	378	308
Net income (loss)	$ 30,154	$ 23,232	$(12,838)

From the balance sheet at January 31, 2009

Inventory $25,529 (in thousands)

From the balance sheet at February 2, 2008

Inventory $31,590

From the balance sheet at February 3, 2007

Inventory $34,231

From the balance sheet at January 28, 2006

Inventory $25,475

FSA5-3. *Analyze inventory management. (LO 6).* Use the following information to analyze the inventory management of Amazon.com, Inc.:

(in millions)	For the year ended December 31, 2008	For the year ended December 31, 2007	At December 31, 2006
Sales	$19,166	$14,835	
Cost of sales	$14,896	$11,482	
Net income	$ 645	$ 476	
Inventory (at year end)	$ 1,399	$ 1,200	$877

Write a short report for Amazon.com's shareholders with your comments about its inventory management.

Critical Thinking Problems

Risks and Controls

In this chapter, you learned that retail firms are at risk that their inventory will become obsolete. What can a firm do to minimize this risk? What types of firms are most at risk? Least at risk?

Ethics

Jim's Music Company uses LIFO for inventory, and the company's profits are quite high this year. The cost of the inventory has been steadily rising all year, and Jim is worried about his taxes. His accountant has suggested that the company make a large purchase of inventory to be received during the last week in December. The accountant has explained to Jim that this would reduce his income significantly.

1. Jim does not understand the logic of the accountant's suggestion. Explain how the purchase would affect taxable income.
2. Is this ethical? Jim is uncertain about the appropriateness of this action from a legal and an ethical standpoint.

Group Assignment

Select a retail firm that you think might be concerned about obsolete inventory and another that you believe would not be very concerned. Then, find the financial statements and calculate the inventory turnover ratio of these two firms for the past two fiscal years. Are your results what you expected? Explain what you expected to find and your results.

Internet Exercise: Gap

The Gap, Inc., was founded in 1969 by Donald and Doris Fisher in San Francisco, California, with a single store and a handful of employees. Today, the company is one of the world's largest specialty retailers with three of the most recognized brands in the apparel industry (Gap, Banana Republic, and Old Navy). The Gap, Inc., has more than 134,000 employees supporting about 3,100 stores in the United States, United Kingdom, Canada, France, and Japan.

Go to www.gapinc.com.

IE5-1. Click on Investors, followed by Financials, and then Annual Reports and Proxy. Download the latest annual report.

1. Which inventory cost flow assumption is used to measure the cost of inventory? Does The Gap, Inc., value inventory at the lower-of-cost-or-market value? If so, how is market value determined? Does this policy comply with GAAP?

2. For the three most recent years, list the amounts reported for net sales and gross profit. Is net sales increasing or decreasing? Is gross profit increasing or decreasing? Are these trends favorable or unfavorable? Explain your answer.

3. Using the financial statements, calculate the inventory turnover ratio for the three most recent years. (You will need inventory values from the 2007 and 2006 10Ks or annual reports, available on the Web site.) Did the inventory turnover ratio increase or decrease? What does this measure? What does The Gap, Inc., do to identify inventory that is slow moving and how is this inventory treated?

4. For cost of goods sold, The Gap, Inc., uses Cost of Goods Sold and Occupancy Expenses. What is included in this amount?

IE5-2. Go back to The Gap, Inc., homepage and click on Social Responsibility.

1. Does The Gap, Inc., do anything to ensure its garment workers are treated fairly? If so, why is this important for the company to do?
   Go back to About Gap Inc.

2. Click on How Our Clothes Are Made. List and briefly describe The Gap, Inc.'s five steps of its product life cycle.

Please note: Internet Web sites are constantly being updated. Therefore, if the information is not found where indicated, please explore the annual report further to find the information.

Appendix 5A

<table>
<tr><td>L.O.8</td></tr>
<tr><td>Describe and calculate the effect of inventory errors on the financial statements.</td></tr>
</table>

Inventory Errors

You know that the cost of the beginning inventory plus the cost of purchases equals the cost of goods available for sale. The cost of goods available for sale is then allocated between the cost of goods sold and the ending inventory. That is,

$$
\begin{aligned}
&\text{Beginning inventory} \\
&\underline{+ \text{ Purchases}} \\
&= \text{Cost of goods available for sale} \\
&\underline{- \text{ Ending inventory}} \\
&= \text{Cost of goods sold}
\end{aligned}
$$

Because inventory directly affects cost of goods sold, a major expense, errors in the calculation of beginning inventory or ending inventory will affect net income. Tracing the effects of errors requires slow, focused deliberation. To show how inventory errors can affect income, here is a simple numerical example that shows an ending inventory error and a beginning inventory error. Read each description and study the related examples.

Ending Inventory Errors

Suppose a firm has the correct amount for beginning inventory and the correct amount for purchases. Then, cost of goods available for sale is correct. If the ending inventory is overstated, cost of goods sold must be understated. Why? Because ending inventory and cost of goods sold are the two parts of cost of goods available for sale. Cost of goods sold is an expense. If the expense deducted from sales is too small, the result is that net income will be too large. Suppose you have correctly calculated the cost of goods available for sale (beginning inventory + purchases) to be $10. Those goods will either be sold and become part of cost of goods sold, or they will not be sold and will still be part of the inventory.

So, the cost of goods available for sale consists of two parts—cost of goods sold and ending inventory. Suppose the correct ending inventory is $2, but you erroneously give it a value of $3. If ending inventory is incorrectly valued at $3, then cost of goods sold will be valued at $7. Remember, the ending inventory and cost of goods sold must add up to $10 in this example. What is wrong with cost of goods sold? If ending inventory is actually $2, then cost of goods sold should be $8. See what happens? You understate cost of goods sold when you overstate the ending inventory. Anytime you understate an expense, you will overstate net income.

If ending inventory is too small (understated), cost of goods sold must be too large (overstated). The result is that net income will be understated. Let us use the same example, in which the cost of goods available for sale was correctly computed at $10. If ending inventory is actually $2 but you erroneously understate it as $1, then cost of goods sold will be valued as $9. It should be $8. So, an understatement in ending inventory has caused an overstatement of cost of goods sold. If you overstate an expense, then you will understate net income.

Beginning Inventory Errors

If ending inventory is overstated in 2009, then beginning inventory in 2010 will be overstated. After all, it is the same number. Errors in the ending inventory will, therefore, affect two consecutive years—ending inventory one year and beginning inventory the following year. If beginning inventory is overstated, then the cost of goods available for sale is overstated. If ending inventory is counted correctly, then cost of goods sold will be overstated. So, net income will be understated. Let us continue the previous example. If you value beginning inventory at $3 (and the correct value is $2) and you correctly add the purchases for the second year—say, $15 worth—then, the cost of goods available for sale will be $18. Keep in mind, the correct amount is $17. At year end, you count the ending inventory correctly at $6. The calculated cost of goods sold would be $12. Ending inventory and cost of goods sold must total $18. However, we know that the true cost of goods available for sale is $17. If the correct ending inventory is $6, then the correct cost of goods sold is $11. The calculated cost of goods sold was overstated by $1. When an expense is overstated, then net income will be understated.

If beginning inventory is understated, then the cost of goods available for sale is understated. If ending inventory is counted correctly, then cost of goods sold will be understated. So, net income will be overstated. Try thinking about the example in the format given in Exhibit 5A.1. As you can see, when you understate the beginning inventory, you will naturally understate cost of goods sold. This understated expense will result in an overstatement of net income.

	Calculated Amounts	Correct Amounts
Beginning inventory	$ 1 (understated from prior year error)	$ 2
+ Purchases	+ $15	+ $15
Cost of goods available for sale	$16	$17
− Ending inventory	$ 6	$ 6
Cost of goods sold	$10	$11

EXHIBIT 5A.1

Error in the Beginning Inventory

Note that over a period of two years the errors will counterbalance—they will cancel each other out. However, it is important that the financial statements be correct each year, not every other year, so a company will correct inventory errors if they are discovered, rather than wait for the errors to cancel each other out.

Your Turn 5A-1

Berry Corporation miscounted the ending inventory at December 31, 2010. The balance sheet reported inventory of $360,000, but $25,000 worth of items were omitted from that amount. Berry reported net income of $742,640 for the year. What effect did this inventory error have on Berry's cost of goods sold for the year? What is the correct net income for the year ended December 31, 2010?

Answer: Ending inventory was understated, so cost of goods sold was overstated. Too much expense was deducted, so net income should have been higher by $25,000 for a correct net income of $767,640.

Short Exercises

SE5A-1A. *Calculate inventory errors. (LO 8).* How would each of the following inventory errors affect net income for the year? Assume each is the only error during the year.
1. Ending inventory is overstated by $3,000.
2. Ending inventory is understated by $1,500.
3. Beginning inventory is understated by $3,000.
4. Beginning inventory is overstated by $1,550.

SE5A-2B. *Calculate inventory errors. (LO 8).* How would each of the following inventory errors affect net income for the year? Assume each is the only error during the year.
1. Ending inventory is overstated by $1,000.
2. Ending inventory is understated by $2,500.
3. Beginning inventory is understated by $4,000.
4. Beginning inventory is overstated by $2,500.

Exercises

E5A-3A. *Calculate inventory errors. (LO 8).* Ian's Small Appliances reported cost of goods sold as follows:

	2009	2010
Beginning inventory	$130,000	$ 50,000
Purchases	275,000	240,000
Cost of goods available for sale	405,000	290,000
Ending inventory	50,000	40,000
Cost of goods sold	$355,000	$250,000

All of the A exercises can be found within MyAccountingLab, an online homework and practice environment.

Ian's made two errors:
1. 2009 ending inventory was understated by $5,000.
2. 2010 ending inventory was overstated by $2,000.

Calculate the correct cost of goods sold for 2009 and 2010.

E5A-4B. *Calculate inventory errors. (LO 8).* Tire Pro Company's records reported the following at the end of the fiscal year:

Beginning inventory	$ 80,000
Ending inventory	85,000
Cost of goods sold	295,000

A physical inventory count showed that the ending inventory was actually $78,000. If this error is not corrected, what effect would it have on the income statement for this fiscal year and the following fiscal year?

Problems

P5A-5A. *Analyze results of physical count of inventory and calculate cost of goods sold. (LO 8).* Matrix Company uses a periodic, weighted average inventory system. The company's accounting records showed the following related to November 2010 transactions:

	Units	Cost
Beginning inventory, November 1	400	$ 900
Purchases during November	1,250	4,275
Goods available for sale	1,650	$5,175
Cost of goods sold	1,300	4,077
Ending inventory, November 30	350	$1,098

On November 30, 2010, Matrix conducted a physical count of its inventory and discovered there were only 300 units of inventory actually on hand.

Requirements
1. Using the information from the physical count, correct the company's cost of goods sold for November.
2. How would this correction change the financial statements for this month?
3. What are some possible causes of the difference between the inventory amounts in the accounting records and the inventory amount from the physical count?

P5A-6B. *Analyze results of physical count of inventory and calculate cost of goods sold. (LO 8).* Paige's Office Paper Company uses a perpetual inventory system, so the cost of goods sold is recorded and the inventory records are updated at the time of every sale. The company's accounting records showed the following related to September 2009 transactions:

	Units	Total Cost
Beginning inventory, September 1	500	$ 1,500
Purchases during September	3,750	11,250
Goods available for sale	4,250	$12,750
Cost of goods sold	2,200	6,600
Ending inventory, September 30	2,050	$ 6,150

On September 30, 2009, Paige conducted a physical count of its inventory and discovered there were actually 1,900 units of inventory on hand.

Requirements
1. Using the information from the physical count, correct Paige's Office Paper's cost of goods sold for September.
2. How would this correction change the financial statements for the month?
3. What are some possible causes of the difference between the inventory amounts in the company's accounting records and the inventory amount from the physical count?

Appendix 5B

Gross Profit Method of Estimating Ending Inventory

L.O.9
Estimate inventory using the gross profit method.

There are times when a company might want to *estimate* the cost of the ending inventory rather than count the units to calculate the cost. For example, if a company prepares monthly or quarterly financial statements, GAAP allow ending inventory to be estimated for reporting on those financial statements. This saves a company the trouble of counting the inventory every quarter. Also, if the inventory is destroyed or stolen, the company will have a reliable estimate of the cost of the destroyed inventory for the insurance claim.

First, you must know the usual gross profit percentage—the gross profit ratio you learned about in Chapter 5—for the company. Gross profit percentage is gross profit divided by sales. You can calculate the gross profit ratio using prior years' sales and cost data. Then, you multiply that percentage by the sales for the period, which gives the estimated gross profit. You then subtract the estimated gross profit from sales to get the estimated cost of goods sold. Because you know (a) beginning inventory (from the last period's financial statements), (b) purchases (from your records), and (c) an estimate for cost of goods sold, you can estimate ending inventory.

For example, suppose Super Soap Company lost its entire inventory in a flood on April 16. Super Soap had prepared a set of financial statements on March 31, when the inventory on hand was valued at $2,500. During the first part of April, purchases amounted to $3,500. The usual gross profit percentage in this business is 40%. If Super Soap had sales of $8,200 during the first 16 days of April, how much inventory was lost?

1. If sales were $8,200 and the usual gross profit percentage is 40%, then the gross profit would be $3,280.
2. If sales were $8,200 and gross profit is $3,280, then cost of goods sold would be $4,920. In other words, if the gross profit percentage is 40%, then the other 60% must be the cost of goods sold. So 60% of $8,200 = cost of goods sold = $4,920.
3. Beginning inventory + purchases − cost of goods sold = ending inventory. $2,500 + $3,500 − $4,920 = $1,080. This is our best estimate of the lost inventory.

Your Turn 5B-1

Suppose Base Company began May with inventory of $2,000 and purchased $8,000 worth of inventory during the first half of May. Sales for the first half of May amounted to $12,000.

Then, a fire destroyed the remaining inventory. Base Company has had a gross profit ratio of approximately 30% for the first four months of the year. Approximately how much inventory did Base Company lose in the fire?

Answer: $12,000 × 0.7 + Cost of goods sold, so $8,400 worth of inventory has been sold. $10,000 − $8,400 = $1,600 worth of inventory must have been lost in the fire.

Short Exercise

All of the A exercises can be found within MyAccountingLab, an online homework and practice environment.

SE5B-1A. *Estimate inventory. (LO 9).* Fantasy Games, Inc., wants to estimate its ending inventory balance for its quarterly financial statements for the first quarter of the year. Given the following, what is your best estimate?

Beginning inventory	$75,800
Net sales	$92,500
Net purchases	$50,500
Gross profit ratio	20%

SE5B-2B. *(Estimate inventory. (LO 9).* Knick-Knacks wants to estimate its ending inventory balance for its quarterly financial statements for the first quarter of the year. Given the following, what is your best estimate?

Beginning inventory	$3,800
Net sales	$9,500
Net purchases	$5,500
Gross profit ratio	20%

Exercises

E5B-3A. *Estimate inventory. (LO 9).* The following information is available for the Arizona Chemical Supply Company:

Inventory, January 1, 2009	$240,000
Net purchases for the month of January	750,000
Net sales for the month of January	950,000
Gross profit ratio (historical)	40%

Estimate the cost of goods sold for January and the ending inventory at January 31, 2009.

E5B-4B. *Estimate inventory. (LO 9).* The records of Florida Tool Shop revealed the following information related to inventory destroyed in Hurricane Frances:

Inventory, beginning of period	$300,000
Purchases to date of hurricane	140,000
Net sales to date of hurricane	885,000
Gross profit ratio	55%

The company needs to file a claim for lost inventory with its insurance company. What is the estimated value of the lost inventory?

Problems

P5B-5A. *Estimate inventory. (LO 9).* Hines Fruit Corp. sells fresh fruit to tourists on Interstate 75 in Florida. A tornado destroyed the entire inventory in late June. In order to file an insurance claim, Hazel and Gene, the owners of the company, must estimate the value of the lost inventory. Records from January 1 through the date of the tornado in June indicated that Hines Fruit Corp. started the year with $4,000 worth of inventory on hand. Purchases for the year amounted to $9,000, and sales up to the date of the tornado were $16,000. Gross profit percentage has traditionally been 30%.

Requirements

1. How much should Hazel and Gene request from the insurance company?
2. Suppose that one case of fruit was spared by the tornado. The cost of that case was $700. How much was the inventory loss under these conditions?

P5B-6B. *Estimate inventory. (LO 9).* Carrie's Cotton Candy Company sells cotton candy to visitors at a traveling county fair. During a drought a fire destroyed the entire inventory in late July. In order to file an insurance claim, Carrie, the owner of the company, must estimate the value of the lost inventory. Records from January 1 through the date of the fire in July indicated that Carrie's Cotton Candy Company started the year with $4,250 worth of inventory on hand. Purchases for the year amounted to $8,000, and sales up to the date of the fire were $17,500. Gross profit percentage has traditionally been 35%.

Requirements

1. How much should Carrie request from the insurance company?
2. Suppose that one bag of cotton candy mix was spared by the fire. The cost of that bag was $50. How much was the inventory loss under these conditions?

6

Acquisition and Use of Long-Term Assets

ETHICS Matters

Anyone Need a Forklift?

Most thieves prefer cash; some may even prefer jewelry. However, very few prefer forklifts. Large, expensive assets that a firm uses over a period of years are often difficult to steal. It's impossible to sneak out of the factory building with a forklift in your briefcase. These assets, however, can be stolen. The challenge with these types of assets is to make sure that the people who have access to them have the appropriate authorization.

In June 2009, three contract employees for the Metropolitan Transportation Authority (New York's MTA) were charged with stealing eight forklifts and other equipment from a warehouse in Queens. The employees who were in charge of the warehouse thought that the three contract workers were authorized to dispose of the equipment. Why? Because the three wore the uniforms of the firm that has the maintenance contract with the MTA. The accused thieves sold the forklifts to a scrap yard for a little over $7,000. The cost to replace the stolen property was more than $250,000.

According to the Association of Certified Fraud Examiners' 2008 Report to the Nation on Occupational Fraud & Abuse, 16.3% of all occupational fraud is due to misappropriation of noncash assets. Some of those assets were obviously taken in broad daylight. The lesson is that all assets, no matter how unlikely to be stolen, need appropriate safeguarding.

LEARNING OBJECTIVES

When you are finished studying Chapter 6, you should be able to:

1. Explain how long-term assets are classified and how their costs are computed.

2. Explain and compute how tangible assets are written off over their useful lives and reported on the financial statements.

3. Explain and compute how intangible assets are written off over their useful lives and reported on the financial statements.

4. Explain how decreases in value, repairs, changes in productive capacity, and changes in estimates of useful life and salvage value of long-term assets affect the financial statements.

5. Explain how the disposal of a long-term asset is reflected in the financial statements.

6. Recognize and explain how long-term assets are reported on the financial statements, and prepare financial statements that include long-term assets.

7. Use return on assets (ROA) and the asset turnover ratio to help evaluate a firm's performance.

8. Identify and describe the business risks associated with long-term assets and the controls that can minimize those risks.

9. (Appendix 6) Explain how depreciation for financial statements differs from depreciation for taxes.

L.O.1
Explain how long-term assets are classified and how their costs are computed.

Acquiring Long-Term Assets

So far, you have learned how a firm provides goods and services to its customers and the related collection of the payments. In this chapter, we will look at the purchase of long-term assets, also called long-lived assets or fixed assets, which are used in the operation of a business.

All businesses purchase long-term operational assets, such as computers, copy machines, and furniture, as well as short-term assets, such as folders, paper, and pens. Acquiring long-term assets is usually more complicated than acquiring short-term assets. Purchasing long-term assets is complex for several reasons. With long-term assets, a firm must put a great deal of care in selecting the vendor because the relationship could last for a significant amount of time. In addition, the monetary investment in long-term assets is typically much greater than the investment in short-term assets and it is more difficult to dispose of long-term assets if the company makes a bad decision. For example, a new computer system for tracking inventory would cost a firm like Staples thousands of dollars more than the purchase of a new telephone for the employee lounge. If the Staples manager did not like the kind of phone that was purchased, he or she would simply give the phone away or donate it to the local Goodwill and buy another. What happens if the manager decides that the company purchased the wrong computerized inventory system? It is significantly harder to get rid of the long-term asset, and it could reflect poorly on the manager who made the decision to purchase the system in the first place.

Before a firm purchases a long-term asset, it must determine how much revenue that asset will generate and how much the asset will cost. The cost of a long-term asset must include all of the costs to get the asset ready for use. Long-term assets often require extensive setup and preparation before they become operational, and employees need to be trained to use them. If Staples purchases a new computerized inventory system, it may require new hardware and software, and employees will need to be trained to use the new system. All of these costs will be recorded as part of the cost of the asset.

Considering all of these costs is part of the business process of acquiring a long-term asset. Accountants then use these costs to account for the purchase and use of the asset. What assets to buy and how to pay for them are decisions that do not affect the income statement at the time of the purchase. Recording the purchase of a long-term asset affects the balance sheet and potentially the statement of cash flows. As you saw in Chapter 3, a business defers recognizing the expense of a long-term asset until the asset is actually used in the business. When the asset is used and the expense is recognized, the expense is called depreciation expense. This deferral is an example of a timing difference. We have purchased a long-term asset at one point in time in the past, and we will use that asset over a subsequent period of time.

Types of Long-Lived Assets: Tangible and Intangible

Tangible assets are assets with physical substance; they can be seen and touched.

There are two categories of long-term assets used in a business: **tangible assets** and **intangible assets**. Exhibit 6.1 shows the long-term asset section of Staples' balance sheet, where you will see both types of long-term assets.

Common tangible assets are property, plant, and equipment (PPE). Common intangible assets are trademarks, patents, and copyrights. We will discuss these in detail later in the chapter.

Intangible assets are rights, privileges, or benefits that result from owning long-lived assets that do not have physical substance.

Acquisition Costs

Consider the purchase of a long-term asset. The historical cost principle requires a company to record an asset at the amount paid for the asset—its cost. The cost for property, plant, and equipment includes all expenditures that are reasonable and necessary to get an asset in place and ready for use. The reason for reporting all of these costs on the balance sheet, as part of the cost of the asset, is to defer recognition of the expense until the asset is actually used to generate revenue. This is, as you know, the matching principle, which provides the foundation for accrual basis accounting. The assets are put on the balance sheet and then written off as expenses over the accounting periods in which they are used to generate revenue. Following are some common components of the cost of property, plant, and equipment:

1. When a firm purchases land to use as the location of a building or factory, the acquisition cost includes the following:
   a. Price paid for the land
   b. Real estate commissions

From the Balance Sheet of Staples, Inc.
(in thousands)

	January 31, 2009	February 2, 2008
Property and equipment:		
Land and buildings	$1,040,754	$ 859,751
Leasehold improvements	1,183,879	1,135,132
Equipment	1,949,646	1,819,381
Furniture and fixtures	926,702	871,361
Total property and equipment	5,100,981	4,685,625
Less accumulated depreciation and amortization	2,810,355	2,524,486
Net property and equipment	2,290,626	2,161,139
Lease acquisition costs net of accumulated amortization	26,931	31,399
Intangible assets net of accumulated amortization	701,918	231,310
Goodwill	3,780,169	1,764,928
Other assets	476,153	292,186
Total long-term assets	$7,275,797	$4,480,962

These are *tangible* assets: (Land and buildings, Leasehold improvements, Equipment, Furniture and fixtures)

These are *intangible* assets: (Lease acquisition costs, Intangible assets, Goodwill)

EXHIBIT 6.1

From the Balance Sheet of Staples

You won't know the meaning of some terms Staples has used, but you will learn about many of them in this chapter.

c. Attorneys' fees
d. Costs of preparing the land for use, such as clearing or draining
e. Costs of tearing down existing structures

In general, land is not depreciated. Because land typically retains its usefulness and is not consumed to produce revenue, its cost remains unchanged on the balance sheet as a long-term asset. Even if the land's value increases, financial statements prepared under U.S. GAAP will show the land at cost.

2. When a firm purchases a physical plant, the acquisition cost includes the following:
   a. Purchase cost of buildings or factories
   b. Costs to update or remodel the facilities
   c. Any other costs to get the plant operational
3. When a firm purchases equipment, the acquisition cost includes the following:
   a. Purchase cost
   b. Freight-in—cost to have the equipment delivered
   c. Insurance while in transit
   d. Installation costs, including test runs
   e. Cost of training employees to use the new equipment
4. When a firm constructs or renovates a building, the acquisition cost includes the following:
   a. Architects' or contractors' fees
   b. Construction costs
   c. Cost of renovating the building

In contrast to the accounting treatment of land, even if a firm expects a building to increase in value, the asset will be depreciated. In practice, most assets used in a business to generate revenues will decrease in value as they are used. Recall that depreciation is not meant to value an asset at its market value. Rather, it is the systematic allocation of the cost of an asset to the periods in which the asset is used by the firm to generate revenue.

Your Turn 6-1

For each of the following costs, indicate whether it should be recorded as an asset or recorded as an expense at the time of the transaction:

1. Payment for employee salaries
2. Purchase of new delivery truck
3. Rent paid in advance
4. Rent paid in arrears (after use of the building)

Basket Purchase Allocation

Calculating the acquisition cost of certain assets can be difficult. Buying a building with the land it occupies is an example of a "basket purchase" because two assets are acquired for a single price. For the accounting records, the firm must calculate a separate cost for each asset. Why? The firm will depreciate the building but it will not depreciate the land. The firm divides the purchase price between the building and land by using the **relative fair market value method**. Suppose a company purchased a building and its land together for one price of $100,000. The company would obtain a market price, usually in the form of an appraisal, for each item separately. Then, the company uses the relative amounts of the individual appraisals to allocate the purchase price of $100,000 between the two assets. Suppose the building was appraised at $90,000 and the land was appraised at $30,000. The total appraised value is $120,000 ($90,000 + $30,000).

> **Relative fair market value method** is a way to allocate the total cost for several assets purchased together to each of the individual assets. This method is based on the assets' individual market values.

The building accounts for three-quarters of the total appraised value.

$$\$90,000 \div \$120,000 = 3/4$$

So, the accountant records the building at three-fourths of the total cost of the basket purchase.

$$3/4 \times \$100,000 = \$75,000$$

The cost assigned to the land will be the remaining $25,000.

$$\$100,000 - \$75,000 = \$25,000$$

Or if you want to calculate it,

$$1/4 \times \$100,000 = \$25,000$$

This same method—using an asset's proportion of the total appraised value of a group of assets—can be used for any number of assets purchased together for a single price.

Your Turn 6-2

Bargain Company paid $480,000 for a building and the land on which it is located. Independent appraisals valued the building at $400,000 and the land at $100,000. How much should Bargain Company record as the cost of the building and how much as the cost of the land? Why does the company need to record the costs separately?

L.O.2
Explain and compute how tangible assets are written off over their useful lives and reported on the financial statements.

Using Long-Term Tangible Assets: Depreciation and Depletion

Now that you are familiar with the types of assets a firm may have and the costs associated with their acquisition, we are ready to talk about using the assets. Until property, plant, and equipment are put into use, their costs remain as assets on the balance sheet. As soon as the firm uses the asset to help generate revenue, the financial statements will show some amount of expense on the income statement. Recording a cost as an asset, rather than recording it as an expense, is called **capitalizing** the cost. That cost will be recognized as an expense during the periods in which the asset is used. Recall from Chapter 3 that depreciation is a systematic and rational allocation process to recognize the expense of long-term assets over the periods in which the assets are used. Depreciation is an example of the matching principle—matching the cost of an asset with the revenue it helps generate. For each year a company plans to use an asset, the company will recognize depreciation expense on the income statement.

> To **capitalize** is to record a cost as an asset rather than to record it as an expense.

If you hear or read, "The asset is worth $10,000 on our books," that does not mean the asset is actually worth that amount if it were sold. Instead, it means that $10,000 is the carrying value or book value of the asset in the accounting records—it is the amount not yet depreciated. It is called the carrying value because that is the amount at which we carry our assets on the balance sheet. The amount not yet depreciated is also known as the book value because it is the value of the asset in the accounting records. As you read about the specific methods of depreciating assets, refer to the vocabulary of depreciation in Exhibit 6.2.

> **Amortization** means to write off the cost of a long-term asset over more than one accounting period.

Accountants primarily use three terms to describe how a cost is written off over several accounting periods. **Amortization** is the most general expression for writing off the cost of a

EXHIBIT 6.2

Depreciation Terminology

Term	Definition	Example
Cost or **acquisition cost**	The amount paid for the asset, including all amounts necessary to get the asset up and running	Staples purchases computer cash registers for its new store for $21,000.
Estimated useful life	How long the company plans to use the asset; may be measured in years or in units that the asset will produce	Staples plans to use these cash registers for 10 years.
Salvage value or **residual value**	Estimated value the asset will have when the company is done with it—the salvage value is the estimated market value on the anticipated disposal date	When Staples is done using the cash registers, the company plans to sell them for $1,000.
Depreciable base	*Cost* minus *salvage value*	The depreciable base is $21,000 − $1,000 = $20,000.
Book value or **carrying value**	*Cost* less accumulated *depreciation*	If Staples uses the straight-line method, the company's depreciation expense will be $2,000 per year. After the first year, the book value will be $19,000 (= $21,000 − $2,000).

long-term asset. **Depreciation** is the specific word that describes the amortization of certain kinds of property, plant, or equipment. **Depletion** is the specific term that describes the amortization of a natural resource. There is no specific term for writing off intangible assets, so accountants use the general term *amortization* to describe writing off the cost of intangible assets.

All of these terms—amortization, depreciation, and depletion—refer to allocating the cost of an asset to more than one accounting period.

Accountants use several methods of depreciation for the financial statements. We will discuss three of the most common methods:

1. Straight-line depreciation
2. Activity (units-of-production) depreciation
3. Declining balance depreciation

> **Depreciation** is a systematic and rational allocation process to recognize the expense of long-term assets over the periods in which the assets are used.
>
> **Depletion** is the amortization of a natural resource.

For each of the following, give the term for writing off the cost of the asset:

Your Turn 6-3

1. Equipment
2. Building
3. Oil well

Straight-Line Depreciation

Straight-line depreciation is a depreciation method in which the depreciation expense is the same each period.

Salvage value (also known as *residual value*) is the estimated value of an asset at the end of its useful life.

Straight-line depreciation is the simplest way to allocate the cost of an asset to the periods in which the asset is used. This is the method we used in Chapter 3. Using this method, the depreciation expense is the same every period. To calculate the appropriate amount of depreciation expense for each accounting period, you follow several steps.

1. Estimate the useful life of the asset. The firm should consider this estimate when purchasing an asset and use the estimate after the purchase to properly account for the cost of that asset.
2. Estimate the **salvage value**, the amount you believe the asset will be worth when the company is finished using it. Salvage value is the amount you think someone will pay you for the used asset. Someone who knows a lot about the asset and the relationship between the use of the asset and its market value will estimate the salvage value. Salvage value is an estimate that you may need to revise more than once during the life of the asset. The useful life and the salvage value are related, and the firm should have made these estimates as part of the acquisition decision.
3. Calculate the depreciable base—the amount you want to depreciate—by deducting the salvage value from the acquisition cost of the asset.
4. Divide the depreciable base—the difference between the asset's cost and its estimated salvage value—by the estimate of the number of years of the asset's useful life. This gives you the annual depreciation expense.

$$[\text{Acquisition cost} - \text{Salvage value}] \div \text{Estimated useful life in years}$$
$$= \text{Annual depreciation expense}$$

We will use an orange juice machine purchased by Holiday Hotels to demonstrate all of the depreciation methods. Exhibit 6.3 summarizes the information we need for all three depreciation methods.

EXHIBIT 6.3

Holiday Hotels' Orange Juice Machine

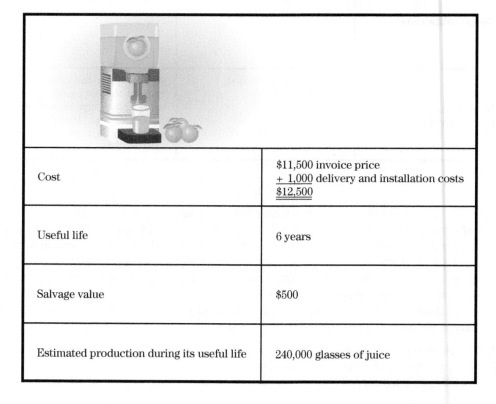

Cost	$11,500 invoice price + 1,000 delivery and installation costs $12,500
Useful life	6 years
Salvage value	$500
Estimated production during its useful life	240,000 glasses of juice

Suppose Holiday Hotels purchases a new squeeze-your-own orange juice machine for its self-service breakfast bar. Such a machine is expensive and requires large supplies of fresh oranges. After considering the risks and rewards of purchasing the machine and evaluating the effect such a purchase would have on the financial statements, Holiday Hotels decides to purchase an $11,500 machine with an estimated useful life of six years. In addition to the invoice price of $11,500, delivery and installation costs amount to $1,000. Holiday will capitalize these costs as part of the acquisition cost of the asset. Holiday estimates that the machine will have a salvage value of $500 at the end of six years. After someone in the firm who is knowledgeable about the characteristics of the asset reviews and confirms the judgments about useful life and salvage value, Holiday will calculate the yearly depreciation expense.

First, Holiday calculates the depreciable base by subtracting the salvage value from the cost.

$$\text{Cost} = \$11,500 + \$1,000 = \$12,500$$
$$\text{Salvage value} = \$500$$
$$\text{Depreciable base} = \$12,500 - \$500 = \$12,000$$

Then, Holiday divides the depreciable base by the number of years of useful life.

$$\text{Annual depreciation expense} = \$12,000/6 \text{ years} = \$2,000 \text{ per year}$$

Each year the income statement will include depreciation expense of $2,000, and each year the carrying value of the asset will be reduced by $2,000. This reduction in carrying value is accumulated over the life of the asset. A company's accounting records always preserve the acquisition cost of the asset and disclose the cost on the balance sheet or in the notes, so Holiday will keep the total accumulated depreciation in a separate account and subtract it from the acquisition cost of the asset on the balance sheet. If Holiday bought the machine on January 1, 2010, and the company's fiscal year ends on December 31, then the income statement for the year ended December 31, 2010, would include depreciation expense of $2,000. The balance sheet would show the acquisition cost of $12,500 and the accumulated depreciation at December 31, 2010 of $2,000. This is how the adjustment for depreciation expense would look in the accounting equation:

Assets	=	Liabilities	+	Shareholders' equity		
				Contributed capital	+	Retained earnings
Accumulated depreciation— Equipment (2,000)						Depreciation expense (2,000)

The equipment account will have a balance of $12,500 during the entire life of the asset. The accumulated depreciation account, a contra-asset, will have a balance of $2,000 after the 2010 depreciation is recorded. Here is how the asset is reported on the balance sheet at December 31, 2010:

	December 31, 2010
Equipment	$12,500
Less: accumulated depreciation	(2,000)
Net book value	$10,500

In the following year, 2011, the income statement for the year would again include $2,000 depreciation expense. The straight-line method gets its name from the fact that the same amount is depreciated each year, so the depreciation expense could be graphed as a straight horizontal line across the life of the asset. The adjustment at the end of 2011 will be identical to the adjustment at the end of 2010. It will add $2,000 to the accumulated depreciation account, so the new balance is $4,000. Because the income statement is only for a single year, the depreciation expense will again be $2,000. The balance sheet at December 31, 2011, would show how the carrying value of our asset is declining, because on that date Holiday has used it for two years.

	December 31, 2011
Equipment	$12,500
Less: accumulated depreciation	(4,000)
Net book value	$ 8,500

Exhibit 6.4 shows the depreciation expense and accumulated depreciation amounts for the year-end financial statements during the entire life of the asset. At the end of the useful life of the

asset, the carrying value will equal the salvage value. Holiday has previously estimated that it could sell the asset at the end of its useful life for a price equal to its carrying value—$500.

EXHIBIT 6.4

Straight-Line Depreciation

The depreciation expense each year is always $2,000, as shown in the table and accompanying graph. The carrying value decreases over time, from $10,500 at December 31, 2010, to $500 at December 31, 2015.

Year	Depreciation Expense for the Year on the Income Statement	Accumulated Depreciation on Year-End Balance Sheet	Carrying or Book Value on the Year-End Balance Sheet
2010	$2,000	$ 2,000	$10,500
2011	$2,000	$ 4,000	$ 8,500
2012	$2,000	$ 6,000	$ 6,500
2013	$2,000	$ 8,000	$ 4,500
2014	$2,000	$10,000	$ 2,500
2015	$2,000	$12,000	$ 500

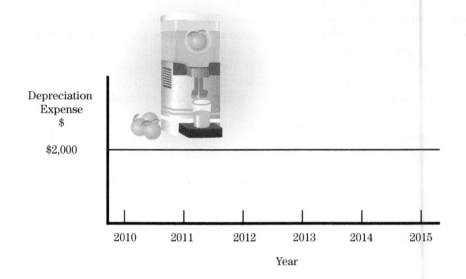

Your Turn

On January 1, 2010, Access Company purchased a new computer system for $15,000. The estimated useful life of the computer system was five years, with an estimated salvage value of $3,000. Using straight-line depreciation, how much depreciation expense will Access Company include on the income statement for the year ended December 31, 2011? Determine the book value of the asset on December 31, 2011.

Activity (Units-of-Production) Depreciation

Another way a firm determines depreciation expense is by estimating the productivity of the asset—how much the asset will produce during its useful life. How many units will the asset produce or how much work will the asset do during its useful life? This way of determining depreciation expense is called the **activity method of depreciation**, also known as the units-of-production method. Examples of activities are miles driven or units produced. If a company buys a car, it may decide to use it for 100,000 miles before trading it in. The activity method is similar to the straight-line method. The difference is that an estimate of the number of units of activity over the asset's life is used as the allocation base instead of an estimate of the number of years of useful life.

> **Activity method of depreciation** is the method of depreciation in which useful life is expressed in terms of the total units of activity or production expected from the asset, and the asset is written off in proportion to its activity during the accounting period.

$$\frac{\text{Acquisition cost } - \text{ Salvage value}}{\text{Estimated useful life in activity units}} = \text{Rate per activity unit}$$

Rate × Actual activity level for the year = Annual depreciation expense

To use the activity method of depreciation, Holiday needs to estimate how many units the machine will be able to produce during its useful life. Suppose Holiday estimates the machine will be able to produce 240,000 glasses of juice during its useful life. You calculate the depreciable base in exactly the same way when using the activity method of depreciation as when using straight-line depreciation—subtract the expected salvage value from the cost. In this example, the depreciable base is $12,000 ($12,500 – $500). You then divide the depreciable base by the total number of units you expect to produce with the machine during its useful life.

Here is how the activity method of depreciation can be applied to Holiday's orange juice machine. Start by dividing the depreciable base—$12,000—by the estimated number of glasses of orange juice the machine will produce. That gives the depreciation rate.

$$\$12,000 \div 240,000 \text{ glasses} = \$0.05 \text{ per glass}$$

Holiday will use this rate of $0.05 per glass to depreciate the machine for each glass of juice it produces. Suppose the machine has a built-in counter that showed 36,000 glasses of juice were squeezed during the first year. The depreciation expense shown on the income statement for that year would be $1,800.

$$36,000 \text{ glasses} \times \$0.05 \text{ per glass} = \$1,800 \text{ depreciation expense}$$

That is the depreciation expense for the year, and the book value of the asset would decline by that amount when the year-end adjustment is made. It is important to keep a record of the book value of the asset so that Holiday Hotels does not depreciate the asset lower than its $500 estimated salvage value. The salvage value will equal the carrying value when the asset has reached the end of Holiday's estimate of the useful life.

Exhibit 6.5 shows the depreciation schedule for the orange juice machine, given the production levels for each year as shown.

EXHIBIT 6.5

Activity Method of Depreciation

Year	Production Each Year— Number of Glasses of Orange Juice	Depreciation Rate × Number of Glasses of Juice *Rate: $0.05 per Glass	Depreciation Expense for the Year (Income Statment)	Accumulated Depreciation (Balance Sheet at the End of the Year)	Book Value of the Asset (Balance Sheet at the End of the Year)
2010	36,000	$0.05 × 36,000	$1,800	$ 1,800	$10,700
2011	41,000	$0.05 × 41,000	$2,050	$ 3,850	$ 8,650
2012	39,000	$0.05 × 39,000	$1,950	$ 5,800	$ 6,700
2013	46,000	$0.05 × 46,000	$2,300	$ 8,100	$ 4,400
2014	43,000	$0.05 × 43,000	$2,150	$10,250	$ 2,250
2015	35,000	$0.05 × 35,000	$1,750	$12,000	$ 500

Cost of machine of $12,500 minus salvage value of $500, gives a depreciable base of $12,000.
Total estimated production is 240,000 glasses. *Rate = $12,000 ÷ 240,000 = $0.05 per glass.

With the activity depreciation method, the depreciation expense each year depends on how many units the asset produces each year. This method matches the expense to the amount of work performed by the asset. Although the book value is decreasing each year, the amount of depreciation expense will likely vary from year-to-year, as shown in both the table and graph. As always, accumulated depreciation is working its way up until it reaches the depreciable base—cost minus salvage value. That means the book value will be equal to the estimated salvage value at the end of its useful life.

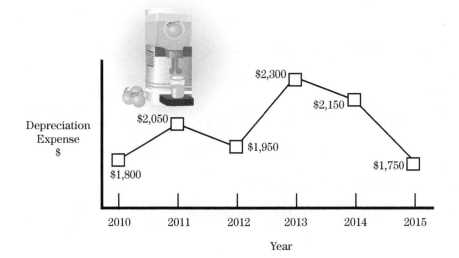

Your Turn 6-5

Hopper Company purchased a weaving machine on January 1, 2009, for $44,000. The expected useful life is 10 years or production of 100,000 rugs, and its salvage value is estimated at $4,000. In 2009, 13,000 rugs were made, and in 2010, 14,000 rugs were made. Calculate the depreciation expense for 2009 and 2010 using activity depreciation.

Declining Balance Depreciation

Declining balance depreciation is an accelerated depreciation method in which depreciation expense is based on the declining book value of the asset.

Accelerated depreciation is a depreciation method in which more depreciation expense is taken in the early years of the asset's life and less in the later years.

You have learned about the straight-line depreciation method and the activity method of depreciation. The third method is **declining balance depreciation**. This method is considered an **accelerated depreciation** method, one that allows more depreciation in the early years of an asset's life and less in the later years. The higher depreciation charges will occur in the early, more productive years when the equipment is generating more revenue. Depreciating more of the asset in the first few years also helps even out the total expenses related to an asset. In later years, the depreciation expense is lower but repair expenses are likely to increase.

The declining balance method speeds up an asset's depreciation by applying a constant rate to the declining book value of an asset. Frequently, firms use a version of the declining balance method called double-declining balance. The firm takes 200% of the straight-line rate to use as the annual depreciation rate. For example, if the useful life of an asset were five years, the straight-line rate would be one-fifth, or 20%. That is because 20% of the asset would be depreciated each year for five years using straight-line depreciation. The rate used for double-declining balance depreciation would be 40%, which is 200%, or twice the straight-line rate. Here is how this method works and why it is called double-declining balance. Every year, the accountant depreciates the carrying value, or book value, of the asset by an amount equal to twice the straight-line rate.

$$\text{Book value} \times (2 \times \text{Straight-line rate}) = \text{Yearly expense}$$

An example will help you see how this method works. Suppose the useful life of an asset is four years. The double-declining rate would be 50%:

$$100\% \div 4 \text{ years} = 25\% \text{ per year} = \text{Straight-line rate}$$

$$\text{Double it: } 50\% = \text{Double-declining balance rate}$$

Using this depreciation method for Holiday Hotels' orange juice machine, the book value at the beginning of the first year is $12,500—its acquisition cost. Notice that the calculation of the annual depreciation expense when using double-declining balance ignores any salvage value. Remember that book value equals cost minus accumulated depreciation. Recall that the useful life of the juice machine is six years. So the depreciation rate is $2 \times (1/6)$, which is 1/3.

The depreciation expense for the first year is

$$1/3 \times \$12,500 = \$4,167$$

The book value on the balance sheet at December 31, 2010, will be

$$\$12,500 - \$4,167 = \$8,333$$

For the second year, the accountant again calculates the amount of depreciation as one-third of the *book value* (not the *cost*). For the second year, the depreciation expense is

$$1/3 \times \$8,333 = \$2,778 \text{ (rounded)}$$

The accumulated depreciation at the end of the second year is

$$\$4,167 + \$2,778 = \$6,945$$

The book value on the December 31, 2011, balance sheet is

$$\$12,500 - \$6,945 = \$5,555$$

Although salvage value is ignored in the calculation of each year's expense, you must always keep the salvage value in mind so that the book value of the asset is never lower than its salvage value. Exhibit 6.6 shows how Holiday Hotels' orange juice machine would be depreciated using double-declining balance depreciation.

EXHIBIT 6.6

Double-Declining Balance Depreciation

Year	Depreciation Rate = 1/3 or 33.333%	Book Value before Depreciating the Asset for the Year	Depreciation Expense for the Year	Accumulated Depreciation (At the End of the Year)	Book Value at the End of the Year: $12,500– Accumulated Depreciation
2010	0.33333	$12,500	$4,167	$ 4,167	$8,333
2011	0.33333	$ 8,333	$2,778	$ 6,945	$5,555
2012	0.33333	$ 5,555	$1,852	$ 8,797	$3,703
2013	0.33333	$ 3,703	$1,234	$10,031	$2,469
2014	0.33333	$ 2,469	$ 823	$10,854	$1,646
2015	0.33333	$ 1,646	$1,146*	$12,000	$ 500**

*The calculation of (0.33333 × $1,646) indicates depreciation expense of $549. Because this is the last year of its useful life and the book value after this year's depreciation should be $500, the depreciation expense must be $1,146 to bring the total accumulated depreciation to $12,000.
**The depreciation expense for 2015 must be calculated to make this the book value at the end of the useful life—because the book value should be the estimated salvage value.

With double-declining depreciation, depreciation expense is larger in the early years of the asset's life and smaller in the later years. The book value is decreasing at a decreasing rate. Still, the balance in Accumulated Depreciation is working its way up until it reaches the cost minus salvage value. A firm always wants the book value of the asset to be equal to the estimated salvage value at the end of its useful life.

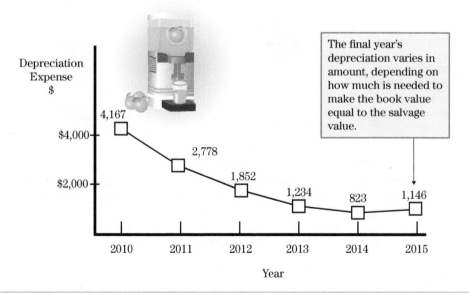

Sometimes depreciation expense for the last year of the asset's useful life is more than the amount calculated by multiplying the book value by the double-declining rate, and sometimes it is less. When the asset has a large salvage value, the depreciation expense in the last year of the asset's life will be less than the amount calculated using the double-declining depreciation rate and the carrying value. When the asset has no salvage value, the depreciation expense in the last year will be more than the calculated amount. The last year's depreciation expense will be the amount needed to get the book value of the asset equal to the salvage value.

Exhibit 6.7 summarizes the calculations for the three depreciation methods.

EXHIBIT 6.7

Depreciation Methods

Method	Formula for Depreciation Expense
Straight-line	$\dfrac{\text{Acquisition cost} - \text{Salvage value}}{\text{Estimated useful life in years}} = \text{Yearly depreciation expense}$
Activity	$\dfrac{\text{Acquisition cost} - \text{Salvage value}}{\text{Estimated useful life in activity units}} = \text{Unit depreciation rate}$ Rate × Actual activity level for the year = Yearly depreciation expense
Double-declining balance	Beginning-of-the-year book value × (2/Estimated useful life in years) = Yearly depreciation expense

Over the useful life of the asset, the same total depreciation expense will be recognized no matter which method is used. Exhibit 6.8 compares the depreciation expense of the orange juice machine with the three different depreciation methods.

EXHIBIT 6.8

Comparison of Depreciation Expense by Year over the Life of the Orange Juice Machine for Holiday Hotels

Notice that the annual depreciation expense differs among the three methods, but the total depreciation expense taken over the life of the asset is the same for all methods.

Year	Straight-Line	Activity	Double-Declining Balance
2010	$ 2,000	$ 1,800	$ 4,167
2011	$ 2,000	$ 2,050	$ 2,778
2012	$ 2,000	$ 1,950	$ 1,852
2013	$ 2,000	$ 2,300	$ 1,234
2014	$ 2,000	$ 2,150	$ 823
2015	$ 2,000	$ 1,750	$ 1,146
Total depreciation expense during the life of the asset	$12,000	$12,000	$12,000

Your Turn 6-6

An asset costs $50,000, has an estimated salvage value of $5,000, and has a useful life of five years. Calculate the amount of depreciation expense for the second year using the double-declining balance method.

Depletion

Now that you know how equipment and similar kinds of fixed assets are written off using various depreciation methods, we turn our attention to the way natural resources are written off. When a company uses a natural resource to obtain benefits for the operation of its business, the write-off of the asset is called *depletion*. Often, all amounts of accumulated depreciation, accumulated depletion, and accumulated amortization are captured in a single total on the balance sheet.

Depletion is similar to the activity method of depreciation, but it applies only to writing off the cost of natural resources. Examples of such natural resources are land being used for oil wells and mines. A depletion cost per unit is calculated by dividing the cost of the natural resource less any salvage value by the estimated units of activity or output available from that natural resource.

The depletion cost per unit is then multiplied by the units pumped, mined, or cut per period to determine the total depletion related to the activity during the period.

Suppose that, on January 1, 2011, a company purchases the rights to an oil well in Texas for $100,000, estimating that the well will produce 200,000 barrels of oil during its life. The depletion rate per barrel is

$$\$100,000 \div 200,000 \text{ barrels} = \$0.50 \text{ per barrel}$$

If 50,000 barrels are produced in the year 2011, then the depletion related to the 50,000 barrels produced in 2011 will be

$$\$0.50 \text{ per barrel} \times 50,000 \text{ barrels} = \$25,000$$

On the December 31, 2011, balance sheet, the book value of the oil rights will be

$$\$100,000 - \$25,000 = \$75,000$$

Using Intangible Assets: Amortization

In addition to tangible assets, most firms have intangible assets, which are rights, privileges, or benefits that result from owning long-lived assets. Intangible assets have long-term value to the firm, but they are not visible or touchable. Their value resides in the rights and privileges given to the owners of the asset. These rights are often represented by contracts. Like tangible assets, they are recorded at cost, which includes all of the costs a firm incurs to obtain the asset.

If an intangible asset has an indefinite useful life, the asset is not amortized. However, the firm will periodically evaluate the asset for any permanent decline in value and then write it down if necessary. The idea here is that the balance sheet should include any asset that has future value to produce revenue for the firm, but the asset should never be valued at more than its fair value. Writing down an asset due to a permanent decline in value means reducing the amount of the asset and recording an expense on the income statement.

Intangible assets that have a limited life are written off over their useful or legal lives, whichever is shorter, using straight-line amortization. That means an equal amount is expensed each year. Accumulated depreciation and accumulated amortization are often added together for the balance sheet presentation.

Copyrights

Copyright is a form of legal protection for authors of "original works of authorship," provided by U.S. law. When you hear the term copyright, you probably think of written works such as books and magazine articles. Copyright protection extends beyond written works to musical and artistic works and is available to both published and unpublished works. According to the 1976 Copyright Act, the owner of the copyright can

- copy the work.
- use the work to prepare related material.
- distribute copies of the work to the public by selling, renting, or lending it.
- perform the work publicly, in the case of literary, musical, dramatic, and choreographic works.
- perform the work publicly by means of a digital audio transmission, in the case of sound recordings.

All costs to obtain and defend copyrights are part of the cost of the asset. Copyrights are amortized using straight-line amortization over their legal or useful lives, whichever is shorter.

Patents

A **patent** is a property right that the U.S. government grants to an inventor "to exclude others from making, using, offering for sale, or selling the invention throughout the United States or importing the invention into the United States for a specified period of time in exchange for public disclosure of the invention when the patent is granted." In 2009, IBM announced that it shattered the 2008 record for the number of patents granted in a single year—4,186. This was more than the number issued to Microsoft, Hewlett Packard, Oracle, Apple, and Google combined.

As with copyrights, costs to defend patents are *capitalized* as part of the cost of the asset. Patents are amortized using straight-line amortization over their useful or legal lives, whichever

L.O.3
Explain and compute how intangible assets are written off over their useful lives and reported on the financial statements.

A **copyright** is a form of legal protection for authors of "original works of authorship," provided by U.S. law.

A **patent** is a property right that the U.S. government grants to an inventor "to exclude others from making, using, offering for sale, or selling the invention throughout the United States or importing the invention into the United States for a specified period of time."

is shorter. For example, most patents have a legal life of 20 years. However, a company may believe the useful life of a patent is less than that. If the company believes the patent will provide value for only 10 years, the company should use the shorter time period for amortizing the asset.

Trademarks

A **trademark** is a symbol, word, phrase, or logo that legally distinguishes one company's product from any others.

A **trademark** is a symbol, word, phrase, or logo that legally distinguishes one company's product from any others. One of the most recognized trademarks is Nike's swoosh symbol. In many cases, trademarks are not amortized because their useful lives are indefinite. Registering a trademark with the U.S. Patent and Trademark Office provides 10 years of protection, renewable as long as the trademark is in use.

Franchises

A **franchise** is an agreement that authorizes someone to sell or distribute a company's goods or services in a certain area.

A **franchise** is an agreement that authorizes someone to sell or distribute a company's goods or services in a certain area. The initial cost of buying a franchise is the franchise fee, and this is the intangible asset that is capitalized. It is amortized over the life of the franchise if there is a limited life. If the life of the franchise is indefinite, it will not be amortized. In addition to the initial fee, franchise owners pay an ongoing fee to the company that is usually a percentage of sales. You might be surprised at some of the top franchises for 2009. Number 1 was Subway; others include McDonald's and Pizza Hut.

Goodwill

Goodwill is the excess of cost over market value of the net assets when one company purchases another company.

Goodwill is the excess of cost over market value of the net assets when one company purchases another company. When the term *goodwill* is used in everyday conversation, it refers to favorable qualities. However, when you see goodwill on a company's balance sheet you know that it is a result of purchasing another company for more than the fair market value of its net assets. Goodwill is an advanced topic for intermediate or advanced accounting courses. However, you should have a general understanding of goodwill because it appears on the balance sheet of many firms.

Suppose that The Home Depot purchased Pop's Hardware store for $950,000 cash. The inventory and building—all of Pop's assets—were appraised at $750,000; and the small hardware store had no debt. Why would The Home Depot pay more than the market value for the net tangible assets of Pop's Hardware? Pop's Hardware store had been in business for many years, and the store had a terrific location and a loyal customer base. All of this is goodwill that Pop's had developed over years of business. GAAP do not allow a company to recognize its internally developed goodwill, so Pop's financial statements do not include goodwill. Now that The Home Depot has decided to purchase Pop's Hardware, however, the goodwill will be recorded. Here is how the transaction affects the accounting equation for The Home Depot:

Assets	=	Liabilities	+	Shareholders' equity		
				Contributed capital	+	Retained earnings
(950,000) Cash						
750,000 Various assets						
200,000 Goodwill						

What happens to the intangible asset goodwill? Goodwill is not amortized because it is assumed to have an indefinite life. Even though goodwill is not amortized, companies must evaluate goodwill to make sure it is not overvalued on the balance sheet. This is called evaluating it for impairment, and we will come back to this topic later in the chapter. Goodwill that has lost some of its value must be written down—that is, the asset is reduced and an expense is recorded. You can read about a firm's goodwill in the notes to the financial statements.

Research and Development Costs

Research and development (R&D) costs have benefits to the firm—at least that is the goal of R&D. However, R&D costs are expensed and are not capitalized as part of the cost of an asset because it is not clear that these costs represent something of value. Software development costs are considered research costs until they result in a product that is technologically feasible, so these costs must also be expensed as they are incurred. However, once the software is considered technologically feasible, the costs incurred from that point on are capitalized as part of the cost of the software. Deciding when a piece of software is technologically feasible is another example of how firms need to use judgment when making accounting decisions. The firm's developers and computer experts would make this judgment.

Changes after the Purchase of the Asset

L.O.4
Explain how decreases in value, repairs, changes in productive capacity, and changes in estimates of useful life and salvage value of long-term assets affect the financial statements.

We started the chapter with a discussion of the types and costs of long-term assets. Then, we discussed how the accounting records show the firm's use of those assets. Now we discuss how to adjust financial statements to record three things that may take place after an asset has been in use. First, the asset may lose value due to circumstances outside the firm's control. Second, the firm may make expenditures to maintain or improve the asset during its useful life. And third, the firm may need to revise its prior estimates of an asset's estimated life and salvage value.

Asset Impairment

By now you know that accountants want to avoid overstating assets on the balance sheet or revenue on the income statement. A firm that is getting ready to prepare its financial statements must evaluate its long-term assets, including goodwill and other intangible assets, for impairment—a permanent reduction in the fair market value of an asset below its book value—if certain changes have occurred. Such changes include

Impairment is a permanent decline in the fair market value of an asset such that its book value exceeds its fair market value.

1. a downturn in the economy that causes a significant decrease in the market value of a long-lived asset.
2. a change in how the company uses an asset.
3. a change in the business climate that could affect the asset's value.

An asset is considered impaired when the book value of the asset or group of assets is greater than its fair market value. Impairment is not easy to measure, but you will read about it in the notes to almost every set of financial statements. Because testing an asset for impairment can be quite difficult, it is a topic reserved for more advanced courses. However, you should be familiar with the terminology because you will see it in almost every annual report.

Exhibit 6.9 shows a portion of the disclosure made by Darden Restaurants, Inc., regarding its reported asset impairment charges (losses) in 2007 and 2008. A company must disclose in the notes to the financial statements a description of the impaired asset and the facts and circumstances leading to the impairment.

EXHIBIT 6.9

Disclosure about Asset Impairment in Darden Restaurants' Notes to the Financial Statements

The Notes to the Financial Statements provide important information about the amounts in the financial statements.

> From the Notes to the Financial Statements
> of Darden Restaurants, Inc.

During fiscal 2008 we recorded less than $0.1 million of long-lived asset impairment charges. During fiscal 2007, we recorded $2.6 million of long-lived asset impairment charges primarily related to the permanent closure of one Red Lobster and one Olive Garden restaurant.

Expenditures to Improve an Asset or Extend Its Useful Life

Another change in the value of an asset may be the result of the firm spending money to improve its assets. Any expenditure that will benefit more than one accounting period is called a **capital expenditure**. A capital expenditure is recorded as an asset when it is incurred, and it is expensed or amortized over the accounting periods in which it is used.

A **capital expenditure** is a cost that is recorded as an asset, not an expense, at the time it is incurred. This is also called *capitalizing* a cost.

Just the opposite of a capital expenditure is an expenditure that does *not* extend the useful life or improve the quality of the asset. Any expenditure that will benefit only the current accounting period is expensed in the period in which it is incurred. It is sometimes called a *revenue expenditure*, although *expense* really captures its meaning in a more logical way.

Many companies establish policies that categorize purchased items as capital expenditures or revenue expenditures—expenses, often based on dollar amounts. The accounting constraint of materiality applies here so that small dollar amounts can simply be expensed.

Remodeling and improvement projects are capital expenditures because they will offer firms benefits over a number of years. An example of remodeling would be a new wiring system to increase the efficiency of the electrical system of a building. Improvements might include items such as a more energy-efficient air-conditioning system.

Ordinary repairs are recognized as current expenses because they are routine and do not increase the useful life of the asset or its efficiency. Ordinary repairs, such as painting, tune-ups for vehicles, or cleaning and lubricating equipment, are expenditures that are necessary to maintain an asset in good operating condition and are expensed as incurred.

Suppose the computer terminals at Staples' corporate offices need a monthly tune-up and cleaning. The cost of this maintenance would be an expense—recognized in the period the work was done. But suppose Staples upgraded its computer hardware to expand its capacity or its useful life. This cost would be considered a capital expenditure and capitalized—recorded as part of the cost of the asset and depreciated along with the asset over its remaining useful life.

Revising Estimates of Useful Life and Salvage Value

Sometimes after an asset has been used for a period of time, managers realize that they need to revise their estimates of the useful life or the salvage value of the asset. Evaluating estimates related to fixed assets is an ongoing part of accounting for those assets. In accounting for long-term assets, revising an estimate is not treated like an error—you do not go back and correct any previous records or financial statements. Those amounts were correct at the time—because the best estimates at that time were used for the calculation. Suppose managers believe that a smoothly running machine will offer a useful life beyond the original estimate. The undepreciated balance—the book value of the asset—reduced by the estimated salvage value would be spread over the new estimated remaining useful life. Similarly, if managers come to believe that the salvage value of the machine will be greater than their earlier estimate, the depreciation expense in the future will be recalculated with the new salvage value. This approach is similar to treating the undepreciated balance like the cost of the asset at the time of the revised estimates and using the new estimates of useful life and salvage value to calculate the depreciation expense for the remaining years of the asset's life.

Suppose Staples purchased a copy machine that cost $50,000, with an estimated useful life of four years and an estimated salvage value of $2,000. Using straight-line depreciation, a single year's depreciation is

$$\frac{\$50,000 - \$2,000}{4 \text{ years}} = \frac{\$48,000}{4 \text{ years}} = \$12,000 \text{ per year}$$

Suppose Staples has depreciated the machine for two years. That would make the book value $26,000.

$$\begin{array}{ccccc} \$50,000 & - & \$12,000 & - & \$12,000 & = & \$26,000 \\ \text{Cost} & - & \text{Depreciation} & - & \text{Depreciation} & = & \text{Book value} \\ & & \text{year 1} & & \text{year 2} \end{array}$$

As Staples begins the third year of the asset's life, the manager realizes that Staples will be able to use it for *three* more years (rather than two more years as originally estimated), but now believes that the salvage value at the end of that time will be $1,000 (not $2,000 as originally estimated).

The depreciation expense for the first two years will not be changed. For the next three years, however, the depreciation expense will be different than it was for the first two years. The acquisition cost of $50,000 less $24,000 of accumulated depreciation gives us the undepreciated balance of $26,000. This amount is treated as if it were now the cost of the asset. The estimated salvage value is $1,000, and the estimated remaining useful life is three years. The calculation is

$$\frac{\$26,000 - 1,000}{3 \text{ years}} = \frac{\$25,000}{3 \text{ years}} = \$8,333.33 \text{ per year}$$

The asset will now be depreciated for three years at $8,333.33 per year. At the end of that time the book value of the asset will be $1,000 [$26,000 − ($8,333.33 per year × 3 years)].

At the beginning of 2010, White Company hired a mechanic to perform a major overhaul of its main piece of equipment at a cost of $2,400. The equipment originally cost $10,000 at the beginning of 2006, and the book value of the equipment on the December 31, 2009, balance sheet was $6,000. At the time of the purchase, White Company estimated that the equipment would have a useful life of 10 years and no salvage value. The overhaul at the beginning of 2010 extended the useful life of the equipment. White Company's new estimate is that the equipment will now last until the end of 2017—eight years from the date of the overhaul. Expected salvage value is still zero. White uses straight-line depreciation for all of its assets. Calculate the depreciation expense for White's income statement for the year ended December 31, 2011.

Your Turn 6-7

Selling Long-Term Assets

We have bought the long-term asset and used it—depreciating, depleting, or amortizing it over its useful life. Now, we deal with getting rid of an asset. Disposing of an asset means to sell it, trade it in, or simply toss it in the trash (please recycle!). When would a company sell an asset? Sometimes an asset is sold because it is no longer useful to the company. Other times an asset is replaced with a newer model, even though there is remaining productive capacity in the current asset. You calculate the gain or loss on the disposal of an asset by comparing the cash received for the sale of the asset—also known as cash proceeds—and the asset's book value at the time of disposal. One of three situations will exist:

L.O.5
Explain how the disposal of a long-term asset is reflected in the financial statements.

1. Cash proceeds are greater than the book value. There will be a gain.
2. Cash proceeds are less than the book value. There will be a loss.
3. Cash proceeds are equal to the book value. There will be no gain or loss.

Suppose you decide to sell equipment that was purchased seven years ago. At the time of the purchase, you estimated it would last 10 years. The asset cost $25,000, and you used straight-line depreciation with an estimated salvage value of zero. The depreciation expense each year was $2,500. Now, seven years later, you sell the asset for $8,000. Is there a gain or loss on the sale? First, calculate the book value on the date you sold the asset:

Book value = Cost   − Accumulated depreciation
Book value = $25,000 − (7 years × $2,500 per year)
Book value = $25,000 − $17,500 = $7,500

Then, subtract the book value from the cash proceeds to calculate the gain or loss on the sale.

$8,000 − $7,500 = $500

Because the proceeds of $8,000 are larger than the book value of $7,500, there is a gain on the sale. The gain from the sale will be shown on the income statement as revenue. A gain has this special name because it is not a normal part of business operations. You are not in business to buy and sell the equipment you use in your business, so the income from such a transaction is called a gain rather than simply called revenue.

Another way to calculate the gain or loss on the sale of an asset is to record the three amounts you know.

1. Record the receipt of cash.
2. Remove the asset and its accumulated depreciation.

3. Balance the transaction in the accounting equation with a gain or loss.

Assets	=	Liabilities	+	Shareholders' equity		
				Contributed capital	+	Retained earnings
8,000 Cash						
(25,000) Equipment						500
17,500						Gain on sale
Accumulated depreciation						of equipment

Now suppose instead that you sell the asset after seven years for $5,000 rather than $8,000. Is there a gain or loss on the sale? You already know the book value is $7,500 at the date of the sale. Subtract the book value from the cash proceeds.

$$\$5,000 - \$7,500 = -\$2,500$$

Because the proceeds are less than the book value, there is a loss on the sale. A loss is an expense, and it is shown on the income statement.

Suppose you sold the asset for exactly the book value, $7,500. There would be no gain or loss on the sale. Look at the following accounting equation to see the effect of selling an asset for its book value.

Assets	=	Liabilities	+	Shareholders' equity		
				Contributed capital	+	Retained earnings
7,500 Cash						
(25,000) Equipment						
17,500						
Accumulated depreciation						

There is no gain or loss. Selling an asset for its book value, therefore, does not affect the income statement.

UNDERSTANDING Business

Selling Assets to Raise Cash

Firms invest in long-term assets to use them for generating revenue for a significant amount of time, often decades. For example, the average age of an airplane in Delta's fleet is 13.8 years. Buildings and equipment can have useful lives of 40 years or longer. Firms sell assets when newer, more productive assets become available or when the assets wear out and need to be replaced. However, it's very uncommon for a firm to sell its long-term assets simply to raise money.

During a serious recession, that could change. In a recent survey of 1,275 chief financial officers of firms in the United States, Asia, and Europe, researchers from Duke University and the University of Illinois found that 59% of U.S. firms reported that the tight credit market had directly affected their firms' plans for investing in new projects. Of those firms, 70% reported that they were selling more corporate assets in order to raise cash than they did before the start of the credit crisis that began in 2008.

State governments are also looking at the possibility of selling assets to help meet budget deficits predicted for 2009 and beyond. For example, the governor of Arizona announced a plan that includes selling state office buildings and prisons to investors. The state would then lease them back from the investors.

When you examine a firm's financial statements, be sure to look at what is happening with its long-term assets. Failing to invest in new projects as well as selling off productive assets could be a sign of bad times ahead.

Source: "Firms Take Drastic Actions in Response to Credit Crisis," News Release, Duke University, Fuqua School of Business, February 3, 2009. www.fuqua.duke.edu/news_events/releases/credit_crisis_cash

Your Turn 6-8

Perry Plants Company owned an asset that originally cost $24,000. The company sold the asset on January 1, 2010, for $8,000 cash. Accumulated depreciation on the day of sale was $18,000. Determine whether Perry should recognize a gain or a loss on the sale. If so, how much?

Presentation of Long-Term Assets on the Financial Statements

Reporting Long-Term Assets

L.O.6
Recognize and explain how long-term assets are reported on the financial statements, and prepare financial statements that include long-term assets.

In this chapter you have seen that both tangible and intangible long-term assets are recorded at the amount the firm paid for them. The assets are shown on the balance sheet in the last half of the asset section, after current assets. Because the carrying value of property, plant, and equipment (PPE) is the difference between the cost of the asset and its accumulated depreciation, accountants say that PPE is reported at its *amortized cost* or its *depreciated cost*. The notes to the financial statements are a good place to learn the types of assets, approximate age of the assets, and depreciation method(s) used.

The use of long-term assets is shown on the income statement with depreciation, depletion, and amortization expense. Often, the amount is included in the total of several accounts for presentation on the income statement, so you may not see it as a separate line item.

The statement of cash flows will indicate any cash expenditures for PPE as cash used for investing activities. Any cash received from the sale of long-term assets will be shown as an inflow in the same section—cash from investing activities—of the statement. Remember that the gain or loss on the sale of a long-term asset, reported on the income statement, is *not* the cash related to the sale. The cash collected from the sale will appear on the statement of cash flows (investing activities).

Exhibit 6.10 shows the asset section of Best Buy's balance sheet. The firm shows the various categories of fixed assets at their cost and then shows the deduction for accumulated depreciation. This is all the depreciation that the firm has taken on its property, plant, and

EXHIBIT 6.10

Presentation of Long-Term Assets

This shows how Best Buy presents information about its fixed assets on the balance sheet.

Best Buy Co., Inc.
Consolidated Balance Sheets (partial)

($ in millions)	February 28, 2009	March 1, 2008
Assets		
Current assets		
Cash and cash equivalents	$ 498	$ 1,438
Short-term investments	11	64
Receivables	1,868	549
Merchandise inventories	4,753	4,708
Other current assets	1,062	583
Total current assets	8,192	7,342
Property and Equipment		
Land and buildings	755	732
Leasehold improvements	2,013	1,752
Fixtures and equipment	4,060	3,057
Property under capital lease	112	67
	6,940	5,608
Less accumulated depreciation	2,766	2,302
Net property and equipment	4,174	3,306
Goodwill	2,203	1,088
Tradenames	173	97
Other Assets	1,084	925
Total Assets	$15,826	$12,758

equipment since the purchase of the items. Some firms show only the net amount, leaving the details for the notes to the financial statements. In any case, you should be able to find or calculate the cost of a firm's long-term assets.

IFRS and Long-Lived Assets

U.S. GAAP value long-term assets at historical cost less accumulated depreciation. International Financial Reporting Standards (IFRS) allow revaluation of assets to their fair value if fair value can be measured reliably. Then, accumulated depreciation would be deducted. Notice that IFRS do not *require* revaluation.

Another significant difference between IFRS and U.S. GAAP relates to impairment. Under GAAP, when assets are written down due to impairment, the impairment losses cannot be reversed even if conditions change. However, under IFRS, impairment losses can be reversed (except those related to goodwill) if circumstances change.

There are many other differences in accounting for long-lived assets between IFRS and U.S. GAAP, but they are quite technical. If you major in accounting, you'll learn more about these in an advanced accounting course.

Preparing Statements for Team Shirts

Since beginning in January 2010, Team Shirts has now finished five months of business. Refresh your memory by reviewing the June 1 balance sheet in Exhibit 6.11, before Team Shirts begins the month of June.

EXHIBIT 6.11

Balance Sheet for Team Shirts at June 1, 2010

Team Shirts
Balance Sheet
At June 1, 2010

Assets		Liabilities and Shareholder's Equity	
Current assets		Current liabilities	
Cash	$12,805	Accounts payable	$ 9,000
Accounts receivable		Unearned revenue	4,950
(net of allowance of $176) . .	8,624	Total current liabilities	13,950
Inventory	5,100	Shareholder's equity	
Prepaid expenses	1,100	Common stock	5,000
Total current assets	27,629	Retained earnings	12,379
Computer (net of $300		Total shareholder's equity . .	17,379
accumulated			
depreciation)	3,700	Total liabilities and	
		shareholder's equity	$31,329
Total assets	$31,329		

The company has been struggling along, but Sara believes that she can make a big profit breakthrough if she can expand the business. Her research indicates a large demand for her T-shirts, so she plans a major expansion in June. Read through each of the transactions and study how they have been entered in the accounting equation worksheet in Exhibit 6.12. Then, we will make the end-of-the-month adjustments and prepare the four financial statements.

Transaction 1: On June 1, Team Shirts purchased a van for $25,000. The company paid an additional $5,000 to have it equipped with the racks for T-shirts. Team Shirts financed the $30,000 with a note payable at 6% per year for five years with a local bank. On May 31 of each year beginning in 2011, Team Shirts will pay the bank the interest it owes for the year plus $6,000 of the $30,000 with a note payable principal. Team Shirts expects the van to be driven for approximately 200,000 miles and have a residual value of $1,000 at the end of its useful life. The company decided to depreciate the van using the activity method, based on miles.

Transaction 2: Team Shirts received cash payments on accounts receivable of $8,000.

Transaction 3: Team Shirts found several big sporting goods stores to buy its shirts, so the firm must increase the inventory. Team Shirts purchases 3,000 T-shirts at $4.20 each on account.

Transaction 4: Team Shirts paid $9,000 on accounts payable.

Transaction 5: Team Shirts paid rent in advance on the warehouse. On June 1, the company still had half a month of prepaid rent ($600). In June, the company paid in advance for six more months of rent, from June 15 to December 15, in the amount of $7,200 ($1,200 × 6 months).

Transaction 6: Team Shirts sold and delivered 2,000 shirts for $10 each to several different sports shops on June 15 on account.

Transaction 7: Team Shirts paid cash for $2,300 worth of general operating expenses.

Transaction 8: Team Shirts found out that one of its customers, B&B Sports, had declared bankruptcy, so the firm wrote off B&B's outstanding balance of $150.

After you understand each of the transactions shown in Exhibit 6.12, you are ready to make the needed adjustments before the June financial statements can be prepared. As you read each of the explanations for the adjustments, follow along on the bottom part of the worksheet in Exhibit 6.12.

Adjustment 1: Team Shirts needs to adjust prepaid insurance. On June 1, there was $250 worth of prepaid insurance on the balance sheet. Recall, Team Shirts purchased three months of insurance in May for a total cost of $300, which is $100 per month. (Only half a month's worth expired in May.)

Adjustment 2: Another item that needs to be adjusted is prepaid rent. Team Shirts monthly rent is $1,200.

Adjustment 3: Prepaid Web costs must be adjusted for the June expense of $50.

Adjustment 4: Unearned revenue at the beginning of the month has now been earned. The sales revenue of $4,950 must be recognized and the cost of goods sold of $1,890 (450 shirts at $4.20 each) must be recorded.

Adjustment 5: Depreciation expense for the computer needs to be recorded. Recall, it is being depreciated at $100 per month.

Adjustment 6: Depreciation expense for the new van needs to be recorded. It cost $30,000 and has an estimated residual value of $1,000. It is being depreciated using the activity method based on an estimated 200,000 miles. During June, the van was driven 5,000 miles. The rate is $0.145 per mile ($29,000 depreciable base divided by 200,000 miles). The depreciation expense for June is $0.145 per mile × 5,000 miles = $725.

Adjustment 7: Interest expense on the note for the van needs to be accrued. The $30,000 note at 6% was signed on June 1. Interest for June will be $150 ($30,000 × 0.06 × 1/12).

Adjustment 8: The allowance for bad debts must be recorded. The current balance in accounts receivable (AR) is $20,650, and Team Shirts wants an allowance of 2% of ending AR. That would be $413. However, the allowance has a current balance of $26 (beginning balance $176 minus $150 write off). That means the firm must record bad debts expense (and an increase to the allowance) of $387 ($413 − $26).

Using the accounting equation worksheet in Exhibit 6.12, you can see how the financial statements are derived. Study each of them by tracing the numbers from the worksheet to the appropriate financial statement, shown in Exhibit 6.13.

EXHIBIT 6.12

Accounting Equation Worksheet for Team Shirts for June

All of the transactions for June and adjustments needed at the end of the month are shown in this accounting equation worksheet.

	Cash	All other assets	(Account)	All liabilities	(Account)	Common Stock	Retained Earnings	(Account)
Assets				**= Liabilities**		**+ Shareholder's Equity** (Contributed Capital / Retained Earnings)		
Beginning Balances	$12,805	$8,800 (176) 5,100 250 600 250 4,000 (300)	Accounts receivable / Allowance for bad debts / Inventory / Prepaid insurance / Prepaid rent / Prepaid Web design / Computer / Accumulated depreciation	$9,000 4,950	Accounts payable / Unearned revenue	$5,000	$12,379	
Transactions 1		30,000	Truck	30,000	Notes payable			
2	8,000	(8,000)	Accounts receivable					
3		12,600	Inventory	12,600	Accounts payable			
4	(9,000)			(9,000)	Accounts payable			
5	(7,200)	7,200	Prepaid rent					
6		20,000 (8,355)	Accounts receivable / Inventory				20,000 (8,355)	Sales / Cost of goods sold*
7	(2,300)						(2,300)	Operating expenses
8		(150) 150	Accounts receivable / Allowance for bad debts					
A-1		(100)	Prepaid insurance				(100)	Insurance expense
A-2		(1,200)	Prepaid rent				(1,200)	Rent expense
A-3		(50)	Prepaid Web design				(50)	Web design expense
A-4		(1,890)	Inventory	(4,950)	Unearned revenue		4,950 (1,890)	Sales / Cost of goods sold
A-5		(100)	Accumulated depreciation computer				(100)	Depreciation expense
A-6		(725)	Accumulated depreciation truck				(725)	Depreciation expense
A-7				150	Interest payable		(150)	Interest expense
A-8		(387)	Allowance for bad debts				(387)	Bad debts expense
	$2,305 +	**$67,517**		**= $42,750 +**		**$5,000 +**	**$22,072**	

━ Income statement   ━ Statement of changes in shareholder's equity   ━ Balance sheet   ━ Statement of cash flows

*Cost of goods sold: (225 shirts × $4.00) + (1,775 shirts × $4.20)

Assets (non cash)		Liabilities	
Accounts receivable	$20,650	Accounts payable	$12,600
Allowance for bad debts	(413)	Interest payable	150
Inventory	7,455	Notes payable	30,000
Prepaid insurance	150		
Prepaid rent	6,600	Total	$42,750
Prepaid Web design	200		
Computer	4000		
Accumulated depreciation	(400)		
Truck	30,000		
Accumulated depreciation	(725)		
Total	$67,517		

EXHIBIT 6.13

Financial Statements for Team Shirts for June 2010

The arrows should help you see the relationships among the financial statements.

Team Shirts
Income Statement
For the Month Ended June 30, 2010

Sales revenue		$24,950
Expenses:		
Cost of goods sold	$10,245	
Operating expenses	2,300	
Bad debts expense	387	
Insurance expense	100	
Rent expense	1,200	
Web design expenses	50	
Depreciation expense	825	
Interest expense	150	
Total expenses		15,257
Net income		$ 9,693

Team Shirts
Statement of Changes in Shareholder's Equity
For the Month Ended June 30, 2010

Beginning common stock	$ 5,000
Common stock issued during month	0
Ending common stock	$ 5,000
Beginning retained earnings	$12,379
Net income	9,693
Dividends	0
Ending retained earnings	$22,072
Total shareholder's equity	$27,072

Team Shirts
Statement of Cash Flows
For the Month Ended June 30, 2010

Cash from operating activities	
Cash collected from customers	$ 8,000
Cash paid to vendors	(9,000)
Cash paid for operating expenses	(9,500)
Net cash used by operating activities	$(10,500)
Cash from investing activities*	0
Cash from financing activities	0
Decrease in cash	(10,500)
Beginning cash balance	12,805
Ending cash balance	$ 2,305

*Note: The firm purchased a $30,000 truck by issuing
a $30,000 note payable.

Team Shirts
Balance Sheet
At June 30, 2010

Assets

Current Assets		
Cash		$ 2,305
Accounts receivable (net of allowance of $413)		20,237
Inventory		7,455
Prepaid expenses		6,950
Total current assets		36,947
Property and equipment		
Computer	$ 4,000	
Truck	30,000	34,000
Accumulated depreciation		(1,125)
Net property and equipment		32,875
Total assets		$69,822

Liabilities and Shareholder's Equity

Current Liabilities	
Accounts payable	$12,600
Notes payable (due 5/31/11)	6,000
Interest payable	150
Total current liabilities	18,750
Notes payable	24,000
Total Liabilities	42,750
Shareholder's Equity	
Common stock	5,000
Retained earnings	22,072
Total shareholder's equity	27,072
Total liabilities and shareholder's equity	$69,822

Applying Your Knowledge—Ratio Analysis

At this point, you have learned how a firm records the purchase of long-term assets and how it accounts for the use of those assets. Now we will look at how you can use the information about long-term assets to help evaluate the performance of the firm.

L.O.7
Use return on assets (ROA) and the asset turnover ratio to help evaluate a firm's performance.

Return on Assets

A company purchases assets to help generate future revenue. Recall the definition of an asset—something of value used by a business to generate revenue. A ratio that measures how well a company is using its assets to generate income is **return on assets** (ROA). ROA is an overall measure of a company's profitability. Like much of the terminology in accounting, the name of this ratio is descriptive. A company's return is what the company is getting back. We want to measure that return as a percentage of assets. So return on assets is literally *return*—net income—divided by *assets*.

Return on assets is a ratio that measures how well a company is using its assets to generate income. It is defined as net income divided by average total assets.

$$\text{Return on assets} = \frac{\text{Net income}}{\text{Average total assets}}$$

This ratio measures a company's success in using its assets to earn income for investors. This is a simplified version of ROA, so you may encounter the more complex version of ROA that adds back interest expense, net of tax, to net income in the numerator. Because interest expense is part of what has been earned to pay creditors, adding it back to net income makes the ratio a more specific measure of return to all investors, both shareholders and creditors, before either is paid. Because it is not always straightforward to calculate the tax effect of the interest payment, however, we will use the simpler version of the ratio with net income by itself as the numerator. The denominator is average total assets.

Using a ratio such as ROA gives financial statement users a way to standardize net income across companies. Exhibit 6.14 provides an example. For the fiscal year ended September 27, 2008, Apple Inc. had a net income of $4,834 million and average assets of $32,460 million. For the fiscal year ended January 30, 2009, Dell Inc. had net income of $2,478 million and average assets of $27,031 million. It appears that Apple is outperforming Dell. But that comparison does not tell us how well each company is using its assets to make that net income. If we divide net income by average total assets, we will get the return on assets for the year, which enables us to better compare the performance of the two companies.

EXHIBIT 6.14

Return on Assets for Apple and Dell

	Apple Inc. For the Year Ended September 27, 2008	Dell Inc. For the Year Ended January 30, 2009

(dollars in millions)

Net income	$ 4,834	$ 2,478
Average assets	$32,460	$27,031
Return on assets	14.89%	9.17%

This comparison shows that Apple is earning a better return with its total assets than Dell is earning with its assets. The industry average for firms in this industry for return on assets is 12.6%. Apple's ROA is 14.89% and Dell's ROA is 9.17% using the results from the fiscal years shown in Exhibit 6.14. You can find up-to-date information on the firms' ROA at www.moneycentral.msn.com.

Asset Turnover Ratio

Asset turnover ratio measures how efficiently a company is using its assets to generate sales. It is defined as net sales divided by average total assets.

Another ratio that helps us evaluate a firm's use of its assets is the **asset turnover ratio**. This ratio indicates how efficiently a company is using its assets to generate sales. The ratio is defined as net sales divided by average total assets. The ratio answers the question: *How many dollars of sales are generated by each dollar invested in assets?*

$$\text{Asset turnover ratio} = \frac{\text{Net sales}}{\text{Average total assets}}$$

Look at Apple and Dell again. Sales for Apple for the fiscal year ended September 27, 2008, were $32,479 million; sales for Dell for the fiscal year ended January 30, 2009, totaled almost twice that at $61,101 million. The asset turnover ratio for each is as follows:

(dollars in millions)	Apple	Dell
Sales	$32,479	$61,101
Average assets	$32,460	$27,031
Asset turnover ratio	1.00	2.26

Asset turnover ratios vary significantly from industry to industry, so it is important to compare firms only in the same industry. Dell's use of its assets to generate revenue was quite a bit better than that of Apple during this time period. It is interesting to note, however, that Apple's net income for the year was $4,834 million, while Dell's was only $2,478 million.

Remember that all ratios have this in common: To be meaningful, ratios must be compared to the ratios from other years with the same company or with other companies. Industry standards are also often available for common ratios to help investors and analysts evaluate a company's performance using ratio analysis. Also, one or two ratios will not give you a clear picture of any firm's performance. Ratio analysis is just one tool among many needed to understand a firm's financial statements.

Business Risk, Control, and Ethics

A firm risks losing long-term assets due to theft. This risk is not a problem with some large assets, such as a factory, but it is a very serious problem with smaller, mobile, fixed assets—such as cars, computers, and furniture and fixtures. Even large assets, such as buildings and factories, are at risk for damage due to vandalism, hurricanes, or terrorist activities. One of the major functions of any company's internal control system is to safeguard all assets from theft and damage—whether intentional or unintentional. The cost of safeguarding assets can be tremendous, as can the cost of replacing them if they are destroyed.

Physical controls to safeguard assets may be as simple as a lock on a warehouse door, a video camera in a retail store, or a security guard who remains in an office complex overnight. Even when assets are protected in a secure facility with guards, fences, or alarms, the company must be sure that only the appropriate people have access to the assets. As you learned in the story about the forklifts at the beginning of the chapter, the proper authorization for access to assets is crucial.

Complete and reliable record keeping for the assets is also part of safeguarding assets. With assets such as cash and inventory, the people who are responsible for the record keeping for long-term assets should be different than the people who have physical custody of the assets. As you learned in earlier chapters, this is called segregation of duties and is a very common control.

Monitoring is another control to safeguard assets. This means that someone needs to make sure the other controls—physical controls, segregation of duties, and any other policies and procedures related to protecting assets—are operating properly. Often, firms have internal auditors—their own employees—who perform this function as part of their job responsibilities. You may recall that it was an internal auditor who first blew the whistle on the WorldCom fraud.

L.O.8
Identify and describe the business risks associated with long-term assets and the controls that can minimize those risks.

Chapter Summary Points

- Assets that last longer than a year are classified as noncurrent (or long-term) on the balance sheet. They are recorded at cost, including all of the costs necessary to get the asset ready for use.
- Long-term assets are written off over their useful lives. For plant and equipment, an asset may be written off using either straight-line, activity, or double-declining balance depreciation methods. Intangible assets with a definite life are written off, or amortized, using the straight-line method.
- Routine repair and maintenance costs are expensed as incurred, whereas improvements to the productive capacity or the useful life of an asset are capitalized as part of the cost of the asset.
- Any revisions in the useful life or the estimated salvage value of an asset are implemented at the time of the revision and in future periods. Any past depreciation expense is *not* revised.
- When an asset is sold, the gain or loss is calculated as the difference between the proceeds (sales amount) and the book value (cost − accumulated depreciation) of the asset.

Chapter Summary Problems

Suppose Pencils Office Supply started the fiscal year with the following balance sheet:

Pencils Office Supply
Balance Sheet
At January 1, 2008

Assets

Cash	$390,000
Accounts receivable	136,000
Inventory	106,350
Prepaid insurance	3,000
Equipment	261,000
Accumulated depreciation—equipment	(75,800)
Total assets	$820,550

Liabilities & Shareholders' Equity

Accounts payable	26,700
Salaries payable	13,500
Unearned revenue	35,000
Long-term note payable	130,000
Other long-term liabilities	85,000
Common stock	250,000
Retained earnings	280,350
Total liabilities and shareholders' equity	$820,550

Suppose the company engaged in the following transactions during its fiscal year ended December 31, 2008:

a. The company purchased new equipment at the beginning of the fiscal year. The invoice price was $158,500, but the manufacturer of the equipment gave Pencils a 3% discount for paying cash for the equipment on delivery. Pencils paid shipping costs of $1,500 and paid $700 for a special insurance policy to cover the equipment while in transit. The installation cost was $3,000, and Pencils spent $6,000 training employees to use the new equipment. Additionally, Pencils hired a new supervisor at an annual salary of $40,000 to be responsible for the printing services area where the new equipment will be used. All payments were made in cash as the costs were incurred.

b. The company sold some old equipment with an original cost of $12,300 and related accumulated depreciation of $11,100. Proceeds from the sale amounted to $1,500.

c. The company collected cash of $134,200 on accounts receivable.

d. The company purchased $365,500 worth of inventory during the year, paying $200,000 cash, with the remainder purchased on account.

e. The company paid insurance premiums of $12,000.

f. The company paid $170,000 on accounts payable.

g. The company paid employees total cash for salaries of $72,250. (This includes the amount owed at the beginning of the year and the salary expense for the new supervisor.)

h. The company made sales to customers in the amount of $354,570. They collected $200,000 in cash, and the remainder was on account. (Inventory sold cost $110,000.) The company uses only one revenue account: sales and service revenue.

i. The company paid $50,000 to reduce principal of the long-term note and paid interest of $10,400.

j. The company paid operating expenses in the amount of $30,000 in cash.

Other Information

- The company owed salaries of $10,250 to employees at year end (earned but not paid).
- Insurance left unused at year end amounted to $2,000.
- The company estimates that the new equipment will last for 20 years and have a salvage value of $2,945 at the end of its useful life. The company uses the straight-line depreciation method.
- Previously purchased fixed assets are being depreciated at a rate of 10% per year.
- Unearned service revenue of $21,000 has been earned at year end.

Requirement

Set up an accounting equation worksheet. Enter the beginning balances, the transactions, and any needed adjustments at year end. Then, prepare an income statement, statement of changes in shareholders' equity, the statement of cash flows (all for the fiscal year), and the balance sheet at December 31, 2008.

Solution

	Assets			=	Liabilities	+	Shareholders' Equity		
							Contributed Capital	Retained Earnings	
	Cash	All other assets	(Account)	All liabilities	(Account)		Common stock	(Account)	
Beginning Balances	$ 390,000	$136,000 106,350 3,000 261,000 (75,800)	Accounts receivable Inventory Prepaid insurance Equipment Accumulated depreciation	$ 26,700 13,500 35,000 130,000 85,000	Accounts payable Salaries payable Unearned revenue Long-term notes payable Other long-term liabilities		$250,000	$280,350	
Transaction a.	(164,945)	164,945	Equipment						
b.	1,500	(12,300) 11,100	Equipment Accumulated depreciation					300	Gain on sale of property, plant, and equipment
c.	134,200	(134,200)	Accounts receivable						
d.	(200,000)	365,500	Inventory	165,500	Accounts payable				
e.	(12,000)	12,000	Prepaid insurance						
f.	(170,000)			(170,000)	Accounts payable				
g.	(72,250)			(13,500)	Salaries payable			(58,750)	Salaries expense
h.		154,570	Accounts receivable					354,570	Sales and service revenue
	200,000	(110,000)	Inventory					(110,000)	Cost of goods sold
i.	(50,000) (10,400)			(50,000)	Long-term notes payable			(10,400)	Interest expense
j.	(30,000)							(30,000)	Operating expenses
Adjustment 1				10,250	Salaries payable			(10,250)	Salary expense
Adjustment 2		(13,000)	Prepaid insurance					(13,000)	Insurance expense
Adjustment 3		(8,100)	Accumulated depreciation					(8,100)	Depreciation expense
Adjustment 4		(24,870)	Accumulated depreciation					(24,870)	Depreciation expense
Adjustment 5				(21,000)	Unearned revenue			21,000	Sales
	$ 16,105 + $836,195			=	$211,450	+	$250,000 +	$390,850	

━ Income statement   ━ Statement of changes in shareholders' equity   ━ Balance sheet   ━ Statement of cash flows

---

Pencils Office Supply
Income Statement
For the Year Ended December 31, 2008

Sales and service revenue		$ 375,570
Cost of goods sold		110,000
Gross profit		265,570
Gain on sale of asset		300
Other expenses		
Insurance expense	$13,000	
Salaries expense	69,000	
Depreciation expense	32,970	
Interest expense	10,400	
Other operating expense	30,000	(155,370)
Net income		$ 110,500

Pencils Office Supply
Statement of Changes in Shareholders' Equity
For the Year Ended December 31, 2008

Common stock		
Beginning balance	$250,000	
+ New contributions	–	
Ending balance		$250,000
Retained earnings		
Beginning balance	$280,350	
+ Net income	110,500	
– Dividends	–	
Ending balance		$390,850
Total shareholders' equity		$ 640,850

Pencils Office Supply
Statement of Cash Flows
For the Year Ended December 31, 2008

Cash from operating activities	
Cash collected from customers	$ 334,200
Cash paid to vendors	(370,000)
Cash paid for insurance	(12,000)
Cash paid to employees	(72,250)
Cash paid for interest	(10,400)
Cash paid for other operating expenses	(30,000)
Net cash from (used for) operating activities	(160,450)
Cash from investing activities	
Proceeds from sale of equipment	1,500
Cash paid for purchase of equipment	(164,945)
Net cash from (used for) investing activities	(163,445)
Cash from financing activities	
Cash paid on long-term note payable	(50,000)
Increase (decrease) in cash during the year	(373,895)
Add beginning cash balance	390,000
Cash balance at December 31, 2008	$ 16,105

Pencils Office Supply
Balance Sheet
At December 31, 2008

Assets	
Cash	$16,105
Accounts receivable	156,370
Inventory	361,850
Prepaid insurance	2,000
Total current assets	536,325
Equipment (net of $97,670 accumulated depreciation)	315,975
Total assets	$852,300
Liabilities and Shareholders' Equity	
Liabilities	
Accounts payable	22,200
Salaries payable	10,250
Unearned revenue	14,000
Total current liabilities	46,450
Long-term notes payable	80,000
Other long-term liabilities	85,000
Shareholders' Equity	
Common stock	250,000
Retained earnings	390,850
Total liabilities and shareholders' equity	$852,300

Key Terms for Chapter 6

Accelerated depreciation (p. 276)
Activity method of depreciation (p. 274)
Amortization (p. 270)
Asset turnover ratio (p. 290)
Capital expenditure (p. 281)

Capitalize (p. 270)
Copyright (p. 279)
Declining balance depreciation (p. 276)
Depletion (p. 271)
Depreciation (p. 271)
Franchise (p. 280)

Goodwill (p. 280)
Impairment (p. 281)
Intangible assets (p. 268)
Modified accelerated cost recovery system (MACRS) (p. 316)
Patent (p. 279)

Relative fair market value method (p. 270)
Return on assets ratio (p. 289)

Salvage value (p. 272)
Straight-line depreciation (p. 272)

Tangible assets (p. 268)
Trademark (p. 280)

Answers to YOUR TURN Questions

Chapter 6

Your Turn 6-1

1. Expense
2. Asset
3. Asset
4. Expense

Your Turn 6-2

Four-fifths of the costs [(400,000/500,000) × $480,000 = $384,000] should be recorded as the cost of the building, and one-fifth of the cost [(100,000/500,000) × $480,000 = $96,000] should be recorded as the cost of the land. These two costs need to be separated because the company will depreciate the building but not the land.

Your Turn 6-3

1. Depreciation
2. Depreciation
3. Depletion

Your Turn 6-4

Each year's depreciation is $2,400 [($15,000 − $3,000)/5 years] per year, so that amount will be on the income statement for the year ended December 31, 2011. At December 31, 2011, the company will have taken two years' worth of depreciation, so the book value will be $10,200 ($15,000 − $4,800).

Your Turn 6-5

Rate = ($44,000 − $4,000) ÷ 100,000 = $0.40 per unit
2009: 13,000 units × $0.40 = $5,200
2010: 14,000 units × $0.40 = $5,600

Your Turn 6-6

$50,000 × 2/5 = $20,000 for the first year
New book value = $50,000 − $20,000 = $30,000
$30,000 × 2/5 = $12,000 for the second year

Your Turn 6-7

$6,000 + $2,400 = $8,400 new depreciable amount
$8,400/8 years remaining life = $1,050 per year for each remaining year

Your Turn 6-8

There is a $2,000 gain on the sale. The proceeds of $8,000 are greater than the book value of $6,000.

Questions

1. Describe the difference between tangible and intangible assets.
2. What is the difference between capitalizing and expensing a cost?
3. What is depreciation?
4. What does amortization mean?
5. Explain the difference between depreciation and depletion.
6. How do firms determine the cost of property, plant, and equipment?

7. What is a basket purchase? What accounting problem does this type of purchase create, and how do firms deal with the accounting problem?
8. What is the carrying value, or book value, of an asset? Is this value equal to the market value of the asset? Explain your answer.
9. What is the residual value, or salvage value, of an asset?
10. What is the difference between depreciation expense and accumulated depreciation? On which financial statement(s) do depreciation expense and accumulated depreciation appear?
11. How does the matching principle apply to depreciation?
12. Explain the difference between the three depreciation methods allowed by GAAP.
13. What is a copyright and how is it accounted for?
14. What is a patent and how is it accounted for?
15. What does it mean for an asset to be impaired?
16. What types of costs related to long-term operational assets are capitalized and what types are expensed?
17. How is a gain or loss on the disposal of an asset calculated? On which financial statement(s) would the gain or loss appear?
18. How does goodwill arise?
19. How do you calculate the return on assets (ROA) ratio and what does this ratio measure?
20. How do you calculate the asset turnover ratio and what does this ratio measure?
21. List two types of controls that safeguard assets.

Multiple-Choice Questions

1. Which of the following is an intangible asset?
   a. Franchise
   b. Oil reserves
   c. Land
   d. Repairs
2. Depreciation is the systematic allocation of the cost of an asset
   a. over the periods during which the asset is paid for.
   b. over the periods during which the market value of the asset decreases.
   c. over the periods during which the company uses the asset.
   d. over the life of the company.
3. Writing off a cost means
   a. putting the cost on the balance sheet as an asset.
   b. evaluating the useful life of the asset.
   c. recording the cost as an expense.
   d. deferring the expense.
4. Suppose a firm purchases a new building for $500,000 and spends an additional $50,000 making alterations to it before it can be used. How much will the firm record as the cost of the asset?
   a. $500,000
   b. $550,000
   c. $450,000
   d. It depends on who performed the alterations.
5. Suppose a firm buys a piece of land with a building for $100,000. The firm's accountant wants to divide the cost between the land and building for the firm's financial records. Why?
   a. Land is always more expensive than buildings.
   b. Land will not be depreciated but the building will be depreciated, so the accountant needs two different amounts.
   c. Land will appreciate and its recorded cost will increase over time, whereas the building will be depreciated.
   d. Depreciation expense will be separated from accumulated depreciation after the first year.
6. When an expenditure to repair an existing asset extends the useful life of the asset, the cost should be
   a. classified as a revenue expenditure because it will result in increased revenue.
   b. capitalized and written off over the remaining life of the asset.

    c. expensed in the period of the repair.

    d. presented on the income statement or in the notes.

7. When goodwill is determined to be impaired, a firm will

    a. increase its book value to market value.

    b. sell it immediately.

    c. reduce the value of the goodwill with a charge against income (impairment loss).

    d. reduce the value of the goodwill with a charge to paid-in capital (reduce paid-in capital).

8. When a company's balance sheet shows goodwill for $300,000, what does that mean?

    a. The company has developed a strong reputation valued at $300,000 if the company were to be sold.

    b. The company is worth $300,000 more than the balance sheet indicates.

    c. The company purchased another company and paid $300,000 more than the fair market value of the company's net assets.

    d. The company has invested $300,000 in new equipment during the period.

9. Suppose a firm purchased an asset for $100,000 and estimated its useful life as 10 years with no salvage value on the date of the purchase. The firm uses straight-line depreciation. After using the asset for five years, the firm changes its estimate of the remaining useful life to four years (a total of nine years rather than the original 10 years). How much depreciation expense will the firm recognize in the sixth year of the asset's life?

    a. $12,500

    b. $10,000

    c. $11,111

    d. $31,111

10. Suppose a firm purchased an asset for $50,000 and depreciated it using straight-line depreciation for its 10-year useful life, with no salvage value. At the end of the seventh year of use, the firm decided to sell the asset. Proceeds from the sale were $17,500. What was the gain or loss from the sale of the asset? How did the sale affect the statement of cash flows?

    a. $2,500 loss; $2,500 cash outflow from investing activities

    b. $32,500 loss; $17,500 cash inflow from investing activities

    c. $17,500 gain; $17,500 cash inflow from investing activities

    d. $2,500 gain; $17,500 cash inflow from investing activities

Short Exercises
Set A

SE6-1A. *Calculate the cost of an asset. (LO 1).* Susan's Bake Shop bought a new air-conditioning system when the old one stopped working. The invoice price of the system was $45,000. Susan's also had the following expenses associated with the purchase:

Delivery charge	$1,925
Installation	3,250
Power to run the system for the first year	1,275

What amount should Susan's record on the books for this air-conditioning system?

SE6-2A. *Account for basket purchase. (LO 1).* Marketing Consultants Corporation obtained a building, its surrounding land, and a computer system in a lump-sum purchase for $375,000. An appraisal set the value of land at $189,000, the building at $126,000, and the computer system at $105,000. At what amount should Marketing Consultants record each new asset on its books?

SE6-3A. *Account for basket purchase. (LO 1).* Wrecker Specialist Corporation purchased three new pieces of equipment at a total cost of $415,000. The appraised values of the individual pieces of equipment were as follows:

Equipment 1	$162,750
Equipment 2	116,250
Equipment 3	186,000

What amounts should be recorded as the cost for each of the pieces of equipment in Wrecker Specialist's accounts?

SE6-4A. *Calculate depreciation expense: straight-line. (LO 2).* Calculate the annual straight-line depreciation expense for an asset that cost $20,000, has a useful life of four years, and has an estimated salvage value of $4,000.

SE4-5A. *Calculate depreciation expense: activity method. (LO 2).* Using the activity method, calculate the first two years of depreciation expense for a vehicle that cost $32,000, has an estimated useful life of five years or 125,000 miles, and has an estimated salvage value of $2,500. The number of miles driven each year is as follows:

Year 1	25,000
Year 2	35,000
Year 3	15,000
Year 4	45,000
Year 5	5,000

SE6-6A. *Calculate depreciation expense: double-declining balance. (LO 2).* Using the double-declining balance method, calculate the annual depreciation expense that will be recorded each year for an asset that cost $18,500, has a useful life of four years, and has an estimated salvage value of $3,500. Explain what accounting issue arises, if any, in the third and fourth years.

SE6-7A. *Determine the cost of an asset. (LO 1, 2).* If an asset with a salvage value of $1,500 is being depreciated at a rate of $1,500 per year using the straight-line method over a useful life of four years, how much did the asset cost?

SE6-8A. *Determine the useful life of an asset. (LO 2).* Suppose an asset cost $28,500 and has an estimated salvage value of $3,500. At the end of two years, the carrying value of the asset is $18,500. What is the useful life of the asset? Assume straight-line depreciation.

SE6-9A. *Calculate depletion. (LO 2).* Mining Expedition Company purchased a coal mine on January 1, 2010, for $8,400,000 and expects the mine to produce 3,500,000 pounds of coal over its useful life. In 2010, 1,100,000 pounds of coal were recovered. In 2011, 900,000 pounds of coal were recovered. What is the depletion for each of these years?

SE6-10A. *Amortization of intangible assets. (LO 3).* Unique Quality Recourses purchased a patent for $150,000 on July 1, 2009. The estimated useful life is 20 years. The legal life is 15 years. What is the amortization expense for the fiscal year ended June 30, 2010?

SE6-11A. *Analyze revenue and capital expenditures. (LO 4).* Categorize each of the following as a capital expenditure or a revenue expenditure (expensed) for Dalton & Sons and explain why:

1. In accordance with the long-term maintenance plan, paid for a newly reshingled roof (replacing similar old shingles)
2. Built an annex to the building for the executive offices
3. Improved the ventilation system to increase energy efficiency in the building
4. Replaced parts in major equipment as needed

SE6-12A. *Calculate depreciation expense with change in estimate of salvage value. (LO 4).* On January 1, 2010, the Premium Beer Corporation purchased equipment at a cost of $110,000. It was expected to have a useful life of eight years and no salvage value. The straight-line depreciation method was used. In January 2012, the estimate of salvage value was revised from $0 to $7,500. How much depreciation should Premium Beer Corporation record for 2012?

SE6-13A. *Account for asset impairment. (LO 4, 6).* Delta Airlines has determined that several of its planes are impaired. The book value of the planes is $10 million, but the fair market value of the planes is $9 million. How would this impairment affect the income statement in the period it is recorded?

SE6-14A. *Account for disposal of an asset. (LO 5).* A machine is purchased on July 1, 2009, for $170,000. It has an expected useful life of 10 years and no salvage value. After eight years, the machine is sold for $36,000 cash. What is the gain or loss on the sale?

Set B

SE6-15B. *Calculate the cost of an asset. (LO 1).* Bargain Basement Shopping Corporation purchased new credit card equipment. The invoice price of the equipment was $25,000. Bargain also had the following expenses associated with purchasing this equipment:

Shipping and delivery insurance	$1,750
Staff training to use new equipment	3,175
Electricity costs the first year	125

What amount should Bargain record on the books for this equipment?

SE6-16B. *Account for basket purchase. (LO 1).* Warehouse Supply Corporation obtained land, a factory, and manufacturing equipment in a lump-sum purchase for $495,000. An appraisal set the value of land at $296,400, the factory at $210,900, and the equipment at $62,700. At what amount should Warehouse Supply record each new asset on its books?

SE6-17B. *Account for basket purchase. (LO 1).* Dependable Courier purchased four vehicles at a total cost of $55,500. The appraised values of the individual vehicles were as follows:

Vehicle 1	$12,390
Vehicle 2	13,570
Vehicle 3	15,930
Vehicle 4	17,110

What amounts should be recorded as the cost for each of the vehicles in Dependable Courier's accounts?

SE6-18B. *Calculate depreciation expense: straight-line. (LO 2).* Calculate the annual straight-line depreciation expense for an asset that cost $45,000, has a useful life of eight years, and has an estimated salvage value of $5,000.

SE6-19B. *Calculate depreciation expense: activity method. (LO 2).* Using the activity method, calculate the first two years of depreciation expense for a piece of equipment that cost $85,000, has an estimated useful life of 5,000,000 hours, and has an estimated salvage value of $5,000. The number of hours used each year is as follows:

Year 1	1,250,000
Year 2	1,000,000
Year 3	650,000
Year 4	850,000
Year 5	1,250,000

SE6-20B. *Calculate depreciation expense: double-declining balance. (LO 2).* Using the double-declining balance method, calculate the annual depreciation expense that will be recorded each year for an asset that cost $23,000, has a useful life of eight years, and has an estimated salvage value of $3,500. Explain what accounting issue arises, if any, in the seventh and eighth years.

SE6-21B. *Determine the cost of an asset. (LO 1, 2).* If an asset with a salvage value of $1,000 is being depreciated at a rate of $1,250 per year using the straight-line method over a useful life of eight years, how much did the asset cost?

SE6-22B. *Determine the useful life of an asset. (LO 2).* Suppose an asset cost $28,000 and has an estimated salvage value of $1,000. At the end of four years, the carrying value of the asset is $16,000. What is the useful life of the asset? Assume straight-line depreciation.

SE6-23B. *Calculate depletion. (LO 2).* CNA Enterprises purchases an oil field and expects it to produce 1,000,000 barrels of oil. The oil field, acquired in January 2008, cost CNA $1.5 million. In 2008, the oil field produced 280,000 barrels. In 2009, the oil field produced 350,000 barrels. What is the depletion for each of these years?

SE6-24B. *Amortization of intangible assets. (LO 3).* STAT Research purchased a patent for $120,000 on January 1, 2010. The estimated useful life is five years. The legal life is 10 years. What is the amortization expense for the fiscal year ended December 31, 2010?

SE6-25B. *Analyze revenue and capital expenditures. (LO 4).* Categorize each of the following as a capital expenditure or a revenue expenditure (expense) for Service Enterprises and explain why:

1. In accordance with the long-term maintenance plan, painted the building
2. Purchased land next to the building to expand parking
3. Remodeled building increasing its useful life
4. Performed routine maintenance on the copier machines

SE6-26B. *Calculate depreciation expense with change in estimate of salvage value. (LO 4).* On January 1, 2010, Arbuckle's Carpet Cleaners purchased a machine at a cost of $42,000. The machine was expected to have a useful life of six years and no salvage value. The straight-line depreciation method was used. In January 2013, the estimate of salvage value was revised from $0 to $3,000. How much depreciation should Arbuckle's record for 2013?

SE6-27B. *Account for asset impairment. (LO 4, 6).* Similar Motors has determined that several of its plants are impaired. The book value of the plants is $8.34 billion, but the fair market value of the plants is just $7.56 billion. How would Similar Motors record this decline in the accounting equation worksheet?

SE6-28B. *Account for disposal of an asset. (LO 5).* A machine is purchased on May 10, for $45,000. It has an expected useful life of nine years and no salvage value. After seven years, the machine is sold for $10,000 cash. What is the gain or loss on the sale?

All of the A exercises can be found within MyAccountingLab, an online homework and practice environment.

Exercises
Set A

E6-29A. *Account for basket purchase. (LO 1, 2).* Connor's Tasty Vegan Restaurant purchased an oven and a delivery vehicle from a "going out of business" sale for a combined total of $32,000. An independent appraiser provides the following market values: oven—$15,000; delivery vehicle—$35,000.

1. How much of the purchase price should Connor's allocate to each of the assets?
2. If the oven has a useful life of four years and an estimated salvage value of $1,600, how much depreciation expense should Connor's record each year using the straight-line method?
3. If the delivery vehicle has a useful life of eight years and an estimated salvage value of $2,000, what would the book value of the vehicle be at the end of three years using the double-declining balance method?

E6-30A. *Calculate the cost of an asset and depreciation expense. (LO 1, 2).* True Light Electricity Company purchased land for $180,000 cash and a building for $420,000 cash. The company paid attorney fees of $22,000 associated with the purchase and allocated that cost to the building and the land based on the purchase price. Redesign costs on the building were $52,000.

Use the accounting equation to record the purchase of the property, including all related expenditures. Assume that all transactions were for cash and that all purchases occurred at the beginning of the year.

1. Compute the annual straight-line depreciation, assuming a 25-year estimated useful life and a $17,400 estimated salvage value for the building.
2. What would the book value of the building be at the end of the third year?
3. What would the book value of the land be at the end of the third year?

E6-31A. *Calculate depreciation expense: straight-line and activity methods. (LO 2).* Paper Printing Company purchased a copy machine for $65,000 on January 1, 2010. The copy machine had an estimated useful life of five years or 1,000,000 copies. Paper Printing estimated the copy machine's salvage value to be $5,000. The company made 250,000 copies in 2010 and 190,000 copies in 2011.

1. Compute the depreciation expense for 2010 and 2011, first using the straight-line method, then the activity method.
2. Which method portrays the actual use of this asset more accurately? Explain your answer.

E6-32A. *Calculate depreciation expense: straight-line and double-declining balance methods. (LO 2).* On July 1, 2010, Seminole Construction Corporation purchased equipment for $62,000. Seminole also paid $2,500 to train employees how to use it. The equipment is expected to have a useful life of eight years and a salvage value of $500.

1. Compute the depreciation expense for years ended June 30, 2011–2013, using the straight-line method.
2. Compute the depreciation expense for the years ended June 30, 2011–2013, using the double-declining balance method. (Round your answers to the nearest dollar.)
3. What is the book value of the equipment at the year ended June 30, 2013, under each method?

E6-33A. *Calculate depreciation under alternative methods. (LO 2).* Burgers to Go purchased a new delivery car at the beginning of the year at a cost of $25,700. The estimated useful life of the car is five years, and its estimated productivity is 80,000 miles. Its salvage value is estimated to be $1,700. Miles used yearly are as follows: Year 1, 16,000 miles; Year 2, 20,000 miles; Year 3, 13,000 miles; Year 4, 15,000 miles; and Year 5, 16,000 miles. Complete a separate depreciation schedule for each of the three methods given for all five years. (Round your answers to the nearest dollar.)

1. Straight-line method
2. Activity method
3. Double-declining balance method

E6-34A. *Calculate depreciation under alternative methods. (LO 2).* Soda Pop Bottling Company bought equipment for $75,500 cash at the beginning of 2009. The estimated useful life is four years and the estimated salvage value is $3,500. The estimated productivity is 150,000 units. Units actually produced were 37,500 in 2009 and 40,000 in 2010. Calculate the depreciation expense for 2009 and 2010 under each of the three methods given. (Round your answers to the nearest dollar.)

1. Straight-line method
2. Activity method
3. Double-declining balance method

E6-35A. *Calculate depletion. (LO 2).* On January 1, 2010, USA Oil Corporation purchased the rights to an offshore oil well for $55,000,000. The company expects the oil well to produce 10,000,000 barrels of oil during its life. During 2010, USA Oil removed 675,000 barrels of oil.

1. How much depletion should USA Oil Corporation record for 2010?
2. What is the book value of the oil rights at December 31, 2010, the end of the fiscal year?

E6-36A. *Amortize intangible assets. (LO 3).* Carterette Research Corporation registered a patent with the U.S. Patent and Trademark Office. The total cost of obtaining the patent was $195,000. Although the firm believes the patent will be useful for only 10 years, it has a legal life of 20 years. What will Carterette Research Corporation record for its annual amortization expense? Show how it would be recorded in the accounting equation.

E6-37A. *Calculate goodwill. (LO 3).* International Manufacturing decides to acquire a small local manufacturing company called Township Manufacturing. Township Manufacturing has assets with a market value of $120,000 and no liabilities, but International Manufacturing pays $135,000. Use the accounting equation to record the purchase.

E6-38A. *Evaluate asset impairment. (LO 4).* During its most recent fiscal year, Bargain Airlines grounded 10 of its 747s due to a potential problem with the wing flaps. Although the planes had been repaired by the end of the fiscal year, the company believed the problems indicated the need for an evaluation of potential impairment of these planes. The results of the analysis indicated that the planes had permanently declined in fair value by $120 million below their book value. What effect would this decline in value have on Bargain Airlines' net income for the year?

E6-39A. *Distinguish between capital and revenue expenditures (expenses). (LO 1, 4).* Classify the following items as either a capital expenditure or a revenue expenditure (an expense):

1. Changed oil in the delivery truck
2. Replaced the engine in the delivery truck
3. Paid sales tax on the new delivery truck
4. Installed a new, similar roof on the office building
5. Paid freight and installation charges for a new computer system
6. Repainted the administrative offices
7. Purchased and installed a new toner cartridge in the laser printer
8. Replaced several missing shingles on the roof
9. Trained an employee prior to using the new computer system
10. Replaced the brake pads on the delivery truck

E6-40A. *Account for capital and revenue expenditures (expenses) and calculate depreciation expense. (LO 2, 4).* Pet Food Enterprises has had a machine for five years. At the beginning of the sixth year, the machine was not performing as well as expected. First, Pet Food performed regularly scheduled maintenance on the machine, which cost $170. Then, the company replaced some worn-out parts, which cost $575. Finally, at the beginning of the sixth year, the company completed a major overhaul of the machine that not only fixed the machine but also added new functionality and extended its useful life by four years (to a total of 10 years) with no salvage value. The overhaul cost $25,000. (Originally, the machine cost $100,000, had a salvage value of $7,000, and had an estimated useful life of six years.)

1. Which of these costs are capital expenditures? How would these amounts appear on the financial statements?
2. Which are revenue expenditures? How would these amounts appear on the financial statements?
3. Assuming Pet Food Enterprises uses the straight-line method of depreciation, how much depreciation expense will be reported on the income statements for years 6–10?

E6-41A. *Account for capital and revenue expenditures (expenses) and calculate depreciation expense. (LO 2, 4).* Reengineering Corporation operates a small repair facility for its products. At the beginning of 2009, the accounting records for the company showed the following balances for its only piece of equipment, purchased at the beginning of 2006:

Equipment	$135,000
Accumulated depreciation	45,000

During 2009, the following costs were incurred for repairs and maintenance on the equipment:

Routine maintenance and repairs	$ 815
Major overhaul of the equipment that improved efficiency	32,000

The company uses the straight-line method, and it now estimates the equipment will last for a total of 12 years with $500 estimated salvage value. The company's fiscal year ends on December 31.

1. How much depreciation did Reengineering Corporation record on the equipment at the end of 2008?
2. After the overhaul at the beginning of 2009, what is the remaining estimated life of the equipment?
3. What is the amount of depreciation expense the company will record for 2009?

E6-42A. *Account for disposal of an asset. (LO 5).* Erickson Electricity bought a utility truck for $70,000. The utility truck is expected to have an eight-year useful life and a salvage value of $6,000.

1. If Erickson sells the utility truck after four years for $40,000, would the company realize a gain or loss? How much? (Assume straight-line depreciation.)
2. What would the gain or loss be if the company sold the utility truck for $17,000 after six years?

E6-43A. *Account for disposal of an asset. (LO 5).* Uptown Bakery purchased a grain grinding machine five years ago for $21,000. The machinery was expected to have a salvage value of $1,000 after a 10-year useful life. Assuming straight-line depreciation is used, calculate the gain or loss realized if the machinery was sold after five years for

1. $13,500
2. $8,400

E6-44A. *Account for disposal of an asset. (LO 5).* Gourmet Pizza's Delivery disposed of a delivery car after using it three years. The records of the company provide the following information:

Delivery car	$25,000
Accumulated depreciation	15,000

Calculate the gain or loss on the disposal of the car for each of the following independent situations:

1. Gourmet Pizza's sold the car to Desserts on Wheels for $13,500.
2. Gourmet Pizza's sold the car to Premium Beer Corporation for $10,000.
3. Gourmet Pizza's sold the car to Organic Food Market for $8,250.
4. The car was stolen out of Gourmet Pizza's parking lot, and the company had no insurance.

E6-45A. *Account for disposal of an asset. (LO 5).* Paper Printing Company disposed of a copy machine after using it for two years. The copy machine originally cost $65,000 and had associated accumulated depreciation of $32,500. Calculate the gain or loss on the disposal of the copy machine for each of the following situations:

1. The company sold the copy machine to a church for $27,500.
2. The company sold the copy machine to a local bank for $33,000.
3. The company gave the copy machine to a hauling company in return for hauling it to the local dump. The copy machine was considered worthless.

E6-46A. *Calculate gain or loss and cash flow. (LO 5, 6).* Big Peach Athletics sold assets with an original cost of $21,000 and accumulated depreciation of $11,500. If the cash proceeds from the sale were $10,250, what was the gain or loss on the sale? On which financial statement would that amount be shown? How much would be shown on the statement of cash flows and in which section?

E6-47A. *Identify items on financial statements. (LO 6).* For each of the following, give the financial statement on which it would appear:

1. Book value of fixed assets of $56,900
2. Proceeds from sale of fixed assets of $20,000
3. Loss on sale of fixed assets of $12,500
4. Accumulated depreciation on equipment of $10,000
5. Depreciation expense on equipment of $2,000
6. Impairment write off on assets of $45,000

E6-48A. *Calculate return on assets and asset turnover ratios. (LO 7).* Using the selection from Books-A-Million's annual report in Appendix A at the back of the book, calculate the following ratios for the most recent fiscal year:

1. Return on assets (ROA)
2. Asset turnover ratio

Set B

E6-49B. *Account for basket purchase. (LO 1, 2).* Runnels' Doggie Daycare purchased a building and land for a total cash price of $150,000. An independent appraiser provides the following market values: building, $59,500; land, $110,500.

1. How much of the purchase price should the company allocate to each of the assets?
2. If the building has a useful life of eight years and an estimated salvage value of $10,500, how much depreciation expense should Runnels record each year using the straight-line method?
3. Using the double-declining balance method, what would the book value of the building be at the end of four years?

E6-50B. *Calculate the cost of an asset and depreciation expense. (LO 1, 2).* Top Dollar Realty purchased a building for $157,500 cash and the land for $192,500 cash. The company paid real estate closing costs of $8,000 and allocated that cost to the building and the land based on the purchase price. Renovation costs on the building were $52,500.

Use the accounting equation to record the purchase of the property, including all related expenditures. Assume that all transactions were for cash and that all purchases occurred at the beginning of the year.

1. Compute the annual straight-line depreciation, assuming a 25-year estimated useful life and a $12,600 estimated salvage value for the building.
2. What would the book value of the building be at the end of the seventh year?
3. What would the book value of the land be at the end of the thirteenth year?

E6-51B. *Calculate depreciation expense: straight-line and activity methods. (LO 2).* Treadmill Repair Masters purchased equipment for $34,000 on January 1, 2010. The equipment had an estimated useful life of five years or 400,000 units of production. Treadmill Repair Masters estimated the equipment's salvage value to be $2,000. The equipment was used to produce 80,000 units in the year ended December 31, 2010, and 97,500 units in the year ended December 31, 2011.

1. Compute the depreciation expense for 2010 and 2011, first using the straight-line method, then the activity method.
2. Which method portrays more accurately the actual use of this asset? Explain your answer.

E6-52B. *Calculate depreciation expense: straight-line and double-declining balance methods. (LO 2).* On January 1, 2010, Ocean's Front Restaurant purchased new meat slicing equipment for $37,500. Ocean's Front also paid $1,000 for shipping and $3,500 to train employees to use the new equipment. The equipment is expected to have a useful life of five years and a salvage value of $2,000.

1. Compute the depreciation expense for the years 2010–2012, using the straight-line method. (December 31 is the fiscal year end.)
2. Compute the depreciation expense for the years 2010–2012, using the double-declining balance method. (Round your answers to the nearest dollar.)
3. What is the book value of the equipment at the end of 2010 under each method?

E6-53B. *Calculate depreciation under alternative methods. (LO 2).* Books Unlimited Corporation purchased a new copy machine at the beginning of the year at a cost of $36,500. The estimated useful life of the machine is five years, and its estimated productivity is 250,000 copies. Its salvage value is estimated to be $1,500. Yearly production for Year 1 was 50,000 copies; Year 2 was 45,000 copies; Year 3 was 55,000 copies; Year 4 was 40,500 copies; and Year 5 was 59,500 copies. Complete a separate depreciation schedule for each of the three methods given for all five years. (Round your answers to the nearest dollar.)

1. Straight-line method
2. Activity method
3. Double-declining balance method

E6-54B. *Calculate depreciation under alternative methods. (LO 2).* Pristine Carpet Cleaner bought a new steamer for $137,000 cash at the beginning of 2010. The estimated useful life is eight years and the estimated salvage value is $2,000. The estimated productivity is 225,000 hours. Hours actually used were 30,000 in 2010 and 28,125 in 2011. Calculate the depreciation expense for 2010 and 2011 under each of the three methods given. (Round your answers to the nearest dollar.)

1. Straight-line method
2. Activity method
3. Double-declining balance method

E6-55B. *Calculate depletion. (LO 2).* On July 1, 2010, Premier Paper Company purchased 1,000 acres of timberland for $22,427,500. The land without the timber is valued at $2,427,500. The land contained 5,494,505 board feet of timber. During the year ended June 30, 2011, Premier Paper Company logged and sold 525,000 board feet of timber.

1. How much depletion should Premier Paper Company record for the year ended June 30, 2011?
2. What is the book value of the timber at June 30, 2011, the end of the fiscal year?

E6-56B. *Amortize intangible assets. (LO 3).* Microtech registered a trademark with the U.S. Patent and Trademark Office. The total cost of obtaining the trademark was $55,000. Although the trademark has a legal life of 10 years, the firm believes it will be renewed indefinitely. What will Microtech record for its annual amortization expense?

E6-57B. *Calculate goodwill. (LO 3).* Big Apple Realty has decided to acquire a competing realty firm. The competitor firm has assets with a market value of $375,000 and liabilities with a market value of $110,000, and Big Apple pays $285,000. Use the accounting equation to record the purchase.

E6-58B. *Evaluate asset impairment. (LO 4).* During its fiscal year ended June 30, Super Shippers Delivery Service had to decommission 1,500 delivery trucks due to a potential problem with the fuel tank. Although the trucks had been repaired by the end of the fiscal year, the company determined that the problems required an evaluation of potential impairment of these trucks. The results of the analysis indicated that the trucks had permanently declined in fair value by $7.5 million below their book value. What effect would this decline have on Super Shippers' net income for the year?

E6-59B. *Distinguish between capital and revenue expenditures (expenses). (LO 1, 4).* Classify the following items as either a capital expenditure or a revenue expenditure (expense):

1. Changed the filter in the moving van
2. Painted the moving van
3. Paid sales tax on the new moving van
4. Installed a new energy-efficient air-conditioning system for the office building
5. Cleaned and lubricated sewing equipment
6. Performed routine yearly maintenance on copy machine
7. Purchased and installed a new set of energy-efficient deep fryers
8. Replaced several cracked tiles in company bathroom floor
9. Trained an employee prior to using the new energy-efficient deep fryers
10. Replaced the tires on the moving van

E6-60B. *Account for capital and revenue expenditures (expenses) and calculate depreciation expense. (LO 2, 4).* McKinney Library Services has had a file server (computer) for seven years. At the beginning of the eighth year, it wasn't performing as well as it should have been. First, McKinney had the server cleaned, which cost $125. Then, the company had the annual maintenance performed, which cost $275. Finally, at the beginning of the eighth year, McKinney completed a major upgrade of the server that not only fixed it, but also added new functionality to it and extended the useful life by four years (to a total of 12 years) with no salvage value. The overhaul cost $25,000. (Originally, the server cost $45,000, had a salvage value of $5,000, and an estimated useful life of eight years.)

1. Which of these costs are capital expenditures? How would these amounts appear on the financial statements?
2. Which are revenue expenditures? How would these amounts appear on the financial statements?
3. Assuming McKinney uses the straight-line method of depreciation, how much depreciation expense will be reported on the income statements for years 8–12?

E6-61B. *Account for capital and revenue expenditures (expenses) and calculate depreciation expense. (LO 2, 4).* At the beginning of 2010, the accounting records for Bright Tans showed the following balances for its deluxe high-pressure tanning bed, purchased at the beginning of 2007:

Deluxe high-pressure tanning bed	$65,000
Accumulated depreciation	30,000

During 2010, the following cash costs were incurred for repairs and maintenance on the tanning bed:

Routine maintenance and repairs	$ 350
Major overhaul of the tanning bed that improved efficiency	18,000

The company uses straight-line depreciation and it now estimates the tanning bed will last for a total of 10 years with $150 estimated salvage value. The company's fiscal year ends on December 31.

1. How much did the company record for depreciation on the tanning bed at the end of 2009?
2. After the overhaul, at the beginning of 2010, what is the remaining estimated life?
3. What is the amount of depreciation expense the company will record for 2010?

E6-62B. *Account for disposal of an asset. (LO 5).* Cupcake Factory purchased an industrial oven for $8,000. The company expects the oven to have a six-year useful life and a salvage value of $500. (Assume straight-line depreciation.)

1. If Cupcake sells the oven after three years for $3,500, would it realize a gain or loss? How much?
2. What would the gain or loss be if the oven were sold for $2,500 after five years?

E6-63B. *Account for disposal of an asset. (LO 5).* Industry Leading Manufacturers purchased equipment five years ago for $78,000. The company expects the equipment to have a salvage value of $3,000 after an eight-year useful life. Assuming the company uses straight-line depreciation; calculate the gain or loss realized if the company sells the equipment after four years for

1. $ 42,050.
2. $ 39,875.

E6-64B. *Account for disposal of an asset. (LO 5).* Fast Pizza Delivery disposed of a delivery vehicle that had been used in the business for four years. The records of the company provide the following information:

Delivery vehicle	$35,000
Accumulated depreciation	20,000

Calculate the gain or loss on the disposal of the delivery vehicle for each of the following independent situations:

1. Fast Pizza sold the delivery vehicle to the business manager for $15,000.

2. Fast Pizza sold the delivery vehicle to a homeless shelter for $10,000.
3. Fast Pizza sold the delivery vehicle to a customer for $17,000.
4. Fast Pizza caught on fire and the delivery vehicle was destroyed; Fast Pizza had no insurance.

E6-65B. *Account for disposal of an asset. (LO 5).* Sylvan Manufacturing disposed of equipment that had been used in the business for six years. The equipment originally cost $65,000 and had associated accumulated depreciation of $45,000. Calculate the gain or loss on the disposal of the equipment for each of the following situations:

1. The company sold the equipment to a scrap yard for $10,000.
2. The company sold the equipment to a competitor for $23,525.
3. The company called the city trash collectors to pick up the equipment because it was totally worthless.

E6-66B. *Calculate gain or loss and cash flow. (LO 5, 6).* Vintage Records sold assets with an original cost of $45,000 and accumulated depreciation of $30,000. If the cash proceeds from the sale were $13,500, what was the gain or loss on the sale? On which financial statement would that amount be shown? How much would be shown on the statement of cash flows and in which section?

E6-67B. *Identify items for financial statements. (LO 6).* For each of the following, give the financial statement on which it would appear:

1. Cost of fixed assets of $100,000
2. Proceeds from sale of land of $120,000
3. Gain on sale of fixed assets of $12,500
4. Accumulated depreciation on equipment of $50,000
5. Depreciation expense on equipment of $7,000
6. Impairment write off on assets of $65,000

E6-68B. *Calculate return on assets and asset turnover ratios. (LO 7).* Use the information from the 2008 annual report of Barnes & Noble to calculate the following ratios for the two most recent fiscal years:

(dollars in thousands)	2008	2007	2006
Sales (net)	$5,121,804	$5,286,674	$5,139,618
Net income	$ 75,920	$ 135,799	$ 150,527
Total assets	$2,993,888	$3,249,826	$3,196,798*

*From the 2007 annual report

1. Return on assets (ROA)
2. Asset turnover ratio

Problems
Set A

All of the A problems can be found within MyAccountingLab, an online homework and practice environment.

P6-69A. *Calculate capitalized cost and depreciation expense. (LO 1, 2).* Auto Mechanics, Inc., purchased a new piece of equipment for one of the company's repair shops on January 1, 2010. The invoice price was $64,700, but the salesperson gave Auto a 5% discount for paying cash for the equipment. Delivery costs amounted to $2,500, and Auto paid $300 for a special insurance policy to cover the equipment while in transit. The installation cost was $1,250, and Auto spent $2,500 training the employees to use the new equipment. Additionally, Auto had to spend $7,500 to customize the equipment to fit the shop's needs and hired a special mechanic at an annual salary of $55,000 who had several years experience with this type of equipment.

Requirements

1. What amount should be capitalized for this new asset?
2. To calculate the depreciation expense for 2010, what other information do you need? Do you think the company should gather this information before purchasing the asset? Why or why not?

P6-70A. *Calculate and analyze depreciation under alternative methods. (LO 2).* On January 1, 2010, the Super Fast Subs Company purchased a delivery automobile for $31,000. The estimated useful life of the vehicle is five years, and the estimated salvage value is $1,000. The company expects the automobile to be driven 200,000 miles during its service life. Actual miles driven were:

Year	Miles
2010	35,000
2011	40,000
2012	45,000
2013	39,000
2014	41,000

Requirements

1. Calculate the depreciation expense for each year of the five-year life of the automobile using the following methods. (Round your answers to the nearest dollar.)
   a. Straight-line method
   b. Double-declining balance method
   c. Activity method
2. How does the choice of depreciation methods affect net income in each of the years? How does the choice of depreciation methods affect the balance sheet in each of the years?

P6-71A. *Calculate and analyze depreciation under alternative methods. (LO 2).* Marshall's Dry Cleaning purchased new equipment on January 1, 2010, at a cost of $125,000. The estimated useful life is eight years with a salvage value of $15,000.

Requirements

1. Prepare two different depreciation schedules for the equipment—one using the straight-line method, and the other using the double-declining balance method. (Round to the nearest dollar.)
2. Determine which method would result in the greatest net income for the year 2010.

P6-72A. *Calculate and analyze depreciation under alternative methods. (LO 2).* Schillig & Gray Industries purchased a new machine at the beginning of 2011 for $9,500. The company expected the machine to last for four years and have a salvage value of $500. The productive life of the machine was estimated to be 180,000 units. Yearly production was as follows: in 2011 it produced 50,000 units; in 2012 it produced 45,000 units; in 2013 it produced 30,000 units; and in 2014 it produced 55,000 units.

Requirements

1. Calculate the depreciation expense for each year of the four-year life of the machine using the following methods. (Round to the nearest dollar.)
   a. Straight-line method
   b. Double-declining balance method
   c. Activity method using units
2. For each method, give the amount of accumulated depreciation that would be shown on the balance sheet at the end of each year.
3. Calculate the book value of the machine at the end of each year for each method.

P6-73A. *Account for intangible assets. (LO 3, 6).* Scientific Genius Company had the following balances in its intangible assets accounts at the beginning of the year. The trademarks have a remaining useful life of 15 years, and the copyright has a remaining useful life of nine years.

Trademarks	$45,000
Copyrights	36,000
Goodwill	50,000

Transactions during the year are as follows:

  a. At the beginning of the year, Scientific Genius filed for a new trademark. The costs totaled $30,000. Its useful life is estimated at 15 years.
  b. Scientific Genius incurred R&D costs of $75,000 related to new product development. No new products have been identified.
  c. Scientific Genius evaluated the goodwill for impairment and reduced its book value by $5,000.
  d. Scientific Genius successfully defended one of its copyrights in court. Fees totaled $18,000.

Requirements

  1. Show each of the transactions in the accounting equation, including any adjustments that would need to be made for the year-end financial statements.
  2. Prepare the intangible assets section of the balance sheet at year end.

P6-74A. *Account for change in estimates for depreciation. (LO 4).* In January 2009, Flooring Installation & Repair, Inc., purchased a van that cost $45,000. The firm estimated that the van would last for six years and have a salvage value of $3,000 at the end of 2014. The company uses the straight-line method of depreciation. Analyze each of the following independent scenarios:

  a. Before the depreciation expense is recorded for the year 2012, the mechanic tells Flooring that the van can be used until the end of 2014 as planned, but that it will be worth only $750.
  b. Before depreciation expense is recorded for the year 2012, Flooring decides that the van will last only until the end of 2013. The company anticipates the value of the van at that time will still be $1,500.
  c. Before depreciation expense is recorded for the year 2012, Flooring decides that the van will last until the end of 2015, but that it will be worth nothing at that time.
  d. Before the depreciation expense is recorded for the year 2012, the mechanic tells Flooring that the van can be used until the end of 2017 if the company spends $5,000 on a major overhaul. However, the estimated salvage value at that time (end of 2017) would be $100. Flooring decides to follow the mechanic's advice and has the van overhauled.

Requirement

Calculate the amount of depreciation expense related to the van that Flooring Installation & Repair, Inc., would report on its income statement for the year ended December 31, 2012, for each scenario.

P6-75A. *Account for disposal of an asset. (LO 5).* Analyze each of the following independent scenarios:

  a. A machine that cost $22,000 had an estimated useful life of three years with salvage value of $1,000. After two years of using straight-line depreciation, the company sold the machine for $8,000.
  b. A van that cost $40,000 had an estimated useful life of 10 years and a salvage value of $4,000. After 10 years of using straight-line depreciation, the company sold the completely worn-out van for $1,000 as scrap.
  c. Equipment that cost $45,000 had an estimated useful life of eight years and a salvage value of $3,000. After four years of using double-declining balance depreciation, the company sold the equipment for $14,750. (Round to the nearest dollar.)
  d. An asset that cost $21,000 had an estimated useful life of seven years and no salvage value. After six years of using straight-line depreciation, the company deemed the asset worthless and hauled it to the dump.

Requirement

For each scenario, calculate the gain or loss, if any, that would result upon disposal.

P6-76A. *Calculate depreciation under alternative methods and account for disposal of an asset. (LO 2, 5).* Hope Construction purchased new equipment on January 1, 2011, for $55,000. The company expects the equipment to have a useful life of five years and no salvage value. The company's fiscal year ends on December 31.

Requirements

1. Calculate the depreciation expense for the fiscal years 2011 and 2012 using each of the following methods:
   a. Straight-line method
   b. Double-declining balance method
2. Hope Construction sold the equipment on January 1, 2013, for $33,000. What was the gain or loss on the sale using each of the depreciation methods? On which financial statement would the gain or loss appear?

P6-77A. *Calculate depreciation under alternative methods and account for disposal of an asset. (LO 2, 5).* Book Printing Company bought a machine four years ago for $60,000. The company expects the machine to have a useful life of five years with no salvage value. The company has taken four full years of depreciation expense.

Requirements

1. Assume that the company uses straight-line depreciation. If the machine is sold for $11,000, will there be a gain or loss on the sale? If so, how much will that gain or loss be? How will the sale affect the financial statements for the year?
2. Assume that the company uses double-declining balance depreciation. If the machine is sold for $9,000, will there be a gain or loss on the sale? If so, how much will that gain or loss be? How will the sale affect the financial statements for the year?
3. Assume the company uses straight-line depreciation and sells the machine for $13,000. Would there be a gain or loss on the sale? How would that change if the company had been using double-declining balance depreciation?

P6-78A. *Analyze and correct accounting errors related to long-term assets. (LO 4, 6).* Due to an umpire strike early in 2011, Umpire's Empire had some trouble with its information processing and some errors were made in accounting for certain transactions. Evaluate the following independent situations that occurred during the year:
   a. At the beginning of 2011, a building and land were purchased together for $100,000. Even though the appraisers determined that 90% of the price should be allocated to the building, Umpire's decided to allocate the entire purchase price to the building. The building is being depreciated using the straight-line method over 40 years, with an estimated salvage value of $10,000.
   b. During the year, Umpire's did some R&D on a new gadget to keep track of balls and strikes. The R&D cost $20,000, and Umpire's capitalized it. The company intends to write it off over five years, using straight-line depreciation with no salvage value.
   c. Near the beginning of the year, Umpire spent $10,000 on routine maintenance for its equipment, and the accountant decided to capitalize these costs as part of the equipment. (Equipment is depreciated over five years with no salvage value.)
   d. Umpire spent $5,000 to extend the useful life of some of its equipment. The accountant capitalized the cost.

Requirements

1. For each situation, describe the error made and list the effect, if any, that the uncorrected error would have on the following items for Umpire's 2011 financial statements: net income, long-term assets, and retained earnings. If there is no error, simply write N/A next to the item.
2. Describe the adjustments that would correct the company's accounting records and make the 2011 financial statements accurate. If there is no error, write N/A next to the item.

Set B

P6-79B. *Calculate capitalized cost and depreciation expense. (LO 1, 2).* The executives for Paradise Island resorts bought a piece of property adjacent to the resort with an old medical facility to build a golf course on July 1, 2009. The land with the old medical facility was $1,750,000. Real estate commissions and fees including the title search were $250,750. Paradise paid $45,500 for the medical facility to be demolished and an additional $21,000 for medical and hazard waste cleanup. The company paid $60,000 for vegetation and sand for the new area. Paradise paid $550,000 to an architectural landscaper and contractor to design and build the golf course. Paradise hired two new employees at a salary of $40,000 a year each to maintain the landscaping for the new area.

Requirements

1. What amount should be capitalized for this new asset?
2. Would there be any depreciation expense for land for the year ended June 30, 2010? Explain your answer.

P6-80B. *Calculate and analyze depreciation under alternative methods. (LO 2).* Daniel's Cement Company purchased new cement pouring equipment at a cost of $22,500 at the beginning of July 2009. The equipment was estimated to have a salvage value of $2,500 at the end of its useful life of five years. Equipment like this is supposed to deliver 250,000 hours of service. The actual number of hours that the equipment was used per year is as follows:

Year Ended	Hours
June 30, 2010	44,000
June 30, 2011	50,000
June 30, 2012	39,000
June 30, 2013	57,000
June 30, 2014	60,000

Requirements

1. Calculate the depreciation expense for each year of the five-year life of the cement pouring equipment using the following methods:
   a. Straight-line method
   b. Activity method
   c. Double-declining balance method
2. How does the choice of depreciation method affect net income in each of the years?
3. How does the choice of depreciation method affect the balance sheet in each of the years?

P6-81B. *Calculate and analyze depreciation under alternative methods. (LO 2).* Stanley Lawn Service purchased new equipment on January 1, 2012, at a cost of $45,000. The company estimates the equipment has a useful life of four years with a salvage value of $6,000.

Requirements

1. Prepare two different depreciation schedules for the equipment—one using the straight-line method and the other using the double-declining balance method. (Round to the nearest dollar.)
2. Determine which method would result in the greater net income for the year 2014.

P6-82B. *Calculate and analyze depreciation under alternative methods. (LO 2).* Soft Fabrics Manufacturing purchased new textile machinery at the beginning of 2010 for $150,000. It was expected to last for 10 years and have a salvage value of $10,000. The estimated productive life of the machine was 250,000 units. Yearly production was as follows: in 2010 it produced 25,000 units; in 2011 it produced 28,000 units; in 2012 it produced 18,000 units; in 2013 it produced 29,000 units; in 2014 it produced 23,000 units; in 2015 it produced 15,000 units; in 2016 it produced 40,000 units; in 2017 it produced 25,000 units; in 2018 it produced 21,000 units; and in 2019 it produced 26,000 units.

Requirements

1. Calculate the depreciation for each year using each of these depreciation methods. (Round to the nearest dollar.)
   a. Straight-line method
   b. Activity method based on units
   c. Double-declining balance method
2. For each method, give the amount of accumulated depreciation that would be shown on the balance sheet at the end of each year.
3. Calculate the book value of the textile machinery at the end of each year for each method.

P6-83B. *Account for intangible assets. (LO 3, 6).* Hargrove Dynamics, Inc., had the following balances in its intangible asset accounts at the beginning of the year:

Patents	$65,000
Copyrights	42,000
Goodwill	67,500

The patents have a remaining useful life of 10 years, and the copyright has a remaining useful life of 12 years.

Transactions during the year were as follows:
   a. At the beginning of the year, Hargrove filed for a new patent. The costs totaled $35,000. Its useful life is estimated at 10 years.
   b. Hargrove incurred R&D costs of $45,000, related to new product development. No new products have been identified.
   c. Hargrove evaluated the goodwill for impairment and reduced its book value by $2,500.
   d. Hargrove successfully defended its patents in court. Fees totaled $13,500.

Requirement

Show each of the transactions in the accounting equation, including any adjustments that would need to be made for the year-end financial statements. Then prepare the intangible assets section of the balance sheet at year end.

P6-84B. *Account for change in estimates for depreciation. (LO 4).* In July 2009, Bottling Company purchased equipment that cost $55,000. The company estimates that the equipment will last for four years and will have a salvage value of $5,000. The company uses the straight-line method of depreciation and has a June 30 fiscal year end. Analyze each of the following independent scenarios:
   a. Before depreciation expense is recorded for the fiscal year ended June 30, 2011, Bottling decides that the equipment will last until June 30, 2013, but that it will be worth only $500 at that time.
   b. Before depreciation expense is recorded for the fiscal year ended June 30, 2011, Bottling decides that the equipment will last only until June 30, 2012. The company anticipates the value of the equipment at that time will still be $5,000.
   c. Before depreciation expense is recorded for the fiscal year ended June 30, 2011, Bottling decides that the equipment will last until June 30, 2013, but that it will be worth only $50 at that time.
   d. Before depreciation expense is recorded for the fiscal year ended June 30, 2011, Bottling is told by the manufacturer that with an upgrade, the equipment's estimated life will be extended to June 30, 2016; however, the estimated salvage value at that time would be zero. The company spends $10,000 on upgrades.

Requirement

Calculate the amount of depreciation expense related to the equipment Bottling will report on its income statement for the fiscal year ended June 30, 2011, for each scenario.

P6-85B. *Account for disposal of an asset. (LO 5).* Analyze each of the following independent scenarios:
   a. Equipment that cost $44,000 had an estimated useful life of six years and a salvage value of $2,000. After five years of using straight-line depreciation, the company sold the equipment for $9,500.
   b. A computer system that cost $95,000 had an estimated useful life of four years and no salvage value. After two years of using double-declining balance depreciation, the company sold the computer system for $40,000.
   c. A company truck that cost $32,000 had an estimated useful life of six years and a salvage value of $2,000. After five years of using straight-line depreciation and driving the truck many miles on tough terrain, the company sold the completely worn-out truck for $750 for spare parts.

d. An asset that cost $35,000 had an estimated useful life of five years and a salvage value of $2,500. After three years of using double-declining balance depreciation, the company sold the asset for $7,500.

Requirement

For each scenario, calculate the gain or loss, if any, that would result upon disposal.

P6-86B. *Calculate depreciation under alternative methods and account for disposal of an asset. (LO 2, 5).* Elite Cleaners bought a new machine on January 1, 2010, for $75,000. The company expects the machine to have a useful life of 10 years and a salvage value of $10,000. The company's fiscal year ends on December 31.

Requirements

1. Calculate the depreciation expense for the fiscal years 2010 and 2011 using each of the following methods:
   a. Straight-line method
   b. Double-declining balance method
2. Elite Cleaners sold the machine on January 1, 2012, for $59,000. What was the gain or loss on the sale using each of the depreciation methods? (Round your answers.) On which financial statement would the gain or loss appear?

P6-87B. *Calculate depreciation under alternative methods and account for disposal of an asset. (LO 2, 5).* Whitehouse Air-Conditioning purchased a machine two years ago for $84,000. The company expects the machine to have a useful life of eight years and a $4,000 salvage value. Whitehouse Air has taken two full years of depreciation expense.

Requirements

1. Assume that Whitehouse Air uses straight-line depreciation. If the machine is sold for $70,000, will there be a gain or loss on the sale? If so, how much will the gain or loss be? How will it affect Whitehouse Air's financial statements for the year?
2. Assume that Whitehouse Air uses double-declining balance depreciation. If the machine is sold for $45,000 will there be a gain or loss on the sale? If so, how much will the gain or loss be? How will it affect Whitehouse Air's financial statements for the year?
3. Assume Whitehouse Air uses double-declining balance depreciation and sells the machine for $60,000. Would there be a gain or loss on the sale? How would that change if Whitehouse Air had been using straight-line depreciation?

P6-88B. *Analyze and correct accounting errors related to long-term assets. (LO 4, 6).* During 2009, Jule's Gym had some trouble with its information processing due to several hurricanes, and some errors were made in accounting for certain transactions. The firm uses straight-line depreciation for all of its long-term assets. Evaluate the following independent situations that occurred during the year:
   a. At the beginning of the year, a basket purchase of a building and land was made for $350,000. The appraisers indicated that the market value of the land was $135,000 and the market value of the building was $250,000. So, Jule's Gym allocated $135,000 of the purchase price to the land and the remainder of the purchase price to the building. The building has an estimated useful life of 20 years and an estimated salvage value of $25,000.
   b. The plumber spent a great deal of time repairing broken toilets in one of the gym's buildings this year. Total cost, which Jule's Gym capitalized, was $5,000. Jule's Gym decided it was best to leave it on the books as an asset and not write it off, because the toilets will be used for quite a few more years. (Use 20 years as the estimated remaining useful life of the toilets.)
   c. Jule's Gym purchased a new van. It cost $20,000 and is expected to last three years. It has a salvage value of $2,000. To properly equip it for transporting gym equipment between locations, the inside was customized at a cost of $6,000. The cost of the van was capitalized, and the cost of the customization was expensed.
   d. Jule's Gym spent $5,500 on routine maintenance of its exercise equipment. The cost was expensed.

Requirements

1. For each situation, describe the error made and list the effect, if any, that the uncorrected error would have on the following items for Jule's Gym's 2009 financial statements: net income, long-term assets, and retained earnings. If there is no error, simply write N/A next to the item.
2. Use the accounting equation to show the adjustments that would correct the company's accounting records and make the 2009 financial statements accurate.

Financial Statement Analysis

FSA6-1. *Analyze long-term assets on the balance sheet. (LO 6).* The following information comes from The Home Depot Annual Report:

Information from the Balance Sheet of The Home Depot:

(dollars in millions)	At February 1, 2009	At February 3, 2008
Property and Equipment		
Land	$ 8,301	$ 8,398
Buildings	16,961	16,642
Furniture, fixtures, and equipment	8,741	8,050
Leasehold improvements	1,359	1,390
Construction in progress	625	1,435
Other	490	497
	36,477	36,412
Less: accumulated depreciation and amortization	10,243	8,936
Net property and equipment	$26,234	$27,476

Requirements

1. Can you tell how much The Home Depot paid for the buildings it owns? If so, how do you know?
2. Can you tell how much the buildings are worth (the market value)?
3. Explain what you think is included in each category of Property and Equipment.
4. The Home Depot says it spent less for capital expenditures in fiscal 2008 (FYE February 1, 2009) than it did in fiscal 2007 (FYE February 3, 2008). Is this supported by any of the information given here?

FSA6-2. *Analyze long-term assets on the balance sheet. (LO 2, 3, 5, 6).* Use the selection from Books-A-Million's annual report in Appendix A at the back of the book to help you answer the following questions:

1. What type of depreciable assets does Books-A-Million have? What methods does the company use to depreciate these assets?
2. Does Books-A-Million have any intangible assets? What are they and how does the company account for them?
3. What can you tell about the age and/or condition of Books-A-Million's property and equipment? Is the company continuing to invest in property, plant, and equipment?
4. Is the company making good use of its assets? How can you evaluate this?

Critical Thinking Problems

Risk and Control

What kinds of risks does a firm like Barnes & Noble face with respect to safeguarding its assets? What types of controls do you think it already has in place to minimize these risks? Go to the firm's Web site at www.barnesandnobleinc.com and click on For Investors. You'll be able to find the firm's annual report to help you answer these questions. Are any specific controls mentioned in the annual report?

Ethics

Rachel works in a real estate office that is equipped with up-to-date copiers, scanners, and printers. She is frequently the only employee working in the office in the evenings and often has spare time to do personal work. She has begun to use the office equipment for her children's school reports and for her husband's business. Do you think Rachel's use of the office equipment is harmless, or is she behaving unethically? Why? If you believe her behavior is unethical, what controls could be in place to prevent it? Have you ever used office resources for personal tasks? Under what conditions could such use of office resources be justified?

Group Assignment

Select one of the three depreciation methods presented in the chapter. Discuss reasons why the method should be used and reasons why the method is not a good choice. Determine the method you think is most consistent with the objectives of financial reporting.

Internet Exercise: Best Buy

Best Buy is the number-one specialty retailer of consumer electronics, personal computers, entertainment software, and appliances. Best Buy operates in the United States, Canada, Mexico, Europe, and China, employing over 155,000 people worldwide (at the end of fiscal 2008). Go to www.bestbuy.com and complete the following exercises:

IE6-1. Select For Our Investors near the bottom of the page. Then, select Best Buy's most recent annual report in the PDF format. Use the consolidated balance sheets to answer the following questions. At the most recent year end, examine Property and Equipment.

1. What is the acquisition cost of these assets?
2. What is the book value (carrying value)?
3. What amount of the acquisition cost has already been expensed?
4. Are any of the assets listed not being depreciated?

IE6-2. Use the notes to financial statements to answer the following questions (the information can usually be found in note 1):

1. Find the heading Property and Equipment. What depreciation method does Best Buy use for property and equipment? What is the range of useful lives for buildings and for fixtures and equipment? Do these useful lives make sense?
2. Find the heading Goodwill. What type of an asset is goodwill? Does Best Buy write off this asset? Explain what the company does.

IE6-3. On page 27 of Best Buy's annual report for its fiscal year ended February 28, 2009, there is a five-year summary of financial highlights. (If you have trouble finding this page, you can look on the financial statements for this information.)

1. Identify the amounts reported for total assets at the four most recent year ends.
2. Identify the amounts reported for revenues and net earnings (net income) for the three most recent years.
3. Compute the asset turnover ratio for the two most recent fiscal years. In which fiscal year did the company make best use of its assets? How can you tell?

Appendix 6

Depreciation and Taxes

The accounting information a company presents on its financial statements is not the same information the company reports to the IRS on its federal income tax return. The company follows GAAP reporting standards when preparing financial statements because those statements are provided to shareholders, who are the owners of the company. The information for taxes is determined by the legal rules of the Internal Revenue Code. GAAP and the IRS require different information to be reported, so companies will use an information system that can produce two sets of data.

Modified accelerated cost recovery system (MACRS) is the method that the IRS requires firms to use to depreciate its assets for tax purposes.

For depreciating fixed assets, corporations use a method called the **Modified Accelerated Cost Recovery System (MACRS)** to calculate the deduction for their tax returns. MACRS is allowed for tax purposes but not GAAP. The goal of MACRS is to give companies incentive to invest in new property, plant, and equipment. If an asset can be written off quickly—large depreciation deductions over a small number of years—the tax benefit from the depreciation deductions leaves the company more cash to invest in new assets.

How does more depreciation expense result in lower taxes? Suppose a company's income before depreciation and before taxes is $10,000. If depreciation expense for taxes is $2,000, then the company has taxable income of $8,000. Suppose the company's tax rate is 25%. Then, the company must pay $2,000 (= $8,000 × 0.25) in taxes. (Net income will be $6,000.)

Now, suppose the company can depreciate the assets using a more accelerated depreciation method that results in $4,000 worth of depreciation expense. Income before depreciation and taxes is $10,000, so income before taxes will be $6,000 (= $10,000 − $4,000). With a tax rate of 25%, the company will have to pay $1,500 in taxes. (Net income will be $4,500.)

When depreciation expense is larger, the amount of taxes a company must pay is smaller. A smaller tax bill means less cash has to be paid to the IRS, so the company's net cash flow for the year will be greater. However, as we have seen from comparing straight-line depreciation and double-declining balance depreciation, *over the life of an asset*, the total depreciation expense is the same no matter what method the company uses. The difference between the methods is reflected in the way the total depreciation is allocated to the years the asset is used. The reason a company wants to use an accelerated method like MACRS for tax purposes is so that the largest deductions are taken as soon as possible. Saving tax dollars *this* year is preferred to saving them *next* year because it is cash the company can use to buy assets that can increase production and therefore profits.

Accounting for Shareholders' Equity

LEARNING OBJECTIVES

When you are finished studying Chapter 8, you should be able to:

1. Explain how a company finances its business with equity.

2. Account for the payment of cash dividends and calculate the allocation of dividends between common and preferred shareholders.

3. Define treasury stock, explain why a company would purchase treasury stock, and account for its purchase.

4. Explain stock dividends and stock splits.

5. Define retained earnings and account for its increases and decreases.

6. Prepare financial statements that contain equity transactions.

7. Compute return on equity and earnings per share, and explain what these ratios mean.

8. Recognize the business risks associated with shareholders' equity and the related controls.

ETHICS Matters

Buy Low, Sell High

Imagine that you owned quite a bit of a certain company's stock, and you were getting ready to sell it. You would certainly want to sell it for as high a price as possible. Perhaps you've heard the investment advice "buy low, sell high." Hopefully, you would not be willing to commit a crime to influence the price of the stock. This was not the case for a Seattle attorney and three others who were charged with fraud by the SEC in July 2009. These people were involved in a scheme that attempted to boost the price of a stock through recommendations based on false, misleading, or greatly exaggerated statements. This type of scheme is called "pump and dump." Pump up the stock price with false information and then dump (sell) your stock at the new, higher price. It generally happens with small, publicly-traded firms in which the perpetrator has a significant investment in the firm's stock and can influence others to buy it. The firm has to be small enough for its stock price to be influenced by a small number of buyers.

David Otto and three others have been accused of providing false and misleading press releases and information on Web sites about anti-aging, nutritional supplements that never existed. The chief executive of MitoPharm, the company said to be producing these supplements, was also charged in the crime. After they drove up the stock price with false information, the accused perpetrators sold their own stock in MitoPharm for more than a million dollars.

Source: "SEC Charges Four With Fraud," by Kathy Shwiff, *Wall Street Journal*, July 14, 2009, p. C8.

L.O.1
Explain how a company
finances its business
with equity.

Components of Shareholders' Equity in a Corporation—Contributed Capital

Every business has owners. As you learned in Chapter 1, there are three general forms of business organizations.

1. Sole proprietorships
2. Partnerships
3. Corporations

No matter which form a business takes, it needs money—contributions—from the owners to operate. With sole proprietorships and partnerships, individual owners use their own money or borrow money from family, friends, or banks. Corporations have access to more money because they sell stock to investors. In this chapter, we will focus on how a firm acquires and accounts for money from owners.

The claims of the owners to the assets of the firm are called shareholders' equity or stockholders' equity. Recall that there are two major parts to stockholders' equity—contributed capital and retained earnings. Each part is recorded and reported on the balance sheet as a separate amount. Contributed capital is the amount owners have invested in the corporation. Contributed capital is generally subdivided into two parts: capital stock and additional paid-in capital.

Stock—Authorized, Issued, and Outstanding

In return for their contributions, the owners receive shares of stock, representing units of ownership in the corporation. A corporation may have a variety of different ownership levels, usually known as classes of stock. All shares in the same class of stock have the same rights as every other share in that class. Rights of the shareholders, however, are different for different classes of stock. Every corporation has to have a class of stock that represents the basic ownership interest in the corporation, and that is called **common stock**.

When a corporation is formed, the state in which the firm incorporates requires an agreement called a charter that specifies the characteristics of the firm. For example, the charter sets a maximum number of shares of stock it can issue, called **authorized shares**.

Issued shares are shares offered and sold to shareholders in batches, during times when a company needs capital.

Exhibit 8.1 shows the shareholders' equity section of PetSmart, Inc., at February 1, 2009, and February 3, 2008. Notice that the number of shares of common stock authorized is 625 million and the number of shares issued is 159,770,000 at February 1, 2009. An issued share of

Common stock is the most widespread form of ownership in a corporation; common shareholders have a vote in the election of the firm's board of directors.

Authorized shares are shares of stock that are available for a firm to issue per its corporate charter.

Issued shares are shares of stock that have been offered and sold to shareholders.

EXHIBIT 8.1

Shareholders' Equity Section of the Balance Sheet of PetSmart, Inc.

As you read about the different parts of shareholders' equity, refer to this information from the balance sheet of PetSmart, Inc.

PetSmart, Inc.
Consolidated Balance Sheets (partial)
(in thousands, except par value)

	February 1, 2009	February 3, 2008
Stockholders' equity:		
Preferred stock; $.0001 par value; 10,000 shares authorized, none issued and outstanding	–	–
Common stock; $.0001 par value; 625,000 shares authorized; 159,770 and 158,104 shares issued	16	16
Additional paid-in capital	1,117,557	1,079,190
Retained earnings	936,100	758,674
Accumulated other comprehensive (loss) income	(2,714)	5,585
Less: treasury stock, at cost, 32,408 and 30,066 shares	(906,823)	(856,868)
Total stockholders' equity	1,144,136	986,597
Total liabilities and stockholders' equity	$2,357,653	$2,167,257

stock does not need to remain outstanding. Because firms can purchase their own stock in the stock market, all issued shares may not be outstanding. **Outstanding shares** are owned by stockholders rather than by the corporation.

When a company buys back its stock, those shares of stock are called **treasury stock**. Any stock that has been issued by a company may be either outstanding, which is owned by investors, or treasury stock, which is held in the company's treasury. Notice in Exhibit 8.1 that PetSmart has a significant amount of treasury stock (32,408,000 shares at February 1, 2009), shown at the end of the shareholders' equity section where it is subtracted from total shareholders' equity.

Exhibit 8.2 shows the relationships among authorized shares, issued shares, outstanding shares, and treasury shares.

Outstanding shares are shares of stock that are owned by stockholders.

Treasury stock is stock that has been repurchased by the issuing firm.

EXHIBIT 8.2

Authorized, Issued, and Outstanding Stock

In this example, 1,000,000 shares are authorized, but only 300,000 are issued. Of the issued shares, 290,000 are outstanding, and 10,000 are treasury shares.

Common Stock

Common stock, as the name suggests, is the most common type of capital stock representing ownership of a corporation. All corporations must have common stock. The owners of common stock generally have the right to

1. vote for members of the board of directors.
2. share in the corporation's profits.
3. share in any assets left if the corporation must dissolve (for example, if the company goes out of business due to bankruptcy).
4. acquire more shares when the corporation issues new stock, often referred to as a pre-emptive right (although this right is often given up by the shareholders).

The corporate charter often provides a fixed per-share amount called the **par value** of the stock. Par value is an arbitrary amount and has no real meaning in today's business environment, and most states do not require a par value. The corporation must maintain a specific amount of capital, as determined by the state or contained in the corporate charter. That amount could be the total par value of the outstanding stock. Frequently, however, other means are used to determine the legal capital to protect creditors. Some firms actually issue no-par stock. Exhibit 8.1 shows that PetSmart common stock has a par value of $0.0001 per share. If you know the par value per share of the common stock and you know the dollar amount in the common stock account, you can calculate the number of shares that have been issued. Use the balance sheet in Exhibit 8.1 to see how that can be done. At February 1, 2009, the common stock account has a balance of $16,000, and the par value of the stock is $0.0001 per share. To calculate the number of shares issued, divide the common stock balance by the par value per share to see how many shares are represented by the balance in the common stock account.

Par value is the monetary amount assigned to a share of stock in the corporate charter. It has little meaning in today's business environment.

$$\frac{\$16,000}{\$0.0001} = 160,000,000 \text{ shares}$$

Because the common stock account balance was rounded to $16,000, the number of shares from the calculation will also be rounded. The actual number of shares issued is 159,770,000. Our rounded calculation shows 160,000,000 shares.

Stock is usually sold for more than its par value. In some states, it is a legal requirement that stock sell for at least par value. Suppose the par value of a company's stock is $2 per share, the market price of the stock on the date the stock is issued is $10 per share, and the company issues 100 shares. Here is how to calculate the dollar amount that will be recorded as common stock.

$$\$2 \text{ par value per share} \times 100 \text{ shares} = \$200$$

The amount of $200 will be shown on the balance sheet in an account separate from any contributions in excess of the par value. The remaining $8 per share will be shown in another account called additional paid-in capital.

$$\$8 \text{ excess over par (per share)} \times 100 \text{ shares} = \$800$$

The total par value amount—$200—is called common or capital stock, and the excess contributions amount—$800—is called additional paid-in capital. Both amounts are reported on the balance sheet. Exhibit 8.3 shows how the amount of cash from the issue of stock is divided between the two paid-in capital accounts when the stock has a par value. For no-par stock, the full amount will be recorded in the common stock account. Remember that paid-in capital designates both capital stock and additional paid-in capital. All amounts of contributed capital are called paid-in capital.

UNDERSTANDING Business

Corporate Bankruptcy: Dividing the Spoils

In the United States, there are two ways a firm can file for bankruptcy. The first is called Chapter 7 (for its location in the U.S. Bankruptcy Code), and it signals the end of the business. Operations are stopped, and a trustee is appointed to sell the company's assets and pay off the company's debt. This is called liquidation. There is rarely enough money to repay all of the creditors and also pay the owners their investment or their share of the company's retained earnings. The creditors are first in line for payment. Bondholders will get their share before any of the stockholders. And among the stockholders, the preferred shareholders are first in line. The common shareholders are last.

The second form of bankruptcy is called Chapter 11. This type of bankruptcy signals a reorganization of the business. A firm in Chapter 11 expects to continue in business and return to sound financial condition at some point in the future. Often, a firm files for Chapter 11 when it can no longer pay its debt holders. The debt is restructured—perhaps with a lower interest rate and a longer time horizon—according to the reorganization plan. This plan must be approved by the bankruptcy court and includes a committee to represent the interests of creditors and stockholders. The interests of the creditors continue to have priority over the interests of the stockholders.

Most publicly-traded firms prefer Chapter 11 to Chapter 7 bankruptcy because they want to continue their operations and return to profitable operations in the future.

Here's what the SEC says about investors of a company in bankruptcy:

"During Chapter 11 bankruptcy, bondholders stop receiving interest and principal payments, and stockholders stop receiving dividends. If you are a bondholder, you may receive new stock in exchange for your bonds, new bonds or a combination of stock and bonds. If you are a stockholder, the trustee may ask you to send back your stock in exchange for shares in the reorganized company. The new shares may be fewer in number and worth less. The reorganization plan spells out your rights as an investor and what you can expect to receive, if anything, from the company." (www.sec.gov/investor/pubs/bankrupt.htm)

In the summer of 2009, General Motors became the second largest industrial bankruptcy in history. Bondholders agreed to exchange their portion of the company's $27.1 billion unsecured debts for 10% of the equity of the new GM. The U.S. government is now a common shareholder of GM, owning 60% of the new company. You may want to read about this historic bankruptcy and see how the structure of GM changes when it emerges from Chapter 11. (Start your search for information at www.nytimes.com.)

Cash ($10 per share)	Common Stock at Par ($2 per share)	Additional Paid-In Capital ($8 per share)
Company receives cash from issuing stock	The amount, $10, is divided between two accounts: common stock and additional paid-in capital	
Amount received by the company: 100 × $10 per share = $1,000	Common Stock: 100 × $2 per share = $200 + Additional Paid-In Capital: 100 × ($10 − $2) per share = $800	

EXHIBIT 8.3

Recording the Issue of Stock

One hundred shares of stock are issued for $10 each. Par value is $2 per share. The proceeds from the stock issue, $1,000, are divided between two accounts: common stock and additional paid-in capital.

Suppose the corporate charter of Miles Barkery authorizes 50 shares of common stock at par value $1 per share. Suppose the company issues 30 shares at $15 per share. Here is how the firm would record the transaction.

Assets	=	Liabilities	+	Shareholders' equity	
				Contributed capital	+ Retained earnings
450 cash				30 common stock	
				420 additional paid-in capital	

How would this transaction be shown on Miles Barkery's financial statements? Suppose the company is issuing the stock for the first time. The shareholders' equity section of the balance sheet would show this information in the part of the statement that shows contributed capital.

Contributed capital	
Common stock (par value $1 per share; 50 shares authorized; 30 shares issued and outstanding)	$ 30
Additional paid-in capital	420

Suppose General Mills issued 10,000 shares of $1 par value per share common stock for $20 per share. How would the company record this transaction?

Your Turn 8-1

Preferred Stock

Preferred stock is stock that represents a special kind of ownership in a corporation. Preferred shareholders do not get a vote but they do receive dividends before the common shareholders.

As you read earlier in the chapter, corporations may have other classes of stock in addition to common stock. Many firms have a class of stock called **preferred stock**. Owners of preferred stock must receive their dividends before the common shareholders and also have a preferred claim on assets. If a firm goes out of business, the preferred shareholders have the right to receive assets that remain after the creditors have been paid. The common shareholders then get any remaining assets. However, the owners of preferred stock usually do not have voting rights.

L.O.2
Account for the payment of cash dividends and calculate the allocation of dividends between common and preferred shareholders.

Cash Dividends

Dividends are the distribution of a corporation's earnings to shareholders.

People buy stock in a corporation because they expect the value of the corporation to increase. Selling stock for more than its cost is one way a shareholder can make money on the investment. The other way is by receiving distributions from the firm. The distributions shareholders receive from the earnings of the corporation are called **dividends**. The board of directors decides the amount of dividends to be paid and when they will be paid to the shareholders. Remember that if the corporation has any preferred shareholders, those owners will get their dividends first. The directors are also free not to pay dividends any time they believe it is in the best interest of the corporation. The board of directors may want to reinvest the available cash in the business by buying more equipment or inventory.

Microsoft Corporation, for example, was started in 1975 and did not pay a dividend until 2003. Some firms traditionally pay a dividend, and others have never paid a dividend. Exhibit 8.4 shows how General Electric Company and Papa John's International, Inc., explain their dividend policies. Notice that General Electric pays a dividend and Papa John's does not. Often new companies do not pay any dividends because they want to reinvest all of their earnings in the business. Established companies, on the other hand, often do not have the growth potential of new firms and can use regular dividend payments to attract investors.

EXHIBIT 8.4

Dividend Policies: General Electric Corporation and Papa John's International, Inc.

Some firms, like General Electric, consistently pay a dividend. Other firms, like Papa John's, do not pay dividends. Compare the dividend policy for General Electric (left) and Papa John's (right).

General Electric Corporation	**Papa John's International, Inc.**
WE DECLARED $12.6 BILLION IN DIVIDENDS IN 2008. Common per-share dividends of $1.24 were up 8% from 2007, following a 12% increase from the preceding year. On February 6, 2009, our Board of Directors approved a regular quarterly dividend of $0.31 per share of common stock, which is payable April 27, 2009, to share owners of record at close of business on February 23, 2009. The Board will continue to evaluate the Company's dividend level for the second half of 2009 in light of the growing uncertainty in the economy, including U.S. government actions, rising unemployment, and the recent announcements by the rating agencies. In 2008, we declared $0.1 billion in preferred stock dividends.	*Since our initial public offering of common stock in 1993, we have not paid dividends on our common stock, and have no current plans to do so.*

Important Dates Related to Dividends

When the board of directors decides that a cash dividend will be paid, there are three important dates: the declaration date, the date of record, and the payment date.

DECLARATION DATE. The dividend declaration date is the date on which the board of directors decides a dividend will be paid and announces it to shareholders. On this date, a legal liability called dividends payable is created. The amount of this liability is balanced in the accounting equation with a reduction from retained earnings. Dividends are not deducted from the contributed capital accounts because they are a distribution of earnings, not a distribution of the shareholders' original paid-in capital. Here is how a firm would record the declaration of $50,000 dividends to be divided among its shareholders.

Assets	=	Liabilities	+	Shareholders' equity		
				Contributed capital	+	Retained earnings
		50,000 dividends payable				(50,000) dividends

Remember, dividends are not included as an expense on the income statement because they are not related to generating revenue. Rather than a deduction from a company's earnings, dividends are considered a distribution of a company's earnings to owners in proportion to their share of ownership.

DATE OF RECORD. The date of record is used to determine exactly who will receive the dividends. Anyone owning the stock on this date is entitled to the dividend. After a corporation originally sells stock to investors, they are free to trade—sell and buy—shares of stock with other people. Whoever owns the stock on the date of record will receive the dividend. A stockholder may own the stock for only one day and receive the full dividend amount. After this date, stock is said to be ex-dividend. That is, if it is traded after the date of record, the new owner will not get the dividend. The firm does not record anything in its accounting records on the date of record. Notice GE's reference to this date in its dividend note in Exhibit 8.4.

PAYMENT DATE. The payment date is when the cash is actually paid to the shareholders. This payment has the same effect on the accounting equation as the payment of any liability: Assets (cash) are reduced and liabilities (dividends payable) are reduced.

Assets	=	Liabilities	+	Shareholders' equity		
				Contributed capital	+	Retained earnings
(50,000) cash		(50,000) dividends payable				

Distribution of Dividends between Common and Preferred Shareholders

As you have read, the corporation must give holders of preferred stock a certain amount of dividends before common stockholders can receive any dividends. (Note, however, that bondholders must have received any interest payments due to them before dividends of any kind can be distributed.) Dividends on preferred stock are usually fixed at a percentage of the par value of the stock. For example, preferred stock characterized as 10% preferred ($100 par) will receive a dividend of $10 in any year the corporation's board of directors declares a dividend. The preferred shareholders must get their $10 per preferred share before the common shareholders receive any dividends. The board of directors has discretion about whether or not to pay dividends to the preferred shareholders, but the board does not decide on the amount of the dividend for the preferred shareholders. The dividend for preferred shareholders is typically shown on the face of the preferred stock certificate. There are two types of preferred stock—cumulative and noncumulative.

- Cumulative preferred stock means the fixed dividend amount accumulates from year to year, and the entire amount of all past unpaid dividends must be paid to the preferred shareholders before any dividends can be paid to the common shareholders. Any dividends that are owed to holders of cumulative preferred stock from past years, but are undeclared are called dividends in arrears. The corporation does not consider such dividends liabilities but does disclose them in the notes to the financial statements. Only after a dividend is actually declared is it considered a liability. Most preferred stock is cumulative preferred stock.
- With noncumulative preferred stock, the board determines whether or not to make up any missed dividends to the preferred shareholders.

An Example of a Dividend Payment

Suppose JG Company has the following stock outstanding:

- 1,000 shares of 9%, $100 par, cumulative preferred stock
- 50,000 shares of $0.50 per share par common stock

The company last paid dividends in December 2009. With the 2009 payment, JG paid all dividends through December 31, 2009. There were no dividends in arrears prior to 2010. No dividends were paid in 2010. On October 1, 2011, the board of directors declares a total of $30,000 in dividends for its shareholders to be paid on December 15, 2011, to all shareholders of record on November 1, 2011. How much of the dividend will go to the preferred shareholders, and how much will go to the common shareholders?

First, calculate the annual dividend for the preferred shareholders.

$$1,000 \text{ shares} \times \$100 \text{ par value} \times 0.09 = \$9,000$$

Because the preferred stock is cumulative and no dividends were paid to the preferred shareholders in 2010, JG must first pay the 2010 dividend of $9,000 to the preferred shareholders. Then, JG must pay the current year's (2011) $9,000 dividend to the preferred shareholders. The company pays a total of $18,000 to the preferred shareholders, and the remaining $12,000 goes to the common shareholders. On the date of declaration, October 1, the company incurs the legal liability for the dividend payment. Following is how the company records the transaction:

Assets	=	Liabilities	+	Shareholders' equity		
				Contributed capital	+	**Retained earnings**
		18,000 dividends payable, preferred shareholders 12,000 dividends payable, common shareholders				(30,000) dividends

On the declaration date, the company records the liability. If JG were to prepare its balance sheet, it would show a current liability called dividends payable. This liability is a debt owed to the shareholders for dividends. A corporation may list the liability to common shareholders separately from the liability to preferred shareholders, as shown in the preceding example, or the corporation may combine the preferred and common dividends into one amount for total dividends payable.

On December 15, when JG actually pays the cash to the shareholders to fulfill the obligation, cash is reduced and the liability—dividends payable—is removed from the records. Following is how the company records the transaction:

Assets	=	Liabilities	+	Shareholders' equity		
				Contributed capital	+	**Retained earnings**
(30,000) cash		(18,000) dividends payable, preferred shareholders (12,000) dividends payable, common shareholders				

Suppose the preferred stock was noncumulative. Then, JG would pay only the current year's dividend of $9,000 to the preferred shareholders, and the remaining $21,000 would go to the common shareholders.

Your Turn 8-2

A corporation has 10,000 shares of 8% cumulative preferred stock and 20,000 shares of common stock outstanding. Par value for each is $100. No dividends were paid last year, but this year $200,000 in dividends is paid to stockholders. How much of this $200,000 goes to the holders of preferred stock?

Treasury Stock

L.O.3
Define treasury stock, explain why a company would purchase treasury stock, and account for its purchase.

Companies can trade—buy and sell—their own stock on the open market. (The timing of these transactions is controlled by Securities and Exchange Commission (SEC) rules.) Treasury stock refers to common stock that has been issued and subsequently purchased by the company that issued it. Once it is purchased by the company, the stock is considered treasury stock until it is resold or retired—taken completely out of circulation.

Why Do Firms Buy Their Own Stock?

There are many reasons companies purchase shares of their own stock. Here are a few of the most common ones:

1. *To have stock to distribute to employees for compensation plans.* When a firm wants to give employees or corporate executives shares of stock, the firm will often use treasury shares. Issuing new shares is a costly and time-consuming project, with many requirements set by the SEC, so firms typically issue new shares only to raise a significant amount of money.
2. *To return cash to the shareholders using a way that is more flexible for both the firm and the shareholder than paying cash dividends.* Firms that have a great deal of cash will often buy their own stock as a way to get the cash to the shareholders. The firm has complete flexibility over when to buy the stock and how much to buy, and the individual shareholders have complete flexibility over whether or not they sell their shares back to the company. This flexibility benefits the firm and the shareholder. The firm can control the mix of debt and equity in its capital structure. For example, it can reduce equity by buying back stock. The shareholders can decide when to take cash out of their investment in the firm by deciding whether or not to sell back their stock.
3. *To increase the company's earnings per share.* When a firm decreases the number of shares outstanding, earnings per share will increase with no change in net income due to the mathematics of the EPS calculation. However, a firm must consider that the cash used to buy back the stock would have earned some return—at least interest revenue—that would increase the numerator by some amount.
4. *To reduce the cash needed to pay future dividends.* When a firm reduces the number of shares outstanding, the total cash needed for future dividends decreases. Treasury shares do not receive dividends.
5. *To reduce chances of a hostile takeover.* Top management or the board of directors may help the firm resist a takeover by making sure the treasury stock is distributed or sold to the right people—those who would resist the takeover. Buying stock also reduces cash reserves, which are a popular attraction for takeover attempts.

The board of directors of a firm decides if and when that firm will pursue a strategy to buy back its shares. This has become quite common, and you can read about it in the firm's notes to the financial statements. Exhibit 8.5 shows an excerpt from the notes to the financial statements of PetSmart for the fiscal year ended February 1, 2009. Notice that PetSmart has a very active stock repurchase program. Over half of the firms that trade on the New York Stock Exchange regularly purchase their own stock.

EXHIBIT 8.5

PetSmart, Inc., Purchases Its Own Common Stock

Share Purchase Programs—excerpts from the Notes to the Financial Statements

In August 2007, the Board of Directors approved a new share purchase program authorizing the purchase of up to $300.0 million of our common stock through August 2, 2009.

During 2008, we purchased 2.3 million shares of our common stock for $50.0 million. As of February 1, 2009, the amount remaining under the August 2007 share purchase authorization was $25.0 million.

Accounting for the Purchase

The purchase of treasury stock reduces a company's assets (cash) and reduces shareholders' equity. Suppose Papa John's decided to buy back some of the stock it had previously issued. Treasury stock is most often recorded at cost. Here is what the company will record if it buys back 100 shares at $16 per share.

Assets	=	Liabilities	+	Shareholders' equity		
				Contributed capital	+	Retained earnings
(1,600) cash				(1,600) treasury stock		

The par value and the price at which the stock was previously issued do not matter. Using this method, called the cost method, treasury stock is simply recorded at the amount the firm pays to repurchase it. Under the cost method, the following procedures are used:

- Treasury stock holdings for the company are shown as a reduction in the total of shareholders' equity on the balance sheet. Therefore, treasury stock is a type of shareholders' equity. Unlike other equity accounts, however, the cost of treasury stock reduces shareholders' equity. Due to its presence in the shareholders' equity section of the balance sheet and its negative effect on total equity, the treasury stock account is called a contra-equity account and is subtracted from total shareholders' equity.
- No gains or losses are recorded in the company's financial records when a company purchases treasury stock or later resells it. Even if a company acquired one of its own shares for $4 and later sold it for $6, the company would not show a gain of $2. Instead, the company would have more money from the sale of stock—which is contributed capital.

Your Turn 8-3

Suppose a company originally issued 100,000 shares of $1 par common stock for $15 per share. Several years later, the company decides to buy back 1,000 shares of common stock. The stock is selling for $50 per share at the time of the stock repurchase. (a) How would the transaction be recorded in the accounting equation? (b) After the transaction, how many shares are issued and how many shares are outstanding?

Selling Treasury Stock

If treasury stock is sold, the shares sold will be removed from the treasury stock account at the amount the firm paid for the stock when it was repurchased. If the treasury stock is sold at a price higher than its cost, the excess will be classified as paid-in capital from treasury stock transactions.

Suppose a firm purchased 1,000 treasury shares at $50 per share. A year later, the firm sells half of the shares for $60 each. Removing 500 shares of treasury stock at $50 cost will increase total shareholders' equity by reducing the balance in the treasury stock account, a contra-equity account, and will increase additional paid-in capital. Here is how the firm would record selling 500 shares of stock that cost $50 per share for $60 per share:

Assets	=	Liabilities	+	Shareholders' equity		
				Contributed capital	+	Retained earnings
30,000 cash				25,000 treasury stock		
				5,000 paid-in capital from treasury stock transactions		

There would be 500 shares remaining in the treasury stock account, each at a cost of $50. Suppose the firm sold those shares for $48 per share. As in the previous example, the treasury stock must be removed from the total amount of treasury stock at its cost. In this example, instead of having additional paid-in capital, the firm would reduce a paid-in capital account to balance the accounting equation. The difference between the cost and the reissue price—$2 per share × 500 shares = $1,000—would be deducted from paid-in capital from treasury stock transactions. Here is how a firm would record selling 500 treasury shares—originally costing the company $50 per share—for a reissue price of $48:

Assets	=	Liabilities	+	Shareholders' equity	
				Contributed capital	+ Retained earnings
24,000 cash				25,000 treasury stock	
				(1,000) paid-in capital from treasury stock transactions	

If the amount in the account paid-in capital from treasury stock transactions were insufficient to cover the $2 per share decrease in stock price, then retained earnings would be reduced by the amount needed to balance the accounting equation.

Reporting Treasury Stock

Treasury stock is most often reported as a deduction from shareholders' equity on the balance sheet. As noted previously, this is called the cost method of accounting for treasury stock. Exhibit 8.6 shows how the shares Abercrombie & Fitch Co. has repurchased are reported on its balance sheet.

EXHIBIT 8.6

From the Balance Sheet of Abercrombie & Fitch Co.

Abercrombie & Fitch Co.
Consolidated Balance Sheets (partial)

(dollars in thousands except per share amounts)	January 31, 2009	February 2, 2008
Class A common stock—$0.01 par value: 150,000,000 shares authorized and 103,300,000 shares issued at January 31, 2009 and February 2, 2008, respectively	1,033	1,033
Paid-in capital	328,488	319,451
Retained earnings	2,244,936	2,051,463
Accumulated other Comprehensive (Loss) Income, net of tax	(22,681)	7,118
Treasury stock, at Average cost 15,573,789 and 17,141,116 shares at January 31, 2009 and February 2, 2008, respectively	(706,198)	(760,752)
Total Shareholders' Equity	1,845,578	1,618,313
Total liabilities and Shareholders' Equity	$2,848,181	$2,567,598

From the 10-K:
During Fiscal 2008, A&F repurchased approximately 0.7 million shares of A&F Common Stock with a value of approximately $50.0 million. During Fiscal 2007, A&F repurchased approximately 3.6 million shares of A&F Common Stock with a value of approximately $287.9 million. A&F did not repurchase any shares of A&F Common Stock during Fiscal 2006. Both the Fiscal 2008 and the Fiscal 2007 repurchases were pursuant to A&F Board of Directors' authorizations.

Your Turn 8-4

Surety Corporation started the year 2010 with 125,000 shares of common stock with par value of $1 issued and outstanding. The issue price of these shares averaged $6 per share. During 2010, Surety purchased 1,000 shares of its own stock at an average price of $7 per share. How would Surety report its treasury stock on the balance sheet at December 31, 2010?

L.O.4
Explain stock dividends and
stock splits.

Stock Dividends and Stock Splits

You have learned about issuing stock and buying back stock. There are two other transactions that a company may have with stock: a stock dividend and a stock split.

Stock Dividends

> **Stock dividends** are new shares of stock that are distributed to the company's current shareholders.

A corporation may want to pay a dividend to shareholders but not have sufficient cash on hand. Instead of giving the shareholders cash, the corporation may give the shareholders additional shares of stock in the company. This is called a **stock dividend**. Recording the stock dividend simply reclassifies amounts in the shareholders' equity accounts. The corporation that issues a stock dividend converts retained earnings to contributed capital, thereby giving the stockholders a more direct claim to that portion of equity. A stock dividend is not income to the shareholder. As a matter of fact, theoretically there is no value to the shareholder from receiving a stock dividend. The shareholder still owns the same relative percentage of the company.

Generally accepted accounting principles (GAAP) distinguish between a small stock dividend (usually considered less than 25% of a company's outstanding stock) and a large stock dividend (greater than 25% of a company's outstanding stock). For a small stock dividend, the company uses the market value of the stock to record the transaction because a small stock dividend has a negligible effect on a stock's market price. For a large stock dividend, the company uses the par value of the stock to record the transaction because a large stock dividend puts so much new stock in the market that the market price per share adjusts to the increased number of shares.

Suppose a company declares and issues a 10% stock dividend to its current shareholders. The stock has a par value of $1 per share, and the current market price is $18 per share. The company will record the stock dividend at its market value. Before the stock dividend, the company has 150,000 shares outstanding. Therefore, the company will issue 15,000 new shares (150,000 × 10%) to shareholders. The total amount of retained earnings that will be converted in to contributed capital will be $270,000 (15,000 × $18). Here is how this company will record the stock dividend:

Assets	=	Liabilities	+	Shareholders' equity	
				Contributed capital	+	Retained earnings
				15,000 common stock	(270,000) retained earnings
				255,000 additional paid-in capital	

This is sometimes called capitalizing retained earnings. Exhibit 8.7 shows how the equity section of the balance sheet is affected by a stock dividend. When considering stock dividends, remember that stock dividends do not increase any shareholder's percentage of ownership in the company. If you owned 5% of the company before the stock dividend, you own 5% of the company after the stock dividend. After the dividend, your 5% includes more shares—but every shareholder's portion of ownership remains the same.

EXHIBIT 8.7

Shareholders' Equity before and after a Stock Dividend

A stock dividend does not change total shareholders' equity. It simply takes a small portion of retained earnings and reclassifies it as paid-in capital.

Shareholders' Equity

	Before Stock Dividend	After Stock Dividend
Shareholders' Equity		
Common stock, $1 par	$ 150,000	$ 165,000
Additional paid-in capital	600,000	855,000
Total paid-in capital	750,000	1,020,000
Retained earnings	950,000	680,000
Total shareholders' equity	$1,700,000	$1,700,000

Stock Splits

Stock splits occur when a corporation increases the number of shares outstanding and proportionately decreases the par value per share. The outstanding shares are "split" into two or more shares with a corresponding division of the par value. Sometimes a firm will call in all the old shares and reissue new shares. Other times, the firm will issue additional split shares with a notice to the shareholders of a change in par value of all shares.

Suppose you own 100 shares of Target stock. It has a par value of $1 a share and a market value of $24 a share. Suppose Target's board of directors votes to split the stock 2 for 1. After the split, instead of having 100 shares with a par value of $1 per share, you have 200 shares with a par value of $0.50 per share. Theoretically, a stock split should not affect the stock price beyond splitting the price in the same proportions as the stock split. For example, if a share was trading for $24 before a 2-for-1 split, a new share should trade for $12. Companies record the details of the stock split parenthetically in the shareholders' equity part of the financial statements. There is nothing formally recorded in the accounting records.

> A **stock split** is the division of the current shares of stock by a specific number to increase the number of shares outstanding.

Your Turn 8-5

1. Compare a stock split and a stock dividend.
2. Suppose you own 1,500 shares, which is 3%, of ABC Company's outstanding stock. If ABC declares a 2-for-1 stock split, how many shares will you own? What percentage ownership will your shares now represent?

Retained Earnings

Retained earnings is the amount of all the earnings of the firm—since its beginning—that have not been distributed to the stockholders. Retained earnings may also be called earned capital. As you know, retained earnings are not cash!

Retained earnings includes

1. net incomes since the day the company began, minus
2. any net losses since the day the company began, minus
3. any dividends declared since the company began.

> **L.O.5**
> Define retained earnings and account for its increases and decreases.

> **Retained earnings** is the total earnings of a firm since its inception—all of its net incomes, reduced by any net losses, that have not been distributed to shareholders.

Because retained earnings is a part of shareholders' equity, the change in retained earnings during the period is contained in the statement of changes in shareholders' equity. Sometimes the part of the shareholders' equity statement that provides the details of the changes in retained earnings is shown separately and is called a statement of retained earnings.

In a firm's accounting system, the retained earnings account does not directly receive additions for revenue earned or deductions for expenses incurred during the normal course of business. Technically, those amounts are kept in separate revenue and expense accounts. Then, at the end of the accounting period, when it is time to prepare the financial statements, the income statement is prepared using those balances in the revenue and expense accounts. At that time, those income statement accounts are added to (revenue accounts) and subtracted from (expense accounts) the actual retained earnings account. Remember this important computation:

> Beginning retained earnings
> + Net income for the period (or − net loss)
> − Dividends
> = Ending retained earnings

Your Turn 8-6

Suppose B&B Company started the year with retained earnings of $84,500. During the year, B&B had net income of $25,600 and declared cash dividends of $12,200. What was the ending balance in retained earnings?

L.O.6
Prepare financial
statements that contain
equity transactions.

Team Shirts Issues New Stock

When a privately-owned company decides it wants to offer ownership to the public in order to raise a significant amount of capital, the form of the business organization must be a corporation. (A sole proprietorship or a partnership wanting to offer ownership to the public must first change its form to a corporation.) The first public offering of stock on one of the stock exchanges is called an initial public offering (IPO). Much like the work done before a company issues bonds, a company must do a great deal of work to prepare for an IPO. The SEC requires the company to provide many reports, including a set of financial statements contained in a report called a prospectus. Remember, the job of the SEC is to protect the public.

In August, Sara decides her company could raise a great deal of capital by "going public." Sara decides it would be a good long-term strategy to increase the company's equity to provide more funds for expansion without increasing the company's debt. As you know, a company's creditors and owners have claim to the company's assets, and the relationship between the amount of debt and the amount of equity in a company is called the company's capital structure. To increase the company's equity, Team Shirts will offer the opportunity to the general public to become part owners in the company.

Exhibit 8.8 shows the balance sheet for Team Shirts at the beginning of August. This is the July 31 balance sheet you saw in Chapter 7 (Exhibit 7.15). The first transaction for August is the Team Shirts IPO. Although the form of the company has been a corporation, Team Shirts has a lot of work to do to prepare to go public. The SEC requirements for this IPO are extensive, and we will let the investment bankers do the work behind the scenes. These are finance, accounting,

EXHIBIT 8.8

Balance Sheet for Team Shirts at August 1, 2010

Team Shirts
Balance Sheet
At August 1, 2010

Assets

Current assets		
Cash		$ 44,705
Accounts receivable (net of allowance of $1,125)		55,125
Inventory		9,990
Prepaid expenses		5,600
Total current assets		115,420
Property and equipment		
Land	$ 8,500	
Computer	4,000	
Truck	30,000	
Building	76,500	$119,000
Accumulated depreciation		(1,910)
Net property and equipment		117,090
Total assets		$232,510

Liabilities & Shareholder's Equity

Current liabilities	
Accounts payable	$ 36,000
Interest payable	654
Current portion of note payable	6,000
Current portion of mortgage payable	6,702
Total current liabilities	49,356
Notes payable	24,000
Mortgage payable	78,298
Total liabilities	151,654
Shareholder's equity	
Common stock	$ 5,000
Retained earnings	75,856
Total shareholder's equity	80,856
Total liabilities and shareholder's equity	$232,510

and legal experts in the area of IPOs. The accounting changes in the balance sheet depend on the characteristics of the debt and equity of the company and the agreements the creditors and owners make. We will make it very simple for Team Shirts, but in a real-world IPO, transactions could be much more complicated.

Sara works with an investment banking firm and an accounting firm to prepare the stock offering—the IPO. The investment bankers do the legal work and essentially buy the stock and then offer it to the public. (For simplicity, we will assume that all of their fees have been deducted from the issue price of the stock.) Team Shirts' corporate charter has 100,000 shares of common stock authorized with a par value of $0.01. Sara's personal ownership has been assigned 30,000 shares. Remember that she is the only shareholder at this time, so all of shareholder's equity belongs to her. Sara wants to retain a majority of the stock so that she can retain control of the company, so Team Shirts decides to issue 25,000 additional common shares in this initial offering. The $0.01 par value shares are issued at $3 per share.

Assets	=	Liabilities	+	Shareholders' equity	
				Contributed capital	+ Retained earnings
75,000 cash				250 common stock 74,750 additional paid-in capital	

The remaining August transactions for Team Shirts are given in Exhibit 8.9. Trace each one to the accounting equation worksheet in Exhibit 8.10 on the following page. Then, study the list of adjustments.

1   Issued 25,000 shares of common stock for $75,000, $0.01 par value

2   Paid $30,000 on accounts payable

3   Collected $40,000 on accounts receivable

4   Purchased inventory on account: 25,000 shirts at $3.50 each

5   Found out that Play Ball Sports, one of its customers with an outstanding balance of $1,000, has filed for bankruptcy, so wrote off the account balance

6   Sold 26,119 shirts at $10 each on account

7   Collected $25,000 on accounts receivable

8   Incurred cash operating expenses of $12,000

9   Renewed insurance policy for 12 months for $2,400 cash. The new policy takes effect on August 15, when the old policy expires.

10 Made first mortgage payment of $900. (See amortization schedule in Exhibit 8.11 on page 387 for breakdown of interest and principal. Remember, the interest was accrued at the end of July.)

EXHIBIT 8.9

Transactions for Team Shirts for August

To make the following necessary adjustments, you'll find some additional information included in the descriptions.

1. Depreciation on computer ($100 per month)
2. Team Shirts drove the truck 4,000 miles in August. So the depreciation on the truck is $580 (4,000 miles × 0.145 per mile).
3. Depreciation on building ($250 per month)
4. Insurance—$150 ($50 + $100) for August
5. Rent—$1,200 for August
6. Web design expense—$50 for August

7. Interest on truck loan ($30,000 × 0.06 = $1,800 per year; $150 per month)
8. Interest on mortgage. (See amortization schedule in Exhibit 8.11.)
9. Allowance for uncollectible accounts will remain at 2% of the ending accounts receivable balance.

EXHIBIT 8.10

Accounting Equation Worksheet for Team Shirts for August

	Cash	All other assets	(Account)	All liabilities	(Account)	Contributed Capital	Retained Earnings	(Account)
			Assets	**= Liabilities**		**+**	**Shareholders' Equity**	
Beginning Balances	$ 44,705	$187,805	See details below	$151,654	See details below	$ 5,000	$ 75,856	
Transactions 1	75,000					250 74,750		
2	(30,000)			(30,000)	Accounts payable			
3	40,000	(40,000)	Accounts receivable					
4		87,500	Inventory	87,500	Accounts payable			
5		(1,000) 1,000	Accounts receivable Allowance for bad debts					
6		261,190 (91,694)	Accounts receivable Inventory				261,190 (91,694)	Sales Cost of goods sold
7	25,000	(25,000)	Accounts receivable					
8	(12,000)						(12,000)	Operating expenses
9	(2,400)	2,400	Prepaid insurance					
10	(900)			(546) (354)	Mortgage payable Interest payable			
A-1		(100)	Accumulated depreciation, computer				(100)	Depreciation expense
A-2		(580)	Accumulated depreciation, truck				(580)	Depreciation expense
A-3		(250)	Accumulated depreciation, building				(250)	Depreciation expense
A-4		(150)	Prepaid insurance				(150)	Insurance expense
A-5		(1,200)	Prepaid rent				(1,200)	Rent expense
A-6		(50)	Prepaid web design				(50)	Web design expense
A-7				150	Interest payable		(150)	Interest expense
A-8				352	Interest payable		(352)	Interest expense
A-9		(4,904)	Allowance for bad debts				(4,904)	Bad debts expense
	$139,405 + $374,967			**= $208,756**		**+**	**$80,000 + $225,616**	

Check   514,372   =   514,372

━ Income statement ━ Statement of changes in shareholders' equity ━ Balance sheet ━ Statement of cash flows

Assets (except cash)	Beginning	Ending
Accounts receivable	$ 56,250	$251,440
Allowance for bad debts	(1,125)	(5,029)
Inventory	9,990	5,796
Prepaid insurance	50	2,300
Prepaid rent	5,400	4,200
Prepaid web design	150	100
Computer	4,000	4,000
Accumulated depreciation	(500)	(600)
Truck	30,000	30,000
Accumulated depreciation	(1,160)	(1,740)
Land	8,500	8,500
Building	76,500	76,500
Accumulated depreciation	(250)	(500)
	$187,805	$374,967
Liabilities		
Accounts payable	$ 36,000	$ 93,500
Interest payable	654	802
Notes payable (truck)	30,000	30,000
Mortgage payable	85,000	84,454
	$151,654	$208,756

Depreciation

Computer	$100	
Truck	$580	$0.145 per mile × 4,000 miles
Building	$250	

	$76,500	Cost (90% of purchase)
	(1,500)	Salvage value
	$75,000	Depreciable base
	÷ 300	25 years × 12 months
	$250.00	Monthly depreciation

EXHIBIT 8.11

Details of Team Shirts Computations for August Financial Statements

Cost of goods sold (FIFO)

Beginning inventory	2,775 shirts at $3.60 each	$ 9,990
Purchases	25,000 at $3.50	87,500
Goods available for sale		$97,490
Sale of 26,119 shirts:	2,775 at $3.60	$ 9,990
	23,344 at $3.50	81,704
Cost of goods sold		91,694
Ending inventory	1,656 at $3.50	5,796
		$97,490

Bad debts expense

Beginning allowance for bad debts	$ 1,125
Write-offs during the month	(1,000)
Balance before adjustment	$ 125
Desired balance	
2% of ending AR =	
2% of $251,440	5,029
Needed adjustment = bad debts expense	$ 4,904

Interest expense and current portion of long-term mortgage

This is the amortization schedule for the first 13 months of the mortgage. The annual interest rate of 5% is divided by 12 to get a monthly rate. The difference between the monthly payment and the interest expense will reduce the principal balance. The total principal reduction for the next 12 months will be the current portion of the long-term debt. It is the amount of the principal that will be due in the next year. Remember that the interest won't be recorded as a liability until the time has passed. At the end of the second month of the mortgage, August, Team Shirts accrued the second month's interest of $352.

Beginning balance (monthly)	Interest expense (monthly) 5%/12	Monthly payment given	Reduction in principal	Ending balance
$85,000	$354	$900	$546	$84,454
84,454	352	900	548	83,906
83,906	350	900	550	83,356
83,356	347	900	553	82,803
82,803	345	900	555	82,248
82,248	343	900	557	81,691
81,691	340	900	560	81,131
81,131	338	900	562	80,569
80,569	336	900	564	80,005
80,005	333	900	567	79,438
79,438	331	900	569	78,869
78,869	329	900	571	78,298
78,298	326	900	574	77,724
			$6,730	

▭ The amounts can be found on the financial statements.

Mortgage payable before the second payment	$84,454
Current portion	6,730
Remaining long-term mortgage payable	$77,724

All of the adjustments are shown on the accounting equation worksheet in Exhibit 8.10.

Details of the depreciation, inventory, bad debts expense, and long-term mortgage are shown in Exhibit 8.11.

After you understand all of the entries on the worksheet, trace the numbers to the financial statements shown in Exhibit 8.12.

EXHIBIT 8.12

Financial Statements for Team Shirts for August 2010

Team Shirts
Income Statement
For the Month Ended August 31, 2010

Sales revenue		$261,190
Expenses:		
Cost of goods sold	$91,694	
Operating expenses	12,000	
Bad debts expense	4,904	
Insurance expense	150	
Rent expense	1,200	
Web design expense	50	
Depreciation expense	930	
Interest expense	502	
Total expenses		111,430
Net income		$149,760

Team Shirts
Statement of Changes in Shareholders' Equity
For the Month Ended August 31, 2010

Beginning common stock	$ 5,000
Common stock issued during month	250
Additional paid-in capital from common stock issue	74,750
Ending contributed capital	$ 80,000
Beginning retained earnings	$ 75,856
Net income	149,760
Dividends	0
Ending retained earnings	$225,616
Total shareholders' equity	$305,616

Team Shirts
Statement of Cash Flows
For the Month Ended August 31, 2010

Cash from operating activities	
Cash collected from customers	$ 65,000
Cash paid to vendors	(30,000)
Cash paid for operating expenses	(14,400)
Cash paid for interest	(354)
Net cash from operating activities	$ 20,246
Cash from investing activities	0
Cash from financing activities	
Cash paid on mortgage	$ (546)
Cash from issue of common stock	75,000
Net cash from financing activities	74,454
Increase in cash	94,700
Beginning cash balance	44,705
Ending cash balance	$139,405

Team Shirts
Balance Sheet
At August 31, 2010

Assets		
Current assets		
Cash		$139,405
Account receivable (net of allowance of $5,029)		246,411
Inventory		5,796
Prepaid expenses		6,600
Total current assets		398,212
Property and equipment		
Land	$ 8,500	
Computer	4,000	
Truck	30,000	
Building	76,500	$119,000
Accumulated depreciation		(2,840)
Net property and equipment		116,160
Total assets		$514,372
Liabilities and Shareholders' Equity		
Current liabilities		
Accounts payable		$ 93,500
Interest payable		802
Current portion of note payable		6,000
Current portion of mortgage payable		6,730
Total current liabilities		107,032
Notes payable		24,000
Mortgage payable		77,724
Total liabilities		208,756
Shareholders' equity		
Common stock		$ 5,250
Additional paid-in capital		74,750
Retained earnings		225,616
Total shareholders' equity		305,616
Total liabilities and shareholders' equity		$514,372

L.O.7
Compute return on equity and earnings per share, and explain what these ratios mean.

Applying Your Knowledge: Ratio Analysis

The shareholders' equity of a firm can provide information useful for financial statement analysis. There are two ratios that help us evaluate the return to shareholders.

1. Return on equity
2. Earnings per share

Return on Equity

Return on equity (ROE) measures the amount of income earned with each dollar of common shareholders' investment in the firm. To calculate ROE, we need the amount of common shareholders' equity at the beginning and at the end of the accounting period. Common shareholders' equity is all the equity except the preferred shareholders' equity. The ratio uses common shareholders' equity because common shareholders are considered to be the true owners of the firm. Then, we use the net income, reduced by the amount of preferred dividends declared, for the numerator. The reason for deducting preferred dividends from net income is that we are calculating the return to the common shareholder. The ratio takes preferred shareholders out of both the numerator and denominator. Recall that common shareholders are entitled to the earnings of the firm only after preferred dividends are paid. Return on equity tells us how well the company is using the common shareholders' contributions and earnings retained in the business.

> **Return on equity (ROE)** measures the amount of income earned with each dollar of common shareholders' investment in the firm. To calculate ROE, take net income minus preferred dividends divided by average common shareholders' equity.

$$\text{Return on equity} = \frac{\text{Net income} - \text{preferred dividends}}{\text{Average common shareholders' equity}}$$

Exhibit 8.13 shows the information needed to calculate Papa John's return on equity for two consecutive years. The size of the return needs to be compared to other similar companies or to industry standards for a meaningful analysis of a firm's performance. Notice that Papa John's ROE has increased from about 23.9% to about 28.6%. Any analyst would want to get more information about an increase this large. Remember that when we calculate the ratios, we use a simple average of beginning and ending common shareholders' equity for the denominator.

EXHIBIT 8.13

Return on Equity for Papa John's International, Inc.

(dollars in thousands)	For the Year Ended December 28, 2008	For the Year Ended December 30, 2007
Net income	$36,796	$32,735
Average common equity	($129,986 + 126,903)/2 = $128,445	($126,903 + 146,782)/2 = $136,843
Return on equity	28.6%	23.9%

Earnings Per Share

Earnings per share (EPS) is perhaps the most well-known and most commonly used ratio because analysts and investors use current earnings to predict future dividends and stock prices. This ratio is the per-share portion of net income of each common shareholder.

> **Earnings per share (EPS)** is a commonly used measure of firm performance, defined as net income minus preferred dividends divided by the weighted average number of common shares outstanding.

$$\text{Earnings per share} = \frac{\text{Net income} - \text{Preferred dividends}}{\text{Weighted average number of common shares outstanding}}$$

The "earnings" in the numerator of this ratio begins with net income. Because EPS is designated as the earnings for the common shareholders, preferred dividends must be deducted from net income. An investor, who saw the corporation's net income increase year after year, might be fooled into thinking that he or she was doing better each year. The investor might be worse off, however, if the amount of common stock outstanding has been increasing, because those increases could dilute the investor's portion of the earnings. Even though net income went up, it must be shared among many more owners. The denominator is the weighted average number of common shares outstanding. For example, suppose a firm began the year, January 1, with 100,000 common shares outstanding and issued an additional 10,000 common shares on April 1. The weighted average number of common shares outstanding for the year would be

$$(100,000 \times 3/12) + (110,000 \times 9/12) = 107,500 \text{ shares}$$

The fractions, 3/12 and 9/12, represent the fraction of the year in which that particular number of shares was outstanding. In other words, the number of shares outstanding is weighted by the amount of time those shares were outstanding.

Suppose the firm had net income of $129,000 for the year and did not have any preferred stock. Then, EPS would be

$$\frac{\$129,000}{107,500} = \$1.20 \text{ per share}$$

EPS helps an investor predict stock prices, which is why it is a popular ratio. All publicly-traded firms' financial statements provide EPS (on the income statement) because it is required by GAAP. EPS is the most common indicator of a company's overall performance. EPS is forecast by financial analysts, anticipated by investors, managed by business executives, and announced with great anticipation by major corporations.

Dollar Tree Stores, Inc.'s income statement in Exhibit 8.14 shows two amounts for earnings per share. The first is called basic net income per share. This is a straightforward calculation of net income divided by the weighted average number of common shares outstanding. The second is called diluted net income per share. This is a "what-if" calculation: What if all of the potential securities that could have been converted into common stock actually had been converted to common stock at year end? Those securities could be securities such as convertible bonds or exercised stock options, both of which could be exchanged for shares of common stock. If you were a shareholder, you might want to know the worst-case scenario for your EPS. That is referred to as the diluted EPS. Calculations for diluted EPS can be complicated and are done by a company's accountant when the annual financial statements are prepared. Fortunately, a firm's income statement will always show the firm's EPS because it is a requirement of GAAP. That means we won't have to compute this ratio when we analyze a publicly-traded firm's financial statements. However, should you decide to become an accountant, you will spend lots of time learning the intricacies of the EPS computation.

EXHIBIT 8.14

Presentation of Earnings per Share on an Income Statement (Statement of Operations)

Dollar Tree Stores, Inc.,
and Subsidiaries
Consolidated Statements of Operations

(In millions, except per share data)	Year Ended January 31, 2009	Year Ended February 2, 2008	Year Ended February 3, 2007
Net sales	$4,644.9	$4,242.6	$3,969.4
Cost of sales	3,052.7	2,781.5	2,612.2
Gross profit	1,592.2	1,461.1	1,357.2
Selling, general and administrative expenses	1,226.4	1,130.8	1,046.4
Operating income	365.8	330.3	310.8
Interest income	2.6	6.7	8.6
Interest expense	(9.3)	(17.2)	(16.5)
Income before income taxes	359.1	319.8	302.9
Provision for income taxes	129.6	118.5	110.9
Net income	$ 229.5	$ 201.3	$ 192.0
Basic net income per share	$ 2.54	$ 2.10	$ 1.86
Diluted net income per share	$ 2.53	$ 2.09	$ 1.85

See accompanying Notes to Consolidated Financial Statements.

By now you should be getting used to the variety of terms accountants have for the same thing. Dollar Tree Stores doesn't have anything labeled earnings per share. Instead, the firm calls it net income per share.

Business Risk, Control, and Ethics

Generally, we have been looking at the risks faced by the firm. We will now look at the risks associated with shareholders' equity from an owner's point of view.

L.O.8
Recognize the business risks associated with shareholders' equity and the related controls.

Risks Faced by Owners

Anyone who purchases a share of stock in a company risks losing that money. At the same time, however, there is the potential of earning a corresponding significant return. In the first few months of 2000, technology stocks were booming. It was called the dot-com boom because so many of the new firms were Internet-based. In March 2000, the NASDAQ (National Association of Securities Dealers Automated Quotation system) closed at a peak of 5,048.62, more than double its value just 14 months before. Many investors reaped the rewards of the stock price increases. Then, prices began to fall. One day after reaching its peak, the NASDAQ lost almost 3% of its value. By October 2002, it had dropped to 1,114.11, a loss of 78% of its peak value. The dot-com boom had become the dot-com bust.

Many investors made money in the dot-com boom, and some technology firms did not lose their value. For example, if you bought a share of stock in eBay in July 2002, you paid approximately $14 for that share of stock. You could have sold it in January of 2005 for over $57. This is the reward side of the risk associated with equity ownership for an individual investor.

In 2008, we saw this phenomenon again as the stock market lost over 20% of its value in a single week in October. According to Urban Institute, a nonpartisan economic and social policy research center, the S&P 500 fell by over a third between year end 2007 and year end 2008. This drop has had a negative effect on the economy and on the retirement funds of millions of people. The long-term effects of the 2008 crash will depend on how the market recovers. Anyone near retirement age has much more to be concerned about than those who have many years to restore their lost wealth. What has become quite clear, however, is that there is significant risk in stock ownership.

How can the risk of stock ownership be controlled? The best way to minimize the risks of stock ownership is to diversify your investments. If you own stock in many different types of firms, the stock prices of some should go up when others are going down. For example, if you own stock in a firm in the retail grocery business, such as Kroger, it might be wise to balance that investment with stock in a restaurant, such as Darden, the parent company of Olive Garden and Red Lobster. Then, if the popular trend is to eat at home, the grocery store stock might increase in value. If eating out becomes more popular, then the restaurant stock might become more valuable. This example is quite simplistic, and finance experts have a much more complicated concept of diversification. The bottom line, however, is quite straightforward. Do not put all your eggs in one basket.

Other risks of stock ownership result from the problems associated with the separation of ownership and management that is common in today's corporation. Considering the potential damage that can result from the actions of unethical management, investors considering ownership in a large corporation must take this risk seriously. Controls that monitor the behavior and decisions of management—such as boards of directors and independent audits—will help minimize these risks. Many of these risks are addressed by the Sarbanes-Oxley Act of 2002, which you can read more about in Chapter 11.

Chapter Summary Points

- Corporations raise money by issuing preferred stock and common stock. The number of shares of stock can be classified as authorized, issued, and outstanding.
- Preferred shareholders get their dividends before the common shareholders. The amount of the dividend is fixed by the par value and the percentage given on the stock certificate. The remaining dividends, out of the total declared by the board of directors, go to the common shareholders. Remember, a firm is not required to pay dividends. Some, like Papa John's, have never paid a cash dividend.
- Treasury stock is stock a firm has issued and later repurchased on the open market. A firm might buy its own stock to have shares available for employees and managers as part of compensation packages.

- A stock dividend is a dividend consisting of shares of stock rather than cash. Each shareholder receives an amount of stock that will maintain the pre-dividend proportion of ownership. A stock split is when the company reduces the par value per share and increases the number of shares proportionately. For example, if you own 5 shares of $3 par stock and the company enacts a 3-for-1 split, the new par value of the stock is $1 per share and you will now own 15 shares. This reduces the market price of the stock. (No entry is made in the formal accounting records for stock splits.)
- The balance in retained earnings is the sum of all the net incomes minus any net losses and minus any dividends declared over the entire life of the company. It is the company's earnings that have been kept in the company.
- Return on equity is defined as net income for the common shareholders divided by average common shareholders' equity. It measures a company's profitability. Earnings per share is defined as net income divided by the weighted average number of shares outstanding (again, common shareholders only). This measures each common shareholder's proportionate share of net income.
- The biggest risk related to stock ownership is the potential for a decrease in the value of your stock. Because owners and managers are often different, the owners may have a problem monitoring the decisions of the managers. For firms, the risk of being publicly traded relates to the complicated requirements set forth by the SEC and the Sarbanes-Oxley Act.

Chapter Summary Problems

Suppose that Pia's Pizza engaged in the following transactions in the fiscal year ended December 28, 2011:

Pia's Pizza
Shareholders' Equity Section of the Balance Sheet
(dollars in thousands)

	At 12/28/11	12/28/10
Shareholders' Equity:		
Preferred stock ($0.01 par value per share; authorized 5,000,000 shares; no shares issued)		
Common stock ($0.01 par value per share; authorized 50,000,000 shares; xxxxxx shares issued at December 28, 2011, and 31,716,105 shares issued at December 28, 2010)		$ 317
Additional paid-in capital-common stock		219,584
Accumulated other comprehensive income (loss)	(3,116)	(3,116)
Retained earnings		293,921
Treasury stock (xxxxxx shares at December 28, 2011, and 13,603,587 shares at December 28, 2010, at cost)		(351,434)
Total shareholders' equity		$ 159,272

---

1. The company issued 100,000 shares of common stock, par value of $0.01 per share, for $24 per share.
2. Cash revenues for the year amounted to $100,690,000, and cash expenses amounted to $50,010,000.
3. The company declared cash dividends of $300,000.
4. The company repurchased 25,000 shares of its own stock (treasury stock) for an average cost of $22 per share.

Instructions

Use the accounting equation to show how Pia's Pizza would record each of the transactions. Then, update the shareholders' equity section of Pia's Pizza's balance sheet by filling in the shaded areas.

Solution

Assets	=	Liabilities	+	Shareholders' equity	
				Contributed capital	+ Retained earnings
1. 2,400,000 cash				1,000 common stock 2,399,000 additional paid-in capital	
2. 100,690,000 cash (50,010,000) cash					100,690,000 revenues (50,010,000) expenses
3.		300,000 dividends payable			(300,000) dividends
4. (550,000) cash				(550,000) treasury stock	

Pia's Pizza
Shareholders' Equity Section of the Balance Sheet
(dollars in thousands)

	At 12/28/11	12/28/10
Shareholders' Equity:		
Preferred stock ($0.01 par value per share; authorized 5,000,000 shares; no shares issued)		
Common stock ($0.01 par value per share; authorized 50,000,000 shares; 31,816,105 shares issued at December 28, 2011, and 31,716,105 shares issued at December 28, 2010)	$ 318	$ 317
Additional paid-in capital-common stock	221,983	219,584
Accumulated other comprehensive income (loss)	(3,116)	(3,116)
Retained earnings	344,301	293,921
Treasury stock (13,628,587 shares at December 28, 2011, and 13,603,587 shares at December 28, 2010, at cost)	(351,984)	(351,434)
Total shareholders' equity	$ 211,502	$ 159,272

Key Terms for Chapter 8

Authorized shares (p. 372)
Common stock (p. 372)
Dividends (p. 376)
Earnings per share (EPS) (p. 389)

Issued shares (p. 372)
Outstanding shares (p. 373)
Par value (p. 373)
Preferred stock (p. 376)
Retained earnings (p. 383)

Return on equity (ROE) (p. 389)
Stock dividends (p. 382)
Stock split (p. 383)
Treasury stock (p. 373)

Answers to YOUR TURN Questions

Chapter 8

Your Turn 8-1

Assets	=	Liabilities	+	Shareholders' equity		
				Contributed capital	**+**	**Retained earnings**
200,000 cash				10,000 common stock		
				190,000 additional paid-in capital		

Your Turn 8-2

($100 × 10,000 × 0.08) = $80,000 for last year and $80,000 for this year for a total of $160,000 to the preferred shareholders. The remaining $40,000 goes to the common shareholders.

Your Turn 8-3

a.

Assets	=	Liabilities	+	Shareholders' equity		
				Contributed capital	**+**	**Retained earnings**
(50,000) cash				(50,000) treasury stock		

b. One hundred thousand shares are issued and 99,000 shares are outstanding.

Your Turn 8-4

Treasury stock would be deducted from shareholders' equity. The amount would be $7,000, the cost of repurchasing the shares of stock.

Your Turn 8-5

1. A stock split is a division of the par value of the stock and an increase in the number of shares owned by each shareholder, proportionate to the presplit ownership distribution. A stock dividend is a distribution of stock to the current shareholders as a dividend, similarly maintaining the pre-dividend distribution of ownership.
2. You will own 3,000 shares, which will still be 3% of the outstanding stock.

Your Turn 8-6

$84,500 + $25,600 − $12,200 = $97,900

Questions

1. What are the two primary ways for a company to finance its business?
2. What is the difference between common stock and preferred stock?
3. Explain how par value affects the issuance of common stock and preferred stock.
4. What is the difference between paid-in capital in general and additional paid-in capital on the balance sheet?
5. What are the two ways that shareholders can make money on an investment in a corporation's stock?
6. Are dividends expenses of a corporation? Explain why or why not.
7. What are the three dates corporations consider when issuing a dividend?

8. What is the difference between cumulative and noncumulative preferred stock?
9. What are dividends in arrears?
10. What is treasury stock and why might a company acquire it?
11. What effect does the purchase of treasury stock have on a company's financial statements?
12. Would treasury stock be considered authorized, issued, or outstanding? Explain your answer.
13. Explain the difference between stock dividends and cash dividends.
14. What is the effect of a stock dividend on a company's financial statements?
15. What is a stock split and what effect does it have on a company's shareholders' equity?
16. What are the two sections of the shareholders' equity section of the balance sheet? Explain what each section reports.
17. How is return on equity calculated? What does this ratio measure?
18. Explain how earnings per share (EPS) is calculated. What does this ratio measure?
19. Of all the financial ratios you have studied, which is the only one that is required by U.S. GAAP to be reported in the financial statements? On which financial statement will it appear?

Multiple-Choice Questions

1. Which of the following *does not* affect retained earnings?
   a. Net income for the period
   b. Dividends declared for common shareholders
   c. Repayment of the principal of a loan
   d. All of the above affect retained earnings.
2. Preferred stock is stock that is
   a. traded above the price of common stock.
   b. issued and later repurchased.
   c. bought and sold to smooth a company's earnings.
   d. given priority over common stock for dividends.
3. Treasury stock is
   a. a company's own stock that it has repurchased and added to its short-term trading securities (current assets) as an investment.
   b. a company's own stock that is considered issued but not outstanding.
   c. a company's own stock that may be used to "manage" earnings—it could be sold for a gain when the price of the stock increases to help a company meet its earnings forecast.
   d. booked as an increase to assets and a decrease to shareholders' equity when it is purchased.
4. The two major components of shareholders' equity are
   a. preferred stock and common stock.
   b. contributed capital and paid-in capital.
   c. contributed capital and retained earnings.
   d. common stock and treasury stock.
5. The purchase of treasury stock will
   a. increase assets and shareholders' equity.
   b. decrease assets and shareholders' equity.
   c. have no effect on assets or shareholders' equity.
   d. decrease assets but have no effect on shareholders' equity.
6. If a company purchased 50 shares of its own stock for $10 per share and later sold it for $12 per share, the company would
   a. record a gain of $2 per share.
   b. record an increase to retained earnings of $100.
   c. show a gain on the sale.
   d. show an increase of $100 of paid-in capital.
7. The number of shares of stock designated as *issued* on the year-end balance sheet are those shares that
   a. were issued during the year.
   b. have been issued during the firm's life.
   c. are authorized to be issued.
   d. have been repurchased during the year.

8. When treasury stock is reissued for more than the company paid to buy it, the difference is
   a. a gain that will increase the firm's income.
   b. included in sales revenue for the period.
   c. added to an additional paid-in capital account.
   d. given to the current shareholders as a dividend.
9. The payment of dividends is
   a. required by corporate law.
   b. determined by the firm's board of directors.
   c. related in amount to the firm's earnings per share.
   d. determined by the Securities and Exchange Commission.
10. Return on equity measures how well a firm is using
    a. owners' original contributions to the firm.
    b. creditors' investment in the firm.
    c. shareholders' total investment in the firm, both contributed and earned.
    d. its assets.

All of the A exercises can be found within MyAccountingLab, an online homework and practice environment.

Short Exercises
Set A

SE8-1A. *Classify stock. (LO 1).* Delta Corporation's corporate charter authorizes the company to sell 450,000,000 shares of $1.50 par common stock. As of December 31, 2011, the company had issued 180,915,000 shares of common stock for an average price of $4 each. Delta has 57,000,000 shares of treasury stock. How many shares of common stock will be disclosed as authorized, issued, and outstanding on the December 31, 2011, balance sheet?

SE8-2A. *Record issuance of common stock. (LO 1).* Vest Corporation sells and issues 100 shares of its $10 par value common stock at $11 per share. Show how this transaction would be recorded in the accounting equation.

SE8-3A. *Analyze effect of issuance of common stock on financial statements. (LO 1).* Ice Video Corporation issued 5,000 shares of $0.01 par value common stock for $32.50 per share. How much cash did Ice Video Corporation receive from the stock issue? How will the transaction be shown in the shareholders' equity section of the balance sheet?

SE8-4A. *Analyze effect of dividends on financial statements. (LO 2).* On December 15, 2010, the board of directors of Seat Corporation declared a cash dividend, payable January 8, 2011, of $1.50 per share on the 100,000 common shares outstanding. The accounting period ends December 31. How will this be reflected on the balance sheet at December 31, 2010?

SE8-5A. *Distribute dividend between preferred and common shareholders. (LO 2).* In 2012, the board of directors of Tasty Bakery Corporation declared total dividends of $40,000. The company has 2,000 shares of 6%, $100 par, preferred stock. There are no dividends in arrears. How much of the $40,000 will be paid to the preferred shareholders? How much will be paid to the common shareholders?

SE8-6A. *Record sale of treasury stock. (LO 3).* Suppose Fitness and Fashion Corporation paid $20 per share for 690 shares of its own common stock on August 30, 2011, and then resold these treasury shares for $22.50 per share on September 25, 2011. Show the transaction on September 25, 2011, in the accounting equation. What effect do these transactions have on the shareholders' equity section of the balance sheet at September 30, 2011?

SE8-7A. *Analyze effect of stock dividend on financial statements. (LO 4).* Zorro Company declared and issued a 10% stock dividend on June 1, 2010. Before this dividend was declared and issued, there were 220,000 shares of $0.10 par common stock outstanding. After the stock dividend, how many shares are outstanding? What is the par value of each share?

SE8-8A. *Analyze effect of stock split on financial statements. (LO 4).* Romax Company announced a 2-for-1 stock split on its common stock. Before the announcement, there were

200,000 shares of $1 par common stock outstanding. Determine how many shares of common stock will be outstanding after the stock split. What will be the par value of each share? What effect does the stock split have on total shareholders' equity?

SE8-9A. *Calculate retained earnings balance. (LO 5).* On January 1, 2011, Green Corporation started the year with a $520,000 balance in retained earnings. During 2011, the company earned net income of $89,500 and declared and paid dividends of $10,000. Also, the company received cash of $150,000 from a new issue of common stock. What is the balance in retained earnings on December 31, 2011?

SE8-10A. *Calculate retained earnings balance. (LO 5).* Suppose Hillard Company started the year with a balance of $450,000 in retained earnings. During the year, the company declared and paid dividends of $20,000. If the ending balance in retained earnings was $495,500, how much was net income (or net loss) for the year?

SE8-11A. *Calculate return on equity. (LO 7).* Use the following data to calculate the return on equity for Mighty Motors (MM), Inc. At the beginning of 2010, MM's current assets totaled $57,855; total assets totaled $449,999; and total liabilities totaled $424,424. For the year ended December 31, 2010, net income was $3,822. At the end of 2010, the current assets were $62,397; total assets were $369,053; and total liabilities were $361,960. Mighty Motors has no preferred stock. Calculate the return on equity (ROE) for MM for 2010. Make sure you use *average* shareholders' equity in your calculation.

Set B

SE8-12B. *Classify stock. (LO 1).* Sunshine Corporation began operations on July 1, 2009. When Sunshine's first fiscal year ended on June 30, 2010, the balance sheet showed 200,000 shares of common stock issued and 195,000 shares of common stock outstanding. During the second year, Sunshine repurchased 10,000 shares for the treasury. No new shares were issued in the second year. On the balance sheet at June 30, 2011, how many shares would be classified as issued? How many shares are outstanding?

SE8-13B. *Record issuance of common stock. (LO 1).* Nugget Corporation issues 300 shares of its $1 par value common stock at $3.50 per share. Show how this transaction would be recorded in the accounting equation.

SE8-14B. *Analyze effect of issuance of common stock on financial statements. (LO 1).* If a company issues 10,000 shares of $1 par common stock for $8.50 per share, what is the effect on total paid-in capital? What is the effect on additional paid-in capital (also known as paid-in capital in excess of par)?

SE8-15B. *Analyze effect of dividends on financial statements. (LO 2).* On March 15, 2011, the board of directors of Everyman Corporation declared a cash dividend, payable July 10, 2011, of $0.30 per share on the 120,000 common shares outstanding. The accounting period ends June 30. How will this be reflected on the balance sheet at June 30, 2011?

SE8-16B. *Distribute dividend between preferred and common shareholders. (LO 2).* Bates Corporation has 7,000 shares of 5%, $100 par, cumulative preferred stock outstanding and 50,000 shares of $1 par common stock outstanding. If the board of directors declares $80,000 of total dividends and the company did not pay dividends the previous year, how much will the preferred and common shareholders receive?

SE8-17B. *Record purchase of treasury stock. (LO 3).* If Fitness and Fashion Corporation paid $10 per share for 590 shares of its own stock, how would the transaction be shown in the accounting equation? How would the transaction be reflected in the shareholders' equity section of the balance sheet?

SE8-18B. *Analyze effect of stock dividend on financial statements. (LO 4).* Inter Company declared and issued a 5% stock dividend on May 1, 2011. Before this dividend was declared and issued, there were 120,000 shares of $0.50 par common stock outstanding. After the stock dividend, how many shares are outstanding? What is the par value of each share?

SE8-19B. *Analyze effect of stock split on financial statements. (LO 4).* Rail Company announced a 2-for-1 stock split on its common stock. Before the announcement, there were 300,000 shares of $0.50 par common stock outstanding. Determine how many shares of common stock will be outstanding after the stock split. What will be the par value of each share? What effect does the stock split have on total shareholders' equity?

SE8-20B. *Calculate retained earnings balance. (LO 5).* On January 1, 2010, Harrison Corporation started the year with a $422,000 balance in retained earnings. During 2010, the company earned net income of $130,000 and declared and paid dividends of $20,000. Also, the company received cash of $450,000 from a new issue of common stock. What is the balance in retained earnings on December 31, 2010?

SE8-21B. *Calculate retained earnings balance. (LO 5).* Baltimore Manufacturing, Inc., had net income for 2010 of $58,280. During the fiscal year, which began on January 1, 2010, the company declared and paid dividends of $5,500. On the balance sheet at December 31, 2010, the balance in retained earnings was $295,880. What was the December 31, 2009, balance (i.e., the beginning balance) in retained earnings?

SE8-22B. *Calculate net income amount using return on equity ratio. (LO 7).* Octevo Corporation had a return on shareholders' equity (ROE) of 12% in 2012. If total average shareholders' equity for Octevo Corporation was $500,000 and the company has no preferred stock, what was net income for 2012?

All of the A exercises can be found within MyAccountingLab, an online homework and practice environment.

Exercises
Set A

E8-23A. *Analyze equity section of balance sheet. (LO 1, 5).* Super Retail Corporation reported the following information on the financial statements included with its 2010 annual report:

(dollars in thousands)	March 31, 2010	March 31, 2009
Common stock, par value $0.0005		
Authorized: 370,000,000 shares;		
Issued and outstanding 74,758,500 shares at March 31, 2010	37	
72,406,500 shares at March 31, 2009		36
Paid-in capital	396,200	352,633
Retained earnings	143,190	66,272

Were any new shares of common stock issued between March 31, 2009, and March 31, 2010? Did the company report net income for the year ended March 31, 2010? Explain how you know.

E8-24A. *Classify stock and prepare shareholders' equity section of balance sheet. (LO 1, 6).* Royal Knight Printing Company's corporate charter allows it to sell 400,000 shares of $3 par value common stock. To date, the company has issued 75,000 shares for a total of $337,500. Last month, Royal Knight repurchased 5,000 shares for $4.75 per share.

1. If Royal Knight were to prepare a balance sheet, how many shares would it show as authorized, issued, and outstanding?
2. In addition to the shareholders' equity given previously, Royal Knight also has $295,000 in retained earnings. Using this information, prepare the shareholders' equity section of Royal Knight's balance sheet.

E8-25A. *Record stock transactions. (LO 1, 3).* Show how each of the following transactions affects the accounting equation:

March 1	Issued 75,000 shares of $0.02 par value common stock for cash of $99,750
April 1	Issued 1,000 shares of $95 par value preferred stock for cash at $115 per share
June 30	Purchased 1,000 shares of treasury stock for $3 per share (i.e., the company bought its own common stock in the stock market)

E8-26A. *Analyze effects of stock transactions on financial statements. (LO 1, 3).* Refer to the information in E8-25A. How many shares of common stock will be classified as issued at June 30? How many shares will be classified as outstanding at June 30?

E8-27A. *Analyze effects of dividends on financial statements. (LO 2).* Burlon Printing Company had net income of $175,000 for the year ended June 30, 2009. On July 15, 2009, the board of directors met and declared a dividend of $0.35 per share for each of the 150,000 outstanding shares of common stock. The board voted to make the actual distribution on September 1 to all shareholders of record as of August 1. What is (a) the date of declaration, (b) the date of record, and (c) the date of payment? If Burlon Printing Company were to prepare a balance sheet on July 31, 2009, how would it report the dividends (if at all)?

E8-28A. *Distribute dividend between preferred and common shareholders. (LO 2).* Holly Brown Architectural Company has 5,000 shares of 8%, $70 par, cumulative preferred stock outstanding and 7,500 shares of $2.50 par value common stock outstanding. The company began operations on July 1, 2009. The cash dividends declared and paid during each of the first three years of Holly Brown's operations are shown. Calculate the amounts that went to the preferred and the common shareholders (SHs) each year.

Year Ended	Total Dividends Paid	Dividends to Preferred SHs	Dividends to Common SHs
June 30, 2010	$20,000		
June 30, 2011	36,000		
June 30, 2012	40,000		

E8-29A. *Analyze equity section of balance sheet. (LO 1, 2).* Athletic Endurance Company had the following stockholders' equity section on the December 31, 2010, balance sheet:

Preferred stock, 6%, $120 par, cumulative	$1,170,000
Common stock, $1.50 par value	300,000
Paid-in capital in excess of par, common stock	1,200,000
Retained earnings	2,500,000
Total	$5,170,000

1. How many shares of common stock are classified as issued?
2. How many shares of common stock are outstanding?
3. How many shares of preferred stock are outstanding?
4. What was the average selling price of a share of common stock?
5. If $115,000 of dividends was declared and there were no dividends in arrears, how much of the total would go to the common shareholders?

E8-30A. *Record stock transactions. (LO 1, 2, 3).* Surfing Dewd Corporation is authorized to issue both preferred and common stock. Surfing Dewd's preferred stock is $105 par, 6% preferred stock. During the first month of operations, the company engaged in the following transactions related to its stock. Show each of the following transactions in the accounting equation:

March 1	Issued 16,000 shares of $0.50 par value common stock for cash at $5 per share
March 11	Issued 1,500 shares of preferred stock at par
March 16	Purchased 3,000 shares of common stock to be held in the treasury for $7 per share

March 18	Issued 32,000 shares $0.50 par value common stock for cash at $10 per share
March 20	Sold 2,900 shares of the treasury stock purchased on the 16th for $12 per share
March 31	Declared a $10,000 dividend

E8-31A. *Prepare equity section of the balance sheet. (LO 1, 2, 3, 6).* Use the data from E8-30A to prepare the shareholders' equity section of the balance sheet at March 31. Retained earnings at month end are $75,000.

E8-32A. *Analyze equity accounts. (LO 1, 2, 3, 5).* The following balances were shown on the year-end balance sheets for 2009 and 2010 for Columbia Company. For each item, give the most likely reason for the change from one year to the next.

	December 31, 2009	December 31, 2010	Explanation
Common stock	$ 45,000	$ 50,000	
Paid-in capital	$200,000	$230,000	
Retained earnings	$182,500	*$200,000	
Treasury stock	$ (3,450)	$ (5,450)	

*Net income for the year was $20,000.

E8-33A. *Analyze equity section of balance sheet. (LO 1, 2, 3).* Answer the following questions using the shareholders' equity section of Enthusiastic Learning Corporation's balance sheet at June 30:

Shareholders' equity	
Preferred stock, cumulative, 15,000 shares authorized, 5,000 shares issued and outstanding	$ 525,000
Additional paid-in capital, preferred stock	75,000
Common stock, $1.00 par, 500,000 shares authorized, 375,000 shares issued	375,000
Additional paid-in capital, common stock	750,000
Retained earnings	855,000
	2,580,000
Less: treasury stock (5,000 common shares)	(25,000)
Total shareholders' equity	$2,555,000

1. How many shares of common stock are outstanding?
2. On average, what was the issue price of the common shares issued?
3. What is the par value of the preferred stock?
4. If the total annual dividend on preferred stock is $31,500, what is the dividend rate on preferred stock?
5. On average, how much per share did the company pay for the treasury stock?

E8-34A. *Record stock transactions. (LO 1, 2, 3, 4).* On the first day of the fiscal year, Music Productions Corporation had 210,000 shares of $2 par common stock issued (at par) and outstanding, and the retained earnings balance was $900,000. Show how each of the following transactions would affect the accounting equation:

1. Issued 5,000 additional shares of common stock for $10 per share
2. Declared and distributed a 5% stock dividend when the market price was $10 per share
3. Issued 15,000 additional shares of common stock for $12 per share
4. Declared a cash dividend on outstanding shares of $1.30 per share
5. Paid the dividend declared in item (4)
6. Purchased 5,000 shares of treasury stock for $14 per share
7. Sold 2,000 shares of treasury stock for $16 per share

8. Sold 2,500 shares of treasury stock for $15 per share
9. Declared 2-for-1 stock split

E8-35A. *Prepare equity section of the balance sheet. (LO 1, 2, 3, 4, 6).* Use the data from E8-34A to prepare the shareholders' equity section of the balance sheet at year end. Net income for the year was $150,000.

E8-36A. *Prepare equity section of the balance sheet. (LO 1, 3, 5, 6).* The following account balances can be found in the general ledger of Zebra Enterprises at year end. Prepare the shareholders' equity section of the balance sheet.

Retained earnings	$ 650,000
Treasury stock (10,000 common shares at cost)	85,000
Common stock ($2 par, 500,000 shares authorized, 220,000 shares issued)	440,000
Additional paid-in capital, common stock	1,100,000
Preferred stock ($12 par value, 8%, 75,000 shares authorized, 25,000 shares issued)	300,000
Additional paid-in capital, preferred stock	50,000

E8-37A. *Calculate return on equity and earnings per share. (LO 7).* The following financial information is available for High-Speed Internet Company at the end of its two most recent fiscal years. The company has no preferred stock. Calculate (1) return on equity and (2) earnings per share for 2009 and 2010. What do the ratios indicate about the company's performance during the year?

(amounts in thousands)	2010	2009
Average common shareholders' equity	$3,984	$3,450
Dividends declared for common shareholders	1,500	1,455
Net income	6,045	4,266
Weighted average number of common shares outstanding during the year	6,558	5,850

E8-38A. *Analyze effects of equity transactions on financial statements. (LO 1, 2, 3, 4, 5).* Analyze the following transactions and indicate the dollar increase (+) or decrease (−) each has on the balance sheet. If there is an overall change in shareholders' equity, also indicate whether contributed capital, retained earnings, or treasury stock is affected. If the transaction has no effect on the balance sheet, enter NA for that item. The first row is filled in for you as an example.

	Assets	Liabilities	Shareholders' Equity	Equity Section Affected
Issued 1,000 shares of $1 par common stock at par	+1,000		+1,000	Contributed capital
Issued 1,500 shares of $1 par common stock for $14				
Declared a cash dividend of $0.25 per share				
Paid the $0.25 cash dividend				
Purchased 200 shares of treasury stock for $17 per share				
Sold 100 shares of treasury stock for $17 per share				
Declared and distributed a 10% common stock dividend (when the market price was $17 per share)				
Announced a 2-for-1 stock split				
Issued 2,000 shares of $100 par, 4% noncumulative preferred stock				

Set B

E8-39B. *Analyze equity section of balance sheet. (LO 1, 5).* Shipping Unlimited, Inc., reported the following information on the financial statements included with its 2011 annual report:

(dollars in thousands)		June 30, 2011	June 30, 2010
Common stock, par value $0.02			
Authorized:	200,000 shares;		
Issued:	95,000 shares at June 30, 2011;		
	95,000 shares at June 30, 2010	$2	$2
Outstanding:	85,000 shares at June 30, 2011;		
	75,000 shares at June 30, 2010		
Additional paid-in capital		205,015	195,820
Retained earnings		835,880	705,970

Were any new shares of common stock issued during the year ended June 30, 2011? Did the company report net income for the year ended June 30, 2011? Explain how you know.

E8-40B. *Classify stock and prepare shareholders' equity section of balance sheet. (LO 1, 6).* Soper Classic Music, Inc.'s corporate charter allows it to sell 250,000 shares of $1 par value common stock. To date, the company has issued 150,000 shares for a total of $225,000. Last month, Soper Classic repurchased 1,000 shares for $2.00 per share.

1. If Soper Classic were to prepare a balance sheet, how many shares would it show as authorized, issued, and outstanding?
2. In addition to the shareholders' equity given previously, Soper Classic also has $285,000 in retained earnings. Using this information, prepare the shareholders' equity section of Soper Classic Music, Inc.'s balance sheet.

E8-41B. *Record stock transactions. (LO 1, 3).* Show how each of the following transactions would be recorded in the accounting equation:

August 1	Issued 75,000 shares of $0.05 par value common stock for cash of $750,000
November 1	Issued 2,500 shares of $100 par value preferred stock for cash at $160 per share
December 31	Purchased 5,000 shares of treasury stock (i.e., the company bought its own common stock in the stock market) for $11.00 per share

E8-42B. *Analyze effects of stock transactions on financial statements. (LO 1, 3).* Refer to the information in E8-41B. How many shares of common stock will be classified as issued at December 31? How many shares of common stock will be classified as outstanding at December 31?

E8-43B. *Analyze effects of dividends on financial statements. (LO 2).* Steverson Air Conditioning, Inc., had net income of $210,000 for the year ended December 31, 2009. On January 15, 2010, the board of directors met and declared a dividend of $0.15 per share for each of the 200,000 outstanding shares of common stock. The board voted to make the actual distribution on April 1 to all shareholders of record as of March 1. What is (a) the date of declaration, (b) the date of record, and (c) the date of payment? If Steverson Air were to prepare a balance sheet on January 31, 2010, how would the dividends be reported (if at all)?

E8-44B. *Distribute dividend between preferred and common shareholders. (LO 2).* State of Grace Publishing, Inc., has 6,000 shares of $120 par, 10% cumulative preferred stock outstanding and 10,000 shares of $1.50 par value common stock outstanding. The company began operations on January 1, 2010. The cash dividends declared and paid during each of the first three years of State of Grace's operations are shown next. Calculate the amounts that went to the preferred shareholders and the common shareholders (SHs) each year.

Year	Total Dividends Paid	Dividends to Preferred SHs	Dividends to Common SHs
2010	$100,000		
2011	70,000		
2012	98,000		

E8-45B. *Analyze equity section of balance sheet. (LO 1, 2).* Frozen Entrée Corporation had the following stockholders' equity section on the June 30, 2011, balance sheet:

Preferred stock, $125 par, 8% cumulative	$1,112,500
Common stock, $3 par value	900,000
Paid-in capital in excess of par, common stock	1,500,000
Retained earnings	3,115,000
Total	$6,627,500

1. How many shares of common stock are classified as issued?
2. How many shares of common stock are outstanding?
3. How many shares of preferred stock are outstanding?
4. What was the average selling price of a share of common stock?
5. If $145,000 of dividends was declared and there were $15,000 dividends in arrears at that time, how much of the dividend would go to the common shareholders?

E8-46B. *Record stock transactions. (LO 1, 2, 3).* Minute Magazine Publications, Inc., is authorized to issue both preferred and common stock. Minute Magazine's preferred stock is $155 par, 10% preferred stock. During the first month of operations, the company engaged in the following transactions related to its stock. For each of the following transactions, show how it would be recorded in the accounting equation:

May 1	Issued 50,000 shares of $1.00 par value common stock for cash at $12 per share
May 9	Issued 2,000 shares of preferred stock at par
May 17	Purchased 2,500 shares of common stock to be held in the treasury for $15 per share
May 21	Issued 35,000 shares $1.00 par value common stock for cash at $18 per share
May 28	Sold 2,000 shares of the treasury stock purchased on the 17th for $20 per share
May 31	Declared a $39,000 dividend

E8-47B. *Prepare equity section of the balance sheet. (LO 1, 2, 3, 6).* Use the data from E8-46B to prepare the shareholders' equity section of the balance sheet at May 31. Retained earnings at month-end are $105,000.

E8-48B. *Analyze equity accounts. (LO 1, 2, 3, 5).* The following balances were shown on the year-end balance sheets for 2010 and 2011 for High Note Publishing Company. For each item, give the most likely reason for the change from one year to the next.

	December 31, 2010	December 21, 2011	Explanation
Common stock	$ 35,000	$ 43,000	
Paid-in capital	$115,000	155,000	
Retained earnings	$142,000	*$160,500	
Treasury stock	$ (2,125)	$ (2,625)	

*Net income for the year was $22,750.

E8-49B. *Analyze equity section of balance sheet. (LO 1, 2, 3).* Answer the following questions using the shareholders' equity section of Technical Data Corporation's balance sheet at June 30:

Shareholders' equity	
Preferred stock, cumulative, 20,000 shares authorized, 5,000 shares issued and outstanding	$ 550,000
Additional paid-in capital, preferred stock	50,000
Common stock, $1.25 par, 650,000 shares authorized, 350,000 shares issued	437,500
Additional paid-in capital, common stock	2,012,500
Retained earnings	1,425,000
	4,475,000
Less: treasury stock (6,500 common shares)	(52,000)
Total shareholders' equity	$4,423,000

1. How many shares of common stock are outstanding?
2. On average, what was the issue price of the common shares issued?
3. What is the par value of the preferred stock?
4. If the total annual dividend on preferred stock is $49,500, what is the dividend rate on preferred stock?
5. On average, how much per share did the company pay for the treasury stock?

E8-50B. *Record stock transactions. (LO 1, 2, 3, 4).* On the first day of the fiscal year, TH Construction, Inc., had 150,000 shares of $1.00 par common stock issued (at par) and outstanding, and the retained earnings balance was $275,000. Show each of the following transactions in the accounting equation:

1. Issued 10,000 additional shares of common stock for $5 per share
2. Declared and distributed a 10% stock dividend when the market price was $5 per share
3. Issued 20,000 additional shares of common stock for $7 per share
4. Declared a cash dividend on outstanding shares of $0.75 per share
5. Paid the dividend declared in item (4)
6. Purchased 8,000 shares of treasury stock for $9 per share
7. Sold 6,500 shares of treasury stock for $10 per share
8. Sold 1,400 shares of treasury stock for $8 per share
9. Declared 2-for-1 stock split

E8-51B. *Prepare equity section of the balance sheet. (LO 1, 2, 3, 4, 6).* Use the data from E8-50B to prepare the shareholders' equity section of the balance sheet at year end. Net income for the year was $90,000.

E8-52B. *Prepare equity section of the balance sheet. (LO 1, 3, 5, 6).* The following account balances can be found in the general ledger of McKinney de Garcia Energy Products Corporation at year end. Prepare the shareholders' equity section of the balance sheet.

Retained earnings	$ 320,000
Treasury stock (5,000 common shares at cost)	45,000
Common stock ($1 par, 600,000 shares authorized, 275,000 shares issued)	275,000
Additional paid-in capital, common stock	1,787,500
Preferred stock ($6 par value, 10%, 80,000 shares authorized, 25,000 shares issued)	150,000
Additional paid-in capital, preferred stock	25,000

E8-53B. *Calculate return on equity and earnings per share. (LO 7).* The following financial information is available for Book Publishing Company at the end of its two most recent fiscal years.

The company has no preferred stock. Calculate (1) return on equity and (2) earnings per share for 2010 and 2011. What do the ratios indicate about the company's performance during the year?

(amounts in thousands)	2011	2010
Average common stockholders' equity	$3,120	$2,470
Dividends declared for common stockholders	600	530
Net income	6,020	3,130
Weighted average number of common shares outstanding during the year	4,100	3,270

E8-54B. *Analyze effects of equity transactions on financial statements. (LO 1, 2, 3, 4, 5).* Analyze the following transactions and indicate the dollar increase (+) or decrease (−) each has on the balance sheet. If there is an overall change in shareholders' equity, also indicate whether contributed capital, retained earnings, or treasury stock is affected. If the transaction has no effect on the balance sheet, enter NA for that item. The first row is filled in for you as an example.

	Assets	Liabilities	Shareholders' Equity	Equity Section Affected
Issued 1,000 shares of $0.50 par common stock at par	+500		+500	Contributed capital
Issued 2,500 shares of $0.50 par common stock for $6.50				
Declared a cash dividend of $0.50 per share				
Paid the $0.50 cash dividend				
Purchased 175 shares of treasury stock for $9 per share				
Sold 65 shares of treasury stock for $9 per share				
Declared and distributed a 5% common stock dividend (when the market price was $9 per share)				
Announced a 2-for-1 stock split				
Issued 5,000 shares of $75 par, 6% noncumulative preferred stock at par				

Problems
Set A

P8-55A. *Account for stock transactions. (LO 1, 6).* Runnels Geometric Designs Company was started on January 1, 2009. The company is authorized to issue 50,000 shares of 8%, $105 par value preferred stock and 600,000 shares of common stock with a par value of $2 per share. The following stock transactions took place during 2009:

January 15	Issued 5,000 shares of common stock for cash at $3 per share
March 1	Issued 10,000 shares of preferred stock for cash at $110 per share
July 12	Issued 30,000 shares of common stock for cash at $5 per share
October 10	Issued 5,000 shares of preferred stock for cash at $108 per share
December 1	Issued 20,000 shares of common stock for cash at $7 per share

Requirements

1. Show each transaction in the accounting equation.
2. Prepare the contributed capital portion of the stockholders' equity section of the balance sheet at December 31, 2009.

P8-56A. *Analyze and record stock dividend transactions. (LO 4).* As of December 31, 2010, Hargrove Dynamics, Inc., had 75,000 shares of $5 par value common stock issued and outstanding. The retained earnings balance was $265,000. On January 15, 2011, Hargrove Dynamics declared and issued an 8% stock dividend to its common shareholders. At the time of the dividend, the market value of the stock was $25 per share.

Requirements
1. Show how the stock dividend would affect the accounting equation.
2. How many shares of stock are outstanding after the stock dividend?
3. If you owned 7% of the outstanding common stock of Hargrove Dynamics, Inc., before the stock dividend, what is your percentage ownership after the stock dividend?

P8-57A. *Analyze and record stock transactions and prepare equity section of balance sheet. (LO 1, 2, 3, 4, 5, 6).* The following information pertains to the equity accounts of Bottling Company:
   a. Contributed capital on January 1, 2010, consisted of 80,000 issued and outstanding shares of common stock with par value of $1; additional paid-in capital in excess of par of $480,000; and retained earnings of $560,000.
   b. During the first quarter of 2010, Bottling Company issued an additional 5,000 shares of common stock for $7 per share.
   c. On July 15, the company declared a 3-for-1 stock split.
   d. On October 15, the company declared and distributed a 5% stock dividend. The market price of the stock on that date was $8 per share.
   e. On November 1, the company declared a dividend of $0.90 per share to be paid on November 15.
   f. Near the end of the year, the company's CEO decided the company should buy 1,000 shares of its own stock. At that time, the stock was trading for $9 per share in the stock market.
   g. Net income for 2010 was $75,500.

Requirements
1. Show how each of the transactions would affect the accounting equation.
2. Prepare the shareholders' equity section of the balance sheet at December 31, 2010.

P8-58A. *Record stock transactions, prepare equity section of balance sheet, and calculate ratios. (LO 1, 2, 3, 5, 6, 7).* On January 1, 2011, Classic Clothing Corporation's shareholders' equity account balances were as follows:

Preferred stock (5%, $80 par noncumulative, 35,000 shares authorized)	$ 800,000
Common stock ($1 par value, 750,000 shares authorized)	500,000
Additional paid-in capital, preferred stock	30,000
Additional paid-in capital, common stock	2,000,000
Retained earnings	1,650,000
Treasury stock—common (10,000 shares, at cost)	60,000

During 2011, Classic Clothing Corporation engaged in the following transactions:

January 1	Issued 10,000 shares of common stock for $6 per share
April 1	Purchased 10,000 additional shares of common treasury stock at $8 per share
June 1	Declared the annual cash dividend on preferred stock, payable June 30
December 1	Declared a $0.55 per share cash dividend to common stockholders payable December 31, 2011

Net income for the year was $940,000.

Requirements
1. Show each of the transactions in the accounting equation.
2. Prepare the shareholders' equity section of the balance sheet at December 31, 2011.
3. Calculate return on common stockholders' equity for the year ended December 31, 2011.

P8-59A. *Prepare equity section of balance sheet. (LO 1, 2, 5, 6).* On November 1, 2009, Dazzling Desserts Corporation had 300,000 shares of $1 par common stock issued and outstanding. The shareholders' equity accounts at November 1, 2009, had the following balances:

Common stock	$ 300,000
Additional paid-in capital	2,700,000
Retained earnings	3,500,000

The following transactions occurred during the fiscal year ended October 31, 2010:
a. On November 30, issued 30,000 shares of 7%, $95 par, cumulative preferred stock at $100.
b. On December 31, reacquired 5,000 shares of common stock for $12 per share.
c. On January 1, declared a cash dividend of $0.75 per share on the common stock outstanding, payable on January 31, 2010, to shareholders of record on December 15.
d. Declared and paid dividends to preferred shareholders on March 1, 2010.
e. Net income for the year ended October 31, 2010, was $675,000.

Requirement

Prepare the shareholders' equity section of Dazzling Desserts' balance sheet at October 31, 2010.

P8-60A. *Analyze equity section of balance sheet. (LO 1, 2, 3, 5).* The following information is from the equity sections of the comparative balance sheets for Freedman Cosmetics Company:

	December 31, 2010	December 31, 2009
Common stock ($20 par)	$ 600,000	$500,000
Additional paid-in-capital	800,000	400,000
Retained earnings	105,000	55,000
Total shareholders' equity	$1,505,000	$955,000

Net income for the year ended December 31, 2010, was $250,000.

Requirements

1. How many new shares of common stock were issued during 2010?
2. What was the average issue price of the stock issued during 2010?
3. What was the amount of dividends declared during 2010?
4. Did the company have any treasury shares at the end of 2010?

P8-61A. *Analyze equity section of balance sheet. (LO 1, 2, 5).* At June 30, 2011, Vision Specialty Company reported the following on its comparative balance sheets:

	June 30, 2011	June 30, 2010
Common stock		
Authorized: 1,200 shares		
Issued: 1,000 shares at June 30, 2011	$20,000	
800 shares at June 30, 2010		$16,000
Paid-in capital in excess of par	22,000	16,000
Retained earnings	40,000	29,500

Requirements

1. What is the par value of the company's common stock?
2. Did the company issue any new shares during the fiscal year ended June 30, 2011?
3. What was the approximate (average) issue price of the stock issued during the year ended June 30, 2011?
4. Did Vision Specialty Company earn net income (loss) during the year ended June 30, 2011? Assuming no dividends were declared and paid, how much was net income (loss)?

P8-62A. *Analyze equity section of balance sheet. (LO 1, 2, 3, 4).* The following information is from the equity section of the comparative balance sheets of Veridian Dynamic, Inc.:

Veridian Dynamics, Inc.
From the **Consolidated Balance Sheets**

Shareholders' equity:	June 30, 2010	June 30, 2009
Common stock, $1.00 par value; 500,000 shares issued and _____ shares outstanding at June 30, 2010; and 320,000 shares issued and _____ shares outstanding at June 30, 2009.	$ 500,000	$ 320,000
Additional paid-in-capital	3,180,000	1,920,000
Retained earnings	1,050,000	975,000
Treasury stock, at cost, 15,000 shares at June 30, 2010, and 9,000 shares at June 30, 2009	(105,000)	(54,000)

Requirements

1. What was the average issue price per share of the 500,000 shares classified as "issued" at June 30, 2010? (Round the answer to the nearest cent.)
2. What was the average issue price of the 180,000 shares of common stock issued during the fiscal year ended June 30, 2010?
3. How many shares were outstanding at June 30, 2010? How many shares were outstanding at June 30, 2009?
4. How many shares did the company buy back during the year? What was the average cost of a share of the treasury shares purchased during the year? (Assume no treasury stock was sold during the year.)
5. If no dividends were declared and paid, what was net income for the year ended June 30, 2010?

Set B

P8-63B. *Account for stock transactions. (LO 1, 6).* Clarkson Chivas, Inc., was started on July 1, 2010. The company is authorized to issue 200,000 shares of 6%, $110 par value preferred stock, and 1,500,000 shares of common stock with a par value of $1 per share. The following stock transactions took place during the fiscal year ended June 30, 2011:

July 15	Issued 10,000 shares of common stock for cash at $2 per share
October 1	Issued 5,000 shares of preferred stock for cash at $115 per share
January 12	Issued 15,000 shares of common stock for cash at $4 per share
March 10	Issued 7,500 shares of preferred stock for cash at $120 per share
June 1	Issued 25,000 shares of common stock for cash at $6 per share

Requirements

1. Show each transaction in the accounting equation.
2. Prepare the contributed capital portion of the shareholders' equity section of the balance sheet at June 30, 2011.

P8-64B. *Analyze and record stock dividend transactions. (LO 4).* At June 30, 2010, Soft Fabrics Manufacturing had 150,000 shares of $7 par common stock issued and outstanding. The retained earnings balance was $190,000. On July 15, 2010, Soft Fabrics declared and issued a 5% stock dividend to its common shareholders. At the time of the dividend, the market value of the stock was $15 per share.

Requirements

1. How would the stock dividend be shown in the accounting equation?
2. How many shares of stock are outstanding after the stock dividend?
3. If you owned 10% of the outstanding common stock of Soft Fabrics Manufacturing before the stock dividend, what is your percentage ownership after the stock dividend?

P8-65B. *Analyze and record stock transactions and prepare equity section of balance sheet. (LO 1, 2, 3, 4, 5, 6).* The following information pertains to Books & Calendars, Inc.:

  a. Contributed capital on November 1, 2009, consisted of 75,000 issued and outstanding shares of common stock with par value of $2; additional paid-in capital in excess of par of $375,000; and retained earnings of $525,000.

  b. During the first quarter of the fiscal year, Books & Calendars issued an additional 10,000 shares of common stock for $6 per share.

  c. On April 15, the company declared a 2-for-1 stock split.

  d. On May 31, the company declared and distributed a 10% stock dividend. The market price of the stock on that date was $8 per share.

  e. On June 30, the company declared a dividend of $0.25 per share to be paid on July 15.

  f. During October 2010, Books & Calendars' CEO decided the company should buy 2,000 shares of its own stock. At that time, the stock was trading for $9 per share.

  g. Net income for the year ended October 31, 2010, was $67,500.

Requirements

1. Show each of the transactions in the accounting equation.
2. Prepare the shareholders' equity section of the balance sheet at October 31, 2010.

P8-66B. *Record stock transactions, prepare equity section of balance sheet, and calculate ratios. (LO 1, 2, 3, 5, 6, 7).* On January 1, 2010, the Manny's Make-up Corporation shareholders' equity account balances were as follows:

Preferred stock (7.5%, $110 par noncumulative, 20,000 shares authorized)	$ 550,000
Common stock ($2 par value, 3,000,000 shares authorized)	800,000
Additional paid-in capital, preferred stock	50,000
Additional paid-in capital, common stock	1,600,000
Retained earnings	1,890,000
Treasury stock—common (1,000 shares, at cost)	9,000

During 2010, Manny's Make-up Corporation engaged in the following transactions:

January 1	Issued 10,000 shares of common stock for $10 per share
March 1	Purchased 1,000 additional shares of common treasury stock at $12 per share
June 1	Declared the annual cash dividend on preferred stock, payable June 30
December 1	Declared a $0.50 per share cash dividend to common stockholders payable December 31, 2010

Net income for the year was $641,250.

Requirements

1. Show the transactions in the accounting equation.
2. Prepare the shareholders' equity section of the balance sheet at December 31, 2010.
3. Compute earnings per share and return on common shareholders' equity for the year ended December 31, 2010.

P8-67B. *Prepare equity section of balance sheet. (LO 1, 2, 5, 6).* On July 1, 2009, Pet Supplies Company had 600,000 shares of $0.50 par common stock issued and outstanding. The shareholders' equity accounts at July 1, 2009, had the following balances:

Common stock	$ 300,000
Additional paid-in capital	1,500,000
Retained earnings	2,650,000

The following transactions occurred during the fiscal year ended June 30, 2010:

  a. On July 30, issued 40,000 shares of $75 par value, 5% cumulative preferred stock at $85.

  b. On October 1, reacquired 10,000 shares of common stock for $4 per share.

c. On December 1, declared a cash dividend of $1.00 per share on the common stock outstanding, payable on December 31, 2009, to shareholders of record on November 15.
d. Declared and paid dividends to preferred shareholders on December 31, 2009.
e. Net income for the year ended June 30, 2010, was $925,000.

Requirement

Prepare the shareholders' equity section of Pet Supplies Company's balance sheet at June 30, 2010.

P8-68B. *Analyze equity section of balance sheet. (LO 1, 2, 3, 5).* The following information was shown on the recent comparative balance sheets for Snipes Couriers, Inc.:

	June 30, 2011	June 30, 2010
Common stock ($5 par)	$250,000	$100,000
Additional paid-in-capital	300,000	60,000
Retained earnings	89,000	68,000
Total shareholders' equity	$639,000	$228,000

Net income for the year ended June 3, 2011, was $42,000.

Requirements

1. How many shares of common stock were issued to new shareholders during the year ended June 30, 2011?
2. What was the average issue price of the stock issued during the year ended June 30, 2011?
3. What was the amount of dividends declared during the year ended June 30, 2011?
4. Can you tell if the company had any treasury shares at June 30, 2011?

P8-69B. *Analyze equity section of balance sheet. (LO 1, 2, 5).* At December 31, 2009, Orange Cleaning Supplies Company reported the following on its comparative balance sheet, which included 2008 amounts for comparison:

	December 31	
	2009	2008
Common stock		
Authorized: 5,000 shares		
Issued: 2,900 shares in 2009	$29,000	
2,800 shares in 2008		$28,000
Paid-in capital in excess of par	8,700	5,780
Retained earnings	30,100	28,600

Requirements

1. What is the par value of the company's common stock?
2. Did the company issue any new shares during the fiscal year ended December 31, 2009?
3. What was the approximate (average) issue price of the stock issued during the year ended December 31, 2009?
4. Did Orange Cleaning Supplies Company earn net income (loss) during the year ended December 31, 2009? Assuming no dividends were paid this year, what was net income (loss)?

P8-70B. *Analyze equity section of balance sheet. (LO 1, 2, 3, 4).* The following information is from the equity section of the comparative balance sheets of Shelby Electronics, Inc.:

Shelby Electronics, Inc.
From the **Consolidated Balance Sheets**

	November 30, 2010	November 30, 2009
Common stock, $2.00 par value; 250,000 shares issued and _____ shares outstanding at November 30, 2010; and 175,000 shares issued and _____ shares outstanding at November 30, 2009	500,000	350,000
Additional paid-in capital	2,175,000	1,050,000
Retained earnings	675,000	580,000
Treasury stock at cost, 20,000 shares at November 30, 2010, and 16,000 shares at November 30, 2009	(140,000)	(96,000)

Requirements

1. What was the average issue price per share of the 250,000 shares classified as "issued" at November 30, 2010? (Round the answer to the nearest cent.)
2. What was the average issue price of the 75,000 shares of common stock issued during the fiscal year ended November 30, 2010?
3. How many shares were outstanding at November 30, 2010? How many shares were outstanding at November 30, 2009?
4. How many shares did the company buy back during the year? What was the average cost of a share of the treasury shares purchased during the year? (Assume no treasury stock was sold during the year.)
5. If no dividends were declared and paid, what was net income for the year ended November 30, 2010?

Financial Statement Analysis

FSA8-1. *Analyze equity section of balance sheet. (LO 1, 2, 5).* ConAgra Foods reported the following information on its comparative balance sheet at May 25, 2008 (dollars in millions):

	May 25, 2008	May 27, 2007
Common stock, par value _____		
Authorized: 1.2 billion shares		
Issued: 566,653,605 shares in 2008	$2,833.4	
566,410,152 shares in 2007		$2,832.2
Additional paid-in capital	866.9	816.8
Retained earnings	3,409.5	2,856.0
Accumulated other comprehensive income	286.5	(5.9)
Treasury stock, at cost 82,282,300 and		
76,631,063 shares, respectively	(2,058.9)	(1,916.2)

1. Explain what Additional paid-in capital and retained earnings each represent.
2. What is the approximate par value of ConAgra's common stock?
3. How many new shares of common stock did the company issue during the fiscal year ended May 25, 2008?
4. What was the approximate (average) issue price of the stock issued during the year?
5. Did ConAgra earn a net income during the year?
6. If ConAgra paid dividends of $377.1 (million) total, what would you estimate net income for the year to be?

FSA8-2. *Analyze equity section of balance sheet. (LO 1, 3, 5).* The following information is from the comparative balance sheets of Ameristar Casinos, Inc.:

Adapted from Ameristar Casinos, Inc.
From the **Consolidated Balance Sheets**

(amounts in thousands, except share data)

Shareholders' equity:	December 31, 2008	December 31, 2007
Preferred stock, $0.01 par value, 30,000,000 shares authorized; none issued and outstanding	–	–
Common stock, $0.01 par value; 120,000,000 shares authorized; 58,093,041 shares issued and _____ shares outstanding at December 31, 2008; and 57,946,167 shares issued and _____ shares outstanding at December 31, 2007	$ 581	$ 579
Additional paid-in-capital	246,662	234,983
Retained earnings	136,551	285,238
Other comprehensive gain (loss)	(27,295)	
Treasury stock, at cost, 792,322 shares at December 31, 2008, and 787,236 shares at December 31, 2007	(17,719)	(17,674)
Total shareholders' equity	$338,780	$503,126

1. How many shares of common stock were outstanding at December 31, 2008?
2. How many shares of common stock were outstanding at December 31, 2007?
3. What was the average issue price per share of the 58,093,041 shares classified as "issued" at December 31, 2008? (Round the answer to the nearest cent.)
4. The company paid cash dividends of $18,015 (in thousands) during the year ended December 31, 2008. What was the company's net income or net loss for the year ended December 31, 2008?

FSA8-3. *Analyze equity section of balance sheet. (LO 3, 7).* Use the annual report of Barnes & Noble, Inc., found on the firm's Web site, www.barnesandnobleinc.com/for_investors/for_investors.html, to answer the following:

1. Does Barnes & Noble buy back its own stock? Where, in the financial statements, is this disclosed? Explain the treasury stock transaction(s) that took place during the most recent fiscal year.
2. Compute the return on equity for the two most recent consecutive years. What information do these ratios provide?

Critical Thinking Problems

Business Risk

When the stock market is going up over a long period of time, investors can become complacent about the risks of being a stockholder. After the significant decline of the stock market in 2008, people have begun to rethink the risk involved in owning stock. What kinds of risks do the owners of publicly-traded companies face? What could you do, as an investor, to continue to invest in the market but minimize your risk?

Ethics

AVX Electronics is very close to bringing a revolutionary new computer chip to the market. The company fears that it could soon be the target of a takeover by a giant telecommunications company if this news were to leak before the product is introduced. The current AVX management intends to redistribute the company's stock holdings so its managers will have a larger share of ownership. So, management has decided to buy back 20% of the company's common stock while the price is still quite low and distribute it to the managers—including themselves—as part of the company's bonus plan. Are the actions of AVX management ethical? Explain why this strategy would reduce the risk of a hostile takeover. Was any group hurt by this strategy?

Group Assignment

In groups, select two companies that you would invest in if you had the money. Find their financial statements on the Internet and examine the shareholders' equity section of their balance sheets. What does your analysis tell you about each firm? Is this a good investment? Explain your findings and conclusion.

Internet Exercise: Hershey Foods Corporation

Hershey is the market leader, ahead of Mars, Incorporated, in the U.S. candy market. The company makes such well-known chocolate and candy brands as Hershey's Kisses, Reese's peanut butter cups, Twizzlers licorice, Jolly Rancher, Mounds, Super Bubble gum, and Kit Kat (licensed from Nestlé). Its products are sold throughout North America and exported to over 90 countries.
    Go to www.hersheys.com.

IE8-1. Explore Investor's Relations. In what city is the Hershey factory located? The current stock quote (market price) of Hershey's stock is how much per share? Is this market price reflected on the Hershey balance sheet? If it is, where is it found?

Use the most recent annual report and find the consolidated balance sheets to answer the following questions.

IE8-2. How many types of stock have been authorized and issued? For the most recent year, how many shares are issued and are outstanding?

IE8-3. For the most recent year end, identify total stockholders' equity. Of this total, how much was contributed by shareholders for issued shares? On average, how much did shareholders pay per issued share? Is the average issue price more or less than the current market price? Give an explanation for this difference.

IE8-4. For the most recent year end, what amount of stockholders' equity is earned capital? What is the name of the earned capital account? Did earned capital increase or decrease compared with the previous year? What might cause this change?

IE8-5. Has the company reacquired any of its common stock? How you can tell? What is reacquired stock called? When a company reacquires stock does total stockholders' equity increase or decrease? Why might a company want to reacquire issued shares?

9

Preparing and Analyzing the Statement of Cash Flows

ETHICS Matters

Follow the Cash

In May 2008, a *Wall Street Journal (WSJ)* article emphasized the importance of cash flows in evaluating stocks. Because earnings can be affected by accounting choices, cash flows may be a better gauge than net income of a firm's financial health.

Headline earnings numbers—typically net income—can be massaged by perfectly legal tricks, such as changing a depreciation schedule or the way revenue is recognized. Cash flows—how much actual money a company spits out—are by no means immune from shenanigans, but many analysts consider them a cleaner way to assess a company's health.

In the *WSJ* article, Richard Sloan of Barclays Global Investors used General Electric Co. as an example of a company with a growing gap between net income and cash flow. He was quoted as saying that this "suggested the company had been stretching to meet its numbers."

In August 2009, GE agreed to pay a $50 million fine to the Securities and Exchange Commission (SEC) to settle civil fraud and other charges that GE's financial statements in 2002 and 2003 mislead investors. According to the director of the SEC's Division of Enforcement, "GE bent the accounting rules beyond the breaking point. Overly aggressive accounting can distort a company's true financial condition and mislead investors." In the settlement of these charges, GE did not admit or deny the allegations.

LEARNING OBJECTIVES

When you are finished studying Chapter 9, you should be able to:

1. Explain the importance of the statement of cash flows and the three classifications of cash included on it.

2. Explain the difference between the direct method and the indirect method of preparing the statement of cash flows.

3. Convert accrual amounts to cash amounts.

4. Prepare the *cash flows from operating activities* section of the statement of cash flows using the direct method.

5. Prepare the *cash flows from operating activities* section of the statement of cash flows using the indirect method.

6. Prepare the *cash flows from investing activities* section and the *cash flows from financing activities* section of the statement of cash flows.

7. Perform general analysis of the statement of cash flows and calculate free cash flow.

8. Use the statement of cash flows and the related controls to evaluate the risk of investing in a firm.

415

Did the gap between GE's cash flows and net income, as observed by Sloan, provide some hint about the accounting problems at GE that were yet to be uncovered? Never underestimate the insights to be gained by following the cash. Start by understanding the statement of cash flows, the topic of this chapter.

Sources: "Cash Flow Reigns Once Again," by Tom Lauricella. *Wall Street Journal*, May 12, 2008, p. C1 and "GE Settles Civil-Fraud Charges," by Paul Glader and Kara Scannell. *Wall Street Journal*, August 5, 2009, p. B2.

L.O.1
Explain the importance of the statement of cash flows and the three classifications of cash included on it.

The Importance of the Statement of Cash Flows

The statement of cash flows—one of the four financial statements a company must prepare as part of generally accepted accounting principles (GAAP) and International Financial Reporting Standards (IFRS)—shows all the cash the company has received and all the cash the company has disbursed during a specific accounting period. Each cash flow relates to one of three business activities—operating, investing, or financing activities. Exhibit 9.1 shows a summary of the information presented on the statement of cash flows.

EXHIBIT 9.1

The Statement of Cash Flows

A firm's statement of cash flows will include every cash inflow and outflow for a specific period of time or for a specific accounting period. The cash flows are divided into three categories: operating, investing, and financing.

	Operating	**Investing**	**Financing**
Types of transactions	Cash related to the day-to-day activities of running the business—revenue and expense transactions	Cash related to buying and selling assets that the firm plans to use for longer than one year	Cash receipts and disbursements related to loans (principal only); cash contributions from and distributions to owners
Examples			
Inflows	Cash collections from customers	Cash proceeds from the sale of land or building	Cash proceeds from a new stock issue
Outflows	Cash paid to vendors for inventory	Cash paid for new land or building	Cash dividends paid to shareholders
Cash flows are generally related to these balance sheet accounts	Current assets and current liabilities	Long-term assets	Long-term liabilities and shareholders' equity

Thousands of companies go bankrupt each year because they fail to plan their cash flows effectively. When the time comes to pay their bills, they do not have enough cash on hand. Preparing a cash budget is a crucial activity for all companies. It is more complicated than just estimating cash inflows and outflows for the accounting period. The sources of cash and the uses of cash must be estimated in detail—both the amounts of cash and when cash is needed. Each month, projected cash inflows and outflows must be budgeted by source and use. With this level of detail, a company can plan ahead for any cash shortage by (1) securing a line of credit from a local bank, (2) borrowing the money, or (3) altering the timing of its receipts (tightening up credit policies) or disbursements (postponing purchases).

A cash budget is a detailed plan of a company's estimated cash receipts and estimated cash disbursements, with very specific forecasts of the sources, uses, and the timing of the cash flows. The budgeted cash flows in the cash budget can then be compared with actual cash flows, and the comparison is the basis for planning and evaluating performance. To compare the actual cash flows for an accounting period with the period's cash budget, a company must produce details about the actual sources of cash and actual uses of cash from the company's records. Comparing actual cash flows with budgeted cash flows gets a company ready to prepare the next period's budgeted cash flows. Even though the focus of financial reporting is financial statements for shareholders and investors, the information about cash flows is equally useful to managers of a company.

Since Sara started her T-shirt business in January 2010, we have prepared the four basic financial statements for her business every month, including the statement of cash flows. The way we have prepared the statement of cash flows has been to do the following:

1. Identify every cash transaction on our accounting equation worksheet, and then
2. classify each cash amount as one of three types: operating, investing, or financing.

When we use a separate column in the accounting equation worksheet for cash transactions, we simply take each addition of cash and each subtraction of cash; then we classify each cash flow as cash from operating activities, cash from investing activities, or cash from financing activities. Because a real company has a much more complex accounting system, needed to handle thousands or millions of transactions, examining each transaction is not a feasible way for a company to prepare the statement of cash flows. In this chapter, we will discuss how the statement is actually prepared.

Two Methods of Preparing and Presenting the Statement of Cash Flows

Both GAAP and IFRS describe two ways of preparing the statement of cash flows: the **direct method** and the **indirect method**. These two methods are named for the way in which the operating section of the statement of cash flows (cash from operating activities) is prepared, either directly by presenting major classes of inflows and outflows of cash, or indirectly by starting with net income and adjusting it until you have the net cash from operating activities. For the other two sections, investing and financing, there is only one way to compute the cash flows: The transactions are directly identified. Thus, in any discussion about different methods of preparing a statement of cash flows, the difference between the direct method and the indirect method applies only to cash from operating activities.

Before we discuss the two different methods in detail, we will look at a simple example of the difference between these methods of preparing the statement of cash flows. We will start with the first month of business for a simple company with the following transactions:

1. Purchase of inventory for $250—paid cash of $200 to vendor with the remaining $50 on account (accounts payable)
2. Sales of all inventory for $600—$500 for cash and $100 on account (accounts receivable)
3. Purchase of supplies for cash of $30—used $20 worth of them, with $10 worth remaining for next month

Net income is calculated as follows:

$600	–	$250	–	$20	=	$330
Sales		Cost of goods sold		Supplies expense		Net income

Cash collected and disbursed is calculated next:

$500	–	$200	–	$30	=	$270
Cash sales		Inventory purchases		Supplies purchase		Net cash flow

This change from accrual basis numbers to cash basis numbers can be done in the two ways shown in Exhibit 9.2 on the following page—directly or indirectly. To use the direct method we will examine each item on the income statement, one by one. In contrast, the indirect method is more mechanical: Net income is adjusted for noncash items from the income statement and for all the changes in current assets and current liabilities, excluding cash. Exactly how this is done

L.O.2
Explain the difference between the direct method and the indirect method of preparing the statement of cash flows.

The **direct method** shows every cash inflow and outflow to prepare the statement of cash flows.

The **indirect method** starts with net income and makes adjustments for items that are not cash to prepare the statement of cash flows.

will be discussed later in the chapter. You may want to study the transactions and the exhibit again after you learn more about how to prepare the statements. Notice that the only cash flows in this example are cash flows from operating activities, and that both methods produce the same amount of net cash from operating activities.

Both methods of preparing the operating section of the statement of cash flows require information about the underlying transactions so the cash can be separated from the accrual accounting numbers. For example, the amount of sales must be examined to get the actual cash collected from making those sales. Supplies expense must be examined to get the actual cash paid for supplies. Doing this converts accrual-basis amounts to cash-basis amounts.

EXHIBIT 9.2

Comparison of the Direct and Indirect Methods for the Statement of Cash Flows

Both methods result in the same net cash from operating activities.

Statement of Cash Flows

(cash from operating activities only)

Direct Method		**Indirect Method**	
Cash from operating activities:		Cash from operating activities:	
Cash collected from customers	$500	Net income	$330
Cash paid for supplies	(30)	– increase in accounts receivable	(100)
Cash paid to vendors for inventory	(200)	– increase in supplies	(10)
Net cash from operating activities	$270	+ increase in accounts payable	50
		Net cash from operating activities	$270

Your Turn 9-1

What is the major difference between the direct and indirect methods of presenting the statement of cash flows? What are the similarities?

L.O.3
Convert accrual amounts to cash amounts.

Accrual Accounting versus Cash Basis Accounting

As you know, companies that follow GAAP maintain their accounting records using the accrual basis. Preparing the statement of cash flows actually involves converting the records of the business to cash basis. That is what you see in Exhibit 9.2. There are many reasons why accrual basis accounting and cash basis accounting are not generally the same.

Sales versus Cash Collected from Customers

For example, a company will record a sale and recognize the revenue on the income statement when the merchandise is shipped or delivered. Does the company always receive the cash at that time? No. Thus, the amount of revenue earned from sales for an accounting period may not be the same as the amount of cash collected during the period. At the end of the accounting period, when the company is preparing its financial statements, customers may still owe the company some money—there may be outstanding accounts receivable. That is one reason the cash collected from sales might not equal the amount of the sales for a specific accounting period.

Also, the company may have collected cash during the current period from sales made during the prior accounting period—accounts receivable from the prior year may have been collected in the current year. Thus, to calculate the cash collected from customers for the statement of cash flows, we must make an adjustment for the change in accounts receivable.

Suppose a company began 2011 with accounts receivable of $500. These accounts receivable were recorded during 2010 when the revenue from the sales was recognized. All sales are made on credit; and during 2011 the company had sales of $3,000. At the end of 2011, the balance in accounts receivable was $600. How much cash was collected from customers during 2011? Because accounts receivable started with a balance of $500 and ended with a balance of $600, the increase represents sales that have not been collected from the customers. Therefore, although sales amounted to $3,000, only $2,900 worth of those sales must have been collected in cash.

Beginning accounts receivable	$ 500
+ Sales	+3,000
− Cash collected from customers	− x
= Ending accounts receivable	$ 600

Simply solve this equation for x: $500 + 3,000 - x = 600$

$$x = \$2,900$$

Another way to think about it is first to suppose that customers paid off their old accounts of $500. If total sales were $3,000 and if an ending accounts receivable balance was $600, then $2,400 of the current sales must have been collected. The beginning balance of $500 was collected plus current sales of $2,400 have been collected—making the total cash collected from customers during the period equal to $2,900. This is the sort of reasoning that must be applied to each item on the income statement to prepare the statement of cash flows using the *direct* method.

Salary Expense versus Cash Paid to Employees

The amount for every item on the income statement is potentially different from the cash paid or received for it. As we just discussed, the dollar amount of sales is potentially different from cash collected from customers. For instance, cost of goods sold is potentially different from cash paid for inventory; insurance expense is potentially different from the cash paid to the insurance company; and so on, for all items on the income statement.

The change in a current asset or a current liability will reflect the difference between the accrual-based income statement amount and the cash amount. Consider an expense on the income statement. Suppose salary expense is shown on the year's income statement as $75,000. For the statement of cash flows, we want to show cash paid to employees as an operating cash outflow. What could make salary expense different from cash paid to employees?

First, we could have paid some employees cash that we owed them from last year. The cash payment would reduce the liability salaries payable. If we did pay some salaries we owed at the beginning of the year, that cash paid would be in addition to any current year's salary paid to employees. What else could make *cash paid to employees* different from salary expense? We could have incurred salary expense that will not be paid until next year. In other words, we recognized some salary expense that did not get paid to the employees. We must have recorded it as salaries payable. In both cases, the difference between salary expense and *cash paid to employees* is reflected in the change in salaries payable from the beginning of the year to the end of the year. This is the sort of reasoning that must be applied to each current asset and each current liability (excluding cash) on the balance sheet to prepare the statement of cash flows.

Suppose we started the year with salaries payable of $690. Our salary expense for the year, as shown on the income statement, is $75,000. If the balance in salaries payable is $500 at year end, how much cash was actually paid to employees? First, we must have paid off the amount we owed at the beginning of the year, $690. Then, because the ending balance in salaries payable is $500, we must have paid only $74,500 ($75,000 − $500) of the current year's salary expense. Thus, the total cash paid to employees is $75,190 ($690 + $74,500).

Another way to interpret what happened is to say that we paid the full $75,000 of this year's expense in cash and we paid down our salaries payable by $190 ($690 down to $500). That total is $75,190. It's really just an analysis of the balance sheet account(s) related to the income statement account, where the cash amount is the unknown value we want to find:

Beginning balance in salaries payable	$ 690
Increased by salary expense	+75,000
Decreased by cash paid to employees	− x
Ending balance in salaries payable	$ 500

Solving for x gives $75,190, the cash amount we need for the statement of cash flows.

Your Turn 9-2

Robo Company began the year with $25,000 in accounts receivable. During the year, Robo's sales totaled $50,000. At year end, Robo had an accounts receivable balance of $15,000. How much cash did Robo collect from customers during the year? How is that amount of cash classified on the statement of cash flows?

L.O.4

Prepare the *cash flows from operating activities* section of the statement of cash flows using the direct method.

Preparing the Statement of Cash Flows: Direct Method

Now you are ready to learn the procedures for preparing a statement of cash flows. First, the cash from operating activities section of the statement of cash flows is prepared using one of the following two methods we have already discussed.

1. Direct method: Each item on the accrual-based income statement is converted to cash.
2. Indirect method: Net income is the starting point, and adjustments are made by adding and subtracting amounts necessary to convert net income into net cash from operating activities.

After you have determined the cash flows from operating activities, you determine the cash flows from investing activities and cash flows from financing activities. You will learn about them later in the chapter.

To use the direct method of computing cash flows from operating activities, we will begin with an analysis of the income statement. Item by item, we will analyze every amount on the statement to determine how much cash was actually collected or disbursed related to that item. (Exactly how a firm's accounting system would prepare the data may be different than our method here.)

Revenue → Cash Collected from Customers

The first item on the income statement is usually revenue. What makes revenue on the income statement different from cash collected from customers? Any cash collected for sales in previous periods—that is, accounts receivable—must be counted as cash collected even though it is not included as revenue. Conversely, any sales for the period for which cash has not been collected must be excluded from cash collections. Both cash collected but not counted as revenue and cash not collected but included in revenue can be identified by looking at the change in accounts receivable during the period.

We will use Team Shirts' third month of business—March—to see how this works. We start at the beginning of the income statement, shown in Exhibit 9.3 (first seen as Exhibit 3.13), for the month and analyze each amount to change it from accrual to cash.

EXHIBIT 9.3

Income Statement for Team Shirts for the Month Ended March 31

Team Shirts
Income Statement
For the Month Ended March 31, 2010

Sales revenue		$2,000
Expenses		
Cost of goods sold	$800	
Depreciation expense	100	
Insurance expense	50	
Interest expense	30	(980)
Net income		$1,020

Sales on the income statement for March amounted to $2,000. What we need to know for the statement of cash flows is how much cash was collected from customers during March. We need to see how accounts receivable changed during the month. On March 1, Team Shirts had $150 worth of accounts receivable, and on March 31 the firm had $2,000 worth of accounts receivable.

By comparing the balance sheet at the beginning of the month with the balance sheet at the end of the month, both shown in Exhibit 9.4, we can see accounts receivable increased by $1,850. The amount of the change in accounts receivable came from the current period's sales for which the cash was not collected.

EXHIBIT 9.4

Comparative Balance Sheets for Team Shirts

Team Shirts
Comparative Balance Sheets
At March 1 and March 31, 2010

	March 31	March 1		March 31	March 1
Cash	$ 3,995	$6,695	Accounts payable	$ 0	$ 800
Accounts receivable ...	2,000	150	Other payables	0	50
Inventory	300	100	Interest payable	30	0
Prepaid insurance	75	125	Notes payable	3,000	0
Prepaid rent	0	0	Total liabilities	3,030	850
Computer (net of $100 accumulated depreciation)	3,900	0	Common stock	5,000	5,000
			Retained earnings	2,240	1,220
			Total liabilities and		
Total assets	$10,270	$7,070	shareholder's equity	$10,270	$7,070

Analyze what happened to accounts receivable. It started with $150. Then during the month, credit sales of $2,000 were made (sales on the income statement). The ending balance in accounts receivable is $2,000. Thus, the cash collected from customers must have been $150 ($2,000 − $1,850). If you go back and look at the transactions for Team Shirts during March (in Chapter 3), you will find $150 was exactly the amount of cash the company collected from customers.

Beginning accounts receivable	$ 150
+ Credit sales	+2,000
− Cash collected	− x
= Ending accounts receivable	$ 2,000

Solving for x gives $150, the amount of cash collected from customers.

Cost of Goods Sold → Cash Paid to Vendors

Continuing down the March income statement, the next item is cost of goods sold of $800. This is the cost of the merchandise sold during the month. How does that compare with the amount of cash paid to vendors during the month? Did Team Shirts sell anything it bought the previous month from the beginning inventory, or did the company buy more goods in March than it actually sold in March? We need to look at what happened to the amount of inventory during the month. The beginning inventory balance was $100. The ending inventory balance was $300. That means Team Shirts bought enough inventory to sell $800 worth and to build up the inventory by an additional $200. Thus, purchases of inventory must have been $1,000. Did Team Shirts pay cash for these purchases of inventory?

To see how the purchases of $1,000 worth of inventory compare with the cash paid to vendors, we look at the change in accounts payable (to vendors). The beginning balance in accounts payable was $800, and the ending balance was zero. That means Team Shirts must have paid $1,000 to vendors for the month's purchases and the $800 owed from February. Thus, the total paid to vendors was $1,800.

Beginning inventory	$ 100
+ Purchases	+ x
− Cost of goods sold	−800
= Ending inventory	$ 300

When we solve for x, we find that Team Shirts purchases were $1,000. Now, to see how much cash we paid to vendors, we have to analyze accounts payable:

Beginning accounts payable	$ 800
+ Purchases (on account)	+1,000 (= x from above)
− Cash paid to vendors	− y
= Ending accounts payable	-0-

Solving for y, we find that $1,800 was the amount of cash paid to vendors.

Other Expenses → Cash Paid for Other Expenses

The next expense on the March 31 income statement is depreciation expense. Depreciation expense is a noncash expense. That means we do not have any cash outflow when we record depreciation expense. The cash we spend to buy equipment is considered an investing cash flow, and the periodic depreciation does not involve cash. Depreciation is one expense we can skip when we are calculating cash from operating activities using the direct method.

Insurance expense of $50 is shown on the March 31 income statement. How much cash was actually paid for insurance? When a company pays for insurance, the payment is generally recorded as prepaid insurance. Examining the change in the prepaid insurance account will help us figure out how much cash was paid for insurance during the month. Prepaid insurance started with a balance of $125 and ended with a balance of $75. Because the decrease in prepaid insurance is exactly the same as the insurance expense, Team Shirts did not pay for any insurance this month. All the expense came from insurance that was paid for in a previous period.

The last expense we need to consider is interest expense. On the income statement for March, we see interest expense of $30. Did Team Shirts pay that in cash? On the balance sheet, the company began the month with no interest payable and ended the month with $30 interest payable. If it started the month without owing any interest and ended the month owing $30, how much of the $30 interest expense did the company pay for with cash? None. Team Shirts must not have paid any cash for interest because it owes the entire amount of the expense at year end.

Team Shirts paid out one more amount of cash related to operating activities during the month. Can you find it? On the March 1 balance sheet, there is $50 that Team Shirts owed; it is called *other payables*. By the end of March, that payable has been reduced to zero. Only one thing could have caused that reduction: a cash payment to settle the obligation related to advertising. Thus, we will also put the cash outflow of $50 on the statement of cash flows.

Summary of Direct Method

To summarize, we have "translated" the accrual amounts found on the income statement to cash amounts for the statement of cash flows. The cash collected from customers was $150. Team Shirts paid its vendors cash of $1,800. It also paid $50 of other payables. Net cash flow from operating activities was $(1,700). The operating section of the statement of cash flows using the direct method is shown in Exhibit 9.5.

EXHIBIT 9.5

Cash from Operating Activities—Direct Method

> Team Shirts
> Partial Statement of Cash Flows
> For the Month Ended March 31, 2010

Cash from operating activities

Cash collected from customers	$	150
Cash paid to vendors		(1,800)
Cash paid for advertising		(50)
Net cash from operating activities		**$(1,700)**

Remember, Exhibit 9.5 shows only the cash flows from operating activities. To explain the entire change in cash from March 1 to March 31, the investing and financing cash flows must be included.

Your Turn 9-3

Flex Company began the year 2010 with $350 of prepaid insurance. For 2010, the company's income statement showed insurance expense of $400. If Flex Company ended the year with $250 of prepaid insurance, how much cash was paid for insurance during 2010? On the statement of cash flows, how would that cash be classified?

Preparing the Statement of Cash Flows: Indirect Method

L.O.5
Prepare the *cash flows from operating activities* section of the statement of cash flows using the indirect method.

Even though the Financial Accounting Standards Board (FASB) and the International Accounting Standards Board (IASB) have encouraged companies to use the direct method of preparing the statement of cash flows, more than 90% of companies use the indirect method. That is because most accountants think it is easier to prepare the statement of cash flows using the indirect method. Also, the requirement that a company using the direct method provide a reconciliation of net income to net cash from operating activities means more work for the company using the direct method. Some companies even suggest that their accounting systems do not produce the information needed to prepare the statement using the direct method.

Start with Net Income

Preparing the statement of cash flows using the indirect method—applied just to the operating section of the statement of cash flows—starts with net income. Following net income, any amounts on the income statement that are completely noncash must be added or subtracted to undo their original effect on net income. Typical noncash items are depreciation and amortization expenses and any gains or losses on the sale of assets. Remember that a gain or loss on the sale of a long-term asset is not cash; it is the difference between the book value of the asset and the proceeds from the sale. (We will include the proceeds from the sale in the cash from investing activities section of the statement of cash flows.)

We will start with net income for Team Shirts for March. Exhibits 9.3 and 9.4 show the numbers we need to prepare the statement of cash flows using the indirect method.

The net income for March was $1,020. The first adjustment we make is to add back any noncash expenses such as depreciation. For Team Shirts, we must add back to net income the $100 depreciation expense. When we calculated the net income of $1,020, we subtracted $100 that was not a cash outflow. So, we must add it back to net income in our task of changing net income to a cash number.

Next, we will adjust net income for other amounts on the income statement that are not cash flows. Recall that in the direct method, we use changes in accounts receivable to convert sales revenue into cash collected from customers, and we use changes in inventory and accounts payable to convert cost of goods sold to cash paid to vendors. For the indirect method, if we adjust net income for every change in each current asset—with the exception of cash—and every change in each current liability, we will make every adjustment we need to convert net income into net cash from operating activities.

We will continue preparing the statement of cash flows using the indirect method with Team Shirts for March. We start with net income of $1,020 and add back any noncash expenses. Depreciation expense of $100 is added back. Then, using Exhibit 9.4, we examine each current asset account and each current liability account for changes during the month.

Examine Current Asset and Current Liability Accounts

Accounts receivable increased by $1,850. That increase represents sales for which we did not collect any cash yet. Thus, we need to subtract this increase in accounts receivable from net income to convert net income into a cash number.

The next change in a current asset is the increase in inventory of $200. This $200 represents purchases made that have not yet been reported as part of cost of goods sold on the income statement because the items have not been sold. Still, Team Shirts did buy them (we will take into account any purchases for which the firm did not yet pay when we examine accounts payable), so the amount needs to be deducted from net income because it was a cash outflow.

Prepaid insurance decreased from $125 to $75. This decrease of $50 was deducted as insurance expense on the income statement, but it was not a cash outflow this period. This amount must be added back to net income because it was not a cash outflow.

The last changes in current assets and current liabilities are the changes in payables. Team Shirts started the month with $800 of accounts payable and $50 of other payables. Team Shirts ended the month with a zero amount of each of these. That means $850 was the cash outflow related to these two amounts. The other current liability is interest payable. It started the month with no interest payable but ended the month with $30 of interest payable. That is $30 Team Shirts did not pay out, so $30 must be added back.

Look at the operating section of the statement of cash flows for Team Shirts for March in Exhibit 9.6. The statement starts with net income and makes all the adjustments we discussed. Compare the cash from operating activities section of this statement of cash flows prepared using the indirect method with the same section using the direct method shown in Exhibit 9.5. The net cash flow from operating activities is the same no matter how we prepare it—when we prepare the statement by examining every cash transaction, as we did in Chapter 3; when we prepare it using the direct method, as we did earlier in this chapter; and when we prepare it using the indirect method, as we just did.

EXHIBIT 9.6

Cash from Operating Activities—Indirect Method

Team Shirts
Partial Statement of Cash Flows
For the Month Ended March 31, 2010

Net income	$ 1,020
+ Depreciation expense	100
− Increase in accounts receivable	(1,850)
− Increase in inventory	(200)
+ Decrease in prepaid insurance	50
− Decrease accounts payable	(800)
− Decrease other payables	(50)
+ Increase interest payable	30
Net cash from operating activities	$(1,700)

Exhibit 9.7 provides a summary of how to adjust net income into cash from operating activities. Although these "rules" always hold for the indirect method, be sure you understand the reasons for either adding or subtracting the change in the current asset or current liability account balance.

EXHIBIT 9.7

Indirect Method: Changing Net Income to Cash from Operations

What to Do	Example
Start with net income	net income
Add any noncash expenses	+ depreciation expense
Subtract any gains	− gain on sale of equipment
Add back any losses	+ loss on the sale of equipment
Deduct an increase in a current asset	− increase in accounts receivable
	− increase in prepaid rent
Add a decrease in a current asset	+ decrease in inventory
	+ decrease in prepaid insurance
Add an increase in a current liability	+ increase in accounts payable
	+ increase in salaries payable
Deduct a decrease in a current liability	− decrease in income taxes payable
	− decrease in accrued liabilities

Comparing the Direct and Indirect Methods

Which method is easier to understand? The presentation produced by the direct method—the presentation shown in Exhibit 9.5—gives details about cash that are often considered easier to understand than the details provided by the indirect method. Still, most companies today use the indirect method, which provides information not found on the statement prepared using the direct method. A change in this practice could be a real benefit to users of financial statements. A recent discussion paper (2008) released jointly by the FASB and the IASB has proposed that only the direct method be used in the future. Stay tuned for developments on this issue. It is not likely to be resolved easily or quickly.

Your Turn 9-4

Suppose a company had net income of $50,000 for the year. Depreciation expense, the only noncash item on the income statement, was $7,000. The only current asset that changed during the year was accounts receivable, which began the year at $6,500 and ended the year at $8,500. The only current liability that changed was salaries payable, which began the year at $2,500 and ended the year at $3,000. Assume this is all the relevant information. Calculate net cash from operating activities using the indirect method.

Cash from Investing and Financing Activities

In addition to cash from operating activities, there are two other classifications of cash flows found on the statement of cash flows: cash from investing activities and cash from financing activities. No matter which method you use to prepare the statement of cash flows, direct or indirect, the cash from investing activities and cash from financing activities sections are prepared the same way—by reviewing noncurrent balance sheet accounts. The primary amounts on the balance sheet to review are property, plant, and equipment; notes payable; bonds payable; common stock; and retained earnings.

L.O.6
Prepare the *cash flows from investing activities* section and the *cash flows from financing activities* section of the statement of cash flows.

Investing Activities

Information about cash flows related to investing activities will be found by analyzing the long-term asset section of the balance sheet. For Team Shirts the balance sheet at March 31 shows a computer with a cost of $4,000. The carrying value is $3,900 and the accumulated depreciation is $100, for a total cost of $4,000. The asset representing this computer was not on the March 1 balance sheet, so Team Shirts must have purchased a $4,000 computer during March. The purchase of a computer is an investing cash flow.

When we see that a company purchased a long-term asset, we must investigate how the company paid for the asset. In this case, we find that Team Shirts paid cash of $1,000 and signed a note for $3,000. We include only the $1,000 cash outflow in the statement of cash flows, but we must add a note disclosing the amount of the computer purchase financed by the note payable. All investing and financing activities must be disclosed, even if there was no cash involved.

Financing Activities

Information about cash flows related to financing activities will be found by analyzing the long-term liability section and the equity section of the balance sheet. Notice that on the balance sheet at March 1, Team Shirts shows no notes payable. On the balance sheet at March 31, notes payable shows a balance of $3,000. That means that Team Shirts borrowed $3,000 during March. Again, when we discover such a change, we must find out the details of the transaction before we can decide how the transaction affects the statement of cash flows. Generally, borrowing money using a note would result in a financing cash inflow. However, in this case, the note was given in exchange for a computer. Notice that the loan is disclosed, even though the amount is not included on the statement of cash flows. Whenever a company engages in a financing or investing activity, it must be disclosed on the statement of cash flows, even though the company never actually received or paid out any cash. The cash is considered implicit in the transaction. It is as if Team Shirts received the cash from the loan and immediately turned around and purchased the computer with it.

Other transactions we should look for when preparing the financing section of the statement of cash flows include any principal payments on loans and any new capital contributions—such as stock issued. We should also look for any dividends paid to the stockholders. For Team Shirts for March 2010, none of these transactions took place.

Putting It All Together

When we put the information about investing activities and financing activities with the cash from operating activities we have already prepared, we have all the information we need to complete the statement of cash flows. Look at the two statements in Exhibit 9.8. We used different methods to prepare the statements, but they are similar in form and amounts.

EXHIBIT 9.8A

Statement of Cash Flows (Direct)

Team Shirts
Statement of Cash Flows
For the Month Ended March 31, 2010

Cash from operating activities
Cash collected from customers	$ 150	
Cash paid to vendors	(1,800)	
Cash paid for advertising	(50)	
Net cash from operating activities		$(1,700)

Cash from investing activities
Purchase of computer	$(1,000)ᵃ	
Net cash from investing activities		(1,000)
Cash from financing activities		0
Net increase (decrease) in cash		$(2,700)
Beginning cash balance		6,695
Ending cash balance		$ 3,995

ᵃA computer was purchased for $4,000. A note was signed for $3,000 and cash paid was $1,000.

EXHIBIT 9.8B

Statement of Cash Flows (Indirect)

Team Shirts
Statement of Cash Flows
For the Month Ended March 31, 2010

Cash from operating activities
Net income	$ 1,020	
+ Depreciation expense	100	
− Increase in accounts receivable	(1,850)	
− Increase in inventory	(200)	
+ Decrease in prepaid insurance	50	
− Decrease in accounts payable	(800)	
− Decrease in other payables	(50)	
+ Increase in interest payable	30	
Net cash from operating activities		$(1,700)

Cash from investing activities
Purchase of computer	(1,000)ᵃ	
Net cash from investing activities		(1,000)
Cash from financing activities		0
Net increase (decrease) in cash		$(2,700)
Beginning cash balance		6,695
Ending cash balance		$ 3,995

ᵃA computer was purchased for $4,000. A note was signed for $3,000 and cash paid was $1,000.

Check it out. The balance sheets in Exhibit 9.4 show that cash went from $6,695 on March 1 to $3,995 on March 31. The difference is a $2,700 decrease in cash. Explaining that change in the cash balance is the purpose of the statement of cash flows.

Summary of Direct and Indirect Methods

As you have seen, there are two ways, both acceptable using GAAP, to prepare and present the statement of cash flows: the direct method and the indirect method. The direct method provides more straightforward details about cash from operating activities, because it shows the individual operating cash flows. When a company uses the direct method, GAAP requires that the company also show a reconciliation of net income to net cash from operating activities in a supplemental schedule. That reconciliation looks exactly like the operating section of the statement of cash flows using the indirect method.

The indirect presentation of the statement of cash flows is easier to prepare from the income statement and the beginning and ending balance sheets for the period, but the presentation of the information may not be as easy to understand. A company that uses the indirect method must make separate disclosures for cash paid for interest and cash paid for taxes somewhere in the financial statements. This is required by GAAP. Keep in mind that the investing activities and the financing activities sections for the two methods are identical; and the total change in cash is the same for both methods.

Applying Your Knowledge: Financial Statement Analysis

L.O.7
Perform general analysis of the statement of cash flows and calculate free cash flow.

Look at the statement of cash flows for AutoZone, Inc., shown in Exhibit 9.9 on the following page. First, notice the organization of the statement. The statement has the three required parts: (1) cash flows from operating activities; (2) cash flows from investing activities; and (3) cash flows from financing activities. Second, notice that the first section—cash provided by operating activities—is prepared using the indirect method.

Cash from Operating Activities—AutoZone

The statement starts with the amount for net income and makes several adjustments to that amount. Look at the adjustments and see if you understand what information they provide. For example, depreciation and amortization are added back to net income to work toward net cash from operating activities because the amounts for depreciation and amortization were subtracted in the original computation of net income but they were not cash expenditures. That subtraction is undone by adding the amounts back to net income. There are many other adjustments that are beyond the scope of an introductory accounting course, but you should understand why these adjustments are being made. The adjustments are "undoing" the effect of the noncash amounts that were included in the calculation of net income. Investors are looking for a positive net cash flow from operating activities. In the long run, this is crucial to the continuing success of any business.

Cash from Investing Activities—AutoZone

The cash flows from investing activities section of the statement shows capital expenditures as the first entry. Those are items such as property, plant, and equipment. Recall the discussion in Chapter 6 about capital versus revenue expenditures—capitalizing a cost versus expensing a cost. These are costs that have been capitalized by AutoZone. Other entries in the cash flows from investing activities section include cash inflows and outflows related to the purchase and sale of long-term assets not related to the normal operations of AutoZone. (When AutoZone buys the items that it resells in the normal course of business, the cash flows are included in the first section—cash provided from operating activities.)

The cash flows from investing activities section of the statement of cash flows gives information about the company's plans for the future. Investments in property, plant, and equipment may indicate an expansion or, at the very least, a concern about keeping the company's infrastructure up to date. Over time, a company's failure to invest in the infrastructure may indicate a problem.

EXHIBIT 9.9

AutoZone's Statement of Cash Flows

This statement of cash flows has been prepared using the indirect method.

AutoZone, Inc.
Statement of Cash Flows

(in thousands)	August 30, 2008 (53 Weeks)	August 25, 2007 (52 Weeks)	August 26, 2006 (52 Weeks)
	Year Ended		
Cash flows from operating activities:			
Net income	$ 641,606	$ 595,672	$ 569,275
Adjustments to reconcile net income to net cash provided by operating activities:			
Depreciation and amortization of property and equipment	169,509	159,411	139,465
Amortization of debt origination fees	1,837	1,719	1,559
Income tax benefit from exercise of stock options	(10,142)	(16,523)	(10,608)
Deferred income taxes	67,474	24,844	36,306
Share-based compensation expense	18,388	18,462	17,370
Changes in operating assets and liabilities:			
Accounts receivable	(11,145)	20,487	37,900
Merchandise inventories	(137,841)	(160,780)	(182,790)
Accounts payable and accrued expenses	175,733	186,228	184,986
Income taxes payable	(3,861)	17,587	28,676
Other, net	9,542	(1,913)	608
Net cash provided by operating activities	921,100	845,194	822,747
Cash flows from investing activities:			
Capital expenditures	(243,594)	(224,474)	(263,580)
Purchase of marketable securities	(54,282)	(94,615)	(159,957)
Proceeds from sale of investments	50,712	86,921	145,369
Disposal of capital assets	4,014	3,453	9,845
Net cash used in investing activities	(243,150)	(228,715)	(268,323)
Cash flows from financing activities:			
Net (repayments of) proceeds from commercial paper	(206,700)	84,300	(51,993)
Proceeds from issuance of debt	750,000	—	200,000
Repayment of debt	(229,827)	(5,839)	(152,700)
Net proceeds from sale of common stock	27,065	58,952	38,253
Purchase of treasury stock	(849,196)	(761,887)	(578,066)
Income tax benefit from exercise of stock options	10,142	16,523	10,608
Payments of capital lease obligations	(15,880)	(11,360)	—
Other	(8,286)	(2,072)	(3,778)
Net cash used in financing activities	(522,682)	(621,383)	(537,676)
Effect of exchange rate changes on cash	539	—	—
Net increase (decrease) in cash and cash equivalents	155,807	(4,904)	16,748
Cash and cash equivalents at beginning of year	86,654	91,558	74,810
Cash and cash equivalents at end of year	$ 242,461	$ 86,654	$ 91,558
Supplemental cash flow information:			
Interest paid, net of interest cost capitalized	$ 107,477	$ 116,580	$ 104,929
Income taxes paid	$ 313,875	$ 299,566	$ 267,913
Assets acquired through capital lease	$ 61,572	$ 69,325	$ —

Cash from Financing Activities—AutoZone

The cash flows from financing activities section of the statement of cash flows shows the cash flows related to the way the company is financed. Some of the items should be recognizable—proceeds from issuance of debt and proceeds from the sale of common stock. Notice the large amount that AutoZone spent to repurchase its own stock. All of the items in this section relate to AutoZone's financing. This information, when combined with the information on the balance sheet, gives the financial statement user a complete picture of the way the company is financing the business.

Other Characteristics of the Statement of Cash Flows

We should consider two more characteristics of the statement. First, following the calculation of the net increase or decrease in cash for the year, the statement includes the reconciliation from the year's beginning cash balance to the year's ending cash balance. Second, it also discloses supplementary information concerning the cash paid for interest and the cash paid for taxes during the year. This is required by GAAP. The information is not always on the face of the statement of cash flows, but, if not, it will be included in the notes.

Free Cash Flow

When analyzing the statement of cash flows, managers and analysts often calculate an amount called **free cash flow**. Free cash flow is defined as net cash from operating activities minus dividends and capital expenditures. This gives a measure of a firm's ability to engage in long-term investment opportunities. It is sometimes seen as a measure of a company's financial flexibility. For fiscal year ended August 30, 2008, AutoZone's free cash flow is quite adequate: $921.1 million − $243.6 million = $677.5 million. Looking over the capital expenditures for the past two years, you can see that $677.5 million should be enough for new investment opportunities.

> **Free cash flow** is equal to net cash from operating activities minus dividends and minus capital expenditures.

Your Turn 9-5

DRP Company reported net cash from operating activities of $45,600. Suppose the firm purchased $25,000 worth of new long-term assets for cash and did not pay any dividends during the year. The firm's average current liabilities for the year were $40,000. What was the firm's free cash flow during the year?

UNDERSTANDING
Business

Cash Burn Rate

General Motors had a cash problem. For the third quarter of 2008, the company had a net loss of $4.2 billion and was spending cash at a rate of approximately $6.9 billion per quarter. For the first quarter of 2009, the company reported a net loss of $6 billion and was spending cash at a rate of $10.2 billion per quarter.

The rate at which a firm spends its cash is called the cash burn rate. GM's cash burn rate was alarming in 2008 and early 2009. On June 1, 2009, GM filed for Chapter 11 bankruptcy protection.

Having enough cash is crucial for survival. When a business runs out of cash and cannot borrow any more money, then bankruptcy is a likely outcome. However, there are steps that any business can take to minimize the risk of running out of cash.

First, planning is essential. A cash budget is a crucial component of any budget. Know your cash burn rate! When preparing a cash budget, a firm estimates when it will collect cash and when it will disburse cash. In this process, the potential for experiencing a cash shortfall can be identified. Knowing the timing of cash flows enables a company to secure a line of credit or other short-term borrowing to

navigate the business through a shortfall and plan how to repay the short-term debt when the cash flow is adequate.

Second, managing cash flows is important. A key management function is to make sure that a company's receivables and inventories are being managed efficiently. Making sure there is an adequate level of product availability and appropriate credit polices are part of this function. A company does not want to tie up too much cash in receivables and inventory, so there is a balance that must be achieved. Collecting receivables in a timely manner is a crucial component of managing cash flows.

GM's problems have been complicated and extensive, but the company collapsed when it ran out of cash. Even billions of dollars from the U.S. government wasn't enough cash to keep the company from bankruptcy.

Even though Wall Street puts significant emphasis on a firm's earnings—net income—cash flows are also important. In some ways, managing cash is even more crucial than managing earnings. There is truth to the old adage that "cash is king."

Sources: "GM's Crippling Burn Rate," *BusinessWeek*, November 7, 2008, and "Time To Cut Our Losses? GM's Cash Burn Rate Increases To An Alarming $113 MILLION A Day!" AutoSpies.com, May 7, 2009.

The statement of cash flows provides important information for managers, creditors, and investors. In corporate annual reports, the statement of cash flows is presented with the other three basic financial statements—the income statement, the balance sheet, and the statement of changes in shareholders' equity—to provide information needed to evaluate a company's performance and to provide a basis for predicting a company's future potential.

Business Risk, Control, and Ethics

In Chapter 4, you learned about the controls a company should have to minimize the risks associated with cash. Now we will talk about investors' risks associated with the statement of cash flows. The misleading financial statements that have been at the heart of such failures as Enron and WorldCom have been the income statement and the balance sheet. Managers can rarely falsify cash inflows and outflows, so few people think of the statement of cash flows as a place where the ethics of a firm's management could be tested. However, managers can manipulate the classification of the cash flows. Because analysts are often looking for positive net cash flows from operating activities, especially in established companies, a firm's managers may feel some pressure to make sure that this part of the statement of cash flows is positive. There is an opportunity to engage in the same type of manipulation as WorldCom did when it classified expenses that belonged on the income statement as long-term assets on the balance sheet. Someone could misclassify cash outflows from operating activities as investing cash outflows. This changes the whole nature of such expenditures. Operating expenses are the costs of doing business, so investors want to see a low number. Investing cash outflows are often interpreted as a positive signal for future growth of the firm, so investors want to see a high number.

There is a great deal of information in the statement of cash flows, and it deserves careful consideration when you are analyzing a firm's financial statements. As with the information provided by the other financial statements, the statement of cash flows provides reliable information only when the firm's management is ethical.

Chapter Summary Points

- The statement of cash flows explains the change in cash from the beginning of the accounting period to the end of the accounting period—the amount on one balance sheet and the amount on the subsequent balance sheet.
- Cash flows can be categorized as cash from operating activities, cash from investing activities, or cash from financing activities. The statement of cash flows has a section for each of these categories.
- There are two methods—direct and indirect—for preparing and presenting the statement of cash flows. The direct method simply provides all operating cash inflows and outflows in a straightforward manner. The indirect method starts with net income and adjusts it for all noncash items—depreciation expense and gains or losses on the sale of long-term assets are typical noncash items. It also adjusts for changes in the current assets (excluding cash) and the current liabilities. These two methods describe the cash from the operating activities section of the statement. The other two sections—cash from investing activities and cash from financing activities—are the same on both types of statements of cash flows.
- Free cash flow is the amount of cash left after cash spent on investments in long-term assets and cash paid for dividends are subtracted from net cash from operating activities. It measures how much cash a firm has available for long-term investment opportunities.
- Before you invest in a firm, look at its statement of cash flows. A growing or established firm should be generating positive net cash flows from operating activities. Investing cash flows may provide insights into the firm's plans for the future. Be sure to look at the firm's cash situation over several years and also compare the firm's sources and uses of cash to those of its competitors.

Chapter Summary Problems

Suppose Attic Treasures, a retail store, provided you with the following comparative balance sheets and the related income statement. (Notice the most recent year is in the right column. It is always important to pay attention to the way the years are ordered on a set of comparative financial statements.) Assume the firm did not purchase any property, plant, and equipment (PPE) during the year.

Attic Treasures
Comparative Balance Sheets

At	January 30, 2008	January 30, 2009
Assets		
Cash	$ 23,000	$ 39,200
Accounts receivable	12,000	23,450
Merchandise inventory	25,200	28,100
Prepaid rent..................................	6,000	5,500
Property, plant, and equipment (PP&E)	79,500	70,000
Accumulated depreciation	(24,000)	(29,000)
Total assets	$121,700	$137,250
Liabilities and Shareholders' Equity		
Accounts payable	$ 12,300	$ 26,200
Income taxes payable	10,000	8,100
Long-term notes payable	39,700	25,800
Common stock and additional paid-in capital	18,500	20,000
Retained earnings	41,200	57,150
Total liabilities and shareholders' equity	$121,700	$137,250

Attic Treasures
Income Statement
For the Year Ended January 29, 2009

Sales		$234,900
Cost of goods sold		178,850
Gross margin		56,050
Selling expenses	$24,000	
General expense*	8,500	32,500
Income from operations		23,550
Interest expense		1,200
Income before income taxes		22,350
Income tax expense		3,400
Net income		$ 18,950

* includes rent expense of $2,000 and depreciation expense of $6,000

Instructions

Prepare a statement of cash flows. Your instructor will tell you whether to use the indirect method or the direct method (or both). Solutions for each are provided.

Solution

Direct Method

To prepare the cash from operating activities section using the direct method, go down the income statement and convert the accrual amounts to cash amounts by referring to the related current asset or current liability account.

1. Convert *sales* to *cash collected from customers*.

   Sales = $234,900.

   Increase in accounts receivable (AR) from $12,000 to $23,450 = $11,450.

   The increase in AR is the amount of sales Attic Treasures did NOT collect in cash, so the cash collected from customers is $234,900 − $11,450 = **$223,450**.

2. Convert *cost of goods sold* to *cash paid to vendors*. This takes two steps. First, convert cost of goods sold to total purchases.

   Cost of goods sold = $178,850.

   Increase in inventory from $25,200 to $28,100 = $2,900 of additional purchases.

   The increase in inventory is added to the cost of goods sold to get total purchases = $178,850 + $2,900 = $181,750. Then, convert total purchases to cash paid to vendors.

   Total purchases = $181,750.

   Increase in accounts payable of $12,300 to $26,200 = $13,900 represents purchases that did not get paid for, so cash paid to vendors = $181,750 − $13,900 = **$167,850**.

3. Convert *selling expenses* to *cash paid for selling expenses*. Because there are no current assets or current liabilities related to selling expenses (such as accrued selling expenses), Attic Treasures must have paid cash for this entire amount. So cash paid for selling expenses = **$24,000**.

4. Convert *general expenses* to *cash paid for general expenses*.

   General expenses = $8,500. This includes $2,000 rent expense and $6,000 depreciation expense. So we could break down the general expenses as follows:

Rent expense	$2,000
Depreciation expenses	$6,000
Other expenses	$ 500

   First, rent expense is related to prepaid rent on the balance sheet. Prepaid rent decreased from $6,000 to $5,500. This means the company used rent it had already (last year) paid for, so the decrease in prepaid rent reduces the rent expense by $500 to get cash paid for rent = $2,000 − $500 = $1,500.

   Depreciation expense is a noncash expense, so there is no cash flow associated with it. Other expenses of $500 must have been all cash because there are no associated current assets or current liabilities on the balance sheet. So the total cash paid for general expenses = $1,500 + $500 = **$2,000**.

5. Change *interest expense* to *cash paid for interest*.

   Interest expense = $1,200.

   This must have been all cash because there were no current assets or current liabilities associated with it. Cash paid for interest = **$1,200**.

6. Change *income tax expense* to *cash paid for taxes*:

   Income tax expense = $3,400.

   Decrease in income taxes payable from $10,000 to $8,100 = $1,900, which represents additional taxes the company paid beyond the income tax expense on the income statement. Cash paid for income taxes = $3,400 + $1,900 = **$5,300**.

You have now converted all the income statement items to cash inflows and outflows and are ready to prepare the first part of the statement of cash flows.

Cash from operating activities:	
Cash collected from customers	$223,450
Cash paid to vendors	(167,850)
Cash paid for selling expenses	(24,000)
Cash paid for general expenses	(2,000)
Cash paid for interest	(1,200)
Cash paid for income taxes	(5,300)
Net cash provided by operating activities	$ 23,100

7. Next, calculate cash from investing activities. An analysis of long-term assets shows that property, plant, and equipment decreased by $9,500. A decrease is caused by disposing of assets. Because the income statement showed no gain or loss from disposal of long-term assets, the assets must have been sold for book value. The property, plant, and equipment account decreased by $9,500 (the cost of the PPE sold) and the accumulated depreciation account increased by $5,000. Recall from the income statement that depreciation expense for the year was $6,000. If accumulated depreciation only increased by $5,000, then $1,000 must have been subtracted. That means the PPE sold had a book value of $8,500 ($9,500 − $1,000). Because there was no gain or loss on the disposal, the company must have received proceeds equal to the book value. So the cash inflow—proceeds—from disposal of PPE was an investing cash inflow of **$8,500**.

8. To calculate the cash flows from financing activities, analyze what happened in the long-term liability accounts and the shareholders' equity accounts. Long-term notes payable decreased from $39,700 to $25,800. That must have been a cash outflow of **$13,900**. Common stock and additional paid-in capital increased by **$1,500**. That must have been a cash inflow from the issue of stock of $1,500. Lastly, see if the company declared any dividends during the year. Retained earnings increased from $41,200 to $57,150 = $15,950. How does that compare to net income? Net income was $18,950 but retained earnings only increased by $15,950, so **$3,000** must have been declared as dividends. The absence of dividends payable indicates that the dividends were paid.

You are now ready to put the whole statement together using the direct method.

Attic Treasures
Statement of Cash Flows—Direct Method
For the Year Ended January 29, 2009

Cash from operating activities	
Cash collected from customers	$ 223,450
Cash paid to vendors	(167,850)
Cash paid for selling expenses	(24,000)
Cash paid for general expenses	(2,000)
Cash paid for interest	(1,200)
Cash paid for income taxes	(5,300)
Net cash provided by operating activities	$ 23,100
Cash from investing activities	
Cash proceeds from sale of property, plant, and equipment	$ 8,500
Cash from financing activities	
Cash paid on loan principal	(13,900)
Cash proceeds from stock issue	1,500
Cash paid for dividends	(3,000)
Net cash used for financing activities	$ (15,400)
Net increase in cash during the year	16,200
Cash balance, beginning of the year	23,000
Ending cash balance	$ 39,200

Indirect Method

To prepare the statement using the indirect method, start with net income. Adjust it for any non-cash expenses and the change in every current asset (excluding cash) and every current liability. The other two sections—cash from investing activities and cash from financing activities—are the same as for the direct method.

Attic Treasures
Statement of Cash Flows—Indirect Method
For the Year Ended January 29, 2009

Cash from operating activities	
Net income	$ 18,950
Add depreciation expense	6,000
Deduct increase in accounts receivable	(11,450)
Deduct increase in inventory	(2,900)
Add decrease in prepaid rent	500
Add increase in accounts payable	13,900
Deduct decrease in income taxes payable	(1,900)
Net cash provided by operating activities	$ 23,100
Cash from investing activities	
Cash proceeds from sale of property, plant, and equipment	$ 8,500
Cash from financing activities	
Cash paid on loan principal	$(13,900)
Cash proceeds from stock issue	1,500
Cash paid for dividends	(3,000)
Net cash used for financing activities	$(15,400)
Net increase in cash during the year	$ 16,200
Cash balance, beginning of the year	23,000
Ending cash balance	$ 39,200

Key Terms for Chapter 9

Direct method (p. 417)   Free cash flow (p. 429)   Indirect method (p. 417)

Answers to YOUR TURN Questions

Chapter 9

Your Turn 9-1

The difference is in the section that examines cash flows from operating activities. The direct method identifies each cash flow, whereas the indirect method starts with net income and adjusts it to a cash amount. The net cash flow from operating activities is the same no matter which method is used. The other two sections—cash from investing activities and cash from financing activities—are identical with both methods.

Your Turn 9-2

$50,000 + ($25,000 − $15,000) = $60,000.
This is a cash flow from operating activities.

Your Turn 9-3

$400 − ($350 − $250) = $300.
This is a cash flow from operating activities.

Your Turn 9-4

Begin with net income and add back depreciation expense: $50,000 + $7,000 = $57,000. Then, subtract the $2,000 increase in accounts receivable. Sales on account were included in net income but should be deducted if the cash has not been collected. Next, add the $500 increase in salaries payable. Some of the salaries expense, which was deducted on the income statement, was not paid at the balance sheet date.

$50,000 + $7,000 − $2,000 + $500 =

$55,500 net cash from operating activities.

Your Turn 9-5

Free cash flow = Net cash from operations − Purchase of long-term assets − Dividends = $45,600 − $25,000 − $0 = $20,600.

Questions

1. What is the purpose of the statement of cash flows?
2. Which two financial statements are used to prepare the statement of cash flows?
3. Describe the three categories of cash flows that explain the total change in cash for the year.
4. Why is the statement of cash flows so important?
5. What are the two traditional approaches for preparing and presenting the statement of cash flows? What is the difference between these two approaches?
6. Which types of business transactions would result in cash from operating activities? Give three examples of transactions that would be classified as cash flows from operating activities.
7. Which types of business transactions would result in cash flows from investing activities? Give three examples of transactions that would be classified as cash flows from investing activities.
8. Which types of business transactions would result in cash flows from financing activities? Give three examples of transactions that would be classified as cash flows from financing activities.
9. How is depreciation expense treated when using the direct method of preparing the statement of cash flows? When using the indirect method?
10. Which account(s) must be analyzed to determine the cash collected from customers? How is this cash flow classified?
11. Which account(s) must be analyzed to determine the proceeds from the sale of a building? How is this cash flow classified?
12. Which account(s) must be analyzed to determine the cash paid to vendors? How is this cash flow classified?
13. Which account(s) must be analyzed to determine the cash paid for dividends? How is this cash flow classified?
14. How is interest collected or interest paid classified on the statement of cash flows?
15. Define free cash flow and explain what this amount indicates about a firm.
16. How might a firm misuse the statement of cash flows to give investors a better impression of the firm's operations?

Multiple-Choice Questions

Use the following information to answer questions 1–3.

Quality Products engaged in the following **cash** transactions during May:

Purchase of inventory	$ 5,000
Cash proceeds from loan	$ 7,000
Cash paid for interest	$ 400
Cash collected from sales	$26,500
New stock issued	$25,000
Salaries paid to employees	$ 4,600
Purchase of new delivery van	$20,000

(Note: Answers in parentheses indicate net cash outflows.)

1. How much is net cash from financing activities?
   a. $ 7,000
   b. $25,000
   c. $31,600
   d. $32,000
2. How much is net cash from investing activities?
   a. $(20,000)
   b. $(25,000)
   c. $ 25,000
   d. $ 32,000
3. How much is net cash from operating activities?
   a. $26,500
   b. $ (3,500)
   c. $16,500
   d. $16,900
4. Cash from the sale of treasury stock
   a. would not be included in the statement of cash flows.
   b. would be classified as a contra-equity cash flow.
   c. would be classified as an investing cash flow.
   d. would be classified as a financing cash flow.
5. The cash proceeds from the sale of a building will be
   a. the cost of the building.
   b. the book value of the building.
   c. the book value plus any gain or minus any loss.
   d. shown on the financing portion of the appropriate financial statement.
6. If a firm has net investing cash inflows of $5,000; net financing cash inflows of $24,000; and a net increase in cash for the year of $12,000, how much is net cash from operating activities?
   a. Net cash inflow of $17,000
   b. Net cash inflow of $29,000
   c. Net cash outflow of $17,000
   d. Net cash outflow of $19,000
7. Depreciation for the year was $50,000 and net income was $139,500. If the company's transactions were all cash except those related to long-term assets, how much was net cash from operating activities?
   a. $139,500
   b. $189,500
   c. $ 89,500
   d. It cannot be determined from the given information.

Use the following information to answer questions 8–10.

The income statement and additional data for Frances Company for the year ended December 31, 2011, follow:

> ### Frances Company
> ### Income Statement
> ### For the Year Ended December 31, 2011

Sales revenue		$400,000
Expenses:		
Cost of goods sold	$165,000	
Salary expense	70,000	
Depreciation expense	55,000	
Insurance expense	20,000	
Interest expense	10,000	
Income tax expense	18,000	338,000
Net income		$ 62,000

Accounts receivable decreased by $12,000. Inventories increased by $6,000 and accounts payable decreased by $2,000. Salaries payable increased by $8,000. Prepaid insurance increased by $4,000. Interest expense and income tax expense equal their cash amounts. Frances Company uses the direct method for its statement of cash flows.

8. How much cash did Frances Company collect from customers during 2011?
   a. $400,000
   b. $412,000
   c. $406,000
   d. $388,000
9. How much cash did Frances Company pay its vendors during 2011?
   a. $173,000
   b. $165,000
   c. $167,000
   d. $163,000
10. How much cash did Frances Company pay for insurance during the year?
    a. $20,000
    b. $24,000
    c. $16,000
    d. $48,000

Short Exercises
Set A

All of the A exercises can be found within MyAccountingLab, an online homework and practice environment.

SE9-1A. *Identify cash flows. (LO 1).* Given the following cash transactions, classify each as a cash flow from (1) operating activities, (2) investing activities, or (3) financing activities.
   a. Payment to employees for work done
   b. Dividends paid to shareholders
   c. Payment for new equipment
   d. Payment to supplier for inventory
   e. Interest payment to the bank related to a loan

SE9-2A. *Calculate and identify cash flows. (LO 1, 3, 4).* College Television Company had supplies on its balance sheet at December 31, 2010, of $20,000. The income statement for 2011 showed supplies expense of $50,000. The balance sheet at December 31, 2011, showed supplies of $25,000. If no supplies were purchased on account (all were cash purchases), how much cash did College Television Company spend on supplies during 2011? How would that cash outflow be classified on the statement of cash flows?

SE9-3A. *Calculate and identify cash flows. (LO 3, 6).* A building cost $55,000 and had accumulated depreciation of $15,000 when it was sold for a gain of $5,000. It was a cash sale. How much cash was collected from this transaction and how would it be classified on the statement of cash flows?

SE9-4A. *Calculate and identify cash flows. (LO 1, 3, 4).* Sales for 2010 were $50,000; cost of goods sold was $35,000. If accounts receivable increased by $2,000; inventory decreased by $1,300; accounts payable decreased by $2,000; and other accrued liabilities decreased by $1,000, how much cash was paid to vendors and suppliers during the year? How would the cash from this transaction be classified on the statement of cash flows?

SE9-5A. *Evaluate adjustments to net income using the indirect method. (LO 5).* The income statement for Lilly's Company for the year ended June 30, 2010, showed sales of $50,000. During the year, the balance in accounts receivable increased by $7,500. What adjustment to net income would be shown in the operating section of the statement of cash flows prepared using the indirect method related to this information? How much cash was collected from customers during the fiscal year ended June 30, 2010?

SE9-6A. *Evaluate adjustments to net income using the indirect method. (LO 5).* During 2011, Mail Direct, Inc., incurred salary expense of $67,500, as shown on the income statement. The

January 1, 2011, balance sheet showed salaries payable of $10,450; and the December 31, 2011, balance sheet showed salaries payable of $13,200. What adjustment to net income would be shown in the operating section of the statement of cash flows prepared using the indirect method related to this information? How much cash was paid to employees (for salary) during 2011?

SE9-7A. *Calculate and identify cash flows using the indirect method. (LO 5).* Beta Company spent $40,000 for a new delivery truck during the year. Depreciation expense of $2,000 related to the truck was shown on the income statement. How are the purchase of the truck and the related depreciation reflected on the statement of cash flows prepared using the indirect method?

SE9-8A. *Evaluate adjustments to net income under the indirect method. (LO 1, 5).* In 2012, Jewels Company had net income of $350,000. The depreciation on plant assets during 2012 was $73,000, and the company incurred a loss on the sale of plant assets of $20,000. All other transactions were cash. Compute net cash provided by operating activities under the indirect method.

SE9-9A. *Calculate and identify cash flows. (LO 5).* C&S Supply, Inc., had $125,000 of retained earnings at the beginning of the year and a balance of $150,000 at the end of the year. Net income for the year was $80,000. What caused the change in the retained earnings balance? Other than net income, how would any change in retained earnings be shown on the statement of cash flows?

Set B

SE9-10B. *Identify cash flows. (LO 1).* Given the following cash transactions, classify each as a cash flow from (1) operating activities, (2) investing activities, or (3) financing activities.
   a. Principal payment to the bank for a loan
   b. Collection from customers to whom sales were previously made on account
   c. Collection from customers for cash sales
   d. Collection for sale of land that had been purchased as a possible factory site
   e. Petty cash used to pay for doughnuts for staff

SE9-11B. *Calculate and identify cash flows. (LO 1, 3, 4).* Col Corporation reported credit sales of $150,000 for 2010. Col's accounts receivable from sales were $25,000 at the beginning of 2010 and $38,000 at the end of 2010. What was the amount of cash collected from sales in 2010? How would this cash be classified on the statement of cash flows?

SE9-12B. *Calculate and identify cash flows. (LO 3, 6).* A machine cost $235,000 and had accumulated depreciation of $200,000 when it was sold for a loss of $10,000. It was a cash sale. How much cash did the company collect for the sale and how would it be classified on the statement of cash flows?

SE9-13B. *Calculate and identify cash flow. (LO 1, 3, 4).* During 2011, Cameron Company had $300,000 in cash sales and $3,500,000 in credit sales. The accounts receivable balances were $450,000 and $530,000 at December 31, 2010 and 2011, respectively. What was the total cash collected from all customers during 2011? How should this cash be classified on the statement of cash flows?

SE9-14B. *Evaluate adjustments to net income using the indirect method. (LO 5).* The income statement for Sharp, Inc., for the month of May showed insurance expense of $250. The beginning and ending balance sheets for the month showed an increase of $50 in prepaid insurance. There were no payables related to insurance on the balance sheet. What adjustment to net income, related to this information, would be shown in the operating section of the statement of cash flows prepared using the indirect method? How much cash was paid for insurance during the month?

SE9-15B. *Evaluate adjustments to net income using the indirect method. (LO 5).* Havelen's Road Paving Company had depreciation expense of $43,000 on the income statement for the year. How would this expense be shown on the statement of cash flows prepared using the indirect method? Why?

SE9-16B. *Evaluate adjustments to net income under the indirect method. (LO 5).* B&W, Inc., reported net income of $1.2 million in 2011. Depreciation for the year was $120,000; accounts receivable increased $728,000; and accounts payable decreased $420,000. Compute net cash provided by operating activities using the indirect method.

SE9-17B. *Evaluate adjustments to net income under the indirect method. (LO 5).* The comparative balance sheets for JayCee Company showed the following changes in current asset accounts: accounts receivable decreased by $50,000, prepaid expenses decreased by $23,000, and merchandise inventory increased by $17,000. These were all the changes in the current assets and current liability accounts (except cash). Net income for the year was $275,500. Compute net cash provided by or used by operating activities using the indirect method.

SE9-18B. *Calculate and identify cash flows. (LO 5).* Idea, Inc., had $375,000 of retained earnings at the beginning of the year and a balance of $590,000 at the end of the year. Net income for the year was $320,000. What caused the change in the retained earnings balance? Other than net income, how would any change in retained earnings be shown on the statement of cash flows?

Exercises
Set A

E9-19A. *Identify cash flows. (LO 1).* For each of the following items, tell whether it is a cash inflow or cash outflow and the section of the statement of cash flows in which the item would appear. (Assume the direct method is used.)

Item	Inflow or Outflow	Section of the Statement
a. Cash collected from customers		
b. Proceeds from issue of stock		
c. Interest payment on loan		
d. Principal repayment on loan		
e. Cash paid for advertising		
f. Proceeds from sale of treasury stock		
g. Money borrowed from the local bank		
h. Cash paid to employees (salaries)		
i. Purchase of equipment for cash		
j. Cash paid to vendors for inventory		
k. Taxes paid		

E9-20A. *Identify cash flows. (LO 1, 4, 6).* For each transaction, indicate the amount of the cash flow, indicate whether each results in an inflow or outflow of cash, and give the section of the statement in which each cash flow would appear. Assume the statement of cash flows is prepared using the direct method.

Transaction	Amount	Inflow or Outflow	Section of the Statement
a. Issued 1,000 shares of $1 par common stock for $8 per share			
b. Purchased $800 of supplies for $650 cash and the balance on account			
c. Borrowed $9,500 from a local bank to expand the business			
d. Purchased some office equipment for $5,200 cash			
e. Earned revenue of $16,000, receiving $8,500 cash and the balance on account			
f. Repaid $6,000 of the bank loan along with $500 interest			
g. Hired an office assistant and paid her $750 cash			
h. Declared and paid cash dividends of $875			

E9-21A. *Prepare cash from operating activities section of statement of cash flows using the direct method. (LO 4).* Use the income statement for Hargrove Dynamics, Inc., for the past year ended December 31, 2011, and the information from the comparative balance sheets shown for the beginning and the end of the year to prepare the cash from operating activities section of the statement of cash flows using the direct method.

Hargrove Dynamics, Inc.
Income Statement
For the Year Ended December 31, 2011

Sales		$120,000
Cost of goods sold		40,000
Gross margin		80,000
Operating expenses		
Wages	$ 7,500	
Rent	10,200	
Utilities	4,800	
Insurance	1,500	24,000
Net income		$ 56,000

Selected accounts from the balance sheet:

Account	Beginning of the Year	End of the Year
Accounts receivable	$ 5,000	$15,000
Inventory	32,000	12,500
Prepaid insurance	1,500	500
Accounts payable	12,000	17,500
Wages payable	1,850	1,600
Utilities payable	500	-0-

E9-22A. *Prepare cash from operating activities section of statement of cash flows using the indirect method. (LO 5).* Use the information from E9-21A to prepare the cash from operating activities section of the statement of cash flows using the indirect method. Then, compare it with the statement you prepared for E9-21A. What are the similarities? What are the differences? Which statement do you find most informative?

E9-23A. *Calculate change in cash. (LO 1, 4, 6).* Given the following information, calculate the change in cash for the year:

Cash sales collected from customers	$31,000
Cash received from sale of vehicle	5,000
Goodwill amortization expense for the year	3,200
Cash received from issuance of stock	75,000
Cash paid for salaries	19,800
Cash received from sale of land	21,200
Cash paid for other operating expenses	14,000
Cash paid to vendor for inventory	10,550

E9-24A. *Calculate cash from operating activities. (LO 3, 4).* Use the information given for Very Heavenly Desserts, Inc., to calculate the following:
  a. Cash paid for salaries
  b. Cash paid for income taxes
  c. Cash paid for inventory items

d. Cash collected from customers
e. Cash proceeds from stock issue

From the Financial Statements for Very Heavenly Desserts, Inc.

	Income Statement Amount for the Year	Balance Sheet	
		Beginning of the Year	End of the Year
Sales revenue	$67,000		
Accounts receivable		$ 8,800	$ 3,500
Salary expense	18,750		
Salaries payable		3,000	3,250
Cost of goods sold	31,200		
Inventory		11,600	9,500
Accounts payable		1,500	1,750
Income tax expense	7,500		
Income taxes payable		1,500	1,600
Common stock and additional paid-in capital		500,000	750,000

E9-25A. *Prepare the cash from operating activities section of the statement of cash flows and determine the method used. (LO 2, 4, 6).* Use the information from E9-24A to calculate the cash flow from operations for Very Heavenly Desserts, Inc. Based on the information provided, which method of preparing the statement of cash flows does the company use?

E9-26A. *Calculate cash flows from investing and financing activities. (LO 1, 6).* The following events occurred at Voich Plumbing, Inc., during 2011:

January 10	Issued common stock for $160,000
February 27	Signed a note with Last Local Bank for $15,000
May 12	Sold old service truck for $4,500 resulting in a $500 gain
May 30	Purchased a new service truck for $42,000
August 15	Paid cash dividends of $5,400
October 30	Purchased a new computer server for $25,000 cash
December 31	Paid interest expense with $1,500 cash to Last Local Bank

Compute Voich Plumbing, Inc.'s net cash flow from (1) investing activities and from (2) financing activities for 2011.

E9-27A. *Calculate cash from operating activities using the direct method. (LO 1, 4).* The following information applies to Quality Tech, Inc.:

Quality Tech, Inc.
Income Statement
For the Year Ended June 30, 2009

Sales	$ 75,000
Cost of goods sold	(25,000)
Gross margin	50,000
Insurance expense	(5,000)
Net income	$ 45,000

1. Accounts receivable started the year with a balance of $2,500 and ended the year with a balance of $500.
2. The beginning balance in accounts payable (to vendors) was $5,000, and the ending balance for the year was $3,000. Inventory at the end of the year was $1,000 more than at the beginning of the year.
3. The company started the year with $5,000 of prepaid insurance and ended the year with $5,750 of prepaid insurance.

Determine the following cash flows:
   a. Cash collected from customers for sales during the year
   b. Cash paid to vendors for inventory during the year
   c. Cash paid for insurance during the year

E9-28A. *Calculate cash from operating activities using the indirect method. (LO 5, 6).* Brenda Textiles, Inc., reported net income of $120,000 for 2011. The company also reported depreciation expense of $35,000 and a loss of $2,500 on the sale of sewing equipment. The comparative balance sheet shows a decrease in accounts receivable of $5,000 for the year, a $2,500 decrease in accounts payable, and a $1,980 increase in prepaid expenses. Prepare the cash from operating activities section of the statement of cash flows for 2011 using the indirect method.

E9-29A. *Calculate cash from operating activities using the indirect method. (LO 5).* The following information was taken from Artist, Inc.'s balance sheets at December 31, 2009 and 2010:

	2010	2009
Current assets		
Cash	$ 65,000	$ 60,000
Accounts receivable	10,000	30,000
Inventory	66,000	59,000
Prepaid expenses	50,000	23,500
Total current assets	$191,000	$172,500
Current liabilities		
Accrued expenses payable	$ 8,500	$ 4,500
Accounts payable	30,000	42,000
Total current liabilities	$ 38,500	$ 46,500

Net income for 2010 was $21,000. Depreciation expense was $11,000.

Prepare the cash provided by operating activities section of the company's statement of cash flows for the year ended December 31, 2010, using the indirect method.

E9-30A. *Calculate cash from operating activities using the direct method. (LO 4).* Stackhouse International, Inc., completed its first year of operations on June 30, 2010. The firm's income statement for the year showed revenues of $250,000 and operating expenses of $75,000. Accounts receivable was $71,000 at year end and payables related to operating expense were $35,000 at year end. Compute net cash from operating activities using the direct method.

E9-31A. *Calculate cash from operating activities using the direct method. (LO 1, 4).* During the fiscal year ended March 31, 2009, Fins & Feathers Pet Company engaged in the following transactions:
   a. Collected $125,000 on accounts receivable
   b. Paid interest of $5,000
   c. Made cash sales of $225,000
   d. Paid salaries of $45,000
   e. Paid income taxes of $15,000
   f. Recorded amortization expense of $35,000
   g. Sold vehicle for cash of $12,000
   h. Made payments to vendors of $85,200
   i. Issued bonds for $375,000

j. Purchased new vehicle for cash of $37,000
k. Purchased land for cash of $350,000
l. Paid operating expenses of $29,800

Using the relevant transactions, prepare the cash from operating activities section of the statement of cash flows using the direct method.

E9-32A. *Prepare the statement of cash flows using the indirect method. (LO 5, 6).* Use the following information for Eriksen Sporting Goods, Inc., to prepare a statement of cash flows using the indirect method:

```
                    Eriksen Sporting Goods, Inc.
                    Comparative Balance Sheets
```

	December 31, 2010	December 31, 2009
Assets		
Cash	$ 386,000	$ 241,000
Accounts receivable	128,000	120,000
Inventories	240,000	350,000
Land	190,000	240,000
Equipment	500,000	360,000
Accumulated depreciation	(150,000)	(90,000)
Total assets	$1,294,000	$1,221,000
Liabilities and Shareholders' Equity		
Accounts payable	$ 84,000	$ 100,000
Bonds payable	320,000	440,000
Common stock and additional paid-in capital	400,000	360,000
Retained earnings	490,000	321,000
Total liabilities and shareholders' equity	$1,294,000	$1,221,000

Additional information follows:
a. Net income for the fiscal year ended December 31, 2010, was $190,000.
b. The company declared and paid cash dividends.
c. The company redeemed bonds payable amounting to $120,000 for cash of $120,000.
d. The company issued common stock for $40,000 cash.

E9-33A. *Analyze a statement of cash flows. (LO 7).* The following information has been taken from the most recent statement of cash flows of Expansion Company:

Net cash used by operating activities	$ (932,000)
Net cash provided by investing activities	$1,180,500
Net cash provided by financing activities	$2,107,000

1. What information do these subtotals from the statement of cash flows tell you about Expansion Company?
2. What additional information would you want to see before you analyze Expansion Company's ability to generate positive operating cash flows in the future?
3. Did Expansion have a positive net income for the period? What information would you like to see to help you predict next year's net income?

Set B

E9-34B. *Identify cash flows. (LO 1).* For each of the following items, tell whether it is a cash inflow or cash outflow and the section of the statement of cash flows in which the item would appear. (Assume the direct method is used.)

Item	Inflow or Outflow	Section of the Statement
a. Cash paid to vendor for supplies		
b. Purchase of treasury stock		
c. Principal repayment on bonds		
d. Interest payment on bonds		
e. Cash paid for salaries		
f. Cash from issuance of common stock		
g. Cash dividends paid		
h. Cash paid for rent and utilities		
i. Purchase of computer for cash		
j. Cash paid for company vehicle		
k. Income taxes paid		

E9-35B. *Identify cash flows. (LO 1, 4).* For each transaction, indicate the amount of the cash flow, indicate whether each results in an inflow or outflow of cash, and give the section of the statement in which each cash flow would appear. Assume the statement of cash flows is prepared using the direct method.

Transaction	Amount	Inflow or Outflow	Section of the Statement
a. Issued 5,000 shares of $0.50 par common stock for $25 per share			
b. Paid $15,000 cash for office renovations			
c. Sold $32,000 of inventory, received $27,000 in cash and remaining $5,000 on account			
d. Paid $6,500 for security services			
e. Repaid a $8,000 short-term note along with $800 interest			
f. Purchased a delivery truck for $42,000			
g. Paid salary expenses totaling $7,950			
h. Purchased $8,000 of treasury stock			

E9-36B. *Prepare cash from operating activities using the direct method. (LO 4).* Use the income statement for Arbuckle's Anti-Aging, Inc., for the year ended December 31, 2011, and the information from the comparative balance sheets shown for the beginning and the end of the year to prepare the operating section of the statement of cash flows using the direct method.

Arbuckle's Anti-Aging, Inc.
Income Statement
For the Year Ended December 31, 2011

Sales		$250,000
Cost of goods sold		50,000
Gross margin		200,000
Operating Expenses:		
Wages	$4,750	
Rent	2,050	
Utilities	1,000	
Insurance	2,400	10,200
Net income		$189,800

Account	Beginning of the Year	End of the Year
Accounts receivable	$15,000	$18,000
Inventory	5,000	30,000
Prepaid insurance	100	1,000
Accounts payable	4,000	8,500
Wages payable	375	400
Utilities payable	0	85

E9-37B. *Prepare cash from operating activities using the indirect method. (LO 5).* Use the information from E9-36B to prepare the cash from operating activities section of the statement of cash flows using the indirect method. Then, compare it with the statement you prepared for E9-36B. What are the similarities? What are the differences? Which statement do you find most informative?

E9-38B. *Calculate change in cash. (LO 1, 5).* Given the following information, calculate the change in cash for the year:

Cash received from sale of company equipment	$ 20,000
Cash paid for salaries	8,500
Cash paid for other operating expenses	12,250
Cash paid for purchase of treasury stock	16,000
Cash paid for rent	12,000
Cash received from issuance of bonds	125,000
Cash collected from customers	45,000
Cash paid to do a major repair of delivery van to prolong its useful life for five more years	21,820

E9-39B. *Calculate cash from operating activities. (LO 2, 5).* Use the information given for Pro Consultants, Inc., to calculate the following:
a. Cash paid for utilities
b. Cash paid for interest
c. Cash paid for inventory items
d. Cash collected from customers
e. Cash proceeds from stock issue

From the Financial Statements for Pro Consultants, Inc.

	Income Statement Amount for the Year	Beginning of the Year	End of the Year
Sales revenue	$105,050		
Accounts receivable		$ 10,000	$ 16,500
Utilities expense	8,700		
Utilities payable		2,000	3,500
Cost of goods sold	35,500		
Inventory		10,500	5,500
Accounts payable		2,000	500
Interest expense	2,550		
Interest payable		400	325
Common stock and additional paid-in capital		175,000	260,000

E9-40B. *Prepare cash from operating activities section of statement of cash flows and determine the method used. (LO 2, 4).* Use the information from E9-39B to calculate the cash flow from operating activities for Pro Consultants, Inc. Based on the information provided, which method of preparing the statement of cash flows does Pro Consultants, Inc., use?

E9-41B. Calculate cash flows from investing and financing activities. *(LO 1, 6).* The following events occurred at Electric Research, Inc., during the year ended June 30, 2010:

July 25	Signed a note with Local First Bank for $25,000
August 8	Purchased equipment for $50,000 cash
October 15	Sold old equipment for $20,100, resulting in a $100 gain
January 24	Issued bonds for $150,000
March 20	Purchased new delivery vehicles for $32,000 cash
April 15	Paid cash dividends of $2,500
June 30	Paid interest expense with $2,300 cash to Local First Bank

Compute Electric Research, Inc.'s net cash flow from (1) investing activities and from (2) financing activities for the year ended June 30, 2010.

E9-42B. *Calculate cash from operating activities using the direct method. (LO 1, 4).* The following information applies to Change Corporation:

> ### Change Corporation
> ### Income Statement
> ### For the Year Ended December 31, 2010

Sales	$ 55,000
Cost of goods sold	(17,250)
Gross margin	37,750
Rent expense	(5,750)
Net income	$ 32,000

1. Accounts receivable started the year with a balance of $1,050 and ended the year with a balance of $2,250.
2. The beginning balance in accounts payable (to vendors) was $650, and the ending balance was $1,550. Inventory was $1,000 less at the end of the year than it was at the beginning of the year.
3. The company started the year with $2,000 of prepaid rent and ended the year with $1,500 of prepaid rent.

Determine the following cash flows:
    a. Cash collected from customers for sales during the year
    b. Cash paid to vendors for inventory during the year
    c. Cash paid for rent during the year

E9-43B. *Calculate cash from operating activities using the indirect method. (LO 5).* Anika Book Distributors, Inc., reported net income of $415,000 for 2009. The company also reported depreciation expense of $75,000 and a gain of $6,250 on the sale of machinery. The comparative balance sheet shows an increase in accounts receivable of $1,500 for the year, a $4,100 increase in accounts payable, and a $2,175 decrease in prepaid expenses. Prepare the cash from operating activities section of the statement of cash flows for 2009 using the indirect method.

E9-44B. *Calculate cash from operating activities using the indirect method. (LO 5).* The following information was taken from Hive Marketing, Inc.'s balance sheets at June 30, 2010 and 2011:

	2011	2010
Current assets		
Cash	$ 71,000	$ 65,000
Accounts receivable	50,000	45,000
Inventory	75,000	61,000
Prepaid expenses	$ 35,000	$ 41,000
Total current assets	$231,000	$212,000

Current liabilities		
Accrued expenses payable	$ 9,000	$10,000
Accounts payable	62,000	81,000
Total current liabilities	$ 71,000	$91,000

Net income for the year ended June 30, 2011, was $62,000. Depreciation expense was $12,750.

Prepare the cash provided by operating activities section of the company's statement of cash flows for the year ended June 30, 2011, using the indirect method.

E9-45B. *Calculate cash from operating activities using the direct method. (LO 4).* Health Spa Corporation completed its first year of operations on December 31, 2012. The firm's income statement for the year showed revenues of $210,000 and operating expenses of $78,000. Accounts receivable was $45,000 at year end and payables related to operating expense were $28,750 at year end. Compute net cash from operating activities using the direct method.

E9-46B. *Calculate cash from operating activities using the direct method. (LO 1, 4).* During the fiscal year ended September 30, 2010, Whitehouse Data, Inc., engaged in the following transactions:
 a. Collected $75,000 on accounts receivable
 b. Paid $125,000 on accounts payable related to operating expenses
 c. Made cash sales of $275,000
 d. Declared a 3-for-1 stock split
 e. Paid salaries of $35,000
 f. Recorded depreciation expense of $17,250
 g. Issued common stock for $25,000
 h. Repaid principal of mortgage for $295,000
 i. Sold land for $150,000
 j. Paid interest on mortgage in the amount of $17,800
 k. Purchased new equipment for cash of $61,500
 l. Paid operating expenses of $55,000

Using the relevant transactions, prepare the cash from operating activities section of the statement of cash flows using the direct method.

E9-47B. *Prepare the statement of cash flows using the indirect method. (LO 2, 5).* Use the following information for Professional Athletics, Inc., to prepare a statement of cash flows for the year ended June 30, 2009, using the indirect method:

Professional Athletics, Inc.
Comparative Balance Sheets

	June 30, 2009	June 30, 2008
Assets		
Cash	$ 110,000	$ 47,000
Accounts receivable	156,000	128,000
Inventories	360,000	338,000
Land	270,000	210,000
Equipment	700,000	520,000
Accumulated depreciation	(180,000)	(120,000)
Total assets	$1,416,000	$1,123,000
Liabilities and Shareholders' Equity		
Accounts payable	$ 70,000	$ 80,000
Bonds payable	370,000	430,000
Common stock and additional paid-in capital	450,000	350,000
Retained earnings	526,000	263,000
Total liabilities and shareholders' equity	$1,416,000	$1,123,000

Additional information follows:
  a. Net income for the fiscal year ended June 30, 2009, was $290,000.
  b. The company declared and paid cash dividends.
  c. The company redeemed bonds payable amounting to $60,000 for cash of $60,000.
  d. The company issued common stock for $100,000 cash.

E9-48B. *Analyze a statement of cash flows. (LO 7).* The following information was taken from the most recent statement of cash flows of Innovative Electronics Company:

Net cash provided by operating activities	$ 845,000
Net cash used by investing activities	$ (530,000)
Net cash provided by financing activities	$1,675,000

1. What information do these subtotals from the statement of cash flows tell you about Innovative Electronics Company?
2. What additional information would you want to see before you analyze Innovative Electronics Company's ability to generate positive operating cash flows in the future?
3. Did Innovative Electronics have a positive net income for the period? What information would you like to see to help you predict next year's net income?

MyAccountingLab

All of the A problems can be found within MyAccountingLab, an online homework and practice environment.

Problems
Set A

P9-49A. *Prepare the statement of cash flows (direct or indirect method). (LO 2, 3, 4, 5, 6, 7).* The income statement for the year ended December 31, 2011, and the balance sheets at December 31, 2010, and December 31, 2011, for Craig's Service Company are presented here.

Craig's Service Company
Income Statement
For the Year Ended December 31, 2011

(amounts in thousands, except earnings per share)

Service revenue		$92,000
Expenses:		
Wages and salaries	$60,000	
Advertising	10,000	
Rent	4,800	
Depreciation	3,600	
Supplies	5,200	
Total expenses		83,600
Income before taxes		$ 8,400
Income taxes		2,940
Net income		$ 5,460
Earnings per share		$ 0.55

Craig's Service Company
Comparative Balance Sheets

(amounts in thousands)		December 31, 2011	December 31, 2010
Assets:			
Current assets:			
Cash		$ 6,910	$ 3,500
Accounts receivable		12,000	14,000
Supplies		200	370
Prepaid advertising		800	660
Total current assets		$19,910	$18,530
Property, plant, and equipment			
Equipment	$44,000		$40,000
Less: accumulated depreciation	21,600		18,000
Total property, plant, and equipment		22,400	22,000
Total assets		$42,310	$40,530
Liabilities and Stockholders' Equity:			
Current liabilities:			
Wages and salaries payable		$ 2,700	$ 3,300
Taxes payable		1,900	1,780
Total current liabilities		$ 4,600	$ 5,080
Stockholders' equity:			
Common stock	$30,000		$30,000
Retained earnings	7,710		5,450
		$37,710	$35,450
Total liabilities and stockholders' equity		$42,310	$40,530

Requirements

1. Prepare a statement of cash flows for the year ended December 31, 2011, using (a) the direct method and (b) the indirect method.
2. Why is the statement of cash flows important to the company and to parties external to the company?
3. As a user, which format would you prefer—direct or indirect—and why?
4. Evaluate the way in which the company spent its cash during the year. Do you think the company is in a sound cash position?
5. Calculate the firm's free cash flow for the most recent year.

P9-50A. *Calculate cash from operating activities using the indirect method. (LO 5).* The following information is from the comparative balance sheets of Discovery Tech Corporation at June 30, 2011 and 2010:

(in thousands) At June 30	2011	2010
Current assets:		
Cash	$2,750	$2,115
Accounts receivable	3,000	2,750
Inventory	1,700	1,025
Prepaid insurance	270	320
Total current assets	$7,720	$6,210

Current liabilities:		
Accounts payable	$1,800	$1,750
Salaries payable	$3,750	$3,150
Total current liabilities	$5,550	$4,900

Net income for the year ended June 30, 2011, was $425,000. Depreciation expense of $105,000 was included in the operating expenses for the year.

Requirement

Use the indirect method to prepare the *cash from operations* section of the statement of cash flows for Discovery Tech Corporation for the year ended June 30, 2011.

P9-51A. *Calculate cash from operating activities using the indirect method. (LO 5).* The following information comes from the balance sheets of Moonlight Spa Treatments, Inc., at March 31, 2011 and 2010:

(in thousands)	2011	2010
Current assets:		
Cash	$3,765	$3,005
Accounts receivable	989	1,050
Inventory	1,500	1,000
Prepaid rent	125	250
Total current assets	$6,379	$5,305
Current liabilities:		
Accounts payable	$1,475	$1,105
Wages payable	1,700	1,960
Total current liabilities	$3,175	$3,065

Net income for the year ended March 30, 2011, was $105,700. Included in the operating expenses for the year was depreciation expense of $98,000.

Requirement

Prepare the *cash from operating activities* section of Moonlight Spa Treatments, Inc.'s statement of cash flows for the year March 31, 2011. Use the indirect method.

P9-52A. *Calculate cash from operating activities using the indirect method. (LO 5).* Burke Landscaping Company had the following information available for the year ended June 30, 2009:

	July 1, 2008	June 30, 2009
Accounts receivable	$356,000	$302,000
Prepaid insurance	76,000	32,000
Inventory	132,000	142,000

Burke Landscaping Company reported net income of $675,000 for the year ended June 30, 2009. Depreciation expense, included on the income statement, was $60,500.

Requirement

Assume that the preceding information is all the information relevant to the statement of cash flows. Use the indirect method to prepare the *cash flows from operating activities* section of Burke Landscaping Company's statement of cash flows for the year ended June 30, 2009.

P9-53A. *Calculate investing and financing cash flows. (LO 6).* To prepare its statement of cash flows for the year ended December 31, 2010, Sweet Confections, Inc., gathered the following information:

Gain on sale of land	$ 25,000
Proceeds from sale of land	170,000
Proceeds from bond issue (face value $150,000)	135,000
Amortization of bond discount	3,500
Dividends declared	34,000
Dividends paid	32,000
Issuance of common stock	50,000

Requirements

1. Prepare the *cash from investing* section of the statement of cash flows.
2. Prepare the *cash from financing* section of the statement of cash flows.

P9-54A. *Calculate investing and financing cash flows. (LO 6).* To prepare its statement of cash flows for the year ended June 30, 2011, Glavine Sports Products, Inc., gathered the following information:

Loss on sale of automobile	$ 5,000
Proceeds from sale of automobile	7,500
Purchase of automobile	42,000
Dividends declared	10,000
Dividends paid	5,000
Proceeds from sale of treasury stock	65,000
Repayment of loan principal	17,500
Payment of interest on loan	500

Requirements

1. Prepare the *cash from investing* section of the statement of cash flows.
2. Prepare the *cash from financing* section of the statement of cash flows.

P9-55A. *Calculate investing and financing cash flows. (LO 6).* To prepare its statement of cash flows for the year ended December 31, 2012, McKinney Carterette Cataloging Specialists, Inc., gathered the following information:

Dividends paid	$ 17,750
Purchase of treasury stock	25,000
Proceeds from bank loan	55,000
Gain on sale of equipment	15,000
Proceeds from sale of equipment	30,000
Proceeds from sale of common stock	175,000

Requirements

1. Prepare the *cash from investing* section of the statement of cash flows.
2. Prepare the *cash from financing* section of the statement of cash flows.

P9-56A. *Analyze a statement of cash flows. (LO 5, 6, 7).* Use the following statement of cash flows for the Matlock Company to answer the required questions:

Matlock Company
Statement of Cash Flows
For the Year Ended December 31, 2010

(amounts in thousands)

Cash flows from operating activities:

Net income		$1,500
Depreciation expense	$ 210	
Decrease in accounts receivable	320	
Increase in inventory	(70)	
Increase in prepaid rent	(10)	
Increase in accounts payable	150	600
Net cash provided by operating activities		$2,100
Cash flows from investing activities:		
Purchase of equipment	$(1,000)	
Proceeds from sale of old equipment	200	
Net cash used by investing activities		(800)
Cash flows from financing activities:		
Repayment of long-term mortgage	$(1,350)	
Proceeds from sale of common stock	500	
Payment of cash dividends	(200)	
Net cash used by financing activities		(1,050)
Net increase in cash during 2010		$ 250
Cash balance, January 1, 2010		346
Cash balance, December 31, 2010		$ 596

Requirements

1. How did Matlock Company use the majority of its cash during 2010?
2. What information does this give you about Matlock Company?
3. What was Matlock Company's major source of cash during 2010?
4. Is this an appropriate source of cash for the long run? Explain.
5. Calculate Matlock's free cash flow for 2010.

Set B

P9-57B. *Prepare the statement of cash flows (direct or indirect method). (LO 2, 3, 4, 5, 6, 7).* Following are the income statements for Ocoee Oil Company for the year ended December 31, 2011, and the balance sheets at December 31, 2010 and 2011.

Ocoee Oil Company
Income Statement
For the Year Ended December 31, 2011

Sales revenue		$150,000
Cost of goods sold		63,000
Gross margin		87,000
Other expenses:		
Wages and salaries	$32,000	
Depreciation and depletion	4,500	
Miscellaneous	12,400	
Total other expenses		48,900
Income before taxes		38,100
Income taxes		8,200
Net income		$ 29,900

Ocoee Oil Company
Comparative Balance Sheets

		December 31, 2011		December 31, 2010
Assets				
Current assets:				
Cash		$ 0		$ 6,400
Accounts receivable		2,900		2,700
Inventory		60,000		42,000
Total current assets		$ 62,900		$51,100
Property, plant, and equipment			$ 39,000	
Equipment	$ 82,300			
Less: accumulated depreciation	(20,100)		(15,600)	
Total property, plant, and equipment		62,200		23,400
Total assets		$125,100		$74,500
Liabilities and shareholders' equity				
Current liabilities:				
Accounts payable	$ 6,400		$ 5,700	
Salaries payable	1,500		1,300	
Taxes payable	1,900		2,100	
Total current liabilities	$ 9,800		$ 9,100	
Notes payable	30,000		10,000	
Total liabilities		$ 39,800		$19,100
Shareholders' equity				
Common stock	$ 40,000		$ 40,000	
Retained earnings	45,300		15,400	
Total shareholders' equity		85,300		55,400
Total liabilities and shareholders' equity		$125,100		$74,500

Requirements

1. Prepare a statement of cash flows for the year ended December 31, 2011, using (1) the direct method and (2) the indirect method.
2. Why is the statement of cash flows important to the company and to parties external to the company?
3. As a user, which format—direct or indirect—would you prefer and why?
4. Evaluate the way in which the company spent its cash during the year. Do you think the company is in a sound cash position?
5. Compute the firm's free cash flow.

P9-58B. *Calculate cash from operating activities using the indirect method. (LO 5).* The following information is from the comparative balance sheets of Runnels Cosmetics Company at March 31, 2010 and 2009:

(in thousands) At March 31	2010	2009
Current assets:		
Cash	$4,050	$3,720
Accounts receivable	3,500	3,150
Inventory	1,550	1,800
Prepaid rent	450	520
Total current assets	$9,550	$9,190
Current liabilities:		
Accounts payable	$3,000	$2,275
Salaries payable	3,900	4,700
Total current liabilities	$6,900	$6,975

Net income for the year ended March 31, 2010, was $157,000. Depreciation expense of $54,000 was included in the operating expenses for the year.

Requirement

Use the indirect method to prepare the *cash from operations* section of the statement of cash flows for Runnels Cosmetics Company for the year ended March 31, 2010.

P9-59B. *Calculate cash from operating activities using the indirect method. (LO 5).* The following information comes from the balance sheets of Expert Continuing Education, Inc., at June 30:

(in thousands)	2011	2010
Current assets:		
Cash	$4,075	$3,980
Accounts receivable	2,500	2,250
Inventory	675	725
Prepaid insurance	700	485
Total current assets	$7,950	$7,440
Current liabilities:		
Accounts payable	$4,600	$4,265
Wages payable	1,505	1,869
Total current liabilities	$6,105	$6,134

Net income for the year ended June 30, 2011, was $315,000. Included in the operating expenses for the year was depreciation expense of $134,000.

Requirement

Prepare the *cash from operating activities* section of Expert Continuing Education, Inc.'s statement of cash flows for the year ended June 30, 2011. Use the indirect method.

P9-60B. *Calculate cash from operating activities using the indirect method. (LO 5).* Fitness Elite Corporation had the following information available for 2012:

	January 1	December 31
Accounts receivable	$160,000	$152,000
Prepaid insurance	96,000	52,000
Inventory	152,000	120,000

Fitness Elite Corporation reported net income of $275,000 for the year. Depreciation expense, included on the income statement, was $35,400.

Requirement

Assume that the preceding information is all the information relevant to the statement of cash flows. Use the indirect method to prepare the cash flows from operating activities section of Fitness Elite Corporation's statement of cash flows for the year ended December 31, 2012.

P9-61B. *Calculate investing and financing cash flows. (LO 6).* To prepare its statement of cash flows for the year ended June 30, 2011, Purified Water Company gathered the following information:

Proceeds from bond issue (face value $500,000)	$350,000
Amortization of bond premium	2,750
Dividends declared	19,000
Dividends paid	14,000
Purchase of treasury stock	35,000
Loss on sale of equipment	10,000
Proceeds from sale of equipment	45,000

Requirements

1. Prepare the *cash from investing* section of the statement of cash flows.
2. Prepare the *cash from financing* section of the statement of cash flows.

P9-62B. *Calculate investing and financing cash flows. (LO 6).* To prepare its statement of cash flows for the year ended December 31, 2012, N.C. Lewis Technology International, Inc., gathered the following information:

Dividends declared	$25,000
Dividends paid	18,000
Proceeds from sale of treasury stock	55,000
Repayment of loan principal	27,000
Payment of interest on loan	270
Loss on sale of machinery	1,500
Proceeds from sale of machinery	6,000
Purchase of machinery	48,700

Requirements

1. Prepare the *cash from investing* section of the statement of cash flows.
2. Prepare the *cash from financing* section of the statement of cash flows.

P9-63B. *Calculate investing and financing cash flows. (LO 6).* To prepare its statement of cash flows for the year ended June 30, 2010, Linds Cloud Soft Bedding Company gathered the following information:

Proceeds from bank loan	$225,000
Loss on sale of machinery	5,000
Proceeds from sale of machinery	10,000
Proceeds from bond issuance	275,000
Dividends paid	45,200
Purchase of treasury stock	125,000

Requirements

1. Prepare the *cash from investing* section of the statement of cash flows.
2. Prepare the *cash from financing* section of the statement of cash flows.

P9-64B. *Analyze a statement of cash flows. (LO 5, 6, 7).* Use the following statement of cash flows for the SS&P Company to answer the required questions:

SS&P Company
Statement of Cash Flows
For the Year Ended December 31, 2011

(amounts in thousands)

Cash from operating activities:		
Net income		$ 2,500
Depreciation expense	$ 510	
Decrease in accounts receivable	720	
Increase in inventory	(90)	
Increase in prepaid rent	(20)	
Decrease in accounts payable	(150)	970
Net cash provided by operating activities		$ 3,470
Cash from investing activities:		
Purchase of equipment	$(3,000)	
Proceeds from sale of old equipment	900	
Net cash used by investing activities		(2,100)
Cash from financing activities:		
Repayment of long-term mortgage	$(7,500)	
Proceeds from sale of common stock	2,100	
Payment of cash dividends	(1,200)	
Net cash used by financing activities		$(6,600)
Net increase (decrease) in cash during 2011		(5,230)
Cash balance, January 1, 2011		10,580
Cash balance, December 31, 2011		$ 5,350

Requirements

1. How did SS&P Company use the majority of its cash during 2011?
2. What information does this give you about SS&P Company?
3. How did SS&P Company obtain the majority of its cash during 2011?
4. Is this an appropriate source of cash for the long run? Explain.
5. Calculate SS&P's free cash flow for 2011.

Financial Statement Analysis

FSA9-1. *Analyze a statement of cash flows. (LO 7).* Use the financial statements for Borders Group, Inc., which can be found at www.borders.com, to answer the following questions:

1. What were the major sources and uses of cash during the most recent fiscal year? What does this indicate about Borders' cash position?
2. What evidence, if any, is there that Borders is expanding?

FSA9-2. *Analyze a statement of cash flows. (LO 2, 7).* The following statements of cash flows are from First Solar, Inc.'s 2008 annual report:

FIRST SOLAR, INC., AND SUBSIDIARIES
Consolidated Statements of Cash Flows

	Year Ended		
(in thousands)	December 27, 2008	December 29, 2007	December 30, 2006
Cash flows from operating activities:			
Cash received from customers	$1,203,822	$ 515,994	$ 110,196
Cash paid to suppliers and associates	(723,123)	(276,525)	(111,945)
Interest received	19,138	19,965	2,640
Interest paid, net of amounts capitalized	(4,629)	(2,294)	(712)
Income taxes paid, net of refunds	(1,975)	(19,002)	—
Excess tax benefit from share-based			
compensation arrangements	(28,661)	(30,196)	(45)
Other	(1,505)	(1,991)	(710)
Net cash provided by (used in) operating activities ...	463,067	205,951	(576)
Cash flows from investing activities:			
Purchases of property, plant and equipment	(459,271)	(242,371)	(153,150)
Purchase of marketable securities	(334,818)	(1,081,154)	—
Proceeds from maturities of marketable securities ..	107,450	787,783	—
Proceeds from sales of marketable securities	418,762	—	—
Increase in restricted investments	(15,564)	(6,008)	(6,804)
Investment in related party	(25,000)	—	—
Acquisitions, net of cash acquired	—	(5,500)	—
Other investments in long-term assets	—	—	(40)
Net cash used in investing activities	(308,441)	(547,250)	(159,994)
Cash flows from financing activities:			
Proceeds from issuance of common stock	—	365,969	302,650
Proceeds from notes payable to a related party	—	—	36,000
Repayment of notes payable to a related party	—	—	(64,700)
Repayment of long-term debt	(41,691)	(34,757)	(135)
Other equity contributions	—	—	30,000
Proceeds from stock options exercised	16,036	10,173	100
Proceeds from issuance of debt,			
net of issuance costs	138,887	49,368	130,833
Excess tax benefit from share-based compensation			
arrangements	28,661	30,196	45
Proceeds from economic development funding	35,661	9,475	16,766
Other financing activities	(5)	(3)	(9)
Net cash provided by financing activities	177,549	430,421	451,550
Effect of exchange rate changes on cash and cash			
equivalents	(20,221)	7,050	391
Net increase in cash and cash equivalents	311,954	96,172	291,371
Cash and cash equivalents, beginning of year	404,264	308,092	16,721
Cash and cash equivalents, end of year	$ 716,218	$ 404,264	$ 308,092

Answer the following questions:
1. What was First Solar's main source of cash for the most recent fiscal year?
2. Is First Solar expanding its business? What evidence on the statement of cash flows supports your opinion?
3. Did the company issue any new stock during the most recent fiscal year? Any new debt?
4. When a firm uses the direct method, it must also provide a reconciliation of net income to net cash from operating activities. What does this mean? Do you think this requirement discourages the use of the direct method?

FSA9-3. *Analyze a statement of cash flows. (LO 7, 8).* The statement of cash flows for Chico's FAS, Inc., for the years ended January 31, 2009, February 2, 2008, and February 3, 2007, appears on the following page.

CHICO'S FAS, INC., AND SUBSIDIARIES
CONSOLIDATED STATEMENTS OF CASH FLOWS

	Fiscal Year Ended		
(in thousands)	January 31, 2009	February 2, 2008	February 3, 2007
CASH FLOWS FROM OPERATING ACTIVITIES			
Net (loss) income	$ (19,137)	$ 88,875	$ 166,636
Adjustments to reconcile net (loss) income to net cash provided by operating activities —			
Depreciation and amortization, cost of goods sold	8,782	10,386	7,564
Depreciation and amortization, other	88,790	81,593	61,840
Deferred tax benefit	(20,507)	(6,635)	(22,324)
Stock-based compensation expense, cost of goods sold	2,769	4,909	6,004
Stock-based compensation expense, other	9,821	12,171	15,237
Excess tax benefit from stock-based compensation	(100)	(209)	(2,365)
Deferred rent expense, net	6,060	9,508	6,867
Goodwill impairment	—	—	6,752
Gain on sale of investment	—	(6,833)	—
Impairment of long-lived assets	13,691	—	—
Loss (gain) on disposal of property and equipment	761	(908)	826
Decrease (increase) in assets —			
Receivables, net	3,766	(18,770)	(4,517)
Income tax receivable	12,267	—	—
Inventories	11,847	(32,388)	(14,696)
Prepaid expenses and other	4,224	(3,958)	(3,676)
(Decrease) increase in liabilities —			
Accounts payable	(22,488)	24,119	7,532
Accrued and other deferred liabilities	(1,100)	46,787	57,314
Total adjustments	118,583	119,772	122,358
Net cash provided by operating activities	99,446	208,647	288,994
CASH FLOWS FROM INVESTING ACTIVITIES:			
Purchases of marketable securities	(569,358)	(1,212,894)	(162,690)
Proceeds from sale of marketable securities	587,809	1,190,761	325,894
Purchase of Fitigues assets	—	—	(7,527)
Purchase of Minnesota franchise rights and stores	—	(32,896)	—
Acquisition of other franchise stores	—	(6,361)	(811)
Proceeds from sale of land	—	13,426	—
Proceeds from sale of investment	—	15,090	—
Purchases of property and equipment	(104,615)	(202,223)	(218,311)
Net cash used in investing activities	(86,164)	(235,097)	(63,445)
CASH FLOWS FROM FINANCING ACTIVITIES:			
Proceeds from issuance of common stock	306	3,533	6,402
Excess tax benefit from stock-based compensation	100	209	2,365
Cash paid for deferred financing costs	(629)	—	—
Repurchase of common stock	(311)	(694)	(200,148)
Net cash (used in) provided by financing activities	(534)	3,048	(191,381)
Net increase (decrease) in cash and cash equivalents	12,748	(23,402)	34,168
CASH AND CASH EQUIVALENTS, Beginning of period	13,801	37,203	3,035
CASH AND CASH EQUIVALENTS, End of period	$ 26,549	$ 13,801	$ 37,203
SUPPLEMENTAL DISCLOSURES OF CASH FLOW INFORMATION:			
Cash paid for interest	$ 159	$ 461	$ 107
Cash paid for income taxes, net	$ 13,591	$ 74,563	$ 105,646
NON-CASH INVESTING AND FINANCING ACTIVITIES:			
Receipt of note receivable for sale of land	—	$ 25,834	—
Receivable from sale of equity investment	—	$ 2,161	—

The accompanying notes are an integral part of these consolidated statements.

Answer the following questions:

1. Does Chico's use the direct or the indirect method of preparing the statement of cash flows?
2. Did receivables increase or decrease during the most recent fiscal year?
3. Why is depreciation, a noncash expense, included on the statement of cash flows?
4. On two of the three years' statements, inventory is shown as a negative number (subtracted). Describe what happened to the balance in the inventory account during each of those years.
5. Did the balance in accounts payable increase or decrease during the most recent year? Explain.
6. Do you think Chico's is expanding? Find some numbers to support your answer.
7. Calculate Chico's free cash flow for all three years. What do these values indicate?
8. Do you see any particular risks indicated by Chico's cash flow patterns?

Critical Thinking Problems

Risk and Control

To be successful, a company must anticipate its cash flows. What evidence would help you evaluate whether or not a company does adequate cash planning? Is there any information not available in the company's annual report that would help you make this evaluation?

Ethics

After two years of business, the Lucky Ladder Company decided to apply for a bank loan to finance a new store. Although the company had been very successful, it had never prepared a cash budget. The owner of Lucky Ladder Company used the information from the first two years of business to reconstruct cash forecasts. He presented these new forecasts with his financial statements as though they had been prepared as part of the company's planning. Do you think this behavior was ethical? What would you do in similar circumstances? Why?

Group Assignment

To prepare the class for a debate about the format of the statement of cash flows, assign the direct method to half of the groups in the class and the indirect method to the other half of the groups. Have each group prepare arguments about the superiority of its assigned method of presenting the operating section of the statement of cash flows. Think about both theoretical and practical aspects of the methods. Refer to the cash flow information from First Solar, Inc., provided in FSA9-2.

Internet Exercise: Carnival Corporation

Carnival Corporation prides itself on being "The Most Popular Cruise Line in the World®"—a distinction achieved by offering a wide array of quality cruise vacations. Go to www.carnival.com and locate About Carnival: Investor Relations. You should be able to find the firm's SEC filings. Find the firm's 10-K filed on January 29, 2009, for its 2008 fiscal year.

IE9-1. Use the entire 10-K to answer the following questions:

1. Carnival Corporation operates several cruise lines. Find and list three of them.
2. Within the past five years, how many new ships has Carnival put into service?
3. Are the payments for ships considered capital expenditures or revenue expenditures? On the statement of cash flows, which business activity category will report these payments?

IE9-2. Find the annual statement of cash flows (page F-3 of the 2008 10-K) to answer the following questions:

1. Does Carnival use the direct or the indirect method to prepare the statement of cash flows? How can you tell? Which activity section is affected by this choice of method?
2. For the most recent year, list the amount of net cash inflow or outflow from each of the three major types of activities reported on the statement of cash flows. Which type of activity is providing the most cash? Is this considered favorable or unfavorable?

3. For the most recent year, what amount is reported for net income and net cash from operating activities? Are these amounts the same? Explain why or why not.

4. For the most recent year, did Carnival report cash inflows or outflows for capital expenditures? Is this considered favorable or unfavorable? Explain why. What do you think these capital expenditures are primarily for? What was the net amount of the capital expenditure? Which activity section reports this information?

5. For the most recent year, what amount of cash dividends did Carnival pay out? For the most recent year did Carnival issue or retire any common stock? What was the net amount issued or retired? For the most recent year did Carnival issue or retire any long-term debt? What was the net amount issued or retired? Which activity section reports this information?

6. Does this statement of cash flows indicate a strong or weak position with regard to cash and liquidity? Explain.

10

Using Financial Statement Analysis to Evaluate Firm Performance

LEARNING OBJECTIVES

When you are finished studying Chapter 10, you should be able to:

1. Recognize and explain the components of net income.

2. Perform and interpret a horizontal analysis and a vertical analysis of financial statement information.

3. Perform a basic ratio analysis of a set of financial statements and explain what the ratios mean.

4. Recognize the risks of investing in stocks and explain how to control those risks.

5. (Appendix 10A) Define comprehensive income and explain how it changes.

6. (Appendix 10B) Explain how a firm's investments in other firms' marketable securities are valued and reported.

ETHICS Matters

Getting It Right the First Time

Accounting information is an important part of the financial information investors use to evaluate a firm's performance. As an investor, you need to feel confident in a firm's reported earnings. We count on the people who prepare the financial statements as well as the independent auditors to produce reliable financial information. However, mistakes are inevitable. When a firm has made an error, earnings may need to be restated. Good news for investors: The number of corporate financial restatements dropped from 1,235 in 2007 to 869 in 2008. This was the second year in a row that the number of restatements declined. The number of restatements hit its lowest level since before the passage of the Sarbanes-Oxley Act of 2002. The time period covered by the restatement (479 days) and the size of the required adjustment ($6.1 million on average) were also much lower than in the two previous years.

You might think this very significant improvement in restatement statistics is related to the provisions of the Sarbanes-Oxley Act, which requires firms to have effective internal controls over financial reporting. Maybe it is related to the law's requirements for a code of ethics for managers or to the requirement that firms have a whistle-blower hotline for reporting suspected fraud. Whatever the reasons, this is a trend that brings some welcome favorable news related to corporate accounting and reliable financial statements.

L.O.1
Recognize and explain the
components of net income.

A Closer Look at the Income Statement

You have learned a great deal about the basic financial statements and how accountants record, summarize, and report transactions. There is information you can easily see in the financial statement, but there is also information that is difficult to see. It is important to look beyond the size and source of the numbers to see what the numbers *mean*. We have been examining the individual parts of the financial statements. Now we will examine all of the financial statements together to answer the following questions: What information do financial statements provide? What does the information mean? How can we use it?

Before beginning the detailed analysis of the financial statements, we need to take a closer look at some of the characteristics of the income statement. Because earnings—net income—is the focus of financial reporting, companies worry about how current and potential investors will interpret the announcement of earnings each quarter. It is not uncommon for companies to be accused of manipulating their earnings to make them appear higher than they actually are. In an effort to make the components of earnings clear and to represent exactly what they should to financial statement users, the Financial Accounting Standards Board (FASB) requires that two items be separated from the regular earnings of a company. The major reason for segregating these items is that they should not be considered as part of the ongoing earnings of the firm. Reported earnings is an amount used to predict future earnings, but the following two items are not expected to be repeated in the future:

1. Discontinued operations
2. Extraordinary items

Discontinued Operations

If you pay attention to the financial news, you are bound to hear about a company selling off a division. During 2006, 2007, and 2008, Darden Restaurants, Inc., showed discontinued operations on its income statement. During those years, the firm sold its Smokey Bones restaurants and closed a number of Bahama Breeze restaurants. The gains or losses from these kinds of transactions are shown separately on the income statement. Firms are always evaluating the contribution that the various divisions make to the profits of the firm. If a division is not profitable or no longer fits the strategy of the firm, a firm may sell it to remain profitable or change the firm's focus. Parts of a company's operations that are eliminated are called **discontinued operations**.

Discontinued operations are those parts of the firm that a company has eliminated by selling a division.

When a firm eliminates a division, the financial implications are shown separately from the regular operations of the firm under both U.S. generally accepted accounting principles (GAAP) and International Financial Reporting Standards (IFRS). Why would this separation be useful? Earnings is an important number because it is used to evaluate the performance of a firm and to predict its future performance. To make these evaluations and predictions more meaningful, it is important that one-time transactions be separated from recurring transactions. This separation allows investors to see one-time transactions as exceptions to the normal operations of the firm. In addition to any gain or loss from the sale, the earnings or loss for the accounting period for the discontinued operations must also be shown separately. The tax effects of these items are shown with each individual item rather than being included with the rest of the firm's income taxes. This presentation is called *net of tax*. We will look at an example of a firm with discontinued operations.

In 2010, Muzby Manufacturing sold off a major business segment, the crate-production division, because the firm wanted to focus its operations on its core business, which did not include the crate division. The current year's income or loss from the crate-production division and the gain or loss from the sale of that division is shown separately on the income statement. Suppose the following:

1. Muzby Manufacturing's income from continuing operations before taxes was $395,600, and taxes related to that income were $155,000.
2. The discontinued segment contributed income of $12,000 during the year, and taxes related to that income were $1,900.
3. The discontinued segment was sold for a gain of $63,000, and taxes related to that gain were $28,000.

The first highlighted section of Exhibit 10.1 shows how this information would be presented on the income statement for Muzby Manufacturing.

EXHIBIT 10.1

Showing Discontinued Operations and Extraordinary Items on the Income Statement

The first highlighted portion of the income statement shows how amounts related to discontinued operations are presented, and the second highlighted portion shows how extraordinary items are presented.

Muzby Manufacturing
Income Statement
For the Year Ended December 31, 2010

Income from continuing operations before income taxes		$ 395,600
Income tax expense		155,000
Income from continuing operations		240,600
Discontinued operations		
Income from discontinued crate-production segment (net of taxes of $1,900)	$10,100	
Gain on disposal of crate-production segment (net of taxes of $28,000)	35,000	45,100
Income before extraordinary item		$ 285,700
Loss on extraordinary item		
Expropriation of foreign operation (net of taxes of $67,000)		(133,000)
Net income		$ 152,700

Extraordinary Items

You have learned that the effect of discontinued operations is the first item that accountants disclose separately on the income statement. The second item is the financial effect of any event that is *unusual* in nature and *infrequent* in occurrence. The financial effects of such events are called **extraordinary items** under U.S. GAAP. (IFRS do not allow extraordinary items.) To qualify as extraordinary, the events must be abnormal and must *not* be reasonably expected to occur again in the foreseeable future. There is a great deal of judgment required to decide if an event should be considered extraordinary. Examples of occurrences that have been considered extraordinary include eruptions of a volcano, a takeover of foreign operations by the foreign government, and the effects of new laws or regulations that result in a one-time cost to comply. Each situation is unique and must be considered in light of the environment in which the business operates. Note that the income tax effects of extraordinary items are also reported separately from the rest of the firm's income taxes.

> **Extraordinary items** are events that are unusual in nature and infrequent in occurrence.

Suppose Muzby Manufacturing has a factory in a foreign country, and the government of that country decides to take possession of all American businesses. The value of the lost factory is $200,000. U.S. tax law allows companies to write off this type of extraordinary loss, which means that the company receives a tax savings. Suppose the applicable tax savings is $67,000. The second highlighted portion of Exhibit 10.1 shows how Muzby Manufacturing would present the information on its income statement for the year.

What does it mean for a company to show discontinued operations and extraordinary items *net of tax?* What would be the alternative?

Your Turn 10-1

Horizontal and Vertical Analysis of Financial Information

Now that you are prepared to recognize extraordinary items and discontinued operations that may appear on the income statement, you are ready to analyze an entire statement or set of statements.

There are three primary ways to analyze financial information: horizontal analysis, vertical analysis, and ratio analysis.

L.O.2
Perform and interpret a horizontal analysis and a vertical analysis of financial statement information.

Horizontal Analysis

Horizontal analysis is a technique for evaluating a financial statement item over a period of time. The purpose of horizontal analysis is to express the change in a financial statement item in percentages rather than in dollars. Financial statement users can spot trends more easily with horizontal analysis than by simply looking at the raw numbers. Consider the cash flows for General Mills, Inc. According to its 2009 10-K, General Mills made the following cash expenditures for property, plant, and equipment:

General Mills, Inc.: Capital Expenditures
For Fiscal Years Ended on the Last Sunday in May
(in millions of dollars)

2009	2008	2007	2006	2005
$562.6	$522.0	$460.2	$360.0	$434.0

Often, the analyst selects one of the years, called the base year, as the reference point. The amounts reported for the other years are expressed as a percentage of the chosen base year. Suppose we choose 2005 as the base year. Then, we subtract the 2005 capital expenditures ($434.0) from 2006 capital expenditures ($360.0) and divide by the base year number ($434.0).

$$\frac{\$360.0 - \$434.0}{\$434.0} = -17.1\%$$

Our calculation shows that during the fiscal year ended in May 2006, General Mills decreased its capital expenditures by 17.1% of the base year's capital expenditures. The calculation is done the same way for each year. The percentage change from the base year to 2007 is calculated as follows:

$$\frac{\$460.2 - \$434.0}{\$434.0} = 6.0\%$$

General Mills, Inc.
Capital Expenditures Comparison—Base Year 2005
(in millions of dollars)

	2009	2008	2007	2006	2005
Capital expenditures	$562.6	$522.0	$460.2	$360.0	$434.0
% change	29.6%	20.3%	6.0%	-17.1%	100%

There is more than one way to do a horizontal analysis. Frequently, the analysis is done by comparing one year with the next, rather than using a fixed base year. For example, we could compare the capital expenditures for 2009 with those for 2008. In this case, there would be an increase. How much? Less than 8%, as shown next:

$$\frac{\$562.6 - \$522.0}{\$522.0} = 7.8\%$$

It is usually difficult to understand the significance of a single item such as capital expenditures when viewing the raw numbers. To make trends more apparent, it may be useful to express the changes in spending in percentage form. Horizontal analysis shows the changes in investment in General Mills, Inc.'s property, plant, and equipment in a way that makes it easy to see what's happening.

Suppose Watts Company has sales for the past five years as follows:

2012	2011	2010	2009	2008
$142,600	$138,500	$125,900	$134,500	$125,000

Use 2008 as the base year and perform a horizontal analysis. What does it tell you about the firm's sales for this five-year period?

Vertical Analysis

Vertical analysis is similar to horizontal analysis, but this analysis involves items on a single year's financial statement. Each item on a financial statement is expressed as a percentage of a selected base amount. This is also called **common-sizing** a financial statement. For example, to perform a vertical analysis on the balance sheet, you would take every amount on the statement and convert it to a percentage of total assets. For a vertical analysis of an income statement, sales is almost always used as the base amount because almost all of a firm's expenditures depend on the level of sales. Each amount on the statement is expressed as a percentage of sales. This type of analysis can point out areas in which the costs might be too large or growing without an obvious cause. For example, if managers at General Mills see that certain costs, as a percentage of sales, are increasing, they can investigate the increase and, if necessary, take action to reduce the firm's costs in that area. Internally, General Mills would do a vertical analysis with much more detail. For investors, vertical analysis also allows the meaningful comparison of companies of different sizes. Exhibit 10.2 shows a vertical analysis for General Mills' income statements for the fiscal years ended May 31, 2009, and May 25, 2008.

Vertical analysis is a technique for comparing items on a financial statement in which all items are expressed as a percent of a common amount.

Common-sizing involves converting all amounts on a financial statement to a percentage of a chosen value on that statement; also known as *vertical analysis*.

EXHIBIT 10.2

Vertical Analysis

The analysis for a single year provides some information, but the comparison of two years reveals more about what's going on with General Mills, Inc. The percentages look very consistent across these two years. What item(s) stands out in the analysis? The notes to the financial statements are the first place to look for additional information whenever an analysis reveals something interesting or unusual.

General Mills, Inc.
Consolidated Statements of Earnings
(dollars in millions)

	For the Year Ended			
	May 31, 2009		May 25, 2008	
Net sales	$14,691.30	100.00%	$13,652.10	100.00%
Cost of sales	9,457.80	64.38%	8,778.30	64.30%
Selling, general, and administrative expenses	2,953.90	20.11%	2,625.00	19.23%
Other (gain), net	(84.90)	–0.58%	0	
Restructuring, impairment, and other costs	41.60	0.28%	21.00	0.15%
Operating profit	2,322.90	15.81%	2,227.80	16.32%
Interest, net	390.00	2.65%	421.70	3.09%
Earnings before income taxes and after-tax				
earnings from joint ventures	1,932.90	13.16%	1,806.10	13.23%
Income taxes	720.40	4.90%	622.20	4.56%
After-tax earnings from joint ventures	91.90	0.63%	110.80	0.81%
Net earnings	$ 1,304.40	8.88%	$ 1,294.70	9.48%

Your Turn 10-3

Use the income statements for 2010 and 2009 from Brothers Company to perform a vertical analysis using sales as the base. What information does the analysis provide?

	Brothers Company Income Statements		

		For the Year Ended	
		March 31, 2010	March 31, 2009
Sales revenue		$10,000	$8,000
Expenses:			
Cost of goods sold		3,200	2,800
Operating expenses		300	275
Bad debts expense		100	90
Insurance expense		200	200
Rent expense		600	600
Depreciation expense		250	250
Interest expense		75	75
Total expenses		4,725	4,290
Net income		$ 5,275	$3,710

L.O.3
Perform a basic ratio analysis of a set of financial statements and explain what the ratios mean.

Ratio Analysis

As you have read, a financial ratio is a comparison of different amounts on the financial statements. Throughout this book, you have learned that ratio analysis uses information in the financial statements to formulate specific values that determine some measure of a company's financial position. We will review all the ratios you have learned and then look at an additional category of ratios, market indicators.

A Review of All Ratios

There are four general categories of ratios, named for what they attempt to measure:

Liquidity ratios are used to measure the company's ability to pay its current bills and operating costs.

Solvency ratios are used to measure the company's ability to meet its long-term obligations and to survive over a long period of time.

Profitability ratios are used to measure the operating or income performance of a company.

Market indicators are ratios that relate the current market price of the company's stock to earnings or dividends.

- **Liquidity ratios:** These ratios measure a company's ability to pay its current bills and operating costs—obligations coming due in the next fiscal year. We have previously discussed the current ratio (Chapter 2), the accounts receivable turnover ratio (Chapter 4), and the inventory turnover ratio (Chapter 5). In this chapter, we will learn an additional liquidity ratio: cash from operations to current liabilities.
- **Solvency ratios:** These ratios measure a company's ability to meet its long-term obligations, such as its long-term debt (bank loans), and to survive over a long period of time. We previously discussed the debt-to-equity ratio (Chapter 7).
- **Profitability ratios:** These ratios measure the operating or income performance of a company. Remember, the goal of a business is to make a profit, so this type of ratio examines how well a company is meeting that goal. We've read about the profit margin ratio (Chapter 3), return on assets (Chapter 6), asset turnover ratio (Chapter 6), and return on equity (Chapter 8).
- **Market indicators:** These ratios relate the current market price of the company's stock to earnings or dividends. In this chapter, you'll learn about the price–earnings ratio and the dividend payout ratio.

Exhibits 10.3A on page 467 and 10.3B on page 468 show the three types of ratios you learned about in earlier chapters. Exhibit 10.3B, on page 468, also includes these two new ratios called

EXHIBIT 10.3A

Common Ratios

Ratio	Definition	How to use the ratio	Chapter where you studied the ratio
LIQUIDITY			
Current ratio	$\dfrac{\text{Total current assets}}{\text{Total current liabilities}}$	To measure a company's ability to pay current liabilities with current assets. This ratio helps creditors determine if a company can meet its short-term obligations.	2
Cash from operations to current liabilities	$\dfrac{\text{Net cash from operating activities}}{\text{Average current liabilities}}$	To measure a company's ability to meet its short-term obligations. This ratio is similar to the current ratio. However, only cash generated from operating activities is considered as available to pay the current liabilities.	10
Inventory turnover ratio	$\dfrac{\text{Cost of goods sold}}{\text{Average inventory}}$	To measure how quickly a company is selling its inventory.	5
Accounts receivable turnover ratio	$\dfrac{\text{Net credit sales}}{\text{Average net accounts receivable}}$	To measure how quickly a company collects the cash from its credit sales.	4
SOLVENCY			
Debt-to-equity ratio	$\dfrac{\text{Total liabilities}}{\text{Total shareholders' equity}}$	To compare the amount of debt a company has with the amount the owners have invested in the company.	7

Note: Turnover ratios are sometimes called efficiency ratios.

market indicators. Keep in mind that the ratios introduced in this book are just a few of the dozens of ratios used in the analysis of financial statements.

Your Turn 10-4

Suppose General Mills has a current ratio greater than one and pays off a current liability with cash. What effect would this have on the company's current ratio?

Liquidity Ratio with Cash Flows

The current ratio (current assets divided by current liabilities) was introduced in Chapter 2; it is the most commonly used ratio for measuring liquidity. The new liquidity ratio introduced here uses net cash from operating activities, from the statement of cash flows, in the numerator and average current liabilities in the denominator. This ratio is directed specifically at the amount of cash a firm is generating from its operations to pay its current liabilities. The ratio is called **cash from operations to current liabilities**, and the calculation is straightforward:

$$\frac{\text{Net cash provided by operating activities}}{\text{Average current liabilities}}$$

Cash from operations to current liabilities ratio is the net cash from operating activities divided by average current liabilities.

EXHIBIT 10.3B

Ratio	Definition	How to use the ratio	Chapter where you studied the ratio
PROFITABILITY			
Return on assets	$\dfrac{\text{Net income}}{\text{Average total assets}}$	To measure a company's success in using its assets to earn income for owners and creditors, those who are financing the business. Average total assets are the average of beginning assets and ending assets for the year.	6
Asset turnover ratio	$\dfrac{\text{Net sales}}{\text{Average total assets}}$	To measure how efficiently a company uses its assets.	6
Return on equity	$\dfrac{\text{Net income} - \text{preferred dividends}}{\text{Average common shareholders' equity}}$	To measure how much income is earned with the common shareholders' investment in the company.	8
Profit margin ratio	$\dfrac{\text{Net income}}{\text{Net sales}}$	To measure the amount from each dollar of sales that is bottom-line profit.	3
Gross profit ratio	$\dfrac{\text{Gross profit}}{\text{Net sales}}$	To measure a company's profitability. It is one of the most carefully watched ratios by management because it describes the percentage of the sales price that is gross profit. A small shift usually indicates a big change in the profitability of the company's sales.	5
Earnings per share	$\dfrac{\text{Net income} - \text{preferred dividends}}{\text{Weighted average number of shares of common stock outstanding}}$	To calculate net income per share of common stock.	8
MARKET INDICATORS			
Price–earnings ratio	$\dfrac{\text{Market price per common share}}{\text{Earnings per share}}$	To calculate the market price for $1 of earnings.	10
Dividend yield ratio	$\dfrac{\text{Dividend per share}}{\text{Market price per share}}$	To calculate the percentage return on the investment in a share of stock via dividends.	10

Your Turn 10-5

Company A has a gross profit ratio of 30% and Company B has a gross profit ratio of 60%. Can you tell which company is more profitable? Why or why not?

Market Indicator Ratios

The market price of a share of stock is what an investor is willing to pay for the stock. There are two ratios that use the current market price of a share of stock to help potential investors predict what they might earn by purchasing that stock. One ratio is the **price–earnings (P/E) ratio**. This ratio is defined by its name: It is the price of a share of stock divided by the company's current earnings per share.

Price–earnings (P/E) ratio is the market price of a share of stock divided by that stock's earnings per share.

$$\text{P/E ratio} = \frac{\text{Market price per share}}{\text{Earnings per share}}$$

Investors and financial analysts believe the P/E ratio indicates future earnings potential. A high P/E ratio indicates that the company has the potential for significant growth. When a new firm has no earnings, the P/E ratio has no meaning because the denominator is zero. For the first several years of business Amazon.com had no earnings but a rising stock price. Analysts have varying opinions about the information contained in the P/E ratio.

The other market indicator ratio is the **dividend yield ratio**. This ratio is the dividend per share divided by the market price per share. You may find that the values for the dividend yield ratio are quite low compared to the return an investor would expect on an investment. Investors are willing to accept a low dividend yield when they anticipate an increase in the price of the stock.

Stocks with low growth potential, however, may need to offer a higher dividend yield to attract investors.

$$\text{Dividend yield ratio} = \frac{\text{Dividend per share}}{\text{Market price per share}}$$

Exhibit 10.4 shows the earnings per share, the dividends per share, and the market price per share for Google Inc. and for ExxonMobil. Which stock would be a better buy for long-term growth? Which would be best if you needed regular dividend income?

EXHIBIT 10.4

Price/Earnings and Dividend Yield Ratios

For fiscal years ended	Google Inc. December 31, 2008	ExxonMobil Corporation December 31, 2008
Earnings per share	$ 13.46	$ 8.78
Dividends per share	$ 0.00	$ 1.55
Ending market price per share	$448.89	$79.83
Price/earnings ratio	33.35	9.09
Dividend yield ratio	n/a	1.94%

The types of stock that will appeal to an investor depend on the investor's preferences for income and growth. A young investor, for example, will not need dividends from retirement funds invested in stocks. These long-term investors would prefer to invest in companies with high growth potential, no matter what the dividend yield. Google might be more attractive, with its high P/E ratio of 33.35 (last day of 2008), than ExxonMobil, with its lower P/E ratio of 9.09 (last day of 2008). A retiree who needs dividend income for living expenses will be more concerned with the size of the dividend yield of an investment and less concerned with the investment's long-term growth. For that investor, ExxonMobil would be better than Google for dividends, because ExxonMobil pays regular dividends and Google has never paid a dividend to its shareholders.

These two market-related ratios are very important to management and to investors because analysts and investors use them in evaluating firms' stock. If you examine a company's annual report, you are likely to see these ratios reported, usually for the most recent two or three years.

Understanding Ratios

A ratio by itself does not give much information. To be useful, a ratio must be compared to the same ratios from previous periods, ratios of other companies in the industry, or industry averages. Keep in mind that, with the exception of earnings per share (EPS), the calculations to arrive at a specific ratio may vary from company to company. There are no standard or required formulas to calculate a ratio. One company may calculate a debt ratio as *debt* to *equity*, whereas another company may calculate a debt ratio as *debt* to *debt plus equity*. An analyst can create any ratio that he or she believes will be useful in the analysis of a company's financial statements. When interpreting and using any company's ratios, be sure you know how those ratios have been computed. When you are computing ratios, be sure to be consistent in your calculations so you can make meaningful comparisons among them.

Even though the only ratio that must be calculated and presented as part of the financial statements is EPS, which is shown on the income statement, a firm typically includes many of the ratios we have discussed in this chapter in its annual report. When these ratios are not shown as part of the financial statements, they may be included in other parts of the annual report, often in graphs depicting trends over several years.

Any valuable financial statement analysis requires more than a cursory review of ratios. The analyst must look at trends, components of the values that are part of the ratios, and other information about the company that may not even be contained in the financial statements.

Using Ratio Analysis

We will compute some of the ratios shown in Exhibits 10.3A and 10.3B for Abercrombie & Fitch Co. (A&F) using the company's 2008 annual report. Exhibit 10.5 shows the income statements for three years, and Exhibit 10.6 shows the balance sheets for two years.

EXHIBIT 10.5

Income Statements for Abercrombie & Fitch Co.

Abercrombie & Fitch Co. Consolidated Statements of Net Income (Thousands, except per share amounts)			
	2008	2007	2006*
NET SALES	$3,540,276	$3,749,847	$3,318,158
Cost of Goods Sold	1,178,584	1,238,480	1,109,152
GROSS PROFIT	2,361,692	2,511,367	2,209,006
Stores and Distribution Expense	1,511,511	1,386,846	1,187,071
Marketing, General & Administrative Expense	419,659	395,758	373,828
Other Operating Income, Net	(8,864)	(11,734)	(9,983)
OPERATING INCOME	439,386	740,497	658,090
Interest Income, Net	(11,382)	(18,828)	(13,896)
INCOME BEFORE INCOME TAXES	450,768	759,325	671,986
Provision for Income Taxes	178,513	283,628	249,800
NET INCOME	$ 272,255	$ 475,697	$ 422,186
NET INCOME PER SHARE:			
BASIC	$ 3.14	$ 5.45	$ 4.79
DILUTED	$ 3.05	$ 5.20	$ 4.59
WEIGHTED-AVERAGE SHARES OUTSTANDING:			
BASIC	86,816	87,248	88,052
DILUTED	89,291	91,523	92,010
DIVIDENDS DECLARED PER SHARE	$ 0.70	$ 0.70	$ 0.70

*Fiscal 2006 was a 53-week year.

Other information needed for the analysis follows:

- Net cash from operating activities is $490,836,000 for fiscal year 2008 and $817,524,000 for fiscal year 2007.
- Market price per share at the close of fiscal year is approximately $17.85 per share at January 30, 2009 (the 2008 fiscal year end) and $82.06 per share at February 1, 2008 (the 2007 fiscal year end).
- Dividends declared are shown on the face of the income statement.

The computations for the ratios are shown in Exhibits 10.7A on page 472 and 10.7B on page 473. Even though two years of ratios do not give us enough information for making decisions, use this as an opportunity to practice how to calculate the ratios.

Ratios are relatively easy to calculate; the difficulty comes in interpreting them. Books have been written to try to teach people to do this, and analysts can be paid very large salaries for their expertise in financial statement analysis. In each chapter of this book in which a ratio was introduced, you will find information about how the ratio is calculated, interpreted, and used. Following are some examples of how ratios are related and how information can be gained from looking at them in conjunction with each other.

Liquidity Ratios

CURRENT RATIO. Often, a current ratio greater than one is viewed as adequate, meaning that a firm has enough current assets to meet its current obligations (current liabilities) in the coming year. Recall, however, that the ratio captures current assets and current liabilities at a moment in time—the

EXHIBIT 10.6

Balance Sheets for Abercrombie & Fitch Co.

Abercrombie & Fitch Co.
Consolidated Balance Sheets
(Thousands, except share amounts)

	January 31, 2009	February 2, 2008
ASSETS		
CURRENT ASSETS:		
Cash and Equivalents	$ 522,122	$ 118,044
Marketable Securities	—	530,486
Receivables	53,110	53,801
Inventories	372,422	333,153
Deferred Income Taxes	43,408	36,128
Other Current Assets	93,763	68,643
TOTAL CURRENT ASSETS	1,084,825	1,140,255
PROPERTY AND EQUIPMENT, NET	1,398,655	1,318,291
MARKETABLE SECURITIES	229,081	—
OTHER ASSETS	135,620	109,052
TOTAL ASSETS	$2,848,181	$2,567,598
LIABILITIES AND SHAREHOLDERS' EQUITY		
CURRENT LIABILITIES:		
Accounts Payable	$ 92,814	$ 108,437
Outstanding Checks	56,939	43,361
Accrued Expenses	241,231	280,910
Deferred Lease Credits	42,358	37,925
Income Taxes Payable	16,455	72,480
TOTAL CURRENT LIABILTIES	449,797	543,113
LONG-TERM LIABILITIES:		
Deferred Income Taxes	34,085	22,491
Deferred Lease Credits	211,978	213,739
Debt	100,000	—
Other Liabilities	206,743	169,942
TOTAL LONG-TERM LIABILITIES	552,806	406,172
SHAREHOLDERS' EQUITY:		
Class A Common Stock—$.01 par value: 150,000,000 shares authorized and 103,300,000 shares issued at January 31, 2009 and February 2, 2008, respectively	1,033	1,033
Paid-In Capital	328,488	319,451
Retained Earnings	2,244,936	2,051,463
Accumulated Other Comprehensive (Loss) Income, net of tax	(22,681)	7,118
Treasury Stock at Average Cost 15,664,385 and 17,141,116 shares at January 31, 2009, and February 2, 2008, respectively	(706,198)	(760,752)
TOTAL SHAREHOLDERS' EQUITY	1,845,578	1,618,313
TOTAL LIABILITIES AND SHAREHOLDERS' EQUITY	$2,848,181	$2,567,598

The accompanying notes are an integral part of these consolidated financial statements.

end of the last day of the fiscal year. A&F has a current ratio of 2.41. In isolation, this appears to be quite adequate. However, it is very useful to look at the other liquidity ratios in conjunction with the current ratio to see how quickly A&F is converting its receivables and inventory into cash. If a current ratio is high because of high values in accounts receivable and inventory, rather than cash, the rate at which those current assets are converted into cash, which is what is needed to pay current liabilities, becomes important. Another way to approach that question of adequate cash is to look at the amount of cash the company is generating from its operating activities.

CASH FROM OPERATIONS TO CURRENT LIABILITIES RATIO. For A&F, this ratio has declined. Having a ratio of less than 1 indicates that A&F has more current liabilities, on average, than the cash it generates from its operations. If this is a problem, we should try to identify more specifically why the company is not generating sufficient cash. That takes us to the turnover ratios.

EXHIBIT 10.7A

Ratio Analysis for Abercrombie & Fitch Co.

As you evaluate the ratios, keep in mind that even two years' worth of ratios is rarely enough information to come to any conclusions. Most annual reports provide the data for ten years' worth of ratios. Often, ratio analysis is useful for identifying potential problem areas. No problems are obvious for Abercrombie & Fitch Co. from this analysis.

Ratio	Definition	Computation	Computation	Interpretation
LIQUIDITY		FYE January 31, 2009	FYE February 2, 2008	
Current ratio	$\dfrac{\text{Total current assets}}{\text{Total current liabilities}}$	$\dfrac{\$1,084,825}{\$449,797} = 2.41$	$\dfrac{\$1,140,255}{\$543,113} = 2.10$	Excellent current ratio. Industry (apparel retailers) average is 1.37.
Cash from operations to current liabilities	$\dfrac{\text{Net cash from operating activities}}{\text{Average current liabilities}}$	$\dfrac{\$490,836}{(\$543,113 + \$449,797)/2}$ $= 0.99$	$\dfrac{\$817,524}{(\$510,627^* + \$543,113)/2}$ $= 1.55$ * From the 2007 balance sheet not shown here	The significant decline in this ratio is troublesome. The serious decline in cash generated by operations deserves further analysis.
Inventory turnover ratio	$\dfrac{\text{Cost of goods sold}}{\text{Average inventory}}$	$\dfrac{\$1,178,584}{(\$333,153 + \$372,422)/2}$ $= 3.34$	$\dfrac{\$1,238,480}{(\$427,447^* + \$333,153)/2}$ $= 3.26$ * From the 2007 balance sheet not shown here	The company is turning its inventory over only a little more than 3 times per year. Industry average is 3.3 times per year in 2008.
Accounts receivable turnover ratio	$\dfrac{\text{Net sales}}{\text{Average net accounts receivable}}$	$\dfrac{\$3,540,276}{(\$53,801 + \$53,110)/2} = 66.23$	$\dfrac{\$3,749,847}{(\$43,240^* + \$53,801)/2}$ $= 77.28$ * From the 2007 balance sheet not shown here	The company is turning over its receivables over 66 times per year. When cash and credit card sales are included in the numerator, it inflates this ratio, so it isn't very meaningful without more information.
SOLVENCY				
Debt-to-equity	$\dfrac{\text{Total liabilities}}{\text{Total equity}}$	$\dfrac{\$449,797 + \$552,806}{\$1,845,578} = 0.54$	$\dfrac{\$543,113 + \$406,172}{\$1,618,313} = 0.59$	The firm has made a small decrease in the amount of debt in its capital structure.

INVENTORY TURNOVER RATIO. At first glance, it appears that this is an area that could be a problem for A&F. Turning over inventory only 3.34 times per year translates into over 109 days in inventory. Remember that you can calculate the average number of days in inventory by dividing 365 (days in the year) by the turnover ratio. In other words, it takes, on average, 109 days to sell an inventory item. While this sounds like very slow moving inventory, we'll need more information to reach any conclusion. The Retail Owners Institute (http://retailowner.com) provides some relevant industry data. The average inventory turnover for clothing and accessories stores was 3.4 in 2007 and 3.3 in 2008. As a matter of fact, in 2004 the average was only 3.1. It appears that inventory turnover is not a particular problem for A&F considering the industry. However, improving that ratio could help A&F's cash flow.

ACCOUNTS RECEIVABLE TURNOVER RATIO.   As mentioned in the table, the accounts receivable turnover ratio for a retail store is always high due to the large number of sales made with cash and bank credit cards. Even this ratio has declined for A&F, which is not a good sign. Taken

EXHIBIT 10.7B

PROFITABILITY		FYE January 31, 2009	FYE February 2, 2008	
Return on assets	$\dfrac{\text{Net income}}{\text{Average total assets}}$	$\dfrac{\$272,255}{(\$2,567,598 + \$2,848,181)/2}$ $= 10.1\%$	$\dfrac{\$475,697}{(\$2,248,067^* + \$2,567,598)/2}$ $= 19.8\%$ * From the 2007 balance sheet not shown here	The effect of the recession can easily be seen in this decrease in the firm's ROA.
Asset turnover ratio	$\dfrac{\text{Net sales}}{\text{Average total assets}}$	$\dfrac{\$3,540,276}{(\$2,567,598 + \$2,848,181)/2}$ $= 1.31$	$\dfrac{\$3,749,847}{(\$2,248,067^* + \$2,567,598)/2}$ $= 1.56$ * From the 2007 balance sheet not shown here	The firm's use of its assets to generate sales has decreased. Again, this is not surprising in the economic climate of this particular year.
Return on equity	$\dfrac{\text{Net income} - \text{preferred dividends}}{\text{Average common shareholders' equity}}$	$\dfrac{\$272,255}{(\$1,618,313 + \$1,845,578)/2}$ $= 15.7\%$	$\dfrac{\$475,697}{(\$1,405,297^* + \$1,618,313)/2}$ $= 31.5\%$ * From the 2007 balance sheet not shown here	Again, we see the large decrease in ROE. Still, the return to shareholders is good.
Profit margin ratio	$\dfrac{\text{Net income}}{\text{Net sales}}$	$\dfrac{\$272,255}{\$3,540,276} = 7.7\%$	$\dfrac{\$475,697}{\$3,749,847} = 12.7\%$	Not only have sales decreased, the amount of each sales dollar that makes it all the way to the bottom line has decreased. This indicates increasing costs.
Gross profit ratio	$\dfrac{\text{Gross profit}}{\text{Sales}}$	$\dfrac{\$2,361,692}{\$3,540,276} = 66.7\%$	$\dfrac{\$2,511,367}{\$3,749,847} = 67.0\%$	This ratio has not changed much, so the increasing costs indicated by the profit margin ratio are not due to the cost of the inventory.
Earnings per share	$\dfrac{\text{Net income} - \text{preferred dividends}}{\text{Weighted average \# of common shares outstanding}}$	$\dfrac{\$272,255}{86,816^*} = \$3.14$ *Disclosed on the income statement	$\dfrac{\$475,697}{87,248^*} = \$5.45$ *Disclosed on the income statement	The calculation is shown here, but remember that you will not need to calculate this ratio if you have the income statement. It will be shown on the face of the statement.
MARKET INDICATORS				
Price-earnings ratio	$\dfrac{\text{Market price per share}}{\text{Earnings per share}}$	$\dfrac{\$17.85}{\$3.14} = 5.68$	$\dfrac{\$82.06}{\$5.45} = 15.06$	Earnings have decreased significantly, and the stock price has plummeted. At the beginning of the 2008 fiscal year, investors were willing to pay $15.06 for every dollar of earnings. By year end, they were only willing to pay $5.68 for a dollar of earnings.
Dividend yield	$\dfrac{\text{Dividend per share}}{\text{Market price per share}}$	$\dfrac{\$0.70}{\$17.85} = 3.9\%$	$\dfrac{\$0.70}{\$82.06} = 0.9\%$	Dividends have remained stable, so the yield will vary with stock price. These are the stock prices at fiscal year end.

together, these liquidity ratios indicate that A&F can meet its short-term obligations but that both inventory and accounts receivable could be areas where A&F could increase its efficiency.

Profitability Ratios

Return ratios—ROA and ROE—measure the relationship between the firm's income and the amount of investment that a specific group has made in the company. ROA, for example, measures the return to all investors, both debt and equity holders. ROE, on the other hand, measures the return to common equity investors only. Our analysis showed that A&F had an ROA of 10.1% and an ROE of 15.7% for the 2008 fiscal year. Unfortunately, both have gone down significantly from the 2007 fiscal year (ROA was 19.8% and ROE was 31.5%). Industry data for 2007 indicates that the industry average for apparel (retail) was 11.9 for ROA and 21.4 for ROE (Standard and Poor's Industry Surveys, February 12, 2009). In both cases, A&F's return ratios exceeded the industry averages in 2007.

As you can see, ratio analysis is not an easy task. There are many resources to help you, often provided online or in your school's library. However, there is no substitute for understanding the company you are analyzing. A company's financial history, its market, its management, its strategy, and the general state of the economy all play a role in the interpretation of financial information.

Financial Statement Analysis—More than Numbers

You have probably noticed the following sentence at the end of every actual financial statement you have ever seen, "The accompanying notes are an integral part of these financial statements." Some analysts believe there is more real information about the financial health of a company in the notes than in the statements themselves. Go to the back of the book where you will find the financial statements for Books-A-Million, Inc. Look at the detailed and extensive notes that accompany the statements. The more you learn about analyzing and evaluating a company's performance, whether in subsequent courses or in actual business experience, the more you will understand the information in the notes to the financial statements. When you are comparing two or more firms, you need to know the accounting choices those firms have made—such as depreciation and inventory methods—to make valid comparisons. Often, analysts compute new

UNDERSTANDING Business

What is EBITDA?

If you read much about financial statements and earnings, you will eventually come across the expression "EBITDA" (pronounced íba duh). It is an acronym for *earnings before interest, taxes, depreciation, and amortization*. EBITDA can be calculated from information on the income statement (earnings, taxes, and interest) and the statement of cash flows (depreciation and amortization—added back to net income when calculating cash from operating activities). Eliminating these items—because they involve management discretion and estimates—can make it easier to compare the financial health of various firms. Because it is a result of management's financing choices (debt rather than equity), eliminating interest takes away the effect of a firm's capital structure.

Even though EBITDA has become a popular measure of a firm's performance, it does not tell the whole story. According

to Investopedia.com, there are at least four reasons to be wary of EBITDA.

1. There is no substitute for cash flows. No matter what EBITDA is, a firm cannot operate without sufficient cash.
2. The items that are eliminated from earnings are not avoidable, so ignoring them can be misleading.
3. EBITDA ignores the quality of earnings. You will learn more about that in Chapter 11.
4. Using EBITDA to calculate a price–earnings ratio could make a firm look cheaper than it actually is.

The bottom line is that EBITDA is useful, but it is only one of many measures of a firm's performance. Remember that EBITDA is NOT defined by GAAP, so firms may measure EBITDA in different ways.

amounts using a different method than the one the firm used so that the amounts can be meaning-fully compared to those of another firm. For example, if one company uses LIFO and another uses FIFO, an analyst would convert the LIFO values to FIFO values using the disclosures required in the notes of firms that use LIFO.

To better appreciate the role of accounting information in business, look at a business plan. A business plan is a detailed analysis of what it would take to start and maintain the operation of a successful business. Anyone writing a business plan includes a sales forecast, expense esti-mates, and prospective financial statements. These are "what-if" financial statements, forecasts that are part of the business plan. Banks often require these statements before they will lend money to a new firm.

Because accounting is such an integral part of business, accounting principles will continue to change as business changes. Each year, the FASB and the SEC add and change the rules for valuing items on the financial statements. FASB is also concerned with the continued usefulness and reliability of the accounting data from electronic transactions, e-business, and real-time access to financial data. As competition takes on new dimensions, particularly due to new tech-nology, the scrutiny of a firm's financial information will increase. With the influence of the financial scandals of the early 2000s and the recession that began in 2008, the financial informa-tion needed for good decision making will continue to grow in importance.

Business Risk, Control, and Ethics

L.O.4
Recognize the risks of investing in stocks and explain how to control those risks.

We already discussed, in Chapter 1, the risks associated with starting a business. Now we will take the perspective of an investor. After all, you are very likely to buy stock in a publicly-traded company sometime in your life. Many working people have money in retirement funds that are invested in the stock of publicly-traded companies. Additionally, the movement of the stock market affects a large number of firms and individual investors. How should you, as an investor, minimize the risks associated with stock ownership? That risk, of course, is losing your money!

First, you should be diligent about finding a financial advisor or financial analyst to help you, or you should become an expert from your own study and analysis of available stocks. You also need to know and understand some financial accounting and financial statement analysis, which you have been exposed to in this course. However, being knowledgeable or consulting an expert does not give an investor complete protection against losses.

Between September 30, 2007, and March 6, 2009, the stock market lost 56% of its value, a decline of about $13 trillion.

Source: The Urban Institute, Fact Sheet on Retirement Policy, March 9, 2009.
http://www.urban.org/retirement_policy/url.cfm?ID=411847

That leads to the second and most effective way to minimize the risks associated with stock ownership: diversify. In everyday usage, to diversify means to vary or expand. In the language of investment, diversify means to vary the investments you make—to expand beyond a narrow set of investments. Diversification means not putting all of your eggs in one basket. A diversified set of investments allows an investor to earn a higher rate of return for a given amount of risk.

There is no way to eliminate all of the risks of stock ownership, but having many differ-ent types of investments will help you minimize your risk or, equivalently, increase your return for a given amount of risk. Part of diversification is investing in assets other than stocks. As you might recall from Chapter 7, investors also purchase corporate bonds. Investing in bonds and other debt securities is part of a sound diversification strategy. Real estate is another example of an investment that is often included in a diversified portfolio. The composition of a person's investment portfolio depends on how much risk that person is willing to take. According to Bank One, "A diversified portfolio does not concentrate in one or two investment categories. Instead, it includes some investments whose returns zig while the returns of other investments zag."

Chapter Summary Points

- Components of net income include income from continuing operations, discontinued operations, and extraordinary items. Gains and losses from discontinued operations and from extraordinary items are segregated from other revenues and expenses so that an investor can easily separate these nonrecurring items from those expected to recur in the future.
- Horizontal analysis compares a specific financial statement item across time, often with reference to a chosen base year. A vertical analysis, also known as common-sized statements, shows every item on a single year's financial statement as a percentage of one of the other financial statement items. Most often, a vertical analysis of the income statement calculates all items as a percentage of sales, and a vertical analysis of the balance sheet calculates all items as a percentage of total assets.
- Ratio analysis is a tool used by anyone who wants to evaluate a firm's financial statements. Remember that a ratio is meaningful only when it is compared to another ratio.
- Investing in a firm as an owner, by purchasing a firm's stock, can create risks. The biggest risk is that the firm will not do well and its stock price will decrease. The best protection for an investor is to have a diversified portfolio. That is, buy a variety of stocks and other investments, such as bonds and real estate, so that a decrease in the price of one asset may be offset by an increase in the price of another.

Chapter Summary Problems

Instructions

Use the information on the following income statement and balance sheet for Apple Inc. to perform a ratio analysis on the two most recent fiscal years. Use Exhibits 10.7A and 10.7B as a model. Comment on your results.

Apple Inc.
Consolidated Statements of Operations
(In millions, except share amounts, which are reflected in thousands and per share amounts)

Three Fiscal Years Ended September 27, 2008	2008	2007	2006
Net sales	$ 32,479	$ 24,006	$ 19,315
Cost of sales	21,334	15,852	13,717
Gross margin	11,145	8,154	5,598
Operating expenses:			
Research and development	1,109	782	712
Selling, general, and administrative	3,761	2,963	2,433
Total operating expenses	4,870	3,745	3,145
Operating income	6,275	4,409	2,453
Other income and expense	620	599	365
Income before provision for income taxes	6,895	5,008	2,818
Provision for income taxes	2,061	1,512	829
Net income	$ 4,834	$ 3,496	$ 1,989
Earnings per common share:			
Basic	$ 5.48	$ 4.04	$ 2.36
Diluted	$ 5.36	$ 3.93	$ 2.27
Shares used in computing earnings per share:			
Basic	881,592	864,595	844,058
Diluted	902,139	889,292	877,526

Apple Inc.
Consolidated Balance Sheets
(In millions, except share amounts)

	September 27, 2008	September 29, 2007
ASSETS:		
Current Assets:		
Cash and cash equivalents	$11,875	$ 9,352
Short-term investments	12,615	6,034
Accounts receivable, less allowances of $47 in each period ...	2,422	1,637
Inventories	509	346
Deferred tax assets	1,447	782
Other current assets	5,822	3,805
Total current assets	34,690	21,956
Property, plant, and equipment, net	2,455	1,832
Goodwill	207	38
Acquired intangible assets, net	285	299
Other assets	1,935	1,222
Total assets	$39,572	$25,347
LIABILITIES AND SHAREHOLDERS' EQUITY:		
Current liabilities:		
Accounts payable	$ 5,520	$ 4,970
Accrued expenses	8,572	4,310
Total current liabilities	14,092	9,280
Non-current liabilities	4,450	1,535
Total liabilities	18,542	10,815
Commitments and contingencies		
Shareholders' equity:		
Common stock, no par value; 1,800,000,000 shares authorized; 888,325,973 and 872,328,972 shares issued and outstanding, respectively	7,177	5,368
Retained earnings	13,845	9,101
Accumulated other comprehensive income	8	63
Total shareholders' equity	21,030	14,532
Total liabilities and shareholders' equity	$39,572	$25,347

See accompanying Notes to Consolidated Financial Statements.

Additional information you will need (dollars in millions) follows:

Total assets at September 27, 2006	$17,205
Inventory at September 27, 2006	$ 270
Net accounts receivable at September 27, 2006	$ 1,252
Total current liabilities at September 27, 2006	$ 6,443
Total shareholders' equity at September 27, 2006	$ 9,984
Net cash from operating activities for FYE September 27, 2007	$ 5,470
Net cash from operating activities for FYE September 27, 2008	$ 9,596
Market price of stock on September 27, 2007	$153.47
Market price of stock on September 27, 2008	$128.24

Solution

Ratio	Definition	Computation	Computation	Interpretation
LIQUIDITY		FYE September 27, 2008 (dollars in millions)	FYE September 27, 2007 (dollars in millions)	
Current ratio	$\dfrac{\text{Total current assets}}{\text{Total current liabilities}}$	$\dfrac{34,690}{14,092} = 2.46$	$\dfrac{21,956}{9,280} = 2.37$	Apple has no problem meeting its short-term obligations.
Cash from operations to current liabilities	$\dfrac{\text{Net cash from operating activities}}{\text{Average current liabilities}}$	$\dfrac{\$9,596}{(\$9,280 + \$14,092)/2} = 0.82$	$\dfrac{\$5,470}{(\$6,443^* + \$9,280)/2} = 0.70$ * From the 2006 balance sheet not shown here	The ratio appears to be a bit low, but it has increased during the most recent year.
Inventory turnover ratio	$\dfrac{\text{Cost of goods sold}}{\text{Average inventory}}$	$\dfrac{\$21,334}{(\$346 + \$509)/2} = 49.90$	$\dfrac{\$15,852}{(\$270^* + \$346)/2} = 51.47$ * From the 2006 balance sheet not shown here but provided with the given data	Apple turns over its inventory quickly. For 2008, the average number of days in inventory was only 7.31 days (365/49.90).
Accounts receivable turnover ratio	$\dfrac{\text{Net sales}}{\text{Average net accounts receivable}}$	$\dfrac{\$32,479}{(\$1,637 + \$2,422)/2} = 16.00$	$\dfrac{\$24,006}{(\$1,252^* + \$1,637)/2} = 16.62$ * From the 2006 balance sheet not shown here but provided with the given data	Apple collects its receivables in a reasonable amount of time. Average days to collect AR in 2008 was 22.81 days (365/16.00).
SOLVENCY				
Debt-to-equity	$\dfrac{\text{Total liabilities}}{\text{Total equity}}$	$\dfrac{\$18,542}{\$21,030} = 0.88$	$\dfrac{\$10,815}{\$14,532} = 0.74$	While this looks like a high debt ratio, notice that Apple has very little long-term debt. Some sources will use only long-term debt in the numerator of this ratio.

PROFITABILITY				
Return on assets	Net income / Average total assets	$\frac{\$4,834}{(\$25,347 + \$39,572)/2}$ $= 14.89\%$	$\frac{\$3,496}{(\$17,205^* + \$25,347)/2}$ $= 16.43\%$ * From the 2006 balance sheet not shown here but provided with the given data	Good ROA, although decreasing slightly; not surprising given the recession during this year
Asset turnover ratio	Net sales / Average total assets	$\frac{\$32,479}{(\$25,347 + \$39,572)/2}$ $= 1.00$	$\frac{\$24,006}{(\$17,205^* + \$25,347)/2}$ $= 1.13$ * From the 2006 balance sheet not shown here but provided with the given data	This change indicates a decrease in the efficiency with which the firm's assets are generating sales.
Return on equity	Net income − preferred dividends / Average common shareholders' equity	$\frac{\$4,834}{(\$14,532 + \$21,030)/2}$ $= 27.19\%$	$\frac{\$3,496}{(\$9,984^* + \$14,532)/2}$ $= 28.52\%$ * From the 2006 balance sheet not shown here	This is an excellent ROE, decreasing only very slightly even in a recession.
Profit margin ratio	Net income / Net sales	$\frac{\$4,834}{\$32,479} = 14.88\%$	$\frac{\$3,496}{\$24,006} = 14.57\%$	This is an excellent profit margin ratio. It shows Apple is controlling its costs quite well.
Gross profit ratio	Gross profit / Sales	$\frac{\$11,145}{\$32,479} = 34.31\%$	$\frac{\$8,154}{\$24,006} = 33.97\%$	The slight increase is excellent, especially considering the economy at this time.
Earnings per share	Net income − preferred dividends / Average # of common shares outstanding	$\frac{\$4,834,000}{881,592^*} = \$5.48$ * Disclosed on the income statement. Notice that NI was given in millions while number of shares was given in thousands. Three zeros are added to the net income number to put the numerator and denominator in the same units.	$\frac{\$3,496,000}{864,595^*} = \$4.04$ * Disclosed on the income statement	The calculation is shown here, but remember that you will not need to calculate this ratio if you have the income statement. It will be shown on the face of the statement.
MARKET INDICATORS				
Price–earnings ratio	Market price per share / Earnings per share	$\frac{\$128.24}{\$5.48} = 23.40$	$\frac{\$153.47}{\$4.04} = 37.99$	Even though earnings have gone up, the market price at year end has decreased significantly during this time. That has resulted in a significant decrease in the PE ratio.
Dividend yield	Dividend per share / Market price per share	N/A Apple did not pay any dividends.		

Key Terms for Chapter 10

Available-for-sale securities
(p. 508)
Cash from operations to
current liabilities ratio
(p. 467)
Common-sizing (p. 465)
Comprehensive income
(p. 505)

Discontinued operations
(p. 462)
Dividend yield ratio (p. 468)
Extraordinary items (p. 463)
Held-to-maturity securities
(p. 507)
Horizontal analysis (p. 464)
Liquidity ratios (p. 466)
Market indicators (p. 466)

Price–earnings (PE) ratio
(p. 468)
Profitability ratios (p. 466)
Solvency ratios (p. 466)
Trading securities (p. 507)
Unrealized gain or loss
(p. 507)
Vertical analysis (p. 465)

Answers to YOUR TURN Questions

Chapter 10

Your Turn 10-1

Those items must be shown after the tax consequences have been subtracted because this method of reporting the items net of taxes keeps the tax implications of these items separate from the company's regular tax expense. The alternative is to show the items before the tax implications and then to include the tax savings or tax increases in the company's regular tax expense.

Your Turn 10-2

2008	2009	2010	2011	2012
100%	7.6%	0.7%	10.8%	14.1%

Every year the firm's sales have exceeded sales in the base year. Except for 2010, the percentage increase has been good and continues to increase.

Your Turn 10-3

Brothers Company
Income Statements

| | For the Year Ended | | | |
	March 31, 2010		March 31, 2009	
Sales revenue	$10,000	100.0%	$8,000	100.0%
Expenses:				
Cost of goods sold	3,200	32.0%	2,800	35.0%
Operating expenses	300	3.0%	275	3.4%
Bad debts expense	100	1.0%	90	1.1%
Insurance expense	200	2.0%	200	2.5%
Rent expense	600	6.0%	600	7.5%
Depreciation expense	250	2.5%	250	3.1%
Interest expense	75	0.8%	75	0.9%
Total expenses	4,725	47.3%	4,290	53.6%
Net income	$ 5,275	52.8%	$3,710	46.4%

The company's performance has improved in almost all areas. The higher net income is not just due to the increase in sales. The cost of goods sold as a percentage of sales has gone down, and all the expenses have also decreased as a percent of sales.

Your Turn 10-4

This payoff would increase the current ratio. We can use a simple example to illustrate why: Suppose current assets were $500 million and current liabilities were $250 million. The current ratio would be 2. Now suppose $50 million worth of current liabilities were paid off with current assets. Then current assets would be $450 million, and current liabilities would be $200 million.

The current ratio is now 2.25. When a fraction is greater than 1 and both the numerator and the denominator of a fraction are reduced by the same amount, the value of the fraction will increase.

Your Turn 10-5

No, the gross profit ratio does not tell which company is more profitable because one company may have higher sales than the other. For example 30% of a large number is better than 60% of a small number. Also, the amount of costs the companies must cover beyond the cost of goods sold is unknown. The gross profit ratio is most useful for comparing companies in the same industry or evaluating performance of a single company across time.

Questions

1. Define the items that the Financial Accounting Standards Board requires a firm to report separately on the income statement. Why is this separation useful?
2. What criteria must be met for an event to be considered extraordinary? Give an example of an event that would be considered extraordinary.
3. What does it mean to show an item net of tax? Where is this done and why?
4. What is horizontal analysis? What is the purpose of this method of analysis?
5. What is vertical analysis? What is the purpose of this method of analysis?
6. What is liquidity? Which ratios are useful for measuring liquidity and what does each measure?
7. What is solvency? Which ratios are useful for measuring solvency and what does each measure?
8. What is profitability? Which ratios are useful for measuring profitability and what does each measure?
9. What are market indicators? Which ratios are market indicators and what does each measure?
10. How are financial ratios used to determine how successfully a company is operating?

Multiple-Choice Questions

1. Suppose a firm had an extraordinary loss of $300,000. If the firm's tax rate is 35%, how will the loss be shown in the financial statements?
   a. On the income statement, below income from operations, net of tax savings, for a net loss of $195,000
   b. On the income statement as part of the calculation of income from operations, before taxes, for a loss of $300,000
   c. As supplementary information in the notes to the financial statements
   d. As a cash outflow from financing on the statement of cash flows
2. Current assets for Kearney Company are $120,000 and total assets are $600,000. Current liabilities are $80,000 and total liabilities are $300,000. What is the current ratio?
   a. 2.00
   b. 2.50
   c. 1.90
   d. 1.50
3. Ritchie Company sold some fixed assets for a gain of $100,000. The firm's tax rate is 25%. How would Ritchie Company report this transaction on its financial statements?
   a. On the income statement as part of the calculation of income from continuing operations, net of tax, in the amount of $75,000
   b. As an extraordinary item, net of tax, in the amount of $75,000
   c. As discontinued operations, net of tax, in the amount of $75,000
   d. On the income statement as part of the calculation of income from continuing operations at the before tax amount of $100,000
4. Gerard Company reported sales of $300,000 for 2010; $330,000 for 2011; and $360,000 for 2012. If the company uses 2010 as the base year, what were the percentage increases for 2011 and 2012 compared to the base year?
   a. 10% for 2011 and 10% for 2012
   b. 120% for 2011 and 120% for 2012
   c. 110% for 2011 and 110% for 2012
   d. 10% for 2011 and 20% for 2012

5. On June 30, Star Radio reported total current assets of $45,000; total assets of $200,000; total current liabilities of $42,000; and total liabilities of $80,000. What was the current ratio on this date?
   a. 0.56
   b. 2.50
   c. 1.07
   d. 0.93

6. Talking Puppet Company reported a P/E ratio of 50 on the last day of the fiscal year. If the company reported earnings of $2.50 per share, how much was a share of the company's stock trading for at that time?
   a. $20 per share
   b. $125 per share
   c. $50 per share
   d. $47.50 per share

7. Singleton Company had sales of $2,000,000, cost of sales of $1,200,000, and average inventory of $400,000. What was the company's inventory turnover ratio for the period?
   a. 3.00
   b. 4.00
   c. 5.00
   d. 0.33

8. Suppose a firm had an inventory turnover ratio of 20. Suppose the firm considers a year to be 360 days. How many days, on average, does an item remain in the inventory?
   a. 5.56 days
   b. 18 days
   c. 20 days
   d. 360 days

9. Suppose a new company is trying to decide whether to use LIFO or FIFO in a period of rising inventory costs. The CFO suggests using LIFO because it will give a higher inventory turnover ratio. Is the CFO correct?
   a. Yes, the average inventory will be lower (the ratio's denominator) and the cost of goods sold (the ratio's numerator) will be higher than if FIFO were used.
   b. No, the average inventory would be the same because purchases are the same no matter which inventory method is chosen.
   c. The inventory method has no effect on the inventory turnover ratio.
   d. Without specific inventory amounts, it is not possible to predict the effect of the inventory method.

10. If a firm has $100,000 debt and $100,000 equity, then
    a. the return on equity ratio is 1.
    b. the debt-to-equity ratio is 1.
    c. the return on assets ratio is 0.5.
    d. the firm has too much debt.

All of the A exercises can be found within MyAccountingLab, an online homework and practice environment.

Short Exercises
Set A

SE10-1A. *Discontinued operations. (LO 1).* In 2010, Earthscope Company decided to sell its satellite sales division, even though the division had been profitable during the year. During 2010, the satellite division earned $54,000 and the taxes on that income were $12,500. The division was sold for a gain of $750,000, and the taxes on the gain amounted to $36,700. How would these amounts be reported on the income statement for the year ended December 31, 2010?

SE10-2A. *Extraordinary items. (LO 1).* Sew and Save Company suffered an extraordinary loss of $30,000 last year. The related tax savings amounted to $5,600. How would this tax savings be reported on the income statement?

SE10-3A. *Horizontal analysis. (LO 2).* Olin Copy Corporation reported the following amounts on its 2012 comparative income statement:

(in thousands)	2012	2011	2010
Revenues	$6,400	$4,575	$3,850
Cost of sales	3,900	2,650	2,050

Perform a horizontal analysis of revenues and cost of sales in both dollar amounts and in percentages for 2012 and 2011, using 2010 as the base year.

SE10-4A. *Vertical analysis. (LO 2).* Bessie's Quilting Company reported the following amounts on its balance sheet at December 31, 2010:

Cash	$ 5,000
Accounts receivable, net	40,000
Inventory	35,000
Equipment, net	120,000
Total assets	$200,000

Perform a vertical analysis of the assets of Bessie's Quilting Company. Use total assets as the base. What information does the analysis provide?

SE10-5A. *Ratio analysis. (LO 3).* Fireworks Company reported current assets of $720,000 and a current ratio of 1.2. What were current liabilities?

SE10-6A. *Ratio analysis. (LO 3).* A five-year comparative analysis of Low Light Company's current ratio follows:

	2008	2009	2010	2011	2012
Current ratio	1.19	1.85	2.50	3.40	4.02

What has been happening to the liquidity of Low Light Company over the five years presented?

SE10-7A. *Ratio analysis. (LO 3).* Suppose Company A has an inventory turnover ratio of 25 and a gross margin ratio of 10%, while Company B has an inventory turnover ratio of 3.5 and a gross margin of 50%. Which company is more likely to be a grocery store and which is more likely to be a clothing boutique? Explain why.

Set B

SE10-8B. *Discontinued operations. (LO 1).* In 2011, Office Products decided to sell its furniture division because it had been losing money for several years. During 2011, the furniture division lost $140,000. The tax savings related to the loss amounted to $25,000. The division was sold at a loss of $350,000, and the tax savings related to the loss on the sale was $50,000. How would these amounts be reported on the income statement for the year ended December 31, 2011?

SE10-9B. *Extraordinary items. (LO 1).* RM Inc. suffered an extraordinary loss of $50,000 last year. The related tax savings amounted to $8,600. How would this tax savings be reported on the income statement?

SE10-10B. *Horizontal analysis. (LO 2).* Use the following information about the capital expenditures of Andes Company to perform a horizontal analysis, with 2009 as the base year:

(in millions)	2012	2011	2010	2009
Capital expenditures	$41,400	$45,575	$43,850	$50,600

What information does this provide about Andes Company?

SE10-11B. *Vertical analysis. (LO 2).* Perform a vertical analysis on the following income statement, with sales as the base amount:

Sales	$35,000
Cost of goods sold	14,000
Gross margin	21,000
Other expenses	7,000
Net income	$14,000

What other information would you need to make this analysis meaningful?

SE10-12B. *Ratio analysis. (LO 3).* Ronca Company reported current liabilities of $720,000 and a current ratio of 1.2. What were current assets?

SE10-13B. *Ratio analysis. (LO 3).* The following is a five-year comparative analysis of Accent Company's return on assets and return on equity:

	2007	2008	2009	2010	2011
Return on assets	8%	7.5%	7.12%	6.54%	6%
Return on equity	20%	21%	21.8%	22.2%	23%

1. What does this analysis tell you about the overall profitability of Accent Company over the five-year period?
2. What does this analysis tell you about what has happened to Accent's amount of debt over the past five years?

SE10-14B. Ratio analysis. *(LO 3).* Do you think that Macy's or Wal-Mart has the higher inventory turnover ratio? Why? Which company do you think has the higher gross margin ratio? Why? (Find these firms' financial statements on the Internet and see if you are correct.)

MyAccountingLab

All of the A exercises can be found within MyAccountingLab, an online homework and practice environment.

Exercises
Set A

E10-15A. *Discontinued operations. (LO 1).* Use the following information to construct a partial income statement beginning with income from continuing operations:

Income from continuing operations	$230,000
Loss during the year from operating discontinued operations	60,000
Tax benefit of loss	9,500
Loss from sale of discontinued operations	128,500
Tax savings from loss on the sale	31,000

E10-16A. *Extraordinary items. (LO 1).* Devon's Central Processing Agency suffered a $560,000 loss due to a disaster that qualifies as an extraordinary item for financial statement purposes. The tax benefit of the loss amounts to $123,000. If income from continuing operations (net of tax) amounted to $1,300,500, what is net income?

E10-17A. *Horizontal analysis. (LO 2).* Conway Furniture reported the following amounts for its sales during the past five years:

2010	2009	2008	2007	2006
$30,000	$28,400	$26,300	$24,200	$25,400

Using 2006 as the base year, perform a horizontal analysis. What information does the analysis provide that was not apparent from the raw numbers?

E10-18A. *Vertical analysis. (LO 2).* Use the following income statement from Color Copy to perform a vertical analysis with sales as the base:

Color Copy, Inc.
Income Statement
For the Year Ended September 30, 2011

Sales revenue		$10,228
Cost of goods sold		5,751
Gross profit		4,477
Operating expenses:		
Depreciation—buildings and equipment	$ 100	
Other selling and administrative	2,500	
Total expenses		2,600
Income before interest and taxes		1,877
Interest expense		350
Income before taxes		1,527
Income taxes		150
Net income		$ 1,377

E10-19A. *Current ratio. (LO 3).* Calculate the current ratio for Suzanne's Hotels for the years given in the following comparative balance sheets:

Suzanne's Hotels, Inc.
Balance Sheets

	December 31, 2011	December 31, 2010
Current assets:		
Cash	$ 98,000	$ 90,000
Accounts receivable, net	110,000	116,000
Inventory	170,000	160,000
Prepaid expenses	18,000	16,000
Total current assets	396,000	382,000
Equipment, net	184,000	160,000
Total assets	$580,000	$542,000
Total current liabilities	$206,000	$223,000
Long-term liabilities	119,000	117,000
Total liabilities	325,000	340,000
Common stockholders' equity	90,000	90,000
Retained earnings	165,000	112,000
Total liabilities and stockholders' equity	$580,000	$542,000

Although two years is not much of a trend, what is your opinion of the direction of this ratio?

E10-20A. *Debt-to-equity ratio. (LO 3).* Use the balance sheets from Suzanne's Hotels in E10-19A to compute the debt-to-equity ratio for 2011 and 2010. Suppose you calculated a debt ratio using debt plus equity as the denominator. Which ratio—debt-to-equity or debt-to-debt plus equity— seems easiest to interpret? As an investor, do you view the "trend" in the debt-to-equity ratio as favorable or unfavorable? Why?

E10-21A. *Ratio analysis. (LO 3).* Zap Electronics reported the following for the fiscal years ended January 31, 2011, and January 31, 2010:

January 31	2011	2010
(in thousands)		
Accounts receivable	$ 36,184	$ 24,306
Inventory	106,754	113,875
Current assets	174,369	154,369
Current liabilities	71,616	68,001
Long-term liabilities	12,316	35,200
Shareholders' equity	121,851	198,935
Sales	712,855	580,223
Cost of goods sold	483,463	400,126
Interest expense	335	709
Net income	11,953	4,706

Assume all sales are on credit and the firm has no preferred stock outstanding. Calculate the following ratios:

1. Current ratio (for both years)
2. Accounts receivable turnover ratio (for 2011)
3. Inventory turnover ratio (for 2011)
4. Debt-to-equity ratio (for both years)
5. Return on equity ratio (for 2011)

Do any of these ratios suggest problems for the company?

E10-22A. *Ratio analysis. (LO 3).* Corner Grocers reported the following for its two most recent fiscal years:

December 31	2012	2011
Cash	$ 25,000	$ 20,000
Receivables (net)	60,000	70,000
Merchandise inventory	55,000	30,000
Plant assets (net)	280,000	260,000
Total assets	$420,000	$380,000
Accounts payable	45,000	62,000
Long-term notes payable	75,000	100,000
Common stock	135,000	122,000
Retained earnings	165,000	96,000
Total Liabilities and Shareholders' Equity	$420,000	$380,000
Net income for the year ended 12/31/12	$ 75,000	
Sales (all sales were on account)	450,000	
Cost of goods sold	210,000	
Interest expense	1,500	

Calculate the following for the year ended December 31, 2012:

1. Current ratio
2. Accounts receivable turnover ratio
3. Inventory turnover ratio
4. Return on assets
5. Return on equity

E10-23A. *Ratio analysis. (LO 3).* Furniture Showcase reported the following for its fiscal year ended June 30, 2010:

Sales	$530,000
Cost of sales	300,000
Gross margin	230,000
Expenses	113,000
Net income	$117,000

At the beginning of the year, the company had 50,000 shares of common stock outstanding. At the end of the year, there were 40,000 shares outstanding. The market price of the company's stock at year end was $20 per share. The company declared and paid $80,000 of dividends near year end.

Calculate earnings per share and the price–earnings ratio for Furniture Showcase.

Use the following balance sheets and income statements for Campbell Soup Company for E10-24A through E10-27A:

Campbell Soup Company
Consolidated Balance Sheets
(Millions, except per share amounts)

	August 3, 2008	July 29, 2007
Current Assets		
Cash and cash equivalents	$ 81	$ 71
Accounts receivable (Note 15)	570	581
Inventories (Note 15)	829	775
Other current assets (Note 15)	172	151
Current assets held for sale	41	—
Total current assets	1,693	1,578
Plant Assets, Net of Depreciation (Note 15)	1,939	2,042
Goodwill (Note 5)	1,998	1,872
Other Intangible Assets, Net of		
Amortization (Note 5)	605	615
Other Assets (Note 15)	211	338
Non-current Assets Held for Sale	28	—
Total assets	$ 6,474	$ 6,445
Current Liabilities		
Notes payable (Note 11)	$ 982	$ 595
Payable to suppliers and others	655	694
Accrued liabilities (Note 15)	655	622
Dividend payable	81	77
Accrued income taxes	9	42
Current liabilities held for sale	21	—
Total current liabilities	2,403	2,030
Long-term Debt (Note 11)	1,633	2,074
Other Liabilities (Note 15)	1,119	1,046
Non-current Liabilities Held for Sale	1	—
Total liabilities	5,156	5,150
Shareowners' Equity (Note 13)		
Preferred stock; authorized 40		
shares; none issued	—	—
Capital stock, $.0375 par value; authorized		
560 shares; issued 542 shares	20	20
Additional paid-in capital	337	331
Earnings retained in the business	7,909	7,082
Capital stock in treasury, 186 shares in 2008		
and 163 shares in 2007, at cost	(6,812)	(6,015)
Accumulated other comprehensive loss	(136)	(123)
Total shareowners' equity	1,318	1,295
Total liabilities and shareowners' equity	$ 6,474	$ 6,445

Campbell Soup Company
Consolidated Statements of Earnings
(millions, except per share amounts)

	2008 53 Weeks	2007 52 Weeks	2006 52 Weeks
Net Sales	$7,998	$7,385	$6,894
Costs and expenses			
Cost of products sold	4,827	4,384	4,100
Marketing and selling expenses	1,162	1,106	1,033
Administrative expenses	608	571	552
Research and development expenses	115	111	103
Other expenses/(income) (Note 15)	13	(30)	9
Restructuring charges (Note 7)	175	—	—
Total costs and expenses	6,900	6,142	5,797
Earnings Before Interest and Taxes	1,098	1,243	1,097
Interest expense (Note 15)	167	163	165
Interest income	8	19	15
Earnings before taxes	939	1,099	947
Taxes on earnings (Note 10)	268	307	227
Earnings from continuing operations	671	792	720
Earnings from discontinued operations	494	62	46
Net Earnings	$1,165	$ 854	$ 766
Per Share—Basic			
Earnings from continuing operations	$ 1.80	$ 2.05	$ 1.77
Earnings from discontinued operations	1.32	.16	.11
Net Earnings	$ 3.12	$ 2.21	$ 1.88
Weighted average shares outstanding—basic	373	386	407
Per Share—Assuming Dilution			
Earnings from continuing operations	$ 1.76	$ 2.00	$ 1.74
Earnings from discontinued operations	1.30	.16	.11
Net Earnings	$ 3.06	$ 2.16	$ 1.85
Weighted average shares outstanding—assuming dilution	381	396	414

E10-24A. *Horizontal analysis. (LO 2).* Use the statements of earnings for Campbell Soup Company to perform a horizontal analysis for each item reported for the year from July 29, 2007, to August 3, 2008. What does your analysis tell you about the operations of Campbell Soup Company for the year?

E10-25A. *Vertical analysis. (LO 2).* Use the statements of earnings for Campbell Soup Company to perform a vertical analysis for each item reported for the last two fiscal years using net sales as the base. What does your analysis tell you about the operations for the years reported?

E10-26A. *Liquidity ratios. (LO 3).* Use the financial statements for Campbell Soup Company to calculate the following liquidity ratios for FYE August 3, 2008:

1. Current ratio
2. Inventory turnover ratio
3. Accounts receivable turnover ratio (Assume all sales are credit sales.)

What information does this provide about the firm's liquidity?

E10-27A. *Solvency and profitability ratios. (LO 3).* Use the financial statements for Campbell Soup Company to calculate the following solvency and profitability ratios for FYE August 3, 2008:

1. Debt-to-equity ratio
2. Return on assets
3. Return on equity

4. Gross margin percentage
5. Profit margin percentage

What information does this provide about the firm's solvency and profitability?

Set B

E10-28B. *Discontinued operations. (LO 1).* Use the following information to construct a partial income statement beginning with income from continuing operations:

Income from continuing operations	$310,000
Loss during the year from operation of discontinued operations	75,000
Tax benefit of loss	19,400
Loss from sale of discontinued operations	105,750
Tax savings from loss on the sale	32,000

E10-29B. *Extraordinary items. (LO 1).* Tropical Vacations suffered a $1,070,000 loss due to a tsunami, which qualifies as an extraordinary item for financial statement purposes. The tax benefit of the loss amounts to $155,000. If income from continuing operations (net of tax) amounted to $1,861,250, what is net income?

E10-30B. *Horizontal analysis. (LO 2).* Sunny's Umbrellas reported the following amounts for sales during the past five years:

2012	2011	2010	2009	2008
$27,925	$30,400	$33,525	$26,250	$30,300

Using 2008 as the base year, perform a horizontal analysis. What information does the analysis provide that was not apparent from the raw numbers?

E10-31B. *Vertical analysis. (LO 2).* Use the following income statement from Designers Discount, Inc., to perform a vertical analysis with sales as the base:

Designers Discount, Inc.
Income Statement
For the Year Ended December 31, 2010

Sales revenue		$16,374
Cost of goods sold		7,985
Gross profit on sales		$ 8,389
Operating expenses:		
Depreciation—buildings and equipment	$ 265	
Other selling and administrative	3,750	
Total expenses		4,015
Income before interest and taxes		$ 4,374
Interest expense		254
Income before taxes		$ 4,120
Income taxes		1,236
Net income		$ 2,884

E10-32B. *Current ratio. (LO 3).* Calculate the current ratio for Mike & Kat Racing Company for the years given in the following comparative balance sheets:

Mike & Kat Racing Company
Balance Sheets

	December 31, 2010	December 31, 2009
Current assets:		
Cash	$186,000	$192,000
Accounts receivable, net	94,000	85,000
Inventory	185,000	170,500
Prepaid expenses	17,000	14,000
Total current assets	482,000	461,500
Equipment, net	215,000	195,000
Total assets	$697,000	$656,500
Total current liabilities	$267,000	$269,000
Long-term liabilities	185,000	190,000
Total liabilities	452,000	459,000
Shareholders' equity	163,750	148,250
Retained earnings	81,250	49,250
Total liabilities and shareholders' equity	$697,000	$656,500

Although two years will not show a significant trend, what is your opinion of the direction of this ratio?

E10-33B. *Debt-to-equity ratio. (LO 3).* Use the balance sheets from Mike & Kat Racing Company in E10-32B to compute a debt-to-equity ratio for 2010 and 2009. Suppose you calculated a debt ratio using debt plus equity as the denominator. Which ratio—debt-to-equity or debt-to-debt plus equity—seems easiest to interpret? As an investor, do you view the "trend" in the debt-to-equity ratio as favorable or unfavorable? Why?

E10-34B. *Ratio analysis. (LO 3).* Crystal Cromartie's Frozen Foods reported the following for the fiscal years ended September 30, 2011, and September 30, 2010:

September 30 (in millions)	2011	2010
Accounts receivable	$ 21,265	$ 13,802
Inventory	45,692	47,682
Current assets	185,716	155,716
Current liabilities	80,954	72,263
Long-term liabilities	15,251	17,852
Shareholders' equity	21,871	58,035
Sales	88,455	70,223
Cost of goods sold	60,463	52,750
Interest expense	21.5	43.2
Net income	1,842	1,006

Assume there is no outstanding preferred stock and all sales are credit sales. Calculate the follow-ing ratios:

1. Current ratio (for both years)
2. Accounts receivable turnover ratio (for 2011)
3. Inventory turnover ratio (for 2011)
4. Debt-to-equity ratio (for both years)
5. Return on equity (for 2011)

Do any of these ratios suggest problems for the company?

E10-35B. *Ratio analysis. (LO 3).* Hudson Coffee Shops reported the following for the two most recent fiscal years:

December 31	2010	2009
Cash	$ 34,000	$ 17,000
Receivables (net)	85,000	80,000
Merchandise inventory	74,000	48,000
Fixed assets	365,000	324,000
Total assets	$558,000	$469,000
Accounts payable	65,000	83,000
Long-term notes payable	82,000	112,000
Common stock	176,000	144,000
Retained earnings	235,000	130,000
Total liabilities and shareholders' equity	$558,000	$469,000
Net income for the year ended 12/31/10	$115,000	
Sales (all sales were on account)	620,000	
Cost of goods sold	284,000	
Interest expense	3,000	

Calculate the following for the year ended December 31, 2010:

1. Current ratio
2. Accounts receivable turnover ratio
3. Inventory turnover ratio
4. Return on assets
5. Return on equity

E10-36B. *Ratio analysis. (LO 3).* International Imports Corporation reported the following for its fiscal year ended June 30, 2011:

Sales	$640,000
Cost of sales	470,000
Gross margin	170,000
Expenses	94,000
Net income	$ 76,000

At the beginning of the year, the company had 50,000 shares of common stock outstanding and no preferred stock. At the end of the year, there were 50,000 common shares outstanding and no preferred stock. The market price of the company's stock at year end was $20 per share. The company declared and paid $25,000 of dividends near year end.

Calculate earnings per share, the price–earnings ratio, and dividend yield for International Imports.

Use the following balance sheets and income statements for GameStop Corp. for E10-37B through E10-40B:

GameStop Corp.
Consolidated Balance Sheets
(In thousands)

	January 31, 2009	February 2, 2008
ASSETS		
Current assets:		
Cash and cash equivalents	$ 578,141	$ 857,414
Receivables, net	65,981	56,019
Merchandise inventories, net	1,075,792	801,025
Deferred income taxes — current	23,615	27,481
Prepaid expenses	59,101	48,915
Other current assets	15,411	3,863
Total current assets	1,818,041	1,794,717
Property and equipment:		
Land	10,397	11,870
Buildings and leasehold improvements	454,651	378,611
Fixtures and equipment	619,845	538,738
Total property and equipment	1,084,893	929,219
Less accumulated depreciation and amortization	535,639	417,550
Net property and equipment	549,254	511,669
Goodwill, net	1,862,107	1,402,440
Other intangible assets	247,790	14,214
Deferred taxes	—	26,332
Other noncurrent assets	35,398	26,519
Total noncurrent assets	2,694,549	1,981,174
Total assets	$4,512,590	$3,775,891
LIABILITIES AND STOCKHOLDERS' EQUITY		
Current liabilities:		
Accounts payable	$1,047,963	$ 844,376
Accrued liabilities	514,748	416,181
Total current liabilities	1,562,711	1,260,557
Senior notes payable, long-term portion, net ...	545,712	574,473
Other long-term liabilities	104,486	78,415
Total long-term liabilities	650,198	652,888
Total liabilities	2,212,909	1,913,445
Commitments and contingencies (Notes 10 and 11)		
Stockholders' equity:		
Preferred stock — authorized 5,000 shares; no shares issued or outstanding	—	—
Class A common stock — $.001 par value; authorized 300,000 shares; 163,843 and 161,007 shares issued and outstanding, respectively	164	161
Additional paid-in-capital	1,307,453	1,208,474
Accumulated other comprehensive income (loss)	(28,426)	31,603
Retained earnings	1,020,490	622,208
Total stockholders' equity	2,299,681	1,862,446
Total liabilities and stockholders' equity	$4,512,590	$3,775,891

See accompanying notes to consolidated financial statements.

GameStop Corp.
Consolidated Statements of Operations
(In thousands, except per share data)

	52 Weeks Ended January 31, 2009	52 Weeks Ended February 2, 2008	53 Weeks Ended February 3, 2007
Sales	$8,805,897	$7,093,962	$5,318,900
Cost of sales	6,535,762	5,280,255	3,847,458
Gross profit	2,270,135	1,813,707	1,471,442
Selling, general and administrative			
expenses	1,445,419	1,182,016	1,021,113
Depreciation and amortization	145,004	130,270	109,862
Merger-related expenses	4,593	—	6,788
Operating earnings	675,119	501,421	333,679
Interest income	(11,619)	(13,779)	(11,338)
Interest expense	50,456	61,553	84,662
Debt extinguishment expense	2,331	12,591	6,059
Earnings before income tax expense	633,951	441,056	254,296
Income tax expense	235,669	152,765	96,046
Net earnings	$ 398,282	$ 288,291	$ 158,250
Net earnings per common share — basic	$ 2.44	$ 1.82	$ 1.06
Weighted average shares of common			
stock — basic	163,190	158,226	149,924
Net earnings per common share — diluted	$ 2.38	$ 1.75	$ 1.00
Weighted average shares of common			
stock — diluted	167,671	164,844	158,284

E10-37B. *Horizontal analysis. (LO 2).* Use the statements of income for GameStop Corp. to perform a horizontal analysis for each item reported for the year from February 2, 2008, to January 31, 2009. What does your analysis tell you about the operations of GameStop Corp. for the years reported?

E10-38B. *Vertical analysis. (LO 2).* Use the statements of income for GameStop Corp. to perform a vertical analysis for each item reported for the two most recent years using sales as the base. What does your analysis tell you about the operations of GameStop Corp. for the years reported?

E10-39B. *Liquidity ratios. (LO 3).* Use the financial statements for GameStop Corp. to calculate the following liquidity ratios for the most recent fiscal year:

1. Current ratio
2. Inventory turnover and average days in inventory
3. Accounts receivable turnover and average days to collect AR

What do these ratios tell you about the firm?

E10-40B. *Solvency and profitability ratios. (LO 3).* Use the financial statements for GameStop Corp. to calculate the following solvency ratios and profitability for the most recent fiscal year and provide an interpretation for each ratio:

1. Debt-to-equity ratio
2. Profit margin ratio
3. Return on assets
4. Return on equity
5. Gross margin percentage

Problems
Set A

P10-41A. *Discontinued operations and extraordinary items. (LO 1).* Each of the following items was found on the financial statements for Hartsfield Company for the year ended December 31, 2011:

Net income from continuing operations	$136,500
Gain on the sale of a discontinued segment, net of taxes of $42,000	140,000
Loss from operation of discontinued segment, net of taxes of $24,000	(80,000)
Gain on sale of land	65,000
Extraordinary loss, net of taxes of $6,000	(20,000)

Requirements

1. For the items listed, indicate the financial statement and appropriate section, where applicable, on which each would appear.
2. Provide a description of each item and give as many details of each item's financial statement presentation as possible.
3. Based on the data provided, what is Hartsfield Company's tax rate?

P10-42A. *Prepare an income statement. (LO 1).* The Pops Corporation reported the following for the year ended December 31, 2010:

Sales	$575,000
Cost of goods sold	230,000
Interest income	10,000
Gain on sale of equipment	8,000
Selling and administrative expenses	12,000
Interest expense	5,000
Extraordinary gain	15,000
Loss from discontinued segment operations	(10,500)
Gain on disposal of discontinued segment	28,000

Requirement

Assume the corporation is subject to a 30% tax rate. Prepare an income statement for the year ended December 31, 2010.

P10-43A. *Prepare an income statement. (LO 1).* The following balances appeared in the general ledger for Hacky Sak Corporation at fiscal year end September 30, 2011:

Selling and administrative expenses	$ 15,000
Other revenues and gains	40,000
Operating expenses	65,000
Cost of goods sold	125,000
Net sales	385,000
Other expenses and losses	25,000

In addition, the following occurred during the year:
   a. On April 10, a tornado destroyed one of the company's manufacturing plants, resulting in an extraordinary loss of $55,000.
   b. On July 31, the company discontinued one of its unprofitable segments. The loss from operations was $25,000. The assets of the segment were sold at a gain of $15,000.

Requirements

1. Assume Hacky Sak's income tax rate is 35%; prepare the income statement for the year ended September 30, 2011.
2. Calculate the earnings per share the company would report on the income statement assuming Hacky Sak had a weighted average of 200,000 shares of common stock outstanding during the year and paid no preferred dividends.

P10-44A. *Prepare horizontal and vertical analysis. (LO 2).* Following are the income statements for Alpha Company:

<table>
<tr><td colspan="4" align="center">**Alpha Company**
Income Statements
(in thousands)</td></tr>
<tr><td></td><td colspan="3" align="center">For the Year Ended December 31,</td></tr>
<tr><td></td><td>2010</td><td>2009</td><td>2008</td></tr>
<tr><td>Net sales ....</td><td>$5,003,837</td><td>$4,934,430</td><td>$4,881,103</td></tr>
<tr><td>Cost of goods sold ....</td><td>2,755,323</td><td>2,804,459</td><td>2,784,392</td></tr>
<tr><td>Gross profit ....</td><td>2,248,514</td><td>2,129,971</td><td>2,096,711</td></tr>
<tr><td>Selling, general, and administrative</td><td></td><td></td><td></td></tr>
<tr><td>   expenses ....</td><td>1,673,449</td><td>1,598,333</td><td>1,573,510</td></tr>
<tr><td>Operating income ....</td><td>575,065</td><td>531,638</td><td>523,201</td></tr>
<tr><td>Interest expense ....</td><td>61,168</td><td>71,971</td><td>80,837</td></tr>
<tr><td>Interest and net investment</td><td></td><td></td><td></td></tr>
<tr><td>   expense (income) ....</td><td>(5,761)</td><td>(6,482)</td><td>(8,278)</td></tr>
<tr><td>Other expense—net ....</td><td>29,540</td><td>26,046</td><td>23,365</td></tr>
<tr><td>Income before income taxes ....</td><td>490,118</td><td>440,103</td><td>427,277</td></tr>
<tr><td>Income taxes ....</td><td>186,258</td><td>167,239</td><td>166,663</td></tr>
<tr><td>Net income ....</td><td>$ 303,860</td><td>$ 272,864</td><td>$ 260,614</td></tr>
</table>

Requirements

1. For each of the years shown, prepare a vertical analysis, using sales as the base. Write a paragraph explaining what the analysis shows.
2. Using 2008 as the base year, prepare a horizontal analysis for sales and cost of goods sold. What information does this analysis give you?

P10-45A. *Calculate and analyze financial ratios. (LO 3).* Following is information from a firm's financial statements:

<table>
<tr><td></td><td colspan="3" align="center">Year Ended December 31</td></tr>
<tr><td></td><td>2011</td><td>2010</td><td>2009</td></tr>
<tr><td>Net sales (all on account)</td><td>$5,003,837</td><td>$4,934,430</td><td></td></tr>
<tr><td>Cost of goods sold</td><td>2,755,323</td><td>2,804,459</td><td></td></tr>
<tr><td>Gross profit</td><td>2,248,514</td><td>2,129,971</td><td></td></tr>
<tr><td>Interest expense</td><td>61,168</td><td>71,971</td><td></td></tr>
<tr><td>Income taxes</td><td>186,258</td><td>167,239</td><td></td></tr>
<tr><td>Net income</td><td>303,860</td><td>272,864</td><td></td></tr>
<tr><td>Cash and cash equivalents</td><td>18,623</td><td>19,133</td><td>3,530</td></tr>
<tr><td>Accounts receivable, less allowance</td><td>606,046</td><td>604,516</td><td>546,314</td></tr>
<tr><td>Total current assets</td><td>1,597,377</td><td>1,547,290</td><td>1,532,253</td></tr>
<tr><td>Total assets</td><td>4,052,090</td><td>4,065,462</td><td>4,035,801</td></tr>
<tr><td>Total current liabilities</td><td>1,189,862</td><td>1,111,973</td><td>44,539</td></tr>
<tr><td>Long-term liabilities</td><td>1,163,696</td><td>1,237,549</td><td></td></tr>
<tr><td>Total shareholders' equity*</td><td>1,698,532</td><td>1,715,940</td><td>1,592,180</td></tr>
</table>

*The firm has no preferred stock.

Requirements

1. Calculate the following ratios for 2011 and 2010:
   a. Current ratio
   b. Accounts receivable turnover ratio
   c. Debt-to-equity ratio
   d. Profit margin ratio

    e. Return on equity
    f. Gross profit percentage

2. Suppose the changes from 2010 to 2011 in each of these ratios were consistent with the direction and size of the change for the past several years. For each ratio, explain what the trend in the ratio would indicate about the company.

P10-46A. *Calculate and analyze financial ratios. (LO 3).* The following financial statements were taken from the 2010 annual report of Presentations Company:

Presentations Company
Balance Sheets
(in thousands)

	December 31, 2010	December 31, 2009
ASSETS		
Current assets:		
Cash	$ 1,617	$1,220
Accounts receivable	1,925	3,112
Merchandise inventory	2,070	966
Prepaid expenses	188	149
Total current assets	$ 5,800	$5,447
Plant and equipment:		
Buildings, net	$ 4,457	$2,992
Equipment, net	1,293	1,045
Total plant and equipment	$ 5,750	$4,037
Total assets	$11,550	$9,484
LIABILITIES		
Current liabilities:		
Accounts payable	$ 1,817	$1,685
Notes payable	900	1,100
Total current liabilities	2,717	2,785
Long-term liabilities	3,500	2,000
Total liabilities	$ 6,217	$4,785
STOCKHOLDERS' EQUITY		
Common stock, no par value	$ 3,390	$3,042
Retained earnings	1,943	1,657
Total stockholders' equity	5,333	4,699
Total liabilities and stockholders' equity	$11,550	$9,484

Presentations Company
Income Statement
For the Year Ended December 31, 2010

Sales revenue	$12,228
Cost of goods sold	8,751
Gross profit on sales	3,477
Operating expenses:	
Depreciation—buildings and equipment	102
Other selling and administrative	2,667
Total expenses	2,769
Income before interest and taxes	708
Interest expense	168
Income before taxes	540
Income taxes	114
Net income	$ 426

Requirements

1. Calculate the following ratios for the year ended December 31, 2010.
   a. Debt-to-equity ratio
   b. Gross margin percentage
   c. Current ratio
   d. Profit margin ratio
2. What do the ratios indicate about the success of Presentations? What additional information would help you analyze the overall performance of this company?

P10-47A. *Calculate and analyze financial ratios. (LO 3).* The financial statements of For the Kitchen include the following items:

	At June 30, 2011	At June 30, 2010	At June 30, 2009
Balance sheet:			
Cash	$ 17,000	$ 12,000	$ 14,000
Investments (in trading securities)	10,000	16,000	20,000
Accounts receivable (net)	54,000	50,000	48,000
Inventory	75,000	70,000	73,000
Prepaid expenses	16,000	12,000	10,000
Total current assets	172,000	160,000	165,000
Total current liabilities	$140,000	$ 90,000	$ 75,000
Income statement for the year ended	June 30, 2011	June 30 2010	
Net credit sales	$420,000	$380,000	
Cost of goods sold	250,000	225,000	

Requirements

1. Compute the following ratios for the years ended June 30, 2011, and whenever possible for the year ended June 30, 2010. For each, indicate if the direction is favorable or unfavorable for the company.
   a. Current ratio
   b. Accounts receivable turnover
   c. Inventory turnover ratio
   d. Gross profit percentage (assume net credit sales = total sales)
2. Suppose the industry average for similar retail stores for the current ratio is 1.7. Does this information help you evaluate For the Kitchen's liquidity?

P10-48A. *Calculate and analyze financial ratios. (LO 3).* You are interested in investing in Teddy Company, and you have obtained the following balance sheets for the company for the past two years:

Teddy Company
Balance Sheets

	June 30, 2011	June 30, 2010
Current assets:		
Cash	$198,000	$ 90,000
Accounts receivable, net	210,000	116,000
Inventory	270,000	160,000
Prepaid rent	15,000	16,000
Total current assets	693,000	382,000
Equipment, net	280,000	260,000
Total assets	$973,000	$642,000
Total current liabilities	$306,000	$223,000
Long-term liabilities	219,000	117,000
Total liabilities	525,000	340,000
Common stockholders' equity	150,000	90,000
Retained earnings	298,000	212,000
Total liabilities and stockholders' equity	$973,000	$642,000

The following amounts were reported on the income statement for the year ended June 30, 2011:

Sales	$450,000
Cost of goods sold	215,000
Net income	80,000

Requirements

1. Compute as many of the financial statement ratios you have studied as possible with the information provided for Teddy Company. Some ratios can be computed for both years and others can be computed for only one year.
2. Would you invest in Teddy Company? Why or why not? What additional information would be helpful in making this decision?

Set B

P10-49B. *Discontinued operations and extraordinary item. (LO 1).* Each of the following items was found on the financial statements for Edge Company for the year ended December 31, 2011:

Income from continuing operations	$125,000
Gain on the sale of discontinued segment, net of taxes $9,000	50,000
Loss from operation of discontinued segment, net of taxes of $9,500	(34,500)
Gain on sale of equipment	10,000
Extraordinary loss from earthquake, net of taxes $45,000	(120,000)

Requirements

1. For each item listed, indicate the financial statement and appropriate section, if applicable, on which each would appear.
2. Provide a description of each item and give as many details of each item's financial statement presentation as possible.

P10-50B. *Prepare an income statement. (LO 1).* The Blues Corporation reported the following for the year ended December 31, 2011:

Sales	$425,000
Cost of goods sold	185,000
Interest income	4,000
Gain on sale of equipment	6,000
Selling and administrative expenses	18,000
Interest expense	2,000
Extraordinary gain	23,000
Loss from discontinued segment operations	(9,500)
Gain on disposal of discontinued segment	34,000

Requirement

Assume the corporation is subject to a 30% tax rate. Prepare an income statement for the year ended December 31, 2011.

P10-51B. *Prepare an income statement. (LO 1).* The following balances appeared in the general ledger for Ski Daddle Corporation at fiscal year end December 31, 2012:

Selling and administrative expenses	$ 45,000
Other revenues and gains	80,000
Operating expenses	110,000
Cost of goods sold	185,000
Net sales	325,000
Other expenses and losses	8,000

In addition, the following occurred during the year:
   a. On August 20, a fire destroyed one of the company's warehouses resulting in an extraordinary loss of $35,000.
   b. On October 31, the company discontinued one of its unprofitable segments. The loss from operations was $35,000. The assets of the segment were sold at a gain of $19,000.

Requirements

1. Assume Ski Daddle Corporation's income tax rate is 30%; prepare the income statement for the year ended December 31, 2012.
2. Calculate the earnings per share the company would report on the income statement assuming Ski Daddle had 100,000 shares of common stock outstanding during the year and paid preferred dividends of $15,000.

P10-52B. *Perform horizontal and vertical analysis. (LO 2).* Following are the income statements from Nappy's recent annual report:

Nappy Company
Income Statements

	For the Year Ended December 31,		
	2010	2009	2008
Net revenue	$26,971	$25,112	$23,512
Cost of sales	12,379	11,497	10,750
Selling, general, and administrative expenses	9,460	8,958	8,574
Amortization of intangible assets	145	138	165
Other expenses	204	224	356
Operating profit	4,783	4,295	3,667
Income from investments	323	280	160
Interest expense	(163)	(178)	(219)
Interest income	51	36	67
Income before income taxes	4,994	4,433	3,675
Income taxes	1,424	1,433	1,244
Net income	$ 3,570	$ 3,000	$ 2,431

Requirements

1. For each of the years shown, perform a vertical analysis, using sales as the base. Write a paragraph explaining what the analysis shows.
2. Using 2008 as the base year, perform a horizontal analysis for net revenue and cost of sales. What information does this analysis give you?

P10-53B. *Calculate and analyze financial ratios. (LO 3).* Macy's reported the following results in its 2008 10-K:

Macy's, Inc.
Consolidated Balance Sheets
(millions)

	January 31, 2009	February 2, 2008
ASSETS		
Current Assets:		
Cash and cash equivalents	$ 1,306	$ 583
Receivables	439	463
Merchandise inventories	4,769	5,060
Supplies and prepaid expenses	226	218
Total Current Assets	6,740	6,324
Property and Equipment — net	10,442	10,991
Goodwill	3,743	9,133
Other Intangible Assets — net	719	831
Other Assets	501	510
Total Assets	$22,145	$27,789
LIABILITIES AND SHAREHOLDERS' EQUITY		
Current Liabilities:		
Short-term debt	$ 966	$ 666
Merchandise accounts payable	1,282	1,398
Accounts payable and accrued liabilities	2,628	2,729
Income taxes	28	344
Deferred income taxes	222	223
Total Current Liabilities	5,126	5,360
Long-Term Debt	8,733	9,087
Deferred Income Taxes	1,119	1,446
Other Liabilities	2,521	1,989
Shareholders' Equity:		
Common stock (420.1 and 419.7 shares outstanding)	5	5
Additional paid-in capital	5,663	5,609
Accumulated equity	2,008	7,032
Treasury stock	(2,544)	(2,557)
Accumulated other comprehensive loss	(486)	(182)
Total Shareholders' Equity	4,646	9,907
Total Liabilities and Shareholders' Equity	$22,145	$27,789

Macy's, Inc.
Consolidated Statements of Operations
(millions, except per share data)

	2008	2007	2006
Net sales	$ 24,892	$ 26,313	$ 26,970
Cost of sales	(15,009)	(15,677)	(16,019)
Inventory valuation adjustments – May integration	–	–	(178)
Gross margin	9,883	10,636	10,773
Selling, general and administrative expenses	(8,481)	(8,554)	(8,678)
Division consolidation costs and store closing related costs	(187)	–	–
Asset impairment charges	(211)	–	–
Goodwill impairment charges	(5,382)	–	–
May integration costs	–	(219)	(450)
Gains on the sale of accounts receivable	–	–	191
Operating income (loss)	(4,378)	1,863	1,836
Interest expense	(588)	(579)	(451)
Interest income	28	36	61
Income (loss) from continuing operations before income taxes	(4,938)	1,320	1,446
Federal, state and local income tax benefit (expense)	135	(411)	(458)
Income (loss) from continuing operations	(4,803)	909	988
Discontinued operations, net of income taxes	–	(16)	7
Net income (loss)	$ (4,803)	$ 893	$ 995
Basic earnings (loss) per share:			
Income (loss) from continuing operations	$ (11.40)	$ 2.04	$ 1.83
Income (loss) from discontinued operations	–	(.04)	.01
Net income (loss)	$ (11.40)	$ 2.00	$ 1.84
Diluted earnings (loss) per share:			
Income (loss) from continuing operations	$ (11.40)	$ 2.01	$ 1.80
Income (loss) from discontinued operations	–	(.04)	.01
Net income (loss)	$ (11.40)	$ 1.97	$ 1.81

Requirements

1. Calculate the following ratios for the most recent fiscal year:
   a. Current ratio
   b. Accounts receivable turnover ratio (Uses total sales in the numerator.)
   c. Debt-to-equity ratio
   d. Return on assets
   e. Return on equity
2. Comment on the results of your analysis.

P10-54B. *Calculate and analyze financial ratios. (LO 3).* The following information was taken from the annual report of ROM. The account balances are as of December 31, 2011.

Cash	$ 1,220
Accounts receivable	3,112
Merchandise inventory	966
Prepaid expenses	149
Buildings, net	2,992
Equipment, net	1,045
Accounts payable	1,685
Notes payable	1,100
Long-term liabilities	2,000
Common stock, no par value	3,042
Retained earnings	1,657
Sales for the year	10,200
Cost of goods sold	6,750
Net income	2,500

Requirements

1. Calculate the following ratios for 2011:
   a. Debt-to-equity ratio
   b. Gross profit percentage
   c. Current ratio
   d. Profit margin ratio
2. What do the ratios indicate about the success of ROM? What additional information would be useful to help you analyze the overall performance of this company?

P10-55B. *Calculate and analyze financial ratios. (LO 3).* The financial statements of Builder Bob's include the following items:

From the balance sheet:	At September 30, 2010	At September 30, 2009
Cash	$ 27,000	$ 22,000
Investments (short-term)	15,000	12,000
Accounts receivable (net)	44,000	40,000
Inventory	85,000	75,000
Prepaid rent	6,000	2,000
Total current assets	$177,000	$151,000
Total current liabilities	$120,000	$ 80,000

The income statement for the year ended September 30, 2010, includes the following:

Net credit sales*	$320,000
Cost of goods sold	150,000

*Assume all sales are credit sales.

Requirements

1. Compute the following ratios for the year ended September 30, 2010, and September 30, 2009:
   a. Current ratio (2009 and 2010)
   b. Accounts receivable turnover (2010 only)
   c. Inventory turnover ratio (2010 only)
   d. Gross margin percentage (2010 only)
2. Which financial statement users would be most interested in these ratios?
3. Suppose the industry average for similar retail stores for the current ratio is 1.2. Does this information help you evaluate Builder Bob's liquidity?

P10-56B. *Calculate and analyze financial ratios. (LO 3).* You are interested in investing in Apples and Nuts Company, and you have obtained the following balance sheets for the company for the past two years:

<table>
<tr><td colspan="3" align="center">Apples and Nuts Company
Balance Sheets</td></tr>
<tr><td></td><td align="center">December 31, 2012</td><td align="center">December 31, 2011</td></tr>
<tr><td>Current assets:</td><td></td><td></td></tr>
<tr><td>Cash ....</td><td>$ 98,000</td><td>$ 90,000</td></tr>
<tr><td>Accounts receivable, net ....</td><td>310,000</td><td>216,000</td></tr>
<tr><td>Inventory ....</td><td>275,000</td><td>170,000</td></tr>
<tr><td>Prepaid rent ....</td><td>10,000</td><td>6,000</td></tr>
<tr><td>Total current assets ....</td><td>693,000</td><td>482,000</td></tr>
<tr><td>Equipment, net ....</td><td>180,000</td><td>258,000</td></tr>
<tr><td>Total assets ....</td><td>$873,000</td><td>$740,000</td></tr>
<tr><td></td><td></td><td></td></tr>
<tr><td>Total current liabilities ....</td><td>$206,000</td><td>$223,000</td></tr>
<tr><td>Long-term liabilities ....</td><td>219,000</td><td>217,000</td></tr>
<tr><td>Total liabilities ....</td><td>425,000</td><td>440,000</td></tr>
<tr><td>Common stockholders' equity ....</td><td>250,000</td><td>190,000</td></tr>
<tr><td>Retained earnings ....</td><td>198,000</td><td>110,000</td></tr>
<tr><td>Total liabilities and stockholders' equity ....</td><td>$873,000</td><td>$740,000</td></tr>
</table>

Net income for the year ended December 31, 2012, was $100,000.

Requirements

1. Compute as many of the financial statement ratios you have studied as possible with the information from Apples and Nuts Company. (Compute 2012 ratios.)
2. Would you invest in this company? Why or why not? What additional information would be helpful in making this decision?

Critical Thinking Problems

Risk and Control

Think about the risks of investing in a company and about the information provided by the financial ratios you studied in this chapter. Which financial ratios do you believe might give you information about the risks of investing in a company? Comment on those ratios from Apple Inc., which you calculated at the end of the chapter in the Chapter Summary Problem.

Ethics

Atlantis Company sells computer components and plans on borrowing some money to expand. After reading a lot about earnings management, Andy, the owner of Atlantis, has decided he should try to accelerate some sales to improve his financial statement ratios. He has called his best customers and asked them to make their usual January purchases by December 31. Andy told the customers he would allow them, until the end of February, to pay for the purchases, just as if they had made their purchases in January.

1. What do you think are the ethical implications of Andy's actions?
2. Which ratios will be improved by accelerating these sales?

Group Assignment

In groups, try to identify the type of company that is most likely indicated by the ratios shown next. The four types of companies represented are as follows: retail grocery, heavy machinery, restaurant, and drug manufacturer. Make notes on the arguments to support your position so that you can share them in a class discussion.

	Gross Margin Ratio	(Long-Term) Debt-to-Equity Ratio	Accounts Receivable Turnover Ratio	Inventory Turnover	Return on Equity Ratio
1	82.9%	25%	5.5 times	1.5 times	22.9%
2	33.7%	134%	49.3 times	11.2 times	3.6%
3	25.3%	147%	2.3 times	5.0 times	5.0%
4	37.4%	62%	34.9 times	32.9 times	15.7%

Internet Exercise: Papa John's International

Papa John's Pizza has become a widely recognized name in pizza. Papa John's 3,000 restaurants (about 75% are franchised) are scattered across the United States and 10 other countries. Examine how Papa John's compares with its competition.

IE10-1. Go to www.papajohns.com and click on Company Info at the bottom of the main page. Then select About Us and explore Papa John's Story and Our Pizza Story. What differentiates Papa John's from its competition?

IE10-2. Go to http://moneycentral.msn.com and get the stock quote for PZZA, Papa John's stock symbol. Identify the current price-to-earnings ratio and dividend yield ratio. What do these market indicators mean for Papa John's?

IE10-3. Go to http://moneycentral.msn.com and look up the information for Papa John's. Then, Select Financial Results from the menu on the left, and then select Key Ratios.
   a. Select Financial Condition from the list. Find the current ratio for Papa John's and the industry. Who would find these ratios of primary interest? Identify the debt-to-equity ratio for Papa John's and the industry. Is Papa John's primarily financed by debt or equity? How can you tell?
   b. Select Investment Returns from the list. Identify return on equity and return on assets for Papa John's and the industry. What do these ratios measure?
   c. Select Ten-Year Summary from the list. Review the information provided for return on equity and return on assets. What additional information is revealed about Papa John's financial position? Is this information helpful?

IE10-4. Review the information recorded earlier. Does Papa John's compare favorably with industry averages? Support your judgment with at least two observations.

Appendix 10A

Comprehensive Income

In the chapter, you learned that the Financial Accounting Standards Board (FASB) has defined two items that companies need to separate from regular earnings on financial statements: discontinued operations and extraordinary items. There is a third item—**comprehensive income**.

Even though most transactions that affect shareholders' equity are found on the income statement—revenues and expenses—there are a small number of transactions that affect shareholders' equity that are excluded from the calculation of net income. We already know about two of them:

1. Owners making contributions (paid-in capital)
2. Owners receiving dividends

In addition to these two, there are several other transactions that affect equity without going through the income statement. The most common examples of these transactions are (1) unrealized gains and losses from foreign currency translations and (2) unrealized gains and losses on certain investments. Rather than including either of these kinds of gains and losses on the income statement, they are reported as a direct adjustment to equity. The reason is that these items do not really reflect a firm's performance, so firms have lobbied to have them kept out of the calculation of earnings. To keep these transactions from getting lost among all the financial statement numbers, the FASB requires the reporting of net income plus these other transactions that affect shareholders' equity in an amount called comprehensive income. Comprehensive income includes all changes in shareholders' equity during a period except those changes in equity resulting from contributions by shareholders and distributions to shareholders. There are two parts of comprehensive income: net income and *other comprehensive income*. We know what types of transactions are included in net income—revenues, expenses, discontinued operations, and extraordinary items. Items included in other comprehensive income include unrealized gains and losses from foreign currency translation and unrealized gains and losses on certain types of investments. Exhibit 10A.1 on the following page shows all of the items that affect shareholders' equity.

L.O.5
Define comprehensive income and explain how it changes.

Comprehensive income is the total of all items that affect shareholders' equity except transactions with the owners; comprehensive income has two parts: net income and other comprehensive income.

What is the purpose of having a statement of comprehensive income rather than a simple income statement?

Your Turn 10A

EXHIBIT 10.A1

Comprehensive Income

The items in the left column appear on the financial statements in the equity classifications shown in the right column.

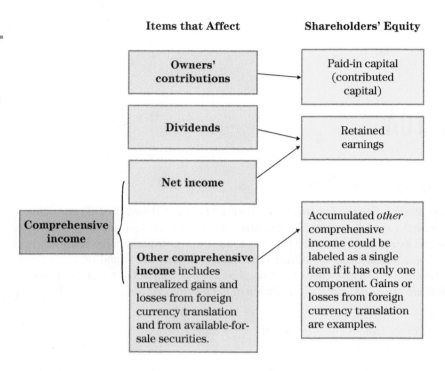

Solution to YOUR TURN Appendix 10A:

The FASB wants to make the changes to shareholders' equity that do not affect net income more apparent to financial statement users.

Short Exercises

SE10A-1A. *Comprehensive income. (LO 5).* Give an example of a gain or loss that would be excluded from the income statement and shown directly on the balance sheet as part of accumulated other comprehensive income.

SE10A-2B. *Comprehensive income. (LO 5).* Give an example of an item (other than a gain or loss) that would be excluded from the income statement and shown directly on the balance sheet as part of accumulated other comprehensive income.

Appendix 10B

Investments in Securities

You have learned that certain gains and losses related to investments may be included in other comprehensive income (Appendix 10A). We will take a closer look at how a firm accounts for its investments in the securities of another firm. You will see how gains and losses on some of these investments are reported as part of comprehensive income.

In addition to assets that a firm uses in its main line of business, a firm will often invest its extra cash in investments in other firms. For example, Apple's 2008 balance sheet shows over $12.6 billion of short-term investments. These are investments in the stocks of other firms. For example, Apple may want to own some stock in Intel. Like individual and other investors, firms can go to the stock market and purchase any of the stocks trading in that market. Firms can have both short- and long-term investments, depending on how long they plan to keep the investments. Although our focus in this chapter has been on long-term assets, we'll take a brief look at both short-term and long-term investments.

When interest rates are low, a company's extra cash—cash not immediately needed—may earn more in the stock market or bond market than it would in a bank savings account or certificate of deposit. That is one reason a company buys stocks and bonds of other companies with its extra cash. For entities such as banks and insurance companies, investing cash in other companies is a crucial part of managing their assets. Stocks are called equity securities and bonds are debt securities. Both may be purchased with a company's extra cash. When a company buys another company's debt securities or less than 20% of its equity securities, the accounting rules require firms to classify their investments in securities into one of three categories: held to maturity, trading, or available for sale.

Held-to-Maturity Securities

Sometimes a company purchases debt securities and intends to keep them until they mature. Bonds have a maturity date, but equity securities do not. If a company has the intention of keeping the debt securities until maturity and their financial condition indicates that they should be able to do this, the securities will be classified as **held-to-maturity securities**. Such investments are recorded at cost, and they are reported on the balance sheet. No matter how much held-to-maturity investments are worth on the market, a company will always report them at cost when preparing its balance sheet.

Trading Securities

If a company buys the securities solely to trade them and make a short-term profit, the company will classify them as **trading securities**. The balance sheet shows trading securities at their market value. A company obtains the current value of the investments from the *Wall Street Journal* or a similar source of market prices. Those values are then shown on the balance sheet. Updating the accounting records to show the securities at their market value is called *marking to market*. If the securities' cost is lower than market value, then the company will record the difference as an unrealized gain. If the securities' cost is higher than market value, then the company will record the difference as an unrealized loss. Remember, *realizing* means actually getting something. Any gain or loss on an investment the company is holding (holding means *not* selling) is something the company does not get (a gain) or does not give up (a loss) until the company sells the securities. **Unrealized gains or losses** are gains or losses on securities that have not been sold. Such a

L.O.6
Explain how a firm's investments in other firms' marketable securities are valued and reported.

Held-to-maturity securities are investments in debt securities that the company plans to hold until they mature.

Trading securities are investments in debt and equity securities that the company has purchased to make a short-term profit.

Unrealized gain or loss is when an increase or decrease in the market value of a company's investments in securities is recognized either on the income statement (for trading securities) or in other comprehensive income in the equity section of the balance sheet (for available-for-sale securities) when the financial statements are prepared, even though the securities have *not* been sold.

gain or loss may also be called a *holding gain* or *loss*. The unrealized gains and losses from trading securities are reported on the income statement.

For example, suppose Avia Company has invested $130,000 of its extra cash in securities—stocks and bonds traded on the stock and bond markets. At the end of the year, the securities that cost Avia $130,000 have a market value of $125,000. On the income statement for the year, Avia will show an unrealized loss of $5,000. The loss is recorded as an adjustment made before the financial statements are prepared.

The securities' new value of $125,000 (originally $130,000 minus loss of $5,000) has replaced their original cost. Now, $125,000 will be the "cost" and will be compared to the market value on the date of the next balance sheet. Remember, the company purchased these trading securities as investments to trade in the short run, so the firm's investment portfolio is likely to look very different at the next balance sheet date.

Available-for-Sale Securities

Available-for-sale securities are investments the company may hold or sell; the company's intention is not clear enough to use one of the other categories—*held to maturity* or *trading*.

Sometimes a company is not sure how long it will keep the securities it has purchased. If the company does not intend to sell the securities in the short term for a quick profit or does not intend to hold them until maturity, the company will classify the securities as **available for sale**. Every year, when it is time to prepare the annual balance sheet, the cost of this group of securities is compared to the market value at the balance sheet date. The book value of the securities is then adjusted to market value, and the corresponding gain or loss is reported in shareholders' equity. Such a gain or loss is called an *unrealized* or *holding* gain or loss, just as it is called for trading securities. But these gains and losses do not go on the income statement. Instead, they are included as part of accumulated other comprehensive income in the shareholders' equity section of the balance sheet.

Your Turn 10B

A corporation has invested $50,000 in the securities of other companies. At the end of the year, that corporation's portfolio has a market value of $52,000. Describe where these securities would be shown on the annual financial statements and at what amount under each of the conditions described.

1. The investment is classified as trading securities.
2. The investment is classified as available for sale.
3. The investment is classified as held to maturity.

Suppose Avia Company classified its portfolio of securities that cost $130,000 as available for sale. If the market value of the securities is $125,000 at the date of the balance sheet, the securities must be shown on the balance sheet at the lower amount. In this case, the unrealized loss will *not* be shown on the income statement. Instead of going through net income to retained earnings, the loss will go directly to the shareholders' equity section of the balance sheet. The loss will be shown after retained earnings, either alone and labeled as an unrealized loss from investments in securities, or combined with other non-income statement gains and losses and labeled as *accumulated other comprehensive income*.

Impairment

When any asset's value has declined permanently below its book value, it must be written down. This is true no matter how the asset is classified. As you know, accountants do not want to overstate assets. This is where the real problem with valuing investments has come in the last few years. Firms with large investments in mortgage-related securities have had to reduce the value of those assets on their balance sheets. The balancing part of the transaction in the accounting equation is a charge to income (i.e., a loss). Both the FASB and the IASB have grappled with this issue, and they have relaxed the rules forcing the write-down of some of these securities.

What happens when the securities stop trading in active markets? How does a firm calculate securities' value for the balance sheet? Should the loss go on the income statement or should it go directly to shareholders' equity? How do you determine if the decline in value is permanent? These are important questions that both the FASB and the IASB continue to debate, and they point out that accounting is not exact. It involves many crucial judgments. Keep an eye out for developments on this topic in the financial press.

Selling the Securities

When a firm sells any of these securities—trading, available for sale, or held to maturity—the gain or loss on the sale is calculated like other accounting gains and losses. The book value of the security at the time of the sale is compared to the selling price. The selling price is often called the proceeds from the sale. If the book value is greater than the proceeds, the firm will record a loss on the sale. If the book value is less than the proceeds, the firm will record a gain on the sale. Gains and losses from the actual sale of the securities are both *realized* (the sale has actually happened) and *recognized* (the relevant amounts are shown on the income statement).

Solution to YOUR TURN Appendix 10B:

1. The securities will be shown in the current asset section of the balance sheet at a value of $52,000. The write-up will be balanced with a $2,000 unrealized gain on the income statement.
2. The securities will be shown in either the current asset or the long-term asset section of the balance sheet (depending on a firm's intent) at a value of $52,000. The write-up will be balanced with a $2,000 unrealized gain that will go directly to equity, as part of accumulated other comprehensive income.
3. The securities will be shown at their cost of $50,000 in the long-term asset section of the balance sheet (unless the debt securities are maturing in the coming year, in which case they would be current assets).

Short Exercises

All of the A exercises can be found within MyAccountingLab, an online homework and practice environment.

SE10B-1A. *Investments. (LO 6).* In January 2010, Bowers Company had some extra cash and purchased the stock of various companies with the objective of making a profit in the short run. The cost of Bowers' portfolio was $36,500. On December 31, 2010, the date of the balance sheet, the market value of the portfolio was $25,200. How would this decrease in value be reflected in Bowers' financial statements for the year ended December 31, 2010?

SE10B-2B. *Investments. (LO 6).* In April 2011, Convey Company had some extra cash and purchased the stock of various companies with the objective of making a profit in the short run. The cost of Convey's portfolio was $79,450. At December 31, 2011, the date of the balance sheet, the market value of the portfolio was $85,200. How would this increase in value be reflected in Convey's financial statements for the year ended December 31, 2011?

Exercises
Set A

E10B-3A. *Investments. (LO 6).* Omicron Corporation invested $125,000 of its extra cash in securities. Under each of the following independent scenarios, (a) calculate the amount at which the investments would be valued for the year-end balance sheet, and (b) indicate how the effect of these scenarios should be reported on the other financial statements, if at all.
1. All the securities were debt securities, with a maturity date in two years. Omicron will hold the securities until they mature. The market value of the securities at year end was $123,000.
2. Omicron purchased the securities for trading, hoping to make a quick profit. At year end the market value of the securities was $120,000.
3. Omicron is uncertain about how long it will hold the securities. At year end the market value of the securities is $126,000.

E10B-4A. *Investments. (LO 6).* Kinsey Scales invested $164,000 of its extra cash in securities. Under each of the following independent scenarios, (a) calculate the amount at which the investments would be valued for the year-end balance sheet, and (b) indicate how these scenarios should be reported on the other financial statements, if at all.

1. All the securities were debt securities, with a maturity date in two years. Kinsey will hold the securities until they mature. The market value of the securities at year end was $158,000.
2. Kinsey purchased the securities for trading, hoping to make a quick profit. At year end the market value of the securities was $162,000.
3. Kinsey is uncertain about how long it will hold the securities. At year end the market value of the securities is $167,000.

Set B

E10B-5B. *Investments. (LO 6).* During 2010, Nike invested $500,000 of extra cash in securities. Of the total amount invested, $275,000 was invested in bonds that Nike plans to hold until maturity (the bonds were issued at par value); $165,000 was invested in various equity securities that Nike plans to hold for an indefinite period of time; and $60,000 was invested in the stock of various companies that Nike intends to trade to make a short-term profit. At the end of the year, the market value of the held-to-maturity securities was $200,000; the market value of the trading securities was $145,000; and the market value of the available-for-sale securities was $75,000. Use the accounting equation to record all adjustments required at year end, and indicate how the effects of each group of securities will be reported on the financial statements.

E10B-6B. *Investments. (LO 6).* During 2009, Arctic Fans & Blowers invested $245,000 of extra cash in securities. Of the total amount invested, $115,000 was invested in bonds that Arctic plans to hold until maturity (the bonds were issued at par); $55,000 was invested in various equity securities that Arctic plans to hold for an indefinite period of time; and $75,000 was invested in the stock of various companies that Arctic intends to trade to make a short-term profit. At the end of the year, the market value of the held-to-maturity securities was $108,000; the market value of the trading securities was $52,000; and the market value of the available-for-sale securities was $85,000. Use the accounting equation to record all adjustments required at year end and indicate how the effects of each group of securities will be reported on the financial statements.

Glossary

A

Accelerated depreciation is a depreciation method in which more depreciation expense is taken in the early years of the asset's life and less in the later years.

The **accounting cycle** begins with the transactions of a new accounting period. It includes recording and posting the transactions, adjusting the books, preparing financial statements, and closing the temporary accounts to get ready for the next accounting period.

Accounts payable are amounts that a company owes its vendors. They are liabilities and are shown on the balance sheet.

Accounts receivable is a current asset that arises from sales on credit; it is the total amount customers owe the firm.

The **accounts receivable (AR) turnover ratio** is a ratio that measures how quickly a firm collects its accounts receivable. It is defined as credit sales divided by average accounts receivable.

An **accrual** is a transaction in which the revenue has been earned or the expense has been incurred, but no cash has been exchanged.

Accrual basis accounting refers to the way we recognize revenues and expenses. Accountants do not rely on the exchange of cash to determine the timing of revenue recognition. Firms recognize revenue when it is earned and expenses when they are incurred—no matter when the cash is received or disbursed. Accrual accounting follows the matching principle.

The **accumulated depreciation** is the reduction to the cost of the asset. Accumulated depreciation is a contra-asset, deducted from the cost of the asset for the balance sheet.

Activity method of depreciation is the method of depreciation in which useful life is expressed in terms of the total units of activity or production expected from the asset, and the asset is written off in proportion to its activity during the accounting period.

An **adjusted trial balance** is a list of all accounts with their debit and credit balances, prepared after adjustments have been made.

Adjusting the books means to make changes in the accounting records, at the end of the period, just before the financial statements are prepared, to make sure the amounts reflect the financial condition of the company at that date.

An **aging schedule** is an analysis of the amounts owed to a firm by the length of time they have been outstanding.

The **allowance for uncollectible accounts** is a contra-asset account, the balance of which represents the total amount the firm believes it will not collect from its total accounts receivable.

The **allowance method** is a method of accounting for bad debts in which the amount of the uncollectible accounts is estimated at the end of each accounting period.

Amortization means to write off the cost of a long-term asset over more than one accounting period.

Amortization schedule is a chart that shows the amount of principal and the amount of interest that make up each payment of a loan.

An **annuity** is a series of equal cash receipts or cash payments over equally spaced intervals of time.

Asset turnover ratio measures how efficiently a company is using its assets to generate sales. It is defined as net sales divided by average total assets.

Assets are economic resources owned or controlled by the business.

Authorized shares are shares of stock that are available for a firm to issue per its corporate charter.

Available-for-sale securities are investments the company may hold or sell; the company's intention is not clear enough to use one of the other categories—*held to maturity* or *trading*.

The **average days in inventory** is the number of days it takes, on average, to sell an item of inventory.

B

Bad debts expense is the expense to record uncollectible accounts receivable.

The **balance sheet** shows a summary of each element of the accounting equation: assets, liabilities, and shareholders' equity.

A **bank reconciliation** is a comparison between the cash balance in the firm's accounting records and the cash balance on the bank statement to identify the reasons for any differences.

A **bank statement** is a summary of the activity in a bank account sent each month to the account holder.

Big bath is an expression that describes a violation of the GAAP matching principle in which more expenses are taken in a bad year than are actually justified, so fewer expenses can be taken in future years.

A **bond** is an interest-bearing, long-term note payable issued by corporations, universities, and governmental agencies.

Bonds issued at a discount are bonds issued for an amount less than the face value of the bond. This happens when the market rate of interest is greater than the bond's stated rate of interest.

Bonds issued at a premium are bonds issued for an amount more than the face value of the bond. This happens when the market rate of interest is less than the bond's stated rate of interest.

Bonds issued at par are bonds issued for the face value of the bond. This happens when the market rate of interest is equal to the bond's stated rate of interest.

The **book value** of an asset is the cost minus the accumulated depreciation related to the asset.

The **books** are a company's accounting records.

C

Capital is the name for the resources used to start and run a business.

A **capital expenditure** is a cost that is recorded as an asset, not an expense, at the time it is incurred. This is also called *capitalizing* a cost.

Capital structure is the combination of debt and equity that a firm uses to finance its business.

To **capitalize** is to record a cost as an asset rather than to record it as an expense.

Carrying value is another expression for book value.

The **carrying value** of a bond is the amount that the balance sheet shows as the net value of the bond, similar in meaning to the carrying value of a fixed asset. It is equal to the face value of the bond minus any discount or plus any premium.

Cash basis accounting is a system based on the exchange of cash. In this system, revenue is recognized only when cash is collected, and an expense is recognized only when cash is disbursed. This is not an acceptable method of accounting under GAAP.

Cash equivalents are highly liquid investments with a maturity of three months or less that a firm can easily convert into a known amount of cash.

The **cash from financing activities** section of the statement of cash flows includes transactions related to how a business is financed. Examples include contributions from owners and amounts borrowed using loans.

The **cash from investing activities** section of the statement of cash flows includes transactions involving the sale and purchase of long-term assets used in the business.

The **cash from operating activities** section of the statement of cash flows includes cash transactions that relate to the everyday, routine transactions needed to run a business.

Cash from operations to current liabilities ratio is the net cash from operating activities divided by average current liabilities.

A **certified public accountant (CPA)** is someone who has met specific education and exam requirements set up by individual states to make sure that only individuals with the appropriate qualifications can perform audits. To sign an audit report, an accountant must be a CPA.

A **classified balance sheet** shows a subtotal for many items, including current assets and current liabilities.

Closing the accounts means bringing the balances in the temporary accounts to zero.

Common stock is the most widespread form of ownership in a corporation; common shareholders have a vote in the election of the firm's board of directors.

Common-sizing involves converting all amounts on a financial statement to a percentage of a chosen value on that statement; also known as *vertical analysis*.

Comparative balance sheets are the balance sheets from consecutive fiscal years for a single company. The ending balance sheet for one fiscal year is the beginning balance sheet for the next fiscal year.

Comprehensive income is the total of all items that affect shareholders' equity except transactions with the owners; comprehensive income has two parts: net income and other comprehensive income.

A **contra-asset** is an amount that is deducted from an asset.

A **contra-revenue** is an account that is an offset to a revenue account and therefore deducted from the revenue for the financial statements.

Contributed capital is an owner's investment in a company.

Cookie jar reserves is an expression that describes an account, usually a liability, that is established by recognizing an estimated expense inaccurately. When the expenditures actually occur, the firm charges them against the reserve rather than against income. This practice is a violation of the matching principle.

Cooking the books is a slang expression that means to manipulate or falsify the firm's accounting records to make the firm's financial performance or position look better than it actually is.

A **copyright** is a form of legal protection for authors of "original works of authorship," provided by U.S. law.

Corporate governance is the way a firm governs itself, as executed by the board of directors. Corporate governance is also described as the set of relationships between the board of directors, management, shareholders, auditors, and any others with a stake in the company.

A **corporation** is a special legal form for a business in which the business is a legal entity separate from the owners. A corporation may have a single owner or a large number of owners.

Cost of goods available for sale is the total of beginning inventory plus the net purchases made during the period (plus any freight-in costs).

Cost of goods sold is the total amount paid by a firm for the goods sold during the period.

Credit means right side of an account.

Current assets are the assets the company plans to turn into cash or use to generate revenue in the next fiscal year.

Current liabilities are liabilities the company will settle—pay off—in the next fiscal year.

Current ratio is a liquidity ratio that measures a firm's ability to meet its short-term obligations.

D

Debit means left side of an account.

Debt-to-equity ratio compares the amount of a firm's liabilities to the amount of its equity, an indication of solvency.

Declining balance depreciation is an accelerated depreciation method in which depreciation expense is based on the declining book value of the asset.

A **deferral** is a transaction in which the cash is exchanged *before* the revenue has been earned or the expense has been incurred.

Definitely determinable liabilities are obligations that can be measured exactly.

Depletion is the amortization of a natural resource.

A **deposit in transit** is a bank deposit the firm has made but is not included on the month's bank statement because the deposit did not reach the bank's record-keeping department in time to be included on the current bank statement.

Depreciation is a systematic and rational allocation process to recognize the expense of long-term assets over the periods in which the assets are used.

The **depreciation expense** is the expense for each period.

The **direct method** shows every cash inflow and outflow to prepare the statement of cash flows.

The **direct write-off method** is a method of accounting for bad debts in which they are recorded as an expense in the period in which they are identified as uncollectible.

Discontinued operations are those parts of the firm that a company has eliminated by selling a division.

Discount on bonds payable is a contra-liability that is deducted from bonds payable on the balance sheet; it is the difference between the face value of the bond and its selling price when the selling price is less than the face (par) value.

The **discount rate** is the interest rate used to compute the present value of future cash flows.

Discounting means to compute the present value of future cash flows.

Dividend yield ratio is dividend per share divided by the current market price per share.

Dividends are the distribution of a corporation's earnings to the owners or shareholders of the corporation.

E

Earnings per share (EPS) is a commonly used measure of firm performance, defined as net income minus preferred dividends divided by the weighted average number of common shares outstanding.

An **enterprise-wide resource planning system (ERP)** is an integrated software program used by large firms to manage all of a firm's information.

Estimated liabilities are obligations that have some uncertainty in the amount, such as the cost to honor a warranty.

Expenses are the costs incurred to generate revenue.

Extraordinary items are events that are unusual in nature and infrequent in occurrence.

F

The **Financial Accounting Standards Board (FASB)** is the group that sets accounting standards. It gets its authority from the SEC.

Financial leverage is the use of borrowed funds to increase earnings.

Financial services companies deal in services related to money.

First-in, first-out (FIFO) is the inventory cost flow method that assumes the first items purchased are the first items sold.

A **fiscal year** is a year in the life of a business. It may or may not coincide with the calendar year.

FOB (free on board) destination means that the vendor (selling firm) pays the shipping costs, so the buyer has no freight-in cost.

FOB (free on board) shipping point means the buying firm pays the shipping costs. The amount is called freight-in and is included in the cost of the inventory.

A **for-profit firm** has the goal of making a profit for its owners.

A **franchise** is an agreement that authorizes someone to sell or distribute a company's goods or services in a certain area.

Free cash flow is equal to net cash from operating activities minus dividends and minus capital expenditures.

The **full-disclosure principle** means that the firm must disclose any circumstances and events that would make a difference to the users of the financial statements.

G

The **general ledger** is the collection of the company's accounts where the information from the financial transactions is organized and stored.

The **general ledger system** is the accountant's traditional way of keeping track of a company's financial transactions and then using those records to prepare the basic financial statements.

Generally accepted accounting principles (GAAP) are the guidelines for financial reporting.

The **going-concern assumption** means that, unless there is obvious evidence to the contrary, a firm is expected to continue operating in the foreseeable future.

Goodwill is the excess of cost over market value of the net assets when one company purchases another company.

Gross profit ratio is equal to the gross profit (sales minus cost of goods sold) divided by sales. It is a ratio for evaluating firm performance.

H

Held-to-maturity securities are investments in debt securities that the company plans to hold until they mature.

The **historical-cost principle** means that transactions are recorded at actual cost.

Horizontal analysis is a technique for evaluating financial statement items across time.

I

Impairment is a permanent decline in the fair market value of an asset such that its book value exceeds its fair market value.

The **income statement** shows all revenues minus all expenses for an accounting period—a month, a quarter, or a year.

The **indirect method** starts with net income and makes adjustments for items that are not cash to prepare the statement of cash flows.

Intangible assets are rights, privileges, or benefits that result from owning long-lived assets that do not have physical substance.

The **interest** is the cost of borrowing money—using someone else's money.

Interest payable is a liability. It is the amount a company owes for borrowing money (after the time period to which the interest applies has passed).

Internal controls are a company's policies and procedures designed to protect the assets of the firm and to ensure the accuracy and reliability of the accounting records.

The **Internal Revenue Service (IRS)** is the federal agency responsible for federal income tax collection.

The **International Accounting Standards Board (IASB)** is the group that sets international financial reporting standards.

The **International Financial Reporting Standards (IFRS)** are international guidelines for financial reporting, used in many places around the world.

The **inventory turnover ratio** is defined as cost of goods sold divided by average inventory. It is a measure of how quickly a firm sells its inventory.

Issued shares are shares of stock that have been offered and sold to shareholders.

J

Business transactions are first recorded in a **journal**. Then they are transferred to accounts in the general ledger through a process called posting.

L

Last-in, first-out (LIFO) is the inventory cost flow method that assumes the last items purchased are the first items sold.

Liabilities are the obligations of a business; amounts owed to creditors.

Liquidity is a measure of how easily an asset can be converted to cash. The more liquid an asset is, the more easily it can be turned into cash.

Liquidity ratios are used to measure the company's ability to pay its current bills and operating costs.

Long-term assets are assets that will last for more than a year.

Long-term liabilities are liabilities that will take longer than a year to settle.

The **lower-of-cost-or-market (LCM) rule** is the rule that requires firms to use the lower of either the cost or the market value (replacement cost) of its inventory on the date of the balance sheet.

M

The **maker** of a note is the person or firm making the promise to pay.

A **manufacturing company** makes the goods it sells.

Market indicators are ratios that relate the current market price of the company's stock to earnings or dividends.

The **market rate of interest** is the interest rate that an investor could earn in an equally risky investment.

The **matching principle** says that expenses should be recognized—shown on the income statement—in the same period as the revenue they helped generate.

A **merchandising company** sells a product to its customers.

Modified accelerated cost recovery system (MACRS) is the method that the IRS requires firms to use to depreciate its assets for tax purposes.

The **monetary-unit assumption** means that the items on the financial statements are measured in monetary units (dollars in the United States).

A **multistep income statement** starts with sales and subtracts cost of goods sold to get a subtotal called gross profit on sales, also known as gross margin. Then, other operating revenues are added and other operating expenses are deducted. A subtotal for operating income is shown before deductions related to nonoperating items and taxes are deducted. Then, income taxes are subtracted, leaving net income.

N

Net income equals all revenues minus all expenses for a specific period of time.

Net profit equals all revenues minus all expenses.

Net realizable value is the amount of its accounts receivable balance that the firm expects to collect.

Noncurrent assets, or long-term assets, are assets that will last for more than a year.

Noncurrent liabilities, or long-term liabilities, are liabilities that will take longer than a year to settle.

A **not-for-profit firm** has the goal of providing goods or services to its clients.

Notes to the financial statements are information provided with the four basic statements that describe the company's major accounting policies and provide other disclosures to help external users better understand the financial statements.

O

On account means *on credit*. The expression applies to either buying or selling on credit.

An **ordinary annuity** is an annuity whose payments are made at the end of each interval or period.

An **outstanding check** is a check the firm has written but that has not yet cleared the bank. That is, the check has not been presented to the bank for payment yet.

Outstanding shares are shares of stock that are owned by stockholders.

P

Paid-in capital, another name for contributed capital, is the owner's investment in the business.

Par value is the monetary amount assigned to a share of stock in the corporate charter. It has little meaning in today's business environment.

A **partnership** is a company owned by two or more individuals.

A **patent** is a property right that the U.S. government grants to an inventor "to exclude others from making, using, offering for sale, or selling the invention throughout the United States or importing the invention into the United States for a specified period of time."

The **payee** of a note is the person or firm receiving the money.

The **periodic inventory system** is a method of record keeping that involves updating the inventory account only at the end of the accounting period.

Permanent accounts or **real accounts** are accounts that are never closed. They are the asset, liability, and shareholders' equity accounts.

The **perpetual inventory system** is a method of record keeping that involves updating the inventory account at the time of every purchase, sale, and return.

A **postclosing trial balance** is a list of all the accounts and their debit balances or credit balances, prepared after the temporary accounts have been closed. Only balance sheet accounts will appear on the postclosing trial balance.

Posting is the process of recording the transactions from the journal into the firm's general ledger so that the transactions will be organized by accounts.

Preferred stock is stock that represents a special kind of ownership in a corporation. Preferred shareholders do not get a vote but they do receive dividends before the common shareholders.

Premium on bonds payable is an adjunct-liability that is added to bonds payable on the balance sheet; it is the difference between the face value of the bond and its selling price, when the selling price is more than the face (par) value.

Prepaid insurance is the name for insurance a business has purchased but not yet used. It is an asset.

Prepaid rent is an asset. It represents amounts paid for rent not yet used. The rent expense is deferred until the rented asset has actually been used—when the time related to the rent has passed.

The **present value** is the value today of a given amount to be invested or received in the future, assuming compound interest.

Price–earnings (P/E) ratio is the market price of a share of stock divided by that stock's earnings per share.

The **principal** of a loan is the amount of money borrowed.

Proceeds are the amount of cash the bond issuer collects from the bondholders when the bonds are issued.

Profit margin on sales is a ratio that measures how much of the firm's sales revenue actually makes its way to the bottom line—net income. To calculate this ratio, simply divide net income by net sales.

Profitability ratios are used to measure the operating or income performance of a company.

A **promissory note** is a written promise to pay a specified amount of money at a specified time.

The **Public Company Accounting Oversight Board (PCAOB)** is a group formed to oversee the auditing profession and the audits of public companies. Its creation was mandated by the Sarbanes-Oxley Act of 2002.

A **purchase discount** is a reduction in the price of an inventory purchase for prompt payment according to terms specified by the vendor.

A **purchase order** is a record of the company's request to a vendor for goods or services. It may be referred to as a P.O.

Purchase returns and allowances are amounts that decrease the cost of inventory due to returned or damaged merchandise.

Q

Quality of earnings refers to how well a reported earnings number communicates the firm's true performance.

R

Realized means the cash is collected. Sometimes revenue is *recognized* before it is *realized*.

Recognized revenue is revenue that has been recorded so that it will show up on the income statement.

Relative fair market value method is a way to allocate the total cost for several assets purchased together to each of the individual assets. This method is based on the assets' individual market values.

Replacement cost is the cost to buy similar items in inventory from the supplier to replace the inventory.

Residual value, also known as salvage value, is the estimated value of an asset at the end of its useful life. With most depreciation methods, residual value is deducted before the calculation of depreciation expense.

Retained earnings is the total of all net income amounts minus all dividends paid in the life of the company. It is descriptively named—it is the earnings that have been kept (retained) in the company. The amount of retained earnings represents the part of the owner's claims that the company has earned (i.e., not contributed). Retained earnings is *not* the same as cash.

Return on assets is a ratio that measures how well a company is using its assets to generate income. It is defined as net income divided by average total assets.

Return on equity (ROE) measures the amount of income earned with each dollar of common shareholders' investment in the firm. To calculate ROE, take net income minus preferred dividends divided by average common shareholders' equity.

Revenue is the amount the company has earned from providing goods or services to customers.

The **revenue-recognition principle** says that revenue should be recognized when it is earned and collection is reasonably assured.

A **risk** is a danger—something that exposes a business to a potential injury or loss.

S

A **sales discount** is a reduction in the sales price of a product offered to customers for prompt payment.

Sales returns and allowances is an account that holds amounts that reduce sales due to customer returns or allowances for damaged merchandise.

Salvage value (also known as *residual value*) is the estimated value of an asset at the end of its useful life.

The **Securities and Exchange Commission (SEC)** is the governmental agency that monitors the stock market and the financial reporting of the firms that trade in the market.

Segregation of duties means that the person who has physical custody of an asset is not the same person who has record-keeping responsibilities for that asset.

The **separate-entity assumption** means that the firm's financial records and financial statements are completely separate from those of the firm's owners.

A **service company** does something for its customers.

Shareholders' equity—the owners' claims to the assets of the company. There are two types: contributed capital and retained earnings.

Shares of common stock are the units of ownership in a corporation.

A **single-step income statement** groups all revenues together and shows all expenses deducted from total revenue.

A **sole proprietorship** is a company with a single owner.

Solvency ratios are used to measure the company's ability to meet its long-term obligations and to survive over a long period of time.

The **specific identification method** is the inventory cost flow method in which the actual cost of the specific goods sold is recorded as cost of goods sold.

The **statement of cash flows** shows all the cash collected and all the cash disbursed during the period. Each cash amount is classified as one of three types: cash from operating activities, cash from investing activities, or cash from financing activities.

The **statement of changes in shareholders' equity** starts with the beginning amount of contributed capital and shows all changes during the accounting period. Then the statement shows the beginning balance in retained earnings with its changes. The usual changes to retained earnings are the increase due to net income and the decrease due to dividends paid to shareholders.

Stock dividends are new shares of stock that are distributed to the company's current shareholders.

A **stock exchange** is a marketplace where buyers and sellers exchange their shares of stock. Buying and selling shares of stock can also be done on the Internet.

The **stock market** is the name for a collection of stock exchanges. It is a term generally used to designate any place where stock is bought and sold.

A **stock split** is the division of the current shares of stock by a specific number to increase the number of shares outstanding.

Stockholders or **shareholders** are the owners of the corporation.

Straight-line depreciation is a depreciation method in which the depreciation expense is the same each period.

In general, **supplies** are not called inventory. Supplies are miscellaneous items used in the business. When purchased, supplies are recorded as an asset. Supplies expense is recognized after the supplies are used. *Inventory* is a term reserved for the items a company purchases to resell.

T

Tangible assets are assets with physical substance; they can be seen and touched.

Temporary accounts are the revenue, expense, and dividends accounts.

The **time-period assumption** means that the life of a business can be divided into meaningful time periods for financial reporting.

Timing differences arise when revenues are earned in one accounting period and collected in a different accounting period. They also arise when expenses are incurred in one accounting period and paid for in another.

A **trademark** is a symbol, word, phrase, or logo that legally distinguishes one company's product from any others.

Trading securities are investments in debt and equity securities that the company has purchased to make a short-term profit.

Treasury stock is stock that has been repurchased by the issuing firm.

A **trial balance** is a list of all the accounts of a company with the related balance.

U

Unearned revenue is a liability. It represents the amount of goods or services that a company owes its customers. The cash has been collected, but the action of *earning* the revenue has not taken place.

Unrealized gain or loss is when an increase or decrease in the market value of a company's investments in securities is recognized either on the income statement (for trading securities) or in other comprehensive income in the equity section of the balance sheet (for available-for-sale securities) when the financial statements are prepared, even though the securities have *not* been sold.

V

Vertical analysis is a technique for comparing items on a financial statement in which all items are expressed as a percent of a common amount.

W

Weighted average cost is the inventory cost flow method in which the weighted average cost of the goods available for sale is used to calculate the cost of goods sold and the ending inventory.

A distribution to the owner of a sole proprietorship is called a **withdrawal**; in a corporation, distributions to the shareholders are called **dividends**.

X

XBRL (Extensible Business Reporting Language) is a technology that enables firms to report information in a standardized way that makes the data immediately reusable and interactive.

Index

A

Abercrombie & Fitch, 233, 381, 470, 471, 472, 474
Accelerated depreciation, 276–277
Accounting assumptions
 going-concern assumption, 55
 monetary-unit assumption, 54
 separate-entity assumption, 54
 time-period assumption, 55
Accounting constraints, 56
Accounting cycle, 568–579
 example (Clint's Consulting Company), 568–579
 review and summary, 580
Accounting equation, 14, 17, 62
 worksheet, 58
Accounting frauds, 27
Accounting information
 characteristics of, 53–56
 comparability, 53–54
 consistency, 54
 relevance, 53
 reliability, 53
 users, 67–68
Accounting jobs, 519
Accounting periods, 67
Accounting principles
 full-disclosure principle, 55
 historical-cost principle, 55
 matching principle, 55
 revenue-recognition principle, 55
Accounting scandals, 515–516
Accounting software, 123
Accounting system
 mechanics of, 563–607
Accounts payable, 56
Accounts receivable, 57, 100, 153–200
 accounts receivable method, 163–165, 167
 aging schedule, 163, 164
 allowance method, 162–165
 balance sheet presentation, 164
 controls, 177–178
 defined, 161
 direct write-off method, 168–169
 estimating bad debt expense, 162–165
 example (Team Shirts), 171–174
 extending credit, 161–162
 managing, 163
 percentage of sales method, 162–163, 167
 ratio analysis, 175–176
 recording uncollectible accounts, 162
 writing off specific account, 165–168
Accounts receivable method, 163–165, 167
Accounts receivable subsidiary ledger, 565
Accounts receivable (AR) turnover ratio, 175–176, 472–474

Accrual accounting information, 67–68
 versus cash basis, 418–419
Accrual basis accounting, 65, 66–67
 cash basis accounting versus, 66–67
Accruals, 66, 99–104, 571–572
 adjustments to accounting records, 115–116
 defined, 99
 example, 119–121
 expenses, 101–104, 571, 572
 financial statements, and, 112–121
 other expenses, 102–104
 real firm examples, 119–121
 revenue, 99–101, 571–572
Accrued expenses, 101–104, 119, 571, 572
Accrued liabilities, 102
Accrued revenue, 571–572
Accumulated amortization, 279
Accumulated depreciation, 110, 111, 115, 119, 328
Accumulated other comprehensive income, 508
Acquiring merchandise for sale, 202–210
Acquisition cost, 271, 272
Activity method depreciation, 274–275
Additional paid-in capital, 374
Adjunct liability, 329
Adjusted trial balance, 574
 preparing, 574
Adjusting the books, 59
ADP. See Automatic Data Processing
Aging method, 163
Aging schedule, 163, 164
Allowance for depreciation, 119
Allowance for obsolescence, 231
Allowance for uncollectible accounts, 162
Allowance method, 162, 163–165
Amazon.com, 76, 469
Amortization
 bonds, 329–333
 defined, 270
 intangible assets, 279–281
Amortization schedule, 324, 330, 331
Amortized costs, 285
Analysis of business transactions, 56–62, 68–72
Analysis of transactions, 56–62, 68–72
Andover Bank, 155
Annuity, 363
Apple Computers, 3, 64, 214, 279, 507
AR turnover ratio. See Accounts receivable turnover ratio
Archway & Mother's Cookie Company, 97
Asset impairment, 281
Asset turnover ratio, 290–291
Assets, 14, 62, 566

Assumptions. See Accounting assumptions
Audit opinion, 25
Auditors, 517
 report, 26
Authorized shares, 372
Auto Zone, 427, 428, 429
Automatic Data Processing (ADP), 318
Available-for-sale securities, 508
Average days in inventory, 232
Avia, 508

B

BAAN, 580
Bad debts expense, 162. See also Accounts receivable
Balance sheet, 13–17, 578
 accounts receivable, 164
 analysis of transactions, 15
 classified, 64
 comparative, 15
 elements, 62–66
 income statement, contrasted, 19
 liabilities, 319
 long-term assets, 285
 sample, 63, 74, 319, 522
 shareholders' equity, 372, 382
Banana Republic, 260
Bank One, 475
Bank reconciliation, 154–160
Bank statement, 154, 160
Bankruptcy, corporate, 374
Barclays Global Investors, 415
Barnes & Noble, 214
Basic earnings per share, 390
Basket purchase, 270
Beginning inventory errors, 262–263
Berenson, Alex, 512
Best Buy, 105, 106, 110, 111, 213, 234, 285, 315
Big bath charges, 513–514
Black & Decker, 204, 206, 318
Bloomingdale's, 201
Board of directors, 517
Boeing, 4, 212
Bond, 325–333
 amortization, 329–333
 calculating proceeds, 365–366
 defined, 325
 getting the money (issuing bonds), 326–327
 issued at discount, 327, 328
 issued at par, 327
 issued at premium, 327, 329
 paying the bondholders, 329–333
 reading a quote, 332
 types, 327
 why used, 325–326

Bond certificate, 325, 326
Bond covenants, 326
Bondholder, 317
Bonds issued at a discount, 327, 328
Bonds issued at a premium, 327, 329
Bonds issued at par, 327
Book value, 110, 115, 271, 276
Bookkeeping, 564
Books, 17
Books-A-Million, 62, 474
Bottom line, 67
Budgeted cash flows, 416
Business
   decision making, 10–13
   how it works, 8–9
   purpose and organization, 2–8
Business description, 5
Business failures, 515–516
Business plan, 5, 475
Business risk, 26–28, 75–77
Business scandals, 1–2, 26, 515–516
Business transactions, 8–9, 56–62, 68–72

C

Cadbury, 521, 522
Callable bond, 327
Campbell Soup Company, 122
Capital, 2, 64, 70
Capital expenditure, 281
Capital stock, 373
Capital structure, 338
Capitalize, 270
Capitalizing retained earnings, 382
Carnival Corp., 459–460
Carrying value, 110, 115, 271, 328
Cash, 73, 153–200, 416
   controlling, 154–160
   paid to employees, 419
Cash and cash equivalents, 160
Cash basis accounting, 66
   versus accrual basis accounting, 66–67
Cash budget, 416, 417
Cash budgeting, 73
Cash burn rate, 429
Cash dividends, 376–378
Cash equivalents, 160
Cash flow projection, 73
Cash flow statement. *See* Statement of
   cash flows
Cash from financing activities, 20
Cash from investing activities, 20
Cash from operating activities, 20
Cash from operations to current liabilities, 471
Cash inflows/outflows, 21
Cash management, 154–160
   bank reconciliation, 154–160
   bank statement, 154, 160
   cash equivalents, 160
   cash flow statement. *See* Statement of
      cash flows
   controls, 154–160, 177–178
   credit/debit memos, 160
   physical controls, 154, 177
   reporting cash, 160–161
Cash reserve, 514
Caterpillar, 215
Catterton Partners, 97
CEO. *See* Chief Executive Officer
Certified public accountant (CPA), 13

CFO. *See* Chief Financial Officer
Chapter 7 bankruptcy, 374
Chapter 11 bankruptcy, 374
Charles Schwab, 7
Chase Manhattan Bank, 1
Chico's, 213
Chief Executive Officer (CEO), 517
Chief Financial Officer (CFO), 517
Chrysler, 53
Classified balance sheet, 64
Clear assignment of responsibility, 177
Closely held corporation, 6
Closing entries
   preparing, 574–577
Closing the account, 574–577, 578
Common stock, 372, 373–375
Common-sizing, 465
Comparability, 52–53
Comparative balance sheets, 15
Compound interest, 361, 362
Comprehensive income, 505–506
Computer Associates, 27, 51, 55, 97
Computerized accounting systems, 123
Computron, 76
Conservatism, 56, 65
Consistency, 54
Constraints, 56
Contra-asset, 110
Contra-liability account, 328
Contra-revenue, 209
Contributed capital, 9, 64, 372–376
Contribution, 9
Controls
   clear assignment of responsibility, 177
   defined, 28
   detective, 76–77
   documentation procedures, 177
   errors in recording transactions,
      122–123
   financial statements, 76–77
   independent internal verification of
      data, 178
   internal, 76–77
   inventory controls, 233–234
   long-term assets, 291
   long-term debt, 339–340
   loss/destruction of data, 123
   monitoring, 291
   physical controls, 291
   stock ownership, 475
   stockholders' equity, 391
   unauthorized access, 123
Convertible bond, 327
Cookie jar reserves, 514–515
Cooking the books, 513. *See also* Earnings
   manipulation
Cooper, Cynthia, 511
Copyright, 279
Corporate bankruptcy, 374
Corporate bonds, 332
Corporate filings, 23
Corporate governance, 511, 516
   evaluating, 520–521
   key players, 517–519
Corporation, 6–8
   advantages of, 7
   disadvantages of, 8
   regulation, 7
Corrective controls, 77

Cost of goods available for sale, 207, 262
Cost of goods sold, 25, 262
Cost of revenue, 25
Costco, 201
Countrywide Financial, 27
Countrywide Mortgage, 4
CPA. *See* Certified public accountant
Credit, 565–567
Credit card sales, 169–170
Credit memo, 160
Credit policies, 163
Cumulative preferred stock, 377
Current assets, 62
Current liabilities, 64
Current ratio, 75, 470–471
Cutoff issues, 67

D

Darden Restaurants, Inc., 53, 75, 152, 281,
   391, 462
Date of record, 377
Debenture, 327
Debit, 565–567
Debit memo, 160
Debt. *See* Liabilities
Debt-to-equity ratio, 338, 469
Decision making, information, 52–53
Declaration date, 376–377
Declining balance depreciation, 276–278
Deferrals, 66, 104–112
   adjustments to accounting records,
      115–116
   defined, 99
   depreciation, 110–111
   equipment, 109–112
   example, 119–121
   expenses, 106–112, 571, 574
   financial statements, and, 112–121
   gift cards, 105
   insurance, 106–107
   magazine subscriptions, 105
   real firm examples, 119–121
   rent, 107–108
   revenue, 104–106, 571, 573
   subscriptions, 105
   supplies, 108–109
   unearned revenue, 104
Deferred expenses, 106–112, 571, 574
Deferred revenue, 104–106, 571, 574
Definitely determinable liabilities, 318
Dell, 3, 7, 8, 23–26, 121
Dell, Michael, 7
Delta, 284
Department, 11
Depletion, 271, 278–279
Deposit in transit, 156, 157
Depreciable base, 271, 272
Depreciated costs, 285
Depreciating an asset, 110
Depreciation
   accelerated, 276
   activity method, 274–275
   declining balance, 276–278
   defined, 271
   double-declining balance, 276, 277
   MACRS, 316
   straight-line, 272–274
   taxes, and, 316
   terminology, 271

Depreciation expense, 110
Destruction of accounting data, 123
Detective controls, 76
Diluted earnings per share, 390
Direct method, 417–418, 420–422, 427
Direct write-off method, 168–169
Disclosure. *See* Notes to financial
    statements
Discontinued operations, 462
Discount
    purchase, 206–207
    sales, 209–210
Discount on bonds payable, 328
Discount rate, 363
Discounting, 363
Diversification, 391, 475
Dividend, 8, 570
    cash, 376–378
    defined, 376
    stock, 382–383
Dividend declaration date, 376–377
Dividend payment date, 377
Dividend payment example, 378
Dividend yield ratio, 469
Documentation procedures, 177
Dollar Tree Stores, 390
Double-declining balance depreciation,
    276, 277
Dow Chemicals, 512
DVD sales, 234

E

Earned capital, 383
Earnings, 512
    importance of, 512
    quality of, 512–513
Earnings manipulation
    big bath charges, 513–514
    cookie jar reserves, 514–515
    revenue recognition, 515
Earnings per share (EPS), 389–390, 512
Earnings restatement, 461
Ebay, 391
Ebbers, Bernard, 27
EBITDA, 474
Effective interest method, 329–333
Employee theft, 201, 211
Employees
    salary expense versus cash paid, 419
Ending inventory errors, 262
Enron, 2, 27, 340, 430, 511, 516
Enterprise-wide resource planning (ERP),
    564, 580
Entrepreneur, 8
EPS. *See* Earnings per share
Equipment, 109–112, 202, 328
Equity, 64
ERP. *See* Enterprise-wide resource planning
    system
Errors in recording transactions, 122–123
Estimated liabilities, 318, 321–322
Estimated useful life, 271, 272
Ex-dividend, 377
Expenses, 10
Extensible Business Reporting Language.
    See XBRL
External auditors, 517
Extraordinary items, 462, 463
ExxonMobil, 469

F

Factor, 163
Factoring, 163
FASB. *See* Financial Accounting Standards
    Board
Fastow, Andrew, 27
FBI, 511
Federal Bureau of Labor Statistics, 519
Fiat, 53
FIFO. *See* First-in, first-out
Financial Accounting Standards Board
    (FASB), 11, 462, 505
Financial advisor, 475
Financial analyst, 475
Financial Executives International, 519
Financial leverage, 338
Financial management plan, 5
Financial ratios. *See* Ratio analysis
Financial risks, 27
Financial scandals, 1–2, 515–516
Financial services companies, 4
Financial statement analysis, 474–475
    continued usefulness, 474–475
    horizontal analysis, 464
    how used, 474–475
    ratio analysis. *See* Ratio analysis
    vertical analysis, 465
Financial statements
    balance sheet. *See* Balance sheet
    elements of, 56–66
    example, 68–72, 576
    income statement. *See* Income statement
    notes. *See* Notes to financial statements
    objectives, 72–75
    preparing, 574
    real company, 23–26
    relationship between, 22
    statement of cash flows. *See* Statement of
        cash flows
    statement of changes in shareholders'
        equity, 19
    type of information provided, 68–72
Financing activities, 9, 20, 417
First-in, first-out (FIFO), 214–215,
    475, 513
    income tax effects, 222
Fiscal year, 15
Fisher, Donald and Doris, 260
Fitch, 317
Fixed assets. *See* Long-term operational assets
FOB (free on board) destination, 204
FOB (free on board) shipping point,
    204, 205
Footnotes, 13. *See also* Notes to financial
    statements
For-profit firm, 2
Forecasts, 475
Forms of business organization. *See*
    Ownership structure
FOSSIL, Inc., 73
Franchise, 280
Free cash flow, 429
Freight costs, 204–205, 210
Friehling & Horowitz, 2
Frito-Lay, 215
Full-disclosure principle, 55, 65
Fuzzy earnings numbers. *See* Earnings
    manipulation

G

GAAP. *See* Generally accepted accounting
    principles
Gap, Inc., 98, 233, 260–261
General Electric, 376, 415
General ledger, 563
    accounting system, 564–565
    posting journal entries to, 570
General ledger system, 563
    example (Team Shirts), 581–587
General Mills, 464, 465
General Motors, 374, 429, 512
General strategic risks, 27
Generally accepted accounting principles
    (GAAP), 11, 51, 52–53, 56, 67, 169,
    208, 212, 340, 416, 462, 463
    versus IFRS, 521–524
Gift cards, 105
    unredeemed, 105
Going-concern assumption, 55, 65
Goodwill, 280, 268
Google, 3, 64, 279, 469
GovernanceMetrics International, 520
Gross margin on sales, 25
Gross profit ratio, 231–233
Guess?, 231, 232

H

Held-to-maturity securities, 507
Hershey Foods, 412–413
Hewlett Packard, 279
Historical-cost principle, 55, 65
Holding gain or loss, 507, 508
Hollander, Jeffrey, 121
Home Depot, 63, 64, 75, 280, 318–320,
    338, 339
Horizontal analysis, 464
Hormel Foods, 119–120, 122
Hostile takeover, 379

I

IASB. *See* International Accounting
    Standards Board
IBM, 208, 279
IFRS. *See* International Financial Reporting
    Standards
Impairment, 281, 508–509
Improvement projects, 282
Income
    measuring, 98–99
Income statement, 17–18, 98–99, 578
    balance sheet, contrasted, 19
    comprehensive income, 505–506
    defined, 17
    discontinued operations, 462–463
    extraordinary items, 462, 463
    time periods, 67
Income taxes. *See* Taxes
Independent internal verification of
    data, 178
Indirect method, 417–418, 423–425, 427
Information risks, 27
Initial public offering (IPO), 384
Input and processing controls, 123
Insull Utility, 516
Insurance, 106–107
Intangible assets
    amortization, 279–281
    copyright, 279

defined, 268
franchise, 280
goodwill, 280
patent, 279–280
research and development costs, 280–281
risks, 291
trademark, 280
Intel, 213, 200, 507
Interest
compound, 361, 362
defined, 9
formula, 101
simple, 361, 362
Interest expense, 102–104
Interest payable, 102
Interest receivable, 100
Internal controls, 76. *See also* Controls
Internal Revenue Service (IRS), 12
International Accounting Standards Board
(IASB), 11, 52
International Financial Reporting Standards
(IFRS), 11, 53, 224, 416, 521–524
Internet, trading stock, 7
Inventory, 201–266
acquiring merchandise for sale, 202–210
controls, 233–234
cost flow assumptions. *See* Inventory cost
flow assumptions
ethics, 234
freight costs, 204–205, 210
LCM rule, 230
obsolescence, 231, 234
over/understatement, 262–263
periodic inventory system, 204, 211
perpetual inventory system, 204, 211
purchase discounts, 206–207
purchase returns and allowances, 206
ratio analysis, 231–233
risks, 233–234
sales discounts, 207, 209–210
sales returns and allowances, 209
sales taxes, 210
selling merchandise, 207–210
shipping costs, 204–205, 209–210
shrinkage, 211
Inventory controls, 233–234
Inventory cost flow assumptions, 211–225
example (Team Shirts), 225–230
FIFO, 214–215, 222
financial statements, and, 217–222
how method chosen, 223
industry usage, 223
LIFO, 215–217, 222, 223
methods, compared, 216–217
specific identification method, 212
taxes, 222, 223, 224
weighted average cost, 213–214
Inventory errors, 262–263
Inventory obsolescence, 231, 234
Inventory shrinkage, 211
Inventory turnover ratio, 232–233, 472, 473
Investing activities, 9, 20, 417
Investments in securities
available-for-sale securities, 508
held-to-maturity securities, 507
impairment, 508
selling the securities, 509
trading securities, 507–508
IPO. *See* Initial public offering

IRS. *See* Internal Revenue Service
Issued shares, 372

J

J. Crew, 2
J.D. Edwards, 580
JetBlue, 56
Journal, 564
Journal entries
adjusting, 570–574
posting to general ledger, 570
recording, 568–570
Junk bond, 327

K

Kearney, A.T., 121
Kroger, 211, 231, 391
Kumar, Sanjay, 27, 51

L

Large stock dividend, 382
Last-in, first-out (LIFO), 215–217, 513, 475
income tax effects, 222, 223
LCM rule. *See* Lower-cost-of-market rule
Leasehold improvements, 269
Ledger. *See* General ledger
Leverage, 338
Levitt, Arthur, 513
Liabilities, 14, 64, 317–370, 567
adjunct, 329
balance sheet presentation, 319
bank loan, 321
bond. *See* Bond
definitely determinable, 318
estimated, 318, 321–322
example (Team Shirts), 333–337
financial statement analysis, 338–339
long-term notes payable, 323–325
mortgage, 323–325
payroll, 318–321
ratio analysis, 338–339
risk, 339–340
types, 318–321
LIFO. *See* Last-in, first-out
LIFO conformity rule, 223
Limited liability, 8
Limited liability corporation (LLC), 8
Limited liability partnership (LLP), 8
Line of credit, 321
Liquidity, 62
Liquidity ratios, 466, 467, 470–474
LLC. *See* Limited liability corporation
LLP. *See* Limited liability partnership
Lockheed Martin, 4
LongHorn Steakhouse, 75
Long-term assets, 62
Long-term liabilities, 64
Long-term notes payable, 323–325
Long-term operational assets, 267–316
acquiring assets, 268–270
acquisition costs, 268–269
asset impairment, 281
balance sheet presentation, 285–286
basket purchase, 270
controls, 291
depletion, 278–279
depreciation. *See* Depreciation
example (Team Shirts), 286–289
improvements, 281–282

intangible assets, 279–280. *See also*
Intangible assets
ratio analysis, 289–291
reporting, 285
revised estimates of useful life, 282–283
risks, 291
selling the assets, 283–284
types of assets, 268
Loss or destruction of accounting data, 123
Lower-of-cost-or-market (LCM) rule, 230
Lowe's, 75, 338

M

MACRS. *See* Modified accelerated cost
recovery system
Macy's, 211, 233
Madoff, Bernie, 1–2, 201
Magazine subscriptions, 105
Mahoney, John, 121
Maker, 170
Management, 517
Management plan, 5
Manipulating earnings. *See* Earnings
manipulation
Manufacturing company, 4
Market indicators, 466–469
Market rate of interest, 327
Marketing plan, 5
Marking to market, 507
Mars, 412
MasterCard, 170
Matching principle, 55, 65
Materiality, 56, 65
McDonald's, 280
McGee, Joanna, 153
McKesson Corporation, 215, 318
Measuring assets, 64–66
Measuring income, 98–99
Merchandise inventory, 202
Merchandising company, 3
Merrill Lynch, 4
Metropolitan Transportation Authority
(MTA), 267
Microsoft, 279, 376
MitoPharm, 371
Modified accelerated cost recovery system
(MACRS), 316
Monetary-unit assumption, 54, 65
Monitoring, 291
Monster Worldwide, Inc., 27
Moody's, 317
Mortgages, 323–325
Mozilo, Angelo, 27
MTA. *See* Metropolitan Transportation
Authority
Multistep income statement, 25

N

NASDAQ (National Association of
Securities Dealers Automated
Quotation), 391
National Retail Federation, 201
Net assets, 14, 64
Net income, 3, 18, 67, 462, 505
Net loss, 67
Net of tax, 462
Net profit, 52
Net realizable value (NRV) of accounts
receivable, 162

Net sales, 209
New York Stock Exchange (NYSE), 7
Nike, 212, 280
Noncumulative preferred stock, 377
Noncurrent assets, 62
Noncurrent liabilities, 64
Non-sufficient-funds (NSF) check, 157, 158
Not-for-profit organization, 2
Notes receivable, 170–171
Notes to financial statements, 13, 25
    asset impairment, 281
    cash, 430
    cash equivalents, 160
    change in inventory cost flow methods, 223
    company purchasing its own stock,
        379–380
    dividend policy, 376
    inventory obsolescence reserve, 234
    LIFO disclosure, 216
    revenue recognition, 208
    uncollectible accounts, 162
    usefulness, 474
NRV. *See* Net realizable value of accounts
    receivable
NSF check. *See* Non-sufficient-funds check
The Number, 512
NYSE. *See* New York Stock Exchange

O

Oakley, 211–212
Obsolescence, 231, 234
Off-balance-sheet financing, 340
Office Depot, 203
Office Max, 202
Old Navy, 260
Olive Garden, 53, 75, 391
On account, 56
Operating activities, 9, 20, 417
Operating cycle, 202
Operating risks, 27
Oracle, 279, 580
Ordinary annuities, 363
Ordinary repairs, 282
Other comprehensive income, 505
Other expenses, 102–104
Other receivables, 100
Otto, David, 371
Outstanding check, 156, 157
Outstanding shares, 373
Over/understatement of inventory, 262–263
Owner's capital, 70
Owner's equity, 14
Ownership structure, 4–8
    corporation, 6–8
    limited liability partnerships and
        corporations, 8
    partnership, 5–6
    sole proprietorship, 4–5
Oxley, Michael, 516

P

P/E ratio. *See* Price-earnings ratio
P&L. *See* Income statement
Paccioli, Fra Luca, 566
Paid-in capital, 64
Papa John's, 376, 380, 389, 504
Par value, 327, 373
Partnership, 5–6
Patent, 279–280

Payee, 170
Payroll deductions, 318–321
Payroll tax expense, 320
PCAOB. *See* Public Company Accounting
    Oversight Board
Pearson Education, 4
Peoplesoft, 580
Pepsico, 215
Percent of accounts receivable method,
    162–163
Percentage of sales method, 162–163, 167
Periodic inventory system, 204, 211
Permanent account, 577
Perpetual inventory system, 204, 211
PetSmart, Inc., 372, 379
Physical controls, 291
Pizza Hut, 280
Plant assets. *See* Long-term operational
    assets
Ponzi scheme, 1–2
Positive financial leverage, 338
Positively correlated, 68
Postclosing trial balance, 578
    preparing, 578–579
Posting, 564
Preferred stock, 376
Premium on bonds payable, 329
Prepaid expenses, 119
Prepaid insurance, 57, 106
Prepaid rent, 107–108
Present value, 361. *See also* Time value of
    money
Present value tables, 369–370
Preventive controls, 76
Price-earnings (P/E) ratio, 468–469
Principal, 9
Principles. *See* Accounting principles
Proceeds, 327, 365–366
Proctor & Gamble, 171
Profit, 52
Profit and loss statement, 98. *See also*
    Income statement
Profit margin on sales, 121
Profitability ratios, 466, 474
Promissory note, 170
Property, plant, and equipment. *See*
    Long-term operational assets
Prospectus, 384
Public Company Accounting Oversight
    Board (PCAOB), 11, 519
Purchase allowance, 206
Purchase discounts, 206–207
Purchase order, 203
Purchase return, 205
Purchase returns and allowances, 206

Q

Quality of earnings, 512

R

R&D costs. *See* Research &
    development costs
Raiter, Frank, 317
Ratio analysis, 466–469
    accounts receivable, 175–176
    AR turnover ratio, 175–176
    asset turnover ratio, 290–291
    current ratio, 75
    debt-to-equity ratio, 338

dividend yield ratio, 469
earnings per share (EPS), 389–390
gross profit ratio, 231–232
inventory, 231–233
inventory turnover ratio, 232–233
liquidity, 75
long-term operational assets, 289–291
overview (ratios, listed), 470–474
P/E ratio, 468–469, 472, 473
profit margin on sales, 121–122
return on assets (ROA), 289, 290
return on equity (ROE), 388–389
shareholders' equity, 388–390
times-interest-earned ratio, 338–339
types of ratios, 466–467
understanding ratios, 469
using, 470–474
Real account, 577
Realized, 100, 509
Receivables, 161. *See also* Accounts
    receivable
Recognized, 509
Recognized revenue, 55
Recognizing revenue and expenses, 65
Reconciliation and control reports, 123
Red Lobster, 53, 75, 391
Relative fair market value method, 270
Relevance, 53
Reliability, 53
Remodeling, 282
Rent, 107–108
Repairs, 282
Replacement cost, 230
Reported earnings, 462
Research and development (R&D) costs,
    280–281
Reserve, 514
Reserve for obsolescence, 231
Residual value, 110, 271, 272
Retained earnings, 14, 19, 64, 383
Return on assets (ROA), 289, 290, 474
Return on equity (ROE), 388–389, 474
Revenue, 10
Revenue expenditure, 282
Revenue recognition, 515
Revenue-recognition principle, 55, 65
Risk, 26–28. *See also* Controls
RiskMetrics, 520
ROA. *See* Return on assets
Robert Half International, 520
Roberts, Keith, 97
Rock Center for Corporate Governance, 520
ROE. *See* Return on equity
Rowley, Coleen, 511

S

Safeway, 211
Salary, 419
Sales discounts, 207, 209–210
Sales returns and allowances, 207, 209
Sales taxes, 210
Salvage value, 110, 271, 272
Sambol, David, 27
SanDisk Corporation, 234
Sanford, John, 201
SAP, 580
Sarbanes, Paul, 516
Sarbanes-Oxley (SOX) Act, 391, 461, 511,
    517–520

SBA. *See* Small Business Administration
Sears, 95
SEC. *See* Securities and Exchange Commission
Secured bond, 327
Securities Acts of 1933 and 1934, 516
Securities and Exchange Commission (SEC), 7, 415, 513
  corporate filings, 23
  defined, 7
  delegation to FASB, 11
  improper reporting, 76
  IPO, 384
Securities, selling, 509
Segregation of duties, 154, 233, 291
Selling merchandise, 207–210
Separate-entity assumption, 54, 65
Serial bond, 327
Service charge, 158
Service company, 3
Shareholder, 6
Shareholders' equity, 14, 64, 371–413, 567
  balance sheet presentation, 372, 382
  cash dividends, 376–378
  common stock, 373–375
  contributed capital, 372–376
  example (Team Shirts), 384–388
  major components, 372–376
  preferred stock, 376
  ratio analysis, 388–390
  retained earnings, 383
  risks faced by owners, 391
  statement of changes, 578
  stock (authorized, issued, outstanding), 372–373
  stock dividend, 382–383
  stock split, 382, 383
  treasury stock, 379–381
Shares of common stock, 6
Sherwin Williams, 338, 339
Shipping costs, 204–205, 209–210
Shipping terms, 204, 205
Shoplifting, 233
Sieracki, Eric, 27
Simple interest, 361, 362
Single-step income statement, 25
Skilling, Jeff, 27
Sloan, Richard, 415
Small Business Administration (SBA), 5
Small stock dividend, 382–383
Social responsibility, 121
Sole proprietorships, 4–5
Solvency ratios, 466
Sony, 231
SOX. *See* Sarbanes-Oxley Act
Specific identification method, 212
Sprint PCS, 234
Standard & Poor's, 317
Standard-setting bodies, 11
Staples, Inc., 121, 202, 268, 269, 282
Starbucks, 213, 360
Stated value, 327
Statement of cash flows, 20–23, 415–460
  cash flows from investing and financing activities, 425–426

cash flows from operating activities— direct method, 420–422
cash flows from operating activities— indirect method, 423–425
classification of cash, 417
convert accrual amounts to cash, 418–419
defined, 20
direct method, 417–418, 420–422, 427
ethics (earnings manipulation), 430
financial statement analysis, 427–430
free cash flow, 429
importance, 416–417, 430
indirect method, 417–418, 423–425, 427
Statement of changes in owner's equity, 19
Statement of changes in shareholders' equity, 19
Statement of earnings, 98. *See also* Income statement
Statement of financial position. *See* Balance sheet
Statement of income. *See* Income statement
Statement of operations, 98. *See also* Income statement
Stiglitz, Joseph, 317
Stock dividend, 382–383
Stock exchange, 7
Stock market, 7
Stock option, 372
Stock ownership, risks, 475
Stock split, 382, 383
Stockbrokers, 7
Stockholder, 6
Stockholders' equity, 14. *See also* Shareholders' equity
Straight-line amortization, 279, 332–333
Straight-line depreciation, 272–274
Subway, 280
Sunglass Hut, 211–212
Supermarket example, 11
Supplies, 108–109, 202
Supporting evidence, 123

T

T-accounts, 566
T-Mobile, 231, 234
Talbots, 100, 101
Tangible assets, 268
Target, 3, 4, 76, 201, 202, 211, 231, 233
Taxes
  corporate income, 8
  depreciation, 316
  inventory cost flow assumptions, 222, 224
  IRS, 13
  LIFO/FIFO, 222, 223, 224
  MACRS, 316
  reporting, 463
  sales, 210
Technology, 475
Temporary account, 574
10-K report, 23
Term bond, 327
3/15, n/45, 206
Time-period assumption, 55, 65

Time value of money, 361–370
  calculating proceeds from issue of bonds, 365–366
  present value of annuity, 363–364
  present value of single amount, 361–363
  present value tables, 369–370
  simple vs. compound interest, 361, 362
Time Warner, 105
Times-interest-earned ratio, 338–339
Timing differences, 99
Tootsie Roll, 216
Trademark, 280
Trading securities, 507–508
Treasury stock, 373, 379–381
Trial balance, 565
  adjusted, 574
  preparing unadjusted, 570
Turco, Preston, 201
2/10, n/30, 206

U

Unauthorized access to accounting information, 123
Uncollectible accounts. *See* Accounts receivable
Under/overstatement of inventory, 262–263
Unearned revenue, 104
Units of production depreciation, 274–275
Unrealized gains and losses, 505, 507, 508
Unsecured bond, 327
Uses of accrual accounting information, 67–68

V

Vertical analysis, 465–466
VHS tapes, 234
Volkswagen, 212

W

Wachovia, 97
Wal-Mart, 203, 211
Walgreens, 318
Walt Disney Company, 49
Warranties, 321–323
Watkins, Sherron, 511
Weighted average cost, 213–214
Wendy's, 214
What-if financial statements, 475
What Matters Most (Hollander), 121
Whistleblowers, 511
Withdrawal, 570
Whole Foods Market, 231, 232
WorldCom, 2, 27, 430, 511, 516
Write-off, 165–168

X

XBRL (Extensible Business Reporting Language), 23
Xerox, 76

Y

Yahoo, 161, 162, 175

Z

Zero coupon, 327
Zero interest bond, 327

Taken from:

Managerial Accounting, Third Edition
by Karen Wilken Braun and Wendy M. Tietz

BRIEF CONTENTS

2   Building Blocks of Managerial Accounting   46

9   The Master Budget   514

6   Cost Behavior   318

7   Cost-Volume-Profit Analysis   394

8   Relevant Costs for Short-Term Decisions   456

12   Capital Investment Decisions and the Time Value of Money   710

Company Index   I-1
Glossary/Index   I-6

CONTENTS

2 Building Blocks of Managerial Accounting 46

What are the Most Common Business Sectors and Their Activities? 48

Service, Merchandising, and Manufacturing Companies 48

Which Business Activities Make up the Value Chain? 50

Coordinating Activities Across the Value Chain 51

Sustainability and the Value Chain 52

How do Companies Define Cost? 53

Cost Objects, Direct Costs, and Indirect Costs 53

Costs for Internal Decision Making and External Reporting 54

Merchandising Companies' Inventoriable Product Costs 56

Review: Inventoriable Product Costs or Period Costs? 58

Prime and Conversion Costs 58

Additional Labor Compensation Costs 59

How are Inventoriable Product Costs and Period Costs Shown in the Financial Statements? 62

Service Companies 62

Merchandising Companies 63

Manufacturing Companies 64

Comparing Balance Sheets 66

What Other Cost Terms are Used by Managers? 66

Controllable Versus Uncontrollable Costs 66

Relevant and Irrelevant Costs 67

Fixed and Variable Costs 68

How Manufacturing Costs Behave 69

Calculating Total and Average Costs 69

End of Chapter 73

9 The Master Budget 514

How and Why do Managers Use Budgets? 516

How are Budgets Used? 516

How are Budgets Developed? 516

What are the Benefits of Budgeting? 518

What is the Master Budget? 519

How are the Operating Budgets Prepared? 520

Sales Budget 520

Production Budget 521

Direct Materials Budget 523

Direct Labor Budget 524

Manufacturing Overhead Budget 525

Operating Expenses Budget 526

Budgeted Income Statement 527

How are the Financial Budgets Prepared? 532

Capital Expenditure Budget 532

Cash Collections Budget 532

Cash Payments Budget 533

Combined Cash Budget 535

Budgeted Balance Sheet 537

Sensitivity Analysis and Flexible Budgeting 538

Sustainability and Budgeting 539

How do the Budgets for Service and Merchandising Companies Differ? 540

Service Companies 540

Merchandising Companies 540

Impact of Credit and Debit Card Sales on Budgeting 542

End of Chapter 547

6 Cost Behavior 318

Cost Behavior: How do Changes in Volume Affect Costs? 320

Variable Costs 320

Fixed Costs 323

Mixed Costs 325

Relevant Range 327

Other Cost Behaviors 329

Sustainability and Cost Behavior 331

How do Managers Determine Cost Behavior? 334

Account Analysis 334

Scatter Plots 334

High-Low Method 336

Regression Analysis 338

Data Concerns 342

What are the Roles of Variable Costing and the Contribution Margin Income Statement? 342

Comparing Absorption Costing and Variable Costing 342

An Alternative Income Statement Format 344

Comparing Operating Income: Variable versus Absorption Costing 346

Reconciling Operating Income Between the Two Costing Systems 348

End of Chapter 355

7 Cost-Volume-Profit Analysis 394

How Does Cost-Volume-Profit Analysis Help Managers? 396

Data and Assumptions Required for CVP Analysis 396

The Unit Contribution Margin 397

The Contribution Margin Ratio 398

How do Managers Find the Breakeven Point? 400

The Income Statement Approach 400

The Shortcut Approach Using the Unit Contribution Margin 401

The Shortcut Approach Using the Contribution Margin Ratio 402

How do Managers Find the Volume Needed to Earn a Target Profit? 403

How Much Must we Sell to Earn a Target Profit? 403

Graphing CVP Relationships 404

How do Managers Use CVP to Plan for Changing Business Conditions? 411

Changing the Sales Price 411

Changing Variable Costs 412

Changing Fixed Costs 414

Sustainability and CVP 415

Changing the Mix of Products Offered for Sale 416

Information Technology and Sensitivity Analysis 419

What are Some Common Indicators of Risk? 420

Margin of Safety 420

Operating Leverage 421

Choosing a Cost Structure 424

End of Chapter 429

8 Relevant Costs for Short-Term Decisions 456

How do Managers Make Decisions? 458

Relevant Information 458

Relevant Nonfinancial Information 459

Keys to Making Short-Term Special Decisions 460

Sustainability and Short-Term Business Decisions 461

How do Managers Make Special Order and Regular Pricing Decisions? 461

Special Order Decisions 462

Regular Pricing Decisions 465

How do Managers Make Other Special Business Decisions? 473

Decisions to Discontinue Products, Departments, or Stores 473

Product Mix Decisions when Resources are Constrained 477

Outsourcing Decisions (Make or Buy) 479

Decisions to Sell As Is or Process Further 483

End of Chapter 488

12 Capital Investment Decisions and the Time Value of Money 710

What is Capital Budgeting? 712

Four Popular Methods of Capital Budgeting Analysis 712

Focus on Cash Flows 713

Capital Budgeting Process 713

Sustainability and Capital Investments 714

How do Managers Calculate the Payback Period and Accounting Rate of Return? 715

Payback Period 715

Accounting Rate of Return (ARR) 718

How do Managers Compute the Time Value of Money? 723

Factors Affecting the Time Value of Money 723

Future Values and Present Values: Points Along the Time Continuum 724

Future Value and Present Value Factors 725

Calculating Future Values of Single Sums and Annuities Using FV Factors 725

Calculating Present Values of Single Sums and Annuities Using PV Factors 727

How do Managers Calculate the Net Present Value and Internal Rate of Return? 730

Net Present Value (NPV) 731

Internal Rate of Return (IRR) 735

How do the Capital Budgeting Methods Compare? 738

APPENDIX 12A 741

Present Value Tables and Future Value Tables 741

Table A Present Value of $1 741

Table B Present Value of Annuity of $1 742

Table C Future Value of $1 743

Table D Future Value of Annuity of $1 744

APPENDIX 12B 745

Using a TI-83, TI-83 Plus, TI-84, or TI-84 Plus Calculator to Perform Time Value of Money Calculations 745

APPENDIX 12C 751

Using Microsoft Excel (2007 and 2010) to Perform Time Value of Money Calculations 751

End of Chapter 757

Company Index I-1

Glossary/Index I-6

Building Blocks of Managerial Accounting

Learning Objectives

■**1** Distinguish among service, merchandising, and manufacturing companies

■**2** Describe the value chain and its elements

■**3** Distinguish between direct and indirect costs

■**4** Identify the inventoriable product costs and period costs of merchandising and manufacturing firms

■**5** Prepare the financial statements for service, merchandising, and manufacturing companies

■**6** Describe costs that are relevant and irrelevant for decision making

■**7** Classify costs as fixed or variable and calculate total and average costs at different volumes

From Chapter 2 of *Managerial Accounting*, Third Edition. Karen W. Braun, Wendy M. Tietz.

With the introduction of the Prius,

Toyota became the front-runner in offering fuel-efficient vehicles with cutting edge technology. Ten years after the Prius's debut, Toyota is still committed to developing new environmentally friendly vehicles that "redefine what it means to be environmentally considerate." Not only has Toyota introduced award-winning vehicles, but also award-winning manufacturing plants. Toyota's use of solar energy, waste-water recycling, and improved manufacturing robotics has decreased the harmful consequences of manufacturing on the environment. At the same time, these "green" initiatives have cut plant energy costs and improved productivity.

To understand whether these and other investments were worth it, Toyota's managers needed to understand their costs across all business functions. They also needed to consider

Dreammediapeel | Dreamstime.com

Sources: Toyota.com, 2008 Annual Report.

which costs should be *increased*, and which costs should be *reduced*. For example, by spending *more* money on green technologies, product quality, and safety improvements, Toyota has increased its market share and decreased warranty and liability costs. On the other hand, Toyota's cost reduction efforts in production saved the company over $1.19 billion dollars in 2008. For example, to offset rising raw material costs, Toyota's engineers have figured out ways to decrease the quantity of materials needed without sacrificing performance and quality. They also work with suppliers to help them reduce their own costs, so that the cost savings can be passed on. In this chapter, we talk about many costs: costs that both managers and management accountants must understand to successfully run a business.

So far, we have seen how managerial accounting provides information that managers use to run their businesses more efficiently. Managers must understand basic managerial accounting terms and concepts before they can use the information to make good decisions. This terminology provides the "common ground" through which managers and accountants communicate. Without a common understanding of these concepts, managers may ask for (and accountants may provide) the wrong information for making decisions. As you will see, different types of costs are useful for different purposes. Both managers and accountants must have a clear understanding of the situation and the types of costs that are relevant to the decision at hand.

What are the Most Common Business Sectors and Their Activities?

Before we talk about specific types of costs, let's consider the three most common types of companies and the business activities in which they incur costs.

Service, Merchandising, and Manufacturing Companies

Recall from Chapter 1 that many companies are beginning to adhere to the notion of a **triple bottom line**, in which the company's performance is evaluated not only in terms of profitability, but also in terms of its impact on people and the planet. Even so, for a business to flourish and grow in the long-run, it will need to generate economic profits that are sufficiently large enough to attract and retain investors, as well as fuel future expansion of operations. Companies typically generate profit through one of three basic business models: they provide a service, they sell merchandise, or they manufacture products.

Service Companies

Service companies are in business to sell intangible services—such as health care, insurance, banking, and consulting—rather than tangible products. Recall from the last chapter that service firms now make up the largest sector of the U.S. economy. Because these types of companies sell services, they generally don't have inventory. Some service providers carry a minimal amount of supplies inventory; however, this inventory is generally used for internal operations—not sold for profit. Service companies incur costs to provide services, develop new services, advertise, and provide customer service. For many service providers, salaries and benefits make up over 70% of their costs.

Merchandising Companies

Merchandising companies such as Walmart and JCPenney resell tangible products they buy from suppliers. For example, Walmart buys clothing, toys, and electronics and resells them to customers at higher prices than what it pays its own suppliers for these goods. Merchandising companies include retailers (such as Walmart) and wholesalers. **Retailers** sell to consumers like you and me. **Wholesalers**, often referred to as "middlemen," buy products in bulk from manufacturers, mark up the prices, and then sell those products to retailers.

Because merchandising companies sell tangible products, they have inventory. The cost of inventory includes the cost merchandisers pay for the goods *plus* all costs necessary to get the merchandise in place and ready to sell, such as freight-in costs and any import duties or tariffs. A merchandiser's balance sheet reports just one inventory account called "Inventory" or "Merchandise Inventory." Besides incurring inventory-related costs, merchandisers also incur costs to operate their retail stores and websites, advertise, research new products and new store locations, and to provide customer service.

Manufacturing Companies

Manufacturing companies use labor, plant, and equipment to convert raw materials into new finished products. For example, Toyota's production workers use the company's factories (production plants and equipment) to transform raw materials, such as steel, into high-performance automobiles. Manufacturers sell their products to retailers or wholesalers at a price that is high enough to cover their costs and generate a profit.

Because of their broader range of activities, manufacturers have three types of inventory (pictured in Exhibit 2-1):

1. **Raw materials inventory**: *All raw materials used in manufacturing.* Toyota's raw materials include steel, glass, tires, upholstery fabric, engines, and other automobile components. It also includes other physical materials used in the plant, such as machine lubricants and janitorial supplies.

2. **Work in process inventory**: *Goods that are partway through the manufacturing process but not yet complete.* At Toyota, the work in process inventory consists of partially completed vehicles.

3. **Finished goods inventory**: *Completed goods that have not yet been sold.* Toyota is in business to sell completed cars, not work in process. Once the vehicles are completed, they are no longer considered work in process, but rather they become part of finished goods inventory. Manufacturers sell units from finished goods inventory to merchandisers or directly to consumers.

EXHIBIT 2-1 Manufacturers' Three Types of Inventory

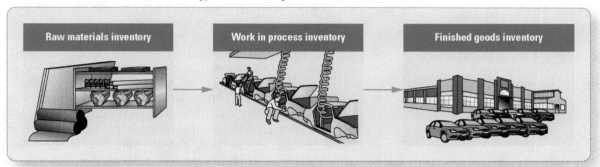

Exhibit 2-2 summarizes the differences among service, merchandising, and manufacturing companies.

EXHIBIT 2-2 Service, Merchandising, and Manufacturing Companies

	Service Companies	Merchandising Companies	Manufacturing Companies
Examples	Advertising agencies Banks Law firms Insurance companies	Amazon.com Kroger Walmart Wholesalers	Procter & Gamble General Mills Dell Computer Toyota
Primary Output	Intangible services	Tangible products purchased from suppliers	New tangible products made as workers and equipment convert raw materials into new finished products
Type(s) of Inventory	None	Inventory (or Merchandise Inventory)	Raw materials inventory Work in process inventory Finished goods inventory

STOP & THINK

What type of company is Outback Steakhouse, Inc.?

Answer: Some companies don't fit nicely into one of the three categories discussed previously. Restaurants are usually considered to be in the service sector. However, Outback has some elements of a service company (it serves hungry patrons), some elements of a manufacturing company (its chefs convert raw ingredients into finished meals), and some elements of a merchandising company (it sells ready-to-serve bottles of wine and beer).

As the "Stop & Think" shows, not all companies are strictly service, merchandising, or manufacturing firms. Recall from Chapter 1 that the U.S. economy is shifting more toward service. Many traditional manufacturers, such as General Electric (GE), have developed profitable service segments that provide much of their company's profits. Even merchandising firms are getting into the "service game" by selling extended warranty contracts on merchandise sold. Retailers offer extended warranties on products ranging from furniture and major appliances to sporting equipment and consumer electronics. While the merchandiser recognizes a liability for these warranties, the price charged to customers for the warranties greatly exceeds the company's cost of fulfilling its warranty obligations.

Which Business Activities Make up the Value Chain?

Many people describe Toyota, General Mills, and Dell as manufacturing companies. But it would be more accurate to say that these are companies that *do* manufacturing. Why? Because companies that do manufacturing also do many other things. Toyota also conducts research to determine what type of new technology to integrate into next year's models. Toyota designs the new models based on its research and then produces, markets, distributes, and services the cars. These activities form Toyota's <u>value chain</u>—the activities that add value to the company's products and services. The value chain is pictured in Exhibit 2-3.

EXHIBIT 2-3 The Value Chain

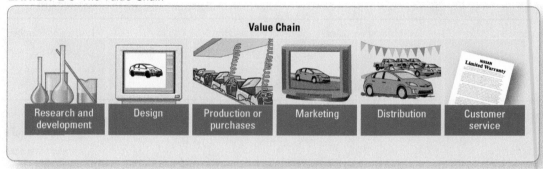

Value Chain

| Research and development | Design | Production or purchases | Marketing | Distribution | Customer service |

2 Describe the value chain and its elements

The value chain activities also cost money. To set competitive, yet profitable selling prices, Toyota must consider all of the costs incurred along the value chain, not just the costs incurred in manufacturing vehicles. Let's briefly consider some of the costs incurred in each element of the value chain.[1]

Research and Development (R&D): *Researching and developing new or improved products or services and the processes for producing them.* Toyota continually engages in researching and developing new technologies to incorporate in its vehicles (such as fuel cells, pre-crash safety systems, and "smart keys,") and in its manufacturing plants (such as environmentally friendly and efficient manufacturing robotics). In 2010, Toyota spent 725 million yen (approximatetly $8 billion dollars) on R&D.

Design: *Detailed engineering of products and services and the processes for producing them.* Toyota's goal is to design vehicles that create total customer satisfaction, including satisfaction with vehicle style, features, safety, and quality. As a result, Toyota updates the design of older models (such as the Corolla) and designs new prototypes (such as the new ultra-energy efficient "iQ" model) on a regular basis. Part of the design process also includes determining how to mass-produce the vehicles. Because Toyota produces nearly 7 million vehicles per year, engineers must design production plants that are efficient, yet flexible enough to allow for new features and models.

[1]Toyota Motor Corp. 2010 annual report and new.yahoo.com/s/ap/as_japan_toyota/print

<u>Production or Purchases</u>:   *Resources used to produce a product or service or to purchase finished merchandise intended for resale.* For Toyota, the production activity includes all costs incurred to *make* the vehicles. These costs include raw materials (such as steel), plant labor (such as machine operators' wages and benefits), and manufacturing overhead (such as factory utilities and depreciation on the factory). As you can imagine, factories are very expensive to build and operate. Toyota earmarked over $1.3 billion dollars just to build and equip a new manufacturing plant in Mississippi.

Production or purchases

For a merchandiser such as Best Buy, this value chain activity includes the cost of purchasing the inventory that the company plans to sell to customers. It also includes all costs associated with getting the inventory to the store, including freight-in costs and any import duties and tariffs that might be incurred if the merchandise was purchased from overseas.

<u>Marketing</u>:   *Promotion and advertising of products or services.* The goal of marketing is to create consumer demand for products and services. Toyota uses print advertisements in magazines and newspapers, billboards, television commercials, and the internet to market its vehicles. Some companies use sponsorship of star athletes and sporting events to market their products. Each method of advertising costs money, but adds value by reaching different target customers.

Marketing

<u>Distribution</u>:   *Delivery of products or services to customers.* Toyota sells most of its vehicles through traditional dealerships. However, more customers are ordering "build-your-own" vehicles through Toyota's website. Toyota's distribution costs include the costs of shipping the vehicles to retailers and the costs of administering Web-based sales portals. Other industries use different distribution mechanisms. For example, Tupperware primarily sells its products through home-based parties while Amazon.com sells only through the internet. Until recently, Lands' End sold only through catalogs and the Web.

Distribution

<u>Customer Service</u>:   *Support provided for customers after the sale.* Toyota incurs substantial customer service costs, especially in connection with warranties on new car sales. Toyota generally warranties its vehicles for the first three years and/or 36,000 miles, whichever comes first. Historically, Toyota has had one of the best reputations in the auto industry for excellent quality. However, 2010 proved to be a costly and difficult year for the company, as recalls were made on over 14 million vehicles. In addition to the cost of repairing the vehicles, the company incurred millions of dollars in costs related to government fines, lawsuits, and public relations campaigns. The company has pledged its commitment to building safe and reliable vehicles.

Customer service

Coordinating Activities Across the Value Chain

Many of the value chain activities occur in the order discussed here. However, managers cannot simply work on R&D and not think about customer service until after selling the car. Rather, cross-functional teams work on R&D, design, production, marketing, distribution, and customer service simultaneously. As the teams develop new model features, they also plan how to produce, market, and distribute the redesigned vehicles. They also consider how the new design will affect warranty costs. Recall from the last chapter that management accountants typically participate in these cross-functional teams. Even at the highest level of global operations, Toyota uses cross-functional teams to implement its business goals and strategy.

The value chain pictured in Exhibit 2-3 also reminds managers to control costs over the value chain as a whole. For example, Toyota spends more in R&D and product design to increase the quality of its vehicles, which, in turn, reduces customer service costs. Even though R&D and design costs are higher, the total cost of the vehicle—as measured throughout the entire value chain—is lower as a result of this trade off. Enhancing its reputation for high-quality products has also enabled Toyota to increase its market share and charge a slightly higher selling price than some of its competitors.

> ### ◼ Why is this important?
>
> "All activities in the **value chain** are important, yet each costs **money** to perform. Managers must understand how **decisions** made in one area of the value chain will **affect the costs** incurred in other areas of the value chain."

Sustainability and the Value Chain

See Exercise
E2-18A and E2-35B

Progressive companies will incorporate sustainability throughout every function of the value chain. However, experts estimate that 90% of sustainability occurs at the design stage. At the design stage, companies determine how the product will be used by customers, how easily the product can be repaired or eventually recycled, and the types of raw materials and manufacturing processes necessary to produce the product. Thus, good design is essential to the creation of environmentally-friendly, safe products that enhance people's lives. For example, companies can integrate sustainability throughout the value chain by:

- *Researching & Developing environmentally safe packaging.* Frito-Lay has developed a compostable bag for its original Sun Chips product. The bag is made out of vegetables, rather than plastic.

- *Designing the product using lifecycle assessment and biomimicry practices.* <u>Life cycle assessment</u> means the company analyzes the environmental impact of a product, from cradle to grave, in an attempt to minimize negative environmental consequences throughout the entire life span of the product. <u>Biomimicry</u> means that a company tries to mimic, or copy, the natural biological process in which dead organisms (plants and animals) become the input for another organism or process. Ricoh's copiers were designed so that at the end of a copier's useful life, Ricoh will collect and dismantle the product for usable parts, shred the metal casing, and use the parts and shredded material to build new copiers. The entire copier was designed so that nothing is wasted, or thrown out, except the dust from the shredding process. Pepsi recently announced the development of a plastic bottle that is made entirely out of non-edible plant materials such as corn husks, pine bark, and switch grass. These byproducts are the result of manufacturing its other food products (Frito-Lay, Quaker Oats, and Tropicana).

- *Adopting sustainable purchasing practices.* Companies can purchase raw materials from suppliers that are geographically proximate or from suppliers that embrace sustainability. For example, Walmart has recently mandated that all of its suppliers conform to certain sustainability requirements. As the leading retailer in the world, Walmart's own purchasing policies are forcing other companies to adopt sustainable practices.

- *Marketing with integrity.* Consumers are driving much of the sustainability movement by demanding that companies produce environmentally-friendly products and limit, or eliminate operational practices that have a negative impact on the environment. Thus, many companies are successfully spotlighting their sustainability initiatives in order to increase market share and attract potential investors and employees. However, <u>greenwashing</u>, the unfortunate practice of *overstating* a company's commitment to sustainability, can ultimately backfire as investors and consumers learn the truth about company operations. Hence, honesty and integrity in marketing is imperative.

- *Distributing using fossil-fuel alternatives and carbon offsets.* While the biofuel industry is still in its infancy, the production and use of biofuels, especially those generated from non-food waste, is expected to grow exponentially in the near future. Biofuels Digest, which tracks corporate-announced biofuel projects, estimates a global production capacity of 718 *million* gallons of advanced biofuel in 2011 growing to a capacity of 4 *billion* gallons by 2015.[2] Companies whose business is heavily reliant upon fossil fuels, such as oil companies (Valero), airlines (Continental), and distribution companies (UPS) are especially interested in the development of biofuel alternatives. In addition, Continental Airlines offers a carbon-offset program that allows companies (and consumers) to calculate the carbon emissions resulting from their business travel and air-freighting activities. The customer has an option of purchasing carbon offsets (reforestation projects, renewable energy projects, etc.,) to mitigate the emissions resulting from shipping and travel.

- *Providing customer service past the warranty date.* Currently, the average life of many home appliances such as dishwashers and refrigerators is less than 10 years.

[2]http://biofuelsdigest.com/bdigest/2011/01/14/10-advanced-biofuelsprojects-now-planned-in-advanced-biofuels/

However, the original manufacturer could provide valuable customer service, prevent appliances from ending up in landfills, while at the same time creating a new revenue stream by offering reasonably-priced repair services for products that have exceeded the warranty date. For those products that are not repairable, the company could institute a policy such as Ricoh's, in which the company takes back the old product and recycles it into new products.

How do Companies Define Cost?

How do companies such as Bank of America and Toyota determine how much it costs to serve a customer or produce a Prius? Before we can answer this question, let's first consider some of the specialized language that accountants use when referring to costs.

3 Distinguish between direct and indirect costs

Cost Objects, Direct Costs, and Indirect Costs

A **cost object** is anything for which managers want a separate measurement of cost. Toyota's cost objects may include the following:

- Individual units (a specific, custom-ordered Prius)
- Different models (the Prius, Rav4, and Corolla)
- Alternative marketing strategies (sales through dealers versus built-to-order Web sales)
- Geographic segments of the business (United States, Europe, Japan)
- Departments (Human Resources, R&D, Legal)
- A "green" initiative (developing fuel cells)

Costs are classified as either direct or indirect with respect to the cost object. A **direct cost** is a cost that can be traced to the cost object. For example, say the cost object is one Prius. Toyota can trace the cost of tires to a specific Prius; therefore, the tires are a direct cost of the vehicle. An **indirect cost** is a cost that relates to the cost object but cannot be traced to it. For example, Toyota incurs substantial cost to run a manufacturing plant, including utilities, property taxes, and depreciation. Toyota cannot build a Prius without incurring these costs, so the costs are related to the Prius. However, it's impossible to trace a specific amount of these costs to one Prius. Therefore, these costs are considered indirect costs of a single Prius.

As shown in Exhibit 2-4, the same costs can be indirect with respect to one cost object yet direct with respect to another cost object. For example, plant depreciation, property taxes, and utilities are indirect costs of a single Prius. However, if management wants to

EXHIBIT 2-4 The Same Cost Can Be Direct or Indirect, Depending on the Cost Object

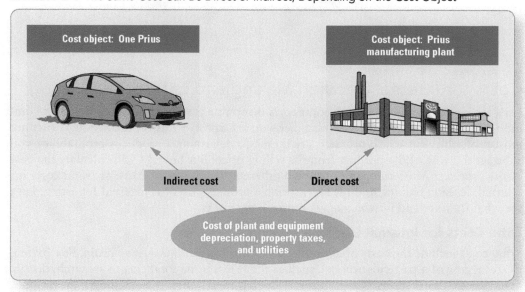

Cost object: One Prius

Cost object: Prius manufacturing plant

Indirect cost

Direct cost

Cost of plant and equipment depreciation, property taxes, and utilities

Why is this important?

"As a manager **making decisions**, you'll need different types of **cost information** for different types of decisions. To get the **information** you really want, you'll have to be able to **communicate** with the accountants using precise **definitions** of cost."

know how much it costs to operate the Prius manufacturing plant, the plant becomes the cost object; so the same depreciation, tax, and utility costs are direct costs of the manufacturing facility. Whether a cost is direct or indirect depends on the specified cost object. In this chapter, we'll be talking about a unit of product (such as one Prius) as the cost object.

If a company wants to know the *total* cost attributable to a cost object, it must **assign** all direct *and* indirect costs to the cost object. Assigning a cost simply means that you are "attaching" a cost to the cost object. Why? Because the cost object caused the company to incur that cost. In determining the cost of a Prius, Toyota assigns both the cost of the tires *and* the cost of running the manufacturing plant to the Priuses built at the plant.

Toyota assigns direct costs to each Prius by **tracing** those costs to specific vehicles. This results in a very precise cost figure, giving managers great confidence in the cost's accuracy. However, because Toyota cannot trace indirect costs to specific vehicles, it must **allocate** these costs between all of the vehicles produced at the plant. The allocation process results in a less precise cost figure being assigned to the cost object (one vehicle). We will discuss the allocation process in more detail in the following two chapters; but for now, think of allocation as dividing up the total indirect costs over all of the units produced, just as you might divide a pizza among friends. Exhibit 2-5 illustrates these concepts.

EXHIBIT 2-5 Assigning Direct and Indirect Costs to Cost Objects

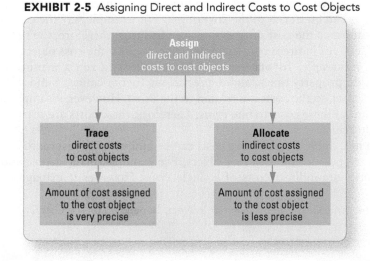

Accounting Simplified

Direct versus Indirect Costs

If your instructor is using MyAccountingLab, go to the Multimedia Library for a quick video on this topic.

Costs for Internal Decision Making and External Reporting

4 Identify the inventoriable product costs and period costs of merchandising and manufacturing firms

Let's look more carefully at how companies determine the costs of one of the most common cost objects: products. As a manager, you'll want to focus on the products that are most profitable. But which products are these? To determine a product's profitability, you subtract the cost of the product from its selling price. But how do you calculate the cost of the product? Most companies use two different definitions of costs: (1) total costs for internal decision making and (2) inventoriable product costs for external reporting. Let's see what they are and how managers use each type of cost.

Total Costs for Internal Decision Making

Total costs include the costs of *all resources used throughout the value chain*. For Toyota, the total cost of a particular model, such as the Prius, is the total cost to research, design, manufacture, market, distribute, and service that model. Before launching a new model, managers predict the total costs of the model to set a selling price that will cover *all costs* plus return a profit. Toyota also compares each model's sale revenue to its total cost to determine which models are most profitable. Perhaps Rav4s are more profitable than Corollas. Marketing can then focus on advertising and promoting the most profitable models. We'll talk more about total costs in Chapter 8, where we discuss many common business decisions. For the next few chapters, we'll concentrate primarily on inventoriable product costs.

Inventoriable Product Costs for External Reporting

GAAP does not allow companies to use total costs to report inventory balances or Cost of Goods Sold in the financial statements. For external reporting, GAAP allows only a *portion* of the total cost to be treated as an inventoriable product cost. GAAP specifies which costs are inventoriable product costs and which costs are not. <u>Inventoriable product costs</u> include *only* the costs incurred during the "production or purchases" stage of the value chain. Inventoriable product costs are treated as an asset (inventory) until the product is sold. Hence, the name "inventoriable" product cost. When the product is sold, these costs are removed from inventory and expensed as cost of goods sold. Since inventoriable product costs include only costs incurred during the production or purchases stage of the value chain, all cost incurred in the *other* stages of the value chain must be expensed in the period in which they are incurred. Therefore, we refer to R&D, design, marketing, distribution, and customer service costs as <u>period costs</u>.

> Period costs are often called "operating expenses" or "selling, general, and administrative expenses" (SG&A) on the company's income statement. Period costs are *always* expensed in the period in which they are incurred and *never* become part of an inventory account.

Exhibit 2-6 shows that a company's total cost has two components: inventoriable product costs (those costs treated as part of inventory until the product is sold) and period costs (those costs expensed in the current period regardless of when inventory is sold). GAAP requires this distinction for external financial reporting. Study the exhibit carefully to make sure you understand how the two cost components affect the income statement and balance sheet.

EXHIBIT 2-6 Total Costs, Inventoriable Product Costs, and Period Costs

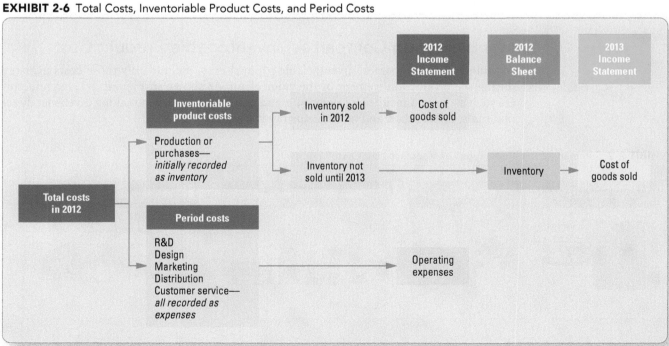

Now that you understand the difference between inventoriable product costs and period costs, let's take a closer look at the specific costs that are inventoriable in merchandising and manufacturing companies.

Merchandising Companies' Inventoriable Product Costs

Merchandising companies' inventoriable product costs include *only* the cost of purchasing the inventory from suppliers plus any costs incurred to get the merchandise to the merchandiser's place of business and ready for sale. Typically, these additional costs include freight-in costs and import duties or tariffs, if the products were purchased from overseas. Why does the cost of the inventory include freight-in charges? Think of the last time you purchased a shirt from a catalog such as L.L.Bean. The catalog may have shown the shirt's price as $30, but by the time you paid the shipping and handling charges, the shirt really cost you around $35. Likewise, merchandising companies pay freight-in charges to get the goods to their place of business (plus import duties if the goods were manufactured overseas). These charges become part of the cost of their inventory.

For instance, Home Depot's inventoriable product costs include what the company paid for its store merchandise plus freight-in and import duties. Home Depot records these costs in an asset account—Inventory—until it *sells* the merchandise. Once the merchandise sells, it belongs to the customer, not Home Depot. Therefore, Home Depot takes the cost out of its inventory account and records it as an expense—the *cost of goods sold*. Home Depot expenses costs incurred in other elements of the value chain as period costs. For example, Home Depot's period costs include store operating expenses (such as salaries, utilities, and depreciation) and advertising expenses.

Some companies, such as Pier 1 Imports, refer to their cost of goods sold as "cost of sales." However, we use the more specific term *cost of goods sold* throughout the text because it more aptly describes the actual cost being expensed in the account—the inventoriable product cost of the goods themselves.

STOP & THINK

What are the inventoriable product costs for a service firm such as H&R Block?

Answer: Service firms such as H&R Block have no inventory of products for sale. Services cannot be produced today and stored up to sell later. Because service firms have no inventory, they have no inventoriable product costs. Instead, they have only period costs that are expensed as incurred.

Manufacturing Companies' Inventoriable Product Costs

Manufacturing companies' inventoriable product costs include *only* those costs incurred during the production element of the value chain. As shown in Exhibit 2-7, manufacturers such as Toyota incur three types of manufacturing costs when making a vehicle: direct materials, direct labor, and manufacturing overhead.

EXHIBIT 2-7 Summary of the Three Types of Manufacturing Costs

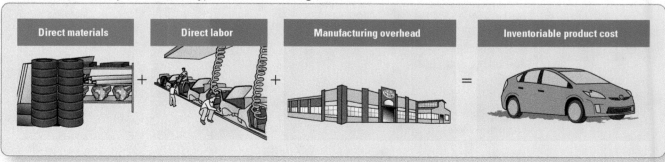

Direct Materials (DM)

Manufacturers convert raw materials into finished products. <u>**Direct materials**</u> are the *primary* raw materials that become a physical part of the finished product. The Prius's direct materials include steel, tires, engines, upholstery, carpet, dashboard instruments, and so forth. Toyota can trace the cost of these materials (including freight-in and import duties) to specific units or batches of vehicles; thus, they are considered direct costs of the vehicles.

Direct Labor (DL)

Although many manufacturing facilities are highly automated, most still require some direct labor to convert raw materials into a finished product. <u>**Direct labor**</u> is the cost of compensating employees who physically convert raw materials into the company's products. At Toyota, direct labor includes the wages and benefits of machine operators and technicians who assemble the parts and wire the electronics to build the completed vehicles. These costs are *direct* with respect to the cost object (the vehicle) because Toyota can *trace* the time each of these employees spends working on specific units or batches of vehicles.

Manufacturing Overhead (MOH)

The third production cost is manufacturing overhead. <u>**Manufacturing overhead**</u> *includes all manufacturing costs other than direct materials and direct labor.* In other words, manufacturing overhead includes *all indirect manufacturing costs.* Manufacturing overhead is also referred to as factory overhead because all of these costs relate to the factory. As shown in Exhibit 2-8, manufacturing overhead has three components: indirect materials, indirect labor, and other indirect manufacturing costs.

EXHIBIT 2-8 Components of Manufacturing Overhead

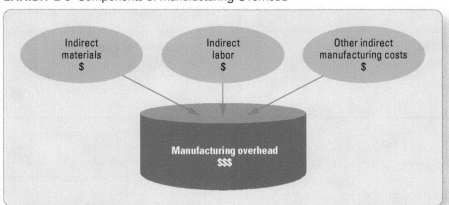

- <u>Indirect materials</u> include materials used in the plant that are not easily traced to individual units. For example, indirect materials often include janitorial supplies, oil and lubricants for the machines, and any physical components of the finished product that are very inexpensive. For example, Toyota might treat the invoice sticker placed on each vehicle's window as an indirect material rather than a direct material. Even though the cost of the sticker *could* be traced to the vehicle, it wouldn't make much sense to do so. Why? Because the cost of tracing the sticker to the vehicle outweighs the benefit management receives from the increased accuracy of the information. Therefore, Toyota treats the cost of the stickers as an indirect material, which becomes part of manufacturing overhead.

- <u>Indirect labor</u> includes the cost of all employees *in the plant* other than those employees directly converting the raw materials into the finished product. For example, at Toyota, indirect labor includes the salaries, wages, and benefits of plant forklift operators, plant security officers, plant janitors, and plant supervisors.

- <u>Other indirect manufacturing costs</u> include such plant-related costs as insurance and depreciation on the plant and plant equipment, plant property taxes, plant repairs and maintenance, and plant utilities. Indirect manufacturing costs have grown in recent years as manufacturers automate their plants with the latest technology.

In summary, *manufacturing overhead includes all manufacturing costs other than direct materials and direct labor.*

Review: Inventoriable Product Costs or Period Costs?

Exhibit 2-9 summarizes the differences between inventoriable product costs and period costs for service, merchandising, and manufacturing companies. Study this exhibit carefully. When are such costs as depreciation, insurance, utilities, and property taxes inventoriable product costs? *Only* when those costs are related to the manufacturing plant. When those costs are related to nonmanufacturing activities such as R&D or marketing, they are treated as period costs. Service companies and merchandisers do no manufacturing, so they always treat depreciation, insurance, utilities, and property taxes as period costs. When you studied financial accounting, you studied nonmanufacturing firms. Therefore, salaries, depreciation, insurance, and taxes were always expensed.

EXHIBIT 2-9 Inventoriable Product Costs and Period Costs for Service, Merchandising, and Manufacturing Companies

	Inventoriable Product Costs	Period Costs
Accounting Treatment	• Initially recorded as inventory • Expensed as *Cost of Goods Sold* only when inventory is sold	• Always recorded as an expense • Never considered part of inventory
Type of Company:		
Service company	• None	• All costs along the value chain • For example, salaries, depreciation expense, utilities, insurance, property taxes, and advertising
Merchandising company	• Purchases of merchandise • Freight-in; customs and duties	• All costs along the value chain *except* for the purchases element • For example, salaries, depreciation expense, utilities, insurance, property taxes, advertising, and freight-out
Manufacturing company	• Direct materials • Direct labor • Manufacturing overhead (including indirect materials, indirect labor, and other indirect manufacturing costs)	• All costs along the value chain *except* for the production element • For example, R&D; freight-out; all expenses for executive headquarters (separate from plant), including depreciation, utilities, insurance, and property taxes; advertising; and CEO's salary

Prime and Conversion Costs

Managers and accountants sometimes talk about certain combinations of manufacturing costs. As shown in Exhibit 2-10, **prime costs** refer to the combination of direct materials and direct labor. Prime costs used to be the primary costs of production. However, as

EXHIBIT 2-10 Prime and Conversion Costs

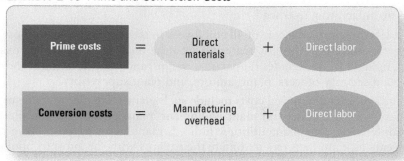

companies have automated production with expensive machinery, manufacturing overhead has become a greater cost of production. **Conversion costs** refer to the combination of direct labor and manufacturing overhead. These are the costs of *converting* direct materials into finished goods.

Additional Labor Compensation Costs

The cost of labor, in all areas of the value chain, includes more than the salaries and wages paid to employees. The cost also includes company-paid fringe benefits such as health insurance, retirement plan contributions, payroll taxes, and paid vacations. These costs are very expensive. Health insurance premiums, which have seen double-digit increases for many years, often amount to $500–$1,500 per month for *each* employee electing family coverage. Many companies also contribute an amount equal to 3% to 6% of their employees' salaries to company-sponsored retirement 401(k) plans. Employers must pay Federal Insurance Contributions Act (FICA) payroll taxes to the federal government for Social Security and Medicare, amounting to 7.65% of each employee's gross pay. In addition, most companies offer paid vacation and other benefits. Together, these fringe benefits usually cost the company an *additional* 35% beyond gross salaries and wages. Thus, an assembly-line worker who makes a $40,000 salary costs Toyota approximately another $14,000 (= $40,000 × 35%) in fringe benefits. Believe it or not, for automobiles manufactured in the United States, the cost of health care assigned to the vehicle is greater than the cost of the steel in the vehicle! Throughout the remainder of this book, any references to wages or salaries also include the cost of fringe benefits.

Decision Guidelines

Building Blocks of Managerial Accounting

Dell engages in *manufacturing* when it assembles its computers, *merchandising* when it sells them on its website, and support *services* such as start-up and implementation services. Dell had to make the following types of decisions as it developed its accounting systems.

Decision	Guidelines

How do you distinguish among service, merchandising, and manufacturing companies? How do their balance sheets differ?	*Service companies:*
	• Provide customers with intangible services
	• Have no inventories on the balance sheet
	
	Merchandising companies:
	• Resell tangible products purchased ready-made from suppliers
	• Have only one category of inventory
	
	Manufacturing companies:
	• Use labor, plant, and equipment to transform raw materials into new finished products
	• Have three categories of inventory:
	  1. Raw materials inventory
	  2. Work in process inventory
	  3. Finished goods inventory

What business activities add value to companies?	All of the elements of the value chain, including the following: • R&D • Design • Production or Purchases • Marketing • Distribution • Customer Service
What costs should be assigned to cost objects such as products, departments, and geographic segments?	Both direct and indirect costs are assigned to cost objects. Direct costs are traced to cost objects, whereas indirect costs are allocated to cost objects.
Which product costs are useful for internal decision making, and which product costs are used for external reporting?	Managers use *total costs* for internal decision making. However, GAAP requires companies to use only *inventoriable product costs* for external financial reporting.
What costs are treated as inventoriable product costs under GAAP?	• *Service companies:* No inventoriable product costs • *Merchandising companies:* The cost of merchandise purchased for resale plus all of the costs of getting the merchandise to the company's place of business (for example, freight-in and import duties) • *Manufacturing companies:* Direct materials, direct labor, and manufacturing overhead
How are inventoriable product costs treated on the financial statements?	Inventoriable product costs are initially treated as assets (inventory) on the balance sheet. These costs are expensed (as cost of goods sold) on the income statements when the products are sold.

SUMMARY PROBLEM **1**

Requirements

1. Classify each of the following business costs into one of the six value chain elements:

    a. Costs associated with warranties and recalls

    b. Cost of shipping finished goods to overseas customers

    c. Costs a pharmaceutical company incurs to develop new drugs

    d. Cost of a 30-second commercial during the SuperBowl™

    e. Cost of making a new product prototype

    f. Cost of assembly labor used in the plant

2. For a manufacturing company, identify the following as either an inventoriable product cost or a period cost. If it is an inventoriable product cost, classify it as direct materials, direct labor, or manufacturing overhead.

    a. Depreciation on plant equipment

    b. Depreciation on salespeoples' automobiles

    c. Insurance on plant building

    d. Marketing manager's salary

    e. Cost of major components of the finished product

    f. Assembly-line workers' wages

    g. Costs of shipping finished products to customers

    h. Forklift operator's salary

▪ SOLUTIONS

Requirement 1
a. Customer service
b. Distribution
c. Research and Development
d. Marketing
e. Design
f. Production

Requirement 2
a. Inventoriable product cost; manufacturing overhead
b. Period cost
c. Inventoriable product cost; manufacturing overhead
d. Period cost
e. Inventoriable product cost; direct materials
f. Inventoriable product cost; direct labor
g. Period cost
h. Inventoriable product cost; manufacturing overhead

How are Inventoriable Product Costs and Period Costs Shown in the Financial Statements?

5 Prepare the financial statements for service, merchandising, and manufacturing companies

The difference between inventoriable product costs and period costs is important because these costs are treated differently in the financial statements. All costs incurred in the production or purchases area of the value chain are inventoriable product costs that remain in inventory accounts until the merchandise is sold—then, these costs become the cost of goods sold. However, costs incurred in all other areas of the value chain (R&D, design, marketing, distribution, and customer service) are period costs, which are expensed on the income statement in the period in which they are incurred. Keep these differences in mind as we review the income statements of service firms (which have no inventory), merchandising companies (which purchase their inventory), and manufacturers (which make their inventory). We'll finish the section by comparing the balance sheets of these three different types of companies.

Service Companies

If your instructor is using MyAccountingLab, go to the Multimedia Library for a quick video on this topic.

Service companies have the simplest income statement. Exhibit 2-11 shows the income statement of eNow!, a group of e-commerce consultants. The firm has no inventory and thus, no inventoriable product costs, so eNow!'s income statement has no Cost of Goods Sold. Rather, all of the company's costs are period costs, so they are expensed in the current period as "operating expenses."

EXHIBIT 2-11 Service Company Income Statement

eNOW!		
Income Statement		
Year Ended December 31		
Revenues		$160,000
Less: Operating expenses		
Salary expense	$106,000	
Office rent expense	18,000	
Depreciation expense—furniture and equipment	3,500	
Marketing expense	2,500	
Total operating expenses		130,000
Operating income		$ 30,000

In this textbook, we always use "operating income" rather than "net income" as the bottom line on the income statement since internal managers are particularly concerned with the income generated through operations. To determine "net income," we would have to deduct interest expense and income taxes from "operating income" and add back interest income. In general, "operating income" is simply the company's income before interest and income taxes.

Merchandising Companies

In contrast with service companies, merchandiser's income statements feature Cost of Goods Sold as the major expense. Exhibit 2-12 illustrates the income statement for Wholesome Foods, a regional grocery store chain. Notice how Cost of Goods Sold is deducted from Sales Revenue to yield the company's gross profit. Next, all operating expenses (*all period costs*) are deducted to arrive at the company's operating income

EXHIBIT 2-12   Merchandiser's Income Statement

Wholesome Foods
Income Statement
For the year ended December 31
(all figures shown in thousands of dollars)

Sales revenues...		$150,000
Less: Cost of goods sold...		106,500
Gross profit..		$ 43,500
Less: Operating expenses		
Salaries and wages	$5,000	
Rent and utilities...	3,000	
Marketing...	1,000	
Total operating expenses..		9,000
Operating income...		$ 34,500

But how does a merchandising company calculate the Cost of Goods Sold?

■ Most likely, the company uses bar coding to implement a **perpetual inventory** system during the year. If so, all inventory is labeled with a unique bar code that reflects 1) the sales price that will be charged to the customer, and 2) the inventoriable cost of the merchandise to the store. Every time a bar-coded product is "scanned" at the checkout counter, the company's accounting records are automatically updated to reflect 1) the sales revenue earned, 2) the cost of goods sold, and 3) the removal of the product from merchandise inventory.

■ However, at the end of the period, merchandisers must also calculate Cost of Goods Sold using the **periodic inventory** method. Why? Because the company's accounting records only reflect those products that were scanned during checkout. Thus, the records would not reflect any breakage, theft, input errors, or obsolescence that occurred during the year. Exhibit 2-13 shows how to calculate Cost of Goods Sold using the periodic method.

EXHIBIT 2-13   Calculation of Cost of Goods Sold for a Merchandising Firm

Calculation of Cost of Goods Sold

Beginning inventory	$ 9,500
Plus: Purchases, freight-in, and any import duties	110,000
Cost of goods available for sale	119,500
Less: Ending inventory	(13,000)
Cost of goods sold	$106,500

In this calculation, we start with the beginning inventory and add to it all of the companies' *inventoriable product costs* for the period: the cost of the merchandise purchased from manufacturers or distributors, freight-in, and any import duties. The resulting total reflects the cost of all goods that were available for sale during the period. Then we subtract the cost of the products still in ending inventory to arrive at the Cost of Goods Sold.

Manufacturing Companies

Exhibit 2-14 shows the income statement for Proquest, a manufacturer of tennis balls. As you can see, the income statement for a manufacturer is essentially identical to that of a merchandising company. The only *real* difference is that the company is selling product that it has *made*, rather than merchandise that it has *purchased*. As a result, the calculation of Cost of Goods Sold is different than that shown in Exhibit 2-13.

EXHIBIT 2-14   Manufacturer's Income Statement

<table>
<tr><td colspan="3" align="center">Proquest
Income Statement
For the year ended December 31
(*all figures shown in thousands of dollars*)</td></tr>
<tr><td>Sales revenues..</td><td></td><td>$65,000</td></tr>
<tr><td>Less: Cost of goods sold..</td><td></td><td>40,000</td></tr>
<tr><td>Gross profit..</td><td></td><td>$25,000</td></tr>
<tr><td>Less: Operating expenses</td><td></td><td></td></tr>
<tr><td>   Selling expenses...</td><td>$8,000</td><td></td></tr>
<tr><td>   General and administrative expenses.................</td><td>2,000</td><td></td></tr>
<tr><td>   Total operating expenses.............................</td><td></td><td>10,000</td></tr>
<tr><td>Operating income..</td><td></td><td>$15,000</td></tr>
</table>

Calculating Cost of Goods Manufactured and Cost of Goods Sold

Exhibit 2-15 illustrates how the manufacturer's *inventoriable product costs* (direct material used, direct labor, and manufacturing overhead) flow through the three inventory accounts before they become part of Cost of Goods Sold. In order to calculate Cost of Goods Sold, a manufacturer must first figure out the amount of direct materials used and the Cost of Goods Manufactured.

EXHIBIT 2-15 Flow of Costs Through a Manufacturer's Financial Statements

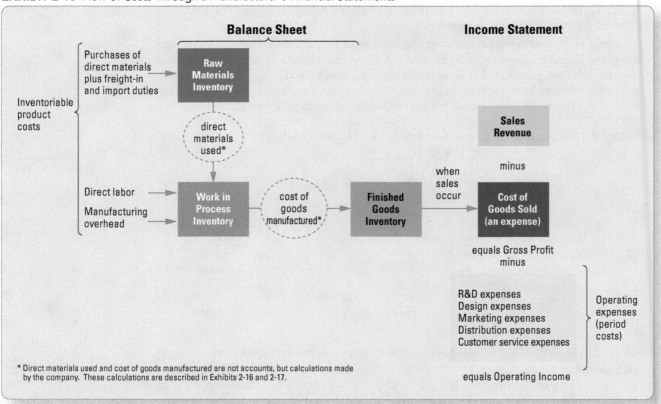

* Direct materials used and cost of goods manufactured are not accounts, but calculations made by the company. These calculations are described in Exhibits 2-16 and 2-17.

As you see in Exhibit 2-15, the **Cost of Goods Manufactured** represents the cost of those goods that were completed and moved to Finished Goods Inventory during the period.

Using Exhibit 2-15 as a guide, let's walk through the calculation of Cost of Goods Sold. We'll use three steps. Each step focuses on a different inventory account: Raw Materials, Work in Process, and Finished Goods.

Step 1: Calculate the cost of the direct materials used during the year

Step 1 simply analyzes what happened in the *Raw Materials Inventory* account during the year. As shown in Exhibit 2-16, we start with the beginning balance in the Raw Materials Inventory account and add to it all of the direct materials purchased during the year, including any freight-in and import duties. This tells us the amount of materials that were available for use during the year. Finally, by subtracting out the ending balance of Raw Materials, we are able to back into the cost of the direct materials that were used[3].

EXHIBIT 2-16   Calculation of Direct Materials Used

Calculation of Direct Materials Used (Analyze the Raw Materials Inventory account)	
Beginning Raw Materials Inventory	$ 9,000
Plus: Purchases of direct materials*, freight-in, and import duties	27,000
Materials available for use	36,000
Less: Ending Raw Material Inventory	(22,000)
Direct materials used	$ 14,000

*For simplicity, we assume that the Raw Materials Inventory account only contains direct materials.

Step 2: Calculate the cost of goods manufactured

Step 2 simply analyzes what happened in the *Work in Process Inventory* account during the year. As shown in Exhibit 2-17, we start with the beginning balance in Work in Process and then add to it all three manufacturing costs that were incurred during the year (DM used, DL, and MOH). Finally, by subtracting out the goods still being worked on at year-end (ending Work in Process Inventory) we are able to back into the Cost of Goods Manufactured. This figure represents the cost of manufacturing the units that were *completed* and sent to Finished Goods Inventory during the year.

EXHIBIT 2-17   Calculation of Cost of Goods Manufactured

Calculation of Cost of Goods Manufactured (Analyze the Work in Process Inventory account)	
Beginning Work in Process Inventory	$ 2,000
Plus: Manufacturing costs incurred	
Direct materials used	14,000
Direct labor	19,000
Manufacturing overhead	12,000
Total manufacturing costs to account for	$47,000
Less: Ending Work in Process Inventory	(5,000)
Cost of goods manufactured (CGM)	$42,000

[3]In this chapter we'll assume that the Raw Materials account only contains direct materials because the company uses indirect materials as soon as they are purchased. In Chapter 3, we expand the discussion to include manufacturers who store both direct and indirect materials in the Raw Materials Inventory account.

Step 3: Calculate the cost of goods sold

Step 3 simply analyzes what happened in the *Finished Goods Inventory* account during the year. As shown in Exhibit 2-18, we start with the beginning balance of Finished Goods Inventory and add to it the product that was manufactured during the year (CGM) to arrive at the total goods available for sale. Finally, just like a merchandiser, we subtract what was left in Finished Goods Inventory to back into the Cost of Goods Sold.

EXHIBIT 2-18   Calculation of Cost of Goods Sold

Calculation of Cost of Goods Sold (Analyze the Finished Goods Inventory account)	
Beginning Finished Goods Inventory	$ 6,000
Plus: Cost of goods manufactured (CGM)	42,000
Cost of goods available for sale	48,000
Less: Ending Finished Goods Inventory	(8,000)
Cost of goods sold	$40,000

By analyzing, step by step, what occurred in each of the three inventory accounts, we were able to calculate the Cost of Goods Sold shown on the company's Income Statement (Exhibit 2-14). Some companies combine Steps 1 and 2 into one schedule called the Schedule of Cost of Goods Manufactured. Others combine all three steps into a Schedule of Cost of Goods Sold.

You may be wondering where all of the data comes from. The beginning inventory balances were simply last year's ending balances. The purchases of direct materials, and the incurrence of direct labor and manufacturing overhead would have been captured in the company's accounting records when those costs were incurred. Finally, the ending inventory balances come from doing a physical count of inventory at the end of the year. In the coming chapters, we'll show you different systems manufacturers use to keep track of the *cost* associated with those units still in the three inventory accounts..

Comparing Balance Sheets

Now that we've looked at the income statement for each type of company, let's consider their balance sheets. The only difference relates to how inventory is shown in the current asset section:

- Service Companies show no inventory
- Merchandising companies show "inventory" or "merchandise inventory"
- Manufacturing companies show Raw Materials, Work in Process, and Finished Goods Inventory

Sometimes manufacturers just show "Inventories" on the face of the balance sheet, but disclose the breakdown of the inventory accounts (Raw Materials, Work in Process, and Finished Goods) in the footnotes to the financial statements.

What Other Cost Terms are Used by Managers?

6 Describe costs that are relevant and irrelevant for decision making

So far in this chapter, we have discussed direct versus indirect costs and inventoriable product costs versus period costs. Now let's turn our attention to other cost terms that managers and accountants use when planning and making decisions.

Controllable Versus Uncontrollable Costs

When deciding to make business changes, management needs to distinguish controllable costs from uncontrollable costs. In the long run, most costs are **controllable**, meaning management is able to influence or change them. However, in the short run, companies are often "locked in" to certain costs arising from previous decisions. These are called **uncontrollable costs**. For example, Toyota has little or no control over the property tax and insurance costs of their existing plants. These costs were "locked in" when Toyota built its plants. Toyota could replace existing production facilities with different-sized plants in different areas of the world that might cost less to operate, but that would take time. To see *immediate* benefits, management must change those costs that are controllable at the present. For example, management can control costs of research and development, design, and advertising. Sometimes Toyota's management chose to *increase* rather than decrease these costs in order to successfully gain market share. However, Toyota was also able to *decrease* other controllable costs, such as the price paid for raw materials, by working with its suppliers.

Relevant and Irrelevant Costs

Decision making involves identifying various courses of action and then choosing among them. When managers make decisions, they focus on those costs and revenues that are relevant to the decision. For example, Toyota plans to build a new state-of-the-art Prius production facility in the United States. After considering alternative locations, management decided to build the facility in Blue Springs, Mississippi. The decision was based on relevant information such as the **differential cost** of building and operating the facility in Mississippi versus building and operating the facility in other potential locations. Differential cost refers to the difference in cost between two alternatives.

Say you want to buy a new car. You narrow your decision to two choices: the Nissan Sentra or the Toyota Corolla. As shown in Exhibit 2-19, the Sentra you like costs $14,480, whereas the Corolla costs $15,345. Because sales tax is based on the sales price, the Corolla's sales tax is higher. However, your insurance agent quotes you a higher price to insure the Sentra ($365 per month versus $319 per month for the Corolla). All of these costs are relevant to your decision because they differ between the two cars.

EXHIBIT 2-19 Comparison of Relevant Information

	Sentra	Corolla	Differential Cost
Car's price	$14,480	$15,345	$ (865)
Sales tax (8%) (rounded to the nearest dollar)	1,158	1,228	(70)
Insurance*	21,900	19,140	2,760
Total relevant costs	$37,538	$35,713	$1,825

*Over the five years (60 months) you plan to keep the car.

Other costs are not relevant to your decision. For example, both cars run on regular unleaded gasoline and have the same fuel economy ratings, so the cost of operating the vehicles is about the same. Likewise, you don't expect cost differences in servicing the vehicles because they both carry the same warranty and have received excellent quality ratings in *Consumer Reports*. Because you project operating and maintenance costs to be the *same* for both cars, these costs are irrelevant to your decision. In other words, they won't influence your decision either way. Based on your analysis, the differential cost is $1,825 in favor of the Corolla. Does this mean that you will choose the Corolla? Not necessarily. The Sentra may have some characteristics you like better, such as a particular paint color, more comfortable seating, or more trunk space. When making decisions, management must also consider qualitative factors (such as effect on employee morale) in addition to differential costs.

Another cost that is irrelevant to your decision is the cost you paid for the vehicle you currently own. Say you just bought a Ford F-150 pickup truck two months ago, but you've decided you need a small sedan rather than a pickup truck. The cost of the truck is a **sunk cost**. Sunk costs are costs that have already been incurred. Nothing you do now can change the fact that you already bought the truck. Thus, the cost of the truck is not relevant to your decision of whether to buy the Sentra versus the Corolla. The only thing you can do now is (1) keep your truck or (2) sell it for the best price you can get.

Management often has trouble ignoring sunk costs when making decisions, even though it should. Perhaps it invested in a factory or a computer system that no longer serves the company's needs. Many times, new technology makes management's past investments in older technology look like bad decisions, even though they weren't at the time. Management should ignore sunk costs because its decisions about the future cannot alter decisions made in the past.

Fixed and Variable Costs

7 Classify costs as fixed or variable and calculate total and average costs at different volumes

Managers cannot make good plans and decisions without first knowing how their costs behave. Costs generally behave as fixed costs or variable costs. We will spend all of Chapter 6 discussing cost behavior. For now, let's look just at the basics. <u>Fixed costs</u> stay constant in total over a wide range of activity levels. For example, let's say you decide to buy the Corolla, so your insurance cost for the year is $3,828 ($319 per month $\times$ 12 months). As shown in Exhibit 2-20, your total insurance cost stays fixed whether you drive your car 0 miles, 1,000 miles, or 10,000 miles during the year.

EXHIBIT 2-20 Fixed Cost Behavior

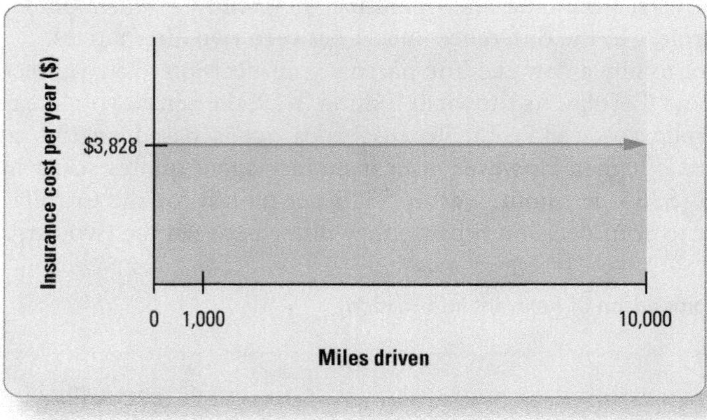

Why is this important?
"Most **business decisions** depend on how costs are **expected** to change at different volumes of **activity**. Managers can't make good decisions without first **understanding** how their costs **behave**."

However, the total cost of gasoline to operate your car varies depending on whether you drive 0 miles, 1,000 miles, or 10,000 miles. The more miles you drive, the higher your total gasoline cost for the year. If you don't drive your car at all, you won't incur any costs for gasoline. Your gasoline costs are <u>variable costs</u>, as shown in Exhibit 2-21. Variable costs change in total in direct proportion to changes in volume. To

EXHIBIT 2-21 Variable Cost Behavior

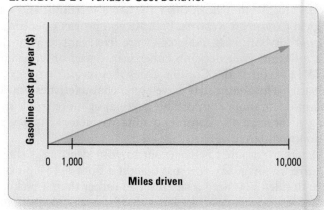

accurately forecast the total cost of operating your Corolla during the year, you need to know which operating costs are fixed and which are variable.

How Manufacturing Costs Behave

Most companies have both fixed and variable costs. Manufacturing companies know that their direct materials are variable costs. The more cars Toyota makes, the higher its total cost for tires, steel, and parts. The behavior of direct labor is harder to characterize. Salaried employees are paid a fixed amount per year. Hourly wage earners are paid only when they work. The more hours they work, the more they are paid. Nonetheless, direct labor is generally treated as a variable cost because the more cars Toyota produces, the more assembly-line workers and machine operators it must employ. Manufacturing overhead includes both variable and fixed costs. For example, the cost of indirect materials is variable, while the cost of property tax, insurance, and straight-line depreciation on the plant and equipment is fixed. The cost of utilities is partially fixed and partially variable. Factories incur a certain level of utility costs just to keep the lights on. However, when more cars are produced, more electricity is used to run the production equipment. Exhibit 2-22 summarizes the behavior of manufacturing costs.

EXHIBIT 2-22 The Behavior of Manufacturing Costs

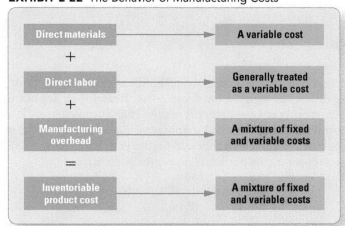

Calculating Total and Average Costs

Why is cost behavior important? Managers need to understand how costs behave to predict total costs and calculate average costs. In our example, we'll look at Toyota's total and average *manufacturing* costs; but the same principles apply to nonmanufacturing costs.

Let's say Toyota wants to estimate the total cost of manufacturing 10,000 Prius cars next year. To do so, Toyota must know 1) its total fixed manufacturing costs, and 2) the variable cost of manufacturing each vehicle. Let's assume total fixed manufacturing costs for the year at the Prius plant are $20,000,000 and the variable cost of manufacturing each Prius is $5,000.[4] How much total manufacturing cost should Toyota budget for the year? Toyota calculates it as follows:

Total fixed cost + (Variable cost per unit × Number of units) = Total cost
$20,000,000   + ($5,000 per vehicle   × 10,000 vehicles) = $70,000,000

[4]All references to Toyota in this hypothetical example were created by the author solely for academic purposes and are not intended in any way to represent the actual business practices of, or costs incurred by, Toyota Motor Corporation.

What is the **average cost** of manufacturing each Prius next year? It's the total cost divided by the number of units:

$$\frac{\text{Total cost}}{\text{Number of units}} = \text{Average cost per unit}$$

$$\frac{\$70,000,000}{10,000 \text{ vehicles}} = \$7,000 \text{ per vehicle}$$

If Toyota's managers decide they need to produce 12,000 Prius cars instead, can they simply predict total costs as follows?

$$\text{Average cost per unit} \times \text{Number of units} = \text{Total cost???}$$
$$\$7,000 \qquad \times \qquad 12,000 \qquad = \$84,000,000???$$

No! They cannot! Why? *Because the average cost per unit is NOT appropriate for predicting total costs at different levels of output.* Toyota's managers should forecast total cost based on cost behavior:

$$\text{Total fixed cost} + (\text{Variable cost per unit} \times \text{Number of units}) = \text{Total cost}$$
$$\$20,000,000 + (\ \$5,000 \text{ per vehicle} \ \times 12,000 \text{ vehicles} \ ) = \$80,000,000$$

Why is the *correct* forecasted cost of $80 million less than the *faulty* prediction of $84 million? The difference stems from fixed costs. Remember, Toyota incurs $20 million of fixed manufacturing costs whether it makes 10,000 vehicles or 12,000 vehicles. As Toyota makes more Prius cars, the fixed manufacturing costs are spread over more vehicles, so the average cost per vehicle declines. If Toyota ends up making 12,000 vehicles, the new average manufacturing cost per Prius decreases as follows:

$$\frac{\text{Total cost}}{\text{Number of units}} = \text{Average cost per unit}$$

$$\frac{\$80,000,000}{12,000 \text{ vehicles}} = \$6,667 \text{ per vehicle (rounded)}$$

The average cost per unit is lower when Toyota produces more vehicles because it is using the fixed manufacturing costs more efficiently—taking the same $20 million of resources and making more vehicles with it.

The moral of the story: The average cost per unit is valid only at ONE level of output—the level used to compute the average cost per unit. Thus, NEVER use average costs to forecast costs at different output levels; if you do, you will miss the mark!

Finally, a **marginal cost** is the cost of making *one more unit*. Fixed costs will not change when Toyota makes one more Prius unless the plant is operating at 100% capacity and simply cannot make one more unit. (If that's the case, Toyota will need to incur additional costs to expand the plant.) So, the marginal cost of a unit is simply its variable cost.

As you have seen, management accountants and managers use specialized terms for discussing costs. They use different costs for different purposes. Without a solid understanding of these terms, managers are likely to make serious judgment errors.

Decision Guidelines

Building Blocks of Managerial Accounting

As a manufacturer, Dell needs to know how to calculate its inventoriable product costs for external reporting. Dell also needs to know many characteristics about its costs (that is, which are controllable, which are relevant to different decisions, which are fixed, and so forth) in order to plan and make decisions.

Decision	Guidelines
How do you compute cost of goods sold?	*Service companies:* No cost of goods sold because they don't sell tangible goods • *Merchandising companies:* Beginning inventory + Purchases plus freight-in and import duties, if any = Cost of goods available for sale − Ending inventory = Cost of goods sold • *Manufacturing companies:* Beginning finished goods inventory + Cost of goods manufactured = Cost of goods available for sale − Ending finished goods inventory = Cost of goods sold
How do you compute the cost of goods manufactured?	Beginning work in process inventory + Total manufacturing costs incurred during year (direct materials used + direct labor + manufacturing overhead) = Total manufacturing costs to account for − Ending work in process inventory = Cost of goods manufactured
How do managers decide which costs are relevant to their decisions?	Costs are relevant to a decision when they differ between alternatives and affect the future. Thus, *differential costs* are relevant, whereas *sunk costs* and costs that don't differ are not relevant.
How should managers forecast total costs for different production volumes?	Total cost = Total fixed costs + (Variable cost per unit × Number of units) Managers should *not* use a product's *average cost* to forecast total costs because it will change as production volume changes. As production increases, the average cost per unit declines (because fixed costs are spread over more units).

SUMMARY PROBLEM 2

Requirements

1. Show how to compute cost of goods manufactured. Use the following amounts: direct materials used ($24,000), direct labor ($9,000), manufacturing overhead ($17,000), beginning work in process inventory ($5,000), and ending work in process inventory ($4,000).

2. Auto-USA spent $300 million in total to produce 50,000 cars this year. The $300 million breaks down as follows: The company spent $50 million on fixed costs to run its manufacturing plants and $5,000 of variable costs to produce each car. Next year, it plans to produce 60,000 cars using the existing production facilities.

   a. What is the current *average cost* per car this year?

   b. Assuming there is no change in fixed costs or variable costs per unit, what is the *total forecasted cost* to produce 60,000 cars next year?

   c. What is the *forecasted average cost* per car next year?

   d. Why does the average cost per car vary between years?

▪ SOLUTIONS

Requirement 1

Cost of goods manufactured:

Calculation of Cost of Goods Manufactured	
Beginning Work in Process Inventory	$ 5,000
Plus: Manufacturing costs incurred	
Direct materials used	24,000
Direct labor	9,000
Manufacturing overhead	17,000
Total manufacturing costs to account for	$55,000
Less: Ending Work in Process Inventory	(4,000)
Cost of goods manufactured (CGM)	$51,000

Requirement 2

a.

Total cost ÷ Number of units = Current average cost

$300 million ÷ 50,000 cars = $6,000 per car

b.

Total fixed costs + Total variable costs = Total projected costs

$50 million + (60,000 cars × $5,000 per car) = $350 million

c.

Total cost ÷ Number of units = Projected average cost

$350 million ÷ 60,000 cars = $5,833 per car

d. The average cost per car decreases because Auto-USA will use the same fixed costs ($50 million) to produce more cars next year. Auto-USA will be using its resources more efficiently, so the average cost per unit will decrease.

END OF CHAPTER

Learning Objectives

- 1 Distinguish among service, merchandising, and manufacturing companies
- 2 Describe the value chain and its elements
- 3 Distinguish between direct and indirect costs
- 4 Identify the inventoriable product costs and period costs of merchandising and manufacturing firms
- 5 Prepare the financial statements for service, merchandising, and manufacturing companies
- 6 Describe costs that are relevant and irrelevant for decision making
- 7 Classify costs as fixed or variable and calculate total and average costs at different volumes

Accounting Vocabulary

Allocate. (p. 54) To assign an *indirect* cost to a cost object.

Assign. (p. 54) To attach a cost to a cost object.

Average cost. (p. 70) The total cost divided by the number of units.

Biomimicry. (p. 52) A means of product design in which a company tries to mimic, or copy, the natural biological process in which dead organisms (plants and animals) become the input for another organism or process.

Controllable Costs. (p. 66) Costs that can be influenced or changed by management.

Conversion Costs. (p. 59) The combination of direct labor and manufacturing overhead costs.

Cost Object. (p. 53) Anything for which managers want a separate measurement of costs.

Cost of Goods Manufactured. (p. 65) The cost of manufacturing the goods that were *finished* during the period.

Customer Service. (p. 51) Support provided for customers after the sale.

Design. (p. 50) Detailed engineering of products and services and the processes for producing them.

Differential Cost. (p. 67) The difference in cost between two alternative courses of action.

Direct Cost. (p. 53) A cost that can be traced to a cost object.

Direct Labor. (p. 57) The cost of compensating employees who physically convert raw materials into the company's products; labor costs that are directly traceable to the finished product.

Direct Materials. (p. 57) Primary raw materials that become a physical part of a finished product and whose costs are traceable to the finished product.

Distribution. (p. 51) Delivery of products or services to customers.

Finished Goods Inventory. (p. 49) Completed goods that have not yet been sold.

Fixed Costs. (p. 68) Costs that stay constant in total despite wide changes in volume.

Greenwashing. (p. 52) The unfortunate practice of *overstating* a company's commitment to sustainability.

Indirect Cost. (p. 53) A cost that relates to the cost object but cannot be traced to it.

Indirect Labor. (p. 57) Labor costs that are difficult to trace to specific products.

Indirect Materials. (p. 57) Materials whose costs are difficult to trace to specific products.

Inventoriable Product Costs. (p. 55) All costs of a product that GAAP requires companies to treat as an asset (inventory) for external financial reporting. These costs are not expensed until the product is sold.

Life cycle assessment. (p. 52) A method of product design in which the company analyzes the environmental impact of a product, from cradle to grave, in an attempt to minimize negative environmental consequences throughout the entire life span of the product.

Manufacturing Company. (p. 48) A company that uses labor, plant, and equipment to convert raw materials into new finished products.

Manufacturing Overhead. (p. 57) All manufacturing costs other than direct materials and direct labor; also called factory overhead and indirect manufacturing cost.

Marginal Cost. (p. 70) The cost of producing one more unit.

Marketing. (p. 51) Promotion and advertising of products or services.

Merchandising Company. (p. 48) A company that resells tangible products previously bought from suppliers.

Other Indirect Manufacturing Costs. (p. 57) All manufacturing overhead costs aside from indirect materials and indirect labor.

Period Costs. (p. 55) Costs that are expensed in the period in which they are incurred; often called Operating Expenses, or Selling, General, and Administrative Expenses.

Perpetual Inventory. (p. 63) An inventory system in which both Cost of Goods Sold and Inventory are updated every time a sale is made.

Periodic Inventory. (p. 63) An inventory system in which Cost of Goods Sold is calulated at the end of the period, rather than every time a sale is made.

Prime Costs. (p. 58) The combination of direct material and direct labor costs.

Production or Purchases. (p. 51) Resources used to produce a product or service, or to purchase finished merchandise intended for resale.

Raw Materials Inventory. (p. 48) All raw materials (direct materials and indirect materials) not yet used in manufacturing.

Research and Development (R&D). (p. 50) Researching and developing new or improved products or services or the processes for producing them.

Retailer. (p. 48) Merchandising company that sells to consumers.

Service Company. (p. 48) A company that sells intangible services rather than tangible products.

Sunk Cost. (p. 67) A cost that has already been incurred.

Total Costs. (p. 54) The cost of all resources used throughout the value chain.

Trace. (p. 54) To assign a *direct* cost to a cost object.

Triple bottom line. (p. 48) Evaluating a company's performance not only by its ability to generate economic profits, but also by its impact on people and the planet.

Uncontrollable Costs. (p. 67) Costs that cannot be changed or influenced in the short run by management.

Value Chain. (p. 50) The activities that add value to a firm's products and services; includes R&D, design, production or purchases, marketing, distribution, and customer service.

Variable Costs. (p. 68) Costs that change in total in direct proportion to changes in volume.

Wholesaler. (p. 48) Merchandising companies that buy in bulk from manufacturers, mark up the prices, and then sell those products to retailers.

Work in Process Inventory. (p. 48) Goods that are partway through the manufacturing process but not yet complete.

MyAccountingLab | **Go to** http://myaccountinglab.com/ **for the following Quick Check, Short Exercises, Exercises, and Problems. They are available with immediate grading, explanations of correct and incorrect answers, and interactive media that acts as your own online tutor.**

Quick Check

1. *(Learning Objective 1)* Walmart is a
   a. service company.
   b. retailer.
   c. wholesaler.
   d. manufacturer.

2. *(Learning Objective 2)* The cost of oranges at a fruit juice manufacturer is an example of a cost from which element in the value chain?
   a. Design
   b. Production
   c. Marketing
   d. Distribution

3. *(Learning Objective 2)* Which is *not* an element of Toyota's value chain?
   a. Administrative costs
   b. Cost of shipping cars to dealers
   c. Salaries of engineers who update car design
   d. Cost of print ads and television commercials

4. *(Learning Objective 3)* For Toyota, which is a direct cost with respect to the Prius?
   a. Depreciation on plant and equipment
   b. Cost of vehicle engine
   c. Salary of engineer who rearranges plant layout
   d. Cost of customer hotline

5. *(Learning Objective 3)* Which one of the following costs would be considered a direct cost of serving a particular customer at a McDonald's restaurant?
   a. The salary of the restaurant manager
   b. The depreciation on the restaurant building
   c. The cost of the hamburger patty in the sandwich the customer ordered
   d. The cost of heating the restaurant

6. *(Learning Objective 4)* Which of the following is *not* part of Toyota's manufacturing overhead?
   a. Insurance on plant and equipment
   b. Depreciation on its North American corporate headquarters
   c. Plant property taxes
   d. Plant utilities

7. *(Learning Objective 4)* The three basic components of inventoriable product costs are direct materials, direct labor, and
   a. cost of goods manufactured.
   b. manufacturing overhead.
   c. cost of goods sold.
   d. work in process.

8. *(Learning Objective 5)* In computing cost of goods sold, which of the following is the manufacturer's counterpart to the merchandiser's purchases?
   a. Direct materials used
   b. Total manufacturing costs incurred during the period
   c. Total manufacturing costs to account for
   d. Cost of goods manufactured

9. (*Learning Objective 6*) Which of the following is irrelevant to business decisions?
    a. Differential costs
    b. Sunk costs
    c. Variable costs
    d. Qualitative factors

10. (*Learning Objective 7*) Which of the following is *true*?
    a. Total fixed costs increase as production volume increases.
    b. Total fixed costs decrease as production volume decreases.
    c. Total variable costs increase as production volume increases.
    d. Total variable costs stay constant as production volume increases.

Quick Check Answers

Short Exercises

S2-1 Identify type of company from balance sheets (*Learning Objective 1*)

The current asset sections of the balance sheets of three companies follow. Which company is a service company? Which is a merchandiser? Which is a manufacturer? How can you tell?

ABC Co.		DEF Co.		GHI Co.	
Cash.............................	$ 2,000	Cash.................................	$ 2,500	Cash..	$3,000
Accounts receivable	5,000	Accounts receivable	5,500	Accounts receivable	6,000
Raw materials inventory	1,000	Inventory	8,000	Prepaid expenses	500
Work in process inventory .	800	Prepaid expenses	300	Total..	$9,500
Finished goods inventory ..	4,000	Total.................................	$16,300		
Total.................................	$12,800				

S2-2 Identify types of companies and inventories (*Learning Objective 1*)

Fill in the blanks with one of the following terms: *manufacturing, service, merchandising, retailer(s), wholesaler(s), raw materials inventory, merchandise inventory, work in process inventory, finished goods inventory, freight-in, the cost of merchandise.*

a. Direct materials are stored in _____.
b. Kmart is a _____ company.
c. Manufacturers sell from their stock of _____.
d. Labor costs usually account for the highest percentage of _____ companies' costs.
e. Partially completed units are kept in the _____.
f. _____ companies generally have no inventory.
g. Intel (computer chips) is a _____ company.
h. Merchandisers' inventory consists of _____ and _____.
i. _____ companies carry three types of inventories: _____, _____, and _____.
j. H&R Block (tax preparation) is a _____ company.
k. Two types of _____ companies include _____ and _____.

S2-3 Classify costs by value chain function *(Learning Objective 2)*

Classify each of Hewlett-Packard's (HP's) costs as one of the six business functions in the value chain.

a. Depreciation on Roseville, California, plant
b. Costs of a customer support center website
c. Transportation costs to deliver laser printers to retailers such as Best Buy
d. Depreciation on research lab
e. Cost of a prime-time TV ad featuring the new HP logo
f. Salary of scientists at HP laboratories who are developing new printer technologies
g. Purchase of plastic used in printer casings
h. Salary of engineers who are redesigning the printer's on-off switch
i. Depreciation on delivery vehicles
j. Plant manager's salary

S2-4 Classify costs as direct or indirect *(Learning Objective 3)*

Classify the following as direct or indirect costs with respect to a local National Rentals equipment rental store (the store is the cost object). In addition, state whether National Rentals would trace or allocate these costs to the store.

a. The wages of store employees
b. The cost of operating the corporate payroll department
c. The cost of carpet steamers offered for rent
d. The cost of gas and oil sold at the store
e. Store utilities
f. The CEO's salary
g. The cost of the chainsaws offered for rent
h. The cost of national advertising

S2-5 Classify inventoriable product costs and period costs
(Learning Objective 4)

Classify each of Georgia-Pacific's costs as either inventoriable product costs or period costs. Georgia-Pacific is a manufacturer of paper, lumber, and building material products.

a. Cost of new software to track inventory during production
b. Cost of electricity at one of Georgia-Pacific's paper mills
c. Salaries of Georgia-Pacific's top executives
d. Cost of chemical applied to lumber to inhibit mold from developing
e. Cost of TV ads promoting environmental awareness
f. Depreciation on the gypsum board plant
g. Purchase of lumber to be cut into boards
h. Life insurance on the CEO
i. Salaries of scientists studying ways to speed forest growth

S2-6 Classify a manufacturer's costs *(Learning Objective 4)*

Classify each of the following costs as a period cost or an inventoriable product cost. If you classify the cost as an inventoriable product cost, further classify it as direct material (DM), direct labor (DL), or manufacturing overhead (MOH).

a. Wages and benefits paid to assembly-line workers in the manufacturing plant
b. Repairs and maintenance on factory equipment
c. Lease payment on administrative headquarters
d. Salaries paid to quality control inspectors in the plant
e. Property insurance—40% of building is used for sales and administration; 60% of building is used for manufacturing
f. Standard packaging materials used to package individual units of product for sale (for example, cereal boxes in which cereal is packaged)
g. Depreciation on automated production equipment
h. Telephone bills relating to customer service call center

S2-7 Classify costs incurred by a dairy processing company
(Learning Objective 4)

Each of the following costs pertains to DairyPlains, a dairy processing company. Classify each of the company's costs as a period cost or an inventoriable product cost. Further classify inventoriable product costs as direct material (DM), direct labor (DL), or manufacturing overhead (MOH).

Cost	Period Cost or Inventoriable Product Cost?	DM, DL, or MOH?
1. Company president's annual bonus		
2. Plastic gallon containers in which milk is packaged		
3. Depreciation on Marketing Department's computers		
4. Wages and salaries paid to machine operators at dairy processing plant		
5. Research and development on improving milk pasteurization process		
6. Cost of milk purchased from local dairy farmers		
7. Lubricants used in running bottling machines		
8. Depreciation on refrigerated trucks used to collect raw milk from local dairy farmers		
9. Property tax on dairy processing plant		
10. Television advertisements for DairyPlains' products		
11. Gasoline used to operate refrigerated trucks delivering finished dairy products to grocery stores		

S2-8 Determine total manufacturing overhead (Learning Objective 4)

Frame Pro manufactures picture frames. Suppose the company's March records include the items described below. What is Frame Pro's total manufacturing overhead cost in March?

Company president's salary	$28,000
Plant supervisor's salary	$ 3,300
Plant janitor's salary	$ 1,500
Oil for manufacturing equipment	$ 110
Wood for frames	$48,000
Glue for picture frames	$ 450
Depreciation expense on company cars used by sales force	$ 4,100
Plant depreciation expense	$ 8,100
Interest expense	$ 3,500

S2-9 Compute Cost of Goods Sold for a merchandiser (Learning Objective 5)

Given the following information for a retailer, compute the cost of goods sold.

Import duties	$ 1,100
Purchases	$42,000
Ending inventory	$ 5,400
Revenues	$71,000
Marketing expenses	$10,000
Beginning inventory	$ 4,200
Website maintenance	$ 7,500
Delivery expenses	$ 1,300
Freight-in	$ 3,600

S2-10 Prepare a retailer's income statement *(Learning Objective 5)*

Gossamer Secrets is a retail chain specializing in salon-quality hair care products. During the year, Gossamer Secrets had sales of $39,300,000. The company began the year with $3,350,000 of merchandise inventory and ended the year with $4,315,000 of inventory. During the year, Gossamer Secrets purchased $23,975,000 of merchandise inventory. The company's selling, general, and administrative expenses totaled $6,150,000 for the year. Prepare Gossamer Secrets' income statement for the year.

S2-11 Calculate direct materials used *(Learning Objective 5)*

You are a new accounting intern at Allterrain Bikes. Your boss gives you the following information and asks you to compute the cost of direct materials used (assume that the company's raw materials inventory contains only direct materials).

Purchases of direct materials	$15,600
Import duties	$ 900
Freight-in	$ 600
Freight-out	$ 500
Ending raw materials inventory	$ 2,000
Beginning raw materials inventory	$ 3,900

S2-12 Compute Cost of Goods Manufactured *(Learning Objective 5)*

Robinson Manufacturing found the following information in its accounting records: $523,000 of direct materials used, $215,000 of direct labor, and $774,500 of manufacturing overhead. The Work in Process Inventory account had a beginning balance of $78,000 and an ending balance of $84,000. Compute the company's Cost of Goods Manufactured.

S2-13 Consider relevant information *(Learning Objective 6)*

You have been offered an entry-level marketing position at two highly respectable firms: one in Los Angeles, California, and one in Sioux Falls, South Dakota. What quantitative and qualitative information might be relevant to your decision? What characteristics about this information make it relevant?

S2-14 Classify costs as fixed or variable *(Learning Objective 7)*

Classify each of the following personal expenses as either fixed or variable. In some cases, your answer may depend on specific circumstances. If so, briefly explain your answer.

a. Water and sewer bill
b. Cell phone bill
c. Health club dues
d. Bus fare
e. Apartment rental
f. Internet cable service
g. Cost of groceries

EXERCISES Group A

E2-15A Identify types of companies and their inventories *(Learning Objective 1)*

Complete the following statements with one of the terms listed here. You may use a term more than once, and some terms may not be used at all.

Finished goods inventory	Inventory (merchandise)	Service companies
Manufacturing companies	Merchandising companies	Work in process inventory
Raw materials inventory	Wholesalers	

Building Blocks of Managerial Accounting   79

a. _____ buy products in bulk from producers, mark them up, and resell to retailers.

b. Most for-profit organizations can be described as being in one (or more) of three categories: _____, _____, and _____.

c. Honda Motors converts _____ into finished products.

d. _____ for a company such as Staples (office supplies) includes all of the costs necessary to purchase products and get them onto the store shelves.

e. Lands' End, Sears Roebuck & Co., and LL Bean are all examples of _____.

f. An insurance company, a health care provider, and a bank are all examples of _____.

g. _____ is composed of goods partially through the manufacturing process (not finished yet).

h. _____ report three types of inventory on the balance sheet.

i. _____typically do not have an inventory account.

E2-16A Classify costs along the value chain for a retailer (Learning Objective 2)

Suppose Radio Shack incurred the following costs at its Atlanta, Georgia, store:

Payment to consultant for advice on location of new store..	$2,100	Research on whether store should sell satellite radio service...	$ 600
Freight-in..	$3,700	Purchases of merchandise...............................	$39,000
Salespeople's salaries....................................	$4,300	Rearranging store layout..................................	$ 700
Customer Complaint Department	$ 800	Newspaper advertisements	$ 5,800
		Depreciation expense on delivery trucks	$ 1,100

Requirements

1. Classify each cost as to which category of the value chain it belongs (R&D, Design, Purchases, Marketing, Distribution, or Customer Service).
2. Compute the total costs for each value chain category.
3. How much are the total inventoriable product costs?

E2-17A Classify costs along the value chain for a manufacturer
(Learning Objectives 2 & 3)

Suppose the cell phone manufacturer Samsung Electronics provides the following information for its costs last month (in hundreds of thousands):

Chip set	$62	Salaries of salespeople..	$ 5
Rearrange production process to accommodate new robot..	$ 1	Depreciation on plant and equipment......................	$70
Assembly-line workers' wages	$12	Exterior case for phone...	$ 6
Technical customer support hotline	$ 3	Salaries of scientists who developed new model...	$11
1-800 (toll-free) line for customer orders..............	$ 5	Delivery expense to customers via UPS...................	$ 8

Requirements

1. Classify each of these costs according to its place in the value chain (R&D, Design, Production, Marketing, Distribution, or Customer Service). (Hint: You should have at least one cost in each value chain function.)
2. Within the production category, break the costs down further into three sub-categories: Direct Materials, Direct Labor, and Manufacturing Overhead.
3. Compute the total costs for each value chain category.
4. How much are the total inventoriable product costs?
5. How much are the total prime costs?
6. How much are the total conversion costs?

E2-18A Value chain and sustainability efforts (*Learning Objective 2*)

Each of the scenarios to follow describes some cost item for organizations in the recycled carpet industry. For each scenario, identify which function of the value chain that cost would represent (R&D, Design, Purchasing/Producing, Marketing, Distributing, or Customer Service.) *Note:* The companies and products used in this exercise are real companies with a strong sustainable practices commitment.

a. Fibre(B)lock® Flooring is manufactured using the waste generated from the manufacture of commercial nylon carpet. The cost of the research into how to create Fibre(B)lock® Flooring would fall into which function in the value chain?

b. Ford Motor Company purchases cylinder head covers made from a nylon resin containing 100% recycled carpet in its 2011 Mustangs. The cost of the cylinder head covers would fall into which function in the value chain?

c. Los Angeles Fiber Company (LAFC) received the EPA/CARE award to recognize Los Angeles Fiber Company's sustainability efforts. Since 2000, LAFC has recycled more than 464 million pounds of post-consumer carpet. Its carpet brand, Reliance Carpet, is made entirely from post-consumer carpet fiber. The cost of promoting the company's products and its sustainability efforts would fall into which function in the value chain?

d. Axminster Carpets offsets the carbon emissions from its carpet distribution process by investing in renewable energy projects such as wind, power, and hydropower plants. This carbon offset is verified independently by the Voluntary Carbon Standard. The cost of these carbon offsets would fall into which function in the value chain?

e. Flor®, a company that produces residential carpet tiles made from recycled carpet, has an R&R (return and recycle) Program. Homeowners can arrange to have old tiles picked up and shipped back to the plant for recycling. The cost of operating this R&R program would fall into which function in the value chain?

f. Shaw Industries is a flooring manufacturer. It has created Cradle to Cradle Silver Certified carpet, which is carpet that can be recycled back into new carpet again and again at the end of its useful life or it can go back into the soil. The costs to develop the production process for the Cradle to Cradle Silver Certified carpet would fall into which function in the value chain?

E2-19A Classify costs as direct or indirect (*Learning Objective 3*)

Classify each of the following costs as a direct cost or an indirect cost assuming that the cost object is the Juniors department (clothing and accessories for teenage and young women) in the Medina Kohl's department store. (Kohl's is a chain of department stores and has stores located across the U.S.)

a. Manager of Juniors Department

b. Cost of Juniors clothing

c. Cost of radio advertising for the store

d. Cost of bags used to package customer purchases at the main registers for the store

e. Juniors Department sales clerks

f. Electricity for the building

g. Depreciation of the building

h. Cost of hangers used to display the clothing in the store

i. The Medina Kohl's store manager's salary

j. Juniors clothing buyers' salaries (these buyers buy for all the Juniors departments of Kohl's stores)

k. Cost of costume jewelry on the mannequins in the Juniors Department

l. Cost of the security staff at the Medina store

E2-20A Define cost terms (*Learning Objectives 3 & 4*)

Complete the following statements with one of the terms listed here. You may use a term more than once, and some terms may not be used at all.

Prime costs	Cost objects	Inventoriable product costs
Assigned	Direct costs	Fringe benefits
Period costs	Assets	Cost of goods sold
Indirect costs	Conversion costs	Total costs

a. Company-paid _____ may include health insurance, retirement plan contributions, payroll taxes, and paid vacations.

b. _____ are the costs of transforming direct materials into finished goods.

c. Direct material plus direct labor equals _____.

d. The allocation process results in a less precise cost figure being _____ to the _____.

e. _____ include the costs of all resources used throughout the value chain.

f. _____ are initially treated as _____ on the balance sheet.

g. Steel, tires, engines, upholstery, carpet, and dashboard instruments are used in the assembly of a car. Since the manufacturer can trace the cost of these materials (including freight-in and import duties) to specific units or batches of vehicles, they are considered _____ of the vehicles.

h. _____ cannot be directly traced to a(n) _____.

i. Costs that can be traced directly to a(n) _____ are called _____.

j. When manufacturing companies sell their finished products, the costs of those finished products are removed from inventory and expensed as _____.

k. _____ include R&D, marketing, distribution, and customer service costs.

l. GAAP requires companies to use only _____ for external financial reporting.

E2-21A Classify and calculate a manufacturer's costs (Learning Objectives 3 & 4)

An airline manufacturer incurred the following costs last month (in thousands of dollars):

a.	Depreciation on forklifts	$ 60
b.	Property tax on corporate marketing office	$ 30
c.	Cost of warranty repairs	$ 220
d.	Factory janitors' wages	$ 10
e.	Cost of designing new plant layout	$ 190
f.	Machine operators' health insurance	$ 40
g.	Airplane seats	$ 270
h.	Depreciation on administrative offices	$ 70
i.	Assembly workers' wages	$ 670
j.	Plant utilities	$ 110
k.	Production supervisors' salaries	$ 160
l.	Jet engines	$1,100
m.	Machine lubricants	$ 20

Requirements

1. Assuming the cost object is an airplane, classify each cost as one of the following: direct material (DM), direct labor (DL), indirect labor (IL), indirect materials (IM), other manufacturing overhead (other MOH), or period cost. (*Hint:* Set up a column for each type of cost.) What is the total for each type of cost?
2. Calculate total manufacturing overhead costs.
3. Calculate total inventoriable product costs.
4. Calculate total prime costs.
5. Calculate total conversion costs.
6. Calculate total period costs.

E2-22A Prepare the current assets section of the balance sheet
(Learning Objective 5)

Consider the following selected amounts and account balances of Knights:

Prepaid expenses	$ 6,100	Cost of goods sold	$102,000
Marketing expense	$27,000	Direct labor	$50,000
Work in process inventory	$42,000	Direct materials used	$20,100
Manufacturing overhead	$22,000	Accounts receivable	$79,000
Finished goods inventory	$59,000	Cash	$15,300
Raw materials inventory	$ 9,800	Cost of goods manufactured	$90,000

Requirement

Show how this company reports current assets on the balance sheet. Not all data are used. Is this company a service company, a merchandiser, or a manufacturer? How do you know?

E2-23A Prepare a retailer's income statement *(Learning Objective 5)*

Ron Rutland is the sole proprietor of Pampered Pets, a business specializing in the sale of high-end pet gifts and accessories. Pampered Pets' sales totaled $1,010,000 during the most recent year. During the year, the company spent $55,000 on expenses relating to website maintenance, $33,000 on marketing, and $28,000 on wrapping, boxing, and shipping the goods to customers. Pampered Pets also spent $639,000 on inventory purchases and an additional $19,900 on freight-in charges. The company started the year with $16,800 of inventory on hand and ended the year with $13,700 of inventory. Prepare Pampered Pets' income statement for the most recent year.

E2-24A Compute direct materials used and cost of goods manufactured
(Learning Objective 5)

Sharpland Industries is calculating its Cost of Goods Manufactured at year-end. Sharpland's accounting records show the following: The Raw Materials Inventory account had a beginning balance of $14,000 and an ending balance of $17,000. During the year, Sharpland purchased $58,000 of direct materials. Direct labor for the year totaled $132,000, while manufacturing overhead amounted to $164,000. The Work in Process Inventory account had a beginning balance of $22,000 and an ending balance of $18,000. Compute the Cost of Goods Manufactured for the year. (*Hint:* The first step is to calculate the direct materials used during the year.)

E2-25A Compute cost of goods manufactured and cost of goods sold
(Learning Objective 5)

Compute the cost of goods manufactured and cost of goods sold for Quality Aquatic Company for the most recent year using the amounts described next. Assume that raw materials inventory contains only direct materials.

	Beginning of Year	End of Year		End of Year
Raw materials inventory	$29,000	$31,000	Insurance on plant	$10,500
Work in process inventory	$36,000	$30,000	Depreciation—plant building and equipment	$13,000
Finished goods inventory	$22,000	$28,000	Repairs and maintenance—plant	$ 4,000
Purchases of direct materials		$73,000	Marketing expenses	$83,000
Direct labor		$89,000	General and administrative expenses	$26,500
Indirect labor		$42,000		

E2-26A Continues E2-25A: Prepare income statement *(Learning Objective 5)*

Prepare the income statement for Quality Aquatic Company in E2-25A for the most recent year. Assume that the company sold 33,000 units of its product at a price of $14 each during the year.

E2-27A Work backward to find missing amounts *(Learning Objective 5)*

JR Electronics manufactures and sells a line of smartphones. Unfortunately, JR Electronics suffered serious fire damage at its home office. As a result, the accounting records for October were partially destroyed—and completely jumbled. JR Electronics has hired you to help figure out the missing pieces of the accounting puzzle. Assume that the raw materials inventory contains only direct materials.

Work in process inventory, October 31	$ 1,800
Finished goods inventory, October 1	$ 4,200
Direct labor in October	$ 3,100
Purchases of direct materials in October	$ 9,200
Work in process inventory, October 1	0
Revenues in October	$27,300
Gross profit in October	$12,700
Direct materials used in October	$ 8,000
Raw materials inventory, October 31	$ 3,300
Manufacturing overhead in October	$ 6,300

Requirement

Find the following amounts:

a. Cost of goods sold in October
b. Beginning raw materials inventory
c. Ending finished goods inventory

E2-28A Determine whether information is relevant *(Learning Objective 6)*

Classify each of the following costs as relevant or irrelevant to the decision at hand and briefly explain your reason.

a. The type of fuel (gas or diesel) used by delivery vans when deciding which make and model of van to purchase for the company's delivery van fleet
b. Depreciation expense on old manufacturing equipment when deciding whether to replace it with newer equipment
c. The fair market value of old manufacturing equipment when deciding whether to replace it with new equipment
d. The interest rate paid on invested funds when deciding how much inventory to keep on hand
e. The cost of land purchased three years ago when deciding whether to build on the land now or wait two more years
f. The total amount of the restaurant's fixed costs when deciding whether to add additional items to the menu
g. Cost of operating automated production machinery versus the cost of direct labor when deciding whether to automate production
h. Cost of computers purchased six months ago when deciding whether to upgrade to computers with a faster processing speed
i. Cost of purchasing packaging materials from an outside vendor when deciding whether to continue manufacturing the packaging materials in-house
j. The property tax rates in different locales when deciding where to locate the company's headquarters

E2-29A Describe other cost terms *(Learning Objectives 6 & 7)*

Complete the following statements with one of the terms listed here. You may use a term more than once, and some terms may not be used at all.

Differential costs	Variable costs	Controllable costs
Marginal cost	Fixed costs	Average cost
Uncontrollable costs	Sunk costs	

a. In the long-run, most costs are _____, meaning that management is able to influence or change the amount of the cost.
b. Gasoline is one of many _____ in the operation of a motor vehicle.
c. Within the relevant range, _____ do not change in total with changes in production volume.
d. Costs that differ between alternatives are called _____.
e. The _____ per unit declines as a production facility produces more units.
f. A _____ is the cost of making one more unit.
g. A product's _____ and _____, not the product's _____, should be used to forecast total costs at different production volumes.
h. _____ are costs that have already been incurred.

E2-30A Classify costs as fixed or variable *(Learning Objective 7)*

Classify each of the following costs as fixed or variable:

a. Shipping costs for Amazon.com
b. Cost of fuel used for a national trucking company
c. Sales commissions at a car dealership
d. Cost of fabric used at a clothing manufacturer
e. Monthly office lease costs for a CPA firm
f. Cost of fruit sold at a grocery store
g. Cost of coffee used at a Starbucks' store
h. Monthly rent for a nail salon
i. Depreciation of exercise equipment at the YMCA
j. Hourly wages paid to sales clerks at Best Buy
k. Property taxes for a restaurant
l. Monthly insurance costs for the home office of a company
m. Monthly flower costs for a florist
n. Monthly depreciation of equipment for a customer service office
o. Monthly cost of French fries at a McDonald's restaurant

E2-31A Compute total and average costs *(Learning Objective 7)*

Smith Soda spends $3 on direct materials, direct labor, and variable manufacturing overhead for every unit (24-pack of soda) it produces. Fixed manufacturing overhead costs $4 million per year. The plant, which is currently operating at only 80% of capacity, produced 20 million units this year. Management plans to operate closer to full capacity next year, producing 25 million units. Management doesn't anticipate any changes in the prices it pays for materials, labor, and manufacturing overhead.

Requirements

1. What is the current total product cost (for the 20 million units), including fixed and variable costs?
2. What is the current average product cost per unit?
3. What is the current fixed cost per unit?
4. What is the forecasted total product cost next year (for the 25 million units)?
5. What is the forecasted average product cost next year?
6. What is the forecasted fixed cost per unit?
7. Why does the average product cost decrease as production increases?

EXERCISES Group B

E2-32B Identify types of companies and their inventories *(Learning Objective 1)*

Complete the following statements with one of the terms listed here. You may use a term more than once, and some terms may not be used at all.

Wholesalers	Work in process inventory	Service companies
Manufacturing companies	Raw materials inventory	Merchandising companies
Finished goods inventory	Inventory (merchandise)	

a. During production, _____ use direct labor and manufacturing overhead to convert direct materials into finished products.

b. _____ have only one category of inventory on their balance sheet.

c. During production as units are completed, they are moved out of _____ into _____.

d. _____ includes all of the costs associated with getting the goods to the store including freight-in costs and import duties if the products for resale were purchased overseas.

e. Merchandising companies can either be _____ or retailers.

f. _____ includes the wood, fasteners, and braces used in building picnic tables at a park furniture manufacturer.

g. _____ sell products to other companies (typically not to individual consumers.)

h. _____ make up the largest sector of the U.S. economy.

i. Ford Motor Company and Post Cereals can be described as _____.

E2-33B Classify costs along the value chain for a retailer *(Learning Objective 2)*

Suppose Radio Shack incurred the following costs at its Charlotte, North Carolina, store.

Payment to consultant for advice on location of new store	$2,500	Research on whether store should sell satellite radio service......	$ 400
Freight-in......	$3,900	Purchases of merchandise......	$30,000
Salespeople's salaries......	$4,000	Rearranging store layout......	$ 950
Customer Complaint Department	$ 700	Newspaper advertisements	$ 5,200
		Depreciation expense on delivery trucks......	$ 1,400

Requirements

1. Classify each cost as to which category of the value chain it belongs (R&D, Design, Purchases, Marketing, Distribution, Customer Service.).
2. Compute the total costs for each value chain category.
3. How much are the total inventoriable product costs?

E2-34B Classify costs along the value chain for a manufacturer

(Learning Objectives 2 & 3)

Suppose the cell phone manufacturer Nokia provides the following information for its costs last month (in hundreds of thousands):

Chip set......	$60	Salaries of salespeople......	$ 7
Rearrange production process to accommodate new robot......	$ 4	Depreciation on plant and equipment......	$75
Assembly-line workers' wages	$12	Exterior case for phone......	$ 6
Technical customer-support hotline	$ 2	Salaries of scientists who developed new model	$10
1-800 (toll-free) line for customer orders	$ 3	Delivery expense to customers via UPS......	$ 5

Requirements

1. Classify each of these costs according to its place in the value chain (R&D, Design, Production, Marketing, Distribution, or Customer Service.)
2. Within the production category, break the costs down further into three sub-categories: Direct Materials, Direct Labor, and Manufacturing Overhead.
3. Compute the total costs for each value chain category.
4. How much are the total inventoriable product costs?
5. How much are the total prime costs?
6. How much are the total conversion costs?

E2-35B Value chain and sustainability efforts *(Learning Objective 2)*

Each of the scenarios to follow describes some cost item for organizations in recent years. For each scenario, identify which function of the value chain that cost would represent (R&D, Design, Purchasing/Producing, Marketing, Distributing, or Customer Service.) *Note: The companies and products used in this exercise are real companies with a strong sustainable practices commitment.*

a. GreenShipping™ is a service that companies can use to purchase carbon offsets for the carbon generated by shipments to customers. Any shipments made with UPS, FedEx, or USPS can be tracked. The GreenShipping™ calculator uses weight, distance traveled and mode of transport to calculate the carbon generated by that shipment. A carbon offset is then purchased so that the shipment becomes carbon neutral. The carbon offset helps to fund the development of renewable energy sources. The cost of these carbon offsets to the company making the shipment to their customer would fall into which function in the value chain?

b. The Red Wing Shoe Company manufactures work boots. The company has a philosophy that products should be repaired, not thrown away. After the twelve month warranty has expired on Red Wing boots, the company offers free oiling, free laces, low-cost replacement insoles, and low-cost hardware repairs. The cost of operating this shoe repair service would fall into which function in the value chain?

c. Ford Motor Company's Rouge Center in Dearborn Michigan has a "living roof" on the Dearborn Truck Plant final assembly building. It is the largest living roof in the world, encompassing 10.4 acres. The living roof is made from living grass and its primary purpose is to collect and filter rainfall as part of a natural storm water management system. It also provides cooler surroundings and offers a longer roof life than a traditional roof. The cost of promoting the company's products and its sustainability efforts would fall into which function in the value chain?

d. Nike Products, an athletic apparel and shoe manufacturer, developed the Environmental Apparel Design Tool over a period of seven years. The Environmental Apparel Design Tools helps apparel and shoe designers to make real-time choices that decrease the environmental impact of their work. With the tool, the designers can see the potential waste resulting from their design and the amount of environmentally preferred materials used by their design. When designers make changes to the preliminary product design, they can see instantly the effect of those changes on waste and input usage. The $6 million investment used to develop the Environmental Apparel Design Tool would fall into which function in the value chain?

e. Nyloboard® produces decking materials made from recycled carpet. The cost of the research into how to create Nyloboard® from recycled carpet would fall into which function in the value chain?

f. Late in 2010, the U.S. National Park Service approved the use of an erosion control system from GeoHay® for a roadway construction project in the Great Smoky Mountains National Park. GeoHay® erosion and sediment control products are produced from recycled carpet fibers. The cost of these erosion and sediment control products would fall into which function in the value chain?

E2-36B Classify costs as direct or indirect *(Learning Objective 3)*

Classify each of the following costs as a *direct cost* or an *indirect cost* assuming the cost object is the new car sales department of a local car dealership.

a. Salary of the manager of the dealership
b. Sales commissions
c. Cost of new cars
d. Cost of car detailing
e. Salary of the receptionist for the dealership
f. Depreciation on the building
g. Advertising in the local newspaper
h. Salary of the sales manager for new car sales
i. Cost of drinks provided in the reception area
j. Cost of gasoline used at the dealership
k. Utilities expense for the building
l. New car brochures provided to prospective buyers

E2-37B Define cost terms *(Learning Objectives 3 & 4)*

Complete the following statements with one of the terms listed here. You may use a term more than once, and some terms may not be used at all.

Assigned	Indirect costs	Cost objects
Assets	Fringe benefits	Total costs
Cost of goods sold	Direct costs	Prime costs
Period costs	Inventoriable product costs	Conversion costs

a. Material and labor costs that can be traced directly to particular units manufactured are _____ if the manufactured product is the _____.
b. _____ are outlays that can be identified with a specific product or department.
c. _____ include the direct costs attributable to the production of the goods.
d. In manufacturing, when goods are sold, costs are transferred from the finished goods inventory account to _____.
e. Allocation is used to _____ the _____ to a product or department.
f. _____ include direct material, direct labor, and manufacturing overhead costs.
g. _____ are the combination of direct materials and direct labor.
h. _____ are expenditures that are not directly associated with the production of a product, such as advertising costs and general administrative costs.
i. Nearly anything of interest to a decision maker can be a _____, including products, stores, and departments.
j. Raw materials inventory, work in process inventory, and finished goods inventory are considered to be _____ on the balance sheet.
k. _____ are those outlays that can be traced to a particular cost object.
l. _____ are the cost of compensation provided employees besides the employees' salaries and wages.

E2-38B Classify and calculate a manufacturer's costs *(Learning Objectives 3 & 4)*

An airline manufacturer incurred the following costs last month (in thousands of dollars).

a. Depreciation on forklifts	$ 80
b. Property tax on corporate marketing offices	$ 35
c. Cost of warranty repairs	$ 235
d. Factory janitors' wages	$ 10
e. Cost of designing new plant layout	$ 185
f. Machine operators' health insurance	$ 70
g. Airplane seats	$ 270
h. Depreciation on administrative offices	$ 50
i. Assembly workers' wages	$ 690
j. Plant utilities	$ 140
k. Production supervisors' salaries	$ 110
l. Jet engines	$1,300
m. Machine lubricants	$ 15

Requirements

1. Assuming the cost object is an airplane, classify each cost as one of the following: direct material (DM), direct labor (DL), indirect labor (IL), indirect materials (IM), other manufacturing overhead (other MOH), or period cost. What is the total for each type of cost?
2. Calculate total manufacturing overhead costs.
3. Calculate total inventoriable product costs.
4. Calculate total prime costs.
5. Calculate total conversion costs.
6. Calculate total period costs.

E2-39B Prepare the current assets section of the balance sheet *(Learning Objective 5)*

Consider the following selected amounts and account balances of Saints:

Prepaid expenses	$ 5,900	Cost of goods sold	$106,000
Marketing expense	$29,000	Direct labor	$ 51,000
Work in process inventory	$40,000	Direct materials used	$ 23,100
Manufacturing overhead	$25,000	Accounts receivable	$ 81,000
Finished goods inventory	$61,000	Cash	$ 14,700
Raw materials inventory	$ 9,600	Cost of goods manufactured	$ 91,000

Requirement

Show how Saints reports current assets on the balance sheet. Not all data are used. Is this company a service company, a merchandiser, or a manufacturer? How do you know?

E2-40B Prepare a retailer's income statement *(Learning Objective 5)*

Roderick Thompson is the sole proprietor of Pretty Pets, a business specializing in the sale of high-end pet gifts and accessories. Pretty Pets' sales totaled $997,000 during the most recent year. During the year, the company spent $56,500 on expenses relating to website maintenance, $33,200 on marketing, and $27,500 on wrapping, boxing, and shipping the goods to customers. Pretty Pets also spent $635,000 on inventory purchases and an additional $19,500 on freight-in charges. The company started the year with $17,350 of inventory on hand, and ended the year with $13,100 of inventory. Prepare Pretty Pets' income statement for the most recent year.

E2-41B Compute direct materials used and cost of goods manufactured
(Learning Objective 5)

Fitzcarron Industries is calculating its Cost of Goods Manufactured at year-end. The company's accounting records show the following: The Raw Materials Inventory account had a beginning balance of $17,000 and an ending balance of $18,000. During the year, the company purchased $58,000 of direct materials. Direct labor for the year totaled $128,000 while manufacturing overhead amounted to $161,000. The Work in Process Inventory account had a beginning balance of $29,000 and an ending balance of $20,000. Compute the Cost of Goods Manufactured for the year. (*Hint:* The first step is to calculate the direct materials used during the year.)

E2-42B Compute cost of goods manufactured and cost of goods sold
(Learning Objective 5)

Compute the cost of goods manufactured and cost of goods sold for Crystal Bay Company for the most recent year using the amounts described next. Assume that raw materials inventory contains only direct materials.

	Beginning of Year	End of Year		End of Year
Raw materials inventory	$26,000	$33,000	Insurance on plant	$10,000
Work in process inventory	$35,000	$31,000	Depreciation—plant building and equipment	$13,200
Finished goods inventory	$14,000	$29,000	Repairs and maintenance—plant	$ 4,200
Purchases of direct materials		$73,000	Marketing expenses	$76,000
Direct labor		$86,000	General and administrative expenses	$27,500
Indirect labor		$40,000		

E2-43B Continues E2-42B: Prepare income statement *(Learning Objective 5)*

Prepare the income statement for Crystal Bay Company using the data in E2-42B for the most recent year. Assume that the company sold 36,000 units of its product at a price of $15 each during the year.

E2-44B Work backward to find missing amounts *(Learning Objective 5)*

LZ Electronics manufactures and sells smartphones. Unfortunately, the company recently suffered serious fire damage at its home office. As a result, the accounting records for October were partially destroyed and completely jumbled. LZ has hired you to help figure out the missing pieces of the accounting puzzle. Assume that LZ Electronics raw materials inventory contains only direct materials.

Work in process inventory, October 31	$ 1,000
Finished goods inventory, October 1	$ 4,900
Direct labor in October	$ 3,400
Purchases of direct materials in October	$ 9,600
Work in process inventory, October 1	0
Revenues in October	$27,900
Gross profit in October	$12,400
Direct materials used in October	$ 8,500
Raw materials inventory, October 31	$ 3,500
Manufacturing overhead in October	$ 6,300

Requirement

Find the following amounts:
a. Cost of goods sold in October
b. Beginning raw materials inventory
c. Ending finished goods inventory

E2-45B Determine whether information is relevant *(Learning Objective 6)*

Classify each of the following costs as relevant or irrelevant to the decision at hand and briefly explain your reason.

a. Fuel economy when purchasing new trucks for the delivery fleet.

b. Real estate property tax rates when selecting the location for a new order processing center.

c. The purchase price of the old computer when replacing it with a new computer with improved features.

d. The average cost of vehicle operation when purchasing a new delivery van.

e. The original cost of the current stove when selecting a new, more efficient stove for a restaurant.

f. The fair market value (trade-in value) of the existing forklift when deciding whether to replace it with a new, more efficient model.

g. The cost of land when determining where to build a new call center.

h. The cost of renovations when deciding whether to build a new office building or to renovate the existing office building.

i. The cost of production when determining whether to continue to manufacture the screen for a smartphone or to purchase it from an outside supplier.

j. Local tax incentives when selecting the location of a new office complex for a company's headquarters.

E2-46B Describe other cost terms *(Learning Objectives 6 & 7)*

Complete the following statements with one of the terms listed here. You may use a term more than once, and some terms may not be used at all.

Variable costs	Sunk costs	Differential costs
Marginal cost	Uncontrollable costs	Average cost
Fixed costs	Irrelevant costs	Controllable costs

a. Costs that change in total in direct proportion to changes in volume are called _____.

b. Costs and benefits that are the same for all alternatives considered and can be ignored are called _____.

c. _____ are irrelevant costs that have already been incurred and cannot be changed or recovered.

d. The _____ at any production level is the cost required to produce the next unit.

e. Research and development and advertising costs are considered to be _____.

f. _____ are costs that stay constant in total over the relevant range despite changes in volume.

g. _____ is equal to the total costs of production divided by the number of units produced.

h. _____ are the differences in costs between two alternative courses of action.

E2-47B Classify costs as fixed or variable *(Learning Objective 7)*

Classify each of the following costs as fixed or variable:

a. Total wages paid to the hourly production workers

b. Property taxes at a manufacturer

c. Freight costs at Ford Motor Company

d. Cost of fuel for the delivery department of a home improvement store

e. Packaging costs for Crate and Barrel's web sales operations

f. Annual salary for a manager of a fast-food restaurant

g. Shipping costs for Amazon.com

h. Building lease cost for a hair care salon

i. Coffee costs for a coffee shop

j.   Monthly straight-line depreciation costs for a factory
k.   Monthly travel expenses for sales people
l.   Property insurance costs on a warehouse
m. Cost of postage for the bills mailed by an electric company
n.   Cost of produce at a grocery store
o.   Monthly lawn maintenance fee for a tenant in an office building

E2-48B Compute total and average costs *(Learning Objective 7)*

Kotlan Soda spends $1 on direct materials, direct labor, and variable manufacturing overhead for every unit (12-pack of soda) it produces. Fixed manufacturing overhead costs $4 million per year. The plant, which is currently operating at only 70% of capacity, produced 20 million units this year. Management plans to operate closer to full capacity next year, producing 25 million units. Management doesn't anticipate any changes in the prices it pays for materials, labor, or manufacturing overhead.

Requirements

1. What is the current total product cost (for the 20 million units), including fixed and variable costs?
2. What is the current average product cost per unit?
3. What is the current fixed cost per unit?
4. What is the forecasted total product cost next year (for the 25 million units)?
5. What is the forecasted average product cost next year?
6. What is the forecasted fixed cost per unit?
7. Why does the average product cost decrease as production increases?

PROBLEMS Group A

P2-49A Classify costs along the value chain *(Learning Objectives 2 & 4)*

Fizz Cola produces a lemon-lime soda. The production process starts with workers mixing the lemon syrup and lime flavors in a secret recipe. The company enhances the combined syrup with caffeine. Finally, the company dilutes the mixture with carbonated water. Fizz Cola incurs the following costs (in thousands):

Lime flavoring	$ 980
Production costs of "cents-off" store coupons for customers	$ 370
Delivery truck drivers' wages	$ 265
Bottles	$ 1,140
Sales commissions	$ 350
Plant janitors' wages	$ 1,000
Wages of workers who mix syrup	$ 7,700
Customer hotline	$ 180
Depreciation on delivery trucks	$ 300
Freight-in on materials	$ 1,500
Plant utilities	$ 850
Depreciation on plant and equipment	$ 3,100
Payment for new recipe	$ 1,140
Salt	$ 25
Replace products with expired dates upon customer complaint	$ 35
Rearranging plant layout	$ 1,400
Lemon syrup	$18,000

Requirements

1. Classify each of the listed costs according to its category in the value chain (R&D, Design, Production, Marketing, Distribution, or Customer Service.)
2. Further breakdown production costs into three subcategories: direct materials, direct labor, or manufacturing overhead.
3. Compute the total costs for each value chain category.
4. How much are the total inventoriable product costs?
5. Suppose the managers of the R&D and design functions receive year-end bonuses based on meeting their unit's target cost reductions. What are they likely to do? How might this affect costs incurred in other elements of the value chain?

P2-50A Prepare income statements *(Learning Objective 5)*

Part One: In 2010, Pam Baker opened Pam's Posies, a small retail shop selling floral arrangements. On December 31, 2011, her accounting records show the following:

Sales revenue	$55,000
Utilities for shop	$ 1,100
Inventory on December 31, 2011	$ 9,800
Inventory on January 1, 2011	$12,200
Rent for shop	$ 3,200
Sales commissions	$ 4,300
Purchases of merchandise	$37,000

Requirement

Prepare an income statement for Pam's Posies, a merchandiser, for the year ended December 31, 2011.

Part Two: Pam's Posies was so successful that Pam decided to manufacture her own brand of floral supplies: Floral Manufacturing. At the end of December 2012, her accounting records show the following:

Utilities for plant	$ 4,200
Delivery expense	$ 3,000
Sales salaries expense	$ 4,500
Plant janitorial services	$ 1,050
Work in process inventory, December 31, 2012	$ 5,000
Finished goods inventory, December 31, 2011	0
Finished goods inventory, December 31, 2012	$ 5,500
Sales revenue	$109,000
Customer service hotline expense	$ 1,600
Direct labor	$ 24,000
Direct material purchases	$ 35,000
Rent on manufacturing plant	$ 8,200
Raw materials inventory, December 31, 2011	$ 18,000
Raw materials inventory, December 31, 2012	$ 9,500
Work in process inventory, December 31, 2011	0

Requirements

1. Calculate the cost of goods manufactured for Floral Manufacturing for the year ended December 31, 2012.
2. Prepare an income statement for Floral Manufacturing for the year ended December 31, 2012.

3. How does the format of the income statement for Floral Manufacturing differ from the income statement of Pam's Posies?

Part Three: Show the ending inventories that would appear on these balance sheets:

1. Pam's Posies at December 31, 2011
2. Floral Manufacturing at December 31, 2012

P2-51A Fill in missing amounts (Learning Objective 5)

Certain item descriptions and amounts are missing from the monthly calculation of cost of goods manufactured and the income statement of Elly Manufacturing. Fill in the missing items.

Calculation of Cost of Goods Manufactured

Beginning _____				$ 21,000
Add: Direct _____:				
Beginning raw materials inventory	$ X			
Purchases of direct materials	53,000			
_____	77,000			
Ending raw materials inventory	(23,000)			
Direct _____		$ X		
Direct _____		X		
Manufacturing overhead			45,000	
Total _____ costs _____				169,000
Total _____ costs _____				X
Less: Ending _____				(27,000)
_____				$ X

ELLY MANUFACTURING COMPANY

_____ June 30

Sales revenue		$ X
Cost of goods sold:		
Beginning _____	$116,000	
_____	X	
Cost of goods _____	X	
Ending _____	X	
Cost of goods sold		210,000
Gross profit		300,000
_____ expenses:		
Marketing expense	$ 94,000	
Administrative expense	X	154,000
Operating income		$ X

P2-52A Identify relevant information (Learning Objective 6)

You receive two job offers in the same big city. The first job is close to your parents' house, and they have offered to let you live at home for a year so you won't have to incur expenses for housing, food, or cable and internet. This job pays $44,000 per year. The second job is far from your parents' house, so you'll have to rent an apartment with parking ($12,000 per year), buy your own food ($2,500 per year), and pay for your own cable and internet ($650 per year). This job pays $49,000 per year. You still plan to do laundry at your parents' house once a week if you live in the city, and you plan to go into the city once a week to visit with friends if you live at home. Thus, the cost of operating your car will be about the same either way. In addition, your parents refuse to pay for your cell phone service ($760 per year), and you can't function without it.

Requirements

1. Based on this information alone, what is the net difference between the two alternatives (salary, net of relevant costs)?
2. What information is irrelevant? Why?
3. What qualitative information is relevant to your decision?
4. Assume that you really want to take Job #2, but you also want to live at home to cut costs. What new quantitative and qualitative information will you need to incorporate into your decision?

P2-53A Calculate the total and average costs (Learning Objective 7)

The owner of Riverdale Restaurant is disappointed because the restaurant has been averaging 5,000 pizza sales per month, but the restaurant and wait staff can make and serve 10,000 pizzas per month. The variable cost (for example, ingredients) of each pizza is $1.20. Monthly fixed costs (for example, depreciation, property taxes, business license, and manager's salary) are $5,000 per month. The owner wants cost information about different volumes so that some operating decisions can be made.

Requirements

1. Fill in the following chart to provide the owner with the cost information. Then use the completed chart to help you answer the remaining questions.

Monthly pizza volume	2,500	5,000	10,000
Total fixed costs	$	$	$
Total variable costs	_____	_____	_____
Total costs	_____	_____	_____
Fixed cost per pizza	$	$	$
Variable cost per pizza	_____	_____	_____
Average cost per pizza	_____	_____	_____
Selling price per pizza	$ 5.50	$ 5.50	$ 5.50
Average profit per pizza	_____	_____	_____

2. From a cost standpoint, why do companies such as Riverdale Restaurant want to operate near or at full capacity?
3. The owner has been considering ways to increase the sales volume. The owner thinks that 10,000 pizzas could be sold per month by cutting the selling price per pizza from $5.50 to $5.00. How much extra profit (above the current level) would be generated if the selling price were to be decreased? (Hint: Find the restaurant's current monthly profit and compare it to the restaurant's projected monthly profit at the new sales price and volume.)

PROBLEMS Group B

P2-54B Classify costs along the value chain (Learning Objectives 2 & 4)

Buzz Cola produces a lemon-lime soda. The production process starts with workers mixing the lemon syrup and lime flavors in a secret recipe. The company enhances the combined syrup with caffeine. Finally, the company dilutes the mixture with carbonated water. Buzz Cola incurs the following costs (in thousands):

Lime flavoring...	$ 920
Production costs of "cents-off" store coupons for customers...........................	$ 530
Delivery truck drivers' wages	$ 295
Bottles	$ 1,190
Sales commissions..	$ 325
Plant janitors' wages	$ 1,000
Wages of workers who mix syrup	$ 7,700
Customer hotline..	$ 190
Depreciation on delivery trucks	$ 225
Freight-in on materials	$ 1,300
Plant utilities..	$ 650
Depreciation on plant and equipment...	$ 3,200
Payment for new recipe	$ 1,190
Salt..	$ 25
Replace products with expired dates upon customer complaint	$ 40
Rearranging plant layout..	$ 1,700
Lemon syrup...	$18,000

Requirements

1. Classify each of the listed costs according to its category in the value chain, (R&D, Design, Production, Marketing, Distribution, or Customer Service.)

		Production					
R&D	Design of Products or Processes	Direct Materials	Direct Labor	Manufacturing Overhead	Marketing	Distribution	Customer Service

2. Further breakdown production costs into three subcategories: Direct Materials, Direct Labor, or Manufacturing Overhead.
3. Compute the total costs for each value chain category.
4. How much are the total inventoriable product costs?
5. Suppose the managers of the R&D and design functions receive year-end bonuses based on meeting their unit's target cost reductions. What are they likely to do? How might this affect costs incurred in other elements of the value chain?

P2-55B Prepare income statements *(Learning Objective 5)*

Part One: In 2011, Lindsey Conway opened Lindsey's Blooms, a small shop selling floral arrangements. On December 31, 2011, her accounting records show the following:

Inventory on December 31, 2011	$ 9,300
Inventory on January 1, 2011	$12,000
Sales revenue	$58,000
Utilities for shop	$ 1,600
Rent for shop	$ 3,800
Sales commissions	$ 4,500
Purchases of merchandise	$38,000

Requirement

Prepare an income statement for Lindsey's Blooms, a merchandiser, for the year ended December 31, 2011.

Part Two: Lindsey's Blooms succeeded so well that Lindsey decided to manufacture her own brand of floral supplies: Floral Manufacturing. At the end of December 2012, her accounting records show the following:

Work in process inventory, December 31, 2012	$ 1,000
Finished goods inventory, December 31, 2011	0
Finished goods inventory, December 31, 2012	$ 5,000
Sales revenue	$101,000
Customer service hotline expense	$ 1,400
Utilities for plant	$ 4,100
Delivery expense	$ 3,000
Sales salaries expense	$ 4,200
Plant janitorial services	$ 1,350
Direct labor	$ 22,000
Direct material purchases	$ 39,000
Rent on manufacturing plant	$ 8,800
Raw materials inventory, December 31, 2011	$ 10,000
Raw materials inventory, December 31, 2012	$ 9,500
Work in process inventory, December 31, 2011	0

Requirements

1. Calculate the cost of goods manufactured for Floral Manufacturing for the year ended December 31, 2012.
2. Prepare an income statement for Floral Manufacturing for the year ended December 31, 2012.
3. How does the format of the income statement for Floral Manufacturing differ from the income statement of Lindsey's Blooms?

Part Three: Show the ending inventories that would appear on these balance sheets:

1. Lindsey's Blooms at December 31, 2011.
2. Floral Manufacturing at December 31, 2012.

P2-56B Fill in missing amounts *(Learning Objective 5)*

Certain item descriptions and amounts are missing from the monthly calculation of cost of goods manufactured and the income statement of Tioga Manufacturing Company. Fill in the missing items.

Calculation of the Cost of Goods Manufactured

Beginning _____			$ 20,000
Add: Direct _____:			
Beginning raw materials inventory	$ X		
Purchases of direct materials	58,000		
_____	83,000		
Ending raw materials inventory	(29,000)		
Direct _____		$ X	
Direct _____		X	
Manufacturing overhead		47,000	
Total _____ costs _____			$171,000
Total _____ costs _____			X
Less: Ending _____			(23,000)
_____			$ X

Tioga Manufacturing Company
_____ June 30

Sales revenue		$ X
Cost of goods sold:		
Beginning _____	$111,000	
_____	X	
Cost of goods _____	X	
Ending _____	X	
Cost of goods sold		216,000
Gross profit		264,000
_____ expenses:		
Marketing expense	$100,000	
Administrative expense	X	167,000
Operating income		$ X

P2-57B Identify relevant information *(Learning Objective 6)*

You receive two job offers in the same big city. The first job is close to your parents' house, and they have offered to let you live at home for a year so you won't have to incur expenses for housing, food, or cable and internet. This job pays $41,000 per year. The second job is far away from your parents' house, so you'll have to rent an apartment with parking ($12,000 per year), buy your own food ($2,500 per year), and pay for your own cable and internet ($800 per year). This job pays $46,000 per year. You still plan to do laundry at your parents' house once a week if you live in the city and plan to go into the city once a week to visit with friends if you live at home. Thus, the cost of operating your car will be about the same either way. Additionally, your parents refuse to pay for your cell phone service ($750 per year), and you can't function without it.

Requirements

1. Based on this information alone, what is the net difference between the two alternatives (salary, net of relevant costs)?

2. What information is irrelevant? Why?

3. What qualitative information is relevant to your decision?

4. Assume you really want to take Job #2, but you also want to live at home to cut costs. What new quantitative and qualitative information will you need to incorporate in your decision?

P2-58B Calculate the total and average costs (Learning Objective 7)

The owner of Staten Island Restaurant is disappointed because the restaurant has been averaging 6,000 pizza sales per month but the restaurant and wait staff can make and serve 7,500 pizzas per month. The variable cost (for example, ingredients) of each pizza is $1.20. Monthly fixed costs (for example, depreciation, property taxes, business license, manager's salary) are $9,000 per month. The owner wants cost information about different volumes so that some operating decisions can be made.

Requirements

1. Fill in the chart to provide the owner with the cost information. Then use the completed chart to help you answer the remaining questions.

Monthly pizza volume	4,500		6,000		7,500	
Total fixed costs						
Total variable costs						
Total costs						
Fixed cost per pizza						
Variable cost per pizza						
Average cost per pizza						
Selling price per pizza	$	6.25	$	6.25	$	6.25
Average profit per pizza						

2. From a cost standpoint, why do companies such as Staten Island Restaurant want to operate near or at full capacity?

3. The owner has been considering ways to increase the sales volume. It is believed that 7,500 pizzas could be sold per month by cutting the selling price from $6.25 per pizza to $5.75. How much extra profit (above the current level) would be generated if the selling price were to be decreased? (Hint: Find the restaurant's current monthly profit and compare it to the restaurant's projected monthly profit at the new sales price and volume.)

CRITICAL THINKING

Discussion & Analysis

A2-59 Discussion Questions

1. Briefly describe a service company, a merchandising company, and a manufacturing company. Give an example of each type of company, but do not use the same examples as given in the chapter.

2. How do service, merchandising, and manufacturing companies differ from each other? How are service, merchandising, and manufacturing companies similar to each other? List as many similarities and differences as you can identify.

3. What is the value chain? What are the six types of business activities found in the value chain? Which type(s) of business activities in the value chain generate costs that go directly to the income statement once incurred? What type(s) of business activities in the value chain generate costs that flow into inventory on the balance sheet?

4. Compare direct costs to indirect costs. Give an example of a cost at a company that could be a direct cost at one level of the organization but would be considered an indirect cost at a different level of that organization. Explain why this same cost could be both direct and indirect (at different levels).

5. What is meant by the term "inventoriable product costs"? What is meant by the term "period costs"? Why does it matter whether a cost is an inventoriable product cost or a period cost?

6. Compare inventoriable product costs to period costs. Using a product of your choice, give examples of inventoriable product costs and period costs. Explain why you categorized your costs as you did.

7. Describe how the income statement of a merchandising company differs from the income statement of a manufacturing company. Also comment on how the income statement from a merchandising company is similar to the income statement of a manufacturing company.

8. How are the cost of goods manufactured, the cost of goods sold, the income statement, and the balance sheet related for a manufacturing company? What specific items flow from one statement or schedule to the next? Describe the flow of costs between the cost of goods manufactured, the cost of goods sold, the income statement, and the balance sheet for a manufacturing company.

9. What makes a cost relevant or irrelevant when making a decision? Suppose a company is evaluating whether to use its warehouse for storage of its own inventory or whether to rent it out to a local theater group for housing props. Describe what information might be relevant when making that decision.

10. Explain why "differential cost" and "variable cost" do *not* have the same meaning. Give an example of a situation in which there is a cost that is a differential cost but *not* a variable cost.

11. Greenwashing, the practice of overstating a company's commitment to sustainability, has been in the news over the past few years. Perform an internet search of the term "greenwashing." What examples of greenwashing can you find?

12. In the chapter, Ricoh was mentioned as a company that has designed its copiers so that at the end of the copier's life, Ricoh will collect and dismantle the product for usable parts, shred the metal casing, and use the parts and shredded material to build new copiers. This product design can be called "cradle to cradle" design. Are there any other products you are aware of that have a "cradle to cradle" design? Perform a search of the internet for "cradle to cradle design" or a related term if you need ideas.

Application & Analysis

A2-60 Costs in the Value Chain at a Real Company and Cost Objects

Choose a company with which you are familiar that manufactures a product. In this activity, you will be making reasonable assumptions about the activities involved in the value chain for this product; companies do not typically publish information about their value chain.

Basic Discussion Questions

1. Describe the product that is being produced and the company that produces it.

2. Describe the six value chain business activities that this product would pass through from its inception to its ultimate delivery to the customer.

3. List at least three costs that would be incurred in each of the six business activities in the value chain.

4. Classify each cost you identified in the value chain as either being an inventoriable product cost or a period cost. Explain your justification.

5. A cost object can be anything for which managers want a separate measurement of cost. List three different potential cost objects *other* than the product itself for the company you have selected.

6. List a direct cost and an indirect cost for each of the three different cost objects in question 5. Explain why each cost would be direct or indirect.

Decision Case

A2-61 Determine ending inventory balances (*Learning Objective 5*)

PowerBox designs and manufactures switches used in telecommunications. Serious flooding throughout North Carolina affected PowerBox's facilities. Inventory was completely ruined, and the company's computer system, including all accounting records, was destroyed.

Before the disaster recovery specialists clean the buildings, Annette Plum, the company controller, is anxious to salvage whatever records she can to support an insurance claim for the destroyed inventory. She is standing in what is left of the Accounting Department with Paul Lopez, the cost accountant.

"I didn't know mud could smell so bad," Paul says. "What should I be looking for?"

"Don't worry about beginning inventory numbers," responds Annette. "We'll get them from last year's annual report. We need first-quarter cost data."

"I was working on the first-quarter results just before the storm hit," Paul says. "Look, my report's still in my desk drawer. But all I can make out is that for the first quarter, material purchases were $476,000 and that direct labor, manufacturing overhead (other than indirect materials), and total manufacturing costs to account for were $505,000; $245,000; and $1,425,000, respectively. Wait, and cost of goods available for sale was $1,340,000."

"Great," says Annette. "I remember that sales for the period were approximately $1.7 million. Given our gross profit of 30%, that's all you should need."

Paul is not sure about that, but decides to see what he can do with this information. The beginning inventory numbers are as follows:

- Raw materials, $113,000
- Work in process, $229,000
- Finished goods, $154,000

He remembers a schedule he learned in college that may help him get started.

Requirements

1. Use exhibits in the chapter to determine the ending inventories of raw materials, work in process, and finished goods.

2. Draft an insurance claim letter for the controller, seeking reimbursement for the flood damage to inventory. PowerBox's insurance representative is Gary Streer, at Industrial Insurance, 1122 Main Street, Hartford, CT 06268. The policy number is #3454340-23. PowerBox's address is 5 Research Triangle Way, Raleigh, NC 27698.

CMA Questions

A2-62

Roberta Johnson is the manager of Sleep-Well Inn, one of a chain of motels located throughout the U.S. An example of an operating cost at Sleep-Well that is both direct and fixed is

a. Johnson's salary.

b. water.

c. toilet tissue.

d. advertising for the Sleep-Well Inn chain.   *(CMA Adapted)*

A2-63

The Profit and Loss Statement of Madengrad Mining, Inc., includes the following information for the current fiscal year:

Sales	$ 160,000
Gross profit	48,000
Year-end finished good inventory	58,300
Opening finished good inventory	60,190

The cost of goods manufactured by Madengrad for the current fiscal year is

a. $46,110.

b. $49,890.

c. $110,110.

d. $113,890.   *(CMA Adapted)*

A2-64

The schedule of cost of goods manufactured of Gruber Fittings, Inc., shows the following balances for its fiscal year-end:

Direct manufacturing labor	$ 280,000
Manufacturing overhead	375,000
Ending work in process inventory	230,000
Raw materials used in production	450,000
Cost of goods manufactured	1,125,000

The value of the work in process inventory at the beginning of the fiscal year was

a. $625,000.

b. $250,000.

c. $210,000.

d. $20,000.   *(CMA Adapted)*

The Master Budget

Learning Objectives

- **1** Describe how and why managers use budgets
- **2** Prepare the operating budgets
- **3** Prepare the financial budgets
- **4** Prepare budgets for a merchandiser

From Chapter 9 of *Managerial Accounting*, Third Edition. Karen W. Braun, Wendy M. Tietz.
Copyright © 2013 by Pearson Education, Inc. All rights reserved.

Campbell Soup Company's

goal is "to win with integrity in the workplace, the marketplace, and the community as the world's most extraordinary food company." How will the company attain this goal? First, it identifies key strategies. Some of Campbell's key strategies include expanding its icon brands (such as Campbell's Soup, V8 Juice, and Pepperidge Farms Snacks), increasing margins through improving productivity, and advancing its commitment to organizational excellence and social responsibility. These strategies require detailed plans be put into place. The company's managers express these plans, in financial terms, through budgets. The

© Profimedia International s.r.o. / Alamy

Sources: Campbell Soup Company, 2010 Annual Report www.gallup.com/consulting/25312/gallup-great-workplace-award.aspx

company's budgets reflect and support each of these key strategies. For example, management has budgeted millions of dollars toward researching new products in order to expand its iconic brands. Management has also budgeted millions of dollars towards new, more productive manufacturing equipment and an ERP information system that should improve profit margins and increase organizational excellence. Is the company on track for reaching its goal of winning in the workplace, marketplace and community? In 2010, Campbell became a four-time winner of Gallup's "Great Workplace Award," for creating an extraordinary workplace environment for its employees. This prestigious award is only given to 25 companies a year, worldwide. For the past five years, Campbell's total shareowner return has exceeded the Standard & Poor's 500 Stock Index and Standard & Poor's Packaged Foods Index. And in 2010, Campbell ranked as one of the 10 most socially responsible U.S. companies and 100 Best Corporate Citizens. The company's budget is a vital tool in making it all happen.

Budgeting is perhaps the most widely used management accounting tool employed by companies, organizations, and governments throughout the world. Even individuals, such as you and I, can benefit from creating a personal budget that shows how we plan to use our resources and to make sure our spending does not get out of control. For example, if your goal is to buy a car directly after college or a house five years after college, then you need to plan for those goals. Your budget should include saving enough money each year to accumulate the down payments you'll need. By carefully planning how you'll spend and save your resources, you'll have a better chance of reaching your goals.

1 Describe how and why managers use budgets

How and Why do Managers Use Budgets?

As you'll see throughout this chapter, management uses budgeting to express its plans and to assess how well it's reaching its goals. In this section, we'll take a closer look at how budgets are used and developed, the benefits of budgeting, and the particular budgets that are prepared as part of the company's master budget.

How are Budgets Used?

All companies and organizations use budgets for the same reasons you would in your personal life—to plan for the future and control the revenues and expenses related to those plans. Exhibit 9-1 shows how managers use budgets in fulfilling their major responsibilities of planning, directing, and controlling operations. Budgeting is an on-going cycle: Company strategies lead to detailed plans, which in turn lead to actions. Results are then compared to the budget to provide managers feedback. This feedback allows managers to take corrective actions and if necessary, revise strategies, which starts the cycle over.

EXHIBIT 9-1 Managers Use Budgets to Plan and Control Business Activities

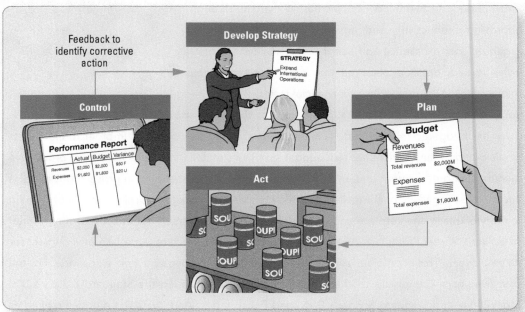

How are Budgets Developed?

A few years ago Campbell was not performing up to expectations. The first step toward getting the company back on track was management's decision to create long-term strategic goals. **Strategic planning** involves setting long-term goals that may extend 5–10 years into the future. Long-term, loosely-detailed budgets are often created to reflect expectations for these long-term goals.

Once the goals are set, management designs key strategies for attaining the goals. These strategies, such as Campbell's expansion of its iconic brands and improvements to production efficiency, are then put into place through the use of shorter-term budgets for an entire fiscal year. However, even a yearly budget is not detailed enough to guide many management decisions. For example, Campbell's soup production managers must know what month of the year they expect to receive and start using new production machinery. They must also decide how much of each raw material (vegetables, chicken, and so forth) to purchase each month to meet production requirements for both existing and new products. In turn, this will affect monthly cash needs. Therefore, companies usually prepare a budget for every month of the fiscal year.

Many companies set aside time during the last two quarters of the fiscal year to create their budget for the upcoming fiscal year. Other companies prepare rolling, or continuous budgets. A **rolling budget** is a budget that is continuously updated so that the next 12 months of operations are always budgeted. For example, as soon as January is over, the next January is added to the budget. The benefit of a rolling budget is that managers always have a budget for the next 12 months.

Who is Involved in the Budgeting Process?

Rather than using a "top-down" approach in which top management determines the budget, most companies use some degree of participative budgeting. As the term implies, **participative budgeting** involves the participation of many levels of management. Participative budgeting is beneficial for the following reasons:

- Lower level managers are closer to the action, and should have a more detailed knowledge for creating realistic budgets.
- Managers are more likely to accept, and be motivated by budgets they helped to create.

However, participative budgeting also has disadvantages:

- The budget process can become much more complex and time consuming as more people participate in the process.
- Managers may intentionally build **slack** into the budget for their area of operation by overbudgeting expenses or underbudgeting revenue. Why would they do this? They would do so for three possible reasons: 1) because of uncertainty about the future, 2) to make their performance look better when actual results are compared against budgeted amounts at the end of the period, and 3) to have the resources they need in the event of budget cuts.

Even with participative budgeting, someone must still have the "final say" on the budget. Often, companies use a **budget committee** to review the submitted budgets, remove unwarranted slack, and revise and approve the final budget. The budget committee often includes upper management, such as the CEO and CFO, as well as managers from every area of the value chain (such as Research and Development, Marketing, Distribution, and so forth). By using a cross-functional budget committee, the final budget is more likely to reflect a comprehensive view of the organization and be accepted by managers than if the budget were prepared by one person or department for the entire organization. The budget committee is often supported by full-time staff personnel devoted to updating and analyzing the budgets.

What is the Starting Point for Developing the Budgets?

Many companies use the prior year's budgeted figures, or actual results, as the *starting point* for creating the budget for the coming year. Of course, those figures will then be modified to reflect

- new products, customers, or geographical areas;
- changes in the marketplace caused by competitors;
- changes in labor contracts, raw material, and fuel costs;
- general inflation;
- and any new strategies.

However, this approach to budgeting may cause year-after-year increases that after time, grow out of control. To prevent perpetual increases in budgeted expenses, many companies intermittently use zero-based budgeting. When a company implements **zero-based budgeting**, all managers begin with a budget of zero and must justify *every dollar* they put in the budget. This budgeting approach is very time-consuming and labor intensive. Therefore, companies only use it from time to time in order to keep their expenses in check.

What are the Benefits of Budgeting?

Exhibit 9-2 summarizes three key benefits of budgeting. Budgeting forces managers to plan, promotes coordination and communication, and provides a benchmark for motivating employees and evaluating actual performance.

EXHIBIT 9-2 Benefits of Budgeting

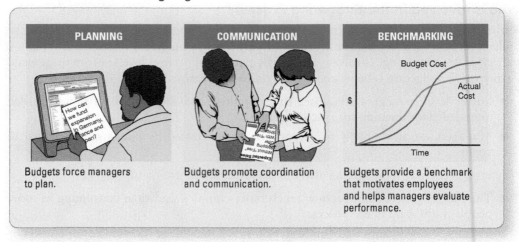

PLANNING	COMMUNICATION	BENCHMARKING
Budgets force managers to plan.	Budgets promote coordination and communication.	Budgets provide a benchmark that motivates employees and helps managers evaluate performance.

Planning

Business managers are extremely busy directing the day-to-day operations of the company. The budgeting process forces managers to spend time planning for the future, rather than only concerning themselves with daily operations. The sooner companies develop a plan and have time to act on the plan, the more likely they will achieve their goals.

Coordination and Communication

The budget coordinates a company's activities. It forces managers to consider relations among operations across the entire value chain. For example, Campbell's decision to expand its iconic brands will first affect the research and development function. However, once new products are developed, the design and production teams will need to focus on how and where the products will be mass produced. The marketing team will need to develop attractive labeling and create a successful advertising campaign. The distribution team may need to alter its current distribution system to accommodate the new products. And customer service will need to be ready to handle any complaints or warranty issues. All areas of the value chain are ultimately affected by management's plans. The budget process helps to communicate and coordinate the effects of the plan.

Benchmarking

Budgets provide a benchmark that motivates employees and helps managers evaluate performance. The budget provides a target that most managers will try to achieve, especially if they participated in the budgeting process and the budget has been set at a realistic level. Budgets should be achievable with effort. Budgets that are too "tight" (too hard to achieve) or too "loose" (too easy to achieve) do not provide managers with much motivation.

Think about exams for a moment. Some professors have a reputation for giving "impossible" exams while others may be known for giving "easy" exams. In either of these cases, students are rarely motivated to put much effort into learning the material because they feel they won't be rewarded for their additional efforts. However, if students feel that a professor's exam can be achieved with effort, they will be more likely to devote themselves to learning the material. In other words, the perceived "fairness" of the exam affects how well the exam motivates students to study. Likewise, if a budget is perceived to be "fair," employees are likely to be motivated by it.

Budgets also provide a benchmark for evaluating performance. At the end of the period, companies use performance reports, such as the one pictured in Exhibit 9-3, to compare "actual" revenues and expenses against "budgeted" revenues and expenses. The **variance**, or difference between actual and budgeted figures, is used to evaluate how well the manager controlled operations and to determine whether the plan needs to be revised. The use of budgets for performance evaluation will be discussed in more detail in Chapters 10 and 11. In this chapter, we'll focus primarily on the use of budgets for planning purposes.

EXHIBIT 9-3 Summary Performance Report

	Actual	Budget	Variance (Actual − Budget)
Sales revenue	$550	$600	$(50)
Less: Total expenses	90	68	(22)
Net income	$460	$532	$(72)

What is the Master Budget?

The **master budget** is the comprehensive planning document for the entire organization. It consists of all of the supporting budgets needed to create the company's budgeted financial statements. Exhibit 9-4 shows all of the components of the master budget for a manufacturer, and the order in which they are usually prepared. The master budgets of service and merchandising firms are less complex, and will be discussed in the final section of the chapter.

EXHIBIT 9-4 Master Budget for a Manufacturing Company

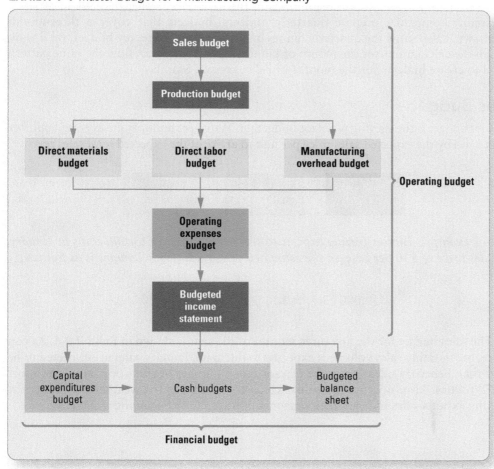

The **operating budgets** are the budgets needed to run the daily operations of the company. The operating budgets culminate in a budgeted income statement. As Exhibit 9-4 shows, the starting point of the operating budgets is the sales budget because it affects most other components of the master budget. After estimating sales, manufacturers prepare the production budget, which determines how many units need to be produced. Once production volume is established, managers prepare the budgets determining the amounts of direct materials, direct labor, and manufacturing overhead that will be needed to meet production. Next, managers prepare the operating expenses budget. After all of these budgets are prepared, management will be able to prepare the budgeted income statement.

As you'll see throughout the chapter, cost behavior will be an important factor in developing many of the operating budgets. Total fixed costs will not change as volume changes within the relevant range. However, total variable costs will fluctuate as volume fluctuates.

The **financial budgets** project the collection and payment of cash, as well as forecast the company's budgeted balance sheet. The capital expenditure budget shows the company's plan for purchasing property, plant, and equipment. The cash budget projects the cash that will be available to run the company's operations and determines whether the company will have extra funds to invest or whether the company will need to borrow cash. Finally, the budgeted balance sheet forecasts the company's position at the end of the budget period.

How are the Operating Budgets Prepared?

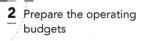

2 Prepare the operating budgets

We will be following the budget process for Tucson Tortilla, a fairly small, independently owned manufacturer of tortilla chips. The company sells its product, by the case, to restaurants, grocery stores, and convenience stores. To keep our example simple, we will just show the budgets for the first three months of the fiscal year, rather than all 12 months. Since many companies prepare quarterly budgets (budgets that cover a three-month period), we'll also show the quarterly figures on each budget. For every budget, we'll walk through the calculations for the month of January. Then we'll show how the same pattern is used to create budgets for the months of February and March.

Sales Budget

The sales budget is the starting place for budgeting. Managers multiply the expected number of unit sales by the expected sales price per unit to arrive at the expected total sales revenue.

For example, Tucson Tortilla expects to sell 30,000 cases of tortilla chips in January, at a sales price of $20 per case, so the estimated sales revenue for January is as follows:

$$30,000 \text{ cases} \times \$20 \text{ per case} = \$600,000$$

The sales budget for the first three months of the year is shown in Exhibit 9-5. As you can see, the monthly sales volume is expected to fluctuate. January sales are expected to be higher than February sales due to the extraordinary number of chips purchased for Super Bowl™ parties. Also, since more tortillas chips are sold when the weather warms up, the company expects sales to begin their seasonal upward climb beginning in March.

As shown in the lower portion of Exhibit 9-5, managers may also choose to indicate the type of sale that will be made. Tucson Tortilla expects 20% of its sales to be cash (COD) sales. Companies often use <u>COD</u> ("collect on delivery"[1]) collection terms if the customer is new, has a poor credit rating, or has not paid on time in the past. Tucson Tortilla will still sell to these customers, but will demand payment immediately when the inventory is delivered.

EXHIBIT 9-5 Sales Budget

Tucson Tortilla Sales Budget For the Quarter Ended March 31				
	Month			
	January	February	March	1st Quarter
Unit sales (cases)	30,000	20,000	25,000	75,000
Unit selling price	× $ 20	× $ 20	× $ 20	× $ 20
Total sales revenue	$600,000	$400,000	$500,000	$1,500,000
Type of Sale:				
Cash sales (20%)	$120,000	$ 80,000	$100,000	$ 300,000
Credit sales (80%)	480,000	320,000	400,000	1,200,000
Total sales revenue	$600,000	$400,000	$500,000	$1,500,000

The remaining 80% of sales will be made on credit. Tucson Tortilla's credit terms are "net 30," meaning the customer has up to 30 days to pay for its purchases. Having this information available on the sales budget will help managers prepare the cash collections budget later.

Production Budget

Once managers have estimated how many units they expect to sell, they can figure out how many units they need to produce. Most manufacturers maintain some ending finished goods inventory, or <u>safety stock</u>, which is inventory kept on hand in case demand is higher than predicted, or the problems in the factory slow production (such as machine break-

> **Why is this important?**
>
> "The **sales budget** is the **basis** for every other budget. If sales are not projected as **accurately** as possible, all other budgets will be **off target**."

down, employees out sick, and so forth). As a result, managers need to factor in the desired level of ending inventory when deciding how much inventory to produce. They do so as follows:

Units Needed for Sales + Desired Ending Inventory = Total Units Needed − Units in Beginning Inventory = Units to Produce

---

[1]In the past, COD meant "cash on delivery." However, as other forms of payment (such as checks, credit cards, and debit cards) have become more common, the word "cash" has been replaced with the word "collect" to incorporate these additional types of payments.

Let's walk through this calculation step-by-step:

■ First, managers figure out how many total units they need. To do this, they add the number of units they plan to sell to the number of units they want on hand at the end of the month. *Let's assume Tucson Tortilla wants to maintain an ending inventory equal to 10% of the next month's expected sales (20,000 cases in February). Thus, the total number of cases needed in January is as follows:*

30,000 cases for January sales + (10% × 20,000) = 32,000 total cases needed

■ Next, managers calculate the amount of inventory they expect to have on hand at the beginning of the month. *Since Tucson Tortilla desires ending inventory to be 10% of the next month's sales, managers expect to have 10% of January's sales on hand on December 31, which becomes the beginning balance on January 1ˢᵗ:*

10% × 30,000 cases = 3,000 cases in beginning inventory on January 1

■ Finally, by subtracting what the company already has in stock at the beginning of the month from the total units needed, the company is able to calculate how many units to produce:

32,000 cases needed − 3,000 cases in beginning inventory = 29,000 cases to produce

Exhibit 9-6 shows Tucson Tortilla's Production Budget for the first three months of the year. As the red arrows show, the ending inventory from one month (January 31) always becomes the beginning inventory for the next month (February 1).

Accounting Simplified

▶

Budgets

If your instructor is using MyAccountingLab, go to the Multimedia Library for a quick video on this topic.

EXHIBIT 9-6 Production Budget

Tucson Tortilla Production Budget For the Quarter Ended March 31				
	Month			
	January	February	March	1st Quarter
Unit sales (from Sales Budget)	30,000	20,000	25,000	75,000
Plus: Desired end inventory	2,000	2,500	3,200*	3,200**
Total needed	32,000	22,500	28,200	78,200
Less: Beginning inventory	(3,000)	(2,000)	(2,500)	(3,000)**
Units to produce	29,000	20,500	25,700	75,200

* April sales are projected to be 32,000 units.
** Since the quarter begins January 1 and ends March 31, the beginning inventory for the quarter is the balance on January 1 and the ending inventory for the quarter is the balance on March 31.

Now that the company knows how many units it plans to produce every month, it can figure out the amount of direct materials, direct labor, and manufacturing overhead that will be needed. As shown in the following sections, the company will create separate budgets for each of these three manufacturing costs. Each budget will be driven by the number of units to be produced each month.

Direct Materials Budget

The format of the direct materials budget is quite similar to the production budget:

Let's walk through the process using January as an example:

■ First, the company figures out the quantity of direct materials (DM) needed for production. *Let's assume Tucson Tortilla's only direct material is masa harina, the special corn flour used to make tortilla chips. Each case of tortilla chips requires 5 pounds of this corn flour. Therefore, the quantity of direct materials needed for January production is as follows:*

> 29,000 cases to be produced × 5 pounds per case = 145,000 pounds

■ Next, the company adds in the desired ending inventory of direct materials. Some amount of direct materials safety stock is usually needed in case suppliers do not deliver all of the direct materials needed on time. *Let's assume that Tucson Tortilla wants to maintain an ending inventory of direct materials equal to 10% of the materials needed for next month's production (102,500 required in February, as shown in Exhibit 9-7):*

> 145,000 pounds + (10% × 102,500) = 155,250 total pounds needed

■ Next, managers determine the direct material inventory they expect to have on hand at the beginning of the month. *Tucson Tortilla expects to have 10% of the materials needed for January's production in stock on December 31, which becomes the opening balance on January 1:*

> 10% × 145,000 pounds = 14,500 pounds in beginning inventory

Finally, by subtracting what the company already has in stock at the beginning of the month from the total quantity needed, the company is able to calculate the quantity of direct materials they need to purchase:

> 155,250 pounds needed − 14,500 pounds in beginning inventory = 140,750 pounds to purchase

■ Finally, the company calculates the expected cost of purchasing those direct materials. *Let's say Tucson Tortilla can buy the masa harina corn flour in bulk for $1.50 per pound.*

> 140,750 pounds × $1.50 = $211,125

Exhibit 9-7 shows Tucson Tortilla's direct materials budget for the first three months of the year.

EXHIBIT 9-7 Direct Materials Budget

<table>
<tr><td colspan="5" align="center">Tucson Tortilla
Direct Materials Budget for Masa Harina Corn Flour
For the Quarter Ended March 31</td></tr>
<tr><td></td><td colspan="3" align="center">Month</td><td></td></tr>
<tr><td></td><td>January</td><td>February</td><td>March</td><td>1st Quarter</td></tr>
<tr><td>Unit to be produced (from Production Budget)</td><td>29,000</td><td>20,500</td><td>25,700</td><td>75,200</td></tr>
<tr><td>× Quantity (pounds) of DM needed per unit</td><td>× 5 lbs</td><td>× 5 lbs</td><td>× 5 lbs</td><td>× 5 lbs</td></tr>
<tr><td>Quantity (pounds) needed for production</td><td>145,000</td><td>102,500</td><td>128,500</td><td>376,000</td></tr>
<tr><td>Plus: Desired end inventory of DM</td><td>10,250</td><td>12,850</td><td>16,150*</td><td>16,150**</td></tr>
<tr><td>Total quantity (pounds) needed</td><td>155,250</td><td>115,350</td><td>144,650</td><td>392,150</td></tr>
<tr><td>Less: Beginning inventory of DM</td><td>(14,500)</td><td>(10,250)</td><td>(12,850)</td><td>(14,500)**</td></tr>
<tr><td>Quantity (pounds) to purchase</td><td>140,750</td><td>105,100</td><td>131,800</td><td>377,650</td></tr>
<tr><td>× Cost per pound</td><td>× $1.50</td><td>× $1.50</td><td>× $1.50</td><td>× $1.50</td></tr>
<tr><td>Total cost of DM purchases</td><td>$211,125</td><td>$157,650</td><td>$197,700</td><td>$566,475</td></tr>
</table>

* 161,500 pounds are needed for production in April.
** Since the quarter begins January 1 and ends March 31, the beginning inventory for the quarter is the balance on January 1 and the ending inventory for the quarter is the balance on March 31.

Direct Labor Budget

The direct labor (DL) budget is determined as follows:

Units to be Produced × DL Hours per Unit = Total DL Hours Required × DL Cost per Hour = Total Direct Labor Cost

Tucson Tortilla's factory is fairly automated, so very little direct labor is required. *Let's assume that each case requires only 0.05 of an hour. Direct laborers are paid $22 per hour. Thus, the direct labor cost for January is projected to be as follows:*

29,000 cases × 0.05 hours per case = 1,450 hours required × $22 per hour = $31,900

The Direct Labor budget for the first three months of the year is shown in Exhibit 9-8:

EXHIBIT 9-8 Direct Labor Budget

<table>
<tr><td colspan="5" align="center">Tucson Tortilla
Direct Labor Budget
For the Quarter Ended March 31</td></tr>
<tr><td></td><td colspan="3" align="center">Month</td><td></td></tr>
<tr><td></td><td>January</td><td>February</td><td>March</td><td>1st Quarter</td></tr>
<tr><td>Units to be produced (from Production Budget)</td><td>29,000</td><td>20,500</td><td>25,700</td><td>75,200</td></tr>
<tr><td>× Direct labor hours per unit</td><td>× 0.05</td><td>× 0.05</td><td>× 0.05</td><td>× 0.05</td></tr>
<tr><td>Total hours required</td><td>1,450</td><td>1,025</td><td>1,285</td><td>3,760</td></tr>
<tr><td>× Direct labor cost per hour</td><td>× $ 22</td><td>× $ 22</td><td>× $ 22</td><td>× $ 22</td></tr>
<tr><td>Total Direct labor cost</td><td>$31,900</td><td>$22,550</td><td>$28,270</td><td>$82,720</td></tr>
</table>

Manufacturing Overhead Budget

The manufacturing overhead budget is highly dependent on cost behavior. Some overhead costs, such as indirect materials, are variable. For example, Tucson Tortilla considers the oil used for frying the tortilla chips to be an indirect material. Since a portion of the oil is absorbed into the chips, the amount of oil required increases as production volume increases. Thus, the cost is variable. The company also considers salt and cellophane packaging to be variable indirect materials. *Tucson Tortilla expects to spend $1.25 on indirect materials for each case of tortilla chips produced, so January's budget for indirect materials is as follows:*

29,000 cases × $1.25 = $36,250 of indirect materials

Costs such as utilities and indirect labor are mixed costs. Mixed costs are usually separated into their variable and fixed components using one of the cost behavior estimation methods already discussed in Chapter 6. *Based on engineering and cost studies, Tucson Tortilla has determined that each case of chips requires $0.75 of variable indirect labor, and $0.50 of variable utility costs as a result of running the production machinery. These variable costs are budgeted as follows for January:*

29,000 cases × $0.75 = $21,750 of variable indirect labor

29,000 cases × $0.50 = $14,500 of variable factory utilities

Finally, many manufacturing overhead costs are fixed. *Tucson Tortilla's fixed costs include depreciation, insurance, and property taxes on the factory. The company also incurs some fixed indirect labor (salaried production engineers that oversee the daily manufacturing operation) and a fixed amount of utilities just to keep the lights, heat, or air conditioning on in the plant regardless of the production volume.*

Exhibit 9-9 shows that the manufacturing overhead budget usually has separate sections for variable and fixed overhead costs so that managers can easily see which costs will change as production volume changes.

Now that we have completed budgets for each of the three manufacturing costs (direct materials, direct labor, and manufacturing overhead), we turn our attention to operating expenses.

EXHIBIT 9-9 Manufacturing Overhead Budget

Tucson Tortilla
Manufacturing Overhead Budget
For the Quarter Ended March 31

	January	February	March	1st Quarter
Units to be Produced (from Production Budget)	29,000	20,500	25,700	75,200
Variable Costs:				
Indirect materials ($1.25 per case)	$ 36,250	$25,625	$32,125	$ 94,000
Indirect labor—variable portion ($0.75 per case)	21,750	15,375	19,275	56,400
Utilities—variable portion ($0.50 per case)	14,500	10,250	12,850	37,600
Total variable MOH	$ 72,500	$51,250	$64,250	$188,000
Fixed MOH Costs:				
Depreciation on factory and production equipment	$ 10,000	$10,000	$10,000	$ 30,000
Insurance and property taxes on the factory	3,000	3,000	3,000	9,000
Indirect labor—fixed portion	15,000	15,000	15,000	45,000
Utilities—fixed portion	2,000	2,000	2,000	6,000
Total fixed MOH	$ 30,000	$30,000	$30,000	$ 90,000
Total manufacturing overhead	$102,500	$81,250	$94,250	$278,000

Operating Expenses Budget

Recall that all costs incurred in every area of the value chain, except production, must be expensed as operating expenses in the period in which they are incurred. Thus all research and development, design, marketing, distribution, and customer service costs will be shown on the operating expenses budget.

Some operating expenses are variable, based on how many units will be *sold* (not produced). *For example, to motivate its sales force to generate sales, Tucson Tortilla pays its sales representatives a $1.50 sales commission for every case they sell.*

30,000 sales units × $1.50 = $45,000 sales commission expense in January

The company also incurs $2.00 of shipping costs on every case sold.

30,000 sales units × $2.00 = $60,000 shipping expense in January

Finally, the company knows that not all of the sales made on credit will eventually be collected. Based on experience, Tucson Tortilla expects monthly bad debt expense to be 1% of its credit sales. Since January credit sales are expected to be $480,000 (from Sales Budget, Exhibit 9-5), the company's bad debt expense for January is as follows:

$480,000 of credit sales in January × 1% = $4,800 bad debt expense for January

Other operating expenses are fixed: They will stay the same each month even though sales volume fluctuates. *For example, Tucson Tortilla's fixed expenses include salaries, office rent, depreciation on office equipment and the company's vehicles, advertising, telephone, and internet service.*

As shown in Exhibit 9-10, operating expenses are usually shown according to their cost behavior.

EXHIBIT 9-10 Operating Expenses Budget

<table>
<tr><td colspan="5" align="center">Tucson Tortilla
Operating Expenses Budget
For the Quarter Ended March 31</td></tr>
<tr><td></td><td colspan="3" align="center">Month</td><td></td></tr>
<tr><td></td><td>January</td><td>February</td><td>March</td><td>1st Quarter</td></tr>
<tr><td>Sales units (from Sales Budget)</td><td>30,000</td><td>20,000</td><td>25,000</td><td>75,000</td></tr>
<tr><td>Variable Operating Expenses:</td><td></td><td></td><td></td><td></td></tr>
<tr><td>Sales commissions expense ($1.50 per case sold)</td><td>$ 45,000</td><td>$ 30,000</td><td>$ 37,500</td><td>$112,500</td></tr>
<tr><td>Shipping expense ($2.00 per case sold)</td><td>60,000</td><td>40,000</td><td>50,000</td><td>150,000</td></tr>
<tr><td>Bad debt expense (1% of credit sales)</td><td>4,800</td><td>3,200</td><td>4,000</td><td>12,000</td></tr>
<tr><td>Variable operating expenses</td><td>$109,800</td><td>$ 73,200</td><td>$ 91,500</td><td>$274,500</td></tr>
<tr><td>Fixed Operating Expenses:</td><td></td><td></td><td></td><td></td></tr>
<tr><td>Salaries</td><td>$ 20,000</td><td>$ 20,000</td><td>$ 20,000</td><td>$ 60,000</td></tr>
<tr><td>Office rent</td><td>4,000</td><td>4,000</td><td>4,000</td><td>12,000</td></tr>
<tr><td>Depreciation</td><td>6,000</td><td>6,000</td><td>6,000</td><td>18,000</td></tr>
<tr><td>Advertising</td><td>2,000</td><td>2,000</td><td>2,000</td><td>6,000</td></tr>
<tr><td>Telephone and internet</td><td>1,000</td><td>1,000</td><td>1,000</td><td>3,000</td></tr>
<tr><td>Fixed operating expenses</td><td>$ 33,000</td><td>$ 33,000</td><td>$ 33,000</td><td>$ 99,000</td></tr>
<tr><td>Total operating expenses</td><td>$142,800</td><td>$106,200</td><td>$124,500</td><td>$373,500</td></tr>
</table>

Budgeted Income Statement

A budgeted income statement looks just like a regular income statement, except for the fact that it uses budgeted data. Recall the general format for an income statement:

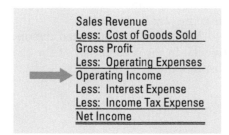

Sales Revenue
Less: Cost of Goods Sold
Gross Profit
Less: Operating Expenses
→ Operating Income
Less: Interest Expense
Less: Income Tax Expense
Net Income

This textbook has focused on a company's operating income, rather than net income. However, a complete income statement would include any interest expense (and/or interest income) as well as a provision for income taxes. These additional costs are subtracted from operating income to arrive at net income.

We have already computed the budgeted sales revenue and operating expenses on separate budgets. But we still need to calculate the Cost of Goods Sold before we can prepare the income statement.

Tucson Tortilla computes its Cost of Goods Sold as follows:

Number of Unit Sales × Manufacturing Cost per Unit = Cost of Goods Sold

This will be relatively simple for Tucson Tortilla since the company produces only one product.

The cost of manufacturing each case of tortilla chips is shown in Exhibit 9-11. Almost all of the information presented has already been presented and used to prepare the budgets for direct materials, direct labor, and manufacturing overhead. The only new piece of information is the total production volume for the year, budgeted to be 400,000 cases.

EXHIBIT 9-11 Budgeted Manufacturing Cost per Unit

Tucson Tortilla Budgeted Manufacturing Cost per Unit	
Direct materials (5 pounds of corn flour per case × $1.50 per pound)[a]	$ 7.50
Direct labor (0.05 hours per case × $22 per hour)[b]	1.10
Manufacturing overhead[c]:	
Variable—indirect materials ($1.25 per case), variable indirect labor ($0.75 per case), and variable utilities ($0.50 per case)	2.50
Fixed—$30,000 per month × 12 months = $360,000 for the year	
So, the fixed cost per unit is $360,000 ÷ 400,000[d] cases	0.90
Cost of manufacturing each case	$12.00

[a] From Exhibit 9-7
[b] From Exhibit 9-8
[c] From Exhibit 9-9
[d] Recall that companies base their predetermined MOH rate on the total estimated cost and volume for the *entire year*, rather than on monthly costs and volumes that will fluctuate.

Why is this important?

"The **budgeted income statement** helps managers know in advance whether their **plans** will result in an **acceptable** level of **income**. If not, **management** will need to consider how it can cut expenses or increase **sales revenues**."

Exhibit 9-12 shows the company's budgeted income statement for January. Interest expense is budgeted to be zero since the company has no outstanding debt. The income tax expense is budgeted to be 35% of income before taxes. The company will prepare budgeted income statements for each month and quarter, as well as for the entire year.

We have now completed the operating budgets for Tucson Tortilla. In the second half of the chapter, we'll prepare Tucson Tortilla's financial budgets.

EXHIBIT 9-12 Budgeted Income Statement

Tucson Tortilla
Budgeted Income Statement
For the month ended January 31

Sales (30,000 cases × $20 per case, from Exhibit 9-5)	$600,000
Less: Cost of goods sold (30,000 cases × $12.00 per case, from Exhibit 9-11)	360,000
Gross profit	240,000
Less: Operating expenses (from Exhibit 9-10)	142,800
Operating income	$ 97,200
Less: Interest expense (or add interest income)	0
Less: Income tax expense*	34,020
Net income	$ 63,180

*The corporate income tax rate for most companies is currently 35% of income before tax ($97,200 × 35% = $34,020).

Decision Guidelines

The Master Budget

Let's consider some of the decisions Campbell Soup Company made as it set up its budgeting process.

Decision	Guidelines
What should be the driving force behind the budgeting process?	The company's long-term goals and strategies drive the budgeting of the company's resources.
What are budgets used for?	Managers use budgets to help them fulfill their primary responsibilities: planning, directing, and controlling operations. Managers use feedback from the budgeting process to take corrective actions and, if necessary, revise strategies.
Who should be involved in the budgeting process?	Budgets tend to be more realistic and more motivational if lower level managers, as well as upper level managers, are allowed to participate in the budgeting process. The budgeting process tends to encompass a more comprehensive view when managers from all areas of the value chain participate in the process and serve on the budget committee.
What period of time should the budgets cover?	Long-term, strategic planning often results in forecasts of revenues and expenses 5–10 years into the future. Monthly and yearly budgets provide much more detailed information to aid management's shorter-term decisions.
How tough should the budget be to achieve?	Budgets are more useful for motivating employees and evaluating performance if they can be achieved with effort. Budgets that are too tight (too hard to achieve) or too loose (too easy to achieve) are not as beneficial.
What benefits should a company expect to obtain from developing a budget?	Benefits include the following: • Planning • Coordination and Communication • Benchmarking (used for both motivation and performance evaluation)
What budgets should be included in a manufacturer's master budget?	The *operating budgets* includes all budgets necessary to create a budgeted income statement. For a manufacturer, this includes the following: • Sales Budget • Production Budget • Direct Materials Budget • Direct Labor Budget • Manufacturing Overhead Budget • Operating Expenses Budget • Budgeted Income Statement The *financial budgets* include the capital expenditures budget, the cash budgets, and the budgeted balance sheet.

SUMMARY PROBLEM 1

Pillows Unlimited makes decorative throw pillows for home use. The company sells the pillows to home décor retailers for $14 per pillow. Each pillow requires 1.25 yards of fabric, which the company obtains at a cost of $6 per yard. The company would like to maintain an ending stock of fabric equal to 10% of the next month's production requirements. The company would also like to maintain an ending stock of finished pillows equal to 20% of the next month's sales. Sales (in units) are projected to be as follows for the first 3 months of the year:

January	100,000
February	110,000
March	115,000

Requirements

Prepare the following budgets for the first three months of the year, as well as a summary budget for the quarter:

1. Prepare the sales budget, including a separate section that details the type of sales made. For this section, assume that 10% of the company's pillows are cash sales, while the remaining 90% are sold on credit terms.

2. Prepare the production budget. Assume that the company anticipates selling 120,000 units in April.

3. Prepare the direct materials purchases budget. Assume the company needs 150,000 yards of fabric for production in April.

▪ SOLUTIONS

Requirement 1

Pillows Unlimited
Sales Budget
For the Quarter ended March 31

	Month			
	January	February	March	1st Quarter
Unit sales	100,000	110,000	115,000	325,000
Unit selling price	×$ 14	×$ 14	×$ 14	×$ 14
Total sales revenue	$1,400,000	$1,540,000	$1,610,000	$4,550,000
Type of Sale:				
Cash sales (10%)	$ 140,000	$ 154,000	$ 161,000	$ 455,000
Credit sales (90%)	1,260,000	1,386,000	1,449,000	4,095,000
Total sales revenue	$1,400,000	$1,540,000	$1,610,000	$4,550,000

Requirement 2

<table>
<tr><td colspan="5" align="center">Pillows Unlimited
Production Budget
For the Quarter ended March 31</td></tr>
<tr><td></td><td colspan="3" align="center">Month</td><td></td></tr>
<tr><td></td><td>January</td><td>February</td><td>March</td><td>1st Quarter</td></tr>
<tr><td>Unit sales</td><td>100,000</td><td>110,000</td><td>115,000</td><td>325,000</td></tr>
<tr><td>Plus: Desired end inventory (20% of next month's unit sales)</td><td>22,000</td><td>23,000</td><td>24,000</td><td>24,000</td></tr>
<tr><td>Total needed</td><td>122,000</td><td>133,000</td><td>139,000</td><td>349,000</td></tr>
<tr><td>Less: Beginning inventory</td><td>(20,000)*</td><td>(22,000)</td><td>(23,000)</td><td>(20,000)</td></tr>
<tr><td>Units to produce</td><td>102,000</td><td>111,000</td><td>116,000</td><td>329,000</td></tr>
</table>

*January 1 balance (equal to December 31 balance) is 20% of the projected unit sales in January (100,000).

Requirement 3

<table>
<tr><td colspan="5" align="center">Pillows Unlimited
Direct Materials Budget
For the Quarter ended March 31</td></tr>
<tr><td></td><td colspan="3" align="center">Month</td><td></td></tr>
<tr><td></td><td>January</td><td>February</td><td>March</td><td>1st Quarter</td></tr>
<tr><td>Units to be produced (from Production Budget)</td><td>102,000</td><td>111,000</td><td>116,000</td><td>329,000</td></tr>
<tr><td>× Quantity (yards) of DM needed per unit</td><td>× 1.25</td><td>× 1.25</td><td>× 1.25</td><td>× 1.25</td></tr>
<tr><td>Quantity (yards) needed for production</td><td>127,500</td><td>138,750</td><td>145,000</td><td>411,250</td></tr>
<tr><td>Plus: Desired end inventory of DM (10% of the amount needed for next month's production)</td><td>13,875</td><td>14,500</td><td>15,000</td><td>15,000</td></tr>
<tr><td>Total quantity (yards) needed</td><td>141,375</td><td>153,250</td><td>160,000</td><td>426,250</td></tr>
<tr><td>Less: Beginning inventory of DM</td><td>(12,750)*</td><td>(13,875)</td><td>(14,500)</td><td>(12,750)</td></tr>
<tr><td>Quantity (yards) to purchase</td><td>128,625</td><td>139,375</td><td>145,500</td><td>413,500</td></tr>
<tr><td>× Cost per pound</td><td>× $ 6.00</td><td>× $ 6.00</td><td>× $ 6.00</td><td>× $ 6.00</td></tr>
<tr><td>Total cost of DM purchases</td><td>$771,750</td><td>$836,250</td><td>$873,000</td><td>$2,481,000</td></tr>
</table>

*January 1 balance (equal to December 31 balance) is 10% of the quantity needed for January's production (127,500).

How are the Financial Budgets Prepared?

In the first half of the chapter, we prepared Tucson Tortilla's operating budgets, culminating with the company's budgeted income statement. In this part of the chapter we turn our attention to Tucson Tortilla's financial budgets. Managers typically prepare a capital expenditures budget as well as three separate cash budgets:

1. Cash collections (or receipts) budget
2. Cash payments (or disbursements) budget
3. Combined cash budget, complete with financing arrangements

Finally, managers prepare the budgeted balance sheet. Each of these budgets is illustrated next.

Capital Expenditure Budget

The capital expenditure budget shows the company's intentions to invest in new property, plant, or equipment (capital investments). When planned capital investments are significant, this budget must be developed early in the process because the additional investments may affect depreciation expense, interest expense (if funds are borrowed to pay for the investments), or dividend payments (if stock is issued to pay for the investments). Chapter 12 contains a detailed discussion of the capital budgeting process, including the techniques managers use in deciding whether to make additional investments.

Exhibit 9-13 shows Tucson Tortilla's capital expenditure budget for the first three months of the year. *Tucson Tortilla expects to invest in new computers, delivery vans, and production equipment in January. The depreciation expense shown in the operating budget and the depreciation shown in the MOH budget reflect these anticipated investments. No other capital investments are planned in the first quarter of the year.*

EXHIBIT 9-13 Capital Expenditure Budget

Tucson Tortilla Capital Expenditure Budget For the Quarter Ended March 31				
	Month			
	January	**February**	**March**	**1st Quarter**
Computers and Printers	$ 15,000			
Delivery Vans	35,000			
Production Equipment	75,000			
Total new investments in property, plant and equipment	$125,000	0	0	$125,000

Cash Collections Budget

The cash collections budget is all about timing: *When* does Tucson Tortilla expect to receive cash from its sales? Of course, Tucson Tortilla will receive cash immediately on its cash (COD) sales. From the Sales Budget (Exhibit 9-5) we see that the company expects the following cash sales in January:

Cash (COD) sales = $120,000

However, most of the company's sales are made on credit. Recall that Tucson Tortilla's credit terms are "net 30 days," meaning customers have 30 days to pay. Therefore, most customers will wait nearly 30 days (a full month) before paying. However, some companies may be experiencing cash flow difficulties and may not be able to pay Tucson Tortilla on time. Because of this, Tucson Tortilla doesn't expect to receive payment on all of its credit sales the month after the sale.

Based on collection history, Tucson Tortilla expects 85% of its credit sales to be collected in the month after sale, and 14% to be collected two months after the sale. Tucson Tortilla expects that 1% of credit sales will never be collected, and therefore, has recognized a 1% bad debt expense in its operating expenses budget. Furthermore, assume that December credit sales were $500,000 and November credit sales were $480,000.

> Anticipated January Collections of Credit Sales:
> 85% × $500,000 (December credit sales) = $425,000
> 14% × $480,000 (November credit sales) = $ 67,200

Exhibit 9-14 shows Tucson Tortilla's expected cash collections for the first three months of the year:

EXHIBIT 9-14 Cash Collections Budget

Tucson Tortilla
Cash Collections Budget
For the Quarter Ended March 31

	January	February	March	1st Quarter
Cash sales (from Sales Budget)	$120,000	$ 80,000	$100,000	$ 300,000
Collections on Credit Sales:				
85% of credit sales made one month ago	425,000	408,000[a]	272,000[c]	1,105,000
14% of credit sales made two months ago	67,200	70,000[b]	67,200[d]	204,400
Total cash collections	$612,200	$558,000	$439,200	$1,609,400

[a] 85% × $480,000 (January credit sales, Exhibit 9-5) = $408,000
[b] 14% × $500,000 (December credit sales, Exhibit 9-5) = $70,000
[c] 85% × $320,000 (February credit sales, Exhibit 9-5) = $272,000
[d] 14% × $480,000 (January credit sales, Exhibit 9-5) = $67,200

Cash Payments Budget

The cash payments budget is also about timing: *When* will Tucson Tortilla pay for its direct materials purchases, direct labor costs, manufacturing overhead costs, operating expenses, capital expenditures, and income taxes? Let's tackle each cost, one at a time.

DIRECT MATERIALS PURCHASES *Tucson Tortilla has been given "net 30 days" payment terms from its suppliers of the corn flour used to make the tortilla chips. Therefore, Tucson Tortilla waits a month before it pays for the direct material purchases shown in the Direct Materials Budget (Exhibit 9-7). So, the company will pay for its December purchases (projected to be $231,845) in January, its January purchases of $211,125 (Exhibit 9-7) in February, its February purchases of $157,650 (Exhibit 9-7) in March, and so forth:*

	January	February	March	1st Quarter
Cash payments for DM purchases	$231,845	$211,125	$157,650	$600,620

DIRECT LABOR *Tucson Tortilla's factory employees are paid twice a month for the work they perform during the month. Therefore, January's direct labor cost of $31,900 (Exhibit 9-8) will be paid in January, and likewise, for each month.*

	January	February	March	1st Quarter
Cash payments for direct labor	$31,900	$22,550	$28,270	$82,720

MANUFACTURING OVERHEAD Tucson Tortilla must consider when it pays for its manufacturing overhead costs. *Let's assume that the company pays for all manufacturing overhead costs except for depreciation, insurance, and property taxes **in the month in which they are incurred.** Depreciation is a non-cash expense, so it never appears on the cash payments budget. Insurance and property taxes are typically paid on a semiannual basis. While Tucson Tortilla budgets a cost of $3,000 per month for factory insurance and property tax, it doesn't actually pay these costs on a monthly basis. Rather, Tucson Tortilla prepays its insurance and property tax twice a year, in January and July. The amount of these semiannual payments is calculated as shown:*

$3,000 monthly cost $\times$ 12 months = $36,000 $\div$ 2 = $18,000 payments in January and July

So, the cash payments for manufacturing overhead costs are expected to be as follows:

	January	February	March	1st Quarter
Total manufacturing overhead (from Exhibit 9-9)	$102,500	$ 81,250	$ 94,250	$278,000
Less: Depreciation (not a cash expense)	(10,000)	(10,000)	(10,000)	(30,000)
Less: Property tax and insurance (paid twice a year, not monthly)	(3,000)	(3,000)	(3,000)	(9,000)
Plus: Semiannual payments for property taxes and insurance	18,000	0	0	18,000
Cash payments for MOH costs	$107,500	$ 68,250	$ 81,250	$257,000

OPERATING EXPENSES *Let's assume that the company pays for all operating expenses, except depreciation and bad debt expense, **in the month in which they are incurred.** Both depreciation and bad debt expense are non-cash expenses, so they never appear on the cash payments budget. Bad debt expense simply recognizes the sales revenue that will never be collected. Therefore, these non-cash expenses need to be deducted from the total operating expenses to arrive at **cash** payments for operating expenses:*

	January	February	March	1st Quarter
Total operating expenses (from Exhibit 9-10)	$142,800	$106,200	$124,500	$373,500
Less: Depreciation expense	(6,000)	(6,000)	(6,000)	(18,000)
Less: Bad debt expense	(4,800)	(3,200)	(4,000)	(12,000)
Cash payments for operating expenses	$132,000	$ 97,000	$114,500	$343,500

CAPITAL EXPENDITURES The timing of these cash payments have already been scheduled on the Capital Expenditures Budget in Exhibit 9-13.

INCOME TAXES Corporations must make quarterly income tax payments for their estimated income tax liability. For corporations like Tucson Tortilla that have a December 31 fiscal year-end, the first income tax payment is not due until April 15. The remaining payments are due June 15, September 15, and December 15. *As a result, Tucson Tortilla will not show any income tax payments in the first quarter of the year.*

DIVIDENDS Like many corporations, Tucson Tortilla pays dividends to its shareholders on a quarterly basis. Tucson Tortilla plans to pay $25,000 in cash dividends in January for the company's earnings in the fourth quarter of the previous year.

Finally, we pull all of these cash payments together onto a single budget, as shown in Exhibit 9-15.

EXHIBIT 9-15 Cash Payments Budget

Tucson Tortilla
Cash Payments Budget
For the Quarter Ended March 31

	January	February	March	1st Quarter
Cash payments for direct materials purchases	$231,845	$211,125	$157,650	$ 600,620
Cash payments for direct labor	31,900	22,550	28,270	82,720
Cash payments for manufacturing overhead	107,500	68,250	81,250	257,000
Cash payments for operating expenses	132,000	97,000	114,500	343,500
Cash payments for capital investments	125,000	0	0	125,000
Cash payments for income taxes	0	0	0	0
Cash dividends	25,000	0	0	25,000
Total cash payments	$653,245	$398,925	$381,670	$1,433,840

Combined Cash Budget

The combined cash budget simply merges the budgeted cash collections and cash payments to project the company's ending cash position. Exhibit 9-16 shows the following:

- Budgeted cash collections for the month are added to the beginning cash balance to determine the total cash available.
- Budgeted cash payments are then subtracted to determine the ending cash balance before financing.
- Based on the ending cash balance before financing, the company knows whether it needs to borrow money or whether it has excess funds with which to repay debt or invest.

By looking at Exhibit 9-16, we see that Tucson Tortilla expects to begin the month with $36,100 of cash. However, by the end of the month, it will be short of cash. Therefore, the company's managers must plan for how they will handle this shortage. One strategy would be to delay the purchase of equipment planned for January. Another strategy would be to borrow money. Let's say Tucson Tortilla has prearranged a line of credit that carries an interest rate of prime plus 1%. A <u>line of credit</u> is a lending arrangement from a bank in which a company is allowed to borrow money as needed, up to a specified maximum amount, yet only pay interest on the portion that is actually borrowed until it is repaid.

EXHIBIT 9-16 Combined Cash Budget

<table>
<tr><td colspan="5" align="center">Tucson Tortilla
Combined Cash Budget
For the Quarter Ended March 31</td></tr>
<tr><td></td><td colspan="3" align="center">Month</td><td></td></tr>
<tr><td></td><td align="center">January</td><td align="center">February</td><td align="center">March</td><td align="center">1st Quarter</td></tr>
<tr><td>Beginning balance of cash</td><td>$ 36,100</td><td>$ 15,055</td><td>$ 153,980</td><td>$ 36,100</td></tr>
<tr><td>Cash collections (Exhibit 9-14)</td><td>612,200</td><td>558,000</td><td>439,200</td><td>1,609,400</td></tr>
<tr><td>Total cash available</td><td>648,300</td><td>573,055</td><td>593,180</td><td>1,645,500</td></tr>
<tr><td>Less: Cash payments (Exhibit 9-15)</td><td>(653,245)</td><td>(398,925)</td><td>(381,670)</td><td>(1,433,840)</td></tr>
<tr><td>Ending cash balance before financing</td><td>(4,945)</td><td>174,130</td><td>211,510</td><td>211,660</td></tr>
<tr><td>Financing:</td><td></td><td></td><td></td><td></td></tr>
<tr><td>Borrowings</td><td>20,000</td><td>0</td><td>0</td><td>20,000</td></tr>
<tr><td>Repayments</td><td>0</td><td>(20,000)</td><td>0</td><td>(20,000)</td></tr>
<tr><td>Interest payments</td><td>0</td><td>(150)</td><td>0</td><td>(150)</td></tr>
<tr><td>End cash balance</td><td>$ 15,055</td><td>$ 153,980</td><td>$ 211,510</td><td>$ 211,510</td></tr>
</table>

The line of credit will enable Tucson Tortilla to borrow funds to meet its short-term cash deficiencies. Let's say that Tucson Tortilla wants to maintain an ending cash balance of at least $15,000. By borrowing $20,000 on its line of credit at the end of January, the company will have slightly more ($15,055) than its minimum desired balance.

The cash budget also shows that Tucson Tortilla will be able to repay this borrowing, along with the accrued interest, in February. Assuming Tucson Tortilla borrows the $20,000 for a full month at an interest rate of 9%, February's interest payment would be calculated as follows:

$20,000 loan × 1/12 of the year × 9% interest rate = $150

Why is this important?

"The combined **cash budget** lets managers know in **advance** when they will be **short** on cash and need to **borrow** money, or when they may have **extra funds** to invest."

Exhibit 9-16 also shows that Tucson Tortilla expects to have a fairly substantial cash balance at the end of both February and March. The company's managers use the cash budgets to determine when this cash will be needed and to decide how to invest it accordingly. Since the first quarterly income tax payment is due April 15, management will want to invest most of this excess cash in a safe, short-term investment, such as a money market fund or short-term certificate of deposit. The company will also need cash in April to pay shareholders a quarterly dividend. Any cash not needed in the short run can be invested in longer-term investments. Managers exercising good cash management should have a plan in place for both cash deficiencies and cash excesses.

Budgeted Balance Sheet

Exhibit 9-17, shows Tucson Tortilla's budgeted balance sheet as of January 31. The company will prepare a budgeted balance sheet for each month of the year.

EXHIBIT 9-17 Budgeted Balance Sheet

Tucson Tortilla
Budgeted Balance Sheet
January 31

Assets

Cash (from Cash Budget, Exhibit 9-16)	$ 15,055	
Accounts receivable, net of allowance^A	549,450	
Raw materials inventory (from Direct Materials Budget: 10,250 lbs end inventory × $1.50)	15,375	
Finished goods inventory (from Production Budget: 2,000 cases × $12.00 unit cost)	24,000	
Prepaid property taxes and insurance^B	15,000	
Total current assets		$ 618,880
Property, plant, and equipment^C	6,350,000	
Less: Accumulated depreciation^D	(1,920,000)	
Property, plant, and equipment, net		4,430,000
Total assets		$5,048,880

Liabilities and Stockholders' Equity

Accounts payable^E	$ 211,125	
Income tax liability (from income statement, Exhibit 9-12)	34,020	
Other current liabilities (line of credit) (from Cash Budget, Exhibit 9-16)	20,000	
Total liabilities		$ 265,145
Stockholders' equity^F		4,783,735
Total liabilities and stockholders' equity		$5,048,880

---

^A Accounts Receivable, Net of Allowance

January credit sales (from Sales Budget, Exhibit 9-5)	$480,000
15% of December's credit sales ($500,000) yet to be collected	75,000
Accounts receivable, January 31	$555,000
Less: Allowance for uncollectible accounts (Assume $750 balance prior to additional $4,800 bad debt expense, Exhibit 9-10)	(5,550)
Accounts receivable, net of allowance for uncollectible accounts	$549,450

---

^B Prepaid Property Tax and Insurance

Semiannual payment made in January (cash payments for MOH, p. 534)	$18,000
Less: January cost (MOH Budget, Exhibit 9-9)	3,000
Prepaid property tax and insurance, January 31	$15,000

C Property, Plant, and Equipment

December 31 balance (assumed)..	$6,225,000
Plus: January's investment in new equipment (Capital Expenditure Budget, Exhibit 9-13)............................	125,000
Property, plant, and equipment, January 31..	$6,350,000

D Accumulated Depreciation

December 31 balance (assumed)..	$1,904,000
Plus: January's depreciation from Manufacturing Overhead Budget, Exhibit 9-9..	10,000
Plus: January's depreciation from Operating Expenses Budget, Exhibit 9-10	6,000
Accumulated depreciation, January 31..	$1,920,000

E Accounts Payable

January's DM purchases to be paid in February (p. 533 and Exhibit 9-15)...	211,125
Accounts payable, January 31...	$211,125

F Stockholders' Equity

December 31 balance of common stock and retained earnings (assumed)	$4,720,555
Plus: January's net income (Budgeted Income Statement, Exhibit 9-12)	63,180
Stockholders' equity, January 31...	$4,783,735

Sensitivity Analysis and Flexible Budgeting

The master budget models the company's *planned* activities. Managers try to use the best estimates possible when creating budgets. However, managers do not have a crystal ball for making predictions. Some of the key assumptions (such sales volume) used to create the budgets may turn out to be different than originally predicted. How do managers prepare themselves for potentially different scenarios? They use sensitivity analysis and flexible budgeting.

As shown in Exhibit 9-18, <u>sensitivity analysis</u> is a *what if* technique that asks *what* a result will be *if* a predicted amount is not achieved or *if* an underlying assumption changes. For example, *what if* shipping costs increase due to increases in gasoline prices? *What if* the cost of the corn flour increases or union workers negotiate a wage increase? *What if* sales are 15% cash and 85% credit, rather than 20% cash and 80% credit? How will any

EXHIBIT 9-18 Sensitivity Analysis

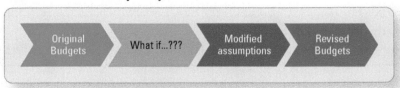

or all of these changes in key assumptions affect Tucson Tortilla's budgeted income and budgeted cash position?

In addition to these "what if" scenarios, management is particularly concerned with sales projections. Why? Because the sales budget is the driving force behind most of the other budgets. If the budgeted sales figures change, then most other budgets will also change. To address this concern, managers often prepare **flexible budgets**, which are budgets prepared for different volumes of activity. Cost behavior is much of the driving force behind flexible budgets. Recall that as volume changes within the relevant range, only total variable costs should change. Fixed costs should remain unaffected. We'll discuss flexible budgets again in Chapter 10, where we show how flexible budgets are often used at the end of the period as the best basis for performance evaluation.

Technology makes it cost-effective to perform comprehensive sensitivity analyses and flexible budgets. Most companies use computer spreadsheet programs or special budget software to prepare the master budget and all of its components. Managers perform sensitivity analysis by simply changing one or several of the underlying assumptions in the budgets, such as sales volume, direct material cost, and collection terms. The budget software automatically computes a complete set of revised budgets based on the changes.

Armed with a better understanding of how changes in key assumption will affect the company's bottom line and cash position, today's managers can be prepared to lead the company when business conditions change.

Sustainability and Budgeting

Budgets reflect and communicate management's goals and objectives. Managers leading their companies towards more sustainable practices will want to reflect those goals in the company's budgets. For example, Campbell Soup Company has set long-term environmental goals for 2020 which include:[1]

- Cutting water use and greenhouse gas emissions in half per ton of food produced
- Recycling 95% of waste generated
- Delivering 75% of packaging from sustainable materials
- Sourcing 40% of energy used from renewable or alternative energy sources

The adoption of these long-term goals will affect most, if not all of the company's shorter-term budgets. For example, the operating expense budget should reflect additional resources devoted to researching and developing more sustainable packaging materials. Once developed, the new packaging will impact the direct materials budget. The operating expense budget should also include additional resources for marketing the sustainably packaged products, which should in turn create additional sales to be included in the sales budget. The capital expenditures budget will reflect plans to purchase new energy saving production equipment, such as the $15.1 million of environmentally related capital investments that Campbell made in 2009. The company's MOH budget will in turn be affected by depreciation of the new equipment, as well as the reduction of water cost, the recycling of waste, and the use of alternative forms of energy. All of these measures will impact the cash budget, as well as the company's projected income statement and balance sheet.

Recall that budgets also serve as benchmarks for judging performance. By developing strategic environmental goals that span several years, and then tracking yearly performance, Campbell can see how well it is working towards achieving those longer-term goals. For example, in 2009, Campbell was able to reduce water use per ton of food produced by 9.5% from what it had been in 2008. In 2009, Campbell also recycled 84% of waste generated (up from 64% for US operations in 2008). These key metrics indicate that Campbell is well on its way towards achieving its longer-term environmental goals.

See Exercises
E9-15A and E9-35B

[1]Campbell Soup Company 2010 Corporate Social Responsibility Report

How do the Budgets for Service and Merchandising Companies Differ?

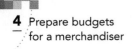

Earlier in this chapter we presented the master budget for a manufacturing company. The components of the master budget for a manufacturing company were summarized in Exhibit 9-4. The master budgets for service companies and merchandising companies are somewhat less complex, and will be described next.

Service Companies

Recall that service companies have no merchandise inventory. Therefore, their operating budgets only include the Sales Budget, the Operating Expenses Budget, and the Budgeted Income Statement, as shown in Exhibit 9-19. Notice that the financial budgets are the same as those a manufacturer would prepare.

EXHIBIT 9-19 Master Budget for a Service Company

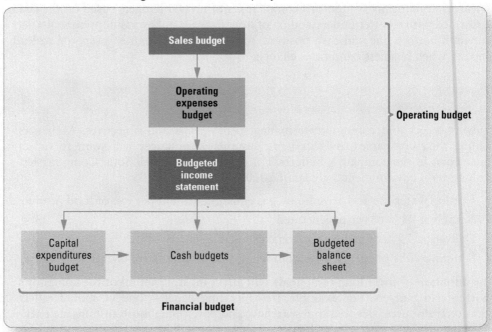

Merchandising Companies

Since merchandising companies purchase ready-made products, they do not need to prepare the Production, Direct Materials, Direct Labor, or Manufacturing Overhead Budgets. Replacing these budgets is a combined **Cost of Goods Sold, Inventory, and Purchases Budget**, as shown in Exhibit 9-20.

The Cost of Goods Sold, Inventory, and Purchases budget follows the same general format as the manufacturer's production budget except that it is calculated at cost (in dollars) rather than in units:[2]

Cost of Goods Sold	(the inventory we plan to sell during the month, at cost)
Plus: Desired Ending Inventory	(the amount of inventory we want on hand at month's end)
Total Inventory Needed	(the total amount of inventory needed)
Less: Beginning Inventory	(the amount of inventory we have on hand)
Purchases of Inventory	(the amount of inventory we need to purchase)

[2]A merchandiser could first prepare this budget in units, and then convert it to dollars. However, merchandisers usually have hundreds or thousands of products for sale, so it is often simpler to directly state it in dollars.

EXHIBIT 9-20 Master Budget for a Merchandising Company

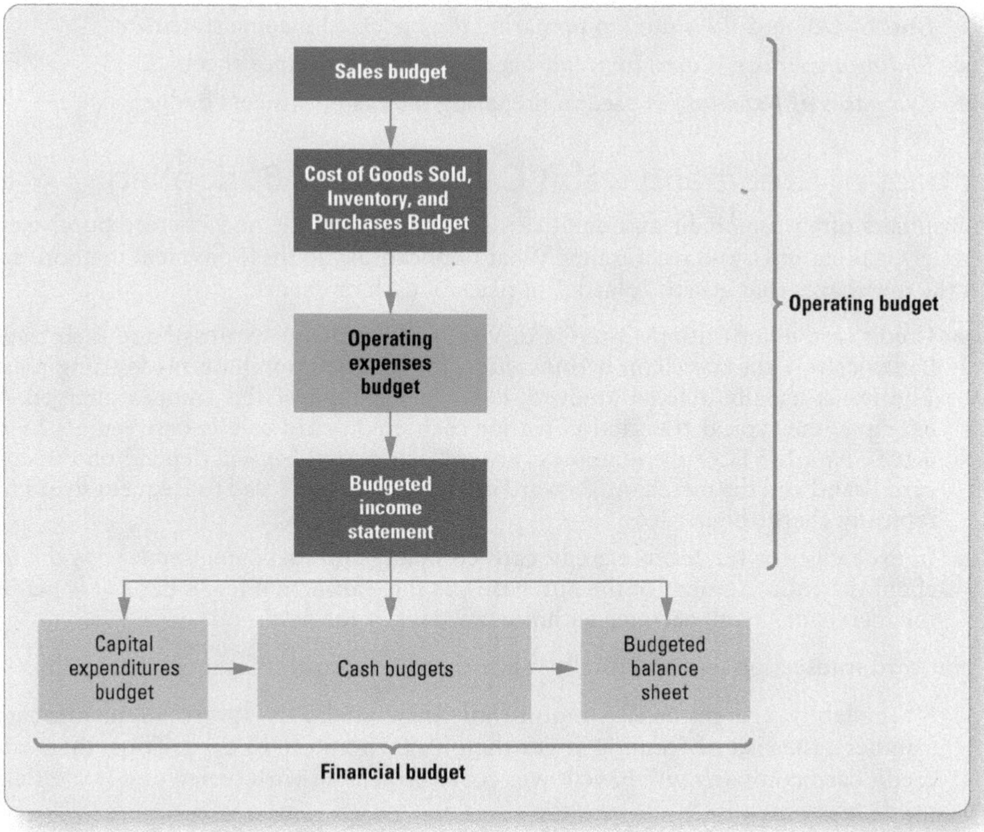

Notice that the format of the budget is easy to remember because it follows the name of the budget: We start with *Cost of Goods Sold*, then consider *inventory* levels, and finally arrive at the amount of *purchases* to be made. Let's try an example:

Let's say one Circle J convenience store expects sales of $500,000 in January, $520,000 in February, $530,000 in March, and $550,000 in April. Let's also assume that management sets its prices to achieve an overall 40% gross profit. As a result, Cost of Goods Sold is 60% of the sales revenue (100% − 40%). Finally, management wishes to have ending inventory equal to 10% of the next month's Cost of Goods Sold. Exhibit 9-21 shows the Cost of Goods Sold, Inventory, and Purchases budget for the first three months of the year. Keep in mind that all figures (other than Sales Revenue) are shown at cost.

EXHIBIT 9-21 Merchandiser's Cost of Goods Sold, Inventory, and Purchases Budget

Circle J Convenience Store
Cost of Goods Sold, Inventory, and Purchases Budget
For the months of January and February

	Month		
	January	February	March
Sales revenue (from Sales Budget)	$500,000	$520,000	$530,000
Cost of goods sold (60% of sales revenue)	$300,000	$312,000	$318,000
Plus: Desired ending inventory 10% of next month's cost of goods sold	31,200	31,800	33,000[b]
Total inventory required	331,200	343,800	351,000
Less: Beginning inventory	(30,000)[a]	(31,200)	(31,800)
Purchases of inventory	$301,200	$312,600	$319,200

[a] December 31 balance (equal to January 1 balance) is 10% of January's Cost of Goods Sold.
[b] April sales of $550,000 × 60% = $330,000; April Cost of Goods Sold × 10% = $33,000

Figures from this budget are then used as follows:

- *Cost of Goods Sold* is used in preparing the budgeted income statement.
- *Ending Inventory* is used in preparing the budgeted balance sheet.
- *Purchases of Inventory* is used in preparing the cash payments budget.

Impact of Credit and Debit Card Sales on Budgeting

Consumers often use credit and debit cards to pay for online and in-store purchases at retailers, gas stations, and restaurants. What implications do these payment methods have on the merchants that accept "plastic" in place of cash or checks?

- Credit card companies (MasterCard, Visa, and American Express)[3] and their issuing banks charge the merchant a transaction fee for each purchase made using plastic. The fee is usually a fixed amount *plus* a percentage of the amount charged. For example, the typical transaction fee for each credit card sale is between $0.25 and $0.50, *plus* 1–5% of the amount charged.[4] The actual fee will depend on the credit card brand and the merchant. Reward cards, such as those tied to frequent flyer miles, typically charge higher fees.
- In exchange for the fee, the credit card company and its issuing bank pays the merchant the entire amount of the purchase *less* the transaction fee. A deposit is made to the merchant's bank account within a few days of the sale.

Debit card transaction fees are usually lower than credit card transaction fees. Why?

1. Since debit card purchases require an associated PIN (personal identification number), the risk of fraud is lower than it is with a credit card. Thus, the issuing credit card company will have lower costs associated with stolen and fraudulently used cards.
2. Debit card sales are paid to the merchant using money that is in the customer's bank account, rather than money that is in essence loaned to the customer by the credit card company. Since the cash used for the deposit is not subject to credit risk, it is made with "cheaper" funds.
3. Beginning October 1, 2011, the Federal Reserve set a cap on the debit card transaction fees that banks can charge merchants. The new limit is as follows:

Limit on *debit* card fees = $0.22 per transaction + 0.05% of the amount of the transaction

Notice that the amount charged on the value of the transaction (0.0005) is substantially less than it is for a typical credit card transaction.[5]

Although credit and debit card transaction fees are costly to merchants, the acceptance of plastic payment methods also has benefits:

- Merchants would lose potential sales if they did not allow customers to pay with credit and debit cards.
- The acceptance of credit cards decreases the costs associated with bounced checks, misappropriation of cash, and the activities associated with preparing and transporting cash deposits (sometimes via armored vehicle collection services).
- Merchants receive the cash quickly, which may improve their cash flow.

---

[3]These three credit card companies control approximately 93% of the credit card transactions in the United States. By 2008, $48 billion in transaction fees were assessed by credit card issuers. www.newrules.org/retail/news/soaring-credit-card-transaction-fees-squeeze-independent-businesses

[4]www.allbusiness.com/sales/internet-e-commerce/3930-1.html

[5]www.federalreserve.gov/newsevents/press/bcreg/20110629a.htm. Banks with less than $10 billion in assets are exempt from the new cap. In addition, if a bank does not have fraud prevention policies and procedures in place, the cap is $0.21 per transaction rather than $0.22 per transaction.

Let's try an example:

Say a customer purchases some clothes at Aeropostale for $50 and uses a MasterCard to pay for the purchase. Let's also assume that MasterCard charges Aeropostale a transaction fee equal to $0.25 + 2% of the amount charged. The transaction fee on this sale would be:

$$\text{Transaction Fee} = \$0.25 + (2\% \times \text{Amount Charged})$$
$$\$1.25 = \$0.25 + (2\% \times \$50)$$

Within a few days, MasterCard would deposit the following amount in Aeropostale's bank account:

$$\text{Cash Deposited} = \text{Amount Charged on Credit Card} - \text{Transaction Fee}$$
$$\$48.75 = \$50.00 - \$1.25$$

The anticipation of this credit card sale would be shown in the budgets as follows:

- The $50 sale would be shown in the Sales Budget, *in the month of sale.*
- The $1.25 transaction fee would be shown in the Operating Expense Budget, *in the month of sale.*
- The $48.75 would be shown as a cash receipt on the Cash Collections Budget, *in the month of collection* (which is typically within one to seven days of the actual sale).

When preparing the master budget, merchants need to consider:

- The percentage of sales that will be made using debit cards and credit cards
- The different transaction fees charged for debit and credit card transactions
- The length of time between the sale and the deposit.

Retail Credit Cards

Many retailers, such as Target, Kohl's, and Old Navy issue their own credit cards in addition to accepting credit cards such as Visa and MasterCard. When a customer uses a store-based credit card, no transaction fee is incurred. However, the risk of collection falls back on the merchant, rather than on a third-party credit card company. The merchant must wait for the customer to make payments on the credit card bill. The cash collection may occur over several months, several years, or never. The cash collections budget will take into account the aging of these receivables. Likewise, the operating expense budget will need to take into consideration possible bad debts. Finally, the company will need to budget for interest income assessed on unpaid balances and any fees charged to the customer for late payments.

Decision Guidelines

The Master Budget

Let's consider some additional decisions with respect to budgeting.

Decision	Guidelines
What is the key to preparing the cash collections and cash payments budgets?	The key to preparing the cash budgets is *timing*. *When* will cash be received, and *when* will cash be paid? The timing of cash collections and cash payments often differs from the period in which the related revenues and expenses are recognized on the income statement.
What can be done to prepare for possible changes in key, underlying budget assumptions?	Management uses sensitivity analysis to understand how changes in key, underlying assumptions might affect the company's financial results. This awareness helps managers cope with changing business conditions when they occur.
How does sustainability impact budgeting?	Companies that are planning on adopting any sustainable practice will want to capture those plans in their budgets. Any or all of the budgets could be impacted by plans to adopt sustainable practices.
How does the master budget of a service company differ from that of a manufacturer?	Service companies have no inventory to make or sell, thus their operating budgets are less complex. The operating budgets include the: • Sales Budget • Operating Expense Budget • Budgeted Income Statement
How does the master budget of a merchandising company differ from that of a manufacturer?	Merchandising companies buy their inventory, rather than make it. In place of the Production budget, they use a "Cost of Goods Sold, Inventory, and Purchases" budget. This budget follows the same basic format as the Production budget. The amounts on the budget are calculated at cost, rather than in units. The operating budgets include the: • Sales budget • Cost of Goods Sold, Inventory, and Purchases budget • Operating Expense budget • Budgeted Income statement
How does the acceptance of debit and credit card payments affect a merchant's budgets?	Merchants must budget for the transaction fees charged by the credit card companies and their issuing banks. The transaction fee needs to be shown on the operating expense budget. The amount of credit and debit card sales, net of the transaction fee, will be shown on the cash receipts budget.
How are credit and debit card transaction fees calculated?	The transaction fee is typically a set dollar amount per transaction, plus a percentage of the amount of sale charged on a credit or debit card. For example: Transaction Fee = $0.25 + (2\% \times$ Amount Charged)
How does the acceptance of debit and credit cards affect the cash collection budget?	The amount of cash shown on the cash collections budget will be the net amount deposited: Cash Deposited = Amount Charged on Credit Card − Transaction Fee

SUMMARY PROBLEM **2**

The following information was taken from Pillows Unlimited Sales Budget, found in Summary Problem 1 on page 530:

		Month		
Pillows Unlimited **Sales Budget—Type of Sale** **For the Quarter Ended March 31**				
Type of Sale:	**January**	**February**	**March**	**1st Quarter**
Cash sales (10%)	$ 140,000	$ 154,000	$ 161,000	$ 455,000
Credit sales (90%)	1,260,000	1,386,000	1,449,000	4,095,000
Total sales revenue	$1,400,000	$1,540,000	$1,610,000	$4,550,000

The company's collection history indicates that 75% of credit sales are collected in the month after the sale, 15% are collected two months after the sale, 8% are collected three months after the sale, and the remaining 2% are never collected.

Assume the following additional information was gathered about the types of sales made in the fourth quarter (October through December) of the previous year:

		Month		
Pillows Unlimited **Sales Budget—Type of Sale** **For the Quarter Ended December 31**				
Type of Sale:	**October**	**November**	**December**	**4th Quarter**
Cash sales (10%)	$ 142,800	$ 151,200	$ 137,200	$ 431,200
Credit sales (90%)	1,285,200	1,360,800	1,234,800	3,880,800
Total sales revenue	$1,428,000	$1,512,000	$1,372,000	$4,312,000

The following information was taken from Pillows Unlimited Direct Materials Budget, found in Summary Problem 1 on page 530:

	January	**February**	**March**	**1st Quarter**
Total cost of DM purchases	$771,750	$836,250	$873,000	$2,481,000

Assume that the total cost of direct materials purchases in December was $725,000. The company pays 40% of its direct materials purchases in the month of purchase, and pays the remaining 60% in the month after purchase.

Requirements

1. Prepare the Cash Collections Budget for January, February, and March, as well as a summary for the first quarter.
2. Prepare the Cash Disbursements Budget for Direct Materials purchases for the months of January, February, and March, as well as a summary for the quarter.

▪ SOLUTIONS

Requirement 1

	January	February	March	1st Quarter
Pillows Unlimited **Cash Collections Budget** For the Quarter Ended March 31		**Month**		
	January	**February**	**March**	**1st Quarter**
Cash sales	$ 140,000	$ 154,000	$ 161,000	$ 455,000
Collections on credit sales:				
75% of credit sales made last month	926,100[A]	945,000[D]	1,039,500[G]	2,910,600
15% of credit sales made two months ago	204,120[B]	185,220[E]	189,000[H]	578,340
8% of credit sales made two months ago	102,816[C]	108,864[F]	98,784[I]	310,464
Total cash collections	$1,373,036	$1,393,084	$1,488,284	$4,254,404

[A] December credit sales ($1,234,800) × 75% = $ 926,100
[B] November credit sales ($1,360,800) × 15% = $ 204,120
[C] October credit sales ($1,285,200) × 8% = $ 102,816

[D] January credit sales ($1,260,000) × 75% = $ 945,000
[E] December credit sales ($1,234,800) × 15% = $ 185,220
[F] November credit sales ($1,360,800) × 8% = $ 108,864

[G] February credit sales ($1,386,000) × 75% = $1,039,500
[H] January credit sales ($1,260,000) × 15% = $ 189,000
[I] December credit sales ($1,234,800) × 8% = $ 98,784

Requirement 2

	January	February	March	1st Quarter
Pillows Unlimited **Cash Payments Budget—Direct Materials** For the Quarter Ended March 31		**Month**		
	January	**February**	**March**	**1st Quarter**
40% of current month DM purchases	$308,700[A]	$334,500[C]	$349,200[E]	$ 992,400
60% of last month's DM purchases	435,000[B]	463,050[D]	501,750[F]	1,399,800
Total cash payments for DM	$743,700	$797,550	$850,950	$2,392,200

[A] January DM purchases ($771,750) × 40% = $308,700
[B] December DM purchases ($725,000) × 60% = $435,000

[C] February DM purchases ($836,250) × 40% = $334,500
[D] January DM purchases ($771,750) × 60% = $463,050

[E] March DM purchases ($873,000) × 40% = $349,200
[F] February DM purchases ($836,250) × 60% = $501,750

END OF CHAPTER

Learning Objectives

- 1 Describe how and why managers use budgets
- 2 Prepare the operating budgets
- 3 Prepare the financial budgets
- 4 Prepare budgets for a merchandiser

Accounting Vocabulary

Budget Committee. (p. 517) A committee comprised of upper management, as well as cross-functional managers, who review, revise, and approve the final budget.

COD. (p. 521) Collect on Delivery, or Cash on Delivery. A sales term indicating that the inventory must be paid for at the time of delivery.

Cost of Goods Sold, Inventory, and Purchases Budget. (p. 540) A merchandiser's budget that computes the Cost of Goods Sold, the amount of desired ending inventory, and amount of merchandise to be purchased.

Financial Budgets. (p. 520) The budgets that project the collection and payment of cash, as well as forecast the company's budgeted balance sheet.

Flexible Budgets. (p. 539) Budgets prepared for different volumes of activity.

Line of Credit. (p. 536) A lending arrangement from a bank in which a company is allowed to borrow money as needed, up to a specified maximum amount, yet only pay interest on the portion that is actually borrowed until it is repaid.

Master Budget. (p. 519) The comprehensive planning document for the entire organization. The master budget includes the operating budgets and the financial budgets.

Operating Budgets. (p. 520) The budgets needed to run the daily operations of the company. The operation budgets culminate in a budgeted income statement.

Participative Budgeting. (p. 517) Budgeting that involves the participation of many levels of management.

Rolling Budget. (p. 517) A budget that is continuously updated so that the next 12 months of operations are always budgeted; also known as a continuous budget.

Safety Stock. (p. 521) Extra inventory kept on hand in case demand is higher than expected or problems in the factory slow production.

Sensitivity Analysis. (p. 538) A *what if* technique that asks what a result will be if a predicted amount is not achieved or if an underlying assumption changes.

Slack. (p. 517) Intentionally overstating budgeted expenses or understating budgeted revenues in order to cope with uncertainty, make performance appear better, or make room for potential budget cuts.

Strategic Planning. (p. 516) Setting long-term goals that may extend 5–10 years into the future.

Variance. (p. 519) The difference between actual and budgeted figures (revenues and expenses).

Zero-Based Budgeting. (p. 517) A budgeting approach in which managers begin with a budget of zero and must justify every dollar put into the budget.

MyAccountingLab Go to http://myaccountinglab.com/ for the following Quick Check, Short Exercises, Exercises, and Problems. They are available with immediate grading, explanations of correct and incorrect answers, and interactive media that acts as your own online tutor.

Quick Check

1. *(Learning Objective 1)* Amazon.com expects to receive which of the following benefits when it uses its budgeting process?
    a. The planning required to develop the budget helps managers foresee and avoid potential problems before they occur.
    b. The budget helps motivate employees to achieve Amazon.com's sales growth and cost reduction goals.
    c. The budget provides Amazon.com's managers with a benchmark against which to compare actual results for performance evaluation.
    d. All of the above.

2. *(Learning Objective 1)* Budgets are
    a. required by Generally Accepted Accounting Principles (GAAP).
    b. future-oriented.
    c. only used by large corporations.
    d. prepared by the controller for the entire company.

3. *(Learning Objective 1)* Technology has made it easier for managers to perform all of the following tasks *except*
   a. sensitivity analyses.
   b. combining individual units' budgets to create the companywide budget.
   c. removing slack from the budget.
   d. preparing responsibility center performance reports that identify variances between actual and budgeted revenues and costs.

4. *(Learning Objective 2)* Which of the following is the starting point for the master budget?
   a. The sales budget
   b. The direct materials budget
   c. The production budget
   d. The operating expenses budget

5. *(Learning Objective 2)* The income statement is part of which element of a company's master budget?
   a. The operating budgets
   b. The capital expenditures budget
   c. The financial budgets
   d. The cash budgets

6. *(Learning Objective 2)* The usual starting point for a direct labor budget for a manufacturer is the
   a. direct materials budget.
   b. sales budget.
   c. cash budget.
   d. production budget.

7. *(Learning Objective 3)* The following budgets are all financial budgets *except* for the
   a. combined cash budget.
   b. budgeted balance sheet.
   c. budgeted income statement.
   d. capital expenditures budget.

8. *(Learning Objective 3)* Which of the following expenses would *not* appear in a cash budget?
   a. Depreciation expense
   b. Wages expense
   c. Interest expense
   d. Marketing expense

9. *(Learning Objective 4)* Which of the following budgets would ordinarily *not* be prepared by a service company?
   a. Sales budget
   b. Operating expense budget
   c. Production budget
   d. Budgeted income statement

10. *(Learning Objective 4)* For a merchandising company, the Cost of Goods Sold, Inventory, and Purchases budget replaces all of the following budgets *except* the:
    a. Production budget
    b. Sales budget
    c. Direct labor budget
    d. Direct materials budget

Quick Check Answers

1. d2. b3. c4. a5. c6. d7. c8. a9. c10. b

Short Exercises

S9-1 Order of preparation and components of master budget
(Learning Objective 1)

Identify the order in which a manufacturer would prepare the following budgets. Also note whether each budget is an operating budget or a financial budget.

a. Budgeted income statement
b. Combined cash budget
c. Sales budget
d. Budgeted balance sheet
e. Cash payments budget
f. Direct materials budget
g. Production budget

S9-2 Understand key terms and definitions *(Learning Objectives 1 & 2)*

Listed next are several terms. Complete the following statements with one of these terms. You may use a term more than once, and some terms may not be used at all.

Operating budgets	Production budget	Master budget	Participative budgeting
Financial budgets	Slack	Zero-based budgeting	Strategic planning
Safety stock	Variance	Budget committee	Rolling budget

a. Managers will sometimes build _____ into their budgets to protect themselves against unanticipated expenses or lower revenues.

b. The _____ is the difference between actual and budgeted figures and is used to evaluate how well the manager controlled operations during the period.

c. _____ are often used by companies to review submitted budgets, make revisions as needed, and approve the final budgets.

d. _____ is extra inventory of finished goods that is kept on hand in case demand is higher than predicted or problems in the factory slow production.

e. The sales budget and production budget are examples of _____.

f. _____ is a budgeting process that begins with departmental managers and flows up through middle management to top management.

g. _____ is a budget that is continuously updated by adding months to the end of the budgeting period.

h. _____ is the comprehensive planning document for the entire organization.

i. These budgets, _____, project both the collection and payment of cash and forecast the company's budgeted balance sheet.

j. The _____ is used to forecast how many units should be made to meet the sales projects.

k. When an organization builds its budgets from the ground up, it is using _____.

l. _____ is the process of setting long-term goals that may extend several years into the future.

S9-3 Prepare a Sales Budget *(Learning Objective 2)*

Sport Physicians, Inc., offers two types of physical exams for students: the basic physical and the extended physical. The charge for the basic physical is $75, while the charge for the extended physical is $140. Sport Physicians expects to perform 200 basic physicals and 160 extended physicals in July, 220 basic and 190 extended in August, and 100 basic and 80 extended in September. Prepare the sales budget for the second quarter (July through September), with a column for each month and for the quarter in total.

S9-4 Production budget *(Learning Objective 2)*

Thomas Cycles manufactures chainless bicycles. On March 31, Thomas Cycles had 280 bikes in inventory. The company has a policy that the ending inventory in any month must be 10% of the following month's expected sales. Thomas Cycles expects to sell the following number of bikes in each of next four months:

April	1,050 bikes
May	1,190 bikes
June	1,360 bikes
July	1,240 bikes

Prepare a production budget for the second quarter, with a column for each month and for the quarter.

S9-5 Direct materials budget *(Learning Objective 2)*

The Bakery on the Riverbank produces organic bread that is sold by the loaf. Each loaf requires 1/2 of a pound of flour. The bakery pays $3.00 per pound of the organic flour used in its loaves. The bakery expects to produce the following number of loaves in each of the upcoming four months:

July	1,480 loaves
August	1,940 loaves
September	1,720 loaves
October	1,400 loaves

The bakery has a policy that it will have 20% of the following month's flour needs on hand at the end of each month. At the end of June, there were 75 pounds of flour on hand. Prepare the direct materials budget for the third quarter, with a column for each month and for the quarter.

S9-6 Direct labor budget *(Learning Objective 2)*

The Production Department of Carrington Manufacturing has prepared the following schedule of units to be produced over the first quarter of the upcoming year:

	January	February	March
Units to be produced	550	640	800

Each unit requires 5.0 hours of direct labor. Direct labor workers are paid an average of $20 per hour. How many hours will be required in January? In February? In March?

S9-7 Manufacturing overhead budget *(Learning Objective 2)*

Poppy Corporation is preparing its manufacturing overhead budget. The direct labor budget for the upcoming quarter is as follows:

	April	May	June
Budgeted direct labor hours...	410	730	680

The company's variable manufacturing overhead rate is $1.20 per direct labor hour and the company's fixed manufacturing overhead is $3,100 per month. How much manufacturing overhead will be budgeted for April? For May? For June?

S9-8 Operating expenses budget *(Learning Objective 2)*

Hyannisport Corporation is preparing its operating expenses budget. The budgeted unit sales for the upcoming quarter are as follows:

	July	August	September
Budgeted unit sales	1,290	1,420	1,730

The company's variable operating expenses are $4.00 per unit. Fixed monthly operating expenses include $5,200 for salaries, $3,800 for office rent, and depreciation of $2,800. How much operating expenses will be budgeted for July? For August? For September?

S9-9 Budgeted income statement *(Learning Objective 2)*

Scandia Scales manufactures a specialty precision scale. For January, Scandia expects to sell 1,400 scales at an average price of $2,360 per unit. Scandia's average manufacturing cost of each unit sold is $1,490. Variable operating expenses for Scandia Scales will be $1.50 per unit sold and fixed operating expenses are expected to be $7,300 for the month. Monthly interest expense is $3,200. Scandia Scales has a tax rate of 40% of income before taxes. Prepare Scandia Scales' budgeted income statement for January.

S9-10 Cash collections budget *(Learning Objective 3)*

Keystone Service anticipates the following sales revenue over a five-month period:

	November	December	January	February	March
Sales revenue	$16,100	$10,900	$15,800	$12,900	$14,200

Keystone Service's sales are 40% cash and 60% credit. Keystone Service's collection history indicates that credit sales are collected as follows:

25% in the month of the sale
50% in the month after the sale
15% two months after the sale
10% are never collected

How much cash will be collected in January? In February? In March?

S9-11 Cash payments budget *(Learning Objective 3)*

Centennial Corporation is preparing its cash payments budget for next month. The following information pertains to the cash payments:

a. Centennial Corporation pays for 50% of its direct materials purchases in the month of purchase and the remainder the following month. Last month's direct material purchases were $75,000, while the company anticipates $87,000 of direct material purchases next month.

b. Direct labor for the upcoming month is budgeted to be $36,000 and will be paid at the end of the upcoming month.

c. Manufacturing overhead is estimated to be 130% of direct labor cost each month and is paid in the month in which it is incurred. This monthly estimate includes $13,000 of depreciation on the plant and equipment.

d. Monthly operating expenses for next month are expected to be $41,000, which includes $2,500 of depreciation on office equipment and $1,600 of bad debt expense. These monthly operating expenses are paid during the month in which they are incurred.

e. Centennial Corporation will be making an estimated tax payment of $7,800 next month. How much cash will be paid out next month?

S9-12 Cash budget *(Learning Objective 3)*

Henderson Services, Inc., has $8,300 cash on hand on January 1. The company requires a minimum cash balance of $7,300. January cash collections are $548,430. Total cash payments for January are $575,160. Prepare a cash budget for January. How much cash, if any, will Henderson need to borrow by the end of January?

S9-13 Estimate credit card fees *(Learning Objective 4)*

The local grocery store expects that customers will use credit cards to pay for a total of 60,000 sales transactions during the month of April. These transactions are expected to amount to $3,000,000 in total sales revenue. The credit card issuers charge the store a transaction fee equal to $0.30 per transaction plus 2% of the amount charged. When budgeting for operating expenses in April, how much should the store expect to incur for credit card transaction fees?

S9-14 Inventory, purchases, and cost of goods sold *(Learning Objective 4)*

Heisler Company sells its smartphone worldwide. Heisler expects to sell 4,600 smartphones for $160 each in January and 4,000 smartphones for $225 each in February. All sales are cash only. Heisler expects cost of goods sold to average 60% of sales revenue and the company expects to sell 4,300 smartphones in March for $300 each. Heisler's target ending inventory is $10,000 plus 50% of the next month's cost of goods sold.

1. Prepare the sales budget for January and February.

2. Prepare Heisler's inventory, purchases, and cost of goods sold budget for January and February.

EXERCISES Group A

E9-15A Budgeting and sustainability *(Learning Objective 1)*

Dudley Beverages manufactures its own soda pop bottles. The bottles are made from polyethylene terephthalate (PET), a lightweight yet strong plastic. Dudley uses as much PET recycled resin pellets in its bottles as it can, both because using recycled PET helps Dudley to meet its sustainability goals and because recycled PET is less expensive than virgin PET.

Dudley is continuing to search for ways to reduce its costs and its impact on the environment. PET plastic is melted and blown over soda bottle molds to produce the bottles. One idea Dudley's engineers have suggested is to retrofit the soda bottle molds and change the plastic formulation slightly so that 20% less PET plastic is used for each bottle. The average kilograms of PET per soda bottle before any redesign is 0.005 kg. The cost of retrofitting the soda bottle molds will result in a one-time charge of $18,000, while the plastic reformulation will cause the average cost per kilogram of PET plastic to change from $2.00 to $2.20.

Dudley's management is analyzing whether the change to the bottle molds to reduce PET plastic usage should be made. Management expects the following number of soda bottles to be used in the upcoming year:

	Quarter 1	Quarter 2	Quarter 3	Quarter 4
Number of soda pop bottles to be produced	2,500,000	2,900,000	3,200,000	2,300,000

For the upcoming year, management expects the beginning inventory of PET to be 1,250 kilograms, while ending inventory is expected to be 1,700 kilograms. During the first three quarters of the year, management wants to keep the ending inventory of PET at the end of each quarter equal to 10% of the following quarter's PET needs.

Requirements

1. Using the original data (before any redesign of soda bottles), prepare a direct materials budget to calculate the cost of PET purchases in each quarter for the upcoming year and for the year in total.

2. Assume that the company retrofits the soda bottle molds and changes the plastic formulation slightly so that less PET plastic is used in each bottle. Now prepare a direct materials budget to calculate the cost of PET purchases in each quarter for the upcoming year and for the year in total for this possible scenario.

3. Compare the cost of PET plastic for Requirement 1 (original data) and for Requirement 2 (making change to using less PET.) What is the direct material cost savings from making the change to using less PET? Compare the total of those savings to the cost of retrofitting the soda bottle molds. Should the company make the change? Explain your rationale.

E9-16A Prepare a sales budget for a retail organization *(Learning Objective 2)*

Upstate College Bookstore is the bookstore on campus for students and faculty. Upstate College Bookstore shows the following sales projections in units by quarter for the upcoming year:

Quarter	Books	School Supplies	Apparel	Miscellaneous
1st	1,590	200	510	690
2nd	850	140	350	580
3rd	1,760	250	880	870
4th	680	120	540	480

The average price of an item in each of the departments is as follows:

	Average sales per unit
Books	$88
School supplies	$10
Apparel	$25
Miscellaneous	$ 8

Requirement
Prepare a sales budget for the upcoming year by quarter for the Upstate College Bookstore, with sales categorized by the four product groupings (books, school supplies, apparel, and miscellaneous).

E9-17A Prepare a sales budget for a not-for-profit organization
(Learning Objective 2)

Copley Preschool operates a not-for-profit morning preschool. Each family pays a non-refundable registration fee of $115 per child per school year. Monthly tuition for the nine-month school year varies depending on the number of days per week that the child attends preschool. The monthly tuition is $125 for the two-day program, $145 for the three-day program, $170 for the four-day program, and $185 for the five-day program. The following enrollment has been projected for the coming year:

Two-day program:	80 children
Three-day program:	36 children
Four-day program:	52 children
Five-day program:	12 children

In addition to the morning preschool, Copley Preschool offers a Lunch Bunch program where kids have the option of staying an extra hour for lunch and playtime. Copley Preschool charges an additional $2 per child for every Lunch Bunch attended. Historically, half the children stay for Lunch Bunch an average of 15 times a month.

Requirement
Calculate Copley Preschool's budgeted revenue for the school year.

E9-18A Production budget *(Learning Objective 2)*

Wolanin Foods produces specialty soup sold in jars. The projected sales in dollars and jars for each quarter of the upcoming year are as follows:

	Total sales revenue	Number of jars sold
1st quarter	$180,000	153,000
2nd quarter	$214,000	184,000
3rd quarter	$257,000	211,000
4th quarter	$196,000	163,500

Wolanin anticipates selling 226,000 jars with total sales revenue of $266,000 in the first quarter of the year *following* the year given in the preceding table. Wolanin has a policy that the ending inventory of jars must be 30% of the following quarter's sales. Prepare a production budget for the year that shows the number of jars to be produced each quarter and for the year in total.

E9-19A Direct materials budget *(Learning Objective 2)*

Milford Industries manufactures a popular interactive stuffed animal for children that requires two computer chips inside each toy. Milford Industries pays $1 for each computer chip. To help to guard against stockouts of the computer chip, Milford Industries has a policy that states that the ending inventory of computer chips should be at least 30% of the following month's production needs. The production schedule for the first four months of the year is as follows:

	Stuffed animals to be produced
January	5,200
February	4,700
March	4,000
April	4,600

Requirement

Prepare a direct materials budget for the first quarter that shows both the number of computer chips needed and the dollar amount of the purchases in the budget.

E9-20A Production and direct materials budgets *(Learning Objective 2)*

Osborne Manufacturing produces self-watering planters for use in upscale retail establishments. Sales projections for the first five months of the upcoming year show the estimated unit sales of the planters each month to be as follows:

	Number of planters to be sold
January	3,900
February	3,200
March	3,700
April	4,400
May	4,900

Inventory at the start of the year was 975 planters. The desired inventory of planters at the end of each month should be equal to 25% of the following month's budgeted sales. Each planter requires 4 pounds of polypropylene (a type of plastic). The company wants to have 30% of the polypropylene required for next month's production on hand at the end of each month. The polypropylene costs $0.20 per pound.

Requirements

1. Prepare a production budget for each month in the first quarter of the year, including production in units for each month and for the quarter.
2. Prepare a direct materials budget for the polypropylene for each month in the first quarter of the year, including the pounds of polypropylene required, and the total cost of the polypropylene to be purchased.

E9-21A Direct labor budget *(Learning Objective 2)*

Valentine Industries manufactures three models of a product in a single plant with two departments: Cutting and Assembly. The company has estimated costs for each of the three product models: the Flash, the Royal, and the Zip models. The company is currently analyzing direct labor hour requirements for the upcoming year.

	Cutting	Assembly
Estimated hours per unit:		
Flashes	1.6	2.0
Royals	1.1	2.6
Zips	1.2	2.7
Direct labor hour rate	$9	$10

Budgeted unit production for each of the products is as follows:

	Number of units to be produced
Product model:	
Flashes	590
Royals	730
Zips	810

Requirement

Prepare a direct labor budget for the upcoming year that shows the budgeted direct labor costs for each department and for the company as a whole.

E9-22A Manufacturing overhead budget *(Learning Objective 2)*

The Donaldson Company is in the process of preparing its manufacturing overhead budget for the upcoming year. Sales are projected to be 40,000 units. Information about the various manufacturing overhead costs follows:

	Variable rate per unit	Total fixed costs
Indirect materials	$1.40	
Supplies	$1.00	
Indirect labor	$0.40	$68,000
Plant utilities	$0.10	$35,000
Repairs and maintenance	$0.60	$14,000
Depreciation on plant and equipment		$42,000
Insurance on plant and equipment		$20,000
Plant supervision		$66,000

Requirement

Prepare the manufacturing overhead budget for the Donaldson Company for the upcoming year.

E9-23A Prepare an operating expenses budget and an income statement
(Learning Objective 2)

Fairlawn Preschool operates a not-for-profit morning preschool that operates nine months of the year. Fairlawn Preschool has 160 kids enrolled in its various programs. The preschool's primary expense is payroll. Teachers are paid a flat salary each of the nine months as follows:

Teachers of two-day program:	$ 430 per month
Teachers of three-day program:	$ 660 per month
Teachers of four-day program:	$ 880 per month
Teachers of five-day program:	$1,050 per month
Preschool director's salary:	$1,980 per month

Fairlawn Preschool has 8 two-day program teachers, 3 three-day program teachers, 5 four-day program teachers, and 4 five-day program teachers. The preschool also has a director.

In addition to the salary expense, the preschool must pay federal payroll taxes (FICA taxes) in the amount of 7.65% of salary expense. The preschool leases its facilities from a local church, paying $5,000 every month it operates. Fixed operating expenses (telephone, internet access, bookkeeping services, and so forth) amount to $900 per month over the nine-month school year. Variable monthly expenses (over the nine-month school year) for art supplies and other miscellaneous supplies are $12 per child. Revenue for the entire nine-month school year from tuition, registration fees, and the lunch program is projected to be $233,400.

Requirements

1. Prepare Fairlawn Preschool's monthly operating budget. Round all amounts to the nearest dollar.
2. Using your answer from Requirement 1, create Fairlawn Preschool's budgeted income statement for the entire nine-month school year. You may group all operating expenses together.
3. Fairlawn Preschool is a not-for-profit preschool. What might the preschool do with its projected income for the year?

E9-24A Budgeted income statement *(Learning Objective 2)*

Irvin Labs performs a specialty lab test for local companies for $50 per test. For the upcoming quarter, Irvin Labs is projecting the following sales:

	January	February	March
Number of lab tests	5,800	4,100	5,700

The budgeted cost of performing each test is $22. Operating expenses are projected to be $60,000 in January, $52,000 in February, and $65,000 in March. Irvin Labs is subject to a corporate tax rate of 30%.

Requirement

Prepare a budgeted income statement for the first quarter, with a column for each month and for the quarter.

E9-25A Prepare a budgeted income statement *(Learning Objective 2)*

Klaben Motors is a chain of car dealerships. Sales in the fourth quarter of last year were $6,000,000. Suppose management projects that its current year's quarterly sales will increase by 3% in quarter 1, by another 4% in quarter 2, by another 6% in quarter 3, and by another 5% in quarter 4. Management expects cost of goods sold to be 50% of revenues every quarter, while operating expenses should be 30% of revenues during each of the first two quarters, 25% of revenues during the third quarter, and 35% during the fourth quarter.

Requirement

Prepare a budgeted income statement for each of the four quarters and for the entire year.

E9-26A Cash collections budget *(Learning Objective 3)*

Grisham Corporation has found that 80% of its sales in any given month are credit sales, while the remainder are cash sales. Of the credit sales, Grisham Corporation has experienced the following collection pattern:

25% paid in the month of the sale
50% paid in the month after the sale
22% paid two months after the sale
3% of the sales are never collected

November sales for last year were $105,000, while December sales were $125,000. Projected sales for the next three months are as follows:

January sales	$165,000
February sales..	$130,000
March sales..	$180,000

Requirement

Prepare a cash collections budget for the first quarter, with a column for each month and for the quarter.

E9-27A Cash payments budget *(Learning Objective 3)*

The St. Germaine Company is preparing its cash payments budget. The following items relate to cash payments the company anticipates making during the second quarter of the upcoming year.

a. The company pays for 45% of its direct materials purchases in the month of purchase and the remainder the following month. The company's direct material purchases for March through June are anticipated to be as follows:

March	April	May	June
$116,000	$132,000	$120,000	$146,000

b. Direct labor is paid in the month in which it is incurred. Direct labor for each month of the second quarter is budgeted as follows:

April	May	June
$46,000	$56,000	$71,000

c. Manufacturing overhead is estimated to be 140% of direct labor cost each month. This monthly estimate includes $33,000 of depreciation on the plant and equipment. All manufacturing overhead (excluding depreciation) is paid in the month in which it is incurred.

d. Monthly operating expenses for March through June are projected to be as follows:

March	April	May	June
$77,000	$86,000	$89,000	$92,000

Monthly operating expenses are paid in the month after they are incurred. Monthly operating expenses include $9,000 for monthly depreciation on administrative offices and equipment, and $3,400 for bad debt expense.

e. The company plans to pay $3,000 (cash) for a new server in May.

f. The company must make an estimated tax payment of $11,500 on June 15.

Requirement

Prepare a cash payments budget for April, May, and June and for the quarter.

E9-28A Combined cash budget *(Learning Objective 3)*

Brimfield Health Center provides a variety of medical services. The company is preparing its cash budget for the upcoming third quarter. The following transactions are expected to occur:

a. Cash collections from services in July, August, and September are projected to be $99,000, $152,000, and $121,000 respectively.

b. Cash payments for the upcoming third quarter are projected to be $148,000 in July, $109,000 in August, and $135,000 in September.

c. The cash balance as of the first day of the third quarter is projected to be $36,000.

d. The health center has a policy that it must maintain a minimum cash balance of $27,000.

The health center has a line of credit with the local bank that allows it to borrow funds in months that it would not otherwise have its minimum balance. If the company has more than its minimum balance at the end of any given month, it uses the excess funds to pay off any outstanding line of credit balance. Each month, Brimfield Health Center pays interest on the prior month's line of credit ending balance. The actual interest rate that the health center will pay floats since it is tied to the prime rate. However, the interest rate paid during the budget period is expected to be 1% of the prior month's line of credit ending balance (if the company did not have an outstanding balance at the end of the prior month, then Brimfield Health Center does not have to pay any interest). All line of credit borrowings are taken or paid off on the first day of the month. As of the first day of the third quarter, Brimfield Health Center did not have a balance on its line of credit.

Requirement

Prepare a combined cash budget for Brimfield Health Center for the third quarter, with a column for each month and for the quarter total.

E9-29A Estimate debit and credit card fees *(Learning Objective 4)*

The local drug store expects to have 30,000 sales transactions in November, amounting to $900,000 in sales revenue. The store expects that 60% of the sales transactions will be made using credit or debit cards. Although customers use credit cards and debit cards with differing transaction fees, the average transaction fee charged to the store amounts to $0.20 per transaction plus 3% of the amount charged.

1. How many sales transactions does the store expect will be paid by customers using credit or debit cards?
2. How much of November's sales revenue is expected to be paid by customers using credit or debit cards?
3. When budgeting for November's operating expenses, how much should the store expect to incur in credit and debit card transaction fees?
4. Assuming the credit and debit card companies process the deposit the same day as the transaction, how much cash does the store expect the credit and debit card companies to deposit in the store's bank account during the month of November?

E9-30A Prepare sales and cash collections budgets *(Learning Objectives 2 & 3)*

Augustine Reeds, a manufacturer of saxophone, oboe, and clarinet reeds, has projected sales to be $900,000 in October, $964,000 in November, $1,040,000 in December, and $922,000 in January. Augustine's sales are 25% cash and 75% credit. Augustine's collection history indicates that credit sales are collected as follows:

20% in the month of the sale
70% in the month after the sale
8% two months after the sale
2% are never collected

Requirements

1. Prepare a sales budget for all four months, showing the breakdown between cash and credit sales.
2. Prepare a cash collections budget for December and January. Round all answers up to the nearest dollar.

E9-31A Prepare a budgeted balance sheet *(Learning Objective 3)*

Use the following information to prepare a budgeted balance sheet for Zucca Corporation at March 31. Show computations for the cash and stockholders' equity amounts.

a. March 31 inventory balance, $13,405.
b. March payments for inventory, $4,300.
c. March payments of accounts payable and accrued liabilities, $8,500.
d. March 31 accounts payable balance, $2,100.
e. February 28 furniture and fixtures balance, $34,600; accumulated depreciation balance, $29,860.
f. February 28 stockholders' equity, $28,520.
g. March depreciation expense, $700.
h. Cost of goods sold, 70% of sales.
i. Other March expenses, including income tax, total $8,000; paid in cash.

j. February 28 cash balance, $11,500.

k. March budgeted sales, $12,500.

l. March 31 accounts receivable balance, one-fourth of March sales.

m. March cash receipts, $14,400.

E9-32A Prepare a cash budget *(Learning Objective 3)*

Helton Medical Supply began October with $10,600 cash. Management forecasts that collections from credit customers will be $12,200 in October and $15,800 in November. The business is scheduled to receive $5,000 cash on a business note receivable in October. Projected cash payments include inventory purchases ($13,200 in October and $13,300 in November) and operating expenses ($3,600 each month).

Helton Medical Supply's bank requires a $10,000 minimum balance in the business' checking account. At the end of any month when the account balance dips below $10,000, the bank automatically extends credit to the business in multiples of $1,000. Helton Medical Supply borrows as little as possible and pays back loans in quarterly installments of $2,000 plus 4% interest on the entire unpaid principal. The first payment occurs three months after the loan.

Requirement

Prepare Helton Medical Supply's cash budget for October and November.

E9-33A Finish an incomplete cash budget *(Learning Objective 3)*

You recently began a job as an accounting intern at Mountain Adventures. Your first task was to help prepare the cash budget for February and March. Unfortunately, the computer with the budget file crashed, and you did not have a backup or even a hard copy. You ran a program to salvage bits of data from the budget file. After entering the following data in the budget, you may have just enough information to reconstruct the budget.

Mountain Adventures eliminates any cash deficiency by borrowing the exact amount needed from State Street Bank, where the current interest rate is 6%. Mountain Adventures pays interest on its outstanding debt at the end of each month. The company also repays all borrowed amounts at the end of the month as cash becomes available.

Requirement

Complete the following cash budget:

MOUNTAIN ADVENTURES
Cash Budget
February and March

	February	March
Beginning cash balance	$ 16,200	$?
Cash collections	?	79,800
Cash from sale of plant assets	0	1,900
Cash available	$106,200	$?
Cash payments:		
Purchase of inventory	$?	$41,000
Operating expenses	47,200	?
Total payments	$ 98,000	$?
(1) Ending cash balance before financing	$?	$27,400
Minimum cash balance desired	23,000	23,000
Cash excess (deficiency)	$?	$?
Financing of cash deficiency:		
Borrowing (at end of month)	$?	$?
Principal repayments (at end of month)	?	?
Interest expense	?	?
(2) Total effects of financing	$?	$?
Ending cash balance (1) + (2)	$?	$?

E9-34A Prepare an inventory, purchases, and cost of goods sold budget
(Learning Objective 4)

Lightning Readers sells eReaders. Its sales budget for the nine months ended September 30 follows:

	Mar 31	Jun 30	Sep 30	Nine-Month Total
		Quarter Ended		
Cash sales, 30%............................	$ 37,500	$ 52,500	$ 45,000	$135,000
Credit sales, 70%...........................	87,500	122,500	105,000	315,000
Total sales, 100%..........................	$125,000	$175,000	$150,000	$450,000

In the past, cost of goods sold has been 70% of total sales. The director of marketing and the financial vice president agree that each quarter's ending inventory should not be below $30,000 plus 20% of cost of goods sold for the following quarter. The marketing director expects sales of $225,000 during the fourth quarter. The January 1 inventory was $15,000.

Requirement
Prepare an inventory, purchases, and cost of goods sold budget for each of the first three quarters of the year. Compute cost of goods sold for the entire nine-month period.

EXERCISES Group B

E9-35B Budgeting and Sustainability *(Learning Objective 1)*

Crawford Beverages manufactures its own soda pop bottles. The bottles are made from polyethylene terephthalate (PET), a lightweight yet strong plastic. Crawford uses as much PET recycled resin pellets in its bottles as it can, both because using recycled PET helps Crawford to meet its sustainability goals and because recycled PET is less expensive than virgin PET.

Crawford is continuing to search for ways to reduce its costs and its impact on the environment. PET plastic is melted and blown over soda bottle molds to produce the bottles. One idea Crawford's engineers have suggested is to retrofit the soda bottle molds and change the plastic formulation slightly so that 20% less PET plastic is used for each bottle. The average kilograms of PET per soda bottle before any redesign is 0.005 kg. The cost of retrofitting the soda bottle molds will result in a one-time charge of $24,000, while the plastic reformulation will cause the average cost per kilogram of PET plastic to change from $2.50 to $2.60.

Crawford's management is analyzing whether the change to the bottle molds to reduce PET plastic usage should be made. Management expects the following number of soda bottles to be used in the upcoming year:

	Quarter 1	Quarter 2	Quarter 3	Quarter 4
Number of soda pop bottles to be produced	2,000,000	3,000,000	2,700,000	2,500,000

For the upcoming year, management expects the beginning inventory of PET to be 1,000 kilograms, while ending inventory is expected to be 1,700 kilograms. During the first three quarters of the year, management wants to keep the ending inventory of PET at the end of each quarter's PET needs.

Requirements

1. Using the original date (before any redesign of soda bottles), prepare a direct materials budget to calculate the cost of PET purchases in each quarter for the upcoming year and for the year in total.

2. Assume that the company retrofits the soda bottle molds and changes the plastic formulation slightly so that less PET plastic is used in each bottle. Now prepare a direct materials budget to calculate the cost of PET purchases in each quarter for the upcoming year and for the year in total for this possible scenario.

3. Compare the cost of PET plastic for Requirement 1 (original data) and for Requirement 2 (making the change to using less PET.) What is the direct material cost saving from making the change to using less PET? Compare the total of those savings to the cost of retrofitting the soda bottle molds. Should the company make the change? Explain your rationale.

E9-36B Prepare a sales budget for a retail organization *(Learning Objective 2)*

Parma College Bookstore is the bookstore on campus for students and faculty. Parma College Bookstore shows the following sales projections in units by quarter for the upcoming year:

Quarter	Books	School Supplies	Apparel	Miscellaneous
1st	1,580	280	550	630
2nd	840	120	390	560
3rd	1,760	290	820	820
4th	680	100	540	490

The average price of an item in each of the departments is as follows:

	Average sales per unit
Books	$87
School supplies	$18
Apparel	$28
Miscellaneous	$ 4

Requirement

Prepare a sales budget for the upcoming year by quarter for the Parma College Bookstore, with sales categorized by the four product groupings (books, school supplies, apparel, and miscellaneous).

E9-37B Prepare a sales budget for a not-for-profit organization *(Learning Objective 2)*

Wadsworth Preschool operates a not-for-profit morning preschool. Each family pays a nonrefundable registration fee of $140 per child per school year. Monthly tuition for the eight-month school year varies depending on the number of days per week that the child attends preschool. The monthly tuition is $130 for the two-day program, $155 for the three-day program, $180 for the four-day program, and $195 for the five-day program. The following enrollment has been projected for the coming year:

Two-day program: 88 children	Four-day program: 54 children
Three-day program: 34 children	Five-day program: 28 children

In addition to the morning preschool, Wadsworth Preschool offers a Lunch Bunch program where kids have the option of staying an extra hour for lunch and playtime. The preschool charges an additional $2 per child for every Lunch Bunch attended. Historically, half the children stay for Lunch Bunch an average of 10 times a month.

Requirement

Calculate Wadsworth Preschool's budgeted revenue for the school year.

E9-38B Production budget *(Learning Objective 2)*

Gable Foods produces specialty soup sold in jars. The projected sales in dollars and jars for each quarter of the upcoming year are as follows:

	Total sales revenue	Number of jars sold
1st quarter	$187,000	150,500
2nd quarter	$216,000	184,000
3rd quarter	$253,000	210,000
4th quarter	$191,000	160,000

Gable anticipates selling 220,000 jars with total sales revenue of $261,000 in the first quarter of the year following the year given in the preceding table. Gable has a policy that the ending inventory of jars must be 30% of the following quarter's sales. Prepare a production budget for the year that shows the number of jars to be produced each quarter and for the year in total.

E9-39B Direct materials budget *(Learning Objective 2)*

Schaeffer Industries manufactures a popular interactive stuffed animal for children that requires three computer chips inside each toy. Schaeffer Industries pays $2 for each computer chip. To help to guard against stockouts of the computer chip, Schaeffer Industries has a policy that states that the ending inventory of computer chips should be at least 30% of the following month's production needs. The production schedule for the first four months of the year is as follows:

	Stuffed animals to be produced
January	5,100
February	4,500
March	4,100
April	4,000

Requirement

Prepare a direct materials budget for the first quarter that shows both the number of computer chips needed and the dollar amount of the purchases in the budget.

E9-40B Production and direct materials budgets *(Learning Objective 2)*

Snyder Manufacturing produces self-watering planters for use in upscale retail establishments. Sales projections for the first five months of the upcoming year show the estimated unit sales of the planters each month to be as follows:

	Number of planters to be sold
January	3,400
February	3,800
March	3,300
April	4,900
May	4,600

Inventory at the start of the year was 850 planters. The desired inventory of planters at the end of each month should be equal to 25% of the following month's budgeted sales. Each planter requires 3 pounds of polypropylene (a type of plastic). The company wants to have 20% of the polypropylene required for next month's production on hand at the end of each month. The polypropylene costs $0.20 per pound.

Requirements

1. Prepare a production budget for each month in the first quarter of the year, including production in units for each month and for the quarter.
2. Prepare a direct materials budget for the polypropylene for each month in the first quarter of the year, including the pounds of polypropylene required, and the total cost of the polypropylene to be purchased.

E9-41B Direct labor budget *(Learning Objective 2)*

Laughton Industries manufactures three models of a product in a single plant with two departments: Cutting and Assembly. The company has estimated costs for each of the three product models, which are the Flash, the Regal, and the Imperial models.

The company is currently analyzing direct labor hour requirements for the upcoming year.

	Cutting	Assembly
Estimated hours per unit:		
Flashes	1.6	2.4
Regals	1.1	2.1
Imperials	1.0	2.0
Direct labor hour rate	$10	$12

Budgeted unit production for each of the products is as follows:

	Number of units to be produced
Product model:	
Flashes	590
Regals	760
Imperials	810

Requirement

Prepare a direct labor budget for the upcoming year that shows the budgeted direct labor costs for each department and for the company as a whole.

E9-42B Manufacturing overhead budget *(Learning Objective 2)*

The Robbins Company is in the process of preparing its manufacturing overhead budget for the upcoming year. Sales are projected to be 44,000 units. Information about the various manufacturing overhead costs follows:

	Variable rate per unit	Total fixed costs
Indirect materials	$0.90	
Supplies	$0.80	
Indirect labor	$0.30	$65,000
Plant utilities	$0.20	$38,000
Repairs and maintenance	$0.40	$14,000
Depreciation on plant and equipment		$40,000
Insurance on plant and equipment		$22,000
Plant supervision		$62,000

Requirement

Prepare the manufacturing overhead budget for the Robbins Company for the upcoming year.

E9-43B Prepare an operating expenses budget and an income statement
(Learning Objective 2)

Hinkley Preschool operates a not-for-profit morning preschool that operates nine months of the year. The preschool has 160 kids enrolled in its various programs. The preschool's primary expense is payroll. Teachers are paid a flat salary each of the nine months as follows:

Salary data	
Teachers of two-day program:	$ 400 per month
Teachers of three-day program:	$ 600 per month
Teachers of four-day program:	$ 800 per month
Teachers of five-day program:	$ 900 per month
Preschool director's salary:	$1,400 per month

Hinkley Preschool has 8 two-day program teachers, 5 three-day program teachers, 7 four-day program teachers, and 3 five-day program teachers. Hinkley Preschool also has a director.

In addition to the salary expense, Hinkley Preschool must pay federal payroll taxes (FICA taxes) in the amount of 7.65% of salary expense. The preschool leases its facilities from a local church, paying $4,000 per month. Fixed operating expenses (telephone, internet access, bookkeeping services, and so forth) amount to $700 per month over the nine-month school year. Variable monthly expenses (over the nine-month school year) for art supplies and other miscellaneous supplies are $12 per child. Revenue for the entire nine-month school year from tuition, registration fees, and the lunch program is projected to be $233,400.

Requirements

1. Prepare Hinkley Preschool's monthly operating budget. Round all amounts to the nearest dollar.
2. Using your answer from Requirement 1, create Hinkley Preschool's budgeted income statement for the entire nine-month school year. You may group all operating expenses together.
3. Hinkley Preschool is a not-for-profit preschool. What might the preschool do with its projected income for the year?

E9-44B Budgeted income statement *(Learning Objective 2)*

Engleman Labs performs a specialty lab test for local companies for $45 per test. For the upcoming quarter, Engleman Labs is projecting the following sales:

	January	February	March
Number of tests	5,600	4,000	5,700

The budgeted cost of performing each test is $20. Operating expenses are projected to be $59,000 in January, $56,000 in February, and $61,000 in March. Engleman Labs is subject to a corporate tax rate of 30%.

Requirement

Prepare a budgeted income statement for the first quarter, with a column for each month and for the quarter in total.

E9-45B Prepare a budgeted income statement *(Learning Objective 2)*

Chesrown Motors is a chain of car dealerships. Sales in the fourth quarter of last year were $8,000,000. Suppose its management projects that its current year's quarterly sales will increase by 4% in quarter 1, by another 5% in quarter 2, by another 5% in quarter 3, and by another 3% in quarter 4. Management expects cost of goods sold to be 50% of revenues every quarter, while operating expenses should be 30% of revenues during each of the first two quarters, 20% of revenues during the third quarter, and 25% during the fourth quarter.

Requirement

Prepare a budgeted income statement for each of the four quarters and for the entire year.

E9-46B Cash collections budget *(Learning Objective 3)*

Majestic Corporation has found that 70% of its sales in any given month are credit sales, while the remainder are cash sales. Of the credit sales, the company has experienced the following collection pattern:

25% paid in the month of the sale

50% paid in the month after the sale

16% paid two months after the sale

9% of the sales are never collected

November sales for last year were $80,000, while December sales were $125,000. Projected sales for the next three months are as follows:

January sales	$150,000
February sales	$130,000
March sales	$170,000

Requirement

Prepare a cash collections budget for the first quarter, with a column for each month and for the quarter.

E9-47B Cash payments budget *(Learning Objective 3)*

Kobe Corporation is preparing its cash payments budget. The following items relate to cash payments Kobe Corporation anticipates making during the second quarter of the upcoming year.

a. Kobe Corporation pays for 50% of its direct materials purchases in the month of purchase and the remainder the following month. The company direct material purchases for March through June are anticipated to be as follows:

March	April	May	June
$116,000	$133,000	$122,000	$147,000

b. Direct labor is paid in the month in which it is incurred. Direct labor for each month of the second quarter is budgeted as follows:

April	May	June
$44,000	$54,000	$69,000

c. Manufacturing overhead is estimated to be 140% of direct labor cost each month. This monthly estimate includes $31,000 of depreciation on the plant and equipment. All manufacturing overhead (excluding depreciation) is paid in the month in which it is incurred.

d. Monthly operating expenses for March through June are projected to be as follows:

March	April	May	June
$74,000	$88,000	$83,000	$93,000

Monthly operating expenses are paid in the month after they are incurred. Monthly operating expenses include $15,000 for monthly depreciation on administrative offices and equipment, and $3,100 for bad debt expense.

e. Kobe Corporation plans to pay $4,000 (cash) for a new server in May.

f. Kobe Corporation must make an estimated tax payment of $11,000 on June 15.

Requirement

Prepare a cash payments budget for April, May, and June and for the quarter.

E9-48B Combined cash budget *(Learning Objective 3)*

Streetsboro Health Center provides a variety of medical services. The company is preparing its cash budget for the upcoming third quarter. The following transactions are expected to occur:

a. Cash collections from services in July, August, and September are projected to be $99,000, $150,000, and $120,000, respectively.

b. Cash payments for the upcoming third quarter are projected to be $146,000 in July, $103,000 in August, and $130,000 in September.

c. The cash balance as of the first day of the third quarter is projected to be $32,000.

Streetsboro Health Center has a policy that it must maintain a minimum cash balance of $25,000. The company has a line of credit with the local bank that allows it to borrow funds in months that it would not otherwise have the minimum balance. If the company has more than the minimum balance at the end of any given month, it uses the excess funds to pay off any outstanding line of credit balance. Each month, Streetsboro Health Center pays interest on the prior month's line of credit ending balance. The actual interest rate that Streetsboro Health Center will pay floats since it is tied to the prime rate. However, the interest rate paid during the budget period is expected to be 1% of the prior month's line of credit ending balance (if it did not have an outstanding balance at the end of the prior month, then the company does not have to pay any interest). All line of credit borrowings are taken or paid off on the first day of the month. As of the first day of the third quarter, Streetsboro Health Center did not have a balance on its line of credit.

Requirement

Prepare a combined cash budget for Streetsboro Health Center for the third quarter, with a column for each month and for the quarter total.

E9-49B Estimate debit and credit card fees *(Learning Objective 4)*

The local hardware store expects to have 40,000 in total sales transactions in November, amounting to $700,000 in sales revenue. The store expects that 60% of the sales transactions will be made using credit or debit cards. Although customers use credit cards and debit cards with differing transaction fees, the average transaction fee charged to the store amounts to $0.30 per transaction plus 2% of the amount charged.

1. How many sales transactions does the store expect will be paid by customers using credit or debit cards?

2. How much of November's sales revenue is expected to be paid by customers using credit or debit cards?

3. When budgeting for November's operating expenses, how much should the store expect to incur in credit and debit card transaction fees?

4. Assuming the credit and debit card companies process the deposit the same day as the transaction, how much cash does the store expect the credit and debit card companies to deposit in the store's bank account during the month of November?

E9-50B Prepare sales and cash collections budgets *(Learning Objectives 2 & 3)*

Goodman Reeds, a manufacturer of saxophone, oboe, and clarinet reeds, has projected sales to be $890,000 in October, $960,000 in November, $1,030,000 in December, and $932,000 in January. Goodman's sales are 30% cash and 70% on credit. Goodman's collection history indicates that credit sales are collected as follows:

20% in the month of the sale
60% in the month after the sale
14% two months after the sale
6% are never collected

Requirements

1. Prepare a sales budget for all four months, showing the breakdown between cash and credit sales.
2. Prepare a cash collection budget for December and January. Round all answers up to the nearest dollar.

E9-51B Prepare a budgeted balance sheet *(Learning Objective 3)*

Use the following information to prepare a budgeted balance sheet for Grimm Corporation at March 31. Show computations for the cash and owners' equity amounts.

a. March 31 inventory balance, $17,965.
b. March payments for inventory, $4,700.
c. March payments of accounts payable and accrued liabilities, $8,500.
d. March 31 accounts payable balance, $2,200.
e. February 28 furniture and fixtures balance,$34,700; accumulated depreciation balance, $29,830.
f. February 28 owners' equity, $28,890.
g. March depreciation expense, $400.
h. Cost of goods sold, 40% of sales.
i. Other March expenses, including income tax, total $6,000; paid in cash.
j. February 28 cash balance, $11,800.
k. March budgeted sales, $12,700.
l. March 31 accounts receivable balance, one-fourth of March sales.
m. March cash receipts, $14,100.

E9-52B Prepare a cash budget, then revise *(Learning Objective 3)*

Donovan Medical Supply began October with $11,200 cash.

Management forecasts that collections from credit customers will be $12,000 in October and $14,800 in November. The business is scheduled to receive $5,000 cash on a business note receivable in October. Projected cash payments include inventory purchases ($13,200 in October and $12,400 in November) and operating expenses ($4,000 each month).

Donovan's bank requires a $10,000 minimum balance in the business's checking account. At the end of any month when the account balance dips below the minimum balance, the bank automatically extends credit to the business in multiples of $1,000. Donovan's borrows as little as possible and pays back loans in quarterly installments of $2,000, plus 2% interest on the entire unpaid principal. The first payment occurs three months after the loan.

Requirement

Prepare Donovan Medical Supply's cash budget for October and November.

E9-53B Finish an incomplete cash budget *(Learning Objective 3)*

You recently began a job as an accounting intern at Rocky Adventures. Your first task was to help prepare the cash budget for February and March. Unfortunately, the computer with the budget file crashed, and you did not have a backup or even a hard copy. You ran a program to salvage bits of data from the budget file. After entering the following data in the budget, you may have just enough information to reconstruct the budget.

Rocky Adventures eliminates any cash deficiency by borrowing the exact amount needed from State Street Bank, where the current interest rate is 6%. Rocky Adventures pays interest on its outstanding debt at the end of each month. The company also repays all borrowed amounts at the end of the month, as cash becomes available.

Requirement
Complete the following cash budget:

		February	March
Rocky Adventures			
Cash Budget			
February and March			
Beginning cash balance		$ 16,400	$?
Cash collections		?	79,600
Cash from sale of plant assets		0	2,100
Cash available		$106,500	?
Cash payments:			
Purchase of inventory		$?	$ 41,400
Operating expenses		47,300	?
Total payments		$ 97,900	?
(1) Ending cash balance before financing		?	$ 25,000
Minimum cash balance desired		(20,000)	(20,000)
Cash excess (deficiency)		$?	$?
Financing of cash deficiency:			
Borrowing (at end of month)		$?	$?
Principal repayments (at end of month)		?	?
Interest expense		?	?
(2) Total effects of financing		$?	$?
Ending cash balance (1) + (2)		$?	$?

E9-54B Prepare an inventory, purchases, and cost of goods sold budget
(Learning Objective 4)

Clear Readers sells eReaders. Its sales budget for the nine months ended September 30 follows:

	Quarter Ended			Nine-Month
	Mar 31	Jun 30	Sep 30	Total
Cash sales, 30%..............................	$ 36,000	$ 51,000	$ 43,500	$130,500
Credit sales, 70%...........................	84,000	119,000	101,500	304,500
Total sales, 100%...........................	$120,000	$170,000	$145,000	$435,000

In the past, cost of goods sold has been 70% of total sales. The director of marketing and the financial vice president agree that each quarter's ending inventory should not be below $25,000 plus 20% of cost of goods sold for the following quarter. The marketing director expects sales of $220,000 during the fourth quarter. The January 1 inventory was $19,000.

Requirement
Prepare an inventory, purchases, and cost of goods sold budget for each of the first three quarters of the year. Compute cost of goods sold for the entire nine-month period.

PROBLEMS **Group A**

P9-55A **Comprehensive budgeting problem** (*Learning Objectives 2 & 3*)

Dudley Manufacturing is preparing its master budget for the first quarter of the upcoming year. The following data pertain to Dudley Manufacturing's operations:

Current Assets as of December 31 (prior year):	
Cash	$ 4,500
Accounts receivable, net	$ 50,000
Inventory	$ 15,000
Property, plant, and equipment, net	$122,500
Accounts payable	$ 42,400
Capital stock	$126,000
Retained earnings	$ 22,920

a. Actual sales in December were $70,000. Selling price per unit is projected to remain stable at $10 per unit throughout the budget period. Sales for the first five months of the upcoming year are budgeted to be as follows:

January	$83,000
February	$92,000
March	$94,000
April	$97,000
May	$89,000

b. Sales are 30% cash and 70% credit. All credit sales are collected in the month following the sale.

c. Dudley Manufacturing has a policy that states that each month's ending inventory of finished goods should be 25% of the following month's sales (in units).

d. Of each month's direct material purchases, 10% are paid for in the month of purchase, while the remainder is paid for in the month following purchase. Two pounds of direct material is needed per unit at $2 per pound. Ending inventory of direct materials should be 10% of next month's production needs.

e. Most of the labor at the manufacturing facility is indirect, but there is some direct labor incurred. The direct labor hours per unit is 0.02. The direct labor rate per hour is $10 per hour. All direct labor is paid for in the month in which the work is performed. The direct labor total cost for each of the upcoming three months is as follows:

> January $1,705
> February $1,850
> March $1,895

f. Monthly manufacturing overhead costs are $5,000 for factory rent, $3,000 for other fixed manufacturing expenses, and $1.20 per unit for variable manufacturing overhead. No depreciation is included in these figures. All expenses are paid in the month in which they are incurred.

g. Computer equipment for the administrative offices will be purchased in the upcoming quarter. In January, Dudley Manufacturing will purchase equipment for $6,200 (cash), while February's cash expenditure will be $12,000 and March's cash expenditure will be $16,800.

h. Operating expenses are budgeted to be $1 per unit sold plus fixed operating expenses of $1,400 per month. All operating expenses are paid in the month in which they are incurred.

i. Depreciation on the building and equipment for the general and administrative offices is budgeted to be $4,700 for the entire quarter, which includes depreciation on new acquisitions.

j. Dudley Manufacturing has a policy that the ending cash balance in each month must be at least $4,000. It has a line of credit with a local bank. The company can borrow in increments of $1,000 at the beginning of each month, up to a total outstanding loan balance of $160,000. The interest rate on these loans is 2% per month simple interest (not compounded). Dudley Manufacturing would pay down on the line of credit balance if it has excess funds at the end of the quarter. The company would also pay the accumulated interest at the end of the quarter on the funds borrowed during the quarter.

k. The company's income tax rate is projected to be 30% of operating income less interest expense. The company pays $11,000 cash at the end of February in estimated taxes.

Requirements

1. Prepare a schedule of cash collections for January, February, and March, and for the quarter in total. Use the following format:

Cash Collections Budget

	January	February	March	Quarter
Cash sales				
Credit sales				
Total cash collections				

2. Prepare a production budget, using the following format:

Production Budget

	January	February	March	Quarter
Unit sales*				
Plus: Desired ending inventory				
Total needed				
Less: Beginning inventory				
Units to be produced				

*Hint: Unit sales = Sales in dollars ÷ Selling price per unit

3. Prepare a direct materials budget, using the following format:

Direct Materials Budget

	January	February	March	Quarter
Units to be produced				
× Pounds of DM needed per unit				
Quantity (pounds) needed for production				
Plus: Desired ending inventory of DM				
Total quantity (pounds) needed				
Less: Beginning inventory of DM				
Quantity (pounds) to purchase				
× Cost per pound				
Total cost of DM purchases				

4. Prepare a cash payments budget for the direct material purchases from Requirement 3, using the following format:

Cash Payments for Direct Material Purchases Budget

	January	February	March	Quarter
December purchases (from Accounts Payable)				
January purchases				
February purchases				
March purchases				
Total cash payments for direct material purchases				

5. Prepare a cash payments budget for direct labor, using the following format:

Cash Payments for Direct Labor Budget

	January	February	March	Quarter
Direct labor				

6. Prepare a cash payments budget for manufacturing overhead costs, using the following format:

Cash Payments for Manufacturing Overhead Budget

	January	February	March	Quarter
Variable manufacturing overhead costs				
Rent (fixed)				
Other fixed MOH				
Total payments for MOH costs				

7. Prepare a cash payments budget for operating expenses, using the following format:

Cash Payments for Operating Expenses Budget

	January	February	March	Quarter
Variable operating expenses				
Fixed operating expenses				
Total payments for operating expenses				

8. Prepare a combined cash budget, using the following format:

Combined Cash Budget

	January	February	March	Quarter
Cash balance, beginning				
Add cash collections				
Total cash available				
Less cash payments:				
Direct material purchases				
Direct labor				
Manufacturing overhead costs				
Operating expenses				
Tax payment				
Equipment purchases				
Total cash payments				
Ending cash balance before financing				
Financing:				
Borrowings				
Repayments				
Interest payments				
Cash balance, ending				

9. Calculate the budgeted manufacturing cost per unit, using the following format (assume that fixed manufacturing overhead is budgeted to be $0.70 per unit for the year):

Budgeted Manufacturing Cost per Unit	
Direct materials cost per unit	
Direct labor cost per unit	
Variable manufacturing overhead costs per unit	
Fixed manufacturing overhead per unit	
Budgeted cost of manufacturing each unit	

10. Prepare a budgeted income statement for the quarter ending March 31, using the following format:

Budgeted Income Statement
For the Quarter Ending March 31

Sales..	
Cost of goods sold*.......................................	_____
Gross profit..	
Operating expenses	
Depreciation...	_____
Operating income..	
Less interest expense	
Less provision for income taxes......................	_____
Net income...	_____

*Cost of goods sold = Budgeted cost of manufacturing each unit × Number of units sold

P9-56A Prepare a budgeted income statement (*Learning Objective 2*)

The budget committee of Greta Fashions, an upscale women's clothing retailer, has assembled the following data. As the business manager, you must prepare the budgeted income statements for May and June.

a. Sales in April were $60,000. You forecast that monthly sales will increase 10% in May and 5% in June.

b. Greta Fashions maintains inventory of $10,000 plus 10% of sales revenues budgeted for the following month. Monthly purchases average 50% of sales revenues in that same month. Actual inventory on April 30 is $16,600. Sales budgeted for July are $70,000.

c. Monthly salaries amount to $7,000. Sales commissions equal 5% of sales for that month. Combine salaries and commissions into a single figure.

d. Other monthly expenses are as follows:

Rent expense	$3,000, paid as incurred
Depreciation expense	$ 300
Insurance expense	$ 200, expiration of prepaid amount
Income tax	20% of operating income

Requirement

Prepare Greta Fashions' budgeted income statements for May and June. Show cost of goods sold computations.

P9-57A Cash budgets *(Learning Objective 3)*

Wendell's Restaurant Supply is preparing its cash budgets for the first two months of the upcoming year. Here is the information about the company's upcoming cash receipts and cash disbursements:

a. Sales are 60% cash and 40% credit. Credit sales are collected 30% in the month of sale and the remainder in the month after sale. Actual sales in December were $57,000. Schedules of budgeted sales for the two months of the upcoming year are as follows:

	Budgeted Sales Revenue
January	$61,000
February	$71,000

b. Actual purchases of direct materials in December were $25,500. The company's purchases of direct materials in January are budgeted to be $22,500 and $27,000 in February. All purchases are paid 40% in the month of purchase and 60% the following month.

c. Salaries and sales commissions are also paid half in the month earned and half the next month. Actual salaries were $7,500 in December. Budgeted salaries in January are $8,500 and February budgeted salaries are $10,000. Sales commissions each month are 10% of that month's sales.

d. Rent expense is $2,700 per month.

e. Depreciation is $2,800 per month.

f. Estimated income tax payments are made at the end of January. The estimated tax payment is projected to be $12,500.

g. The cash balance at the end of the prior year was $21,000.

Requirements

1. Prepare schedules of (a) budgeted cash collections, (b) budgeted cash payments for purchases, and (c) budgeted cash payments for operating expenses. Show amounts for each month and totals for January and February.

2. Prepare a combined cash budget similar to exhibits in the chapter. If no financing activity took place, what is the budgeted cash balance on February 28?

P9-58A Prepare a combined cash budget and a budgeted balance sheet *(Learning Objective 3)*

Towson Medical Supply has applied for a loan. First National Bank has requested a budgeted balance sheet as of April 30, and a combined cash budget for April. As Towson Medical Supply's controller, you have assembled the following information:

a. March 31 equipment balance, $52,400; accumulated depreciation, $41,300.

b. April capital expenditures of $42,800 budgeted for cash purchase of equipment.

c. April depreciation expense, $900.

d. Cost of goods sold, 60% of sales.

e. Other April operating expenses, including income tax, total $13,200, 25% of which will be paid in cash and the remainder accrued at April 30.

f. March 31 owners' equity, $93,700.

g. March 31 cash balance, $40,600.

h. April budgeted sales, $90,000, 70% of which is for cash. Of the remaining 30%, half will be collected in April and half in May.

i. April cash collections on March sales, $29,700.

j. April cash payments of March 31 liabilities incurred for March purchases of inventory, $17,300.

k. March 31 inventory balance, $29,600.

l. April purchases of inventory, $10,000 for cash and $36,800 on credit. Half of the credit purchases will be paid in April and half in May.

Requirements

1. Prepare the budgeted balance sheet for Towson Medical Supply at April 30. Show separate computations for cash, inventory, and owners' equity balances.
2. Prepare the combined cash budget for April.
3. Suppose Towson Medical Supply has become aware of more efficient (and more expensive) equipment than it budgeted for purchase in April. What is the total amount of cash available for equipment purchases in April, before financing, if the minimum desired ending cash balance is $21,000? (For this requirement, disregard the $42,800 initially budgeted for equipment purchases.)
4. Before granting a loan to Towson Medical Supply, First National Bank asks for a sensitivity analysis assuming that April sales are only $60,000 rather than the $90,000 originally budgeted. (While the cost of goods sold will change, assume that purchases, depreciation, and the other operating expenses will remain the same as in the earlier requirements.)
   a. Prepare a revised budgeted balance sheet for Towson Medical Supply, showing separate computations for cash, inventory, and owners' equity balances.
   b. Suppose Towson Medical Supply has a minimum desired cash balance of $23,000. Will the company need to borrow cash in April?
   c. In this sensitivity analysis, sales declined by 33 1/3% ($30,000 ÷ $90,000). Is the decline in expenses and income more or less than 33 1/3%? Explain.

P9-59A Prepare an inventory, purchases, and cost of goods sold budget
(Learning Objective 4)

Radical Logos buys logo-imprinted merchandise and then sells it to university bookstores. Sales are expected to be $2,001,000 in September, $2,230,000 in October, $2,385,000 in November, and $2,570,000 in December. Radical Logos sets its prices to earn an average 40% gross profit on sales revenue. The company does not want inventory to fall below $415,000 plus 20% of the next month's cost of goods sold.

Requirement

Prepare an inventory, purchases, and cost of goods sold budget for the months of October and November.

P9-60A Estimate debit and credit card fees *(Learning Objective 4)*

The local Thai restaurant expects sales to be $500,000 in January. The average restaurant bill is $40. Only 20% of restaurant bills are paid in cash, while 70% are paid with credit cards and 10% are paid with debit cards. The transaction fees charged by the credit and debit card issuers are as follows:

- Credit cards: $0.50 per transaction + 2% of the amount charged
- Debit cards: $0.22 per transaction + 0.05% of the amount charged

Requirements

a. How much of the total sales revenue is expected to be paid with cash?
b. How many customer transactions does the company expect in January?
c. How much of the total sales revenue is expected to be paid with credit cards?
d. How many customer transactions will be paid for by customers using credit cards?
e. When budgeting for January's operating expenses, how much should the restaurant expect to incur in credit card transaction fees?
f. How much of the total sales revenue is expected to be paid with debit cards?
g. How many customer transactions will be paid for by customers using debit cards?
h. When budgeting for January's operating expenses, how much should the restaurant expect to incur in debit card transaction fees?
i. How much money will be deposited in the restaurant's bank account during the month of January related to credit and debit card sales? Assume the credit and debit card issuers deposit the funds on the same day the transactions occur at the restaurant (there is no processing delay).

PROBLEMS Group B

P9-61B Comprehensive budgeting problem *(Learning Objectives 2 & 3)*

Ravenna Manufacturing is preparing its master budget for the first quarter of the upcoming year. The following data pertain to Ravenna Manufacturing's operations:

Current assets as of December 31 (prior year):	
Cash	$ 4,500
Accounts receivable, net	$ 46,000
Inventory	$ 15,000
Property, plant, and equipment, net	$122,000
Accounts payable	$ 42,400
Capital stock	$125,000
Retained earnings	$ 22,920

a. Actual sales in December were $70,000. Selling price per unit is projected to remain stable at $10 per unit throughout the budget period. Sales for the first five months of the upcoming year are budgeted to be as follows:

January	$83,000
February	$99,000
March	$96,000
April	$90,000
May	$86,000

b. Sales are 30% cash and 70% credit. All credit sales are collected in the month following the sale.

c. Ravenna Manufacturing has a policy that states that each month's ending inventory of finished goods should be 25% of the following month's sales (in units).

d. Of each month's direct material purchases, 20% are paid for in the month of purchase, while the remainder is paid for in the month following purchase. Two pounds of direct material is needed per unit at $2.00 per pound. Ending inventory of direct materials should be 10% of next month's production needs.

e. Most of the labor at the manufacturing facility is indirect, but there is some direct labor incurred. The direct labor hours per unit is 0.03. The direct labor rate per hour is $8 per hour. All direct labor is paid for in the month in which the work is performed. The direct labor total cost for each of the upcoming three months is as follows:

January	$2,088
February	$2,358
March	$2,268

f. Monthly manufacturing overhead costs are $5,000 for factory rent, $3,000 for other fixed manufacturing expenses, and $1.20 per unit for variable manufacturing overhead. No depreciation is included in these figures. All expenses are paid in the month in which they are incurred.

g. Computer equipment for the administrative offices will be purchased in the upcoming quarter. In January, the company will purchase equipment for $5,000 (cash), while February's cash expenditure will be $12,000 and March's cash expenditure will be $16,000.

h. Operating expenses are budgeted to be $1.00 per unit sold plus fixed operating expenses of $1,000 per month. All operating expenses are paid in the month in which they are incurred.

i. Depreciation on the building and equipment for the general and administrative offices is budgeted to be $4,900 for the entire quarter, which includes depreciation on new acquisitions.

j. Ravenna Manufacturing has a policy that the ending cash balance in each month must be at least $4,000. The company has a line of credit with a local bank. It can borrow in increments of $1,000 at the beginning of each month, up to a total outstanding loan balance of $125,000. The interest rate on these loans is 1% per month simple interest (not compounded). Ravenna Manufacturing would pay down on the line of credit balance if it has excess funds at the end of the quarter. The company would also pay the accumulated interest at the end of the quarter on the funds borrowed during the quarter.

k. The company's income tax rate is projected to be 30% of operating income less interest expense. The company pays $10,000 cash at the end of February in estimated taxes.

Requirements

1. Prepare a schedule of cash collections for January, February, and March, and for the quarter in total.

Cash Collections Budget

	January	February	March	Quarter
Cash sales				
Credit sales				
Total cash collections				

2. Prepare a production budget. (Hint: Unit sales = Sales in dollars / Selling price per unit.)

Production Budget

	January	February	March	Quarter
Unit sales				
Plus: Desired ending inventory				
Total needed				
Less: Beginning inventory				
Units to be produced				

3. Prepare a direct materials budget.

Direct Materials Budget

	January	February	March	Quarter
Units to be produced				
× Pounds of DM needed per unit				
Quantity (pounds) needed for production				
Plus: Desired ending inventory of DM				
Total quantity (pounds) needed				
Less: Beginning inventory of DM				
Quantity (pounds) to purchase				
× Cost per pound				
Total cost of DM purchases				

4. Prepare a cash payments budget for the direct material purchases from Requirement 3.

Cash Payments for Direct Material Purchases Budget

	January	February	March	Quarter
December purchases (from Accounts Payable)				
January purchases				
February purchases				
March purchases				
Total cash payments for DM purchases				

5. Prepare a cash payments budget for direct labor, using the following format:

Cash Payments for Direct Labor Budget

	January	February	March	Quarter
Direct labor				

6. Prepare a cash payments budget for manufacturing overhead costs.

Cash Payments for Manufacturing Overhead Costs Budget

	January	February	March	Quarter
Variable manufacturing overhead costs				
Rent (fixed)				
Other fixed MOH				
Total payments for MOH costs				

7. Prepare a cash payments budget for operating expenses.

Cash Payments for Operating Expenses Budget

	January	February	March	Quarter
Variable operating expenses				
Fixed operating expenses				
Total payments for operating expenses				

8. Prepare a combined cash budget.

Combined Cash Budget

	January	February	March	Quarter
Cash balance, beginning				
Add cash collections				
Total cash available				
Less cash payments:				
Direct material purchases				
Direct labor costs				
Manufacturing overhead costs				
Operating expenses				
Tax payment				
Equipment purchases				
Total disbursements				
Ending cash balance before financing				
Financing:				
Borrowings				
Repayments				
Interest payments				
Total financing				
Cash balance, ending				

9. Calculate the budgeted manufacturing cost per unit (assume that fixed manufacturing overhead is budgeted to be $0.70 per unit for the year).

Budgeted Manufacturing Cost per Unit

Direct materials cost per unit	
Direct labor cost per unit	
Variable manufacturing overhead costs per unit	
Fixed manufacturing overhead per unit	
Budgeted cost of manufacturing each unit	

10. Prepare a budgeted income statement for the quarter ending March 31. (Hint: Cost of goods sold = Budgeted cost of manufacturing each unit × Number of units sold)

Budgeted Income Statement
For the Quarter Ended March 31

Sales	
Cost of goods sold	
Gross profit	
Operating expenses	
Depreciation expense	
Operating income	
Less interest expense	
Less provision for income taxes	
Net income	

P9-62B Prepare budgeted income statement (Learning Objective 2)

The budget committee of Soventino Fashions, an upscale women's clothing retailer, has assembled the following data. As the business manager, you must prepare the budgeted income statements for May and June.

a. Sales in April were $40,000. You forecast that monthly sales will increase 10% in May and 5% in June.

b. The company maintains inventory of $10,000 plus 10% of the sales revenue budgeted for the following month. Monthly purchases average 50% of sales revenue in that same month. Actual inventory on April 30 is $13,000. Sales budgeted for July are $70,000.

c. Monthly salaries amount to $5,000. Sales commissions equal 5% of sales for that month. Combine salaries and commissions into a single figure.

d. Other monthly expenses are as follows:

Rent expense	$2,000, paid as incurred
Depreciation expense	$ 500
Insurance expense	$ 100, expiration of prepaid amount
Income tax	20% of operating income

Requirement

Prepare Soventino Fashions' budgeted income statements for May and June. Show cost of goods sold computations.

P9-63B Cash budgets *(Learning Objective 3)*

Omega's Restaurant Supply is preparing its cash budgets for the first two months of the upcoming year. Here is the information about the company's upcoming cash receipts and cash disbursements:

a. Sales are 70% cash and 30% credit. Credit sales are collected 30% in the month of sale and the remainder in the month after sale. Actual sales in December were $51,000. Schedules of budgeted sales for the two months of the upcoming year are as follows:

	Budgeted sales revenue
January	$59,000
February	$69,000

b. Actual purchases of materials in December were $24,000. The company's purchases of direct materials in January are budgeted to be $23,000 and $25,500 in February. All purchases are paid 30% in the month of purchase and 70% the following month.

c. Salaries and sales commissions are also paid half in the month earned and half the next month. Actual salaries were $8,000 in December. Budgeted salaries in January are $9,000 and February budgeted salaries are $10,500. Sales commissions each month are 8% of that month's sales.

d. Rent expense is $3,200 per month.

e. Depreciation is $2,900 per month.

f. Estimated income tax payments are made at the end of January. The estimated tax payment is projected to be $13,500.

g. The cash balance at the end of the prior year was $25,000.

Requirements

1. Prepare schedules of (a) budgeted cash collections, (b) budgeted cash payments for purchases, and (c) budgeted cash payments for operating expenses. Show amounts for each month and totals for January and February.

2. Prepare a combined cash budget. If no financing activity took place, what is the budgeted cash balance on February 28?

P9-64B Prepare a combined cash budget and a budgeted balance sheet
(Learning Objective 3)

Hastings Medical Supply has applied for a loan. First National Bank has requested a budgeted balance sheet at April 30 and a combined cash budget for April. As Hastings Medical Supply's controller, you have assembled the following information:

a. March 31 equipment balance, $52,800; accumulated depreciation, $41,900.

b. April capital expenditures of $42,400 budgeted for cash purchase of equipment.

c. April depreciation expense, $800.

d. Cost of goods sold, 45% of sales.

e. Other April operating expenses, including income tax, total $14,000, 35% of which will be paid in cash and the remainder accrued at April 30.

f. March 31 owners' equity, $93,800.

g. March 31 cash balance, $40,900.

h. April budgeted sales, $90,000, 60% of which is for cash; of the remaining 40%, half will be collected in April and half in May.

i. April cash collections on March sales, $29,900.

j. April cash payments of March 31 liabilities incurred for March purchases of inventory, $17,100.

k. March 31 inventory balance, $29,200.

l. April purchases of inventory, $10,300 for cash and $37,000 on credit. Half of the credit purchases will be paid in April and half in May.

Requirements

1. Prepare the budgeted balance sheet for Hastings Medical Supply at April 30. Show separate computations for cash, inventory, and stockholders' equity balances.
2. Prepare the combined cash budget for April.
3. Suppose Hastings Medical Supply has become aware of more efficient (and more expensive) equipment than it budgeted for purchase in April. What is the total amount of cash available for equipment purchases in April, before financing, if the minimum desired ending cash balance is $19,000? (For this requirement, disregard the $42,400 initially budgeted for equipment purchases.)
4. Before granting a loan to Hastings, First National Bank asks for a sensitivity analysis assuming that April sales are only $60,000 rather than the $90,000 originally budgeted. (While the cost of goods sold will change, assume that purchases, depreciation, and the other operating expenses will remain the same as in the earlier requirements.)
   a. Prepare a revised budgeted balance sheet for the company, showing separate computations for cash, inventory, and stockholders' equity balances.
   b. Suppose Hastings has a minimum desired cash balance of $23,000. Will the company need to borrow cash in April?
   c. In this sensitivity analysis, sales declined by 33 1/3% ($30,000/$90,000). Is the decline in expenses and income more or less than 33 1/3%? Explain.

P9-65B Prepare an inventory, purchases, and cost of goods sold budget
(Learning Objective 4)

University Logos buys logo-imprinted merchandise and then sells it to university bookstores. Sales are expected to be $2,004,000 in September, $2,180,000 in October, $2,380,000 in November, and $2,550,000 in December. University Logos sets its prices to earn an average 30% gross profit on sales revenue. The company does not want inventory to fall below $405,000 plus 10% of the next month's cost of goods sold.

Requirement

Prepare an inventory, purchases, and cost of goods sold budget for the months of October and November.

P9-66B Estimate debit and credit card fees (Learning Objective 4)

The local Japanese-style steakhouse expects sales to be $500,000 in January. The average restaurant bill is $50. Only 25% of restaurant bills are paid in cash, while 70% are paid with credit cards and 5% are paid with debit cards. The transaction fees charged by the credit and debit card issuers are as follows:

- Credit cards: $0.50 per transaction + 2% of the amount charged
- Debit cards: $0.22 per transaction + 0.05% of the amount charged

Requirements

a. How much of the total sales revenue is expected to be paid with cash?
b. How many customer transactions does the company expect in January?
c. How much of the total sales revenue is expected to be paid with credit cards?
d. How many customer transactions will be paid for by customers using credit cards?
e. When budgeting for January's operating expenses, how much should the restaurant expect to incur in credit card transaction fees?
f. How much of the total sales revenue is expected to be paid with debit cards?
g. How many customer transactions will be paid for by customers using debit cards?
h. When budgeting for January's operating expenses, how much should the restaurant expect to incur in debit card transaction fees?
i. How much money will be deposited in the restaurant's bank account during the month of January related to credit and debit card sales? Assume the credit and debit card issuers deposit the funds on the same day the transactions occur at the restaurant (there is no processing delay).

CRITICAL THINKING

Discussion & Analysis

A9-67 Discussion Questions

1. "The sales budget is the most important budget." Do you agree or disagree? Explain your answer.

2. List at least four reasons why a company would use budgeting.

3. Describe the difference between an operating budget and a capital budget.

4. Describe the process for developing a budget.

5. Compare and contrast "participative budgeting" with "top-down" budgeting.

6. What is a budget committee? What is the budget committee's role in the budgeting process?

7. What are operating budgets? List at least four operating budgets.

8. What are financial budgets? List at least three financial budgets.

9. Managers may build slack into their budgets so that their target numbers are easier to attain. What might be some drawbacks to building slack into the budgets?

10. How does the master budget for a service company differ from a master budget for a manufacturing company? Which (if any) operating budgets differ and how specifically do they differ? Which (if any) financial budgets differ and how specifically do they differ?

11. Give an example of a sustainable practice, if adopted that would affect a company's budget. How might this sustainable practice, if adopted, impact the company's budget in both the short-term and in the long-term?

12. Why might a company want to state environmental goals for increased sustainability in its budgets? Explain.

Application & Analysis

A9-68 Budgeting for a Single Product

In this activity, you will be creating budgets for a single product for each of the months in an upcoming quarter. Select a product that you could purchase in large quantities (at a Sam's Club or other warehouse retail chain) and repackage into smaller quantities to offer for sale at a sidewalk café, a sporting event, a flea market, or other similar venue. Investigate the price and quantity at which this product is available at the warehouse. Choose a selling price for the smaller (repackaged) package. Make reasonable assumptions about how many of the smaller units you can sell in each of the next four months (you will need the fourth month's sales in units for the operating budgets).

Basic Discussion Questions

1. Describe your product. What is your cost of this product? What size (quantity) will you purchase? At what price will you sell your repackaged product? Make projections of your sales in units in each of the upcoming three months.

2. Estimate how many hours you will spend in each of the upcoming three months doing the purchasing, repackaging, and selling. Select a reasonable wage rate for yourself. What will your total labor costs be in each of the upcoming three months?

3. Prepare a sales budget for each of the upcoming three months.

4. Prepare the direct material budgets for the upcoming three months, assuming that you need to keep 10% of the direct materials needed for next month's sales on hand at the end of each month (this requirement is why you needed to estimate unit sales for four months).

5. Prepare a direct labor budget (for your labor) for each of the upcoming three months.

6. Think about any other expenses you are likely to have (i.e., booth rental at a flea market

or a vendor license). Prepare the operating expenses budget for each of the upcoming three months.

7. Prepare a budgeted income statement that reflects the budgets you prepared, including the sales budget, direct materials budget, direct labor budget, and the operating expenses budget. This budgeted income statement should include one column for each of the three months in the quarter and it should also include a total column that represents the totals of the three months. What is your projected profit by month and for the quarter?

Decision Case

A9-69 Suggest performance improvements (Learning Objective 1)

Angie Hughes recently joined Cycle World, a bicycle store in St. Louis, as an assistant manager. She recently finished her accounting courses. Cycle World's manager and owner, Loretta Harland, asks Hughes to prepare a budgeted income statement for the upcoming year based on the information she has collected. Hughes' budget follows:

CYCLE WORLD
Budgeted Income Statement
For the Year Ending July 31

Sales revenue		$244,000
Cost of goods sold		177,000
Gross profit		$ 67,000
Operating expenses:		
Salary and commission expense	$46,000	
Rent expense	8,000	
Depreciation expense	2,000	
Insurance expense	800	
Miscellaneous expenses	12,000	68,800
Operating loss		$ (1,800)
Interest expense		225
Net loss		$ (2,025)

Requirement

Hughes does not want to give Harland this budget without making constructive suggestions for steps Harland could take to improve expected performance. Write a memo to Harland outlining your suggestions.

A9-70 Prepare cash budgets under two alternatives (Learning Objectives 2 & 3)

Each autumn, as a hobby, Pauline Spahr weaves cotton place mats to sell at a local craft shop. The mats sell for $20 per set of four mats. The shop charges a 10% commission and remits the net proceeds to Spahr at the end of December. Spahr has woven and sold 25 sets in each of the last two years. She has enough cotton in inventory to make another 25 sets. She paid $7 per set for the cotton. Spahr uses a four-harness loom that she purchased for cash exactly two years ago. It is depreciated at the rate of $10 per month. The accounts payable relate to the cotton inventory and are payable by September 30.

Spahr is considering buying an eight-harness loom so that she can weave more intricate patterns in linen. The new loom costs $1,000; it would be depreciated at $20 per month. Her bank has agreed to lend her $1,000 at 18% interest, with $200 principal plus accrued interest payable each December 31. Spahr believes she can weave 15 linen place mat sets in time for the Christmas rush if she does not weave any cotton mats. She predicts that each linen set will sell for $50. Linen costs $18 per set. Spahr's supplier will sell her linen on credit, payable December 31.

Spahr plans to keep her old loom whether or not she buys the new loom. The balance sheet for her weaving business at August 31 is as follows:

PAULINE SPAHR, WEAVER
Balance Sheet
August 31

Current assets:			Current liabilities:		
Cash..	$ 25		Accounts payable		$ 74
Inventory of cotton	175				
	$ 200				
Fixed assets:					
Loom	500		Stockholders' equity..................................		386
Accumulated depreciation...............	(240)				
	$ 260				
Total assets..	$ 460		Total liabilities and stockholders' equity		$460

Requirements

1. Prepare a combined cash budget for the four months ending December 31, for two alternatives: weaving the place mats in cotton using the existing loom and weaving the place mats in linen using the new loom. For each alternative, prepare a budgeted income statement for the four months ending December 31 and a budgeted balance sheet at December 31.

2. On the basis of financial considerations only, what should Spahr do? Give your reason.

3. What nonfinancial factors might Spahr consider in her decision?

Ethical Issue

A9-71 Ethical considerations for padded budgets *(Learning Objectives 1 & 4)*

Residence Suites operates a regional hotel chain. Each hotel is operated by a manager and an assistant manager/controller. Many of the staff who run the front desk, clean the rooms, and prepare the breakfast buffet work part-time or have a second job, so turnover is high.

Assistant manager/controller John Rach asked the new bookkeeper to help prepare the hotel's master budget. The master budget is prepared once a year and submitted to company headquarters for approval. Once approved, the master budget is used to evaluate the hotel's performance. These performance evaluations affect hotel managers' bonuses; they also affect company decisions about which hotels deserve extra funds for capital improvements.

When the budget was almost complete, Rach asked the bookkeeper to increase amounts budgeted for labor and supplies by 15%. When asked why, Rach responded that hotel manager Lauren Romick told him to do this when he began working at the hotel. Romick explained that this budgetary cushion gave her flexibility in running the hotel. For example, because company headquarters tightly controls capital improvement funds, Romick can use the extra money budgeted for labor and supplies to replace broken televisions or to pay "bonuses" to keep valued employees. Rach initially accepted this explanation because he had observed similar behavior at his previous place of employment.

Put yourself in Rach's position. In deciding how to deal with the situation, answer the following questions:

1. What is the ethical issue?

2. What are my options?

3. What are the possible consequences?

4. What should I do?

Team Project

A9-72 Analyzing and discussing budget concerns (Learning Objectives 1, 2, & 3)

PharmSys provides enterprise and information technology consulting services to the pharmaceuticals industry. PharmSys is organized into several divisions. A companywide planning committee sets general strategy and goals for the company and its divisions, but each division develops its own budget.

Rick Watson is the new division manager of wireless communications software. His division has two departments: Development and Sales. Carrie Pronai manages the 20 or so programmers and systems specialists typically employed in the Development Department to create and update the division's software applications. Liz Smith manages the Sales Department.

PharmSys considers the divisions to be investment centers. To earn his bonus next year, Watson must achieve a 30% return on the $3 million invested in his division. This amounts to $900,000 of income (30% × $3 million). Within the wireless division, development is a cost center, while sales are a revenue center.

Budgeting is in progress. Pronai met with her staff and is now struggling with two sets of numbers. Alternative A is her best estimate of next year's costs. However, unexpected problems can arise in the writing of software, and finding competent programmers is an ongoing challenge. She knows that Watson was a programmer before he earned an MBA, so he should be sensitive to this uncertainty. Consequently, she is thinking of increasing her budgeted costs (Alternative B). Her department's bonuses largely depend on whether the department meets its budgeted costs.

PHARMSYS
Wireless Division
Development Budget

	Alternative A	Alternative B
Salaries expense (including overtime and part-time)	$2,400,000	$2,640,000
Software expense	120,000	132,000
Travel expense	65,000	71,500
Depreciation expense	255,000	255,000
Miscellaneous expense	100,000	110,000
Total expense	$2,940,000	$3,208,500

Liz Smith is also struggling with her sales budget. Companies have made their initial investments in communications software, so it is harder to win new customers. If things go well, she believes her sales team can maintain the level of growth achieved over the last few years. This is Alternative A in the sales budget. However, if Smith is too optimistic, sales may fall short of the budget. If this happens, her team will not receive bonuses. Therefore, Smith is considering reducing the sales numbers and submitting Alternative B.

PHARMSYS
Wireless Division
Sales Budget

	Alternative A	Alternative B
Sales revenue	$5,000,000	$4,500,000
Salaries expense	360,000	360,000
Travel expense	240,000	210,500

Split your team into three groups. Each group should meet separately before the entire team meets.

Requirements

1. The first group plays the role of Development Manager Carrie Pronai. Before meeting with the entire team, determine which set of budget numbers you are going to present to Rick Watson. Write a memo supporting your decision. Give this memo to the third group before the team meeting.

2. The second group plays the role of Sales Manager Liz Smith. Before meeting with the entire team, determine which set of budget numbers you are going to present to Rick Watson. Write a memo supporting your decision. Give this memo to the third group before the team meeting.

3. The third group plays the role of Division Manager Rick Watson. Before meeting with the entire team, use the memos that Pronai and Smith provided to prepare a division budget based on the sales and development budgets. Your divisional overhead costs (additional costs beyond those incurred by the Development and Sales Departments) are approximately $390,000. Determine whether the wireless division can meet its targeted 30% return on assets given the budgeted alternatives submitted by your department managers.

During the meeting of the entire team, the group playing Watson presents the division budget and considers its implications. Each group should take turns discussing its concerns with the proposed budget. The team as a whole should consider whether the division budget must be revised. The team should prepare a report that includes the division budget and a summary of the issues covered in the team meeting.

A9-73 CMA-1 Crisper, Inc. plans to sell 80,000 bags of potato chips in June, and each of these bags requires five potatoes. Pertinent data includes:

	Bags of potato chips	Potatoes
Actual June inventory	15,000 bags	27,000 potatoes
Desired June 30 inventory	18,000 bags	23,000 potatoes

What number of units of raw material should Crisper plan to purchase?

a. 381,000
b. 389,000
c. 411,000
d. 419,000

A9-74 CMA-2 Holland Company is in the process of projecting its cash position at the end of the second quarter. Shown below is pertinent information from Holland's records.

Cash balance at end of 1st quarter	$ 36,000
Cash collections from customers for 2nd quarter	1,300,000
Accounts payable at end of 1st quarter	100,000
Accounts payable at end of 2nd quarter	75,000
All 2nd quarter costs and expenses (accrual basis)	1,200,000
Depreciation (accrued expense included above)	60,000
Purchases of equipment (for cash)	50,000
Gain on sale of asset (for cash)	5,000
Net book value of asset sold	35,000
Repayment of notes payable	66,000

From the data above, determine Holland's projected cash balance at the end of the second quarter.

a. Zero
b. $25,000
c. $60,000
d. $95,000

(CMA Adapted)

Cost Behavior

Learning Objectives

- **1** Describe key characteristics and graphs of various cost behaviors
- **2** Use cost equations to express and predict costs
- **3** Use account analysis and scatter plots to analyze cost behavior
- **4** Use the high-low method to analyze cost behavior
- **5** Use regression analysis to analyze cost behavior
- **6** Describe variable costing and prepare a contribution margin income statement

From Chapter 6 of *Managerial Accounting*, Third Edition. Karen W. Braun, Wendy M. Tietz.
Copyright ©2013 by Pearson Education, Inc. All rights reserved.

High above the rushing

waters and mist of Niagara Falls, hundreds of tourists from around the world return to the 512-room Embassy Suites[1] to enjoy a complimentary afternoon refreshment hour, relax in the hotel's pool and spa, and rest in luxurious suites overlooking the falls. A similar scene occurs across the street at the Sheraton, Marriott, and DoubleTree hotels, as well as at thousands of other travel destinations around the world.

How do hotel managers set prices high enough to cover costs and earn a profit, but low enough to fill most rooms each night? How do they plan for higher occupancy during the busy summer months and lower occupancy during the off-season? They know how their costs behave. Some hotel costs, such as the complimentary morning breakfast, rise and fall with the number of guests. But many hotel costs, such as depreciation on the building and furniture, stay the same whether 50 or 2,000 guests stay each night. In this chapter we'll learn more about how costs behave, and how managers can use that knowledge to make better business decisions.

© Profimedia International s.r.o. / Alamy

[1]All references to Embassy Suites in this hypothetical example were created by the author solely for academic purposes and are not intended, in any way, to represent the actual business practices of, or costs incurred by, Embassy Suites.

Up to this point, we have focused our attention on product costing. We have discussed how managers use job costing or process costing to figure out the cost of making a product or providing a service. Product costs are useful for valuing inventory and calculating cost of goods sold. Product costs are also used as a starting place for setting sales prices. However, product costs are not very helpful for planning and making many business decisions. Why? Because they contain a mixture of fixed and variable costs. Some of these costs change as volume changes, but other costs do not. To make good decisions and accurate projections, managers must understand how the company's costs will react to changes in volume.

1 Describe key characteristics and graphs of various cost behaviors

Cost Behavior: How do Changes in Volume Affect Costs?

In order to make good decisions and accurate projections, managers must understand <u>cost behavior</u>—that is, how costs change as volume changes. Embassy Suite's managers need to understand how the hotel's costs will be affected by the number of guests staying at the hotel each night. We first consider three of the most common cost behaviors, some of which were introduced in Chapter 2 (pp. 68–69):

- Variable costs
- Fixed costs
- Mixed costs

Why is this important?

"Cost behavior is a **key** component of most **planning** and operating decisions. Without a thorough understanding of **cost behavior,** managers are apt to make less **profitable** decisions."

Variable Costs

<u>Variable costs</u> are costs that are incurred for every unit of volume. As a result, total variable costs change in direct proportion to changes in volume. For example, every guest at Embassy Suites is entitled to a complimentary morning breakfast and afternoon refreshment hour (drinks and snacks). Guests also receive complimentary toiletries, (shampoo, soap, lotion, and mouthwash) that they typically use or take with them. These costs are considered to be variable because they are incurred for every guest. In addition, the hotel's total cost for the complimentary breakfast and toiletries will increase as the number of guests increases.

Let's assume that the toiletries cost the hotel $3 per guest and that the breakfast and refreshment hour costs the hotel $10 per guest. Exhibit 6-1 graphs these costs in relation to the number of guests staying at the hotel. The vertical axis (y-axis) shows total variable costs, while the horizontal axis (x-axis) shows total volume of activity (thousands of guests, in this case).

EXHIBIT 6-1 Variable Costs

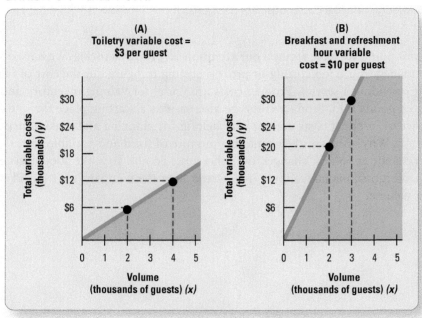

Notice a few things about these graphs:

- Graphs of variable costs always begin at the *origin*, the point that represents zero volume and zero cost. For example, if the hotel has no guests for the night, it will not incur any costs for complimentary toiletries or breakfasts.

- The *slope* of the variable cost line represents the *variable cost per unit of activity*. For example, the slope of the toiletry cost line is $3 per guest while the slope of the breakfast cost line is $10 per guest. As a result, the slope of the line representing the breakfast cost is steeper than that of the toiletry cost.

- Total variable costs change in *direct proportion* to changes in volume. In other words, if volume doubles, then total variable cost doubles. If volume triples then total variable cost triples. For example, Exhibit 6-1(a) shows that if the hotel serves 2,000 guests, it will spend $6,000 on toiletries. However, doubling the number of guests to 4,000 likewise doubles the total variable cost to $12,000.

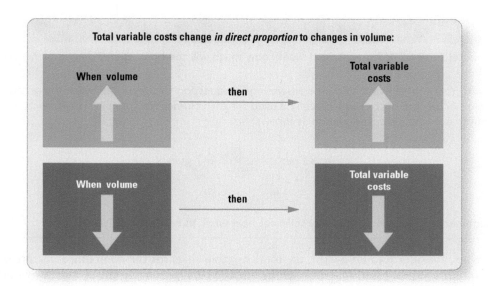

Managers do not need to rely on graphs to predict total variable costs at different volumes of activity. They can use a **cost equation**, a mathematical equation for a straight line, to express how a cost behaves. On cost graphs like the ones pictured in Exhibit 6-1, the vertical (y-axis) always shows total costs, while the horizontal axis (x-axis) shows volume of activity. Therefore, any variable cost line can be mathematically expressed as follows:

2 Use cost equations to express and predict costs

Total variable cost (y) = Variable cost per unit of activity (v) × Volume of activity (x)

Or simply:

$$y = vx$$

The hotel's total toiletry cost is as follows:

$$y = \$3x$$

where,

y = total toiletry cost
$3 = variable cost per guest
x = number of guests

Why is this important?
"Cost **equations** help managers foresee what their **total costs** will be at **different** operating **volumes** so that they can **better** plan for the future."

We can confirm the observations made in Exhibit 6-1(a) using the cost equation. If the hotel has no guests ($x = 0$), total toiletry costs are zero, as shown in the graph. If the hotel has 2,000 guests, total toiletry costs will be as follows:

$$y = \$3 \text{ per guest} \times 2,000 \text{ guests}$$
$$= \$6,000$$

If the hotel has 4,000 guests, managers will expect total toiletry costs to be as follows:

$$y = \$3 \text{ per guest} \times 4,000 \text{ guests}$$
$$= \$12,000$$

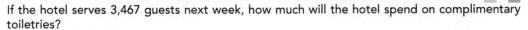

STOP & THINK

If the hotel serves 3,467 guests next week, how much will the hotel spend on complimentary toiletries?

Answer: You would have a hard time answering this question by simply looking at the graph in Exhibit 6-1(a), but cost equations can be used for any volume. We "plug in" the expected volume to our variable cost equation as follows:

$$y = \$3 \text{ per guest} \times 3,467 \text{ guests}$$
$$= \$10,401$$

Management expects complimentary toiletries next week to cost about $10,401.

Now, consider Exhibit 6-1(b), the total variable costs for the complimentary breakfast and refreshment hour. The slope of the line is $10, representing the cost of providing each guest with the complimentary breakfast and refreshments. We can express the total breakfast and refreshment hour cost as follows:

$$y = \$10x$$

where,

$$y = \text{total breakfast and refreshment hour cost}$$
$$\$10 = \text{variable cost per guest}$$
$$x = \text{number of guests}$$

The total cost of the breakfast and refreshment hour for 2,000 guests is as follows:

$$y = \$10 \text{ per guest} \times 2,000 \text{ guests}$$
$$= \$20,000$$

Both graphs in Exhibit 6-1 show how *total* variable costs vary with the number of guests. *But note that the variable cost per guest (v) remains constant in each of the graphs.* That is, Embassy Suites incurs $3 in toiletry costs and $10 in breakfast and refreshment hour costs for each guest no matter how many guests the hotel serves. Some key points to remember about variable costs are shown in Exhibit 6-2.

EXHIBIT 6-2 Key Characteristics of Variable Costs

- *Total* variable costs change in *direct proportion* to changes in volume
- The *variable cost per unit of activity* (*v*) remains constant and is the slope of the variable cost line
- Total variable cost graphs always begin at the origin (if volume is zero, total variable costs are zero)
- Total variable costs can be expressed as follows:

$$y = vx$$

where,

y = total variable cost

v = variable cost per unit of activity

x = volume of activity

Fixed Costs

<u>Fixed costs</u> are costs that do not change in total despite wide changes in volume. Many of Embassy Suites' costs are fixed because the same total cost will be incurred regardless of the number of guests that stay each month. Some of the hotel's fixed costs include the following:

- Property taxes and insurance
- Depreciation and maintenance on parking ramp, hotel, and room furnishings
- Pool, fitness room, and spa upkeep
- Cable TV and wireless internet access for all rooms
- Salaries of hotel department managers (housekeeping, food service, special events, etc.)

Most of these costs are **committed fixed costs**, meaning that the hotel is locked in to these costs because of previous management decisions. For example, as soon as the hotel was built, management became locked in to a certain level of property taxes and depreciation, simply because of the location and size of the hotel, and management's choice of furnishings and amenities (pool, fitness room, restaurant, and so forth). Management has little or no control over these committed fixed costs in the short run.

However, the hotel also incurs **discretionary fixed costs**, such as advertising expenses, that are a result of annual management decisions. Companies have more control over discretionary fixed costs in the short run.

EXHIBIT 6-3 Fixed Costs

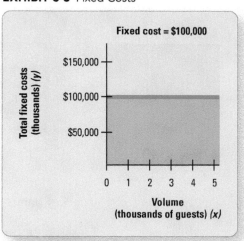

Suppose Embassy Suites incurs $100,000 of fixed costs each month. In Exhibit 6-3, the vertical axis (y-axis) shows total fixed costs while the horizontal axis (x-axis) plots volume of activity (thousands of guests). The graph shows total fixed costs as a *flat line* that intersects the y-axis at $100,000 (this is known as the vertical intercept) because the hotel will incur the same $100,000 of fixed costs regardless of the number of guests that stay during the month.

The cost equation for a fixed cost is as follows:

Total fixed cost (*y*) = Fixed amount over a period of time (*f*)

Or simply,

$$y = f$$

Embassy Suites' *monthly* fixed cost equation is as follows:

$$y = \$100,000$$

where,

$$y = \text{total fixed cost per month}$$

In contrast to the *total fixed costs* shown in Exhibit 6-3, the *fixed cost per guest* depends on the number of guests. If the hotel only serves 2,000 guests during the month, the fixed cost per guest is as follows:

$$\$100,000 \div 2,000 \text{ guests} = \$50/\text{guest}$$

If the number of guests *doubles* to 4,000, the fixed cost per guest is *cut in half*:

$$\$100,000 \div 4,000 \text{ guests} = \$25/\text{guest}$$

The fixed cost per guest is *inversely proportional* to the number of guests. When volume *increases*, the fixed cost per guest *decreases*. When volume *decreases*, the fixed cost per guest *increases*.

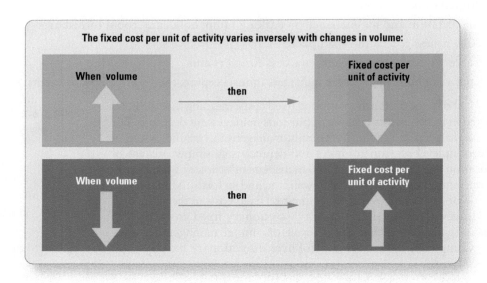

Key points to remember about fixed costs appear in Exhibit 6-4.

EXHIBIT 6-4 Key Characteristics of Fixed Costs

- *Total* fixed costs stay *constant* over a wide range of volume
- Fixed costs *per unit of activity* vary *inversely* with changes in volume:
    - Fixed cost per unit of activity *increases* when volume *decreases*
    - Fixed cost per unit of activity *decreases* when volume *increases*
- Total fixed cost graphs are always flat lines with no slope that intersect the y-axis at a level equal to total fixed costs
- Total fixed costs can be expressed as $y = f$
  where,
    $y = \text{total fixed cost}$
    $f = \text{fixed cost over a given period of time}$

STOP&THINK

Compute the (a) total fixed cost and (b) fixed cost per guest if the hotel has 16,000 guests next month. Compare the fixed cost per guest at the higher occupancy rate to the fixed cost per guest if only 2,000 guests stay during the month. Explain why hotels and other businesses like to operate near 100% capacity.

Answer:

a. Total fixed costs do not react to wide changes in volume; therefore, total fixed costs will still be $100,000.

b. Fixed costs per unit decrease as volume increases. At the higher occupancy, the fixed cost per guest is as follows:

$$\$100,000 \div 16,000 \text{ guests} = \$6.25 \text{ per guest}$$

If only 2,000 guests stay during the month, the fixed cost per guest is much higher ($50). Businesses like to operate near full capacity because it lowers their fixed cost per unit. A lower cost per unit gives businesses the flexibility to lower their prices to compete more effectively.

Mixed Costs

<u>Mixed costs</u> contain both variable and fixed cost components. Embassy Suites' utilities are mixed costs because the hotel requires a certain amount of utilities just to operate. However, the more guests at the hotel, the more water, electricity, and gas required. Exhibit 6-5 illustrates mixed costs.

EXHIBIT 6-5 Mixed Costs

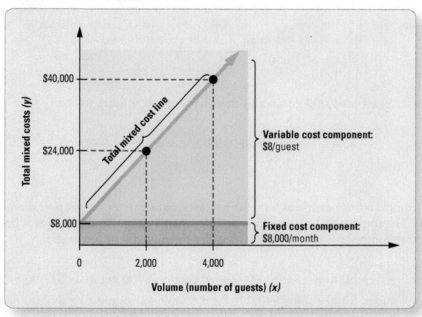

For example, let's assume that utilities for the common areas of the hotel and unoccupied rooms cost $8,000 per month. In addition, these costs increase by $8 per guest as each guest cools or heats his or her room, takes showers, turns on the TV and lights, and uses freshly laundered sheets and towels.

Notice the two components—variable and fixed—of the mixed cost in Exhibit 6-5. Similar to a variable cost, the total mixed cost line increases as the volume of activity increases. However, *the line does not begin at the origin.* Rather, it intersects the y-axis at a level equal to the fixed cost component. Even if no guests stay this month, the hotel will still incur $8,000 of utilities cost.

Managers can once again use a cost equation to express the mixed cost line so that they can predict total mixed costs at different volumes. The mixed cost equation simply *combines* the variable cost and fixed cost equations:

$$\text{Total mixed costs} = \text{Variable cost component} + \text{Fixed cost component}$$
$$y = vx + f$$

Embassy Suites' monthly utilities cost equation is as follows:

$$y = \$8x + \$8,000$$

where,

$$y = \text{total utilities cost per month}$$
$$x = \text{number of guests}$$

If the hotel serves 2,000 guests this month it expects utilities to cost:

$$y = (\$8 \text{ per guest} \times 2,000 \text{ guests}) + \$8,000$$
$$= \$24,000$$

If the hotel serves 4,000 guests this month it expects utilities to cost:

$$y = (\$8 \text{ per guest} \times 4,000 \text{ guests}) + \$8,000$$
$$= \$40,000$$

Total mixed costs increase as volume increases, *but not in direct proportion to changes in volume.* The total mixed cost did *not* double when volume doubled. This is because of the fixed cost component. Additionally, consider the mixed cost *per guest*:

If the hotel serves 2,000 guests: $24,000 total cost ÷ 2,000 guests = $12.00 per guest
If the hotel serves 4,000 guests: $40,000 total cost ÷ 4,000 guests = $10.00 per guest

The mixed cost per guest did *not* decrease by half when the hotel served twice as many guests. This is because of the variable cost component. Mixed costs per unit decrease as volume increases, but *not in direct proportion* to changes in volume. Because mixed costs contain both fixed cost and variable cost components, they behave differently than purely variable costs and purely fixed costs. Key points to remember about mixed costs appear in Exhibit 6-6.

EXHIBIT 6-6 Key Characteristics of Mixed Costs

- *Total* mixed costs increase as volume increases because of the variable cost component
- Mixed costs *per unit* decrease as volume increases because of the fixed cost component
- Total mixed cost graphs slope upward but do *not* begin at the origin—they intersect the y-axis at the level of fixed costs
- Total mixed costs can be expressed as a *combination* of the variable and fixed cost equations:

Total mixed costs = variable cost component + fixed cost component

$$y = vx + f$$

where,

y = total mixed cost

v = variable cost per unit of activity (slope)

x = volume of activity

f = fixed cost over a given period of time (vertical intercept)

STOP&THINK

If your cell phone plan charges $10 per month plus $0.15 for each minute you talk, how could you express the monthly cell phone bill as a cost equation? How much will your cell phone bill be if you (a) talk 100 minutes this month or (b) talk 200 minutes this month? If you double your talk time from 100 to 200 minutes, does your total cell phone bill double? Explain.

Answer: The cost equation for the monthly cell phone bill is as follows:

$$y = \$0.15x + \$10$$

where,

y = total cell phone bill for the month

x = number of minutes used

a. At 100 minutes, the total cost is $25 [= ($0.15 per minute × 100 minutes) + $10].
b. At 200 minutes, the total cost is $40 [= ($0.15 per minute × 200 minutes) + $10].
The cell phone bill does not double when talk time doubles. The variable portion of the bill doubles from $15 ($0.15 × 100 minutes) to $30 ($0.15 × 200 minutes), but the fixed portion of the bill stays constant ($10).

Relevant Range

Managers always need to keep their **relevant range** in mind when predicting total costs. The relevant range is the band of volume where the following remain constant:

- *Total fixed costs*
- *Variable cost per unit*

A change in cost behavior means a change to a different relevant range.

Let's consider how the concept of relevant range applies to Embassy Suites. As shown in Exhibit 6-3, the hotel's current fixed costs are $100,000 per month. However, since the hotel's popularity continues to grow, room occupancy rates continue to increase.

As a result, guests are becoming dissatisfied with the amount of time they have to wait for breakfast tables and elevators. To increase customer satisfaction, management is deciding whether to expand the breakfast facilities and add a 30-passenger elevator to its existing bank of elevators. This expansion, if carried out, will increase the hotel's fixed costs to a new level. Exhibit 6-7 illustrates the hotel's current relevant range and future potential relevant range for fixed costs.

EXHIBIT 6-7 Examples of Different Relevant Ranges for Fixed Costs

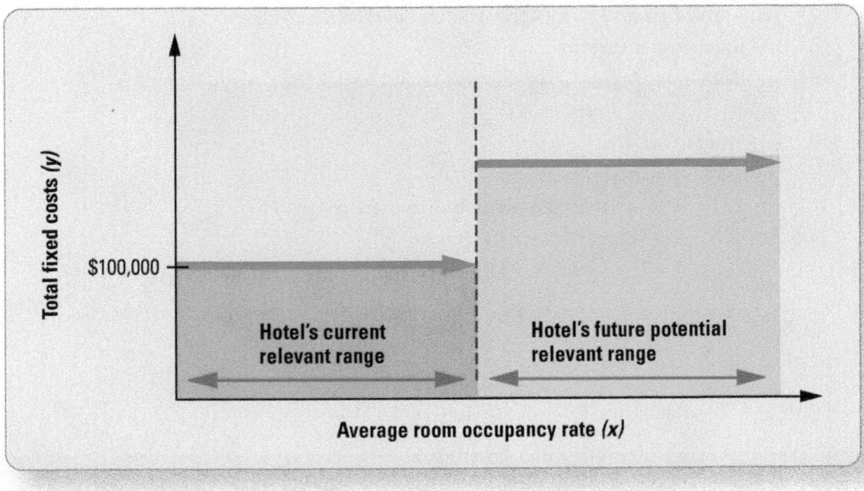

Does the concept of relevant range apply only to fixed costs? No, it also applies to variable costs. As shown in Exhibit 6-1, the hotel's current variable cost for toiletries is $3 per guest. However, as room occupancy rates continue to grow, management hopes to negotiate greater volume discounts on the toiletries from its suppliers. These volume discounts will decrease the variable toiletries cost per guest (for example, down to $2.75 per guest). Exhibit 6-8 illustrates the hotel's current relevant range and future potential relevant range for variable toiletries costs.

EXHIBIT 6-8 Examples of Different Relevant Ranges for Variable Costs

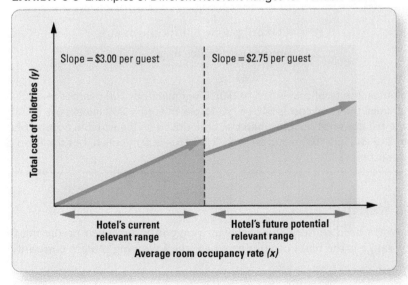

Why is the concept of relevant range important? Managers can predict costs accurately only if they use cost information for the appropriate relevant range. For example, think about your cell phone plan. Many cell phone plans offer a large block of "free" minutes for a set fee each month. If the user exceeds the allotted minutes, the cell phone company charges an additional per-minute fee. Exhibit 6-9 shows a cell phone plan in which the first 1,000 minutes of call time each month cost $50. After the 1,000 minutes are used, the user must pay an additional $0.30 per minute for every minute of call time. This cell phone plan has two relevant ranges. The first relevant range extends from 0 to 1,000 minutes. In this range, the $50 fee behaves strictly as a fixed cost. You could use 0, 100, or 975 minutes and you would still pay a flat $50 fee that month. The second relevant range starts at 1,001 minutes and extends indefinitely. In this relevant range, the cost is mixed: $50 plus $0.30 per minute. To forecast your cell phone bill each month, you need to know in which relevant range you plan to operate. The same holds true for businesses: To accurately predict costs, they need to know the relevant range in which they plan to operate.

EXHIBIT 6-9 Example of Relevant Ranges

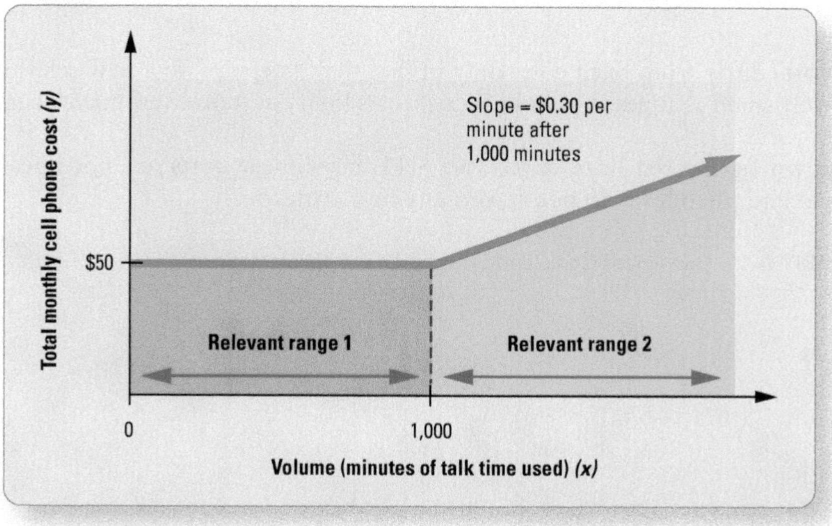

Other Cost Behaviors

While many business costs behave as variable, fixed, or mixed costs, some costs do not neatly fit these patterns. We'll briefly describe other cost behaviors you may encounter.

Step costs resemble stair steps: They are fixed over a small range of activity and then jump up to a new fixed level with moderate changes in volume. Hotels, restaurants, hospitals, and educational institutions typically experience step costs. For example, states usually require day-care centers to limit the caregiver-to-child ratio to 1:7—that is, there must be one caregiver for every seven children. As shown in Exhibit 6-10, a day-care center that takes on an eighth child must incur the cost of employing another caregiver. The new caregiver can watch the eighth through fourteenth child enrolled at the day-care center. If the day-care center takes on a fifteenth child, management will once again need to hire another caregiver, costing another $15,000 in salary. The same step cost patterns occur with hotels (maid-to-room ratio), restaurants (server-to-table ratio), hospitals (nurse-to-bed ratio), and schools (teacher-to-student ratio).

EXHIBIT 6-10 Step Costs

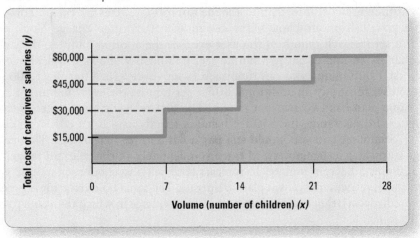

Step costs differ from fixed costs only in that they "step up" to a new relevant range with relatively small changes in volume. Fixed costs hold constant over much larger ranges of volume.

As shown by the red lines in Exhibit 6-11, **curvilinear costs** are not linear (not a straight line) and, therefore, do not fit into any neat pattern.

EXHIBIT 6-11 Curvilinear Costs and Straight-Line Approximations

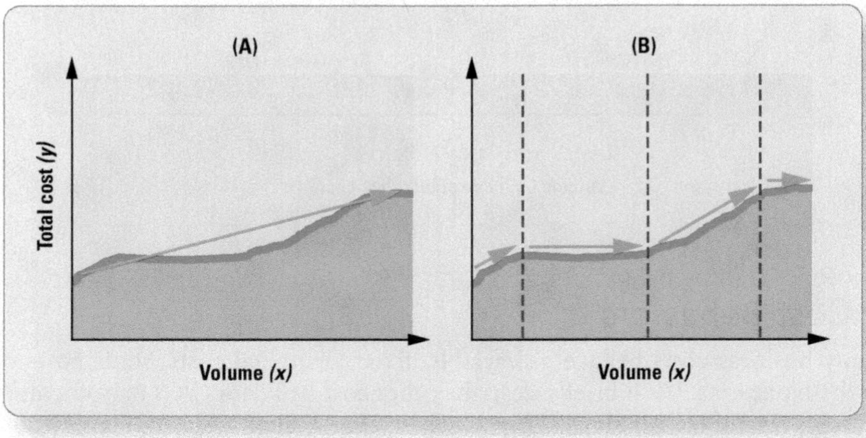

As shown by the straight green arrow in Exhibit 6-11(a), some businesses *approximate* these types of costs as mixed costs, knowing that they will have an estimation error at particular volumes. Sometimes managers also approximate step costs the same way: They simply draw a straight mixed cost line through the steps.

However, as shown in Exhibit 6-11(b), if managers need more accurate predictions, they can simply break these types of costs into smaller relevant ranges and make their predictions based on the particular relevant range. For example, the day-care center may want to predict total caregiver salaries if it enrolls 26 children. The manager knows this enrollment falls into the relevant range of 21 to 28 children, where he or she needs to employ four caregivers. The manager can then predict total caregiver salaries to be $60,000 (four caregivers × $15,000 salary per caregiver).

Sustainability and Cost Behavior

Many companies adopting sustainable business practices experience changes in the way their costs behave. For example, many banks, credit card companies, and utilities offer e-banking and e-billing services as an alternative to sending traditional paper statements and bills through the mail. E-banking and e-billing drive down a company's variable costs.

The environmental consequences of this action are tremendous if you consider the entire production and delivery cycle of the bills and statements, all of the way from the logging of the trees in the forest to the delivery of the bill at the customer's doorstep. Not only are fewer trees cut down, but also less energy is consumed in the transportation of the timber, the processing of the paper, the distribution of the paper, the delivery of the statements via the US Postal Service, and the final disposal of the paper at landfills or recycling centers. In addition, less waste-water is generated and fewer toxic air emissions are produced.

From the customer's perspective, adoption of e-billing and e-banking services provides one means for households to embrace a greener lifestyle. Charter One Bank estimates that, on an annual basis, the average household that receives e-bills and pays bills online reduces paper consumption by 6.6 pounds, saves 4.5 gallons of gasoline, saves 63 gallons of water, and cuts greenhouse gas emissions equal to the amount that would be emitted by driving 176 miles.[2] According to the US Postal Service, in 2009, 24.4 billion bills and statements (equating to 684 million pounds of paper) were delivered across the country.[3] Because of the increasing popularity of e-billing, this volume is actually down by 1.5 billion pieces since 2006. Thus, the adoption of electronic billing by the general public could have a significant positive impact on the environment.

From the company's perspective, this practice also reduces the total variable costs associated with processing, printing, and mailing statements (and cancelled checks) to each customer. In place of these variable costs, the company must incur additional fixed costs to develop secure online banking and billing websites. However, the variable cost savings generated must be substantial and cost effective. We know this because some companies offer cash incentives to customers if they switch to electronic billing. For example, Charter One Bank actually *pays* customers to go paperless: 10 cents per electronic payment made (online bill payments and debit card payments) up to $120 per year.

See Exercises 6-26A and E6-52B

[2]www.charterone.com/greensense/tips.aspx
[3]www.usps.com/householddiary/welcome.htm

We have just described the most typical cost behaviors. In the next part of the chapter, we will discuss methods managers use for determining how their costs behave.

Decision Guidelines

Cost Behavior

Suppose you manage a local fitness club. To be an effective manager, you need to know how the club's costs behave. Here are some decisions you will need to make.

Decision	Guidelines
How can you tell if a *total* cost is variable, fixed, or mixed?	• Total variable costs increase in *direct proportion* to increases in volume. • Total fixed costs stay *constant* over a wide range of volumes. • Total mixed costs increase but *not* in direct proportion to increases in volume.
How can you tell if a *per-unit* cost is variable, fixed, or mixed?	• On a per-unit basis, variable costs stay constant. • On a per-unit basis, fixed costs decrease in proportion to increases in volume (that is to say they are inversely proportional). • On a per-unit basis, mixed costs decrease, but not in direct proportion to increases in volume.
How can you tell by looking at a graph if a cost is variable, fixed, or mixed?	• Variable cost lines slope upward and begin at the origin. • Fixed cost lines are flat (no slope) and intersect the y-axis at a level equal to total fixed costs (this is known as the vertical intercept). • Mixed cost lines slope upward but do *not* begin at the origin. They intersect the y-axis at a level equal to their fixed cost component.
How can you mathematically express different cost behaviors?	• Cost equations mathematically express cost behavior using the equation for a straight line: $$y = vx + f$$ where, y = total cost v = variable cost per unit of activity (slope) x = volume of activity f = fixed cost (the vertical intercept) • For a variable cost, f is zero, leaving the following: $$y = vx$$ • For a fixed cost, v is zero, leaving the following: $$y = f$$ • Because a mixed cost has both a fixed cost component and a variable cost component, its cost equation is: $$y = vx + f$$

SUMMARY PROBLEM **1**

The previous manager of Fitness-for-Life started the following schedule, but left before completing it. The manager wasn't sure but thought the club's fixed operating costs were $10,000 per month and the variable operating costs were $1 per member. The club's existing facilities could serve up to 750 members per month.

Requirements

1. Complete the following schedule for different levels of monthly membership assuming the previous manager's cost behavior estimates are accurate:

Monthly Operating Costs	100 Members	500 Members	750 Members
Total variable costs			
Total fixed costs..............................			
Total operating costs.........................			
Variable cost per member.................			
Fixed cost per member			
Average cost per member			

2. As the manager of the fitness club, why shouldn't you use the average cost per member to predict total costs at different levels of membership?

▪ SOLUTIONS

Requirement 1

As volume increases, fixed costs stay constant in total but decrease on a per-unit basis. As volume increases, variable costs stay constant on a per-unit basis but increase in total in direct proportion to increases in volume:

	100 Members	500 Members	750 Members
Total variable costs	$ 100	$ 500	$ 750
Total fixed costs..................................	10,000	10,000	10,000
Total operating costs...........................	$10,100	$10,500	$10,750
Variable cost per member......................	$ 1.00	$ 1.00	$ 1.00
Fixed cost per member	100.00	20.00	13.33
Average cost per member	$101.00	$ 21.00	$ 14.33

Requirement 2

The average cost per member should not be used to predict total costs at different volumes of membership because it changes as volume changes. The average cost per member decreases as volume increases due to the fixed component of the club's operating costs. Managers should base cost predictions on cost behavior patterns, not on the average cost per member.

How do Managers Determine Cost Behavior?

In real life, managers need to figure out how their costs behave before they can make predictions and good business decisions. In this section, we discuss the most common ways of determining cost behavior.

Account Analysis

When performing **account analysis**, managers use their judgment to classify each general ledger account as a variable, fixed, or mixed cost. For example, by looking at invoices from his or her supplier, the hotel manager knows that every guest packet of toiletries costs $3. Because guests use or take these toiletries, the total toiletries cost rises in direct proportion to the number of guests. These facts allow the manager to classify the complimentary toiletries expense account as a variable cost.

Likewise, the hotel manager uses account analysis to determine how the depreciation expense accounts behave. Because the hotel uses straight-line depreciation on the parking ramp, building, and furnishings, the manager would classify the depreciation expense accounts as fixed costs. Thus, the manager can use this knowledge of cost behavior and his or her judgment to classify many accounts as variable or fixed.

Scatter Plots

The hotel manager also knows that many of the hotel's costs, such as utilities, are mixed. But how does the manager figure out the portion of the mixed cost that is fixed and the portion that is variable? In other words, how does the manager know from looking at the monthly utility bills that the hotel's utilities cost about $8,000 per month plus $8 more for every guest? One way of figuring this out is by collecting and analyzing historical data about costs and volume.

For example, let's assume that the hotel has collected the information shown in Exhibit 6-12 about last year's guest volume and utility costs.

EXHIBIT 6-12 Historical Information on Guest Volume and Utility Costs

Month	Guest Volume (x)	Utility Costs (y)
January	13,250	$114,000
February	15,200	136,000
March	17,600	135,000
April	18,300	157,000
May	22,900	195,400
June	24,600	207,800
July	25,200	209,600
August	24,900	208,300
September	22,600	196,000
October	20,800	176,400
November	18,300	173,600
December	15,420	142,000

As you can see, the hotel's business is seasonal. More people visit in the summer. However, special events such as the annual Festival of Lights, business conferences, and the nearby casino attract people to the hotel throughout the year.

Once the data has been collected, the manager creates a **scatter plot** of the data.

A scatter plot, which graphs the historical cost data on the y-axis and volume data on the x-axis, helps managers visualize the relationship between the cost and the volume of activity (number of guests, in our example). If there is a fairly strong relationship between

3 Use account analysis and scatter plots to analyze cost behavior

Accounting Simplified

▶

Cost Estimation Methods

If your instructor is using MyAccountingLab, go to the Multimedia Library for a quick video on this topic.

the cost and volume, the data points will fall in a linear pattern, meaning they will resemble something close to a straight line. However, if there is little or no relationship between the cost and volume, the data points will appear almost random.

Exhibit 6-13 shows a scatter plot of the data in Exhibit 6-12. Scatter plots can be prepared by hand, but they are simpler to create using Microsoft Excel (see the "Technology Makes It Simple" feature on page 336). Notice how the data points fall in a pattern that resembles something *close* to a straight line. This shows us that there is a strong relationship between the number of guests and the hotel's utility costs. In other words, the number of guests could be considered a driver of the hotel's utilities costs (recall from our discussion of ABC in Chapter 4 that cost drivers are activities that cause costs to be incurred). On the other hand, if there were a *weaker* relationship between the number of guests and the utility costs, the data points would not fall in such a tight pattern. They would be more loosely scattered, but still in a semilinear pattern. If there were *no* relationship between the number of guests and the utility costs, the data points would appear almost random.

EXHIBIT 6-13 Scatter Plot of Monthly Data

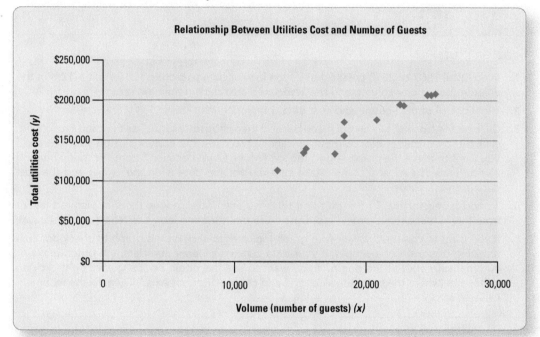

Why is this important? If the data points suggest a fairly weak relationship between the cost and the volume of the chosen activity, any cost equation based on that data will not be very useful for predicting future costs. If this is the case, the manager should consider using a different activity for modeling cost behavior. For example, many hotels use "occupancy rate" (the percentage of rooms rented) rather than number of guests as a basis for explaining and predicting variable and mixed costs.

Scatter plots are also very useful because they allow managers to identify <u>outliers</u>, or abnormal data points. Outliers are data points that do not fall in the same general pattern as the other data points. Since all data points in Exhibit 6-13 fall in the same basic pattern, no outliers appear to exist in our data. However, if a manager sees a potential outlier in the data, he or she should first determine whether the data is correct. Perhaps a clerical error was made when gathering or inputting the data. However, if the data is correct, the manager may need to consider whether to delete that data from any further analysis.

Once the scatter plot has been prepared and examined for outliers, the next step is to determine the cost behavior that best describes the historical data points pictured in the scatter plot. Take a moment and pencil in the cost behavior line that you think best represents the data points in Exhibit 6-13. Where does your line intersect the y-axis? At the origin or above it? In other words, does the utilities cost appear to be a purely variable cost or a mixed cost? If it's a mixed cost, what portion of it is fixed?

Instead of guessing, managers can use one of the following methods to estimate the cost equation that describes the data in the scatter plot:

■ High-low method
■ Regression analysis

The biggest difference between these methods is that the high-low method *uses only two* of the historical data points for this estimate, whereas regression analysis uses *all* of the historical data points. Therefore, regression analysis is theoretically the better of the two methods.

We'll describe both of these methods in the next sections. Before continuing, check out the "Technology Makes It Simple" feature. It shows you just how easy it is to make a scatter plot using Microsoft Excel 2007 or Excel 2010.

Technology makes it simple   Excel 2007 and Excel 2010

Scatter Plots

1. In an Excel 2007 or 2010 spreadsheet, type in your data as pictured in Exhibit 6-12. Put the volume data in one column and the associated cost data in the next column.

2. Highlight all of the volume and cost data with your cursor.

3. Click on the "Insert" tab on the menu bar and then choose "Scatter" as the chart type. Next, click the plain scatter plot (without any lines). You'll see the scatter plot on your screen. If you want to make the graph larger, choose "Move Chart Location" from the menu bar and select "New Sheet" and "OK:" Make sure the volume data is on the x-axis and the cost data is on the y-axis.

4. To add labels for the scatter plot and titles for each axis, choose the first pictured layout from the "Chart Layout" menu tab. Customize the titles and labels to reflect your data set.

5. If you want to change the way your graph looks, right-click on the graph to check out customizing options. For example, if your data consists of large numbers, the graph may not automatically start at the origin. If you want to see the origin on the graph, right-click on either axis (where the number values are) and choose "Format Axis." Then, fix the minimum value at zero.

High-Low Method

The **high-low method** is an easy way to estimate the variable and fixed cost components of a mixed cost. The high-low method basically fits a mixed cost line through the highest and lowest *volume* data points, as shown in Exhibit 6-14, hence the name *high-low*. The high-low method produces the cost equation describing this mixed cost line.

To use the high-low method, we must first identify the months with the highest and lowest volume of activity. Looking at Exhibit 6-12, we see that the hotel served the *most* guests in July and the *fewest* guests in January. *Therefore, we use the data from only these two months in our analysis. We ignore data from all other months.* Even if a month other than July had the highest utility cost, we would still use July. Why? Because we choose the "high" data point based on the month with the highest volume of activity (number of guests)—not the highest cost. We choose the "low" data point in a similar fashion.

STEP 1: The first step is to find *the slope of the mixed cost line* that connects the January and July data points. The slope is the variable cost per unit of activity. We can determine the slope of a line as "rise over run." The *rise* is simply the

4 Use the high-low method to analyze cost behavior

EXHIBIT 6-14 Mixed Cost Line Using High-Low Method

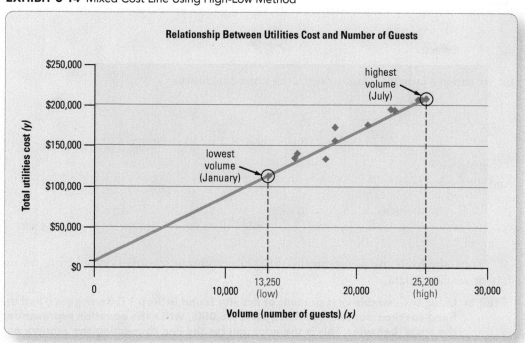

difference in cost between the high and low data points (July and January in our case), while the *run* is the difference in *volume* between the high and low data points:

$$\text{Slope} = \text{Variable cost per unit of activity } (v) = \frac{\text{Rise}}{\text{Run}} = \frac{\text{Change in cost}}{\text{Change in volume}} = \frac{y\,(\text{high}) - y\,(\text{low})}{x\,(\text{high}) - x\,(\text{low})}$$

Using the data from July (as our high) and January (as our low), we calculate the slope as follows:

$$\frac{(\$209{,}600 - \$114{,}000)}{(25{,}200 \text{ guests} - 13{,}250 \text{ guests})} = \$8 \text{ per guest}$$

The slope of the mixed cost line, or variable cost per unit of activity, is $8 per guest.

STEP 2: The second step is to find the vertical intercept—the place where the line connecting the January and July data points intersects the y-axis. This is the fixed cost component of the mixed cost. We insert the slope found in Step 1 ($8 per guest) and the volume and cost data from *either* the high or low month into a mixed cost equation:

$$\text{Total mixed costs} = \text{Variable cost component} + \text{Fixed cost component}$$
$$y \qquad = \qquad vx \qquad + \qquad f$$

For example, we can insert July's cost and volume data as follows:

$$\$209{,}600 = (\$8 \text{ per guest} \times 25{,}200 \text{ guests}) + f$$

And then solve for *f*:

$$f = \$8,000$$

Or we can use January's data to reach the same conclusion:

$$y = vx + f$$
$$\$114,000 = (\$8 \text{ per guest} \times 13,250 \text{ guests}) + f$$

And then solve for *f*:

$$f = \$8,000$$

Thus, the fixed cost component is $8,000 per month regardless of whether we use July or January's data.

STEP 3: **Using the variable cost per unit of activity found in Step 1 ($8 per guest) and the fixed cost component found in Step 2 ($8,000), write the equation representing the costs' behavior. This is the equation for the line connecting the January and July data points on our graph.**

$$y = \$8x + \$8,000$$

where,

$$y = \text{total monthly utilities cost}$$
$$x = \text{number of guests}$$

This is the equation used by the manager in the first half of the chapter to express the hotel's utility costs.

One major drawback of the high-low method is that it uses only two data points: January and July. Because we ignored every other month, the line might not be representative of those months. In our example, the high-low line is representative of the other data points, but in other situations, it may not be. Therefore, the better method to use is regression analysis, which is explained next.

Regression Analysis

Regression analysis is a statistical procedure for determining the line and cost equation that best fits *all of the data points, not just the high-volume and low-volume data points*. In fact, some refer to regression analysis as "the line of best fit." Since the statistical analysis considers all of the data points when forming the line, it is usually more accurate than the high-low method. A statistic (called the R-square) generated by regression analysis also tells us *how well* the line fits the data points. Regression analysis is tedious to complete by hand but simple to do using Microsoft Excel (see the "Technology Makes It Simple" feature on page 341). Many graphing calculators also perform regression analysis.

Regression analysis using Microsoft Excel gives us the output shown in Exhibit 6-15. The output looks complicated, but for our purposes, we only need to consider the three highlighted pieces of information:

1. Intercept coefficient (this refers to the vertical intercept) = 14,538.05
2. X Variable 1 coefficient (this refers to the slope) = 7.85 (rounded)
3. The R-square value (the "goodness-of-fit" statistic) = 0.947 (rounded)

5 Use regression analysis to analyze cost behavior

Accounting Simplified

Regression Analysis

If your instructor is using MyAccountingLab, go to the Multimedia Library for a quick video on this topic.

EXHIBIT 6-15 Output of Microsoft Excel Regression Analysis

	A	B	C	D	E	F	G	H	I
1	SUMMARY OUTPUT								
2									
3		*Regression Statistics*							
4	Multiple R		0.973273						
5	R Square		0.94726						
6	Adjusted R Square		0.941986						
7	Standard Error		8053.744						
8	Observations		12						
9									
10	ANOVA								
11		*df*	*SS*	*MS*	*F*	*Significance F*			
12	Regression	1	11650074512	1.17E + 10	179.6110363	1.02696E-07			
13	Residual	10	648627988.2	64862799					
14	Total	11	12298702500						
15									
16		*Coefficients*	*Standard Error*	*t Stat*	*P-value*	*Lower 95%*	*Upper 95%*	*Lower 95.0%*	*Upper 95.0%*
17	Intercept	14538.05	11898.3624	1.221853	0.249783701	-11973.15763	41049.25	-11973.16	41049.25
18	X Variable 1	7.849766	0.585720166	13.4019	1.02696E-07	6.5446997	9.154831	6.5447	9.154831

Let's look at each piece of information, starting with the highlighted information at the bottom of the output:

1. The "Intercept coefficient" is the vertical intercept of the mixed cost line. It's the fixed cost component of the mixed cost. Regression analysis tells us that the fixed component of the monthly utility bill is $14,538 (rounded). Why is this different from the $8,000 fixed component we found using the high-low method? It's because regression analysis considers *every* data point, not just the high- and low-volume data points, when forming the best fitting line.

2. The "X Variable 1 coefficient" is the line's slope, or our variable cost per guest. Regression analysis tells us that the hotel spends an extra $7.85 on utilities for every guest it serves. This is slightly lower than the $8 per guest amount we found using the high-low method.

Using the regression output, we can write the utilities monthly cost equation as follows:

$$y = \$7.85x + \$14,538$$

where,

$$y = \text{total monthly utilities cost}$$
$$x = \text{number of guests}$$

3. Now, let's look at the R-square statistic highlighted near the top of Exhibit 6-15. The R-square statistic is often referred to as a "goodness-of-fit" statistic because it tells us how well the regression line fits the data points. The R-square can range in value from zero to one, as shown in Exhibit 6-16. If there were no relationship between the number of guests and the hotel's utility costs, the data points would be scattered randomly

> **Why is this important?**
>
> "Regression analysis is **fast** and **easy** to perform using Excel 2007 or Excel 2010. **Regression analysis** usually gives managers the most **representative** cost equations, allowing them to make the most **accurate** cost projections."

(rather than being in a linear pattern) and the R-square would be close to zero. If there were a *perfect* relationship between the number of guests and the hotel's utility cost, a *perfectly* straight line would run through *every* data point and the R-square would be 1.00. In our case, the R-square of 0.947 means that the regression line fits the data quite well (it's very close to 1.00). In other words, the data points *almost* fall in a straight line (as you can see in Exhibit 6-13).

EXHIBIT 6-16 Range of R-square Values

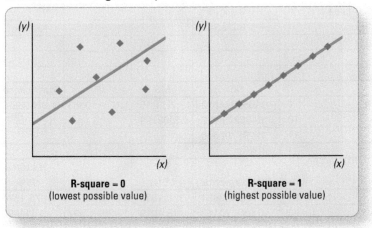

The R-square provides managers with very helpful information. The higher the R-square, the stronger the relationship between cost and volume. The stronger the relationship, the more confidence the manager would have in using the cost equation to predict costs at different volumes within the same relevant range. As a rule of thumb, an R-square over 0.80 generally indicates that the cost equation is very reliable for predicting costs at other volumes within the relevant range. An R-square between 0.50 and 0.80 means that the manager should use the cost equation with caution. However, if the R-square is fairly low (for example, less than 0.50), the manager should try using a different activity base (for example, room occupancy rate) for cost analysis because the current measure of volume is only weakly related to the costs.

Regression analysis can also help managers implement ABC. Recall from Chapter 4 that managers must choose a cost allocation base for every activity cost pool. The cost allocation base should be the primary cost driver of the costs in that pool. Management will use logic to come up with a short list of potential cost drivers for each activity cost pool. Then, management can run a regression analysis for each potential cost driver to see how strongly related it is to the activity costs in the pool. Managers compare the R-squares from each regression to see which one is highest. The regression with the highest R-square identifies the primary cost driver.

Adding a regression line to a scatter plot

Adding a regression line, the regression equation, and the R-square value to a scatter plot is very simple using Excel 2007 or Excel 2010. You'll be amazed at how quickly and easily you can create a professional-quality graph using the instructions found below.

Technology makes it simple

Adding a Regression Line, Equation, and R-square to the Scatter Plot

1. Start with the Excel Scatter plot you created using the directions found on page 336.
2. Point the cursor at any data point on your scatter plot and *right* click on the mouse.
3. Choose "Add Trendline."
4. Check the two boxes: "Display Equation on Chart" and "Display R-squared value on chart." Then "Close."
5. OPTIONAL: To force the regression line stretch back to the y-axis, point the cursor at the regression line and *right* click on the mouse. Choose "format Trendline." Then fill in the "Forecast Backward" box with the *lowest* x-value (volume) in your data set. Then "close."

Technology makes it simple

Regression Analysis

1. If you created a scatter plot, you have already done this first step. In an Excel spreadsheet, type in your data as pictured in Exhibit 6-12. Put the volume data in one column and the associated cost data in the below column.
2. Click on the "Data" tab on the menu bar.
3. Next, click on "Data Analysis." If you don't see it on your menu bar, follow the directions for add-ins given below before continuing.
4. From the list of data analysis tools, select "Regression," then "OK."
5. Follow the two instructions on the screen:
   i.   Highlight (or type in) the y-axis data range (this is your cost data).
   ii. Highlight (or type in) the x-axis data range (this is your volume data).
   iii. Click "OK."
6. That's all. Excel gives you the output shown in Exhibit 6-15.

DIRECTIONS FOR ADD-INs: It's easy and free to add the "Data Analysis Toolpak" if it's not already on your menu bar. You'll need to add it only once, and then it will always be on your menu bar. Simply follow these instructions:

1a. **For Excel 2007:** Click the Microsoft Office button (the colorful button in the upper-left-hand corner) and then click on the "Excel Options" box shown at the bottom.
1b. **For Excel 2010:** Click on the "File" tab on the menu bar. Then select "Options" on the left-hand side of the screen.
2. Click "Add-Ins."
3. In the "Manage" box at the bottom of the screen, select "Excel Add-ins" and click "GO."
4. In the "Add-Ins available" box, select the "Analysis Toolpak" check box and then click "OK."
5. If asked, click "Yes" to install.

Data Concerns

Cost equations are only as good as the data on which they are based. For example, if the hotel's utility bills are seasonal, management may want to develop separate cost equations for each season. For example, it might develop a winter utility bill cost equation using historical data from only the winter months. Management would do likewise for every other season. Inflation can also affect predictions. If inflation is running rampant, managers should adjust projected costs by the inflation rate. Even if the economy has generally low inflation, certain industries (such as health care) or raw material inputs may be experiencing large price changes.

Another cause for concern is outliers, or abnormal data points. Outliers can distort the results of the high-low method and regression analysis. Recall that the high-low method uses only two data points—the data points associated with the highest and lowest volumes of activity. If either of these points is an outlier, the resulting line and cost equation will be skewed. Because regression analysis uses all data points, any outlier in the data will affect the resulting line and cost equation. To find outliers, management should first plot the data like we did in Exhibit 6-13.

What are the Roles of Variable Costing and the Contribution Margin Income Statement?

You have just learned about different cost behaviors. As you'll see in the coming chapters, almost all business decisions are influenced by cost behavior. In the following sections, we'll explain how the accounting system can communicate cost behavior information to managers so that they have it readily available for planning, decision-making, and performance evaluation purposes.

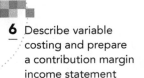

6 Describe variable costing and prepare a contribution margin income statement

Comparing Absorption Costing and Variable Costing

So far in this textbook, we have used a costing concept known as absorption costing. Why? Generally Accepted Accounting Principles (GAAP) requires absorption costing for external financial reporting and the Internal Revenue Service (IRS) requires it for tax preparation. Under **absorption costing**, all manufacturing-related costs, whether fixed or variable, are "absorbed" into the cost of the product. In other words, all direct materials, direct labor, and MOH costs are treated as inventoriable product costs, as described in Chapter 2. We used absorption costing, also known as "traditional" or "full costing" when we illustrated job costing and process costing in Chapters 3, 4, and 5.

Under absorption costing, no distinction is made between manufacturing costs that rise and fall with production volume and manufacturing costs that remain fixed. As a review,

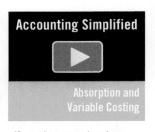

Accounting Simplified

Absorption and Variable Costing

If your instructor is using MyAccountingLab, go to the Multimedia Library for a quick video on this topic.

- variable manufacturing costs would include direct material, direct labor, and variable manufacturing overhead costs (MOH) such as the utilities used during the production process.
- fixed MOH costs would include property taxes and insurance on the plant, straight-line depreciation on the plant, lease payments on the production equipment and the portion of utilities that are not affected by changes in production volume.

Supporters of absorption costing argue that all of these costs—whether variable or fixed—are necessary for production to occur, so *all* of these costs should become part of the inventoriable cost of the product.

On the other hand, many accountants and managers do not agree. They argue that fixed manufacturing costs are related to the available production capacity and will be incurred *regardless* of the actual production volume which occurs during the period. Since these costs will be incurred regardless of volume, they should be treated as period costs and expensed immediately. This argument has led to the development and use of an alternative costing system known as **variable costing** (or **direct costing**) in which only *variable* manufacturing costs are treated as inventoriable product costs. Since GAAP and the IRS require absorption costing for external reporting, variable costing may only be used for internal management purposes.

One benefit of variable costing is that it often leads to better decisions. By assigning only variable manufacturing costs to each unit of product, managers can easily see how much additional manufacturing cost will be incurred every time another unit is produced. In addition, the unit cost of the product will not be affected by the number of units produced during the period, as it is when fixed manufacturing costs are absorbed into the unit cost. As we'll discuss next, another benefit of variable costing is that it provides incentives for better inventory management than does absorption costing.

Let's illustrate this concept using an example. Exhibit 6-17 provides the most recent annual data for ShredCo, a maker of electronic paper shredders.

EXHIBIT 6-17 ShredCo data

Variable costs:	
Direct material cost per unit produced	$35
Direct labor cost per unit produced	$10
Variable MOH cost per unit produced	$5
Variable operating expenses per unit sold	
(selling, general and administrative)	$2
Fixed costs:	
Fixed MOH	$1,000,000
Fixed operating expenses (selling, general and administrative)	$300,000
Other information:	
Units produced	40,000 units
Sales price per unit	$100

Exhibit 6-18 shows the inventoriable product cost of one unit under both absorption costing and variable costing. Notice that the only difference is the treatment of fixed MOH. Absorption costing includes fixed MOH per unit ($25) in the unit cost, whereas variable costing does not. The $75 unit cost shown in Exhibit 6-18 will be used by the company to 1) record the value of inventory on the balance sheet, and 2) record Cost of Goods Sold on the income statement when the inventory is eventually sold.

Notice how variable costing shows managers exactly how much extra cost ($50) will be incurred every time a unit is made. This transparency is not the case with absorption costing, which can easily mislead managers. To illustrate, let's assume that the company decides to produce an extra 5,000 units with its existing capacity. Using variable costing, we see the additional production cost will really be $250,000 (5,000 units × $50).

EXHIBIT 6-18 Comparing inventoriable product costs

Manufacturing Costs	Absorption Costing	Variable Costing
Direct materials	$35	$35
Direct labor	10	10
Variable MOH	5	5
Fixed MOH ($1,000,000 ÷ 40,000 units)	25	–
Unit cost	$75	$50

However, absorption costing could mislead the manager into believing that the extra cost would be $375,000 (5,000 × $75). The fallacy in this erroneous analysis stems from treating the $25 of fixed MOH in the product cost as if it were variable. In fact, the company will *not* incur an additional $25 of fixed cost with every unit produced. Rather, the company will incur $1 million of fixed cost *regardless* of the production volume, as long as the production volume stays within the company's relevant range (which in most cases is its existing production capacity). Variable costing tends be the better costing system for internal decision-making purposes because the reported unit cost is purely variable in nature.

Exhibit 6-19 illustrates period costs under both costing systems. Remember that these are often referred to as "operating expenses" in the income statement. Notice again that the only difference is the treatment of fixed MOH. Under absorption costing, *none* of the fixed MOH is expensed as a period cost. Under variable costing, *all* of the fixed MOH ($1 million) is expensed as a period cost.

EXHIBIT 6-19 Comparing period costs (operating expenses)

Operating Expenses of the Period	Absorption Costing	Variable Costing
Variable operating expenses when 40,000 units are sold (40,000 × $2)	$ 80,000	$ 80,000
Fixed operating expenses	300,000	300,000
Fixed MOH	–	1,000,000
Total period costs	$380,000	$1,380,000

Keep the following rule of thumb in mind:

The ONLY difference between absorption costing and variable costing is the treatment of Fixed MOH, and the *timing* with which it is expensed:

- Under variable costing, fixed MOH is expensed immediately as a period cost (operating expense).
- Under absorption costing, fixed MOH becomes part of the inventoriable cost of the product, which isn't expensed (as Cost of Goods Sold) until the inventory is sold.

An Alternative Income Statement Format

Now that you know the difference between absorption costing and variable costing, let's see how the information is communicated to managers in the income statement.

Comparing Income Statement Formats

Let's start with the situation in which the company sells *exactly* all of the units it produced during the period. In our example, this means that the company sells all 40,000 units it produced during the year. This situation occurs most frequently with lean producers who use Just-in-Time inventory systems. Exhibit 6-20 shows a traditional income statement, which is based on absorption costing. Notice how Cost of Goods Sold is calculated using the $75 unit cost shown in Exhibit 6-18.

EXHIBIT 6-20 Traditional Income Statement based on Absorption Costing

ShredCo
Traditional Income Statement (Absorption costing)
For the year ending December 31

Sales revenue (40,000 × $100)	$4,000,000
Less: Cost of goods sold (40,000 × $75)	3,000,000
Gross profit	$1,000,000
Less: Operating expenses [300,000 + (40,000 × $2)]	380,000
Operating income	$ 620,000

In contrast, Exhibit 6-21 shows a **contribution margin income statement**, which is an income statement organized by cost behavior. When manufacturers use variable costing, they report income internally using a contribution margin income statement format.

EXHIBIT 6-21 Contribution Margin Income Statement using Variable Costing

ShredCo
Contribution Margin Income Statement (Variable costing)
For the year ending December 31

Sales revenue (40,000 × $100)	$4,000,000
Less: Variable expenses	
Variable cost of goods sold (40,000 × $50)	2,000,000
Variable operating expenses (40,000 × $2)	80,000
Contribution margin	$1,920,000
Less: Fixed expenses	
Fixed MOH	1,000,000
Fixed operating expenses	300,000
Operating income	$620,000

Notice the following in Exhibit 6-21:

- The contribution margin income statement is organized by cost behavior.
- All variable costs are expensed *above* the contribution margin line. As a result, only the *variable* product cost ($50, from Exhibit 6-18) is used when calculating Variable Cost of Goods Sold.
- All fixed costs, including fixed MOH, are expensed *below* the contribution margin line.
- The **contribution margin** is equal to sales revenue minus variable expenses. It shows managers how much profit has been made on sales before considering fixed costs.
- The operating income ($620,000) is the *same* in both statements. For manufacturers, this equality will *only* occur when all of units produced during a period are also sold during that same period, resulting in no change in inventory levels.
- For service and merchandising companies, operating income will *always* be the same regardless of the income statement format used.

The contribution margin income statement may only be used for internal management purposes, never for external reporting. Managers like the contribution margin format because it allows them to quickly see which costs will change with fluctuations in volume, and which costs will remain the same. For example, if sales volume increases 10%, managers would expect

Why is this important?

"The **contribution margin** income statement allows **managers** to **quickly** see which costs will **change** with **volume,** and which will remain **fixed.**"

sales revenue and variable costs to increase by 10%. As a result, the contribution margin should also increase 10%. On the other hand, all fixed costs shown below the contribution margin should not change.

Service and Merchandising Companies

Variable costing only applies to manufacturing companies since they are the only type of company that incurs manufacturing overhead costs. However, many service and merchandising companies like to use the contribution margin format of the income statement for internal management purposes. Why? Because the contribution margin income statement clearly communicates cost behavior information to managers who need this information for planning and decision making purposes. Just as shown in Exhibit 6-21, all variable expenses are deducted from revenue to arrive at the company's contribution margin. Next, all fixed expenses are subtracted from the contribution margin to arrive at operating income.

For merchandising companies, Cost of Goods Sold is considered to be a variable cost because it rises and falls with the amount of inventory sold. Service companies have no Cost of Goods Sold. Since neither of these types of companies have fixed manufacturing overhead, operating income will always be the same regardless of the income statement format used.

Comparing Operating Income: Variable versus Absorption Costing

For manufacturers, operating income will not always be the same between the two costing systems. In fact, it will *only* be the same if the manufacturer sells *exactly* what it produced during the period, as was the case in Exhibits 6-20 and 6-21. This scenario is typical of a lean producer. However, traditional manufacturers in a growing economy often produce extra safety stock, *increasing* their inventory levels to ensure against unexpected demand. On the other hand, in periods of economic recession (such as in the years 2008–2009) companies often *reduce* their inventory levels to decrease costs, build cash reserves, and adjust for lower sales demand.

We will discuss how inventory levels impact operating income, for both absorption and variable costing, under three possible scenarios:

1. Inventory levels remain constant
2. Inventory levels increase
3. Inventory levels decrease

As we discuss each scenario, keep in mind that in our example, absorption costing assigned $25 of fixed MOH to each unit of product produced by ShredCo (Exhibit 6-18).

Scenario 1: Inventory levels remain constant

As shown in Exhibits 6-20, 6-21, and 6-22, when inventory levels remain constant, both absorption costing and variable costing result in the same operating income. This scenario usually occurs at lean manufacturers since they only produce enough inventory to fill existing customer orders.

EXHIBIT 6-22 Inventory levels remain constant

In this situation, *all* fixed MOH incurred during the period ($1,000,000) is expensed under both costing systems. Under variable costing, it is expensed as a period cost ($1,000,000), as shown in Exhibit 6-21. Under absorption costing, it is first absorbed into the product's cost ($25 of the $75 unit cost), and then expensed as Cost of Goods Sold when the product is sold.

When all product is sold in the same period as it is produced, exactly $1 million of fixed MOH is expensed as part of Cost of Goods Sold (40,000 × $25) as shown in Exhibit 6-20.

Scenario 2: Inventory levels increase

As shown in Exhibit 6-23, when inventory levels increase, operating income will be greater under absorption costing than it is under variable costing. This scenario typically occurs at traditional manufacturers during times of economic growth.

EXHIBIT 6-23 Inventory levels increase

If units produced > units sold, then... → Inventory levels **increase**, and... → Absorption income > variable costing income

In this situation, all fixed MOH incurred during the period is expensed as a period cost under variable costing ($1,000,000). However, under absorption costing, some of the fixed MOH remains "trapped" on the balance sheet as part of the cost of inventory. For example, let's say only 30,000 of the 40,000 units are sold, leaving 10,000 units still in ending inventory. As a result, $750,000 of fixed MOH is expensed as part of Cost of Goods Sold (30,000 units × $25) while $250,000 of fixed MOH (10,000 units × $25) remains in inventory. As a result, *more* cost is expensed under variable costing than under absorption costing, leading to a higher operating income under absorption costing.

Thus, under absorption costing, managers can misuse their powers by continuing to build up unwarranted levels of inventory simply to increase operating income. The more inventory builds up, the more favorable operating income will be. Unfortunately, as we learned in Chapter 4, building unnecessary inventory is wasteful and should be avoided. Because of this drawback to absorption costing, many companies prefer to use variable costing to evaluate managers' performance. Since variable costing expenses all fixed MOH in the current period regardless of the amount of inventory produced, managers have no incentive to build unnecessary inventory.

Scenario 3: Inventory levels decrease

As shown in Exhibit 6-24, when inventory levels decrease, operating income will be greater under variable costing than it is under absorption costing. This scenario typically occurs at traditional manufacturers during times of economic recession. It also occurs when traditional manufacturers are in the process of switching to lean operations, which carry little to no inventory.

EXHIBIT 6-24 Inventory levels decrease

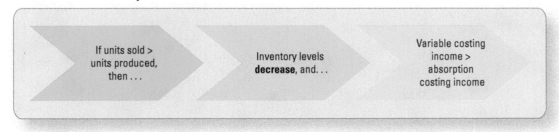

If units sold > units produced, then . . . → Inventory levels **decrease**, and . . . → Variable costing income > absorption costing income

In this situation, all fixed MOH incurred during the period is expensed under variable costing ($1,000,000). However, under absorption costing, all of the fixed MOH of the period is expensed as part of Cost of Goods Sold *plus* some of the fixed MOH from the previous period. For example, let's say that 45,000 units are sold, comprised of the 40,000 units produced in the current period and 5,000 units produced in the previous period. For the sake of simplicity, we'll assume the same unit costs were incurred in the previous period. As a result of selling 45,000 units this year, $1,125,000 of fixed MOH is expensed as Cost of Goods Sold (45,000 × $25). This figure consists of $1,000,000 from the current year (40,000 × $25) and $125,000 from the previous year (5,000 × $25). As a result, *more* cost is expensed under absorption costing than under variable costing, leading to a lower net income under absorption costing.

Managers who are evaluated based on absorption income have every incentive to *avoid* the situation in which inventory levels decline. However, sometimes it is in the company's best interest to decrease inventory levels. For example, companies switching over to lean production methods should experience long-run benefits from lean practices, but in the short-run, inventory reductions will cause absorption-based operating income to decline. Managers switching over to lean production should be fully aware that absorption income will be temporarily affected as the company sheds itself of unnecessary inventory. The challenge for managers is to avoid thinking that lean operations are having a negative effect on the company's earnings, when, in fact, the temporary decrease in operating income is simply a result of the costing system. Again, variable costing is not affected by inventory fluctuations, making it the better costing system for evaluating performance.

Reconciling Operating Income Between the Two Costing Systems

As discussed, absorption costing is required by GAAP and the IRS, yet variable costing is preferred for internal decision-making and performance evaluation purposes. Thus, managers are often exposed to both sets of information. For manufacturers, the costing systems will yield different results for operating income when inventory levels increase or decline. Managers can easily reconcile the difference between the two income figures using the following formula:

Difference in operating income = (Change in inventory level, in units) × (Fixed MOH per unit)

We'll illustrate the use of this formula next.

Reconciling Income When Inventory Levels Increase

Let's try this formula with the example in which 40,000 units are produced, yet only 30,000 are sold. Using the formula, we predict the difference in operating income will be:

Difference in operating income = (Change in inventory level, in units) × (Fixed MOH per unit)
$250,000 = 10,000 units × $ 25

Since the inventory level has *grown*, we would expect operating income under absorption costing to be *greater* than it is under variable costing by $250,000 (see Exhibit 6-23). Exhibit 6-25, which presents comparative income statements, verifies this prediction: Absorption costing income ($390,000) is *higher* than variable costing income ($140,000) by $250,000.

EXHIBIT 6-25 Comparing Income when Inventory Levels Increase

Panel A: Absorption Costing:

ShredCo
Traditional Income Statement (Absorption Costing)
For the year ending December 31

Sales revenue (30,000 × $100)..	$3,000,000
Less: Cost of goods sold (30,000 × $75)...................................	2,250,000
Gross profit...	$ 750,000
Less: Operating expenses [300,000 + (30,000 × $2)]..................	360,000
Operating income..	$ 390,000

Panel B: Variable Costing:

ShredCo
Contribution Margin Income Statement (Variable Costing)
For the year ending December 31

Sales revenue (30,000 × $100)..	$3,000,000
Less: Variable expenses	
Variable cost of goods sold (30,000 × $50)	1,500,000
Variable operating expenses (30,000 × $2).......................	60,000
Contribution margin	$1,440,000
Less: Fixed expenses	
Fixed MOH	1,000,000
Fixed operating expenses	300,000
Operating income..	$ 140,000

Reconciling Income When Inventory Levels Decrease

Now let's briefly consider the situation in which inventory decreases, rather than increases. Let's assume that 45,000 units are sold, comprised of 40,000 that were produced in the current period plus 5,000 units that were produced in the previous period. The formula used to reconcile income suggests that operating income under absorption costing will be *lower* than it is under variable costing (see Exhibit 6-24) by $125,000:

Difference in operating income = (change in inventory level, in units) × (Fixed MOH per unit)
$125,000 = 5,000 units × $ 25

Exhibit 6-26 verifies the truth of this prediction. Operating income under absorption costing ($735,000) is $125,000 *lower* than operating income under variable costing ($860,000).

Key points to remember

You have just learned about variable costing and the contribution margin income statement. Some key points to remember are summarized in Exhibit 6-27.

EXHIBIT 6-26 Comparing Income when Inventory Levels Decrease

Panel A: Absorption Costing:

ShredCo
Traditional Income Statement (Absorption Costing)
For the year ending December 31

Sales revenue (45,000 × $100)...	$4,500,000
Less: Cost of goods sold (45,000 × $75)...	3,375,000
Gross profit..	$1,125,000
Less: Operating expenses [300,000 + (45,000 × $2)]...........................	390,000
Operating income...	$ 735,000

Panel B: Variable Costing:

ShredCo
Contribution Margin Income Statement (Variable Costing)
For the year ending December 31

Sales revenue (45,000 × $100)...	$4,500,000
Less: Variable expenses	
Variable cost of goods sold (45,000 × $50)	2,250,000
Variable operating expenses (45,000 × $2).................................	90,000
Contribution margin	$2,160,000
Less: Fixed expenses	
Fixed MOH	1,000,000
Fixed operating expenses	300,000
Operating income...	$ 860,000

EXHIBIT 6-27 Key Points about Variable Costing and the Contribution Margin Income Statement

Variable Costing

- treats all fixed MOH costs as operating expenses in the period incurred, rather than treating fixed MOH as an inventoriable product cost.
- can only be used for internal management purposes; never for external financial reporting or tax purposes.
- is often better for decision making than absorption costing because it clearly shows managers the additional cost of making one more unit of product (the variable cost per unit).
- is often better for performance evaluation than absorption costing because it gives managers no incentive to build unnecessary inventory.
- will result in a different operating income than absorption costing for manufacturers whose inventory levels *increase* or *decrease* from the previous period.

The Contribution Margin Income Statement

- is organized by cost behavior. First, all variable expenses are deducted from sales revenue to arrive at the company's contribution margin. Next, all fixed expenses are deducted from the contribution margin to arrive at operating income.
- is often more useful than a traditional income statement for planning and decision making because it clearly distinguishes the costs that will be affected by changes in volume (the variable costs) from the costs that will be unaffected (fixed costs).
- can only be used for internal management purposes, and never for external financial reporting.
- will show the same operating income as a traditional income statement for 1) service firms, 2) merchandising companies, and 3) manufacturers *only* if their inventory levels remain stable.

Decision Guidelines

Cost Behavior

As the manager of a local fitness club, Fitness-for-Life, you'll want to plan for operating costs at various levels of membership. Before you can make forecasts, you'll need to make some of the following decisions.

Decision	Guidelines
How can I separate the fixed and the variable components of a mixed cost?	• Managers typically use the high-low method or regression analysis. • The high-low method is fast and easy but uses only two historical data points to form the cost equation and, therefore, may not be very indicative of the cost's true behavior. • Regression analysis uses every data point provided to determine the cost equation that best fits the data. It is simple to do with Excel, but tedious to do by hand.
I've used the high-low method to formulate a cost equation. Can I tell how well the cost equation fits the data?	The only way to determine how well the high-low cost equation fits the data is by (1) plotting the data, (2) drawing a line through the data points associated with the highest and lowest volume, and (3) "visually inspecting" the resulting graph to see if the line is representative of the other plotted data points.
I've used regression analysis to formulate a cost equation. Can I tell how well the cost equation fits the data?	The R-square is a "goodness-of-fit" statistic that tells how well the regression analysis cost equation fits the data. The R-square ranges from 0 to 1, with 1 being a perfect fit. When the R-square is high, the cost equation should render fairly accurate predictions.
Do I need to be concerned about anything before using the high-low method or regression analysis?	Cost equations are only as good as the data on which they are based. Managers should plot the historical data to see if a relationship between cost and volume exists. In addition, scatter plots help managers identify outliers. Managers should remove outliers before further analysis. Managers should also adjust cost equations for seasonal data, inflation, and price changes.
Can I present the club's financial statements in a manner that will help with planning and decision making?	Managers often use contribution margin income statements for internal planning and decision making. Contribution margin income statements organize costs by *behavior* (fixed versus variable) rather than by *function* (product versus period).
What is the difference between absorption and variable costing?	Fixed manufacturing costs are treated as: • inventoriable product costs under absorption costing. • period costs under variable costing.

How are inventoriable product costs calculated under absorption costing and variable costing?	*Absorption Costing*		*Variable Costing*
	Direct materials		Direct materials
	+ Direct labor		+ Direct labor
	+ Variable MOH		+ Variable MOH
	+ Fixed MOH		
	= Product cost		= Product cost

| Why is variable costing often used for internal management purposes? | • Variable costing and the contribution margin income statement help managers easily predict the cost of operating at different volumes within the relevant range.
• Variable costing helps managers with decision making, because it allows them to easily see the cost of making one more unit of product.
• Variable costing does not give managers incentives to build up unnecessary inventory. |

SUMMARY PROBLEM 2

As the new manager of a local fitness club, Fitness-for-Life, you have been studying the club's financial data. You would like to determine how the club's costs behave in order to make accurate predictions for next year. Here is information from the last 6 months:

Month	Club Membership (number of members)	Total Operating Costs	Average Operating Costs per Member
July	450	$ 8,900	$19.78
August	480	$ 9,800	$20.42
September	500	$10,100	$20.20
October	550	$10,150	$18.45
November	560	$10,500	$18.75
December	525	$10,200	$19.43

Requirements

1. By looking at the "Total Operating Costs" and the "Operating Costs per Member," can you tell whether the club's operating costs are variable, fixed, or mixed? Explain your answer.

2. Use the high-low method to determine the club's monthly operating cost equation.

3. Using your answer from Requirement 2, predict total monthly operating costs if the club has 600 members.

4. Can you predict total monthly operating costs if the club has 3,000 members? Explain your answer.

5. Prepare the club's traditional income statement and its contribution margin income statement for the month of July. Assume that your cost equation from Requirement 2 accurately describes the club's cost behavior. The club charges members $30 per month for unlimited access to its facilities.

6. *Optional*: Perform regression analysis using Microsoft Excel. What is the monthly operating cost equation? What is the R-square? Why is the cost equation different from that in Requirement 2?

▪ SOLUTIONS

Requirement 1

By looking at "Total Operating Costs," we can see that the club's operating costs are not purely fixed; otherwise, total costs would remain constant. Operating costs appear to be either variable or mixed because they increase in total as the number of members increases. By looking at the "Operating Costs per Member," we can see that the operating costs aren't purely variable; otherwise, the "per-member" cost would remain constant. Therefore, the club's operating costs are mixed.

Requirement 2

Use the high-low method to determine the club's operating cost equation:

STEP 1: The highest volume month is November, and the lowest volume month is July. Therefore, we use *only these 2 months* to determine the cost equation. The first step is to find the variable cost per unit of activity, which is the slope of the line connecting the November and July data points:

$$\frac{\text{Rise}}{\text{Run}} = \frac{\text{Change in } y}{\text{Change in } x} = \frac{y\text{ (high)} - y\text{ (low)}}{x\text{ (high)} - x\text{ (low)}} = \frac{(\$10,500 - \$8,900)}{(560 - 450 \text{ members})} = \$14.55 \text{ per member (rounded)}$$

STEP 2: The second step is to find the fixed cost component (vertical intercept) by plugging in the slope and either July or November data to a mixed cost equation:

$$y = vx + f$$

Using November data:

$$\$10,500 = (\$14.55/\text{member} \times 560 \text{ guests}) + f$$

Solving for *f*:

$$f = \$2,352$$

Or we can use July data to reach the same conclusion:

$$\$8,900 = (\$14.55/\text{members} \times 450 \text{ guests}) + f$$

Solving for *f*:

$$f = \$2,352 \text{ (rounded)}$$

STEP 3: Write the monthly operating cost equation:

$$y = \$14.55x + \$2,352$$

where,

$$x = \text{number of members}$$
$$y = \text{total monthly operating costs}$$

Requirement 3

Predict total monthly operating costs when volume reaches 600 members:

$$y = (\$14.55 \times 600) + \$2,352$$
$$y = \$11,082$$

Requirement 4

Our current data and cost equation are based on 450 to 560 members. If membership reaches 3,000, operating costs could behave much differently. That volume falls outside our current relevant range.

Requirement 5

The club had 450 members in July and total operating costs of $8,900. Thus, its traditional income statement is as follows:

FITNESS-FOR-LIFE
Income Statement
Month Ended July 31

Club membership revenue (450 × $30)	$13,500
Less: Operating expenses (given)	(8,900)
Operating income	$ 4,600

To prepare the club's contribution margin income statement, we need to know how much of the total $8,900 operating costs is fixed and how much is variable. If the cost equation from Requirement 2 accurately reflects the club's cost behavior, fixed costs will be $2,352 and variable costs will be $6,548 (= $14.55 × 450). The contribution margin income statement would look like this:

FITNESS-FOR-LIFE
Contribution Margin Income Statement
Month Ended July 31

Club membership revenue (450 × $30)	$13,500
Less: Variable expenses (450 × $14.55)	(6,548)
Contribution margin	6,952
Less: Fixed expenses	(2,352)
Operating income	$ 4,600

Requirement 6

Regression analysis using Microsoft Excel results in the following cost equation and R-square:

$$y = \$11.80x + \$3,912$$

where,

$$x = \text{number of members}$$
$$y = \text{total monthly operating costs}$$

R-square = 0.8007

The regression analysis cost equation uses all of the data points, not just the data from November and July. Therefore, it better represents all of the data. The high R-square means that the regression line fits the data well and predictions based on this cost equation should be quite accurate.

END OF CHAPTER

Learning Objectives

- 1 Describe key characteristics and graphs of various cost behaviors
- 2 Use cost equations to express and predict costs
- 3 Use account analysis and scatter plots to analyze cost behavior
- 4 Use the high-low method to analyze cost behavior
- 5 Use regression analysis to analyze cost behavior
- 6 Describe variable costing and prepare a contribution margin income statement

Accounting Vocabulary

Absorption Costing. (p. 342) The costing method where products "absorb" both fixed and variable manufacturing costs.

Account Analysis. (p. 334) A method for determining cost behavior that is based on a manager's judgment in classifying each general ledger account as a variable, fixed, or mixed cost.

Committed Fixed Costs. (p. 323) Fixed costs that are locked in because of previous management decisions; management has little or no control over these costs in the short run.

Contribution Margin. (p. 345) Sales revenue minus variable expenses.

Contribution Margin Income Statement. (p. 345) Income statement that organizes costs by *behavior* (variable costs or fixed costs) rather than by *function*.

Cost Behavior. (p. 320) Describes how costs change as volume changes.

Cost Equation. (p. 321) A mathematical equation for a straight line that expresses how a cost behaves.

Curvilinear Costs. (p. 330) A cost behavior that is not linear (not a straight line).

Discretionary Fixed Costs. (p. 323) Fixed costs that are a result of annual management decisions; fixed costs that are controllable in the short run.

Fixed Costs. (p. 323) Costs that do not change in total despite wide changes in volume.

High-Low Method. (p. 336) A method for determining cost behavior that is based on two historical data points: the highest and lowest volume of activity.

Mixed Cost. (p. 325) Costs that change, but *not* in direct proportion to changes in volume. Mixed costs have both variable cost and fixed cost components.

Regression Analysis. (p. 338) A statistical procedure for determining the line that best fits the data by using *all of the historical data points, not just the high and low data points*.

Relevant Range. (p. 327) The band of volume where total fixed costs remain constant at a certain level and where the variable cost *per unit* remains constant at a certain level.

Scatter Plot. (p. 334) A graph that plots historical cost and volume data.

Step Costs. (p. 329) A cost behavior that is fixed over a small range of activity and then jumps to a different fixed level with moderate changes in volume.

Outliers. (p. 335) Abnormal data points; data points that do not fall in the same general pattern as the other data points.

Variable Costs. (p. 320) Costs incurred for every unit of activity. As a result, total variable costs change in direct proportion to changes in volume.

Variable Costing. (p. 343) The costing method that assigns only *variable* manufacturing costs to products. All fixed manufacturing costs (Fixed MOH) are expensed as period costs.

MyAccountingLab Go to http://myaccountinglab.com/ for the following **Quick Check, Short Exercises, Exercises, and Problems. They are available with immediate grading, explanations of correct and incorrect answers, and interactive media that acts as your own online tutor.**

Quick Check

1. *(Learning Objective 1)* If a *per-unit* cost remains constant over a wide range of volume, the cost is most likely a
   - a. variable cost.
   - b. fixed cost.
   - c. mixed cost.
   - d. step cost.

2. *(Learning Objective 1)* The cost per unit decreases as volume increases for which of the following cost behaviors?
   - a. Variable costs and fixed costs
   - b. Variable costs and mixed costs
   - c. Fixed costs and mixed costs
   - d. Only fixed costs

3. *(Learning Objective 2)* In the following mixed cost equation, what amount represents the **total variable cost component**: $y = vx + f$?
   a. y
   b. v
   c. f
   d. vx

4. *(Learning Objective 2)* Which of the following would generally be considered a committed fixed cost for a retailing firm?
   a. Cost of a trip to Cancun given to the employee who is "Employee of the Year"
   b. Lease payments made on the store building
   c. Cost of sponsoring the local golf tournament for charity
   d. Cost of annual sales meeting for all employees

5. *(Learning Objective 3)* Which method is used to see if a relationship between the cost driver and total cost exists?
   a. Scatter plot
   b. Variance analysis
   c. Outlier
   d. Account analysis

6. *(Learning Objective 4)* When choosing the high point for the high-low method, how is the high point selected?
   a. The point with the highest total cost is chosen.
   b. The point with the highest volume of activity is chosen.
   c. The point that has the highest cost and highest volume of activity is always chosen.
   d. Both the high point and the low point are selected at random.

7. *(Learning Objective 5)* What is the advantage of using regression analysis to determine the cost equation?
   a. The method is objective.
   b. All data points are used to calculate the equation for the cost equation.
   c. It will generally be more accurate than the high-low method.
   d. All of the above statements are true about regression analysis.

8. *(Learning Objective 5)* Which of the following statements about using regression analysis is *true*?
   a. Regression analysis always ignores outliers.
   b. Regression analysis uses two points of data to arrive at the cost estimate equation.
   c. The R-square generated by the regression analysis is a measure of how well the regression analysis cost equation fits the data.
   d. Regression analysis is a subjective cost estimation method.

9. *(Learning Objective 6)* The only difference between variable costing and absorption costing lies in the treatment of
   a. fixed manufacturing overhead costs.
   b. variable manufacturing overhead costs.
   c. direct materials and direct labor costs.
   d. variable nonmanufacturing costs.

10. *(Learning Objective 6)* When inventories decline, operating income under variable costing is
   a. lower than operating income under absorption costing.
   b. the same as operating income under absorption costing.
   c. higher than operating income under absorption costing.

Quick Check Answers

1.a 2.c 3.d 4.b 5.a 6.b 7.d 8.c 9.a 10.c

Short Exercises

S6-1 Identify cost behavior *(Learning Objective 1)*

The following chart shows three different costs: Cost A, Cost B, and Cost C. For each cost, the chart shows the total cost and cost per unit at two different volumes within the same relevant range. Based on this information, identify each cost as fixed, variable, or mixed. Explain your answers.

	At 5,000 units		At 6,000 units	
	Total Cost	**Cost per Unit**	**Total Cost**	**Cost per Unit**
Cost A..............	$30,000	$6.00	$36,000	$6.00
Cost B..............	$30,000	$6.00	$30,000	$5.00
Cost C..............	$30,000	$6.00	$33,000	$5.50

S6-2 Sketch cost behavior graphs *(Learning Objective 1)*

Sketch graphs of the following cost behaviors. In each graph, the y-axis should be "total costs" and the x-axis should be "volume of activity."

a. Fixed
b. Step
c. Mixed
d. Curvilinear
e. Variable

S6-3 Computer fixed costs per unit *(Learning Objective 2)*

First Equipment produces high-quality basketballs. If the fixed cost per basketball is $5 when the company produces 15,000 basketballs, what is the fixed cost per basketball when it produces $18,750 basketballs? Assume that both volumes are in the same relevant range.

S6-4 Define various cost equations *(Learning Objective 2)*

Write the cost equation for each of the following cost behaviors. Define the variables in each equation.

a. Fixed
b. Mixed
c. Variable

S6-5 Predict total mixed costs *(Learning Objective 2)*

Cutting Edge Razors produces deluxe razors that compete with Gillette's Mach line of razors. Total manufacturing costs are $300,000 when 10,000 packages are produced. Of this amount, total variable costs are $20,000. What are the total production costs when 20,000 packages of razors are produced? Assume the same relevant range.

S6-6 Predict and graph total mixed costs *(Learning Objectives 1 & 2)*

Suppose T-Call offers an international calling plan that charges $5.00 per month plus $0.40 per minute for calls outside the United States.

1. Under this plan, what is your monthly international long-distance cost if you call Europe for

   a. 25 minutes?
   b. 50 minutes?
   c. 100 minutes?

2. Draw a graph illustrating your total cost under this plan. Label the axes and show your costs at 25, 50, and 100 minutes.

S6-7 Classify cost behavior *(Learning Objective 3)*

Carlson Sound builds innovative speakers for home theater systems. Identify the following costs as variable or fixed:

a. Depreciation on equipment used to cut wood enclosures

b. Wood for speaker enclosures

c. Patents on crossover relays (internal components)

d. Crossover relays

e. Grill cloth

f. Glue

g. Quality inspector's salary

S6-8 Prepare and analyze a scatter plot *(Learning Objective 3)*

Speedy Lube is a car care center specializing in ten-minute oil changes. Speedy Lube has two service bays, which limits its capacity to 3,600 oil changes per month. The following information was collected over the past six months:

Month	Number of Oil Changes	Operating Expenses
January	3,100	$36,000
February	2,500	$31,500
March	2,700	$32,500
April	2,600	$32,100
May	3,500	$36,600
June	2,800	$33,300

1. Prepare a scatter plot graphing the volume of oil changes (x-axis) against the company's monthly operating expenses (y-axis). Graph by hand or use Excel.

2. How strong of a relationship does there appear to be between the company's operating expenses and the number of oil changes performed each month? Explain. Do there appear to be any outliers in the data? Explain.

3. Based on the graph, do the company's operating costs appear to be fixed, variable, or mixed? Explain how you can tell.

4. Would you feel comfortable using this information to project operating costs for a volume of 4,000 oil changes per month? Explain.

S6-9 Use the high-low method *(Learning Objective 4)*

Refer to the Speedy Lube data in S6-8. Use the high-low method to determine the variable and fixed cost components of Speedy Lube's operating costs. Use this information to project the monthly operating costs for a month in which the company performs 3,600 oil changes.

S6-10 Use the high-low method *(Learning Objective 4)*

Two Sisters Catering uses the high-low method to predict its total overhead costs. Past records show that total overhead cost was $25,300 when 840 hours were worked and $27,500 when 940 hours were worked. If Two Sisters Catering has 865 hours scheduled for next month, what is the expected total overhead cost for next month?

S6-11 Predicting costs in a health care setting *(Learning Objective 4)*

The Surgical Care Unit of Ultra Care Health Group uses the high-low method to predict its total surgical unit supplies costs. It appears that nursing hours worked is a good predictor of surgical unit supplies costs in the unit. The supervisor for the unit has gone through the records for the past year and has found that June had the fewest nursing hours worked at 1,000 hours, while September had the most nursing hours worked at 1,500 hours. In June, total surgical unit supplies cost $30,000 and in September, total surgical unit supplies cost $38,000. If the Surgical Care Unit plans to have 1,025 nursing hours worked next month, what is the expected surgical unit supplies cost for the month?

S6-12 Critique the high-low method *(Learning Objective 4)*

You have been assigned an intern to help you forecast your firm's costs at different volumes. He thinks he will get cost and volume data from the two most recent months, plug them into the high-low method equations, and turn in the cost equation results to your boss before the hour is over. As his mentor, explain to him why the process isn't quite as simple as he thinks. Point out some of the concerns he is overlooking, including your concerns about his choice of data and method.

S6-13 Analyze a scatter plot *(Learning Objectives 3 & 4)*

The local Holiday Inn collected seven months of data on the number of room-nights rented per month and the monthly utilities cost. The data was graphed, resulting in the following scatter plot:

Number of room-nights rented and utilities cost

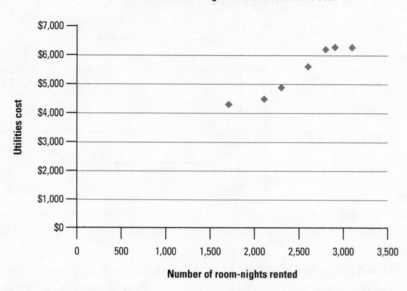

1. Based on this scatter plot, how strong of a relationship does there appear to be between the number of room-nights rented per month and the monthly utilities cost?
2. Do there appear to be any outliers in the data? Explain.
3. Suppose management performs the high-low method using this data. Do you think the resulting cost equation would be very accurate? Explain.

S6-14 Theoretical comparison of high-low and regression analysis
(Learning Objectives 4 & 5)

Refer to the Holiday Inn scatter plot in S6-13.

1. Would the high-low method or regression analysis result in a more accurate cost equation for the data pictured in the scatter plot? Explain.
2. A regression analysis of the data revealed an R-squared figure of 0.939. Interpret this figure in light of the lowest and highest possible R-squared values.
3. As a manager, would you be confident predicting utilities costs for other room-night volumes within the same relevant range?

S6-15 Write a cost equation given regression output (*Learning Objective 5*)

An advertising agency wanted to determine the relationship between its monthly operating costs and a potential cost driver, professional hours. The output of a regression analysis performed using Excel showed the following information:

	A	B	C	D	E	F	G	H	I
1	**SUMMARY OUTPUT**								
2									
3	*Regression Statistics*								
4	Multiple R		0.85						
5	R Square		0.72						
6	Adjusted R Square		0.66						
7	Standard Error		207.23						
8	Observations		12						
9									
10	**ANOVA**								
11		*df*	*SS*	*MS*	*F*	*Significance F*			
12	Regression	1	545,878.49	545,878.49	12.71	0.02			
13	Residual	10	214,721.51	42,944.3					
14	Total	11	760,600						
15									
16		*Coefficients*	*Standard Error*	*t Stat*	*P-value*	*Lower 95%*	*Upper 95%*	*Lower 95.0%*	*Upper 95.0%*
17	Intercept	947.2	1,217.79	0.78	47.19	-2,183.23	4,077.64	-2,183.23	4,077.64
18	X Variable 1	0.27	0.08	3.57	0.02	0.02	0.08	0.02	0.08

a. Given this output, write the advertising agency's monthly cost equation.

b. Should management use this equation to predict monthly operating costs? Explain your answer.

S6-16 Prepare a contribution margin income statement (*Learning Objective 6*)

Patricia's Quilt Shoppe sells homemade Amish quilts. Patricia buys the quilts from local Amish artisans for $230 each, and her shop sells them for $380 each. Patricia also pays a sales commission of 10% of sales revenue to her sales staff. Patricia leases her country-style shop for $800 per month and pays $1,200 per month in payroll costs in addition to the sales commissions. Patricia sold 75 quilts in February. Prepare Patricia's traditional income statement and contribution margin income statement for the month.

S6-17 Prepare income statements using variable costing and absorption costing with no change in inventory levels (*Learning Objective 6*)

O'Malley's Products manufactures a single product. Cost, sales, and production information for the company and its single product is as follows:

- Selling price per unit is $60
- Variable manufacturing costs per unit manufactured (includes DM, DL & variable MOH) $32
- Variable operating expenses per unit sold $1
- Fixed manufacturing overhead (MOH) in total for the year $120,000
- Fixed operating expenses in total for the year $90,000
- Units manufactured and sold for the year 10,000 units

Requirements

1. Prepare an income statement for the upcoming year using variable costing.
2. Prepare an income statement for the upcoming year using absorption costing.

S6-18 Prepare income statements using variable costing and absorption costing when inventory units increase (*Learning Objective 6*)

Augustine Manufacturing manufactures a single product. Cost, sales, and production information for the company and its single product is as follows:

- Sales price per unit $40
- Variable manufacturing costs per unit manufactured (DM, DL & variable MOH) $23

- Variable operating expenses per unit sold $2
- Fixed manufacturing overhead (MOH) in total for the year $180,000
- Fixed operating expenses in total for the year $50,000
- Units manufactured during the year 20,000 units
- Units sold during the year 16,000 units

Requirements

1. Prepare an income statement for the upcoming year using variable costing.
2. Prepare an income statement for the upcoming year using absorption costing.
3. What causes the difference in income between the two methods?

EXERCISES Group A

E6-19A Graph specific costs *(Learning Objective 1)*

Graph these cost behavior patterns over a relevant range of 0–10,000 units:

a. Variable expenses of $10 per unit
b. Mixed expenses made up of fixed costs of $15,000 and variable costs of $3 per unit
c. Fixed expenses of $25,000

E6-20A Identify cost behavior graph *(Learning Objective 1)*

Following are a series of cost behavior graphs. The total cost is shown on the vertical (y) axis and the volume (activity) is shown on the horizontal (x) axis.

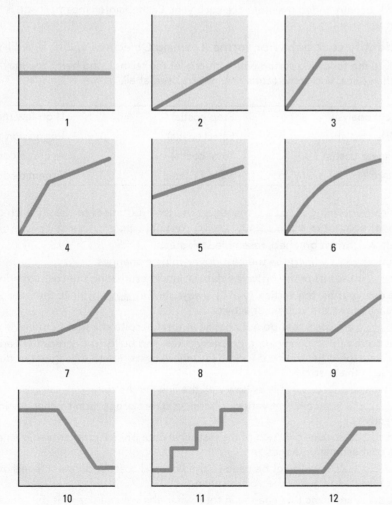

For each of the following situations, identify the graph that most closely represents the cost behavior pattern of the cost in that situation. Some graphs may be used more than once or not at all.

a. Customer service staff is paid $12.50 per hour

b. Depreciation on the company fleet of trucks (the units of production method is used with miles driven as the depreciation base)

c. Property taxes for a warehouse

d. Fuel costs for the delivery vehicles used by a local document delivery firm; assume the price per gallon is fixed at $3.10 per gallon

e. Utility costs for a production facility that is charged a fixed monthly charge of $250 by the local electrical co-op plus the following usage fees (implemented to encourage conservation):

Up to 10,000 kilowatts	$0.0020 per kilowatt
10,001–20,000 kilowatts	$0.0025 per kilowatt
More than 20,000 kilowatts	$0.0028 per kilowatt

f. Food costs for Meals on Wheels; the cost of direct materials (food) in each meal delivered is $3

g. Advertising costs for a grocery store; the store runs a four page color insert in the local newspaper once per week

h. Sales salary costs for a clothing store; each member of the sales staff is paid $400 per week plus 4% of net sales

i. Property insurance costs for an office building

j. Annual maintenance costs for the vans in a service fleet; each van is taken in for standard recommended maintenance each year. Each maintenance package is $200 per van per year.

E6-21A Identify cost behavior terms (*Learning Objectives 1, 2, 3, 4, & 5*)

Complete the following statements with one of the terms listed here. You may use a term more than once, and some terms may not be used at all.

Account analysis	Step cost(s)	High-low method
Variable cost(s)	Fixed cost(s)	Regression analysis
Curvilinear cost(s)	Total cost(s)	Average cost per unit
R-square	Mixed cost(s)	Committed fixed costs

a. When performing _____, managers use their judgment to classify each general ledger account as a _____, _____, or _____.

b. _____, when graphed, resemble stair steps.

c. Total _____ change as the cost driver volume changes.

d. _____ uses all of the historical data points in estimating the cost equation.

e. On cost graphs, the vertical (y-axis) always shows _____ while the horizontal axis (x-axis) shows the volume of activity.

f. _____ are costs that do not change in total despite changes in the level of activity.

g. The costs of occupancy (rent, property taxes, and building depreciation) are _____, because the organization is locked into these costs due to management decisions made in the past.

h. A statistic, _____, tells us how well the line fits the data.

i. A _____ is a cost that varies, in total, in direct proportion to changes in the level of activity.

j. The _____ uses only two of the historical data points in determining an estimate of the cost estimation equation.

k. The _____ should not be used to predict total costs at different levels of activity because it changes as the volume changes.

l. _____ are costs that change in total when the volume changes, but not in direct proportion to that change in volume.

m. _____ are not linear and, therefore, do not fit into a straight line.

E6-22A Forecast costs at different volumes *(Learning Objectives 1 & 2)*

Preston Drycleaners has capacity to clean up to 7,500 garments per month.

Requirements

1. Complete the following schedule for the three volumes shown.

	4,500 Garments	6,000 Garments	7,500 Garments
Total variable costs		$5,100	
Total fixed costs	___	___	___
Total operating costs	___	___	___
Variable cost per garment			
Fixed cost per garment	___	$2.40	___
Average cost per garment	___	___	___

2. Why does the average cost per garment change?
3. Suppose the owner, Dan Preston, erroneously uses the average cost per unit *at full capacity* to predict total costs at a volume of 4,500 garments. Would he overestimate or underestimate his total costs? By how much?

E6-23A Prepare income statement in two formats *(Learning Objective 6)*

Refer to the Preston Drycleaners in E6-22A. Assume that Preston charges customers $7 per garment for dry cleaning. Prepare Preston's *projected* income statement if 4,252 garments are cleaned in March. First, prepare the income statement using the traditional format; then prepare Preston's contribution margin income statement.

E6-24A Use the high-low method *(Learning Objective 4)*

Schaffer Company, which uses the high-low method to analyze cost behavior, has determined that machine hours best predict the company's total utilities cost. The company's cost and machine hour usage data for the first six months of the year follow:

Month	Total Cost	Machine Hours
January	$3,460	1,070
February	$3,760	1,170
March	$3,500	1,000
April	$3,780	1,200
May	$4,700	1,330
June	$4,200	1,400

Requirements

Using the high-low method, answer the following questions:

1. What is the variable utilities cost per machine hour?
2. What is the fixed cost of utilities each month?
3. If Schaffer Company uses 1,210 machine hours in a month, what will its total costs be?

E6-25A Use unit cost data to forecast total costs *(Learning Objective 2)*

Freedom Mailbox produces decorative mailboxes. The company's average cost per unit is $24.43 when it produces 1,300 mailboxes.

Requirements

1. What is the total cost of producing 1,300 mailboxes?
2. If $21,359 of the total costs is fixed, what is the variable cost of producing each mailbox?
3. Write Freedom Mailbox's cost equation.

4. If the plant manager uses the average cost per unit to predict total costs, what would the forecast be for 1,700 mailboxes?

5. If the plant manager uses the cost equation to predict total costs, what would the forecast be for 1,700 mailboxes?

6. What is the dollar difference between your answers to questions 4 and 5? Which approach to forecasting costs is appropriate? Why?

E6-26A Sustainability and cost estimation *(Learning Objective 4)*

Star Entertainment is a provider of cable, internet, and on-demand video services. Star currently sends monthly bills to its customers via the postal service. Because of a concern for the environment and recent increases in postal rates, Star management is considering offering an option to its customers for paperless billing. In addition to saving printing, paper, and postal costs, paperless billing will save energy and water (through reduced paper needs, reduced waste disposal, and reduced transportation needs.) While Star would like to switch to 100% paperless billing, many of its customers are not comfortable with paperless billing or may not have web access, so the paper billing option will remain regardless of whether Star adopts a paperless billing system or not.

The cost of the paperless billing system would be $140,000 per quarter with no variable costs since the costs of the system are the salaries of the clerks and the cost of leasing the computer system. The paperless billing system being proposed would be able to handle up to 900,000 bills per quarter (more than 900,000 bills per quarter would require a different computer system and is outside the scope of the current situation at Star.)

Star has gathered its cost data for the past year by quarter for paper, toner cartridges, printer maintenance costs, and postage costs for its billing department. The cost data is as follows:

	Quarter 1	Quarter 2	Quarter 3	Quarter 4
Total paper, toner, printer maintenance, and postage costs	$627,500	$635,000	$770,000	$650,000
Total number of bills mailed	575,000	605,000	725,000	625,000

Requirements

1. Calculate the variable cost per bill mailed under the current paper-based billing system.

2. Assume that the company projects that it will have a total of 700,000 bills to mail in the upcoming quarter. If enough customers choose the paperless billing option so that 25% of the mailings can be converted to paperless, how much would the company save from the paperless billing system (be sure to consider the cost of the paperless billing system)?

3. What if only 20% of the mailings are converted to the paperless option (assume a total of 700,000 bills)? Should the company still offer the paperless billing system? Explain your rationale.

E6-27A Create a scatter plot *(Learning Objective 3)*

Kelsey Gerbig, owner of Flowers 4 You, operates a local chain of floral shops. Each shop has its own delivery van. Instead of charging a flat delivery fee, Gerbig wants to set the delivery fee based on the distance driven to deliver the flowers. Gerbig wants to separate the fixed and variable portions of her van operating costs so that she has a better idea how delivery distance affects these costs. She has the following data from the past seven months:

Month	Miles Driven	Van Operating Costs
January	16,500	$5,260
February	18,500	$5,730
March	16,100	$4,960
April	17,100	$5,420
May	17,500	$5,790
June	15,800	$5,300
July	15,500	$5,040

Requirements

1. Prepare a scatter plot of Flowers 4 You's volume (miles driven) and van operating costs.
2. Does the data appear to contain any outliers? Explain.
3. How strong of a relationship is there between miles driven and van operating costs?

E6-28A High-low method *(Learning Objective 4)*

Refer to Flowers 4 You's data in E6-27A. Use the high-low method to determine Flowers 4 You's cost equation for van operating costs. Use your results to predict van operating costs at a volume of 16,000 miles.

E6-29A Continuation of E6-27A: Regression analysis *(Learning Objective 5)*

Refer to the Flowers 4 You data in E6-27A. Use Microsoft Excel to do the following:

Requirements

1. Run a regression analysis.
2. Determine the company's cost equation (use the output from the Excel regression).
3. Determine the R-square (use the output from the Excel regression). What does Flowers 4 You's R-square indicate?
4. Predict van operating costs at a volume of 16,900 miles.

E6-30A Regression analysis using Excel output *(Learning Objective 5)*

Assume that Flowers 4 You does a regression analysis on the next year's data using Excel. The output generated by Excel is as follows:

	A	B	C	D	E	F	G	H	I
1	SUMMARY OUTPUT								
2									
3		*Regression Statistics*							
4	Multiple R		0.81						
5	R Square		0.65						
6	Adjusted R Square		0.58						
7	Standard Error		202.91						
8	Observations		7						
9									
10	ANOVA								
11		*df*	*SS*	*MS*	*F*	*Significance F*			
12	Regression	1	379,674.00	379,674.00	9.22	0.0289			
13	Residual	5	205,868.85	41,173.77					
14	Total	6	585,542.85						
15									
16		*Coefficients*	*Standard Error*	*t Stat*	*P-value*	*Lower 95%*	*Upper 95%*	*Lower 95.0%*	*Upper 95.0%*
17	Intercept	478.30	1,538.00	0.31	0.77	-3,475.25	4,431.85	-3,475.25	4,431.85
18	X Variable 1	0.30	0.10	3.04	0.03	0.05	0.55	0.05	0.55

Requirements

1. Determine the firm's cost equation (use the output from the Excel regression).
2. Determine the R-square (use the output from the Excel regression). What does Flowers 4 You's R-square indicate?
3. Predict van operating costs at a volume of 16,000 miles.

E6-31A Create a scatter plot for a hospital laboratory *(Learning Objective 3)*

The manager of the main laboratory facility at MetroHealth Center is interested in being able to predict the overhead costs each month for the lab. The manager believes that total overhead varies with the number of lab tests performed but that some costs remain the same each month regardless of the number of lab tests performed.

The lab manager collected the following data for the first seven months of the year:

Month	Number of Lab Tests Performed	Total Laboratory Overhead Costs
January	2,500	$26,800
February	2,400	$25,700
March	3,200	$25,900
April	3,650	$28,900
May	3,800	$28,500
June	1,800	$20,900
July	1,900	$19,600

Requirements

1. Prepare a scatter plot of the lab's volume (number of lab tests performed) and total laboratory overhead costs.
2. Does the data appear to contain any outliers? Explain.
3. How strong of a relationship is there between the number of lab tests performed and laboratory overhead costs?

E6-32A Using the high-low method to predict overhead for a hospital laboratory *(Learning Objective 4)*

Refer to the laboratory overhead cost and activity data for MetroHealth Center in E6-31A. Use the high-low method to determine the laboratory's cost equation for total laboratory overhead. Use your results to predict total laboratory overhead if 2,900 lab tests are performed next month.

E6-33A Using regression analysis output to predict overhead for a hospital laboratory *(Learning Objective 5)*

Using the data provided in E6-31A, the laboratory manager performed a regression analysis to predict total laboratory overhead costs. The output generated by Excel is as follows:

	A	B	C	D	E	F	G	H	I
1	SUMMARY OUTPUT								
2									
3		*Regression Statistics*							
4	Multiple R		0.88053406						
5	R Square		0.77534024						
6	Adjusted R Square		0.73040829						
7	Standard Error		1868.82221						
8	Observations		7						
9									
10	ANOVA								
11		*df*	*SS*	*MS*	*F*	*Significance F*			
12	Regression	1	60266089.17	60266089.17	17.255877	0.008875395			
13	Residual	5	17462482.26	3492496.451					
14	Total	6	77728571.43						
15									
16		*Coefficients*	*Standard Error*	*t Stat*	*P-value*	*Lower 95%*	*Upper 95%*	*Lower 95.0%*	*Upper 95.0%*
17	Intercept	14409.92	2688.512	5.359	0.003	7498.875	21320.960	7498.875	21320.960
18	X Variable 1	3.92	0.943	4.154	0.008	1.493	6.343	1.493	6.343

Requirements

1. Determine the lab's cost equation (use the output from the Excel regression).
2. Determine the R-square (use the output from the Excel regression).
3. Predict the total laboratory overhead for the month if 2,900 tests are performed.

E6-34A Performing a regression analysis to predict overhead for a hospital laboratory *(Learning Objective 5)*

The manager of the main laboratory facility at MetroHealth Center (from E6-31A) collects seven additional months of data after obtaining the regression results in E6-33A. The number of tests performed and the total monthly overhead costs for the lab follow:

Month	Number of Lab Tests Performed	Total Laboratory Overhead
August	2,900	$26,700
September	3,100	$26,200
October	2,800	$25,800
November	2,500	$24,300
December	3,600	$27,650
January	2,600	$23,700
February	3,200	$25,900

Use the Excel to do the following:

Requirements

1. Run a regression analysis.
2. Determine the lab's cost equation (use the output from the regression analysis you performed using Excel).
3. Determine the R-square using the Excel output you obtain. What does the lab's R-square indicate?
4. Predict the lab's total overhead costs for the month if 2,500 tests are performed.

E6-35A Prepare and interpret a scatter plot *(Learning Objective 3)*

Rick's Golden Pancake Restaurant features sourdough pancakes made from a strain of sourdough dating back to the Alaskan Gold Rush. To plan for the future, Rick needs to figure out his cost behavior patterns. He has the following information about his operating costs and the number of pancakes served:

Month	Number of Pancakes	Total Operating Costs
July	3,900	$2,340
August	4,200	$2,530
September	3,600	$2,440
October	3,700	$2,290
November	4,000	$2,560
December	3,850	$2,510

Requirements

1. Prepare a scatter plot of Rick's pancake volume and operating costs. (*Hint*: If you use Excel, be sure to force the vertical axis to zero.)
2. Does the data appear sound, or do there appear to be any outliers? Explain.
3. Based on the scatter plot, do operating costs appear to be variable, fixed, or mixed costs?
4. How strong of a relationship is there between pancake volume and operating costs?

E6-36A High-low method *(Learning Objective 4)*

Refer to Rick's Golden Pancake Restaurant in E6-35A.

Requirements

1. Use the high-low method to determine Rick's operating cost equation.
2. Use your answer from Requirement 1 to predict total monthly operating costs if Rick serves 4,300 pancakes in one month.
3. Can you predict total monthly operating costs if Rick serves 14,000 pancakes a month? Explain.

E6-37A Regression analysis *(Learning Objective 5)*

Refer to Rick's Golden Pancake Restaurant in E6-35A.

Requirements

1. Use Microsoft Excel to perform regression analysis on Rick's monthly data. Based on the output, write Rick's monthly operating cost equation.
2. Based on the R-square shown on the regression output, how well does this cost equation fit the data?

E6-38A Regression analysis using Excel output *(Learning Objective 5)*

Assume that Rick's Golden Pancake Restaurant does a regression analysis on the next year's data using Excel. The output generated by Excel is as follows:

	A	B	C	D	E	F	G	H	I
1	**SUMMARY OUTPUT**								
2									
3	*Regression Statistics*								
4	Multiple R		0.88						
5	R Square		0.83						
6	Adjusted R Square		0.78						
7	Standard Error		107.42						
8	Observations		6						
9									
10	**ANOVA**								
11		*df*	*SS*	*MS*	*F*	*Significance F*			
12	Regression	1	13,643.22	13,643.22	4.01	0.02			
13	Residual	4	46,156.78	11,539.19					
14	Total	5	59,800.00						
15									
16		*Coefficients*	*Standard Error*	*t Stat*	*P-value*	*Lower 95%*	*Upper 95%*	*Lower 95.0%*	*Upper 95.0%*
17	Intercept	1,787.23	574.41	3.11	0.04	192.40	3,382.06	192.40	3,382.06
18	X Variable 1	0.17	0.16	1.09	0.34	-0.26	0.60	-0.26	0.60

Requirements

1. What is the fixed cost per month?
2. What is the variable cost per pancake?
3. If Rick's Golden Pancake Restaurant serves 3,800 pancakes in a month, what would the company's total operating costs be?

E6-39A Determine cost behavior and predict operating costs
(Learning Objective 4)

Seaside Apartments is a 600-unit apartment complex. When the apartments are 90% occupied, monthly operating costs total $204,240. When occupancy dips to 80%, monthly operating costs fall to $200,880. The owner of the apartment complex is worried because many of the apartment residents work at a nearby manufacturing plant that has just announced that it will close in three months. The apartment owner fears that occupancy of her apartments will drop to 55% if residents lose their jobs and move away. Assuming the same relevant range, what can the owner expect her operating costs to be if occupancy falls to 55%?

E6-40A Prepare a contribution margin income statement *(Learning Objective 6)*

Two Turtles is a specialty pet gift store selling exotic pet-related items through its website. Two Turtles has no physical store; all sales are through its website.
    Results for last year are shown next:

TWO TURTLES Income Statement Year Ended December 31		
Sales revenue		$1,011,000
Cost of goods sold		(673,000)
Gross profit		$ 338,000
Operating expenses:		
Selling and marketing expenses	$65,000	
Website maintenance expenses	60,000	
Other operating expenses	17,000	
Total operating expenses		(142,000)
Operating income		$ 196,000

For internal planning and decision-making purposes, the owner of Two Turtles would like to translate the company's income statement into the contribution margin format. Since Two Turtles is web-based, all of its cost of goods sold is variable. A large portion of the selling and marketing expenses consists of freight-out charges ($19,000), which were also variable. Only 20% of the remaining selling and marketing expenses and 25% of the website expenses were variable. Of the other operating expenses, 90% were fixed.
    Based on this information, prepare Two Turtles' contribution margin income statement for last year.

E6-41A Prepare a contribution margin income statement *(Learning Objective 6)*

Cranmore Carriage Company offers guided horse-drawn carriage rides through historic Charleston, South Carolina. The carriage business is highly regulated by the city. Cranmore Carriage Company has the following operating costs during April:

Monthly depreciation expense on carriages and stable	$2,200
Fee paid to the City of Charleston	15% of ticket revenue
Cost of souvenir set of postcards given to each passenger	$0.75/set of postcards
Brokerage fee paid to independent ticket brokers (60% of tickets are issued through these brokers; 40% are sold directly by the Cranmore Carriage Company)	$1.40/ticket sold by broker
Monthly cost of leasing and boarding the horses	$46,000
Carriage drivers (tour guides) are paid on a per passenger basis	$3.20 per passenger
Monthly payroll costs of non–tour guide employees	$7,550
Marketing, website, telephone, and other monthly fixed costs	$7,100

During April (a month during peak season), Cranmore Carriage Company had 13,030 passengers. Eighty-five percent of passengers were adults ($23 fare) while 15% were children ($15 fare).

Requirements

1. Prepare the company's contribution margin income statement for the month of April. Round all figures to the nearest dollar.

2. Assume that passenger volume increases by 12% in May. Which figures on the income statement would you expect to change, and by what percentage would they change? Which figures would remain the same as in April?

E6-42A Prepare income statements using variable costing and absorption costing with changing inventory levels *(Learning Objective 6)*

Henderson Manufacturing manufactures a single product that it will sell for $80 per unit. The company is looking to project its operating income for its first two years of operations. Cost information for the single unit of its product is as follows:

- Direct material per unit produced $35
- Direct labor cost per unit produced $12
- Variable manufacturing overhead (MOH) per unit produced $6
- Variable operating expenses per unit sold $3

Fixed manufacturing overhead (MOH) for each year is $200,000, while fixed operating expenses for each year will be $85,000.

During its first year of operations, the company plans to manufacture 20,000 units and anticipates selling 15,000 of those units. During the second year of its operations, the company plans to manufacture 20,000 units and anticipates selling 24,000 units (it has units in beginning inventory for the second year from its first year of operations).

Requirements

1. Prepare an absorption costing income statement for the following:

   a. Henderson's first year of operations

   b. Henderson's second year of operations

2. Before you prepare the variable costing income statements for Henderson, predict Henderson's operating income using variable costing for both its first year and its second year without preparing the variable costing income statements. *Hint:* Calculate the variable costing operating income for a given year by taking that year's absorption costing operating income and adding or subtracting the difference in operating income as calculated using the following formula:

   Difference in operating income = (Change in inventory level in units x Fixed MOH per unit)

3. Prepare a variable costing income statement for each of the following years:

   a. Henderson's first year of operations

   b. Henderson's second year of operations

E6-43A Prepare a variable costing income statement given an absorption costing income statement *(Learning Objective 6)*

Wronkovich Industries manufactures and sells a single product. The controller has prepared the following income statement for the most recent year:

Wronkovich Industries	
Income Statement (Absorption costing)	
For the year ending December 31	
Sales revenue	$420,000
Less: Cost of goods sold	343,000
Gross profit	$ 77,000
Less: Operating expenses	67,000
Operating income	$ 10,000

The company produced 10,000 units and sold 7,000 units during the year ending December 31. Fixed manufacturing overhead (MOH) for the year was $200,000, while fixed operating expenses were $60,000. The company had no beginning inventory.

Requirements

1. Will the company's operating income under variable costing be higher, lower, or the same as its operating income under absorption costing? Why?
2. Project the company's operating income under variable costing without preparing a variable costing income statement.
3. Prepare a variable costing income statement for the year.

E6-44A Absorption and variable costing income statements
(Learning Objective 6)

The annual data that follows pertain to See Underwater, a manufacturer of swimming goggles (the company had no beginning inventories):

Sales price	$ 44
Variable manufacturing expense per unit	$ 15
Sales commission expense per unit	$ 6
Fixed manufacturing overhead	$2,475,000
Fixed operating expenses	$ 250,000
Number of goggles produced	225,000
Number of goggles sold	205,000

Requirements

1. Prepare both conventional (absorption costing) and contribution margin (variable costing) income statements for See Underwater for the year.
2. Which statement shows the higher operating income? Why?
3. The company marketing vice president believes a new sales promotion that costs $145,000 would increase sales to 225,000 goggles. Should the company go ahead with the promotion? Give your reason.

EXERCISES Group B

E6-45B Graph specific costs *(Learning Objective 1)*

Graph these cost behavior patterns over a relevant range of 0–10,000 units:
a. Variable expenses of $9 per unit
b. Mixed expenses made up of fixed costs of $15,000 and variable costs of $6 per unit
c. Fixed expenses of $20,000

E6-46B Identify cost behavior graph *(Learning Objective 1)*

Following are a series of cost behavior graphs. The total cost is shown on the vertical (y) axis and the volume (activity) is shown on the horizontal (x) axis.

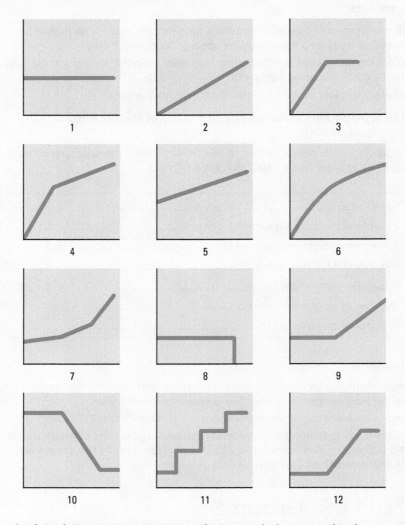

For each of the following situations, identify the graph that most closely represents the cost behavior pattern of the cost in that situation. Some graphs may be used more than once or not at all.

a. Monthly gas bill for the restaurant's delivery vehicles; cost of gas is constant at $3.10 per gallon

b. Monthly factory equipment depreciation, straight-line method is used

c. Monthly electric cost for a florist; $30 base monthly fee plus $.005 per kilowatt used

d. Total salary costs for an office; managers are paid a salary and the other workers are paid by the hour

e. Oil disposal fees for an automotive maintenance company. The oil disposal fee is based on two components: a $100 base fee plus a usage fee (to encourage reduction of waste):

Up to 10 barrels	$10 per barrel
11–25 barrels................	$12 per barrel
More than 26 barrels....	$16 per barrel

f. Monthly cell phone expense for a mobile grooming business; the cell phones are billed at a rate of $50 for unlimited voice and text for each cell phone

g. Monthly copier costs; the lease is $350 per month with a fee of $0.02 per copy for any copies over 100,000 copies in that month

h. Wood costs for a chair manufacturer; the cost of direct materials per chair is $8.40
i. Customer service representatives are paid $13.25 per hour
j. Monthly vehicle lease costs for a company that pays $280 month plus $.11 per mile for any miles driven over 1,500 per month

E6-47B Identify cost behavior terms *(Learning Objectives 1, 2, 3, 4, & 5)*

Complete the following statements with one of the terms listed here. You may use a term more than once, and some terms may not be used at all.

R-square	Committed fixed costs	Regression analysis
Average cost per unit	Curvilinear cost(s)	Fixed cost(s)
Variable cost(s)	Total cost(s)	Mixed cost(s)
Step cost(s)	Account analysis	High-low method

a. The total _____ line increases as the volume of activity increases, but the line does not begin at the origin.
b. The slope of the total _____ line is the variable cost per unit of activity.
c. The _____ uses two data points to arrive at a cost equation to describe a mixed cost.
d. _____ is a method for determining cost behavior that is based on a manager's judgment.
e. _____ are a type of cost behavior that is fixed over a small range of activity and then jumps to a different fixed level with moderate changes in volume.
f. The _____ per unit is inversely related to the volume of activity.
g. An s-shaped line would represent a _____.
h. The _____ value is referred to as the "goodness-of-fit" statistic.
i. As the activity level rises and falls, _____ remain constant in total.
j. _____ are fixed costs that management has little or no control over in the short run.
k. _____ is equal to the sum of _____ plus _____.
l. _____ is the cost to produce a single unit of production as calculated by dividing the total cost by the total number of units produced.
m. The cost equation resulting from using _____ is described as "this line of best fit."

E6-48B Forecast costs at different volumes *(Learning Objectives 1 & 2)*

Corbin Drycleaners has the capacity to clean up to 6,000 garments per month.

Requirements
1. Complete the following schedule for the three volumes shown.

	3,000 Garments	4,500 Garments	6,000 Garments
Total variable costs		$3,825	
Total fixed costs	___	___	___
Total operating costs	___	___	___
Variable cost per garment			
Fixed cost per garment	___	$2.00	___
Average cost per garment	___	___	___

2. Why does the average cost per garment change?
3. The owner, Yvonne Corbin, uses the average cost per unit *at full capacity* to predict total costs at a volume of 3,000 garments. Would she overestimate or underestimate total costs? By how much?

E6-49B Prepare income statement in two formats *(Learning Objective 6)*

Refer to the Corbin Drycleaners in E6-48B. Assume that Corbin charges customers $7 per garment for dry cleaning. Prepare Corbin's *projected* income statement if 4,220 garments are cleaned in March. First, prepare the income statement using the traditional format; then, prepare Corbin's contribution margin income statement.

E6-50B Use the high-low method *(Learning Objective 4)*

Chen Company, which uses the high-low method to analyze cost behavior, has determined that machine hours best predict the company's total utilities cost. The company's cost and machine hour usage data for the first six months of the year follow:

Month	Total Cost	Machine Hours
January	$3,400	1,090
February	$3,730	1,170
March	$3,385	1,070
April	$3,750	1,250
May	$4,700	1,380
June	$3,985	1,470

Requirements

Using the high-low method, answer the following questions:

1. What is the variable utilities cost per machine hour?
2. What is the fixed cost of utilities each month?
3. If Chen Company uses 1,260 machine hours in a month, what will its total costs be?

E6-51B Use unit cost data to forecast total costs *(Learning Objective 2)*

Rollins Mailboxes produces decorative mailboxes. The company's average cost per unit is $20.43 when it produces 1,600 mailboxes.

Requirements

1. What is the total cost of producing 1,600 mailboxes?
2. If $24,688 of the total costs are fixed, what is the variable cost of producing each mailbox?
3. Write Rollins Mailboxes' cost equation.
4. If the plant manager uses the average cost per unit to predict total costs, what would the forecast be for 1,900 mailboxes?
5. If the plant manager uses the cost equation to predict total costs, what would the forecast be for 1,900 mailboxes?
6. What is the dollar difference between your answers to Requirements 4 and 5? Which approach to forecasting costs is appropriate? Why?

 ### E6-52B Sustainability and cost estimation *(Learning Objective 4)*

Bright Entertainment is a provider of cable, internet, and on-demand video services. Bright currently sends monthly bills to its customers via the postal service. Because of a concern for the environment and recent increases in postal rates, Bright's management is considering offering an option to its customers for paperless billing. In addition to saving printing, paper, and postal costs, paperless billing will save energy and water (through reduced paper needs, reduced waste disposal, and reduced transportation needs.) While Bright would like to switch to 100% paperless billing, many of its customers are not comfortable with paperless billing or may not have web access, so the paper billing option will remain regardless of whether Bright adopts a paperless billing system or not.

The cost of the paperless billing system would be $125,000 per quarter with no variable costs since the costs of the system are the salaries of the clerks and the cost of leasing the computer system. The paperless billing system being proposed would be able to handle up to 900,000 bills per quarter (more than 900,000 bills per quarter would require a different computer system and is outside the scope of the current situation at Bright.)

Bright has gathered its cost data for the past year by quarter for paper, toner cartridges, printer maintenance costs, and postage costs for its billing department. The cost data is as follows:

	Quarter 1	Quarter 2	Quarter 3	Quarter 4
Total paper, toner, printer maintenance, and postage costs	$622,000	$770,000	$670,000	$642,500
Total number of bills mailed	614,000	725,000	625,000	575,000

Requirements

1. Calculate the variable cost per bill mailed under the current paper-based billing system.
2. Assume that the company projects that it will have a total of 700,000 bills to mail in the upcoming quarter. If enough customers choose the paperless billing option so that 25% of the mailing can be converted to paperless, how much would the company save from the paperless billing system (be sure to consider the cost of the paperless billing system)?
3. What if only 20% of the mailings are converted to the paperless option (assume a total of 700,000 bills)? Should the company still offer the paperless billing system? Explain your rationale.

E6-53B Create a scatter plot (Learning Objective 3)

Tony Long, owner of Flowers Direct, operates a local chain of floral shops. Each shop has its own delivery van. Instead of charging a flat delivery fee, Long wants to set the delivery fee based on the distance driven to deliver the flowers. Long wants to separate the fixed and variable portions of his van operating costs so that he has a better idea how delivery distance affects these costs. He has the following data from the past seven months:

Month	Miles Driven	Van Operating Costs
January................	15,900	$5,430
February.............	17,300	$5,740
March	14,600	$4,940
April....................	16,300	$5,270
May.....................	17,200	$5,820
June....................	15,200	$5,400
July	14,300	$4,990

Requirements

1. Prepare a scatter plot of Long's volume (miles driven) and van operating costs.
2. Do the data appear to contain any outliers? Explain.
3. How strong of a relationship is there between miles driven and van operating expenses?

E6-54B High-low method (Learning Objective 4)

Refer to Long's Flowers Direct data in E6-53B. Use the high-low method to determine Flowers Direct's cost equation for van operating costs. Use your results to predict van operating costs at a volume of 15,500 miles.

E6-55B Continuation of E6-53B: Regression analysis *(Learning Objective 5)*

Refer to the Flowers Direct data in E6-53B. Use Microsoft Excel to run a regression analysis, then do the following calculations:

Requirements

1. Determine the firm's cost equation (use the output from the Excel regression).
2. Determine the R-square (use the output from the Excel regression). What does Flowers Direct's R-square indicate?
3. Predict van operating costs at a volume of 15,500 miles.

E6-56B Regression analysis using Excel output *(Learning Objective 5)*

Assume that Flowers Direct does a regression analysis on the next year's data using Excel. The output generated by Excel is as follows:

	A	B	C	D	E	F	G	H	I
1									
2									
3		*Regression Statistics*							
4	Multiple R		0.96						
5	R Square		0.92						
6	Adjusted R Square		0.90						
7	Standard Error		112.91						
8	Observations		7						
9									
10	**ANOVA**								
11		*df*	*SS*	*MS*	*F*	*Significance F*			
12	Regression	1	689,408.19	689,408.19	54.08	0.0007			
13	Residual	5	63,745.52	12,749.10					
14	Total	6	753,153.71						
15									
16		*Coefficients*	*Standard Error*	*t Stat*	*P-value*	*Lower 95%*	*Upper 95%*	*Lower 95.0%*	*Upper 95.0%*
17	Intercept	826.04	629.77	1.31	0.25	-792.83	2,444.91	-792.83	2,444.91
18	X Variable 1	0.28	0.04	7.35	0.00	0.18	0.37	0.18	0.37

Requirements

1. Determine the firm's cost equation (use the output from the Excel regression).
2. Determine the R-square (use the output from the Excel regression). What does Flowers Direct's R-square indicate?
3. Predict van operating costs at a volume of 15,000 miles.

E6-57B Create a scatter plot for a hospital laboratory *(Learning Objective 3)*

The manager of the main laboratory facility at CitiHealth Center is interested in being able to predict the overhead costs each month for the lab. The manager believes that total overhead varies with the number of lab tests performed but that some costs remain the same each month regardless of the number of lab tests performed.

The lab manager collected the following data for the first seven months of the year.

Month	Number of Lab Tests Performed	Total Laboratory Overhead Costs
January	3,100	$22,800
February	2,750	$21,700
March	3,350	$23,900
April	3,750	$28,100
May	4,000	$27,500
June	2,000	$19,500
July	3,900	$27,100

Requirements

1. Prepare a scatter plot of the lab's volume (number of lab tests performed) and total laboratory overhead costs.
2. Does the data appear to contain any outliers? Explain.
3. How strong of a relationship is there between the number of lab tests performed and laboratory overhead costs?

E6-58B Using the high-low method to predict overhead for a hospital laboratory *(Learning Objective 4)*

Refer to the laboratory overhead cost and activity data for CitiHealth Center in E6-57B. Use the high-low method to determine the laboratory's cost equation for total laboratory overhead. Use your results to predict total laboratory overhead if 3,200 lab tests are performed next month.

E6-59B Using regression analysis output to predict overhead for a hospital laboratory *(Learning Objective 5)*

Using the data provided in E6-57B, the laboratory manager performed a regression analysis to predict total laboratory overhead costs. The output generated by Excel is as follows:

	A	B	C	D	E	F	G	H	I
1	SUMMARY OUTPUT								
2									
3	*Regression Statistics*								
4	Multiple R		0.963524797						
5	R Square		0.928380034						
6	Adjusted R Square		0.914056041						
7	Standard Error		962.6424624						
8	Observations		7						
9									
10	ANOVA								
11		*df*	*SS*	*MS*	*F*	*Significance F*			
12	Regression	1	60060883.16	60060883.16	64.81293443	0.000478529			
13	Residual	5	4633402.552	926680.5104					
14	Total	6	64694285.71						
15									
16		*Coefficients*	*Standard Error*	*t Stat*	*P-value*	*Lower 95%*	*Upper 95%*	*Lower 95.0%*	*Upper 95.0%*
17	Intercept	9953.28	1827.515	5.446	0.002	5255.505	14651.060	5255.505	14651.060
18	X Variable 1	4.42	0.548	8.050	0.000	3.006	5.827	3.006	5.827

Requirements

1. Determine the lab's cost equation (use the output from the Excel regression).
2. Determine the R-square (use the output from the Excel regression).
3. Predict the total laboratory overhead for the month if 2,900 tests are performed.

E6-60B Performing a regression analysis to predict overhead for a hospital laboratory *(Learning Objective 5)*

The manager of the main laboratory facility at CitiHealth Center (from E6-57B) collects seven additional months of data after obtaining the regression results in the prior period. The number of tests performed and the total monthly overhead costs for the lab follows:

Month	Number of Lab Tests Performed	Total Laboratory Overhead Costs
August	3,050	$22,300
September	2,800	$22,100
October	3,600	$25,100
November	3,800	$26,700
December	4,200	$27,300
January	2,200	$20,300
February	3,950	$28,500

Use Excel to perform the requirements.

Requirements

1. Run a regression analysis.
2. Determine the lab's cost equation (use the output from the regression analysis you perform using Excel).
3. Determine the R-square using the Excel output you obtain. What does the lab's R-square indicate?
4. Predict the lab's total overhead costs for the month if 3,000 tests are performed.

E6-61B Prepare and interpret a scatter plot *(Learning Objective 3)*

Devon's Yukon Pancake Restaurant features sourdough pancakes made from a strain of sourdough dating back to the Alaskan Gold Rush. To plan for the future, Devon needs to figure out his cost behavior patterns. He has the following information about his operating costs and the number of pancakes served:

Month	Number of Pancakes	Total Operating Costs
July	3,700	$2,330
August	4,100	$2,410
September	3,200	$2,320
October	3,400	$2,260
November	3,800	$2,520
December	3,500	$2,500

Requirements

1. Prepare a scatter plot of Devon's pancake volume and operating costs.
2. Do the data appear sound, or do there appear to be any outliers? Explain.
3. Based on the scatter plot, do operating costs appear to be variable, fixed, or mixed costs?
4. How strong of a relationship is there between pancake volume and operating costs?

E6-62B High-low method *(Learning Objective 4)*

Refer to Devon's Yukon Pancake Restaurant in E6-61B.

Requirements

1. Use the high-low method to determine Devon's operating cost equation.
2. Use your answer from Requirement 1 to predict total monthly operating costs if Devon serves 4,200 pancakes a month.
3. Can you predict total monthly operating costs if Devon serves 15,000 pancakes a month? Explain.

E6-63B Regression analysis *(Learning Objective 5)*

Refer to Devon's Yukon Pancake Restaurant in E6-61B.

Use Microsoft Excel to run a regression analysis, then perform the following calculations:

Requirements

1. Determine Devon's monthly operating cost equation (use the output from the Excel regression).
2. Based on the R-square shown on the regression output, how well does this cost equation fit the data?

E6-64B Regression analysis using Excel output *(Learning Objective 5)*

Assume that Devon's Yukon Pancake Restaurant does a regression analysis on the next year's data using Excel. The output generated by Excel is as follows:

	A	B	C	D	E	F	G	H	I
1									
2									
3		*Regression Statistics*							
4	Multiple R		0.38						
5	R Square		0.14						
6	Adjusted R Square		-0.07						
7	Standard Error		76.49						
8	Observations		6						
9									
10	**ANOVA**								
11		*df*	*SS*	*MS*	*F*	*Significance F*			
12	Regression	1	3,945.34	3,945.34	0.67	0.46			
13	Residual	4	23,404.66	5,851.16					
14	Total	5	27,350.00						
15									
16		*Coefficients*	*Standard Error*	*t Stat*	*P-value*	*Lower 95%*	*Upper 95%*	*Lower 95.0%*	*Upper 95.0%*
17	Intercept	2,116.41	316.45	6.69	0.00	1,237.80	2,995.03	1,237.80	2,995.03
18	X Variable 1	0.07	0.09	0.82	0.46	-0.17	0.32	-0.17	0.32

Requirements

1. What is the fixed cost per month?

2. What is the variable cost per pancake?

3. If Devon's Yukon Pancake Restaurant serves 3,500 pancakes in a month, what would its total operating costs be?

E6-65B Determine cost behavior and predict operating costs

(Learning Objective 4)

SeaView Apartments is a 1000-unit apartment complex. When the apartments are 90% occupied, monthly operating costs total $228,400. When occupancy dips to 80%, monthly operating costs fall to $222,800. The owner of the apartment complex is worried because many of the apartment residents work at a nearby manufacturing plant that has just announced it will close in three months. The apartment owner fears that occupancy of her apartments will drop to 65% if residents lose their jobs and move away. Assuming the same relevant range, what should the owner expect operating costs to be if occupancy falls to 65%?

E6-66B Prepare a contribution margin income statement *(Learning Objective 6)*

Hoffwood Gifts is a specialty pet gift shop selling exotic pet-related items over the internet. Results for last year are shown next:

HOFFWOOD GIFTS
Income Statement
Year Ended December 31

Sales revenue		$ 999,000
Cost of goods sold		(670,000)
Gross profit		$ 329,000
Operating expenses:		
Selling and marketing expenses	$65,500	
Website maintenance expenses	57,500	
Other operating expenses	18,600	
Total operating expenses		(141,600)
Operating income		$ 187,400

For internal planning and decision-making purposes, the owner of Hoffwood Gifts would like to translate the company's income statement into the contribution margin format. Since Hoffwood Gifts is a web retailer and has no physical presence, all of its cost of goods sold is variable. A large portion of the selling and marketing expenses consists of freight-out charges $19,600, which were also variable. Only 20% of the remaining selling and marketing expenses and 25% of the website expenses were variable. Of the other operating expenses, 90% were fixed. Based on this information, prepare Hoffwood Gifts' contribution margin income statement for last year.

E6-67B Prepare a contribution margin income statement *(Learning Objective 6)*

Curt Carriage Company offers guided horse-drawn carriage rides through historic Charleston, South Carolina. The carriage business is highly regulated by the city. Curt Carriage Company has the following operating costs during April:

Monthly depreciation expense on carriages and stable........................	$2,000
Fee paid to the City of Charleston...	15% of ticket revenue
Cost of souvenir set of postcards given to each passenger	$0.95/set of postcards
Brokerage fee paid to independent ticket brokers (60% of tickets are issued through these brokers; 40% are sold directly by the Curt Carriage Company)	$1.80/ticket sold by broker
Monthly cost of leasing and boarding the horses...................................	$51,000
Carriage drivers (tour guides) are paid on a per passenger basis	$3.40 per passenger
Monthly payroll costs of non–tour guide employees.............................	$7,600
Marketing, website, telephone, and other monthly fixed costs	$7,100

During April (a month during peak season), Curt Carriage Company had 12,960 passengers. Eighty-five percent of passengers were adults ($20 fare) while 15% were children ($12 fare).

Requirements

1. Prepare the company's contribution margin income statement for the month of April. Round all figures to the nearest dollar.

2. Assume that passenger volume increases by 17% in May. Which figures on the income statement would you expect to change and by what percentage would they change? Which figures would remain the same as in April?

E6-68B Prepare income statements using variable costing and absorption costing with changing inventory levels *(Learning Objective 6)*

Fagan Manufacturing manufactures a single product that it will sell for $120 per unit. The company is looking to project its operating income for its first two years of operations. Cost information for the single unit of its product is as follows:

- Direct material per unit produced $50
- Direct labor cost per unit produced $12
- Variable manufacturing overhead (MOH) per unit produced $10
- Variable operating expenses per unit sold $4

Fixed manufacturing overhead (MOH) for each year is $1,200,000, while fixed operating expenses for each year will be $250,000.

During its first year of operations, the company plans to manufacture 50,000 units and anticipates selling 40,000 of those units. During the second year of its operations, the company plans to manufacture 50,000 units and anticipates selling 55,000 units (it has units in beginning inventory for the second year from its first year of operations.)

Requirements

1. Prepare an absorption costing income statement for:
   a. The first year of operations
   b. The second year of operations

2. Before you prepare the variable costing income statements for Fagan, predict Fagan's operating income using variable costing for both its first year and its second year without preparing the variable costing income statements. *Hint*: Calculate the variable costing operating income for a given year by taking that year's absorption costing operating income and adding or subtracting the difference in operating income as calculated using the following formula:

   Difference in operating income = (Change in inventory level in units × Fixed MOH per unit)

3. Prepare a variable costing income statement for:

a. The first year of operations

b. The second year of operations

E6-69B Prepare a variable costing income statement given an absorption costing income statement *(Learning Objective 6)*

McFall Industries manufactures and sells a single product. The controller has prepared the following income statement for the most recent year:

McFall Industries Income Statement (Absorption costing) For the year ending December 31	
Sales revenue	$1,050,000
Less: Cost of goods sold	675,000
Gross profit	$ 375,000
Less: Operating expenses	260,000
Operating income	$ 115,000

The company produced 20,000 units and sold 15,000 units during the year ending December 31. Fixed manufacturing overhead (MOH) for the year was $240,000, while fixed operating expenses were $200,000. The company had no beginning inventory.

Requirements

1. Will the company's operating income under variable costing be higher, lower, or the same as its operating income under absorption costing? Why?
2. Project the company's operating income under variable costing without preparing a variable costing income statement.
3. Prepare a variable costing income statement for the year.

E6-70B Absorption and variable costing income statements *(Learning Objective 6)*

The annual data that follow pertain to Swimmerz, a manufacturer of swimming goggles (Swimmerz has no beginning inventories):

Sale price..	$	39
Variable manufacturing expense per unit	$	16
Sales commission expense per unit	$	7
Fixed manufacturing overhead	$2,820,000	
Fixed operating expense	$ 240,000	
Number of goggles produced	235,000	
Number of goggles sold	225,000	

Requirements

1. Prepare both conventional (absorption costing) and contribution margin (variable costing) income statements for Swimmerz for the year.
2. Which statement shows the higher operating income? Why?
3. Swimmerz's marketing vice president believes a new sales promotion that costs $150,000 would increase sales to 235,000 goggles. Should the company go ahead with the promotion? Give your reason.

PROBLEMS Group A

P6-71A Analyze cost behavior at a hospital using various cost estimation methods (*Learning Objectives 1, 2, 3, 4, & 5*)

Suzanne Spahr is the Chief Operating Officer at Union Hospital in Forest Lake, Minnesota. She is analyzing the hospital's overhead costs but is not sure whether nursing hours or the number of patient days would be the best cost driver to use for predicting the hospital's overhead. She has gathered the following information for the last six months of the most recent year:

Month	Hospital Overhead Costs	Nursing Hours	Number of Patient Days	Overhead Cost per Nursing Hour	Overhead Cost per Patient Day
July....................	$485,000	25,000	3,800	$19.40	$127.63
August...............	$540,000	26,700	4,360	$20.22	$123.85
September.........	$420,000	20,000	4,210	$21.00	$ 99.76
October.............	$462,000	21,900	3,450	$21.10	$133.91
November	$579,000	32,000	5,600	$18.09	$103.39
December..........	$455,000	20,400	3,270	$22.30	$139.14

Requirements

1. Are the hospital's overhead costs fixed, variable, or mixed? Explain.
2. Graph the hospital's overhead costs against nursing hours. Use Excel or graph by hand.
3. Graph the hospital's overhead costs against the number of patient days. Use Excel or graph by hand.
4. Do the data appear to be sound or do you see any potential data problems? Explain.
5. Use the high-low method to determine the hospital's cost equation using nursing hours as the cost driver. Predict total overhead costs if 26,000 nursing hours are predicted for the month.
6. Ms. Spahr runs a regression analysis using nursing hours as the cost driver to predict total hospital overhead costs. The Excel output from the regression analysis is shown next.

	A	B	C	D	E	F	G	H	I
1	SUMMARY OUTPUT – Nursing hours as cost driver								
2									
3		*Regression Statistics*							
4	Multiple R		0.967848203						
5	R Square		0.936730144						
6	Adjusted R Square		0.92091268						
7	Standard Error		16568.3268						
8	Observations		6						
9									
10	ANOVA								
11		*df*	*SS*	*MS*	*F*	*Significance F*			
12	Regression	1	16256795521	16256795521	59.2212594	0.001533989			
13	Residual	4	1098037812	274509453					
14	Total	5	17354833333						
15									
16		*Coefficients*	*Standard Error*	*t Stat*	*P-value*	*Lower 95%*	*Upper 95%*	*Lower 95.0%*	*Upper 95.0%*
17	Intercept	187378.980	39923.061	4.694	0.009	76534.789	298223.164	76534.789	298223.164
18	X Variable 1	12.440	1.617	7.696	0.002	7.954	16.933	7.954	16.993

If 26,000 nursing hours are predicted for the month, what is the total predicted hospital overhead?

7. Ms. Spahr then ran the regression analysis using number of patient days as the cost driver. The Excel output from the regression is shown here:

	A	B	C	D	E	F	G	H	I
1	**SUMMARY OUTPUT – Using number of patient days as cost driver**								
2									
3		*Regression Statistics*							
4	Multiple R		0.75770497						
5	R Square		0.574116821						
6	Adjusted R Square		0.467646026						
7	Standard Error		42985.84532						
8	Observations		6						
9									
10	**ANOVA**								
11		*df*	*SS*	*MS*	*F*	*Significance F*			
12	Regression	1	9963701742	9963701742	5.392246976	0.08094813			
13	Residual	4	7391131591	1847782898					
14	Total	5	17354833333						
15									
16		*Coefficients*	*Standard Error*	*t Stat*	*P-value*	*Lower 95%*	*Upper 95%*	*Lower 95.0%*	*Upper 95.0%*
17	Intercept	271537.440	95772.174	2.835	0.047	5631.253	537443.620	5631.253	537443.620
18	X Variable 1	53.130	22.880	2.322	0.081	-10.395	116.655	-10.395	116.655

If 3,700 patient days are predicted for the month, what is the total predicted hospital overhead?

8. Which regression analysis (using nursing hours or using number of patient days as the cost driver) produces the best cost equation? Explain your answer.

P6-72A Analyze cost behavior (*Learning Objectives 1, 2, 3, & 4*)

Renkas Industries is in the process of analyzing its manufacturing overhead costs. Renkas Industries is not sure if the number of units produced or number of direct labor (DL) hours is the best cost driver to use for predicting manufacturing overhead (MOH) costs. The following information is available:

Month	Manufacturing Overhead Costs	Direct Labor Hours	Units Produced	MOH Cost per DL Hour	MOH Cost per Unit Produced
July	$457,000	23,200	3,580	$19.70	$127.65
August	$512,000	26,600	4,290	$19.25	$119.35
September	$421,000	19,000	4,240	$22.16	$ 99.29
October	$449,000	21,500	3,430	$20.88	$130.90
November	$571,000	31,000	5,730	$18.42	$ 99.65
December	$434,000	19,700	3,220	$22.03	$134.78

Requirements

1. Are manufacturing overhead costs fixed, variable, or mixed? Explain.
2. Graph Renkas Industries' manufacturing overhead costs against DL hours. Use Excel or graph by hand.
3. Graph Renkas Industries' manufacturing overhead costs against units produced. Use Excel or graph by hand.

4. Do the data appear to be sound, or do you see any potential data problems? Explain.
5. Use the high-low method to determine Renkas Industries' manufacturing overhead cost equation using DL hours as the cost driver. Assume that management believes all data to be accurate and wants to include all of it in the analysis.
6. Estimate manufacturing overhead costs if Renkas Industries incurs 25,000 DL hours in January.

P6-73A Continuation of P6-72A: Regression analysis *(Learning Objective 5)*

Refer to Renkas Industries in P6-72A.

Requirements

1. Use Excel regression analysis to determine Renkas Industries' manufacturing overhead cost equation using DL hours as the cost driver. Comment on the R-square. Estimate manufacturing overhead costs if Renkas Industries incurs 25,500 DL hours in January.
2. Use Excel regression analysis to determine Renkas manufacturing overhead cost equation using number of units produced as the cost driver. Use all of the data provided. Project total manufacturing overhead costs if Renkas Industries produces 4,900 units. Which cost equation is better—this one or the one from Requirement 1? Why?
3. Use Excel regression analysis to determine Renkas Industries' manufacturing overhead cost equation using number of units produced as the cost driver. This time, remove any potential outliers before performing the regression. How does this affect the R-square? Project total manufacturing overhead costs if 4,900 units are produced.
4. In which cost equation do you have the most confidence? Why?

P6-74A Prepare traditional and contribution margin income statements
(Learning Objective 6)

The Old Tyme Ice Cream Shoppe sold 9,400 servings of ice cream during June for $4 per serving. Old Tyme purchases the ice cream in large tubs from the Golden Ice Cream Company. Each tub costs Old Tyme $11 and has enough ice cream to fill 20 ice cream cones. Old Tyme purchases the ice cream cones for $0.10 each from a local warehouse club. Old Tyme Ice Cream Shoppe is located in a local strip mall, and rent for the space is $1,900 per month. Old Tyme expenses $230 a month for the depreciation of the Shoppe's furniture and equipment. During June, Old Tyme incurred an additional $2,100 of other operating expenses (75% of these were fixed costs).

Requirements

1. Prepare Old Tyme's June income statement using a traditional format.
2. Prepare Old Tyme's June income statement using a contribution margin format.

P6-75A Determine financial statement components *(Learning Objective 6)*

Violins and More produces student-grade violins for beginning violin students. The company produced 2,300 violins in its first month of operations. At month-end, 600 finished violins remained unsold. There was no inventory in work in process. Violins were sold for $125.00 each. Total costs from the month are as follows:

Direct materials used	$99,500
Direct labor	$65,000
Variable manufacturing overhead	$31,000
Fixed manufacturing overhead	$41,400
Variable selling and administrative expenses	$10,000
Fixed selling and administrative expenses	$12,500

The company prepares traditional (absorption costing) income statements for its bankers. Violins and More would also like to prepare contribution margin income statements for management use. Compute the following amounts that would be shown on these income statements:

1. Gross profit
2. Contribution margin
3. Total expenses shown **below** the **gross profit** line
4. Total expenses shown **below** the **contribution margin** line
5. Dollar value of ending inventory under absorption costing
6. Dollar value of ending inventory under variable costing

Which income statement will have a higher operating income? By how much? Explain.

P6-76A Absorption and variable costing income statements *(Learning Objective 6)*

Owen's Foods produces frozen meals, which it sells for $9 each. The company uses the FIFO inventory costing method, and it computes a new monthly fixed manufacturing overhead rate based on the actual number of meals produced that month. All costs and production levels are exactly as planned. The following data are from the company's first two months in business:

	January	February
Sales	1,400 meals	1,600 meals
Production..	2,000 meals	1,400 meals
Variable manufacturing expense per meal.........................	$ 4	$ 4
Sales commission expense per meal.................................	$ 1	$ 1
Total fixed manufacturing overhead	$ 700	$ 700
Total fixed marketing and administrative expenses...........	$ 400	$ 400

Requirements

1. Compute the product cost per meal produced under absorption costing and under variable costing. Do this first for January and then for February.
2. Prepare separate monthly income statements for January and for February, using the following:
   a. Absorption costing
   b. Variable costing
3. Is operating income higher under absorption costing or variable costing in January? In February? Explain the pattern of differences in operating income based on absorption costing versus variable costing.

PROBLEMS Group B

P6-77B Analyze cost behavior at a hospital using various cost estimation methods *(Learning Objectives 1, 2, 3, 4 & 5)*

Freida Dudley is the Chief Operating Officer at Memorial Hospital in Scandia, Minnesota. She is analyzing the hospital's overhead costs but is not sure whether nursing hours or the number of patient days would be the best cost driver to use for predicting the hospital's overhead. She has gathered the following information for the last six months of the most recent year:

Month	Hospital Overhead Costs	Nursing Hours	Number of Patient Days	Overhead Cost per Nursing Hour	Overhead Cost per Patient Day
July	$462,000	22,900	3,610	$20.17	$127.98
August	$510,000	26,300	4,330	$19.39	$117.78
September	$401,000	17,500	4,250	$22.91	$ 94.35
October	$445,000	21,700	3,460	$20.51	$128.61
November	$556,000	30,000	5,740	$18.53	$ 96.86
December	$430,000	19,000	3,230	$22.63	$133.13

Requirements

1. Are the hospital's overhead costs fixed, variable, or mixed? Explain.
2. Graph the hospital's overhead costs against nursing hours. Use Excel or graph by hand.
3. Graph the hospital's overhead costs against the number of patient days. Use Excel or graph by hand.
4. Do the data appear to be sound or do you see any potential data problems? Explain
5. Use the high-low method to determine the hospital's cost equation using nursing hours as the cost driver. Predict total overhead costs if 23,500 nursing hours are predicted for the month.
6. Ms. Dudley runs a regression analysis using nursing hours as the cost driver to predict total hospital overhead costs. The Excel output from the regression analysis is shown next:

	A	B	C	D	E	F	G	H	I
1	**SUMMARY OUTPUT**								
2									
3		*Regression Statistics*							
4	Multiple R		0.9938						
5	R Square		0.9876						
6	Adjusted R Square		0.9845						
7	Standard Error		7027.6715						
8	Observations		6						
9									
10	**ANOVA**								
11		*df*	*SS*	*MS*	*F*	*Significance F*			
12	Regression	1	1580578	1580578	320.031	3.0254			
13	Residual	4	19755	49388167.25					
14	Total	5	1600333						
15									
16		*Coefficients*	*Standard Error*	*t Stat*	*P-value*	*Lower 95%*	*Upper 95%*	*Lower 95.0%*	*Upper 95.0%*
17	Intercept	190017.690	15764.911	12.053	0.000	146247.280	233788.101	146247.280	233788.101
18	X Variable 1	12.110	0.677	17.889	0.000	10.230	13.989	10.230	13.989

If 23,500 nursing hours are predicted for the month, what is the total predicted hospital overhead?

7. Ms. Dudley then ran the regression analysis using number of patient days as the cost driver. The Excel output from the regression is shown here:

	A	B	C	D	E	F	G	H	I
1	SUMMARY OUTPUT								
2									
3		Regression Statistics							
4	Multiple R		0.75340						
5	R Square		0.5676						
6	Adjusted R Square		0.45953						
7	Standard Error		41591.550						
8	Observations		6						
9									
10	ANOVA								
11		df	SS	MS	F	Significance F			
12	Regression	1	908390	908390	5.25124	0.08371			
13	Residual	4	691942	172985					
14	Total	5	1600333						
15									
16		Coefficients	Standard Error	t Stat	P-value	Lower 95%	Upper 95%	Lower 95.0%	Upper 95.0%
17	Intercept	275852.530	85266.887	3.235	0.032	39113.700	512591.364	39113.700	512591.364
18	X Variable 1	46.660	20.364	2.292	0.084	-9.874	103.203	-9.874	103.203

If 3,300 patient days are predicted for the month, what is the total predicted hospital overhead?

8. Which regression analysis (using nursing hours or using number of patient days as the cost driver) produces the best cost equation? Explain your answer.

P6-78B Analyze cost behavior *(Learning Objectives 1, 2, 3, & 4)*

Wythe Industries is in the process of analyzing its manufacturing overhead costs. Wythe Industries is not sure if the number of units produced or the number of direct labor (DL) hours is the best cost driver to use for predicting manufacturing overhead (MOH) costs. The following information is available:

Month	Manufacturing Overhead Costs	Direct Labor Hours	Units Produced	MOH Cost per DL Hour	MOH Cost per Unit Produced
July	$470,000	22,800	3,630	$20.61	$129.48
August	$517,000	26,200	4,340	$19.73	$119.12
September	$428,000	19,000	4,190	$22.53	$102.15
October	$453,000	21,800	3,420	$20.78	$132.46
November	$557,000	29,000	5,770	$19.21	$ 96.53
December	$439,000	19,500	3,260	$22.51	$134.66

Requirements

1. Are manufacturing overhead costs fixed, variable, or mixed? Explain.
2. Graph Wythe Industries' manufacturing overhead costs against DL hours.
3. Graph Wythe Industries' manufacturing overhead costs against units produced.
4. Do the data appear to be sound or do you see any potential data problems? Explain.

5. Use the high-low method to determine Wythe Industries' manufacturing overhead cost equation using DL hours as the cost driver. Assume that management believes all the data to be accurate and wants to include all of it in the analysis.

6. Estimate manufacturing overhead costs if Wythe Industries incurs 23,000 DL hours in January.

P6-79B Continuation of P6-78B: Regression analysis (Learning Objective 5)

Refer to Wythe Industries in P6-78B.

Requirements

1. Use Excel regression analysis to determine Wythe Industries' manufacturing overhead cost equation using DL hours as the cost driver. Comment on the R-square. Estimate manufacturing overhead costs if Wythe Industries incurs 24,000 DL hours in January.

2. Use Excel regression analysis to determine Wythe's manufacturing overhead cost equation using number of units produced as the cost driver. Use all of the data provided. Project total manufacturing overhead costs if Wythe Industries produces 5,100 units. Which cost equation is better—this one or the one from Requirement 1? Why?

3. Use Excel regression analysis to determine Wythe Industries' manufacturing overhead cost equation using number of units produced as the cost driver. This time, remove any potential outliers before performing the regression. How does this affect the R-square? Project total manufacturing overhead costs if 5,100 units are produced.

4. In which cost equation do you have the most confidence? Why?

P6-80B Prepare traditional and contribution margin income statements
(Learning Objective 6)

Marlo's Ice Cream Shoppe sold 9,500 servings of ice cream during June for $2 per serving. Marlo purchases the ice cream in large tubs from the Georgia Ice Cream Company. Each tub costs Marlo $11 and has enough ice cream to fill 20 ice cream cones. Marlo purchases the ice cream cones for $0.10 each from a local warehouse club. The shop is located in a local strip mall, and she pays $1,750 a month to lease the space. Marlo expenses $230 a month for the depreciation of the shop's furniture and equipment. During June, Marlo incurred an additional $2,900 of other operating expenses (75% of these were fixed costs).

Requirements

1. Prepare Marlo's June income statement using a traditional format.
2. Prepare Marlo's June income statement using a contribution margin format.

P6-81B Determine financial statement components (Learning Objective 6)

Violins-by-Lucy produces student-grade violins for beginning violin students. The company produced 2,400 violins in its first month of operations. At month-end, 550 finished violins remained unsold. There was no inventory in work in process. Violins were sold for $115.00 each. Total costs from the month are as follows:

Direct materials used	$139,400
Direct labor	$ 35,000
Variable manufacturing overhead	$ 32,000
Fixed manufacturing overhead	$ 52,800
Variable selling and administrative expenses	$ 9,000
Fixed selling and administrative expenses	$ 13,000

The company prepares traditional (absorption costing) income statements for its bankers.

Lucy would also like to prepare contribution margin income statements for her own management use. Compute the following amounts that would be shown on these income statements:

1. Gross profit
2. Contribution margin
3. Total expenses shown **below** the **gross profit** line
4. Total expenses shown **below** the **contribution margin** line
5. Dollar value of ending inventory under absorption costing
6. Dollar value of ending inventory under variable costing

Which income statement will have a higher operating income? By how much? Explain.

P6-82B Absorption and variable costing income statements *(Learning Objective 6)*

Jason's Meals produces frozen meals, which it sells for $10 each. The company uses the FIFO inventory costing method, and it computes a new monthly fixed manufacturing overhead rate based on the actual number of meals produced that month. All costs and production levels are exactly as planned. The following data are from the company's first two months in business:

	January	February
Sales	1,500 meals	1,900 meals
Production	2,000 meals	1,600 meals
Variable manufacturing expense per meal	$ 4	$ 4
Sales commission expense per meal	$ 1	$ 1
Total fixed manufacturing overhead	$ 800	$ 800
Total fixed marketing and administrative expenses	$ 300	$ 300

Requirements

1. Compute the product cost per meal produced under absorption costing and under variable costing. Do this first for January and then for February.
2. Prepare separate monthly income statements for January and for February, using (a) absorption costing and (b) variable costing.
3. Is operating income higher under absorption costing or variable costing in January? In February? Explain the pattern of differences in operating income based on absorption costing versus variable costing.

CRITICAL THINKING

Discussion & Analysis

A6-83 Discussion Questions

1. Briefly describe an organization with which you are familiar. Describe a situation when a manager in that organization could use cost behavior information and how the manager could use the information.

2. How are fixed costs similar to step fixed costs? How are fixed costs different from step fixed costs? Give an example of a step fixed cost and describe why that cost is not considered to be a fixed cost.

3. Describe a specific situation when a scatter plot could be useful to a manager.

4. What is a mixed cost? Give an example of a mixed cost. Sketch a graph of this example.

5. Compare discretionary fixed costs to committed fixed costs. Think of an organization with which you are familiar. Give two examples of discretionary fixed costs and two examples of committed fixed costs which that organization may have. Explain why the costs you have chosen as examples fit within the definitions of "discretionary fixed costs" and "committed fixed costs."

6. Define the terms "independent variable" and "dependent variable," as used in regression analysis. Illustrate the concepts of independent variables and dependent variables by selecting a cost a company would want to predict and what activity it might use to predict that cost. Describe the independent variable and the dependent variable in that situation.

7. Define the term "relevant range." Why is it important to managers?

8. Describe the term "R-square." If a regression analysis for predicting manufacturing overhead using direct labor hours as the dependent variable has an R-square of 0.40, why might this be a problem? Given the low R-square value, describe the options a manager has for predicting manufacturing overhead costs. Which option do you think is the best option for the manager? Defend your answer.

9. Over the past year, a company's inventory has increased significantly. The company uses absorption costing for financial statements, but internally, the company uses variable costing for financial statements. Which set of financial statements will show the highest operating income? What specifically causes the difference between the two sets of financial statements?

10. A company has adopted a lean production philosophy and, as a result, has cut its inventory levels significantly. Describe the impact on the company's external financial statements as a result of this inventory reduction. Also describe the impact of the inventory reduction on the company's internal financial statements which are prepared using variable costing.

11. What costs might a business incur by not adopting paperless services? Is paperless only profitable to large businesses or is it applicable to small businesses? Explain what factors might be involved in changing over to paperless billing.

12. How might the principles of sustainability (such as increased efficiency) affect cost behavior overall? Think of an example of a sustainable change in process or material that could impact the cost equation for that cost (i.e., the total fixed cost versus the variable cost per unit). Describe this example in detail and what might happen to total fixed costs and per unit variable costs.

Application & Analysis

A6-84 Cost Behavior in Real Companies

Choose a company with which you are familiar that manufactures a product or provides a service. In this activity, you will be making reasonable estimates of the costs and activities associated with this company; companies do not typically publish internal cost or process information.

Basic Discussion Questions

1. Describe the company you selected and the products or services it provides.

2. List ten costs that this company would incur. Include costs from a variety of departments within the company, including human resources, sales, accounting, production (if a manufacturer), service (if a service company), and others. Make sure that you have at least one cost from each of the following categories: fixed, variable, and mixed.

3. Classify each of the costs you listed as either fixed, variable, or mixed. Justify why you classified each cost as you did.

4. Describe a potential cost driver for each of the variable and mixed costs you listed. Explain why each cost driver would be appropriate for its associated cost.

5. Discuss how easy or difficult it was for you to decide whether each cost was fixed, variable, or mixed. Describe techniques a company could use to determine whether a cost is fixed, variable, or mixed.

Decision Cases

A6-85 Appendix *(Learning Objective 6)*

Suppose you serve on the board of directors of American Faucet, a manufacturer of bathroom fixtures that recently adopted a lean production philosophy. Part of your responsibility is to develop a compensation contract for Toni Moen, the vice president of manufacturing. To give her the incentive to make decisions that will increase the company's profits, the board decides to give Moen a year-end bonus if American Faucet meets a target operating income.

Write a memo to Chairperson of the Board Herbert Kohler explaining whether the bonus contract should be based on absorption costing or variable costing.

A6-86 Analyze cost behavior using a variety of methods
(Learning Objectives 1, 2, 3, 4, & 5)

Braunhaus Microbrewery is in the process of analyzing its manufacturing overhead costs. Braunhaus Microbrewery is not sure if the number of cases or the number of processing hours is the best cost driver of manufacturing overhead (MOH) costs. The following information is available:

Month	Manufacturing Overhead Costs	Processing Hours	Cases	MOH Cost per Processing Hour	MOH Cost per Case
January	$29,500	680	8,000	$43.38	$3.69
February	27,800	575	6,750	48.35	4.12
March	24,500	500	5,500	49.00	4.45
April	29,000	600	7,250	48.33	4.00
May	28,000	650	7,800	43.08	3.59
June	29,750	710	5,600	41.90	5.31

Requirements

1. Are manufacturing overhead costs fixed, variable, or mixed? Explain.
2. Graph Braunhaus Microbrewery's manufacturing overhead costs against processing hours. Use Excel or graph by hand.
3. Graph Braunhaus Microbrewery's manufacturing overhead costs against cases produced. Use Excel or graph by hand.
4. Does the data appear to be sound, or do you see any potential data problems? Explain.

5. Use the high-low method to determine Braunhaus Microbrewery's manufacturing overhead cost equation using processing hours as the cost driver. Assume that management believes all of the data to be accurate and wants to include all of it in the analysis.

6. Estimate manufacturing overhead costs if Braunhaus Microbrewery incurs 550 processing hours in July, using the results of the high-low analysis in Requirement 5.

7. Use Excel regression analysis to determine Braunhaus Microbrewery's manufacturing overhead cost equation using processing hours as the cost driver. Comment on the R-square. Estimate manufacturing overhead costs if Braunhaus Microbrewery incurs 550 processing hours in July.

8. Use Excel regression analysis to determine Braunhaus Microbrewery's manufacturing overhead cost equation using number of cases produced as the cost driver. Use all of the data provided. Project total manufacturing overhead costs if Braunhaus Microbrewery produces 6,000 cases. Which cost equation is better—this one or the one from Requirement 7? Why?

9. Use Excel regression analysis to determine Braunhaus Microbrewery's manufacturing overhead cost equation using number of cases produced as the cost driver. This time, remove any potential outliers before performing the regression. How does this affect the R-square? Project total manufacturing overhead costs if Braunhaus Microbrewery produces 6,000 cases.

10. In which cost equation do you have the most confidence? Why?

CMA Questions

A6-87

Ace, Inc., estimates its total materials handling costs at two production levels as follows.

Cost	Gallons
$160,000	80,000
$132,000	60,000

What is the estimated total cost for handling 75,000 gallons?

a. $146,000

b. $150,000

c. $153,000

d. $165,000   (CMA Adapted)

A6-88

Huntington Corporation pays bonuses to its managers based on operating income, as calculated under variable costing. It is now two months before year-end, and earnings have been depressed for some time. Which one of the following should Wanda Richards, production manager, **definitely** implement if she desires to maximize her bonus for this year?

a. Step up production so that more manufacturing costs are deferred into inventory.

b. Cut $2.3 million of advertising and marketing costs.

c. Postpone $1.8 million of discretionary equipment maintenance until next year.

d. Implement, with the aid of the controller, an activity-based costing and activity-based management system.   (CMA Adapted)

Cost-Volume-Profit Analysis

Learning Objectives

- **1** Calculate the unit contribution margin and the contribution margin ratio

- **2** Use CVP analysis to find breakeven points and target profit volumes

- **3** Perform sensitivity analysis in response to changing business conditions

- **4** Find breakeven and target profit volumes for multiproduct companies

- **5** Determine a firm's margin of safety, operating leverage, and most profitable cost structure

From Chapter 7 of *Managerial Accounting*, Third Edition. Karen W. Braun, Wendy M. Tietz.

Art.com, Inc., has become

the world's largest online retailer of fine art, photography, post-ers, and other wall décor. The company offers over 850,000 differ-ent products to customers ranging from budget-minded college students to professional decorators searching for high-end art. Using a domestic website, as well as 22 localized websites across five continents, the company has been able to generate sales from over 10 million customers in 120 countries. Each localized website uses the country's native language and currency, and offers local e-mail support. In addition, the company now offers free iPhone and Facebook apps that allow customers to turn personal photos into professionally-framed art, as well as preview art by importing it into a photo of their own living space. Innovations such as these continue to expand the company's marketing reach.

Even though Art.com doesn't face many of the fixed costs of traditional retail outlets, the company still incurs fixed costs related to its websites, distribution centers, and custom-framing facilities. It also incurs variable costs for each piece of art. The bottom line is, e-tail or retail, every business faces fixed and variable costs, and Art.com is no exception. Before they launched the company, how did Art.com managers figure out what sales volume they had to reach to break even? How did they forecast the volume needed to achieve their target profit? And as the company continues to operate, how do managers respond to fluctuating business conditions, changing variable and fixed costs, and pricing pressure from new competitors? Cost-volume-profit (CVP) analysis helps managers answer such questions.

In the last chapter, we discussed cost behavior patterns and the methods managers use to determine how the company's costs behave. We showed how managers use the contri-bution margin income statement to separately display the firm's variable and fixed costs. In this chapter, we show how managers identify the volume of sales necessary to achieve breakeven or a target profit. We also look at how changes in costs, sales price, and volume affect the firm's profit. Finally, we discuss ways to identify the firm's risk level, including ways to gauge how easily a firm's profits could turn to loss if sales volume declines.

How Does Cost-Volume-Profit Analysis Help Managers?

Cost-volume-profit analysis, or CVP, is a powerful tool that helps managers make important business decisions. **Cost-volume-profit analysis** expresses the relationships among costs, volume, and the company's profit. Entrepreneurs and managers use CVP analysis to determine the sales volume that will be needed just to break even, or cover costs. They also use CVP to determine the sales volume that will be needed to earn a target profit, such as $100,000 per month. And because business conditions are always changing, CVP can help managers prepare for and respond to economic changes, such as increases in costs from suppliers.

Let's begin our discussion by looking at the data needed for CVP analysis.

Data and Assumptions Required for CVP Analysis

CVP analysis relies on the interdependency of five components, or pieces of information, shown in Exhibit 7-1.

EXHIBIT 7-1 Components of CVP Analysis

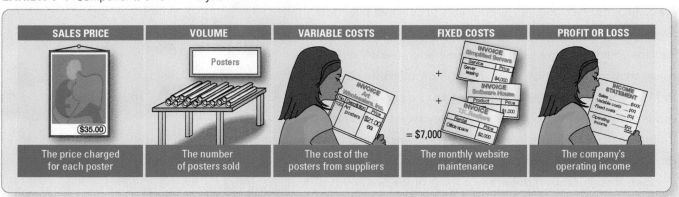

Let's examine this information in terms of a simple company example. Kay Martin, an entrepreneur, has just started an e-tail business selling art posters on the internet. Kay is a "virtual retailer" and carries no inventory. Kay's software tabulates all customer orders each day and then automatically places the order to buy posters from a wholesaler. Kay buys only what she needs to fill the prior day's sales orders. The posters cost $21 each, and Kay sells them for $35 each. Customers pay the shipping costs, so there are no other variable selling costs. Monthly fixed costs for server leasing and maintenance, software, and office rental total $7,000. Kay's relevant range extends from 0 to 2,000 posters a month. Beyond this volume, Kay will need to hire an employee and upgrade her website software in order to handle the increased volume.

Thus, we know the following:

- Sales price = $35 per poster
- Variable cost = $21 per poster
- Fixed costs = $7,000 per month

For CVP to be accurate, certain assumptions must be met. We'll itemize each of these assumptions, and discuss whether Kay's business meets the assumptions.

1. **A change in volume is the only factor that affects costs.** In Kay's business, costs are expected to increase only if volume increases. ✓

2. **Managers can classify each cost (or the components of mixed costs) as either variable or fixed. These costs are linear throughout the relevant range of volume.** In Kay's business, variable costs are $21 per poster and fixed costs are $7,000 per month. These costs are expected to remain the same unless Kay's volume exceeds 2,000 posters per month. Thus, we could draw each of these costs as straight lines on a graph. ✓

3. **Revenues are linear throughout the relevant range of volume.** In Kay's business, each poster generates $35 of sales revenue, with no volume discounts. Therefore, revenue could be graphed as a straight line beginning at the origin and sloping upwards at a rate of $35 per poster sold. ✓

4. **Inventory levels will not change.** Kay keeps no inventory. If she did, CVP analysis would still work as long as Kay did not allow her inventory levels to greatly fluctuate from one period to the next. ✓

5. **The sales mix of products will not change.** Sales mix is the combination of products that make up total sales. For example, Art.com may sell 15% posters, 25% unframed photographs, and 60% framed prints. If profits differ across products, changes in sales mix will affect CVP analysis. Kay currently offers only one size of poster, so her sales mix is 100% posters. Later in this chapter we will expand her product offerings to illustrate how sales mix impacts CVP analysis. ✓

Now that we know Kay's business meets these assumptions, we can proceed with confidence about the CVP results we will obtain. When assumptions are not met perfectly, managers should consider the results of CVP analysis to be approximations, rather than exact figures.

The Unit Contribution Margin

The last chapter introduced the **contribution margin income statement**, which separates costs on the income statement by cost behavior rather than function. Many managers prefer the contribution margin income statement because it gives them the information for CVP analysis in a "ready-to-use" format. On these income statements, the contribution margin is the "dividing line"—all variable expenses go above the line, and all fixed expenses go below the line. The results of Kay's first month of operations is shown in Exhibit 7-2.

1 Calculate the unit contribution margin and the contribution margin ratio

EXHIBIT 7-2 Contribution Margin Income Statement

KAY MARTIN POSTERS	
Contribution Margin Income Statement	
Month Ended August 31	
Sales revenue (550 posters)	$ 19,250
Less: Variable expenses	(11,550)
Contribution margin	7,700
Less: Fixed expenses	(7,000)
Operating income	$ 700

Notice that the **contribution margin** is the excess of sales revenue over variable expenses. The contribution margin tells managers how much revenue is left—after paying variable expenses—for *contributing* toward covering fixed costs and then generating a profit. Hence the name contribution margin.

The contribution margin is stated as a *total* amount on the contribution margin income statement. However, managers often state the contribution margin on a *per unit* basis and as a *percentage,* or *ratio.* A product's **contribution margin per unit**—or unit contribution margin—is the excess of the selling price per unit over the variable cost of obtaining *and* selling each unit. Some businesses pay a sales commission on each unit or have other variable costs, such as shipping costs, for each unit sold. However, Kay's

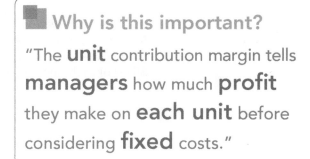

Why is this important?

"The **unit** contribution margin tells **managers** how much **profit** they make on **each unit** before considering **fixed** costs."

variable cost per unit is simply the price she pays for each poster. Therefore, her unit contribution margin is as follows:

Sales price per poster..	$ 35
Less: Variable cost per poster.........................	(21)
Contribution margin per poster....................	$ 14

The unit contribution margin indicates how much profit each unit provides *before* fixed costs are considered. Each unit *first* contributes this profit toward covering the firm's fixed costs. Once the company sells enough units to cover its fixed costs, the unit contribution margin contributes *directly* to operating income. For example, every poster Kay sells generates $14 of contribution margin that can be used to pay for the monthly $7,000 of fixed costs. After Kay sells enough posters to cover fixed costs, each additional poster she sells will generate $14 of operating income.

Managers can use the unit contribution margin to quickly forecast income at any volume within their relevant range. First, they project the total contribution margin by multiplying the unit contribution margin by the number of units they expect to sell. Then, they subtract fixed costs. For example, let's assume that Kay hopes to sell 650 posters next month. She can project her operating income as follows:

Contribution margin (650 posters × $14 per poster).....................	$ 9,100
Less: Fixed expenses..	(7,000)
Operating income...	$ 2,100

If Kay sells 650 posters next month, her operating income should be $2,100.

The Contribution Margin Ratio

In addition to computing the unit contribution margin, managers often compute the **contribution margin ratio**, which is the ratio of contribution margin to sales revenue. Kay can compute her contribution margin ratio at the unit level as follows:

$$\text{Contribution margin ratio} = \frac{\text{Unit contribution margin}}{\text{Sales price per unit}} = \frac{\$14}{\$35} = 40\%$$

Kay could also compute the contribution margin ratio using any volume of sales. Let's use her current sales volume, pictured in Exhibit 7-2:

$$\text{Contribution margin ratio} = \frac{\text{Contribution margin}}{\text{Sales revenue}} = \frac{\$7,700}{\$19,250} = 40\%$$

The contribution margin ratio is the percentage of each sales dollar that is available for covering fixed expenses and generating a profit. As shown in Exhibit 7-3, each *$1.00* of sales revenue contributes $0.40 toward fixed expenses and profit while the remaining $0.60 of each sales dollar is used to pay for variable costs.

EXHIBIT 7-3 Breakdown of $1 of Sales Revenue

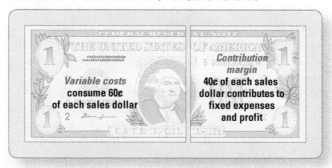

Managers can also use the contribution margin ratio to quickly forecast operating income within their relevant range. When using the contribution margin ratio, managers project income based on sales revenue (*dollars*) rather than sales *units*. For example, if Kay generates $70,000 of sales revenue one month, what operating income should she expect? To find out, Kay simply multiplies her projected sales revenue by the contribution margin ratio to arrive at the total contribution margin. Then she subtracts fixed expenses:

Contribution margin ($70,000 sales × 40%)..................	$28,000
Less: Fixed expenses...	(7,000)
Operating income..	$21,000

Let's verify. If Kay has $70,000 of sales revenue, she has sold 2,000 posters ($70,000 ÷ $35 per poster). Her complete contribution margin income statement would be calculated as follows:

Sales revenue (2,000 posters × $35/poster).....................................	$ 70,000
Less: Variable expenses (2,000 posters × $21/poster)	(42,000)
Contribution margin (2,000 posters × $14/poster)	$ 28,000
Less: Fixed expenses...	(7,000)
Operating income...	$ 21,000

The contribution margin per unit and contribution margin ratio help managers quickly and easily project income at different sales volumes. However, when projecting profits, managers must keep in mind the relevant range. For instance, if Kay wants to project income at a volume of 5,000 posters, she shouldn't use the existing contribution margin and fixed costs. Her current relevant range extends to only 2,000 posters per month. At a higher volume of sales, her variable cost per unit may be lower than $21 (due to volume discounts from her suppliers) and her monthly fixed costs may be higher than $7,000 (due to upgrading her system and hiring an employee to handle the extra sales volume).

Rather than using the individual unit contribution margins on each of their products, large companies that offer hundreds or thousands of products (like Art.com) use their contribution margin *ratio* to predict profits. As long as the sales mix remains constant (one of our CVP assumptions), the contribution margin ratio will remain constant.

We've seen how managers use the contribution margin to project income; but managers use the contribution margin for other purposes too, such as motivating the sales force. Salespeople who know the contribution margin of each product can generate more profit for the company by emphasizing high-margin products. This is why many companies base sales commissions on the contribution margins produced by sales rather than on sales revenue alone.

In the next section, we'll see how managers use CVP analysis to determine the company's breakeven point.

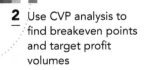

2 Use CVP analysis to find breakeven points and target profit volumes

How do Managers Find the Breakeven Point?

A company's **breakeven point** is the sales level at which *operating income is zero*. Sales below the breakeven point result in a loss. Sales above the breakeven point provide a profit. Before Kay started her business, she wanted to figure out how many posters she would have to sell just to break even.

There are three ways to calculate the breakeven point. All of the approaches are based on the income statement, so they all reach the same conclusion. The first two methods find breakeven in terms of sales *units*. The last approach finds breakeven in terms of sales revenue (sales dollars).

1. The income statement approach
2. The shortcut approach using the *unit* contribution margin
3. The shortcut approach using the contribution margin *ratio*

Let's examine these three approaches in detail.

The Income Statement Approach

The income statement approach starts with the contribution margin income statement, and then breaks it down into smaller components:

> **■ Why is this important?**
>
> "Businesses **don't** want to operate at a **loss**. CVP analysis helps **managers** determine how many units they need to sell *just* to **break even**."

SALES REVENUE	−	VARIABLE EXPENSES	−	FIXED EXPENSES	=	OPERATING INCOME
$\left(\dfrac{\text{Sales price}}{\text{per unit}} \times \text{Units sold}\right)$	−	$\left(\dfrac{\text{Variable cost}}{\text{per unit}} \times \text{Units sold}\right)$	−	Fixed expenses	=	Operating income

Let's use this approach to find Kay's breakeven point. Recall that Kay sells her posters for $35 each and that her variable cost is $21 per poster. Kay's fixed expenses total $7,000. At the breakeven point, operating income is zero. We use this information to solve the income statement equation for the number of posters Kay must sell to break even.

SALES REVENUE	−	VARIABLE EXPENSES	−	FIXED EXPENSES	=	OPERATING INCOME
$\left(\dfrac{\text{Sales price}}{\text{per unit}} \times \text{Units sold}\right)$	−	$\left(\dfrac{\text{Variable cost}}{\text{per unit}} \times \text{Units sold}\right)$	−	Fixed expenses	=	Operating income
($35 × Units sold) −		($21 × Units sold) −		$7,000	=	$ 0
($35	−	$21) × Units sold −		$7,000	=	$ 0
		$14 × Units sold			=	$7,000
		Units sold			=	$7,000/$14
		Sales in units			=	500 posters

Kay must sell 500 posters to break even. Her breakeven point in sales revenue is $17,500 (500 posters × $35).

You can check this answer by creating a contribution margin income statement using a sales volume of 500 posters:

Sales revenue (500 posters × $35)..	$ 17,500
Less: Variable expenses (500 posters × $21)...................	(10,500)
Contribution margin	$ 7,000
Less: Fixed expenses..	(7,000)
Operating income..	$ 0

Notice that at breakeven, a firm's fixed expenses ($7,000) equal its contribution margin ($7,000). In other words, the firm has generated *just* enough contribution margin to cover its fixed expenses, but *not* enough to generate a profit.

The Shortcut Approach Using the Unit Contribution Margin

To develop the shortcut approach, we start with the contribution margin income statement, and then rearrange some of its terms:

SALES REVENUE − VARIABLE EXPENSES − FIXED EXPENSES = OPERATING INCOME

Contribution margin	− Fixed expenses	= Operating income
Contribution margin		= Fixed expenses + Operating income
(Contribution margin per unit × Units sold)		= Fixed expenses + Operating income

As a final step, we divide both sides of the equation by the contribution margin per unit. Now we have the shortcut formula:

$$\text{Sales in units} = \frac{\text{Fixed expenses} + \text{Operating income}}{\text{Contribution margin per unit}}$$

Kay can use this shortcut approach to find her breakeven point in units. Kay's fixed expenses total $7,000, and her unit contribution margin is $14. At the breakeven point, operating income is zero. Thus, Kay's breakeven point in units is as follows:

$$\text{Sales in units} = \frac{\$7,000 + \$0}{\$14}$$

$$= 500 \text{ posters}$$

Why does this shortcut approach work? Recall that each poster provides $14 of contribution margin. To break even, Kay must generate enough contribution margin to cover $7,000 of fixed expenses. At the rate of $14 per poster, Kay must sell 500 posters ($7,000/$14) to cover her $7,000 of fixed expenses. Because the shortcut formula simply rearranges the income statement equation, the breakeven point is the same under both methods (500 posters).

Accounting Simplified

Cost-Volume-Profit Analysis

If your instructor is using MyAccountingLab, go to the Multimedia Library for a quick video on this topic.

STOP & THINK

What would Kay's operating income be if she sold 501 posters? What would it be if she sold 600 posters?

Answer: Every poster sold provides $14 of contribution margin, which first contributes toward covering fixed costs, then profit. Once Kay reaches her breakeven point (500 posters), she has covered all fixed costs. Therefore, each additional poster sold after the breakeven point contributes $14 *directly to profit*. If Kay sells 501 posters, she has sold one more poster than breakeven. Her operating income is $14. If she sells 600 posters, she has sold 100 more posters than breakeven. Her operating income is $1,400 ($14 per poster × 100 posters). We can verify this as follows:

Contribution margin (600 posters × $14 per poster)	$ 8,400
Less: Fixed expenses...	(7,000)
Operating income...	$ 1,400

Once a company achieves breakeven, each additional unit sold contributes its unique unit contribution margin directly to profit.

The Shortcut Approach Using the Contribution Margin Ratio

It is easy to compute the breakeven point in *units* for a simple business like Kay's that has only one product. But what about companies that have thousands of products such as Art.com, Home Depot, and Amazon.com? It doesn't make sense for these companies to determine the number of each various product they need to sell to break even. Can you imagine a Home Depot manager describing breakeven as 100,000 wood screws, two million nails, 3,000 lawn mowers, 10,000 gallons of paint, and so forth? It simply doesn't make sense. Therefore, multiproduct companies usually compute breakeven in terms of *sales revenue* (dollars).

This shortcut approach differs from the other shortcut we've just seen in only one way: Fixed expenses plus operating income are divided by the contribution margin *ratio* (not by contribution margin *per unit*) to yield sales in *dollars* (not *units*):

$$\text{Sales in dollars} = \frac{\text{Fixed expenses} + \text{Operating income}}{\text{Contribution margin ratio}}$$

Recall that Kay's contribution margin ratio is 40%. At the breakeven point, operating income is $0, so Kay's breakeven point in sales revenue is as follows:

$$\text{Sales in dollars} = \frac{\$7,000 + \$0}{0.40}$$

$$= \$17,500$$

This is the same breakeven sales revenue we calculated earlier (500 posters × $35 sales price = $17,500).

Why does the contribution margin ratio formula work? Each dollar of Kay's sales contributes $0.40 to fixed expenses and profit. To break even, she must generate enough contribution margin at the rate of $0.40 per sales dollar to cover the $7,000 fixed expenses ($7,000 ÷ 0.40 = $17,500).

When determining which formula to use, keep the following rule of thumb in mind:

> *Dividing fixed costs by the **unit** contribution margin provides breakeven in sales **units**. Dividing fixed costs by the contribution margin **ratio** provides breakeven in sales **dollars**.*

How do Managers Find the Volume Needed to Earn a Target Profit?

For established products and services, managers are more interested in the sales level needed to earn a target profit than in the breakeven point. Managers of new business ventures are also interested in the profits they can expect to earn. For example, Kay doesn't want to just break even—she wants her business to be her sole source of income. She would like the business to earn $4,900 of profit each month. How many posters must Kay sell each month to reach her target profit?

> **Why is this important?**
>
> "**Companies** want to make a profit. **CVP** analysis helps **managers** determine **how many** units they need to sell to earn a **target** amount of **profit**."

How Much Must we Sell to Earn a Target Profit?

The only difference from our prior analysis is that instead of determining the sales level needed for *zero profit* (breakeven), Kay now wants to know how many posters she must sell to earn a $4,900 profit. We can use the income statement approach or the shortcut approach to find the answer. Because Kay wants to know the number of *units*, we'll use the shortcut formula based on the *unit* contribution margin. This time, instead of an operating income of zero (breakeven), we'll insert Kay's target operating income of $4,900:

$$\text{Sales in } \textit{units} = \frac{\text{Fixed expenses + Operating income}}{\text{Contribution margin } \textit{per unit}}$$

$$= \frac{\$7,000 + \$4,900}{\$14}$$

$$= \frac{\$11,900}{\$14}$$

$$= 850 \text{ posters}$$

This analysis shows that Kay must sell 850 posters each month to earn profits of $4,900 a month. Notice that this level of sales falls within Kay's current relevant range (0–2,000 posters per month), so the conclusion that she would earn $4,900 of income at this sales volume is valid. If the calculation resulted in a sales volume outside the current relevant range (greater than 2,000 units), we would need to reassess our cost assumptions.

Assume that Kay also wants to know how much sales revenue she needs to earn $4,900 of monthly profit. Because she already knows the number of units needed (850), she can easily translate this volume into sales revenue:

$$850 \text{ posters} \times \$35 \text{ sales price/poster} = \$29,750 \text{ sales revenue}$$

If Kay only wanted to know the sales revenue needed to achieve her target profit rather than the number of units needed, she could have found the answer directly by using the shortcut formula based on the contribution margin *ratio*:

$$\text{Sales in } dollars = \frac{\text{Fixed expenses} + \text{Operating income}}{\text{Contribution margin } ratio}$$

$$= \frac{\$7,000 + \$4,900}{0.40}$$

$$= \frac{\$11,900}{0.40}$$

$$= \$29,750$$

Finally, Kay could have used the income statement approach to find the same answers:

SALES REVENUE	−	VARIABLE EXPENSES	−	FIXED EXPENSES	=	OPERATING INCOME
($35 Units sold)	−	($21 Units sold)	−	$7,000	=	$ 4,900
($35	−	$21) Units sold	−	$7,000	=	$ 4,900
		$14 Units sold			=	$11,900
				Units sold	=	$11,900/$14
				Units sold	=	850 posters

We can prove that our answers (from any of the three approaches) are correct by preparing Kay's income statement for a sales volume of 850 units:

Sales revenue (850 posters × $35)...................................	$ 29,750
Less: Variable expenses (850 posters × $21)....................	(17,850)
Contribution margin	$ 11,900
Less: Fixed expenses..	(7,000)
Operating income...	$ 4,900

Graphing CVP Relationships

By graphing the CVP relationships for her business, Kay can see at a glance how changes in the levels of sales will affect profits. As in the last chapter, the volume of units (posters) is placed on the horizontal x-axis, while dollars is placed on the vertical y-axis. Then, she follows five steps to graph the CVP relations for her business, as illustrated in Exhibit 7-4. This graph also shows the linear nature of Kay's costs and revenues. Recall that CVP analysis assumes costs and revenues will be linear throughout the relevant range.

EXHIBIT 7-4 Cost-Volume-Profit Graph

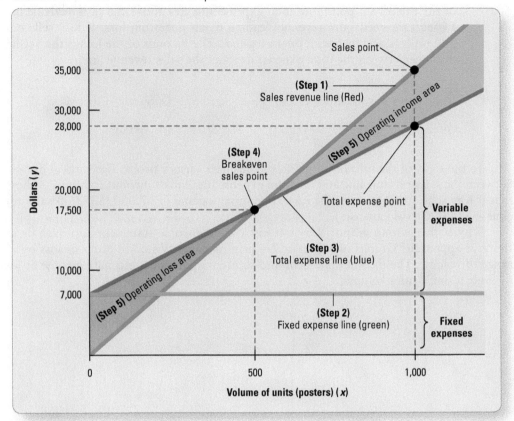

STEP 1: Choose a sales volume, such as 1,000 posters. Plot the point for total sales revenue at that volume: 1,000 posters × $35 per poster = sales of $35,000. Draw the *sales revenue line* from the origin (0) through the $35,000 point. Why does the sales revenue line start at the origin? If Kay does not sell any posters, there is no sales revenue.

STEP 2: Draw the *fixed expense line*, a horizontal line that intersects the y-axis at $7,000. Recall that the fixed expense line is flat because fixed expenses are the same ($7,000) no matter how many posters Kay sells within her relevant range (up to 2,000 posters per month).

STEP 3: Draw the *total expense line*. Total expense is the sum of variable expense plus fixed expense. Thus, total expense is a *mixed* cost. So, the total expense line follows the form of the mixed cost line. Begin by computing variable expense at the chosen sales volume: 1,000 posters × $21 per poster = variable expense of $21,000. Add variable expense to fixed expense: $21,000 + $7,000 = $28,000. Plot the total expense point ($28,000) for 1,000 units. Then, draw a line through this point from the $7,000 fixed expense intercept on the dollars axis. This is the *total expense line*. Why does the total expense line start at the fixed expense line? If Kay sells no posters, she still incurs the $7,000 fixed cost for the server leasing, software, and office rental, but she incurs no variable costs.

STEP 4: Identify the *breakeven point*. The breakeven point is the point where the sales revenue line intersects the total expense line. This is the point where sales revenue equals total expenses. Our previous analyses told us that Kay's breakeven point is 500 posters, or $17,500 in sales. The graph shows this information visually.

STEP 5: Mark the *operating income* and the *operating loss* areas on the graph. To the left of the breakeven point, the total expense line lies above the sales revenue line. Expenses exceed sales revenue, leading to an operating loss. If Kay sells only 300 posters, she incurs an operating loss. The amount of the loss is the vertical distance between the total expense line and the sales revenue line:

Sales revenue − Variable expenses − Fixed expenses = Operating income (Loss)
$(300 \times \$35) - \quad (300 \times \$21) \quad - \quad \$7,000 \quad = \quad \$(2,800)$

To the right of the breakeven point, the business earns a profit. The vertical distance between the sales revenue line and the total expense line equals income. Exhibit 7-4 shows that if Kay sells 1,000 posters, she earns operating income of $7,000 ($35,000 sales revenue − $28,000 total expenses).

Why bother with a graph? Why not just use the income statement approach or the shortcut approach? Graphs like Exhibit 7-4 help managers visualize profit or loss over a range of volume. The income statement and shortcut approaches estimate income or loss for only a single sales volume.

Decision Guidelines

CVP Analysis

Your friend wants to open her own ice cream parlor after college. She needs help making the following decisions:

Decision	Guidelines
How much will I earn on every ice cream cone I sell?	The unit contribution margin shows managers how much they earn on each unit sold after paying for variable *costs but before considering fixed expenses.* The unit contribution margin is the amount each unit earns that contributes toward covering fixed expenses and generating a profit. It is computed as follows:

Sales price per unit

Less: Variable cost per unit

Contribution margin per unit

The contribution margin ratio shows managers how much contribution margin is earned on every $1 of sales. It is computed as follows:

$$\text{Contribution margin ratio} = \frac{\text{Contribution margin}}{\text{Sales revenue}}$$

Can I quickly forecast my income without creating a full income statement?	The contribution margin concept allows managers to forecast income quickly at different sales volumes. First, find the total contribution margin (by multiplying the forecasted number of units by the unit contribution margin *or* by multiplying the forecasted sales revenue by the contribution margin ratio) and then subtract all fixed expenses.

How can I compute the *number of ice cream cones* I'll have to sell to break even or earn a target profit?

Income Statement Approach:

$$\text{SALES REVENUE} - \text{VARIABLE EXPENSES} - \frac{\text{FIXED}}{\text{EXPENSE}} = \frac{\text{OPERATING}}{\text{INCOME}}$$

$$\frac{\text{Sales price per unit}}{\times \text{Units sold}} - \frac{\text{Variable cost per unit}}{\times \text{Units sold}} - \frac{\text{Fixed}}{\text{expenses}} = \frac{\text{Operating}}{\text{income}}$$

Shortcut Unit Contribution Margin Approach:

$$\text{Sales in } units = \frac{\text{Fixed expenses} + \text{Operating income}}{\text{Contribution margin } per \; unit}$$

How can I compute the *amount of sales revenue* (in dollars) I'll have to generate to break even or earn a target profit?

Shortcut Contribution Margin Ratio Approach:

$$\text{Sales in } dollars = \frac{\text{Fixed expenses} + \text{Operating income}}{\text{Contribution margin } ratio}$$

What will my profits look like over a range of volumes?	CVP graphs show managers, at a glance, how different sales volumes will affect profits.

SUMMARY PROBLEM 1

Fleet Foot buys hiking socks for $6 a pair and sells them for $10. Management budgets monthly fixed expenses of $10,000 for sales volumes between 0 and 12,000 pairs.

Requirements

1. Use the income statement approach and the shortcut unit contribution margin approach to compute monthly breakeven sales in units.

2. Use the shortcut contribution margin ratio approach to compute the breakeven point in sales revenue (sales dollars).

3. Compute the monthly sales level (in units) required to earn a target operating income of $14,000. Use either the income statement approach or the shortcut contribution margin approach.

4. Prepare a graph of Fleet Foot's CVP relationships, similar to Exhibit 7-4. Draw the sales revenue line, the fixed expense line, and the total expense line. Label the axes, the breakeven point, the operating income area, and the operating loss area.

▪ SOLUTIONS

Requirement 1
Income Statement Approach:

SALES REVENUE	−	VARIABLE EXPENSES	− FIXED EXPENSES	= OPERATING INCOME
$\left(\begin{array}{l}\text{Sales price}\\\text{per unit}\end{array} \times \text{Units sold}\right)$	−	$\left(\begin{array}{l}\text{Variable cost}\\\text{per unit}\end{array} \times \text{Units sold}\right)$ −	Fixed expenses	= Operating income
($10 × Units sold) −		($6 × Units sold) −	$10,000	= $ 0
($10	−	$6)	× Units sold	= $10,000
		$4	× Units sold	= $10,000
			Units sold	= $10,000 ÷ $4
			Breakeven sales in units	= 2,500 units

Shortcut Unit Contribution Margin Approach:

$$\text{Sales in units} = \frac{\text{Fixed expenses} + \text{Operating income}}{\text{Contribution margin per unit}}$$

$$= \frac{\$10,000 + \$0}{(\$10 - \$6)}$$

$$= \frac{\$10,000}{\$4}$$

$$= 2,500 \text{ units}$$

Requirement 2

$$\text{Sales in dollars} = \frac{\text{Fixed expenses} + \text{Operating income}}{\text{Contribution margin ratio}}$$

$$= \frac{\$10,000 + \$0}{0.40^*}$$

$$= \$25,000$$

$$^*\text{Contribution margin ratio} = \frac{\text{Contribution margin per unit}}{\text{Sales price per unit}} = \frac{\$4}{\$10} = 0.40$$

Requirement 3

Income Statement Equation Approach:

SALES REVENUE	−	VARIABLE EXPENSES	− FIXED EXPENSES	= OPERATING INCOME
$\left(\begin{matrix}\text{Sales price} \\ \text{per unit}\end{matrix} \times \text{Units sold}\right)$	−	$\left(\begin{matrix}\text{Variable cost} \\ \text{per unit}\end{matrix} \times \text{Units sold}\right)$	− Fixed expenses	= Operating income
(\$10 × Units sold) −		(\$6 × Units sold) −	\$10,000	= \$14,000
(\$10	−	\$6) × Units sold		= \$10,000 + \$14,000
		\$4 × Units sold		= \$24,000
		Units sold		= \$24,000 ÷ \$4
		Units sold		= 6,000 units

Shortcut Unit Contribution Margin Approach:

$$\text{Sales in units} = \frac{\text{Fixed expenses} + \text{Operating income}}{\text{Contribution margin per unit}}$$

$$= \frac{\$10,000 + \$14,000}{(\$10 - \$6)}$$

$$= \frac{\$24,000}{\$4}$$

$$= 6,000 \text{ units}$$

Requirement 4

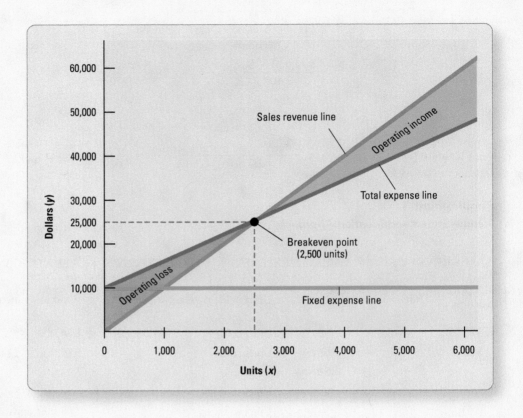

How do Managers Use CVP to Plan for Changing Business Conditions?

In today's fast-changing business world, managers need to be prepared for increasing costs, pricing pressure from competitors, and other changing business conditions.

Managers use CVP analysis to conduct <u>sensitivity analysis</u>. Sensitivity analysis is a "what-if" technique that asks what results will be if actual prices or costs change or if an underlying assumption such as sales mix changes. For example, increased competition may force Kay to lower her sales price, while at the same time her suppliers increase poster costs. How will these changes affect Kay's breakeven and target profit volumes? What will happen if Kay changes her sales mix by offering posters in two different sizes? We'll tackle these issues next.

3 Perform sensitivity analysis in response to changing business conditions

Changing the Sales Price

Let's assume that Kay has now been in business for several months. Because of competition, Kay is considering cutting her sales price to $31 per poster. If her variable expenses remain $21 per poster and her fixed expenses stay at $7,000, how many posters will she need to sell to break even? To answer this question, Kay calculates a new unit contribution margin using the new sales price:

New sales price per poster....................................	$ 31
Less: Variable cost per poster.............................	(21)
New contribution margin per poster..................	$ 10

She then uses the new unit contribution margin to compute breakeven sales in units:

$$\text{Sales in units} = \frac{\text{Fixed expenses} + \text{Operating income}}{\text{Contribution margin per unit}}$$

$$= \frac{\$7,000 + \$0}{\$10}$$

$$= 700 \text{ posters}$$

With the original $35 sale price, Kay's breakeven point was 500 posters. If Kay lowers the sales price to $31 per poster, her breakeven point increases to 700 posters. The lower sales price means that each poster contributes *less* toward fixed expenses ($10 versus $14 before the price change), so Kay must sell 200 *more* posters to break even. Each dollar of sales revenue would contribute $0.32 ($10/$31) rather than $0.40 toward covering fixed expenses and generating a profit.

If Kay reduces her sales price to $31, how many posters must she sell to achieve her $4,900 monthly target profit? Kay again uses the new unit contribution margin to determine how many posters she will need to sell to reach her profit goals:

$$\text{Sales in units} = \frac{\$7,000 + \$4,900}{\$10}$$

$$= 1,190 \text{ posters}$$

> **Why is this important?**
>
> "**CVP analysis** helps managers prepare for and respond to **economic** changes, such as increasing costs and **pressure** to drop sales prices, so companies can remain **competitive** and **profitable**."

With the original sales price, Kay needed to sell only 850 posters per month to achieve her target profit level. If Kay cuts her sales price (and, therefore, her contribution margin), she must sell more posters to achieve her financial goals. Kay could have found the same results using the income statement approach. Exhibit 7-5 shows the effect of changes in sales price on breakeven and target profit volumes.

EXHIBIT 7-5 The Effect of Changes in Sales Price on Breakeven and Target Profit Volumes

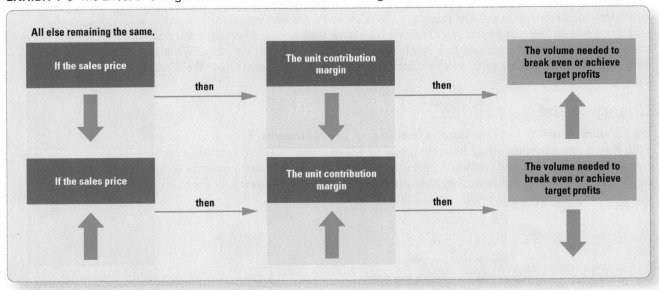

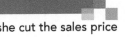

STOP&THINK

Kay believes she could dominate the e-commerce art poster business if she cut the sales price to $20. Is this a good idea?

Answer: No. The variable cost per poster is $21. If Kay sells posters for $20 each, she loses $1 on each poster. Kay will incur a loss if the sales price is less than the variable cost.

Changing Variable Costs

Let's assume that Kay does *not* lower her sales price. However, Kay's supplier raises the price for each poster to $23.80 (instead of the original $21). Kay does not want to pass this increase on to her customers, so she holds her sales price at the original $35 per poster. Her fixed costs remain $7,000. How many posters must she sell to break even after her supplier raises the prices? Kay's new contribution margin per unit drops to $11.20 ($35 sales price per poster – $23.80 variable cost per poster). So, her new breakeven point is as follows:

$$\text{Sales in units} = \frac{\text{Fixed expenses} + \text{Operating income}}{\text{Contribution margin per unit}}$$
$$= \frac{\$7,000 + \$0}{\$11.20}$$
$$= 625 \text{ posters}$$

Higher variable costs per unit have the same effect as lower selling prices per unit—they both reduce the product's unit contribution margin. As a result, Kay will have to sell *more* units to break even and achieve target profits. As shown in Exhibit 7-6, a *decrease* in variable costs would have just the opposite effect. Lower variable costs increase the contribution margin each poster provides and, therefore, lowers the breakeven point.

EXHIBIT 7-6 The Effect of Changes in Variable Costs on Breakeven and Target Profit Volumes

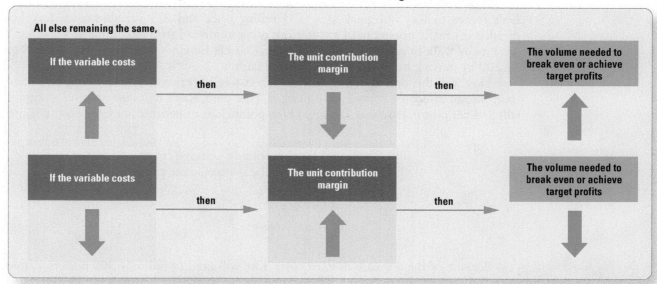

STOP & THINK

Suppose Kay is squeezed from both sides: Her supply costs have increased to $23.80 per poster, yet she must lower her price to $31 in order to compete. Under these conditions, how many posters will Kay need to sell to achieve her monthly target profit of $4,900? If Kay doesn't think she can sell that many posters, how else might she attempt to achieve her profit goals?

Answer: Kay is now in a position faced by many companies—her unit contribution margin is squeezed by both higher supply costs and lower sales prices:

New sales price per poster....................................	$ 31.00
Less: New variable cost per poster......................	(23.80)
New contribution margin per poster...................	$ 7.20

Kay's new contribution margin is about half of what it was when she started her business ($14). To achieve her target profit, her volume will have to increase dramatically (yet, it would still fall within her current relevant range for fixed costs—which extends to 2,000 posters per month):

$$\text{Sales in units} = \frac{\text{Fixed expenses} + \text{Operating income}}{\text{Contribution margin per unit}}$$

$$= \frac{\$7,000 + \$4,900}{\$7.20}$$

$$= 1,653 \text{ posters (rounded)}$$

Based on her current volume, Kay may not believe she can sell so many posters. To maintain a reasonable profit level, Kay may need to take other measures. For example, she may try to find a different supplier with lower poster costs. She may also attempt to lower her fixed costs. For example, perhaps she could negotiate a cheaper lease on her office space or move her business to a less expensive location. She could also try to increase her volume by spending *more* on fixed costs, such as advertising. Kay could also investigate selling other products, in addition to her regular-size posters, that would have higher unit contribution margins. We'll discuss these measures next.

Changing Fixed Costs

Let's return to Kay's original data ($35 selling price and $21 variable cost). Kay has decided she really doesn't need a storefront office at a retail strip mall because she doesn't have many walk-in customers. She could decrease her monthly fixed costs from $7,000 to $4,200 by moving her office to an industrial park.

How will this decrease in fixed costs affect Kay's breakeven point? *Changes in fixed costs do not affect the contribution margin.* Therefore, Kay's unit contribution margin is still $14 per poster. However, her breakeven point changes because her fixed costs change:

$$\text{Sales in units} = \frac{\text{Fixed expenses} + \text{Operating income}}{\text{Contribution margin per unit}}$$

$$= \frac{\$4,200 + \$0}{\$14.00}$$

$$= 300 \text{ posters}$$

Because of the decrease in fixed costs, Kay will need to sell only 300 posters, rather than 500 posters, to break even. The volume needed to achieve her monthly $4,900 target profit will also decline. However, if Kay's fixed costs *increase*, she will have to sell *more* units to break even. Exhibit 7-7 shows the effect of changes in fixed costs on breakeven and target profit volumes.

EXHIBIT 7-7 The Effect of Changes in Fixed Costs on Breakeven and Target Profit Volumes

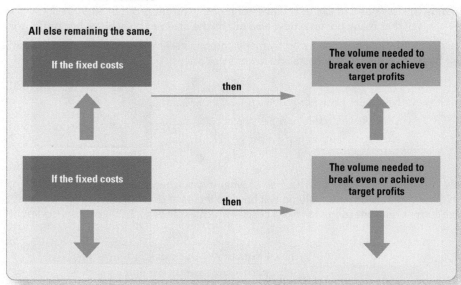

We have seen that changes in sales prices, variable costs, and fixed costs can have dramatic effects on the volume of product that companies must sell to achieve breakeven and target profits. Companies often turn to automation to decrease variable costs (direct labor); but this, in turn, increases their fixed costs (equipment depreciation). Companies often move production overseas to decrease variable and fixed production costs, feeling forced to take these measures to keep their prices as low as their competitors. For example, Charbroil, the maker of gas grills, said that if it didn't move production overseas, profits would decline, or worse yet, the company would go out of business.

STOP & THINK

Kay has been considering advertising as a means to increase her sales volume. Kay could spend an extra $3,500 per month on website banner ads. How many *extra* posters would Kay have to sell *just to pay for the advertising?* (Use Kay's original data.)

Answer: Instead of using *all* of Kay's fixed costs, we can isolate *just* the fixed costs relating to advertising. This will allow us to figure out how many *extra* posters Kay would have to sell each month to break even on (or pay for) the advertising cost. Advertising is a fixed cost, so Kay's contribution margin remains $14 per unit.

$$\text{Sales in units} = \frac{\text{Fixed expenses} + \text{Operating income}}{\text{Contribution margin per unit}}$$

$$= \frac{\$3,500 + \$0}{\$14.00}$$

$$= 250 \text{ posters}$$

Kay must sell 250 *extra* posters each month just to pay for the cost of advertising. If she sells fewer than 250 extra posters, she'll increase her volume but lose money on the advertising. If she sells more than 250 extra posters, her plan will have worked—she'll increase her volume *and* her profit.

Sustainability and CVP

Sustainability initiatives can have a significant bearing on the cost information used in CVP analysis. For example, Coca-Cola[1], a recognized leader in corporate sustainability, has been able to reduce the size of the cap on its PET plastic bottles by 38%, saving 40 million pounds of plastic annually in the U.S. alone. The company has also reduced the PET in its Coke and Dasani bottles by 23% and 35%, respectively. In addition to *reducing* the PET content, the company has *increased* the percentage of recycled plastic used in these containers. The company is also working to reduce the amount of water needed for each unit of its product. As a result of these initiatives, the variable cost of packaging each unit of product has decreased. For example, the company reports that its new ultra glass contour bottle is not only 40% stronger and 20% lighter, but also 10% cheaper to produce than its traditional contour bottle.

Coca-Cola's redesign of product packaging has had favorable environmental and financial ramifications. For example, the new ultra glass contour bottle has reduced annual CO_2 emissions by an amount equivalent to planting 8,000 acres of trees. From a financial standpoint, the 10% variable cost savings on the ultra glass contour design results in a 10% increase in each bottle's contribution margin. As a result, one might assume that Coca-Cola needs to sell fewer units of product to achieve its target profit. However, keep in mind that the company had to incur many fixed costs to research, develop and design these new bottles. In addition, they probably had to invest in new production equipment to handle the new packaging design.

As the Coca-Cola example shows, sustainability initiatives often result in both cost savings *and* additional costs. These costs and cost savings may be fixed or variable in nature. Managers use CVP analysis to determine how these initiatives will impact the volume needed to achieve the company's operating income goals.

See Exercises E7-25A and E7-49B

[1]The Coca-Cola Company website. www.thecoca-colacompany.com/citizenship/package_design.html Section on Sustainable Packaging. Subsection: Reduce

Changing the Mix of Products Offered for Sale

4 Find breakeven and target profit volumes for multiproduct companies

So far, we have assumed that Kay sold only one size poster. What would happen if she offered different types of products? Companies that sell more than one product must consider their *sales mix* when performing CVP analysis. All else being equal, a company earns more income by selling high-contribution margin products than by selling an equal number of low-contribution margin products.

The same CVP formulas that are used to perform CVP analysis for a company with a single product can be used for any company that sells more than one product. However, the formulas use the *weighted-average contribution margin* of all products, rather than the contribution margin of a sole product. Each unit's contribution margin is *weighted* by the relative number of units sold. As before, the company can find the breakeven or the target profit volume in terms of units, or in terms of sales revenue. We'll consider each in turn.

Multiproduct Company: Finding Breakeven in Terms of Sales Units

Suppose Kay plans to sell two types of posters. In addition to her regular-size posters, Kay plans to sell large posters. Let's assume that none of Kay's original costs have changed. Exhibit 7-8 shows that each regular poster will continue to generate $14 of contribution margin, while each large poster will generate $30 of contribution margin. Kay is adding the large-poster line because it carries a higher unit contribution margin.

EXHIBIT 7-8 Calculating the Weighted-Average Contribution Margin per Unit

	Regular Posters	Large Posters	Total
Sales price per unit	$ 35	$ 70	
Less: Variable cost per unit	(21)	(40)	
Contribution margin per unit	$ 14	$ 30	
Sales mix	× 5	× 3	8
Contribution margin	$ 70	$ 90	$160
Weighted-average contribution margin per unit ($160/8)			$ 20

For every five regular posters sold, Kay expects to sell three large posters. In other words, she expects 5/8 of the sales to be regular posters and 3/8 to be large posters. This is a 5:3 sales mix. Exhibit 7-8 shows how Kay uses this expected sales mix to find the weighted-average contribution margin per unit.

Notice that none of Kay's products actually generates $20 of contribution margin. However, if the sales mix is 5:3, as expected, it is *as if* the contribution margin is $20 per unit. Once Kay has computed the weighted-average contribution margin per unit, she uses it in the shortcut formula to determine the total number of posters that would need to be sold to break even:

$$\text{Sales in total units} = \frac{\text{Fixed expenses} + \text{Operating income}}{\text{Weighted-average contribution margin per unit}}$$

$$= \frac{\$7,000 + \$0}{\$20}$$

$$= 350 \text{ posters}$$

In total, Kay must sell 350 posters to breakeven. However, this is only the case if 5/8 of those sold are regular posters and 3/8 are large posters. Therefore, we must take still figure out how many of *each type* of poster must be sold to breakeven.

As a final step, Kay splits the total number of posters into the regular and large sizes using the same sales mix ratios she assumed previously:

Breakeven sales of regular posters (350 × 5/8)..................... <u>218.75</u> regular posters
Breakeven sales of large posters (350 × 3/8) .... <u>131.25</u> large posters

As is often the case in real situations, these computations don't yield round numbers. Because Kay cannot sell partial posters, she must sell 219 regular posters and 132 large posters to avoid a loss. Using these rounded numbers would lead to a small rounding error in our check figures, however, so the rest of our computations will use the exact results: 218.75 regular posters and 131.25 large posters.

If Kay wants, she can now use the number of units to find her breakeven point in terms of sales revenue (amounts rounded to the nearest dollar):

218.75 regular posters at $35 each.................... $ 7,656
131.25 large posters at $70 each...................... 9,188
Total revenues $16,844

We can prove this breakeven point as follows:

	Total
Contribution margin:	
Regular posters (218.75 × $14).................	$ 3,063
Large posters (131.25 × $30)	3,937
Contribution margin	$ 7,000
Less: Fixed expenses...	(7,000)
Operating income...	$ 0

We just found Kay's *breakeven* point, but Kay can also use the same steps to calculate the number of units she must sell to achieve a target profit. The only difference, as before, is that she would use *target profit*, rather than *zero*, as the operating income in the short-cut formula.

STOP & THINK

Suppose Kay would still like to earn a monthly profit of $4,900. Recall that she needed to sell 850 posters to achieve this profit level when she was selling only regular posters. If her sales mix is 5:3, as planned, will she need to sell *more than* or *fewer than* 850 posters to achieve her target profit? Why?

Answer: Kay will need to sell *fewer* than 850 posters because she is now selling some large posters that have a higher unit contribution margin. We can verify this as follows:

$$\text{Sales in total units} = \frac{\text{Fixed expenses} + \text{Operating income}}{\text{Weighted-average contribution margin per unit}}$$

$$= \frac{\$7,000 + \$0}{\$20}$$

$$= 350 \text{ posters}$$

Kay would have to sell a *total* of 595 posters—372 regular posters (595 × 5/8) and 223 large posters (595 × 3/8)—to achieve her target profit.

Multiproduct Company: Finding Breakeven in Terms of Sales Revenue

Companies that offer hundreds or thousands of products (such as WalMart and Amazon.com) will not want to find the breakeven point in terms of units. Rather, they'll want to know breakeven (or target profit volumes) in terms of sales revenue. To find this sales volume, the company needs to know, or estimate, its weighted-average contribution margin ratio. If a company prepares contribution margin income statements, it easily calculates the contribution margin ratio by dividing the total contribution margin by total sales. The contribution margin ratio is *already* weighted by the company's *actual* sales mix! The following "Stop and Think" illustrates how Amazon.com would use this approach to calculating breakeven.

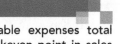

STOP & THINK

Suppose Amazon.com's total sales revenue is $4.50 billion, its variable expenses total $3.15 billion, and its fixed expenses total $1.1 billion. What is the breakeven point in sales revenue?

Answer: First, Amazon computes its total contribution margin:

Sales revenue..................................	$4.50 billion
Less: Variable expenses	3.15 billion
Contribution margin	$1.35 billion

Now Amazon is able to compute its overall contribution margin ratio, which is already weighted by the company's actual sales mix: $1.35 billion ÷ 4.50 billion = 30%.

Finally, Amazon uses the contribution margin ratio in the shortcut formula to predict the breakeven point:

$$\text{Sales in dollars} = \frac{\text{Fixed expenses} + \text{Operating income}}{\text{Contribution margin ratio}}$$

$$= \frac{\$1.1 \text{ billion} + \$0}{0.30}$$

$$= \$3.667 \text{ billion (rounded)}$$

Amazon.com must achieve sales revenue of $3.667 billion just to break even.

Unlike Amazon, Kay's business to this point has been limited to a sole product (regular posters), which had a 40% contribution margin ratio. Once Kay starts selling large posters in addition to the regular posters, her overall weighted-average contribution margin ratio will change. Recall that Kay expects to sell five regular posters for every three large posters. Exhibit 7-9 shows how Kay weights the individual contribution margins and sales revenue, using the anticipated sales mix, to arrive at her anticipated weighted-average contribution margin ratio for this particular sales mix:

EXHIBIT 7-9 Estimating the Weighted-Average Contribution Margin Ratio

Expected contribution margin:		
Regular posters (5 × $14)	$ 70	
Large posters (3 × $30)	$ 90	
Expected contribution margin		$160
Divided by expected sales revenue:		
Regular posters (5 × $35)	$175	
Large posters (3 × $70)	$210	
Expected sales revenue		÷ 385
Weighted-average contribution margin ratio		= 41.558%

Notice how Kay's weighted-average contribution margin ratio (41.558%) will be higher than it was when she sold only regular posters (40%). That's because she expects to sell some large posters that have a 42.9% contribution margin ratio ($30/$70) in addition to the regular-sized posters. Because her sales mix is changing, she now has a different contribution margin ratio.

Once Kay knows her weighted-average contribution margin ratio, she can use the shortcut formula to estimate breakeven in terms of sales revenue:

$$\text{Sales in dollars} = \frac{\text{Fixed expenses} + \text{Operating income}}{\text{Contribution margin ratio}}$$

$$= \frac{\$7,000 + \$0}{0.41558}$$

$$= \$16,844 \text{ (rounded)}$$

Notice that this is the same breakeven point in sales revenue we found earlier by first finding breakeven in *units*. Kay could also use the formula to find the total sales revenue she would need to meet her target monthly operating income of $4,900.

If Kay's actual sales mix is not five regular posters to three large posters, her actual operating income will differ from the projected amount. The sales mix greatly influences the breakeven point. When companies offer more than one product, they do not have a unique breakeven point. Every sales mix assumption leads to a different breakeven point.

STOP & THINK

Suppose Kay plans to sell 800 total posters in the 5:3 sales mix (500 regular posters and 300 large posters). She actually does sell 800 posters—375 regular and 425 large. The sale prices per poster, variable costs per poster, and fixed expenses are exactly as predicted. Without doing any computations, is Kay's actual operating income greater than, less than, or equal to her expected income?

Answer: Kay's actual sales mix did not turn out to be the 5:3 mix she expected. She actually sold more of the higher-margin large posters than the lower-margin regular posters. This favorable change in the sales mix causes her to earn a higher operating income than she expected.

Information Technology and Sensitivity Analysis

We have just seen that Kay's breakeven point and target profit volumes are very sensitive to changes in her business environment, including changes in sales prices, variable costs, fixed costs, and sales mix assumptions. Information technology allows managers to perform a wide array of sensitivity analyses before committing to decisions. Managers of small- to medium-sized companies use Excel spreadsheets to perform sensitivity analyses like those we just did for Kay. Spreadsheets allow managers to estimate how one change (or several simultaneous changes) affects business operations. Managers also use spreadsheet software to create CVP graphs like the one in Exhibit 7-4.

Many large companies use sophisticated enterprise resource planning (ERP) software such as SAP and Oracle to provide detailed data for CVP analysis. For example, after Sears stores lock their doors at 9 P.M., records for each individual transaction flow into a massive database. From a DieHard battery sold in Texas to a Trader Bay polo shirt sold in New Hampshire, the system compiles an average of 1.5 million transactions a day. With the click of a mouse, managers access sales price, variable cost, and sales volume for individual products to conduct breakeven or profit planning analyses.

What are Some Common Indicators of Risk?

A company's level of risk depends on many factors, including the general health of the economy and the specific industry in which the company operates. In addition, a firm's risk depends on its current volume of sales and the relative amount of fixed and variable costs that make up its total costs. Next, we discuss how a firm can gauge its level of risk, to some extent, by its margin of safety and its operating leverage.

Margin of Safety

The **margin of safety** is the excess of actual or expected sales over breakeven sales. This is the "cushion," or drop in sales, the company can absorb without incurring a loss. The higher the margin of safety, the greater the cushion against loss and the less risky the business plan. Managers use the margin of safety to evaluate the risk of current operations as well as the risk of new plans.

Let's continue to assume that Kay has been in business for several months and that she generally sells 950 posters a month. Kay's breakeven point in our original data is 500 posters. Kay can express her margin of safety in units, as follows:

$$
\begin{aligned}
\text{Margin of safety in units} &= \text{Expected sales in units} - \text{Breakeven sales in units} \\
&= \quad\quad 950 \text{ posters} \quad\quad - \quad\quad 500 \text{ posters} \\
&= \quad\quad 450 \text{ posters}
\end{aligned}
$$

Kay can also express her margin of safety in sales revenue (sales dollars):

$$
\begin{aligned}
\text{Margin of safety in dollars} &= \text{Expected sales in dollars} - \text{Breakeven sales in dollars} \\
&= \quad (950 \text{ posters} \times \$35) \quad - (500 \text{ posters} \times \$35) \\
&= \quad\quad\quad \$33{,}250 \quad\quad\quad - \quad\quad\quad \$17{,}500 \\
&= \quad\quad\quad \$15{,}750
\end{aligned}
$$

Sales would have to drop by more than 450 posters, or $15,750 a month, before Kay incurs a loss. This is a fairly comfortable margin.

Managers can also compute the margin of safety as a percentage of sales. Simply divide the margin of safety by sales. We obtain the same percentage whether we use units or dollars.

In units:

$$
\begin{aligned}
\text{Margin of safety as a percentage} &= \frac{\text{Margin of safety in units}}{\text{Expected sales in units}} \\
&= \frac{450 \text{ posters}}{950 \text{ posters}} \\
&= 47.4\% \text{ (rounded)}
\end{aligned}
$$

In dollars:

$$
\begin{aligned}
\text{Margin of safety as a percentage} &= \frac{\text{Margin of safety in dollars}}{\text{Expected sales in dollars}} \\
&= \frac{\$15{,}750}{\$33{,}250} \\
&= 47.4\% \text{ (rounded)}
\end{aligned}
$$

5 Determine a firm's margin of safety, operating leverage, and most profitable cost structure

Accounting Simplified

Risk Measurement

If your instructor is using MyAccountingLab, go to the Multimedia Library for a quick video on this topic.

The margin of safety percentage tells Kay that sales would have to drop by more than 47.4% before she would incur a loss. If sales fall by less than 47.4%, she would still earn a profit. If sales fall exactly 47.4%, she would break even. This ratio tells Kay that her business plan is not unduly risky.

Operating Leverage

A company's <u>operating leverage</u> refers to the relative amount of fixed and variable costs that make up its total costs. Most companies have both fixed and variable costs. However, companies with *high* operating leverage have *relatively more fixed costs* and relatively fewer variable costs. Companies with high operating leverage include golf courses, airlines, and hotels. Because they have fewer variable costs, their contribution margin ratio is relatively high. Recall from the last chapter that Embassy Suites' variable cost of servicing each guest is low, which means that the hotel has a high contribution margin ratio and high operating leverage.

What does high operating leverage have to do with risk? If sales volume decreases, the total contribution margin will drop significantly because each sales dollar contains a high percentage of contribution margin. Yet, the high fixed costs of running the company remain. Therefore, the operating income of these companies can easily turn from profit to loss if sales volume declines. For example, airlines were financially devastated after September 11, 2001, because the number of people flying suddenly dropped, creating large reductions in contribution margin. Yet, the airlines had to continue paying their high fixed costs. High operating leverage companies are at *more* risk because their income declines drastically when sales volume declines.

Why is this important?

"The margin of safety and **operating leverage** help managers understand their **risk** if **volume** decreases due to a recession, **competition,** or other **changes** in the **marketplace**."

What if the economy is growing and sales volume *increases*? High operating leverage companies will reap high rewards. Remember that after breakeven, each unit sold contributes its unit contribution margin directly to profit. Because high operating leverage companies have high contribution margin ratios, each additional dollar of sales will contribute more to the firm's operating income. Exhibit 7-10 summarizes these characteristics.

EXHIBIT 7-10 Characteristics of High Operating Leverage Firms

- High operating leverage companies have the following:
    - —*Higher* levels of fixed costs and *lower* levels of variable costs
    - —*Higher* contribution margin ratios
- For high operating leverage companies, changes in volume significantly affect operating income, so they face the following:
    - —*Higher* risk
    - —*Higher* potential for reward
  Examples include golf courses, hotels, rental car agencies, theme parks, airlines, cruise lines, etc.

However, companies with low operating leverage have relatively *fewer* fixed costs and relatively *more* variable costs. As a result, they have much lower contribution margin ratios. For example, retailers incur significant levels of fixed costs, but more of every sales dollar is used to pay for the merchandise (a variable cost), so less ends up as contribution margin. If sales volume declines, these companies have relatively fewer fixed costs to cover, so they are at *less* risk of incurring a loss. If sales volume increases, their relatively small contribution margins ratios add to the bottom line, but in smaller increments. Therefore, they reap less reward than high operating leverage companies experiencing the same volume increases. *In other words, at low operating leverage companies, changes in sales volume do not have as much impact on operating income as they do at high operating leverage companies.* Exhibit 7-11 summarizes these characteristics.

EXHIBIT 7-11 Characteristics of Low Operating Leverage Firms

- Low operating leverage companies have the following:
    —*Higher* levels of variable costs and *lower* levels of fixed costs
    —*Lower* contribution margin ratios
- For low operating leverage companies, changes in volume do NOT have as significant an effect on operating income, so they face the following:
    —*Lower* risk
    —*Lower* potential for reward

Examples include merchandising companies and fast-food restaurants.

A company's **operating leverage factor** tells us how responsive a company's operating income is to changes in volume. The greater the operating leverage factor, the greater the impact a change in sales volume has on operating income.

The operating leverage factor, *at a given level of sales*, is calculated as follows:

$$\text{Operating leverage factor} = \frac{\text{Contribution margin}}{\text{Operating income}}$$

Why do we say, "at a given level of sales"? A company's operating leverage factor will depend, to some extent, on the sales level used to calculate the contribution margin and operating income. Most companies compute the operating leverage factor at their current or expected volume of sales, which is what we'll do in our examples.

What does the operating leverage factor tell us?

The operating leverage factor, at a given level of sales, indicates the percentage change in operating income that will occur from a 1% change in volume. In other words, it tells us how responsive a company's operating income is to changes in volume.

The *lowest* possible value for this factor is 1, which occurs only if the company has *no* fixed costs (an *extremely low* operating leverage company). *For a minute, let's assume that Kay has no fixed costs.* Given this scenario, her unit contribution margin ($14 per poster) contributes directly to profit because she has no fixed costs to cover. In addition, she has *no* risk. The worst she can do is break even, and that will occur only if she doesn't sell any posters. Let's continue to assume that she generally sells 950 posters a month, so this will be the level of sales at which we calculate the operating leverage factor:

Sales revenue (950 posters × $35/poster)	$ 33,250
Less: Variable expenses (950 posters × $21/poster)	(19,950)
Contribution margin (950 posters × $14/poster)	$ 13,300
Less: Fixed expenses	(0)
Operating income	$ 13,300

Her operating leverage factor is as follows:

$$\text{Operating leverage factor} = \frac{\$13,300}{\$13,300}$$
$$= 1$$

What does this tell us?

- If Kay's volume changes by 1%, her operating income will change by 1% (= 1% × a factor of 1).
- If Kay's volume changes by 15%, her operating income will change by 15% (= 15% × a factor of 1).

Let's now see what happens if we assume, as usual, that Kay's fixed expenses are $7,000. We'll once again calculate the operating leverage factor given Kay's current level of sales (950 posters per month):

Contribution margin (950 posters × $14/poster)	$13,300
Less: Fixed expenses...	(7,000)
Operating income...	$ 6,300

Now that we have once again assumed that Kay's fixed expenses are $7,000, her operating leverage factor is as follows:

$$\text{Operating leverage factor} = \frac{\$13,300}{\$6,300}$$
$$= 2.11 \text{ (rounded)}$$

Notice that her operating leverage factor is *higher* (2.11 versus 1) when she has *more* fixed costs ($7,000 versus $0). Kay's operating leverage factor of 2.11 tells us how responsive her income is to changes in volume.

- If Kay's volume changes by 1%, her operating income will change by 2.11% (= 1% × a factor of 2.11).
- If Kay's volume changes by 15%, her operating income will change by 31.65% (= 15% × a factor of 2.11).

Managers use the firm's operating leverage factor to determine how vulnerable their operating income is to changes in sales volume—both positive and negative.

> The larger the operating leverage factor is, the greater the impact a change in sales volume has on operating income. This is true for both increases *and* decreases in volume.

Therefore, companies with higher operating leverage factors are particularly vulnerable to changes in volume. In other words, they have *both* higher risk of incurring losses if volume declines *and* higher potential reward if volume increases. Hoping to capitalize on the reward side, many companies have intentionally increased their operating leverage by lowering their variable costs while at the same time increasing their fixed costs. This strategy works well during periods of economic growth but can be detrimental when sales volume declines.

Choosing a Cost Structure

Managers often have some control over how the company's costs are structured—as fixed, variable, or a combination of the two. For example, let's assume that in addition to selling posters online, Kay has decided to lease a small retail kiosk at the local mall. To keep things simple, let's assume Kay will only be selling her regular-size posters, which sell for $35 each. Let's also assume the mall leasing agent has given Kay the following two options for leasing the space:

- Option 1: Pay $300 per month plus 10% of the sales revenue generated at the kiosk.
- Option 2: Pay $1,000 per month.

Which option should Kay choose? The answer depends on how many posters Kay thinks she will sell from the kiosk each month. As we see above, Option 1 has fewer fixed costs and more variable costs than Option 2. Thus, Kay's operating leverage would be lower under Option 1 than under Option 2. As a result, Option 1 carries less financial risk if sales volume is low, but less financial reward if sales volume is high. But how high must sales volume be to make Option 2 the better choice?

To answer this question Kay will need to figure out her **indifference point,** the point at which she would be indifferent between the two options because they both would result in the same total cost. Once Kay knows the indifference point, she can better judge which option is preferable. Let's see how this is done.

First, Kay calculates the variable and fixed costs associated with each option, as shown in Exhibit 7-12. Notice that Kay does not need to consider any of her other business expenses (such as the cost of the posters themselves or the website maintenance costs), because they will not differ between the two leasing options. In deciding which lease option to take, Kay only needs to consider those costs that are associated with the lease.

EXHIBIT 7-12 Costs associated with each leasing option

	Option 1	Option 2
Variable cost component:		
10% of sales revenue (= 10% × $35 per poster)	$3.50 per poster	-0-
Fixed Cost component:	$300	$1,000

Next, Kay develops an equation in which she sets the cost of each leasing option equal to the other. She then fills in the appropriate information and solves for number of units:

Costs under Option 1	=	Costs under Option 2

Variable Costs + Fixed Costs = Variable Costs + Fixed Costs

(# Units × Variable cost per unit) + Fixed Costs = (# Units × Variable cost per unit) + Fixed Costs

(# Units × $3.50) + $300 = (# Units × $0) + $1,000

(# Units × $3.50) = $700

Units = 200

Based on this analysis, Kay will be *indifferent* between the two leasing options if she sells *exactly* 200 posters per month at the kiosk. At a volume of 200 units, she would pay $1,000 for the lease under Option 1 [(200 × $3.50) + $300 = $1,000] and $1,000 for the lease under Option 2. Both options would result in the same cost.

But what if sales volume is lower or higher than 200 posters per month? As shown in Exhibit 7-13, Kay will prefer the lower operating leverage alternative (Option 1) if she sells *fewer* than 200 posters a month. However, she will prefer the higher operating leverage alternative (Option 2) if she sells *more* than 200 posters a month. Her decision will be based on whether she expect sales volume to be lower, or higher, than the indifference point.

EXHIBIT 7-13 Using an indifference point to choose the most profitable cost structure

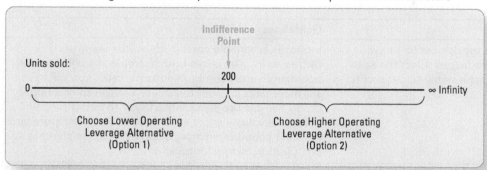

We can verify the conclusion presented in Exhibit 7-13 by calculating the lease costs at *any* volume of sales. First, let's assume that Kay expects to sell 100 posters a month at the kiosk. The lease cost under each option is calculated as follows:

Lease cost under Option 1: $300 + [10% × (100 units × $35 sales price)] = **$650**

Lease cost under Option 2: **$1,000**

As expected, when the sales volume is *lower* than the indifference point, the lease cost is lower under Option 1 than under Option 2.

Next, let's assume Kay expects to sell 500 posters a month. The lease cost is calculated as follows:

Lease cost under Option 1: $300 + [10% × (500 units × $35 sales price)] = **$2,050**

Lease cost under Option 2: **$1,000**

As expected, when the sales volume is *higher* than the indifference point, the lease cost is lower under Option 2 than under Option 1.

The following rule of thumb summarizes the conclusions presented in Exhibit 7-13:

*When faced with a choice between cost structures, choose the **lower** operating leverage option when sales volume is expected to be **lower** than the indifference point. Choose the **higher** operating leverage option when sales volume is expected to be **higher** than the indifference point.*

Managers can use this rule of thumb whenever they are faced with choices about how to structure their costs.

In this chapter, we have discussed how managers use the contribution margin and CVP analysis to predict profits, determine the volume needed to achieve breakeven or a target profit, and assess how changes in the business environment affect their profits. In the next chapter, we look at several types of short-term decisions managers must make. Cost behavior and the contribution margin will continue to play an important role in these decisions.

Decision Guidelines

CVP Analysis

Your friend opened an ice cream parlor. But now she's facing changing business conditions. She needs help making the following decisions:

Decision	Guidelines
The cost of ice cream is rising, yet my competitors have lowered their prices. How will these factors affect the sales volume I'll need to break even or achieve my target profit?	Increases in variable costs (such as ice cream) and decreases in sales prices both decrease the unit contribution margin and contribution margin ratio. You will have to sell more units in order to achieve breakeven or a target profit. You can use sensitivity analysis to better pinpoint the actual volume you'll need to sell. Simply compute your new unit contribution margin and use it in the shortcut unit contribution margin formula.
Would it help if I could renegotiate my lease with the landlord?	Decreases in fixed costs do not affect the firm's contribution margin. However, a decrease in fixed costs means that the company will have to sell fewer units to achieve breakeven or a target profit. Increases in fixed costs have the opposite effect.
I've been thinking about selling other products in addition to ice cream. Will this affect the sales volume I'll need to earn my target profit?	Your contribution margin ratio will change as a result of changing your sales mix. A company earns more income by selling higher-margin products than by selling an equal number of lower-margin products. If you can shift sales toward higher contribution margin products, you will have to sell fewer units to reach your target profit.
If the economy takes a downturn, how much risk do I face of incurring a loss?	The margin of safety indicates how far sales volume can decline before you would incur a loss: Margin of safety = Expected sales − Breakeven sales The operating leverage factor indicates the percentage change in operating income that will occur from a 1% change in volume. It tells you how sensitive your company's operating income is to changes in volume. At a given level of sales, the operating leverage factor is as follows: $$\text{Operating leverage factor} = \frac{\text{Contribution margin}}{\text{Operating income}}$$
If given a choice between alternative cost structures, how do I choose the most profitable one?	Choose the *lower* operating leverage option when sales volume is expected to be *lower* than the indifference point. Choose the *higher* operating leverage option when sales volume is expected to be *higher* than the indifference point.
How do I find the indifference point?	The indifference point is found by setting the total costs of one option equal to the total costs of another option, and then solving for the volume that equates the two options.

SUMMARY PROBLEM **2**

Recall from Summary Problem 1 that Fleet Foot buys hiking socks for $6 a pair and sells them for $10. Monthly fixed costs are $10,000 (for sales volumes between 0 and 12,000 pairs), resulting in a breakeven point of 2,500 units. Assume that Fleet Foot has been selling 8,000 pairs of socks per month.

Requirements

1. What is Fleet Foot's current margin of safety in units, in sales dollars, and as a percentage? Explain the results.

2. At this level of sales, what is Fleet Foot's operating leverage factor? If volume declines by 25% due to increasing competition, by what percentage will the company's operating income decline?

3. Competition has forced Fleet Foot to lower its sales price to $9 a pair. How will this affect Fleet's breakeven point?

4. To compensate for the lower sales price, Fleet Foot wants to expand its product line to include men's dress socks. Each pair will sell for $7.00 and cost $2.75 from the supplier. Fixed costs will not change. Fleet expects to sell four pairs of dress socks for every one pair of hiking socks (at its new $9 sales price). What is Fleet's weighted-average contribution margin per unit? Given the 4:1 sales mix, how many of each type of sock will it need to sell to break even?

▪ SOLUTIONS

Requirement 1

$$\text{Margin of safety in units} = \text{Expected sales in units} - \text{Breakeven sales in units}$$
$$= \quad 8{,}000 \quad\quad - \quad\quad 2{,}500$$
$$= \quad 5{,}500 \text{ units}$$

$$\text{Margin of safety in dollars} = \text{Expected sales in dollars} - \text{Breakeven sales in dollars}$$
$$= \quad (8{,}000 \times \$10) \quad - \quad (2{,}500 \times \$10)$$
$$= \quad \$55{,}000$$

$$\text{Margin of safety as a percentage} = \frac{\text{Margin of safety in units}}{\text{Expected sales in units}}$$
$$= \frac{5{,}500 \text{ pairs}}{8{,}000 \text{ pairs}}$$
$$= \quad 68.75\%$$

Fleet Foot's margin of safety is quite high. Sales have to fall by more than 5,500 units (or $55,000) before Fleet incurs a loss. Fleet will continue to earn a profit unless sales drop by more than 68.75%.

Requirement 2

At its current level of volume, Fleet's operating income is as follows:

Contribution margin (8,000 pairs × $4/pair).....................	$ 32,000
Less: Fixed expenses..	(10,000)
Operating income...	$ 22,000

Fleet's operating leverage factor at this level of sales is computed as follows:

$$\text{Operating leverage factor} = \frac{\text{Contribution margin}}{\text{Operating income}}$$

$$= \frac{\$32,000}{\$22,000}$$

$$= 1.45 \text{ (rounded)}$$

If sales volume declines by 25%, operating income will decline by 36.25% (Fleet's operating leverage factor of 1.45 multiplied by 25%).

Requirement 3

If Fleet drops its sales price to $9 per pair, its contribution margin per pair declines to $3 (sales price of $9 – variable cost of $6). Each sale contributes less toward covering fixed costs. Fleet's new breakeven point *increases* to 3,334 pairs of socks ($10,000 fixed costs ÷ $3 unit contribution margin).

Requirement 4

	Hiking Socks	Dress Socks	Total
Sales price per unit	$ 9.00	$ 7.00	
Deduct: Variable expense per unit......................................	(6.00)	(2.75)	
Contribution margin per unit...	$ 3.00	$ 4.25	
Sales mix	× 1	× 4	5
Contribution margin	$ 3.00	$17.00	$20.00
Weighted-average contribution margin per unit ($20/5)......			$ 4.00

$$\text{Sales in total units} = \frac{\text{Fixed expenses} + \text{Operating income}}{\text{Weighted-average contribution margin per unit}}$$

$$= \frac{\$10,000 + \$0}{\$4}$$

$$= 2,500 \text{ pairs of socks}$$

Breakeven sales of dress socks (2,500 × 4/5)......................	2,000 pairs dress socks
Breakeven sales of hiking socks (2,500 × 1/5)....................	500 pairs hiking socks

By expanding its product line to include higher-margin dress socks, Fleet is able to decrease its breakeven point back to its original level (2,500 pairs). However, to achieve this breakeven point, Fleet must sell the planned ratio of four pairs of dress socks to every one pair of hiking socks.

Learning Objectives

■ 1 Calculate the unit contribution margin and the contribution margin ratio

■ 2 Use CVP analysis to find breakeven points and target profit volumes

■ 3 Perform sensitivity analysis in response to changing business conditions

■ 4 Find breakeven and target profit volumes for multiproduct companies

■ 5 Determine a firm's margin of safety, operating leverage, and most profitable cost structure

Accounting Vocabulary

Breakeven Point. (p. 400) The sales level at which operating income is zero: Total revenues = Total expenses.

Contribution Margin. (p. 397) Sales revenue minus variable expenses.

Contribution Margin Income Statement. (p. 397) An income statement that groups costs by behavior rather than function; it can be used only by internal management.

Contribution Margin Per Unit. (p. 397) The excess of the unit sales price over the variable cost per unit; also called unit contribution margin.

Contribution Margin Ratio. (p. 398) Ratio of contribution margin to sales revenue.

Cost-Volume-Profit (CVP) Analysis. (p. 396) Expresses the relationships among costs, volume, and profit or loss.

Indifference Point. (p. 424) The volume of sales at which a company would be indifferent between

alternative cost structures because they would result in the same total cost.

Margin of Safety. (p. 420) Excess of expected sales over breakeven sales; the drop in sales a company can absorb without incurring an operating loss.

Operating Leverage. (p. 421) The relative amount of fixed and variable costs that make up a firm's total costs.

Operating Leverage Factor. (p. 422) At a given level of sales, the contribution margin divided by operating income; the operating leverage factor indicates the percentage change in operating income that will occur from a 1% change in sales volume.

Sales Mix. (p. 397) The combination of products that make up total sales.

Sensitivity Analysis. (p. 411) A "what-if" technique that asks what results will be if actual prices or costs change or if an underlying assumption changes.

MyAccountingLab   Go to http://myaccountinglab.com/ for the following Quick Check, Short Exercises, Exercises, and Problems. They are available with immediate grading, explanations of correct and incorrect answers, and interactive media that acts as your own online tutor.

Quick Check

1. *(Learning Objective 1)* When a company is operating at its breakeven point,
   a. its selling price will be equal to its variable expense per unit.
   b. its contribution margin will be equal to its variable expenses.
   c. its fixed expenses will be equal to its variable expenses.
   d. its total revenues will be equal to its total expenses.

2. *(Learning Objective 1)* If a company sells one unit above its breakeven sales volume, then its operating income would be equal to
   a. the unit selling price.
   b. the unit contribution margin.
   c. the fixed expenses.
   d. zero.

3. *(Learning Objective 2)* How is the unit sales volume necessary to reach a target profit calculated?
   a. Target profit / unit contribution margin
   b. Target profit / contribution margin ratio
   c. (Fixed expenses + target profit)/unit contribution margin
   d. (Fixed expenses + target profit)/contribution margin ratio

4. *(Learning Objective 2)* The number of units to be sold to reach a certain target profit is calculated as
   a. target profit / unit contribution margin.
   b. target profit / contribution margin ratio.
   c. (fixed expenses + target profit)/unit contribution margin.
   d. (fixed expenses + target profit)/contribution margin ratio.

5. *(Learning Objective 3)* The breakeven point on a CVP graph is
   a. the intersection of the sales revenue line and the total expense line.
   b. the intersection of the fixed expense line and the total expense line.
   c. the intersection of the fixed expense line and the sales revenue.
   d. the intersection of the sales revenue line and the y-axis.

6. *(Learning Objective 3)* If the sales price of a product increases while everything else remains the same, what happens to the breakeven point?
   a. The breakeven point will increase.
   b. The breakeven point will decrease.
   c. The breakeven point will remain the same.
   d. The effect cannot be determined without further information.

7. *(Learning Objective 4)* Target profit analysis is used to calculate the sales volume that is needed to
   a. cover all fixed expenses.
   b. cover all expenses.
   c. avoid a loss.
   d. earn a specific amount of net operating income.

8. *(Learning Objective 4)* A shift in the sales mix from a product with a high contribution margin ratio toward a product with a low contribution margin ratio will cause the breakeven point to
   a. increase.
   b. decrease.
   c. remain the same.
   d. increase or decrease, but the direction of change cannot be determined from the information given.

9. *(Learning Objective 5)* If the degree of operating leverage is 3, then a 2% change in the number of units sold should result in a 6% change in
   a. sales.
   b. variable expense.
   c. unit contribution margin.
   d. operating income.

10. *(Learning Objective 5)* What is the margin of safety?
    a. The amount of fixed and variable costs that make up a company's total costs
    b. The difference between the sales price per unit and the variable cost per unit
    c. The excess of expected sales over breakeven sales
    d. The sales level at which operating income is zero

Quick Check Answers

1.d 2.b 3.c 4.c 5.a 6.b 7.d 8.a 9.d 10.c

Short Exercises

Luxury Cruiseline Data Set used for S7-1 through S7-12:

Luxury Cruiseline offers nightly dinner cruises off the coast of Miami, San Francisco, and Seattle. Dinner cruise tickets sell for $120 per passenger. Luxury Cruiseline's variable cost of providing the dinner is $48 per passenger, and the fixed cost of operating the vessels (depreciation, salaries, docking fees, and other expenses) is $270,000 per month. The company's relevant range extends to 15,000 monthly passengers.

S7-1 Compute unit contribution margin and contribution margin ratio
(Learning Objective 1)

Use the information from the Luxury Cruiseline Data Set to compute the following:
a. What is the contribution margin per passenger?
b. What is the contribution margin ratio?
c. Use the unit contribution margin to project operating income if monthly sales total 10,000 passengers.
d. Use the contribution margin ratio to project operating income if monthly sales revenue totals $650,000.

S7-2 Project change in income *(Learning Objective 1)*

Use the information from the Luxury Cruiseline Data Set. If Luxury Cruiseline sells an additional 300 tickets, by what amount will its operating income increase (or operating loss decrease)?

S7-3 Find breakeven *(Learning Objective 2)*

Use the information from the Luxury Cruiseline Data Set to compute the number of dinner cruise tickets it must sell to break even and the sales dollars needed to break even.

S7-4 Find target profit volume *(Learning Objective 2)*

Use the information from the Luxury Cruiseline Data Set. If Luxury Cruiseline has a target operating income of $97,200 per month, how many dinner cruise tickets must the company sell?

S7-5 Prepare a CVP graph *(Learning Objective 2)*

Use the information from the Luxury Cruiseline Data Set. Draw a graph of Luxury Cruiseline's CVP relationships. Include the sales revenue line, the fixed expense line, and the total expense line. Label the axes, the breakeven point, the income area, and the loss area.

S7-6 Interpret a CVP graph *(Learning Objective 2)*

Describe what each letter stands for in the CVP graph.

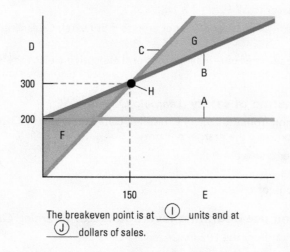

The breakeven point is at ⓘ units and at
ⓙ dollars of sales.

S7-7 Changes in sales price and variable costs *(Learning Objective 3)*

Use the information from the Luxury Cruiseline Data Set.

1. Suppose Luxury Cruiseline cuts its dinner cruise ticket price from $120 to $96 to increase the number of passengers. Compute the new breakeven point in units and in sales dollars. Explain how changes in sales price generally affect the breakeven point.

2. Assume that Luxury Cruiseline does *not* cut the price. Luxury Cruiseline could reduce its variable costs by no longer serving an appetizer before dinner. Suppose this operating change reduces the variable expense from $48 to $30 per passenger. Compute the new breakeven point in units and in dollars. Explain how changes in variable costs generally affect the breakeven point.

S7-8 Changes in fixed costs *(Learning Objective 3)*

Use the information from the Luxury Cruiseline Data Set. Suppose Luxury Cruiseline embarks on a cost-reduction drive and slashes fixed expenses from $270,000 per month to $180,000 per month.

1. Compute the new breakeven point in units and in sales dollars.

2. Is the breakeven point higher or lower than in S7-3? Explain how changes in fixed costs generally affect the breakeven point.

S7-9 Compute weighted-average contribution margin *(Learning Objective 4)*

Use the information from the Luxury Cruiseline Data Set. Suppose Luxury Cruiseline decides to offer two types of dinner cruises: regular cruises and executive cruises. The executive cruise includes complimentary cocktails and a five-course dinner on the upper deck. Assume that fixed expenses remain at $270,000 per month and that the following ticket prices and variable expenses apply:

	Regular Cruise	Executive Cruise
Sales price per ticket..	$120	$240
Variable expense per passenger...........................	$ 48	$180

Assuming that Luxury Cruiseline expects to sell four regular cruises for every executive cruise, compute the weighted-average contribution margin per unit. Is it higher or lower than a *simple* average contribution margin? Why? Is it higher or lower than the regular cruise contribution margin calculated in S7-1? Why? Will this new sales mix cause Luxury Cruiseline's breakeven point to increase or decrease from what it was when it sold only regular cruises?

S7-10 Continuation of S7-9: Breakeven *(Learning Objective 4)*

Refer to your answer to S7-9.

a. Compute the total number of dinner cruises that Luxury Cruiseline must sell to break even.

b. Compute the number of regular cruises and executive cruises the company must sell to break even.

S7-11 Compute margin of safety *(Learning Objective 5)*

Use the information from the Luxury Cruiseline Data Set. If Luxury Cruiseline sells 10,000 dinner cruises, compute the margin of safety

a. in units (dinner cruise tickets).

b. in sales dollars.

c. as a percentage of sales.

S7-12 Compute and use operating leverage factor *(Learning Objective 5)*

Use the information from the Luxury Cruiseline Data Set.

a. Compute the operating leverage factor when Luxury Cruiseline sells 12,000 dinner cruises.

b. If volume increases by 10%, by what percentage will operating income increase?

c. If volume decreases by 5%, by what percentage will operating income decrease?

S7-13 Compute margin of safety *(Learning Objective 5)*

Sarah has an online poster business. Suppose Sarah expects to sell 1,000 posters. Her average sales price per poster is $31 and her average cost per poster is $21. Her fixed expenses total $6,000. Compute her margin of safety

a. in units (posters).

b. in sales dollars.

c. as a percentage of expected sales.

S7-14 Compute and use operating leverage factor *(Learning Objective 5)*

Suppose Sarah sells 1,000 posters. Use the original data from S7-13 to compute her operating leverage factor. If sales volume increases 10%, by what percentage will her operating income change? Prove your answer.

S7-15 Calculating total costs under two different scenarios *(Learning Objective 5)*

The Cupcake Factory plans to open a new retail store in Medina, Ohio. The Cupcake Factory will sell specialty cupcakes for $5 per cupcake (each cupcake has a variable cost of $2.) The company is negotiating its lease for the new Medina location. The landlord has offered two leasing options: 1) a lease of $2,000 per month; or 2) a monthly lease cost of $1,000 plus 4% of the company's monthly sales revenue.

Requirements

1. If the Cupcake Factory plans to sell 1,000 cupcakes a month, which lease option would cost less each month? Why?
2. If the company plans to sell 1,800 cupcakes a month, which lease option would be more attractive? Why?

S7-16 Calculating total costs under two different scenarios
(Learning Objective 5)

Keely owns a hair salon. She gives her hairdressers two options for using her facility, equipment, and salon products: 1) they can pay Keely a flat "chair rental" of $1,200 per month or 2) they can pay her $5 per haircut plus 20% of their revenue. The hairdressers charge their customers $35 per haircut. The hairdressers incur no other expenses.

Requirements

1. At what point (number of haircuts per month) will the hairdressers be indifferent between the two payment options?
2. Because of the poor economic outlook, the hairdressers expect that people will wait longer between haircuts and start cutting their kids hair, rather than bringing them in for a trim. If volume is expected to drop below the indifference point, which payment option of the two described above will the hairdressers prefer?

EXERCISES Group A

E7-17A Prepare contribution margin income statements *(Learning Objective 1)*

Western Travel uses the contribution margin income statement internally. Western's first-quarter results are as follows:

WESTERN TRAVEL Contribution Margin Income Statement Three Months Ended March 31	
Sales revenue	$500,000
Less: Variable expenses	100,000
Contribution margin	$400,000
Less: Fixed expenses	174,000
Operating income	$226,000

Western's relevant range is sales of between $100,000 and $700,000.

Requirements

1. Prepare contribution margin income statements at sales levels of $255,000 and $363,000. (*Hint*: Use the contribution margin ratio.)
2. Compute breakeven sales in dollars.

E7-18A Work backward to find missing information *(Learning Objectives 1 & 2)*

Bentfield Dry Cleaners has determined the following about its costs: Total variable expenses are $32,000, total fixed expenses are $25,200, and the sales revenue needed to break even is $42,000. Determine the company's current 1) sales revenue and 2) operating income. (*Hint*: First, find the contribution margin ratio; then prepare the contribution margin income statement.)

E7-19A Find breakeven and target profit volume *(Learning Objectives 1 & 2)*

Happy Feet produces sports socks. The company has fixed expenses of $150,000 and variable expenses of $3.50 per package. Each package sells for $5.00.

Requirements

1. Compute the contribution margin per package and the contribution margin ratio.
2. Find the breakeven point in units and in dollars.
3. Find the number of packages Happy Feet needs to sell to earn a $22,500 operating income.

E7-20A Continuation of E7-19A: Changing costs (Learning Objective 3)

Refer to Happy Feet in E7-19A. If Happy Feet can decrease its variable costs to $3.00 per package by increasing its fixed costs to $160,000, how many packages will it have to sell to generate $22,500 of operating income? Is this more or less than before? Why?

E7-21A Find breakeven and target profit volume (Learning Objectives 1 & 2)

Owner Lei Wong is considering franchising her Global Chopsticks restaurant concept. She believes people will pay $5.75 for a large bowl of noodles. Variable costs are $2.30 a bowl. Wong estimates monthly fixed costs for franchisees at $8,400.

Requirements

1. Find a franchisee's breakeven sales in dollars.
2. Is franchising a good idea for Wong if franchisees want a minimum monthly operating income of $6,000 and Wong believes that most locations could generate $26,000 in monthly sales?

E7-22A Continuation of E7-21A: Changing business conditions
(Learning Objective 3)

Refer to Global Chopsticks in E7-21A. Wong did franchise her restaurant concept. Because of Global Chopsticks' success, Noodles-n-More has come on the scene as a competitor. To maintain its market share, Global Chopsticks will have to lower its sales price to $5.25 per bowl. At the same time, Happy Wok hopes to increase each restaurant's volume to 6,500 bowls per month by embarking on a marketing campaign. Each franchise will have to contribute $400 per month to cover the advertising costs. Prior to these changes, most locations were selling 6,000 bowls per month.

Requirements

1. What was the average restaurant's operating income before these changes?
2. Assuming that the price cut and advertising campaign are successful at increasing volume to the projected level, will the franchisees still earn their target profit of $6,000 per month? Show your calculations.

E7-23A Compute breakeven and project income (Learning Objectives 1 & 2)

Stewart's Steel Parts produces parts for the automobile industry. The company has monthly fixed expenses of $640,000 and a contribution margin of 80% of revenues.

Requirements

1. Compute Stewart's Steel Parts' monthly breakeven sales in dollars.
2. Use the contribution margin ratio to project operating income (or loss) if revenues are $530,000 and if they are $1,050,000.
3. Do the results in Requirement 2 make sense given the breakeven sales you computed in Requirement 1? Explain.

E7-24A Continuation of E7-23A: Changing business conditions
(Learning Objective 3)

Refer to Stewart's Steel Parts in E7-23A. Stewart feels like he's in a giant squeeze play: The automotive manufacturers are demanding lower prices, and the steel producers have increased raw material costs. Stewart's contribution margin has shrunk to 50% of revenues. Stewart's monthly operating income, prior to these pressures, was $200,000.

Requirements

1. To maintain this same level of profit, what sales volume (in sales revenue) must Stewart now achieve?

2. Stewart believes that his monthly sales revenue will go only as high as $1,050,000. He is thinking about moving operations overseas to cut fixed costs. If monthly sales are $1,050,000, by how much will he need to cut fixed costs to maintain his prior profit level of $200,000 per month?

 E7-25A Sustainability and CVP concepts *(Learning Objective 3)*

Kingston Garage Doors manufactures a premium garage door. Currently, the price and cost data associated with the premium garage door is as follows:

Average selling price per premium garage door...	$ 1,500
Average variable manufacturing cost per door	$ 600
Average variable selling cost per door	$ 150
Total annual fixed costs...	$250,000

Kingston Garage Doors has undertaken several sustainability projects over the past few years. Management is currently evaluating whether to develop a comprehensive software control system for its manufacturing operations that would significantly reduce scrap and waste generated during the manufacturing process. If the company were to implement this software control system in its manufacturing operations, the use of the software control system would result in an increase of $60,000 in its annual fixed costs while the average variable manufacturing cost per door would drop by $50.

Requirements

1. What is the company's current breakeven in units and in dollars?

2. If the company expects to sell 400 premium garage doors in the upcoming year, and it does not develop the software control system, what is its expected operating income from premium garage doors?

3. If the software control system were to be developed and implemented, what would be the company's new breakeven point in units and in dollars?

4. If the company expects to sell 400 premium garage doors in the upcoming year, and it develops the software control system, what is its expected operating income from premium garage doors?

5. If the company expects to sell 400 premium garage doors in the upcoming year, do you think the company should implement the software control system? Why or why not? What factors should the company consider?

E7-26A Prepare a CVP graph *(Learning Objective 2)*

Suppose that Murray Stadium, the home of the Upstate Cardinals, earns total revenue that averages $30 for every ticket sold. Assume that annual fixed expenses are $32 million and that variable expenses are $5 per ticket.

Requirements

1. Prepare the ballpark's CVP graph under these assumptions. Label the axes, sales revenue line, fixed expense line, total expense line, operating loss area, and operating income area on the graph.

2. Show the breakeven point in dollars and in tickets.

E7-27A Work backward to find new breakeven point *(Learning Objectives 2 & 3)*

Empire Industries is planning on purchasing a new piece of equipment that will increase the quality of its production. It hopes the increased quality will generate more sales. The company's contribution margin ratio is 40%, and its current breakeven point is $400,000 in sales revenue. If the company's fixed expenses increase by $55,000 due to the equipment, what will its new breakeven point be (in sales revenue)?

E7-28A Find consequence of rising fixed costs *(Learning Objectives 1 & 3)*

Elizabeth Miller sells homemade knit scarves for $14 each at local craft shows. Her contribution margin ratio is 62.5%. Currently, the craft show entrance fees cost Elizabeth $1,400 per year. The craft shows are raising their entrance fees by 25% next year. How many *extra* scarves will Elizabeth have to sell next year just to pay for rising entrance fee costs?

E7-29A Extension of E7-28A: Multiproduct firm *(Learning Objective 4)*

John Miller admired his wife's success at selling scarves at local craft shows (E7-28A), so he decided to make two types of plant stands to sell at the shows. John makes twig stands out of downed wood from his backyard and the yards of his neighbors, so his variable cost is minimal (wood screws, glue, and so forth). However, John has to purchase wood to make his oak plant stands. His unit prices and costs are as follows:

	Twig Stands	Oak Stands
Sales price	$18.00	$38.00
Variable cost	$ 3.00	$ 8.00

The twig stands are more popular, so John sells four twig stands for every one oak stand. Elizabeth charges her husband $360 to share her booth at the craft shows (after all, she has paid the entrance fees). How many of each plant stand does John need to sell to break even? Will this affect the number of scarves Elizabeth needs to sell to break even? Explain.

E7-30A Find breakeven for a multiproduct firm *(Learning Objective 4)*

Rally Scooters plans to sell a motorized standard scooter for $50 and a motorized chrome scooter for $60. Rally Scooters purchases the standard scooter for $35 and the chrome scooter for $40. Rally Scooters expects to sell two chrome scooters for every three standard scooters. The company's monthly fixed expenses are $14,450. How many of each type of scooter must Rally Scooters sell monthly to break even? To earn $11,900?

E7-31A Work backward to find missing data *(Learning Objective 4)*

Ambrose Manufacturing manufactures two styles of watches—the Digital and the Classic. The following data pertain to the Digital:

Variable manufacturing cost..	$130
Variable operating cost	$ 20
Sale price...	$230

Ambrose's monthly fixed expenses total $220,000. When Digitals and Classics are sold in the mix of 6:4, respectively, the sale of 2,500 total watches results in an operating income of $90,000. Compute the contribution margin per watch for the Classic.

E7-32A Breakeven and an advertising decision at a multiproduct company *(Learning Objectives 3, 4, & 5)*

Ghent Medical Supply is a retailer of home medical equipment. Last year, Ghent's sales revenues totaled $6,300,000. Total expenses were $2,200,000. Of this amount, approximately $1,260,000 were variable, while the remainder were fixed. Since Ghent's offers thousands of different products, its managers prefer to calculate the breakeven point in terms of sales dollars rather than units.

Requirements

1. What is Ghent's current operating income?
2. What is Ghent's contribution margin ratio?
3. What is Ghent's breakeven point in sales dollars (*Hint*: The contribution margin ratio calculated in Requirement 2 is already weighted by Ghent's actual sales mix.)
4. Ghent's top management is deciding whether to embark on a $200,000 advertisement campaign. The marketing firm has projected annual sales volume to increase by 20% as a result of this campaign. Assuming that the projections are correct, what effect would this advertising campaign have on the company's annual operating income?

E7-33A Work backward through margin of safety (*Learning Objective 5*)

Bob's Bait Shop had budgeted bait sales for the season at $18,000, with a $10,500 margin of safety. However, due to unseasonable weather, bait sales reached only $17,050. Actual sales exceeded breakeven sales by what amount?

E7-34A Compute margin of safety and operating leverage
(*Learning Objective 5*)

Foster's Repair Shop has a monthly target operating income of $10,500. *Variable expenses* are 50% of sales, and monthly fixed expenses are $7,000.

Requirements

1. Compute the monthly margin of safety in dollars if the shop achieves its income goal.
2. Express Foster's margin of safety as a percentage of target sales.
3. What is Foster's operating leverage factor at the target level of operating income?
4. Assume that the company reaches its target. By what percentage will the company's operating income fall if sales volume declines by 9%?

E7-35A Use operating leverage factor to find fixed costs (*Learning Objective 5*)

Guinty Manufacturing had a 1.50 operating leverage factor when sales were $50,000. Guinty Manufacturing's contribution margin ratio was 30%. What were Guinty Manufacturing's fixed expenses?

E7-36A Calculating total costs under two different scenarios
(*Learning Objective 5*)

The Candle Company plans to open a new retail store in Forest Lake, Minnesota. The Candle Company will sell specialty candles for an average of $20 each. The average variable costs per candle are as follows?

- Wax $6
- Other additives $1
- Base $2

The company is negotiating its lease for the new location. The landlord has offered two leasing options:

Option A) a lease of $2,500 per month; or

Option B) a monthly lease cost of $1,200 plus 10% of the company's monthly sales revenue.

The company expects to sell approximately 900 candles per month.

Requirements

1. Which lease option is more attractive for the company under its current sales expectations? Calculate the total lease cost under:
   - Option A
   - Option B
2. At what level of sales (in units) would the company be indifferent between the two lease options? Show your proof.
3. If the company's expected sales were 500 candles instead of the projection listed in the exercise, which lease options would be more favorable for the company? Why?

E7-37A Calculating total costs under two different scenarios
(Learning Objective 5)

Hannah sells custom-ordered, fabric headbands over the internet for $10 each. The fabric and elastic used to make the headbands will cost $1 per headband. Hannah has contracted with a local seamstress to make the headbands using the seamstress's own equipment at a price of $3 per headband. Hannah has also hired an internet marketing firm to maintain the website and place banner ads on search engines and other websites. This firm charges Hannah $1,000 per month plus 20% of sales revenue. Hannah also spends $500 per month traveling to different fabric suppliers to research possible new fabrics. (Hannah's costs are expected to remain as stated, unless she sells more than 4,000 headbands per month.)

The internet firm that will be maintaining her website has offered Hannah two contract options to retain their services for the coming year. She can either pay them 1) $1,000 per month plus 20% of revenue, or 2) $2,000 per month plus 10% of revenue.

Requirements

1. Which alternative will provide her with a lower operating leverage? Briefly explain why.
2. At what level of sales (in units) will Hannah be indifferent between the two contract options?
3. If Hannah expects to sell 1,500 headbands per month during the coming year, which contract term should she choose (which would be the most profitable for her)?

E7-38A Comprehensive CVP analysis *(Learning Objectives 1, 2, 3, 4, & 5)*

Scott Cole is evaluating a business opportunity to sell grooming kits at dog shows. Scott can buy the grooming kits at a wholesale cost of $29 per set. He plans to sell the grooming kits for $84 per set. He estimates fixed costs such as travel costs, booth rental cost, and lodging to be $880 per dog show.

Requirements

1. Determine the number of grooming kits Scott must sell per show to break even.
2. Assume Scott wants to earn a profit of $1,320 per show.
   a. Determine the sales volume in units necessary to earn the desired profit.
   b. Determine the sales volume in dollars necessary to earn the desired profit.
   c. Using the contribution margin format, prepare an income statement (condensed version) to confirm your answers to parts a and b.
3. Determine the margin of safety between the sales volume at the breakeven point and the sales volume required to earn the desired profit. Determine the margin of safety in both sales dollars, units, and as a percentage.

E7-39A Comprehensive CVP analysis *(Learning Objectives 1, 2, 3, 4, & 5)*

Preston Company manufactures and sells a single product. The company's sales and expenses for last year follow:

	Total	Per Unit	%
Sales	$116,000	$40	?
Variable expenses	87,000	30	?
Contribution margin	?	?	?
Fixed expenses	11,000		
Operating income	$ 18,000		

Requirements

1. Fill in the missing numbers in the preceding table. Use the table to answer the following questions:
   a. What is the total contribution margin?
   b. What is the per unit contribution margin?
   c. What is the operating income?
   d. How many units were sold?

2. Answer the following questions about breakeven analysis:
   a. What is the breakeven point in units?
   b. What is the breakeven point in sales dollars?

3. Answer the following questions about target profit analysis and safety margin:
   a. How many units must the company sell in order to earn a profit of $55,000?
   b. What is the margin of safety in units?
   c. What is the margin of safety in sales dollars?
   d. What is the margin of safety in percentage?

E7-40A Comprehensive CVP analysis (Learning Objectives 1, 2, 3, 4, & 5)

Wolf Manufacturing manufactures 16 GB flash drives (jump drives). Price and cost data for a relevant range extending to 200,000 units per month are as follows:

Sales price per unit (current monthly sales volume is 120,000 units)	$ 20.00
Variable costs per unit:	
Direct materials	$ 6.00
Direct labor	$ 7.00
Variable manufacturing overhead	$ 1.80
Variable selling and administrative expenses	$ 1.20
Monthly fixed expenses:	
Fixed manufacturing overhead	$182,000
Fixed selling and administrative expenses	$267,000

Requirements

1. What is the company's contribution margin per unit? Contribution margin percentage? Total contribution margin?

2. What would the company's monthly operating income be if the company sold 150,000 units?

3. What would the company's monthly operating income be if the company had sales of $4,000,000?

4. What is the breakeven point in units? In sales dollars?

5. How many units would the company have to sell to earn a target monthly profit of $260,000?

6. Management is currently in contract negotiations with the labor union. If the negotiations fail, direct labor costs will increase by 10% and fixed costs will increase by $28,500 per month. If these costs increase, how many units will the company have to sell each month to break even?

7. Return to the original data for this question and the rest of the questions. What is the company's current operating leverage factor (round to two decimals)?

8. If sales volume increases by 5%, by what percentage will operating income increase?

9. What is the company's current margin of safety in sales dollars? What is its margin of safety as a percentage of sales?

10. Say the company adds a second line of flash drives (32 GB rather than 16 GB). A unit of the 32 GB flash drives will sell for $45 and have variable cost per unit of $21 per unit. The expected sales mix is three of the small flash drives (16 GB) for every one large flash drive (32 GB). Given this sales mix, how many of each type of flash drive will the company need to sell to reach its target monthly profit of $260,000? Is this volume higher or lower than previously needed (in Question 5) to achieve the same target profit? Why?

EXERCISES Group B

E7-41B Prepare contribution margin income statements *(Learning Objective 1)*

Worldwide Travel uses the contribution margin income statement internally. Worldwide's first quarter results are as follows:

Worldwide Travel Contribution Margin Income Statement Three Months Ended March 31	
Sales revenue	$316,500
Less: Variable expenses	126,600
Contribution margin	$189,900
Less: Fixed expenses	174,000
Operating income	$ 15,900

Worldwide's relevant range is sales of between $100,000 and $700,000.

Requirements

1. Prepare contribution margin income statements at sales levels of $220,000 and $361,000. (*Hint:* Use the contribution margin ratio.)
2. Compute breakeven sales in dollars.

E7-42B Work backward to find missing information *(Learning Objectives 1 & 2)*

Alderman's Dry Cleaners has determined the following about its costs: Total variable expenses are $37,500, total fixed expenses are $33,000, and the sales revenue needed to break even is $44,000. Determine Alderman's current 1) sales revenue and 2) operating income. (*Hint:* First, find the contribution margin ratio; then prepare the contribution margin income statement.)

E7-43B Find breakeven and target profit volume *(Learning Objectives 1 & 2)*

Trendy Toes produces sports socks. The company has fixed expenses of $85,000 and variable expenses of $1.20 per package. Each package sells for $2.00.

Requirements

1. Compute the contribution margin per package and the contribution margin ratio.
2. Find the breakeven point in units and in dollars.
3. Find the number of packages that Trendy Toes needs to sell to earn a $26,000 operating income.

E7-44B Continuation of E7-43B: Changing costs *(Learning Objective 3)*

Refer to Trendy Toes in E7-43B. If Trendy Toes can decrease its variable costs to $1.00 per package by increasing its fixed costs to $90,000, how many packages will it have to sell to generate $26,000 of operating income? Is this more or less than before? Why?

E7-45B Find breakeven and target profit volume (Learning Objectives 1 & 2)

Owner Jackie Long is considering franchising her Oriental Express restaurant concept. She believes people will pay $4.50 for a large bowl of noodles. Variable costs are $1.80 a bowl. Long estimates monthly fixed costs for franchisees at $9,000.

Requirements

1. Find a franchisee's breakeven sales in dollars.
2. Is franchising a good idea for Long if franchisees want a minimum monthly operating income of $7,350 and Long believes most locations could generate $23,000 in monthly sales?

E7-46B Continuation of E7-45B: Changing business conditions
(Learning Objective 3)

Refer to Oriental Express in E7-45B. Since franchising Oriental Express, the restaurant has not been very successful due to Noodles Unlimited coming on the scene as a competitor. To increase its market share, Oriental Express will have to lower its sales price to $4.00 per bowl. At the same time, Oriental Express hopes to increase each restaurant's volume to 7,000 bowls per month by embarking on a marketing campaign. Each franchise will have to contribute $500 per month to cover the advertising costs. Prior to these changes, most locations were selling 6,500 bowls per month.

Requirements

1. What was the average restaurant's operating income before these changes?
2. Assuming the price cut and advertising campaign are successful at increasing volume to the projected level, will the franchisees earn their target profit of $7,350 per month?

E7-47B Compute breakeven and project income (Learning Objectives 1 & 2)

Rodger's Steel Parts produces parts for the automobile industry. The company has monthly fixed expenses of $660,000 and a contribution margin of 75% of revenues.

Requirements

1. Compute Rodger's Steel Parts' monthly breakeven sales in dollars.
2. Project operating income (or loss) if revenues are $560,000 and if they are $1,030,000.
3. Do the results in Requirement 2 make sense given the breakeven sales you computed in Requirement 1? Explain.

E7-48B Continuation of E7-47B: Changing business conditions
(Learning Objective 3)

Refer to Rodger's Steel Parts in E7-47B. Rodger feels like he's in a giant squeeze play: The automotive manufacturers are demanding lower prices, and the steel producers have increased raw material costs. Rodger's contribution margin has shrunk to 60% of revenues. Rodger's monthly operating income, prior to these pressures, was $112,500.

Requirements

1. To maintain this same level of profit, what sales volume (in sales revenue) must Rodger now achieve?
2. Rodger believes that his monthly sales revenue will only go as high as $1,030,000. He is thinking about moving operations overseas to cut fixed costs. If monthly sales are $1,030,000, by how much will he need to cut fixed costs to maintain his prior profit level of $112,500 per month?

E7-49B Sustainability and CVP *(Learning Objective 3)*

Lopez Garage Doors manufactures a premium garage door. Currently, the price and cost data associated with the premium garage door is as follows:

Average selling price per premium garage door	$ 1,300
Average variable manufacturing cost per door	$ 550
Average variable selling cost per door	$ 150
Total annual fixed costs	$240,000

Lopez Garage Doors has undertaken several sustainability projects over the past few years. Management is currently evaluating whether to develop a comprehensive software control system for its manufacturing operations that would significantly reduce scrap and waste generated during the manufacturing process. If the company were to implement this software control system in its manufacturing operations, the use of the software control system would result in an increase of $61,000 in its annual fixed costs while the average variable manufacturing cost per door would drop by $100.

Requirements

1. What is the company's current breakeven in units and in dollars?
2. If the company expects to sell 450 premium garage doors in the upcoming year, and it does not develop the software control system, what is its expected operating income from premium garage doors?
3. If the software control system were to be developed and implemented, what would be the company's new breakeven point in units and in dollars?
4. If the company expects to sell 450 premium garage doors in the upcoming year, and it develops the software control system, what is its expected operating income from premium garage doors?
5. If the company expects to sell 450 premium garage doors in the upcoming year, do you think the company should implement the software control system? Why or why not? What factors should the company consider?

E7-50B Prepare a CVP graph *(Learning Objective 2)*

Suppose that Donovan Park, the home of the Highland Hornets, earns total revenue that averages $35 for every ticket sold. Assume that annual fixed expenses are $24 million, and that variable expenses are $5 per ticket.

Requirements

1. Prepare the ballpark's CVP graph under these assumptions. Label the axes, sales revenue line, fixed expense line, total expense line, operating loss area, and operating income area on the graph.
2. Show the breakeven point in dollars and in tickets.

E7-51B Work backward to find new breakeven point *(Learning Objectives 2 & 3)*

Edward Industries is planning on purchasing a new piece of equipment that will increase the quality of its production. It hopes the increased quality will generate more sales. The company's contribution margin ratio is 20%, and its current breakeven point is $300,000 in sales revenue. If Edward Industries' fixed expenses increase by $40,000 due to the equipment, what will its new breakeven point be (in sales revenue)?

E7-52B Find consequence of rising fixed costs *(Learning Objectives 1 & 3)*

Ramona Brown sells homemade knit scarves for $20 each at local craft shows. Her contribution margin ratio is 62.5%. Currently, the craft show entrance fees cost Ramona $500 per year. The craft shows are raising their entrance fees by 10% next year. How many *extra* scarves will Ramona have to sell next year just to pay for rising entrance fee costs?

E7-53B Extension of E7-52B: Multiproduct firm *(Learning Objective 4)*

Mike Brown admired his wife's success at selling scarves at local craft shows (E7-52B), so he decided to make two types of plant stands to sell at the shows. Mike makes twig stands out of downed wood from his backyard and the yards of his neighbors, so his variable cost is minimal (wood screws, glue, and so forth). However, Mike has to purchase wood to make his oak plant stands. His unit prices and costs are as follows.

	Twig Stands	Oak Stands
Sales price	$14.00	$40.00
Variable cost	$ 2.00	$18.00

The twig stands are more popular so Mike sells four twig stands for every one oak stand. Ramona charges her husband $350 to share her booths at the craft shows (after all, she has paid the entrance fees). How many of each plant stand does Mike need to sell to break even? Will this affect the number of scarves Ramona needs to sell to break even? Explain.

E7-54B Find breakeven for a multiproduct firm *(Learning Objective 4)*

Zippy Scooters plans to sell a motorized standard scooter for $45 and a motorized chrome scooter for $65. Zippy Scooters purchases the standard scooter for $30 and the chrome scooter for $35. Zippy Scooters expects to sell two chrome scooters for every three standard scooters. The company's monthly fixed expenses are $17,850. How many of each type of scooter must the company sell monthly to break even? To earn $14,700?

E7-55B Work backward to find missing data *(Learning Objective 4)*

Martin Timepieces manufactures two styles of watches—the Digital and the Classic. The following data pertain to the Digital:

Variable manufacturing cost	$145
Variable operating cost	$ 10
Sale price	$225

The company's monthly fixed expenses total $180,000. When Digitals and Classics are sold in the mix of 6:4, respectively, the sale of 2,500 total watches results in an operating income of $70,000. Compute the contribution margin per watch for the Classic.

E7-56B Breakeven and an advertising decision at a multiproduct company *(Learning Objectives 3, 4, & 5)*

Helton Medical Supplies is a retailer of home medical equipment. Last year, Helton's sales revenues totaled $6,500,000. Total expenses were $2,700,000. Of this amount, approximately $1,560,000 were variable, while the remainder were fixed. Since Helton offers thousands of different products, its managers prefer to calculate the breakeven point in terms of sales dollars, rather than units.

Requirements

1. What is Helton's current operating income?
2. What is Helton's contribution margin ratio?
3. What is Helton's breakeven point in sales dollars? (*Hint:* The contribution margin ratio calculated in Requirement 2 is already weighted by Helton's actual sales mix.) What does it mean?
4. Top management is deciding whether to embark on a $230,000 advertisement campaign. The marketing firm has projected annual sales volume to increase by 10% as a result of this campaign. Assuming that the projections are correct, what effect would this advertising campaign have on Helton's annual operating income?

E7-57B Work backward through margin of safety *(Learning Objective 5)*

Bennett's Bait Shop had budgeted bait sales for the season at $20,000, with a $11,700 margin of safety. However, due to unseasonable weather, bait sales only reached $18,400. Actual sales exceeded breakeven sales by what amount?

E7-58B Compute margin of safety and operating leverage *(Learning Objective 5)*

Samantha's Repair Shop has a monthly target operating income of $12,500. *Variable expenses* are 50% of sales, and monthly fixed expenses are $10,000.

Requirements

1. Compute the monthly margin of safety in dollars if the shop achieves its income goal.
2. Express Samantha's margin of safety as a percentage of target sales.
3. What is Samantha's operating leverage factor at the target level of operating income?
4. Assume that the company reaches its target. By what percentage will the company's operating income fall if sales volume declines by 8%?

E7-59B Use operating leverage factor to find fixed costs *(Learning Objective 5)*

Welch Manufacturing had a 1.25 operating leverage factor when sales were $60,000. Welch Manufacturing's contribution margin ratio was 25%. What were Welch Manufacturing's fixed expenses?

E7-60B Calculating total costs under two different scenarios
(Learning Objectives 5)

Candles Unlimited plans to open a new retail store in White Bear Lake, Minnesota. Candles Unlimited will sell specialty candles for an average of $25 each. The average variable costs per candle are as follows:

- Wax $7
- Other additives $2
- Base $3

The company is negotiating its lease for the new location. The landlord has offered two leasing options:

> Option A) a lease of $2,000 per month; or
> Option B) a monthly lease cost of $1,500 plus 5% of the company's monthly sales revenue.

The company expects to sell approximately 500 candles per month.

Requirements

1. Which lease option is more attractive for the company under its current sales expectations? Calculate the total lease cost under:
   a. Option A
   b. Option B
2. At what level of sales (in units) would the company be indifferent between the two lease options? Show your proof.
3. If the company's expected sales were 300 candles instead of the projection listed in the exercise, which lease option would be more favorable for the company? Why?

E7-61B Comprehensive CVP analysis *(Learning Objectives 1, 2, 3, 4, & 5)*

Rachel sells custom-ordered, fabric headbands over the internet for $20 each. The fabric and elastic used to make the headbands will cost $4 per headband. Rachel has contracted with a local seamstress to make the headbands using the seamstress's own equipment, at a price of $8 per headband. Rachel has also hired an internet marketing firm to maintain the website and banner ads on search engines and other websites. This firm charges Rachel $1,200 per month plus 25% of sales revenue. Rachel also spends $300 per month traveling to different fabric suppliers to research possible new fabrics. (Rachel's costs are expected to remain as stated, unless she sells more than 4,000 headbands per month.)

The internet firm that will be maintaining her website has offered Rachel two contract options to retain their services for the coming year. She can either pay them 1) $1,200 per month plus 25% of revenue, or, 2) $2,400 per month plus 15% of revenue.

Requirements

1. Which alternative will provide her with a lower operating leverage? Briefly explain why.
2. At what level of sales (in units) will Rachel be indifferent between the two contract options?
3. If Rachel expects to sell 1,000 headbands per month during the coming year, which contract term should she choose (which would be the most profitable for her)?

E7-62B Comprehensive CVP analysis (Learning Objectives 1, 2, 3, 4, & 5)

Brett Stenback is evaluating a business opportunity to sell grooming kits at dog shows. Brett can buy the grooming kits at a wholesale cost of $37 per set. He plans to sell the grooming kits for $70 per set. He estimates fixed costs such as travel costs, booth rental cost, and lodging to be $759 per dog show.

Requirements

1. Determine the number of grooming kits Brett must sell per show to break even.
2. Assume Brett wants to earn a profit of $627 per show.
    a. Determine the sales volume in units necessary to earn the desired profit.
    b. Determine the sales volume in dollars necessary to earn the desired profit.
    c. Using the contribution margin format, prepare an income statement (condensed version) to confirm your answers to parts a and b.
3. Determine the margin of safety between the sales volume at the breakeven point and the sales volume required to earn the desired profit. Determine the margin of safety in both sales dollars, units, and as a percentage.

E7-63B Comprehensive CVP analysis (Learning Objectives 1, 2, 3, 4, & 5)

Gable Company manufactures and sells a single product. The company's sales and expenses for last year follow:

	Total	Per Unit	%
Sales	$110,000	$20	?
Variable expenses	82,500	15	?
Contribution margin	?	?	?
Fixed expenses	14,000		
Operating income	$ 13,500		

Requirements

1. Fill in the missing numbers in the table. Use the table to answer the following questions:
    a. What is the total contribution margin?
    b. What is the per unit contribution margin?
    c. What is the operating income?
    d. How many units were sold?
2. Answer the following questions about breakeven analysis:
    a. What is the breakeven point in units?
    b. What is the breakeven point in sales dollars?
3. Answer the following questions about target profit analysis and safety margin:
    a. How many units must the company sell in order to earn a profit of $52,000?
    b. What is the margin of safety in units?
    c. What is the margin of safety in sales dollars?
    d. What is the margin of safety in percentage?

E7-64B Comprehensive CVP analysis *(Learning Objectives 1, 2, 3, 4, & 5)*

Behr Manufacturing manufactures 16 GB flash drives (jump drives). Price and cost data for a relevant range extending to 200,000 units per month are as follows:

Sales price per unit	
(current monthly sales volume is 130,000 units)	$ 20.00
Variable costs per unit:	
Direct materials..	$ 5.20
Direct labor..	$ 6.00
Variable manufacturing overhead...	$ 2.50
Variable selling and administrative expenses...............................	$ 1.30
Monthly fixed expenses:	
Fixed manufacturing overhead...	$191,700
Fixed selling and administrative expenses....................................	$287,300

Requirements

1. What is the company's contribution margin per unit? Contribution margin percentage? Total contribution margin?
2. What would the company's monthly operating income be if it sold 160,000 units?
3. What would the company's monthly operating income be if it had sales of $4,000,000?
4. What is the breakeven point in units? In sales dollars?
5. How many units would the company have to sell to earn a target monthly profit of $260,000?
6. Management is currently in contract negotiations with the labor union. If the negotiations fail, direct labor costs will increase by 10% and fixed costs will increase by $27,000 per month. If these costs increase, how many units will the company have to sell each month to break even?
7. Return to the original data for this question and the rest of the questions. What is the company's current operating leverage factor (round to two decimal places)?
8. If sales volume increases by 5%, by what percentage will operating income increase?
9. What is the firm's current margin of safety in sales dollars? What is its margin of safety as a percentage of sales?
10. Say Behr Manufacturing adds a second line of flash drives (32 GB rather than 16 GB). A unit of the 32 GB flash drives will sell for $45 and have variable cost per unit of $20 per unit. The expected sales mix is six of the smaller flash drives (16 GB) for every one larger flash drive (32 GB). Given this sales mix, how many of each type of flash drive will Behr need to sell to reach its target monthly profit of $260,000? Is this volume higher or lower than previously needed (in Question 5) to achieve the same target profit? Why?

PROBLEMS Group A

P7-65A Find missing data in CVP relationships (Learning Objectives 1 & 2)

The budgets of four companies yield the following information:

	Company			
	Q	**R**	**S**	**T**
Target sales..................................	$720,000	$328,750	$190,000	$ _____
Variable expenses........................	216,000	_____	_____	270,000
Fixed expenses............................	_____	$153,000	$ 90,000	_____
Operating income (loss)...............	$154,000	$ _____	$ _____	$133,000
Units sold....................................	_____	$131,500	12,000	18,000
Contribution margin per unit	$ 6.00	_____	$ 9.50	$ 35.00
Contribution margin ratio	_____	0.80	_____	_____

Requirements

1. Fill in the blanks for each company.
2. Compute breakeven, in sales dollars, for each company. Which company has the lowest breakeven point in sales dollars? What causes the low breakeven point?

P7-66A Find breakeven and target profit and prepare income statements (Learning Objectives 1 & 2)

A traveling production of *Jersey Boys* performs each year. The average show sells 1,000 tickets at $60 a ticket. There are 120 shows each year. The show has a cast of 75, each earning an average of $300 per show. The cast is paid only after each show. The other variable expense is program printing costs of $9 per guest. Annual fixed expenses total $969,000.

Requirements

1. Compute revenue and variable expenses for each show.
2. Use the income statement equation approach to compute the number of shows needed annually to break even.
3. Use the shortcut unit contribution margin approach to compute the number of shows needed annually to earn a profit of $3,078,000. Is this goal realistic? Give your reason.
4. Prepare *Jersey Boys'* contribution margin income statement for 100 shows each year. Report only two categories of expenses: variable and fixed.

P7-67A Comprehensive CVP problem (Learning Objectives 1, 2, & 5)

University Calendars imprints calendars with college names. The company has fixed expenses of $1,065,000 each month plus variable expenses of $3.50 per carton of calendars. Of the variable expense, 65% is Cost of Goods Sold, while the remaining 35% relates to variable operating expenses. The company sells each carton of calendars for $13.50.

Requirements

1. Compute the number of cartons of calendars that University Calendars must sell each month to break even.
2. Compute the dollar amount of monthly sales University Calendars needs in order to earn $304,000 in operating income (round the contribution margin ratio to two decimal places).
3. Prepare the company's contribution margin income statement for June for sales of 470,000 cartons of calendars.
4. What is June's margin of safety (in dollars)? What is the operating leverage factor at this level of sales?
5. By what percentage will operating income change if July's sales volume is 12% higher? Prove your answer.

P7-68A Compute breakeven, prepare CVP graph, and respond to change
(Learning Objectives 1, 2, & 3)

Market Time Investors is opening an office in Orlando, Florida. Fixed monthly expenses are office rent ($2,100), depreciation on office furniture ($260), utilities ($280), special telephone lines ($600), a connection with an online brokerage service ($640), and the salary of a financial planner ($5,220). Variable expenses include payments to the financial planner (14% of revenue), advertising (7% of revenue), supplies and postage (3% of revenue), and usage fees for the telephone lines and computerized brokerage service (6% of revenue).

Requirements

1. Compute the investment firm's breakeven revenue in dollars. If the average trade leads to $520 in revenue for Market Time, how many trades must it make to break even?
2. Compute dollar revenues needed to earn monthly operating income of $3,640.
3. Graph Market Time's CVP relationships. Assume that an average trade leads to $520 in revenue for the firm. Show the breakeven point, sales revenue line, fixed expense line, total expense line, operating loss area, operating income area, and sales in units (trades) and dollars when monthly operating income of $3,640 is earned. The graph should range from 0 to 40 units (trades).
4. Assume that the average revenue that Market Time Investors earns decreases to $420 per trade. How does this affect the breakeven point in number of trades?

P7-69A CVP analysis at a multiproduct firm *(Learning Objectives 4 & 5)*

The contribution margin income statement of Pepperpike Coffee for February follows:

PEPPERPIKE COFFEE
Contribution Margin Income Statement
For the Month Ended February 29

Sales revenue		$103,000
Variable expenses:		
Cost of goods sold	$28,000	
Marketing expense	10,000	
General and administrative expense	3,000	41,000
Contribution margin		$62,000
Fixed expenses:		
Marketing expense	$34,650	
General and administrative expense	7,350	42,000
Operating income		$20,000

Pepperpike Coffee sells three small coffees for every large coffee. A small coffee sells for $3.00, with a variable expense of $1.50. A large coffee sells for $5.00, with a variable expense of $2.50.

Requirements

1. Determine Pepperpike Coffee's monthly breakeven point in the numbers of small coffees and large coffees. Prove your answer by preparing a summary contribution margin income statement at the breakeven level of sales. Show only two categories of expenses: variable and fixed.
2. Compute Pepperpike Coffee's margin of safety in dollars.
3. Use Pepperpike Coffee's operating leverage factor to determine its new operating income if sales volume increases 15%. Prove your results using the contribution margin income statement format. Assume that sales mix remains unchanged.

PROBLEMS Group B

P7-70B Find missing data in CVP relationships (Learning Objectives 1 & 2)

The budgets of four companies yield the following information:

	Company			
	Q	R	S	T
Target sales...	$687,500	$480,000	$171,875	$ _____
Variable expenses.................................	192,500	_____	_____	156,000
Fixed expenses.....................................	_____	165,000	88,000	_____
Operating income (loss)........................	$ 90,000	$ _____	$ _____	$131,000
Units sold..	_____	110,000	11,000	16,000
Contribution margin per unit	$ 6.60	_____	$ 10.00	$ 39.00
Contribution margin ratio	_____	0.55	_____	_____

Requirements

1. Fill in the blanks for each company.
2. Compute breakeven, in sales dollars, for each company. Which company has the lowest breakeven point in sales dollars? What causes the low breakeven point?

P7-71B Find breakeven and target profit and prepare income statements
(Learning Objectives 1 & 2)

A traveling production of *Shrek* performs each year. The average show sells 1,000 tickets at $45 per ticket. There are 120 shows a year. The show has a cast of 45, each earning an average of $300 per show. The cast is paid only after each show. The other variable expense is program printing expenses of $9 per guest. Annual fixed expenses total $787,500.

Requirements

1. Compute revenue and variable expenses for each show.
2. Compute the number of shows needed annually to break even.
3. Compute the number of shows needed annually to earn a profit of $3,262,500. Is this goal realistic? Give your reason.
4. Prepare *Shrek's* contribution margin income statement for 120 shows each year. Report only two categories of expenses: variable and fixed.

P7-72B Comprehensive CVP problem (Learning Objectives 1, 2, & 5)

College Calendars imprints calendars with college names. The company has fixed expenses of $1,115,000 each month plus variable expenses of $6.00 per carton of calendars. Of the variable expense, 67% is Cost of Goods Sold, while the remaining 33% relates to variable operating expenses. College Calendars sells each carton of calendars for $18.50.

Requirements

1. Compute the number of cartons of calendars that College Calendars must sell each month to break even.
2. Compute the dollar amount of monthly sales College Calendars needs in order to earn $330,000 in operating income (round the contribution margin ratio to two decimal places).
3. Prepare College Calendar's contribution margin income statement for June for sales of 455,000 cartons of calendars.
4. What is June's margin of safety (in dollars)? What is the operating leverage factor at this level of sales?
5. By what percentage will operating income change if July's sales volume is 11% higher? Prove your answer.

P7-73B Compute breakeven, prepare CVP graph, and respond to change
(Learning Objectives 1, 2, & 3)

Dolson Investors is opening an office in Stow, Ohio. Fixed monthly costs are office rent ($2,900), depreciation on office furniture ($330), utilities ($280), special telephone lines ($690), a connection with an online brokerage service ($700), and the salary of a financial planner ($2,700). Variable expenses include payments to the financial planner (10% of revenue), advertising (5% of revenue), supplies and postage (2% of revenue), and usage fees for the telephone lines and computerized brokerage service (3% of revenue).

Requirements

1. Compute the investment firm's breakeven revenue in dollars. If the average trade leads to $475 in revenue for Dolson Investors, how many trades must be made to break even?
2. Compute dollar revenues needed to earn monthly operating income of $3,040.
3. Graph Dolson's CVP relationships. Assume that an average trade leads to $475 in revenue for Dolson Investors. Show the breakeven point, sales revenue line, fixed expense line, total expense line, operating loss area, operating income area, and sales in units (trades) and dollars when monthly operating income of $3,040 is earned. The graph should range from 0 to 40 units (trades).
4. Assume that the average revenue Dolson Investors earns decreases to $375 per trade. How does this affect the breakeven point in number of trades?

P7-74B CVP analysis at a multiproduct firm *(Learning Objectives 4 & 5)*

The contribution margin income statement of Hemingway Coffee for February follows:

Hemingway Coffee **Contribution Margin Income Statement** For the Month Ended February 29		
Sales revenue		$94,000
Variable expenses:		
Cost of goods sold	$30,000	
Marketing expense	8,000	
General and administrative expense	2,000	40,000
Contribution margin		$54,000
Fixed expenses:		
Marketing expense	$24,750	
General and administrative expense	5,250	30,000
Operating income		$24,000

Hemingway Coffee sells three small coffees for every large coffee. A small coffee sells for $2.00, with a variable expense of $1.00. A large coffee sells for $4.00, with a variable expense of $2.00.

Requirements

1. Determine Hemingway Coffee's monthly breakeven point in numbers of small coffees and large coffees. Prove your answer by preparing a summary contribution margin income statement at the breakeven level of sales. Show only two categories of expenses: variable and fixed.
2. Compute Hemingway Coffee's margin of safety in dollars.
3. Use Hemingway Coffee's operating leverage factor to determine its new operating income if sales volume increases by 15%. Prove your results using the contribution margin income statement format. Assume the sales mix remains unchanged.

CRITICAL THINKING

Discussion & Analysis

A7-75 Discussion Questions

1. Define breakeven point. Why is the breakeven point important to managers?

2. Describe four different ways cost-volume-profit analysis could be useful to management.

3. The purchasing manager for Rockwell Fashion Bags has been able to purchase the material for its signature handbags for $2 less per bag. Keeping everything else the same, what effect would this reduction in material cost have on the breakeven point for Rockwell Fashion Bags? Now assume that the sales manager decides to reduce the selling price of each handbag by $2. What would the net effect of both of these changes be on the breakeven point in units for Rockwell Fashion Bags?

4. Describe three ways that cost-volume-profit concepts could be used by a service organization.

5. "Breakeven analysis isn't very useful to a company because companies need to do more than break even to survive in the long run." Explain why you agree or disagree with this statement.

6. What conditions must be met for cost-volume-profit analysis to be accurate?

7. Why is it necessary to calculate a weighted-average contribution margin ratio for a multi-product company when calculating the breakeven point for that company? Why can't all of the products' contribution margin ratios just be added together and averaged?

8. Is the contribution margin ratio of a grocery store likely to be higher or lower than that of a plastics manufacturer? Explain the difference in cost structure between a grocery store and a plastics manufacturer. How does the cost structure difference impact operating risk?

9. Alston Jewelry had sales revenues last year of $2.4 million, while its breakeven point (in dollars) was $2.2 million. What was Alston Jewelry's margin of safety in dollars? What does the term margin of safety mean? What can you discern about Alston Jewelry from its margin of safety?

10. Rondell Pharmacy is considering switching to the use of robots to fill prescriptions that consist of oral solids or medications in pill form. The robots will assist the human pharmacists and will reduce the number of human pharmacy workers needed. This change is expected to reduce the number of prescription filling errors, to reduce the customer's wait time, and to reduce the total overall costs. How does the use of the robots affect Rondell Pharmacy's cost structure? Explain the impact of this switch to robotics on Rondell Pharmacy's operating risk.

11. Suppose a company can replace the packing material it currently uses with a biodegradable packing material. The company believes this move to biodegradable packing materials will be well-received by the general public. However, the biodegradable packing materials are more expensive than the current packing materials and the contribution margin ratios of the related products will drop. What are the arguments for the company to use the biodegradable packing materials? What are the arguments for the company to not use the biodegradable materials? What do you think the company should do?

12. How can CVP techniques be used in supporting a company's sustainability efforts? Conversely, how might CVP be a barrier to sustainability efforts?

Application & Analysis

A7-76 CVP for a Product

Select one product that you could make yourself. Examples of possible products could be cookies, birdhouses, jewelry, or custom t-shirts. Assume that you have decided to start a small business producing and selling this product. You will be applying the concepts of cost-volume-profit analysis to this potential venture.

Basic Discussion Questions

1. Describe your product. What market are you targeting this product for? What price will you sell your product for? Make projections of your sales in units over each of the upcoming five years.

2. Make a detailed list of all of the materials needed to make your product. Include quantities needed of each material. Also include the cost of the material on a per-unit basis.

3. Make a list of all of the equipment you will need to make your product. Estimate the cost of each piece of equipment that you will need.

4. Make a list of all other expenses that would be needed to create your product. Examples of other expenses would be rent, utilities, and insurance. Estimate the cost of each of these expenses per year.

5. Now classify all of the expenses you have listed as being either fixed or variable. For mixed expenses, separate the expense into the fixed component and the variable component.

6. Calculate how many units of your product you will need to sell to break even in each of the five years you have projected.

7. Calculate the margin of safety in units for each of the five years in your projection.

8. Now decide how much you would like to make in before-tax operating income (target profit) in each of the upcoming five years. Calculate how many units you would need to sell in each of the upcoming years to meet these target profit levels.

9. How realistic is your potential venture? Do you think you would be able to break even in each of the projected five years? How risky is your venture (use the margin of safety to help answer this question). Do you think your target profits are achievable?

Decision Cases

A7-77 Determine the feasibility of a business plan (Learning Objective 2)

Brian and Nui Soon live in Macon, Georgia. Two years ago, they visited Thailand. Nui, a professional chef, was impressed with the cooking methods and the spices used in the Thai food. Macon does not have a Thai restaurant, and the Soons are contemplating opening one. Nui would supervise the cooking, and Brian would leave his current job to be the maître d'. The restaurant would serve dinner Tuesday through Saturday.

Brian has noticed a restaurant for lease. The restaurant has seven tables, each of which can seat four. Tables can be moved together for a large party. Nui is planning two seatings per evening, and the restaurant will be open 50 weeks per year.

The Soons have drawn up the following estimates:

Average revenue, including beverages and dessert	$ 40 per meal
Average cost of the food	$ 12 per meal
Chef's and dishwasher's salaries	$50,400 per *year*
Rent (premises, equipment)	$ 4,000 per month
Cleaning (linen and premises)	$ 800 per month
Replacement of dishes, cutlery, glasses	$ 300 per month
Utilities, advertising, telephone	$ 1,900 per month

Requirement

Compute *annual* breakeven number of meals and sales revenue for the restaurant. Also, compute the number of meals and the amount of sales revenue needed to earn operating income of $75,600 for the year. How many meals must the Soons serve each night to earn their target income of $75,600? Should the couple open the restaurant? Support your answer.

Ethical Issue

A7-78 Ethical dilemma with CVP analysis error *(Learning Objective 2)*

You have just begun your summer internship at Tmedic. The company supplies sterilized surgical instruments for physicians. To expand sales, Tmedic is considering paying a commission to its sales force. The controller, Jane Hewitt, asks you to compute 1) the new breakeven sales figure and 2) the operating profit if sales increase 15% under the new sales commission plan. She thinks you can handle this task because you learned CVP analysis in your accounting class.

You spend the next day collecting information from the accounting records, performing the analysis, and writing a memo to explain the results. The company president is pleased with your memo. You report that the new sales commission plan will lead to a significant increase in operating income and only a small increase in breakeven sales.

The following week, you realize that you made an error in the CVP analysis. You overlooked the sales personnel's $2,500 monthly salaries, and you did not include this fixed marketing expense in your computations. You are not sure what to do. If you tell Hewitt of your mistake, she will have to tell the president. In this case, you are afraid Tmedic might not offer you permanent employment after your internship.

Requirements

1. How would your error affect breakeven sales and operating income under the proposed sales commission plan? Could this cause the president to reject the sales commission proposal?
2. Consider your ethical responsibilities. Is there a difference between (a) initially making an error and (b) subsequently failing to inform the controller?
3. Suppose you tell Hewitt of the error in your analysis. Why might the consequences not be as bad as you fear? Should Hewitt take any responsibility for your error? What could Hewitt have done differently?
4. After considering all of the factors, should you inform Hewitt or simply keep quiet?

Team Project

A7-79 Advertising campaign and production level decisions *(Learning Objectives 1 & 3)*

EZPAK Manufacturing produces filament packaging tape. In 2012, EZPAK Manufacturing produced and sold 15 million rolls of tape. The company has recently expanded its capacity, so it can now produce up to 30 million rolls per year. EZPAK Manufacturing's accounting records show the following results from 2012:

Sale price per roll	$ 3.00
Variable manufacturing expenses per roll...	$ 2.00
Variable marketing and administrative expenses per roll	$ 0.50
Total fixed manufacturing overhead costs	$8,400,000
Total fixed marketing and administrative expenses........................	$ 600,000
Sales	15 million rolls
Production..	15 million rolls

There were no beginning or ending inventories in 2012.

In January 2013, EZPAK Manufacturing hired a new president, Kevin McDaniel. McDaniel has a one-year contract specifying that he will be paid 10% of EZPAK Manufacturing's 2013 operating income (based on traditional absorption costing) instead of a salary. In 2013, McDaniel must make two major decisions:

1. Should EZPAK Manufacturing undertake a major advertising campaign? This campaign would raise sales to 25 million rolls. This is the maximum level of sales that EZPAK Manufacturing can expect to make in the near future. The ad campaign would add an additional $3.5 million in marketing and administrative costs. Without the campaign, sales will be 15 million rolls.

2. How many rolls of tape will EZPAK Manufacturing produce?

At the end of the year, EZPAK Manufacturing's board of directors will evaluate McDaniel's performance and decide whether to offer him a contract for the following year.

Requirements

Within your group form two subgroups. The first subgroup assumes the role of Kevin McDaniel, EZPAK Manufacturing's new president. The second subgroup assumes the role of EZPAK Manufacturing's board of directors. McDaniel will meet with the board of directors shortly after the end of 2013 to decide whether he will remain at EZPAK Manufacturing. Most of your effort should be devoted to advance preparation for this meeting. Each subgroup should meet separately to prepare for the meeting between the board and McDaniel. (*Hint:* Keep computations [other than per-unit amounts] in millions.) Kevin McDaniel should do the following:

1. Compute EZPAK Manufacturing's 2012 operating income.

2. Decide whether to adopt the advertising campaign by calculating the projected increase in operating income from the advertising campaign. Do not include the executive bonus in this calculation. Prepare a memo to the board of directors explaining this decision.

3. Assume that EZPAK Manufacturing adopts the advertising campaign. Decide how many rolls of tape to produce in 2013. Assume that no safety stock is considered necessary to EZPAK's business.

4. Given your response to Question 3, prepare an absorption costing income statement for the year ended December 31, 2013, ending with operating income before bonus. Then compute your bonus separately. The variable cost per unit and the total fixed expenses (with the exception of the advertising campaign) remain the same as in 2012. Give this income statement and your bonus computation to the board of directors as soon as possible (before your meeting with the board).

5. Decide whether you want to remain at EZPAK Manufacturing for another year. You currently have an offer from another company. The contract with the other company is identical to the one you currently have with EZPAK Manufacturing—you will be paid 10% of absorption costing operating income instead of a salary.

The board of directors should do the following:

1. Compute EZPAK Manufacturing's 2012 operating income.

2. Determine whether EZPAK Manufacturing should adopt the advertising campaign by calculating the projected increase in operating income from the advertising campaign. Do not include the executive bonus in this calculation.

3. Determine how many rolls of tape EZPAK Manufacturing should produce in 2013. Assume that no safety stock is considered necessary to EZPAK's business.

4. Evaluate McDaniel's performance based on his decisions and the information he provided to the board. (*Hint:* You may want to prepare a variable costing income statement.)

5. Evaluate the contract's bonus provision. Are you satisfied with this provision? If so, explain why. If not, recommend how it should be changed.

After McDaniel has given the board his memo and income statement and after the board has had a chance to evaluate McDaniel's performance, McDaniel and the board should meet. The purpose of the meeting is to decide whether it is in everyone's mutual interest for McDaniel to remain with EZPAK Manufacturing and, if so, the terms of the contract EZPAK Manufacturing will offer McDaniel.

Relevant Costs for Short-Term Decisions

Learning Objectives

- **1** Describe and identify information relevant to short-term business decisions
- **2** Decide whether to accept a special order
- **3** Describe and apply different approaches to pricing
- **4** Decide whether to discontinue a product, department, or store
- **5** Factor resource constraints into product mix decisions
- **6** Analyze outsourcing (make or buy) decisions
- **7** Decide whether to sell a product "as is" or process it further

From Chapter 8 of *Managerial Accounting*, Third Edition. Karen W. Braun, Wendy M. Tietz.
Copyright © 2013 by Pearson Education, Inc. All rights reserved.

Most Major Airlines, including Delta,

outsource work. Delta estimates it has been able to cut maintenance costs by $240 million over a five-year period by outsourcing much of its airplane maintenance to Miami- and Canadian-based firms. Delta also has a ten-year arrangement to outsource its European finance and accounting functions to Accenture and a seven-year contract to outsource much of its domestic human resource functions to ACS. But why would Delta outsource so much of its work? Primarily to cut costs. Due to rising fuel costs and cut-throat competition, airlines need to find ways to cut costs, and one way is through outsourcing. However, costs are not everything. Even though Delta used to save $25 million per year by outsourcing its call center work to India, customer dissatisfaction prompted Delta to bring its call center work back to the U.S. in 2009.

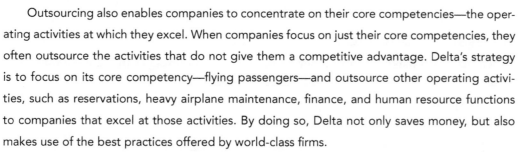

© Bayne Stanley / Alamy

Outsourcing also enables companies to concentrate on their core competencies—the operating activities at which they excel. When companies focus on just their core competencies, they often outsource the activities that do not give them a competitive advantage. Delta's strategy is to focus on its core competency—flying passengers—and outsource other operating activities, such as reservations, heavy airplane maintenance, finance, and human resource functions to companies that excel at those activities. By doing so, Delta not only saves money, but also makes use of the best practices offered by world-class firms.

Sources:
Harry Weber, "Delta no longer sending calls to India", *USA Today*, April 17, 2009. www.usatoday.com/travel/flights/2009-04-17-delta-outsourcing_N.htm
www.allbusiness.com, "Outsourcing of HR Functions to Regain Momentum in 2008, According to Everest Research Institute", Nov. 2, 2007
www.newratings.com, "Delta AirLines to reduce costs through maintenance outsourcing", March 30, 2005
www.accenture.com, "Helping Delta Air Lines Achieve High Performance Through Financial Outsourcing", 2006

In the last chapter, we saw how managers use cost behavior to determine the company's breakeven point and to estimate the sales volume needed to achieve target profits. In this chapter, we'll see how managers use their knowledge of cost behavior to make six special business decisions, such as whether to outsource operating activities. The decisions we'll discuss in this chapter usually pertain to short periods of time, so managers do not need to worry about the time value of money. In other words, they do not need to compute the present value of the revenues and expenses relating to the decision. In Chapter 12, we will discuss longer-term decisions (such as buying equipment and undertaking plant expansions) in which the time value of money becomes important. Before we look at the six business decisions in detail, let's consider a manager's decision-making process and the information managers need to evaluate their options.

How do Managers Make Decisions?

Exhibit 8-1 illustrates how managers decide among alternative courses of action. Management accountants help gather and analyze *relevant information* to compare alternatives. Management accountants also help with the follow-up: comparing the actual results of a decision to those originally anticipated. This feedback helps management as it faces similar types of decisions in the future. It also helps management adjust current operations if actual results of its decision are markedly different from those anticipated.

EXHIBIT 8-1 How Managers Make Decisions

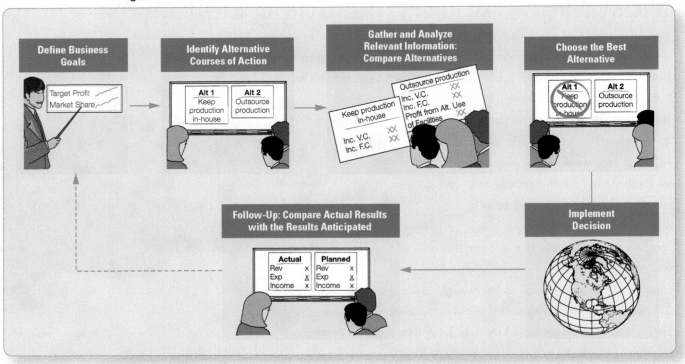

Relevant Information

When managers make decisions, they focus on costs and revenues that are relevant to the decisions. Exhibit 8-2 shows that **relevant information**

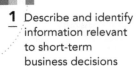

1 Describe and identify information relevant to short-term business decisions

1. is expected *future* data.
2. *differs* among alternatives.

Recall our discussion of relevant costs in Chapter 2. In deciding whether to purchase a Toyota Corolla or Nissan Sentra, the cost of the car, the sales tax, and the insurance premium are relevant because these costs

- are incurred in the *future* (after you decide to buy the car).
- *differ between alternatives* (each car has a different invoice price, sales tax, and insurance premium).

These costs are *relevant* because they affect your decision of which car to purchase. *Irrelevant* costs are costs that *do not* affect your decision. For example, because the Corolla and Sentra both have similar fuel efficiency and maintenance ratings, we do not expect the car operating costs to differ between alternatives. Because these costs do not differ, they do not affect your decision. In other words, they are *irrelevant* to the decision. Similarly, the cost of a campus parking sticker is also irrelevant because the sticker costs the same whether you buy the Sentra or the Corolla.

Sunk costs are also irrelevant to your decision. Sunk costs are costs that were incurred in the *past* and cannot be changed regardless of which future action is taken. Perhaps you

EXHIBIT 8-2 Relevant Information

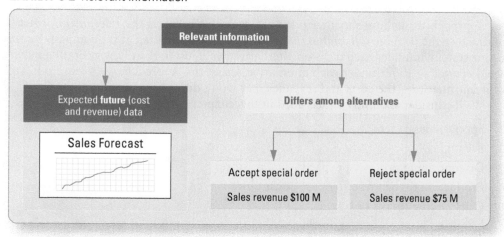

want to trade in your current truck when you buy your new car. The amount you paid for the truck—which you bought for $15,000 a year ago—is a sunk cost. In fact, it doesn't matter whether you paid $15,000 or $50,000—it's still a sunk cost. No decision made *now* can alter the past. You already bought the truck, so *the price you paid for it is a sunk cost*. All you can do *now* is keep the truck, trade it in, or sell it for the best price you can get, even if that price is substantially less than what you originally paid for the truck.

What *is* relevant is what you can get for your truck in the future. Suppose the Nissan dealership offers you $8,000 for your truck. The Toyota dealership offers you $10,000. Because the amounts differ and the transaction will take place in the future, the trade-in value is relevant to your decision.

The same principle applies to all situations—*only relevant data affect decisions*.

Relevant Nonfinancial Information

Nonfinancial, or qualitative factors, also play a role in managers' decisions. For example, closing manufacturing plants or laying off employees can seriously hurt the local community and employee morale. Outsourcing can reduce control over delivery time and product quality. Offering discounted prices to select customers can upset regular customers and tempt them to take their business elsewhere. Managers must think through the likely quantitative *and* qualitative effects of their decisions.

Managers who ignore qualitative factors can make serious mistakes. For example, the City of Nottingham, England, spent $1.6 million on 215 solar-powered parking meters after seeing how well the parking meters worked in countries along the Mediterranean Sea. However, the city did not adequately consider that British skies are typically overcast. The result? The meters didn't always work because of the lack of sunlight. The city *lost* money because people ended up parking for free! Relevant qualitative information has the same characteristics as relevant financial information: The qualitative factor occurs in the *future*, and it *differs* between alternatives. The amount of *future* sunshine required *differed* between alternatives: The mechanical meters didn't require any sunshine, but the solar-powered meters needed a great deal of sunshine.

Likewise, in deciding between the Corolla and Sentra, you will likely consider qualitative factors that differ between the cars (legroom, trunk capacity, dashboard design, and so forth) before making your final decision. Since you must live with these factors in the future, they become relevant to your decision.

 **Why is this important?**

"The accounting information used to make **business decisions** in this chapter considers only one factor: **profitability**. However in real life, managers should consider **many** more **factors**, including the effect of the decision on **employees**, the local **community**, and the **environment**."

Keys to Making Short-Term Special Decisions

Our approach to making short-term special decisions is called the *relevant information approach* or the *incremental analysis approach*. Instead of looking at the company's *entire* income statement under each decision alternative, we'll just look at how operating income would *change or differ* under each alternative. Using this approach, we'll leave out irrelevant information—the costs and revenues that won't differ between alternatives.

We'll consider six kinds of decisions in this chapter:

1. Special sales orders
2. Pricing
3. Discontinuing products, departments, or stores
4. Product mix when resources are constrained
5. Outsourcing (make or buy)
6. Selling as is or processing further

As you study these decisions, keep in mind the two keys in analyzing short-term special business decisions shown in Exhibit 8-3:

1. **Focus on relevant revenues, costs, and profits.** Irrelevant information only clouds the picture and creates information overload. That's why we'll use the incremental analysis approach.

2. **Use a contribution margin approach that separates variable costs from fixed costs.** Because fixed costs and variable costs behave differently, they must be analyzed separately. Traditional (absorption costing) income statements, which blend fixed and variable costs, can mislead managers. Contribution margin income statements, which isolate costs by behavior (variable or fixed), help managers gather the cost-behavior information they need. Recall from Chapter 6 that unit manufacturing costs based on absorption costing are mixed costs, so they can also mislead managers. That's why variable costing is often better for decision-making purposes. If you use unit manufacturing costs in your analysis, make sure you separate the cost's fixed and variable components first.

Keep in mind that every business decision is unique. What might be a relevant cost in one decision might not be relevant in another decision. Each unique business decision needs to be assessed to determine what pieces of information are relevant. Just because a piece of information is relevant in one decision doesn't mean it will be relevant in the next. Because of this, accountants often follow the adage that different costs are used for different purposes.

EXHIBIT 8-3 Two Keys to Making Short-Term Special Decisions

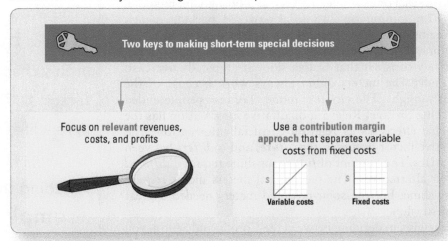

Sustainability and Short-Term Business Decisions

For companies that embrace sustainability and the triple bottom line, almost every decision will be viewed through the lens of its impact on people and the planet, as well as profitability. For example, let's look at Timberland, a company with $1.4 billion in annual revenue that specializes in outdoor shoes and clothing. Timberland is intentionally "focusing the resources, energy and profits of a publicly traded...company to combat social ills, help the environment, and improve conditions of laborers around the globe."[1]

In the words of Jeffrey Swartz, President and CEO, "Timberland believes, and has always believed, that we have a responsibility to help effect change in the communities where we work and live." The company is committed to "doing well and doing good". But how does the company work toward such lofty goals? Here are a few examples:[2]

- Employees are given up to 40 hours of paid leave each year to perform community service work.
- For the last 13 years, the company has sponsored an annual day-long employee service event. In 2010 alone, over 4,800 employees participated, generating over 35,000 hours of service to local community projects.
- The company's strict "Code of Conduct" ensures that domestic and overseas workers are employed at fair wage rates, work reasonable shifts, and work in safe factories.
- The company is committed to being environmentally conscious in the production of its products. By the end of 2012, the company hopes to label all of its footwear with a "Green Index" rating system. The index will educate consumers about the product's climate impact, chemicals used, and materials used (percentage of organic, recycled, or renewable materials used).
- The company is committed to planting 5 million trees in the next 5 years in regions of Haiti and China suffering from the effects of deforestation. Acting as carbon offsets, these trees will also help the company achieve its goal of becoming carbon neutral in all operations under its control.
- The company has earned LEED (Leadership in Energy and Environmental Design) certification on several of its retail outlets.
- The company uses solar panels on its California distribution center to provide 60% of its energy. This $3.5 million investment was made, even though cost models showed it might take 20 years for the investment to earn a return.
- In 2010, Timberland ranked #2 on Climate Count's list of companies making aggressive strides in fighting climate change.

These initiatives, as well as others, are costly. The company's financial performance, while profitable, has lagged the S&P 500 Footwear and Apparel Index over the past 5 years. However, the company does not measure its success strictly in terms of stock market returns. Rather, it adheres to the notion of the triple bottom line. Perhaps as a result, Timberland has been named one of *Fortune* magazine's "100 Best Companies to Work For" for 10 consecutive years.

See Exercises
E8-17A and E8-31B

How do Managers Make Special Order and Regular Pricing Decisions?

We'll start our discussion on the six business decisions by looking at special sales order decisions and regular pricing decisions. In the past, managers did not consider pricing to be a short-term decision. However, product life cycles are shrinking in most industries. Companies often sell products for only a few months before replacing them with an

2 Decide whether to accept a special order.

[1]Reingold, Jennifer, "Walking the Walk," *Fast Company*, November, 2005. http://www.fastcompany.com/magazine/100/timberland.html?page=0%2C0
[2]Timberland.com

updated model. The clothing and technology industries have always had short life cycles. Even auto and housing styles change frequently. Pricing has become a shorter-term decision than it was in the past.

Let's examine a special sales order in detail; then we will discuss regular pricing decisions.

Special Order Decisions

A special order occurs when a customer requests a one-time order at a *reduced* sales price. Often, these special orders are for large quantities. Before agreeing to the special deal, management must consider the questions shown in Exhibit 8-4.

EXHIBIT 8-4 Special Order Considerations

- Do we have excess capacity available to fill this order?

- Will the reduced sales price be high enough to cover the *incremental* costs of filling the order (the variable costs of filling the order and any additional fixed costs)?

- Will the special order affect regular sales in the long run?

First, managers must consider available capacity. If the company is already making as many units as possible and selling them all at its *regular* sales price, it wouldn't make sense to fill a special order at a *reduced* sales price. Therefore, available excess capacity is a necessity for accepting a special order. This is true for service firms (law firms, caterers, and so forth) as well as manufacturers.

Second, managers need to consider whether the special reduced sales price is high enough to cover the incremental costs of filling the order. The special price *must* exceed the variable costs of filling the order or the company will lose money on the deal. In other words, the special order must provide a positive contribution margin.

Next, the company must consider fixed costs. If the company has excess capacity, fixed costs probably won't be affected by producing more units (or delivering more service). However, in some cases, management may need to hire a consultant or incur some other fixed cost to fill the special order. If so, management will need to consider whether the special sales price is high enough to generate a positive contribution margin *and* cover the additional fixed costs.

Finally, managers need to consider whether the special order will affect regular sales in the long run. Will regular customers find out about the special order and demand a lower price or take their business elsewhere? Will the special order customer come back *again and again*, asking for the same reduced price? Will the special order price start a price war with competitors? Managers must gamble that the answers to these questions are "no" or consider how customers will respond. Managers may decide that any profit from the special sales order is not worth these risks.

Special Order Example

Let's consider a special sales order example. Suppose ACDelco sells oil filters for $3.20 each. Assume that a mail-order company has offered ACDelco $35,000 for 20,000 oil filters, or $1.75 per filter ($35,000 ÷ 20,000 = $1.75). This sale will

- use manufacturing capacity that would otherwise be idle.
- not change fixed costs.
- not require any variable marketing or administrative expenses.
- not affect regular sales.

We have addressed every consideration except one: Is the special sales price of $1.75 high enough to cover the incremental costs of filling the order. Let's take a look.

Exhibit 8-5 shows a contribution margin income statement for the current volume of oil filters sold (250,000 units). As discussed in Chapters 6 and 7, this format is much better for decision making than a traditional income statement format because it shows variable and fixed costs separately. Managers can easily see the variable cost of *manufacturing* each oil filter ($1.20) the variable cost of *selling* each oil filter ($0.30).

EXHIBIT 8-5 Contribution Margin Income Statement for Current Volume of Oil Filters

Contribution Margin Income Statement	Per Unit	Total (current volume of 250,000)
Sales revenue (at normal sales price)	$3.20	$800,000
Less variable expenses:		
Variable manufacturing costs	1.20	300,000
(DM, DL, and Variable MOH)		
Variable marketing and administrative costs	0.30	75,000
Contribution margin	$1.70	$425,000
Less fixed expenses:		
Fixed manufacturing costs (Fixed MOH)		200,000
Fixed marketing and administrative costs		125,000
Operating Income		$100,000

We'll use this information to determine whether ACDelco should accept the special order. Exhibit 8-6 illustrates an incremental analysis in which the revenue associated with the order is compared against the additional costs that will be incurred to fill the order. The analysis shows that the special order sales price of $1.75 is high enough to cover all incremental costs, and will provide the company with an additional $11,000 in operating income. Therefore, the order should be accepted unless managers have reason to suspect accepting the order would adversely affect regular sales in the long-run.

EXHIBIT 8-6 Incremental Analysis of Special Sales Order

Incremental Analysis for Special Order	Per Unit	Total Special Order (20,000 units)
Revenue from special order (at special order price)	$1.75	$35,000
Less variable expenses associated with the order:		
Variable manufacturing costs (DM, DL, and Variable MOH)	1.20	24,000
Contribution margin from the special order	$0.55	$11,000
Less additional fixed expenses associated with the		
order: (none in this example)		0
Increase in operating income from the special order		$11,000

Remember that in this particular example, ACDelco doesn't expect to incur any variable marketing or administrative costs associated with the special order. Therefore, they weren't included in Exhibit 8-6. However, this won't always be the case. Many times, companies will incur variable operating expenses on special orders, such as freight-out or sales commissions. *Only those incremental costs associated with the order should be included in the analysis.*

As shown in Exhibit 8-6, managers also need to consider any incremental fixed costs that will be incurred as a result of the order. Since the company has excess capacity with which to produce this order, fixed manufacturing overhead costs are not expected to change. Likewise, fixed selling and administrative expenses are not expected to change. Therefore, Exhibit 8-6 shows zero incremental fixed costs as a result of this order. However, if a company expects to incur a new fixed cost as a result of the order, the additional fixed cost needs to be included in the analysis.

Notice that the analysis follows the two keys to making short-term special business decisions discussed earlier: (1) focus on relevant data (revenues and costs that *will change* if ACDelco accepts the special order) and (2) use a contribution margin approach that separates variable costs from fixed costs.

To summarize, for special sales orders, the decision rule is as follows:

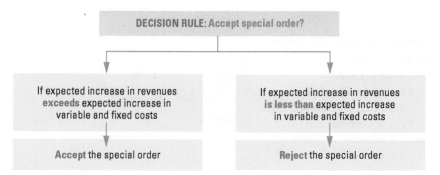

Pitfall to Avoid on Special Order Decisions

One of the most common mistakes managers make when analyzing special orders is to base their decision on the unit cost provided by absorption costing. Recall from Chapter 6 that under absorption costing, all manufacturing costs, including fixed MOH, are "absorbed" into the unit cost of the product. Absorption costing was used when we studied job costing and process costing in Chapters 3, 4, and 5 because GAAP requires it for external financial reporting purposes. Using the figures found in Exhibit 8-5, we see that the unit cost of each oil filter under absorption costing is $2.00:

Inventoriable Product Cost Using Absorption Costing	Unit Cost
Variable manufacturing costs (DM, DL, Variable MOH) per unit	$1.20
Fixed manufacturing costs (Fixed MOH) per unit at current volume	
$200,000 ÷ 250,000 units	0.80
Cost per unit using absorption costing	$2.00

The $2.00 unit cost, which GAAP mandates for inventory and cost of goods sold valuation, is *not* a good basis for making a special order decision. Why? Because it is a mixed cost, which includes both fixed and variable components. Since there is excess capacity in the plant, fixed MOH will remain $200,000 in total, regardless of whether ACDelco accepts the special order. Producing 20,000 more oil filters will *not* increase total fixed costs by $0.80 per unit. The incremental cost incurred to make each additional filter is the variable cost of $1.20 per unit, not $2.00 per unit.

STOP & THINK

In addition to the facts presented in the text, assume ACDelco will pay its sales staff a commission of $0.15 per unit on the special order. Also assume ACDelco will incur an additional $2,000 in legal fees to draw up the contract for the order. Given these additional facts, should ACDelco still accept the special order?

Answer: The special order sales price ($1.75) is still higher than the variable costs associated with filling the order ($1.20 + $0.15). As a result, the special order for 20,000 units will provide a contribution margin of $0.40 per unit, or $8,000 in total. By subtracting the incremental fixed expenses associated with the special order ($2,000) from the contribution margin, we see that the special order will increase the company's operating income by $6,000. Therefore, ACDelco should still accept the order.

Consider this: Since the special order price of $1.75 is less than the absorption cost of $2.00, a manager falling into this decision pitfall would have turned down the special order, thinking that the company would lose money on it. In reality, by not accepting the special order, this manager just cost the company $11,000 in additional profit.

Regular Pricing Decisions

In the special order decision, ACDelco decided to sell a limited quantity of oil filters for $1.75 each even though the normal price was $3.20 per unit. But how did ACDelco decide to set its regular price at $3.20 per filter? Exhibit 8-7 shows that managers start with three basic questions when setting regular prices for their products or services.

3 Describe and apply different approaches to pricing

EXHIBIT 8-7 Regular Pricing Considerations

- What is our target profit?
- How much will customers pay?
- Are we a price-taker or a price-setter for this product?

The answers to these questions are often complex and ever-changing. Stockholders expect the company to achieve certain profits. Economic conditions, historical company earnings, industry risk, competition, and new business developments all affect the level of profit that stockholders expect. Stockholders usually tie their profit expectations to the amount of assets invested in the company. For example, stockholders may expect a 10% annual return on their investment. A company's stock price tends to decline if the company does not meet target profits, so managers must keep costs low while generating enough revenue to meet target profits.

This leads to the second question: How much will customers pay? Managers cannot set prices above what customers are willing to pay or sales will decline. The amount customers will pay depends on the competition, the product's uniqueness, the effectiveness of marketing campaigns, general economic conditions, and so forth.

To address the third pricing question, imagine a continuum with price-takers at one end and price-setters at the other end. A company's products and services fall somewhere along this continuum, shown in Exhibit 8-8. Companies are price-takers when they have little or no control over the prices of their products or services. This occurs when their products and services are *not* unique or when competition is heavy. Examples include food commodities (milk and corn), natural resources (oil and lumber), and generic consumer products and services (paper towels, dry cleaning, and banking).

EXHIBIT 8-8 Price-Takers Versus Price-Setters

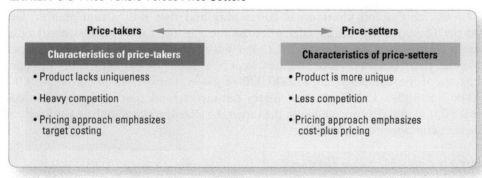

Companies are price-setters when they have more control over pricing—in other words, they can "set" prices to some extent. Companies are price-setters when their products are unique, which results in less competition. Unique products such as original art and jewelry, specially manufactured machinery, patented perfume scents, and custom-made furniture can command higher prices.

Obviously, managers would rather be price-setters than price-takers. To gain more control over pricing, companies try to differentiate their products. They want to make their products unique in terms of features, service, or quality—or at least make you *think* their product is unique or somehow better even if it isn't. How do they do this? Primarily through advertising. Consider Nike's tennis shoes, Starbucks' coffee, Hallmark's wrapping paper, Nexus' shampoo, Tylenol's acetaminophen, General Mills' cereal, Capital One's credit cards, Shell's gas, Abercrombie and Fitch's jeans—the list goes on and on. Are these products really better or significantly different from their lower-priced competitors? Possibly. If these companies can make you think so, they've gained more control over their pricing because you are willing to pay *more* for their products or services. The downside? These companies must charge higher prices or sell more just to cover their advertising costs.

A company's approach to pricing depends on whether its product or service is on the price-taking or price-setting side of the spectrum. Price-takers emphasize a target costing approach. Price-setters emphasize a cost-plus pricing approach. Keep in mind that many products fall somewhere along the continuum. Therefore, managers tend to use both approaches to some extent. We'll now discuss each approach in turn.

Target Costing

When a company is a price-taker, it emphasizes a target costing approach to pricing. **Target costing** starts with the market price of the product (the price customers are willing to pay) and subtracts the company's desired profit to determine the product's target total cost—the *total* cost to develop, design, produce, market, deliver, and service the product. In other words, the total cost includes *every* cost incurred throughout the value chain relating to the product.

> Revenue at market price
> Less: Desired profit
> Target total cost

In this relationship, the market price is "taken." If the product's current cost is higher than the target cost, the company must find ways to reduce costs, otherwise it will not meet its profit goals. Managers often use ABC, value engineering, and lean thinking (as discussed in Chapter 4) to find ways to cut costs. Let's look at an example of target costing.

Let's assume that oil filters are a commodity and that the current market price is $3.00 per filter (not the $3.20 sales price assumed in the earlier ACDelco example). Because the oil filters are a commodity, ACDelco will emphasize a target costing approach. Let's assume that ACDelco's stockholders expect a 10% annual return on the company's assets. If the company has $1,000,000 of assets, the desired profit is $100,000 ($1,000,000 × 10%). Exhibit 8-9 calculates the target total cost at the current sales volume (250,000 units). Once we know the target total cost, we can analyze the fixed and variable cost components separately.

EXHIBIT 8-9 Calculating Target Full Cost

	Calculations	Total
Revenue at market price	250,000 units × $3.00 price =	$ 750,000
Less: Desired profit	10% × $1,000,000 of assets	(100,000)
Target total cost		$ 650,000

Can ACDelco make and sell 250,000 oil filters at a target total cost of $650,000 or less? We know from ACDelco's contribution margin income statement (Exhibit 8-5) that the company's variable costs are $1.50 per unit. This variable cost per unit includes both manufacturing costs ($1.20 per unit) and marketing and administrative expenses ($0.30 per unit). From Exhibit 8-5 we also know that the company incurs $325,000 in fixed costs in its current relevant range. Again, some fixed cost stems from manufacturing ($200,000) and some from marketing and administrative activities ($125,000). *In setting regular sales prices, companies must cover **all** of their costs—it doesn't matter if these costs are inventoriable product costs or period costs, or whether they are fixed or variable.*

Making and selling 250,000 filters currently costs the company $700,000 [(250,000 units × $1.50 variable cost per unit) + $325,000 of fixed costs], which is more than the target total cost of $650,000 (shown in Exhibit 8-9). So, what are ACDelco's options?

1. Accept a lower profit.
2. Cut fixed costs.
3. Cut variable costs.
4. Use other strategies. For example, ACDelco could attempt to increase sales volume. Recall that the company has excess capacity, so making and selling more units would affect only variable costs. The company could also consider changing or adding to its product mix. Finally, it could attempt to differentiate its oil filters (or strengthen its name brand) to gain more control over sales prices.

Let's look at some of these options. ACDelco may first try to cut fixed costs. As shown in Exhibit 8-10, the company would have to reduce fixed costs to $275,000 to meet its target profit. Since current fixed costs are $325,000 (Exhibit 8-5), that means the company would have to cut fixed costs by $50,000.

EXHIBIT 8-10 Calculating Target Fixed Cost

	Calculations	Total
Target total cost		$ 650,000
Less: Current variable costs	250,000 units × $1.50	(375,000)
Target fixed cost		$ 275,000

The company would start by considering whether any discretionary fixed costs could be eliminated without harming the company. Since committed fixed costs are nearly impossible to change in the short run, ACDelco will probably not be able to reduce this type of fixed cost.

If the company can't reduce its fixed costs by $50,000, it would have to lower its variable cost to $1.30 per unit, as shown in Exhibit 8-11.

EXHIBIT 8-11 Calculating Target Unit Variable Cost

	Total
Target total cost	$ 650,000
Less: Current fixed costs	(325,000)
Target total variable costs	$ 325,000
Divided by number of units	÷ 250,000
Target variable cost per unit	$ 1.30

Perhaps the company could renegotiate raw materials costs with its suppliers or find a less costly way of packaging or shipping the air filters.

However, if ACDelco can't reduce variable costs to $1.30 per unit, could it meet its target profit through a combination of lowering both fixed costs and variable costs?

STOP & THINK

Suppose ACDelco can reduce its current fixed costs, but only by $25,000. If it wants to meet its target profit, by how much will it have to reduce the variable cost of each unit? Assume that sales volume remains at 250,000 units.

Answer: Companies typically try to cut both fixed and variable costs. Because ACDelco can cut its fixed costs only by $25,000, to meet its target profit, it would have to cut its variable costs as well:

Target total cost	$ 650,000
Less: Reduced fixed costs ($325,000 − $25,000)...........	(300,000)
Target total variable costs	$ 350,000
Divided by number of units..	÷ 250,000
Target variable cost per unit...	$ 1.40

In addition to cutting its fixed costs by $25,000, the company must reduce its variable costs by $0.10 per unit ($1.50 – $1.40) to meet its target profit at the existing volume of sales.

Another strategy would be to increase sales. ACDelco's managers can use CVP analysis, as you learned in Chapter 7, to figure out how many oil filters the company would have to sell to achieve its target profit. How could the company increase demand for the oil filters? Perhaps it could reach new markets or advertise. How much would advertising cost—and how many extra oil filters would the company have to sell to cover the cost of advertising? These are only some of the questions managers must ask. As you can see, managers don't have an easy task when the current total cost exceeds the target total cost. Sometimes, companies just can't compete given the current market price. If that's the case, they may have no other choice than to exit the market for that product.

Cost-Plus Pricing

When a company is a price-setter, it emphasizes a cost-plus approach to pricing. This pricing approach is essentially the *opposite* of the target-pricing approach. <u>Cost-plus pricing</u> starts with the product's total costs (as a given) and *adds* its desired profit to determine a cost-plus price.

Total cost
Plus: Desired profit
Cost-plus price

When the product is unique, the company has more control over pricing. However, the company still needs to make sure that the cost-plus price is not higher than what customers are willing to pay. Let's go back to our original ACDelco example. This time, let's assume that the oil filters benefit from brand recognition, so the company has some control over the price it charges for its filters. Exhibit 8-12 takes a cost-plus pricing approach assuming the current level of sales.

EXHIBIT 8-12 Calculating Cost-Plus Price

	Calculations	Total
Current variable costs	250,000 units × $1.50 per unit =	$375,000
Plus: Current fixed costs		+ 325,000
Current total costs		$700,000
Plus: Desired profit	10% × $1,000,000 of assets	+ 100,000
Target revenue		$800,000
Divided by number of units		÷ 250,000
Cost-plus price per unit		$ 3.20

If the current market price for generic oil filters is $3.00, as we assumed earlier, can ACDelco sell its brand-name filters for $3.20 apiece? The answer depends on how well the company has been able to differentiate its product or brand name. The company may use focus groups or marketing surveys to find out how customers would respond to its cost-plus price. The company may find out that its cost-plus price is too high, or it may find that it could set the price even higher without jeopardizing sales.

STOP & THINK

Which costing system (job costing or process costing) do you think price-setters and price-takers typically use?

Answer: Companies tend to be price-setters when their products are unique. Unique products are produced as single items or in small batches. Therefore, these companies use job costing to determine the product's cost. However, companies are price-takers when their products are high-volume commodities. Process costing better suits this type of product.

Notice how pricing decisions used our two keys to decision making: (1) focus on relevant information and (2) use a contribution margin approach that separates variable costs from fixed costs. In pricing decisions, all cost information is relevant because the company must cover *all* costs along the value chain before it can generate a profit. However, we still needed to consider variable costs and fixed costs separately because they behave differently at different volumes.

Our pricing decision rule is as follows:

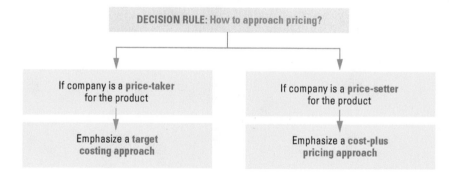

Decision Guidelines

Relevant Information for Business Decisions

Nike makes special order and regular pricing decisions. Even though it sells mass-produced tennis shoes and sports clothing, Nike has differentiated its products with advertising. Nike's managers consider both quantitative and qualitative factors as they make pricing decisions. Here are key guidelines that Nike's managers follow in making their decisions.

Decision	Guidelines
What information is relevant to a short-term special business decision?	Relevant information is as follows: 1. Pertains to the *future* 2. *Differs* between alternatives
What are two key guidelines in making short-term special business decisions?	1. Focus on *relevant* data. 2. Use a *contribution margin* approach that separates variable costs from fixed costs.
How does a company's committment to sustainability affect decision making?	Companys that are committed to sustainability will judge every decision through the lens of the triple bottom line, assessing the impact of the decision not only on company profit, but also on its consequences for people and the planet.
Should Nike accept a lower sales price than the regular price for a large order from a customer in São Paulo, Brazil?	If the revenue from the order exceeds the incremental variable and fixed costs incurred to fill the order, then accepting the order will increase operating income.
What should Nike consider in setting its regular product prices?	Nike considers the following: 1. What profit stockholders expect 2. What price customers will pay 3. Whether it is a price-setter or a price-taker
What approach should Nike take to pricing?	Nike has differentiated its products through advertising its brand name. Thus, Nike tends to be a price-setter. Nike's managers can emphasize a cost-plus approach to pricing.
What approach should discount shoe stores such as Payless ShoeSource take to pricing?	Payless ShoeSource sells generic shoes (no-name brands) at low prices. Payless is a price-taker, so managers use a target-costing approach to pricing.

SUMMARY PROBLEM **1**

Linger Industries makes tennis balls. Linger's only plant can produce up to 2.5 million cans of balls per year. Current production is two million cans. Annual manufacturing, selling, and administrative fixed costs total $700,000. The variable cost of making and selling each can of balls is $1. Stockholders expect a 12% annual return on the company's $3 million of assets.

Requirements

1. What is Linger Industries' current total cost of making and selling two million cans of tennis balls? What is the current cost per unit of each can of tennis balls?

2. Assume that Linger Industries is a price-taker and the current market price is $1.45 per can of balls (this is the price at which manufacturers sell to retailers). What is the *target* total cost of producing and selling two million cans of balls? Given Linger Industries' current total costs, will the company reach stockholders' profit goals?

3. If Linger Industries cannot reduce its fixed costs, what is the target variable cost per can of balls?

4. Suppose Linger Industries could spend an extra $100,000 on advertising to differentiate its product so that it could be more of a price-setter. Assuming the original volume and costs plus the $100,000 of new advertising costs, what cost-plus price will Linger Industries want to charge for a can of balls?

5. Nike has just asked Linger Industries to supply 400,000 cans of balls at a special order price of $1.20 per can. Nike wants Linger Industries to package the balls under the Nike label (Linger will imprint the Nike logo on each ball and can). As a result, Linger Industries will have to spend $10,000 to change the packaging machinery. Assuming the original volume and costs, should Linger Industries accept this special order? (Unlike the chapter problem, assume that Linger will incur variable selling costs as well as variable manufacturing costs related to this order.)

▪ SOLUTION

Requirement 1
The current total cost, and cost per unit are calculated as follows:

Fixed costs	$ 700,000
Plus: Total variable costs (2 million cans × $1 per unit)	+ 2,000,000
Current total costs	$2,700,000
Divided by number of units	÷ 2,000,000
Current cost per can	$ 1.35

Requirement 2
The target total cost is as follows:

Revenue at market price (2,000,000 cans × $1.45 price)	$2,900,000
Less: Desired profit (12% × $3,000,000 of assets)	(360,000)
Target total cost	$2,540,000

Linger Industries' *current* total costs ($2,700,000 from Requirement 1) are $160,000 higher than the *target* total costs ($2,540,000). If Linger Industries can't cut costs, it won't be able to meet stockholders' profit expectations.

Requirement 3

Assuming that Linger Industries cannot reduce its fixed costs, the target variable cost per can is as follows:

Target total cost (from Requirement 2)	$ 2,540,000
Less: Fixed costs..	(700,000)
Target total variable costs	$ 1,840,000
Divided by number of units...............................	÷ 2,000,000
Target variable cost per unit..............................	$ 0.92

Since Linger Industries cannot reduce its fixed costs, it needs to reduce variable costs by $0.08 per can ($1.00 – $0.92) to meet its profit goals. This would require an 8% cost reduction in variable costs, which may not be possible.

Requirement 4

If Linger Industries can differentiate its tennis balls, it will gain more control over pricing. The company's new cost-plus price would be as follows:

Current total costs (from Requirement 1).............	$ 2,700,000
Plus: Additional cost of advertising	+ 100,000
Plus: Desired profit (from Requirement 2)............	+ 360,000
Target revenue...	$ 3,160,000
Divided by number of units..................................	÷ 2,000,000
Cost-plus price per unit...	$ 1.58

Linger Industries must study the market to determine whether retailers would pay $1.58 per can of balls.

Requirement 5

First, Linger determines that it has enough extra capacity (500,000 cans) to fill this special order (400,000). Next, Linger compares the revenue from the special order with the extra costs that will be incurred to fill the order. Notice that Linger shouldn't compare the special order price ($1.20) with the current unit cost of each can ($1.35) because the unit cost contains both a fixed and variable component. Since the company has excess capacity, the existing fixed costs won't be affected by the order. The correct analysis is as follows:

Revenue from special order (400,000 × $1.20 per unit)	$ 480,000
Less: Variable cost of special order (400,000 × $1.00)	(400,000)
Contribution margin from special order....................................	$ 80,000
Less: Additional fixed costs of special order.............................	(10,000)
Operating income provided by special order.............................	$ 70,000

Linger Industries should accept the special order because it will increase operating income by $70,000. However, Linger Industries also needs to consider whether its regular customers will find out about the special price and demand lower prices, too. If Linger had simply compared the special order price of $1.20 to the current unit cost of each can ($1.35), it would have rejected the special order and missed out on the opportunity to make an additional $70,000 of profit.

How do Managers Make Other Special Business Decisions?

In this part of the chapter we'll consider four more special business decisions:

- Whether to discontinue a product, department, or store
- How to factor constrained resources into product mix decisions
- Whether to make a product or outsource it (buy it)
- Whether to sell a product as is or process it further

Decisions to Discontinue Products, Departments, or Stores

Managers often must decide whether to discontinue products, departments, stores, or territories that are not as profitable as desired. Newell Rubbermaid—maker of Sharpie markers, Graco strollers, and Rubbermaid plastics—recently discontinued some of its European products lines. Home Depot closed its Expo stores. Kroger food stores replaced some in-store movie rental departments with health food departments. How do managers make these decisions? Exhibit 8-13 shows some questions managers must consider when deciding whether to discontinue a product line, department, or retail store location.

4 Decide whether to discontinue a product, department, or store

EXHIBIT 8-13 Considerations for Discontinuing Products, Departments, or Stores

- Does the product provide a positive contribution margin?
- Are there any fixed costs that can be avoided if we discontinue the product?
- Will discontinuing the product affect sales of the company's other products?
- What could we do with the freed capacity?

Accounting Simplified

Discontinuing a Product

If your instructor is using MyAccountingLab, go to the Multimedia Library for a quick video on this topic.

In the first half of the chapter we assumed ACDelco offered only one product—oil filters. Now let's assume the company makes both oil filters and air cleaners. Exhibit 8-14 illustrates a product line income statement in contribution margin format. As you can see, a **product line income statement** shows the operating income of each product line, as well as the company as a whole.

EXHIBIT 8-14 Product Line Income Statement

Product Line Income Statement	Company Total (312,500 units)	Oil Filters (250,000 units)	Air Cleaners (62,500 units)
Sales revenue	$925,000	$800,000	$125,000
Less variable expenses:			
Variable manufacturing costs (DM, DL, and Variable MOH)	362,500	300,000	62,500
Variable marketing and administrative costs	87,500	75,000	12,500
Contribution margin	$475,000	$425,000	$ 50,000
Less fixed expenses:			
Fixed manufacturing costs (Fixed MOH)	200,000	160,000	40,000
Fixed marketing and administrative costs	125,000	100,000	25,000
Operating income	$150,000	$165,000	$ (15,000)

In this exhibit, notice that the contribution margin provided by oil filters ($425,000) is the same as shown in Exhibit 8-6. What differs is that the fixed costs have now been allocated between the two product lines. Since 80% of the units produced are oil filters (250,000 ÷ 312,500 total units) and since each unit takes about the same amount of time to produce, management has allocated 80% of the fixed costs to the oil filters. The remaining 20% of fixed costs have been allocated to air cleaners. Keep in mind that management could have chosen another allocation system which would have resulted in a different allocation of fixed costs.

Further notice that the air cleaner product line appears to be unprofitable. Currently, the air cleaners have an operating loss of $15,000 per period. Without this loss, management believes the company's operating income could be $15,000 higher each period. Therefore, management is considering whether to discontinue the product line. Let's now consider how management should approach this decision.

Consider the Product's Contribution Margin and Avoidable Fixed Costs

In making this decision, management should consider the questions raised in Exhibit 8-13. The first question addresses the product line's contribution margin: is it positive or negative? Exhibit 8-14 shows that the air cleaners provide $50,000 of contribution margin. This positive contribution margin means the product line is generating enough revenue to cover its own variable costs, plus provide another $50,000 that can be used to cover some of the company's fixed costs.

Had the contribution margin been negative, management would either need to raise the price of the product, if possible, cut variable costs, or discontinue the line. Management would only keep a product line with a negative contribution margin if they expected the sales of a companion product to decline as a result of discontinuing the product. For example, if customers alway buy one oil filter every time they buy an air cleaner, then sales of oil filters might decline as a result of discontinuing the air cleaners. As a result, the total contribution margin earned from the oil filters would decline. This potential loss in contribution margin on the oil filters would need to be weighed against the savings generated from eliminating the product line with a negative contribution margin.

After assessing the contribution margin, managers need to consider fixed costs. The important question is this: Can any fixed costs be eliminated if the product line is discontinued? Any fixed costs that can be eliminated as a result of discontinuing the product are known as **avoidable fixed costs**. These costs are relevant to the decision, because they will be incurred *only* if the product line is retained.

On the other hand, **unavoidable fixed costs** are those fixed costs that will continue to be incurred even if the product line is discontinued. Unavoidable fixed costs are irrelevant to the decision because they will be the same regardless of whether the product line is kept or discontinued.

Exhibit 8-15 shows the company's fixed costs in more detail. Notice that total fixed costs ($200,000 of manufacturing and $125,000 of marketing and administrative) are the same as shown in Exhibit 8-14. Managers will assess each fixed cost to determine how much, if any, is avoidable.

Exhibit 8-15 shows that management has identified $8,000 of fixed manufacturing and $10,000 of fixed marketing and administrative costs that can be eliminated if the air cleaners are discontinued. The avoidable fixed costs consist of a cancellable lease on equipment used to manufacture the air cleaners, advertisements for the air cleaners, and salaried employees who work solely on the air cleaner product line. Most of the fixed costs, such as property taxes, insurance, depreciation and so forth are unavoidable: they will continue even if the air cleaners are discontinued.

EXHIBIT 8-15 Analysis of the Company's Fixed Costs

Detailed listing of fixed expenses	Total Cost	Avoidable
Fixed manufacturing (Fixed MOH):		
Property taxes	18,000	0
Insurance	5,000	0
Depreciation on plant and production equipment	130,000	0
Fixed portion of utilities	7,000	0
Salaries of indirect labor (supervisors, janitors, etc.)	35,000	3,000
Equipment lease (cancellable)	5,000	5,000
Total fixed manufacturing costs	$200,000	$8,000
Fixed marketing and administrative:		
Building lease	17,000	0
Telephone, internet, utilities	8,000	0
Depreciation on sales vehicles and office equipment	20,000	0
Advertisements	25,000	6,000
Sales and administrative salaries	55,000	4,000
Total fixed marketing and administrative costs	$125,000	$10,000

With this information in hand, management can now determine whether or not to discontinue the air cleaner product line. Exhibit 8-16 presents management's analysis of the decision. In this analysis, managers compare the contribution margin that would be lost from discontinuing the air cleaners with the fixed cost savings that could be generated.

EXHIBIT 8-16 Incremental Analysis for Discontinuing a Product Line

Incremental Analysis—Discontinuation Decision	(Costs)/Savings
Contribution margin lost if air cleaners are discontinued (from Exhibit 8-14)	$(50,000)
Less: Cost savings from eliminating avoidable fixed costs	18,000
Decrease in company's operating income	$(32,000)

This analysis shows that the company's operating income would actually *decrease* by $32,000 if the air cleaners are discontinued. Therefore, the air cleaners should not be discontinued. The company would only eliminate the air cleaners if it could use the freed capacity to make a different product that is more profitable than the air cleaners.

Other Considerations

As noted in Exhibit 8-13, management must consider at least two other issues when making the decision to discontinue a product line, department, or store.

First, will discontinuing the product line affect sales of the company's other products? As discussed previously, some products have companion products whose sales would be hurt through discontinuing a particular product. This is also true about store departments. Can you imagine a grocery store discontinuing its produce department? Sales of every other department in the store would decline as a result of shoppers' inability to purchase fruits and vegetables at the store. On the other hand, sometimes discontinuing a product, such as one particular camera model, can increases the sales of the other company products (other camera models). The same holds true for retail stores. For example, assume two Starbucks are located close to one other. If one store is closed, then sales at the other location might increase as a result.

The second question concerns freed capacity. If a product line, department, or store is discontinued, management needs to consider what it would do with the newly freed capacity. As mentioned in the opening story, Kroger recently replaced some of its in-store movie rental departments with health food departments. Why? Managers must have determined that a health food department would be more profitable than a movie rental department. However, they could have used the space to house a sushi bar, or display other products. Management must consider which alterative use of the freed capacity will be most profitable. Finally, management should consider what to do with any newly freed labor capacity. To exercise corporate responsibility, management should do all it can to retrain employees for other areas of its operations rather than laying off employees.

Business decisions should take into account all costs affected by the choice of action.

STOP & THINK

Unlike the text example, assume that all of ACDelco's fixed costs are *unavoidable*. If the company discontinues the air cleaners, it could use the freed capacity to make spark plugs. The spark plugs are expected to provide a contribution margin of $70,000 but will require $5,000 of new fixed costs. Should ACDelco drop the air cleaners and use the freed capacity to make spark plugs?

Answer: The following incremental analysis shows that the company would be more profitable if it discontinued the air cleaners and used the freed capacity to make spark plugs.

Incremental Analysis: Product Replacement Decision	(Costs)/Savings
Contribution margin lost if air cleaners are discontinued (from Exhibit 8-14)...	$(50,000)
Plus: Contribution margin gained from spark plugs	70,000
Less: New fixed costs	(5,000)
Increase in company's operating income	$ 15,000

Managers must ask what total costs—variable and fixed—will change. The key to deciding whether to discontinue products, departments, or stores is to compare the lost revenue against the costs that can be saved and to consider what would be done with the freed capacity. The decision rule is as follows:

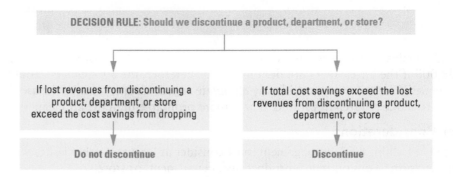

DECISION RULE: Should we discontinue a product, department, or store?

If lost revenues from discontinuing a product, department, or store exceed the cost savings from dropping → Do not discontinue

If total cost savings exceed the lost revenues from discontinuing a product, department, or store → Discontinue

Pitfall to Avoid on Discontinuation Decisions

One of the most common mistakes managers make when analyzing whether or not to discontinue a product is to base the decision on a product line income statement that contains an allocation of common fixed expenses. **Common fixed expenses** are those expenses that *cannot* be traced directly to a product line. For example, in Exhibits 8-14 and 8-15, we see that fixed MOH costs such as property taxes, insurance, and depreciation are all common production costs that have been allocated between the product lines. While appropriate for product costing purposes, the allocation of common fixed costs is not appropriate for making product discontinuation decisions. Nor is the allocation of common fixed costs related to marketing and administration, such as the building lease, utilities, internet, or depreciation of office equipment.

As shown in Exhibit 8-14, the allocation of common fixed costs suggests the company's overall operating income could be $15,000 higher if the company stopped making the air cleaners. However, based on the correct analysis in Exhibit 8-16 we know the company's operating income would actually decline by $32,000 if the air cleaners were discontinued.

Since income statements with allocated common costs can potentially mislead managers, some companies prepare **segment margin income statements**, which contain no allocation of common fixed costs. Segment margin income statements look similar to Exhibit 8-14, except for two differences:

1. Only direct fixed costs that can be traced to specific product lines are deducted from the product line's contribution margin. The resulting operating income or loss for each individual product line is known as a **segment margin**.

2. All common fixed costs are shown under the company "total" column, but are not allocated among product lines.

We discuss and illustrate segment margin income statement in more detail in Chapter 10.

Product Mix Decisions when Resources are Constrained

Companies do not have unlimited resources. **Constraints** that restrict production or sale of a product vary from company to company. For a manufacturer, the production constraint is often the number of available machine hours. For a merchandiser such as Walmart, the primary constraint is cubic feet of display space. In order to determine which products to emphasize displaying or producing, companies facing constraints consider the questions shown in Exhibit 8-17.

5 Factor resource constraints into product mix decisions

EXHIBIT 8-17 Product Mix Considerations

- What constraint(s) stops us from making (or displaying) all of the units we can sell?
- Which products offer the highest contribution margin per unit of the constraint?
- Would emphasizing one product over another affect fixed costs?

Consider Union Bay, a manufacturer of shirts and jeans. Let's say the company can sell all of the shirts and jeans it produces, but it has only 2,000 machine hours of capacity. The company uses the same machines to produce both jeans and shirts. In this case, machine hours is the constraint. Note that this is a short-term decision, because in the long run, Union Bay could expand its production facilities to meet sales demand if it made financial sense to do so. The following data suggest that shirts are more profitable than jeans:

	Per Unit	
	Shirts	**Jeans**
Sale price	$ 30	$ 60
Less: Variable expenses	(12)	(48)
Contribution margin	$ 18	$ 12
Contribution margin ratio:		
Shirts—$18 ÷ $30	60%	
Jeans—$12 ÷ $60		20%

However, an important piece of information is missing—the time it takes to make each product. Let's assume that Union Bay can produce either 20 pairs of jeans *or* 10 shirts per machine hour. *The company will incur the same fixed costs either way, so fixed costs are irrelevant.* Which product should it emphasize?

To maximize profits when fixed costs are irrelevant, follow this decision rule:

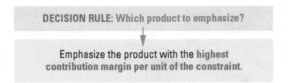

Because *machine hours* is the constraint, Union Bay needs to figure out which product has the *highest contribution margin per machine hour*. Exhibit 8-18 shows the contribution margin per machine hour for each product.

EXHIBIT 8-18 Product Mix—Which Product to Emphasize

	Shirts	Jeans
(1) Units that can be produced each machine hour	10	20
(2) Contribution margin per unit	× $18	× $12
Contribution margin per machine hour (1) × (2)	$180	$240
Available capacity—number of machine hours	× 2,000	× 2,000
Total contribution margin at full capacity	$360,000	$480,000

Jeans have a higher contribution margin per machine hour ($240) than shirts ($180). Therefore, Union Bay will earn more profit by producing jeans. Why? Because even though jeans have a lower contribution margin *per unit*, Union Bay can make twice as many jeans as shirts in the available machine hours. Exhibit 8-18 also proves that Union Bay earns more total profit by making jeans. Multiplying the contribution margin per machine hour by the available number of machine hours shows that Union Bay can earn $480,000 of contribution margin by producing jeans but only $360,000 by producing shirts.

To maximize profit, Union Bay should make 40,000 jeans (2,000 machine hours × 20 jeans per hour) and zero shirts. Why zero shirts? Because for every machine hour spent making shirts, Union Bay would *give up* $60 of contribution margin ($240 per hour for jeans versus $180 per hour for shirts).

Changing Assumptions: Product Mix When Demand is Limited

We made two assumptions about Union Bay: (1) Union Bay's sales of other products, if any, won't be hurt by this decision and (2) Union Bay can sell as many jeans and shirts as it can produce. Let's challenge these assumptions. First, how could making only jeans (and not shirts) hurt sales of the company's other products? Using other production equipment, Union Bay also makes ties and jackets that coordinate with their shirts. Tie and jacket sales might fall if Union Bay no longer offers coordinating shirts.

Let's challenge our second assumption. A new competitor has decreased the demand for Union Bay's jeans. Now, the company can sell only 30,000 pairs of jeans. Union Bay should make only as many jeans as it can sell and use the remaining machine hours to produce shirts. Let's see how this constraint in sales demand changes profitability.

Recall from Exhibit 8-18 that Union Bay will earn $480,000 of contribution margin from using all 2,000 machine hours to produce jeans. However, if Union Bay makes only 30,000 jeans, it will use only 1,500 machine hours (30,000 jeans ÷ 20 jeans per machine hour). That leaves 500 machine hours available for making shirts. Union Bay's new contribution margin will be as follows:

	Shirts	Jeans	Total
Contribution margin per machine hour (from Exhibit 8-18)...........	$ 180	$ 240	
Machine hours devoted to product...	× 500	× 1,500	2,000
Total contribution margin at full capacity......................................	$90,000	$360,000	$450,000

Because of the change in product mix, Union Bay's total contribution margin will fall from $480,000 to $450,000, a $30,000 decline. Union Bay had to give up $60 of contribution margin per machine hour ($240 − $180) on the 500 hours it spent producing shirts rather than jeans. However, Union Bay had no choice—the company would have incurred an *actual loss* from producing jeans that it could not sell. If Union Bay had produced 40,000 jeans but sold only 30,000, the company would have spent $480,000 to make the unsold jeans (10,000 jeans × $48 variable cost per pair of jeans) yet would have received no sales revenue from them.

What about fixed costs? In most cases, changing the product mix emphasis in the short run will not affect fixed costs, so fixed costs are irrelevant. However, fixed costs could differ when a different product mix is emphasized. What if Union Bay had a month-to-month lease on a zipper machine used only for making jeans? If Union Bay made only shirts, it could *avoid* the lease cost. However, if Union Bay makes any jeans, it needs the machine. In this case, the fixed costs become relevant because they differ between alternative product mixes (shirts only *versus* jeans only or jeans and shirts).

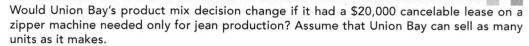

STOP&THINK

Would Union Bay's product mix decision change if it had a $20,000 cancelable lease on a zipper machine needed only for jean production? Assume that Union Bay can sell as many units as it makes.

Answer: We would compare the profitability as follows:

	Shirts	Jeans
Total contribution margin at full capacity (from Exhibit 8-18)	$360,000	$480,000
Less: Avoidable fixed costs	-0-	(20,000)
Net benefit	$360,000	$460,000

Even considering the zipper machine lease, producing jeans is more profitable than producing shirts. Union Bay would prefer producing jeans over shirts unless demand for jeans drops so low that the net benefit from jeans is less than $360,000 (the benefit gained from solely producing shirts).

Notice that the analysis again follows the two guidelines for special business decisions: (1) focus on relevant data (only those revenues and costs that differ) and (2) use a contribution margin approach, which separates variable from fixed costs.

Outsourcing Decisions (Make or Buy)

Outsourcing decisions are sometimes called <u>make-or-buy</u> decisions because managers must decide whether to make a product or service in-house or buy it from another company. Sometimes people confuse the term "outsourcing" with the term "offshoring."

6 Analyze outsourcing (make or buy) decisions

- <u>Outsourcing</u> refers to contracting an outside company to produce a product or perform a service. Outsourced work could be done domestically or overseas.

- <u>Offshoring</u> refers to having work performed overseas. Companies offshore work by either 1) operating their own manufacturing plants and call centers overseas or 2) outsourcing the overseas work to another company. Thus, offshored work is not necessarily outsourced work.

Outsourcing is not new. For years, companies have outsourced specialized services such as marketing, payroll processing, and legal work to firms that have expertise in those areas. More and more, brand-name companies such as Nike, IBM, and Sara Lee are outsourcing the production of their products so that they can concentrate on their core competencies of marketing and product development. In fact, so much production is outsourced that contract manufacturing has become an entire industry. <u>**Contract manufacturers**</u> are manufacturers who only make products for other companies, not for themselves.

Let's see how managers make outsourcing decisions. The heart of these decisions is how to best use available resources. Let's assume that Apple, the developer of iPods, is deciding whether to continue making the earbuds that are sold with the product or outsource production to Skullcandy, a company that specializes in earbuds. Let's assume Apple's cost to produce 2 million earbuds each period is as shown in Exhibit 8-19:[3]

EXHIBIT 8-19 Production Costs and Volume

Manufacturing Cost	Variable Cost per Unit	Total Cost for 2 million units
Direct materials	$4.00	8,000,000
Direct labor	0.50	1,000,000
Variable MOH	1.50	3,000,000
Total variable cost	$6.00	12,000,000
Plus: Fixed MOH		4,000,000
Total cost		$16,000,000
Divide by: Number of units		÷2,000,000
Cost per unit (absorption)		$ 8.00

Let's further assume that Skullcandy is willing to provide earbuds to Apple for $7.00 each. Should Apple make the earbuds or buy them from Skullcandy? The $7.00 price is less than the full absorption cost per unit ($8.00), but greater than Apple's variable cost per unit ($6.00). The answer isn't as easy as simply comparing unit costs. In deciding what to do, managers should consider the questions outlined in Exhibit 8-20.

Why is this important?

"Almost any **business activity** can be **outsourced** (for example, manufacturing, marketing, and payroll). **Companies** often choose to retain only their **core competencies**—things they are *really* good at doing—and **outsource** just about everything else to companies that can do it *better* for them."

EXHIBIT 8-20 Outsourcing Considerations

- How do our variable costs compare to the outsourcing cost?
- Are any fixed costs avoidable if we outsource?
- What could we do with the freed capacity?

Let's see how these considerations apply to our example:

1. **Variable costs:** The variable cost of producing each earbud ($6.00) is less than the outsourcing cost ($7.00). Based on variable costs alone, Apple should manufacture the earbuds in-house. However, managers must still consider fixed costs.

2. **Fixed costs:** Let's assume that Apple could save $500,000 of fixed costs each period by outsourcing. This savings would primarily result from laying off salaried indirect labor, such as production supervisors. However, most of the fixed manufacturing cost relates to plant capacity, and will continue to exist even if the company stops making earbuds. These costs might include property tax on the plant and non-cancellable lease payments made on the production equipment.

[3]The hypothetical cost information was created solely for academic purposes, and is not intended in any way, to represent the actual costs incurred by Apple or the price that would be charged by Skullcandy.

3. **Use of freed capacity:** We'll start by assuming that Apple has no other use for the production capacity, so it will remain idle. We will change this assumption later.

Given this information, what should Apple do? Exhibit 8-21 compares the two alternatives.

EXHIBIT 8-21 Incremental Analysis for Outsourcing Decisions

Manufacturing Costs	Make Earbuds	Outsource Earbuds	Difference: Additional Cost/ (Savings) From Outsourcing
Variable Costs:			
If Make: $6.00 × 2,000,000 units	$12,000,000		
If Buy: $7.00 × 2,000,000 units		$14,000,000	$2,000,000
Fixed Costs	4,000,000	3,500,000	(500,000)
Total cost of producing 2,000,000 units	$16,000,000	$17,500,000	$1,500,000

This analysis shows that Apple should continue to make the earbuds. Why is this the case? As shown in the last column of Exhibit 8-21, the company would spend $2,000,000 more in variable costs to outsource the earbuds, but only save $500,000 in fixed costs. The net result is a $1,500,000 increase in total costs if the company outsources production.

The analysis shown in Exhibit 8-21 is partially dependent on production volume. If Apple needed fewer than 500,000 earbuds each period, then the decision would be reversed because the savings on fixed costs would outweigh the additional $1 per unit spent on variable costs. At volumes lower than 500,000, it would be cheaper for Apple to outsource production than produce in-house.

Notice how Exhibit 8-21 uses our two keys for decision making: 1) focus on relevant data (costs that differ between alternatives), and 2) use a contribution margin approach that separates variable costs from fixed costs. Our decision rule for outsourcing is as follows:

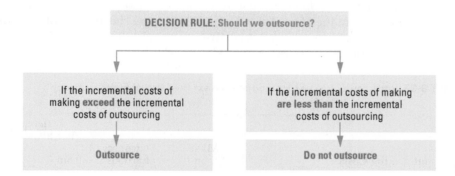

DECISION RULE: Should we outsource?

If the incremental costs of making **exceed** the incremental costs of outsourcing	If the incremental costs of making **are less than** the incremental costs of outsourcing
Outsource	Do not outsource

Determining an Acceptable Outsourcing Price

In Chapter 7, we used the concept of an indifference point to help managers decide how to structure costs. We can use the same concept here to determine the maximum outsourcing price Apple would be willing to pay to have another manufacturer make the earbuds. By knowing up front how much Apple would be willing to pay, the company can proactively seek bids from multiple companies, such as contract manufacturers.

Exhibit 8-22 shows how to calculate the indifference point. The exhibit begins by equating the costs of making the earbuds with the costs of outsourcing the earbuds. Next, all of the information from Exhibit 8-21 is inserted into the equations, with the exception of the variable cost per unit under the outsourcing alternative. The variable cost of outsourcing each unit is the cost we wish to solve for.

EXHIBIT 8-22 Using an Indifference Point to Find an Acceptable Outsourcing Price

Costs of making earbuds	=	Costs of outsourcing earbuds
Variable Costs + Fixed Costs	=	Variable Costs + Fixed Costs
(2,000,000 units × $6) + $4,000,000	=	(2,000,000 units × Variable cost per unit) + $3,500,000
$16,000,000	=	(2,000,000 × Variable cost per unit) + $3,500,000
$12,500,000	=	(2,000,000 × Variable cost per unit)
Variable cost per unit	=	$6.25

This analysis shows that, all else being equal, Apple would be *indifferent* between making and outsourcing 2 million earbuds if the outsourcing price was exactly $6.25 a unit. Therefore, the most Apple would be willing to pay for this volume of earbuds would be just under $6.25 a unit.

Notice, again, that this analysis is dependent on production volume. For example, if Apple needs 3 million units, the most they would be willing to pay would be $6.17 per unit. Why the difference? By producing more units, Apple's fixed costs are being utilized more efficiently, driving down the average cost of making each unit. As Apple's own unit cost falls, so will the price they are willing to pay some other company to make the earbuds. The opposite is also true: The fewer units Apple needs, the more they will be willing to pay another company to make the earbuds.

Alternative use of Freed Capacity

Now let's change one of our original assumptions. Instead of assuming that the production capacity will remain idle, let's assume that Apple could lease it out to another company for $2.5 million per period. In this case, Apple must consider its **opportunity cost**, which is the benefit foregone by choosing a particular course of action. If Apple continues to make its own earbuds, it will be losing out on the opportunity to earn lease income of $2.5 million per period.

Exhibit 8-23 incorporates this information into our analysis by showing lease income as additional income that *could be made* if the company outsources production. Thus, we show the lease income in the "Outsource Earbuds" column. This income offsets some of the cost associated with outsourcing. Alternatively, we could show the $2.5 million as an *additional* cost (an opportunity cost) in the "Make Earbuds" column.

EXHIBIT 8-23 Incremental Analysis Incorporating Next Best Use of Freed Capacity

Manufacturing Costs	Make Earbuds	Outsource Earbuds	Difference: Additional Cost/ (Savings) from Outsourcing
Variable Costs:			
If Make: $6.00 × 2,000,000 units	$12,000,000		
If Buy: $7.00 × 2,000,000 units		$14,000,000	$ 2,000,000
Fixed Costs	$ 4,000,000	$ 3,500,000	(500,000)
Total cost	$16,000,000	$17,500,000	$ 1,500,000
Less: Lease income	-0-	(2.500,000)	(2,500,000)
Net Cost	$16,000,000	15,000,000	($1,000,000)

This analysis shows that Apple will save $1,000,000 each period by outsourcing production of the earbuds. This result holds regardless of whether we treat the $2.5 million lease as income in the "outsource earbuds" column or as an opportunity cost in the "make earbuds" column. Again, notice that a different production volume could potentially result in a different outcome.

Potential Drawbacks of Outsourcing

While outsourcing often provides cost savings, it is not without drawbacks. When a company outsources, it gives up control of the production process, including control over quality and production scheduling. Rather, it must rely on the supplier to provide the product or service at an agreed-upon level of quality, at agreed-upon delivery dates. Often, one or more employees are needed just to manage the relationship with the outsourcing company to make sure that everything runs smoothly. The cost of employing any such additional personnel should also be considered when comparing the cost of outsourcing versus the cost of producing in-house.

In addition, for those companies embracing the triple bottom line, outsourcing is often not viewed as a viable alternative. Why? Because outsourcing often results in laying off employees. In addition, companies will want to thoroughly investigate and monitor the labor practices and working conditions of offshored contract work to make sure laborers are treated fairly and work in a safe environment. While overseas labor is often cheap and readily available, the exploitation of any people, in any country, is not an acceptable business practice.

Decisions to Sell As Is or Process Further

At what point in processing should a company sell its product? Many companies, especially in the food processing and natural resource industries, face this business decision. Companies in these industries process a raw material (milk, corn, livestock, crude oil, lumber, and so forth) to a point before it is saleable. For example, Kraft pasteurizes raw milk before it is saleable. Kraft must then decide whether it should sell the pasteurized milk as is or process it further into other dairy products (reduced-fat milk, butter, sour cream, cottage cheese, yogurt, blocks of cheese, shredded cheese, and so forth). Managers consider the questions shown in Exhibit 8-24 when deciding whether to sell as is or process further.

7 Decide whether to sell a product "as is" or process it further

EXHIBIT 8-24 Sell As Is or Process Further Considerations

- How much revenue will we receive if we sell the product as is?
- How much revenue will we receive if we sell the product *after* processing it further?
- How much will it cost to process the product further?

Let's consider Bertolli, the manufacturer of Italian food products. Suppose Bertolli spends $100,000 to process raw olives into 50,000 quarts of plain virgin olive oil. Should Bertolli sell the olive oil as is or should it spend more to process the olive oil into gourmet dipping oils, such as a Basil and Garlic Infused Dipping Oil? In making the decision, Bertolli's managers consider the following relevant information[2]:

- Bertolli could sell the plain olive oil for $5 per quart, for a total of $250,000 (50,000 × $5).
- Bertolli could sell the gourmet dipping oil for $7 per quart, for a total of $350,000 (50,000 × $7).
- Bertolli would have to spend $0.75 per quart, or $37,500 (50,000 × $0.75), to further process the plain olive oil into the gourmet dipping oil. This cost would include the extra direct materials required (such as basil, garlic, and the incremental cost of premium glass containers) as well as the extra conversion costs incurred (the cost of any

Why is this important?

"Some companies are able to sell their products at **different points** of completion. For example, some furniture **manufacturers** sell flat-packed bookshelves, TV stands, and home office furniture that the consumer must **finish assembling**. A **cost-benefit analysis** helps managers choose the most **profitable point** at which to sell the company's products."

[2]All references to Bertolli in this hypothetical example were created by the author solely for academic purposes and are not intended, in any way, to represent the actual business practices of, or costs incurred by Bertolli.

additional machinery and labor that the company would need to purchase in order to complete the extra processing).

By examining the incremental analysis shown in Exhibit 8-25, Bertolli's managers can see that they can increase operating income by $62,500 by further processing the plain olive oil into the gourmet dipping oil. The extra $100,000 of revenue greatly exceeds the incremental $37,500 of cost incurred to further process the olive oil.

EXHIBIT 8-25 Incremental Analysis for Sell As Is or Process Further Decision

	Sell As Is	Process Further	Difference: Additional Revenue/(Costs) from Processing Further
Expected revenue from selling 50,000 quarts of plain olive oil at $5.00 per quart	$250,000		
Expected revenue from selling 50,000 quarts of gourmet dipping oil at $7.00 per quart		$350,000	$100,000
Additional costs of $0.75 per quart to convert 50,000 quarts of plain olive oil into gourmet dipping oil		(37,500)	(37,500)
Total net benefit	$250,000	$312,500	$ 62,500

Notice that Bertolli's managers do *not* consider the $100,000 originally spent on processing the olives into olive oil. Why? It is a sunk cost. Recall from our previous discussion that a sunk cost is a past cost that cannot be changed regardless of which future action the company takes. Bertolli has incurred $100,000 regardless of whether it sells the olive oil as is or processes it further into gourmet dipping oils. Therefore, the cost is *not* relevant to the decision.

Thus, the decision rule is as follows:

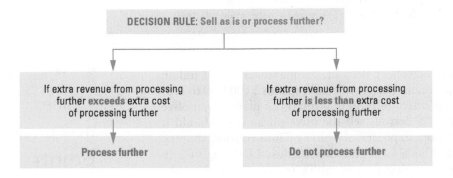

Decision Guidelines

Short-Term Special Business Decisions

Amazon.com has confronted most of the special business decisions we've covered. Here are the key guidelines Amazon.com's managers follow in making their decisions.

Decision	Guidelines
Should Amazon.com discontinue its electronics product line?	If the cost savings exceed the lost revenues from dropping the electronics product line, then dropping will increase operating income.
Given limited warehouse space, which products should Amazon.com focus on selling?	Amazon.com should focus on selling the products with the highest contribution margin per unit of the constraint, which is cubic feet of warehouse space
Should Amazon.com outsource its warehousing operations?	If the incremental costs of operating its own warehouses exceed the costs of outsourcing, then outsourcing will increase operating income.
How should a company decide whether to sell a product as is or process further?	Process further only if the extra sales revenue (from processing further) exceeds the extra costs of additional processing.

SUMMARY PROBLEM 2

Requirements

1. Aziz produces Standard and Deluxe sunglasses:

	Per Pair	
	Standard	Deluxe
Sale price...	$20	$30
Variable expenses...	16	21

The company has 15,000 machine hours available. In one machine hour, Aziz can produce 70 pairs of the Standard model or 30 pairs of the Deluxe model. Assuming machine hours is a constraint, which model should Aziz emphasize?

2. Just Do It! incurs the following costs for 20,000 pairs of its high-tech hiking socks:

Direct materials..	$ 20,000
Direct labor..	80,000
Variable manufacturing overhead	40,000
Fixed manufacturing overhead..	80,000
Total manufacturing cost	$220,000
Cost per pair ($220,000 ÷ 20,000)..	$ 11

Another manufacturer has offered to sell Just Do It! similar socks for $10 a pair, a total purchase cost of $200,000. If Just Do It! outsources *and* leaves its plant idle, it can save $50,000 of fixed overhead cost. Or the company can use the released facilities to make other products that will contribute $70,000 to profits. In this case, the company will not be able to avoid any fixed costs. Identify and analyze the alternatives. What is the best course of action?

▪ SOLUTION

Requirement 1

	Style of Sunglasses	
	Standard	Deluxe
Sale price per pair...................................	$ 20	$ 30
Variable expense per pair	(16)	(21)
Contribution margin per pair	$ 4	$ 9
Units produced each machine hour	× 70	× 30
Contribution margin per machine hour.....	$ 280	$ 270
Capacity—number of machine hours	× 15,000	× 15,000
Total contribution margin at full capacity...........	$4,200,000	$4,050,000

Decision: Emphasize the Standard model because it has the higher contribution margin per unit of the constraint—machine hours—resulting in a higher contribution margin for the company.

Requirement 2

	Make Socks	Outsource Socks	
		Facilities Idle	Make Other Products
Relevant costs:			
Direct materials	$ 20,000	—	—
Direct labor	80,000	—	—
Variable overhead...	40,000	—	—
Fixed overhead	80,000	$ 30,000	$ 80,000
Outsourcing cost (20,000 × $10)	—	200,000	200,000
Total cost of obtaining socks	220,000	230,000	280,000
Profit from other products......................................	—	—	(70,000)
Net cost of obtaining 20,000 pairs of socks.............	$220,000	$230,000	$210,000

Decision: Just Do It! should outsource the socks from the outside supplier and use the released facilities to make other products.

END OF CHAPTER

Learning Objectives

- 1 Describe and identify information relevant to short-term business decisions
- 2 Decide whether to accept a special order
- 3 Describe and apply different approaches to pricing
- 4 Decide whether to discontinue a product, department, or store
- 5 Factor resource constraints into product mix decisions
- 6 Analyze outsourcing (make or buy) decisions
- 7 Decide whether to sell a product "as is" or process it further

Accounting Vocabulary

Avoidable fixed costs. (p. 476) Fixed costs that can be eliminated as a result taking a particular course of action.

Constraint. (p. 479) A factor that restricts production or sale of a product.

Contract manufacturers. (p. 470) Manufacturers who make products for other companies, not for themselves.

Cost-Plus Pricing. (p. 481) An approach to pricing used by price-setters; cost-plus pricing begins with the product's total costs and adds the company's desired profit to determine a cost-plus price.

Offshoring. (p. 481) Having work performed overseas. Offshored work can either be performed by the company itself or by outsourcing the work to another company.

Opportunity Cost. (p. 484) The benefit forgone by choosing a particular alternative course of action.

Outsourcing. (p. 481) A make-or-buy decision: Managers decide whether to buy a product or service or produce it in-house.

Product line income statement. (p. 475) An income statement that shows the operating income of each product line, as well as the company as a whole.

Relevant Information. (p. 460) Expected *future* data that *differs* among alternatives

Segment margin. (p. 479) The income resulting from subtracting only the direct fixed costs of a product line from its contribution margin. The segment margin contains no allocation of common fixed costs.

Segment margin income statement. (p. 479) A product line income statement that contains no allocation of common fixed costs. Only direct fixed costs that can be traced to specific product lines are subtracted from the product line's contribution margin. All common fixed costs remain unallocated, and are shown only under the company total.

Sunk Cost. (p. 460) A past cost that cannot be changed regardless of which future action is taken.

Target Costing. (p. 468) An approach to pricing used by price-takers; target costing begins with the revenue at market price and subtracts the company's desired profit to arrive at the target total cost.

Unavoidable fixed costs. (p. 476) Fixed costs that will continue to be incurred even if a particular course of action is taken.

MyAccountingLab | Go to http://myaccountinglab.com/ **for the following Quick Check, Short Exercises, Exercises, and Problems. They are available with immediate grading, explanations of correct and incorrect answers, and interactive media that acts as your own online tutor.**

Quick Check

1. (*Learning Objective 1*) In making short-term special decisions, you should
   - a. focus on total costs.
   - b. separate variable from fixed costs.
   - c. use a traditional absorption costing approach.
   - d. focus only on quantitative factors.

2. (*Learning Objective 1*) When making decisions, managers should
   - a. consider sunk costs.
   - b. consider costs that do not differ between alternatives.
   - c. consider only variable costs.
   - d. consider revenues that differ between alternatives.

3. (*Learning Objective 1*) Which of the following costs are irrelevant to business decisions?
   a. Sunk costs
   b. Costs that differ between alternatives
   c. Variable costs
   d. Avoidable costs

4. (*Learning Objective 2*) Which of the following is relevant to Amazon.com's decision to accept a special order at a lower sales price from a large customer in China?
   a. The cost of Amazon.com's warehouses in the United States
   b. Amazon.com's investment in its website
   c. The cost of shipping the order to the customer
   d. Founder Jeff Bezos's salary

5. (*Learning Objective 3*) When companies are price-setters, their products and services
   a. are priced by managers using a target-pricing emphasis.
   b. tend to be unique.
   c. tend to have a great many competitors.
   d. tend to be commodities.

6. (*Learning Objective 3*) When pricing a product or service, managers must consider which of the following?
   a. Only variable costs
   b. Only period costs
   c. Only manufacturing costs
   d. All costs

7. (*Learning Objective 4*) In deciding whether to drop its electronics product line, Amazon.com would consider
   a. the costs it could save by discontinuing the product line.
   b. the revenues it would lose from discontinuing the product line.
   c. how discontinuing the electronics product line would affect sales of its other products, such as mp3s.
   d. all of the above.

8. (*Learning Objective 5*) In deciding which product lines to emphasize, Amazon.com should focus on the product line that has the highest
   a. contribution margin per unit of the constraining factor.
   b. contribution margin per unit of product.
   c. contribution margin ratio.
   d. profit per unit of product.

9. (*Learning Objective 6*) When making outsourcing decisions
   a. the manufacturing full unit cost of making the product in-house is relevant.
   b. the variable cost of producing the product in-house is relevant.
   c. avoidable fixed costs are irrelevant.
   d. expected use of the freed capacity is irrelevant.

10. (*Learning Objective 7*) When deciding whether to sell as is or process a product further, managers should ignore which of the following?
    a. The revenue if the product is processed further
    b. The cost of processing further
    c. The costs of processing the product thus far
    d. The revenue if the product is sold as is

Quick Check Answers

1. b 2. d 3. a 4. c 5. b 6. d 7. d 8. a 9. b 10. c

Short Exercises

S8-1 Determine relevance of information (*Learning Objective 1*)

You are trying to decide whether to trade in your laser printer for a more recent model. Your usage pattern will remain unchanged, but the old and new printers use different toner cartridges. Are the following items relevant or irrelevant to your decision?
a. The price of the new printer
b. The price you paid for the old printer
c. The trade-in value of the old printer
d. Paper costs
e. The difference between the cost of toner cartridges

S8-2 Special order decision (*Learning Objective 2*)

Forst Manufacturing produces and sells oil filters for $3.30 each. A retailer has offered to purchase 20,000 oil filters for $1.55 per filter. Of the total manufacturing cost per filter of $1.95, $1.50 is the variable manufacturing cost per filter. For this special order, Forst would have to buy a special stamping machine that costs $8,500 to mark the customer's logo on the special-order oil filters. The machine would be scrapped when the special order is complete. This special order would use manufacturing capacity that would otherwise be idle. No variable nonmanufacturing costs would be incurred by the special order. Regular sales would not be affected by the special order.

Would you recommend that Forst accept the special order under these conditions?

S8-3 Determine pricing approach and target price *(Learning Objective 3)*

SnowCastles operates a Rocky Mountain ski resort. The company is planning its lift ticket pricing for the coming ski season. Investors would like to earn a 14% return on the company's $100 million of assets. The company incurs primarily fixed costs to groom the runs and operate the lifts. SnowCastles projects fixed costs to be $34,000,000 for the ski season. The resort serves about 800,000 skiers and snowboarders each season. Variable costs are about $8 per guest. Currently, the resort has such a favorable reputation among skiers and snowboarders that it has some control over the lift ticket prices.

1. Would SnowCastles emphasize target costing or cost-plus pricing. Why?
2. If other resorts in the area charge $60 per day, what price should SnowCastles charge?

S8-4 Use target costing to analyze data *(Learning Objective 3)*

Consider SnowCastles from S8-3. Assume that SnowCastles' reputation has diminished and other resorts in the vicinity are charging only $60 per lift ticket. SnowCastles has become a price-taker and won't be able to charge more than its competitors. At the market price, SnowCastles' managers believe they will still serve 800,000 skiers and snowboarders each season.

1. If SnowCastles can't reduce its costs, what profit will it earn? State your answer in dollars and as a percent of assets. Will investors be happy with the profit level? Show your analysis.
2. Assume that SnowCastles has found ways to cut its fixed costs to $31 million. What is its new target variable cost per skier/snowboarder? Compare this to the current variable cost per skier/snowboarder. Comment on your results.

S8-5 Decide whether to discontinue a department *(Learning Objective 4)*

Zena Fashion in New York operates three departments: Men's, Women's, and Accessories. Zena Fashion allocates all fixed expenses (unavoidable building depreciation and utilities) based on each department's square footage. Departmental operating income data for the third quarter of the current year are as follows:

	Department			
	Men's	Women's	Accessories	Total
Sales revenue	$106,000	$54,000	$100,000	$260,000
Variable expenses.	58,000	28,000	88,000	174,000
Fixed expenses.	26,000	21,000	25,000	72,000
Total expenses	$ 84,000	$49,000	$113,000	$246,000
Operating income (loss).	$ 22,000	$ 5,000	$ (13,000)	$ 14,000

The store will remain in the same building regardless of whether any of the departments are discontinued. Should Zena Fashion discontinue any of the departments? Give your reason.

S8-6 Discontinue a department: Revised information *(Learning Objective 4)*

Consider Zena Fashion from S8-5. Assume that the fixed expenses assigned to each department include only direct fixed costs of the department (rather than unavoidable fixed costs as given in S8-5):

• Salary of the department's manager
• Cost of advertising directly related to that department

If Zena Fashion discontinues a department, it will not incur these fixed expenses. Under these circumstances, should Zena Fashion discontinue any of the departments? Give your reason.

S8-7 Replace a department *(Learning Objective 4)*

Consider Zena Fashion from S8-5. Assume once again that all fixed costs are unavoidable. If Zena Fashion discontinues one of the current departments, it plans to replace the discontinued department with a Shoe Department. The company expects the Shoe

Department to produce $77,000 in sales and have $47,000 of variable costs. Because the shoe business would be new to Zena Fashion, the company would have to incur an additional $7,100 of fixed costs (advertising, new shoe display racks, and so forth) per quarter related to the department. What should Zena Fashion do now?

S8-8 Product mix decision: Unlimited demand (Learning Objective 5)

Boxes Unlimited produces plastic storage bins for household storage needs. The company makes two sizes of bins: Large (50 gallon) and Regular (35 gallon). Demand for the product is so high that Boxes Unlimited can sell as many of each size as it can produce. The company uses the same machinery to produce both sizes. The machinery can be run for only 3,500 hours per period. The company can produce 11 Large bins every hour compared to 15 Regular bins in the same amount of time. Fixed expenses amount to $100,000 per period. Sales prices and variable costs are as follows:

	Regular	Large
Sales price per unit.	$8.50	$10.60
Variable cost per unit	$3.50	$ 4.60

1. Which product should Boxes Unlimited emphasize? Why?
2. To maximize profits, how many of each size bin should the company produce?
3. Given this product mix, what will the company's operating income be?

S8-9 Product mix decision: Limited demand (Learning Objective 5)

Consider Boxes Unlimited in S8-8. Assume that demand for Regular bins is limited to 30,000 units and demand for Large bins is limited to 25,000 units.

1. How many of each size bin should the company make now?
2. Given this product mix, what will be the company's operating income?
3. Explain why the operating income is less than it was when the company was producing its optimal product mix.

S8-10 Outsourcing production decision (Learning Objectives 1 & 6)

Suppose an Olive Garden restaurant is considering whether to (1) bake bread for its restaurant in-house or (2) buy the bread from a local bakery. The chef estimates that variable costs of making each loaf include $0.50 of ingredients, $0.20 of variable overhead (electricity to run the oven), and $0.70 of direct labor for kneading and forming the loaves. Allocating fixed overhead (depreciation on the kitchen equipment and building) based on direct labor assigns $1.00 of fixed overhead per loaf. None of the fixed costs are avoidable. The local bakery would charge Olive Garden $1.80 per loaf.

1. What is the unit cost of making the bread in-house (use absorption costing)?
2. Should Olive Garden bake the bread in-house or buy from the local bakery? Why?
3. In addition to the financial analysis, what else should Olive Garden consider when making this decision?

S8-11 Relevant information for outsourcing delivery function (Learning Objectives 1 & 6)

Grier Food in Lexington, Kentucky, manufactures and markets snack foods. Deela Riley manages the company's fleet of 180 delivery trucks. Riley has been charged with "reengineering" the fleet-management function. She has an important decision to make.

- Should she continue to manage the fleet in-house with the five employees reporting to her? To do so, she will have to acquire new fleet-management software to streamline Grier Food's fleet-management process.

- Should she outsource the fleet-management function to Fleet Management Services, a company that specializes in managing fleets of trucks for other companies? Fleet Management Services would take over the maintenance, repair, and scheduling of Grier Food's fleet (but Grier Food would retain ownership). This alternative would require Riley to lay off her five employees. However, her own job would be secure, as she would be Grier Food's liaison with Fleet Management Services.

Assume that Riley's records show the following data concerning Grier Food's fleet:

Book value of Grier Food's trucks, with an estimated five-year life.	$3,100,000
Annual leasing fee for new fleet-management software	$ 8,600
Annual maintenance of trucks	$ 166,000
Fleet Supervisor Riley's annual salary.	$ 57,000
Total annual salaries of Grier Food's five other fleet-management employees.	$ 150,000

Suppose that Fleet Management Services offers to manage Grier Food's fleet for an annual fee of $280,000.

Which alternative will maximize Grier Food's short-term operating income?

S8-12 Outsourcing qualitative considerations *(Learning Objectives 1 & 6)*

Refer to Grier Food in S8-11. What qualitative factors should Riley consider before making a final decision?

S8-13 Scrap or process further decision *(Learning Objective 7)*

Paulson Auto Components has an inventory of 490 obsolete remote entry keys that are carried in inventory at a manufacturing cost of $79,870. Production Supervisor Ricky Lewis must decide to do one of the following:

- Process the inventory further at a cost of $19,000, with the expectation of selling it for $31,000
- Scrap the inventory for a sale price of $6,000

What should Lewis do? Present figures to support your decision.

S8-14 Determine most profitable final product *(Learning Objective 7)*

Cocoalicious processes cocoa beans into cocoa powder at a processing cost of $9,600 per batch. Cocoalicious can sell the cocoa powder as is, or it can process the cocoa powder further into chocolate syrup or boxed assorted chocolates. Once processed, each batch of cocoa beans would result in the following sales revenue:

Cocoa powder	$ 12,000
Chocolate syrup	$103,000
Boxed assorted chocolates	$202,000

The cost of transforming the cocoa powder into chocolate syrup would be $68,000. Likewise, the company would incur $176,000 to transform the cocoa powder into boxed assorted chocolates. The company president has decided to make boxed assorted chocolates owing to its high sales value and to the fact that the $9,600 cost of processing cocoa beans "eats up" most of the cocoa powder profits. Has the president made the right or wrong decision? Explain your answer.

EXERCISES **Group A**

E8-15A Determine relevant and irrelevant information *(Learning Objective 1)*

Swenson's Meats is considering whether it should replace a meat grinder patty shaper machine. The new machine will produce 25% more hamburger patties than the old machine in the same amount of time. (This machine is the bottleneck of the hamburger patty process for Swenson's.) The purchase of the new machine will cause fixed selling costs to increase, but variable selling costs will not be affected. The new machine will require installation by a specialty engineering firm. If the new machine is purchased, the old machine can be sold to an overseas meat processing company. The old machine requires frequent (quarterly) repairs and maintenance to keep it running. The new machine will require maintenance only once per year. The new machine will be paid for by signing a note payable with the bank that will cover the cost of the machine and its installation. Swenson's will have to pay interest monthly on the note payable for the new machine. The note payable that was used to purchase the old machine was fully paid off two years ago.

For each of the following costs, indicate whether each of the costs described would be relevant or not to Swenson's Meats' decision about whether to purchase the new machine or to keep the old machine.

Item	Relevant	Not Relevant
a. Cost of new machine		
b. Cost of old machine		
c. Added profits from increase in production resulting from new machine		
d. Fixed selling costs.		
e. Variable selling costs		
f. Sales value of old machine.		
g. Interest expense on new machine		
h. Interest expense on old machine		
i. Book value of old machine.		
j. Maintenance cost of new machine.		
k. Repairs and maintenance costs of old machine		
l. Installation costs of new machine.		
m. Accumulated depreciation on old machine		
n. Cost per pound of hamburger		
o. Installation cost of old machine		

E8-16A Special order decisions given two scenarios *(Learning Objective 2)*

Suppose the Baseball Hall of Fame in Cooperstown, New York, has approached Collectible Cards with a special order. The Hall of Fame wants to purchase 57,000 baseball card packs for a special promotional campaign and offers $0.40 per pack, a total of $22,800. Collectible Cards' total production cost is $0.60 per pack, as follows:

Variable costs:	
Direct materials.	$0.13
Direct labor.	0.06
Variable overhead.	0.11
Fixed overhead	0.30
Total cost	$0.60

Collectible Cards has enough excess capacity to handle the special order.

Requirements

1. Prepare an incremental analysis to determine whether Collectible Cards should accept the special sales order assuming fixed costs would not be affected by the special order.
2. Now assume that the Hall of Fame wants special hologram baseball cards. Collectible Cards must spend $5,000 to develop this hologram, which will be useless after the special order is completed. Should Collectible Cards accept the special order under these circumstances? Show your analysis.

E8-17A Sustainability and short-term decision making *(Learning Objective 2)*

Over the past several years, decommissioned U.S. warships have been turned into artificial reefs in the ocean by towing them out to sea and sinking them. The thinking was that sinking the ship would conveniently dispose of it while providing an artificial reef environment for aquatic life. In reality, some of the sunken ships have released toxin into the ocean and have been costly to decontaminate. Now the U.S. government is taking bids to instead dismantle and recycle ships that have recently been decommissioned (but have not been sunk yet.)

Assume that a recently decommissioned aircraft carrier, the USS *Forrestal*, is estimated to contain approximately 40 tons of recyclable materials able to be sold for approximately $32.3 million. The low bid for dismantling and transporting the ship materials to appropriate facilities is $33.7 million. Recycling and dismantling the ship would create about 500 jobs for about a year in the Rust Belt. This geographic area has been experiencing record-high unemployment rates in recent years.

1. Is it more financially advantageous to sink the ship (assume that it costs approximately $1.2 million to tow a ship out to sea and sink it) or to dismantle and recycle it? Show your calculations.

2. From a sustainability standpoint, what should be done with the decommissioned aircraft carrier? List some of the qualitative factors that should enter into this analysis.

3. As a taxpayer, which action would you prefer (sink or recycle)? Defend your answer.

E8-18A Special order decision and considerations *(Learning Objective 2)*

Coco Bradley Sunglasses sell for about $150 per pair. Suppose the company incurs the following average costs per pair:

Direct materials	$40
Direct labor	14
Variable manufacturing overhead	11
Variable marketing expenses	2
Fixed manufacturing overhead	16*
Total costs	$83

*$\frac{2,000,000 \text{ total fixed manufacturing overhead}}{125,000 \text{ pairs of sunglasses}}$

Coco Bradley has enough idle capacity to accept a one-time-only special order from Oceanside Resorts for 20,000 pairs of sunglasses at $71 per pair. Coco Bradley will not incur any variable marketing expenses for the order.

Requirements

1. How would accepting the order affect Coco Bradley's operating income? In addition to the special order's effect on profits, what other (longer-term qualitative) factors should Coco Bradley's managers consider in deciding whether to accept the order?

2. Coco Bradley's marketing manager, Jim Revo, argues against accepting the special order because the offer price of $71 is less than Coco Bradley's $83 cost to make the sunglasses. Revo asks you, as one of Coco Bradley's staff accountants, to write a memo explaining whether his analysis is correct.

E8-19A Pricing decisions given two scenarios *(Learning Objective 3)*

Smith Builders builds 1,500-square-foot starter tract homes in the fast-growing suburbs of Chicago. Land and labor are cheap, and competition among developers is fierce. The homes are "cookie-cutter," with any upgrades added by the buyer after the sale. Smith Builders' costs per developed sublot are as follows:

Land	$ 57,000
Construction	$124,000
Landscaping	$ 5,000
Variable marketing costs	$ 4,000

Smith Builders would like to earn a profit of 14% of the variable cost of each home sale. Similar homes offered by competing builders sell for $206,000 each.

Requirements

1. Which approach to pricing should Smith Builders emphasize? Why?

2. Will Smith Builders be able to achieve its target profit levels? Show your computations.

3. Bathrooms and kitchens are typically the most important selling features of a home. Smith Builders could differentiate the homes by upgrading bathrooms and kitchens. The upgrades would cost $18,000 per home but would enable Smith Builders to increase the selling prices by $31,500 per home (in general, kitchen and bathroom upgrades typically add at least 150% of their cost to the value of any home). If Smith Builders upgrades, what will the new cost-plus price per home be? Should the company differentiate its product in this manner? Show your analysis.

E8-20A Decide whether to discontinue a product line (Learning Objective 4)

Top managers of Entertainment Plus are alarmed by their operating losses. They are considering dropping the DVD product line. Company accountants have prepared the following analysis to help make this decision:

	Total	Blu-ray Discs	DVDs
Sales revenue	$437,000	$301,000	$136,000
Variable expenses	244,000	158,000	86,000
Contribution margin	$193,000	$143,000	$ 50,000
Fixed expenses:			
Manufacturing	134,000	77,000	57,000
Marketing and administrative	64,000	53,000	11,000
Total fixed expenses	$198,000	$130,000	$ 68,000
Operating income (loss)	$ (5,000)	$ 13,000	$ (18,000)

Total fixed costs will not change if the company stops selling DVDs.

Requirements

1. Prepare an incremental analysis to show whether Entertainment Plus should discontinue the DVD product line. Will discontinuing DVDs add $18,000 to operating income? Explain.
2. Assume that the company can avoid $20,000 of fixed expenses by discontinuing the DVD product line (these costs are direct fixed costs of the DVD product line). Prepare an incremental analysis to show whether the company should stop selling DVDs.
3. Now, assume that all $68,000 of fixed costs assigned to DVDs are direct fixed costs and can be avoided if the company stops selling DVDs. However, marketing has concluded that Blu-ray disc sales would be adversely affected by discontinuing the DVD line (retailers want to buy both from the same supplier). Blu-ray disc production and sales would decline 10%. What should the company do?

E8-21A Discontinuing a product line (Learning Objective 4)

Suppose General Mills is considering discontinuing its organic cereal product line. Assume that during the past year, the organic cereal's product line income statement showed the following:

Sales	$7,500,000
Cost of goods sold	6,500,000
Gross profit	$1,000,000
Operating expenses	1,250,000
Operating loss	$ (250,000)

Fixed manufacturing overhead costs account for 40% of the cost of goods, while only 30% of the operating expenses are fixed. Since the organic cereal line is only one of General Mills' breakfast cereals, only $780,000 of direct fixed costs (the majority of which is advertising) will be eliminated if the product line is discontinued. The remainder of the fixed costs will still be incurred by General Mills. If the company decides to discontinue the product line, what will happen to the company's operating income? Should General Mills discontinue the product line?

E8-22A Identify constraint, then determine product mix *(Learning Objective 5)*

Get Fit produces two types of exercise treadmills: Regular and Deluxe. The exercise craze is such that Get Fit could use all of its available machine hours producing either model. The two models are processed through the same production department.

	Per Unit	
	Deluxe	Regular
Sale price	$1,010	$560
Costs:		
Direct materials.	$ 310	$ 90
Direct labor.	88	184
Variable manufacturing overhead.	264	88
Fixed manufacturing overhead*	114	38
Variable operating expenses	119	65
Total cost	$ 895	$465
Operating income	$ 115	$ 95

* Allocated on the basis of machine hours.

What product mix will maximize operating income? (*Hint:* Use the allocation of fixed manufacturing overhead to determine the proportion of machine hours used by each product.)

E8-23A Determine product mix for retailer *(Learning Objective 5)*

Honacker Fashions sells both designer and moderately priced fashion accessories. Top management is deciding which product line to emphasize. Accountants have provided the following data:

	Per Item	
	Designer	Moderately Priced
Average sale price	$205	$83
Average variable expenses	95	28
Average fixed expenses (allocated)	20	10
Average operating income	$ 90	$45

The Honacker store in Charleston, South Carolina, has 14,000 square feet of floor space. If Honacker emphasizes moderately priced goods, it can display 840 items in the store. If Honacker emphasizes designer wear, it can display only 560 designer items to create more of a boutique-like atmosphere. These numbers are also the average monthly sales in units. Prepare an analysis to show which product to emphasize.

E8-24A Determine product mix for retailer—two stocking scenarios *(Learning Objective 5)*

Each morning, Nick Ivery stocks the drink case at Nick's Beach Hut in Newark, New Jersey. Nick's Beach Hut has 115 linear feet of refrigerated display space for cold drinks. Each linear foot can hold either five 12-ounce cans or four 20-ounce plastic or glass bottles. Nick's Beach Hut sells three types of cold drinks:

1. Cola in 12-oz. cans for $1.55 per can
2. Energy drink in 20-oz. plastic bottles for $1.80 per bottle
3. Orange soda in 20-oz. glass bottles for $2.15 per bottle

Nick's Beach Hut pays its suppliers the following:

1. $0.25 per 12-oz. can of cola
2. $0.40 per 20-oz. bottle of energy drink
3. $0.65 per 20-oz. bottle of orange soda

Nick's Beach Hut's monthly fixed expenses include the following:

Hut rental	$ 375
Refrigerator rental	75
Nick's salary	1,550
Total fixed expenses.	$2,000

Nick's Beach Hut can sell all drinks stocked in the display case each morning.

Requirements

1. What is Nick's Beach Hut's constraining factor? What should Nick stock to maximize profits? What is the maximum contribution margin he could generate from refrigerated drinks each day?

2. To provide variety to customers, suppose Nick refuses to devote more than 70 linear feet and no less than 15 linear feet to any individual product. Under this condition, how many linear feet of each drink should Nick stock? How many units of each product will be available for sale each day?

3. Assuming the product mix calculated in Requirement 2, what contribution margin will Nick generate from refrigerated drinks each day?

E8-25A Make-or-buy product component (Learning Objective 6)

OptiSystems manufactures an optical switch that it uses in its final product. OptiSystems incurred the following manufacturing costs when it produced 72,000 units last year:

Direct materials	$ 720,000
Direct labor	180,000
Variable overhead	216,000
Fixed overhead	468,000
Total manufacturing cost for 72,000 units	$1,584,000

OptiSystems does not yet know how many switches it will need this year; however, another company has offered to sell OptiSystems the switch for $17 per unit. If OptiSystems buys the switch from the outside supplier, the manufacturing facilities that will be idle cannot be used for any other purpose, yet none of the fixed costs are avoidable.

Requirements

1. Given the same cost structure, should OptiSystems make or buy the switch? Show your analysis.

2. Now, assume that OptiSystems can avoid $100,000 of fixed costs a year by outsourcing production. In addition, because sales are increasing, OptiSystems needs 77,000 switches a year rather than 72,000. What should the company do now?

3. Given the last scenario, what is the most OptiSystems would be willing to pay to outsource the switches?

E8-26A Make-or-buy with alternative use of facilities (Learning Objective 6)

Refer to E8-25A. OptiSystems needs 84,000 optical switches next year (assume same relevant range). By outsourcing them, OptiSystems can use its idle facilities to manufacture another product that will contribute $120,000 to operating income, but none of the fixed costs will be avoidable. Should OptiSystems make or buy the switches? Show your analysis.

E8-27A Determine maximum outsourcing price (Learning Objective 6)

Henderson Containers manufactures a variety of boxes used for packaging. Sales of its Model A20 box have increased significantly to a total of 420,000 A20 boxes. Henderson has enough existing production capacity to make all of the boxes it needs. The variable cost of making each A20 box is $0.70. By outsourcing the manufacture of these A20 boxes, Henderson can reduce its current fixed costs by $84,000. There is no alternative use for the factory space freed up through outsourcing, so it will just remain idle.

What is the maximum Henderson will pay per Model A20 box to outsource production of this box?

E8-28A Sell as is or process further *(Learning Objective 7)*

Naturalmaid processes organic milk into plain yogurt. Naturalmaid sells plain yogurt to hospitals, nursing homes, and restaurants in bulk, one-gallon containers. Each batch, processed at a cost of $800, yields 600 gallons of plain yogurt. The company sells the one-gallon tubs for $6.00 each and spends $0.10 for each plastic tub. Naturalmaid has recently begun to reconsider its strategy. Management wonders if it would be more profitable to sell individual-sized portions of fruited organic yogurt at local food stores. Naturalmaid could further process each batch of plain yogurt into 12,800 individual portions (3/4 cup each) of fruited yogurt. A recent market analysis indicates that demand for the product exists. Naturalmaid would sell each individual portion for $0.50. Packaging would cost $0.05 per portion, and fruit would cost $0.15 per portion. Fixed costs would not change. Should Naturalmaid continue to sell only the gallon-sized plain yogurt (sell as is) or convert the plain yogurt into individual-sized portions of fruited yogurt (process further)? Why?

EXERCISES Group B

E8-29B Determine relevant and irrelevant information *(Learning Objective 1)*

Zippy Frozen Foods purchased new computer-controlled production machinery last year from Advanced Design. The equipment was purchased for $4.1 million and was paid for with cash. A representative from Advanced Design recently contacted Zippy management because Advanced Design has an even more efficient piece of machinery available. The new design would double the production output of the equipment purchased last year but would cost Zippy another $5.0 million. The old machinery was installed by an engineering firm; the same firm would be required to install the new machinery. Fixed selling costs would not change if the new machinery were to be purchased. The variance selling cost per unit would decrease. Raw material costs (i.e., food ingredients) would remain the same with either machine. The new machinery would be purchased by signing a note payable at the bank and interest would be paid monthly on the note payable. Maintenance costs on the new machine would be the same as the maintenance costs on the machinery purchased last year. Advanced Design is offering a trade-in on the machinery purchased last year against the purchase price of the new machinery.

For each of the following costs, indicate whether each of the costs described would be relevant or not to Zippy Frozen Foods' decision about whether to purchase the new machinery or not.

Item	Relevant	Not Relevant
a. Book value of old machine		
b. Maintenance cost of new machine		
c. Maintenance cost of old machine		
d. Installation cost of new machine		
e. Accumulated depreciation on old machine		
f. Cost per pound of pizza dough		
g. Installation cost of old machine		
h. Cost of the new machine		
i. Cost of the old machine		
j. Added profits from the increase in production resulting from the new machine		
k. Fixed selling costs		
l. Variable selling costs		
m. Trade-in value of old machine		
n. Interest expense on new machine		
o. Sales tax paid on old machine		

E8-30B Special order decisions given two scenarios *(Learning Objective 2)*

Suppose the Baseball Hall of Fame in Cooperstown, New York, has approached SportCardz with a special order. The Hall of Fame wishes to purchase 50,000 baseball card packs for a special promotional campaign and offers $0.35 per pack, a total of $17,500. SportCardz total production cost is $0.55 per pack, as follows:

Variable costs:	
Direct materials.	$0.12
Direct labor.	0.07
Variable overhead.	0.11
Fixed overhead	0.25
Total cost	$0.55

SportCardz has enough excess capacity to handle the special order.

Requirements

1. Prepare an incremental analysis to determine whether SportCardz should accept the special sales order assuming fixed costs would not be affected by the special order.
2. Now assume that the Hall of Fame wants special hologram baseball cards. SportCardz will spend $5,400 to develop this hologram, which will be useless after the special order is completed. Should SportCardz accept the special order under these circumstances? Show your analysis.

E8-31B Sustainability and short-term decision making *(Learning Objective 2)*

Over the past several years, decommissioned U.S. warships have been turned into artificial reefs in the ocean by towing them out to sea and sinking them. The thinking was that sinking the ship would conveniently dispose of it while providing an artificial reef environment for aquatic life. In reality, some of the sunken ships have released toxins into the ocean and have been costly to decontaminate. Now the U.S. government is taking bids to instead dismantle and recycle ships that have recently been decommissioned (but have not been sunk yet.)

Assume that a recently decommissioned aircraft carrier, the USS *Independence*, is estimated to contain approximately 40 tons of recyclable materials able to be sold for approximately $30.8 million. The low bid for dismantling and transporting the ship materials to appropriate facilities is $32.3 million. Recycling and dismantling the ship would create about 500 jobs for about a year in the Rust Belt. This geographic area has been experiencing record-high unemployment rates in recent years.

Requirements

1. Is it more financially advantageous to sink the ship (assume that it costs approximately $1.2 million to tow a ship out to sea and sink it) or to dismantle and recycle it? Show your calculations.
2. From a sustainability standpoint, what should be done with the decommissioned aircraft carrier? List some of the qualitative factors that should enter into this analysis.
3. As a taxpayer, which action would you prefer (sink or recycle)? Defend your answer.

E8-32B Special order decision and considerations *(Learning Objective 2)*

Sera Shade Sunglasses sell for about $151 per pair. Suppose the company incurs the following average costs per pair:

Direct materials	$40
Direct labor	12
Variable manufacturing overhead	7
Variable marketing expenses	4
Fixed manufacturing overhead	16*
Total costs	$79

*$2,100,000 total fixed manufacturing overhead / 131,250 pairs of sunglasses

Sera Shade has enough idle capacity to accept a one-time-only special order from Oceanview Hotels for 23,000 pairs of sunglasses at $64 per pair. Sera Shade will not incur any variable marketing expenses for the order.

Requirements

1. How would accepting the order affect Sera Shade's operating income? In addition to the special order's effect on profits, what other (longer-term, qualitative) factors should the company's managers consider in deciding whether to accept the order?
2. Sera Shade's marketing manager argues against accepting the special order because the offer price of $64 is less than the cost to make the sunglasses. The marketing manager asks you, as one of Sera Shades' staff accountants, to explain whether this analysis is correct.

E8-33B Pricing decisions given two scenarios *(Learning Objective 3)*

Johnson Builders builds 1,500-square-foot starter tract homes in the fast-growing suburbs of Atlanta. Land and labor are cheap, and competition among developers is fierce. The homes are "cookie-cutter," with any upgrades added by the buyer after the sale. Johnson Builders' costs per developed sublot are as follows:

Land	$ 53,000
Construction	$125,000
Landscaping	$ 6,000
Variable marketing costs	$ 1,000

Johnson Builders would like to earn a profit of 16% of the variable cost of each home sale. Similar homes offered by competing builders sell for $201,000 each.

Requirements

1. Which approach to pricing should Johnson Builders emphasize? Why?
2. Will Johnson Builders be able to achieve its target profit levels? Show your computations.
3. Bathrooms and kitchens are typically the most important selling features of a home. Johnson Builders could differentiate the homes by upgrading bathrooms and kitchens. The upgrades would cost $24,000 per home but would enable Johnson Builders to increase the selling prices by $42,000 per home (in general, kitchen and bathroom upgrades typically add at least 150% of their cost to the value of any home.) If Johnson Builders upgrades, what will the new cost-plus price per home be? Should the company differentiate its product in this manner? Show your analysis.

E8-34B Decide whether to discontinue a product line *(Learning Objective 4)*

Top managers of Movies Plus are alarmed by their operating losses. They are considering discontinuing the DVD product line. Company accountants have prepared the following analysis to help make this decision:

	Total	Blu-ray Discs	DVDs
Sales revenue	$429,000	$305,000	$124,000
Variable expenses.	240,000	152,000	88,000
Contribution margin.	$189,000	$153,000	$ 36,000
Fixed expenses:			
Manufacturing	128,000	73,000	55,000
Marketing and administrative.	64,000	53,000	11,000
Total fixed expenses.	$192,000	126,000	$ 66,000
Operating income (loss).	$ (3,000)	$ 27,000	$ (30,000)

Total fixed costs will not change if the company stops selling DVDs.

Requirements

1. Prepare an incremental analysis to show whether Movie Plus should discontinue the DVD product line. Will discontinuing the DVDs add $30,000 to operating income? Explain.

2. Assume that Movies Plus can avoid $32,000 of fixed expenses by discontinuing the DVD product line (these costs are direct fixed costs of the DVD product line). Prepare an incremental analysis to show whether Movies Plus should stop selling DVDs.

3. Now, assume that all $66,000 of fixed costs assigned to DVDs are direct fixed costs and can be avoided if the company stops selling DVDs. However, marketing has concluded that Blu-ray disc sales would be adversely affected by discontinuing the DVD line (retailers want to buy both from the same supplier). Blu-ray disc production and sales would decline 10%. What should the company do?

E8-35B Discontinuing a product line *(Learning Objective 4)*

Suppose Post Cereals is considering discontinuing its maple cereal product line. Assume that during the past year, the maple cereal product line income statement showed the following:

Sales	$ 5,200,000
Cost of goods sold.	6,350,000
Gross profit.	$ (1,150,000)
Operating expenses.	1,500,000
Operating loss	$ (2,650,000)

Fixed manufacturing overhead costs account for 40% of the cost of goods, while only 30% of the operating expenses are fixed. Since the maple cereal line is only one of Post Cereals' breakfast cereals, only $755,000 of direct fixed costs (the majority of which is advertising) will be eliminated if the product line is discontinued. The remainder of the fixed costs will still be incurred by Post Cereals. If the company decides to discontinue the product line, what will happen to the company's operating income? Should Post Cereals discontinue the maple cereal product line?

E8-36B Identify constraint, then determine product mix (Learning Objective 5)

TreadMile produces two types of exercise treadmills: Regular and Deluxe. The exercise craze is such that TreadMile could use all of its available machine hours producing either model. The two models are processed through the same production department.

	Per Unit	
	Deluxe	Regular
Sale price	$990	$550
Costs:		
Direct materials.	$300	$100
Direct labor.	82	182
Variable manufacturing overhead.	252	84
Fixed manufacturing overhead*.	126	42
Variable operating expenses	115	67
Total cost	$875	$475
Operating income	$115	$ 75

*Allocated on the basis of machine hours.

What product mix will maximize operating income? (Hint: Use the allocation of fixed manufacturing overhead to determine the proportion of machine hours used by each product.)

E8-37B Determine product mix for retailer (Learning Objective 5)

Melanie Fashions sells both designer and moderately priced fashion accessories. Top management is deciding which product line to emphasize. Accountants have provided the following data:

	Per Item	
	Designer	Moderately Priced
Average sale price	$210	$85
Average variable expenses	75	25
Average fixed expenses (allocated).	15	10
Average operating income	$120	$50

The Melanie Fashions store in Reno, Nevada, has 15,000 square feet of floor space. If Melanie emphasizes moderately priced goods, it can display 900 items in the store. If Melanie emphasizes designer wear, it can display only 600 designer items to create more of a boutique-like atmosphere. These numbers also are the average monthly sales in units. Prepare an analysis to show which product to emphasize.

E8-38B Determine product mix for retailer—two stocking scenarios (Learning Objective 5)

Each morning, Mark Johnston stocks the drink case at Mark's Beach Hut in Myrtle Beach, South Carolina. Mark's Beach Hut has 120 linear feet of refrigerated display space for cold drinks. Each linear foot can hold either five 12-ounce cans or three 20-ounce plastic or glass bottles.

Mark's Beach Hut sells three types of cold drinks:

1. Cola in 12-oz. cans, for $1.50 per can
2. Juice in 20-oz. plastic bottles, for $1.65 per bottle
3. Diet cola in 20-oz. glass bottles, for $2.15 per bottle

Mark's Beach Hut pays its suppliers the following:

1. $0.10 per 12-oz. can of cola
2. $0.45 per 20-oz. bottle of juice
3. $0.65 per 20-oz. bottle of diet cola

Mark's Beach Hut's monthly fixed expenses include the following:

Hut rental	$ 370
Refrigerator rental	85
Mark's salary	1,400
Total fixed expenses	$1,855

Mark's Beach Hut can sell all the drinks stocked in the display case each morning.

Requirements

1. What is Mark's Beach Hut's constraining factor? What should Mark stock to maximize profits? What is the maximum contribution margin he could generate from refrigerated drinks each day?

2. To provide variety to customers, suppose Mark refuses to devote more than 70 linear feet and no less than 20 linear feet to any individual product. Under this condition, how many linear feet of each drink should Mark stock? How many units of each product will be available for sale each day?

3. Assuming the product mix calculated in Requirement 2, what contribution margin will Mark generate from refrigerated drinks each day?

E8-39B Make-or-buy product component (Learning Objective 6)

World Systems manufactures an optical switch that it uses in its final product. World Systems incurred the following manufacturing costs when it produced 66,000 units last year:

Direct materials	$ 726,000
Direct labor	99,000
Variable overhead	132,000
Fixed overhead	363,000
Total manufacturing cost for 66,000 units	$1,320,000

World Systems does not yet know how many switches it will need this year; however, another company has offered to sell World Systems the switch for $12.50 per unit. If World Systems buys the switch from the outside supplier, the manufacturing facilities that will be idle cannot be used for any other purpose, yet none of the fixed costs are avoidable.

Requirements

1. Given the same cost structure, should World Systems make or buy the switch? Show your analysis.

2. Now, assume that World Systems can avoid $99,000 of fixed costs a year by outsourcing production. In addition, because sales are increasing, World Systems needs 71,000 switches a year rather than 66,000. What should World Systems do now?

3. Given the last scenario, what is the most World Systems would be willing to pay to outsource the switches?

E8-40B Make-or-buy with alternative use of facilities (Learning Objective 6)

Refer to E8-39B. World Systems needs 80,000 optical switches next year (assume same relevant range). By outsourcing them, World Systems can use its idle facilities to manufacture another product that will contribute $120,000 to operating income, but none of the fixed costs will be avoidable. Should World Systems make or buy the switches? Show your analysis.

E8-41B Determine maximum outsourcing price (Learning Objective 6)

Augustine Containers manufactures a variety of boxes used for packaging. Sales of its Model A30 box have increased significantly to a total of 360,000 A30 boxes. Augustine has enough existing production capacity to make all of the boxes it needs. The variable cost of making each A30 box is $0.80. By outsourcing the manufacture of these A30 boxes, Augustine can reduce its current fixed costs by $54,000. There is no alternative use for the factory space freed up through outsourcing, so it will just remain idle.

What is the maximum Augustine will pay per Model A30 box to outsource production of this box?

E8-42B Sell as is or process further (Learning Objective 7)

Dairyfood processes organic milk into plain yogurt. Dairyfood sells plain yogurt to hospitals, nursing homes, and restaurants in bulk, one-gallon containers. Each batch, processed at a cost of $800, yields 570 gallons of plain yogurt. Dairyfood sells the one-gallon tubs for $6.00 each, and spends $0.10 for each plastic tub. Management has recently begun to reconsider its strategy. Dairyfood wonders if it would be more profitable to sell individual-sized portions of fruited organic yogurt at local food stores. Dairyfood could further process each batch of plain yogurt into 12,160 individual portions (3/4 cup each) of fruited yogurt. A recent market analysis indicates that demand for the product exists. Dairyfood would sell each individual portion for $0.50. Packaging would cost $0.08 per portion, and fruit would cost $0.12 per portion. Fixed costs would not change. Should Dairyfood continue to sell only the gallon-sized plain yogurt (sell as is) or convert the plain yogurt into individual-sized portions of fruited yogurt (process further)? Why?

PROBLEMS Group A

P8-43A Special order decision and considerations (Learning Objective 2)

Summer Fun manufactures flotation vests in Atlanta, Georgia. Summer Fun's contribution margin income statement for the most recent month contains the following data:

Sales in units.	31,000
Sales revenue	$496,000
Variable expenses:	
Manufacturing	$ 93,000
Marketing and administrative.	104,000
Total variable expenses	197,000
Contribution margin.	$299,000
Fixed expenses:	
Manufacturing	130,000
Marketing and administrative.	87,000
Total fixed expenses	$217,000
Operating income	$ 82,000

Suppose Luxury Cruiselines wants to buy 5,700 vests from Summer Fun. Acceptance of the order will not increase Summer Fun's variable marketing and administrative expenses or any of its fixed expenses. The Summer Fun plant has enough unused capacity to manufacture the additional vests. Luxury Cruiseline has offered $10 per vest, which is below the normal sale price of $16.

Requirements

1. Prepare an incremental analysis to determine whether Summer Fun should accept this special sales order.

2. Identify long-term factors Summer Fun should consider in deciding whether to accept the special sales order.

P8-44A Pricing of nursery plants *(Learning Objective 3)*

Nature House operates a commercial plant nursery where it propagates plants for garden centers throughout the region. Nature House has $4.9 million in assets. Its yearly fixed costs are $682,000, and the variable costs for the potting soil, container, label, seedling, and labor for each gallon-sized plant total $1.30. Nature House's volume is currently 480,000 units. Competitors offer the same quality plants to garden centers for $4.00 each. Garden centers then mark them up to sell to the public for $9 to $11, depending on the type of plant.

Requirements

1. Nature House's owners want to earn a 14% return on the company's assets. What is Nature House's target full cost?
2. Given Nature House's current costs, will its owners be able to achieve their target profit? Show your analysis.
3. Assume that Nature House has identified ways to cut its variable costs to $1.15 per unit. What is its new target fixed cost? Will this decrease in variable costs allow the company to achieve its target profit? Show your analysis.
4. Nature House started an aggressive advertising campaign strategy to differentiate its plants from those grown by other nurseries. Nature House doesn't expect volume to be affected, but it hopes to gain more control over pricing. If Nature House has to spend $110,400 this year to advertise and its variable costs continue to be $1.15 per unit, what will its cost-plus price be? Do you think Nature House will be able to sell its plants to garden centers at the cost-plus price? Why or why not?

P8-45A Prepare and use contribution margin statements for discontinuing a line decision *(Learning Objective 4)*

Members of the board of directors of Security One have received the following operating income data for the year just ended:

| | Product Line | | |
	Industrial Systems	Household Systems	Total
Sales revenue	$320,000	$330,000	$650,000
Cost of goods sold:			
Variable	$ 39,000	$ 42,000	$ 81,000
Fixed	220,000	67,000	287,000
Total cost of goods sold	$259,000	$109,000	$368,000
Gross profit	$ 61,000	$221,000	$282,000
Marketing and administrative expenses:			
Variable	65,000	73,000	138,000
Fixed	40,000	22,000	62,000
Total marketing and administrative expenses	$105,000	$95,000	$200,000
Operating income (loss)	$ (44,000)	$126,000	$ 82,000

Members of the board are surprised that the industrial systems product line is losing money. They commission a study to determine whether the company should discontinue the line. Company accountants estimate that discontinuing industrial systems will decrease fixed cost of goods sold by $83,000 and decrease fixed marketing and administrative expenses by $13,000.

Requirements

1. Prepare an incremental analysis to show whether Security One should discontinue the industrial systems product line.
2. Prepare contribution margin income statements to show Security One's total operating income under the two alternatives: (a) with the industrial systems line and (b) without the line. Compare the *difference* between the two alternatives' income numbers to your answer to Requirement 1. What have you learned from this comparison?

P8-46A Product mix decision under constraint (Learning Objective 5)

Brett Products, located in Buffalo, New York, produces two lines of electric toothbrushes: Deluxe and Standard. Because Brett can sell all of the toothbrushes it produces, the owners are expanding the plant. They are deciding which product line to emphasize. To make this decision, they assemble the following data:

	Per Unit	
	Deluxe Toothbrush	Standard Toothbrush
Sale price	$92	$45
Variable expenses.....................................	23	18
Contribution margin...................................	$69	$27
Contribution margin ratio	75%	60%

After expansion, the factory will have a production capacity of 4,700 machine hours per month. The plant can manufacture either 56 Standard electric toothbrushes or 25 Deluxe electric toothbrushes per machine hour.

Requirements

1. Identify the constraining factor for Brett.
2. Prepare an analysis to show which product line to emphasize.

P8-47A Outsourcing decision given alternative use of capacity (Learning Objective 6)

Outdoor Life manufactures snowboards. Its cost of making 1,890 bindings is as follows:

Direct materials	$18,000
Direct labor	3,200
Variable manufacturing overhead	2,340
Fixed manufacturing overhead	6,700
Total manufacturing costs	$30,240
Cost per pair ($30,240 ÷ 1,890)..	$ 16.00

Suppose an outside supplier will sell bindings to Outdoor Life for $13 each. Outdoor Life will pay $2.00 per unit to transport the bindings to its manufacturing plant, where it will add its own logo at a cost of $0.40 per binding.

Requirements

1. Outdoor Life's accountants predict that purchasing the bindings from the outside supplier will enable the company to avoid $2,000 of fixed overhead. Prepare an analysis to show whether Outdoor Life should make or buy the bindings.

2. The facilities freed by purchasing bindings from the outside supplier can be used to manufacture another product that will contribute $3,300 to profit. Total fixed costs will be the same as if Outdoor Life had produced the bindings. Show which alternative makes the best use of Outdoor Life's facilities: (a) make bindings, (b) buy bindings and leave facilities idle, or (c) buy bindings and make another product.

P8-48A Sell or process further decisions (Learning Objective 7)

Root Chemical has spent $244,000 to refine 70,000 gallons of acetone, which can be sold for $2.30 a gallon. Alternatively, Root Chemical can process the acetone further. This processing will yield a total of 60,000 gallons of lacquer thinner that can be sold for $3.00 a gallon. The additional processing will cost $0.60 per gallon of lacquer thinner. To sell the lacquer thinner, Root Chemical must pay shipping of $0.19 a gallon and administrative expenses of $0.11 a gallon on the thinner.

Requirements

1. Diagram Root's decision.
2. Identify the sunk cost. Is the sunk cost relevant to Root's decision? Why or why not?
3. Should Root sell the acetone or process it into lacquer thinner? Show the expected net revenue difference between the two alternatives.

PROBLEMS Group B

P8-49B Special order decision and considerations (Learning Objective 2)

Nautical Products, Inc., manufactures flotation vests in San Diego, California. Nautical Products' contribution margin income statement for the most recent month contains the following data:

Sales in units...	29,000
Sales revenue..	$435,000
Variable expenses:	
Manufacturing	$ 87,000
Marketing and administrative....................	102,000
Total variable expenses	$189,000
Contribution margin.................................	$246,000
Fixed expenses:	
Manufacturing	124,000
Marketing and administrative.....................	88,000
Total fixed expenses...............................	$212,000
Operating income (loss)............................	$ 34,000

Suppose Royal Cruiselines wishes to buy 5,600 vests from Nautical Products. Acceptance of the order will not increase Nautical Products' variable marketing and administrative expenses. The Nautical Products plant has enough unused capacity to manufacture the additional vests. Royal Cruiselines has offered $6 per vest, which is below the normal sale price of $15.

Requirements

1. Prepare an incremental analysis to determine whether Nautical Products should accept this special sales order.
2. Identify long-term factors Nautical Products should consider in deciding whether to accept the special sales order.

P8-50B Pricing of nursery plants (Learning Objective 3)

Garden House operates a commercial plant nursery where it propagates plants for garden centers throughout the region. Garden House has $4.4 million in assets. Its yearly fixed costs are $580,000, and the variable costs for the potting soil, container, label, seedling, and labor for each gallon-sized plant total $1.15. Garden House's volume is currently 480,000 units. Competitors offer the same quality plants to garden centers for $3.40 each. Garden centers then mark them up to sell to the public for $8 to $10, depending on the type of plant.

Requirements

1. Garden House's owners want to earn a 13% return on the company's assets. What is Garden House's target full cost?
2. Given Garden House's current costs, will its owners be able to achieve their target profit? Show your analysis.
3. Assume that Garden House has identified ways to cut its variable costs to $1.00 per unit. What is its new target fixed cost? Will this decrease in variable costs allow the company to achieve its target profit? Show your analysis.

4. Garden House started an aggressive advertising campaign strategy to differentiate its plants from those grown by other nurseries. Garden House doesn't expect volume to be affected, but it hopes to gain more control over pricing. If Garden House has to spend $120,000 this year to advertise and its variable costs continue to be $1.00 per unit, what will its cost-plus price be? Do you think Garden House will be able to sell its plants to garden centers at the cost-plus price? Why or why not?

P8-51B Prepare and use contribution margin statements for discontinuing a line decision (Learning Objective 4)

Members of the board of directors of Safety Systems have received the following operating income data for the year just ended:

	Product Line		
	Industrial Systems	Household Systems	Total
Sales revenue	$330,000	$360,000	$690,000
Cost of goods sold:			
Variable	$ 35,000	$ 44,000	$ 79,000
Fixed	250,000	67,000	317,000
Total cost of goods sold	$285,000	$111,000	$396,000
Gross profit	$ 45,000	$249,000	$294,000
Marketing and administrative expenses:			
Variable	62,000	76,000	138,000
Fixed	39,000	23,000	62,000
Total marketing and administrative expenses	$101,000	$ 99,000	$200,000
Operating income (loss)	$(56,000)	$150,000	$ 94,000

Members of the board are surprised that the industrial systems product line is losing money. They commission a study to determine whether the company should discontinue the line. Company accountants estimate that discontinuing industrial systems will decrease fixed cost of goods sold by $81,000 and decrease fixed marketing and administrative expenses by $14,000.

Requirements

1. Prepare an incremental analysis to show whether Safety Systems should discontinue the industrial systems product line.

2. Prepare contribution margin income statements to show Safety Systems' total operating income under the two alternatives: (a) with the industrial systems line and (b) without the line. Compare the *difference* between the two alternatives' income numbers to your answer to Requirement 1. What have you learned from this comparison?

P8-52B Product mix decision under constraint (Learning Objective 5)

Branson Products, Inc., located in Orlando, Florida, produces two lines of electric toothbrushes: Deluxe and Standard. Because Branson can sell all the toothbrushes it can produce, the owners are expanding the plant. They are deciding which product line to emphasize. To make this decision, they assemble the following data:

	Per Unit	
	Deluxe Toothbrush	Regular Toothbrush
Sale price	$80	$50
Variable expenses	22	16
Contribution margin	$58	$34
Contribution margin ratio	72.5%	68%

After expansion, the factory will have a production capacity of 4,600 machine hours per month. The plant can manufacture either 68 Standard electric toothbrushes or 28 Deluxe electric toothbrushes per machine hour.

Requirements

1. Identify the constraining factor for Branson.
2. Prepare an analysis to show which product line to emphasize.

P8-53B Outsourcing decision given alternative use of capacity (Learning Objective 6)

Snowtime Sports manufactures snowboards. Its cost of making 20,000 bindings is as follows:

Direct materials	$ 20,000
Direct labor	80,000
Variable manufacturing overhead	40,000
Fixed manufacturing overhead	80,000
Total manufacturing costs	$220,000
Cost per pair ($220,000 / 20,000)	$ 11.00

Suppose an outside supplier will sell bindings to Snowtime Sports for $9 each. Snowtime Sports would pay $1.00 per unit to transport the bindings to its manufacturing plant, where it would add its own logo at a cost $0.20 of per binding.

Requirements

1. Snowtime Sports' accountants predict that purchasing the bindings from an outside supplier will enable the company to avoid $2,100 of fixed overhead. Prepare an analysis to show whether Snowtime Sports should make or buy the bindings.
2. The facilities freed by purchasing bindings from the outside supplier can be used to manufacture another product that will contribute $2,900 to profit. Total fixed costs will be the same as if Snowtime Sports had produced the bindings. Show which alternative makes the best use of Snowtime Sports' facilities: (a) make bindings, (b) buy bindings and leave facilities idle, or (c) buy bindings and make another product.

P8-54B Sell or process further decisions (Learning Objective 7)

Stenbeck Chemical has spent $244,000 to refine 71,000 gallons of acetone, which can be sold for $2.00 a gallon. Alternatively, Stenbeck Chemical can process the acetone further. This processing will yield a total of 60,000 gallons of lacquer thinner that can be sold for $3.40 a gallon. The additional processing will cost $0.85 per gallon of lacquer thinner. To sell the lacquer thinner, Stenbeck Chemical must pay shipping of $0.19 a gallon and administrative expenses of $0.11 a gallon on the thinner.

Requirements

1. Diagram Stenbeck's decision.
2. Identify the sunk cost. Is the sunk cost relevant to Stenbeck's decision? Why or why not?
3. Should Stenbeck sell the acetone or process it into lacquer thinner? Show the expected net revenue difference between the two alternatives.

CRITICAL THINKING

Discussion & Analysis

A8-55 Discussion Questions

1. A beverage company is considering whether to discontinue its line of grape soda. What factors will affect the company's decision? What is a qualitative factor? Which of the factors you listed are qualitative?

2. What factors would be relevant to a restaurant that is considering whether to make its own dinner rolls or to purchase dinner rolls from a local bakery?

3. How would outsourcing change a company's cost structure? How might this change in cost structure help or harm a company's competitive position?

4. What is an opportunity cost? List possible opportunity costs associated with a make-or-buy decision.

5. What undesirable result can arise from allocating common fixed costs to product lines?

6. Why could a manager be justified in ignoring fixed costs when making a decision about a special order? When would fixed costs be relevant when making a decision about a special order?

7. What is the difference between segment margin and contribution margin? When would each be used?

8. Do joint costs affect a sell or process further decision? Why or why not?

9. How can "make-or-buy" concepts be applied to decisions at a service organization? What types of "make-or-buy" decisions might a service organization face?

10. Oscar Company builds outdoor furniture using a variety of woods and plastics. What is a constraint? List at least four possible constraints at Oscar Company.

11. Do a web search on the terms "carbon offset" and "carbon footprint." What is a carbon footprint? What is a carbon offset? Why would carbon offsets be of interest to a company? What are some companies that offer (sell) carbon offsets?

12. A computer manufacturer is considering outsourcing its technical support call center to India. Its current technical support call center is located in Dellroy, Ohio. The current call center is one of the top employers in Dellroy and employs about 10% of the townspeople in Dellroy. The town has experienced high unemployment rates in the past two decades and oftentimes the call employees are the sole breadwinners in their households. If the technical support call center were to be moved to India, the company would be able to pay about 50% less per hour than they currently pay in Dellroy, Ohio. From a triple bottom line perspective (people, planet, and profit), what factors are relevant to the company's decision to outsource its technical support call center? Be sure to discuss both quantitative and qualitative factors.

Application & Analysis

A8-56 Outsourcing Decision at a Real Company

Go to the New York Times website (www.nytimes.com/) or to USA Today (www.usatoday.com/) and search for the term "outsource." Find an article about a company making a decision to outsource a part of its business operations.

Basic Discussion Questions

1. Describe the company that is making the decision to outsource. What area of the business is the company either looking to outsource or did it already outsource?

2. Why did the company decide to outsource (or is considering outsourcing)?

3. List the revenues and costs that might be impacted by this outsourcing decision. The article will not list many, if any, of these revenues and costs; you should make reasonable guesses about what revenues and/or costs would be associated with the business operation being outsourced.

4. List the qualitative factors that could influence the company's decision whether to outsource this business operation or not. Again, you need to make reasonable guesses about the qualitative factors that might influence the company's decision to outsource or not.

Decision Case

A8-57 Outsourcing e-mail *(Learning Objective 6)*

AI Banking provides banks web access to sophisticated financial information and analysis systems. The company combines these tools w ith benchmarking data access, including e-mail and wireless communications, so that banks can instantly evaluate individual loan applications and entire loan portfolios. All information is encrypted and is available 24/7.

AI Banking's CEO, Amanda Duncan, is happy with the company's growth. To better focus on client service, Duncan is considering outsourcing some functions. CFO Sarabeth Miracle suggests that the company's e-mail may be the place to start. She recently attended a conference and learned that companies such as Continental Airlines, DellNet, GTE, and NBC were outsourcing their e-mail function. Duncan asks Miracle to identify costs related to AI Banking's in-house Microsoft Exchange e-mail application, which has 2,400 mailboxes. This information follows:

Variable costs:	
E-mail license	$7 per mailbox per month
Virus protection license	$1 per mailbox per month
Other variable costs	$4 per mailbox per month
Fixed costs:	
Computer hardware costs	$94,300 per month
$8,050 monthly salary for two information technology staff members who work only on e-mail.	$16,100 per month

Requirements

1. Compute the *total cost* per mailbox per month of AI Banking's current e-mail function.
2. Suppose Mail.com, a leading provider of email services, offers to host AI Banking's e-mail function for $7 per mailbox per month. If AI Banking outsources its e-mail to Mail.com, AI Banking will still need the virus protection software; its computer hardware; and one information technology staff member who would be responsible for maintaining virus protection, quarantining suspicious e-mail, and managing content (e.g., screening e-mail for objectionable content). Should CEO Duncan accept Mail.com's offer? Why or why not?
3. Suppose for an additional $5 per mailbox per month, Mail.com will also provide virus protection, quarantine, and content-management services. Outsourcing these additional functions would mean that AI Banking would not need an e-mail information technology staff member or the separate virus protection license. Should CEO Duncan outsource these extra services to Mail.com? Why or why not?

Ethical Issue

A8-58 Outsourcing and ethics *(Learning Objective 6)*

Mary Tan is the controller for Duck Associates, a property management company in Portland, Oregon. Each year, Tan and payroll clerk Toby Stock meet with the external auditors about payroll accounting. This year, the auditors suggest that Tan consider outsourcing Duck Associates' payroll accounting to a company specializing in payroll processing services. This would allow Tan and her staff to focus on their primary responsibility: accounting for the properties under management. At present, payroll requires 1.5 employee positions—payroll clerk Toby Stock and a bookkeeper who spends half her time entering payroll data in the system.

Tan considers this suggestion and she lists the following items relating to outsourcing payroll accounting:

a. The current payroll software that was purchased for $4,000 three years ago would not be needed if payroll processing were outsourced.
b. Duck Associates' bookkeeper would spend half her time preparing the weekly payroll input form that is given to the payroll processing service. She is paid $450 a week.
c. Duck Associates would no longer need payroll clerk Toby Stock, whose annual salary is $42,000.
d. The payroll processing service would charge $2,000 a month.

Requirements

1. Would outsourcing the payroll function increase or decrease Duck Associates' operating income?
2. Tan believes that outsourcing payroll would simplify her job, but she does not like the prospect of having to lay off Stock, who has become a close personal friend. She does not believe there is another position available for Stock at his current salary. Can you think of other factors that might support keeping Stock rather than outsourcing payroll processing? How should each of the factors affect Tan's decision if she wants to do what is best for Duck Associates and act ethically?

Team Project

A8-59 Relevant information to outsourcing decision *(Learning Objective 6)*

John Menard is the founder and sole owner of Menards. Analysts have estimated that his chain of home improvement stores scattered around nine midwestern states generate about $3 billion in annual sales. But how can Menards compete with giant Home Depot?

Suppose Menard is trying to decide whether to invest $45 million in a state-of-the-art manufacturing plant in Eau Claire, Wisconsin. Menard expects the plant would operate for 15 years, after which it would have no residual value. The plant would produce Menards's own line of Formica countertops, cabinets, and picnic tables.

Suppose Menards would incur the following unit costs in producing its own product lines:

	Per Unit		
	Countertops	Cabinets	Picnic Tables
Direct materials	$15	$10	$25
Direct labor	10	5	15
Variable manufacturing overhead	5	2	6

Rather than Menard making these products, assume that he can buy them from outside suppliers. Suppliers would charge Menards $40 per countertop, $25 per cabinet, and $65 per picnic table.

Whether Menard makes or buys these products, assume that he expects the following annual sales:

-   Countertops—487,200 at $130 each
-   Picnic tables—100,000 at $225 each
-   Cabinets—150,000 at $75 each

If "making" is sufficiently more profitable than outsourcing, Menard will build the new plant. John Menard has asked your consulting group for a recommendation. Menard uses the straight-line depreciation method.

Requirements

1. Are the following items relevant or irrelevant in Menard's decision to build a new plant that will manufacture his own products?
    a. The unit sale prices of the countertops, cabinets, and picnic tables (the sale prices that Menards charges its customers)
    b. The prices that outside suppliers would charge Menards for the three products if Menards decides to outsource the products rather than make them
    c. The $45 million to build the new plant
    d. The direct materials, direct labor, and variable overhead that Menards would incur to manufacture the three product lines
    e. Menard's salary

2. Determine whether Menards should make or outsource the countertops, cabinets, and picnic tables assuming that the company has already built the plant and, therefore, has the manufacturing capacity to produce these products. In other words, *what is the annual difference in cash flows* if Menards decides to make rather than outsource each of these three products?

3. Write a memo giving your recommendation to Menard. The memo should clearly state your recommendation and briefly summarize the reasons for your recommendation.

A8-60 CMA Question

Breegle Company produces three products (B-40, J-60, and H-102) from a single process. Breegle uses the physical volume method to allocate joint costs of $22,500 per batch to the products. Based on the following information, which product(s) should Breegle continue to process after the split-off point in order to maximize profit?

	B-40	J-60	H-102
Physical units produced per batch	1,500	2,000	3,200
Sales value per unit at splitoff	$10.00	$4.00	$7.25
Cost per unit of further processing after splitoff	3.05	1.00	2.50
Sales value per unit after further processing	12.25	5.70	9.75

a. B-40 only.

b. J-60 only.

c. H-102 only.

d. B-40 and H-102 only.

(*CMA Adapted*)

Capital Investment Decisions and the Time Value of Money

Learning Objectives

- **1** Describe the importance of capital investments and the capital budgeting process

- **2** Use the payback and accounting rate of return methods to make capital investment decisions

- **3** Use the time value of money to compute the present and future values of single lump sums and annuities

- **4** Use discounted cash flow models to make capital investment decisions

- **5** Compare and contrast the four capital budgeting methods

From Chapter 12 of *Managerial Accounting*, Third Edition. Karen W. Braun, Wendy M. Tietz.

Cedar Fair Entertainment

Company is the leading operator of amusement parks in the United States and Canada, entertaining over 22 million guests each year. The company's flagship park, Cedar Point, in Sandusky, Ohio, is known as the "Roller Coaster Capital of the World." The park has a world-record breaking collection of 17 roller coasters, as well as an abundance of non-coaster rides and activities. These roller coasters include some of the *fastest* and *tallest* roller coasters in North America. The newest roller coaster, "Maverick," cost over $21 million to build. The company doesn't mind paying that kind of money for a new ride, as long as it is expected to generate handsome returns in years to come. According to Cedar Fair's chief executive officer, the company "remains committed to investing in new rides and attractions...on an annual basis." The CEO views these "strategic investments" as one of the keys to the company's success. In the eyes of customers, the strategy has worked: Cedar Point has been voted the "Best Amusement Park in the World" for 13 consecutive years, by *Amusement Today's* international survey.

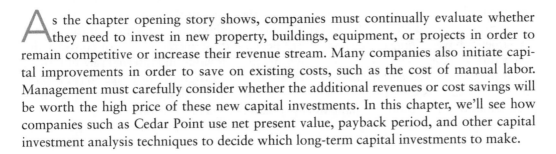

© Dennis MacDonald / Alamy

Source: Cedarpoint.com

As the chapter opening story shows, companies must continually evaluate whether they need to invest in new property, buildings, equipment, or projects in order to remain competitive or increase their revenue stream. Many companies also initiate capital improvements in order to save on existing costs, such as the cost of manual labor. Management must carefully consider whether the additional revenues or cost savings will be worth the high price of these new capital investments. In this chapter, we'll see how companies such as Cedar Point use net present value, payback period, and other capital investment analysis techniques to decide which long-term capital investments to make.

1 Describe the importance of capital investments and the capital budgeting process

What is Capital Budgeting?

The process of making capital investment decisions is often referred to as **capital budgeting**. Companies make capital investments when they acquire *capital assets*—assets used for a long period of time. Capital investments include buying new equipment, building new plants, automating production, and developing major commercial websites. In addition to affecting operations for many years, capital investments usually require large sums of money. Cedar Point's decision to spend $21 million on the Maverick roller coaster will tie up resources for years to come—as will Marriott's decision to spend $187 million to renovate its Marco Island Marriott Beach Resort, Golf Club, and Spa.

Capital investment decisions affect all types of businesses as they try to become more efficient by automating production and implementing new technologies. Grocers and retailers such as Walmart have invested in expensive self-scan check-out machines, while airlines such as Delta and Continental have invested in self-check-in kiosks. These new technologies cost money. How do managers decide whether these expansions in plant and equipment will be good investments? They use capital budgeting analysis. Some companies, such as Georgia Pacific, employ staff dedicated solely to capital budgeting analysis. They spend thousands of hours a year determining which capital investments to pursue.

Four Popular Methods of Capital Budgeting Analysis

In this chapter, we discuss four popular methods of analyzing potential capital investments:

1. Payback period
2. Accounting rate of return (ARR)
3. Net present value (NPV)
4. Internal rate of return (IRR)

The first two methods, payback period and accounting rate of return, are fairly quick and easy to calculate and work well for capital investments that have a relatively short life span, such as computer equipment and software that may have a useful life of only two to three years. Management often uses the payback period and accounting rate of return to screen potential investments from those that are less desirable. The payback period provides management with valuable information on how fast the cash invested will be recouped. The accounting rate of return shows the effect of the investment on the company's accrual-based income. However, these two methods are inadequate if the capital investments have a longer life span. Why? Because these methods do not consider the time value of money. The last two methods, net present value and internal rate of return, factor in the time value of money, so they are more appropriate for longer-term capital investments such as Cedar Point's new roller coasters and rides. Management often uses a combination of methods to make final capital investment decisions.

Capital budgeting is not an exact science. Although the calculations these methods require may appear precise, remember that they are based on predictions about an uncertain future. These predictions must consider many unknown factors, such as changing consumer preferences, competition, and government regulations. The further into the future the decision extends, the more likely actual results will differ from predictions. Long-term decisions are riskier than short-term decisions.

> ■ **Why is this important?**
>
> "Each of these **four methods** help managers **decide** whether it would be wise to **invest** large sums of money in **new projects**, buildings, or equipment."

Focus on Cash Flows

Generally Accepted Accounting Principles (GAAP) are based on accrual accounting, but capital budgeting focuses on cash flows. The desirability of a capital asset depends on its ability to generate *net cash inflows*—that is, inflows in excess of outflows—over the asset's useful life. Recall that operating income based on accrual accounting contains noncash expenses such as depreciation expense and bad-debt expense. The capital investment's *net cash inflows*, therefore, will differ from its operating income. Of the four capital budgeting methods covered in this chapter, only the accounting rate of return method uses accrual-based accounting income. The other three methods use the investment's projected *net cash inflows*.

What do the projected net cash inflows include? Cash *inflows* include future cash revenue generated from the investment, any future savings in ongoing cash operating costs resulting from the investment, and any future residual value of the asset. To determine the investment's *net* cash inflows, the inflows are *netted* against the investment's future cash *outflows*, such as the investment's ongoing cash operating costs and refurbishment, repairs, and maintenance costs. The initial investment itself is also a significant cash outflow. However, in our calculations, *we refer to the amount of the investment separately from all other cash flows related to the investment.* The projected net cash inflows are "given" in our examples and in the assignment material. In reality, much of capital investment analysis revolves around projecting these figures as accurately as possible using input from employees throughout the organization.

Capital Budgeting Process

As shown in Exhibit 12-1, the first step in the capital budgeting process is to identify potential investments—for example, new technology and equipment that may make the company more efficient, competitive, and profitable. Employees, consultants, and outside sales vendors often offer capital investment proposals to management. After identifying potential capital investments, managers next estimate the investments' net cash inflows. As discussed previously, this step can be very time-consuming and difficult. However, managers make the best projections possible given the information they have. The third step is to analyze the investments using one or more of the four methods listed previously. Sometimes the analysis involves a two-stage process. In the first stage, managers screen the investments using one or both of the methods that do *not* incorporate the time value of money: payback period or accounting rate of return. These simple methods quickly weed out undesirable investments. Potential investments that "pass the initial test" go on to a second stage of analysis. In the second stage, managers further analyze the potential investments using the net present value or internal rate of return method. Because these methods consider the time value of money, they provide more accurate information about the potential investment's profitability. Since each method evaluates the potential investment from a different angle, some companies use all four methods to get the most "complete picture" they can about the investment.

Some companies can pursue all of the potential investments that meet or exceed their decision criteria. However, because of limited resources, other companies must engage in **capital rationing** and choose among alternative capital investments. This is the fourth step pictured in Exhibit 12-1. Based on the availability of funds, managers determine if and when to make specific capital investments. For example, management may decide to wait three years to buy a certain piece of equipment because it considers other investments to be more important. In the intervening three years, the company will reassess whether it should still invest in the equipment. Perhaps technology has changed and even better equipment is available. Perhaps consumer tastes have changed, so the company no longer needs the equipment. Because of changing factors, long-term capital budgets are rarely set in stone.

As a final step, most companies perform **post-audits** of their capital investments. After investing in the assets, they compare the actual net cash inflows generated from the investment to the projected net cash inflows. Post-audits help companies determine whether the investments are going as planned and deserve continued support or whether

EXHIBIT 12-1 Capital Budgeting Process

Step 1: Identify potential capital investments

Step 2: Estimate future net cash inflows

Step 3: Analyze potential investments
i) Screen out undesirable investments using payback and/or ARR
ii) Further analyze investments using NPV and/or IRR

Step 4: Engage in capital rationing, if necessary, to choose among alternative investments

Step 5: Perform post-audits after making capital investments

they should abandon the project and sell the assets (if possible). Managers also use feedback from post-audits to better estimate net cash inflow projections for future projects. If managers expect routine post-audits, they will more likely submit realistic net cash inflow estimates with their capital investment proposals.

 Sustainability and Capital Investments

Investments in "green" technologies often require large capital outlays that are subject to capital investment analysis. Investments in clean energy have risen dramatically in recent years, especially with respect to wind and solar power projects. In 2010 alone, $243 billion was invested globally in clean energy.[1] Companies deciding whether to invest in solar paneling on retail outlets (Target)[2], a fleet of electric vehicles (Continental Airlines)[3], or LEED certified buildings (Best Buy)[4] will want to assess how quickly payback will occur and how prudent the investment will be. Their analysis should consider all of the future revenues and cost savings that may occur as a result of using greener technology.

See Exercises E12-22A and E12-42B

For example, companies need to be aware of grants and tax breaks offered by governmental agencies for investing in green technology. These government-sponsored incentives should be treated as reductions in the initial cost of the investment or as periodic cost savings, depending on how the incentive is structured and when it is received. Companies should also factor in future cost savings from having fewer lawsuits, regulatory fines, and clean-up costs as a result of investing in green technology. Furthermore, as the supply of fossil fuels decreases and the cost of it rises, greener technology may also result in lower annual operating costs.

[1]"China leads in clean-energy investing," Christopher Martin, Plain Dealer, March 30, 2011.
[2]http://www.environmentalleader.com/2007/04/30/target-begins-solar-power-rollout/
[3]https://www.continental.com/web/en-US/content/company/globalcitizenship/environment.aspx
[4]http://www.jetsongreen.com/2007/08/best-buy-to-bui.html

When renovating existing facilities, or constructing new facilities, <u>**LEED certification**</u> should be considered. LEED, which stands for "Leadership in Energy and Environmental Design," is a certification system developed by the U.S. Green Building Council as a way of promoting and evaluating environmentally friendly construction projects. Five factors are assessed as part of the certification process:[5]

1. Site development
2. Water efficiency
3. Energy efficiency
4. Materials selection
5. Indoor environmental quality

Why do companies care about LEED certification? Besides being better for the planet and the people who work in the buildings, LEED certified buildings typically have lower operating costs which often result in higher returns on the investment. Additionally, LEED certified buildings have a competitive advantage over non-certified buildings. As a result, LEED certified buildings often attract more potential buyers and command higher lease prices.

How do Managers Calculate the Payback Period and Accounting Rate of Return?

Payback Period

<u>**Payback**</u> is the length of time it takes to recover, in net cash inflows, the cost of the capital outlay. The payback model measures how quickly managers expect to recover their investment dollars. The shorter the payback period, the more attractive the asset, *all else being equal.* Why? The quicker an investment pays itself back, the less inherent risk that the investment will become unprofitable. Computing the payback period depends on whether net cash inflows are equal each year or whether they differ over time. We consider each in turn.

2 Use the payback and accounting rate of return methods to make capital investment decisions

Payback with Equal Annual Net Cash Inflows

Tierra Firma makes camping gear. The company is considering investing $240,000 in hardware and software to develop a business-to-business (B2B) portal. Employees throughout the company will use the B2B portal to access company-approved suppliers. Tierra Firma expects the portal to save $60,000 each year for the six years of its useful life. The savings will arise from a reduction in the number of purchasing personnel the company employs and from lower prices on the goods and services purchased. Net cash inflows arise from an increase in revenues, a decrease in expenses, or both. In Tierra Firma's case, the net cash inflows result from lower expenses.

When net cash inflows are equal each year, managers compute the payback period as follows:

Why is this important?

"Companies want to **recover their cash** as quickly as possible. The **payback period** tells managers **how long** it will take before the investment is **recouped.**"

$$\text{Payback period} = \frac{\text{Amount invested}}{\text{Expected annual net cash inflow}}$$

Tierra Firma computes the investment's payback as follows:

$$\text{Payback period for B2B portal} = \frac{\$240,000}{\$60,000} = 4 \text{ years}$$

[5]http://www.usgbc.org

The left side of Exhibit 12-2 verifies that Tierra Firma expects to recoup the $240,000 investment in the B2B portal by the end of Year 4, when the accumulated net cash inflows total $240,000.

EXHIBIT 12-2 Payback—Equal Annual Net Cash Inflows

| | | Net Cash Inflows | | | |
| | | B2B Portal | | Website Development | |
Year	Amount Invested	Annual	Accumulated	Annual	Accumulated
0	$240,000	—	—	—	—
1	—	$60,000	$ 60,000	$80,000	$ 80,000
2	—	60,000	120,000	80,000	160,000
3	—	60,000	180,000	80,000	240,000
4	—	60,000	240,000		
5	—	60,000	300,000		
6	—	60,000	360,000		

Tierra Firma is also considering investing $240,000 to develop a website. The company expects the website to generate $80,000 in net cash inflows each year of its three-year life. The payback period is computed as follows:

$$\text{Payback period for website development} = \frac{\$240{,}000}{\$80{,}000} = 3 \text{ years}$$

The right side of Exhibit 12-2 verifies that Tierra Firma will recoup the $240,000 investment for website development by the end of Year 3, when the accumulated net cash inflows total $240,000.

Payback with Unequal Net Cash Inflows

The payback equation works only when net cash inflows are the same each period. When periodic cash flows are unequal, you must accumulate net cash inflows until the amount invested is recovered. Assume that Tierra Firma is considering an alternate investment, the Z80 portal. The Z80 portal differs from the B2B portal and website in two respects: (1) it has *unequal* net cash inflows during its life, and (2) it has a $30,000 residual value at the end of its life. The Z80 portal will generate net cash inflows of $100,000 in Year 1, $80,000 in Year 2, $50,000 each year in Years 3–5, $30,000 in Year 6, and $30,000 when it is sold at the end of its life. Exhibit 12-3 shows the payback schedule for these unequal annual net cash inflows.

By the end of Year 3, the company has recovered $230,000 of the $240,000 initially invested and is only $10,000 short of payback. Because the expected net cash inflow in Year 4 is $50,000, by the end of Year 4, the company will have recovered *more* than the initial investment. Therefore, the payback period is somewhere between three and four years. Assuming that the cash flow occurs evenly throughout the fourth year, the payback period is calculated as follows:

$$\text{Payback} = 3 \text{ years} + \frac{\$10{,}000 \text{ (amount needed to complete recovery in Year 4)}}{\$50{,}000 \text{ (projected net cash inflow in Year 4)}}$$

$$= 3.2 \text{ years}$$

EXHIBIT 12-3 Payback—Unequal Annual Net Cash Inflows

		Net Cash Inflows Z80 Portal		
Year	Amount Invested	Annual		Accumulated
0	$240,000	—		—
1	—	100,000	Useful Life	$100,000
2	—	80,000		180,000
3	—	50,000		230,000
4	—	50,000		280,000
5	—	50,000		330,000
6	—	30,000		360,000
Residual Value		30,000		390,000

Criticism of the Payback Period Method

A major criticism of the payback method is that it focuses only on time, not on profitability. The payback period considers only those cash flows that occur *during* the payback period. This method ignores any cash flows that occur *after* that period, including any residual value. For example, Exhibit 12-2 shows that the B2B portal will continue to generate net cash inflows for two years after its payback period. These additional net cash inflows amount to $120,000 ($60,000 × 2 years), yet the payback method ignores this extra cash. A similar situation occurs with the Z80 portal. As shown in Exhibit 12-3, the Z80 portal will provide an additional $150,000 of net cash inflows, including residual value, after its payback period of 3.2 years. In contrast, the website's useful life, as shown in Exhibit 12-2, is the *same* as its payback period (three years). Since no additional cash flows occur after the payback period, the website will merely cover its cost and provide no profit. Because this is the case, the company has little or no reason to invest in the website even though its payback period is the shortest of all three investments.

Exhibit 12-4 compares the payback period of the three investments. As the exhibit illustrates, the payback method does not consider the asset's profitability. *The method only tells management how quickly it will recover its cash.* Even though the website has the shortest payback period, both the B2B portal and the Z80 portal are better investments because they provide profit. The key point is that the investment with the shortest payback period is best *only when all other factors are the same*. Therefore, managers usually use the payback method as a screening device to "weed out" investments that will take too long to recoup. They rarely use payback period as the sole method for deciding whether to invest in the asset.

EXHIBIT 12-4   Comparing Payback Periods Between Investments

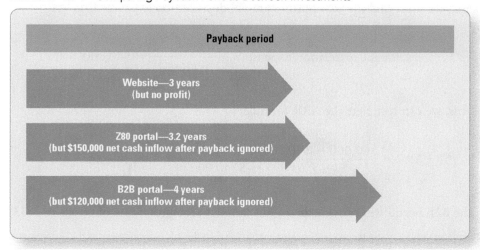

When using the payback period method, managers are guided by the following decision rule:

DECISION RULE: Payback Period

↓

Investments with **shorter** payback periods are more desirable, *all else being equal.*

Accounting Rate of Return (ARR)

Companies are in business to earn profits. One measure of profitability is the **accounting rate of return (ARR)** on an asset:[6]

$$\text{Accounting rate of return} = \frac{\text{Average annual operating income from asset}}{\text{Initial investment}}$$

The ARR focuses on the *operating income, not the net cash inflow*, that an asset generates. The ARR measures the average annual rate of return over the asset's life. Recall that operating income is based on *accrual accounting*. Therefore, any noncash expenses such as depreciation expense must be subtracted from the asset's net cash inflows to arrive at its operating income. Assuming that depreciation expense is the only noncash expense relating to the investment, we can rewrite the ARR formula as follows:

$$\text{ARR} = \frac{\text{Average annual net cash flow} - \text{Annual depreciation expense}}{\text{Initial investment}}$$

Exhibit 12-5 reviews how to calculate annual depreciation expense using the straight-line method.

EXHIBIT 12-5 Review of Straight-Line Depreciation Expense Calculation

$$\text{Annual depreciation expense} = \frac{\text{Initial cost of asset} - \text{Residual value}}{\text{Useful life of asset (in years)}}$$

Investments with Equal Annual Net Cash Inflows

Recall that the B2B portal, which costs \$240,000, has equal annual net cash inflows of \$60,000, a six-year useful life, and no residual value.

First, we must find the B2B portal's annual depreciation expense:

$$\text{Annual depreciation expense} = \frac{\$240{,}000 - 0}{6 \text{ years}} = \$40{,}000$$

Now, we can complete the ARR formula:

$$\text{ARR} = \frac{\$60{,}000 - \$40{,}000}{\$240{,}000} = \frac{\$20{,}000}{\$240{,}000} = 8.33\% \text{ (rounded)}$$

The B2B portal will provide an average annual accounting rate of return of 8.33%.

[6]Some managers prefer to use the average investment, rather than the initial investment, as the denominator. For simplicity, we will use the initial investment.

Investments with Unequal Net Cash Inflows

Now, consider the Z80 portal. Recall that the Z80 portal would also cost $240,000 but it had unequal net cash inflows during its life (as pictured in Exhibit 12-3) and a $30,000 residual value at the end of its life. Since the yearly cash inflows vary in size, we need to first calculate the Z80's *average* annual net cash inflows:[7]

Total net cash inflows *during* operating life of asset	
(does not include the residual value at the end of life)[7]	
(Year 1 + Year 2, and so forth) from Exhibit 12-3...................	$360,000
Divide by: Asset's operating life (in years)...	÷ 6 years
Average annual net cash inflow from asset..	$ 60,000

Now, let's calculate the asset's annual depreciation expense:

$$\text{Annual depreciation expense} = \frac{\$240,000 - \$30,000}{6 \text{ years}} = \$35,000$$

Finally, we can complete the ARR calculation:

$$\text{ARR} = \frac{\$60,000 - \$35,000}{\$240,000} = \frac{\$25,000}{\$240,000} = 10.42\% \text{ (rounded)}$$

Notice that the Z80 portal's average annual operating income ($25,000) is higher than the B2B portal's average operating income ($20,000). Since the Z80 asset has a residual value at the end of its life, less depreciation is expensed each year, leading to a higher average annual operating income and a higher ARR.

Companies that use the ARR model set a minimum required accounting rate of return. If Tierra Firma required an ARR of at least 10%, its managers would not approve an investment in the B2B portal but would approve an investment in the Z80 portal.

The decision rule is as follows:

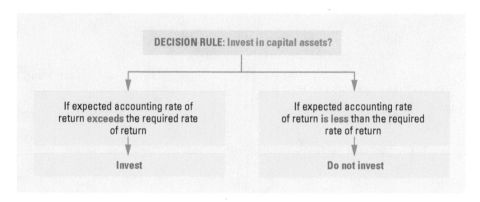

In summary, the payback period focuses on the time it takes for the company to

---

[7]The residual value is not included in the net cash inflows *during* the asset's operating life because we are trying to find the asset's average *annual operating* income. We assume that the asset will be sold for its expected residual value ($30,000) at the *end* of its life, resulting in no additional accounting gain or loss.

recoup its cash investment but ignores all cash flows occurring after the payback period. Because it ignores any additional cash flows (including any residual value), the method does not consider the profitability of the project.

The ARR, however, measures the profitability of the asset over its entire life using accrual accounting figures. It is the only method that uses accrual accounting rather than net cash inflows in its computations. As discussed in Chapter 10, company divisions are often evaluated based on accounting income. Therefore, the investment's ARR helps managers see how the investment will impact their division's profitability. The payback period and ARR methods are simple and quick to compute, so managers often use them to screen out undesirable investments and to gain a more complete picture of the investment's desirability. However, both methods ignore the time value of money.

Decision Guidelines

Capital Budgeting

Amazon.com started as a virtual retailer. It held no inventory. Instead, it bought books and CDs only as needed to fill customer orders. As the company grew, its managers decided to invest in their own warehouse facilities. Why? Owning warehouse facilities allows Amazon.com to save money by buying in bulk. Also, shipping all items in the customer's order in one package from one location saves shipping costs. Here are some of the guidelines Amazon.com's managers used as they made the major capital budgeting decision to invest in building warehouses.

Decision	Guidelines
Why is this decision important?	Capital budgeting decisions typically require large investments and affect operations for years to come.
What method shows us how soon we will recoup our cash investment?	The payback method shows how quickly managers will recoup their investment. The method highlights investments that are too risky due to long payback periods. However, it doesn't reveal any information about the investment's profitability.
Does any method consider the impact of the investment on accrual-based accounting income?	The accounting rate of return is the only capital budgeting method that shows how the investment will affect accrual-based accounting income, which is important to financial statement users. All other methods of capital investment analysis focus on the investment's net cash inflows.
How do we compute the payback period if cash flows are *equal*?	$$\text{Payback period} = \frac{\text{Amount invested}}{\text{Expected annual net cash inflow}}$$
How do we compute the payback period if cash flows are *unequal*?	Accumulate net cash inflows until the amount invested is recovered.
How do we compute the ARR?	$$\text{Accounting rate of return} = \frac{\text{Average annual operating income from asset}}{\text{Initial investment}}$$ We can also write this formula as follows: $$\text{ARR} = \frac{\text{Average annual net cash flow} - \text{Annual depreciation expense}}{\text{Initial investment}}$$

SUMMARY PROBLEM 1

Zetamax is considering buying a new bar-coding machine for its Austin, Texas plant. The company screens its potential capital investments using the payback period and accounting rate of return methods. If a potential investment has a payback period of less than four years and a minimum 7% accounting rate of return, it will be considered further. The data for the machine follow:

Cost of machine	$48,000
Estimated residual value	$ 0
Estimated annual net cash inflow (each year for five years)	$13,000
Estimated useful life	5 years

Requirements

1. Compute the bar-coding machine's payback period.
2. Compute the bar-coding machine's ARR.
3. Should Zetamax turn down this investment proposal or consider it further?

▪ SOLUTIONS

Requirement 1

$$\text{Payback period} = \frac{\text{Amount invested}}{\text{Expected annual net cash inflow}} = \frac{\$48,000}{\$13,000} = 3.7 \text{ years (rounded)}$$

Requirement 2

$$\text{Accounting rate of return} = \frac{\text{Average annual net cash inflow} - \text{Annual depreciation expense}}{\text{Initial investment}}$$

$$= \frac{\$13,000 - \$9,600^*}{\$48,000}$$

$$= \frac{\$3,400}{\$48,000}$$

$$= 7.08\%$$

*Depreciation expense = $48,000 ÷ 5 years = $9,600

Requirement 3

The bar-coding machine proposal passes both initial screening tests. The payback period is slightly less than four years, and the accounting rate of return is slightly higher than 7%. Zetamax should further analyze the proposal using a method that incorporates the time value of money.

How do Managers Compute the Time Value of Money?

A dollar received today is worth more than a dollar to be received in the future. Why? Because you can invest today's dollar and earn extra income. The fact that invested money earns income over time is called the **time value of money**, and this explains why we would prefer to receive cash sooner rather than later. The time value of money means that the timing of capital investments' net cash inflows is important. Two methods of capital investment analysis incorporate the time value of money: the NPV and IRR. This section reviews time value of money concepts to make sure you have a firm foundation for discussing these two methods.

3 Use the time value of money to compute the present and future values of single lump sums and annuities

Factors Affecting the Time Value of Money

The time value of money depends on several key factors:

1. The principal amount (*p*)
2. The number of periods (*n*)
3. The interest rate (*i*)

The principal (*p*) refers to the amount of the investment or borrowing. Because this chapter deals with capital investments, we'll primarily discuss the principal in terms of investments. However, the same concepts apply to borrowings (which you probably discussed in your financial accounting course when you studied bonds payable). We state the principal as either a single lump sum or an annuity. For example, if you want to save money for a new car after college, you may decide to invest a single lump sum of $10,000 in a certificate of deposit (CD). However, you may not currently have $10,000 to invest. Instead, you may invest funds as an annuity, depositing $2,000 at the end of each year in a bank savings account. An **annuity** is a stream of *equal installments* made at *equal time intervals*. An *ordinary annuity* is an annuity in which the installments occur at the *end* of each period.[8]

The number of periods (*n*) is the length of time from the beginning of the investment until termination. All else being equal, the shorter the investment period, the lower the total amount of interest earned. If you withdraw your savings after four years rather than five years, you will earn less interest. If you begin to save for retirement at age 22 rather than age 45, you will earn more interest before you retire. In this chapter, the number of periods is stated in years.[9]

The interest rate (*i*) is the annual percentage earned on the investment. **Simple interest** means that interest is calculated *only* on the principal amount. **Compound interest** means that interest is calculated on the principal *and* on all interest earned to date. *Compound interest assumes that all interest earned will remain invested at the same interest rate, not withdrawn and spent.* Exhibit 12-6 compares simple interest (6%) on a five-year, $10,000 CD with interest compounded yearly. As you can see, the amount of compound interest earned each year grows as the base on which it is calculated (principal plus cumulative interest to date) grows. Over the life of this particular investment, the total amount of compound interest is about 13% more than the total amount of simple interest. Most investments yield compound interest, so we assume compound interest rather than simple interest for the rest of this chapter.

Why is this important?

"The **time value of money** is a critical factor in many management **decisions**. In addition to its use in capital investment analysis, it's also used for **personal financial planning** (such as retirement planning), **business valuation** (for purchasing businesses), and financing decisions **(borrowing and lending)**."

[8]In contrast to an *ordinary annuity*, an *annuity due* is an annuity in which the installments occur at the *beginning* of each period. Throughout this chapter we use ordinary annuities since they are better suited to capital budgeting cash flow assumptions.
[9]The number of periods can also be stated in days, months, or quarters. If so, the interest rate needs to be adjusted to reflect the number of time periods in the year.

EXHIBIT 12-6 Simple Versus Compound Interest for a Principal Amount of $10,000 at 6% over Five Years

Year	Simple Interest Calculation	Simple Interest	Compound Interest Calculation	Compound Interest*
1	$10,000 × 6% =	$ 600	$10,000 × 6% =	$ 600
2	$10,000 × 6% =	600	($10,000 + 600) × 6% =	636
3	$10,000 × 6% =	600	($10,000 + 600 + 636) × 6% =	674
4	$10,000 × 6% =	600	($10,000 + 600 + 636 + 674) × 6% =	715
5	$10,000 × 6% =	600	($10,000 + 600 + 636 + 674 + 715) × 6% =	758
	Total interest	$3,000	Total interest	$3,383

*Rounded

Fortunately, time value calculations involving compound interest do not have to be as tedious as shown in Exhibit 12-6. Formulas and tables (or proper use of business calculators or Excel applications) simplify the calculations. In the next sections, we will discuss how to use these tools to perform time value of money calculations.

Future Values and Present Values: Points Along the Time Continuum

Consider the time line in Exhibit 12-7. The future value or present value of an investment simply refers to the value of an investment at different points in time.

EXHIBIT 12-7 Present Value and Future Value Along the Time Continuum

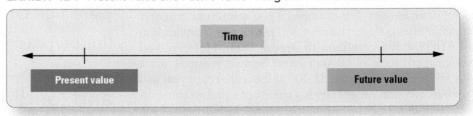

We can calculate the future value or the present value of any investment by knowing (or assuming) information about the three factors listed earlier: (1) the principal amount, (2) the period of time, and (3) the interest rate. For example, in Exhibit 12-6, we calculated the interest that would be earned on (1) a $10,000 principal (2) invested for five years (3) at 6% interest. The future value of the investment is its worth at the end of the five-year time frame—the original principal *plus* the interest earned. In our example, the future value of the investment is as follows:

Future value = Principal + Interest earned
= $10,000 + $3,383
= $13,383

If we invest $10,000 *today*, its *present value* is simply the $10,000 principal amount. So, another way of stating the future value is as follows:

Future value = Present value + Interest earned

We can rearrange the equation as follows:

$$\text{Present value} = \text{Future value} - \text{Interest earned}$$
$$\$10,000 \quad = \quad \$13,383 \quad - \quad \$3,383$$

The only difference between present value and future value is the amount of interest that is earned in the intervening time span.

Future Value and Present Value Factors

Calculating each period's compound interest, as we did in Exhibit 12-6, and then adding it to the present value to determine the future value (or subtracting it from the future value to determine the present value) is tedious. Fortunately, mathematical formulas simplify future value and present value calculations. Mathematical formulas have been developed that specify future values and present values for unlimited combinations of interest rates (i) and time periods (n). Separate formulas exist for single lump-sum investments and annuities.

The formulas have been calculated using various interest rates and time periods. The results are displayed in tables. The formulas and resulting tables are shown in Appendix 12A at the end of this chapter:

1. Present Value of $1 (Table A, p. 741)—*used for lump-sum amounts*
2. Present Value of Annuity of $1 (Table B, p. 742)—*used for annuities*
3. Future Value of $1 (Table C, p. 743)—*used for lump-sum amounts*
4. Future Value of Annuity of $1 (Table D, p. 744)—*used for annuities*

Take a moment to look at these tables because we are going to use them throughout the rest of the chapter. Note that the columns are interest rates (i) and the rows are periods (n).

The data in each table, known as future value factors (FV factors) and present value factors (PV factors), are for an investment (or loan) of $1. To find the future value of an amount other than $1, you simply multiply the FV factor found in the table by the principal amount. To find the present value of an amount other than $1, you multiply the PV factor found in the table by the principal amount.

Rather than using these tables, you may want to use a business calculator that has been programmed with time value of money functions or Microsoft Excel. Business calculators and Excel make time value of money computations much easier because you do not need to find the correct PV and FV factors in the tables. Rather, you simply enter the principal amount, interest rate, and number of time periods and instruct the calculator or Excel to solve for the present or future value.

Appendix 12B shows how to use the TI-83(Plus) and TI-84 (Plus) to perform basic time value of money computations as well as NPV and IRR computations. Appendix 12C shows how to use Excel for present value, future value, NPV and IRR calculations. Instructions for operating other programmed calculators can usually be found on the manufacturer's website.

Appendix 12B and 12C also show how to compute every problem illustrated throughout the rest of the chapter using either a programmed calculator or Excel. As you will see in Appendix 12B and 12C, using a programmed calculator or Excel results in slightly different answers than those presented in the text when using the tables. The differences are due to the fact that the PV and FV factors found in the tables have been rounded to three digits. Finally, all end-of-chapter material has been solved using the tables, Excel, and programmed calculators so that you will have the exact solution for the method you choose to use.

Calculating Future Values of Single Sums and Annuities Using FV Factors

Let's go back to our $10,000 lump-sum investment. If we want to know the future value of the investment five years from now at an interest rate of 6%, we determine the FV factor from the table labeled Future Value of $1 (Appendix 12A, Table C). We use this table for lump-sum amounts. We look down the 6% column and across the 5 periods row and find that the future value factor is 1.338. We finish our calculations as follows:

> Future value = Principal amount × (FV factor for $i = 6\%$, $n = 5$)
> $\qquad$ = \$10,000 × (1.338)
> $\qquad$ = \$13,380

This figure agrees with our earlier calculation of the investment's future value (\$13,383) in Exhibit 12-6. (The difference of \$3 is due to two facts: (1) the tables round the FV and PV factors to three decimal places, and (2) we rounded our earlier yearly interest calculations in Exhibit 12-6 to the nearest dollar.)

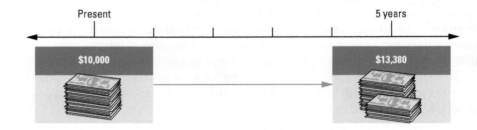

Let's also consider our alternative investment strategy: investing \$2,000 at the end of each year for five years. The procedure for calculating the future value of an annuity is similar to calculating the future value of a lump-sum amount. This time, we use the Future Value of Annuity of \$1 table (Appendix 12A, Table D). Assuming 6% interest, we once again look down the 6% column. Because we will be making five annual installments, we look across the row marked 5 periods. The Annuity FV factor is 5.637. We finish the calculation as follows:

> Future value = Amount of each cash installment × (Annuity FV factor for $i = 6\%$, $n = 5$)
> $\qquad$ = \$2,000 × (5.637)
> $\qquad$ = \$11,274

This is considerably less than the future value (\$13,380) of the lump sum of \$10,000 even though we invested \$10,000 out of pocket either way.

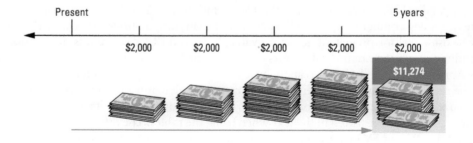

STOP & THINK

Explain why the future value of the annuity ($11,274) is less than the future value of the lump sum ($13,380). Prove that the $11,274 future value is correct by calculating interest using the "longhand" method shown earlier.

Answer: Even though you invested $10,000 out of pocket under both investments, the timing of the investment significantly affects the amount of interest earned. The $10,000 lump sum invested immediately earns interest for the full five years. However, the annuity doesn't begin earning interest until Year 2 (because the first installment isn't made until the *end* of Year 1). In addition, the amount invested begins at $2,000 and doesn't reach a full $10,000 until the end of Year 5. Therefore, the base on which the interest is earned is smaller than the lump-sum investment for the entire five-year period. As shown here, the $11,274 future value of a $2,000 annuity for five years is correct.

Year	Interest Earned During Year (6%) (rounded)	Investment Installment (end of year)	Cumulative Balance at End of Year (investments plus interest earned to date)*
1	$ 0	$2,000	$ 2,000
2	120	2,000	4,120
3	247	2,000	6,367
4	382	2,000	8,749
5	525	2,000	11,274

*This is the base on which the interest is earned the next year.

Calculating Present Values of Single Sums and Annuities Using PV Factors

The process for calculating present values—often called discounting cash flows—is similar to the process for calculating future values. The difference is the point in time at which you are assessing the investment's worth. Rather than determining its value at a future date, you are determining its value at an earlier point in time (today). For our example, let's assume that you've just won the lottery after purchasing one $5 lottery ticket. The state offers you three payout options for your after-tax prize money:

Option #1: $1,000,000 now

Option #2: $150,000 at the end of each year for the next 10 years

Option #3: $2,000,000 10 years from now

Which alternative should you take? You might be tempted to wait 10 years to "double" your winnings. You may be tempted to take the money now and spend it. However, let's assume that you plan to prudently invest all money received—no matter when you receive it—so that you have financial flexibility in the future (for example, for buying a house, retiring early, and taking vacations). How can you choose among the three payment alternatives when the *total amount* of each option varies ($1,000,000 versus $1,500,000 versus $2,000,000) and the *timing* of the cash flows varies (now versus some each year versus later)? Comparing these three options is like comparing apples to oranges—we just can't do it—unless we find some common basis for comparison. Our common basis for comparison will be the prize money's worth at a certain point in time—namely, today. In other words, if we convert each payment option to its *present value*, we can compare apples to apples.

We already know the principal amount and timing of each payment option, so the only assumption we'll have to make is the interest rate. The interest rate will vary depending on the amount of risk you are willing to take with your investment. Riskier investments (such as stock investments) command higher interest rates; safer investments (such as FDIC-insured bank deposits) yield lower interest rates. Let's assume that after investigating possible investment alternatives, you choose an investment contract with an 8% annual return.

We already know that the present value of Option #1 is $1,000,000. Let's convert the other two payment options to their present values so that we can compare them. We'll need to use the Present Value of Annuity of $1 table (Appendix 12A, Table B) to convert payment Option #2 (since it's an annuity) and the Present Value of $1 table (Appendix 12A, Table A) to convert payment Option #3 (since it's a single lump sum). To obtain the PV factors, we look down the 8% column and across the 10 period row. Then, we finish the calculations as follows:

Option #1

Present value = $1,000,000

Option #2

Present value = Amount of each cash installment × (Annuity PV factor for $i = 8\%$, $n = 10$)
Present value = $150,000 × (6.710)
Present value = $1,006,500

Option #3

Present value = Principal amount × (PV factor for $i = 8\%$, $n = 10$)
Present value = $2,000,000 × (0.463)
Present value = $926,000

Exhibit 12-8 shows that we have converted each payout option to a common basis—its worth today—so we can make a valid comparison of the options. Based on this comparison, we should choose Option #2 because its worth, in today's dollars, is the highest of the three options.

Now that we have studied time value of money concepts, we will discuss the two capital budgeting methods that incorporate the time value of money: net present value (NPV) and internal rate of return (IRR).

EXHIBIT 12-8 Comparing Present Values of Lottery Payout Options at i = 8%

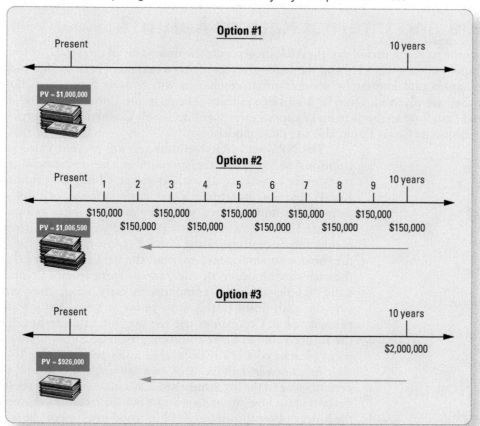

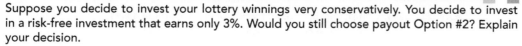

STOP & THINK

Suppose you decide to invest your lottery winnings very conservatively. You decide to invest in a risk-free investment that earns only 3%. Would you still choose payout Option #2? Explain your decision.

Answer: Using a 3% interest rate, the present values of the payout options are as follows:

Payment Options	Present Value of Lottery Payout (Present value calculation, $i = 3\%$, $n = 10$)
Option #1	$1,000,000 (already stated at its present value)
Option #2	$1,279,500 (= $150,000 × 8.530)
Option #3	$1,488,000 (= $2,000,000 × .744)

When the lottery payout is invested at 3% rather than 8%, the present values change. Option #3 is now the best alternative because its present value is the highest. Present values and future values are extremely sensitive to changes in interest rate assumptions, especially when the investment period is relatively long.

How do Managers Calculate the Net Present Value and Internal Rate of Return?

Neither the payback period nor the ARR incorporate the time value of money. *Discounted cash flow models*—the NPV and the IRR—overcome this weakness. These models incorporate compound interest by assuming that companies will reinvest future cash flows when they are received. Over 85% of large industrial firms in the United States use discounted cash flow methods to make capital investment decisions. Companies that provide services, such as Cedar Point, also use these models.

Why is this important?

"The **NPV method** lets managers make an **'apples-to-apples' comparison** between the **cash flows** they will receive in the **future** from the investment and the **price** they must **currently pay** to 'purchase' those future cash flows (the cost of the **investment**)."

The NPV and IRR methods rely on present value calculations to *compare* the amount of the investment (the investment's initial cost) with its expected net cash inflows. Recall that an investment's *net cash inflows* includes all *future* cash flows related to the investment, such as future increased sales and cost savings netted against the investment's future cash operating costs. Because the cash outflow for the investment occurs *now* but the net cash inflows from the investment occur in the *future*, companies can make valid "apple-to-apple" comparisons only when they convert the cash flows to the *same point in time*—namely, the present value. Companies use the present value rather than the future value to make the comparison because the investment's initial cost is already stated at its present value.[10]

As shown in Exhibit 12-9, in a favorable investment, the present value of the investment's net cash inflows exceeds the initial cost of the investment. In terms of our earlier lottery example, the lottery ticket turned out to be a "good investment" because the present value of its net cash inflows (the present value of the lottery payout under *any* of the three payout options) exceeded the cost of the investment (the $5 lottery ticket). Let's begin our discussion by taking a closer look at the NPV method.

EXHIBIT 12-9 Comparing the Present Value of an Investment's Net Cash Inflows Against the Investment's Initial Cost

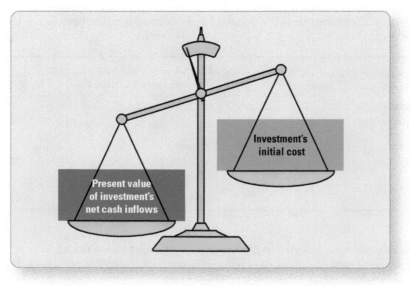

[10]If the investment is to be purchased through lease payments, rather than a current cash outlay, we would still use the current cash price of the investment as its initial cost. If no current cash price is available, we would discount the future lease payments back to their present value to estimate the investment's current cash price.

Net Present Value (NPV)

Allegra is considering producing MP3 players and digital video recorders (DVRs). The products require different specialized machines, each costing $1 million. Each machine has a five-year life and zero residual value. The two products have different patterns of predicted net cash inflows:

	Annual Net Cash Inflows	
Year	MP3 Players	DVRs
1	$ 305,450	$ 500,000
2	305,450	350,000
3	305,450	300,000
4	305,450	250,000
5	305,450	40,000
Total	$1,527,250	$1,440,000

The MP3 project generates more net cash inflows, but the DVR project brings in cash sooner. To decide how attractive each investment is, we find its **net present value (NPV)**. The NPV is the *difference* between the present value of the investment's net cash inflows and the investment's cost. We *discount* the net cash inflows to their present value—just as we did in the lottery example—using Allegra's minimum desired rate of return. This rate is called the **discount rate** because it is the interest rate used for the present value calculations. It's also called the **required rate of return** or **hurdle rate** because the investment must meet or exceed this rate to be acceptable. The discount rate depends on the riskiness of investments. The higher the risk, the higher the discount rate. Allegra's discount rate for these investments is 14%.

We compare the present value of the net cash inflows to the investment's initial cost to decide which projects meet or exceed management's minimum desired rate of return. In other words, management is deciding whether the $1 million is worth more (because the company would have to give it up now to invest in the project) or whether the project's future net cash inflows are worth more. Managers can make a valid comparison between the two sums of money only by comparing them at the *same* point in time—namely at their present value.

NPV with Equal Annual Net Cash Inflows (Annuity)

Allegra expects the MP3 project to generate $305,450 of net cash inflows each year for five years. Because these cash flows are equal in amount and occur every year, they are an annuity. Therefore, we use the Present Value of Annuity of $1 table (Appendix 12A, Table B) to find the appropriate Annuity PV factor for $i = 14\%, n = 5$.

The present value of the net cash inflows from Allegra's MP3 project is as follows:

Present value = Amount of each cash inflow × (Annuity PV factor for $i = 14\%, n = 5$)
= $305,450 × (3.433)
= $1,048,610

Next, we subtract the investment's initial cost ($1 million) from the present value of the net cash inflows ($1,048,610). The difference of $48,610 is the net present value (NPV), as shown in Exhibit 12-10 (on the next page).

EXHIBIT 12-10 NPV of Equal Net Cash Inflows—MP3 Project

	Annuity PV Factor ($i = 14\%$, $n = 5$)	Net Cash Inflow	Present Value
Present value of annuity of equal annual net cash inflows for 5 years at 14%	3.433* ×	$305,450 =	$ 1,048,610
Investment			(1,000,000)
Net present value of the MP3 project			$ 48,610

*Annuity PV factor is found in Appendix 12A, Table B.

A *positive* NPV means that the project earns *more* than the required rate of return. A *negative* NPV means that the project fails to earn the required rate of return. This leads to the following decision rule:

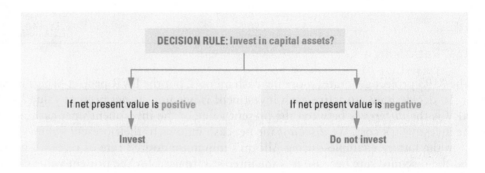

In Allegra's case, the MP3 project is an attractive investment. The $48,610 positive NPV means that the MP3 project earns *more than* Allegra's 14% target rate of return. In other words, management would prefer to give up $1 million today to receive the MP3 project's future net cash inflows. Why? Because those future net cash inflows are worth more than $1 million in today's dollars (they are worth $1,048,610).

Another way managers can use present value analysis is to start the capital budgeting process by computing the total present value of the net cash inflows from the project to determine the *maximum* the company can invest in the project and still earn the target rate of return. For Allegra, the present value of the net cash inflows is $1,048,610. This means that Allegra can invest a maximum of $1,048,610 and still earn the 14% target rate of return. Because Allegra's managers believe they can undertake the project for $1 million, the project is an attractive investment.

NPV with Unequal Annual Net Cash Inflows

In contrast to the MP3 project, the net cash inflows of the DVR project are unequal—$500,000 in Year 1, $350,000 in Year 2, and so forth. Because these amounts vary by year, Allegra's managers *cannot* use the annuity table to compute the present value of the DVR project. They must compute the present value of each individual year's net cash inflows *separately, as separate lump sums received in different years,* using the Present Value of $1 table (Appendix 12A, Table A).

Exhibit 12-11 shows that the $500,000 net cash inflow received in Year 1 is discounted using a PV factor of $i = 14\%$, $n = 1$, while the $350,000 net cash inflow received in Year 2 is discounted using a PV factor of $i = 14\%$, $n = 2$, and so forth. After separately discounting each of the five year's net cash inflows, we find that the *total* present value of the DVR project's net cash inflows is $1,078,910. Finally, we subtract the investment's cost ($1 million) to arrive at the DVR project's NPV: $78,910.

Because the NPV is positive, Allegra expects the DVR project to earn more than the 14% target rate of return, making this an attractive investment.

EXHIBIT 12-11 NPV with Unequal Net Cash Inflows—DVR Project

	PV Factor (i = 14%)		Net Cash Inflow		Present Value
Present value of each year's net cash inflows discounted at 14%:					
Year 1 (n = 1)	0.877*	×	$500,000	=	$ 438,500
Year 2 (n = 2)	0.769	×	350,000	=	269,150
Year 3 (n = 3)	0.675	×	300,000	=	202,500
Year 4 (n = 4)	0.592	×	250,000	=	148,000
Year 5 (n = 5)	0.519	×	40,000	=	20,760
Total present value of net cash inflows					1,078,910
Investment					(1,000,000)
Net present value of the DVR project					$ 78,910

*PV factors are found in Appendix 12A, Table A.

Capital Rationing and the Profitability Index

Exhibits 12-10 and 12-11 show that both the MP3 and DVR projects have positive NPVs. Therefore, both are attractive investments. Because resources are limited, companies are not always able to invest in all capital assets that meet their investment criteria. For example, Allegra may not have the funds to invest in both the DVR and MP3 projects at this time. In this case, Allegra should choose the DVR project because it yields a higher NPV. The DVR project should earn an additional $78,910 beyond the 14% required rate of return, while the MP3 project returns an additional $48,610.

This example illustrates an important point. The MP3 project promises more *total* net cash inflows. But the *timing* of the DVR cash flows—loaded near the beginning of the project—gives the DVR investment a higher NPV. The DVR project is more attractive because of the time value of money. Its dollars, which are received sooner, are worth more now than the more distant dollars of the MP3 project.

If Allegra had to choose between the MP3 and DVR project, it would choose the DVR project because that project yields a higher NPV ($78,910). However, comparing the NPV of the two projects is valid *only* because both projects require the same initial cost—$1 million.

In contrast, Exhibit 12-12 summarizes three capital investment options that Raycor, a sporting goods manufacturer, faces. Each capital project requires a different initial investment. All three projects are attractive because each yields a positive NPV. Assuming that Raycor can invest in only one project at this time, which one should it choose? Project B yields the highest NPV, but it also requires a larger initial investment than the alternatives.

> ■ **Why is this important?**
> "The **profitability index** allows managers to **compare** potential investments of **different sizes** so that they can choose the **most profitable** investment."

EXHIBIT 12-12 Raycor's Capital Investment Options

	Project A	Project B	Project C
Present value of net cash inflows	$150,000	$238,000	$182,000
Investment	(125,000)	(200,000)	(150,000)
Net present value (NPV)	$ 25,000	$ 38,000	$ 32,000

To choose among the projects, Raycor computes the **profitability index** (also known as the **present value index**). The profitability index is computed as follows:

Profitability index = Present value of net cash inflows ÷ Investment

The profitability index computes the number of dollars returned for every dollar invested, *with all calculations performed in present value dollars*. It allows us to compare alternative investments in present value terms, like the NPV method, but also considers differences in the investments' initial cost. Let's compute the profitability index for all three alternatives.

	Present value of net cash inflows	÷ Investment	= Profitability index
Project A:	$150,000	÷ $125,000 =	1.20
Project B:	$238,000	÷ $200,000 =	1.19
Project C:	$182,000	÷ $150,000 =	1.21

The profitability index shows that Project C is the best of the three alternatives because it returns $1.21 in present value dollars for every $1.00 invested. Projects A and B return slightly less.

Let's also compute the profitability index for Allegra's MP3 and DVR projects:

	Present value of net cash inflows	÷ Investment	= Profitability index
MP3:	$1,048,610	÷ $1,000,000 =	1.049
DVR:	$1,078,910	÷ $1,000,000 =	1.079

The profitability index confirms our prior conclusion that the DVR project is more profitable than the MP3 project. The DVR project returns $1.079 (in present value dollars) for every $1.00 invested. This return is beyond the 14% return already used to discount the cash flows. We did not need the profitability index to determine that the DVR project was preferable because both projects required the same investment ($1 million).

NPV of a Project with Residual Value

Many assets yield cash inflows at the end of their useful lives because they have residual value. Companies discount an investment's residual value to its present value when determining the *total* present value of the project's net cash inflows. The residual value is discounted as a single lump sum—not an annuity—because it will be received only once, when the asset is sold.

Suppose Allegra expects the MP3 project equipment to be worth $100,000 at the end of its five-year life. This represents an additional *lump sum* future cash inflow from the MP3 project. To determine the MP3 project's NPV, we discount the residual value ($100,000) using the Present Value of $1 table ($i = 14\%$, $n = 5$) (see Appendix 12A, Table A). We then *add* its present value ($51,900) to the present value of the MP3 project's other net cash inflows ($1,048,610) as shown in Exhibit 12-13:

EXHIBIT 12-13 NPV of a Project with Residual Value

	PV Factor ($i = 14\%$, $n = 5$)	Net Cash Inflow	Present Value
Present value of annuity	3.433	× $305,450 =	$ 1,048,610
Present value of residual value (single lump sum)	0.519	× 100,000 =	51,900
Total present value of net cash inflows			$ 1,100,510
Investment			$(1,000,000)
Net present value (NPV)			$ 100,510

Because of the expected residual value, the MP3 project is now more attractive than the DVR project. If Allegra could pursue only the MP3 or DVR project, it would now choose the MP3 project because its NPV ($100,510) is higher than the DVR project ($78,910) and both projects require the same investment ($1 million).

Sensitivity Analysis

Capital budgeting decisions affect cash flows far into the future. Allegra's managers might want to know whether their decision would be affected by any of their major assumptions. For example consider the following:

- Changing the discount rate from 14% to 12% or to 16%
- Changing the net cash flows by 10%
- Changing an expected residual value

Managers can use spreadsheet software or programmed calculators to quickly perform sensitivity analysis.

Internal Rate of Return (IRR)

The NPV method only tells management whether the investment exceeds the hurdle rate. Since both the MP3 player and DVR projects yield positive NPVs, we know they provide *more* than a 14% rate of return. But what exact rate of return would these investments provide? The IRR method answers that question.

The **internal rate of return (IRR)** is the rate of return, based on discounted cash flows, that a company can expect to earn by investing in the project. *It is the interest rate that makes the NPV of the investment equal to zero:*

$$NPV = 0$$

Let's look at this concept in another light by inserting the definition of NPV:

Present value of the investment's net cash inflows − Investment's cost = 0

Or if we rearrange the equation:

Investment's cost = Present value of the investment's net cash inflows

In other words, the IRR is the *interest rate* that makes the cost of the investment equal to the present value of the investment's net cash inflows. The higher the IRR, the more desirable the project. Like the profitability index, the IRR can be used in the capital rationing process.

IRR computations are very easy to perform on programmed calculators and Microsoft Excel (see Appendix 12B and 12C). However, IRR computations are much more cumbersome to perform using the tables.

IRR with Equal Annual Net Cash Inflows (Annuity)

When the investment is an annuity, we can develop a formula that will tell us the Annuity PV factor associated with the investment's IRR. We start with the equation given previously and then substitute in as follows:

Investment's cost = Present value of the investment's net cash inflows

Investment's cost = Amount of each equal net cash inflow × Annuity PV factor ($i = ?, n =$ given)

Finally, we rearrange the equation to obtain the following formula:

$$\frac{\text{Investment's cost}}{\text{Amount of each equal net cash inflow}} = \text{Annuity PV factor } (i = ?, n = \text{given})$$

Let's use this formula to find the Annuity PV factor associated with Allegra's MP3 project. Recall that the project would cost $1 million and result in five equal yearly cash inflows of $305,450:

$$\frac{\$1,000,000}{\$305,450} = \text{Annuity PV factor } (i = ?, n = 5)$$

$$3.274 = \text{Annuity PV factor } (i = ?, n = 5)$$

Next, we find the interest rate that corresponds to this Annuity PV factor. Turn to the Present Value of Annuity of $1 table (Appendix 12A, Table B). Scan the row corresponding to the project's expected life—five years, in our example. Choose the column(s) with the number closest to the Annuity PV factor you calculated using the formula. The 3.274 annuity factor is in the 16% column.

Therefore, the IRR of the MP3 project is 16%.

Allegra expects the project to earn an internal rate of return of 16% over its life. Exhibit 12-14 confirms this result: Using a 16% discount rate, the project's NPV is zero. In other words, 16% is the discount rate that makes the investment cost equal to the present value of the investment's net cash inflows.

EXHIBIT 12-14 IRR–MP3 Project

	Annuity PV Factor ($i = 16\%, n = 5$)		Net Cash Inflow		Total Present Value
Present value of annuity of equal annual net cash inflows for 5 years at 16%	3.274	×	$305,450	=	$ 1,000,000†
Investment					(1,000,000)
Net present value of the MP3 project					$ 0‡

†Slight rounding error.
‡The zero difference proves that the IRR is 16%.

To decide whether the project is acceptable, compare the IRR with the minimum desired rate of return. The decision rule is as follows:

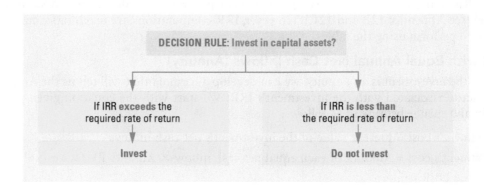

DECISION RULE: Invest in capital assets?

If IRR exceeds the required rate of return → Invest

If IRR is less than the required rate of return → Do not invest

Recall that Allegra's hurdle rate is 14%. Because the MP3 project's IRR (16%) is higher than the hurdle rate (14%), Allegra would invest in the project.

In the MP3 project, the exact Annuity PV factor (3.274) appears in the Present Value of an Annuity of $1 table (Appendix 12A, Table B). Many times, the exact factor will not appear in the table. For example, let's find the IRR of Tierra Firma's B2B Portal. Recall that the B2B portal had a six-year life with annual net cash inflows of $60,000. The investment cost $240,000. We find its Annuity PV factor using the formula given previously:

$$\frac{\text{Investment's cost}}{\text{Amount of each equal net cash inflow}} = \text{Annuity PV factor } (i = ?, n = \text{given})$$

$$\frac{\$240,000}{\$60,000} = \text{Annuity PV factor } (i = ?, n = 6)$$

$$4.00 = \text{Annuity PV factor } (i = ?, n = 6)$$

Now, look in the Present Value of Annuity of $1 table in the row marked 6 periods (Appendix 12A, Table B). You will not see 4.00 under any column. The closest two factors are 3.889 (at 14%) and 4.111 (at 12%).

Thus, the B2B portal's IRR is somewhere between 12% and 14%.

If we used a calculator programmed with the IRR function, we would find the exact IRR is 12.98%. If Tierra Firma had a 14% hurdle rate, it would *not* invest in the B2B portal because the portal's IRR is less than 14%.

IRR with Unequal Annual Net Cash Inflows

Because the DVR project has unequal cash inflows, Allegra cannot use the Present Value of Annuity of $1 table to find the asset's IRR. Rather, Allegra must use a trial-and-error procedure to determine the discount rate that makes the project's NPV equal to zero. Recall from Exhibit 12-11 that the DVR's NPV using a 14% discount rate is $78,910. Since the NPV is *positive*, the IRR must be *higher* than 14%. Allegra performs the trial-and-error process using *higher* discount rates until it finds the rate that brings the net present value of the DVR project to *zero*. Exhibit 12-15 shows that at 16%, the DVR has an NPV of $40,390; therefore, the IRR must be higher than 16%. At 18%, the NPV is $3,980, which is very close to zero. Thus, the IRR must be slightly higher than 18%. If we use a calculator programmed with the IRR function rather than the trial-and-error procedure, we would find that the IRR is 18.23%.

EXHIBIT 12-15 Finding the DVR's IRR Through Trial and Error

	Net Cash Inflow	PV Factor (for $i = 16\%$)	Present Value at 16%	Net Cash Inflow	PV Factor (for $i = 18\%$)	Present Value at 18%
Year 1 ($n = 1$)	$500,000 ×	0.862* =	$ 431,000	$500,000 ×	0.847* =	$ 423,500
Year 2 ($n = 2$)	350,000 ×	0.743 =	260,050	350,000 ×	0.718 =	251,300
Year 3 ($n = 3$)	300,000 ×	0.641 =	192,300	300,000 ×	0.609 =	182,700
Year 4 ($n = 4$)	250,000 ×	0.552 =	138,000	250,000 ×	0.516 =	129,000
Year 5 ($n = 5$)	40,000 ×	0.476 =	19,040	40,000 ×	0.437 =	17,480
Total present value of net cash inflows			$ 1,040,390			$ 1,003,980
Investment			(1,000,000)			(1,000,000)
Net present value (NPV)			$ 40,390			$ 3,980

*PV factors are found in Appendix 12A, Table A.

The DVR's internal rate of return is higher than Allegra's 14% hurdle rate, so the DVR project is attractive.

How do the Capital Budgeting Methods Compare?

5   Compare and contrast the four capital budgeting methods

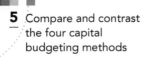

Capital Budgeting Methods

If your instructor is using MyAccountingLab, go to the Multimedia Library for a quick video on this topic.

We have discussed four capital budgeting methods commonly used by companies to make capital investment decisions—two that ignore the time value of money (payback period and ARR) and two that incorporate the time value of money (NPV and IRR). Exhibit 12-16 summarizes the similarities and differences between the two methods that ignore the time value of money.

EXHIBIT 12-16 Capital Budgeting Methods That *Ignore* the Time Value of Money

Payback Period	ARR
• Simple to compute	• The only method that uses accrual accounting figures
• Focuses on the time it takes to recover the company's cash investment	• Shows how the investment will affect operating income, which is important to financial statement users
• Ignores any cash flows occurring after the payback period, including any residual value	• Measures the average profitability of the asset over its entire life
• Highlights risks of investments with longer cash recovery periods	• Ignores the time value of money
• Ignores the time value of money	

Exhibit 12-17 considers the similarities and differences between the two methods that incorporate the time value of money.

EXHIBIT 12-17 Capital Budgeting Methods That *Incorporate* the Time Value of Money

NPV	IRR
• Incorporates the time value of money and the asset's net cash flows over its entire life	• Incorporates the time value of money and the asset's net cash flows over its entire life
• Indicates whether the asset will earn the company's minimum required rate of return	• Computes the project's unique rate of return
• Shows the excess or deficiency of the asset's present value of net cash inflows over its initial investment cost	• No additional steps needed for capital rationing decisions
• The profitability index should be computed for capital rationing decisions when the assets require different initial investments	

Keep in mind that managers often use more than one method to gain different perspectives on the risks and returns of potential capital investments.

STOP & THINK

A pharmaceutical company is considering two research projects that require the same initial investment. Project A has an NPV of $232,000 and a 3-year payback period. Project B has an NPV of $237,000 and a payback period of 4.5 years. Which project would you choose?

Answer: Many managers would choose Project A even though it has a slightly lower NPV. Why? The NPV is only $5,000 lower, yet the payback period is significantly shorter. The uncertainty of receiving operating cash flows increases with each passing year. Managers often forgo small differences in expected cash inflows to decrease the risk of investments.

Decision Guidelines

Capital Budgeting

Here are more of the guidelines Amazon.com's managers used as they made the major capital budgeting decision to invest in building warehouses.

Decision	Guidelines
Which capital budgeting methods are best?	No one method is best. Each method provides a different perspective on the investment decision.
Why do the NPV and IRR models calculate the present value of an investment's net cash flows?	Because an investment's cash inflows occur in the future, yet the cash outlay for the investment occurs now, all of the cash flows must be converted to a common point in time. These methods use the *present* value as the common point in time.
How do we know if investing in warehouse facilities will be worthwhile?	Investment in warehouse facilities may be worthwhile if the NPV is positive or the IRR exceeds the required rate of return.
How do we compute the net present value (NPV) if the investment has equal annual cash inflows?	Compute the present value of the investment's net cash inflows using the Present Value of an Annuity of $1 table and then subtract the investment's cost.
How do we compute the net present value (NPV) if the investment has unequal annual cash inflows?	Compute the present value of each year's net cash inflows using the Present Value of $1 (lump sum) table, sum the present value of the inflows, and then subtract the investment's cost.
How do we compute the internal rate of return (IRR) if the investment has equal annual cash inflows?	Find the interest rate that yields the following Annuity PV factor: $$\text{Annuity PV factor} = \frac{\text{Investment's cost}}{\text{Amount of each equal net cash inflow}}$$
How do we compute the internal rate of return (IRR) if the investment has unequal annual cash inflows?	Use trial and error, a business calculator, or spreadsheet software to find the IRR. See Appendix 12B and 12C for instructions.

SUMMARY PROBLEM 2

Recall from Summary Problem 1 that Zetamax is considering buying a new bar-coding machine. The investment proposal passed the initial screening tests (payback period and accounting rate of return), so the company now wants to analyze the proposal using the discounted cash flow methods. Recall that the bar-coding machine costs $48,000, has a five-year life, and has no residual value. The estimated net cash inflows are $13,000 per year over its life. The company's hurdle rate is 16%.

Requirements

1. Compute the bar-coding machine's NPV.

2. Find the bar-coding machine's IRR (exact percentage not required).

3. Should Zetamax buy the bar-coding machine? Why or why not?

▪ SOLUTIONS

Requirement 1

Present value of annuity of equal annual net cash inflows at 16% ($13,000 × 3.274*)...	$ 42,562
Investment...	(48,000)
Net present value	$ (5,438)

*Annuity PV factor ($i = 16\%, n = 5$).

Requirement 2

$$\frac{\text{Investment's cost}}{\text{Amount of each equal net cash inflow}} = \text{Annuity PV factor } (i = ?, n = \text{given})$$

$$\frac{\$48,000}{\$13,000} = \text{Annuity PV factor } (i = ?, n = 5)$$

$$3.692 = \text{Annuity PV factor } (i = ?, n = 5)$$

Because the cash inflows occur for five years, we look for the PV factor 3.692 in the row marked $n = 5$ on the Present Value of Annuity of $1 table (Appendix 12A, Table B). The PV factor is 3.605 at 12% and 3.791 at 10%. Therefore, the bar-coding machine has an IRR that falls between 10% and 12%. (*Optional:* Using a programmed calculator, we find an 11.038% internal rate of return.)

Requirement 3

Decision: Do not buy the bar-coding machine. It has a negative NPV and its IRR falls below the company's required rate of return. Both methods show that this investment does not meet management's minimum requirements for investments of this nature.

Appendix 12A

Present Value Tables and Future Value Tables
Table A Present Value of $1

Present Value of $1

Periods	1%	2%	3%	4%	5%	6%	8%	10%	12%	14%	16%	18%	20%
1	0.990	0.980	0.971	0.962	0.952	0.943	0.926	0.909	0.893	0.877	0.862	0.847	0.833
2	0.980	0.961	0.943	0.925	0.907	0.890	0.857	0.826	0.797	0.769	0.743	0.718	0.694
3	0.971	0.942	0.915	0.889	0.864	0.840	0.794	0.751	0.712	0.675	0.641	0.609	0.579
4	0.961	0.924	0.888	0.855	0.823	0.792	0.735	0.683	0.636	0.592	0.552	0.516	0.482
5	0.951	0.906	0.863	0.822	0.784	0.747	0.681	0.621	0.567	0.519	0.476	0.437	0.402
6	0.942	0.888	0.837	0.790	0.746	0.705	0.630	0.564	0.507	0.456	0.410	0.370	0.335
7	0.933	0.871	0.813	0.760	0.711	0.665	0.583	0.513	0.452	0.400	0.354	0.314	0.279
8	0.923	0.853	0.789	0.731	0.677	0.627	0.540	0.467	0.404	0.351	0.305	0.266	0.233
9	0.914	0.837	0.766	0.703	0.645	0.592	0.500	0.424	0.361	0.308	0.263	0.225	0.194
10	0.905	0.820	0.744	0.676	0.614	0.558	0.463	0.386	0.322	0.270	0.227	0.191	0.162
11	0.896	0.804	0.722	0.650	0.585	0.527	0.429	0.350	0.287	0.237	0.195	0.162	0.135
12	0.887	0.788	0.701	0.625	0.557	0.497	0.397	0.319	0.257	0.208	0.168	0.137	0.112
13	0.879	0.773	0.681	0.601	0.530	0.469	0.368	0.290	0.229	0.182	0.145	0.116	0.093
14	0.870	0.758	0.661	0.577	0.505	0.442	0.340	0.263	0.205	0.160	0.125	0.099	0.078
15	0.861	0.743	0.642	0.555	0.481	0.417	0.315	0.239	0.183	0.140	0.108	0.084	0.065
20	0.820	0.673	0.554	0.456	0.377	0.312	0.215	0.149	0.104	0.073	0.051	0.037	0.026
25	0.780	0.610	0.478	0.375	0.295	0.233	0.146	0.092	0.059	0.038	0.024	0.016	0.010
30	0.742	0.552	0.412	0.308	0.231	0.174	0.099	0.057	0.033	0.020	0.012	0.007	0.004
40	0.672	0.453	0.307	0.208	0.142	0.097	0.046	0.022	0.011	0.005	0.003	0.001	0.001

The factors in the table were generated using the following formula:

$$\text{Present Value of } \$1 = \frac{1}{(1+i)^n}$$

where:
  i = annual interest rate
  n = number of periods

Table B Present Value of Annuity of $1

Periods	1%	2%	3%	4%	5%	6%	8%	10%	12%	14%	16%	18%	20%
1	0.990	0.980	0.971	0.962	0.952	0.943	0.926	0.909	0.893	0.877	0.862	0.847	0.833
2	1.970	1.942	1.913	1.886	1.859	1.833	1.783	1.736	1.690	1.647	1.605	1.566	1.528
3	2.941	2.884	2.829	2.775	2.723	2.673	2.577	2.487	2.402	2.322	2.246	2.174	2.106
4	3.902	3.808	3.717	3.630	3.546	3.465	3.312	3.170	3.037	2.914	2.798	2.690	2.589
5	4.853	4.713	4.580	4.452	4.329	4.212	3.993	3.791	3.605	3.433	3.274	3.127	2.991
6	5.795	5.601	5.417	5.242	5.076	4.917	4.623	4.355	4.111	3.889	3.685	3.498	3.326
7	6.728	6.472	6.230	6.002	5.786	5.582	5.206	4.868	4.564	4.288	4.039	3.812	3.605
8	7.652	7.325	7.020	6.733	6.463	6.210	5.747	5.335	4.968	4.639	4.344	4.078	3.837
9	8.566	8.162	7.786	7.435	7.108	6.802	6.247	5.759	5.328	4.946	4.607	4.303	4.031
10	9.471	8.983	8.530	8.111	7.722	7.360	6.710	6.145	5.650	5.216	4.833	4.494	4.192
11	10.368	9.787	9.253	8.760	8.306	7.887	7.139	6.495	5.938	5.553	5.029	4.656	4.327
12	11.255	10.575	9.954	9.385	8.863	8.384	7.536	6.814	6.194	5.660	5.197	4.793	4.439
13	12.134	11.348	10.635	9.986	9.394	8.853	7.904	7.103	6.424	5.842	5.342	4.910	4.533
14	13.004	12.106	11.296	10.563	9.899	9.295	8.244	7.367	6.628	6.002	5.468	5.008	4.611
15	13.865	12.849	11.938	11.118	10.380	9.712	8.559	7.606	6.811	6.142	5.575	5.092	4.675
20	18.046	16.351	14.878	13.590	12.462	11.470	9.818	8.514	7.469	6.623	5.929	5.353	4.870
25	22.023	19.523	17.413	15.622	14.094	12.783	10.675	9.077	7.843	6.873	6.097	5.467	4.948
30	25.808	22.396	19.600	17.292	15.373	13.765	11.258	9.427	8.055	7.003	6.177	5.517	4.979
40	32.835	27.355	23.115	19.793	17.159	15.046	11.925	9.779	8.244	7.105	6.234	5.548	4.997

The factors in the table were generated using the following formula:

$$\text{Present value of annuity of \$1} = \frac{1}{i}\left[1 - \frac{1}{(1+i)^n}\right]$$

where:
i = annual interest rate
n = number of periods

Table C Future Value of $1

							Future Value of $1							
Periods	1%	2%	3%	4%	5%	6%	8%	10%	12%	14%	16%	18%	20%
1	1.010	1.020	1.030	1.040	1.050	1.060	1.080	1.100	1.120	1.140	1.160	1.180	1.200
2	1.020	1.040	1.061	1.082	1.103	1.124	1.166	1.210	1.254	1.300	1.346	1.392	1.440
3	1.030	1.061	1.093	1.125	1.158	1.191	1.260	1.331	1.405	1.482	1.561	1.643	1.728
4	1.041	1.082	1.126	1.170	1.216	1.262	1.360	1.464	1.574	1.689	1.811	1.939	2.074
5	1.051	1.104	1.159	1.217	1.276	1.338	1.469	1.611	1.762	1.925	2.100	2.288	2.488
6	1.062	1.126	1.194	1.265	1.340	1.419	1.587	1.772	1.974	2.195	2.436	2.700	2.986
7	1.072	1.149	1.230	1.316	1.407	1.504	1.714	1.949	2.211	2.502	2.826	3.185	3.583
8	1.083	1.172	1.267	1.369	1.477	1.594	1.851	2.144	2.476	2.853	3.278	3.759	4.300
9	1.094	1.195	1.305	1.423	1.551	1.689	1.999	2.358	2.773	3.252	3.803	4.435	5.160
10	1.105	1.219	1.344	1.480	1.629	1.791	2.159	2.594	3.106	3.707	4.411	5.234	6.192
11	1.116	1.243	1.384	1.539	1.710	1.898	2.332	2.853	3.479	4.226	5.117	6.176	7.430
12	1.127	1.268	1.426	1.601	1.796	2.012	2.518	3.138	3.896	4.818	5.936	7.288	8.916
13	1.138	1.294	1.469	1.665	1.886	2.133	2.720	3.452	4.363	5.492	6.886	8.599	10.669
14	1.149	1.319	1.513	1.732	1.980	2.261	2.937	3.798	4.887	6.261	7.988	10.147	12.839
15	1.161	1.346	1.558	1.801	2.079	2.397	3.172	4.177	5.474	7.138	9.266	11.974	15.407
20	1.220	1.486	1.806	2.191	2.653	3.207	4.661	6.728	9.646	13.743	19.461	27.393	38.338
25	1.282	1.641	2.094	2.666	3.386	4.292	6.848	10.835	17.000	26.462	40.874	62.669	95.396
30	1.348	1.811	2.427	3.243	4.322	5.743	10.063	17.449	29.960	50.950	85.850	143.371	237.376
40	1.489	2.208	3.262	4.801	7.040	10.286	21.725	45.259	93.051	188.884	378.721	750.378	1,469.772

The factors in the table were generated using the following formula:

Future Value of $1 $= (1 + i)^n$

where:
i = annual interest rate
n = number of periods

Table D Future Value of Annuity of $1

Periods	1%	2%	3%	4%	5%	6%	8%	10%	12%	14%	16%	18%	20%
1	1.000	1.000	1.000	1.000	1.000	1.000	1.000	1.000	1.000	1.000	1.000	1.000	1.000
2	2.010	2.020	2.030	2.040	2.050	2.060	2.080	2.100	2.120	2.140	2.160	2.180	2.200
3	3.030	3.060	3.091	3.122	3.153	3.184	3.246	3.310	3.374	3.440	3.506	3.572	3.640
4	4.060	4.122	4.184	4.246	4.310	4.375	4.506	4.641	4.779	4.921	5.066	5.215	5.368
5	5.101	5.204	5.309	5.416	5.526	5.637	5.867	6.105	6.353	6.610	6.877	7.154	7.442
6	6.152	6.308	6.468	6.633	6.802	6.975	7.336	7.716	8.115	8.536	8.977	9.442	9.930
7	7.214	7.434	7.662	7.898	8.142	8.394	8.923	9.487	10.089	10.730	11.414	12.142	12.916
8	8.286	8.583	8.892	9.214	9.549	9.897	10.637	11.436	12.300	13.233	14.240	15.327	16.499
9	9.369	9.755	10.159	10.583	11.027	11.491	12.488	13.579	14.776	16.085	17.519	19.086	20.799
10	10.462	10.950	11.464	12.006	12.578	13.181	14.487	15.937	17.549	19.337	21.321	23.521	25.959
11	11.567	12.169	12.808	13.486	14.207	14.972	16.645	18.531	20.655	23.045	25.733	28.755	32.150
12	12.683	13.412	14.192	15.026	15.917	16.870	18.977	21.384	24.133	27.271	30.850	34.931	39.581
13	13.809	14.680	15.618	16.627	17.713	18.882	21.495	24.523	28.029	32.089	36.786	42.219	48.497
14	14.947	15.974	17.086	18.292	19.599	21.015	24.215	27.975	32.393	37.581	43.672	50.818	59.196
15	16.097	17.293	18.599	20.024	21.579	23.276	27.152	31.772	37.280	43.842	51.660	60.965	72.035
20	22.019	24.297	26.870	29.778	33.066	36.786	45.762	57.275	72.052	91.025	115.380	146.630	186.690
25	28.243	32.030	36.459	41.646	47.727	54.865	73.106	98.347	133.330	181.870	249.210	342.600	471.980
30	34.785	40.568	47.575	56.085	66.439	79.058	113.280	164.490	241.330	356.790	530.310	790.950	1,181.900
40	48.886	60.402	75.401	95.026	120.800	154.760	259.060	442.590	767.090	1,342.000	2,360.800	4,163.200	7,343.900

The factors in the table were generated using the following formula:

$$\text{Future Value of Annuity of \$1} = \frac{(1+i)^n - 1}{i}$$

where:
  i = annual interest rate
  n = number of periods

Appendix 12B

Using a TI-83, TI-83 Plus, TI-84, or TI-84 Plus Calculator to Perform Time Value of Money Calculations

Technology makes it simple

Time Value of Money Calculations

Using a TI-83, TI-83 Plus, TI-84, or TI-84 Plus Calculator to Perform Time Value of Money Calculations

Steps to perform basic present value and future value calculations:

1. On the TI-83 Plus or TI-84 Plus: Press [APPS] *to show the applications menu.*

    On the TI-83 or TI-84: Press [2nd] [X⁻¹] [ENTER] *to show the applications menu.*

2. Choose **Finance** *to see the finance applications menu.*

3. Choose **TVM solver** *to obtain the list of time value of money (TVM) variables:*

    N = *number of periods (years)*

    I% = *interest rate per year* (**do not convert percentage to a decimal**)

    PV = *present value*

    PMT = *amount of each annuity installment*

    FV = *future value*

    P/Y = *number of compounding periods per year* (**leave setting at 1**)

    C/Y = *number of coupons per year* (**leave setting at 1**)

    PMT: **End** or Begin *(leave setting on* **End** *to denote an ordinary annuity)*

4. **Enter the known variables** and **set all unknown variables to zero** (except P/Y and C/Y, which need to be left set at 1).

5. To compute the unknown variable, scroll to the line for the variable you want to solve and then press [ALPHA] [ENTER].

6. The answer will now appear on the calculator.

7. Press [2nd] [QUIT] *to exit the TVM solver when you are finished.* **If you would like to do more TVM calculations, you do not need to exit. Simply repeat Steps 4 and 5 using the new data.**

Comments:

i.   The order in which you input the variables does not matter.

ii. The answer will be shown as a negative number unless you input the original cash flow data as a negative number. **Use the [(-)] key to enter a negative number, not the minus key; otherwise you will get an error message.** The calculator follows a cash flow sign convention that assumes that all positive figures are cash inflows and all negative figures are cash outflows.

iii. The answers you get will vary slightly from those found using the PV and FV tables in Appendix A. Why? Because the PV and FV factors in the tables have been rounded to three digits.

Example 1: Future Value of a Lump Sum

Let's use our lump-sum investment example from the text. Assume that you invest $10,000 for five years at an interest rate of 6%. Use the following procedure to find its future value five years from now:

1. On the TI-83 Plus or TI-84 Plus: Press [APPS] *to show the applications menu.*

    On the TI-83 or TI-84: Press [2nd] [X⁻¹] [ENTER] *to show the applications menu.*

2. Choose **Finance** *to see the finance applications menu.*
3. Choose **TVM solver** *to obtain the list of time value of money (TVM) variables.*
4. Fill in the variables as follows:

   N = **5**

   I% = **6**

   PV = **–10000** *(Be sure to use the negative number (-) key, not the minus sign.)*

   PMT = **0**

   FV = **0**

   P/Y = 1

   C/Y = 1

   PMT: **End** or Begin

5. To compute the unknown future value, scroll down to **FV** and press [ALPHA] [ENTER].
6. The answer will now appear as **FV = 13,382.26** (rounded).

If you forgot to enter the $10,000 principal as a negative number (in Step 4), the FV will be displayed as a negative.

Example 2: Future Value of an Annuity

Let's use the annuity investment example from the text. Assume that you invest $2,000 at the end of each year for five years. The investment earns 6% interest. Use the following procedure to find the investment's future value five years from now:

1. On the TI-83 Plus or TI-84 Plus: Press [APPS] *to show the applications menu.*

   On the TI-83 or TI-84: Press [2nd] [X⁻¹] [ENTER] *to show the applications menu.*
2. Choose **Finance** *to see the finance applications menu.*
3. Choose **TVM solver** *to obtain the list of time value of money (TVM) variables.*
4. Fill in the variables as follows:

   N = **5**

   I%= **6**

   PV = **0**

   PMT = **–2000** *(Be sure to use the negative number (-) key, not the minus sign.)*

   FV = **0**

   P/Y = 1

   C/Y = 1

   PMT: **End** or Begin

5. To compute the unknown future value, scroll down to **FV** and press [ALPHA] [ENTER].
6. The answer will now appear as **FV = 11,274.19 (rounded).**

If you forgot to enter the $2,000 annuity as a negative number (in Step 4), the FV will be displayed as a negative.

Example 3: Present Value of an Annuity—Lottery Option #2

Let's use the lottery payout Option #2 from the text for our example. Option #2 was to receive $150,000 at the end of each year for the next ten years. The interest rate was assumed to be 8%. Use the following procedure to find the present value of this payout option:

1. On the TI-83 Plus or TI-84 Plus: Press [APPS] *to show the applications menu.*

   On the TI-83 or TI-84: Press [2nd] [X⁻¹] [ENTER] *to show the applications menu.*
2. Choose **Finance** *to see the finance applications menu.*
3. Choose **TVM solver** *to obtain the list of time value of money (TVM) variables.*
4. Fill in the variables as follows:

N = **10**

I%= **8**

PV = **0**

PMT = **–150000** *(Be sure to use the negative number (-) key, not the minus sign.)*

FV = **0**

P/Y = 1

C/Y = 1

PMT: **End** or Begin

5. To compute the unknown future value, scroll down to **PV** and press [ALPHA] [ENTER].

6. The answer will now appear as **PV = 1,006,512.21** (rounded).

Had we not entered the annuity as a negative figure, the present value would have been shown as a negative.

Example 4: Present Value of a Lump Sum—Lottery Option #3

Let's use the lottery payout Option #3 from the text as our example. Option #3 was to receive $2 million ten years from now. The interest rate was assumed to be 8%. Use the following procedure to find the present value of this payout option:

1. On the TI-83 Plus or TI-84 Plus: Press [APPS] *to show the applications menu.*

    On the TI-83 or TI-84: Press [2nd] [X⁻¹] [ENTER] *to show the applications menu.*

2. Choose **Finance** *to see the finance applications menu.*

3. Choose **TVM solver** *to obtain the list of time value of money (TVM) variables.*

4. Fill in the variables as follows:

    N = **10**

    I%= **8**

    PV = **0**

    PMT = **0**

    FV = **–2000000** *(Be sure to use the negative number (-) key, not the minus sign.)*

    P/Y = 1

    C/Y = 1

5. PMT: **End** or Begin

6. To compute the unknown future value, scroll down to **PV** and press [ALPHA] [ENTER].

7. The answer will now appear as **PV = 926,386.98** (rounded).

Had we not entered the $2 million future cash flow as a negative, the present value would have been shown as a negative.

Technology makes it simple

NPV Calculations

Using a TI-83, TI-83 Plus, TI-84, or TI-84 Plus calculator to perform NPV calculations

Steps to performing NPV calculations:

If you are currently in the TVM solver mode, exit by pressing [2nd] [Quit].

1. On the TI-83 Plus or TI-84 Plus: Press [APPS] *to show the applications menu.*

    On the TI-83 or TI-84: Press [2nd] [X⁻¹] [ENTER] *to show the applications menu.*

2. Choose **Finance** *to see the finance applications menu.*

3. Choose **npv** *to obtain the NPV prompt:* **npv(**.

4. Fill in the following information, paying close attention to using the correct symbols:
npv (hurdle rate, initial investment˚, {cash flow in Year 1, cash flow in Year 2, etc.})

5. To compute the NPV, press [ENTER].

6. The answer will now appear on the calculator.

7. To exit the worksheet, press [CLEAR]. Alternatively, if you would like to change any of the assumptions for sensitivity analysis, you may press [2nd] [ENTER] to recall the formula, edit any of the values, and then recompute the new NPV by pressing [ENTER].

Note: If you would like to find just the present value (not the NPV) of a stream of unequal cash flows, use a zero (0) for the initial investment.

Example 1: NPV of Allegra's MP3 Project—An Annuity

Recall that the MP3 project required an investment of $1 million and was expected to generate equal net cash inflows of $305,450 each year for five years. The company's discount, or hurdle rate, was 14%.

1. On the TI-83 Plus or TI-84 Plus: Press [APPS] *to show the applications menu.*

   On the TI-83 or TI-84: Press [2nd] [X⁻¹] [ENTER] *to show the applications menu.*

2. Choose **Finance** *to see the finance applications menu.*

3. Choose **npv** *to obtain the NPV prompt:* **npv(.**

4. Fill in the following information, paying close attention to using the correct symbols:
npv (14, −1000000, {305450, 305450, 305450, 305450, 305450}) *(Be sure to use the negative number (-) key, not the minus sign.)*

5. To compute the NPV, press [ENTER].

6. The answer will now appear on the calculator: **48,634.58** (rounded).

7. [CLEAR] the worksheet or recall it [2nd] [ENTER] for sensitivity analysis.

Example 2: NPV of Allegra's DVR Project—Unequal Cash Flows

Recall that the DVR project required an investment of $1 million and was expected to generate the unequal periodic cash inflows shown in Exhibit 12-11.

1. On the TI-83 Plus or TI-84 Plus: Press [APPS] *to show the applications menu.*

   On the TI-83 or TI-84: Press [2nd] [X⁻¹] [ENTER] *to show the applications menu.*

2. Choose **Finance** *to see the finance applications menu.*

3. Choose **npv** *to obtain the NPV prompt:* **npv(.**

4. Fill in the following information, paying close attention to using the correct symbols:
npv (14, −1000000, {500000, 350000, 300000, 250000, 40000}) *(Be sure to use the negative number (-) key, not the minus sign.)*

5. To compute the NPV, press [ENTER].

6. The answer will now appear on the calculator: **79,196.40** (rounded).

7. [CLEAR] the worksheet or recall it [2nd] [ENTER] for sensitivity analysis.

Example 3: Investment with a Residual Value

If an investment has a residual value, simply add the residual value as an additional cash inflow in the year in which it is to be received. For example, assume as we did in Exhibit 12-13 that the MP3 project equipment will be worth $100,000 at the end of its five-year life. This represents an additional expected cash inflow to the company in Year 5, so we'll show the cash inflow in Year 5 to be $405,450 (= $305,450 + $100,000).

1. On the TI-83 Plus or TI-84 Plus: Press [APPS] *to show the applications menu.*

   On the TI-83 or TI-84: Press [2nd] [X⁻¹] [ENTER] *to show the applications menu.*

2. Choose **Finance** *to see the finance applications menu.*

3. Choose **npv** *to obtain the NPV prompt:* **npv(.**

*The initial investment must be entered as a negative number.

4. Fill in the following information, paying close attention to using the correct symbols:
    npv (14, –1000000, {305450, 305450, 305450, 305450, 405450}) *(Be sure to use the negative number (-) key, not the minus sign.)*

5. To compute the NPV, press [ENTER].

6. The answer will now appear on the calculator: **100,571.45** (rounded).

7. [CLEAR] the worksheet or recall it [2nd] [ENTER] for sensitivity analysis.

Technology makes it simple

IRR Calculations

Using a TI-83, TI-83 Plus, TI-84, or TI-84 Plus calculator to perform IRR calculations

The procedure for finding the IRR is virtually identical to the procedure used to find the NPV. The only differences are that we choose IRR rather than NPV from the Finance menu and we don't insert a given hurdle rate.

Steps to performing IRR calculations:

If you are currently in the TVM solver mode, exit by pressing [2nd] [Quit].

1. On the TI-83 Plus or TI-84 Plus: Press [APPS] *to show the applications menu.*

    On the TI-83 or TI-84: Press [2nd] [X⁻¹] [ENTER] *to show the applications menu.*

2. Choose **Finance** *to see the finance applications menu.*

3. Choose **irr** *to obtain the IRR prompt:* **irr(.**

4. Fill in the following information, paying close attention to using the correct symbols:
    irr (initial investment*, {cash flow in Year 1, cash flow in Year 2, etc.})

5. To compute the IRR press [ENTER].

6. The answer will now appear on the calculator.

7. To exit the worksheet, press [CLEAR]. Alternatively, if you would like to change any of the assumptions for sensitivity analysis, you may press [2nd] [ENTER] to recall the formula, edit any of the values, and then recompute the new IRR by pressing [ENTER].

Example 1: IRR of Allegra's MP3 Project—An Annuity

Recall that the MP3 project required an investment of $1 million and was expected to generate equal net cash inflows of $305,450 each year for five years. Use the following procedure to find the investment's IRR:

1. On the TI-83 Plus or TI-84 Plus: Press [APPS] *to show the applications menu.*

    On the TI-83 or TI-84: Press [2nd] [X⁻¹] [ENTER] *to show the applications menu.*

2. Choose **Finance** *to see the finance applications menu.*

3. Choose **irr** *to obtain the IRR prompt:* **irr(.**

4. Fill in the following information, paying close attention to using the correct symbols:
    irr (–1000000, {305450, 305450, 305450, 305450, 305450}) *(Be sure to use the negative number (-) key, not the minus sign.)*

5. To compute the IRR, press [ENTER].

6. The answer will now appear on the calculator: **16.01** (rounded).

7. [CLEAR] the worksheet or recall it [2nd] [ENTER] for sensitivity analysis.

---

*The initial investment must be entered as a negative number.

Example 2: IRR of Allegra's DVR Project—Unequal Cash Flows

Recall that the DVR project required an investment of $1 million and was expected to generate the unequal periodic cash inflows shown in Exhibit 12-11. Use the following procedures to find the investment's IRR:

1. On the TI-83 Plus or TI-84 Plus: Press [APPS] *to show the applications menu.*

   On the TI-83 or TI-84: Press [2nd] [X⁻¹] [ENTER] *to show the applications menu.*

2. Choose **Finance** *to see the finance applications menu.*

3. Choose **irr** *to obtain the IRR prompt:* **irr(.**

4. Fill in the following information, paying close attention to using the correct symbols:

   irr (–1000000, {500000, 350000, 300000, 250000, 40000}) *(Be sure to use the negative number (-) key, not the minus sign.)*

5. To compute the IRR, press [ENTER].

6. The answer will now appear on the calculator: **18.23** (rounded).

7. [CLEAR] the worksheet or recall it [2nd] [ENTER] for sensitivity analysis.

Example 3: Investment with a Residual Value

If an investment has a residual value, simply add the residual value as an additional cash inflow in the year in which it is to be received. For example, assume as we did in Exhibit 12-13 that the MP3 project equipment will be worth $100,000 at the end of its five-year life. This represents an additional expected cash inflow to the company in Year 5, so we'll show the cash inflow in Year 5 to be $405,450 (= $305,450 + $100,000).

1. On the TI-83 Plus or TI-84 Plus: Press [APPS] *to show the applications menu.*

   On the TI-83 or TI-84: Press [2nd] [X⁻¹] [ENTER] *to show the applications menu.*

2. Choose **Finance** *to see the finance applications menu.*

3. Choose **irr** *to obtain the IRR prompt:* **irr(.**

4. Fill in the following information, paying close attention to using the correct symbols:

   irr (–1000000, {305450, 305450, 305450, 305450, 405450}) *(Be sure to use the negative number (-) key, not the minus sign.)*

5. To compute the IRR, press [ENTER].

6. The answer will now appear on the calculator: **17.95** (rounded).

7. [CLEAR] the worksheet or recall it [2nd] [ENTER] for sensitivity analysis.

Appendix 12C

Using Microsoft Excel (2007 and 2010) to Perform Time Value of Money Calculations

Technology makes it simple

Future Value Computations

1. In an Excel spreadsheet click on **Formulas**.
2. Click on **Financial**.
3. Choose **FV** from the drop down list. The following will appear as a dialog box:

   Rate

   Nper

   Pmt

   Pv

   Type

4. Fill in the interest **Rate**, in decimal format (for example 14% would be input as .14).
5. Fill in the number of periods (for example, five years would be input as 5 in the space by **Nper**).
6. If the amount is an annuity, fill in the yearly installment as negative number in the space by **Pmt.**
7. If the amount is a lump sum, fill in the lump sum as a negative number in the space by **Pv.**
8. Leave the space by **Type** blank.
9. The future value is shown under the dialog box.

Example 1: Future Value of a Lump Sum

Let's use our lump-sum investment example from page 724 of the text. Assume that you invest $10,000 for five years at an interest rate of 6%. Use the following procedure to find its future value five years from now:

1. In an Excel spreadsheet click on **Formulas**.
2. Click on **Financial**.
3. Choose **FV** from the drop down list. The following will appear as a dialog box. Fill in the variables as follows:

   Rate = **.06**

   Nper = **5**

   Pmt = (leave blank since this is used for annuities)

   PV = -**10000** (the negative sign indicates that the amount is a cash outflow, not inflow)

   Type = (leave blank)

4. The future value now appears under the dialog box as = $13,382.26 (rounded).

Example 2: Future Value of an Annuity

Let's use the annuity investment example from page 724 of the text. Assume that you invest $2,000 at the end of each year for five years. The investment earns 6% interest. Use the following procedures to find the investment's future value five years from now.

1. In an Excel spreadsheet click on **Formulas**.
2. Click on **Financial**.

3. Choose **FV** from the drop down list. The following will appear as a dialog box. Fill in the variables as follows:

Rate = **.06**

Nper = **5**

Pmt = **-2000** (the negative sign indicates that the amount is a cash outflow, not inflow)

PV = (leave blank since this is used for lump-sum amounts)

Type = (leave blank)

4. The future value now appears under the dialog box as = $11,274.19 (rounded).

Technology makes it simple

Present Value Computations

1. In an Excel spreadsheet click on **Formulas**.

2. Click on **Financial**.

3. Choose **PV** from the drop down list. The following will appear as a dialog box:

   Rate

   Nper

   Pmt

   FV

   Type

4. Fill in the interest **Rate**, in decimal format (for example, 14% would be input as .14).

5. Fill in the number of periods (for example, five years would be input as 5).

6. If the amount is an annuity, fill in the yearly installment as negative number in the space by **Pmt**.

7. If the amount is a lump sum, fill in the lump sum as a negative number in the space by **FV**.

8. Leave the space by **Type** blank.

9. The present value is shown under the dialog box.

Example 1: Present Value of an Annuity-Lottery Option #2

Let's use the lottery payout Option #2 from page 727–728 of the text for our example. Option #2 was to receive $150,000 at the end of each year for the next ten years. The interest rate was assumed to be 8%. Use the following procedures to find the present value of the payout option:

1. In an Excel spreadsheet click on **Formulas**.

2. Click on **Financial**.

3. Choose **PV** from the drop down list. The following will appear as a dialog box. Fill in the variables as follows:

   Rate = **.08**

   Nper = **10**

   Pmt = **-150000**

   Fv = (leave blank since this is used for lump sums)

   Type = (leave blank)

4. The present value answer now appears under the dialog box as= $1,006,512.21 **(rounded)**.

Example 2: Present Value of a Lump Sum-Lottery Option #3

Let's use the lottery payout Option #3 from page 727–728 of the text for our example. Option #3 was to receive $2 million ten years from now. The interest rate was assumed to be 8%. Use the following procedures to find the present value of the payout option:

1. In an Excel spreadsheet click on **Formulas**.
2. Click on **Financial**.
3. Choose **PV** from the drop down list. The following will appear as a dialog box. Fill in the variables as follows:

   Rate = **.08**

   Nper = **10**

   Pmt = (leave blank since this is used for annuities)

   FV= **-2000000**

   Type = (leave blank)
4. The present value answer now appears under the dialog box as = $926,386.98 (rounded).

Technology makes it simple

Net Present Value (NPV) Calculations

1. In an Excel spreadsheet, type in the future cash flows expected from the investment. Begin with the cash flow expected in Year 1. In the next cell type in the cash flow expected in Year 2. Continue in the same fashion until all future cash flows are shown in separate cells, in the order in which they are expected to be received.
2. Click on **Formulas**.
3. Click on **Financial.**
4. Choose **NPV** from the drop down list. The following will appear as a dialog box:

   Rate

   Value 1
5. Fill in the interest **Rate**, in decimal format (for example, 14% would be input as .14)
6. Next to **Value 1**, highlight the array of cells containing the cash flow data from Step 1.
7. The **"Formula result"** will appear at the bottom of the dialog box. The result is the present value of the future cash flows.
8. Finally, subtract the initial cost of the investment to obtain the NPV.

Example 1: NPV of Allegra's MP3 Project—An annuity

Recall from pages 731–732 of the text that the MP3 project required an investment of $1 million and was expected to generate equal net cash inflows of $305,450 each year for five years. The company's discount rate was 14%.

1. In an Excel spreadsheet, type in the future cash flows expected from the investment in the order in which they are expected to be received. Your spreadsheet should show five consecutive cells as follows: 305450, 305450, 305450, 305450, 305450.
2. Click on **Formulas**.

3. Click on **Financial**.

4. Choose **NPV** from the drop down list. The following will appear as a dialog box. Fill in the variables as follows:

    Rate = .14

    Value 1 = (Highlight array of cells containing the cash flow data from Step 1)

5. The present value of the cash flows appears at the bottom of the dialog box as = **1,048,634.58.**

6. Finally, subtract the initial cost of the investment ($1 million) to obtain the NPV = $48,634.58.

Example 2: NPV of Allegra's DVR Project-Unequal Cash Flows

Recall from pages 731–733 of the text that the DVR project required an investment of $1 million and was expected to generate the unequal periodic cash inflows shown in Exhibit 12-11. The company's discount rate was 14%.

1. In an Excel spreadsheet, type in the future cash flows expected from the investment in the order in which they are expected to be received. Your spreadsheet should show five consecutive cells with the following values in them: 500000, 350000, 300000, 250000, 40000.

2. Click on **Formulas**.

3. Click on **Financial**.

4. Choose **NPV** from the drop down list. The following will appear as a dialog box. Fill in the variables as follows:

    Rate = .14

    Value 1 = (Highlight array of cells containing the cash flow data from Step 1)

5. The present value of the cash flows appears at the bottom of the dialog box as = **1,079,196.40 (rounded).**

6. Finally, subtract the initial cost of the investment ($1 million) to obtain the NPV = $79,196.40 (rounded).

Example 3: Investment with a residual value

If an investment has a residual value, simply add the residual value as an additional cash inflow in the year in which it is to be received. For example, assume as we did in Exhibit 12-13 on page 734 that the MP3 project equipment will be worth $100,000 at the end of its five-year life. This represents an additional expected cash inflow to the company in Year 5.

1. In an Excel spreadsheet, type in the future cash flows expected from the investment in the order in which they are expected to be received. Your spreadsheet should show five consecutive cells with the following values in them: 305450, 305450, 305450, 305450, 405350

2. Click on **Formulas**.

3. Click on **Financial**.

4. Choose **NPV** from the drop down list. The following will appear as a dialog box. Fill in the variables as follows:

    Rate = .14

    Value 1 = (Highlight array of cells containing the cash flow data from Step 1)

5. The present value of the cash flows appears at the bottom of the dialog box as = **1,100,571.45 (rounded).**

6. Finally, subtract the initial cost of the investment ($1 million) to obtain the NPV = $100,571.45 (rounded).

Technology makes it simple

Internal Rate of Return (IRR) Calculations

1. In an Excel spreadsheet, first type in the initial investment as a negative number. For example, -1000000 for a $1 million investment. In the next cell, type in the cash flow expected in Year 1. In the following cell type in the cash flow expected in Year 2. Continue in the same fashion until all future cash flows are shown in separate cells, in the order in which they are expected to be received.
2. Click on **Formulas**.
3. Click on **Financial**.
4. Choose **IRR** from the drop down list. The following will appear as a dialog box:
   Value 1
5. Next to **Value 1**, highlight the array of cells containing the data from Step 1.
6. The **"Formula result"** will appear at the bottom of the dialog box. The result is the Internal Rate of Return (IRR).

Example 1: IRR of Allegra's MP3 Project-An annuity
Recall that the MP3 project required an investment of $1 million and was expected to generate equal net cash inflows of $305,450 each year for five years.

1. In an Excel spreadsheet, first type in the initial investment as a negative number and then type in the future cash flows expected from the investment in the order in which they are expected to be received. Your spreadsheet should show the following consecutive cells: **-1000000, 305450, 305450, 305450, 305450, 305450.**
2. Click on **Formulas**.
3. Click on **Financial**.
4. Choose **IRR** from the drop down list. The following will appear as a dialog box. Fill in the variables as follows:
   Value 1 = (Highlight array of cells containing the data from Step 1)
5. The IRR appears at the bottom of the dialog box as = 16.01% (rounded).

Example 2: IRR of Allegra's DVR Project-Unequal Cash Flows
Recall that the DVR project required an investment of $1 million and was expected to generate the unequal periodic cash inflows shown in Exhibit 12-11.

1. In an Excel spreadsheet, first type in the initial investment as a negative number and then type in the future cash flows expected from the investment in the order in which they are expected to be received. Your spreadsheet should show the following consecutive cells: **-1000000, 500000, 350000, 300000, 250000, 40000.**
2. Click on **Formulas**.
3. Click on **Financial**.
4. Choose **IRR** from the drop down list. The following will appear as a dialog box. Fill in the variables as follows:
   Value 1 = (Highlight array of cells containing the data from Step 1)
5. The IRR appears at the bottom of the dialog box as = **18.23% (rounded).**

Example 3: Investment with a residual value

If an investment has a residual value, simply add the residual value as an additional cash inflow in the year in which it is to be received. For example, assume as we did in Exhibit 12-13 that the MP3 project equipment will be worth $100,000 at the end of its five-year life. This represents an additional expected cash inflow to the company in Year 5.

1. In an Excel spreadsheet, type in the future cash flows expected from the investment in the order in which they are expected to be received. Your spreadsheet should show six consecutive cells with the following values in them: **-1000000, 305450, 305450, 305450, 305450, 405350.**

2. Click on **Formulas**.

3. Click on **Financial**.

4. Choose **IRR** from the drop down list. The following will appear as a dialog box. Fill in the variables as follows:

   Value 1 = (Highlight array of cells containing the data from Step 1)

5. The IRR appears at the bottom of the dialog box as = **17.95% (rounded)**.

END OF CHAPTER

Learning Objectives

■ 1 Describe the importance of capital investments and the capital budgeting process

■ 2 Use the payback and accounting rate of return methods to make capital investment decisions

■ 3 Use the time value of money to compute the present and future values of single lump sums and annuities

■ 4 Use discounted cash flow models to make capital investment decisions

■ 5 Compare and contrast the four capital budgeting methods

Accounting Vocabulary

Accounting Rate of Return. (p. 718) A measure of profitability computed by dividing the average annual operating income from an asset by the initial investment in the asset.

Annuity. (p. 723) A stream of equal installments made at equal time intervals.

Capital Budgeting. (p. 712) The process of making capital investment decisions. Companies make capital investments when they acquire *capital assets—*assets used for a long period of time.

Capital Rationing. (p. 713) Choosing among alternative capital investments due to limited funds.

Compound Interest. (p. 723) Interest computed on the principal *and* all interest earned to date.

Discount Rate. (p. 731) Management's minimum desired rate of return on an investment; also called the hurdle rate and required rate of return.

Hurdle Rate. (p. 731) Management's minimum desired rate of return on an investment; also called the discount rate and required rate of return.

Internal Rate of Return (IRR). (p. 735) The rate of return (based on discounted cash flows) that a company can expect to earn by investing in a capital asset. The interest rate that makes the NPV of the investment equal to zero.

LEED certification. (p.715) LEED, which stands for "Leadership in Energy and Environmental Design," is a certification system developed by the U.S. Green Building Council as a way of promoting and evaluating environmentally friendly construction projects.

Net Present Value (NPV). (p. 731) The *difference* between the present value of the investment's net cash inflows and the investment's cost.

Payback. (p. 715) The length of time it takes to recover, in net cash inflows, the cost of a capital outlay.

Post-Audits. (p. 713) Comparing a capital investment's actual net cash inflows to its projected net cash inflows.

Present Value Index. (p. 733) An index that computes the number of dollars returned for every dollar invested, *with all calculations performed in present value dollars*. It is computed as present value of net cash inflows divided by investment; also called profitability index.

Profitability Index. (p. 733) An index that computes the number of dollars returned for every dollar invested, *with all calculations performed in present value dollars*. Computed as present value of net cash inflows divided by investment; also called present value index.

Required Rate of Return. (p. 731) Management's minimum desired rate of return on an investment; also called the discount rate and hurdle rate.

Simple Interest. (p. 723) Interest computed *only* on the principal amount.

Time Value of Money. (p. 723) The fact that money can be invested to earn income over time.

Quick Check

1. (Learning Objective 1) Examples of capital budgeting investments could include all of the following except
   a. building a new store.
   b. installing a new computer system.
   c. paying bonuses to the sales force.
   d. developing a new website.

2. (Learning Objective 2) Suppose Amazon.com is considering investing in warehouse-management software that costs $500,000, has $50,000 residual value, and should lead to cost savings of $120,000 per year for its five-year life. In calculating the ARR, which of the following figures should be used as the equation's denominator?
   a. $225,000
   b. $500,000
   c. $250,000
   d. $275,000

3. (Learning Objective 2) Using the information from Question 2, which of the following figures should be used in the equation's numerator (average annual operating income)?
   a. $120,000
   b. $20,000
   c. $30,000
   d. $10,000

4. (Learning Objective 3) Which of the following affects the present value of an investment?
   a. The interest rate
   b. The number of time periods (length of the investment)
   c. The type of investment (annuity versus single lump sum)
   d. All of the above

5. (Learning Objective 5) When making capital rationing decisions, the size of the initial investment required may differ between alternative investments. The profitability index can be used in conjunction with which of the following methods to help managers choose between alternatives?
   a. IRR
   b. ARR
   c. Payback Period
   d. NPV

6. (Learning Objective 4) The IRR is
   a. the same as the ARR.
   b. the firm's hurdle rate.
   c. the interest rate at which the NPV of the investment is zero.
   d. none of the above.

7. (Learning Objective 5) Which of the following methods uses accrual accounting rather than net cash flows as a basis for calculations?
   a. Payback
   b. ARR
   c. NPV
   d. IRR

8. (Learning Objective 5) Which of the following methods does not consider the investment's profitability?
   a. Payback
   b. ARR
   c. NPV
   d. IRR

9. (Learning Objective 4) Which of the following is true regarding capital rationing decisions?
   a. Companies should always choose the investment with the shortest payback period.
   b. Companies should always choose the investment with the highest NPV.
   c. Companies should always choose the investment with the highest ARR.
   d. None of the above

10. (Learning Objective 4) Which of the following is the most reliable method for making capital budgeting decisions?
    a. NPV method
    b. ARR method
    c. Payback method
    d. Post-audit method

CHAPTER 12

Short Exercises

S12-1   Order the capital budgeting process *(Learning Objective 1)*

Place the following activities in order from first to last to illustrate the capital budgeting process:

a. Budget capital investments

b. Project investments' cash flows

c. Perform post-audits

d. Make investments

e. Use feedback to reassess investments already made

f. Identify potential capital investments

g. Screen/analyze investments using one or more of the methods discussed

Medley Products Data Set used for S12-2 through S12-5:

Medley Products is considering producing MP3 players and digital video recorders (DVRs). The products require different specialized machines, each costing $1 million. Each machine has a five-year life and zero residual value. The two products have different patterns of predicted net cash inflows:

	Annual Net Cash Inflows	
Year	MP3 Players	DVRs
1	$ 332,000	$ 500,000
2	332,000	380,000
3	332,000	320,000
4	332,000	280,000
5	332,000	25,000
Total	$1,660,000	$1,505,000

Medley will consider making capital investments only if the payback period of the project is less than 3.5 years and the ARR exceeds 8%.

S12-2   Compute payback period—equal cash inflows *(Learning Objective 2)*

Refer to the Medley Products Data Set. Calculate the MP3-player project's payback period. If the MP3 project had a residual value of $125,000, would the payback period change? Explain and recalculate if necessary. Does this investment pass Medley's payback period screening rule?

S12-3   Compute payback period—unequal cash inflows *(Learning Objective 2)*

Refer to the Medley Products Data Set. Calculate the DVR project's payback period. If the DVR project had a residual value of $125,000, would the payback period change? Explain and recalculate if necessary. Does this investment pass Medley's payback period screening rule?

S12-4   Compute ARR—equal cash inflows *(Learning Objective 2)*

Refer to the Medley Products Data Set. Calculate the MP3-player project's ARR. If the MP3 project had a residual value of $125,000, would the ARR change? Explain and recalculate if necessary. Does this investment pass Medley's ARR screening rule?

S12-5   Compute ARR—unequal cash inflows *(Learning Objective 2)*

Refer to the Medley Products Data Set. Calculate the DVR project's ARR. If the DVR project had a residual value of $125,000, would the ARR change? Explain and recalculate if necessary. Does this investment pass Medley's ARR screening rule?

S12-6   Compute annual cash savings *(Learning Objective 2)*

Suppose Medley Products is deciding whether to invest in a DVD-HD project. The payback period for the $10 million investment is two years, and the project's expected life is seven years. What equal annual net cash inflows are expected from this project?

S12-7 Find the present values of future cash flows *(Learning Objective 3)*

Your grandmother would like to share some of her fortune with you. She offers to give you money under one of the following scenarios (you get to choose):

1. $7,000 a year at the end of each of the next eight years
2. $45,000 (lump sum) now
3. $75,000 (lump sum) eight years from now

Calculate the present value of each scenario using a 6% interest rate. Which scenario yields the highest present value? Would your preference change if you used a 12% interest rate?

S12-8 Show how timing affects future values *(Learning Objective 3)*

Assume that you make the following investments:

a. You invest a lump sum of $8,000 for four years at 14% interest. What is the investment's value at the end of four years?
b. In a different account earning 14% interest, you invest $2,000 at the end of each year for four years. What is the investment's value at the end of four years?
c. What general rule of thumb explains the difference in the investments' future values?

S12-9 Compare payout options at their future values *(Learning Objective 3)*

Listed below are three lottery payout options.
Option 1: $1,000,000 now
Option 2: $150,000 at the end of each year for the next ten years
Option 3: $2,000,000 ten years from now
Rather than compare the payout options at their present values (as is done in the chapter), compare the payout options at their future value ten years from now.

a. Using an 8% interest rate, what is the future value of each payout option?
b. Rank your preference of payout options.
c. Does computing the future value rather than the present value of the options change your preference of payout options? Explain.

S12-10 Relationship between the PV tables *(Learning Objective 3)*

Use the Present Value of $1 table (Appendix 12A, Table A) to determine the present value of $1 received one year from now. Assume a 14% interest rate. Use the same table to find the present value of $1 received two years from now. Continue this process for a total of five years.

a. What is the *total* present value of the cash flows received over the five-year period?
b. Could you characterize this stream of cash flows as an annuity? Why or why not?
c. Use the Present Value of Annuity of $1 table (Appendix 12A, Table B) to determine the present value of the same stream of cash flows. Compare your results to your answer in Part A.
d. Explain your findings.

S12-11 Compute NPV—equal net cash inflows *(Learning Objective 4)*

Munyon Music is considering investing $675,000 in private lesson studios that will have no residual value. The studios are expected to result in annual net cash inflows of $100,000 per year for the next nine years. Assuming that Munyon Music uses an 8% hurdle rate, what is net present value (NPV) of the studio investment? Is this a favorable investment?

S12-12 Compute IRR—equal net cash inflows *(Learning Objective 4)*

Refer to Munyon Music in S12-11. What is the approximate internal rate of return (IRR) of the studio investment?

S12-13 Compute NPV—unequal net cash inflows *(Learning Objective 4)*

The local Red Owl supermarket is considering investing in self-checkout kiosks for its customers. The self-checkout kiosks will cost $47,000 and have no residual value. Management expects the equipment to result in net cash savings over three years as customers grow accustomed to using the new technology: $17,000 the first year; $22,000 the second year; $24,000 the third year. Assuming a 14% discount rate, what is the NPV of the kiosk investment? Is this a favorable investment? Why or why not?

S12-14 Compute IRR—unequal net cash inflows (Learning Objective 4)

Refer to Red Owl in S12-13. What is the approximate internal rate of return (IRR) of the kiosk investment?

S12-15 Compare the capital budgeting methods (Learning Objective 5)

Fill in each statement with the appropriate capital budgeting method: payback period, ARR, NPV, or IRR.

a. In capital rationing decisions, the profitability index must be computed to compare investments requiring different initial investments when the _____ method is used.

b. _____ ignores salvage value.

c. _____ uses discounted cash flows to determine the asset's unique rate of return.

d. _____ highlights risky investments.

e. _____ measures profitability but ignores the time value of money.

f. _____ and _____ incorporate the time value of money.

g. _____ focuses on time, not profitability.

h. _____ uses accrual accounting income.

i. _____ finds the discount rate that brings the investment's NPV to zero.

EXERCISES   Group A

E12-16A Identify capital investments (Learning Objective 1)

Which of the following purchases would be considered to be capital investments?

Purchase Item	Capital Investment?
a. The construction of a new office complex for $1,850,000.	
b. The projected cost of productivity bonuses for the coming year is $900,000.	
c. The advertising campaign to launch a new product is estimated at $400,000.	
d. Purchase and installation of new manufacturing equipment for $4,500,000.	
e. The installation of new computer terminals and software in all retail outlets is estimated to cost $1,400,000.	
f. The purchase and customization of a new production facility for $2,650,000.	
g. The new customer service training is budgeted to cost $450,000.	
h. New tablet computers for the sales force will cost $300,000.	
i. New telecommunication software for the customer response center will cost $890,000.	
j. The cost of the quality program for the upcoming year is estimated at $250,000.	

E12-17A Compute payback period—equal cash inflows (Learning Objective 2)

Lodi Products is considering acquiring a manufacturing plant. The purchase price is $2,320,000. The owners believe the plant will generate net cash inflows of $290,000 annually. It will have to be replaced in seven years. To be profitable, the investment payback must occur before the investment's replacement date. Use the payback method to determine whether Lodi Products should purchase this plant.

E12-18A Compute payback period—unequal cash inflows (Learning Objective 2)

West Hill Hardware is adding a new product line that will require an investment of $1,500,000. Managers estimate that this investment will have a 10-year life and generate net cash inflows of $310,000 the first year, $300,000 the second year, and $250,000 each year thereafter for eight years. The investment has no residual value. Compute the payback period.

E12-19A ARR with unequal cash inflows *(Learning Objective 2)*

Refer to the West Hill Hardware information in E12-18A. Compute the ARR for the investment.

E12-20A Compute and compare ARR *(Learning Objective 2)*

Donofrio Products is considering whether to upgrade its equipment. Managers are considering two options. Equipment manufactured by Smith costs $850,000 and will last six years and have no residual value. The Smith equipment will generate annual operating income of $161,500. Equipment manufactured by Kyler costs $1,375,000 and will remain useful for seven years. It promises annual operating income of $247,500, and its expected residual value is $100,000.

Which equipment offers the higher ARR?

E12-21A Compare retirement savings plans *(Learning Objective 3)*

Assume that you want to retire early at age 54. You plan to save using one of the following two strategies: (1) save $4,200 a year in an IRA beginning when you are 24 and ending when you are 54 (30 years) or (2) wait until you are 39 to start saving and then save $8,400 per year for the next 15 years. Assume that you will earn the historic stock market average of 10% per year.

Requirements

1. How much out-of-pocket cash will you invest under the two options?
2. How much savings will you have accumulated at age 54 under the two options?
3. Explain the results.
4. If you let the savings continue to grow for eight more years (with no further out-of-pocket investments), under each scenario, what will the investment be worth when you are age 62?

E12-22A Calculate the payback and NPV for a sustainable energy project *(Learning Objective 1 and 3)*

Terra Industries is evaluating investing in solar panels to provide some of the electrical needs of its main office building in Tempe, Arizona. The solar panel project would cost $540,000 and would provide cost savings in its utility bills of $60,000 per year. It is anticipated that the solar panels would have a life of 20 years and would have no residual value.

Requirements

1. Calculate the payback period in years of the solar panel project.
2. If the company uses a discount rate of 10%, what is the net present value of this project?
3. If the company has a rule that no projects will be undertaken that have a payback period of more than five years, would this investment be accepted? If not, what arguments could the energy manager make to try to obtain approval for the solar panel project?
4. What would you do if you were in charge of approving capital investment proposals?

E12-23A Fund future cash flows *(Learning Objective 3)*

Lily wants to take the next five years off work to travel around the world. She estimates her annual cash needs at $40,000 (if she needs more, she'll work odd jobs). Lily believes she can invest her savings at 8% until she depletes her funds.

Requirements

1. How much money does Lily need now to fund her travels?
2. After speaking with a number of banks, Lily learns she'll be able to invest her funds only at 6%. How much does she need now to fund her travels?

E12-24A Choosing a lottery payout option *(Learning Objective 3)*

Congratulations! You've won a state lotto! The state lottery offers you the following (after-tax) payout options:

Option #1: $14,500,000 five years from now

Option #2: $2,050,000 at the end of each year for the next five years

Option #3: $13,000,000 three years from now

Requirement

Assuming that you can earn 8% on your funds, which option would you prefer?

E12-25A Solve various time value of money scenarios *(Learning Objective 3)*

1. Suppose you invest a sum of $3,000 in an account bearing interest at the rate of 14% per year. What will the investment be worth six years from now?

2. How much would you need to invest now to be able to withdraw $6,000 at the end of every year for the next 20 years? Assume a 12% interest rate.

3. Assume that you want to have $160,000 saved seven years from now. If you can invest your funds at a 6% interest rate, how much do you currently need to invest?

4. Your aunt Betty plans to give you $2,000 at the end of every year for the next ten years. If you invest each of her yearly gifts at a 12% interest rate, how much will they be worth at the end of the ten-year period?

5. Suppose you want to buy a small cabin in the mountains four years from now. You estimate that the property will cost $61,250 at that time. How much money do you need to invest each year in an account bearing interest at the rate of 6% per year to accumulate the $61,250 purchase price?

E12-26A Calculate NPV—equal annual cash inflows *(Learning Objective 4)*

Use the NPV method to determine whether Princeton Products should invest in the following projects:

- *Project A* costs $280,000 and offers eight annual net cash inflows of $64,000. Princeton Products requires an annual return of 12% on projects like A.

- *Project B* costs $385,000 and offers nine annual net cash inflows of $74,000. Princeton Products demands an annual return of 14% on investments of this nature.

Requirement

What is the NPV of each project? What is the maximum acceptable price to pay for each project?

E12-27A Calculate IRR—equal cash inflows *(Learning Objective 4)*

Refer to Princeton Products in E12-26A. Compute the IRR of each project and use this information to identify the better investment.

E12-28A Calculate NPV—unequal cash flows *(Learning Objective 4)*

Monette Industries is deciding whether to automate one phase of its production process. The manufacturing equipment has a six-year life and will cost $900,000. Projected net cash inflows are as follows:

Year 1	$260,000
Year 2	$253,000
Year 3	$225,000
Year 4	$215,000
Year 5	$204,000
Year 6	$178,000

Requirements

1. Compute this project's NPV using Monette Industries' 14% hurdle rate. Should Monette Industries invest in the equipment? Why or why not?

2. Monette Industries could refurbish the equipment at the end of six years for $100,000. The refurbished equipment could be used one more year, providing $76,000 of net cash inflows in Year 7. In addition, the refurbished equipment would have a $52,000 residual value at the end of Year 7. Should Monette Industries invest in the equipment and refurbish it after six years? Why or why not? (*Hint*: In addition to your answer to Requirement 1, discount the additional cash outflow and inflows back to the present value.)

E12-29A Compute IRR—unequal cash flows (*Learning Objective 4*)

Baskette Products is considering an equipment investment that will cost $920,000. Projected net cash inflows over the equipment's three-year life are as follows: Year 1: $492,000; Year 2: $402,000; and Year 3: $290,000. Baskette wants to know the equipment's IRR.

Requirement

Use trial and error to find the IRR within a 2% range. (*Hint*: Use Baskette's hurdle rate of 12% to begin the trial-and-error process.)

Optional: Use a business calculator spreadsheet to compute the exact IRR.

E12-30A Capital rationing decision (*Learning Objective 4*)

Liverpool Manufacturing is considering three capital investment proposals. At this time, Liverpool Manufacturing has funds available to pursue only one of the three investments.

	Equipment A	Equipment B	Equipment C
Present value of net cash inflows	$1,700,000	$1,950,000	$2,200,000
Investment	($1,360,000)	($1,875,000)	($2,000,000)
NPV	$ 340,000	$ 75,000	$ 200,000

Requirement

Which investment should Liverpool Manufacturing pursue at this time? Why?

Frost Valley Expansion Data Set used for E12-31A through E12-34A:

Assume that Frost Valley's managers developed the following estimates concerning a planned expansion to its Waterfall Park Lodge (all numbers assumed):

Number of additional skiers per day	100
Average number of days per year that weather conditions allow skiing at Flint Valley	150
Useful life of expansion (in years)	8
Average cash spent by each skier per day	$ 250
Average variable cost of serving each skier per day	$ 150
Cost of expansion	$6,000,000
Discount rate	12%

Assume that Frost Valley uses the straight-line depreciation method and expects the lodge expansion to have a residual value of $600,000 at the end of its eight-year life.

E12-31A Compute payback and ARR with residual value (Learning Objective 2)

Consider how Frost Valley, a popular ski resort, could use capital budgeting to decide whether the $6 million Waterfall Park Lodge expansion would be a good investment.

Requirements

1. Compute the average annual net cash inflow from the expansion.
2. Compute the average annual operating income from the expansion.
3. Compute the payback period.
4. Compute the ARR.

E12-32A Continuation of E12-31A: Compute payback and ARR with no residual value (Learning Objective 2)

Refer to the Frost Valley Expansion Data Set. *Assume that the expansion has zero residual value.*

Requirements

1. Will the payback period change? Explain and recalculate if necessary.
2. Will the project's ARR change? Explain and recalculate if necessary.
3. Assume that Frost Valley screens its potential capital investments using the following decision criteria: Maximum payback period = 5 years and minimum accounting rate of return = 10%.

   Will Frost Valley consider this project further or reject it?

E12-33A Calculate NPV with and without residual value (Learning Objective 4)

Refer to the Frost Valley Expansion Data Set.

Requirements

1. What is the project's NPV? Is the investment attractive? Why or why not?
2. Assume that the expansion has no residual value. What is the project's NPV? Is the investment still attractive? Why or why not?

E12-34A Calculate IRR with no residual value (Learning Objective 4)

Refer to the Frost Valley Expansion Data Set. Assume that the expansion has no residual value. What is the project's IRR? Is the investment attractive? Why or why not?

E12-35A Comparing capital budgeting methods (Learning Objective 5)

The following table contains information about four projects in which Rhodes Corporation has the opportunity to invest. This information is based on estimates that different managers have prepared about their potential project.

Project	Investment Required	Net Present Value	Life of Project	Internal Rate of Return	Profitability Index	Payback Period in Years	Accounting Rate of Return
A	$ 220,000	$ 61,190	5	23%	1.28	2.82	18%
B	$ 410,000	$ 37,744	6	22%	1.09	3.20	14%
C	$1,030,000	$191,498	3	18%	1.19	2.17	13%
D	$1,545,000	$ 52,680	4	12%	1.03	3.07	23%

Requirements

1. Rank the four projects in order of preference by using the
   a. net present value.
   b. project profitability index.
   c. internal rate of return.
   d. payback period.
   e. accounting rate of return.
2. Which method(s) do you think is best for evaluating capital investment projects in general? Why?

EXERCISES   Group B

E12-36B   Identify capital investments *(Learning Objective 1)*

Which of the following purchases would be considered capital investments?

Purchase Item	Capital Investment?
a. The replacement of the engine on one of the company's aircraft is $190,000 (this will not increase the useful life of the plane).	
b. The delivered, installed cost of a new production line is $140,000.	
c. The cost of raw materials for the year is estimated at $980,000.	
d. All of the computers at the help desk are being upgraded at a cost of $123,000.	
e. To support the launch of the new product line, staff training costs are $100,000.	
f. The cost to develop and implement the new Facebook retail app is $565,000.	
g. The upgrade of the customer service fleet to new fuel-efficient vehicles has a cost of $300,000.	
h. The total cost of the management succession program for the coming year is projected to be $230,000.	
i. The cost to retrofit one of a company's closed retail outlets into a customer service center is projected to be $100,000.	
j. The cost of workers' compensation insurance for the coming year is projected to be $200,000.	

E12-37B   Compute payback period—equal cash inflows *(Learning Objective 2)*

Preston Products is considering acquiring a manufacturing plant. The purchase price is $1,890,000. The owners believe the plant will generate net cash inflows of $315,000 annually. It will have to be replaced in nine years. To be profitable, the investment payback must occur before the investment's replacement date. Use the payback method to determine whether Preston should purchase this plant.

E12-38B   Compute payback period—unequal cash inflows *(Learning Objective 2)*

Archer Hardware is adding a new product line that will require an investment of $2,000,000. Managers estimate that this investment will have a 10-year life and generate net cash inflows of $650,000 the first year, $490,000 the second year, and $250,000 each year thereafter for eight years. The investment has no residual value. Compute the payback period.

E12-39B   ARR with unequal cash inflows *(Learning Objective 2)*

Refer to the Archer Hardware information in E12-38B. Compute the ARR for the investment.

E12-40B   Compute and compare ARR *(Learning Objective 2)*

Miguel Products is considering whether to upgrade its manufacturing equipment. Managers are considering two options. Equipment manufactured by McKnight costs $940,000 and will last for four years with no residual value. The McKnight equipment will generate annual operating income of $141,000. Equipment manufactured by Logan costs $1,125,000 and will remain useful for five years. It promises annual operating income of $236,250, and its expected residual value is $105,000. Which equipment offers the higher ARR?

E12-41B   Compare retirement savings plans *(Learning Objective 3)*

Assume you want to retire early at age 52. You plan to save using one of the following two strategies: (1) save $3,000 a year in an IRA beginning when you are 27 and ending when you are 52 (25 years) or (2) wait until you are 37 to start saving and then save $5,000 per year for the next 15 years. Assume you will earn the historic stock market average of 10% per year.

Requirements

1. How much out-of-pocket cash will you invest under the two options?
2. How much savings will you have accumulated at age 52 under the two options?

3. Explain the results.

4. If you were to let the savings continue to grow for 10 more years (with no further out-of-pocket investments), under each scenario, what will the investments be worth when you are age 62?

 E12-42B Calculate the payback and NPV for a sustainable energy project
(Learning Objectives 1 & 3)

Terra Industries is evaluating investing in solar panels to provide some of the electrical needs of its main building in Tempe, Arizona. The solar panel project would cost $540,000 and would provide cost savings in its utility bills of $67,500 per year. It is anticipated that the solar panels would have a life of 20 years and would have no residual value.

Requirements

1. Calculate the payback period in years of the solar panel project.

2. If the company uses a discount rate of 8%, what is the net present value of this project?

3. If the company has a rule that no projects will be undertaken that would have a payback period of more than five years, would this investment be accepted? If not, what arguments could the energy manager make to try to obtain approval for the solar panel project?

4. What would you do if you were in charge of approving capital investment proposals?

E12-43B Fund future cash flows *(Learning Objective 3)*

Rachel wants to take the next four years off work to travel around the world. She estimates her annual cash needs at $29,000 (if she needs more, she'll work odd jobs). Rachel believes she can invest her savings at 10% until she depletes her funds.

Requirements

1. How much money does Rachel need now to fund her travels?

2. After speaking with a number of banks, Rachel learns she'll only be able to invest her funds at 4%. How much does she need now to fund her travels?

E12-44B Choosing a lottery payout option *(Learning Objective 3)*

Congratulations! You've won a state lotto! The state lottery offers you the following (after-tax) payout options:

Option #1: $12,000,000 six years from now

Option #2: $2,250,000 at the end of each year for the next six years

Option #3: $10,500,000 three years from now

Requirement

Assuming that you can earn 8% on your funds, which option would you prefer?

E12-45B Solve various time value of money scenarios *(Learning Objective 3)*

Solve these various time value of money scenarios.

1. Suppose you invest a sum of $5,000 in an account bearing interest at the rate of 10% per year. What will the investment be worth six years from now?

2. How much would you need to invest now to be able to withdraw $10,000 at the end of every year for the next 20 years? Assume a 12% interest rate.

3. Assume that you want to have $170,000 saved seven years from now. If you can invest your funds at an 8% interest rate, how much do you currently need to invest?

4. Your aunt Betty plans to give you $2,000 at the end of every year for the next 10 years. If you invest each of her yearly gifts at a 12% interest rate, how much will they be worth at the end of the 10-year period?

5. Suppose you would like to buy a small cabin in the mountains four years from now. You estimate that the property will cost $56,875 at that time. How much money would you need to invest each year in an account bearing interest at the rate of 6% per year in order to accumulate the $56,875 purchase price?

E12-46B   Calculate NPV—equal annual cash inflows *(Learning Objective 4)*

Use the NPV method to determine whether Gendron Products should invest in the following projects:

- *Project A* costs $285,000 and offers eight annual net cash inflows of $60,000. Gendrons Products requires an annual return of 14% on projects like A.
- *Project B* costs $385,000 and offers nine annual net cash inflows of $70,000. Gendron Products demands an annual return of 12% on investments of this nature.

Requirement

What is the NPV of each project? What is the maximum acceptable price to pay for each project?

E12-47B   Calculate IRR—equal cash inflows *(Learning Objective 4)*

Refer to Gendron Products in E12-46B. Compute the IRR of each project and use this information to identify the better investment.

E12-48B   Calculate NPV—unequal cash flows *(Learning Objective 4)*

Bobbin Industries is deciding whether to automate one phase of its production process. The manufacturing equipment has a six-year life and will cost $920,000.

Projected net cash inflows are as follows:	
Year 1	$265,000
Year 2	$254,000
Year 3	$222,000
Year 4	$211,000
Year 5	$205,000
Year 6	$174,000

Requirements

1. Compute this project's NPV using Bobbin Industries' 14% hurdle rate. Should Bobbin Industries invest in the equipment? Why or why not?
2. Bobbin Industries could refurbish the equipment at the end of six years for $100,000. The refurbished equipment could be used for one more year, providing $73,000 of net cash inflows in Year 7. Additionally, the refurbished equipment would have a $52,000 residual value at the end of Year 7. Should Bobbin Industries invest in the equipment and refurbish it after six years? Why or why not? (*Hint:* In addition to your answer to Requirement 1, discount the additional cash outflows and inflows back to the present value.)

E12-49B   Compute IRR—unequal cash flows *(Learning Objective 4)*

Chandler Chairs is considering an equipment investment that will cost $955,000. Projected net cash inflows over the equipment's three-year life are as follows: Year 1: $494,000; Year 2: $390,000; and Year 3: $304,000. Chandler wants to know the equipment's IRR.

Requirement

Use trial and error to find the IRR within a 2% range. (*Hint:* Use Chandler's hurdle rate of 10% to begin the trial-and-error process.)

E12-50B   Capital rationing decision *(Learning Objective 4)*

Whiston Manufacturing is considering three capital investment proposals. At this time, Whiston Manufacturing only has funds available to pursue one of the three investments.

	Equipment A	Equipment B	Equipment C
Present value of net cash inflows	$1,710,000	$1,960,000	$2,210,000
Investment...	($1,425,000)	($1,750,000)	($2,125,000)
NPV	$ 285,000	$ 210,000	$ 85,000

Requirement

Which investment should Whiston Manufacturing pursue at this time? Why?

Hope Valley Data Set used for E12-51B–E12-54B.

Assume that Hope Valley's managers developed the following estimates concerning a planned expansion of its Blizzard Park Lodge (all numbers assumed):

Number of additional skiers per day	110
Average number of days per year that weather conditions allow skiing at Hope Valley	125
Useful life of expansion (in years)	8
Average cash spent by each skier per day	$ 230
Average variable cost of serving each skier per day	$ 130
Cost of expansion	$5,500,000
Discount rate	12%

E12-51B   Compute payback and ARR with residual value *(Learning Objective 2)*

Consider how Hope Valley, a popular ski resort, could use capital budgeting to decide whether the $10 million Blizzard Park Lodge expansion would be a good investment.

Requirements

1. Compute the average annual net cash inflow from the expansion.
2. Compute the average annual operating income from the expansion.
3. Compute the payback period.
4. Compute the ARR.

E12-52B   Continuation of E12-51B: Compute payback and ARR with no residual value *(Learning Objective 2)*

Refer to the Hope Valley data in E12-51B. Now assume the expansion has zero residual value.

Requirements

1. Will the payback period change? Explain and recalculate if necessary.
2. Will the project's ARR change? Explain and recalculate if necessary.
3. Assume Hope Valley screens its potential capital investments using the following decision criteria: maximum payback period of five years, minimum accounting rate of return of 10%. Will Hope Valley consider this project further or reject it?

E12-53B　Calculate NPV with and without residual value *(Learning Objective 4)*

Refer to the Hope Valley data in E12-51B. Assume that Hope Valley uses the straight-line depreciation method and expects the lodge expansion to have a residual value of $1,100,000 at the end of its eight-year life. It has already calculated the average annual net cash inflow per year to be $1,375,000.

Requirements

1. What is the project's NPV? Is the investment attractive? Why or why not?
2. *Assume the expansion has no residual value.* What is the project's NPV? Is the investment still attractive? Why or why not?

E12-54B　Calculate IRR with no residual value *(Learning Objective 4)*

Refer to the Hope Valley data in E12-51B. Assume that Hope uses the straight-line depreciation method and expects the lodge expansion to have no residual value at the end of its eight-year life. The company has already calculated the average annual net cash inflow per year to be $1,375,000 and the NPV of the expansion to be $1,775,400. What is the project's IRR? Is the investment attractive? Why?

E12-55B　Comparing capital budgeting methods *(Learning Objective 5)*

The following table contains information about four projects in which Morales Corporation has the opportunity to invest. This information is based on estimates that different managers have prepared about the company's potential project.

Project	Investment Required	Net Present Value	Life of Project	Internal Rate of Return	Profitability Index	Payback Period in Years	Accounting Rate of Return
A	$ 225,000	$ 35,908	5	20%	1.16	2.96	19%
B	$ 405,000	$ 49,740	6	23%	1.12	3.12	14%
C	$1,030,000	$151,325	3	18%	1.15	2.17	13%
D	$1,530,000	$ 18,870	4	13%	1.01	3.00	22%

Requirements

1. Rank the four projects in order of preference by using the
   a. net present value.
   b. project profitability index.
   c. internal rate of return.
   d. payback period.
   e. accounting rate of return.
2. Which method(s) do you think is best for evaluating capital investment projects in general? Why?

PROBLEMS　Group A

P12-56A　Solve various time value of money scenarios *(Learning Objectives 3 & 4)*

1. Irving just hit the jackpot in Las Vegas and won $45,000! If he invests it now at a 14% interest rate, how much will it be worth in 20 years?
2. Forrest would like to have $4,000,000 saved by the time he retires in 30 years. How much does he need to invest now at a 10% interest rate to fund his retirement goal?
3. Assume that Vivian accumulates savings of $2 million by the time she retires. If she invests this savings at 12%, how much money will she be able to withdraw at the end of each year for 20 years?
4. Donna plans to invest $3,000 at the end of each year for the next eight years. Assuming a 10% interest rate, what will her investment be worth eight years from now?
5. Assuming a 6% interest rate, how much would Vanna have to invest now to be able to withdraw $13,000 at the end of each year for the next ten years?

6. Ray is considering a capital investment that costs $510,000 and will provide the following net cash inflows:

Year	Net Cash Inflow
1	$308,000
2	$200,000
3	$102,000

Using a hurdle rate of 10%, find the NPV of the investment.

7. What is the IRR of the capital investment described in Question 6?

P12-57A Retirement planning in two stages (Learning Objective 3)

You are planning for a very early retirement. You would like to retire at age 40 and have enough money saved to be able to draw $230,000 per year for the next 45 years (based on family history, you think you'll live to age 85). You plan to save for retirement by making 20 equal annual installments (from age 20 to age 40) into a fairly risky investment fund that you expect will earn 14% per year. You will leave the money in this fund until it is completely depleted when you are 85 years old. To make your plan work, answer the following:

1. How much money must you accumulate by retirement? (Hint: Find the present value of the $230,000 withdrawals. You may want to draw a time line showing the savings period and the retirement period.)

2. How does this amount compare to the total amount you will draw out of the investment during retirement? How can these numbers be so different?

3. How much must you pay into the investment each year for the first 20 years? (Hint: Your answer from Requirement 1 becomes the future value of this annuity.)

4. How does the total out-of-pocket savings compare to the investment's value at the end of the 20-year savings period and the withdrawals you will make during retirement?

P12-58A Evaluate an investment using all four methods
(Learning Objectives 2 & 4)

Ocean World is considering purchasing a water park in San Antonio, Texas for $2,400,000. The new facility will generate annual net cash inflows of $600,000 for eight years. Engineers estimate that the facility will remain useful for eight years and have no residual value. The company uses straight-line depreciation. Its owners want payback in less than five years and an ARR of 10% or more. Management uses a 12% hurdle rate on investments of this nature.

Requirements

1. Compute the payback period, the ARR, the NPV, and the approximate IRR of this investment. (If you use the tables to compute the IRR, answer with the closest interest rate shown in the tables.)

2. Recommend whether the company should invest in this project.

P12-59A Compare investments with different cash flows and residual values
(Learning Objectives 2 & 4)

Abrahms operates a chain of sandwich shops. The company is considering two possible expansion plans. Plan A would open eight smaller shops at a cost of $9,450,000. Expected annual net cash inflows are $1,890,000 with zero residual value at the end of 10 years. Under Plan B, Abrahms would open three larger shops at a cost of $9,400,000. This plan is expected to generate net cash inflows of $1,175,000 per year for 10 years, the estimated life of the properties. Estimated residual value is $1,880,000. Abrahms uses straight-line depreciation and requires an annual return of 8%.

Requirements

1. Compute the payback period, the ARR, and the NPV of these two plans. What are the strengths and weaknesses of these capital budgeting models?

2. Which expansion plan should Abrahms choose? Why?

3. Estimate Plan A's IRR. How does the IRR compare with the company's required rate of return?

PROBLEMS Group B

P12-60B Solve various time value of money scenarios *(Learning Objectives 3 & 4)*

1. Harold just hit the jackpot in Las Vegas and won $25,000! If he invests it now, at a 10% interest rate, how much will it be worth 15 years from now?

2. Curtis would like to have $3,000,000 saved by the time he retires 40 years from now. How much does he need to invest now at a 12% interest rate to fund his retirement goal?

3. Assume that Ramona accumulates savings of $1.0 million by the time she retires. If she invests this savings at 12%, how much money will she be able to withdraw at the end of each year for 15 years?

4. Ivana plans to invest $3,000 at the end of each year for the next eight years. Assuming a 12% interest rate, what will her investment be worth eight years from now?

5. Assuming a 12% interest rate, how much would Amanda have to invest now to be able to withdraw $13,000 at the end of every year for the next nine years?

6. Chuck is considering a capital investment that costs $510,000 and will provide the following net cash inflows:

Year	Net Cash Inflow
1	$300,000
2	$198,000
3	$106,000

Using a hurdle rate of 10%, find the NPV of the investment.

7. What is the IRR of the capital investment described in Question 6?

P12-61B Retirement planning in two stages *(Learning Objective 3)*

You are planning for an early retirement. You would like to retire at age 40 and have enough money saved to be able to draw $225,000 per year for the next 35 years (based on family history, you think you'll live to age 75). You plan to save by making 10 equal annual installments (from age 30 to age 40) into a fairly risky investment fund that you expect will earn 10% per year. You will leave the money in this fund until it is completely depleted when you are 75 years old.

To make your plan work, answer the following:

1. How much money must you accumulate by retirement? *(Hint:* Find the present value of the $225,000 withdrawals. You may want to draw a time line showing the savings period and the retirement period.)

2. How does this amount compare to the total amount you will draw out of the investment during retirement? How can these numbers be so different?

3. How much must you pay into the investment each year for the first 10 years? *(Hint:* Your answer from Requirement 1 becomes the future value of this annuity.)

4. How does the total out-of-pocket savings compare to the investment's value at the end of the 10-year savings period and the withdrawals you will make during retirement?

P12-62B Evaluate an investment using all four methods
(Learning Objectives 2 & 4)

Aquatic Fun is considering purchasing a water park in Cleveland, Ohio for $2,500,000. The new facility will generate annual net cash inflows of $625,000 for ten years. Engineers estimate that the facility will remain useful for ten years and have no residual value. The company uses straight-line depreciation. Its owners want payback in less than five years and an ARR of 10% or more. Management uses a 12% hurdle rate on investments of this nature.

Requirements

1. Compute the payback period, the ARR, the NPV, and the approximate IRR of this investment.

2. Recommend whether the company should invest in this project.

E12-63B Compare investments with different cash flows and residual values
(Learning Objectives 2 & 4)

Martinson Restaurant Group operates a chain of sub shops. The company is considering two possible expansion plans. Plan A would involve opening eight smaller shops at a cost of $7,500,000. Expected annual net cash inflows are $1,500,000, with zero residual value at the end of ten years. Under Plan B, Martinson would open three larger shops at a cost of $7,425,000. This plan is expected to generate net cash inflows of $1,237,500 per year for ten years, the estimated life of the properties. Estimated residual value for Plan B is $990,000. Martinson uses straight-line depreciation and requires an annual return of 8%.

Requirements

1. Compute the payback period, the ARR, and the NPV of these two plans. What are the strengths and weaknesses of these capital budgeting models?
2. Which expansion plan should Martinson choose? Why?
3. Estimate Plan A's IRR. How does the IRR compare with the company's required rate of return?

CRITICAL THINKING

Discussion & Analysis

A12-64 Discussion Questions

1. Describe the capital budgeting process in your own words.

2. Define capital investment. List at least three examples of capital investments other than the examples provided in the chapter.

3. "As the required rate of return increases, the net present value of a project also increases." Explain why you agree or disagree with this statement.

4. Summarize the net present value method for evaluating a capital investment opportunity. Describe the circumstances that create a positive net present value. Describe the circumstances that may cause the net present value of a project to be negative. Describe the advantages and disadvantages of the net present value method.

5. Net cash inflows and net cash outflows are used in the net present value method and in the internal rate of return method. Explain why accounting net income is not used instead of cash flows.

6. Suppose you are a manager and you have three potential capital investment projects from which to choose. Funds are limited, so you can only choose one of the three projects. Describe at least three methods you can use to select the one project in which to invest.

7. The net present value method assumes that future cash inflows are immediately reinvested at the required rate of return, while the internal rate of return method assumes that future cash inflows are immediately invested at the internal rate of return rate. Which assumption is better? Explain your answer.

8. The decision rule for NPV analysis states that the project with the highest NPV should be selected. Describe at least two situations when the project with the highest NPV may not necessarily be the best project to select.

9. List and describe the advantages and disadvantages of the internal rate of return method.

10. List and describe the advantages and disadvantages of the payback method.

11. Oftentimes, investments in sustainability projects do not meet traditional investment selection criteria. Suppose you are a manager and have prepared a proposal to install solar panels to provide lighting for the office. The payback period for the project is longer than the company's required payback period and the project's net present value is slightly negative. What arguments could you offer to the capital budgeting committee for accepting the solar energy project in spite of it not meeting the capital selection criteria?

12. Think of a company with which you are familiar. What are some examples of possible sustainable investments that company may be able to undertake? How might the company management justify these possible investments?

Application & Analysis

A12-65 Evaluating the Purchase of an Asset with Various Capital Budgeting Methods

In this activity, you will be evaluating whether you should purchase a hybrid car or its gasoline-engine counterpart. Select two car models that are similar, with one being a hybrid model and one being the non-hybrid model. (For example, the Honda Civic is available as a hybrid or a gasoline-engine model.) Assume that you plan on keeping your car for 10 years and that at the end of the 10 years, the resale value of both models will be negligible.

Basic Discussion Questions

1. Research the cost of each model (include taxes and title costs). Also, obtain an estimate of the miles per gallon fuel efficiency of each model.

2. Estimate the number of miles you drive each year. Also estimate the cost of a gallon of fuel.

3. Given your previous estimates from 1 and 2, estimate the total cost of driving the hybrid model for one year. Also estimate the total cost of driving the non-hybrid model for one year. Calculate the savings offered by the hybrid model over the non-hybrid model.

4. Calculate the NPV of the hybrid model, using the annual fuel savings as the annual cash inflow for the 10 years you would own the car.

5. Compare the NPV of the hybrid model with the cost of the gasoline-engine model. Which model has the lowest cost (the lowest NPV)? From a purely financial standpoint, does the hybrid model make sense?

6. Now look at the payback period of the hybrid model. Use the difference between the cost of the hybrid model and the gasoline-engine model as the investment. Use the annual fuel savings as the expected annual net cash inflow. Ignoring the time value of money, how long does it take for the additional cost of the hybrid model to pay for itself through fuel savings?

7. What qualitative factors might affect your decision about which model to purchase?

Decision Case

A12-66 Apply time value of money to a personal decision (Learning Objective 3)

Kelsey Gerbig, a second-year business student at the University of Utah, will graduate in two years with an accounting major and a Spanish minor. Gerbig is trying to decide where to work this summer. She has two choices: work full-time for a bottling plant or work part-time in the accounting department of a meat-packing plant. She probably will work at the same place next summer as well. She is able to work twelve weeks during the summer.

The bottling plant would pay Gerbig $380 per week this year and 7% more next summer. At the meat-packing plant, she would work 20 hours per week at $8.75 per hour. By working only part-time, she could take two accounting courses this summer. Tuition is $225 per hour for each of the four-hour courses. Gerbig believes that the experience she gains this summer will qualify her for a full-time accounting position with the meat-packing plant next summer. That position will pay $550 per week.

Gerbig sees two additional benefits of working part-time this summer. First, she could reduce her studying workload during the fall and spring semesters by one course each term. Second, she would have the time to work as a grader in the university's accounting department during the fifteen-week fall term. Grading pays $50 per week.

Requirements

1. Suppose that Gerbig ignores the time value of money in decisions that cover this short of a time period. Suppose also that her sole goal is to make as much money as possible between now and the end of next summer. What should she do? What non-quantitative factors might Gerbig consider? What would you do if you were faced with these alternatives?

2. Now, suppose that Gerbig considers the time value of money for all cash flows that she expects to receive one year or more in the future. Which alternative does this consideration favor? Why?

COMPANY NAMES INDEX

Note: Company names in bold-face indicate real companies.

A

Abbott Laboratories, 8, 9, 10, 43
Abercrombie and Fitch, 466, 638
Able Plastics, 902
Abrahms Sandwich Shops, 771
Abrose Manufacturing, 436
Accenture, 287, 457
ACDelco, 462–469, 473, 476
Ace, Inc., 393
Ace Appliance, 148
Acme supermarket, 623
AI Banking, 511
Alderman's Dry Cleaners, 440
ALDI, 601
Allegra
  IRR with equal annual net
    cash inflows, 735–737,
    748–749, 753, 756
  IRR with unequal annual
    net cash inflows, 737,
    748, 750, 754, 756
  NPV (net present value), 731–733
  NPV of project with
    residual value, 734–735
Allied Signal, 193
All Natural, 175–176
Alloy Technology, 221–222
Allterrain Bikes, 78
Allyson Corporation, 806
Alston Jewelry, 451
Amazing Beans, 288
Amazon.com, 49, 51, 84,
  90, 287, 402, 418, 485,
  489, 547, 721, 739, 758
Ambrose Department
  Stores, Inc., 877–878
American Airlines, 176
American Express, 188, 541
American Faucet, 392
American Greetings, 636
**American Institute of Certified
  Public Accountants,** 22
American Red Cross, 33
American Traveler
  magazine, 46, 874
Anderson Company, 631
Anderson Plastics, 902
Anderson Travel Services,
  Inc., 815–816
Apple, Inc., 480–482, 641, 655
Aquatic Fun, 772
Archer Hardware, 766
Arness Containers, 907–908
Art.com, Inc., 395, 397, 399, 402
Arthur Andersen & Co., 211
Arvind Manufacturing, 703
ATV Corporation,
  167–168, 171–172

Audobon International, 889
Audrey Corporation, 811
Augustine Containers, 503–504
Augustine Furniture, 154
Augustine Manufacturing,
  360–361
Augustine Reeds, 558
Automax, 31
Auto-USA, 72
Axis Systems, 251–252
Axminster Carpets, 80
Aziz, 486
Azul, 860

B

Baily and Choi, 175
Bakery on Riverbank, 549–550
Bank of America, 53
Banner Corporation, 689
BarnaCo, 650–651
Barnes & Noble, 636
Barnett & Associates,
  141–144, 146
Barrett Associates, 149
Baseball Hall of Fame, 493, 499
Baskette Products, 764
Bauer Manufacturing, 687
Baxter Corporation, 807
Beatty Industries, 631
Behr Manufacturing, 446
Bellweather Ceramics, 686
Benedict Industries, 912
Bennett's Bait Shop, 443
Bentfield Dry Cleaners, 433
Bergeron's Fine Furnishings, 234
Bertolli, 483–484
Bert's Bees, 910
Best Buy, 51, 76, 84, 714
Best Engine, 169
Best Tire, 171–172
Best Value Stores, Inc., 866
Betsy Ross Flag Company,
  882–883
Blizzard Park Lodge, 769
Bluebird Design, 167
BlueSky Airlines, Inc., 629
Blueson Industries, 305
Blue Stone Corporation, 872
Boat Guard, 690
Boatsburg, 226
Bobbin Industries, 768
Bob's Bait Shop, 437
Boeing, 105, 107, 154, 256
Boxes Unlimited, 491
BP (British Petroleum), 893
Branson Products, Inc., 508–509
Braunhaus Microbrewery,
  392–393
Breegle Company, 513
Brett Products, 506
Bright Entertainment, 374–375

Brimfield Health Center, 557–558
Brooke Landscaping, 686
Brooklyn Corporation, 816
Brookman Semiconductors, 306
Brooks Foundry, 155
Brunswick Corporation, 103, 119
Burpee.com, 624
Buzz Cola, 95

C

Caldrone Industries, 630
Callaway Golf, 260–261
Campbell Soup Company,
  515–516, 518, 529, 539,
  589–594, 596, 597,
  601, 606–607, 618
Candle Company, 437
Candles Unlimited, 444
Capital One, 466
Cardinal.com, 166–167
Cardinal Corporation, 634
Carlson Sounds, 358
Carmen, Inc., 631
Carolina Power and Light, 180
Carol's Music, 706
Carrier, 208
Carrington Manufacturing, 550
Castle Industries, 235
Catering by Design, 150
Caterpillar, Inc., 9, 10, 43
**Cedar Fair Entertainment
  Company,** 711
Cedar Point, 711, 712, 730
Centennial Corporation, 551
Central City Hospital, 13
Chance Consulting, 157
Chandler Chairs, 768
Charles Sports Company,
  647–648
CharterNow Airlines, Inc., 636
Charter One Bank, 331
Chen Company, 374
Chesrown Motors, 564
Chicago Bears, 107, 119
**Chipotle Mexican Grill
  Inc.,** 3–7, 15, 629
Christine's Music, 703
Chrome Accessories, 308–309
Circle J Convenience Store, 541
Circuit Pro, 40
CitiHealth Center, 377–378
Clarke Corp., 234
Clear Optical Corporation, 873
Clear Readers, 568
Cleveland Roping, 305
Coca-Cola, 37, 188, 193,
  415, 622, 623, 893, 902
Cocoalicious, 492
Coco Bradley Sunglasses, 494
Cold Springs, 292–293
Colgate-Palmolive, 653

Collectable Cards, 493
College Calendars, 449
Colors, 40
Continental Airlines, 52,
  176, 511, 712, 714, 893
Cool Springs Luxury
  Resorts, 920–921
Copley Preschool, 553
Corbett Company, 244
Corbin Drycleaners, 373–374
Costco, 636
Craft Supplies & More, 636
Cranmore Carriage
  Company, 369–370
Crate & Barrel, 90
Crawford Beverages, 560–561
Crayton Digital Services,
  Inc., 821
Creative Construction
  Toys Corp., 245–246
Creighton Corp., 242
Crisper, Inc., 587
Crispy Potato Chips, 289
Crystal Bay Company, 89
Crystal Creations, 149
Crystal Vision Corporation, 877
Cupcake Factory, 432–433
Curt Carriage Company, 381
Cusak Recycling, 155
Cutting Edge Razors, 357
Cycle World, 584

D

Dairyfood, 504
DairyPlains, 77
DaisyMate, 695, 699–700
**Damon's Grill and
  Sports Bar,** 623
Daniels Furniture, Inc., 636
Danno's Bakery, 695
Dansfield, Inc., 875–876
Dazzle Entertainment, 904
Dean Foods Company, 636
Decadent Chocolates, 626
Dell Computer, 49, 50, 60,
  71, 105, 107, 146, 180,
  199, 208, 209, 214, 218
DellNet, 511
Delta Airlines, 176–177, 457, 712
Devon's Yukon Pancake
  Restaurant, 378–380
Donaldson Company, 555
Donofrio Products, 762
Donovan Medical Supply, 567
Donovan Park, 442
Donovan's Fine Furnishings, 227
Dorsey Foods, 698
DoubleTree, 319, 889, 899
Douglas Graphics Company,
  Inc., 822–823
Dove Design, 170–171

Doyle Corporation, 291
DuBois Enterprises, 868
Duck Associates, 511–512
Dudley Beverages, 552
Dudley Manufacturing, 569–570
Duke Energy, 899
Duncan Corporation, 810
DuPont, 888

E

Early Start Bakery, 301–302
Eastern Outfitters, 694
EDU Software, 38
Edward Industries, 442
Elk Industries, 177
Elkton Restaurant Supply, 161
Elly Manufacturing, 93
Embassy Suites, 319–320, 322–323, 325–327, 421
Empire Industries, 436
Engineered Plastic Systems, LLC, 901–902
Engleman Labs, 564
eNow!, 62
Enron, 17, 43, 50, 211
Entertainment Plus, 495
Entreé Computer, 12–13
Erks Garage Doors, 905
Everlasting Bubbles, 648–649
Extreme Sports Company, 625
E-Z-Boy Furniture, 124
EZPAK Manufacturing, 454–455
EZ-Rider Motorcycles, 24

F

Fagan Manufacturing, 381–382
Fairlawn Preschool, 555–556
Fairmont Hotels & Resorts, 636
Fashion Fabrics, 138–140
Faucher Foods, 692
FedEx, 86
Festival Corporation, 816–817
Fibre(B)lock® Flooring, 80
FirstEnergy, 629
First Equipment, 357
First National Bank, 574–575, 581–582
Fitness-for-Life, 333, 351–354
Fitzcarron Industries, 89
Fizz Cola, 91–92
Fleet Foot, 408–409, 427–428
Fleet Managing Services, 491–492
Flor®, 80
Floral Manufacturing, 92–93, 96
Florida Tile Industries, 272–273, 284–286
FlowerMate, 689, 692–693
Flowers Direct, 375–376
Flowers 4 You, 364–365
Ford Motor Company, 80, 85, 86, 90, 200, 208, 308, 311, 623, 633, 899, 901, 919, 922
Ford Volunteer Corps, 901
Forst Manufacturing, 489
Fortunado Company, 235

Foster's Repair Shop, 437
Fourth Street Muffins, 640
Frame Pro, 77
Franklin Department Stores, Inc., 873–874
Franklin Fabricators, 232
Franklin Pharmacy, 236–237
Freedom Digital Services, Inc., 826
Freedom Mailbox, 363–364
Fresh Springs, 293–294
Frito-Lay, 52
Frost Valley, 764–765
Frugal Car, 173
Fulton Holdings, 636

G

Gable Company, 445
Gable Foods, 562
Garden House, 507–508
Garnett, 704
Gendron Products, 768
General Allied Conglomerates (GAC), 882
General Electric (GE), 19, 49, 602, 889
General Mills, 49, 50, 466, 495, 911
General Motors, 308, 311
GenPak, LLC, 902
GeoHay®, 86
Georgia Ice Cream Company, 389
Georgia-Pacific, 76, 712
Gerbig Containers, 697
Gerbig Snacks, 220
Get Fit, 496
Ghent Medical Supply, 436–437
Giant Eagle, 623
Gibson Industries, 818–819
Gillette, 357
Global Chopsticks, 434
Global Fitness, 211–213
Golden Corporation, 641
Golden Ice Cream Company, 385
Goodman Reeds, 566–567
Goodyear Tire & Rubber Company, 636
Gossamer Secrets, 78
Grand Lips, 309–310
Grandma Jones's Cookie Company, 624
Grandma's Bakery, 294–295
Great Bubbles, Inc., 644–645
Great Lips, 307
Great Northern Furniture Company, 310
Greene Motors, 632
GreenShipping, 86
Gregg Industries, 908
Greta Fashions, 573
Grier Food, 491–492
Grimm Corporation, 567
Grisham Corporation, 556–557
Gruber Fittings, Inc., 101
GTE, 511
Guinty Manufacturing, 437
Gutierrez Sports Company, 640–641

H

Hajjar's, 861–862
Halliwell Manufacturing, 222
Hallmark, 466
Hamstein Semiconductors, 300, 309
Happy Feet, 433–434
Hasentree™, 889
Hastings Medical Supply, 581–582
Have Fun Industries, 161
Hazelton Sports Company, 629
Healthy Snacks Corp., 233
Heese Corporation, 688
Hegy Chocolate, 175
Heisler Company, 551
Heisler Corporation, 631–632
Helton Medical Supply, 443, 559
Hemingway Coffee, 450
Henderson Containers, 497
Henderson Industries, Inc., 823–824
Henderson Manufacturing, 370
Henderson Services, Inc., 551
Hermiston Food Processors, 316–317
Hershey Company, 629
Hewlett-Packard (HP), 76, 209, 623, 902
Hinkley Preschool, 564
Hoffwood Gifts, 380
Holiday Inn, 359, 624
Holland Company, 587
Hollings Paper Supply, 155
Hollister Mills, 862
Home Depot, 56, 402, 473, 512, 645, 649
Honacker Fashions, 496
Honda Motor Company, 79, 623, 774, 815, 818, 909
Hope Valley, 769–770
Hopkins Music, 38
H&R Block, 56, 75, 629
Huntington Corporation, 393
Huntsman, 706
Hyannisport Corporation, 550

I

IBM, 479
Ice Rides, 37
IDG Consulting, 39, 41
IKEA, 204, 208, 887
Indianapolis Auto Parts (IAP), 200–201, 215
Intel, 75, 209
Irvin Chemical Corporation, 630
Irvin Labs, 556

J

Jacobson Pharmaceuticals, 245
Janasko Garage Doors, 914
Jane's Fudge, 299
Jason's Meals, 390
JCPenney, 48, 636, 844–850, 855, 857

Jelly Belly, 255–260, 274, 288
JetBlue, 176–177
Jimmy's Cricket Farm, 314–315
J.M. Smucker Company, 33, 636, 659, 885, 899
Johnson Awnings, 705
Johnson Builders, 500
Johnson Controls, 886
Johnson & Johnson (J&J), 899, 909
Jones, Inc., 230–231, 238
JR Electronics, 83
JT Electronics, 876
Juda Resources, 157
Jungle Jim Industries, 153
Just Do It!, 486–487

K

Karen's Fudge, 306
Kay Martin Posters, 396–406, 411–425
Keely's Hair Salon, 433
Keener Sports Company, 643–644
Keen Industries, 903–904
Kellogg Company, 910–911
Kelly Fabrics, 702
Kerwin Co., 694
Keystone Service, 550–551
Kia, 162
King, Corp, 231–232
Kingston Garage Doors, 435
KitchenAid, 625
Klaben Motors, 556
Kmart, 75
Kobe Corporation, 565
Kohl's Corporation, 80, 543, 601
Kormic Co., 291
Kotlan Soda, 91
Kraft, 483, 659
Krampf Corporation, 628
Kristal Recycling, 163
Kroger, 49, 473, 475

L

Lambert & Company, 236
Landeau Sports Company, 633
Lansbury, 865
Lands' End, 51, 79
Laughton Industries, 563
Leisure Heating & Cooling, 152
Life Fitness, 103, 179, 255
  activity-based costing allocation, 188–189, 194–195
  allocating manufacturing overhead to jobs, 132
  balance sheet, 109, 111
  closing manufacturing overhead, 135
  cost allocation systems, 179
  cost of quality report, 211
  cost-plus pricing, 119
  discounts, 119
  income statement, 136
  inventory types, 106

job costing system, 105–107, 111, 123, 256–258
job cost record, 118–119
journal entries for, 128, 132–135
manufacturing costs, 114–115
manufacturing overhead, 114–118, 126–128
non-manufacturing costs, 121–122
operating expenses, 134
plantwide overhead rate cost allocation, 181–186
raw materials purchasing, 109, 129
sale of units, 134
Lightning Readers, 560
Lincoln Plastics, 153–154
Lindsey's Blooms, 96
Linger Industries, 471–472
Liverpool Manufacturing, 764
L.L. Bean, 56, 79
Lodi Products, 761
Lopez Garage Doors, 442
Los Angeles Fiber Company (LAFC), 80
Lounge Lizard, 163
Lowe's, 645, 649
Lundy Paper Supply, 163
Luxury Cruiselines, 430–432, 504
LZ Electronics, 89

M

Macy's, Inc., 623
Madengrad Mining Inc., 101
Mail.com, 511
Main Street Muffins, 632–633
Majestic Corporation, 565
Mansfield Heating & Cooling, 161
Maplebrook Spas, 817
Maple Street Furniture, 219
Marcus Interiors, 817
Market Time Investors, 448
Mark's Beach Hut, 502–503
Marlo's Ice Cream Shoppe, 389
Marriott, 319, 591, 712
Martha Stewart, 14
Martin Company, 808–810
Martinson Restaurant Group, 773
Martin Timepieces, 443
MasterCard, 542–543
Mayflower Corporation, 636
Maynard's Mayonnaise, 295
Maytag, 209
McCloud Industries, 807
McCormick Optical Company, 860
McDermott Foods, 629
McDonald's, 74, 84, 316–317, 622
McFall Industries, 382
McGregor's Mayonnaise, 302
McKnight Ceramics, 639
McKnight Corp., 243
McMillan Furniture, 247
McNeil Pharmaceuticals, 248

Meals on Wheels, 362
Medley Products, 759
Melanie Fashions, 502
Memoirs, Inc., 670–671, 678–679
Memorial Hospital, 387–388
Menards, 512–513
Meriweather Entertainment, 913
Metal Accessories, 311
Metal Foundry, 163–164
Metro Bank, 846
MetroHealth Center, 365–367
Mid-West Gas, 41
Miguel Products, 766
Mikhail Manufacturing, 705–706
Milford Industries, 554
Millan & Co., 226
Millson Soda, 289
Minute Maid, 154
Miracle Industries, 687
Mission Industries, 633
Monette Industries, 763–764
Morgan Restaurant Group, 696
Moulton Flooring Company, 816
Mountain Adventures, 559
Movie Plus, 501
Mueller Imports, 44
Munyon Music, 760
Murray Stadium, 435

N

NASCAR, 37
National Graphics, 869
National Rentals, 56
Naturalmaid, 498
Nature Frames, 865
Nature House, 505
Nautical Products, Inc., 507
NBC, 511
Nelson State Bank, 866
NewArt Company, 811
Newell Rubbermaid, 473
New York Stock Exchange, 8, 28
Nexus, 466
Nick's Beach Hut, 496–497
Nike, Inc., 86, 466, 470–471, 479, 623, 918
Nissan, 67, 209, 458–459
Noble Industries, 637–638
Nokia, 85
NT Electronics, 880
Nyloboard®, 86

O

Oceanside Resorts, 494
Ocean World, 39, 771
Old Navy, 543
Old Tyme Ice Cream Shoppe, 385
Olive Garden, 491
O'Malley's Products, 360
Omega's Restaurant Supply, 581
One of a Kind Designs, 157–158
Only LCD, 165
OptiSystems, 497
Oracle, 20, 419

Oriental Express, 441
Osborne Manufacturing, 554
Oscar Company, 290, 510
Outback Steakhouse, Inc., 49
Outdoor Life, 506
Outdoor Living, 294
Owen's Foods, 386

P

Pace Foods, 104, 287, 593, 595–596
Pacific Lumber, 316
PackRite, 149
Paint by Number, 296–297
Pampered Pets, 82
Pam's Posies, 92–93
Parker's Wood Amenities, 147
Parma College Bookstore, 561
Patagonia, 911
Patricia's Quilt Shoppe, 360
Patty's Pumpkin Pies, 302
Paulson Auto Components, 492
Paulson Roping, 299
Pella, 709
Pennsylvania Furniture Company, 307
Pepperpike Coffee, 448
PepsiCo, 52, 851, 867–868, 872
Pesarchick & Company, 228–229
Peterson Awning, 702–703
Pettigrew Tax Services, 696
PharmSys, 584, 586–587
Phelps Motors, 639–640
Philips Corporation, 636
Pier 1 Imports, 56
Pillows Unlimited, 530–531, 545–546
Pioneer Corporation, 631
Piper Corporation, 639
Plantson, 860
Plastic Lumber Company, Inc. (PLC), 628, 636, 814–815, 917
Poppins Corporation, 805
Poppy Corporation, 550
Post Cereals, 85, 501
PowerBox, 100
Premium Company, 166
Preston Company, 438–439
Preston Drycleaners, 363
Preston Products, 766
Pretty Pets, 88
Princeton Products, 763
Proctor & Gamble (P&G), 892, 910
Progressive Insurance, 624, 636
Proquest, 64

Q

Quaint Homes, 172
Quaker Oats, 52
Quality Aquatic Company, 82–83
QuickCo, 646–647
Quigby's, 289
Quinn Corporation, 639

R

Radical Logos, 575
Radio Shack, 79, 85
Rally Scooters, 436
Ramirez, 860
Ravenna Manufacturing, 576–577
Raymond Restaurant Supply, 153
Recycled Packaging, 252
Red Bull, 888
Red Owl, 760–761
Red Wing Shoe Company, 86
Renew-it Plastics, 908–909
Renkas Industries, 384–385
Residence Suites, 585
Rhodes Corporation, 765
Rickett Corp., 239
Rick's Golden Pancake Restaurant, 367–368
Ricoh, 52–53, 99
Riley Company, Inc., 826–827
Risingsun, 231
Riverdale Restaurant, 94
River Rock Corporation, 867
River Sports Company, 637
Road Trip magazine, 878
Robbins Company, 563
Robert Half International Inc., 11
Robillard Products, 242–243
Robinson Manufacturing, 78
Rocco's Bakery, 688
Rockwell Fashion Bags, 451
Rocky Adventures, 567–568
Rodger's Steel Parts, 441
Roland Films, 653
Rolling Hills Corporation, 806–807
Rolling Hills Realtors, 868
Rollins Chemical Corporation, 624
Rollins Mailboxes, 374
Romaine Company, 289
Rondell Company, 628
Rondell Pharmacy, 451
Root Chemical, 506–507
Rose & Rose, 287
Royal Corporation, 641–642
Royal Cruiselines, 507
Royal Fabrics, 704
Royalton Consultants, Inc., 920
Ruby Designs, 864
Russel Corporation, 696

S

Sabatini Industries, 912–913
Sacco Pretzel Company, 806
Safety Shutters, 301
Safety Systems, 508
Saints, 88
Samantha's Repair Shop, 444
Sam's Club, 583
Samson, 148
Samson Winery, 298
Samsung Electronics, 79
Sangood Kitchens, 35

SANSCOM Corporation, 253
SAP, 20, 419
Sarah's Posters, 432
Sara Lee, 479
Sarhan Corporation, 859
Saturn, 882
Scandia Scales, 550
Scenic Frames, 870
Schaeffer Industries, 562
Schaffer Company, 363
Scofield Industries, 228
Sears, 79, 419, 645, 649
Seaside Apartments, 369
SeaView
  insertion department data, 275
  insertion department
    time line, 274
  journal entries for process
    costing, 269–270
  process costing, 262–264,
    266–268, 274–283, 289–290
  product cost reports, 280–281
  production process, 262
  sustainability and process
    costing, 268–269
SeaView Apartments, 380
Secaur Tax Services, 689
Security One, 505
Sedlak Interiors, 814
See Underwater, 371
Sera Shade Sunglasses, 500
Sesnie Co., 700–701
Sharp Corporation, 902
Sharpland Industries, 82
Shasta's Restaurants, 624
Shaw Industries, 80
Shell Oil, 256, 466
Shelton Winery, 304–305
Sheraton, 319
Sherwin-Williams, 590,
  629, 645–646, 649
ShredCo, 343–346, 349–350
Shroath Company, 628
Sidchrome, 311–312
Silla Industries, 687
Sinclair Ceramics, 631–632
Skinny Treats Corp., 241
Skylark.com, 170
Sleep-Well Inn, 101
Smith Builders, 494–495
Smith Soda, 84
Smythe Resorts and
  Hotels, Inc., 636
SnowCastles, 490
Snow Rides, 32
Snowtime Sports, 509
Snyder Manufacturing, 562–563
Southwest Airlines, 176, 177
Soventino Fashions, 580
Spahr Confections, 686
Sparkle Beverages, 906
Sparkling Spring Luxury
  Resorts, 918–919
Specialty Motors Inc., 628
Speedway, 623, 624
Speedy Lube, 358
Speedy Oil, 686
Spellbound Designs, 863–864

SportCardz, 499
Sport Physicians, Inc., 549
SportsTime, Inc.
  balance sheets, 785–787
  income statements, 785–787, 799
  statement of cash flows,
    778–790, 793–796, 797
Springtown Corporation, 813
Square-Tile, 290
St. Germaine Company, 557
Stacy's Strawberry Pies, 295
Starbucks, 84, 466, 475, 889
Star Entertainment, 364
Star Resources, 165
Staten Island Restaurant, 98
State Street Bank, 559, 567
Stenbeck Chemical, 509
Step-by-Step Painting, 303–304
Stewart's Steel Parts, 434–435
Streeter Recycling, 155
Streetsboro Health Center, 566
Subdury Industries, 870
Sugarcreek Spas, 814
Summer Fun, 504
Sun Coast, 708
Sunflower, Inc., 223–224
Sun Gas, 39
Sunny Day Designs, 868, 869
Sunset Homes, 168–169
Sunshine Pools, 626
Superior Tire, 167–168
Superior Value Stores, Inc., 871
Supermart, 831
  accounts receivable turnover, 845
  acid-test ratio, 844
  balance sheet, 833, 837, 843
  book value per share of
    common stock, 850
  common-size income
    statement, 838
  comparative balance sheet, 835
  comparative income
    statement, 834
  current ratio, 843–844
  days' sales in receivables,
    845–846
  debt ratio, 846
  dividend yield, 850
  earnings per share, 848–849
  income statement,
    832, 837, 843
  inventory turnover, 844–845
  price/earnings ratio, 849
  rate of return on common
    stockholders' equity, 848
  rate of return on net sales, 847
  rate of return on total
    assets, 847–848
  sales trend, 835–836
  times-interest-earned,
    846–847
  working capital, 843
SUPERVAU, 636
Susan G. Komen, 901
Sustainable Travel
  International, 893
Swanson, 593
Swenson's Meats, 492–493

Swimmerz, 382
Sylvan Industries, 298–299

T

Target Corporation, 543,
  623, 636, 714, 831, 838
  balance sheets, 854
  horizontal analysis of
    comparative statement, 841
  income statements,
    840–842, 854–857
  sustainability practices of, 911
  vertical analysis of comparative
    income statement, 842
Tasty Chicken, 308
T-Call, 357
Terra Industries, 762, 767
Thomas Cycles, 549
3M Company, 636
Tierra Firma, 715–716, 719, 737
Timberland, 461, 893
Tiny Toys, 249
Tioga Manufacturing Company, 97
Tmedic, 453
Today's Fashion, 801–803
Tom White Automotive, 44
Tongish Beverages, 915
Top-Flight, 12
Topsfield, Inc., 879
Toro, 630–631, 638
Touch Enterprises, 156
Towson Medical Supply, 574–575
Toyota, 7, 20, 25, 47–51,
  53–57, 59, 74, 202,
  207–208, 210, 458–459
  fixed costs, 68–70
  indirect material costs, 57
  lean production philosophy of, 20
  manufacturing costs, 56
  Prius hybrid automobile,
    47, 53–54, 57, 67, 69–70
TreadMile, 502
Trek Bicycle Corporation, 629
Trendy Toes, 440
Tropicana, 52
Tucker Manufacturing, 287
Tucson Tortilla, 520–528
  budgeted balance
    sheet, 537–538
  budgeted income
    statement, 527–528
  budgeted manufacturing
    cost per unit, 527
  capital expenditure budget, 532
  cash collections
    budget, 532–533
  cash payments budget, 533–535
  combined cash budget,
    535–536
  direct labor budget, 524
  direct materials budget,
    523–524
  direct materials variance, 661
  flexible budget performance
    reports, 609–611
  flexible budget variance, 672

manufacturing overhead
    budget, 525
  master budget performance
    report, 608
  operating expenses budget, 526
  production budget, 521–522
  sales budget, 520–521
  standard cost income
    statement, 683
  standard costs, 655–666,
    680–683
Tupperware, 51
Two Sisters Catering, 358
Two Turtles, 369, 628

U

U-Haul, 911
Ultra Care Health Group, 358
Union Hospital, 383–384
United Nations, 886
United Parcel Service (UPS),
  52, 86, 589, 590
University Calendars, 447
University Logos, 582
University of Georgia, 261
University Rings, 689
Upstate College
  Bookstore, 552–553
U.S. Census Bureau, 19
U.S. government, 493–494
U.S. Marine Corps, 180
U.S. National Park Service, 86
U.S. Postal Service (USPS),
  86, 196, 331

V

Valentine Industries, 554–555
Valero, 52
Value Surge Protectors, 297
Value World, 310–311
Varsity Rings, 695
Verizon Communications,
  Inc., 629
Victor Industries, 903
Violins and More, 385–386
Violins-by-Lucy, 389–390
Visa, 542–543
Vittorio Restaurant Group,
  687–688, 690
Voisine Products, 246

W

Wadsworth Preschool, 561–562
Wagner Corporation, 177
Waldman Pools, 147–148
Wallace Corporation, 824–825
Walmart, 48–49, 52, 196, 418,
  477, 712, 831, 844–850,
  855, 857, 888–889
Walt Disney Company, 629, 893
Walton Plastics, 911
Wasick Company, 628
Waterfall Travel Services,
  Inc., 812–813

WaterSpray Marine, 41
Wave Guard, 696
Webster Recycling, 163
Webster State Bank, 871
Wedge Industries, 221
Weekly News Group, 863
Weiters Company, 169–170
Welch Manufacturing, 444
Wendell Chemical
    Corporation, 637
Wendell's Restaurant Supply, 574
West Corporation, 819–820
Western Outfitters, 701
Western Travel, 433
West Hill Hardware, 761–762
West Horizon, 227

Whiston Manufacturing, 769
White Consulting, 165
Wholesome Foods, 63
Whooley Fabricators, 164
Wild Birds, Inc., 150–152,
    159–160
Williams Group, 860
Williamson Fabricators, 240
Williamson Feeders, 150–152
Willis Benchmarking
    Associates, 708
Willitte Company, 247–248
Wilson Feeders, 159–160
Winder corporation, 813
Wolanin Containers, 690–691
Wolanin Foods, 553

Wolanin Pharmacy, 229–230
Wolf Manufacturing, 439–440
Woodfree Plastics, 162
WorldCom, 17, 211
World Systems, 503
Worldwide Travel, 440
Wronkovich Industries, 370–371
Wythe Industries, 388–389

X

Xerox, 910
Xoom Corporation, 880

Z

Zena Fashion, 490–491
Zeta Applications, 223
Zetamax, 722, 740
Zippy Frozen Foods, 498
Zippy Scooters, 443
Zip Surge Protectors, 304
Zucca Corporation,
    558–559
Zylo Electronics, 876

GLOSSARY/INDEX

A Combined Glossary/Subject Index

A

ABC. *See* Activity-based costing (ABC)

ABM. *See* Activity-based management (ABM)

Absorption costing. The costing method where products "absorb" both fixed and variable manufacturing costs, 342–350, 464

Absorption costing income statement, 344–345

Account analysis. A method for determining cost behavior that is based on a manager's judgment in classifying each general ledger account as a variable, fixed, or mixed cost, 334

cost hierarchy for, 193–194
decision guidelines for, 199

Accounting for Sustainability (A4S), 894

Accounting rate of return (ARR). A measure of profitability computed by dividing the average annual operating income from an asset by the initial investment in the asset, 712, 715, 718–720, 738

Accounts receivable, 788

Accounts receivable turnover. Measures a company's ability to collect cash from credit customers. To compute accounts receivable turnover, divide net credit sales by average net accounts receivable, 845, 852

Accrual basis of accounting. Revenues are recorded when they are earned (when the sale takes place), rather than when cash is received on the sale. Likewise, expenses are recorded when they are incurred, rather than when they are paid, 781

Accumulated depreciation, 792

Acid-test ratio. Ratio of the sum of cash plus short-term investments plus net current receivables to total current liabilities. It tells whether the entity can pay all of its current liabilities if they come due immediately; also called the *quick ratio,* 844, 852

Activity allocation bases, 189–191

Activity-based costing (ABC). Focuses on *activities* as the fundamental cost objects. The costs of those activities become building blocks for compiling the indirect costs of products, services, and customers, 188, 194

allocating indirect costs with, 188–194
circumstances favoring, 197
in merchandising companies, 196
results of, 195
in service companies, 196
using to improve operations, 194–198

Activity-based management (ABM). Using activity-based cost information to make decisions that increase profits while satisfying customers' needs, 194–197

Activity cost pools, 188–189, 193–194

Allocate. To assign an *indirect* cost to a cost object, 54. *See also* Cost allocation

American Institute of Certified Public Accountants, 22

Annuity. A stream of equal installments made at equal time intervals, 723

future value of, 725–727

net present value with, 731–732
present value of, 727–729, 742

Appraisal costs. Costs incurred to detect poor-quality goods or services, 209–214

Assets

return on, 847–848
total, 601–602

Assign. To attach a cost to a cost object, 54

Attainable standards. Standards based on currently attainable conditions that include allowances for normal amounts of waste and inefficiency; also known as practical standards, 656

Audit committee. A subcommittee of the board of directors that is responsible for overseeing both the internal audit function and the annual financial statement audit by independent CPAs, 8, 17

Average cost. The total cost divided by the number of units, 69–70

Average unit costs, 267–268

Avoidable fixed costs. Fixed costs that can be eliminated as a result of taking a particular course of action, 474–475

B

Balanced scorecard. A performance evaluation system designed by Kaplan and Norton that integrates financial and operational performance measures along four perspectives: financial, customer, internal business, and learning and growth, 589, 613–619

Balance sheets

budgeted, 537–538
comparative, 785, 786
comparing, 66
horizontal analysis of, 834
vertical analysis of, 837

Bar coding technology, 63, 189, 197

Batch-level activities. Activities and costs incurred for every batch, regardless of the number of unites in the batch, 193

Benchmarking. The practice of comparing a company with other companies or industry averages, 838

budgets and, 518–519

Billing rate. The labor rate charged to the customer, which includes both cost and profit components, 143–144

Bill of materials. A list of all of the raw materials needed to manufacture a job, 108

Biomimicry. A means of product design in which a company tries to mimic, or copy, the natural biological process in which dead organisms (plants and animals) become the input for another organism or process, 52

Blame, placing, 597

Board of directors. The body elected by shareholders to oversee the company, 7–8

Book value per share of common stock. Common stockholders' equity divided by the number of shares of common stock outstanding. It is the recorded amount for each share of common stock outstanding, 850, 853

Breakeven point. The sales level at which operating income is zero: Total revenues = Total expenses, 400

changing fixed costs and, 414
changing sales prices and, 411–412
changing variable costs and, 412–413
finding, using CVP analysis, 400–403
in terms of sales revenue, 418–419
in terms of sales units, 416–417

Budget. Quantitative expression of a plan that helps managers coordinate and implement the plan, 4. *See also* Capital budgeting; Flexible budgets

benefits of, 518–519
capital expenditure, 532
cash collections, 532–533
cash payments, 533–535
combined cash, 535–536
credit and debit cards sales, impact of, 542–543
development of, 516–517
direct labor, 524
direct materials, 523–524
financial, 532–539
flexible, 539
manufacturing overhead, 525
master, 519–520, 540–543
operating, 520
participative, 517
persons involved in, 517
production, 521–522
rolling, 517
sales, 520–521
sensitivity analysis and, 538–539
sustainability and, 539
used for planning, 4, 516–518
use of, 516–520

Budget committee. A committee composed of upper management, as well as cross-functional managers, who review, revise, and approve the final budget, 517

Budgeted balance sheet, 537–538

Budgeted income statement, 527–528

Budget variance. *See* Flexible budget variance; Variance

Business activities, in value chains, 50–51

Business conditions, planning for changing, with CVP analysis, 411–419

Business decisions. *See* Decision making; Decisions

Business Energy Tax Credit (BETC), 888

Business environment, 19–23

Business sectors, 48–50

C

Capital budgeting. The process of making capital investment decisions. Companies make capital investments when they acquire *capital assets*—assets used for a long period of time, 711–715

comparison of methods, 738
decision guidelines for, 721, 739
methods of, 712
process, 713–715
sensitivity analysis and, 735
using accounting rate of return, 712, 715, 718–720
using payback period, 712, 715–720

Capital expenditure budget, 532

Capital expenditures, 535

Capital investments, sustainability and, 714–715

Capital rationing. Choosing among alternative capital investments due to limited funds, 713
profitability index and, 733–734

Capital turnover. Sales revenue divided by total assets. The capital turnover shows how much sales revenue is generated with every $1.00 of assets, 598–599, 601

Carbon Disclosure Project (CDP), 894

Carbon footprint. A measure of the total emissions of carbon dioxide and other greenhouse gases (GHGs), often expressed for simplicity as tons of equivalent carbon dioxide, 893

Cash collections budget, 532–533

Cash equivalents. Very safe, highly liquid assets that are readily convertible into cash, such as money market funds, certificates of deposit that mature in less than three months, and U.S. treasury bills, 779

Cash flows. *See also* Statement of cash flows
capital budgeting and, 713
from financing activities, 779–782, 793–794
free cash flow, 795
from investing activities, 779–782, 791–793
net cash inflows, 713, 715–720
from operating activities, 779–782, 785–791, 799

Cash payments
determining, 797–799
for income taxes, 799
for insurance, 798
interest expense, 798
for inventory, 797
for operating expenses, 799
for salaries and wages, 798

Cash payments budget, 533–535

Cash receipts, from customers, 797

Centralized decision making, 590

Centralized services, 591

Certified Management Accountant (CMA). A professional certification issued by the IMA to designate expertise in the areas of managerial accounting, economics, and business finance, 11
IMA standards for, 14

Certified public accountants (CPAs), 7–8

Chief Executive Officer (CEO). The position hired by the board of directors to oversee the company on a daily basis, 7–8

Chief Financial Officer (CFO). The position responsible for all of the company's financial concerns, 7–8

Chief Operating Officer (COO). The position responsible for overseeing the company's operations, 7–8

Climate Change Act of 2008 (U.K), 888

COD. Collect on Delivery, or Cash on Delivery. A sales term indicating that the inventory must be paid for at the time of delivery, 521

Combined cash budget, 535–536

Committed fixed costs. Fixed costs that are locked in because of previous management decisions; management has little or no control over these costs in the short run, 323

Common fixed expenses. Fixed expenses that *cannot* be traced to the segment. Rather, these are fixed expenses incurred by a higher level segment that have been allocated to the underlying segments, 476–477, 595

Common-size statement. A financial statement that reports only percentages (no dollar amounts), 838

Common stock, 793, 850

Communication, budgets for, 518

Comparative balance sheets. A comparison of the balance sheets from the end of two fiscal periods; usually highlighting the changes in each account, 785–786

Competition
globalization and, 20
pricing pressure from, 119
sustainability and competitive strategy, 887, 889–890

Completion, job, 133

Compound interest. Interest computed on the principal *and* all interest earned to date, 723–724

Constraint. A factor that restricts production or sale of a product, 477

Continuous flow, 206

Contract manufacturers. Manufacturers who make products for other companies, not for themselves, 480–481

Contribution margin. Sales revenue minus variable expenses, 345, 397–398
weighted-average, 416–419

Contribution margin income statement. Income statement that organizes costs by *behavior* (variable costs or fixed costs) rather than by *function*, 342, 345–350, 397–398, 401–402, 463, 474

Contribution margin per unit. The excess of the unit sales price over the variable cost per unit; also called unit contribution margin, 397–398, 401–402

Contribution margin ratio. Ratio of contribution margin to sales revenue, 398–399, 402–403

Control decisions, 195

Controllable costs. Costs that can be influenced or changed by management, 66–67

Controller. The position responsible for general financial accounting, managerial accounting, and tax reporting, 8

Controlling. One of management's primary responsibilities; evaluating the results of business operations against the plan and making adjustments to keep the company pressing toward its goals, 4–5

Conversion costs. The combination of direct labor and manufacturing overhead costs, 58–59, 260–261

Coordination
budgets for, 518
performance evaluation and, 591

Corporate social responsibility, 19

Cost allocation
activity allocation bases, 189–191
activity-based costing for, 188–194
departmental overhead rates for, 182–187

plantwide overhead rate for, 181–182, 186–187

Cost allocation systems
comparison of, 192
more-refined *vs.* less-refined, 181
refinement of, 180–194

Cost behavior. Describes how costs change as volume changes, 229–330, 319–320
curvilinear costs, 330
decision guidelines for, 332, 351
determining, 333–342
fixed costs, 68, 320, 323–325
high-low method for, 336–338
mixed costs, 320, 325–327
operating budgets and, 520–528
regression analysis for, 338–341
relevant range, 327–329
step costs, 329–330
sustainable business practices and, 331
variable costs, 68–69, 320–323

Cost-benefit analysis. Weighing costs against benefits to help make decisions, 21

Cost-benefit test, 197

Cost center. A responsibility center in which managers are responsible for controlling costs, 592–593

Cost distortion. Overcosting some products while undercosting other products, 180–181, 187, 192, 198

Cost driver. The primary factor that causes a cost, 115, 335

Cost equation. A mathematical equation for a straight line that expresses how a cost behaves, 321–322, 326, 336–340

Cost hierarchy, 193

Costing. *See also* Activity-based costing; Job costing; Process costing
absorption, 342–345
decision guidelines for, 199
overcosting/underscosting, 181, 194
standard, 676, 680–683
sustainability and, 196
target costing, 466–468
variable, 343–350

Cost object. Anything for which managers want a separate measurement of costs, 53–54

Cost of goods manufactured. The cost of manufacturing the goods that were *finished* during the period, 65
calculating, 64–66

Cost of goods sold. Anything for which managers want a separate measurement of costs, 62
calculating, 64–66
correcting for underallocated and overallocated MOH, 128
for manufacturing companies, 64
for merchandising companies, 63

Cost of goods sold, inventory, and purchases budget. A merchandiser's budget that computes the Cost of Goods Sold, the amount of desired ending inventory, and amount of merchandise to be purchased, 540–542

Cost per equivalent unit, 266–267, 277–278

Cost-plus pricing. An approach to pricing used by price-setters; cost-plus pricing begins with the product's total costs and adds the company's desired profit to determine a cost-plus price 119–120, 468–469

Cost reduction sustainability programs, 887

Costs
allocating, 54

appraisal, 209–213
assigning, 54
assigning to client jobs, 141
average, 69–70
calculating, 69–70
controllable, 66–67
conversion, 58–59, 260–261
curvilinear, 330
cutting, 194–195
defining, 53–59
differential, 67
direct, 53–54, 141–142
duplicate, 591
external failure, 209–213
in financial statements, 62–66
fixed, 68–69, 323–325, 325–327, 414–416
flow of, through inventory accounts, 106–107
indirect, 53–54, 57, 142–143, 181–187
internal failure, 209–213
inventoriable product, 55–59, 62–66, 343, 464
irrelevant, 67–68
labor, 56–59
manufacturing, 56–59, 69
marginal, 70
mixed, 325–327
non-conformance, 210, 212
non-manufacturing, 121–122
opportunity, 482
period, 55, 58, 62–66, 344
prevention, 209–213
prime, 58–59
quality, 209–214
relevant, 67–68, 458–460
step costs, 329–330
sunk, 67–68, 459
for sustainability, 889–890
total, 54–55, 69–70
transfer pricing and, 604
transferred-in, 274
uncontrollable, 66–67
unit, 266–267
variable, 68–69, 320–322, 412–413
Costs of quality reports. A report that lists the costs incurred by the company related to quality. The costs are categorized as prevention costs, appraised costs, internal failure costs, and external failure costs, 209–212
Cost structures, choosing, 424–425
Cost-volume-profit (CVP) analysis. Expresses the relationships among costs, volume, and profit or loss, 396
for changing business conditions, 411–419
choosing cost structures with, 424–425
contribution margin ratio, 398–399, 402–403
data and assumptions required for, 396–397
decision guidelines for, 407, 426
effect of sales mix in, 416–419
finding target profit using, 403–404
graphing relationships, 404–406
risk indicators, 420–425
sustainability and, 415
unit contribution margin, 397–398
usefulness of, 396
using to find breakeven point, 400–403
Credit and debit cards sales, 542–543
Credit card debt, 777
Cross-functional teams. Corporate teams whose members represent various functions of the organization, such as R&D, Design, Production, Marketing, Distribution and Customer Service, 8
Current asset accounts, 787–789
Current liability accounts, 789–790

Current ratio. Current assets divided by current liabilities. It measures the ability to pay current liabilities with current assets, 843–844, 852
Curvilinear costs. A cost behavior that is not linear (not a straight line), 330
Customer perspective, of balanced scorecard, 613–616
Customer relations, decentralization and, 590
Customer response time. The time that elapses between receipt of a customer order and delivery of the product or service, 202
Customer service. Support provided for customers after the sale, 51
sustainability and, 52–53
Custom orders, bidding on, 119–120
Cutting costs, 194–195

D

Data. See also Information
concerns about, 342
for CVP analysis, 396
scatter plots of, 334–336, 340
Days' sales in receivables. Ratio of average net accounts receivable to one day's sale. It indicates how many days' sales remain in Accounts Receivable awaiting collection, 845–846, 852
Debit card sales, 542–543
Debt ratio. Ratio of total liabilities to total assets. It shows the proportion of a company's assets that is financed with debt, 846, 852
Decentralize. Companies that split their operations into different operating segments, 590
advantages and disadvantages of, 590–591
Decision making. One of management's primary responsibilities; identifying possible courses of action and choosing among them
costs of quality for, 211–213
decision guidelines for, 4–5, 54–55, 470, 485
internal, 54–55
job costing information for, 118–122
by managers, 458–469
relevant information for, 458–459, 470
sustainable business practices and, 461
total costs for internal decisions, 54–55
using activity-based management, 195
Decisions. See also Capital budgeting
discontinuation decisions, 473–477
outsourcing, 457, 479–483
pricing decisions, 194, 461–469
product mix, 194, 477–479
sell as is or process further, 483–484
short-term special, 460–461
special sales order, 461–465
sustainability and short-term business, 461
Defects, as waste, 202
Departmental overhead rates. Separate manufacturing overhead rates established for each department, 182–187
Departments, discontinuation decisions, 473–477
Depreciation, accumulated, 792
Depreciation expense, 786
Design. Detailed engineering of products and services and the processes for producing them, 50
sustainability and, 52

Differential cost. The difference in cost between two alternative courses of action, 67
Direct cost. A cost that can be traced to a cost object, 53–54
job costing and, 122
in service companies, 141–142
Direct costing. See Variable costing
Direct fixed expenses. Fixed expenses that can be traced to the segment, 595
Directing. One of management's primary responsibilities; running the company on a day-to-day basis, 4–5
Direct labor budget, 524
Direct labor (DL). The cost of compensating employees who physically convert raw materials into the company's products; labor costs that are directly traceable to the finished product, 57
in job costing, 130–131
recording, 680–681
standard costs of, 657
tracing cost to jobs, 112–114, 533
Direct labor efficiency variance. This variance tells managers how much of the total labor variance is due to using a greater or lesser amount of time than anticipated. It is calculated as follows: $SR \times (AH - SHA)$, 665–667
Direct labor rate variance. This variance tells managers how much of the total labor variance is due to paying a higher or lower hourly wage rate than anticipated. It is calculated as follows: $AH \times (AR - SR)$, 665–667
Direct labor variances, 659–660, 664–667
Direct materials budget, 523–524
Direct materials (DM). Primary raw materials that become a physical part of a finished product and whose costs are traceable to the finished product, 56–57
calculating use of, 65
in job costing, 129
recording, 680
standard cost of, 657
tracing cost to jobs, 111–112, 533
Direct materials price variance. This variance tells managers how much of the total direct materials variance is due to paying a higher or lower price than expected for the direct materials it purchased. It is calculated as follows: $AQP \times (AP - SP)$, 661–662, 667
Direct materials quantity variance. This variance tells managers how much of the total direct materials variance is due to using a larger or smaller quantity of direct materials than expected. It is calculated as follows: $SP \times (AQU - SQA)$, 663–664, 667
Direct material variances, 659–664, 667
Direct method. A method of presenting cash flows from operating activities that separately lists the receipt and payment of cash for specific operating activities, 781–782
preparing statement of cash flows using, 796–800
Discontinuation decisions, 473–477
Discounting cash flows, 727
Discount rate. Management's minimum desired rate of return on an investment; also called the hurdle rate and required rate of return, 731
Discounts, 119
Discretionary fixed costs. Fixed costs that are a result of annual management decisions;

fixed costs that are controllable in the short run, 323

Distribution. Delivery of products or services to customers, 51

sustainability and, 52

Dividends, 535

Dividend Yield. Ratio of dividends per share of stock to the stock's market price per share. It tells the percentage of a stock's market value that the company returns to stockbrokers annually as dividends, 850, 853

Dow Jones Sustainability Index, 888

DOWNTIME. An acronym for the eight wastes: Defects, Overproduction, Waiting, Not utilizing people to their fullest potential, Transportation, Inventory, Movement, Excess processing, 202–204

E

Earnings per share (EPS). Amount of a company's net income for each share of its outstanding common stock, 848–849, 853

Earnings per share of common stock, 848–849, 853

E-billing/e-banking, 21, 331

Economic Value Added (EVA), 602

Eight Wastes. Defects, Overproduction, Waiting, Not utilizing people to their fullest potential, Transportation, Inventory, Movement, Excess processing, 202–204

Employee roles, in lean operations, 205–206

Enterprise Resource Planning (ERP). Software systems that can integrate all of a company's worldwide functions, departments, and data into a single system, 20–21

Environmental management accounting (EMA). A system used for the identification, collection, analysis and use of two types of information for internal decision making. These two types of information include monetary and physical information, 885, 890

challenges to implementing, 894–895

future of, 895–896

uses of, 891–894

Environmental reporting standards, 894

Environmental sustainability. *See* Sustainability

EPR. *See* Extended producer responsibility

EPS. *See* Earnings per share

Equivalent units. Express the amount of work done during a period in terms of fully completed units of output, 260–261, 264–267, 276–278

ERP systems, 20–21

Ethical dilemmas, 11–14

illegal *vs.* unethical behavior, 14

Excess processing, as waste, 202, 204

Expenses

common fixed, 476–477

direct fixed, 595

interest, 798

noncash, 785–786

Expert knowledge, 590

Extended producer responsibility (EPR), 121, 891

Extended warranties, 50

Extensible Business Reporting Language (XBRL). A data tagging system that enables companies to release financial and business information in a format that can be quickly, efficiently, and cost-effectively accessed, sorted, and analyzed over the internet, 18–19

External failure costs. Costs incurred when the company does not detect poor-quality goods or services until *after* delivery is made to customers, 209–214

F

Facility-level activities. Activities and costs incurred no matter how many units, batches, or products are produced in the plant, 193

Favorable variance. A variance that causes operating income to be higher than budgeted, 594

Federal Insurance Contributions Act (FICA), 59

Financial accounting, 4, 6–7

historical orientation of, 895

Financial Accounting Standards Board (FASB), 782, 796, 799

Financial budgets. The budgets that project the collection and payment of cash, as well as forecast the company's budgeted balance sheet, 520, 532–539

Financial performance measurement of investment centers, 597–604

limitations of, 590–591, 602

Financial perspective of balanced scorecard, 613–615

Financial ratios, 843–850

Financial statement analysis, 832

decision guidelines for, 839, 852–853

horizontal analysis, 832–836, 838–839

methods of, 832

ratio analysis, 832

ratios for, 843–850, 852

red flags in, 851

sustainability and, 851

vertical analysis, 832, 836–839

Financial statements. *See also* Balance sheets; Income statements

common-size, 838

costs in, 62–66

flow of costs through, 64

for manufacturing companies, 64–66

for merchandising companies, 63

preparation of, 120

for service companies, 62

Financing activities. Activities that either generate capital for the company or pay it back, such as issuing stock or long-term debt, paying dividends, and repaying principal amounts on loans; this includes all activities that affect long-term liabilities and owner's equity, 779–782

preparing cash flows from, 793–794

Finished goods (FG) inventory. Completed goods that have not yet been sold, 49, 106–107

First-in, first-out (FIFO) method, 261

5S. A workplace organization system composed of the following steps: Sort, Set in order, Shine, Standardize, and Sustain, 206

Fixed costs. Costs that stay constant in total despite wide changes in volume, 68–69, 320, 323–325

avoidable, 474–475

changing, and CVP analysis, 414–416

committed, 323

discretionary, 323

outsourcing considerations and, 480–481

relevant ranges for, 327–329

vs. step costs, 329–330

unavoidable, 474–475

Fixed overhead budget variance. This variance measures the difference between the actual fixed overhead costs incurred and the budgeted fixed overhead costs. This variance is sometimes referred to as the fixed overhead spending variance, because it specifically looks at whether the company spent more or less than anticipated on fixed overhead costs, 674

Fixed overhead spending variance, 674

Fixed overhead volume variance. This variance is the difference between the budgeted fixed overhead and the *standard fixed overhead* cost allocated to production. In essence, the fixed overhead volume variance measures the utilization of the fixed capacity costs. If volume is higher than originally anticipated, the variance will be favorable. If volume is lower than originally anticipated, the variance will be unfavorable, 675–676

Flexible budget. Budgets prepared for different volumes of activity, 539, 608–609

for performance evaluation, 608–612

sensitivity analysis and, 538–539

using standard costs to develop, 659–660

Flexible budget variance. The difference arising because the company actually earned more or less revenue or incurred more or less cost than expected for the actual level of output, 610–611

causes of variances, 611–612

decomposing, 612

direct labor variance, 659–660, 664–667

direct material variance, 659–664, 667

Free cash flow. The amount of excess cash a business generates after taking into consideration the capital expenditures necessary to maintain its business. It is calculated as cash flows from operating activities minus capital expenditures, 795

Freed capacity, 473, 475–477, 480–482

Fringe benefits, 59

FTSE4Good Index, 888

Full potential, underutilization of, 202–203

Future value, 724–727, 741, 743–744

G

Generally Accepted Accounting Principles (GAAP), 7

absorption costing and, 342, 348

vs. IFRS, 18

inventoriable product costs and, 55

manufacturing overhead and, 114

special order decisions and, 464

Global considerations, transfer pricing and, 604

Globalization, 20

Global Lamp 60 Index, 888

Global Reporting Initiative (GRI), 894

Goal congruence. When the goals of the segment managers align with the goals of top management, 591, 601

Graphs

of CVP relationships, 404–406

scatter plots, 334–336, 340

Green technologies. *See* Sustainability

Greenwashing. The unfortunate practice of *overstating* a company's commitment to sustainability, 52

Gross book value. Historical cost of assets, 601–602

Gross profit, 279

H

Health insurance premiums, 59, 113

High-low method. A method for determining cost behavior that is based on two historical data points: the highest and lowest volume of activity, 336–338

High operating leverage firms, 421–422

High-volume sales, discounts on, 119

Horizontal analysis. Study of percentage changes in comparative financial statements, 832–836, 838–839

Hurdle rate. Management's minimum desired rate of return on an investment; also called the discount rate and required rate of return, 731

I

Ideal standards. Standards based on perfect or ideal conditions that do not allow for any waste in the production process, machine breakdown, or other inefficiencies; also known as perfection standards, 656

IFRS. *See* International Financial Reporting Standards

Illegal *vs.* unethical behavior, 14

Income
    net, 62
    operating, 62
Income statement approach, to finding breakeven point, 400–401
Income statements
    absorption costing, 344–345, 464
    budgeted, 527–528
    comparing formats for, 344–346
    contribution margin, 342 401–402, 345–346, 397–398
    horizontal analysis of, 834
    manufacturing companies, 64
    merchandising companies, 63
    product line, 473–474
    segment margin, 477
    service companies, 62
    standard costing, 683
    traditional, 345
    vertical analysis, 836–837
Income taxes, 535, 799
Incremental analysis approach, 460, 463, 475–476
    for outsourcing decision, 481–482
    for product discontinuation, 476
    for sell as is or process further decision, 483–484
    of special sales orders, 464
Indifference point. The volume of sales at which a company would be indifferent between alternative cost structures because they would result in the same total cost, 424–425

Indirect cost. A cost that relates to the cost object but cannot be traced to it, 53–54, 57

allocating, 181–187
    in service companies, 142–143
Indirect labor. Labor costs that are difficult to trace to specific products, 56–57
    in job costing, 131
Indirect manufacturing costs, 57
Indirect materials. Materials whose costs are difficult to trace to specific products, 57
    in job costing, 129–130
Indirect method. A method of presenting the cash flows from operating activities that begins with the company's net income, which is prepared on an accrual basis, and then reconciles it back to the cash basis through a series of adjustments, 781–782
    preparing statement of cash flows using, 785–795, 800
Inflation, 342
Information. *See also* Data
    for developing and updating standards, 656–657
    monetary, 890
    nonfinancial relevant, 459
    physical, 890
    relevant, 458–459
    sustainability and use of EMA, 892–894
Information systems, advanced, 20–21
Information technology, sensitivity analysis and, 419–420
Institute of Management Accountants (IMA). The professional organization that promotes the advancement of the management accounting profession, 11–14
Insurance, 798
Interest, 723–724
Interest-coverage ratio. Ratio of income from operations to interest expense. It measures the number of times that operating income can cover interest expense; also called the *times-interest-earned ratio*, 846–847, 852
Interest expense, 798
Interest payable, 789
Interest rate, 723
Internal audit function. The corporate function charged with assessing the effectiveness of the company's internal controls and risk management policies, 8
Internal business perspective, of balanced scorecard, 613–614, 616–617
Internal decision making, 54–55
Internal failure costs. Costs incurred when the company detects and corrects poor-quality goods or services *before* making delivery to customers, 209–214
Internal rate of return (IRR). The rate of return (based on discounted cash flows) that a company can expect to earn by investing in a capital asset. The interest rate that makes the NPV of the investment equal to zero, 712, 730, 735
    calculating, 735–737, 749–750, 756
    vs. net present value, 738
Internal Revenue Service (IRS)
    absorption costing and rules, 342, 348
International Accounting Standards Board (IASB), 781, 894
International Financial Reporting Standards (IFRS). The SEC has recently moved to adopt IFRS for all publicly traded companies within the next few years. In many instances, IFRS vary from GAAP, 18

International Organization for Standardization (ISO), 22, 208, 894
Inventoriable product costs. All costs of a product that GAAP requires companies to treat as an asset (inventory) for external financial reporting. These costs are not expensed until the product is sold, 55–59
    absorption costing and, 464
    comparing, 342–344
    in financial statements, 62–66
    GAAP and, 55
    for manufacturing companies, 56–58, 64–66
    for merchandising companies, 56, 58, 63
    vs. period costs, 62
    for service companies, 58, 62
Inventory
    under absorption *vs.* variable costing, 346–348
    cash payments for, 797
    decrease in, 788
    finished goods, 49, 106–107
    flow assumptions, 261
    flow of, through manufacturing system, 106–107
    just-in-time, 21, 204, 344
    periodic, 63
    perpetual, 63
    raw materials, 48–49, 106–107
    recording, 682
    safety stock, 521
    stock, 107
    in traditional production system, 205
    types of, 48–49
    as waste, 202–203
    work in process, 48, 49, 106–107, 278–279
Inventory turnover. Ratio of cost of goods sold to average inventory. It indicates how rapidly inventory is sold, 844–845, 852
Investing activities. Activities that involve buying or selling long-term assets, such as buying or selling property, plant, or equipment; buying or selling stock in other companies (if the stock is meant to be held for the long term); or loaning money to other companies with the goal of earning interest income from the loan, 779–782
    preparing cash flows from, 791–793
Investment appraisal, 892
Investment center. A responsibility center in which managers are responsible for generating revenues, controlling costs, and efficiently managing the division's assets, 592–593
    financial performance evaluation of, 597–604
Investment decisions. *See also* Capital budgeting
    net present value, 730–735
    sustainability and, 714–715
    using accounting rate of return, 712, 715, 718–720
    using payback period, 712, 715–720
Investments, 792–793
    stock investments, 849–850
Invoice. Bill from a supplier, 109
Invoicing, 143–144
Irrelevant costs, 67–68
ISO 9001:2008. A quality-related certification issued by the International Organization for Standardization (ISO). Firms may become ISO 9001:2008 certified by complying with the quality management standards set forth by the ISO and undergoing extensive audits of their quality management processes, 22, 208

J

Job costing. A system for assigning costs to products or services that differ in the amount of materials, labor, and overhead required. Typically used by manufacturers that produce unique, or custom-ordered products in small batches; also used by professional service firms, 104–106
- accounting for manufacturing overhead, 114–118, 122, 126–128, 131–132
- accounting for materials, 111–112
- allocating manufacturing overhead to jobs, 132–133
- closing manufacturing overhead, 135–136
- decision guidelines for, 123, 137
- decision making and, 118–122
- direct and variable costing, 122
- direct labor used in, 130–131
- direct materials used in, 129
- indirect labor used in, 131
- indirect materials used in, 129–130
- journal entries for, 128–136, 144
- in manufacturing companies, 106–120
- for non-manufacturing costs, 121–122
- vs. process costing, 105–106, 256–259
- in service companies, 141–144
- sustainability and, 120–121
- tracing direct labor cost to jobs, 112–114, 533
- tracing direct materials to job costs, 111–112, 533

Job cost record. A written or electronic document that lists the direct materials, direct labor, and manufacturing overhead costs assigned to each individual job, 110–111, 113–114, 117, 125
- used to make business decisions, 118–122

Job costs, reducing future, 118

Jobs
- allocating manufacturing overhead to, 114–118, 132–133
- completion of, 133

Journal entries
- in manufacturer's job costing system, 128–136
- in process costing, 269–270, 281–282
- in service firm's job costing system, 144
- for standard cost accounting systems, 680–683

Just-in-time (JIT). An inventory management philosophy that focuses on purchasing raw materials just in time for production and completing finished goods just in time for delivery to customers, 21, 204, 344

K

Kaizen. A Japanese word meaning "change for the better," 202

Key performance indicators (KPIs). Summary performance metrics that allow managers to assess how well the company's objectives are being met, 613–618

L

Labor
- direct, 56–57, 130–131
- indirect, 56–57, 131
Labor costs, 56–59

Labor time record. A written or electronic document that identifies the employee, the amount of time spent on a particular job, and the labor cost charged to a job, 112–114, 130–131

Lag indicators. Performance indicators that reveal the results of past actions and decisions, 613

Lead indicators. Performance measures that predict future performance, 613

Lean operations
- characteristics of, 204–208
- decision guidelines for, 214
- eight wastes and, 202–204
- employee roles in, 205–206
- equipment arrangement in, 205
- manufacturing cycle times, 207
- in service and merchandising companies, 208
- sustainability and, 208

Lean thinking. A management philosophy and strategy focused on creating value for the customer by eliminating waste, 21, 202, 668

Learning and growth perspective
- of balanced scorecard, 613–614, 616–617

LEED certification. LEED, which stands for "Leadership in Energy and Environmental Design," is a certification system developed by the U.S. Green Building Council as a way of promoting and evaluating environmentally friendly construction projects, 714–715

Leverage. Earning more income on borrowed money than the related interest expense, thereby increasing the earnings for the owners of the business; also called *trading on equity*, 848

Life cycle assessment. A method of product design in which the company analyzes the environmental impact of a product, from cradle to grave, in an attempt to minimize negative environmental consequences throughout the entire life span of the product, 52

Line of credit. A lending arrangement from a bank in which a company is allowed to borrow money as needed, up to a specified maximum amount, yet only pay interest on the portion that is actually borrowed until it is repaid, 536

Living roof, 86, 818, 908, 920, 922

London Climate Exchange, 888

Long-term debt ability to pay, 846–847, 852

Long-term liabilities, 793

Low operating leverage firms, 421–422

M

Make-or-buy decisions, 479–483

Management
- activity-based, 194–196
- quality, 207–208

Management accountants
- decision guidelines for, 15
- ethical challenges for, 11–14
- professional association of, 10–11
- roles of, 7–9
- salaries for, 11
- skills required of, 9–10

Management by exception. A management technique in which managers only investigate budget variances that are relatively large, 594–595, 611

Managerial accounting
- business trends affecting, 19–21
- decision guidelines for, 15, 60, 71
- vs. financial accounting, 4, 6–7
- globalization and, 20–21
- overview, 4–7, 60
- regulatory and business issues affecting, 17–19

Managers
- decision making by, 5, 473–484
- motivation and retention of, 590–591
- responsibilities of, 4–5, 15–16
- use of budgets by, 516–520

Manager's incentives
- absorption costing and, 347–348

Manufacturing company. A company that uses labor, plant, and equipment to convert raw materials into new finished products, 48–50
- balance sheets, 66
- economic shift away from, 19–20
- flow of costs through, 64
- flow of inventory through, 106–107
- income statements, 64
- inventoriable product costs, 56–58, 64–66
- job costing in, 106–120
- master budget for, 519–520

Manufacturing costs, 56–59

Manufacturing cycle time. The time that elapses between the start of production and the product's completion, 207

Manufacturing overhead budget, 525

Manufacturing overhead (MOH). All manufacturing costs other than direct materials and direct labor; also called factory overhead and indirect manufacturing cost, 56–57, 69, 534
- allocating, using activity-based costing, 188–194
- allocating, using plantwide overhead rate, 181–182, 186–187
- allocating to jobs, 114–118, 132–133
- closing, 135–136, 682
- departmental overhead rates for, 182–187
- incurring, 132, 534
- overallocated, 126–128
- predetermined rate, 116
- recording, 681–682
- standard cost of, 657–658
- steps in allocating, 182–184
- underallocated, 126–128

Manufacturing overhead rates standard, 657–658

Manufacturing overhead variances, 672–676

Marginal cost. The cost of producing one more unit, 70

Margin of safety. Excess of expected sales over breakeven sales; the drop in sales a company absorb without incurring an operating loss, 420–421

Marketing. Promotion and advertising of product services, 51
- sustainability and, 51

Market price, 603

Master budget. The comprehensive planning document for the entire organization. The master budget includes the operating budgets and the financial budgets, 519–520
- decision guidelines for, 529, 544
- for service and merchandising companies, 540–543

Master budget performance reports, 608

Master budget variance. The difference between actual results and the master budget, 608–609, 612

Materials
direct, 56–57, 65, 111–112, 129, 533, 657, 680
indirect, 57, 129–130

Materials flow accounting (MFA). An accounting system in which all physical inputs to an organization's operations are reconciled with output generated. The goal is to track where all physical inputs are going, 891

Materials requisition. A written or electronic document that requests specific materials be transferred from the raw materials inventory storeroom to the production floor, 111–112

Merchandising company. A company that resells tangible products previously bought from suppliers, 48–50
activity-based costing in, 196
balance sheets, 66
contribution margin, 346
cost of goods sold for, 63
costs of quality in, 210–211
income statements, 63
inventoriable product costs, 57, 58, 63
lean operations in, 208
master budget for, 540–543

Microsoft Excel
regression analysis using, 338–339
scatter plots using, 336, 340
for time value of money calculations, 751–756

Mixed cost. Costs that change, but not in direct proportion to changes in volume. Mixed costs have both variable cost and fixed cost components, 320, 325–327

Monetary information. The type of information traditionally used in accounting systems, 890

Money, time value of. See Time value of money

Motivation, 590–591

Movement, as waste, 202–203, 205

N

Negotiated price, 603

Net book value. Historical costs of assets less accumulated depreciation, 786–787, 601–602

Net cash inflows, 713, 715–720, 731–732

Net income. See Operating income

Net present value (NPV). The difference between the present value of the investment's net cash inflows and the investment's costs, 712, 731
with annuities, 731–732
calculating, 730–735
vs. internal rate of return, 738
with residual value, 734–735
with unequal net cash inflows, 732–733

Noncash expenses, 785–786

Noncash investing, 781

Noncash revenues, 785–787

Non-conformance costs, 210, 212

Nonfinancial information, 459

Non-manufacturing costs, 121–122

Non-value-added activities. Activities that neither enhance the customer's image of

the product or service nor provide a competitive advantage; also known as waste activities, 195

Number of periods, 723

O

Offshoring. Having work performed overseas. Offshored work can either be performed by the company itself or by outsourcing the work to another company, 479

Operating activities. The day-to-day profit-making activities of the company, such as making or buying inventory, selling inventory, selling services, paying employees, advertising, and so forth; This also includes any other activity that affects net income (not just operating income), current assets, or current liabilities, 779–781
direct method, 781–782, 799
indirect method, 781–782, 799
preparing cash flows from, 779–782, 785–791, 799
sustainability and, 782

Operating budgets. The budgets needed to run the daily operations of the company. The operation budgets culminate in a budgeted income statement, 520
preparation of, 520–528

Operating expenses, 62, 134, 141, 534, 799

Operating expenses budget, 526

Operating income, 62
in variable vs. absorption costing, 346–350

Operating leverage. The relative amount of fixed and variable costs that make up a firm's total costs, 421–423

Operating leverage factor. At a given level of sales, the contribution margin divided by operating income; the operating leverage factor indicates the percentage change in operating income that will occur from a 1% change in sales volume, 422–423

Opportunity cost. The benefit forgone by not choosing an alternative course of action, 482

Organizational charts, 593

Organizational structure, 7–8

Organization-wide performance reports, 596–597

Other indirect manufacturing costs. All manufacturing overhead costs aside from indirect materials and indirect labor, 57

Outliers. Abnormal data points; data points that do not fall in the same general pattern as the other data points, 335–336, 342, 351

Outsourcing. A make-or-buy decision: Managers decide whether to buy a product or service or produce it in-house, 457, 479–483

Overallocated manufacturing overhead. The amount of manufacturing overhead allocated to jobs is more than the amount of manufacturing overhead costs actually incurred; results in jobs being overcosted, 126–128

Overcosting, 181, 194

Overhead. See Manufacturing overhead (MOH)

Overproduction, as waste, 202

P

Packaging, sustainability and, 52, 887–889

Participative budgeting. Budgeting that involves the participation of many levels of management, 517

Payback. The length of time it takes to recover, in net cash inflows, the cost of a capital outlay, 715

Payback period, 712, 715–720, 738

Perfection standards. Standards based on perfect or ideal conditions that do not allow for any waste in the production process, machine breakdown, or other inefficiencies; also known as ideal standards, 656

Performance evaluation
balanced scorecard and, 613–619
decentralization and, 591
decision guidelines for, 605
flexible budgets for, 608–612
global considerations, 604
of investment centers, 597–604
of profit centers, 595–597
of revenue centers, 594
sustainability and, 618
transfer pricing and, 602–604

Performance evaluation systems, 591

Performance management, 893–894

Performance reports. Reports that compare actual results against budgeted figures, 594–597
flexible budget performance reports, 609–611
master budget performance reports, 608
organization-wide performance reports, 596–597
profit center performance reports, 595–597
responsibility centers, 594–597
revenue center performance reports, 594
summary performance report, 519

Performance scorecard or dashboard. A report displaying the measurement of KPIs, as well as their short-term and long-term targets. The report allows managers to visually monitor and focus on managing the company's key activities and strategies as well as business risks, 613

Period costs. Costs that are expensed in the period in which they are incurred; often called Operating Expenses, or Selling, General, and Administrative Expenses, 55, 58, 62–66, 344

Periodic inventory. An inventory system in which Cost of Goods Sold is calculated at the end of the period, rather than every time a sale is made, 63

Perpetual inventory. An inventory system in which both Cost of Goods Sold and Inventory are updated every time a sale is made, 63

Physical information. A vital part of environmental management accounting systems. Examples include: quantity of air emissions; tons of solid waste generated; gallons of wastewater generated; pounds of packaging recycled; and total amount of water consumed, 890

Pick. Storeroom workers remove items from raw materials inventory that are needed by production, 112

Planning. One of management's primary responsibilities; setting goals and objectives for the company and deciding how to achieve them, 4–5
activity-based costing and, 195
budgets used for, 4, 516–518
flexible budgets for, 538–539
strategic, 516

Plantwide overhead rate. When overhead is allocated to every product using the same manufacturing overhead rate, 181–182, 186–187

Point of use storage (POUS). A storage system used to reduce the waste of transportation and movement in which tools, materials, and equipment are stored in proximity to where they will be used most frequently, 206

Post-audits. Comparing a capital investment's actual net cash inflows to its projected net cash inflows, 713–714

Practical standards. Standards based on currently attainable conditions that include allowances for normal amounts of waste and inefficiency; also known as attainable standards, 656

   sustainability and, 268–269

Predetermined manufacturing overhead rate. The rate used to allocate manufacturing overhead to individual jobs; calculated before the year begins as follows: total estimated manufacturing overhead costs divided by total estimated amount of allocation base, 116

Prepaid insurance, 788

Present value, 724–725, 727–729, 741–742

   net, 712, 733–734

Present value index. An index that computes the number of dollars returned for every dollar invested, *with all calculations performed in present value dollars*. It is computed as present value of net cash inflows divided by investment; also called profitability index, 733–734

Prevention costs. Costs incurred to *avoid* poor-quality goods or services, 209–214

Price/earnings (P/E) ratio. Ratio of the market price of a share of common stock to the company's earnings per share. It measures the value that the stock market places on $1 of a company's earnings, 849, 853

Price-setters, 465–466, 469

Price standards, 656–658

Price-takers, 465–466, 469

Pricing

   cost-plus approach, 119–120, 468–469
   incremental analysis approach, 460, 463, 464, 475–476
   outsourcing prices, 481–482
   target costing approach, 466–469
   transfer pricing, 602–604

Pricing decisions, 194, 461–469

Pricing pressure, 119

Prime costs. The combination of direct material and direct labor costs, 58–59

Principal, 723

Process costing. A system for assigning costs to a large numbers of identical units that typically pass through a series of uniform production steps. Costs are averaged over the units produced such that each unit bears the same unit cost, 104–106

   building blocks of, 260–261
   decision guidelines for, 271, 283
   FIFO method, 261

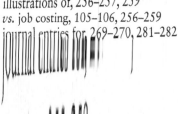

   flow of costs in, 257–260
   illustrations of, 256–257, 259
   vs. job costing, 105–106, 256–259
   journal entries for, 269–270, 281–282

   steps in second/later department, 274–283
   transferred-in costs and, 274
   weighted-average method, 261

Product costing, 5, 104–105. *See also* Job costing; Process costing

Product costs, inventoriable, 55–59, 62–66, 343, 464

Production. Resources used to produce a product or service, or to purchase finished merchandise intended for resale, 51

   in lean operations, 204–208
   scheduling, 107
   traditional systems, 205–206

Production budget, 521–522

Production cost report. Summarizes a processing department's operations for a period, 280–281

Production or purchases. Resources used to produce a product or service, or to purchase finished merchandise intended for resale, 51

Production schedule. A written or electronic document indicating the quantity and types of inventory that will be manufactured during a specified time frame, 107

Product-level activities. Activities and costs incurred for a particular product, regardless of the number of units or batches of the product produced, 193

Product life cycles, 602

Product line income statement. An income statement that shows the operating income of each product line, as well as the company as a whole, 473–474

Product mix, CVP analysis and, 416–419

Product mix decisions, 194, 477–479

Products, discontinuation decisions, 473–477

Profit

   gross, 279
   target, 403–404
   zero, 403

Profitability

   job cost assessments and comparisons, 118–119
   measuring, 847–849, 852

Profitability index. An index that computes the number of dollars returned for every dollar invested, *with all calculations performed in present value dollars*. It is computed as present value of net cash inflows divided by investment; also called present value index, 733–734

Profit center. A responsibility center in which managers are responsible for both revenues and costs, therefore, profits, 592

Profit center performance reports, 595–597

Property, plant, and equipment, 791–792

Pull systems, 206

Purchase order. A written or electronic document authorizing the purchase of specific raw materials from a specific supplier, 109

Purchases. Resources used to produce a product or service, or to purchase finished merchandise intended for resale, 51, 109–110, 129

Q

Quality

   costs of, 209–214

   improving, 209–213
   total quality management, 209–210

Quantity standards, 656–658

Quick ratio. Ratio of the sum of cash plus short-term investments plus net current receivables to total current liabilities. It tells whether the entity can pay all its current liabilities if they come due immediately; also called the *acid-test ratio*, 844, 852

R

Rate of return on common stockholders' equity. Net income minus preferred dividends divided by average common stockholders' equity. It is a measure of profitability; also called *return on equity*, 848, 853

Rate of return on net sales. Ratio of net income to net sales. It is a measure of profitability; also called *return on sales*, 847, 853

Rate of return on total assets. Net income plus interest expense divided by average total assets. This ratio measures a company's success in using its assets to earn income for the people who finance the business; also called *return on assets*, 847–848, 853

Ratio analysis. Evaluating the relationships between two or more key components of the financial statements, 832

Ratios

   accounts receivable turnover, 845, 852
   acid-test, 844, 852
   book value per share of common stock, 850, 853
   contribution margin, 398–399, 402–403
   current ratio, 843–844, 852
   days' sales in receivables, 845–846, 852
   debt ratio, 846, 852
   dividend yield, 850, 853
   earnings per share, 848–849, 853
   inventory turnover, 844–845, 852
   price/earnings, 849, 853
   rate of return on net sales, 847, 853
   return on assets, 847–848, 853
   return on equity, 848
   times-interest-earned, 846–847, 852
   working capital, 843

Raw materials

   purchasing, 109–110, 129
   recording, 680–681

Raw materials inventory. All raw materials (direct materials and indirect materials) not yet used in manufacturing, 48–49, 106–107

Raw materials record. A written or electronic document listing the number and cost of all units used and received, and the balance currently in stock; a separate record is maintained for each type of raw material kept in stock, 108–109, 112

Receiving report. A written or electronic document listing the quantity and type of raw materials received in an incoming shipment; the report is typically a duplicate of the purchase order without the quantity prelisted on the form, 109

Refined costing systems. *See* Activity-based

costing; Costing systems

Regression analysis. A statistical procedure for determining the line that best fits the data by using *all of the historical data points, not*

Regulatory compliance

accounting practices and, 17–19, 23
sustainability and, 887–888, 892

Relevant costs, 67–68, 458–460

Relevant information. Expected *future* data that *differs* among alternatives, 458–459, 470

Relevant information approach, 460, 463, 475–476

Relevant Range. The band of volume where total fixed costs remain constant at a certain level and where the variable cost *per unit* remains constant at a certain level, 327–329

Reporting, environmental performance, 894

Required rate of return. Management's minimum desired rate of return on an investment; also called the discount rate and hurdle rate, 731

Research and development (R&D). Researching and developing new or improved products or services or the processes for producing them, 50

sustainability and, 52

Residual income (RI). Operating income minus the minimum acceptable operating income given the size of the division's assets. Residual income shows whether the division is earning income above or below management's expectations, 597, 599–601

Residual value, 734–735

Responsibility accounting. A system for evaluating the performance of each responsibility center and its manager, 591–594

Responsibility center. A part of an organization whose manager is accountable for planning and controlling certain activities, 591–594

Retail credit cards, 543

Retailer. Merchandising company that sells to consumers, 48

importing and economic shift, 20

Retained earnings, 794

Retirement plans, 59

Return on assets. Net income plus interest expense divided by average total assets. This ratio measures a company's success in using its assets to earn income for the people who finance the business; also called *rate of return on total assets*, 847–848, 853

Return on equity. Net income minus preferred dividends divided by average common stockholders' equity. It is a measure of profitability; also called *rate of return on common stockholders' equity*, 848, 853

Return on investment (ROI). Operating income divided by total assets. The ROI measures the profitability of a division relative to the size of its assets, 597–599, 601–602

Return on sales. Ratio of net income to net sales. It is a measure of profitability; also called *rate of return on net sales*, 847, 853

Revenue center. A responsibility center in which managers are responsible for generating revenue, 592, 594

Revenue center performance reports, 594

Revenues, noncash, 785–787

Risk indicators, 420–425

margin of safety, 420–421
operating leverage, 421–423

Rolling budget. A budget that is continuously updated so that the next 12 months of operations are always budgeted; also known as a continuous budget, 517

Routine planning, 195

R-square, 338–341, 351

S

Safety stock. Extra inventory kept on hand in case demand is higher than expected or problems in the factory slow production, 521

Salaries, 11, 798

Sale of units, 134

Sales budget, 520–521

Sales margin. Operating income divided by sales revenue. The sales margin shows how much income is generated for every $1.00 of sales, 598–599, 601

Sales mix. The combination of products that make up total sales, 397

CVP analysis and, 416–419

Sales price, changing, and CVP analysis, 411–413

Sales revenue line, 404

Sarbanes-Oxley Act of 2002 (SOX). A congressional act that enhances internal control and financial reporting requirements and establishes new regulatory requirements for publicly traded companies and their independent auditors, 17–18

Scatter plot. A graph that plots historical cost and volume data, 334–336, 340

Securities and Exchange Commission (SEC), 7, 19

Segment margin. The income resulting from subtracting only the direct fixed costs of a product line from its contribution margin. The segment margin contains no allocation of common fixed costs, 477, 595

Segment margin income statement. A product line income statement that contains no allocation of common fixed costs. Only direct fixed costs that can be traced to specific product lines are subtracted from the product line's contribution margin. All common fixed costs remain unallocated, and are shown only under the company total, 477

Sensitivity analysis. A *what if* technique that asks what a result will be if a predicted amount is not achieved or if an underlying assumption changes, 411, 538

budgeting and, 538–539
capital budgeting and, 735
CVP analysis and, 411–419
information technology and, 419–420

Service company. A company that sells intangible services rather than tangible products, 48–50

activity-based costing in, 196
balance sheets, 66
contribution margin, 346
costs of quality in, 210–211
economic shift toward, 19–20
income statements, 62
indirect costs in, 142–143
inventoriable product costs, 58, 62
job costing in, 141–144
lean operations in, 208
master budget for, 540–543

Short-term special decisions, 460–461, 485

Simple interest. Interest computed *only* on the principal amount, 723–724

Slack. Intentionally overstating budgeted expense or understating budgeted revenues in order to cope with uncertainty, make performance appear better, or make room for potential budget cuts, 517

Social responsibility, 19. *See also* Sustainability

SOX. *See* Sarbanes-Oxley Act of 2002

Special sales order decisions, 461–465

Stakeholder influence, 887–889

Standard cost. The budget for a single unit of product, 655–656

advantages and disadvantages of, 667–668
analyzing direct labor variances with, 659–660, 664–667
analyzing direct material variances with, 659–664, 667
analyzing manufacturing overhead variances with, 657–658
computing, 657–659
decision guidelines for, 669, 677
direct labor, 657
direct materials, 657
information for developing and updating, 656–657
journal entries for, 680–683
manufacturing overhead rates, 657–658
of one unit, 658–659
price standards, 656–658
quantity standards, 656–658
sustainability and, 659

Standard cost accounting. Another common name for Standard Costing, 680

Standard cost accounting systems, 680–683

Standard cost income statement, 683

Standard costing. Also known as standard cost accounting. A method of accounting in which product costs are entered into the general ledger inventory accounts at standard cost, rather than actual cost. The variances are captured in their own general ledger accounts and displayed on a standard costing income statement prior to being closed out at the end of the period, 676, 680–683

Standard manufacturing overhead rates, 657–658

Standards. Another common name for standard costs, 656

Statement of cash flows. One of the four basic financial statements; the statement shows the overall increase or decrease in cash during the period as well as how the company generated and used cash during the period, 778–782

activities on, 779–781
decision guidelines for, 783, 800
direct method of preparing, 796–800
indirect method of preparing, 785–795, 800
information needed to prepare, 785
interpreting, 790, 795
sustainability and, 782

Statement on Ethical Professional Practice, 11–13

Step costs. A cost behavior that is fixed over a small range of activity and then jumps to a different fixed level with moderate changes in volume, 329–330

Stock inventory. Products normally kept on hand in order to quickly fill customer orders, 107

Stock investments, 849–850

Stores, discontinuation decisions, 473–477

Straight-line approximations, 330

Plantwide overhead rate. When overhead is allocated to every product using the same manufacturing overhead rate, 181–182, 186–187

Point of use storage (POUS). A storage system used to reduce the waste of transportation and movement in which tools, materials, and equipment are stored in proximity to where they will be used most frequently, 206

Post-audits. Comparing a capital investment's actual net cash inflows to its projected net cash inflows, 713–714

Practical standards. Standards based on currently attainable conditions that include allowances for normal amounts of waste and inefficiency; also known as attainable standards, 656

sustainability and, 268–269

Predetermined manufacturing overhead rate. The rate used to allocate manufacturing overhead to individual jobs; calculated before the year begins as follows: total estimated manufacturing overhead costs divided by total estimated amount of allocation base, 116

Prepaid insurance, 788

Present value, 724–725, 727–729, 741–742

net, 712, 733–734

Present value index. An index that computes the number of dollars returned for every dollar invested, *with all calculations performed in present value dollars.* It is computed as present value of net cash inflows divided by investment; also called profitability index, 733–734

Prevention costs. Costs incurred to *avoid* poor-quality goods or services, 209–214

Price/earnings (P/E) ratio. Ratio of the market price of a share of common stock to the company's earnings per share. It measures the value that the stock market places on $1 of a company's earnings, 849, 853

Price-setters, 465–466, 469

Price standards, 656–658

Price-takers, 465–466, 469

Pricing
cost-plus approach, 119–120, 468–469
incremental analysis approach, 460, 463, 464, 475–476
outsourcing prices, 481–482
target costing approach, 466–469
transfer pricing, 602–604

Pricing decisions, 194, 461–469

Pricing pressure, 119

Prime costs. The combination of direct material and direct labor costs, 58–59

Principal, 723

Process costing. A system for assigning costs to a large numbers of identical units that typically pass through a series of uniform production steps. Costs are averaged over the units produced such that each unit bears the same unit cost, 104–106

building blocks of, 260–261
decision guidelines for, 271, 283
FIFO method, 261
flow of costs in, 257–260
illustrations of, 256–257, 259
vs. job costing, 105–106, 256–259
journal entries for, 269–270, 281–282
overview, 255–259
steps in first department, 262–268, 271

steps in second/later department, 274–283
transferred-in costs and, 274
weighted-average method, 261

Product costing, 5, 104–105. *See also* Job costing; Process costing

Product costs, inventoriable, 55–59, 62–66, 343, 464

Production. Resources used to produce a product or service, or to purchase finished merchandise intended for resale, 51

in lean operations, 204–208
scheduling, 107
traditional systems, 205–206

Production budget, 521–522

Production cost report. Summarizes a processing department's operations for a period, 280–281

Production or purchases. Resources used to produce a product or service, or to purchase finished merchandise intended for resale, 51

Production schedule. A written or electronic document indicating the quantity and types of inventory that will be manufactured during a specified time frame, 107

Product-level activities. Activities and costs incurred for a particular product, regardless of the number of units or batches of the product produced, 193

Product life cycles, 602

Product line income statement. An income statement that shows the operating income of each product line, as well as the company as a whole, 473–474

Product mix, CVP analysis and, 416–419

Product mix decisions, 194, 477–479

Products, discontinuation decisions, 473–477

Profit
gross, 279
target, 403–404
zero, 403

Profitability
job cost assessments and comparisons, 118–119
measuring, 847–849, 852

Profitability index. An index that computes the number of dollars returned for every dollar invested, *with all calculations performed in present value dollars.* It is computed as present value of net cash inflows divided by investment; also called present value index, 733–734

Profit center. A responsibility center in which managers are responsible for both revenues and costs, therefore, profits, 592

Profit center performance reports, 595–597

Property, plant, and equipment, 791–792

Pull systems, 206

Purchase order. A written or electronic document authorizing the purchase of specific raw materials from a specific supplier, 109

Purchases. Resources used to produce a product or service, or to purchase finished merchandise intended for resale, 51, 109–110, 129

Q

Quality
costs of, 209–214
emphasis on, 207–208

improving, 209–213
total quality management, 209–210

Quantity standards, 656–658

Quick ratio. Ratio of the sum of cash plus short-term investments plus net current receivables to total current liabilities. It tells whether the entity can pay all its current liabilities if they come due immediately; also called the *acid-test ratio,* 844, 852

R

Rate of return on common stockholders' equity. Net income minus preferred dividends divided by average common stockholders' equity. It is a measure of profitability; also called *return on equity,* 848, 853

Rate of return on net sales. Ratio of net income to net sales. It is a measure of profitability; also called *return on sales,* 847, 853

Rate of return on total assets. Net income plus interest expense divided by average total assets. This ratio measures a company's success in using its assets to earn income for the people who finance the business; also called *return on assets,* 847–848, 853

Ratio analysis. Evaluating the relationships between two or more key components of the financial statements, 832

Ratios
accounts receivable turnover, 845, 852
acid-test, 844, 852
book value per share of common stock, 850, 853
contribution margin, 398–399, 402–403
current ratio, 843–844, 852
days' sales in receivables, 845–846, 852
debt ratio, 846, 852
dividend yield, 850, 853
earnings per share, 848–849, 853
inventory turnover, 844–845, 852
price/earnings, 849, 853
rate of return on net sales, 847, 853
return on assets, 847–848, 853
return on equity, 848
times-interest-earned, 846–847, 852
working capital, 843

Raw materials
purchasing, 109–110, 129
recording, 680–681

Raw materials inventory. All raw materials (direct materials and indirect materials) not yet used in manufacturing, 48–49, 106–107

Raw materials record. A written or electronic document listing the number and cost of all units used and received, and the balance currently in stock; a separate record is maintained for each type of raw material kept in stock, 108–109, 112

Receiving report. A written or electronic document listing the quantity and type of raw materials received in an incoming shipment; the report is typically a duplicate of the purchase order without the quantity prelisted on the form, 109

Refined costing systems. *See* Activity-based costing; Costing systems

Regression analysis. A statistical procedure for determining the line that best fits the data by using *all of the historical data points, not just the high and low data points,* 338–341

Regular pricing decisions, 461–462, 465–469

Regulatory compliance
    accounting practices and, 17–19, 23
    sustainability and, 887–888, 892
Relevant costs, 67–68, 458–460
Relevant information. Expected *future* data that *differs* among alternatives, 458–459, 470
Relevant information approach, 460, 463, 475–476
Relevant Range. The band of volume where total fixed costs remain constant at a certain level and where the variable cost *per unit* remains constant at a certain level, 327–329
Reporting, environmental performance, 894
Required rate of return. Management's minimum desired rate of return on an investment; also called the discount rate and hurdle rate, 731
Research and development (R&D). Researching and developing new or improved products or services or the processes for producing them, 50
    sustainability and, 52
Residual income (RI). Operating income minus the minimum acceptable operating income given the size of the division's assets. Residual income shows whether the division is earning income above or below management's expectations, 597, 599–601
Residual value, 734–735
Responsibility accounting. A system for evaluating the performance of each responsibility center and its manager, 591–594
Responsibility center. A part of an organization whose manager is accountable for planning and controlling certain activities, 591–594
Retail credit cards, 543
Retailer. Merchandising company that sells to consumers, 48
    importing and economic shift, 20
Retained earnings, 794
Retirement plans, 59
Return on assets. Net income plus interest expense divided by average total assets. This ratio measures a company's success in using its assets to earn income for the people who finance the business; also called *rate of return on total assets,* 847–848, 853
Return on equity. Net income minus preferred dividends divided by average common stockholders' equity. It is a measure of profitability; also called *rate of return on common stockholders' equity,* 848, 853
Return on investment (ROI). Operating income divided by total assets. The ROI measures the profitability of a division relative to the size of its assets, 597–599, 601–602
Return on sales. Ratio of net income to net sales. It is a measure of profitability; also called *rate of return on net sales,* 847, 853
Revenue center. A responsibility center in which managers are responsible for generating revenue, 592, 594
Revenue center performance reports, 594
Revenues, noncash, 785–787
Risk indicators, 420–425
    margin of safety, 420–421
    operating leverage, 421–423
Rolling budget. A budget that is continuously updated so that the next 12 months

of operations are always budgeted; also known as a continuous budget, 517
Routine planning, 195
R-square, 338–341, 351

S

Safety stock. Extra inventory kept on hand in case demand is higher than expected or problems in the factory slow production, 521
Salaries, 11, 798
Sale of units, 134
Sales budget, 520–521
Sales margin. Operating income divided by sales revenue. The sales margin shows how much income is generated for every $1.00 of sales, 598–599, 601
Sales mix. The combination of products that make up total sales, 397
    CVP analysis and, 416–419
Sales price, changing, and CVP analysis, 411–413
Sales revenue line, 404
Sarbanes-Oxley Act of 2002 (SOX). A congressional act that enhances internal control and financial reporting requirements and establishes new regulatory requirements for publicly traded companies and their independent auditors, 17–18
Scatter plot. A graph that plots historical cost and volume data, 334–336, 340
Securities and Exchange Commission (SEC), 7, 19
Segment margin. The income resulting from subtracting only the direct fixed costs of a product line from its contribution margin. The segment margin contains no allocation of common fixed costs, 477, 595
Segment margin income statement. A product line income statement that contains no allocation of common fixed costs. Only direct fixed costs that can be traced to specific product lines are subtracted from the product line's contribution margin. All common fixed costs remain unallocated, and are shown only under the company total, 477
Sensitivity analysis. A *what if* technique that asks what a result will be if a predicted amount is not achieved or if an underlying assumption changes, 411, 538
    budgeting and, 538–539
    capital budgeting and, 735
    CVP analysis and, 411–419
    information technology and, 419–420
Service company. A company that sells intangible services rather than tangible products, 48–50
    activity-based costing in, 196
    balance sheets, 66
    contribution margin, 346
    costs of quality in, 210–211
    economic shift toward, 19–20
    income statements, 62
    indirect costs in, 142–143
    inventoriable product costs, 58, 62
    job costing in, 141–144
    lean operations in, 208
    master budget for, 540–543
Short-term special decisions, 460–461, 485
Simple interest. Interest computed *only* on the principal amount, 723–724

Slack. Intentionally overstating budgeted expense or understating budgeted revenues in order to cope with uncertainty, make performance appear better, or make room for potential budget cuts, 517
Social responsibility, 19. See also Sustainability
SOX. *See* Sarbanes-Oxley Act of 2002
Special sales order decisions, 461–465
Stakeholder influence, 887–889
Standard cost. The budget for a single unit of product, 655–656
    advantages and disadvantages of, 667–668
    analyzing direct labor variances with, 659–660, 664–667
    analyzing direct material variances with, 659–664, 667
    analyzing manufacturing overhead variances with, 657–658
    computing, 657–659
    decision guidelines for, 669, 677
    direct labor, 657
    direct materials, 657
    information for developing and updating, 656–657
    journal entries for, 680–683
    manufacturing overhead rates, 657–658
    of one unit, 658–659
    price standards, 656–658
    quantity standards, 656–658
    sustainability and, 659
Standard cost accounting. Another common name for Standard Costing, 680
Standard cost accounting systems, 680–683
Standard cost income statement, 683
Standard costing. Also known as standard cost accounting. A method of accounting in which product costs are entered into the general ledger inventory accounts at standard cost, rather than actual cost. The variances are captured in their own general ledger accounts and displayed on a standard costing income statement prior to being closed out at the end of the period, 676, 680–683
Standard manufacturing overhead rates, 657–658
Standards. Another common name for standard costs, 656
Statement of cash flows. One of the four basic financial statements; the statement shows the overall increase or decrease in cash during the period as well as how the company generated and used cash during the period, 778–782
    activities on, 779–781
    decision guidelines for, 783, 800
    direct method of preparing, 796–800
    indirect method of preparing, 785–795, 800
    information needed to prepare, 785
    interpreting, 790, 795
    sustainability and, 782
Statement on Ethical Professional Practice, 11–13
Step costs. A cost behavior that is fixed over a small range of activity and then jumps to a different fixed level with moderate changes in volume, 329–330
Stock inventory. Products normally kept on hand in order to quickly fill customer orders, 107
Stock investments, 849–850
Stores, discontinuation decisions, 473–477
Straight-line approximations, 330

Strategic Finance journal, 11

Strategic planning. Setting long-term goals that may extend 5-10 years into the future, 516

Strategy development, sustainability and, 891–892

Subsidiary ledger. Supporting detail for a general ledger account, 129

Summary performance report, 519

Sunk cost. A cost that has already been incurred, 67–68, 458–459

Supply-chain management, 208

Sustainability. The ability to meet the needs of the present without compromising the ability of future generations to meet their own needs, 19, 886

   biofuel industry, 52

   business reason for adopting, 886–890

   as business trend, 19

   capital investments and, 714–715

   challenges to implementing EMA, 894–895

   cost behaviors and, 331

   costing for, 892–894

   cost-volume analysis and, 415

   decision guidelines for, 897

   EMA information used for, 891–894

   environmental performance reporting, 893–894

   environmental reporting standards, 893–894

   extended producer responsibility (EPR), 121

   financial statement analysis and, 851

   fuel-efficient vehicles, 47, 53–54, 57, 67, 69–70

   greenwashing, 52

   importance of, 886–896

   information used to support, 890–891

   job costing and, 120–121

   lean thinking and, 208

   LEED certification, 714–715

   living roof, 86, 818, 908, 920, 922

   performance evaluation and KPIs, 618

   process costing and, 268–269

   refined costing systems and, 196

   regulatory compliance and, 887–888, 891

   short-term business decisions and, 461

   standards costs and, 659

   statement of cash flows and, 782

   value chains and, 52–53

T

Takt time. The rate of production needed to meet customer demand yet avoid overproduction, 206

Target costing. An approach to pricing used by price-takers; target costing begins with the revenue at market price and subtracts the company's desired profit to arrive at the target total cost, 466–469

Target profit

   changing fixed costs and, 414

   changing sales prices and, 411–412

   changing variable costs and, 412–413

   finding, using CVP analysis, 403–404

Taxes, income, 535

Teams

   cross-functional teams, 8

   use of in lean production, 205–206

Throughput time. The time between buying raw materials and selling finished products, 21

Time, wasting, 202–203, 205

Times-interest-earned ratio. Ratio of income from operations to interest expense. It measures the number of times that operating income can cover interest expense; also called the *interest-coverage ratio*, 846–847, 852

Time value of money. The fact that money can be invested to earn income over time, 723

   calculating, 745–756

   calculating with Microsoft Excel, 751–756

   computing, 723–729

   factors affecting, 723–724

   future value, 724–727

   present value, 724–725, 727–729

TI-83 Plus calculator, 725, 745–750

TI-84 Plus calculator, 725, 745–750

Total assets, 601–602

Total costs. The cost of all resources used throughout the value chain, 54–55, 69–70, 128–129

   assigning, 267, 278–279

   finding, in service company, 143

   summarizing, 266–267, 277–278

Total Quality Management (TQM). A management philosophy of delighting customers with superior products and services by continually setting higher goals and improving the performance of every business function, 22, 209–210

Trace. To assign a *direct* cost to a cost object, 54

Trading on equity. Earning more income on borrowed money that the related interest expense, thereby increasing the earnings for the owners of the business; also called *leverage*, 848

Traditional production systems, 205–206

Training, decentralization and, 590

Transfer pricing, 602–604

Transferred-in costs. Costs incurred in a previous process that are carried forward as part of the product's cost when it moves to the next process, 274

Transportation, as waste, 202–203, 205

Trash audit. Studying the contents of a company's trash in order to identify solid waste and scraps that could potentially be recycled, repurposed, or sold to create a new revenue stream; also known as waste audit or waste sort, 268–269

Treasurer. The position responsible for raising the firm's capital and investing funds, 8

Trend percentages. A form of horizontal analysis in which percentages are computed by selecting a base year as 100% and expressing amounts for following years as a percentage of the base amount, 834–836, 838–839

Triple bottom line. Evaluating a company's performance not only by its ability to generate economic profits, but also by its impact on people and the planet, 19, 48, 886

U

Unavoidable fixed costs. Fixed costs that will continue to be incurred even if a particular course of action is taken, 474–475

Uncontrollable costs. Costs that cannot be changed or influenced in the short run by management, 66–67

Underallocated manufacturing overhead. The amount of manufacturing overhead allocated to jobs is less than the amount of manufacturing overhead costs actually incurred; this results in jobs being undercosted, 126–128

Undercosting, 181, 194

Unethical *vs.* illegal behavior, 14

Unfavorable variance. A variance that causes operating income to be lower than budgeted, 594

Unit contribution margin, 397–398, 401–402

Unit costs

   determining, 5

   gross profit and, 279

   in process costing, 267–268, 279–280

Unit-level activities. Activities and costs incurred for every unit produced, 193

U.S economy, shifts in, 19–20

V

Value-added activities. Activities for which the customer is willing to pay because these activities add value to the final product or service, 195

Value chain. The activities that add value to a firm's products and services; includes R&D, design, production or purchases, marketing, distribution, and customer service, 50

   business activities in, 50–51

   coordinating activities across, 51–53

   sustainability and, 52–53, 892

Value engineering. Eliminating waste in the system by making the company's processes as effective and efficient as possible, 195

Value stream maps (VSM), 204–205

Variable costing. The costing method that assigns only *variable* manufacturing costs to products. All fixed manufacturing costs (Fixed MOH) are expensed as period costs, 122, 342–350

   vs. absorption costing, 342–350

Variable costs. Costs incurred for every unit of activity. As a result, total variable costs change in direct proportion to changes in volume, 68–69, 320–323

   changing, and CVP analysis, 412–413

   outsourcing considerations and, 480–481

   relevant ranges for, 327–329

Variable overhead efficiency variance. This variance tells managers how much of the total variable MOH variance is due to using more or fewer hours of the allocation base (usually machine hours or DL hours) than anticipated for the actual volume of output. It is calculated as follows: SR × (AH − SHA), 673

Variable overhead rate variance. Also called the variable overhead spending variance. This variance tells managers whether more or less was spent on variable overhead than they expected would be spent for the hours worked. It is calculated as follows: AH × (AR − SR), 672–673

Variable overhead spending variance. Another common name for variable overhead rate variance, 672

Variance. The difference between an actual amount and the budget, 519, 594

   advantages and disadvantages of, 667–668

   decision guidelines for, 669, 677

   direct labor, 659–660, 664–667

   direct material, 659–664, 667

   fixed manufacturing, 674–676

   flexible budget, 610–612, 659–667

   manufacturing overhead, 672–676

Vertical analysis. Analysis of a financial statement that reveals the relationship of each statement item to a specified base, which is the 100% figure, 832, 836–839

Vertical integration. The practice of purchasing other companies within one's supply chain; predicated by the notion that a company's profits can be maximized by owning one's supplier, 603

Vertical intercept, 337

Volume variance. The difference between the master budget and the flexible budget. The volume variance arises *only* because the volume of cases actually sold differs from the volume originally anticipated in the master budget, 610

VSM. *See* value stream maps

W

Wages, 798

Wages payable, 130–131, 789

Waiting, as waste, 202–203, 205–206

Waste activities. Activities that neither enhance the customer's image of the product nor provide a competitive advantage; also known as non-value-added activities, 195

Water footprint. The total volume of water use associated with the processes and products of a business, 893

Weighted-average contribution margin, 416–419

Weighted-average method of process costing. A process costing method that *combines* any beginning inventory units (and costs) with the current period's units (and costs) to get a weighted-average cost, 261

Wholesaler. Merchandising companies that buy in bulk from manufacturers, mark up the prices, and then sell those products to retailers, 48

Working capital. Current assets minus current liabilities; measures a business's ability to meet its short-term obligations with its current assets, 843

Work in process (WIP) inventory. Goods that are partway through the manufacturing process but not yet complete, 48–49, 106–107, 278–279

Z

Zero-based budgeting. A budgeting approach in which managers begin with a budget of zero and must justify every dollar put into the budget, 517

Zero profit, 403